INSIDE THE SYSTEM
CULTURE, INSTITUTIONS, AND POWER
IN AMERICAN POLITICS

To My Students

INSIDE THE SYSTEM
CULTURE, INSTITUTIONS, AND POWER IN AMERICAN POLITICS

W. LANCE BENNETT
University of Washington

Harcourt Brace College Publishers

Fort Worth   Philadelphia   San Diego   New York   Orlando   Austin   San Antonio
Toronto   Montreal   London   Sydney   Tokyo

Publisher	Ted Buchholz
Acquisitions Editor	David Tatom
Developmental Editor	Fritz Schanz
Senior Project Editor	Cliff Crouch
Production Manager	Erin Gregg
Senior Art Director	Diana Jean Parks
Permissions Editor	Sheila Shutter
Photo Research	Cindy Robinson

Library of Congress Cataloging-in-Publication Data
Bennett, W. Lance.
   Inside the system: culture, institutions, and power in American politics / W. Lance Bennett.
     p. cm.
   Includes bibliographical references and index.
   ISBN 0-15-500042-X
   1. United States—Politics and government.   I. Title.
JK274.B49   1994
320.973—dc20   93-27322
                                                                     CIP

International Standard Book Number: 0-15-500042-X

Address for editorial correspondence: Harcourt Brace College Publishers
                                                301 Commerce Street, Suite 3700
                                                Fort Worth, Texas 76102

Address for orders: Harcourt Brace, Inc.
                        6277 Sea Harbor Drive
                        Orlando, Florida, 32887
Phone: 800/782-4479, or
                      (in Florida only) 800/433-0001

Cover photo © 1992 by Steve Hathaway

This book is printed on acid-free paper.

Printed in the United States of America

3 4 5 6 7 8 9 0 1 2 3   048   9 8 7 6 5 4 3 2 1

CONTENTS IN BRIEF

Preface   vii

PART I—THE AMERICAN DEMOCRACY: A USER'S MANUAL

CHAPTER 1   *The American Democracy:*
             Culture, Institutions, and Power   **3**

PART II—CONSTITUTIONAL FOUNDATIONS

CHAPTER 2   *From Revolution to Constitution:*
             The Struggle for Government   **33**

CHAPTER 3   *The Constitutional Design of Power*   **71**

CHAPTER 4   *The Politics of Federalism*   **107**

CHAPTER 5   *The Personal Constitution:*
             Civil Liberties and Civil Rights   **145**

PART III—THE CIVIC CULTURE: PARTICIPATION AND POWER

CHAPTER 6   *Public Opinion: Culture, Society,*
             and the Individual   **189**

CHAPTER 7   *Participation: The Forms of*
             Political Action   **227**

CHAPTER 8   *Interest-Group Politics*   **269**

v

CHAPTER 9   *Political Parties: Engines of Government*   **311**

CHAPTER 10   *Campaigns and Elections: The Political Guidance System*   **345**

CHAPTER 11   *Mass Mediated Democracy*   **387**

PART IV—INSTITUTIONS AT WORK

CHAPTER 12   *Congress: The Legislative Process*   **429**

CHAPTER 13   *Congress: Power and Organization*   **463**

CHAPTER 14   *The Executive: Presidential Power and National Leadership*   **501**

CHAPTER 15   *The Executive: Managing the Bureaucracy*   **537**

CHAPTER 16   *The Judiciary: Courts, Law, and Justice*   **567**

PART V—POLICY: THE SUM OF THE PARTS

CHAPTER 17   *The Policy Process*   **605**

CHAPTER 18   *Social Policy: Managing the Quality of Life*   **631**

CHAPTER 19   *Economic Policy: Paying for It All*   **669**

CHAPTER 20   *Foreign and Defense Policy: National Security and World Power*   **701**

Appendices   **737**

Glossary   **755**

Indexes   **799**

PREFACE

Like most teachers of the introductory course in American government, my goal is to bring the material to life for the students. It can be challenging to grasp the logic behind a complex government design that includes separate national institutions, strong state governments, and a host of unique features—from filibusters to the electoral college. If presented as a vast collection of facts to be memorized, government often remains a distant and puzzling abstraction. Yet the classroom comes alive when topical discussions are held on issues such as abortion, the deficit, affirmative action, bureaucratic mismanagement, or balancing environmental protection with economic growth. For many students, learning begins when they see the connections between these political issues and the workings of the government. This textbook sets the workings of government in the broader context of politics in American society.

POLITICS AS PERSPECTIVE

Is it possible to talk about politics in a mainstream text without introducing a narrow point of view? My experience in the classroom suggests that it is, if one pursues an approach that might be termed "political realism." Clearly, there are and have always been profound political conflicts in society. Rather than dismiss or even shy away from these conflicts, the first step for a political realist is to recognize these as signs of democracy at work. The next step is to move beyond debates over who is right or wrong about an issue and analyze how political players advance or defend their positions. When developed like this, the approach links politics and government; it enables students to evaluate hotly contested issues, and it motivates learning about how government actually works. Thus, this text strikes a balance between political science and politics, using each to explain and explore the other.

INSIDE THE SYSTEM

To help students see how political situations develop, this book introduces the idea of government in the context of a larger political system. The simple framework of a political system presented here involves three core elements: institutions, culture, and power. First, institutions are presented as the foundation of the system. Next, the political culture that *shapes* these institutions and that serves as a source for much political behavior is emphasized. Bringing political culture into play reminds us that politics begins with enduring conflicts and tensions over core values: freedom, social order, equal rights, morality, patriotism, and the role of government in society. Explaining our distinctive political culture is made easy by addressing familiar struggles that most citizens experience firsthand: the eternal question of how much individual freedom we can tolerate before social order is lost; the problem of making sure individual freedoms do not deprive others of an equal opportunity to compete for the American Dream; deciding how much government involvement is desirable in working out these conflicts. These and other themes from the political culture put students squarely into the political picture.

Finally, our overview of the political system is completed by describing patterns of power in society. When citizens make their demands on government, they also mobilize what power they have to make government officials act. One of the most fascinating aspects of politics is how people who lack one political resource, such as money, may make up for it by mobilizing other resources, such as voter movements or political protests. Understanding the ways in which power is mobilized by different groups in society helps explain how government responds to different people and their causes. This book introduces students to three leading models of power in the U.S. political system: majoritarianism, the idea of majority rule; pluralism, the idea that many groups exercise influence and compete with one another; and elitism, the idea that wealthy or well-connected elites often gain a political advantage. Rather than promote a single picture of power, however, this book shows readers that each perspective on power can be useful in understanding particular situations. By weighing these theories, then, students are encouraged to think critically about what makes the government work and thus come to terms with the ultimate question of democratic theory: *Who governs?*

ORGANIZATION OF THE TEXT

The basic organization of this book remains fairly conventional; it covers all the major topics of an introductory course in much the same order and with similar attention to research and factual detail found in most major textbooks. Departures from basic organization are minor and are intended to enhance students' grasp of the material.

The idea of a political system and a simple definition of politics are presented in the first chapter. Instructors who wish to present their own perspective (or to emphasize the general theme of politics over the specific ideas of culture, institutions, and power) may wish to start their reading assignments with Chapter 2. The nation's founding and the Constitution are presented over two chapters instead of the usual one. Chapter 2 explains the politics that shaped the Constitution, and Chapter 3 emphasizes the workings of the Constitution and its impact on contemporary politics. Chapter 4 enlivens the sometimes dull subject of federalism with a broad look at the historical conflicts and struggles over race, economy, and rights that have been played out in the balance between states and the national government. The emphasis in Chapter 5 on rights as the American citizen's most personal political resource explains the decision to introduce rights and liberties early in the book.

The civic culture of participation is covered fully in chapters 6–11, on, respectively, opinion, participation, interest groups, parties, elections, and the media. I am pleased that this coverage of participation and political interest organization has been so well received by pre-publication reviewers. The media chapter is, I believe, the most extensive of any text, featuring standard First Amendment issues along with sections on how the news is produced and how its status as a commercial product affects political content.

The treatment of institutions in chapters 12–16 follows the conventional organization of these topics presented in most major textbooks—with two exceptions. First, the topic of Congress has been divided into two chapters. Chapter 12 covers the workings of the legislative process, and chapter 13 evaluates the inside politics that affects the performance of the institution. A highlight of Chapter 13 is an in-depth look at how the career calculations of individual members affect what Congress does. Second, the topic of the executive branch is also divided into two chapters. Chapter 14 focuses on the president as a national leader, and Chapter 15 explores the politics inside the bureaucracy from the standpoint of how presidents try to manage a vast set of organizations that have independent political ties to Congress and interest groups. Chapter 16, on the judiciary, explains the unique role of law and courts in the American system, with special attention to how the Supreme Court operates.

The concluding chapters on public policy (chapters 17–20) emphasize how all of the above-mentioned parts of the system work together (and sometimes do not) to create the guidelines for government action that we know as policy. There are several departures here from most traditional textbooks. First, an overview chapter (17) helps students to think about policy as a political process. This chapter integrates themes presented throughout the book, and provides a simple framework for understanding how government policies develop. Chapter 18, on social policy, compares three broad areas (health, education, and welfare) and shows the different political forces at work in each. Chapter 19, on economic policy, introduces the economic terms and theories that are increasingly heard in national debates about economic issues, and it explains the inner workings of fiscal, monetary, and regulatory policies. Chapter 20, on military and foreign policy, looks to future domestic and international issues that may be raised by an emerging new world order.

FEATURES

One goal of this journey inside the U.S. political system is to make basic facts and concepts memorable by giving readers a satisfying taste of political analysis. Another goal is to make the material useful to student readers as citizens long after the course itself is over. To reinforce these goals, this book contains these features:

- All chapters open with a *political issue or conflict* that has appeared prominently in the news. This creates a real-world reference for the material in the chapter. Also, the opening raises questions of enduring political importance, and can serve as a guide to help students to recognize similar situations in the future.

- At the close of each chapter is a *Revisited* section that re-examines the main concepts, relates these concepts to broader issues, and reveals their relevance to the reader's life today.

- All chapters conclude with *A Citizen's Question,* to promote thinking about how material from the chapter may be incorporated into a personal philosophy of citizen participation. Some of these questions are, naturally, more philosophical—involving personal questions about dealing with authority or carrying out a citizen's obligations—while others are more practical—informing readers on how to contact political parties or join interest organizations.

- Every chapter contains at least one *Inside the System* feature essay that illustrates various examples of culture, institutions, or power in action.

- Every chapter contains at least one *How We Compare* feature essay that relates important features of the U.S. system to those of other nations. Comparison enriches the learning experience and provides critical understanding of how various systems solve similar problems.

- Whenever possible, historical perspectives show students how American politics has changed, often through the involvement and participation of "ordinary" citizens.

- Each chapter contains a photo essay, *The Players*, which depicts people involved in significant issues—people who represent various forms of power and interest. Also, many captioned photographs throughout the book illustrate and comment on such concepts at work.

- *Suggested Readings* at the end of each chapter combine key works in political science with complementary works— both classic and current—by sociologists, economists, historians, journalists, and political commentators of diverse viewpoints. This section is designed to broaden the student reader's interest in contemporary political issues.

SUPPLEMENTS

The editorial team at Harcourt Brace Publishers has worked with me and with a number of reviewers to develop supplementary materials that will help in presenting the above-mentioned ideas inside the classroom. Particular attention has been paid to integrating the instructor's manual with the test bank, the study guide, the *Getting Involved* supplement, and the overhead transparencies.

Instructor's Manual (printed, IBM, and Mac). Provides the following information for each chapter: Overview, learning objectives, key points, topical outline, key terms, additional lecture suggestions, interjection of "multiculturalism," and additional readings. Free to adopters.

Study Guide (printed, IBM, and Mac). Includes chapter outline, learning objectives, key concepts, terms to identify, self-test with questions from the test bank, answers to self-test, "multicultural" issues, and citizen participation.

Test Bank (printed) and ExaMaster+ software program (IBM and Mac). Provides 2,000 questions in multiple-choice, true/false, and essay formats. ExaMaster+ allows the instructor to add and edit questions, select questions according to several criteria, link related questions, block questions from random selection, and create and print up to 99 versions of the same test and answer sheet. It also includes on-line testing, grading, and scoring features. Free to adopters.

Exam Record. A grade-book program that calculates grades, converts letter grades to numeric, prints grades for posting, and determines distributions and curves. Free to adopters.

Getting Involved. Complements the citizen involvement orientation of the book. Provides assignments and discusses, step by step, how to make contact with public officials on a range of issues. May be used as a citizenship exercise, a self-paced research project, or both. Helps students to make contact with government and to learn from the experience.

Color Transparencies (with an Instructor's Guide). More than 50 four-color transparencies from the book. Free to adopters.

Annenberg Video Cassette Series. The series *The Constitution: That Delicate Balance.* Free to adopters, subject to Harcourt Brace video policy.

American Government Software Simulators (IBM and Mac). Provides simulations of topics such as the Constitution, political participation, campaigning, the presidency, and public policy.

Guide for Writing in Political Science. Discusses doing library research, using sources, developing an outline, observing conventions of style and format, and noting documentation styles. Provides student sample papers.

The New Republic. Free to adopters.

Video Newsletter. A quarterly video news magazine drawn from segments of *The MacNeil/Lehrer News Hour.* These videotapes contain features that reflect current issues in American politics.

ACKNOWLEDGMENTS

Writing a text on American government is a huge job, and writing this one would have been impossible without the help and encouragement of many people along the way. The support network begins with the thousands of students who have taken my introductory courses over the years and helped me to become a better teacher. A number of colleagues at the University of Washington also inspired me through their commitment to undergraduate teaching—a commitment that is truly extraordinary at a large research university. My growth and continuing enthusiasm as a teacher have been inspired by many stimulating exchanges with Don McCrone, David Olson, Michael McCann, Stu Scheingold, Dan Lev, Nancy Hartsock, Christine DiStefano, and Don Matthews, among others. I owe a great debt of gratitude to two people who read every word of the manuscript and offered helpful criticism along the way: Bill Haltom and Regina Lawrence. Regina also assisted mightily with the background research and fact-checking that went into this project. Also helpful at various points along the way were John Gilliom, Steve Livingston, Murray Edelman, Jerry Manheim, and the authors of several competing texts, who privately offered advice and commiseration on the trials involved in undertaking such a large project.

I am indebted to the many people who responded to my phone calls and letters requesting the latest research data unavailable in the published literature. Special thanks to Patti Jo Baber, executive director of the American League of Lobbyists; to Larry Makinson, of the Center for Responsive Politics; and to numerous employees of the Republican and Democratic national committees, for tracking down important bits of information.

The editors and other staff at Harcourt Brace provided tremendous support and guidance. In particular, I thank Drake Bush, acquisitions editor, who shared my vision of this project; David Tatom, acquisitions editor, who provided guidance; Fritz Schanz, developmental editor, who helped to pull it together; Cindy Robinson, photo researcher, who helped me to visualize it; Clifford Crouch, senior project editor, who oversaw the final editing and the production process, and who also researched and drafted an excellent set of photo captions; Diana Jean Parks, senior art director, who created the design; and Erin Gregg, production manager, who made the bound book happen. To my agent, Irv Rockwood, I can only say that your loyalty and continued involvement made all the difference. Finally, Ann Buscherfeld was there all along with word-processing and computer assistance. Thanks for being so helpful.

In closing, my heartfelt appreciation goes to the many instructors at colleges and universities around the country who read the manuscript with great care, offering helpful suggestions on how to present the material in way that would help them to teach it to their students. While the final responsibility for the book's content remains mine, the guidance of the following people has been of great value: Patricia Bodelson, *St. Cloud State University*; Joe Cammerano, *Syracuse University*; Ann H. Cohen, *Illinois State University*; Paige Cubbison, *Miami Dade Community College*; E. B. Duffee, *Anne Arundel Community College*; Craig Emmert, *Texas Tech University*; John H. Gauger, *Lehigh County Community College*; Michael Gilbert, *Pensacola Junior College*; Stephen D. Haag, *Austin Community College*; Scott Hays, *Southern Illinois University*; Richard Allen hays, *University of Northern Iowa*; Brian D. Humes, *University of Nebraska*; Jonathan Hurwitz, *University of Pittsburgh*; Daniel P. Gregory, *El Camino Community College*; Thomas Keating, *Arizona State University*; Doris R. Knight, *Holyoke Community College*; Joseph Kunkel, *Mankato State University*; Michael D. Martinez, *University of Florida*; Michael LeMay, *California State University at San Bernardino*; Arthur Levy, *University of South Florida*; R. M. Peterson, *California State Polytechnic University at Pomona*; James Puetz, *North Harris County Community College*; Robert Miewald, *University of Nebraska*; Andrew Milnor, *State University of New York at Binghamton*; Richard Millsap, *Texas Christian University*; Farzeen Nasri, *Ventura College*; Albert Nelson, *University of Wisconsin at La Crosse*; Charles Noble, *California State University at Long Beach*; Anthony Nownes, *University of Utah*; James W. Riddlesperger, *Texas Christian University*; John Shockly, *Western Illinois University*; Frederick I. Solop, *Northern Arizona University*; Mark Somma, *Texas Tech University*; Priscilla Southwell, *University of Oregon*; A. J. Stevens, *California State University at Long Beach*; Jacqueline Switzer, *Southern Oregon State College*; C. Neal Tate, *University of North Texas*; Thomas D. Ungs, *University of Tennessee*; J. David Woodard, *Clemson University*; Alan S. Wyner, *University of California at Santa Barbara*.

About the Author

W. LANCE BENNETT is professor of political science at the University of  Washington in Seattle. He has published widely on American politics, particularly on the topics of mass media, public opinion, elections, and U.S. foreign policy. Among his other books are *Public Opinion in American Politics, News: The Politics of Illusion,* and *The Governing Crisis: Media, Money, and Marketing in American Politics.* Professor Bennett holds a Ph.D. in political science from Yale University, and has been awarded a Woodrow Wilson Fellowship, the E. E. Schattschneider Award (of the American Political Science Association), a Kellogg Foundation Fellowship, a National Science Foundation research grant, and a Fulbright Research Fellowship.

CONTENTS

PREFACE   vii

FEATURE ESSAYS   xxv

PHOTO ESSAYS: *THE PLAYERS*   xxix

PART I—THE AMERICAN DEMOCRACY: A USER'S MANUAL   1

Chapter 1– *The American Democracy: Culture, Institutions, and Power*   3

A NEWS STORY FOR ALL SEASONS: THE BUDGET   4
THE POLITICAL SYSTEM:CULTURE, INSTITUTIONS, AND POWER   6
POLITICAL CULTURE   8
   Culture and Ideology   10
   Cultural Politics   12
INSTITUTIONS   14
   Institutions and American Democracy   14
   Institutional Gridlock   15
   What Makes the Institutions Go?   17
POWER IN SOCIETY   18
   Majority Rule: The Majoritarian Theory of Power   18
   Group Power: The Pluralist Theory of Power   20
   Rule By the Few: The Elitist Theory of Power   21
   Who Governs?   23
THE POLITICAL SYSTEM REVISITED   26
A CITIZEN'S QUESTION: Power   28
KEY TERMS   29
SUGGESTED READINGS   29

PART II—CONSTITUTIONAL FOUNDATIONS   30

Chapter 2–   *From Revolution to Constitution: The Struggle for Government*   33

THE BIG NEWS OF 1786: THE REVOLUTION IS NOT OVER YET   34
THE POLITICS OF COMPROMISE: AN ENDURING TRADITION   36
   The Constitution as Politics and Political Philosophy   38
IN THE BEGINNING: THIRTEEN COLONIES IN SEARCH OF A REVOLUTION   38
   A Brief History of Rebellion   40
   The Politics of Colonialism   41
THE POLITICS OF REVOLUTION   43
   "No Taxation Without Representation"   48
   The Declaration of Independence   50
AFTER THE REVOLUTION: ONE NATION OR THIRTEEN?   51
   The Articles of Confederation   51
THE POLITICS OF THE CONSTITUTION   52
   Scrap the Articles: The Virginia Plan   56
   Save the Articles: The New Jersey Plan   56
   Representation: The Great Compromise   57
   The Unkindest Compromise: Slavery   58
   The President: Avoiding Demigods and Demagogues   59
   The Supreme Court, etc.: The Rest Was Easy   60
   How the Delegates Saw It   60
SELLING THE CONSTITUTION: THE *FEDERALIST* PAPERS   61
THE BILL OF RIGHTS   64
THE POLITICS OF COMPROMISE REVISITED   67
A CITIZEN'S QUESTION: Authority   68
KEY TERMS   69
SUGGESTED READINGS   69

Chapter 3–   *The Constitutional Design of Power*   71

GOVERNMENTAL GRIDLOCK: NEW STORY OR OLD?   72
THE CONSTITUTIONAL POWER CHART   74
INSTITUTIONAL DESIGN: SEPARATING THE BRANCHES   75
   A System of Checks and Balances   75
   The Legislative Article   78
   The Executive Article   80
   The Judicial Article   81
   Making Government Difficult by Design   83
FEDERAL DESIGN: DIVIDING POWERS WITH THE STATES   83
   National Supremacy vs. States Rights   84
   Interstate Relations   85
   The Supremacy Clause   85
   The Denial of Powers   85
THE "LIVING CONSTITUTION"   85
   The Bill of Rights   85
   Amending the Constitution   91
   A Flexible Interpretation Process   98

WHAT KIND OF GOVERNMENT: THE STRUCTURE OF POWER   99
  Who Governs?   99
THE CONSTITUTIONAL POWER CHART REVISITED   102
A CITIZEN'S QUESTION: The Constitution   104
KEY TERMS   105
SUGGESTED READINGS   105

Chapter 4– *The Politics of Federalism*   107

THE NEWS ABOUT A NEW FEDERALISM   108
WHY FEDERALISM MATTERS   109
WHAT IS FEDERALISM? DEFINITIONS AND CONCEPTS   110
  Federalism and Big Government: Disarming A Loaded Concept   111
THE CONSTITUTIONAL DEBATE: COMPETING THEORIES OF FEDERAL POWER   114
  Victories for the Nation-Centered View   115
  Victories for the State-Centered View   117
  The Civil War and the Deadlock of Federalism   118
THREE MODELS OF FEDERALISM   120
POLITICAL LIFE IN THREE ERAS OF FEDERAL POWER   122
  Dual Federalism (1800–1937)   122
  Cooperative Federalism (1937–1968)   127
  A New Federalism? (1968–Today)   130
WHY FEDERALISM MATTERS REVISITED   138
  State Experimentation   138
  Local Governments Take the Lead   140
  The Problem of Growing Inequalities   141
A CITIZEN'S QUESTION: State and National Citizenship   142
KEY TERMS   142
SUGGESTED READINGS   143

Chapter 5– *The Personal Constitution: Civil Liberties and Civil
            Rights*   145

THE NEWS ABOUT HARASSMENT   146
THE POLITICS OF RIGHTS   148
  How Americans Think About Rights   148
  A Political Culture Based on Rights   150
CLARIFYING THE CONCEPTS: CIVIL LIBERTIES AND CIVIL RIGHTS   150
  The American Rights Tradition   151
  A Working Definition of Liberties and Rights   152
CIVIL LIBERTIES   152
  Dual Citizenship   154
  Freedom of Speech and the First Amendment   155
  Freedom of Religion   160
  Freedom from Injustice   163
  The Right to Privacy   165
  The Civil Liberties Scorecard   168
CIVIL RIGHTS   168
  A Second American Revolution   168
  The Civil Rights Movement   171
  Expanding the Definition of Civil Rights   177
  The Difficulty of Righting Social Wrongs   178

THE POLITICS OF RIGHTS REVISITED   181
A CITIZEN'S QUESTION: Rights   184
KEY TERMS   185
SUGGESTED READINGS   185

PART III—THE CIVIC CULTURE: PARTICIPATION AND POWER   187

Chapter 6– *Public Opinion: Culture, Society, and the Individual*   189

OPINION POLLS IN THE NEWS   190
OPINION, POWER, AND DEMOCRACY   192
    Defining Public Opinion   192
    Opinion and Democracy   193
    The Power of Opinion   193
    The Politics of Public Opinion   197
OPINION FORMATION AND CHANGE   198
    Socialization and Political Learning   198
    Social Characteristics and Opinion   202
    How Opinions Change   206
POLITICAL CULTURE AND IDEOLOGY   208
    Ideology   208
    American Pragmatism   212
THE BATTLE FOR PUBLIC OPINION   212
    Climates of Opinions   212
    The Uses of Political Symbols   214
    The Media   215
DESCRIBING AND MEASURING OPINION   215
    Describing Opinion Formations   215
    Opinion Measurement   218
OPINION, POWER, AND DEMOCRACY REVISITED   221
A CITIZEN'S QUESTION: Forming More Effective Opinions   224
KEY TERMS   223
SUGGESTED READINGS   225

Chapter 7– *Participation: The Forms of Political Action*   227

GOOD NEWS AND BAD NEWS ABOUT VOTING   228
VARIETIES OF PARTICIPATION AND THE NEEDS OF DEMOCRACY   230
    Participation and Personal Commitment   231
    Conventional and Unconventional Participation   232
VOTING   237
    The Psychological Basis of Voting   238
    The Social Basis of Voting   245
    Election Laws and Procedures   249
    How Does It All Add Up?   252
JOINING GROUPS   254

PARTICIPATING IN SOCIAL MOVEMENT ACTIVITIES 254
    Making a Commitment to Unconventional Participation 257
    Mobilizing People: What it Takes 257
    Movements and Elections 262
NONPARTICIPATION 263
VARIETIES OF PARTICIPATION AND THE NEEDS OF DEMOCRACY REVISITED 264
A CITIZEN'S QUESTION: Getting Involved 266
KEY TERMS 267
SUGGESTED READINGS 267

Chapter 8– *Interest-Group Politics* 269

WINNING AND LOSING: THE INTEREST-GROUP STORY 270
DEMOCRACY AND INTEREST-GROUP POLITICS 271
    The Turbulent History of Organized Interests 273
    The Dilemmas of Interest-Group Democracy 275
WHO ARE THE INTERESTS? 278
    How Many Are There? 278
    Reasons for the Growth of Groups 281
    How Groups Keep Their Members 282
HOW INTEREST GROUPS OPERATE POLITICALLY 284
    Lobbying 284
    Campaign Contributions 290
    Litigation 293
    Mobilizing Public Opinion 295
    Mixed Strategies: The Auto Lobby and Fuel Economy Laws 298
GROUP ORGANIZATION AND RESOURCES 302
DEMOCRACY AND INTEREST-GROUP POLITICS REVISITED 303
    The Future of Interests 306
    The Public Interest 306
A CITIZEN'S QUESTION: Joining Interest Groups 308
KEY TERMS 309
SUGGESTED READINGS 309

Chapter 9– *Political Parties: Engines of Government* 311

HEARD THE NEWS? THE PARTY'S OVER 312
A DEFINITION OF PARTIES 314
PARTIES ON TRIAL: THE CHARGES 315
A BRIEF HISTORY OF PARTIES 316
    Controlling Parties by Constitutional Design 316
    The Two-Party System 318
    Third-Party Politics 320
THE POLITICS BEHIND THE TWO-PARTY SYSTEM 324
    Strong Culture, Weak Parties 324
    The Institutional Basis of Two-Party Democracy 324
    Social Power and the Party System 324
WHAT THE PARTIES DO AND HOW THEY DO IT 326
    The Functions of Political Parties 326
    Choices and Channels for Political Demands 326
    Developing Leaders, Nominating Candidates 329
    Governing 335

POLITICAL CRISIS, VOTER ALIGNMENTS, AND PARTY GOVERNMENT   336
  The Parties and Political Change   336
  The Party System Today   337
THE CHARGES AGAINST THE PARTIES REVISITED   339
A CITIZEN'S QUESTION: Party Activism   342
KEY TERMS   341
SUGGESTED READINGS   343

Chapter 10–*Campaigns and Elections: The Political Guidance System*   345

CAMPAIGNS TRY TO BEAT, NOT MEET, THE PRESS   346
ELECTIONS AND AMERICAN DEMOCRACY   348
  Direct *vs.* Representative Democracy   348
A BRIEF HISTORY OF ELECTIONS   350
GETTING ELECTED: THE NUTS AND BOLTS   353
  The Nomination   353
  The Convention   356
  The Campaign   357
GETTING ELECTED: THE POLITICAL REALITY   360
  The Great Money Chase   362
  Marketing the Candidates   369
  Media Management   371
THE SELLING OF THE PRESIDENT 1988   375
THE SELLING OF THE PRESIDENT 1992   377
REFORMING THE SYSTEM   380
ELECTIONS AND AMERICAN DEMOCRACY REVISITED   383
A CITIZEN'S QUESTION: Elections Beyond Voting   384
KEY TERMS   383
SUGGESTED READINGS   384

Chapter 11–*Mass Mediated Democracy*   387

THE MEDIA GO TO WAR   388
INFORMATION, POWER, AND DEMOCRACY   391
  What's News?   392
  The Medium and the Message   395
  Information Characteristics of Mass Media News   396
THE PRESS AND THE GOVERNMENT   399
  Government Regulation of the Press   399
  Truth and the First Amendment   402
MAKING THE NEWS   403
  The Working Relations Between Press and Politicians   404
  How to Make the News   405
  How Do Outsiders Make the News?   409
PUBLIC OPINION AND THE NEWS   410
  The Battle for Public Opinion   410
  Setting the Agenda   413
INSIDE THE NEWS ORGANIZATION: THE ECONOMICS OF INFORMATION   414
  A Social and Economic History of the American Press   414
  How Journalists Work   416
  Routine News: Deadlines, Beats, and Packs   417
  Popular Tastes and News   420

INFORMATION, POWER, AND DEMOCRACY REVISITED   422
A CITIZEN'S QUESTION: Political Information   424
KEY TERMS   423
SUGGESTED READINGS   425

PART IV—INSTITUTIONS AT WORK   427

Chapter 12–*Congress: The Legislative Process*   429

AN END TO GRIDLOCK? MORE OF THE STORY   430
LAWS, LEGISLATURES, AND REPRESENTATION   431
    Constitutional Design: Legislation and Representation   432
    A Brief History of Legislatures   433
    The Logic Behind the American Legislature   435
    Congress Then and Now   436
    Representation Revisited   437
CONGRESS, SOCIETY, AND PUBLIC OPINION   439
    The Social Composition of Congress   439
HOW CONGRESS USES ITS POWERS   442
    Making Laws   442
    Overseeing the Executive   452
    The Politics of Pork   455
    Delivering Services (from Our House to Yours)   456
    Getting Reelected, Of Course   457
LAWS, LEGISLATURES, AND REPRESENTATION REVISITED   459
A CITIZEN'S QUESTION: Evaluating Congress   460
KEY TERMS   460
SUGGESTED READINGS   461

Chapter 13–*Congress: Power and Organization*   463

NO NEWS IS GOOD NEWS: WHY CONGRESS HAS AN IMAGE PROBLEM   464
SOME GOOD REASONS WHY CONGRESS LOOKS BAD   465
THE POWER STRUCTURE OF CONGRESS   466
THE INDIVIDUAL VERSUS THE ORGANIZATION   468
    The Career Management System   468
    Congress in the Media Age   470
TWO CULTURES: NORMS AND RULES IN THE HOUSE AND SENATE   473
    The Senate Club   473
    The House Fraternity   475
    Fighting Styles: The Rules for Debates   476
    The Breakdown in Tradition   478
POWER IN COMMITTEES   478
    A Map of the Committee World   478
    Power to the Subcommittees   482
    Pros and Cons of the Committee System   484
PARTY POLITICS AND CONGRESSIONAL LEADERSHIP   484
    The Problem of Party Loyalty   485
    How the Parties Govern Congress   486

REFORMING CONGRESS   490
   Reforming the Party Machine   490
   Reforming the Staff   491
   Reforming the Committee System   492
   Reforming Campaign Finance   493
   The Results of a Hundred Years of Reform   494
   Term Limits: Reform from the Outside   494
THE POWER STRUCTURE OF CONGRESS REVISITED   495
A CITIZEN'S QUESTION: Term Limits and Other Reforms   498
KEY TERMS   497
SUGGESTED READINGS   499

Chapter 14–*The Executive: Presidential Power and National Leadership*   501

THE GREATEST POLITICAL JUGGLING ACT   502
PRESIDENTS, PUBLICS, AND POWER   503
   The Opinion Rally   505
   Presidential Approval   506
TOO MANY RESPONSIBILITIES, TOO LITTLE POWER?   507
THE HISTORY OF AN OFFICE   508
   Going Public   509
THE VICE PRESIDENT   513
WHAT PRESIDENTS DO: THE CONSTITUTIONAL JOB DESCRIPTION   514
   The Powers of Office   515
THE REST OF THE JOB: TRADITIONAL PRESIDENTIAL ROLES   517
   Chief National Symbol   517
   Party Leader   518
THE PRESIDENT IN ACTION: FORMAL POWERS VS. INSIDE POLITICS   518
   The Executive Arena   519
   The Legislative Arena   520
   The Military and Foreign Policy Arena   524
THE SECRET OF SUCCESS: THE POWER TO PERSUADE   528
   The Media Spotlight   528
THE PRESIDENTIAL CHARACTER   530
   Searching for the Ideal Presidential Personality   532
TOO MANY RESPONSIBILITIES, TOO LITTLE POWER REVISITED   533
A CITIZEN'S QUESTION: Presidential Performance   534
KEY TERMS   535
SUGGESTED READINGS   535

Chapter 15–*The Executive: Managing the Bureaucracy*   537

OLD NEWS: CONTROLLING THE BUREAUCRACY IS HARD TO DO   538
A POLITICAL HOTBED   539
   Bureaucratic Politics: The Case of Environmental Regulation   540
IMPLEMENTING THE LAW: THE BUREAUCRATIC MISSION   542
BUREAUCRATIC ORGANIZATION   543
   Decoding the Alphabet Soup   544
   The Command System   547
HISTORICAL CHANGES IN BUREAUCRATIC POLITICS   549
   The Spoils System   550
   The Rise of a Professional Civil Service   551
   The Rise of an Activist Bureaucracy   551
   The Rise of the Bureaucratic State   552

THE POLITICS OF BUREAUCRATIC INTERESTS   552
  Iron Triangles Revisited   553
POLITICS IN THE DEPARTMENTS AND THE CABINET   554
THE EXECUTIVE OFFICE OF THE PRESIDENT   558
  A Secret Government?   559
  Shrinking the White House Establishment   560
THE PRESIDENT'S PERSONAL STAFF   562
THE POLITICAL HOTBED REVISITED   563
A CITIZEN'S QUESTION: Bureaucratic Politics   563
KEY TERMS   564
SUGGESTED READINGS   565

Chapter 16–*The Judiciary: Courts, Law, and Justice*   567

A DAY IN COURT: A STORY FOR ALL CITIZENS   568
LAW AND SOCIETY   570
  Types of Law   572
  Jurisdiction   574
LAW AND POLITICS   574
  Judicial Review   575
  Separation of Powers Cases   578
LAW AND PROCEDURE IN THE FEDERAL COURTS   581
  Cases, Trials, and Procedures   581
  The Basis of Legal Judgment   582
  Courtroom Ritual   582
CONGRESS AND THE ORGANIZATION OF THE FEDERAL COURTS   583
  The Politics of Judicial Organization   585
HOW THE SUPREME COURT WORKS   586
  Jurisdiction and Paths to the Court   586
  Case Selection   588
  Judicial Philosophy: Activism vs. Self-Restraint   589
  The Endless Debate: What the Framers Intended   590
  Deciding Cases and Writing Opinions   592
  Inside the Court   594
  The Politics of Nominations   598
LAW AND SOCIETY REVISITED   599
A CITIZEN'S QUESTION: Justice   600
KEY TERMS   601
SUGGESTED READINGS   601

PART V—POLICY: THE SUM OF THE PARTS   603

Chapter 17–*The Policy Process*   605

NEWS FEATURE: THE AMERICAN AGENDA   606
THE MANY PATHS TO POLICY   608
  Policy and Politics   608
  The Politics of Compromise   609

POLICY INSIDE THE SYSTEM   612
  Power and Policy   613
  Culture and Symbolic Politics   613
  Constitutional Design: Institutions and Federalism   614
BUILDING THE POLICY AGENDA   616
  The Bottom-Up Path to Policy   619
  The Top-Down Path to Policy   620
  Getting Health Care on the Agenda Again   622
THE REST OF THE PROCESS: FROM GOVERNMENT TO SOCIETY   624
  The Decision Process   624
  Policy Logjams   625
  Looking for Windows of Opportunity   626
  Implementation and Evaluation   626
THE MANY PATHS TO POLICY REVISITED   627
A CITIZEN'S QUESTION: Policy   628
KEY TERMS   629
SUGGESTED READINGS   629

Chapter 18–*Social Policy: Managing the Quality of Life*   631

A STORY OF NATIONAL RENEWAL   632
POLITICS AND SOCIAL POLICIES   633
  The Problems, The Politics, The Proposals   634
MEDICAL ALERT: THE NATIONAL HEALTH CARE CRISIS   636
  The Problem: Soaring Costs, Human Needs   637
  The Politics: The Power of Interests   640
  The Proposals: Who Pays, Who Regulates   644
EDUCATING THE NATION: KEEPING UP WITH THE COMPETITION   647
  The Problem: Preparing People for Life   647
  The Politics: Maximum Federalism   649
  The Proposals: Getting Around Federal Obstacles   651
FULL SYSTEM ALERT: POVERTY, WELFARE, AND SOCIETY   652
  The Problem: Is Poverty Political?   654
  The Politics: A Deep Cultural Divide   656
  The Proposals: Crossing the Cultural Divide   659
POLITICS AND SOCIAL POLICIES REVISITED   664
A CITIZEN'S QUESTION: Social Responsibility   665
KEY TERMS   666
SUGGESTED READINGS   667

Chapter 19–*Economic Policy: Paying For It All*   669

THIS NEWS STORY JUST COST YOU $5,000   670
ECONOMY, GOVERNMENT, AND SOCIETY   673
  Economic Policy: What's Similar, What's Different?   673
A SHORT LESSON IN POLITICAL ECONOMY   676
  From Laissez Faire to Government Activism   676
  The Economy Defies the Theories   679
  Contemporary Economic Theory   680
POLITICS AND ECONOMIC POLICIES   682
THE LEVERS OF ECONOMIC POLICY   682
  Fiscal Policy   682
  Monetary Policy   688
  Regulatory Policy   692

ECONOMY, GOVERNMENT, AND SOCIETY REVISITED   694
    New Economic Ideas   697
A CITIZEN'S QUESTION: Economic Involvement   698
KEY TERMS   698
SUGGESTED READINGS   699

Chapter 20–*Foreign and Defense Policy: National Security and
                    World Power*   701

THE NEW WORLD ORDER   702
THE RISE OF THE UNITED STATES AS A WORLD POWER   704
    Culture, Ideology, and History   704
    Economic Interests and Military Power   708
THE COLD WAR   710
    Foreign Policy in the National Security State   714
    The Great Nuclear Poker Game   715
MAKING FOREIGN POLICY IN THE COLD WAR WORLD   715
    Ideological Consensus and Presidential Leadership   716
    The Foreign Policy Establishment   716
    Congress, the Interests, and the Public   718
THE DOMESTICATION OF THE FOREIGN POLICY PROCESS   719
    Vietnam and the Breakdown of Consensus   719
    Searching for New Doctrines   721
    A Policy Breakdown?   722
DEFENSE: A SOLUTION LOOKING FOR A PROBLEM?   725
    The Peace Dividend   726
    The Defense Establishment and the Economy   728
    New Roles for the Military?   730
THE NEW WORLD ORDER REVISITED   731
    Power in a Multipolar World   732
    Is U.S. Power in Decline?   734
A CITIZEN'S QUESTION: Foreign Policy Participation   733
KEY TERMS   734
SUGGESTED READINGS   735
    Appendices
    Federalist Paper No. 10   739
    Federalist Paper No. 51   742
    President and Party Control of Congress   745
    Twentieth-Century Supreme Court Justices   751

    Glossary   755
    Notes   775
    Reference Index   799
    Subject and Name Index   805
    Literary and Photo Credits   827

FEATURE ESSAYS

BOX 1.1: HOW WE COMPARE
Attitudes About Individual Responsibility in Five Cultures   11
BOX 1.2: HOW WE COMPARE
Government Responsibility to Take Care of the Poor   13
BOX 1.3: INSIDE THE SYSTEM
Supporting Bill Clinton's Budget Plan: A "Patriotic Duty"?   27

BOX 2.1: INSIDE THE SYSTEM
Governing Ideas: The Foundations of Political Culture   39
BOX 2.2: HOW WE COMPARE
The Unwritten British Constitution   49
BOX 2.3: INSIDE THE SYSTEM
A Constitution Written by a "Power Elite"? Or. . .   54
BOX 2.4: INSIDE THE SYSTEM
A Constitution Designed to Promote Pluralism?   55

BOX 3.1: INSIDE THE SYSTEM
Why Sharing Constitutional Powers Is Not Easy But It Is Important: The
    "Iran-*contra*" Affair   77
BOX 3.2: INSIDE THE SYSTEM
The Importance of Loopholes in Constitutions: The "Elastic Clause" as Interpreted
    by the Supreme Court in the Case of *McCulloch v. Maryland* (1819)   79
BOX 3.3: INSIDE THE SYSTEM
The Principle of Judicial Review: The Case of *Marbury v. Madison*   82
BOX 3.4: INSIDE THE SYSTEM
A Cure for Gridlock?: Political Parties as Means of Coordinating Power
    Among the Separate Branches   83
BOX 3.5: HOW WE COMPARE
The Organization of Government Power in England   103

BOX 4.1: HOW WE COMPARE
Federal and Unitary Systems of Government   111
BOX 4.2: INSIDE THE SYSTEM
Political Culture and Big Government: Clarifying Some Myths about American
    Federalism   115
BOX 4.3: HOW WE COMPARE
Canadian Federalism   121
BOX 4.4: INSIDE THE SYSTEM
Social Power in One Era of Federalism: Elite Rule and Dual Federalism   125
BOX 4.5: INSIDE THE SYSTEM
The Political Struggle for a New Federalism   133

BOX 5.1: INSIDE THE SYSTEM
Cultural Themes and Personal Views of Rights   151
BOX 5.2: HOW WE COMPARE
American Civil Liberties: A Comparative Luxury?   153
BOX 5.3: INSIDE THE SYSTEM
Incorporating Civil Liberties and Civil Rights into National Life, *Selectively*   155
BOX 5.4: INSIDE THE SYSTEM
Why Civil Liberties Matter: The Case of John Henry Faulk   157
BOX 5.5: INSIDE THE SYSTEM
U.S. Flag: Tussle Over the National Icon   159
BOX 5.6: INSIDE THE SYSTEM
The Power of Ordinary People: Rosa Parks   177

BOX 6.1: INSIDE THE SYSTEM
Opinion and Power in Environmental Politics   197
BOX 6.2: HOW WE COMPARE
The Importance of Religion in Five Democracies   207
BOX 6.3: HOW WE COMPARE
Ranking of Different Nations: How Citizens Place Themselves Ideologically   211
BOX 6.4: INSIDE THE SYSTEM
Focus Groups: A Power Tool for Opinion Management   221

BOX 7.1: INSIDE THE SYSTEM
Participation and Political Change   235
BOX 7.2: HOW WE COMPARE
Voter Turnout in Eight Industrial Democracies   239
BOX 7.3: INSIDE THE SYSTEM
Gerrymandering: A Way of Making Votes Count Unequally   251
BOX 7.4: INSIDE THE SYSTEM
Some Social Movements In Contemporary America   256

BOX 8.1: HOW WE COMPARE
Corporatism: Another Kind of Interest System   277
BOX 8.2: INSIDE THE SYSTEM
What Shapes the American Interest-Group System and How Well Does It Work?   279
BOX 8.3: INSIDE THE SYSTEM
Regulating the Lobbyists   287
BOX 8.4: INSIDE THE SYSTEM
Saving the Osprey: An Endangered Species?   292

BOX 9.1: HOW WE COMPARE
Small Parties, Big Power: Why Small Parties Can Thrive with Proportional
    Representation   319
BOX 9.2: INSIDE THE SYSTEM
The Politics Behind the Differences in the Republican and Democratic Party
    Platforms, 1992   327

BOX 10.1: HOW WE COMPARE
Direct Democracy, Anyone?   351
BOX 10.2: INSIDE THE SYSTEM
The Forces That Shape Campaigning Today   361
BOX 10.3: INSIDE THE SYSTEM
The Media Cover the Ad Campaigns   372

BOX 11.1: HOW WE COMPARE
Public and Private Broadcasting Systems in Other Nations   401
BOX 11.2: INSIDE THE SYSTEM
Outsiders and Insiders Battle for Public Opinion Through News Coverage   411

BOX 12.1: INSIDE THE SYSTEM
The Enduring Limits on the Powers of Congress   433
BOX 12.2: INSIDE THE SYSTEM
Home-Style Representation   437
BOX 12.3: HOW WE COMPARE
Percentage of Woman in the Legislatures of Twenty-Five Democratic Nations 441
BOX 12.4: INSIDE THE SYSTEM
Some Power Brokers Still Remain: John (The Truck) Dingell   450

BOX 13.1: INSIDE THE SYSTEM
How Outside Political Forces Affect Politics Inside the Congress   469
BOX 13.2: INSIDE THE SYSTEM
The Political World of Congress: Norms and Customs   479
BOX 13.3: HOW WE COMPARE
Committees in the French National Assembly   483

BOX 14.1: INSIDE THE SYSTEM
The President as Focal Point of the System   507
BOX 14.2: HOW WE COMPARE
The Presidency in France   509
BOX 14.3: INSIDE THE SYSTEM
Going Public: A Way of Expanding Weak Institutional Powers   512
BOX 14.4: INSIDE THE SYSTEM
Contrasting the Persuasion Styles of Franklin Roosevelt and Bill Clinton 529

BOX 15.1: INSIDE THE SYSTEM
Why Americans Hate Bureaucracy   541
BOX 15.2: HOW WE COMPARE
The Political Bureaucracy in Mexico   551
BOX 15.3: INSIDE THE SYSTEM
Power in the Bureaucratic State   553

BOX 16.1: INSIDE THE SYSTEM
Why the Judicial Branch Is So Important in American Politics   572
BOX 16.2: HOW WE COMPARE
The Judiciary in Denmark, Canada, and Germany   573
BOX 16.3: INSIDE THE SYSTEM
One Legal System or Many? Why Jurisdiction Can Be Complicated   575
BOX 16.4: INSIDE THE SYSTEM
The Politics of the Rehnquist Court as the Sum of Individual Legal Philosophies 597

BOX 17.1: INSIDE THE SYSTEM
The Politics of Policy Compromise: Energy *vs.* Environment *vs.* the Economy 611
BOX 17.2: HOW WE COMPARE
Making Environmental Policy in France   612
BOX 17.3: INSIDE THE SYSTEM
Why Simple Policy Questions Can Become Complex: the Case of Military
Policy on Homosexuals   617

BOX 18.1: HOW WE COMPARE
What Can We Learn from German Health Care?   645
BOX 18.2: INSIDE THE SYSTEM
How Federalism Affects National Education Policy   650

BOX 19.1: INSIDE THE SYSTEM
How Elite Influence Contributed to the Greatest Financial Scandal of the 1800s   675
BOX 19.2: HOW WE COMPARE
The Tax Structures of the Seven Leading Industrial Nations   685

BOX 20.1: INSIDE THE SYSTEM
The Great Cultural Debate: Was Rebuilding the World Economy After
World War II Self-Interest or Foolish Generosity?   711
BOX 20.2: HOW WE COMPARE
Government Investments in Research and Development in the United States
and Europe   727

PHOTO ESSAYS: *The Players*

CHAPTER 1   *Who Governs?*   19

CHAPTER 2   *Reconciling Differences*   53

CHAPTER 3   *An Ever-Expanding Charter*   97

CHAPTER 4   *Whither the Welfare State?*   139

CHAPTER 5   *Parties in the Struggle*   173

CHAPTER 6   *A Division of Supporters*   213

CHAPTER 7   *Unconventional Means. . .*   259

CHAPTER 8   *The Faces of Influence*   301

CHAPTER 9   *Political Pathfinders*   332

CHAPTER 10   *Of Candidates and Consultants*   376

CHAPTER 11   *Anchoring the Ship of State*   393

CHAPTER 12   *Commanders within Congress*   451

CHAPTER 13   *Cardinals of Capitol Hill*   480

CHAPTER 14   *A Presence on the World Stage*   516

CHAPTER 15   *A Diverse Cabinet?*   557

CHAPTER 16   *Judging the Constitution*   593

CHAPTER 17   *Operation Policy Storm*   618

CHAPTER 18   *Some Health(y) Policy Debate*   643

CHAPTER 19   *Negotiating an Economic Policy*   683

CHAPTER 20   *Domesticating Foreign Policy?*   723

INSIDE THE SYSTEM
CULTURE, INSTITUTIONS, AND POWER
IN AMERICAN POLITICS

Part I

THE AMERICAN DEMOCRACY:
A USER'S MANUAL

CHAPTER 1

The American Democracy: Culture, Institutions, and Power

• • •

The happiness of the people is the sole end of government.
—*JOHN ADAMS*

• • •

In an autocracy one person has his way; in an aristocracy a
few people have their way; in a democracy no one has his way.
—*CELIA GREEN*

• • •

If liberty and equality, as is thought by some, are chiefly to be
found in democracy, they will be best attained when all
persons alike share in the government to the utmost.
—*ARISTOTLE*

• • •

The American Democracy: Culture, Institutions, and Power

- **A NEWS STORY FOR ALL SEASONS: THE BUDGET**

- **THE POLITICAL SYSTEM: CULTURE, INSTITUTIONS, AND POWER**

- **POLITICAL CULTURE**
  Culture and Ideology
  Cultural Politics

- **INSTITUTIONS**
  Institutions and American Democracy
  Institutional Gridlock?
  What Makes the Institutions Go?

- **POWER IN SOCIETY**
  Majority Rule: The Majoritarian Theory of Power
  Group Power: The Pluralist Theory of Power
  Rule By the Few: The Elitist Theory of Power
  Who Governs?

- **THE POLITICAL SYSTEM REVISITED**

- **A CITIZEN'S QUESTION: Power**

- **KEY TERMS**

- **SUGGESTED READINGS**

It was the subject of Bill Clinton's first major speech to the nation after he became president in 1993. Before that, candidate Ross Perot surprised the experts by turning this dull subject into half-hour "infomercials" during his 1992 presidential campaign. Perot's folksy talks drew better ratings than entertainment programs scheduled on the other networks. Talk shows have been crowded with people giving their advice on this subject. What is this political topic, once known for making eyes glaze over, that has become the talk of the nation? The answer is the national budget.

The figures on this "National Debt Clock," overlooking vacant office space in midtown Manhattan, advance continuously to reflect the mounting government deficit. Unfortunately, clashing views on how to handle this crisis make reducing the federal deficit a considerably more difficult task than tracking it.

Budget battles in Washington have captured an increasing share of the news in recent years. Dramatic headlines tell tales of neglected social needs, failing public services, empty tills, and politicians who seem unable to deal with it all. Each year the failure to raise enough in revenues to meet expenses adds more weight to the national debt. The debt is the sum of budget deficits from past years—a figure that now exceeds four trillion dollars. These dramatic developments are delivered in the daily news with headlines like these: THE BUDGET DEFICIT SLOWLY EATS AWAY AT U.S. PROSPERITY;[1] CONGRESS PREDICTS RECORD DEFICIT;[2] and HOW TO BUILD A BOGUS BUDGET.[3] Although the news may seem alarming, it is a good idea to understand the politics behind the budget before drawing any conclusions. This chapter illustrates how complex issues like budgets reflect the workings of the American political system.

To begin with, it helps to remember that the stories told in the news about personal battles between Congress and the president over taxes and spending are fragments of a much larger political scene. There is valuable information in news stories, but, like all information, it should be used selectively and analyzed on the basis of broader understandings of how the government works. One of the morals of news stories about the budget was explained by political humorist Russell Baker:

> This week we had the budget. The budget is a big story in Washington, which is probably why we have it. To understand the budget, remember: The budget is not a budget. It is a story.
>
> Naturally the news industry loves it. It sets up so many stories to get the news industry over the dull patches in the coming year. Examples:
>
> "President Accuses Congress of Busting Budget."
> "Congress Accuses president of Budget Fakery."
> "GOP Blames Dems for Budget Overruns."
> "Dems Charge GOP With Etcetera . . ."[4]

Truly a story for all seasons, the annual budget news breaks first in the grey days of winter when the White House submits its budget proposal to Capitol Hill. This budget request is for funds to keep programs running, along with suggestions about cuts and proposals for new initiatives. Fearful of upsetting their own political fortunes, presidents ask their top budget advisor, the Director of the Office of Management and Budget, how much cutting the budget can take without damaging the economy or angering political supporters. The answer seldom comes close to the amount needed to balance the budget. Thus, the winter season closes as the president hands the budget bomb to Congress, often with great fanfare in the news about how the proposal will reduce the deficit and move the country toward a more balanced budget.

Congress has its own budget department called the Congressional Budget Office, which runs its own economic forecasts. Although congressional forecasts are usually less optimistic than presidential ones, Bill Clinton proposed the bold idea of Congress and the executive both using congressional estimates so they could at least start their negotiations from the same set of figures. Even with a common starting point, however, there are other political pressures that keep Congress from getting carried away with budget-balancing. The curtain goes up (and the news cameras roll) on Act II: the Spring Budget Hearing Season. Rows of bureaucrats, experts, and cabinet officers troop up Capitol Hill to testify at various committee and subcommittee hearings about the importance of saving pet programs and to warn of dire consequences if they are cut. Take military spending, for example: Despite the end of the Cold War, generals still express their concerns inside the hearing chambers of Congress. Old warnings of Soviet aggression have been replaced with new ones about more exotic threats, ranging from narco-terrorism to destabilizing third-world insurgencies. When the generals are backed up by lobbyists, who are in turn backed up by campaign contributions from defense industries, which employ large numbers of voters in home districts, it can be tough to cut military programs even in peacetime.

Somewhere else in the Capitol, phone calls and postcards pour in promising voter revenge if senior citizens' health and retirement benefits are cut. And so, another huge chunk of the budget escapes another year's deficit reduction plan. Down the hall, a closed-door session within the small, wood-paneled chamber of the Senate Agriculture Committee finds a farm expert warning of foreign domination of food supplies if cuts are made in government price support payments to farmers. Speaking in political code, farm lobbyists also remind senators in private about their campaign contributions. Critics charge that interest-group pressures pull government in different directions, undermining the coherence of national policies in many areas like agriculture and farming. Conservative humorist P. J. O'Rourke has quipped that "farm policy, while complex, can be explained. What it can't be is believed."[5]

By the end of the spring budget hearing season, lawmakers begin twitching nervously and seem to be searching for a place to hide when reporters ask where the big cuts will be made and whether the budget will be any closer to balanced this year. If all goes well, the legislators make it to summer recess without sustaining too much media damage. Basking in a few weeks of relief after the spring hearings, the House and Senate finally produce their respective versions of the budget bill. The news spotlight then turns to House and Senate bills that are usually out of line with each other and at odds with the budget proposed by the president.

Afraid of automatic, across-the-board cuts that would endanger favorite programs and anger voters, weary politicians often return to the nation's capital for emergency summer budget conferences. If the deadlock is serious, the curtain goes up on the "summer reruns" of that endless political soap opera, *Budget or Bust.* In a favorite episode, the news camera closes in on the unhappy faces of lawmakers who would rather be out of the public eye and spending time with families and constituents back home. Instead, they swelter in the heat of Washington, the thermostat pushed up a few degrees by political pressures to save their programs while finding someone else's to cut. The news camera typically shows a group of powerful congressional leaders meeting in the Oval Office with the president. They stare politely at one another waiting for someone to sacrifice a sacred cow or break down and utter the fateful call to raise taxes. After applying the latest accounting wizardry, the leaders pronounce the most powerful magic incantation of all, saying they acted in the interest of "keeping the economy going." And so the curtain descends mercifully on Act III.

In a good year, Congress avoids a fall budget season by finishing up work on a compromise that both House and Senate can pass, and the president will sign in time to keep the paychecks and contracts flowing when the new fiscal year begins on October 1. In most years, an agreement is reached before the deadline. In a bad year, there is a political deadlock,

Applause initially met the Clinton–Gore economic program, as seen here in the response to President Clinton's February 1993 address to a joint session of Congress (chaired by House Speaker Thomas Foley, upper right). But praise soon gave way to behind-the-scenes wrangling, as members of Congress struggled to assert their institutional power to protect favored programs, raise taxes, or slash spending; in August, Congress approved a compromise plan by a one-vote margin in each chamber.

no agreement emerges, the treasury runs out of money, and news stories are filled with alarming talk of shutting down the government. When this happens, as it did in 1990, emergency funding bills must be passed until wrangling over the budget finally

produces an agreement. Once a budget bill passes Congress and is signed by the president, the budget news generally subsides for the next several months as politicians try to put the best light (or "spin") on the results. However, if it is an election year, candidates from each party can be counted on to go out on the campaign trail blaming each other for the mess in Washington. And so ends the annual budget news.

While the budget news can be interesting to read or watch, it seldom contains much explanation about *why* budget problems have become so politically difficult to work out. The news may not provide enough information or analysis for deciding how serious the budget crisis is, or even if it is serious enough to qualify as a true crisis. Some economists argue that the problem is not the size of the annual deficits or even the total national debt. The more fundamental problem may have to do with the political wrangling that makes budget agreement so difficult to reach and with the patchwork quality of government spending patterns.

To better understand the budget, we need to ask what features of politics and government are at work inside the system. The budget touches a number of core features of the American political system: *the attitudes of citizens* about government and what it should do; *the relations between government institutions* (in this case, Congress and the executive branch); and *the distribution of power in society*, as reflected in the pressure behind the various spending programs that make up the budget. This chapter introduces a simple way of thinking about a political system that makes it easier to keep track of the concepts encountered throughout this book, and to use them in thinking about actual political topics like the budget.

The Political System: Culture, Institutions, and Power

To understand budget battles and other political issues, it is helpful to start with a broad view of politics, society, and government. Politics involves *what people do to get what they want from government*. Political scientist Harold Lasswell defined politics this way in the title of a classic book on the subject, *Politics: Who Gets What, When, How*.[6] Politics has been called something of an art form because there are so many ways to express demands and resolve conflicts. People can rely on persuasion, bargaining, threats, protests, financial contributions, lawsuits, sending messages with their votes, and other ways of making their demands felt by government officials.

Without the constant pressure of politics, government might be rather dull. The main point of this book is to show how government works. The workings of government are easier to grasp, however, if we understand that politics is almost always operating somewhere in the picture. To help you remember this, we begin by placing the institutions of government inside a surrounding system of politics. The **political system** of the United States is characterized by a distinctive mix of *culture*, *governmental institutions*, and *power relations*; this mix distinguishes it from other nations and explains a great deal about how political issues develop and become resolved.

Political culture consists of the most broadly shared values and beliefs that affect what people want from government and how they express those political demands. Political scientist Byron Shafer defines political culture as "a set of public values about the way that politics should be conducted and the things that government should produce."[7]

When viewed as the basic language of politics that people use to communicate what they want from government, culture becomes easier to see. Demands for specific things like tax reforms or certain kinds of abortion policies become politically charged because they are expressed in cultural terms. Lower taxes may be promoted as good for *free enterprise*. Abortion conflicts lead to passionate debates about the *freedom to choose* and *the right to life*. Many of the programs in the budget reflect basic cultural values like security (social security insurance) or equality (programs to counteract discrimination), along with guidelines about how government should translate those values into action.

Culture is difficult to see as clearly as institutions, but impossible to ignore. Byron Shafer explains that one could not transplant American institutions to Britain or Japan and get anything close to American politics. "For that, you must have American political culture, too."[8] If culture is an important ingredient of a political system, equally important are the government institutions that respond to the demands of different groups in society.

Government institutions, such as courts, legislatures, and bureaucracies, are forums for hearing and responding to political demands. The design of institutions may be inspired by political philosophers and models from other nations, but institutions also

Cultural values are a major factor in determining what people want and expect from government. One group (left), protesting outside New York's Lincoln Center, suggests that spending on the arts deserves precedence over the military budget; but the second group (right), welcoming home captives of the 1979–81 Iranian hostage crisis, might argue that a strong defense is the foundation on which our liberties stand.

reflect cultural attitudes about power and procedure. For example, the national institutions of the United States were inspired by French and English philosophers, but were built upon practical American experience, including cultural concerns about limiting the powers of the central government. As a result, there is greater separation of powers among the three branches of the American government than is encountered in most other nations. It is common to describe the three branches of government as **separate institutions sharing powers**. While this design reflects the popular American attitude that power should be limited, it also creates problems for coordinating political actions like passing budgets. The division of budgetary powers among two legislative chambers and an independent executive explains, in part, why the annual budget battles are so difficult to work out.

Power in society is generally defined as the ability to get people, including decision makers, to do something they might not have done on their own. Power can come in the form of using wealth or personal connections to try to sway the decisions of government officials. Power also comes from the grass roots by organizing interest groups, voters' initiatives, or protesters pushing their issues onto the government agenda. In the case of the budget, the clash of power at different levels affects how much money the government spends on what kinds of things each year.

Because *culture, institutions,* and *power* all operate in political situations, it pays to understand each in a bit more detail. The distinctive features of culture, institutions, and power that define the American political system are useful for deciding *how the American government works, how well it works for different groups,* and in the end, just *how democratic it is.* Recognizing these simple concepts in action also enriches understanding of the politics operating in situations like the annual budget battles between the White House and Capitol Hill.

Political Culture

The cultural mix of political values and expectations about government makes political life unique in each country. For example, relatively few Swedes, whether they are of the left, center, or right, can imagine living in a society where the government does not provide substantial amounts for basic social welfare, including health care, education, housing, and support for raising children. In fact, an enduring image associated with government in Sweden is the responsibility for maintaining society as the "people's home" *(folkhem).* By contrast, Americans have long been divided politically over maintaining a social welfare system that is very modest by Swedish and most other (Canadian, Japanese, or European) standards. These characteristic political patterns reflect basic differences between the Swedish and American political cultures. Such differences roll through the political process, defining problems, and filling the agendas of government institutions. In Sweden, a more conservative government took power in the early 1990s only to discover that many of the people who had just elected it were not prepared to give up the benefits of the welfare state. In the United States, by contrast, even liberal politicians must be careful not to appear too supportive of the idea of welfare.

The American political culture has changed over the years, but there has been a remarkable durability in many of the core values and beliefs noted by observers of the American scene since the early 1800s.[9] Perhaps the most enduring characteristic of the American political culture is the claim to being a nation dedicated to the *freedom* of individuals who value life, liberty, property, and the "pursuit of happiness." These values affect the way many people think about living their lives. It is not surprising that a great deal of political attention is paid to promoting individual *freedoms* in society and to making sure that government protects the *liberty* widely regarded as essential for the "good

People's views on political topics are often influenced by the broad and some-times conflicting cultural themes with which those topics are associated—for example, the rights to "Life, Liberty, and the Pursuit of Happiness" asserted in the Declaration of Independence. In the ongoing battle over abortion, one side views "life" (that of the unborn child) as the overriding issue of the debate, while the other side perceives "liberty" (as implied by the "pro-choice" label) as the crucial theme.

life." Many Americans—more than citizens of other nations—believe that hard work and competition make life more rewarding, build character, and lead to other measures of individual recognition and success. (See "How We Compare" Box 1.1.) Not surprisingly, many Americans also oppose government welfare programs that give people a "free ride" and thereby undermine character, destroy the work ethic, and create a society of people who don't respect the hard work and the hard-won property of others. In many of the European democracies, by contrast, welfare is less contested because cultural ideals emphasize less individual responsibility and greater government responsibility for society.

In addition to freedom and the related ideals of liberty and individual expression, there are other important ideas in the American culture that define our political goals and conflicts. Here is a more detailed set of the **cultural themes** that motivate thought and action in American politics:

> **Freedom–liberty–individualism:** The cluster of ideas associated with liberty is probably the most popular and widely used symbolism in American politics. Many issues are defined as matters of personal freedom. Conflicts often erupt when the government or other people do things that individuals interpret as restricting their personal freedoms or civil liberties.
>
> **Volunteerism–altruism:** The enduring idea that many social problems can be solved by voluntary efforts involving charity or community-based action to help others in need.
>
> **Popular sovereignty–government by the people:** The ultimate power belongs to the people. Elected officials and bureaucrats must be accountable, answering ultimately to the will of the people.
>
> **Equality–equality of opportunity:** At the time of the Revolution, many Americans were concerned with the elimination of nobility and social status differences. Over the years, pressures for *political equality* came from women and minorities. In recent years, *economic equality* has become a more acceptable idea, usually taking the form of demands for *equal opportunity* and equal pay for equal jobs. Many Americans balance their feelings about equality against their concerns for individual freedoms.
>
> **Order–social control:** Based on the belief that too much freedom and social diversity can result in lawlessness and immorality. Many people advocate government restrictions on individual actions that harm or offend others. The origins of "law and order" politics begin here.
>
> **Patriotism–national unity:** Allegiance to the flag and the country may balance individualism and diversity. Surveys show Americans to be more patriotic than most other peoples and more willing to support their country whether it is right or wrong.

Because the above cultural themes condense so many different experiences for people, the ideals of culture motivate a great deal of political action and conflict in society. Ideas like freedom, liberty, and equality become powerful ways of thinking about and expressing political feelings. What we call **ideologies** generally draw upon some combination of the cultural themes outlined above.

Culture and Ideology

Depending on how they grow up, what they are taught, and how their social surroundings changed in adult life, people draw different lessons from this heritage of cultural ideas. Most people are fairly loose about how they apply these cultural ideals,

Attitudes About Individual Responsibility in Five Cultures

T he emphasis on individual responsibility is one of the most important themes in the American political culture. Compared to people in other societies, Americans are much more likely to take responsibility for *their* own successes and failures. This affects how social policies are debated, and how people think about solutions for problems like poverty, homelessness, and unemployment.

These opinion poll data compare responses in five nations to the proposition that "**Success in life is pretty much determined by forces outside our control.**" The figures show the percent who *disagree* with that idea.

SOURCE: Times Mirror Center for the People and the Press. Polling conducted in 1990–1991.

1.1

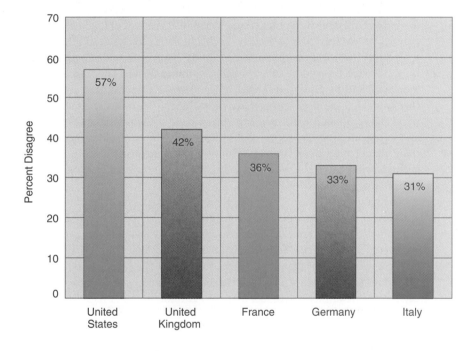

sounding more liberal about some subjects and more conservative about others. Not surprisingly, more people describe themselves as political moderates than as either liberals or conservatives. However, our national political debates are often led by political party leaders and political commentators who are more consistently ideological. Being ideological means emphasizing one set of cultural ideals over all others and applying those chosen ideals consistently to all issues. The two most familiar types of ideologies in society are **liberalism** and **conservatism**. Although they may differ among themselves on many specific issues, the two ideological camps tend to cluster around the following cultural values:

Conservatives tend to emphasize individualism and freedom over equality. They favor *voluntary* solutions over government solutions for social and economic problems. In the area of social order, conservatives are more likely to see an important role for government in establishing law and order and instilling moral values.

Liberals tend to emphasize social equality or equality of opportunity over individual freedom. They tend to be more supportive of government solutions for social and economic problems, yet less willing to impose moral standards or law-and-order solutions through the government.

Around the edges of these two dominant ideologies are a number of even more sharply defined political belief systems. At one extreme is *libertarianism,* based on a nearly exclusive emphasis on the ideals of individualism–freedom–liberty, with very little concern for other cultural themes like equality or the need for government imposition of moral order. At another extreme is *socialism,* which emphasizes imposing equality of social conditions and places a high degree of responsibility on the government for filling the needs and wants of individuals.

Relatively few people can be classified as **libertarians** or **socialists.** Most Americans fall somewhere in the broad range from liberalism to conservatism, with many preferring to think of themselves as moderates. Because there is a pragmatic streak in American culture, people tend to be relatively flexible in their use of cultural themes to understand the political world. In addition, people often change their ideological emphasis as they move through life and as society changes around them. (The formation and change of ideologies will be discussed further in Chapter 6.) For now, it is enough to understand that compared to many, and perhaps most, other societies, the American cultural tradition is rather fluid. Most Americans subscribe to the core principles of individual liberty and economic free enterprise. Conservatives promote those principles more ardently than liberals, and liberals advocate more government activism in society, but neither group is willing to endorse serious restrictions on individual freedoms or major limits to free enterprise.

The modern-day Democratic and Republican parties have broadly adopted these general liberal and conservative positions and differ accordingly on some social and economic policies. However, the lines between liberals and conservatives, and Republicans and Democrats, are less sharply drawn than the ideological and party lines in many other political systems, An important illustration of this is a higher level of agreement in the United States on the idea that the government should not take care of poor people who can't take care of themselves, compared to attitudes in other nations shown in "How We Compare" Box 1.2.

Cultural Politics

These areas of ideological conflict and consensus account for very interesting patterns in American politics. In the case of the budget process, as discussed at the beginning of this chapter, a certain amount of ideological conflict is built in every year. Since both voters and parties tend to disagree over what areas of society the government should fund and regulate, there are recurring battles over support for education, health care, aid to poor families, and other broad social welfare programs. At the same time, there is more agreement on the belief that high taxes restrict personal lifestyles and inhibit the incentive to work and invest. As a result, Americans make more of an issue of their taxes, and end up paying lower income tax rates, than citizens in many other democracies. Thus, even if politicians win battles to fund programs in the budget, they may not be willing to anger voters by raising taxes to pay for them. This makes budget deficits hard to control.

Cultural forces behind the scenes of budget politics also explain why people began talking about a "crisis" when annual budget deficits soared in the early 1990s, hitting

HOW WE COMPARE

Government Responsibility to Take Care of the Poor

1.2

An important foundation of a political culture is the degree to which people believe it is the responsibility of the government to solve social problems.

The data below compare the responses of people in different nations to the proposition "**It is the responsibility of the State** [in Europe] **or the government** [in the U.S.] **to take care of very poor people who cannot take care of themselves.**" The figures show the percentages who *agree* with this idea.

SOURCE: Times Mirror Center for the People and the Press. Polling conducted in 1990–1991.

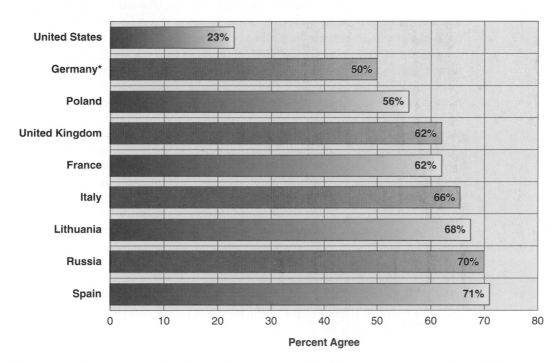

Nation	Percent Agree
United States	23%
Germany*	50%
Poland	56%
United Kingdom	62%
France	62%
Italy	66%
Lithuania	68%
Russia	70%
Spain	71%

Percent Agree

*The average derived from polling done in both eastern and western Germany, where substantial differences were found, reflecting the different cultures existing before unification of the two Germanies. In the west, 45 percent agreed with the proposition, compared to 64 percent in the east, whose people were educated in the former Communist system.

records of $269 billion in 1991, $290 billion in 1992 and $320 billion in 1993. What makes this a crisis? When compared to other industrial democracies in the 1980s and 1990s, the American battle of the budget looks worse than some, about the same as others, and better than many. Standard measures used by economists indicate that the United States' budget problem has been worse than in nations like Norway, Switzerland, or Finland, but not nearly as bad as the numbers posted by Austria, Belgium, Italy, the Netherlands, or Spain.[10] By similar measures, the American debt structure is no worse than that of Japan or England. Even Germany, once the world model of sound government financing, has joined the same debt league (relative to the size of its economy) with

Japan and America due to the huge costs of unifying the former East and West Germanies into a single nation.[11]

If the American debt and deficits are not grossly out of line with the rest of the world, why has it become such a tremendous political issue? Why have some politicians vowed to support a constitutional amendment to balance the national budget? Why did independent presidential candidate Ross Perot win so many votes in 1992 by turning the complex and somewhat dull topic of budgets into a major campaign issue? Part of the answer has to do with the importance of culture in politics.

A traditional American fear of big government can be heard in the background of many discussions of the budget and the national debt. Politicians easily arouse voters by saying the government spends too much and has become too big and irresponsible. Cultural attitudes about controlling big government may lead Americans and their leaders to make a big issue of budget deficits. At the same time, the cultural resistance to taxes works from another direction to further complicate the budget issue.

The point here is not to minimize the debt problem. The world economy is under added pressure because the leading industrial nations are in debt. The U.S. government could be doing other things with the huge sums paid out in interest payments that have consumed roughly 15 percent of the national budgets, on average, over the past decade.[12] In short, there is little doubt that debts and deficits place strains on domestic and world economies. The point is that we get a much better understanding of the politics behind the budget by recognizing the cultural dilemma of a people who make competing demands on government, resist the idea of paying more taxes, and then become alarmed about the size of the debt and the big government looming behind that debt.

Although this section has made a strong case for the importance of culture in American politics, cultural factors are by no means the only keys to understanding the political system. The next section examines the all-important institutional sphere through which cultural demands are processed, and conflicts and issues become resolved. While culture for many observers appears to be an almost invisible component of the political system, institutions are so evident that they can easily be mistaken for the whole of it.

Institutions

As every student has heard a thousand times, the United States government is a **democracy.** The Founders referred to the system they designed as a **republic,** meaning that the institutions specified in the Constitution favored *indirect* or *representative* government over *direct* democracy. *Representative democracies* conduct most of their political business through elected representatives. Although there have been few *direct democracies* in history, the idea refers to people meeting together to decide in person or vote directly on ballot propositions. In the electronic age, direct democracy could occur over television and telephone hookups.[13] Although American institutions have changed over the years, the system remains committed to the idea of representative democracy.

Institutions and American Democracy

At the time the U.S. Constitution was drafted, the term *democracy* was much more controversial than it is today. A spirited philosophical debate went on over the question of how much direct democracy a society could tolerate and still maintain order. As Chapter 2 explains in more detail, the majority of delegates to the Constitutional Convention in Philadelphia in 1787 were opposed to direct democracy for various reasons. Many felt that direct democracies were simply impractical because of the size of the emerging new nation. Although the United States was not large in population in 1787, the ordeals of travel and communication made geographic size a convincing obstacle to direct democracy. Even more important to the thinking of the founders, however, was the instability of the revolutionary society and the divergent interests in it. Direct democracy (indeed, even the term *democracy*) seemed to many who gathered at the convention in Philadelphia a recipe for constant turmoil.

Cultural concerns about order and liberty also figured into the design of American institutions. For some, the idea of liberty involved freedoms of thought and action. For others, liberty meant separation from the old system of monarchy and the creation of a new ideal of popular sovereignty. For still others, liberty had economic aspects like private property and free enterprise, which required enough government order to protect property from those who might threaten it. These and other strains in the revolutionary culture led to a set of political compromises at the Constitutional Convention. (These compromises and the political logic behind them are described more fully in Chapter 2.) The important idea is that the founders designed a system in which at least three major political safety valves were built into the institutions of government:

- First, the conflicts among competing groups were limited by representation, and by different kinds of election and representation schemes for the House, the Senate, and the president.

- Second, the power of elected representatives was limited by a clever system of checks and balances among the three branches of government, creating the separate institutions sharing powers described fully in Chapter 3.

- Third, the already limited power of this national government was limited further by creating a federal system in which many powers were granted to the states.

This government has been called exceptional among the world's democracies largely for the degree to which the powers of the institutions have been limited and dispersed. (The actual workings of these institutions are explored in Chapters 12–16.)

What Americans see when they look elsewhere in the democratic world to Canada, Australia, New Zealand, Japan, or most of Europe can appear very confusing. Americans often puzzle over a world full of prime ministers who seem a bit like our president but belong to the legislative branch, presidents who are more ceremonial leaders than powerful executives, and legislatures that are called parliaments rather than congresses. Their confusion is not reduced by seeing courts that have little or no constitutional authority and discovering few other nations that rely so heavily on their constitutions for guidance in the governing process. Our institutions look pretty confusing to the rest of the world, too. Pointing to the unique American mix of culture and institutions, Byron Shafer has concluded:

> When these [cultural and institutional features] are put together—when they are stacked on top of each other and when they interact—the result is a political life which is reliably baffling to the rest of the world.[14]

The design of this exceptional set of institutions can be explained, in part, by an historical uneasiness about the concentration of power in any one institution or level of government. This complex institutional design for power affects political issues and conflicts as they pass through the congressional, the executive, or the judicial branches. The impact of these separated institutions on everyday politics is one of the most important features to grasp about the American system.

Institutional Gridlock?

The separation of powers among the American institutions is consistent with a philosophy popular at the time of the founding: *that government is best which governs least.* In recent years, however, there has been growing concern among political scientists that

Public concern over institutional "gridlock" has mounted as voters have watched their congressional represen-tatives take the oath of office in January (above) then take recess in August (as in Pat Oliphant's cartoon, opposite page), with few welcome results perceptible from the interval between.

the demands of a large and complex industrial society may require less separation of the institutions of government. The founders, it is suggested, simply could not have imagined the problem of how to get this collection of institutions to act in concert to meet the demands of today's society. *One of the great dilemmas of American politics is that the system is hard to get moving, and once it gets going, it may be even harder to stop.*

All of this offers an interesting insight about the politics of problems like annual budget battles and the national debt. Consider a bold proposition: Given the different institutions and the separation of powers involved in putting a budget together, it may be less surprising that budgets are difficult to pass or that they contain deficits and compromises, than that they are passed at all. Even if this way of thinking is something of an exaggeration, it highlights the institutional dilemma of having to pass legislation through two separate and equally powerful institutions, Congress and the executive. As if this were not difficult enough, each of those institutions, in turn, has internal divisions and splits that hinder consensus and swift action. Congress has two chambers with different constituencies, pressures, and agendas that can make agreement difficult. And inside each chamber, there are two political parties that often pull in different directions. The executive branch includes not just the president, but a vast bureaucracy with entrenched programs to defend and its own relations to Congress and interest groups that can make it difficult for presidents to get the bureaucrats to line up behind a common budgetary pact. The politics inside the bureaucracy are discussed in Chapter 15. To top it all, when one political party controls Congress and the other controls the executive (as happened for most of the period from 1968 to 1992) it is not surprising that budget battles often become nasty affairs that are hard to control. These complicating factors of institutional life make it difficult to put plans for controlling the budget into action.

What Makes the Institutions Go?

If these unwieldy branches of government are to move coherently in the same direction, the forces that make them go are **voters, parties, and elections.** At critical moments in American history, one political party or the other has proposed ideas and promised solutions that attracted loyal voter support for long enough periods to push the nation in one direction or another. (The importance of parties is discussed in Chapter 9, and elections are covered in Chapter 10.)

In recent decades, the parties have lacked broadly appealing governing ideas, and voter loyalty has been weak. The electorate sent Democrat Bill Clinton to the White House in 1992, and the Democratic leadership in Congress promised to tighten party discipline to tackle an agenda of big national problems, from health care and education to the budget. However, there were few signs that voters were shifting their long-term support to the Democrats. The 1992 election more resembled a cautious experiment to see if having the same party in power at both ends of Pennsylvania Avenue might ease some of the gridlock on economic issues, social programs, and the budget. A sure sign of voter unease in 1992 was the nearly 19 percent of the vote delivered to Ross Perot, the blunt billionaire populist who convinced millions that neither party had the will or the way to get the country moving.

The problem with getting the parties to use the institutions effectively is not just a matter of weak parties or poor leadership. The voters, themselves, have sent notoriously mixed signals to Washington over the years. As Senator Jay Rockefeller of West Virginia put it candidly, "Voters . . . are angry with politicians like me. And they're angry with you in the media. Well, let me tell you something. The voters are no bargains, either."[15] Polls show that people do not want politicians to cut their favorite programs, and they want other people to be taxed to pay for them.[16] Most people are mad at Congress, yet they want other people's representatives to be tossed out while they continue to vote for their own. (Such patterns of behavior are explained in Chapters 6–10, which explore the behavioral connections between the political culture and the institutions of government.)

As if the mixed signals among voters, representatives, and parties were not enough to make government sluggish, the pressures of thousands of interest groups do not encourage government to move in consistent or united directions, either. As explained in Chapter 8, interests are a fundamental and often useful feature of the American system, but they may make it difficult for grand political visions to take form. Interest groups take up a large chunk of the national agenda and deliver important programs and benefits to many sectors of society. People are understandably reluctant to give up the gains of interest-group politics, but the price may be living with a budget that is the sum of those interests. If the political course of the nation seems unclear to many people, as is often indicated in the polls (see Chapter 6), this may simply reflect the different directions in which interest groups and voters, alike, pull the institutions of government.

In light of these institutional forces inside the system, it is not surprising that the last time the United States produced a balanced budget was in 1968 (for fiscal year 1969), when a single party was in control of both Congress and the executive, and the nation was riding the crest of one of its greatest periods of economic prosperity. Such good political and economic fortune cannot be counted on very often. It seems reasonable to ask if some of the budget troubles and other problems that worry people about government may not be due to the original institutional design. At the time the Constitution was adopted, less was expected of government, and a government that did less was more likely to win approval. In recent years there have been many suggestions for redesigning the institutions to improve coordination and centralize power. Most of these proposals run up against enduring *cultural* objections to a government with too much power. Can you imagine fundamental changes in the governing institutions?

Power in Society

One moral of this story is that the design of institutions places certain limits on government power and political action. However, it is important to recognize that power also comes from other places in a political system. *Power is generally defined as having (and using) the resources to get others, including government officials, to do something they might not do on their own.* There are many resources that can be converted into political power: money, votes, friendship, information, communication skills, group organization, and physical force, just to name a few. The key questions about power in society are: Who has more? Who has less? What kind do they have? How do they use it? The distribution of power among the citizens in a democracy tells us how much equality there is in that democracy, and more generally, *who governs*. The ultimate question about power, then, is: **Who governs?** There are three broad theories about power in American society: **majoritarian, pluralist,** and **elitist.** Each offers an important perspective on how the political system operates.

Majority Rule: The Majoritarian Theory of Power

Majoritarian theory is the basic theory that most citizens learn in grade school: Majorities rule. People accept this principle of power in many areas of everyday life. When groups form to do almost anything from sports to community activities, decisions are generally made by a majority vote. In many aspects of national government, the power of the majority is also evident. In elections, the will or power of a majority of voters is sufficient to send one candidate into office and another to defeat. In addition, many states and localities offer voters direct ballot propositions on important questions related to schools, development, environmental policies, taxes, and a variety of other issues. In these cases, the major resource operating in the power relationship between citizens and representatives is the vote itself.

Beyond electoral politics, some important issues on the agendas of the executive, Congress, and even the courts may be influenced by majority opinion. For example, politicians consult opinion polls carefully on such matters as taxes, abortion, civil rights, economic policy, and spending decisions that directly affect jobs and personal security.

Who Governs?

The American government is designed, in theory, to make all its citizens "players" at some level in the "power game" of who governs. There are three predominant theories on the topic. In majoritarian theory, the people themselves ultimately decide the issues by exercising their franchise at the voting booth (*above*) and electing delegates who represent them. In pluralist theory, diverse groups exert influence by organizing and lobbying on those issues that concern them the most (as with the AIDS activists *below*). According to elitist theory, power is wielded by a comparatively few wealthy and well-connected individuals; one current example might be Ron Brown (right), formerly a lawyer and lobbyist, later chairman of the Democratic party, and most recently Secretary of Commerce in the Clinton administration.

The Players

There is no precise equation that tells us how majority opinion translates into the decisions of elected representatives on specific issues, but research makes it clear that some issues are important enough to citizens that representatives take their view into account when making government decisions.[17]

When issues clearly matter to the public (as discussed in Chapters 7, 10, and 12), representatives may feel that they are **delegates,** bound to carry out the wishes of the people who voted for them. Whether these delegates feel morally obligated to follow the majority or simply fear reprisal from those voters at the next election, the result is that some issues seem to be decided according to how majorities of citizens feel about them. However, other government decisions are made well out of the view of broad publics. In some cases, the subjects are so technical that few citizens care enough or know enough to become involved in them. In these and other cases, representatives may feel that their role is not to follow the will of a possibly uninformed or uninvolved majority, but to act as a **trustee:** someone who protects the public interest by making decisions on some other basis than the will of the majority. When majoritarian theories of power do not explain how decisions are made, we must look elsewhere to decide who governs. Other theories provide better explanations for these situations.

Group Power: The Pluralist Theory of Power

Many observers of the American political system have been struck by the intense activity of groups, big and small, promoting thousands of causes. There are groups to clean up environments, groups to stop abortion or protect abortion rights, groups to promote the interests of snack-food companies, and groups to get government to educate the public about the health risks of eating snack foods. There are groups to amend the Constitution, limit the terms of elected representatives, promote or stop the sale of military weapons, and to create national days for the recognition of various fruits, vegetables, and local heroes.

To many observers of this scene, it appears that even if majorities do not hold power over many questions, there are interested and diverse groups of citizens who do. This *pluralist* theory of power points to political competition among diverse (plural) groups as a reasonable distribution of power in a democracy. Pluralists say that an open, competitive interest-group democracy may not always, or even very often, be majoritarian, but it still allows us to answer the question of who governs by saying that the people do. At least, that is the basic assumption of the pluralist theory of power as expressed by a

The pluralist theory of power suggests that, while majorities may not always govern, "the people" still do—in the form of those groups that are most concerned and active on behalf of their interests. Here members of a Little League baseball team in Brooklyn protest the elimination of summer youth programs as a budget-cutting measure by the New York city government.

number of leading political scientists, most notably Robert Dahl.[18] Central to the idea of pluralism is the existence of many power centers in society. The same groups who exercise power in health-care issues probably do not exercise power in defense spending, and an entirely different set of interest groups holds sway in questions related to religious freedom and prayer in school.

There are some critics of this idea of interest-group democracy, notably political scientists such as Theodore Lowi, Benjamin Ginsberg, and Martin Shefter, who agree that pluralism is an accurate description of power in society, but they are concerned that it ends up fragmenting the national agenda and threatening the very idea of majoritarian politics.[19] However, most pluralists have argued that plural centers of power in society are the most realistic and reasonable form for modern democracy to take. The pluralists base their case on several arguments:

- First, it is unreasonable to expect majorities to become involved in every issue. Interested groups have the knowledge and motivation to stake out sound positions and apply power wisely.

- Second, as long as many different groups participate in decisions that interest large numbers of people, the system is responding to the will of many of the people, most of the time, on the issues that matter the most to them.

- Finally, as long as the system is open to new groups whenever people feel strongly about an issue, democracy is working as well as can be expected. It is asking too much of human nature to expect people to become involved in issues that are not of great personal concern.

Robert Dahl summed up these arguments by saying that a pluralistic distribution of power in society is:

a relatively effective system for reinforcing agreement, encouraging moderation, and maintaining social peace in a restless and immoderate people operating a gigantic, powerful, diversified, and incredibly complex society.[20]

This bold claim may be acceptable if the *openness, competitiveness,* and *effectiveness* assumptions about pluralism hold true: *if government is open to new groups who enter the competition for power; if all groups have equal chance to compete effectively;* and *if people can organize effectively and be heard when they feel their interests are on the line.* However, a number of critics of these assumptions have argued that in many important areas of politics, people have a great deal of trouble exercising much power at all, either because the government is closed to them, or because they lack the resources to compete and gain effective access. The advocates of these views propose another theory of power called *elitism.* The basic idea of *elitism* is that, contrary to the assumptions of *pluralism,* there are many issue areas in which power is greatly restricted to a relatively small number of elites. These well-connected economic and political insiders use advantages like wealth, information, and direct access to government officials to control important decisions and block access by other groups who want to share power.

Rule by the Few: The Elitist Theory of Power

The power-elite theorists say the American political system is prone to *elitism,* or the *concentration of power in the hands of a small number of very powerful, economically and socially privileged people.*[21] One of the early works on elite theory by historian Charles Beard argued that the men who wrote the Constitution were disproportionately wealthy property owners who designed a set of institutions that protected private property and severely restricted participation by the majority of average people.[22] Other elite theorists claim that from the Revolution to the present day, the most important economic and foreign policy decisions of government have been made of, by, and for a wealthy and privileged class of American elites.

As evidence for their views, the elitists often cite a relatively small number of wealthy individuals who float back and forth between the top jobs in business and government. They also point out that large corporations and the powerful individuals who own and run them have privileged access to top bureaucrats, presidents, and members of Congress. Not only do the economic elite and important politicians run in the same social circles, but leaders of business can gain the ear of politicians through large campaign contributions and personal favors, including the offer of lucrative employment in the private sector after such government officials leave public service. The members of this "power elite," it is said, also cement their social and political ties through periods of government service as cabinet officers, ambassadors, or presidential advisors, while taking time off from their corporate duties.

Some theorists argue that elite rule is inevitable in *all* societies. One conservative American tradition going back to Alexander Hamilton at the time of the Constitution argues that government by elites may be preferable to rule by uninformed, capricious, and apathetic masses.[23] However, most elite theorists disagree, arguing that the elites keep majorities and weaker interest groups alike out of the most important national decisions involving economics, banking, investment, trade, military spending, foreign policy, technology, and other crucial areas that affect economic growth, the distribution of wealth, and national commitments abroad. This more common perspective among elite theorists argues that elites dominate the decision process in one of several ways that subvert the ideals of democracy:

- First, political competition in many areas is discouraged because most people simply lack the resources that elites use to gain access to the inner circles of power.

- Second, elites use their power advantages to promote policies and decisions that advance narrow business or economic interests over the interests of the general public.

- Finally, when issues are discussed by elites in private, decisions become closed to debate and input from larger numbers of people who might become involved if given the chance.

Elite theorists contend that most "real" power in society is controlled by a small group of privileged people, who move back and forth between the corporate and governmental power structures, making important decisions behind the scenes while excluding the majority from influence. One exemplary figure commonly cited by such theorists is Robert McNamara, who rose to the top of the Ford Motor Company, served as Secretary of Defense in both the Kennedy and Johnson administrations, and later became president of the World Bank. Here Secretary McNamara gives reporters details of an August 1964 attack by the North Vietnamese on U.S. ships in the Gulf of Tonkin; a few days later, Congress granted President Johnson broad authority to escalate the war in Vietnam. (Some political figures have since alleged that the attack itself was a fabrication.)

Early studies often claimed that elites shared uniform class interests that pushed government in a single direction. More recent thinking acknowledges the existence of conflicting objectives even among the powerful that may result in a less than monolithic government. However, the key idea of elite theorists is that elites dominate some areas of government decision making, and limit broader public participation. For this reason, elitist theories of power present a direct challenge to both majoritarian and pluralist views of the American democracy. The student of American government cannot afford to ignore this three-way debate about power. *Simply learning how government institutions work on paper is of little help in understanding how power flows through them.* Putting institutions and power together is essential for answering the question of who governs.

Who Governs?

The question of "Who has the power?" is such an obvious and important one that it continues to capture the imagination of political scientists as well as the general public. Ask someone who has the power in the system and you are likely to open up an interesting conversation. Views on power do not always follow predictable liberal or conservative lines. For example, the popular Republican president and military hero Dwight Eisenhower left office in 1961 with a warning to

guard against the acquisition of unwarranted influence, whether sought or unsought, by the military-industrial complex. The potential for the disastrous rise of misplaced power exists and will persist.

He referred to the *iron triangle* of Defense Department (Pentagon) officials, defense industry chiefs, and congressional boosters pushing the government into military commitments that would tip the national economy more in the direction of arms technology than civilian values. (We will discuss iron triangles further in Chapters 8, 12, and 15.) Some argue that today the United States is now living with the effects of an economy geared to produce roughly 30 percent of the world's military outlays, while other industrialized nations have cornered the production of consumer goods that create more jobs and better economic balance.[24]

At the time President Eisenhower issued his warning, only 25 percent of Americans worried about the capture of government by too-powerful interests. By 1970, however—after the nation had suffered several years of war in Vietnam and bitter conflicts over the government's role in reducing poverty—fully 50 percent of those polled in opinion surveys agreed with the statement that "the government is run for the benefit of a few big interests." By 1980, after the scandals marking the Nixon years and a widespread sense of being exploited by "Big Oil" during a series of oil crises, the numbers favoring the elitist view of government jumped to 70 percent. And polls opening the 1990s recorded a 77 percent level of belief in the domination of government by big business.[25]

Part of the problem with simply letting public opinion decide who is running the country is that Americans are willing to condemn what other people do as "special interest" politics, while ignoring their own interest-group activities. Citizens of the United States join an astonishing number of interest groups and receive benefits of various sorts from those groups, regarding their own group interests as reasonable, but *not* the kinds of negative "special interests" that others practice. Indeed, if we add up all the organized interests, the number would be huge. The exact number of registered lobbyists actually in Washington merely hints at the trend, but it does suggest the magnitude of the situation: During peak legislative periods of 1992 and 1993, an average of 6,104 lobbyists registered with the House of Representatives and 8,019 registered with the Senate.[26]

The proliferation of interest-group politics complicates the question of who governs, whether we are looking at the opinion polls or the literature in political science. Since people tend to be kind to their own interest activities and more critical of others' behavior, it is not clear what people would propose to do about the "government by special interests" that they condemn in the polls. Moreover, since some of those interests are clearly more powerful and better connected inside the corridors of power than others, there is evidence that at least some interest-group politics tends to be elitist. Yet, at the same time, the more competitive and less concentrated activities of grass-roots groups provides evidence in favor of a pluralist interpretation.

Critics within both the elitist and pluralist camps argue that the issue is not so much how narrowly or broadly power is concentrated among interest groups, but the fact that so many competing groups simply make a mess of government policy. On the elitist side, sociologist William Domhoff has argued that the major problems with elites these days is that they seldom agree on their common interests, yet have enough power to pull the government in different and often competing directions, leaving the nation with little coherent sense of policy.[27] On the critical pluralist side, political scientists Benjamin Ginsberg and Martin Shefter argue that the proliferation of groups, large and small, has virtually replaced the party system and undermined the purpose of elections. In this view, citizens are left with only the narrowest sort of representation on a few issues they care about and little hope for broad social representation or national leadership from parties or elected officials.[28]

With these interesting points of debate in mind, it may help to consider the possibility that no single theory of power explains fully who governs in America, but each one offers some useful insights about how different aspects of the political system operate. Let's take a closer look at the budget example and see which theories of power apply to what aspects of the politics inside the system.

A MAJORITARIAN VIEW OF THE BUDGET.   Both pluralists and elitists agree that the majoritarian theory explains only a limited range of actual situations in the American system. Consider the case of the budget. Only a few of the specific items in the annual budget make enough difference to enough voters to bring voter pressure into the thinking of representatives. For example, politicians have learned not to threaten entitlement programs such as social security retirement benefits because senior citizens vote in large numbers and tend to have long memories about who threatened their interests. However, even this turns out not to be a good example of pure majoritarian power in action because senior citizens do not represent a majority of the national electorate, although they are important voting blocks in some states. Rather, the power of seniors over entitlement programs in the budget may be better explained by a pluralistic theory of interest-group politics. Retired persons have formed one of the largest and most active interest-organizations in the nation, as described in Chapter 8.

Majoritarian politics does, however, provide some explanation for the more general problem of growing budget deficits and the national debt. Majorities of citizens continue to cite deficits and debts among the top problems facing the nation, yet majorities are very sensitive about raising taxes to keep the government out of the red. Voters may not pay much attention to how representatives vote on many of the small spending items that make up the budget, but they do react when representatives raise taxes. Even Bill Clinton's budget plan was fairly circumspect (in *his* view, at least) in imposing new taxes. Few elected officials have been willing to talk seriously about major tax increases as a way to balance the budget. Thus, fear of voter reprisal discourages government officials from taking the single most direct step (along with slashing spending across the board) toward solving the problem.

What the majoritarian model does not explain very well, then, is the spending side. What keeps the money flowing to the thousands of government programs, big and small, despite the alleged desires of majorities of citizens for the government to reduce spending? Here we turn to both pluralist and elitist explanations to fill in the answer.

A PLURALIST VIEW OF THE BUDGET.   The image of a budget out of control seems made for a pluralist analysis. The idea of thousands of groups pressuring representatives with campaign contributions and other power resources would seem to account for both the proliferation of programs and the difficulty of stopping the spiraling debt. While lawmakers might like to cut the budget back, they simply cannot say no to the many groups who provide them with political resources from campaign money to the technical reports and information that are helpful in writing legislation.

Pluralism may drive up spending, but the result may be less radical than if majorities voted on every government program. It is conceivable that majorities could end up wiping out almost everything the government does, simply because relatively few programs would be seen as benefiting majorities of the people. If majorities ruled, perhaps most people would feel threatened by the *tyranny of the majority* that the American system was designed, in part, to prevent. Just which of the typical programs below do you think should be cut from the budget?[29]

- The $2.3 billion in funding for sewerage plant construction that is a paltry sum considering the chronic levels of pollution being pumped by many cities into rivers and oceans?

- The $358 million for highway safety that has been shown to be effective in reducing traffic accidents and fatalities?

- The $116 million for emergency shelters and transitional housing for the homeless, which is not even close to the amount needed to address the problem?

- The $6.3 billion in loan money and other financial assistance spent so students from poor and middle-class families can attend college? This amount is already projected to be cut in half by the late 1990s. Should it be cut more? If, as many students and their families argue, it should be restored, whose benefits should be cut? The homeless? The sick? Senior citizens on small pensions? Should taxes be increased to pay for student loans? Who should pay those taxes?

These and many similar examples make the politics of pluralism fairly obvious. Many groups have good cases for government programs, and many of those groups also have the resources to get the attention and win the support of government officials. Once funded, each group gains a political support base that makes it difficult to cut, making it much easier to go deeper into debt than to cut real programs for real people. Meanwhile, there is relatively less organized group opposition to the budget deficit itself. Thus a multitude of programs gets funded, and the government borrows money to make up the difference.

Does this mean that pluralism offers the best or most complete look at the politics behind the budget? Pluralist ideas about power seem to explain some aspects of budgetary politics very well. However, there are important questions that the pluralist theory cannot answer completely: What explains government spending priorities, and the vast differences in the amounts spent in different areas? Why are some programs so much easier to cut than others when pressures mount to "trim the fat"? Why do some programs persist even when there is considerable public pressure to cut them? There are reasons to think that the power and political connections of some interests are considerably greater then others.

AN ELITIST VIEW OF THE BUDGET.   One of the challenges to a purely pluralist explanation of budget politics is that some people clearly have much better access to key decision makers than others. Homeless people, for example, have fewer resources to employ than defense contractors. Homeless people seldom attend Washington parties or play golf with politicians. Not only do the homeless lack the money to hire lawyers and lobbyists and make campaign contributions, but they are dispersed, transient, and poorly organized, making it difficult to carry out effective protests or wield other forms of grass-roots power. While we cannot say that this accounts for the whole difference between the $100 million spent on shelter for the homeless and the $100 billion in defense contracts awarded to big corporations, it is probably not an incidental fact that companies manufacturing missiles and bombers have better representation than homeless people and many others in society.

Indeed, there are many anomalies in the budget that are easier to explain with elitist than pluralist models. For example, under a pluralist explanation, defense spending would be expected to decrease quickly if groups organized to lobby against it. With the end of the Cold War, grass-roots lobbying for substantial reductions in military operations has intensified, and plans have been proposed to use the money for social problems. Although defense budgets have been cut significantly in the wake of the Cold War, critics still charge that insider connections and elite politics continue to waste billions on unnecessary but profitable weapons systems and other military programs. One-time congressional critics of military expenditures now oppose the closing of military bases in their home district or state for economic reasons: Such bases mean jobs for large numbers of their constituents. The point here is not to argue the pros and cons of such spending, but to suggest that neither majoritarian nor pluralist models may fully explain some of the power politics at work to protect the defense budget from substantial attempts to cut it further.

What is the answer to the ultimate question of who governs? There is considerable controversy surrounding which theory of power best explains what goes on inside the decision arenas of politics. As the budget process suggests, each view of power offers some useful insights about the political process. Yet each fails to explain everything that goes on. While it may be tempting to choose one theory simply because it feels better or agrees with our personal beliefs and political ideology, this is not a good way to do science. A safer position is to keep an open mind while gathering more information from this book and the class. For the time being, consider that power in the American system operates in different ways in different situations. Rather than force acceptance of one theory of power over the others, it may make more sense to think of these theories rather as lenses that bring different features of the American political system into focus, enabling us to explain more by using all three of them than we could explain by using any one of them exclusively.

The Political System Revisited

The *institutions of government* are the most obvious and central aspects of a political system. However, it is important to remember that institutions are part of a larger system of politics that makes them go. Surrounding the institutions, for example, is a political culture that shapes what people ask for in politics and what they expect government to do about those requests. The values and political practices that define American political culture are important for understanding what the government institutions are asked to do. The groups that make demands on government have various kinds of power available to them to try to influence or control what the government institutions actually do. *At times,* majorities rule. In other situations, the competition among (plural) groups seems to determine the course of government action. In still other cases, government decision makers appear to respond to the demands of a few powerful (elite) actors operating out of public view. When Bill Clinton appealed to the nation to support his budget control plan, he made important references to culture, institutions, and power in his speeches, as illustrated in "Inside the System" Box 1.3.

By the time Bill Clinton took office, there was enormous public pressure to end so-called "political gridlock"—which many blamed for the budget crisis and other breakdowns in effective government. Both chambers of Congress began in the spring budget

INSIDE THE SYSTEM

Supporting Bill Clinton's Budget Plan: A "Patriotic Duty"?

1.3

Bill Clinton made the budget the main topic in his first two major addresses to the nation, one televised directly from the Oval Office and the other before a joint session of Congress. In the intimate setting of the Oval Office, he reached deep into the collection of *cultural themes* that draw people together and drew out the grand concept of patriotism. He also called upon those time-tested cultural ideals of hard work and individual sacrifice:

> If you will join with me, we can create an economy in which all Americans work hard and prosper. This is nothing less than a call to arms to restore the vitality of the American dream. When I was a boy, we had a name for the belief that we should all pull together to build a better, stronger nation. We called it patriotism. And we still do.*

Mr. Clinton also talked about *power,* saying that it was time for "special interests" to step aside so that government could be returned to the majority of the people. He charged that opponents of his plan "have already lined the corridors of power with high-priced lobbyists."* His proposals called for wealthy elites to pay more and ask for less from government because they could afford it.

In addressing the joint session of Congress, the new president claimed that his election was a mandate from the people to end the *institutional gridlock* that blocked so many earlier plans to balance the budget.** He called on the leadership of the Congress to join him and respond to the will of the people who elected them to solve the nation's problems.

There were objections to the president's plan. Republican leaders of the House and Senate

*Oval Office speech of February 15, 1993.
**Speech before a joint session of Congress, February 17, 1993.

responded that there was far too much new taxing and spending and not enough old-fashioned budget-cutting. They reminded the public that liberal Democrats still favored big-spending solutions to problems, which resulted in the continued growth of big government. Meanwhile, Mr. Clinton and the members of his cabinet barnstormed around the country promoting his program and urging all Americans to forget party and ideology and join together in a great patriotic fight to make the nation's economic future secure. It was a classic example of the interplay of culture, institutions, and power in American politics.

season of 1993 with a resolution promising to raise enough in taxes and cut enough in spending over five years to lower the deficit below the $200 billion-per-year mark by 1997. While that would still leave much red ink on the books, it was a sign of movement in the direction of fiscal responsibility. Pessimists pointed out that Congress had passed budget resolutions in the past. In the end, however, short-term political pressures had always prevailed, and Congress had suspended its own laws each year, resulting in soaring deficits and mounting debt—blamed on the executive branch. Would similar political pressures break this latest attempt? Could congressional Republicans, through traditional attacks on tax-and-spend Democrats, insist on greater cuts in "pork-barrel" spending? Could the Democrats sustain the party unity required to resist interest-group pressures and follow through on their resolution this time? By the time the summer budget season arrived, the House and Senate were embroiled in conferences about how to reconcile two differing compromise versions of the budget bill. In August, a final version of the bill was approved by the narrowest possible margin—one-vote majorities in both the House and Senate. Even so, much more action remained to follow through on this initial

A CITIZEN'S QUESTION Power

*W*here do I fit into the political system? What kind of power do I have? These questions are related. Unless you recognize some personal connections to power, your place in the political system will seem small and mysterious. You may even feel left out of it entirely. In fact, many Americans say they have little or no power. Others go so far as to avoid thinking about their relationship to power because they see power and politics as inherently negative things that should be avoided. There are strong cultural themes warning against power and its abuses. People may resent not having power or having power used against them. There is also a common tendency to associate power with corruption. Whatever the reasons for the bad name associated with power, there are good reasons for both students and citizens to keep an open mind about power and its uses.

To begin with, politics is so completely wrapped up with the use of power that it's hard to imagine the government doing anything without power being applied from somewhere, whether from voters, interest groups, or wealthy elites. This leads to an even larger observation about politics. The real issue about power in politics may not be *whether* it should be used, but *how* it should be used, for what ends, and with what considerations about ethics, morality, and the spirit of democracy. These are the considerations about power that most affect the quality of life in society.

In cases where the realities of power do not live up to our personal ideals, the solution is not to become cynical, either by rejecting politics or by accepting corruption simply because others have abused power. On the contrary, citizens who keep an open mind about power will recognize that if they want to get anything done in politics (including cleaning up corruption or changing things they do not like), they need to develop some base of power to get the institutions moving in the direction they want. Perhaps developing your own base of power involves joining with other voters, or joining an interest group, or using personal connections to meet with government officials. The forms and uses of power vary with the situation and with the resources people have. Rejecting power as a bad thing in itself is an effective way to neutralize oneself as a citizen, and, at the same time, turn over the political franchise to others.

Questions about how to act politically and what kinds of power you can exercise become easier to answer after more of the basic workings of the political system are understood. Thinking critically and realistically about how the political system works is the first step toward defining your place in it as a citizen. At the same time, thinking about what kind of citizen to become may motivate learning about how the political system works. What kinds of power do you now have available for action? What does this say about your current place in the political system? What kinds of power would you like to develop in the future? What does this say about your future in politics?

vote. You can follow the development of this great political story of the 1990s because you now have the tools to understand the political forces that will shape its outcome: the interplay of culture, institutions, and power in the national government.

Understanding these simple working parts of the political system allows us to go beyond just memorizing facts about government, and see how government actually operates in different situations. Each chapter of this book deals with a different aspect of the system. This means that the whole framework of culture, institutions, and power will not be rolled out in every chapter. In some cases this would be forced, and, in any event, too much for the reader to manage all at once. Only the most important links between the topic of each chapter and the larger political system will be emphasized. Thus, cultural issues are emphasized most in the chapters on the civic culture (6–11) in which we see how public demands are formed, expressed, and channeled into the institutions of government. Institutional arrangements are explored in great detail in Chapters 12–16, dealing with Congress, the executive, and the judiciary. Power is an important underlying theme throughout the book, reminding us that government is, after all, a political affair. In the chapters on government policy that conclude the book (17–20), we once again see how aspects of culture, institutions, and power all affect what happens in various areas such as health, education, welfare, the environment, and foreign affairs.

Along the way, we will encounter interesting people and dramatic situations that remind us that, above all, politics is about how people work out the issues of living together in society. In every chapter, there is a section reserved for one very important person in this society: you, the reader. To drive this aspect home, and to provide you with ideas for thinking and discussion, each chapter closes with "A Citizen's Question." These questions and the discussions that follow are intended to start the connection between learning about government and your own development as a citizen.

Key Terms

political system

democracy

republic

political culture

cultural themes: liberty–freedom; order–control; equality–equality of opportunity; popular sovereignty; volunteerism; patriotism–national unity

ideology: liberal, conservative, libertarian, socialist

institutional separation and sharing of power

voting, parties, and elections as unifying forces in government

theories of power: majoritarian, pluralist, elitist

types of representation: trustee, delegate

Suggested Readings

Dahl, Robert A. *Democracy and Its Critics.* New Haven: Yale University Press, 1989.

Domhoff, William. *The Power Elite and the State: How Policy Is Made in America.* New York: Aldine de Gruyter, 1990.

Ginsberg, Benjamin and Martin Shefter. *Politics by Other Means: The Declining Importance of Elections in America.* New York: Basic Books, 1990.

Lasswell, Harold D. *Politics: Who Gets What, When, How.* New York: McGraw-Hill, 1938.

McClosky, Herbert and John Zaller. *The American Ethos.* Cambridge: Harvard University Press, 1984.

Smith, Hedrick. *The Power Game: How Washington Works.* New York: Ballantine Books, 1989.

Part II

CONSTITUTIONAL FOUNDATIONS

CHAPTER 2

From Revolution to Constitution: The Struggle for Government

CHAPTER 3

The Constitutional Design of Power

CHAPTER 4

The Politics of Federalism

CHAPTER 5

The Personal Constitution: Civil Liberties and Civil Rights

•••

A little rebellion, now and then, is a good thing, as necessary in the political world as storms in the physical.
—*THOMAS JEFFERSON*

•••

There, King George will be able to read that without his spectacles.
—*JOHN HANCOCK (AFTER PUTTING HIS "KING-SIZED" SIGNATURE ON THE DECLARATION OF INDEPENDENCE)*

•••

This country, with its institutions, belongs to the people who inhabit it. Whenever they shall grow weary of the existing Government, they can exercise their constitutional rights of amending it, or their revolutionary rights to dismember or overthrow it.
—*ABRAHAM LINCOLN*

•••

From Revolution to Constitution: The Struggle for Government

- **THE BIG NEWS OF 1786: THE REVOLUTION IS NOT OVER YET**
- **THE POLITICS OF COMPROMISE: AN ENDURING TRADITION**
  The Constitution as Politics and Political Philosophy
- **IN THE BEGINNING: THIRTEEN COLONIES IN SEARCH OF A REVOLUTION**
  A Brief History of Rebellion
  The Politics of Colonialism
- **THE POLITICS OF REVOLUTION**
  "No Taxation Without Representation"
  The Declaration of Independence
- **AFTER THE REVOLUTION: ONE NATION OR THIRTEEN?**
  The Articles of Confederation
- **THE POLITICS OF THE CONSTITUTION**
  Scrap the Articles: The Virginia Plan
  Save the Articles: The New Jersey Plan
  Representation: The Great Compromise
  The Unkindest Compromise: Slavery
  The President: Avoiding Demigods and Demagogues
  The Supreme Court, Etc.: The Rest Was Easy
  How the Delegates Saw It
- **SELLING THE CONSTITUTION: THE *FEDERALIST* PAPERS**
- **THE BILL OF RIGHTS**
- **THE POLITICS OF COMPROMISE REVISITED**
- **A CITIZEN'S QUESTION: Authority**
- **KEY TERMS**
- **SUGGESTED READINGS**

The Big News of 1786: The Revolution Is Not Over Yet

Ten years after the Declaration of Independence was issued by the Continental Congress as a call to revolution, another sort of unrest began to stir in the land. This time, the rebellions and tensions were aimed not at England, which had been defeated in the Revolution, but against some of the state governments themselves. Politicians and ordinary citizens alike joined often fiery debates about the very future of government. Great differences existed among the people over what kind of government to have, how much power to grant to the central government, and how to protect various individual, group, and regional interests from that power. The outbreak of rebellions in 1786 and 1787 added a strong incentive to resolve these differences at the Constitutional Convention in Philadelphia during the summer of 1787.

It is important to understand the politics of that time in order to understand the document we live with today, because the political compromises reached at that convention affect American politics today. Many cultural tensions and power struggles that shaped the constitutional design of institutions still appear in our modern political life; and today's conflicts involving *cultural values, institutional responsibilities,* and *power in society* still resonate from the solutions worked out more than two centuries ago.

Most readers of newspapers of the time would have received the impression that the rebels of 1786–1787 were a lawless, dangerous element. Leading newspaper publishers and the government officials whose views filled their pages portrayed the rebels as threats to the very order of society.[1] It is true, of course, that surrounding courthouses to keep judges from seizing property was an illegal act. However, it was also a political act by people who felt that they were not being represented by the government that made the laws. The rebellion was the last resort for many angry veterans who had returned

from fighting the Revolution to discover the economy in a shambles and their homes and farms threatened by high taxes and loans they could not pay. In many states, political tensions soared as farms, livestock, and personal belongings were seized by the courts to pay such debts. The most notorious incidents occurred in Massachusetts, where bands of angry farmers, led by veterans of the Revolution, marched on courthouses to stop legal proceedings against their property.

Echoing that old revolutionary slogan "No taxation without representation," the rebels vowed to keep judges from entering county courthouses and ruling on their cases until the state legislature met in Boston to hear their demands. Their demands included relief from steep taxes, along with printing a state-backed currency they could use to pay their debts. Others said that if poor people like them were expected to pay taxes they should be allowed to vote, too. One radical proposal even called for lowering the property requirements for political participation, so that men like the rebels could run for office. The dissidents were well aware of the fine line they walked between allowable protest and treason. They debated whether they should take the step across the line into civil disobedience and, perhaps, armed insurrection. Some called for a peaceful petition to the government in Boston to hear their grievances before armed action was taken. However, many others angrily said it was too late to petition the government, and they reminded their moderate neighbors of the futile efforts of the First Continental Congress to petition King George before the Revolution.

Advocates of rebellion won the day at farmers' meetings with statements like this one attributed to a rebel named Plough Jogger:

> I have been greatly abused, have been obliged to do more than my part in the war;

been loaded with class [tax] rates, town rates, province rates, continental rates and all rates . . . been pulled and hauled by sheriffs, constables and collectors, and had my cattle sold for less than they were worth. . . .

The great men are going to get all we have and I think it is time for us to rise and put a stop to it, and have no more courts, nor sheriffs, nor collectors, nor lawyers.[2]

Inspired by words like these, armed rebels began closing courthouses around Massachusetts. In New Hampshire, an angry mob of farmers surrounded the State House demanding tax relief and paper money. Many state government officials feared that the rebels wanted their states to become more like Rhode Island, where radical elements had won seats in the legislature and delivered on promises of tax relief and paper money. Eager to avoid what happened in so-called "Rogue Island," the legislatures of seven other states yielded to popular pressures for tax cuts and paper currency. Conservative politicians and members of the business community condemned these moves as damaging their efforts to get struggling state economies going again.

Massachusetts Governor James Bowdoin addressed the state assembly with a stirring call to "vindicate the insulted dignity of government."[3] He did not say that his private appeals to the National Congress for troops to put down the rebellion were answered by quiet reminders that, under the Articles of Confederation, the central government had no money to pay for an army. He also knew that it would be difficult to get authorization under the weak Articles of Confederation to send national troops even if the means existed to pay for them. In short, Massachusetts, birthplace of the Revolution and a key economic center of the new nation, was on the verge of chaos.

There was widespread feeling in Boston that the authority of government itself was on the line. Samuel Adams, one of the organizers of the Boston Tea Party protest in 1773, was not on the side of the rebels this time. He was busily at work in legislative committee drawing up a Riot Act to be read by local sheriffs to anyone attempting to shut down county courts. However, the situation worsened as local militias refused orders by sheriffs, judges, and even the governor himself to move against the rebels. Groups of merchants and bankers began to meet in houses and private clubs around Boston, pledging contribu-

tions to hire a temporary army under the command of State Militia General Benjamin Lincoln.

The grass-roots nature of the uprising, however, made it hard to organize a unified military response against it. In fact, dozens of uprisings were going on around the state. Some observers identified the leader as Luke Day in Springfield. Others said the biggest rebel group was headed by a friend of Day named Daniel Shays. Rumor spread that Shays planned to capture the Springfield militia arsenal and arm farmers all the way to Boston. Some reports reached Boston that he was on his way with as many as 1,200 men. The hope among the authorities was that the state could put up a good military bluff, a

During Shays' Rebellion of 1786–1787, Massachusetts rebels (including many veterans of the War of Independence) blocked off county courthouses, demanding that the state legislature cut the tax rate, issue paper currency, and consider electoral reforms. Although the rebellion faded, the potential chaos it augured gave impetus to the Constitutional Convention that began the following May in Philadelphia.

show of force to buy time, after which the long winter would finish off the rebellion. Nobody expected the "Shaysites," as people began calling the rebels, to be able to put up a stand like Washington's troops did at Valley Forge.

With the help of Boston merchants, Massachusetts raised an army and a few small battles were fought. As hoped, winter proved decisive, and the uprising was frozen out by spring. Several leaders were captured and hanged for treason. Daniel Shays escaped and hid in Vermont until he was pardoned, in keeping with his standing as a "brave and good" veteran of the Revolutionary battles of Bunker Hill, Lexington, and Saratoga.[4] The Massachusetts legislature bought some breathing room by lowering taxes that year, waiting expectantly as delegates to the Constitutional Convention began their long, hot summer of deliberations in Philadelphia at the end of May. More important than the specific incidents involved, however, the rebellions in Massachusetts and elsewhere became galvanizing symbols for much larger questions about power, authority, and the need for new political institutions.

Coverage in the newspapers was colored, as it often is, with enduring themes and images from the political culture. Major newspapers highlighted the speeches of officials who urged citizens to protect the *freedom* won in the Revolution by granting government the power to maintain *order*. On January 17, 1787, the front page of the *Massachusetts Centinel* ran a speech by Governor Bowdoin announcing that he had called out the militia to defend the laws, protect the government, and apprehend "all disturbers of the publick [*sic*] peace." His speech put the focus on the enduring cultural tension between freedom and order by claiming that freedom required order. He closed his speech with a question echoed in different forms many times since in American history: "Is then the goodly fabrick [*sic*] of freedom, which cost us so much blood and treasure, so soon to be thrown into ruins?"[5]

Although the newspapers tended to emphasize the views of officials, there was coverage of the rebels' activities, including descriptions of printed handbills they were circulating to call the people to arms.[6] An exchange of letters between General Benjamin Lincoln and Daniel Shays outlined the rebels' demands and the government position.[7] Newspapers, both large and small, circulated throughout the towns and cities carrying news of the rebellion and raising larger political questions that had not been resolved after the Revolution.[8] The overwhelming impression in the news was that the rebels were a lawless element that threatened the legitimate political order, and that the government had to be strengthened somehow to preserve that order.[9]

Were the rebels a small angry fringe, out of step with the consensus of the great leaders of the day? It turns out that there was not all that much political consensus among the many delegates at the Convention in Philadelphia, who were charged with protecting different state interests and authorized only to amend the existing Articles of Confederation. If the delegates who came to Philadelphia were not in agreement about what kind of government to create, how did they produce such an enduring and generally respected governmental design? The answers to these questions require understanding the politics behind the Constitution.

This chapter explores many of the political conflicts behind the Constitution. It will show why a number of compromises were required to pass it and why the resulting document contains many curious—or, better yet, *exceptional*—features that continue to affect our politics to this day. A good place to begin exploring the politics behind the Constitution is with the cultural themes that guided people in their approaches to designing the institutions of a new government. Many of those cultural themes still influence modern-day thinking about power and government.

The Politics of Compromise: An Enduring Tradition

News of the rebellions of 1786 and 1787 did not travel by newspaper alone, but by word of mouth, song, tall tale, handbills, and privately printed news sheets. The national political elite, or the "Founders," as we have come to call them, were among the leading news transmitters of the day. They kept each other informed through a rich exchange of letters that crossed state boundaries, oceans, and even political philosophies. Many of the founders had deep political disagreements about what government should do and how it should be organized. However, they also recognized that times of crisis called for political compromise and creativity. This creative insight eventually enabled them to work out the remarkable set of compromises that we know today as the United States Constitution.

Abigail Adams was probably the first to inform Thomas Jefferson of the rebellions. Sending a letter to Paris, where Jefferson was Ambassador to France, Mrs. Adams branded Shays and other rebel leaders as "ignorant, restless, desperadoes, without conscience of principles . . . mobbish insurgents . . . sapping the foundation [of the weak government]."[10] Jefferson, in turn, wrote his reaction to another friend back home: "I hold that a little rebellion now and then is a good thing. . . . It is the medicine necessary for the sound health of government. . . . God forbid that we should ever be twenty years without such a rebellion. . . . The tree of liberty must be refreshed from time to time with the blood of patriots and tyrants. It is its natural manure."[11] When Abigail Adams heard about Jefferson's response, she became so angry that she refused to write him for months afterwards.

Meanwhile, fellow Virginian James Madison also wrote to the more radical Jefferson, arguing that the rebels had taken the core cultural idea of liberty well beyond anything Jefferson might have intended in the Declaration of Independence a decade earlier. George Washington, the elder statesman from Virginia, also shared Madison's views and feared that the loosely drawn Articles of Confederation were adopted with too naive a view of human nature in mind. Surveying the scene on the eve of the Philadelphia Convention, Washington wrote, "There are combustibles in every state which a spark might set fire to."[12]

From Jefferson to Madison and Washington, we have a lively debate about the *cultural balance* between *freedom* and *political order*. Other influential thinkers of the day were even less disposed toward freedom and more concerned about preserving order than any of the three Virginians. The conservative—some would say aristocratic—end of the cultural spectrum was anchored by Alexander Hamilton of New York, who would propose in Philadelphia that the president and the Senate should rule for life to protect the government from the passions of the mob. He based this vision of ordered government on this analysis of the turmoil and rebellion that rocked post-revolutionary America: "All communities divide themselves into the few and the many. The first are the rich and well-born, the other the mass of the people. . . . The people are turbulent and changing; they seldom judge or determine right. Give therefore to the first class a . . . permanent share in the government. . . . Nothing but a permanent body can check the imprudence of democracy."[13]

Somehow, out of this swirl of contrasting views—with the problems of slavery, competing concerns about private property, and disparities in state interests and sizes thrown in—the Constitution emerged. It was not just any constitution, but one that has served the country well (with the important exception of the Civil War) for more than two hundred years. Yet few of those looking ahead to the **Constitutional Convention** in Philadelphia that summer of 1787 were optimistic about the chances of success. Even after the Convention had finished its business and produced that short but remarkable document, many remained pessimistic about its chances for survival. Washington, for example, turned to a fellow delegate at the close of the convention and said, "I do not expect the Constitution to last for more than twenty years."[14]

The Constitution has lasted because the political compromises struck among the delegates not only solved their immediate political problems as well as could be done, but created a system of broadly dispersed powers flexible enough (again, with the exception of the Civil War) to ease the pressures of future conflicts, and in many cases, resolve those conflicts fairly well. The framers created a political document that worked not just for their particular problems, but for future generations as well. *In part this adaptability resulted because enduring cultural debates about freedom, order, and government power were written into the document through compromises that kept those competing ideals alive. Those same political compromises created the potential for very different interpretations of that Constitution in the future and for different political uses of the document by opposing factions in society to this day.*

The Constitution as Politics and Political Philosophy

One factor allowing the compromises that eventually produced the Constitution was the grand cultural ideal of *liberty,* with which most political leaders of the day, whether rebels or state governors, were captivated. Liberty was (and still is) a concept so broad that different visions of society and government often take its name. For conservatives such as Alexander Hamilton, who saw liberty as tied to the protection of private property, the main task of government was to impose the order necessary to protect those with property from those without it. Others, such as Jefferson, saw the burden of government and taxes as precisely the thing ordinary people were rebelling against in Massachusetts, New Hampshire, and elsewhere. Despite these differences, the idea of liberty drew the founders together in common debate. Most of the founders were familiar with the latest European philosophers writing on the subject of political liberty, as explained in "Inside the System" Box 2.1. These philosophical views provided many of the ideas that swirled around the Constitution.

While *liberty* and *order* provided a focus for debates about what kind of government to invent, there were still profound political differences to be overcome. Some historians think that without the crisis of authority brought on by the rebellions, the pressure for compromise would have been less and a weaker national government might have emerged. To appreciate how great the compromises were, it helps to trace the history of political divisions from the colonial period, through the Revolution, and during the years thereafter. Understanding the compromises written into the Constitution makes it easier to see why, to this day, this great national charter remains a source of both consensus and conflict in American politics.

In the Beginning: Thirteen Colonies in Search of a Revolution

The colonies were turbulent places from the beginning. Many of the first settlers had been religious dissidents back home. For those immigrants who could not find work or land near the coast, life on the frontier produced constant clashes with the native peoples (that is, the American Indians), leading "backwoods farmers" to demand more protection from England. During its first century of American colonialism, England was unprepared either militarily or economically to develop the frontier, much less to further anger Indian groups that were already becoming allies with France, England's arch-rival and another great colonial power in North America.

To this discontented mix of opinionated, rugged individuals came waves of immigrants who swelled the population, adding to miserable conditions in the big cities and putting more pressures on migration to the frontier. In 1700, the population of the

Governing Ideas: The Foundations of Political Culture

2.1

Those who came together to design a government agreed that the freedom of individuals was the thing to promote—freedom from tyrannical monarchs as well as tyrannical mobs. But how to promote it? European philosophies of liberty were both widely read and hotly debated by the American elite. Yet those philosophers offered an amazing range of solutions for the problem of liberty. On the authoritarian extreme was the Englishman Thomas Hobbes, whose classic *Leviathan* (1651) decried the English Civil War and the potential for class conflict to reduce society to a "state of nature" in which life became "solitary, poor, nasty, brutish, and short." Some Americans such as Alexander Hamilton embraced Hobbes' solution of an enlightened sovereign bound to the people by a social contract that respected basic rights and liberties. Since the idea of a monarchy, even an enlightened one, was unsellable in America, Hamilton pushed instead for a president and Senate for life—a plan also rejected by most as too authoritarian and aristocratic. At the other, more democratic, extreme were the ideas of French philosophers like Jean-Jacques Rousseau (1712–1778) who called for a more grass-roots or egalitarian social contract between the people and a broadly representative government. These ideas were brought back to America by people like Franklin and Jefferson, but most other American leaders found them dangerously democratic and too close to inviting mob rule, which, in fact, brought on the downfall of the French Revolution of 1789.

In the middle of the philosophical spectrum of thinking about liberty were the ideas of English philosopher John Locke. In his influential *Second Treatise on Government* (1690), Locke stated three powerful guidelines that shaped the broad outlines of the American Constitution: 1) *the power of the state must be limited*, 2) *the freedom of individuals must be maximized*, and 3) *private property (the eco-nomic engine of the good society) must be protected*. But how to do this? As for limiting the powers of government, the founders quickly latched onto the proposals of the French philosopher Montesquieu, whose book *The Spirit of the Laws* (1748) recommended a constitution that separated the powers of governing between an executive, a legislative, and a judiciary branch. (Sound familiar?) As for protecting property, Madison's schemes for limiting popular participation and representation guaranteed that most of the voters and most of the office holders would be propertied. What better protection for property and the growth of capitalism was there than that? As for individual freedoms, separating and checking the power of government was a start, and the addition of a Bill of Rights added grass-roots support. To this day, a broad range of ideas about liberty, order, and government continue to be expressed in American politics. Can you spot them in contemporary political debates?

---

colonies was about 250,000. By 1760, it had exploded to two million. By 1790, the numbers had doubled again to around four million.[15] Life in the cities became a grinding clash between a prospering middle class and growing ranks of homeless people, beggars, and the down-and-out. One account in Peter Zenger's pesky New York paper *The Journal* described street children in the city as objects that were human in shape, but "half starv'd with cold, with cloathes out at the Elbos, Knees through the Breeches, Hair standing on end. . . . From the age about four to fourteen they spend their days in the streets. . . . then they are put out as Apprentices, perhaps four, five or six years."[16]

Yet life was not much easier for those who tried it on the frontier. A hundred years before the Revolution, resentment boiled over at local colonial governors who had become wealthy through land grants from the king. These colonial land barons cynically encouraged the poor folk to go west, where they received little protection or help from

The plight of the homeless and urban poor is not unique to modern times, as this nineteenth-century drawing of New York squatters illustrates. Indeed, by passing the Quebec Act of 1774—which trapped poor immigrants in the slums of east-coast cities by closing off the frontier from further settlement—Britain's Parliament contributed significantly to colonial discontent and the American desire for independence from England.

those same officials. In 1676 Nathaniel Bacon led the first large-scale rebellion against a colonial government (in Virginia), burning the capital of Jamestown, and prompting Governor Berkeley to describe his political fortunes like this shortly before he fled the scene: "How miserable that man is that Governs a People where six parts of seaven [*sic*] at least are Poore Endebted Discontented and Armed."[17]

A Brief History of Rebellion

In the hundred years between Bacon's rebellion in 1676 and the Declaration of Independence in 1776, there were an estimated eighteen uprisings against colonial governments, six major slave rebellions, and forty urban riots.[18] Yet no more than fifteen years before the War of Independence broke out, the idea of revolution was as remote as one could imagine. Poor peoples' uprisings in those days "came with the territory" in colonies owned by aristocratic governments. Excluded from power and the exchange of ideas, there was no other way for the common folk to make their opinions heard, and their grievances felt, than to stir up trouble now and then.

Why was this not a scene ripe for full-scale revolution? Without the support of people like the wealthy and educated founders who eventually supported the Declaration of Independence and organized an army, there was little chance of the people at the bottom of society joining together in a revolutionary movement. *The whole colonial system—at least when it was functioning according to design—worked against sustained, organized resistance*. In fact, the colonial legacy continued to divide the former colonies well after the Revolution and created bitter fights among the state delegations at the Convention.

The Politics of Colonialism

The colonial system worked against revolution for several basic reasons:

- *Divide-and-conquer economic relations between the colonies.* Under colonialism, each colony had its own economic (and political) arrangement with England. Trade occurred across the Atlantic, not across colonial borders. In fact, many neighboring colonies were virtually cut off by rugged terrain and lacked encouragement from London to form local ties. The results? Even on the eve of revolution, leaders from different colonies often regarded one another with suspicion and distrust—as competitors rather than compatriots. All of this made the eventual design of a constitution a highly challenging problem.[19]

- *Political and economic divisions within the colonies.* Colonial society was complex. First, there were the English administrators and the lucky recipients of royal land grants and licenses to do business. These people had an interest in staying with the king. Then there were small merchants and manufacturers, whose interests rose and fell with the king's economic policies. In the agricultural sector, big planters had interests quite separate from those of small farmers. And people on the frontier had needs quite different from those of city-dwellers. All of these factors made a convergence of revolutionary, much less governmental, interests seem unlikely. Even after the fighting broke out, it is likely (according to the estimate of John Adams) that no more than one-third of the colonists strongly favored the Revolution, another third strongly opposed it, and the middle third were divided in their loyalties. As later events like Shays' Rebellion and the debate over the need for a Bill of Rights suggest, these internal divisions persisted after the Revolution as well, further complicating the politics of the Constitution.

- *A relatively contented colonial elite created an uncertain leadership situation.* Seven in ten signers of the Declaration of Independence held elected political office under the British royal administration. Until the later disputes over taxation and representation erupted, the founders enjoyed the "rights and liberties of Englishmen," as citizens of the most liberal political system in Europe. And most were wealthy. George Washington, on paper at least, was probably the richest man in America.

Until the fighting broke out, many of the colonial elite still hoped that the king would step in, clear up those misunderstandings over taxes imposed by a corrupt Parliament, and restore their once perfect union. In fact, those hopes were written down in the "humble and dutiful" petition to the king by "his majesty's subjects in America" that was issued from the First Continental Congress under the pen of Thomas Jefferson in 1774. After the fighting broke out the next year, Jefferson drafted the Declaration of Independence and the colonial leadership finally broke with the king.

Although some of the leading politicians and thinkers of the day joined the revolutionary cause, they were careful about how they stirred up the masses of poor people.

Thomas Jefferson reads a draft of the Declaration of Independence to Benjamin Franklin. In October of 1774, on behalf of the First Continental Congress, Jefferson had written the Declaration of Rights, calling upon King George III to redress American grievances according to the "principles of the English Constitution." Britain's refusal to do so—to acknowledge the traditional, established rights of the colonists as English subjects—finally led to a reluctant break with the mother country. Wrote Jefferson in 1776: "We have petitioned for redress in the most humble terms: Our repeated petitions have been answered only by repeated injury."

Supporters of the *power-elite thesis* (described in Chapter 1) claim that this thesis applies even to the politics of the Revolution and the Constitution, because many of the leaders of the revolt against the king were also wealthy, propertied individuals who were careful not to let the Revolution or the government afterwards turn against their interests.[20] Tensions between leaders and masses remained evident throughout the revolutionary process. It was Samuel Adams who cautioned the angry mobs of Boston's poor against "confusion and tumult" in favor of more orderly actions like the Tea Party. During Shays' Rebellion, the same Samuel Adams helped draft the Riot Act that was read to poor farmers still seeking economic relief—this time from their own government. *Pluralist* analysts respond that the colonial elite were as mistrustful of one another as they were of tyranny by the majority, resulting in a governing system that limited the power of *all* groups.

The Politics of Revolution

What brought the disorganized colonial scene to a revolutionary climax and later to a new constitutional beginning? To quote the great opening line of the Declaration of Independence, we must look to "the course of human events." In particular, history points to the repeated blunders of King George III, who, as a noted historian observed in a grand understatement, "was not the most astute politician."[21] Had British politics been better conducted, the United States might have experienced a more gradual, peaceful

George III (1738–1820), monarch of England, after a portrait by Sir Thomas Lawrence. A twist of fate placed an unstable ruler on the throne at a crucial time in Anglo-American relations. Beginning in 1765, King George suffered periodic bouts of mental illness (perhaps stemming from physical causes), which doubtless contributed to the swift and unexpected deterioration in political amity. Years later, however, he would tell American president John Adams, "I have done nothing in the late contest but what I thought myself indispensably bound to do by the duty which I owed my people. . . . I was the last to consent to the separation, but the separation having been made. . . . I would be the first to meet the friendship of the United States as an independent power."

separation from England (more like Canada, perhaps), and ended up with quite a different political system. It was due largely to the king's bungling and contempt that the revolutionary upheaval took place.

As late as 1760, however, it was hard to imagine a group happier with its situation than the colonial leadership that eventually threw its weight behind the independence movement. If we go back just fifteen years before "the shot heard around the world" was fired in Massachusetts, the scene looked something like this: The colonial economies were booming, the middle class was growing, and local leaders had considerable influence in colonial assemblies that were granted wide governing powers. To top it off, the British army had just defeated the French and their Indian allies in Montreal, giving the English king claim to vast French territories in North America. (France would later get its revenge on Britain by helping the colonies during the Revolution.)

The great irony of this historical moment is that at no time since settlement began had the future seemed so bright for so many Americans. Huge land grants were given to leaders such as Washington as their reward for services to the king. Poor people began moving in large numbers to the greatly expanded frontier in search of relief from their urban miseries. Although the American Indian peoples understandably resisted the settlement of their lands, the westward movement now had support from the top levels of the colonial administration. For the first time, diverse colonial interests, both rich and poor, looked to prosper from the new development opportunities.

But none of the rosy economic forecasts took into account a Parliament corrupted by the success (and political excess) of empire, or the budgetary crisis that England suffered because of the huge military costs of winning and defending its New World holdings. Most of all, nobody foresaw the consequences of King George III taking the throne in 1760. Into the historical moment stepped a man who even his own father described as "half-witted." To make matters worse, the new king's political ambitions were as sizeable as his lack of intelligence. It was a recipe for disaster.

The king used his ministers to run a series of short-sighted laws through Parliament. Prior to the Peace of Paris in 1763 (which made England's North American territories far too big to neglect), London's general lack of interest in colonial affairs had given the Americans a great deal of autonomy. Afterward, London's insensitive interventions in colonial matters became a source of tremendous friction.

Because the sudden flurry of new rules, regulations, taxes, and orders came officially from Parliament, the legislative arm of England's evolving "parliamentary monarchy," many colonial leaders believed for years that their real dispute was with Parliament, not the king. It was an easy mistake to make, given the corruption and weakness of that legislature. More importantly, blaming the king was difficult to imagine because it ultimately meant breaking with the concept of monarchy itself, which was still the reigning political philosophy of the time. Making this break would eventually require the revolutionaries to embrace the radical new doctrines of popular sovereignty, or self-government. All of this was a tall order for a not very united people.

Such "revolutionary" changes could occur only with constant provocation, and the royal government seemed only too happy to oblige. The first act that got the attention of the colonists was sending thousands of troops to "defend" the colonies following the Peace of Paris. The colonists were not accustomed to an English military presence; the leaders fancied themselves as voluntary subjects and prided themselves on their own defense and internal government. What began as the idle speculation about an unfriendly "military occupation" by England was taken even more seriously when taxes were charged to the colonists to pay for it.

You know the story from this point: The Sugar Act was followed by the Stamp Act; the Stamp Act was followed by the Quartering Act; the Quartering Act was followed by

"Bostonians Paying the Excise-Man, Or, Tarring & Feathering." This 1774 lithograph, showing the harbor's customs commissioner being tarred, feathered, and forced to drink tea, closely reflects the Boston Tea Party of December 16, 1773, in which colonists destroyed hundreds of crates of British tea in an attempt to forestall the imposing of import taxes. When Parliament retaliated by closing down the port in June 1774, this action and the other "Coercive Acts" served only to unite the colonies, leading to the convening of the First Continental Congress that fall.

the Townshend Acts; and on and on. Acts that increased the British military presence were followed by tax laws requiring the colonists to pay for their own "protection." And those acts were followed by acts requiring the local housing and feeding of troops. All in all, this military "protection" program seemed less and less friendly.

The core of the English blunder was the new tax system imposed upon the colonies. The colonies already contributed greatly to England's economy through the production of raw materials (exported to England) and the purchase of processed consumer goods (imported *from* England). However, they were not accustomed to paying large taxes on top of what was already a highly profitable trading system for the English. The multitude of new taxes had two "revolutionary" effects:

- First, the new taxes hit all of the diverse interests in the colonies in one way or another. Small merchants were squeezed. Printers and lawyers had their activities and profits cut. Consumers paid higher prices. The money supply was restricted (in part by new prohibitions on local currencies). Even the thriving industry of smugglers and black marketeers was pinched by increased tax collection and enforcement measures. In short, many of those divided groups mentioned earlier were drawn gradually into a common anger at England.

- Second, the burden of taxes on the colonies created a small ideological opening through which eventually the whole philosophy of representative democracy and popular sovereignty would emerge to replace the idea of monarchy. Although the colonies had not been represented in Parliament, they had not been taxed like this before either. Suddenly, with the new tax system, people began to echo the oldest battle cry in the English political tradition: "No taxation without representation."

THE DECLARATION OF INDEPENDENCE

THE UNANIMOUS DECLARATION OF THE THIRTEEN UNITED STATES OF AMERICA

When in the Course of human events it becomes necessary for one people to dissolve the political bands which have connected them with another, and to assume among the Powers of the earth, the separate and equal station to which the Laws of Nature and of Nature's God entitle them, a decent respect to the opinions of mankind requires that they should declare the causes which impel them to the separation.

We hold these truths to be self-evident, that all men are created equal, that they are endowed by their Creator with certain unalienable Rights, that among these are Life, Liberty and the pursuit of Happiness. That to secure these rights, Governments are instituted among Men, deriving their just Powers from the consent of the governed. That whenever any Form of Government become destructive of these ends, it is the Right of the People to alter or to abolish it, and to institute new Government, laying its foundation on such principles and organizing its Powers in such form, as to them shall seem most likely to effect their Safety and Happiness. Prudence, indeed, will dictate that Governments long established should not be changed for light and transient causes; and accordingly all experience hath shewn, that mankind are more disposed to suffer, while evils are sufferable, than to right themselves by abolishing the forms to which they are accustomed. But when a long train of abuses and usurpation, pursuing invariably the same Object, evinces a design to reduce them under absolute Despotism, it is their right, it is their duty, to throw off such Government, and to provide new Guards for their future security. Such has been the patient sufferance of these Colonies; and such is now the necessity which constrains them to alter their former Systems of Government. The history of the present King of Great Britain is a history of repeated injuries and usurpations, all having in direct object the establishment of an absolute Tyranny over these States. To prove this, let Facts be submitted to a candid world.

He has refused his Assent to Laws, the most wholesome and necessary for the public good.

He has forbidden his Governors to pass Laws of immediate and pressing importance, unless suspended in their operation till his Assent should be obtained; and when so suspended, he has utterly neglected to attend to them.

He has refused to pass other Laws for the accommodation of large districts of people, unless those people would relinquish the right of Representation in the Legislature, a right inestimable to them and formidable to tyrants only.

He has called together legislative bodies at places unusual, uncomfortable, and distant from the depository of their Public Records, for the sole Purpose of fatiguing them into compliance with his measures.

He has dissolved Representative Houses repeatedly, for opposing with manly firmness his invasions on the rights of the People.

He has refused for a long time, after such dissolutions, to cause others to be elected; whereby the Legislative Powers, incapable of Annihilation, have returned to the People at large for their exercise; the State remaining in the mean time exposed to all the dangers of invasion from without, and convulsions within.

He has endeavored to prevent the Population of these States; for that purpose obstructing the Laws for Naturalization of Foreigners; refusing to pass others to encourage their migrations hither, and raising the conditions of new Appropriations of Lands.

He has obstructed the Administration of Justice, by refusing his Assent to Laws for establishing Judiciary Powers.

He has made Judges dependent on his Will alone, for the tenure of their offices, and the amount and payment of their salaries.

He has erected a multitude of New Offices, and sent higher swarms of Officers to harass our People, and eat out their substance.

He has kept among us, in times of peace, Standing Armies without the Consent of our legislatures.

He has affected to render the Military independent of and superior to the Civil Power.

He has combined with others to subject us to a jurisdiction foreign to our constitution, and unacknowledged by our laws; giving his Assent to their Acts of pretended Legislation:

For Quartering large bodies of armed troops among us:

For protecting them, by a mock Trial, from Punishment for any Murders which they should commit on the Inhabitants of these States:

For cutting off our Trade with all parts of the world:

For imposing Taxes on us without our Consent:

For depriving us in many cases, of the benefits of Trial by Jury:

For transporting us beyond Seas to be tried for pretended offences:

For abolishing the free System of English Laws in a neighboring Province, establishing therein an Arbitrary government, and enlarging its Boundaries so as to render it at once an example and fit instrument for introducing the same absolute rule into these Colonies:

For taking away our Charters, abolishing our most valuable Laws, and layering fundamentally the Forms of our Governments:

For suspending our own Legislatures, and declaring themselves invested with Power to legislate for us in all cases whatsoever.

He has abdicated Government here, by declaring us out of his Protection, and waging War against us.

He has plundered our seas, ravaged our Coasts, burnt our towns, and destroyed the lives of our people.

He is at this time transporting large Armies of foreign Mercenaries to compleat the works of death, desolation and tyranny, already begun with circumstances of Cruelty and perfidy scarcely paralleled in the most barbarous ages, and totally unworthy the Head of a civilized nation.

He has constrained our fellow Citizens taken Captive on the high Seas to bear Arms against their Country, to become the executioners of their friends and Brethren, or to fall themselves by their Hands.

He has excited domestic insurrections amongst us, and has endeavored to bring on the inhabitants of our frontiers, the merciless Indian Savages, whose known rule of warfare, is an undistinguished destruction of all ages, sexes and conditions.

In every stage of these Oppressions We have Petitioned for Redress in the most humble terms: Our repeated Petitions have been answered only by repeated injury. A Prince, whose character is thus marked by every act which may define a Tyrant, is unfit to be the ruler of a free People.

Nor have We been wanting in attentions to our British brethren. We have warned them from time to time of attempts by their legislature to extend an unwarrantable jurisdiction over us. We have reminded them of the circumstances of our emigration and settlement here. We have appealed to their native justice and magnanimity, and we have conjured them by the ties of our common kindred to disavow these usurpations, which, would inevitably interrupt our connections and correspondence. They too have been deaf to the voice of justice and of consanguinity. We must, therefore, acquiesce in the necessity, which denounces our Separation, and hold them, as we hold the rest of mankind, Enemies in War, in Peace Friends.

WE, THEREFORE, the Representatives of the UNITED STATES OF AMERICA, in General Congress, Assembled, appealing to the supreme Judge of the world for the rectitude of our intentions, do, in the Name, and by authority of the good People of these Colonies, solemnly publish and declare, That these United Colonies are, and of Right ought to be FREE AND INDEPENDENT STATES; that they are Absolved from all Allegiance to the British Crown, and that all political connection between them and the State of Great Britain, is and ought to be totally dissolved; and that, as Free and Independent States, they have full Power to levy War, conclude Peace, contract Alliances, establish Commerce, and to do all other Acts and Things which Independent States may of right do. And for the support of this Declaration, with a firm reliance on the protection of divine Providence, we mutually pledge to each other our Lives, our Fortunes and our sacred Honor.

Signed by ORDER and BEHALF of the CONGRESS,

JOHN HANCOCK, *President*

Attest.

CHARLES THOMSON, Secretary

Adams, John (Mass.)	Hancock, John (Mass.)	Lynch, Thomas Jr. (S.C.)	Sherman, Roger (Conn.)
Adams, Samuel (Mass.)	Harrison, Benjamin (Va.)	McKean, Thomas (Del.)	Smith, James (Pa.)
Bartlett, Josiah (N.H.)	Hart, John (N.J.)	Middleton, Arthur (S.C.)	Stockton, Richard (N.J.)
Braxton, Carter (Va.)	Hewes, Joseph (N.C.)	Morris, Lewis (N.Y.)	Stone, Thomas (Md.)
Carroll, Chas. of Carrollton (Md.)	Heyward, Thos. Jr. (S.C.)	Morris, Robert (Pa.)	Taylor, George (Pa.)
Chase, Samuel (Md.)	Hooper, William (N.C.)	Morton, John (Pa.)	Thornton, Matthew (N.H.)
Clark, Abraham (N.J.)	Hopkins, Stephen (R.I.)	Nelson, Thos. Jr. (Va.)	Walton, George (Ga.)
Clymer, George (Pa.)	Hopkinson, Francis (N.J.)	Paca, William (Md.)	Whipple, William (N.H.)
Ellery, William (R.I.)	Huntington, Samuel (Conn.)	Paine, Robert Treat (Mass.)	Williams, William (Conn.)
Floyd, William (N.Y.)	Jefferson, Thomas (Va.)	Penn, John (N.C.)	Wilson, James (Pa.)
Franklin, Benjamin (Pa.)	Lee, Francis Lightfoot (Va.)	Read, George (Del.)	Witherspoon, John (N.J.)
Gerry, Elbridge (Mass.)	Lee, Richard Henry (Va.)	Rodney, Caesar (Del.)	Wolcott, Oliver (Conn.)
Gwinnett, Button (Ga.)	Lewis, Francis (N.Y.)	Ross, George (Pa.)	Wythe, George (Va.)
Hall, Lyman (Ga.)	Livingston, Philip (N.Y.)	Rush, Benjamin (Pa.)	
		Rutledge, Edward (S.C.)	

"No Taxation Without Representation": That Revolutionary Slogan of . . . 1215?

The slow movement from the absolute, divine right of monarchy to the popular sovereignty of modern democracy began not in 1776 but long before—more than five hundred years before. The American revolution greatly speeded up the pace of change by fully replacing the rights of royal families with the rights of individuals. However, the first step in this long process came in the year 1215, the year the barons of England met at Runnymede and petitioned King John to stop taxing them without hearing their views first, among other provisions. The king had just spent the royal treasury on another costly war with France and raised taxes to pay for it. As a result of that dispute, the king, the Archbishop of Canterbury, and the barons agreed in **Magna Carta** (the Great Charter) to share certain rights and powers.

Beginning with the idea of representation in taxation, the rights of English subjects expanded gradually over the next four centuries to include the right, if arrested, to trial by a jury of peers (established in the Habeas Corpus Act of 1679); and the right (for men of property) to representation and freedom of speech in Parliament. The greatest expansion of rights came after the "Glorious Revolution," in which Prince William of Orange forced King James II from the throne after a bloodless political struggle in 1688. William and his wife Mary then assumed power with the consent of Parliament, thus ending the concept of divinely ordained monarchy. This was followed by the signing of the English Bill of Rights in 1689—a document that looks very much like the later American version. Although England does not have a formal, written constitution, the existence of Magna Carta and an early bill of rights, among other documents, leads many to classify England as having a "constitutional tradition,"or as some put it, an "unwritten constitution." (See "How We Compare" Box 2.2.)

The point of this story is that when the colonists complained about "taxation without representation," they were upset about a clear violation of their traditional rights as English citizens—or so they thought. The refusal of Parliament or the king to hear their appeals alarmed many colonial leaders who always assumed they were real English citizens with full rights and protections. As taxes increased, so did the level of protest, leading

Crispus Attucks (center), *a sailor and ex-slave, was one of the first casualties of Anglo-American hostilities resulting from the Quartering Acts and Townshend Acts of the late 1760s. Yet the so-called Boston Massacre of March 1770, in which five colonists were killed outright, was at least partly an act of self-defense by eight British soldiers who had been surrounded by a shouting, club-wielding mob. The soldiers were defended in court by no less than John Adams, later a signer of the Declaration of Independence and ultimately the second president of the United States. Six of the eight were acquitted; the remaining two received light sentences. It would take several more years of hostility to bring about a tenuous coalition uniting the various strands of colonial society against the British.*

The Unwritten British Constitution

2.2

The British constitutional tradition is unique for what it lacks: a single written document that spells out the power relationships among various political institutions. Instead, what many observers refer to as the "unwritten" British constitution is a collection of separate documents, common law principles, and political traditions. This collection of chartering ideals began with the Magna Carta agreement, signed in 1215 between King John and a group of nobles seeking representation in matters of taxation.

The absence of a single charter of government means that the force of *tradition* has become, along with the vigilance of the people, politicians, and the press, the binding force of government. Although it is hard to imagine such things happening, the monarchy is not legally bound to assent to measures passed by Parliament, nor is the majority party in power required by law to resign when it receives a no-confidence vote from the House of Commons.

What is the secret of this binding but unwritten constitution? Some political scientists say that the absence of a written charter makes it easier to write ordinary laws in response to crises and changing social conditions. In addition, a cohesive culture with a strong tradition of rights and popular sovereignty creates a strong set of expectations from citizens about the behaviors of their representatives.

Will the British ever attempt to write a constitution? The movement toward unification in Europe in the 1980s and 1990s created conflicts between some British laws and various European agreements. For example,

Britain has tangled with the European Court of Human Rights for keeping prisoners in jail without trial under provisions of the Prevention of Terrorism Act. Proposals have been circulated by various think tanks and political parties for a constitution to streamline legal disputes and clarify institutional powers. Suggestions include a formal bill of rights, a freedom of information act, a streamlined proportional representation system in elections, and making membership in the House of Lords elective rather than by appointment. One proposal even calls for abolishing the monarchy and having an elected president as head of state. These ideas have generated considerable disagreement. Any proposal will have to overcome traditional sentiments that Britain has done perfectly well without a written constitution.

eventually to boycotts of English goods and blatant disregard of the tax laws themselves. Printers, for example, often stamped a small skull and crossbones in the space where the tax stamps were supposed to be placed on all printed materials, including legal contracts, newspapers, and even playing cards.

Instead of taking advantage of many offers to negotiate, the king and his succession of ministers regarded colonial reactions as blatant threats to government authority itself. Soon the tax acts were backed up by laws intended purely to discipline and punish the colonies. The so-called "Coercive Acts," for example, closed the Port of Boston (after the Tea Party), allowed dissidents to be arrested and sent directly to England without trial, and closed the new territories to immigration (which bottled up more poor people in the cities while shutting down the economy at the same time). It is little wonder that many colonists took to renaming the "Coercive Acts" the "Intolerable Acts," and escalated their protests against them.

In the space of fifteen short years the seemingly impossible had happened: Once-prosperous colonial economies were all but shut down. Once-happy colonial leaders now sensed that they were second-class citizens. Seemingly incompatible interests (including the unlikely alliance of rich and poor) were drawn into a common hatred of the English government.

Boston, which had suffered the greatest hostilities, boiled over into mass violence shortly before the outbreak of warfare on April 19, 1775. (One month earlier, Parliament had rejected an eloquent final plea by Englishman Edmund Burke for conciliation with the colonies and the repeal of the various taxes and punitive acts imposed on them.) The rest of the colonies soon joined the fight begun at Lexington, aided by the timely publication of Thomas Paine's popular pamphlet *Common Sense*. Paine spelled out what even the most reluctant colonial leaders were coming to believe: The root problem was with the monarchy itself. So long as there remained a central figure of authority with such great powers, the rights and liberties of individuals were always in danger. That was, for Paine, the inescapable political lesson of the last fifteen years of unrepresentative taxes and unreasonable punishments. According to Paine, common sense told freedom-loving people that, with the idea of monarchy, "'Tis time to part."

The Declaration of Independence

For many of the colonists, Paine's argument was too radical to embrace. However, for the hundreds of thousands who bought *Common Sense* and shared its arguments with their friends, the revolution was on. Thomas Paine was raised from obscurity to the most widely read author of his day. The idea of "natural" and "inalienable" individual rights was raised from a questionable philosophical idea to the key phrase of Jefferson's Declaration of Independence.[22]

Inspired by the Declaration's broad promise of "life, liberty, and the pursuit of happiness," enough Americans rallied to the revolutionary cause to defeat the British (with more than a little help from the French, who finally got their revenge against their old enemies). Throughout the ordeal, however, the revolutionary coalition of rich and poor, urban and rural, north and south was an uneasy one. Washington had trouble keeping his army fed, clothed, armed, and paid. Many farmers preferred to sell their produce to the English army for real payment than to donate to the Continental troops on the promise of future compensation. And colonial governments differed widely in their levels of moral and material support.

In the beginning, the Continental Congress—which began as an informal, secret organization to try to work out the differences with the king—did not even have formal pow-

The Second Continental Congress votes for independence in this painting jointly credited to British-American painter Robert Edge Pine (1730–1788) and American painter Edward Savage (1761–1817). Delegates actually voted twice: On July 2, 1776, they approved a resolution introduced by Richard Henry Lee; two days later, they issued a final version of the Declaration of Independence that had been drafted by Thomas Jefferson.

ers to conduct the war. The embarrassing possibility of having to sign thirteen separate treaties of alliance with France finally goaded the Continental Congress to adopt (in 1777) the Articles of Confederation, so that foreign policy, at least, could be conducted in the name of one nation. Yet the formal ratification of the Articles by all the states did not occur until 1781, leaving in some doubt the authority for much of the governing that went on during the Revolution.

After the war ended, the government operating under the Articles of Confederation worked out a successful peace treaty and began the development of western land. However, in many other areas facing the nation, the governing vacuum that had plagued the Revolution only became worse afterwards, when many of the states, freed from the outside threat that had drawn them together, withdrew into their own political and economic worlds. The political divisions behind the Revolution continued to complicate the struggle to create a stronger government after the Revolution.

After the Revolution: One Nation or Thirteen? ———

The factors that had divided the colonies before the Revolution came back to haunt them as states afterwards:

- The separate economies created by colonial trading relations with England continued to look more to England than to one another for economic exchange.

- The divided internal interests of rich and poor, urban and backwoods, small farm and big plantation, slave and free, continued to project vastly different meanings onto the concept of liberty and the ideas about what kind of government would best promote it.

- The leadership that joined the revolutionary coalition was pulled in different directions by different philosophies of government (as outlined in Box 2.1).

- There were local pressures to maintain strong state governments.

For a time, it seemed that America might resemble Europe, as a multitude of small, squabbling nations emerging in the wake of revolution. The postwar era of government under the Articles of Confederation illustrates both what drove the colonies apart and why they eventually had to join together again under a stronger constitution.

The Articles of Confederation

The **Articles of Confederation** that forged political union from the chaos of revolution were probably not as much a failure as some detractors would suggest. The government operating under the Articles accomplished some important things, including negotiating treaties with foreign powers, setting up a small national bureaucracy, and making policies on how to develop new territories.[23] However, as the state officials of Massachusetts found out when they requested military assistance to put down local rebellions, the powers of the Confederation of States were severely limited. Those limits reflected the many divisions of opinion about just what a central government should do.

Probably the greatest limitation of the national government under the Articles was the absence of tax powers, forcing the Confederation to beg for money from the states. This illustrates *the defining difference between a confederation and a federation: A* **confederation** *is a largely voluntary association of sovereign states, while a federation is a binding association of subordinate states that give up some degree of autonomy*. The Articles of Confederation clearly called for a "league of friendship" that would not threaten the "sovereignty, freedom, and independence" of the member states.

In addition to the absence of tax powers, the Articles of Confederation contained other weaknesses. For example, the Confederate Congress had little means of enforcing its decisions. In addition, there was a provision for a military commander, a role filled during the Revolution by George Washington, but there was no army. The separate states had to authorize Congress to hire an army. Although this authorization was granted to fight the Revolution, the states went deeply into debt to pay for it, removing any later thought of maintaining a standing army. As a result, when Massachusetts called for help to put down Shays' Rebellion, there was none to send.

The Articles placed what governing power there was almost entirely in the Confederation Congress. However, the Congress had to persuade the states to accept and (even more difficult) to pay for its decisions. Worse still, there was no chief executive to coordinate and implement decisions. What this meant, then, was that the Articles left government decisions without an independent executive to implement them, no money to pay for them, and no reliable means to enforce them. To make governing even more difficult, there was not a centralized means of regulating commerce, transportation, or the use of common waterways between the states.

To say the least, many politicians in the newly independent states were mistrustful of centralized authority. United out of necessity against a common enemy during their war for independence, the states quickly reverted to their underlying isolation and mistrust afterward. All in all, it was not a good beginning for a government. Not surprisingly, things fell apart. State economies plunged into depression. State governments were unable to pay debts or raise taxes. Legislatures that issued worthless currency bought temporary relief for poor farmers, who used it to pay debts, but angered businesses that often refused to accept the worthless payments. On the other hand, states that tried to hold the economic line faced open rebellion from poor people and farmers. The problem became increasingly clear: In an atmosphere of growing chaos, there was no central authority to step in, restore order, issue money, raise taxes, pay debts, or settle disputes over rights. The states could not even rely on the Confederation government to resolve fishing squabbles on Chesapeake Bay.

In light of the political divisions among the states, it is not surprising that things had to start falling apart before state leaders were compelled to think about the idea of stronger national government. The outbreak of rebellions led to calls from the press to redesign the government, but there were great differences in philosophy, interests, and power that had to be overcome at the Constitutional Convention in Philadelphia. The politics at that convention continue to affect our lives today.

The Politics of the Constitution

Philadelphia was the natural site for the Convention. It had been the meeting place of the Continental Congresses that petitioned the king, declared independence, and conducted the war. It was the nation's largest city by far (pop. 40,000), and the most refined, whether one wanted to buy fine imported wares or study science and medicine. The heat of summer in Philadelphia did not invite lengthy gatherings inside closed buildings, but it was a time of crisis. And so, the delegates came, and they met.

The fifty-five delegates who came to Philadelphia at one time or another during that long summer of 1787 were among the wealthiest, most politically prominent, and best educated people in the land. Eight had signed the Declaration of Independence, eleven were officers in Washington's army, forty-two had been in the Congress under the Articles of Confederation, and forty held state government positions at the time. The group included thirty-three lawyers, eight businessmen, six plantation owners, three physicians, and two college presidents. At least one third had been to college, and perhaps most notably, "They were generally men of considerable wealth."[24] Considerable debate

Reconciling Differences

The uniting of thirteen colonies into one nation was achieved only through compromise among widely diverging viewpoints. James Madison (*right*) helped to forge the Constitution "to secure the public good, and private rights, against the danger of faction and at the same time to preserve the spirit and form of popular government." The conservative Alexander Hamilton (*above*) supported the document despite his own concerns about "the extremes of democracy." At the opposite end of the political spectrum was Thomas Paine (*below*), who held that "moderation in principle is always a vice." Many of the Founders were relieved that, by 1787, Paine had returned to his native England to urge the monarchy's overthrow, later emigrating to France at the peak of its revolutionary terror. Contemplating his colleague's "career of mischief," John Adams sardonically punned that this era of bloodshed and upheaval should be remembered as "the Age of Paine."

The Players

INSIDE THE SYSTEM

A Constitution Written by a "Power Elite"? Or. . .

2.3

One view of the Constitution is that it is a document written of, by, and for the wealthy, propertied minority. Although divided in many ways, these elites finally overcame their regional and economic differences when the threat of poor people's rebellions and state economic collapses drove them to try to form a stronger central government. According to this view, the conflicts at the convention reflected different interests within the elite, but the compromises that emerged spread broad economic benefits among the wealthy and powerful at the expense of the majority, who were restrained from directly challenging the elites who would be elected to most of the offices of government. In addition, the new government was also given broad tax and revenue powers enabling economic development and paying off loans which elites had made to the old government.

The evidence offered to support this analysis includes the following data:

• No delegate to the Philadelphia convention represented the small farmer or mechanic (working) classes.

• Forty delegates held "public securities," representing government promises to repay money loaned by those delegates to finance the Revolution or later activities of the government under the Articles of Confederation. A stronger federal government with tax and revenue powers greatly increased the chances of repaying those debts.

• Fourteen delegates owned land for speculation that might increase in value under a stronger government dedicated to building roads and other development projects.

• Eleven owned investments in large industries (trading, manufacturing, shipping) that would prosper under a more active government.

• Fifteen owned slaves and wielded enough power to protect the slave system under the new Constitution.

SOURCES: Charles A. Beard, *An Economic Interpretation of the Constitution of the United States.* New York: The Free Press, 1986, pp. 149–151. Howard Zinn, *A People's History of the United States.* New York: Harper & Row, 1980.

has been sparked among historians and political scientists about whether or not these elites designed a government to protect their interests by limiting *majority power* and the interests of the common people.

On the *power elite* (see Chapter 1) side of this controversy are those who follow historian Charles Beard's 1913 contention that wealthy interests from the state legislatures selected like-minded delegates to design a government that would protect property, have the authority to raise money to repay loans they had made to finance the Revolution, and generally limit the power of the unruly and poor majority—like those rebelling in Massachusetts and elsewhere.[25] (See "Inside the System" Box 2.3 for an illustration of this analysis of the politics behind the scenes of the Convention.) Beard's thesis has been criticized by many historians since, largely for ignoring the fact that as many state elites *opposed* a stronger central government as favored it.[26] However, his point about restrictions on majority power continues to be acknowledged and has been developed by other elite theorists.

On the other side of the controversy are the *pluralists* (see Chapter 1), who emphasize the philosophical differences among the delegates and point out that they were guided less by personal interests than by the ideas contained in the French and English philosophies of democratic government reviewed in Box 2.1. In their time, the philoso-

A Constitution Designed to Promote Pluralism?

2.4

Rejecting elitist views of the Constitution are pluralist analyses, which emphasize the philosophical concerns and democratic ideals of the founders. Pluralist historians and political scientists argue that the founders were taken with great ideas and philosophies. They promoted ideals and theories of government as actively as the elitists claim they promoted their class interests.

In addition, the pluralists note that the founders were divided in their specific economic interests, making it difficult to write those interests directly into the document. The goal of compromise was to keep any group from dominating the new government. Pluralists point to examples from the *Federalist* papers to show that the intent of the Constitution was to promote group competition, while spreading power broadly through institutions and levels of government so that no group or class would be able to rule in its exclusive interest. Central to the concern of James Madison, for example, was designing a government that would contain conflicts among "factions" and promote political stability. (See the discussion of *Federalist* No. 10 on page 63.)

Looking for ways to promote liberty by limiting group power, the Founders actively debated the leading political theorists of the day. They borrowed ideas from Montesquieu, who wrote convincingly about separating governing powers among different institutions, and from Locke, who stressed the importance of limited government and rights to life, liberty, and property. These grand ideas, say pluralist analyses, are not aimed at promoting narrow class politics, but at creating the enduring competition among groups called pluralism.

SOURCES: Forrest McDonald, *E Pluribus Unum: The Formation of the American Republic*. Indianapolis: Liberty Press, 1979. Robert A. Dahl, *A Preface to Democratic Theory*. Chicago: University of Chicago Press, 1956. Robert E. Brown, *Charles Beard and the Constitution*. New York: Norton, 1965.

---

phies of Locke, Montesquieu, and others were not only radical, but full of different ideas about how to design a stable democratic government. The pluralists argue that the Constitution was guided largely by concerns for promoting liberty through limiting destructive social conflicts and preventing *any* single group, whether elite or majority, from dominating government. (This pluralist interpretation of the Constitution is sketched in "Inside the System" Box 2.4.)

Whether their motives were more pluralistic or elitist, their concerns about economic chaos and local rebellions kept the delegates inside the hall an average of five or six hours a day, six days a week, for nearly four months. On many of those days, the windows were kept closed against the clouds of flies that visited Philadelphia in the summer.[27] Because of the uncomfortable conditions and a variety of problems back home, many of the delegates were not present the whole time. Of the more than seventy men nominated by twelve state legislatures (Rhode Island sent no delegation), fifty-five showed up at one time or another to participate in the debates. A core of twenty-nine attended nearly every session, and thirty-nine were present to sign the document on September 17, 1787.

The delegations varied in size, with New York being the smallest with three members, and Pennsylvania the largest with eight. The announced purpose of the Convention was simply to revise the Articles of Confederation, and most of the delegates came with that goal in mind. No sooner had the group assembled, however, than a radical idea was proposed. The Virginia delegation introduced a plan that invited the group to consider writing a whole new constitution and scrapping the Articles entirely.

Scrap the Articles:
The Virginia Plan

The Virginians were master politicians. As soon as the delegates settled into their lodgings and held their first organizational meeting on Tuesday, May 29, Edmund Randolph proposed James Madison's plan for a new government. Although loosely defended as a "revision" of the Articles, Randolph would later admit that the plan was in fact a design for a wholly different system. Although many of its specific provisions were changed over the next several months, the **Virginia Plan** set the agenda for the entire convention. It is ironic that Madison and other Virginians regarded the eventual compromises and changes in their plan as catastrophic; their grand vision prevailed, throughout the process, as the guiding inspiration for much of the government that finally emerged. Among the familiar aspects of the original Virginia plan are:

- Separating the powers of government among three branches: a *legislative branch* to make laws, an *executive branch* to implement and enforce laws, and a *judicial branch* to interpret the laws.

- A two-house (or *bicameral)* legislature, with the first house chosen by popular vote and the second house chosen by the first. (Not only would the method of selecting the second house be changed, but the method of representing the states would trigger the most intense debate of the convention. Under the Virginia Plan, the number of legislative seats for each state in both chambers was based on state population and tax contributions. This idea of basing all legislative power on state size and wealth alienated the smaller states.)

- A one-person executive chosen by the legislature. (The method of selection was subsequently debated and changed.)

- A strong judiciary composed of a Supreme Court and federal courts with judges appointed for life. (The Supreme Court provisions were adopted, but Congress was given the power to design the rest of the court system at a later date.)

- Greater powers for the national government than for the states in a range of areas. (Although the federal division of powers was hotly debated, the "supremacy" of the national government was established in numerous places in the Constitution.)

There were many disputed details, but the genius of the Virginia plan was enough to eventually sweep the Articles away and push an entirely different government into place. Such a radical change did not come without bitter fights. Those fights forced the great compromises that shaped the Constitution.

Save the Articles:
The New Jersey Plan

Although the convention immediately began discussing the Virginia plan, there was soon another proposal on the floor. The delegation from New Jersey arrived two weeks late, and its members did not like what they heard when they entered the hall. On June 15, William Paterson, head of that state's delegation, introduced an alternative plan to strengthen the Articles to create a stronger central government without giving up too many state powers. This plan clearly protected small states such as New Jersey. Among the provisions of the **New Jersey Plan** were:

- The core institution of government would continue to be a one-chamber (or *unicameral*) Congress, but with more tax powers and authority to regulate interstate disputes.
- All states would have equal representation in this legislature.
- Congress would have powers to force states to obey its laws.
- There would be a weak, multimember executive committee elected by Congress (not a separate executive branch).
- There would be a weak judicial branch with very limited duties.

The New Jersey plan was clearly a "quick fix" on the obvious governmental defects of the Articles. It was also clear that it gave the small states as much power as the big ones. The Convention quickly polarized. Small states such as Connecticut and Delaware backed the New Jersey plan, while large states such as Pennsylvania, Georgia, Massachusetts, and North Carolina fell in with the Virginians. Choosing between the plans was like deciding between night and day, or, better yet, weak and strong central governments. It was pointless for the Convention to debate all of the differences between the plans since there were so many. Besides, it was clear that the political sides were drawn not so much around the issue of saving or scrapping the Articles, but around the question of how the states would be represented in the new central government.

Representation: The Great Compromise

A divided Convention battling over two seemingly irreconcilable plans was not a happy event. It was an event made even less pleasant by the full-force arrival of summer in Philadelphia. It was a summer the likes of which delegates from rural farm country farther north or south had never experienced. Letters home describe a summer in Hell for the New Englanders, who wore their wool suits each day into the steamy chamber. The question of whether to open the windows or close them against the swarms of biting flies was debated almost as hotly as the two plans before the convention.

Tempers flared by day and were soothed very little at night. There were, in those days, no screens on boarding-house windows, and hordes of mosquitoes visited the delegates in their beds. Philadelphia was infamous for its summer outbreaks of malaria, whooping cough, scarlet fever, and smallpox. One delegate became so desperate that he carefully brought a hornets' nest into the house in hopes the hornets would control the mosquitoes and flies.[28]

By early July the delegates agreed unanimously on one thing: They needed a break. They recessed for two days—July 3 and 4—to honor the day of their Independence. Fearing that they might have reached an impasse, they assigned the task of reconciling the two plans to a small committee composed of one member from each state who stayed behind in Philadelphia while the others fled to the countryside for relief. The most difficult work of the convention was done in committee, and this greatest of all the compromises was no exception.

On July 3, with the Convention in recess, the committee of twelve met on a clear, 90-degree day. Perhaps recognizing that the small states would have their way, the full Convention elected a committee that excluded the arch-defenders of the Virginia Plan. To complete the chemistry of this key committee, the convention added Benjamin Franklin, the man the French had dubbed "the crafty old chameleon" for his skillful extraction of millions of dollars from King Louis XVI to pay for an American revolution that would hasten the decline of European monarchy, beginning in France.

When the delegates returned to Philadelphia, they were greeted with a committee compromise on the representation issue. This "Great Compromise" (also called the Connecticut Compromise, for the political skills of Connecticut members on the committee) enabled them to break the deadlock and leave behind the Articles of Confederation once and for all. Although many of the younger delegates (the average age was forty-two) laughed at Franklin as a doddering old man, the aging and ailing Dr. Franklin found the language that carried the day. The notes of a committee member reveal the key to the compromise:

> That in the first branch of the legislature, each of the states now in the union, be allowed one member for every 40,000 inhabitants [later changed to 30,000].

> That in the second branch of the legislature, *each* state shall have an equal vote.[29]

Madison and others from Virginia issued a last call for support of their original idea. Madison argued that small states could not survive on their own and would be forced back into the union, anyway. On the other side, several delegates from the small states were so upset at compromising their demand for equal representation in both chambers that they left the Convention entirely. In the end, however, the spirit of compromise prevailed, and the most influential leaders at the Convention stepped up to support the Great Compromise.

Outside the hall, the summer heat was showing no signs of breaking, and there were still many other issues to decide. The weary delegates finally voted in favor of the compromise that gave the big states more representation in the House and the small states equal representation in the Senate. There was still one more question of representation that had to be resolved before the convention could finish the legislature and turn to designing the other branches of government: how to count (and tax) the sizeable population of slaves. As it turned out, the problem of slavery and the legacy of race relations in America would be the most painful and volatile unresolved political issues written into the Constitution.

The Unkindest Compromise: Slavery

Complicating the representation problem was the fact that a substantial part of the population (around 30 percent) of the southern states were slaves. If the slaves were "counted," the slave states would gain much more representation in the House of Representatives. Many northern delegates objected, however, saying that slaves were not treated like people in any social, political, or legal sense. Slaves were economic commodities: in a word, property. Southerners, meanwhile, rejected northern proposals that if slaves were counted in state populations, then other kinds of property in the north should be counted, too.

The debate became so heated that delegates on both sides claimed that North and South did not have enough in common to form a union. The Civil War would eventually prove them right. However, the pressures of the moment favored compromise, and the creative search for solutions. When southern delegates threatened to leave the convention if slaves were not counted, it became clear that another bargain would have to be struck. The two sides eventually agreed to count slave populations as "three-fifths" the number of "free" populations. This brute number was settled on because it offered less than full, one-for-one representation, which was unacceptable to most in the North, and it was greater than one-half, which seemed too hard a bargain to many in the South. Not much more can be said for its logic, except that the delegates once again demonstrated their willingness to do what had to be done to create a new government.

As a result of this so-called "Three-fifths Compromise," the seats in the House of Representatives were divided up according to an equation that added "the whole number of free persons" and "three fifths of all other persons" and divided by 30,000, the number at last settled upon to form a representation district in the House. The southern states agreed to pay taxes and other population-based fees to the national government according to the same formula. The nation's racial time-bomb was then set ticking by a final compromise that prevented Congress from stopping the slave trade until at least 1808.

With two compromises on representation in Congress finally worked out, the most difficult political conflicts of the convention were resolved, and the design of the legislative branch went forward fairly quickly. No sooner had the remaining tasks been assigned to committees, however, than the matter of the chief executive returned the Convention to conflict. But by the middle of July, however, the energy for conflict was lower, and the spirit of compromise even greater. And so they created a president elected by a college.

The President: Avoiding Demigods and Demagogues

Most of the delegates wished to avoid their unpleasant pre-Revolutionary experience with a too-powerful chief executive. Yet many agreed that a separate executive, rather than one chosen by the Congress, would also limit the power of the legislature. At the same time, nearly everyone present wanted to avoid the possibility that an independent executive would become too popular, providing a rallying point for the masses. What was not clear was how to choose such a president and how to limit the term in office. There were no precedents and certainly no magic formulas for deciding these things. The solutions that were finally agreed upon bear the telltale marks of more compromises worked out in committee. Indeed, the **electoral college** "solution" is such a curious mechanism that one wonders if it might have been invented by the same committee that set out to design a horse and ended up with a camel.

Since the electoral college is another exceptional feature that we continue to live with in the American government, it is important to understand the political reasons behind its creation, even if the creation itself remains a bit baffling. Despite many differences of opinion among the delegates about the executive, there was a slow drift toward two points of agreement: 1) The people should not elect the president because that would be too much democracy, and 2) Congress should not elect the president (as the Virginia Plan proposed) because that would invite too much coziness between the two branches, while giving too much power to the large states once again. The eventual compromise was to allow each state legislature to devise a plan for choosing "electors." Each state would have a number of electors equal to its number of representatives in Congress. The members of this *electoral college* would then vote for two candidates. The person with the most votes would be president, and the second on the list would be vice president. However, if the top person did not receive a majority, then the House of Representatives would decide the election with each state delegation in the House casting one vote.

As for the term in office, there was wide debate ranging from limiting a president to one term of four, five, or seven years, all the way to Hamilton's stunning suggestion that the chief executive serve for life. The delegates eventually settled on a four-year term with no explicit prohibition against reelection. (The unlimited number of terms in office was not changed until the Twenty-second Amendment was ratified in 1951, limiting presidents to two four-year terms.)

The electoral college never really worked as the delegates intended it. The first unexpected problem was the rise of political parties, something the founders did not imagine.

In 1800 when both Thomas Jefferson and Aaron Burr ran for president and vice president, respectively, on the same party ticket, they each received the same number of electoral votes and the election was promptly thrown into the House. Although it was clear that Jefferson was running for president and Burr for vice president, and the electors cast votes for both of them for that reason, the electoral ballots did not distinguish between votes for the two offices. Jefferson's old Federalist enemies in Congress saw a chance to deny him the presidency, and Aaron Burr saw an unexpected opportunity to advance his political fortunes. After a bitter battle in the House and some political heroics by Alexander Hamilton, Jefferson was properly voted in as president. This incident led to the Twelfth Amendment (1804) that required separate electoral votes for the two offices. However, the electoral college remains to this day a curious and not entirely comfortable feature of American politics, but one that the political parties have preserved for reasons explained in Chapter 9.

The Supreme Court, Etc.: The Rest Was Easy

Most of the work and sweat at the Convention went into designing the Congress and the presidency. After these first two long articles of the Constitution, the rest of the document flows crisply and cleanly through articles defining the Judiciary (Article III), Interstate Relations (IV), Amending Procedures (V), the Supremacy of the Constitution (VI), and Ratification Procedures (VII). (These specific articles and powers will be explained in more detail in Chapter 3.)

It may seem surprising that designing the courts produced so little political heat. Although the delegates eventually backed away from the Virginia Plan's call for a federal court system, they did empower Congress to add such "inferior Courts" as it saw fit. Federal courts were established later. But the Supreme Court was agreed upon early in the Convention between the rounds of unproductive debates over the design of Congress. Perhaps the Convention's preoccupation with other problems made the Supreme Court seem like a simpler matter. It is also clear that greater unity existed on principles of law and justice than on matters of power and representation. Moreover, few of the delegates probably imagined how important the great Court would become within such a short time. If they had imagined the series of landmark cases that would change society, the Court might have been debated as hotly as Congress and the executive. As it was, the judicial branch was laid out in six short and somewhat vague paragraphs.

How the Delegates Saw It

The most remarkable aspect of the Convention may be that the delegates left Philadelphia generally unimpressed with their own work. At one extreme, Benjamin Franklin felt the new government was much too elitist in design, falling short of the level of democracy already achieved in his own Pennsylvania state constitution. At the other extreme, Alexander Hamilton was equally distressed at how much democracy the document allowed. Several delegates walked out on the proceedings altogether, and nearly everyone who remained saw the compromises as necessary but far from perfect. Perhaps George Washington summed it up best in a letter to Patrick Henry: "I wish the Constitution which is offered had been made more perfect, but I sincerely believe it is the best that could be obtained at this time."[30]

What finally brought the group together into a final vote of unity was an outrageous proposal from the most discontented group of all, which wanted to have another convention. Edmund Randolph, who had introduced the original Virginia Plan, called for a second convention and was shouted down so loudly that there was no effort made to count the vote on his motion. Following this unusual moment of agreement came the

The signing of the Constitution on September 17, 1787. Notable among the delegates are the dominating figure of George Washington, who served as president of the Constitutional Convention, and Benjamin Franklin (front row, far left), *who had helped to draft the Declaration of Independence more than a decade before. The Bill of Rights, comprising the Constitution's first ten amendments, would not be written for another two years and would not be ratified for another two years after that.*

final motion of the Convention: "to agree to the Constitution." This time a large majority of the states voiced an "Aye," making it close to unaminous. It was six o'clock on Saturday evening, September 15, 1787. The business of designing a government was done. The Convention adjourned while a writer recorded the results of more than three months of negotiations, compromises, and agreements on just four parchment pages for signing. On September 17, thirty-nine of the forty-two delegates present signed the document.

While many of the signers had reservations about their results, they echoed Washington's feeling that they had done the best they could. Most of them shared the conviction that a government containing great compromises was still considerably better than the one they were living with at the time. As a result, delegates who fought on different sides of issues during the Convention went forth afterwards to sell the idea to the leaders, influential citizens, and legislatures of the states that had to ratify the new government plan.

Selling the Constitution: The *Federalist* Papers _____

James Madison was the workhorse of the Philadelphia Convention, pushing delicate compromises through, drafting much of the document's language, and somehow finding time to take a rich set of notes that provide the most complete record of what went on there.

The Founders managed to conceive and frame our fundamental national political charters largely without the sort of pervasive media scrutiny that attends American politics today. While contemporary newspapers certainly reported at length, and editorialized fervently upon, the Declaration of Independence and Constitution, our primary records of those documents' originating bodies and their deliberations were written by the delegates themselves.

BY JIM BORGMAN FOR THE CINCINNATI ENQUIRER

"AWRIGHT, WHO TOLD 'NIGHTLINE'?"

He was a small, frail intellectual not given to speechifying because of his still-boyish voice; yet this thirty-six-year-old political genius impressed the gathering with his sheer knowledge and analytical abilities. Madison was America's first, and perhaps still greatest, political scientist. He won the day in Philadelphia by persuading conservative delegates that some degree of popular representation—diluted, to be sure, over a vast territory and many levels of government—was the only way to control conflicts among the great political factions. He also argued convincingly that this *republican* form of government, as *a system of limited popular representation* was generally called at the time, could work in a large, socially diverse nation like the emerging United States. Many American politicians felt that some form of *republic* was an acceptable compromise between crumbling *monarchical* and *aristocratic* systems, on the one hand, and on the other, the fearful prospect of pure *democracy* (defined then as direct popular rule). The proposal they sent to the states for ratification (approval) was regarded as daring, however, since it was widely believed that republics would work only in small territories such as Switzerland.

Convincing the fifty-five delegates who showed up in Philadelphia at one time or another during the summer of 1787 was one thing. Persuading state leaders and restless publics who watched from the sidelines was something else again. The most troublesome state was New York, where conservative elements in the legislature and the business community believed they could go it alone as a nation—a move that would have cut the geographical and economic heart out of the emerging United States. Gathering up the arguments that had played in Philadelphia, Hamilton, Madison, and John Jay wrote (under the pseudonym of "Publius") a series of essays called **The Federalist.** Because of the critical situation in Hamilton's own state, these *"Federalist* Papers," as they are often called, appeared first in New York newspapers between the fall of 1787 and the summer of 1788. Key arguments from *The Federalist* series soon made their way around the other states, fueling the pro-federalist (pro-Constitution) side of heated debates over ratification.

Some of these essays, such as Madison's *Federalist* No. 10, and *Federalist* No. 51, have become classics of American political thought. These arguments are often cited in *pluralist* analyses of the Constitution to support the claim that the design of the government was intended to equalize group conflict and minimize the chance that any single group or faction would dominate the government. At the time, however, the arguments of *The Federalist* were not offered up just as abstract political science, but also as political rhetoric; they aimed to convince opinion leaders and state legislators to throw in their lot with a stronger (i.e., federal) national union. In the brilliantly argued *Federalist* No. 10, for example, Madison addressed several key questions very persuasively:

- Why was there a need for a stronger national government? To prevent chaos from below—chaos which Madison described with veiled references to the causes of Shays' Rebellion and other uprisings around the land: "A rage for paper money, for an abolition of debts, for an equal division of property, or for any other improper or wicked project."

- Why was this strong government at the same time resistant to takeover or tyranny from above? The answer: Creating a government with so many internal checks on its own authority made it unlikely to be taken over by any particular faction of either an aristocratic or a democratic persuasion.

- Why would a government of competing interests sharing power at many levels and over a large territory make for an even stronger, more stable republic? Because the limits on power would hold the most divisive issues in check, yet offer groups access to government at many levels to work out their conflicts.

T H E

FEDERALIST:

A COLLECTION

O F

E S S A Y S,

WRITTEN IN FAVOUR OF THE

NEW CONSTITUTION,

AS AGREED UPON BY THE FEDERAL CONVENTION, SEPTEMBER 17, 1787.

IN TWO VOLUMES.

VOL. I.

NEW-YORK:

PRINTED AND SOLD BY J. AND A. M'LEAN, No. 41, HANOVER-SQUARE. M·DCC, LXXXVIII.

The title page to a 1788 volume gathering the essays known collectively as The Federalist. *Originally published in newspapers to cultivate public support for the newly signed Constitution, these articles—written by Alexander Hamilton, James Madison, and John Jay— remain classic works of American political theory.*

While the *Federalist* essays were circulating in the states, most local newspapers were also promoting the Constitution. Even before the Constitution was announced, many of the leading newspapers dramatized the rebellions and economic chaos facing the nation. One newspaper owner of the day described his coverage of the Convention as intended "to prepare the minds of the citizens for the favorable reception of *whatever* might be the result."[31] Some critical stories appeared in the press, most notably in the *Pennsylvania Herald*, which raised questions about the undemocratic tone of the convention debates, but few other papers reprinted them. By contrast, essays and opinions that proclaimed the wisdom and the unity inside the Convention were reprinted widely. In reality, the delegates observed fairly strict secrecy about their deliberations and came forth afterward with a unified argument designed to put the best political interpretation on what they had done.

Despite the persuasive efforts of *The Federalist*, and most newspaper accounts, it was nearly two and a half years before the last state, "Rogue Island," signed on and made the Union unanimous on May 29, 1790. Part of the problem was that the more the Constitution's proponents persuaded conservative elite elements of the advantages of stability and order in a stronger federal republic, the more worried the unruly majority of poor farmers became about losing their rights of free speech, protest, and legal protections to a distant and too strong central government. Even though the nation's majority of poor farmers and city workers could not vote, much less run for office, they relied on the long British-American tradition of civil liberties to express their opinions and protect their interests in other ways, including protests, public demonstrations, and the occasional rebellion. A loud cry from the majority emerged during this period of public debate over the Constitution. It was a cry for a Bill of Rights.

The Bill of Rights

The concerns of the rebels in Massachusetts, New Hampshire, and Rhode Island were mirrored throughout the other states, including Virginia, where radical politicians such as Patrick Henry brought their case before the state legislature. Henry's argument was a

A parade through downtown Manhattan celebrates New York's ratification of the Constitution, approved on July 26, 1788. Actually, New Hampshire's ratification of the document a month earlier had established its adoption, but New York's support was nonetheless considered critical because of that state's economic and political influence. In this drawing, the procession pauses to salute George Washington and other dignitaries, standing upon the fortification wall at left.

simple one: What was the point of ratifying the Constitution if it had no more support from the majority of people than the old government? No matter how elaborate the system of checks and balances, political order would not be created if the common folk continued to rebel because they felt unrepresented and deprived of basic political rights. Henry was persuasive. He said he "smelt a rat" in Philadelphia and even called for an investigation of the Convention as an illegal conspiracy. Cranking the pressure to the maximum, he also called for a second Constitutional Convention—a prospect that must have been a nightmare for those who had just struggled through the first.

At the very least, Henry and the other "Anti-Federalists" who spoke for the poor farmers wanted a Bill of Rights added to the Constitution. Ratification votes in Virginia and several other key states were held up until the "Federalists"—as the pro-Constitution forces were called—promised to draft a Bill of Rights as one of the first acts of the new Congress. Since the states would have to approve these additions to the Constitution as amendments, those who demanded the Bill of Rights would have a chance to make sure the language suited them. Moreover, there was little chance of the "Federalists" breaking their promise. Not only was domestic tranquility on the line in many states, but at least two states (North Carolina and Rhode Island) threatened to withhold ratification of the Constitution altogether until the Bill of Rights went through the new Congress.

By the beginning of the summer of 1788, enough states (nine) had ratified the Constitution to start up a new government—at least in theory. However, there was very little sense in trying to hold elections and form the government until the key states of Virginia and New York finally came on board—which they did later in the summer, after assurances had been given (particularly in Virginia) that a Bill of Rights would be one of the first items of business for the new Congress. With the ratification of eleven states, and the important inclusion of the key states, the old Confederation Congress at last put itself out of business in October, and elections were held in the states that had ratified. (North Carolina and Rhode Island would not join the new Union until November of 1789, and May of 1790, respectively.) Table 2.1 shows the order in which the original states ratified the Constitution.

TABLE 2.1

The Order in Which the States Ratified the Constitution

1.	Delaware	December 7, 1787
2.	Pennsylvania	December 12, 1787
3.	New Jersey	December 18, 1787
4.	Georgia	January 2, 1788
5.	Connecticut	January 9, 1788
6.	Massachusetts	February 6, 1788
7.	Maryland	April 28, 1788
8.	South Carolina	May 23, 1788
9.	New Hampshire	June 21, 1788
10	Virginia	June 25, 1788
11.	New York	July 26, 1788
12.	North Carolina	November 21, 1789
13.	Rhode Island	May 29, 1790

SOURCE: *The New York Public Library Desk Reference.*

The newly elected Congress of the United States met for the first time on March 4, 1789 in New York, which was the national capital at the time. Madison followed up his performance at the Convention and his authorship of a substantial part of *The Federalist* by stepping forward to play a leading role in the first Congress of the United States. For Madison, it seemed, there would be no rest. No sooner did the Virginian arrive in New York to take up his seat in the House than he began working on the Bill of Rights. By day, he dealt with pressing and long-neglected national problems such as taxation and trade relations with England. By night, he trudged back to Mrs. Elsworth's boarding house on the waterfront to resume work on the pesky problem of rights.

Although the Bill of Rights remains for many the greatest achievement of the Constitution, for Madison (and even more for other Federalists, including Washington) it did not merit the same importance as the main document. Madison and the other Federalists wanted the rights problem kept at the state level. In part this was out of fear that volatile questions of rights and freedoms might spark national political conflicts, undermining the main intent of the Constitution to limit such instability. More immediately, Madison saw little point in attaching a list of rights to a document that gave such broad law-making powers to the states. Since the Bill of Rights would apply only to abuses by the national government, many of the concerns of the "Anti-Federalists" who demanded the Rights amendments to the Constitution would not be satisfied anyway. In this vision, Madison proved accurate: The meaningful "incorporation" of the Bill of Rights into the everyday lives of people in the different states did not happen until well into the twentieth century.

The politics behind the slow and selective incorporation of provisions of the Bill of Rights will be explained in Chapter 5. For now, the important point is that Madison correctly saw the most important struggles over rights and liberties involving citizens' relations to their *state* governments, and it would be a long time before the Supreme Court would be willing to intrude in this domain of state powers. In the long run, however, Patrick Henry also proved correct: The **Bill of Rights** *has turned out to be the poor person's and, perhaps, the average individual's most important political resource.* It simply took far longer to come into play than Henry imagined. As we will see in Chapter 5, incorporating provisions from the Bill of Rights into everyday life required a Civil War and another amendment (the Fourteenth) to the Constitution.

Despite the disagreements between the Federalists and the Anti-Federalists about rights and other issues, the spirit of liberty was still strong from the Revolution, and it would not do to deny that spirit its place in the new government. The recent memory of the farmers' rebellions in Massachusetts was still vivid. Thus, James Madison labored those many nights in his room at Mrs. Elsworth's. Madison ended up taking most of the language for the first eight amendments from the Virginia Bill of Rights, written by George Mason in 1776. In the end, the Federalists in Congress honored their promise to deliver the Bill of Rights to the states for ratification as amendments to the original Constitution. And so it came to pass that a document just born of great compromises in Philadelphia was amended ten times before it won final acceptance as the basis for a more broadly legitimate government.

As the politics behind the Constitution shows, winning the support of the people is not automatic. People have different concerns about government powers that must be satisfied before they will grant that government the *legitimate* authority to rule over them. **Legitimacy** *refers to the voluntary acceptance of government powers, which is sometimes referred to as granting* **authority** *to the government.* The great triumph of the Constitutional Convention was the willingness to compromise in ways that created a government widely accepted as legitimate.

The Politics of Compromise Revisited

When you read the Constitution in Chapter 3, you can now read it as a political docu- ment. This is a good thing. Politics is what governments deal with, and the big question is how well they do it. Considering the many differences among the colonies before the Revolution and among the states afterwards, there is no way a central government could have emerged except through compromise. The tradition of **compromise** that began with the Constitution endures to this day as one of the strengths of the American system. Today, many Americans regard compromise as a virtue of the political culture and give it a valued name: **pragmatism,** meaning the ability to sacrifice a bit of principle, when that principle is not working, to achieve something that works.

As you contemplate the politics behind the Constitution, it helps to recognize that without a willingness to compromise there would have been no Constitution at all. Most of the delegates in Philadelphia recognized that they had not solved all the nation's prob- lems with the new charter, but they at least made it possible for life to go on as a nation. In compromising over the issue of slavery, for example, some of the northern delegates felt that they were merely postponing a crisis that was sure to come. They were right. However, there was little political basis in 1787 for forcing the southern states to aban- don slavery. There was a greater call to preserve the Union in 1861, when the issue fi- nally led to war between the states.

In politics, it is not always easy to decide in advance which compromises are work- able and which ones are not. People do well to develop all their judgment skills possible in order to play the game of politics. The delegates who came to Philadelphia in 1787 were aided by general ideas about what a *political system* should be. To begin with, most of the founders were moved by the *cultural ideal* of liberty. Despite the different conno- tations that liberty held for different minds, it provided a common focus for their de- bates. In addition, many of the leaders of the day were familiar with thinkers such as Locke and Montesquieu, who provided ideas about the kinds of *institutions* that might best promote liberty. Finally, the Founders' debates were sharpened by clear but con- trasting views of *power in society*. Those who favored rule by propertied elites over rule by majorities favored centralized institutions. Those who resisted the possibility of any dominant group holding power advocated a system of separate institutions sharing powers.

The struggle over power, and how to best channel it into government, has continued ever since. Many of the voices that spoke loudly in 1787 still echo today. This is a sign that the original compromises may have achieved as much as could be expected, given the diversity of American society and the different views about how best to govern it. Today, as two hundred years ago, there are still those who think we have too much democracy and those who think we have too little. There are those who believe the elites have too much power and those who think the broad majority are incapable of properly exercising any more power than they already have. These competing views continue to promote compromises in government, on issues such as environmental protection, wel- fare, health care, and the annual budgets that pay for it all.

When people feel that the compromises are about the best that can be achieved, the government remains *legitimate*, as it continues to be for most Americans. However, there are always those who cannot accept the results of government action because their interests appear to have been compromised too much. Viewed from one side of the legit- imacy line, those who protest, burn flags, or commit crimes against property are acting in lawless, even criminal, fashion. From the other side, these same acts appear to be rea- sonable rebellions against a system that does not work. In any system built upon com- promise, as most stable governments are, one of the most difficult issues is when it

A CITIZEN'S QUESTION Authority

*W*hen is it proper to resist government authority? This is the oldest question in American politics. The American Revolution was, for many of its leaders, a painful uprising because they were prominent citizens who had once regarded themselves as dutiful subjects of the king. Each generation of citizens faces issues and problems that challenge its sense of obligation and duty. After the Revolution, many honored veterans of the fight against the king took up arms against their own state governments to protect their farms. In a later era, the fight was against a system of slavery that continued to be protected by the Constitution. More recently, citizens have challenged the authority of the government by resisting wars they felt were unjust. Today, citizens continue to face arrest because they reject the laws of the land pertaining to abortion.

In their lifetime, many, and perhaps most, citizens face moral dilemmas about why to obey the law: Do I obey the law because it is an obligation? Do I obey because I fear punishment? Or, do I obey because, most of the time, I truly think it is fair? To the extent that most people of the time find the laws and demands of government fair, they grant legitimacy to the government. Thus, legitimate authority is what keeps government working fairly smoothly most of the time. When people feel that laws or the actions of the government representatives are not legitimate, however, tensions grow in society. Deciding how to respond to unjust situations is one of the most difficult issues citizens face.

There is no blanket rule about civil disobedience. Without those who vigorously opposed earlier governments there would be no United States of America as we know it today. Yet with too much disobedience, no society is safe enough to live in. Once again, we are talking about striking the balance between freedom and order, but this time on a very personal level. Although there is no formula that works for everyone, it is important to begin by considering the goals of political protest or disobedience. Some of the most positive and most lasting changes in American politics have come from those who protested or resisted the powers of government with an aim toward creating new institutions or changing old ones in ways that corrected problems of injustice, misrepresentation, or abuse of power. Some of the Founders, such as Thomas Jefferson, supported acts of disobedience as a necessary part of the process of changing institutions that were not working. (Recall his reactions to the rebellions in Massachusetts from earlier in this chapter.) However, every case involves personal soul-searching and difficult decisions, as indicated by Jefferson's own behavior when he first dutifully petitioned the king before he wrote the Declaration of Independence.

In thinking about the political disobedience that created this nation, put yourself into the picture. For what reasons would you have supported the Revolution? What kind of government would you have promoted afterwards? Do you think our government continues to solve most of the nation's problems as well as can be expected? If not, can you imagine anything that would make you disobey its authority?

becomes reasonable to question and rebel against authority. The proper limits of dissent have been debated from Shays' Rebellion to the present day. Yet for those who feel that government does not represent them, dissent remains a powerful instrument for political change. It was against a background of dissent, after all, that the compromises necessary to create the Constitution were made. The strength of the Constitution is seen in the fact that most Americans since that time have exercised their politics inside rather than outside the system.

Key Terms

Shays' Rebellion

colonialism, and the divisions among the colonies

the political issues leading to the Revolution

differences between the states after the Revolution

Articles of Confederation

confederation

Constitutional Convention

democracy

republic

Connecticut Compromise or Great Compromise

electoral college

The Federalist ("Federalist Papers")

Virginia Plan

New Jersey Plan

compromises on slavery

Bill of Rights

authority, legitimacy

compromise, pragmatism

Suggested Readings

Beard, Charles A. *An Economic Interpretation of the Constitution of the United States*. New York: The Free Press, 1986. (Originally published 1913.)

Hamilton, Alexander, James Madison, and John Jay. *The Federalist Papers*, ed. Isaac Kramnick. New York: Viking, 1987.

Hyneman, Charles S., and Donald S. Lutz, eds. *American Political Writing During the Founding Era: 1760–1805* (2 vols.). Indianapolis: Liberty Press, 1983.

Levy, Leonard W., ed. *Essays on the Making of the Constitution*. New York: Oxford University Press, 1969.

Lipset, Seymour M. *The First New Nation: The United States in Historical and Comparative Perspective*. New York: Basic Books, 1963.

McDonald, Forrest. *We the People: The Economic Origins of the Constitution*. New Brunswick, N.J.: Transaction Publishers, 1992. (Originally published 1958.)

————. *Novus Ordo Seclorum: The Intellectual Origins of the Constitution*. Lawrence: University Press of Kansas, 1985.

Mee, Charles L., Jr. *The Genius of the People*. New York: Harper & Row, 1987.

Morgan, Edmund S. *Inventing the People: The Rise of Popular Sovereignty in England and America*. New York: Norton, 1988.

Nathanson, Stephen. *Should We Consent to Be Governed*? Belmont, Calif.: Wadsworth, 1992.

Wills, Garry. *Inventing America: Jefferson's Declaration of Independence*. New York: Doubleday, 1978.

Wood, Gordon S. *The Radicalism of the American Revolution*. New York: Knopf, 1992.

• • •

In framing a government. . . the great difficulty lies in this:
You must first enable the government to control the governed;
and in the next place oblige it to control itself.
—*James Madison, Federalist No. 51*

• • •

Our Constitution is in actual operation and everything appears
to promise that it will last; but in this world nothing is certain
but death and taxes.
—*Benjamin Franklin*

• • •

The Constitutional

Design of Power

- **GOVERNMENTAL GRIDLOCK: NEW STORY OR OLD?**
- **THE CONSTITUTIONAL POWER CHART**
- **INSTITUTIONAL DESIGN: SEPARATING THE BRANCHES**
  A System of Checks and Balances
  The Legislative Article
  The Executive Article
  The Judicial Article
  Making Government Difficult by Design
- **FEDERAL DESIGN: DIVIDING POWERS WITH THE STATES**
  National Supremacy vs. States' Rights
  Interstate Relations
  The Supremacy Clause
  The Denial of Powers
- **THE "LIVING CONSTITUTION"**
  The Bill of Rights
  Amending the Constitution
  A Flexible Interpretation Process
- **WHAT KIND OF GOVERNMENT?: THE STRUCTURE OF POWER**
  Who Governs?
- **THE CONSTITUTIONAL POWER CHART REVISITED**
- **A CITIZEN'S QUESTION: The Constitution**
- **KEY TERMS**
- **SUGGESTED READINGS**

Governmental Gridlock: New Story or Old?

In recent years a new word has entered news accounts of government: *gridlock*. Headlines proclaim THE POLITICS OF GRIDLOCK[1] and CAPITOL GRIDLOCK.[2] Editorials and news analyses chime in with supporting images of DIVIDED GOVERNMENT[3] and SERIOUS TIMES, TRIVIAL POLITICS.[4] The mention of governmental gridlock evokes the image of institutions standing still with their engines running, unable to move, like traffic frozen at rush hour.

People who expect faster government solutions to their own problems, or greater unity of purpose from the leaders of government, may accept the metaphor of gridlock as a simple way of thinking about problems in Washington. While it may be poetic, the gridlock image explains little about what, if anything, is wrong with government. Indeed, the system of government designed by the Founders may be performing just as they intended: slowly, with great changes requiring broad consensus in society, and with great resistance to the whims and passions of any particular group.

In evaluating the performance of government, a good place to begin is by *avoiding* simple, dramatic news images like gridlock. Instead, put the information from news reports to the political test of what you now know about how the government was designed to work. Consider this passage:

> From the White House to Capitol Hill, Washington seems paralyzed on matters vital to the nation's economic health. On taxes and banking, energy and even unemployment benefits, the combination of a fractious Congress, a disengaged administration and the intractable demands of interest groups has brought action to a halt.[5]

What does this mean? How serious are these problems? Are there reforms that would help? Can the voters straighten things out by making different calculations in the voting booth? Such questions arise from news accounts like this one:

> As president. . . and Congress prepare for the November elections, few can recall a time when relations between the two branches of government have been more contentious in manner, barren of substance and infuriating to the American people.
>
> Their legislative scorecard might read:
>
> - The soaring federal deficit—gridlock.
> - Violent crime—gridlock.
> - Campaign finance reform—gridlock.
> - Revitalizing the nation's public schools—gridlock.
>
> As a way to describe it, Americans have embraced a word more often associated with traffic jams than governance—"gridlock."[6]

Many think the solution is to send the same party to Congress and the White House for a long enough period to develop a coherent legislative agenda. In addition, a party must govern long enough to appoint enough judges to the federal courts to protect that agenda from legal challenges. Some argue that voters in the past have deliberately helped to create party gridlock to keep government in check and prevent it from doing things they don't want. ABC News correspondent Cokie Roberts expressed this view on the eve of the 1992 elections:

> When pollsters ask, is it better for the same party to control both Congress and the Presidency, usually no more than one third of the respondents answer yes. Even right now, with all the attacks on Congress, that figure has only climbed to 43 percent, according to a Wall Street Journal/NBC News poll. . . And in hundreds of interviews all over the country. . . I have found voters readily explaining that they split their tickets with malice aforethought, consciously curbing what they see as the excesses of both parties.[7]

BY JIM BORGMAN FOR THE CINCINNATI ENQUIRER

Even domination of the government by a single political party may prove insufficient to get major legislation passed, as conflicts and concessions between the executive and legislative branches weaken controversial measures. Here President Bill Clinton, House Speaker Thomas Foley, and Senate Majority Leader George Mitchell— all Democrats—stand shoulder to shoulder, and yet the impetus of "change" dies away in their hands.

As it turned out, that 43 percent plurality was enough to elect Bill Clinton. With his election, the Democrats controlled the White House and both houses of Congress, but some observers argued that the cure for gridlock was not that easy. As it turned out, Bill Clinton was unable to get his first major piece of legislation (an economic stimulus package) passed in Congress in 1993.

Understanding the Constitution is an important first step in thinking about how government is performing today. Before leaping to any conclusions, it is good to look behind the headlines about government gridlock to see how the government was designed to work more than two hundred years ago. If more Americans thought about the many separations and divisions of power intentionally written into the Constitution, they might be less surprised to find that the current government works slowly, or inefficiently, or with constant compromises, than to find that it continues to work at all.

At the very least, understanding the design of constitutional power is necessary for thinking realistically about what would be required to increase the speed or broaden the scope of government action. Creating a government capable of more rapid or more sweeping actions would come with a price. The price might not be paid in dollars, but in power and

control. People may grant greater powers to a more centralized government; at the same time, people may have to sacrifice their own interests to do so.

All of this suggests that one of a citizen's first requirements is to form realistic expectations about what the government is capable of doing, as outlined in the Constitution. After attaining a realistic grasp of the limits and capabilities of our constitutional design, citizens can then think more productively about what is required to get the system going in directions they want. For example, if electing the same party to run both the Congress and the executive (and thus to make appointments to the courts) *is* a way around what some observers call gridlock, then this is something citizens can do. If, on the other hand, this is not always enough, then overcoming some forms of gridlock may require amending the Constitution to create more centralized power. Given the latter possibility, many Americans might decide that the current system is not so bad, after all. This chapter examines the design for power contained in the original Constitution against the backdrop of contemporary concerns about government action. Citizens are in a better position to evaluate government performance when they have realistic expectations about what government was designed to do.

The Constitutional Power Chart

Why do people form a government? The rationale for the American government is explained in the preamble to the Constitution, a short, poetic, and abstract paragraph. As you read these words, try to read into them the history and politics of the times, both the founders' times and ours:

We the People of the United States, in Order to form a more perfect Union, establish Justice, insure domestic Tranquility, provide for the common defence, promote the general Welfare, and secure the Blessings of Liberty to ourselves and our Posterity, do ordain and establish this Constitution for the United States of America.

There are many different ways to accomplish such goals of government as domestic order or tranquility, common defense, general welfare, liberty, and justice. Some democratic societies have adopted more centralized governments with concentrated powers, while others spread the powers more broadly among institutions and levels of government. The government created by the Constitution of the United States was designed to broadly disperse governing powers. This government was intended to be flexible by providing many channels for social demands, and by remaining open to amendments that adapt the government to changing social conditions.

What is a **constitution?** It is an outline of the general organization of government institutions, along with the specific duties and procedures that define the operation of those institutions. Also specified in a constitution are the obligations between citizens and government. For example, one of the most significant aspects of the Constitution for many Americans today is the Bill of Rights, which offers individual citizens grounds for protection from various governmental and social actions that may harm them.

What constitutions cannot do, however, is anticipate all the future situations that arise in the course of everyday governing. Rather, the idea of a constitution is to provide general guidelines to help the officers of government approach specific problems. In his ruling in the landmark case of *McCulloch v. Maryland* in 1819, Chief Justice John Marshall explained that a constitution is not supposed to cover every situation the government might face. To the contrary, he said that the very nature of a constitution "requires

Homeless men solicit aid from Congress in a parkground protest. However, the Constitution requires Congress to share powers on such matters with the executive. In the modern era, housing issues have often been spearheaded by the executive branch's Department of Housing and Urban Development (HUD), under such administrators as Jack Kemp, a Republican, and Henry Cisneros, a Democrat.

that only its great outlines should be marked, its important objects designated."[8] (See "Inside the System" Box 3.2 on page 79 for the details of the particular case in which Marshall elucidated this and other principles of constitutions.) Justice Marshall's wisdom about the vagaries of constitutions notwithstanding, people often expect more of a constitution and look to it for specific answers. Creative readings of the Constitution lead different people to see in it quite different solutions for their problems. In the end, the courts interpret and apply the general rules of the political game based on the "great outlines," as Marshall called them. (The process of legal interpretation will be explored more fully in Chapter 16.)

To start thinking about how this constitutional system works, it is helpful to imagine a simple chart that contains just two broad patterns of power. First, power is *separated* among three sets of institutions that we call branches of government. Second, power is *divided* between the national government comprised of the three branches and the governments of the fifty states. The states have been given considerable power under this arrangement, known as **federalism,** that will be introduced in this chapter and explored in more detail in Chapter 4. Understanding these basic **separations and divisions of powers** is an important beginning point for evaluating government performance and thinking about the politics behind modern issues like governmental gridlock.

Institutional Design: Separating the Branches

As noted in Chapter 2, the delegates to the Philadelphia convention generally wanted to avoid creating a government that was too centralized. While many agreed that the Articles of Confederation left the government too weak to enforce or execute the laws, there was fear of placing too much power in any single institution. Among the framers, as those who designed the Constitution are called, the Virginians in particular had become interested in the French political philosopher Montesquieu, who advocated separate institutions to balance the power of law and create a spirit of limited government. In his classic work *The Spirit of the Laws,* Montesquieu recommended independent legislative, executive, and judiciary branches of government. This was the broad design that the delegates in Philadelphia tailored through many compromises into the Constitution. It is common to refer to this separation of powers in the Constitution as a system of **checks and balances** between the branches of government.

A System of Checks and Balances

Under the Constitution, there is a *balance* of power among the three branches: Congress is primarily responsible for making the laws; the executive has primary responsibility for carrying out and enforcing the laws; and the judiciary has the main responsibility for reviewing the laws and the manner of their administration. Requiring three different branches to work toward agreement was intended to reduce the chance of a tyrannical government running out of the control of the people. Whether intended or not, this separation of powers also introduced considerable problems of coordination and agreement into the governing process, making contemporary concerns about gridlock a much more lively issue in the U.S. than it is in many other countries.

To maintain the balance of power among the three branches, the Constitution also gave each branch important *checks* or limits on the primary responsibilities of the others. This is often referred to as a system of checks and balances. For example, an uncooperative Supreme Court can be *checked* either by the president's power to appoint new justices (when current ones die or retire) or by congressional power to reject presidential

French political philosopher Charles-Louis de Secondat (1689–1755), better known as (the Baron) Montesquieu. Montesquieu promoted the idea of separation of powers—the theory that liberty is best served when the power of the state is divided evenly among independent political bodies. A 1750 English translation of his work became a seminal influence on the institutional design of the U.S. Constitution.

appointments that might be seen as unsuitable. In another example, presidential military powers are checked by giving Congress the power to declare war and the ultimate power to shut off the money to military adventures that seem improper. An interesting example of a dispute between Congress and the president over shared military and foreign policy powers occurred in the so-called "Iran-*contra*" affair during the Reagan administration (see "Inside the System" Box 3.1).

This system of broadly separated powers, with many cross-checks to promote the balance, can be thought of as a system of *shared* powers that leaves no unit of government truly independent of the others. Political scientist Richard Neustadt concluded that the idea of "separation of powers" is a bit misleading because what we really have is "separate institutions sharing powers."[9] *The basic idea behind that timeworn phrase "checks and balances" is this: The separation of powers creates an (always shifting) balance of power among the three branches of national government. At the same time, the many*

FIGURE 3.1

Checks and Balances: How the Constitutional System of Separate Institutions Sharing Powers Works

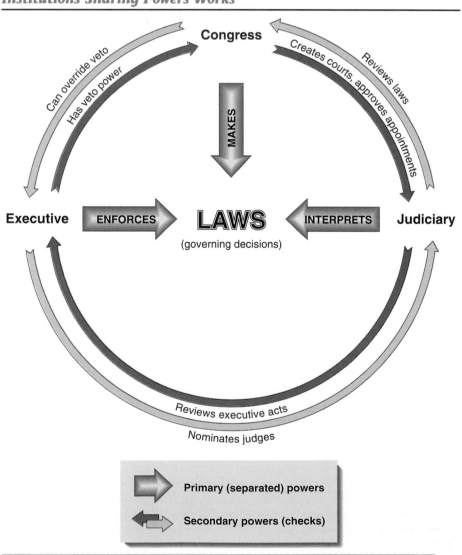

Why Sharing Constitutional Powers Is Not Easy But It Is Important: The "Iran-contra" Affair

3.1

The war-making and foreign-policy powers shared by Congress and the president have seldom meshed easily—especially when the two branches are controlled by different political parties. Presidents eager to take charge of a strong and clear foreign policy have resorted to a variety of ways of getting around partnerships with Congress: fighting "undeclared wars" (Korea, Vietnam), funding native armies whose goals coincided with U.S. interests (Afghanistan, Angola, Nicaragua), and using the Central Intelligence Agency (CIA) to back covert military operations (supporting the overthrow of hostile governments in Iran and Chile). Occasionally Congress looks the other way, and sometimes it finds out too late to do anything. However, there are times when Congress learns about such activities and decides that more than being politically unwise, they are damaging to the constitutional principle of shared powers.

In the early 1980s, Congress learned that President Reagan was employing the CIA to support the opposition in a civil war against the Sandinista government of Nicaragua—a revolu-tionary socialist regime whose actions (and ties to Cuba and the Soviet Union) made Mr. Reagan "see Red." When Congress learned of CIA involvement in "warlike acts" such as mining Sandinista harbors and working with the Nicaraguan rebel army (called *contras* because they were "against" the Sandinista regime), various committees responsible for overseeing the CIA objected, saying they had been excluded from the constitutional picture.

The president agreed to seek formal congressional funding for these actions, but the money he requested was then denied by a Democratic opposition in Congress. Some members of the White House staff, however, were determined to continue the fight against the Sandinista government despite congressional objections. U.S. Marine colonel Oliver North and Admiral John Poindexter, among others, came up with an illegal scheme to help support the *contra* army. Military weapons were sold to a hostile government (Iran, which was then at war with Iraq), and the profits were channeled through Swiss bank accounts to help fund and equip the *contras*.

After the Sandinista military shot down a private American pilot making arms deliveries to the *contras*, the operation was uncovered, and Congress engaged the president and his staff in a lengthy battle over restoring shared military and foreign-policy powers. (A special prosecutor was appointed by Congress, and his staff investigated the affair for several years after Reagan's second term of office had ended.) President Reagan said the rogue operation had been carried on without his approval or knowledge, but Congress's inquiry into the "Iran-*contra*" affair ended up costing him several of his most valued aides, as well as considerable personal prestige, while checking the abuse of power by the executive branch. At least until the next time.

NOTE: For two differing views of the Iran-*contra* affair and the resulting political fallout, see *A Very Thin Line: The Iran-*contra *Affairs,* by Theodore Draper (New York: Hill & Wang, 1991), and *Undue Process: A Story of How Political Differences Are Turned into Crimes,* by Elliott Abrams (New York: The Free Press, 1992).

checks between the branches guard against abuses and permanent imbalances. The re-sult is the sharing of governing powers. See Figure 3.1 for an illustration of this system of power.

The result of this system of checks and balances is that when various branches of government agree on how to use their shared powers, governing becomes a smoother, better coordinated, and, perhaps, even more intelligent process. When units of government ignore power sharing, the prospects occur for abuses of power at one extreme and gridlock at another. Governing is both a matter of each branch doing its primary tasks and exercising its checks on the other branches. The next sections review primary responsibilities of each branch.

The Capitol building, meeting place of the United States Congress. The division of Congress into two chambers and the question of how the states were to be represented in them were among the most controversial topics of the 1787 Constitutional Convention. The article elucidating the legislative branch makes up the longest section of the Constitution itself.

The Legislative Article

The legislative article, Article I, is by far the longest article of the Constitution, taking up more than half the original document. To some extent, the length reflects the great conflict that went into the debates over representation, slavery, and the sharing of state powers described in Chapter 2. For the most part, however, this long article lays out what the delegates saw as the centerpiece of government: making laws. No fewer than ten "sections" in Article I were required to explain how the legislature would work. The key points are:

The House of Representatives (Section 2): Two-year terms. Chosen by the people in each state according to the rules used in the state for choosing the largest branch of the state legislature. Representatives assigned to the states according to population (as worked out in the "Great Compromise"). The House has the power to impeach (place on trial and remove certain officials from office).

The Senate (Section 3): Six-year terms. Chosen by the legislature of each state (later amended). Each state has two senators. The Senate holds the trial in impeachment cases.

Internal Organization (Section 5): Each house is given wide room to organize its own committees, leadership, and decision procedures. Each chamber has the responsibility for supervising and punishing its own members.

How a Bill Becomes a Law (Section 7): The House originates revenue bills, but the Senate may amend them, as with other legislation. All legislation must pass both House and Senate in the same form and then be signed by the president. Overriding a presidential veto requires a two-thirds vote in both chambers.

The Importance of Loopholes in Constitutions: The "Elastic Clause" as Interpreted by the Supreme Court in the Case of McCulloch v. Maryland (1819)

3.2

Perhaps the biggest political conflict in the first half century of government under the Constitution was Congress's authorizing a Bank of the United States. "The Bank" was seen by many as an unfair means for northern business interests to gain control of the national economy. To make matters worse, the Federalist party adopted the Bank as its instrument for making national economic policy and, opponents argued, making fortunes for party loyalists who ran the congressionally chartered operation.

Several states began taxing bank branches in an effort to limit its growth and profits. The conflict finally produced a "constitutional crisis" when the Baltimore branch refused to pay Maryland state taxes, and the state appealed its case all the way to the Supreme Court. On the specific question of paying state taxes, the Court ruled that states have no constitutional powers to tax federal institutions.

In the section of the Court's opinion that made this case a *landmark,* Chief Justice John Marshall went beyond the specific tax issue to use the case to interpret the Constitution itself. Writing for the majority of other justices, Marshall acknowledged that Article I, Section 8 gave Congress no specific power to charter a national bank. However, Congress did have specific powers to regulate the value of money and credit. Since the Bank was one of the means Congress used to carry out its specified monetary powers, Marshall reasoned that the Bank charter fell under the last paragraph of Section 8 which authorized Congress the *elastic* power to make ". . .all laws which shall be necessary and proper, for carrying into Execution the foregoing Powers." In other words, although the bank was not on the list of specified powers granted to Congress, it was a "necessary and proper" means of carrying out duties that were on the list.

Specific or "Formal" Powers Granted to Congress (Section 8): This most explicit section of the Constitution specifically grants to Congress a long list of powers, including the powers to borrow money on the credit of the United States (according to most Americans, the power that has been exercised too often in recent years); coin money; lay and collect taxes; establish post offices and roads; declare war, raise and maintain an army and navy; and carry out many lesser duties. This list has become known as the **expressed powers** of Congress. At the end of this list, the Constitution also provides something of a loophole which has become known as the **elastic clause**. This gives Congress the power "to make all Laws *necessary and proper* for carrying into Execution the foregoing powers." (See "Inside the System" Box 3.2.)

Specific Powers Denied to Congress (Section 9): A catch-all, miniature Bill of Rights: Congress cannot suspend the writ of habeas corpus, or the right to a trial following arrest; no taxation without representation; no taking money from the Treasury without legislative authorization; and no granting (or accepting) titles of nobility.

Specific Powers Denied to the States (Section 10): Prohibits states from making treaties; coining money; taxing imports and exports; keeping troops without the consent of Congress; waging war; or otherwise acting in ways that would compete with the "exclusive powers" of the central government.

The Executive Article

As explained in Chapter 2, there were various proposals for an executive, including Hamilton's idea of an executive for life. The plan introduced by the Virginia delegation would have granted Congress the right to elect the executive in order to improve coordination with the legislature. In the end, the small states prevailed with a plan that, to this day, places considerable emphasis on state politics in electing presidents. The electoral college system gave state legislatures power to choose electors and to decide which citizens could vote. As political parties evolved and promised voters that electors would honor their wishes, the electoral college became, by tradition, less prone to exercise independent judgment. At the same time, more citizens were granted the vote as restrictions were lifted on property, race, gender, age, and literacy. This broad evolution of elections has made the president more accountable to more people.

Although the representative nature of the office and its informal powers and responsibilities have changed over the years, the basic job description remains much the same as outlined in Article II:

Selection Procedures (Section 1): Covers the term in office (four years). Also outlines in detail the procedures of the *electoral college* (later amended by the Twelvth Amendment in 1804). Explains candidate eligibility requirements. Provides the procedures for succession in case the president leaves office before the term is up (amended under the Twenty-fifth Amendment in 1967).

Powers and Duties (Section 2): Commander in chief of the military. Power to make treaties (with the advice and consent of the Senate). Appoints ambassadors, judges, and other government officers (also with Senate approval). Section 3: Required to inform Congress on the State of the Union. Recommends legislation. Takes care that the laws be faithfully executed. Section 4: Specifies grounds for impeachment.

The general idea behind this executive design was to provide a central authority to implement the laws and act decisively in areas where Congress might be slow or divided.

The White House serves as both the residence and working headquarters of the president, head of the executive branch. The figurative nucleus of this three-story mansion is the chief executive's Oval Office. The building itself was completed in 1800, but had to be rebuilt after it was burned in 1814 during a conflict with the British.

Traditionally, the president has been given greater control in military decisions and foreign policy. Other design features were intended to keep the president from becoming a demagogue or an instrument of public opinion. The electoral college was intended to provide a second screening against public passions in selecting the top officer. With the early atrophy of the electoral college and the latter-day attention by the media and public opinion, the presidency may have changed more than any of the branches envisioned by the framers. (These changes will be explored in detail in Chapter 14.)

The Judicial Article

The main contribution of the short and often vague Article III was to create a Supreme Court. This article also instructs that all federal judges shall be appointed for life to ensure their impartiality and independence from the politicians who appoint them. Congress was given the power to create federal courts and define their jurisdictions.

Organization (Section 1): Judicial power "vested in one supreme Court, and in such inferior Courts as the Congress may from time to time ordain and establish." Life terms for judges, assuming good behavior.

Power and jurisdiction (Section 2): Judicial power extends to all cases arising under the Constitution, the laws of the United States, treaties, maritime issues, and controversies between states. The Supreme Court has original jurisdiction in cases involving ambassadors, ministers, and states. Appellate jurisdiction in other cases, subject to congressional regulation.

It was clear at the time of the founding that the full role of the courts in the national government was not anticipated, and the extent of court powers was not well defined. As

The U.S. Supreme Court Building. Judge Ruth Ginsburg's confirmation as an associate justice in 1993 made her only the second woman to serve on the august nine-member Court in its history; the first is her colleague Justice Sandra Day O'Connor, appointed in 1981 by President Ronald Reagan.

The Principle of Judicial Review: The Case of Marbury v. Madison

3.3

In many countries the legislature itself is the supreme guardian of the constitution. Nations such as Sweden and England, which use parliamentary systems, employ "constitutional committees" in parliament to interpret the legality of various laws and government actions. However, in the United States the Supreme Court quickly claimed a constitutional mandate to *review* and rule on the constitutionality of the law itself.

The first case that used this power of judicial review was *Marbury v. Madison* (1803). The issue in question involved the bitter election of 1800 that saw Thomas Jefferson and his party defeat John Adams and the Federalists. The Federalists were so angered with the defeat that they took revenge by creating fifty-nine new federal judgeships and appointing Federalists to all of them for lifetime terms. Jefferson took office before all of the commissions had been delivered. Infuriated at the "court-packing" scheme of the Federalists, Jefferson ordered his secretary of state not to deliver the remaining commissions. As a result, several

of the judges were deprived of the documents they needed for taking office.

One of the denied judges was William Marbury, a clever fellow who located a section of the Judiciary Act of 1789 in which Congress had authorized the Supreme Court to issue a *writ of mandamus,* a court order requiring public officials to perform their legal duties. Marbury asked the Supreme Court to order Jefferson's new secretary of state, James Madison, to hand over his undelivered commission. As coincidence would have it, the new chief justice was John Marshall, who was the former secretary of state who ran out of time to deliver the last of the Federalist commissions. Aside from his personal feelings about the matter, Marshall faced a larger dilemma: If the Court ordered Madison to hand over the commission, President Jefferson might decide to instruct his secretary of state to ignore the order, thereby sabotaging the Court's first attempt to exercise judicial review. On the other hand, a denial of Marbury's request might be interpreted as giving the president the power to ignore an act of Congress, supporting the president's claim that

the Court could not force the executive to obey it.

The unanimous opinion of the Court, written by Marshall, was sheer genius. First, the Court upheld Marbury's claim to the *writ of mandamus,* saying that this was, indeed, a case under the Judiciary Act of 1789 in which a government officer should be ordered to fulfill his duty. Next, Marshall turned around and declared the relevant section of the Judiciary Act unconstitutional! It was unconstitutional, he reasoned, because the operative clause of the Constitution (in Article III defining the judiciary) said that the Supreme Court has jurisdiction in such matters only if they involve ambassadors, diplomats, or states. Since Marbury was none of the three, the law applying to him was unconstitutional and could not be enforced. Thus in one stroke, Marshall asserted the precedent of judicial review by declaring a law unconstitutional. Since Madison did not have to deliver the commission, the president was not able to defy the ruling and undermine the Court's newly claimed powers. It was a ruling that infuriated both sides, but established what may be the Court's most important power.

a result of the relatively vague definition of the judiciary in the Constitution, what is perhaps the most important power of the courts today was not stated explicitly in Article III. There is no explicit mention of the power of **judicial review,** the principle that gives the Supreme Court the power to review the constitutionality of laws.

Many scholars believe that the idea of *judicial review* is implied by the very existence of a "Supreme Court" granted power over "all cases. . . arising under the Constitution." Indeed, without the principle of judicial review, the system of *checks and balances* set up in the Constitution would not give the judicial branch an equal weight with the other branches. The fact remains, however, that the document did not outline a judicial review power for the Court. As a result, the Court quickly addressed the question of its own

A Cure for Gridlock?: Political Parties as Means of Coordinating Power Among the Separate Branches

3.4

Many observers equate gridlock in government with different parties dominating different institutions. It makes sense that the same party in the White House and in both chambers of Congress might be better able to coordinate the activities of the two branches. However, that party would have to be united around a legislative agenda and be able to discipline its members to support that agenda. Even then, there is no guarantee that the Supreme Court would support that agenda, meaning that true one-party government in this system could also require holding power long enough to appoint a majority of justices to the Court (with no guarantee that their legal philosophies would translate into ideological support). In the 1930s, for example, the Democratic party captured the White House and Congress during the Great Depression and pushed a bold agenda of reform through new legislation. However, a Supreme Court appointed by previous Republican administrations rejected many of the key provisions of those laws. To resolve the conflict, President Franklin Roosevelt threatened to increase the number of seats on the Court (which is decided by Congress) so that more liberals could be appointed. Although this "court-packing" scheme was never implemented, it illustrates that sending the same party to Congress and the White House may not always be enough to create the kind of sweeping government action that some people see as the cure for gridlock.

"power balance" with the other branches by claiming its power of **judicial review** in the 1803 landmark case of *Marbury v. Madison* discussed in "Inside the System" Box 3.3.

Making Government Difficult by Design

The Constitution created a government that was not capable of much breathtaking action without tremendous mobilization of political support. It is hardly surprising that one of the first developments on the American political scene was the rise of parties as the most obvious means of coordinating power among the three branches. As we will see in Chapters 9 and 10, many observers blame a breakdown of strong parties for much of the gridlock in Washington. (See "Inside the System" Box 3.4.)

Adding to the possibility of gridlock in government is another important feature of the American system: the great powers granted to the states. Federalism imposes many limits on the actions of the national government. The political workings of federalism are explained in Chapter 4. The constitutional design of federal power is outlined in the next section.

Federal Design: Dividing Powers With the States

In addition to *separating* the primary national government activities among three branches, the Constitution *divides* power further between the national government and the states. The Constitution grants states considerable autonomy to govern their own citizens in most areas of criminal behavior and public order; business dealings; health, education, and safety; and basic citizenship and identity matters such as voting requirements, recording births, and licensing marriages. To an important degree Americans are citizens of both the United States and the state in which they live. While national powers are supreme in many areas, the powers granted to states continue to limit the activities of the national government in many ways.

More will be said in Chapter 4 about the ways in which different states have used their constitutional powers. For now, just remember that *the name of a system that divides governing powers between national and subnational units* (called states in the United States) *is* **federalism.** This system can magnify the tensions and conflicts in American government and contribute to some aspects of what people have come to call governmental gridlock.

National Supremacy vs. States' Rights

From the opening minutes of the Constitutional Convention to the present day, there have been two hotly contested views of federalism: the *state-centered* or *states' rights* position, which favors stronger state governments, and the *nation-centered* or *nationalist* position, favoring a stronger national government. Supporters of both views always find good defenses for their positions in the Constitution. How can this be? Recall from the last chapter that the Constitution was a series of compromises between groups who favored different power arrangements. These compromises gave both states' rights and national power advocates something of what they wanted and left plenty of grey areas open to interpretation. As a result, proponents of both views have believed ever since that theirs is the correct interpretation of the document.

It can even be argued that the state-centered view had an edge in the beginning. Consider, for example, the opinion of no less a constitutional expert than James Madison, who wrote in *Federalist* No. 45: "The powers delegated by the proposed Constitution to the federal government are few and defined. Those which are to remain in the state governments are numerous and indefinite." Madison goes on to point out that most things pertaining to "lives, liberties and properties of the people," as well as matters related to "order, improvement and prosperity" are left to the states. To the national government go the charmless tasks of economic coordination, defense, and dispute resolution. Perhaps the states really had the edge when the bargaining finally stopped in Philadelphia, and the Constitution sealed the deal. Then again, remember that for Madison *The Federalist* was not only a theoretical explanation of the Constitution, it was a sales effort as well. Madison was trying to persuade those opposed to a strong national government that the Constitution was in their interest.

The moral of the story is that whether one's position on power is state-centered or nation-centered, it is possible to read the Constitution and see that position confirmed in it. "Surely," each side reasons, "if my side is so close to the original intent of the Founders, and so well supported by the words of the Constitution itself, then one more Supreme Court victory in this area and another piece of key legislation, and we have won the decisive battle." With the disastrous exception of the Civil War, this reasoning has produced a share of victories for both sides, while encouraging the losers on a variety of issues to rally and fight again to defend their endangered interpretations.

The fight over state and national powers can be seen today in many areas, including environmental quality, abortion, business and banking practices, civil rights, social morality, sexual behavior, religion, and prayer. At stake are fundamental political questions of where the basic qualities of social life will be decided. This explains why appointments of justices to the Supreme Court are so important: The constitutional philosophies of presidents and their appointees are important to the way Americans will live their lives.

Interstate Relations

After the three branches of government are defined in the first three articles, Article IV outlines a rather broad and often disputed set of divisions of power between national and state governments and between the states themselves. This article also coordinates relations among the states to ensure that citizenship, criminal justice proceedings, transportation, and other basic ingredients of "national" life flow smoothly across state boundaries. Among the particular provisions are authorization for states to extradite people fleeing from justice; procedures for admitting new states into the Union; and requirements for each state to have a republican form of government.

The Supremacy Clause

Article VI establishes the Constitution as "the Supreme Law of the Land." All public officials at both the state and national level are bound to follow it and obey the acts of government that flow from it. This is known as the **supremacy clause.** However, as the discussion in Chapter 4 makes clear, the Supreme Court was extremely cautious in asserting this principle. Its application was limited during most of the first century of the Republic to the necessary regulation of trade and commerce. Although the supremacy clause appears very clear in declaring the national government the supreme power of the land, the many provisions for state powers in the Constitution have not made that supremacy easy to establish or to maintain in many areas of political life.

The Denial of Powers

The Constitution specifically *denies* a whole list of powers to the national government and another whole list to the states. Read the Constitution for yourself to see if you can spot these **denied powers.** (Hint: Check Article I, Sections 9 and 10.) The Constitution gives the national government an edge in taxes, along with a near monopoly over the use of force by denying a list of powers in these areas to the states. However, there is still room for states to raise certain taxes, employ police, and (with the consent of Congress) maintain militias. At the same time, there is another list of powers denied to the national government aimed at keeping its taxing (and spending) within bounds. While you are trying to find the above prohibitions or limits on the national government in Article I, Section 9, you will notice a long list of other powers specifically denied Congress.

The "Living Constitution"

The Constitution is what authorizes various institutions, states, and leaders to do what they do. Why do most Americans continue to have faith in this document and accept its authority? Among other reasons, the Constitution is remarkably accessible to ordinary people. Consider three features of our constitutional order that keep the document alive in contemporary politics.

The Bill of Rights

The ten amendments added to secure ratification of the original document have become increasingly vital as resources for individual political action. People have used the provisions of the Bill to address a variety of important concerns ranging from protection of property, to confronting discrimination in jobs and education, to the struggle for and

Text continued on page 91

THE CONSTITUTION
OF THE UNITED STATES OF AMERICA

We the People of the United States, in Order to form a more perfect Union, establish Justice, insure domestic Tranquility, provide for the common defence, promote the general Welfare, and secure the Blessings of Liberty to ourselves and our Posterity, do ordain and establish this Constitution for the United States of America.

Article. I.

Section. 1. All legislative Powers herein granted shall be vested in a Congress of the United States, which shall consist of a Senate and House of Representatives.

Section. 2. The House of Representatives shall be composed of Members chosen every second Year by the People of the several States, and the Electors of the most numerous Branch of the State Legislature.

No Person shall be a Representative who shall not have attained to the Age of twenty five Years, and been seven Years a Citizen of the United States, and who shall not, when elected, be an Inhabitant of that State in which he shall be chosen.

Representatives and direct Taxes shall be apportioned among the several States which may be included within this Union, according to their respective Numbers, which shall be determined by adding to the whole Number of free Persons, including those bound to Service for a Term of Years, and excluding Indians not taxed, three fifths of all other Persons. The actual Enumeration shall be made within three Years after the first Meeting of the Congress of the United States, and within every subsequent Term of ten Years, in such Manner as they shall by Law direct. The Number of Representatives shall not exceed one for every thirty Thousand, but each State shall have at least one Representative; and until such enumeration shall be made, the State of New Hampshire shall be entitled to chuse three; Massachusetts eight; Rhode Island and Providence Plantations one; Connecticut five; New York six; New Jersey four; Pennsylvania eight; Delaware one; Maryland six; Virginia ten; North Carolina five; South Carolina five; and Georgia three.

When vacancies happen in the Representation from any State, the Executive Authority thereof shall issue Writs of Election to fill such Vacancies.

The House of Representatives shall chuse their Speaker and other Officers; and shall have the sole Power of Impeachment.

Section. 3. The Senate of the United States shall be composed of two senators from each State, chosen by the Legislature thereof, for six Years; and each Senator shall have one Vote.

Immediately after they shall be assembled in Consequence of the first Election, they shall be divided as equally as may be into three Classes. The Seats of the Senators of the first Class shall be vacated at the Expiration of the second Year, of the second class at the Expiration of the fourth Year, and of the third Class at the Expiration of the sixth Year, so that one third may be chosen every second Year; and if Vacancies happen by Resignation, or otherwise, during the Recess of the Legislature of any State, the Executive thereof may make temporary Appointments until the next Meeting of the Legislature, which shall then fill such Vacancies.

No Person shall be a Senator who shall not have attained to the Age of thirty Years, and been nine Years a Citizen of the United States, and who shall not, when elected, be an Inhabitant of that State for which he shall be chosen.

The Vice President of the United States shall be President of the Senate, but shall have no Vote, unless they be equally divided.

The Senate shall chuse their other Officers, and also a President pro tempore, in the Absence of the Vice President, or when he shall exercise the Office of President of the United States.

The Senate shall have the sole Power to try all Impeachments. When sitting for that Purpose, they shall be on Oath or Affirmation. When the President of the United States is tried, the Chief Justice shall preside: And no Person shall be convicted without the Concurrence of two thirds of the Members present.

Judgment in Cases of Impeachment shall not extend further than to removal from Office, and disqualification to hold and enjoy any Office of honor, Trust of Profit under the United States: but the Party convicted shall nevertheless be liable and subject to Indictment, Trial, Judgment and Punishment, according to law.

Section. 4. The Times, Places and Manner of holding Elections for Senators and Representatives, shall be prescribed in each State by the Legislature thereof, but the Congress may at any time by Law make or alter such Regulation, except as to the Places of chusing Senators.

The Congress shall assemble at least once in every Year, and such Meeting shall be on the first Monday in December, unless they shall by Law appoint a different Day.

Section. 5. Each House shall be the Judge of the Elections, Returns and Qualifications of its own Members, and a Majority of each shall constitute a Quorum to do Business; but a smaller Number may adjourn from day to day, and may be authorized to compel the Attendance of absent members, in such manner, and under such Penalties as each House may provide.

Each House may determine the Rules of its Proceedings, punish its Members for disorderly Behaviour, and, with the Concurrence of two thirds, expel a Member.

Each House shall keep a Journal of its Proceedings, and from time to time publish the same, excepting such Parts as may in their Judgment require Secrecy; and the Yeas and Nays of the Members of either House on any question shall, at the Desire of one fifth of those Present, be entered on the Journal.

Neither House, during the Session of Congress, shall, without the Consent of the other, adjourn for more than three days, nor to any other Place than that in which the two Houses shall be sitting.

Section. 6. The Senators and Representatives shall receive a Compensation for their Services, to be ascertained by Law, and paid out of the Treasury of the United States. They shall in all Cases, except Treason, Felony and Breach of the Peace, be privileged from Arrest during their Attendance at the Session of their respective Houses, and in going to and returning from the same; and for any Speech or Debate in either House, they shall not be questioned in any other Place.

No Senator or Representative shall, during the Time for which he was elected, be appointed to any civil Office under the Authority of the United States, which shall have been created, or the Emoluments whereof shall have been increased during such time; and no Person holding any Office under the United States, shall be a Member of either House during his Continuance in Office.

Section. 7. All Bills for raising Revenue shall originate in the House of Representatives; but the Senate may propose or concur with Amendments as on other bills.

Every Bill which shall have passed the House of Representatives and the Senate shall, before it become a Law, be presented to the President of the United States; if he approve he shall sign it, but if not he shall return it, with his Objections to that House in which it shall have originated, who shall enter the Objections at large on their Journal, and proceed to reconsider it. If after such Reconsideration two thirds of that House shall agree to pass the Bill, it shall be sent, together with the Objections, to the other House, by which it shall likewise be reconsidered, and if approved by two thirds of that House, it shall become a Law. But in all such Cases the Votes of both Houses shall be determined by yeas and Nays, and the Names of the Persons voting for and against the Bill shall be entered on the Journal of each House respectively. If any Bill shall not be returned by the President within ten Days (Sundays excepted) after it shall have been presented to him, the Same shall be a Law, in Manner as if he had signed it, unless the Congress by their Adjournment prevent its Return, in which Case it shall not be a Law.

Every Order, Resolution, or Vote to which the Concurrence of the Senate and House of Representatives may be necessary (except on a question of Adjournment) shall be presented to the President of the United States; and before the Same shall take Effect, shall be approved by him, or being disapproved by him shall be repassed by two thirds of the Senate and House of Representatives, according to the rules and Limitations prescribed in the Case of a Bill.

Section. 8. The Congress shall have Power to lay and collect Taxes, Duties, Imposts and Excises, to pay the Debts and provide for the common Defence and general Welfare of the United States; but all Duties, Imposts and Excises shall be uniform throughout the United States;

To borrow Money on the credit of the United States;

To regulate Commerce with foreign Nations, and among the several States, and with the Indian Tribes;

To establish an uniform Rule of Naturalization, and uniform Laws on the subject of Bankruptcies throughout the United States;

To coin Money, regulate the Value thereof, and of foreign Coin, and fix the Standard of Weights and Measures;

To provide for the Punishment of counterfeiting the Securities and current Coin of the United States;

To establish Post Offices and Post Roads;

To promote the Progress of Science and useful Arts, by securing for limited Times to Authors and Inventors the exclusive Right to their respective Writings and Discoveries;

To constitute Tribunals inferior to the supreme Court;

To define and punish Piracies and Felonies committed on the high Seas, and Offences against the Law of Nations;

To declare War, grant Letters of Marque and Reprisal, and make Rules concerning Captures on Land and Water;

To raise and support Armies, but no Appropriation of Money to that Use shall be for a longer Term than two Years;

To provide and maintain a Navy;

To make Rules for the government and Regulation of the land and naval Forces;

To provide for calling forth the Militia to execute the Laws of the Union, suppress Insurrections and repel Invasions;

To provide for organizing, arming, and disciplining, the Militia, and for governing such Part of them as may be employed in the Service of the United States, reserving to the States respectively, the Appointment of the Officers, and the Authority of training the Militia according to the discipline prescribed by Congress;

To exercise exclusive Legislation in all Cases whatsoever, over such District (not exceeding ten Miles square) as may, by Cession of particular States, and the Acceptance of Congress, become the Seat of the Government of the United States, and to exercise like Authority over all Places purchased by the consent of the Legislature of the State in which the Same shall be, for the Erection of Forts,

Magazines, Arsenals, dock-Yards, and other needful Buildings;—And

To make all Laws which shall be necessary and proper for carrying into Execution the foregoing Powers, and all other Powers vested by this Constitution in the Government of the United States, or in any Department or Officer thereof.

Section. 9. The Migration or Importation of such Persons as any of the States now existing shall think proper to admit, shall not be prohibited by the Congress prior to the Year one thousand eight hundred and eight, but a Tax or Duty may be imposed on such Importation, not exceeding ten dollars for each Person.

The Privilege of the Writ of Habeas Corpus shall not be suspended, unless when in Cases of Rebellion or Invasion the public Safety may require it.

No Bill of Attainder or ex post fact Law shall be passed.

No Capitation, or other direct, Tax shall be laid, unless in Proportion to the Census or Enumeration herein before directed to be taken.

No Tax or Duty shall be laid on Articles exported from any State.

No Preference shall be given by any Regulation of commerce or Revenue to the Ports of one State over those of another: nor shall Vessels bound to, or from, one State, be obliged to enter, clear, or pay Duties in another.

No Money shall be drawn from the Treasury, but in Consequence of Appropriations made by Law, and a regular Statement and Account of the receipts and Expenditures of all public Money shall be published from time to time.

No Title of Nobility shall be granted by the United States: And no Person holding any Office or Profit or Trust under them, shall, without the Consent of the Congress, accept of any present, Emolument, Office, or Title, of any kind whatever, from any King, Prince, or foreign State.

Section. 10. No State shall enter into any Treaty, Alliance, or Confederation; grant Letters of Marque and Reprisal; coin Money; emit bills of Credit; make any Thing but gold and silver Coin a Tender in Payment of Debts; pass any Bill of Attainder, ex post facto Law, or Law impairing the Obligation of Contracts, or grant any Title of Nobility.

No state shall, without the Consent of the Congress, lay any Imposts or Duties on Imports or Exports, except what may be absolutely necessary for executing its inspection Laws: and the net Produce of all Duties and Imposts, laid by any State on Imports or Exports, shall be for the Use of the Treasury of the United States; and all such Laws shall be subject to the Revision and Controul of the Congress.

No State shall, without the Consent of Congress, lay any Duty of Tonnage, keep Troops or Ships of War in time of peace, enter into any Agreement or Compact with another State, or with a foreign Power, or engage in War, unless actually invaded, or in such imminent Danger as will not admit of delay.

Article. II.

The executive Power shall be vested in a President of the United States of America. He shall hold his Office during the Term of four Years, and together with the Vice President, chosen for the same Term, be elected, as follows:

Each State shall appoint, in such Manner as the Legislature thereof may direct, a Number of Electors, equal to the whole Number of Senators and representatives to which the State may be entitled in the Congress: but no Senator or Representative, or Person holding an Office of Trust or Profit under the United State, shall be appointed an Elector.

The Electors shall meet in their respective States, and vote by Ballot for two Persons, of whom one at least shall not be an Inhabitant of the same State with themselves. And they shall make a List of all the Persons voted for and of the Number of Votes for each; which List they shall sign and certify, and transmit sealed to the Seat of the Government of the United States, directed to the President of the Senate. The President of the Senate shall, in the Presence of the Senate and House of Representatives, open all the Certificates, and the Votes shall then be counted. The Person having the greatest Number of votes shall be the President, if such Number be a Majority of the whole Number of electors appointed; and if there be more than one who have such Majority, and have an equal Number of Votes, then the House of Representatives shall immediately chuse by Ballot one of them for President; and if no Person have a Majority, then from the five highest on the List the said House shall in like Manner chuse the President. But in chusing the President, the Votes shall be taken by States, the Representation from each State having on Vote; A quorum for this Purpose shall consist of a Member or Members from two thirds of the States, and a Majority of all the States shall be necessary to a Choice. In every Case, after the Choice of the President, the Person having the greatest Number of Votes of the Electors shall be the Vice President. But if there should remain two or more who have equal Votes, the Senate shall chuse from them by Ballot the Vice President.

The Congress may determine the Time of chusing the Electors, and the Day on which they shall give their Votes; which Day shall be the same throughout the United States.

No Person except a natural born Citizen, or a Citizen of the United States, at the time of the Adoption of this Constitution, shall be eligible to the Office of President, neither shall any Person be eligible to that Office who shall not have attained to the Age of thirty five Years, and been fourteen Years a Resident within the United States.

In Case of the Removal of the President from Office, or of his Death, Resignation, or Inability to discharge the

Powers and duties of the said Office, the Same shall devolve on the Vice President, and the Congress may by Law provide for the Case of Removal, Death, Resignation or Inability, both of the President and Vice President, declaring what Officer shall then act as President, and such Officer shall act accordingly, until the Disability be removed, or a President shall be elected.

The President shall, at stated Times, receive for his Services, a Compensation, which shall neither be encreased nor diminished during the Period for which he shall have been elected, and he shall not receive within that Period any other emolument from the United States, or any of them.

Before he enter on the Execution of his Office, he shall take the following Oath or Affirmation:—"I do solemnly swear (or affirm) that I will faithfully execute the Office of President of the United States, and will to the best of my Ability, preserve, protect and defend the Constitution of the United States."

Section. 2. The President shall be Commander in Chief of the Army and Navy of the United States, and of the Militia of the several States, when called into the actual Service of the United States; he may require the Opinion, in writing, of the principal Officer in each of the executive Departments, upon any Subject relating to the Duties of their respective Offices, and he shall have Power to grant Reprieves and Pardons for Offences against the United States, except in cases of Impeachment.

He shall have Power, by and with the Advice and Consent of the Senate, to make Treaties, provided two thirds of the Senators present concur; and he shall nominate, and by and with the Advice and Consent of the Senate, shall appoint Ambassadors, other public Ministers and Consuls, Judges of the supreme Court, and all other Officers of the United States, whose Appointments are not herein otherwise provided for, and which shall be established by Law; but the Congress may by Law vest the Appointment of such inferior Officers, as they think proper, in the President alone, in the Courts of Law, or in the Heads of Departments.

The President shall have Power to fill up all Vacancies that may happen during the recess of the Senate, by granting Commissions which shall expire at the End of their next Session.

Section. 3. He shall from time to time give to the Congress Information of the State of the Union, and recommend to their Consideration such measures as he shall judge necessary and expedient; he may, on extraordinary Occasions, convene both Houses, or either of them, and in Case of disagreement between them, with respect to the Time of Adjournment, he may adjourn them to such Time as he shall think proper; he shall receive Ambassadors and other public Ministers; he shall take Care that the Laws be faithfully executed, and shall Commission all the Officers of the United States.

Section. 4. The President, Vice President and all civil Officers of the United States, shall be removed from Office on Impeachment for, and Conviction of, Treason, Bribery, or other high Crimes and Misdemeanors.

Article. III.

Section. 1. The judicial Power of the United States, shall be vested in one supreme Court, and in such inferior Courts as the Congress may from time to time ordain and establish. The Judges, both of the supreme and inferior Courts, shall hold their Offices during good Behaviour, and shall, at stated Times, receive for their Services, a Compensation, which shall not be diminished during their Continuance in Office.

Section. 2. The judicial Power shall extend to all Cases, in Law Equity, arising under this Constitution, the Laws of the United States, and Treaties made, or which shall be made, under their Authority;—to all Cases affecting Ambassadors, other public Ministers and Consuls;—to all Cases of admiralty and maritime Jurisdiction;—to Controversies to which the United States shall be a Party;—to Controversies between two or more States;—between a State and Citizens of another State,—between Citizens of different States,—between Citizens of the same State claiming Lands under Grants of different States, and between a State, or the Citizens thereof, and foreign States, Citizens or subjects.

In all Cases affecting ambassadors, other public Ministers and Consuls, and those in which a State shall be Party, the supreme Court shall have original Jurisdiction. In all the other Cases before mentioned, the supreme Court shall have appellate Jurisdiction, both as to Law and Fact, with such Exceptions, and under such Regulations as the Congress shall make.

The Trial of all Crimes, except in Cases of Impeachment, shall be by Jury; and such Trial shall be held in the State where the said Crimes shall have been committed, but when not committed within any State, the trial shall be at such Place or Places as the Congress may by Law have directed.

Section. 3. Treason against the United States, shall consist only in levying war against them, or in adhering to their Enemies, giving them aid and Comfort. No Person shall be convicted of Treason unless on the Testimony of two Witnesses to the same overt Act, or on confession in open Court.

The Congress shall have Power to declare the Punishment of Treason, but no Attainder of Treason shall work Corruption of Blood, or Forfeiture except during the Life of the Person attainted.

Article. IV.

Section. 1. Full Faith and Credit shall be given in each State to the public Acts, Records, and judicial Proceedings of every other State. And the Congress may by general Laws prescribe the Manner in which such Acts, Records and Proceedings shall be proved, and the Effect thereof.

Section. 2. The Citizens of each State shall be entitled to all Privileges and Immunities of Citizens in the several States.

A Person charged in any State with Treason, Felony, or other Crime, who shall flee from Justice, and be found in another State, shall on Demand of the executive authority of the State from which he fled, be delivered up, to be removed to the State having Jurisdiction of the Crime.

No Person held to Service or Labour in one State, under the Laws thereof, escaping into another, shall, in Consequence of any Law or Regulation therein, be discharged from such Service or Labour, but shall be delivered up on Claim of the Party to whom such Service or Labour may be due.

Section. 3. New States may be admitted by the Congress into this Union; but no new State shall be formed or erected within the Jurisdiction of any other State, nor any State be formed by the Junction of two or more States, or Parts of States, without the Consent of the Legislatures of the States concerned as well as of the Congress.

The Congress shall have Power to dispose of and make all needful Rules and Regulations respecting the Territory or other Property belonging to the United States; and nothing in this Constitution shall be so construed as to Prejudice any Claims of the United States, or of any particular State.

Section. 4. The United States shall guarantee to every State in this Union a Republican Form of Government, and shall protect each of them against Invasion; and on Application of the Legislature, or of the Executive (when the Legislature cannot be convened) against domestic Violence.

Article. V.

The Congress, whenever two thirds of both Houses shall deem it necessary, shall propose Amendments to this Constitution, or, on the Application of the Legislatures of two thirds of the several States, shall call a Convention for proposing Amendments, which, in either Case, shall be valid to all Intents and Purposes, as Part of this Constitution, when ratified by the Legislatures of three fourths of the several States, or by Conventions in three fourths thereof, as the one or the other Mode of Ratification may be proposed by the Congress; Provided that no amendment which may be made prior to the Year One thousand eight hundred and eight shall in any Manner affect the first and fourth Clauses in the Ninth Section of the first Article; and that no State, without its Consent, shall be deprived of its equal Suffrage in the Senate.

Article. VI.

All Debts contracted and Engagements entered into, before the Adoption of this Constitution, shall be as valid against the United States under this Constitution, as under the Confederation.

This Constitution, and the Laws of the United States which shall be made in Pursuance thereof; and all Treaties made, or which shall be made, under the Authority of the United States, shall be the supreme Law of the Land; and the Judges in every State shall be bound thereby, any Thing in the Constitution or Laws of any State to the Contrary notwithstanding.

The Senators and Representatives before mentioned, and the Members of the several State Legislatures, and all executive and judicial Officers, both of the United States and of the several States, shall be bound by Oath or Affirmation, to support this Constitution; but no religious Test shall ever be required as a Qualification to any Office or public Trust under the United States.

Article. VII.

The Ratification of the Conventions of nine States, shall be sufficient for the Establishment of this Constitution between the States so ratifying the Same.

Done in convention by the Unanimous Consent of the States present the Seventeenth Day of September in the Year of our Lord on thousand seven hundred and Eighty seven and of the Independence of the United States of America the twelfth. In witness whereof We have hereunto subscribed our Names,

George Washington, President and deputy from Virginia

Attest: William Jackson, Secretary

New Hampshire—John Landon, Nicholas Gilman

Massachusetts—Nathaniel Gorham, Rufus King

Connecticut—Wm. Saml. Johnson, Roger Sherman

New York—Alexander Hamilton

New Jersey—Wil: Livingston, David Brearley, Wm. Paterson, Jona: Dayton

Pennsylvania—B. Franklin, Thomas Mifflin, Robt. Morris, Geo. Clymer, Thos FitzSimons, Jared Ingersoll, James Wilson, Gouv. Morris

Delaware—Geo: Read, Gunning Bedford Jun., John Dickinson, Richard Bassett, Jaco: Broom

Maryland—James McHenry, Daniel of Saint Thomas' Jenifer, Danl. Carroll

Virginia—John Blair, James Madison Jr.

North Carolina—Wm. Blount, Rich'd. Dobbs Spaight, Hugh Williamson

South Carolina—J. Rutledge, Charles Cotesworth Pinckney, Charles Pinckney, Pierce Butler.

Georgia—William Few, Abr. Baldwin

against abortion. As we will see in Chapter 5, it was not easy to "incorporate" the Bill of Rights into the everyday lives of citizens in the states, nor have the battles always had happy outcomes. Despite or perhaps because of this struggle, however, most Americans know that, above all, they have rights.

The first eight of these ten amendments spell out protections against national violations of specific rights. You should read these amendments now. The Ninth Amendment says that the rights listed above do not deny the existence of other rights that might be retained in the future by the people. The Tenth Amendment says that any powers not delegated to the national government or prohibited to the states are "reserved" to the states "or to the people." We will return to the importance of the so-called **reserved powers** in the discussion of federalism in Chapter 4.

Amending the Constitution

Amending the Constitution adds to its flexibility. For example, the Thirteenth Amendment, prohibiting slavery (ratified in 1865), was a major step toward creating a society more in keeping with its own stated ideals of liberty and justice for all. The Fourteenth Amendment promised equal protection and application of the laws to all citizens—another important part of the democratic ideal. Even with these amendments paving the way, it took nearly a century more for the political struggle to convert the spirit of the Constitution into the force of national laws, as described in Chapter 5. There is still much to be done to create "a more perfect Union," but the power to amend the Constitution and the power to then use those amendments as political resources are important political tools.

Not all amendments, however, are as important to social life as the Thirteenth and Fourteenth are. For example, the latest amendment to the Constitution is such a minor matter that it actually became lost and took over two hundred years to be ratified. This Twenty-seventh Amendment could well have been the twelfth amendment with a bit more support when it was submitted to the states for approval. Written by the ever-present James Madison in 1789, the proposed amendment prevented pay raises passed by one Congress from taking effect until after the next election. Although submitted to the states in the same package that included the Bill of Rights, there was little interest in the pay raise amendment at the time, and only six states ratified it by the time the Bill of Rights was passed. Interest was not revived until two centuries later, when voters began expressing anger at Congress and seeking ways to express that anger. The first state to ratify the amendment was Maryland in 1789 and the necessary thirty-eighth state did not complete the ratification process until Michigan did so in 1992.

Because of the unprecedented length of time involved, there was some concern about whether to accept the amendment as valid. Although some members of Congress doubted that the amendment should be accepted because of its two-century ordeal, constitutional law scholars argued that since the original Congress did not place a time limit on the amendment, it was not the business of later Congresses to do so.[10] In modern times, Congresses have attached time limits (generally of seven years) to complete the ratification process, failing which the amendment is dead.

Although the strange case of the Twenty-seventh Amendment is unusual, all amendments go through the same general procedure outlined in Article V of the Constitution. By a two-thirds votes in both houses of Congress, amendments can be proposed to the states for **ratification** (approval). Congress can send the proposed amendments to either state legislatures or specially called state conventions for ratification. In actual practice, Congress has sent all proposed amendments except one (the repeal of Prohibition) to the

Text continued on page 96

AMENDMENTS TO THE UNITED STATES CONSTITUTION

(The first ten amendments are collectively known as the Bill of Rights.)

Amendment I

Congress shall make no law respecting an establishment of religion, or prohibiting the free exercise thereof; or abridging the freedom of speech, or of the press; or the right of the people peaceably to assemble, and to petition the Government for a redress of grievances.

[effective December 15, 1791]

Amendment II

A well regulated Militia, being necessary to the security of a free State, the right of the people to keep and bear Arms shall not be infringed.

[December 15, 1791]

Amendment III

No Soldier shall, in time of peace, be quartered in any house, without the consent of the Owner, nor in time of war, but in a manner to be prescribed by law.

[December 15, 1791]

Amendment IV

The right of the people to be secure in their persons, houses, papers, and effects, against unreasonable searches and seizures, shall not be violated, and no Warrants shall issue, but upon probable cause, supported by Oath or affirmation, and particularly describing the place to be searched, and the persons or things to be seized.

[December 15, 1791]

Amendment V

No person shall be held to answer for a capital or otherwise infamous crime, unless on a presentment or indictment of a Grand Jury, except in cases arising in the land or naval forces, or in the Militia, when in actual service in time of War or public danger; nor shall any person be subject for the same offence to be twice put in jeopardy of life or limb; nor shall be compelled in any criminal case to be a witness against himself, nor be deprived of life, liberty, or property, without due process of law; nor shall private property be taken for public use, without just compensation.

[December 15, 1791]

Amendment VI

In all criminal prosecutions, the accused shall enjoy the right to a speedy and public trial, by an impartial jury of the State and district wherein the crime shall have been committed, which district shall have been previously ascertained by law, and to be informed of the nature and cause of the accusation; to be confronted with the witnesses against him; to have compulsory process for obtaining witnesses in his favor, and to have the Assistance of Counsel for his defence.

[December 15, 1791]

Amendment VII

In suits at common law, where the value in controversy shall exceed twenty dollars, the right of trial by jury shall be preserved, and no fact tried by a jury, shall be otherwise reexamined in any Court of the United States, than according to the rules of the common law.

[December 15, 1791]

Amendment VIII

Excessive bail shall not be required, no excessive fines imposed, nor cruel and unusual punishments inflicted.

[December 15, 1791]

Amendment IX

The enumeration in the Constitution, of certain rights, shall not be construed to deny or disparage others retained by the people.

[December 15, 1791]

Amendment X

The powers not delegated to the United States by the Constitution; nor prohibited by it to the States, are reserved to the States respectively, or to the people.

[December 15, 1791]

Amendment XI

The Judicial power of the United States shall not be construed to extend to any suit in law or equity, commenced or prosecuted against one of the United States by citizens of another State, or by Citizens or Subjects of any foreign State.

[February 7, 1795]

Amendment XII

The Electors shall meet in their respective States and vote by ballot for President and Vice-President, one of whom, at least, shall not be an inhabitant of the same State with themselves; they shall name in their ballots the person voted for as President, and in distinct ballots the person voted for as Vice-President, and they shall make distinct lists of all persons voted for as President, and of all persons voted for as Vice-President, and of the number of votes for each, which lists they shall sign and certify, and transmit sealed to the seat of the government of the United States, directed to the President of the Senate;—The President of the Senate shall, in the presence of the Senate and House of Representatives, open all the certificates and the votes shall then be counted;—The person having the greatest number of votes for President, shall be the President, if such number be a majority of the whole number of Electors appointed; and if no person have such majority, then from the persons having the highest numbers not exceeding three on the list of those voted for as President, the House of Representatives shall choose immediately, by ballot, the President. But in choosing the President, the votes shall be taken by states, the representation from each state having one vote; a quorum for this purpose shall consist of a member or members from two-thirds of the states, and a majority of all the states shall be necessary to a choice. And if the House of Representatives shall not choose a President whenever the right of choice shall devolve upon them, before the fourth day of March next following, then the Vice-President shall act as President, as in the case of the death or other constitutional disability of the President.—The person having the greatest number of votes as Vice-President, shall be the vice-President, if such number be a majority of the whole number of Electors appointed, and if no person have a majority, then from the two highest numbers on the list, the Senate shall choose the Vice-President; a quorum for the purpose shall consist of two-thirds of the whole number of Senators, and a majority of the whole number shall be necessary to a choice. But no person constitutionally ineligible to the office of President shall be eligible to that of Vice-President of the United States.

[June 15, 1804]

Amendment XIII

Section. 1. Neither slavery nor involuntary servitude, except as a punishment for crime whereof the party shall have been duly convicted, shall exist within the United States, or any place subject to their jurisdiction.

Section. 2. Congress shall have power to enforce this article by appropriate legislation.

[December 18, 1865]

Amendment XIV

Section. 1. All persons born or naturalized in the United States, and subject to the jurisdiction thereof, are citizens of the United States and of the State wherein they reside. No State shall make or enforce any law which shall abridge the privileges or immunities of citizens of the United States; nor shall any State deprive any person of life, liberty, or property, without due process of law; nor deny to any person within its jurisdiction the equal protection of the laws.

Section. 2. Representatives shall be apportioned among the several States according to their respective numbers, counting the whole number of persons in each State, excluding Indians not taxed. But when the right to vote at any election for the choice of electors for President and Vice-President of the United States, Representatives in Congress, the Executive and Judicial officers of a State, or the members of the Legislature thereof, is denied to any of the male inhabitants of such State, being twenty-one years of age, and citizens of the United States, or in any way abridged, except for participation in rebellion, or other crime, the basis of representation therein shall be reduced in the proportion which the number of such male citizens shall bear to the whole number of male citizens twenty-one years of age in such State.

Section. 3. No person shall be a Senator or Representative in Congress, or elector of President and Vice-President, or hold any office, civil or military, under the United States, or under any State, who, having previously taken an oath, as a member of Congress, or as an officer of the United States, or as a member of any State legislature, or as an executive or judicial officer of any State, to support the Constitution of the United States, shall have engaged in insurrection or rebellion against the same, or given aid or comfort to the enemies thereof. But Congress may by a vote of two-thirds of each House, remove such disability.

Section. 4. The validity of the public debt of the United States, authorized by law, including debts incurred for payment of pensions and bounties for services in suppressing insurrection or rebellion, shall not be questioned. But neither the United States nor any State shall assume or pay any debt or obligation incurred in aid of insurrection or rebellion against the United States, or any claim for the loss or emancipation of any slave; but all such debts, obligations, and claims shall be held illegal and void.

Section. 5. The Congress shall have the power to enforce, by appropriate legislation, the provisions of this article.

[July 28, 1868]

Amendment XV

Section. 1. The right of citizens of the United States to vote shall not be denied or abridged by the United States or by any State on account of race, color, or previous condition of servitude—

Section. 2. The Congress shall have power to enforce this article by appropriate legislation.

[March 30, 1870]

Amendment XVI

The Congress shall have power to lay and collect taxes on incomes, from whatever source derived, without apportionment among the several States, and without regard to any census or enumeration.

[February 25, 1913]

Amendment XVII

The Senate of the United States shall be composed of two Senators from each State, elected by the people thereof, for six years; and each Senator shall have one vote. The electors in each State shall have the qualifications requisite for electors of the most numerous branch of the State legislatures.

When vacancies happen in the representation of any State in the Senate, the executive authority of such State shall issue writs of election to fill such vacancies: Provided, That the legislature of any State may empower the executive thereof to make temporary appointments until the people fill the vacancies by election as the legislature may direct. This amendment shall not be so construed as to affect the election or term of any Senator chosen before it becomes valid as part of the Constitution.

[May 31, 1913]

Amendment XVIII

Section. 1. After one year from the ratification of this article the manufacture, sale, or transportation of intoxicating liquors within, the importation thereof into, or the exportation thereof from the United States and all territory subject to the jurisdiction thereof for beverage purposes is hereby prohibited.

Section. 2. The Congress and the several States shall have concurrent power to enforce this article by appropriate legislation.

Section. 3. This article shall be inoperative unless it shall have been ratified as an amendment to the Constitution by the legislatures of the several States, as provided in the Constitution, within seven years from the date of the submission hereof to the States by the Congress.

[January 29, 1919; repealed December 5, 1933]

Amendment XIX

The right of citizens of the United States to vote shall not be denied or abridged by the United States or by any State on account of sex.

Congress shall have power to enforce this article by appropriate legislation.

[August 26, 1920]

Amendment XX

Section. 1. The terms of the President and vice-President shall end at noon on the 20th day of January, and the terms of Senators and Representatives at noon on the 3d day of January, of the years in which such terms would have ended if this article had not been ratified; and the terms of their successors shall then begin.

Section. 2. The Congress shall assemble at least once in every year, and such meeting shall begin at noon the 3d day of January, unless they shall by law appoint a different day.

Section. 3. If, at the time fixed for the beginning of the term of the President, the President elect shall have died, the Vice-President elect shall become President. If a President shall not have been chosen before the time fixed for the beginning of his term, or if the President elect shall have failed to qualify, then the Vice-President elect shall act as President until a President shall have qualified; and the Congress may by law provide for the case wherein neither a President elect not a Vice-President elect shall have qualified, declaring who shall then act as President, or the manner in which one who is to act shall be selected, and such person shall act accordingly until a President or vice-President shall have qualified.

Section. 4. The Congress may by law prvide for the case of the death of any of the persons from whom the House of Representatives may choose a President whenever the right of choice shall have devolved upon them, and for the case of the death of any of the persons from whom the Senate may choose a Vice-President whenever the right of choice shall have devolved upon them.

Section. 5. Sections 1 and 2 shall take effect on the 15th day of October following the ratification of this article.

Section. 6. This article shall be inoperative unless it shall have been ratified as an amendment to the Constitution by the legislatures of three-fourths of the several States within seven years from the date of its submission.

[January 23, 1933]

Amendment XXI

Section. 1. The eighteenth article of amendment to the Constitution of the United States is hereby repealed.

Section. 2. The transportation or importation into any State, Territory, or possession of the United States for delivery or use therein of intoxicating liquors, in violation of the laws thereof, is hereby prohibited.

Section. 3. This article shall be inoperative unless it shall have been ratified as an amendment of the Constitution by conventions in the several States, as provided in the Constitution, within seven years from the date of the submission hereof to the States by the Congress.

[December 5, 1933]

Amendment XXII

No person shall be elected to the office of the President more than twice, and no person who has held the office of

President, or acted as President, for more than two years of a term to which some other person was elected President shall be elected to the office of the President more than once.

But this Article shall not apply to any person holding the office of President when this Article was proposed by the Congress, and shall not prevent any person who may be holding the office of President, or acting as President, during the term within this Article becomes operative from holding the office of President or acting as President during the remainder of such term.

[February 27, 1951]

Amendment XXIII

Section. 1. The district constituting the seat of Government of the United States shall appoint in such manner as the Congress may direct:

A number of electors of President and Vice President equal to the whole number of Senators and Representatives in Congress to which the District would be entitled if it were a State, but in no event more than the least populous State; they shall be in addition to those appointed by the States, but they shall be considered, for the purposes of the election of President and Vice President, to be electors appointed by the State; and they shall meet in the district and perform such duties as provided by the twelfth article of amendment.

Section. 2. The Congress shall have power to enforce this article by appropriate legislation.

[March 29, 1961]

Amendment XXIV

Section. 1. The right of citizens of the United States to vote in any primary or other election for President or Vice President, or for Senator or Representative in Congress, shall not be denied or abridged by the United States or any State by reason of failure to pay any poll tax or other tax.

Section. 2. The Congress shall have power to enforce this article by appropriate legislation.

[January 23, 1964]

Amendment XXV

Section. 1. In case of the removal of the President from office or of his death or resignation, the Vice President shall become President.

Section. 2. Whenever there is a vacancy in the office of the Vice President, the President shall nominate a Vice President who shall take office upon confirmation by a majority vote of both Houses of Congress.

Section. 3. Whenever the President transmits to the President pro tempore of the Senate and the Speaker of

the House of Representatives his written declaration that he is unable to discharge the powers and duties of his office, and until he transmits to them a written declaration to the contrary, such powers and duties shall be discharged by the Vice President as Acting President.

Section. 4. Whenever the Vice President and a majority of either the principal officers of the executive department or of such other body as Congress may by law provide, transmit to the President pro tempore of the Senate and the Speaker of the House of Representative their written declaration that the President is unable to discharge the powers and duties of his office, the Vice President shall immediately assume the powers and duties of the office of Acting President.

Thereafter, when the President transmits to the President pro tempore of the Senate and the Speaker of the House of Representatives his written declaration that no inability exists, he shall resume the powers and duties of his office unless the Vice President and a majority of either the principal officers of the executive department or of such other body as Congress may by law provide, transmit within four days to the President pro tempore of the Senate and the Speaker of the House of Representatives their written declaration that the President is unable to discharge the powers and duties of his office. Thereupon Congress shall decide the issue, assembling within forty-eight hours for that purpose if not in session. If the Congress, within twenty-one days after receipt of the latter written declaration, or, if Congress is not in session, within twenty-one days after Congress is required to assemble, determines by two-thirds vote of both Houses that the President is unable to discharge the powers and duties of his office, the Vice President shall continue to discharge the same as Acting President; otherwise, the President shall resume the powers and duties of his office.

[February 10, 1967]

Amendment XXVI

Section. 1. The right of citizens of the United States, who are eighteen years of age or older, to vote shall not be denied or abridged by the United States or by any State on account of age.

Section. 2. The Congress shall have power to enforce this article by appropriate legislation.

[July 1, 1971]

Amendment XXVII

No law, varying the compensation for the services of the Senators and Representatives, shall take effect, until an election of Representatives shall have intervened.

[May 7, 1992]

state legislatures. Ratification requires approval by *three-fourths* of the states, whether the legislature method or the convention method of ratification is chosen by Congress. Table 3.1 shows when each amendment was added to the Constitution and the length of time required for ratification.

Another, and as yet unused, amendment procedure allows two-thirds of the state legislatures to petition Congress to call a national constitutional convention. In recent years there have been many petitions by state legislatures to hold conventions on various matters. A serious effort has been made to call a convention to draft an amendment requiring Congress to balance the federal budget. Opponents of this idea argue that such a convention might easily turn into a "Trojan Horse" affair in which various groups arrive with plans for other amendments as well. (Remember that delegates went to Philadelphia in 1787 with the purpose of amending the Articles of Confederation, but had designed an entirely new government by the time they left!) Changing the Constitution is not something that is taken lightly or easily done. During the 1970s and early 1980s, a strong battle was fought in state legislatures over an "Equal Rights Amendment" aimed at legislating equal rights for women in all areas of society. This amendment did not win support in three-fourths of the state legislatures by 1979, the end of the seven-year time limit specified by Congress for ratification. However, proponents argued that approval by only three more states was needed to ratify. After heated debate, Congress extended the time limit to 1982. The necessary states still did not support it, and the amendment died, avoiding a possible legal challenge about whether a later Congress can extend the time limit imposed by an earlier one.

TABLE 3.1

Interval Between Congressional Approval and State Ratification of Amendments to the U. S. Constitution

AMENDMENT NUMBER AND SUBJECT MATTER		INTERVAL BETWEEN APPROVAL AND RATIFICATION	YEAR RATIFIED
I-X	Bill of Rights	2 years, $2^1/_2$ months	1791
XI	Lawsuits against states	11 months	1795
XII	Presidential elections	$6^1/_2$ months	1804
XIII	Abolition of slavery	10 months	1865
XIV	Civil rights	2 years, 1 month	1868
XV	Suffrage for all races	11 months	1870
XVI	Income tax	3 years, $6^1/_2$ months	1913
XVII	Senatorial elections	11 months	1913
XVIII	Prohibition	1 year, 1 month	1919
XIX	Women's suffrage	1 year, 2 months	1920
XX	Terms of office	11 months	1933
XXI	Repeal of Prohibition	$9^1/_2$ months	1933
XXII	Limit on presidential terms	3 years, 11 months	1951
XXIII	Washington, D.C., vote	9 months	1961
XXIV	Abolition of poll taxes	1 year, 4 months	1964
XXV	Presidential succession	1 year, 10 months	1967
XXVI	Eighteen-year-old suffrage	3 months	1971
XXVII	Congressional pay raises	202 years, $4^1/_2$ months	1992

SOURCE: Harold W. Stanley and Richard Niemi, *Vital Statistics on American Politics,* 3rd ed. Washington, D.C.: Congressional Quarterly Press, 1992. Information on the 27th Amendment provided by the Congressional Research Service.

An Ever-Expanding Charter

Whatever its flaws, its champions argue, the Constitution has provided our nation with a substantial political framework which has evolved to embrace once-slighted members of society. While women had gained the right to vote in several western territories as early as 1869, it took a constitutional amendment (ratified in 1920) to make this a nationwide right. The Twenty-sixth Amendment, ratified in 1971, lowered the voting age to eighteen. One impetus for this move came from the Vietnam War; youthful protestors were indignant at being considered old enough for combat but too young for the franchise.

Black Americans were guaranteed the vote by the Fifteenth Amendment (ratified in 1870), and have since made use of it to combat discrimination. At right, members of the Southern Christian Leadership Conference march in support of civil-rights bills before the Senate in 1990.

The Players

Please read the list of amendments following the original body of the Constitution. You will see the range of issues that have become attached to the national charter, including clarifying the line of succession in case something happens to the president (Twenty-fifth Amendment in 1967); prohibiting the manufacture, sale, or transportation of "intoxicating liquors" (Eighteenth Amendment, in 1919); the later repeal of that amendment (Twenty-first Amendment, in 1933); providing for the direct election of senators (Seventeenth Amendment, 1913); and extending the vote to women (Nineteenth Amendment, 1920). The main point here is that the Constitution has been changed in important ways that affect how we live our lives.

A Flexible Interpretation Process

With the principle of judicial review established early in the nation's history, the constitutional tradition has developed into a lively political forum. The competing views and interpretations of the document are inevitable aspects of constitutional politics. Without a flexible interpretation process, using the Constitution would be a frustrating experience because it is such a short and frequently vague document. The judicial interpretation process is discussed in detail in Chapter 16. For now, the important point is that, over the years, interpretations of the document have changed in important ways. This flexibility in using the national charter highlights what it means to say that it is "a living Constitution" that continues to hold our society and government together. The Constitution lives not because this piece of parchment is an object of worship (although there is power in its near-sacred symbolism). The Constitution lives mainly because "we, the people" have pushed for new amendments and new interpretations when our society required room to grow and change.

The Constitution's worst crisis came with the Civil War, when the explosive issue of slavery led to conflicts over constitutional questions such as states' rights, the supremacy clause, and the nature of the Union itself—questions that were ultimately resolved only by bloodshed unparalleled in the nation's history. Here Union soldiers lounge outside a defunct slave dealers' headquarters in Alexandria, Virginia, after the city was taken by the Northern army.

For every Supreme Court ruling that grants victory to one side in a political battle, there is the challenge given to the other side: inventing a new argument, designing a new law, or rising to the challenge of accepting new views of society and justice. In the best of cases, society moves closer to living with itself and its conflicts. In the worst cases, the opposing sides are at least invited to come back and go another round using a common set of political rules. The Civil War stands as a reminder that working out conflicts within this constitutional order may not be so bad.

What Kind of Government? The Structure of Power

The Constitution has left its lasting stamp on the design of government and continues to be the focal point of many important national conflicts. At this point, we can return to a key debate from Chapters 1 and 2 and ask how *power in society* flows through the *institutions of government* created by this Constitution. How well does the Constitution fulfill its promise to limit the powers of government so that the balance of power among groups in society is preserved? This returns us to one of the most important questions about politics inside the American system: Who governs?

Who Governs?

A shrewd observer of our politics once pointed out that those who write constitutions and organize governments are quite simply creating the rules of the political game.[11] The rules determine the nature of the game itself: who plays and who does not (for example, the election game is for players of ages eighteen and older); what resources count and which ones do not (one can play a different political strategy with money than without it); what playing skills are required (knowing how the government works is essential, whatever the chosen political strategy); and, above all, what combinations of moves result in winning.

In August of 1988, more than 50,000 people gathered at the Lincoln Memorial to mark the twenty-fifth anniversary of the "I Have a Dream" speech by the Reverend Martin Luther King, Jr., leader of the 1960s' civil-rights movement. The three so-called "Reconstruction" amendments to the Constitution (ratified in 1865, 1868, and 1870) have served as a touchstone for African Americans—and others—seeking to exercise their rights.

As anyone who has played games knows, players who are given the power to invent, change, or interpret the rules gain a considerable advantage. It might be argued that any government, including ours, will favor some of society's players over others. Why is this so? No matter what the political system, not everyone's or every group's interests are represented equally, either because they are excluded by the specific design of the government or because, in practice, the government game happens to be easier for some people to play than for others. For example, it has been argued that starting with the constitutional compromise over slavery and the great powers given to states under the rules of federalism, America's black population has been disadvantaged at virtually every turn in the political game. After the Thirteenth, Fourteenth and Fifteenth Amendments, the problem was less the constitutional design itself, than political maneuvering in many states to make it difficult for African Americans to gain access to government to have their problems redressed.[12]

A different kind of critique says that blacks are just one of many groups disadvantaged by the political game. In this view, the constitutional rule system as a whole has historically favored those with money, status, and connections. This elitist view is countered by the pluralists who contend that with so many separations and divisions of power, it is still easier for people to gain a personal share of power in America than in other democracies. On the issues that are closest to people's lives, things like education, morality, and the environment, there are points of political access available to nearly everyone and ways for nearly everyone to exercise some kind of power. Let's rejoin this debate and explore the issues using what we have learned about the Constitution in this chapter.

A GOVERNMENT OF, BY, AND FOR THE PRIVILEGED FEW?

Recall from Chapter 2 the charge by Patrick Henry that he "smelt a rat" at the Constitutional Convention in Philadelphia. Assembled there, he argued, were some of the wealthiest men in the land. They produced a constitution that guaranteed payments on their government notes that the Confederation could not pay back. Worse still, argued Henry and his fellow critics, there was little room in the new government for common people like Daniel Shays and his followers—the people who fought the Revolution with another vision of liberty in mind. Henry and company were finally appeased by adding a Bill of Rights that has become an important resource for individuals and disadvantaged groups.

As discussed in Chapters 1 and 2, the debate about who the government favors goes on to this day. The *power-elite* thesis has been hotly debated and revised by historians, sociologists, and political scientists ever since. More recently, for example, historian Edmund Morgan argued that Madison's one gesture toward popular sovereignty (allowing popular election of the House) created electoral districts so large that only people of considerable wealth could ever campaign successfully in them. At the same time, Morgan also conceded that the idea of *popular sovereignty* (one of the cultural ideals discussed in Chapter 1) has become so powerful that it has inspired more real democracy in America than Madison or any of the other Federalists ever imagined.[13]

Like Morgan, most later proponents of the elitist view of the Constitution admit that although the founders represented the privileged strata in American society, they took the ideas of liberty and popular sovereignty seriously. Nor were they so politically foolish as to shut the majority of people completely out of the political game. However, they argue, even if the broad limits on government power reflect a mixture of idealism and political realism, the result may still be a system of government that favors elite interests. This more subtle twist in the elitist view of constitutional politics goes something like this: With power so broadly dispersed, the advantage continues to go to people with the means to hire lawyers and lobbyists to influence parties and candidates to promote their interests. The broad dispersal of power may favor ordinary people in some areas like school-board politics or in getting popular initiatives on the ballot in some states. However, connecting up all of the points of power necessary to affect areas like investment and banking policy, trade decisions, and tax laws leaves many of the most important decisions of government today subject to the power of elites.

As noted in Chapter 2, there is also a more conservative elitist position that agrees with the above analysis but concludes that, far from being unjust or wrong, this is the necessary and proper way for government to work. Conservative elite theorists adopt something of a Hamiltonian view, saying that, in important areas like economic issues, it is not only proper but inevitable that "political insiders" should exercise their better judgment and greater interest.[14]

Adding still another twist to contemporary elitist interpretations of American politics, observers such as sociologist William Domhoff argue that elite rule does not imply anything like a conspiracy or even a common set of (class) interests among those with greatest access to government. To the contrary, Domhoff has argued that the gridlock we complain about in recent times is largely the result of different self-interested elites successfully getting very different things from government institutions. In the process, they fill up the agenda of government with narrow and often conflicting demands at the expense of broader visions that might better serve the public interest.[15]

A GOVERNMENT OF, BY, AND FOR THE PEOPLE?   To recapitulate the debate from Chapter 2, pluralist opponents point out two problems with the idea that some power elite has been favored by the very design of the government itself.[16] First, the founders were too deeply divided to create a government that benefited all of them to any great extent. Second, the founders were inspired by the ideals of the liberal political philosophers of the day—ideals that presented quite a range of different governmental solutions for the problem of how to promote individual liberty and prevent tyranny by any group or faction.

Those who believe that the founders were more idealistic than self-interested, and more divided than united in their interests, have been joined by many observers of the contemporary scene who see a modern government that is broadly responsive to many different interests in society. Pluralists continue to argue that the separations and divisions of power create so many points of pressure that many, and perhaps most, people have access to government at some level on the issues that really matter to them.

Then why, counter the elitists, do most people in the 1990s feel the national government represents special interests and not "people like them"? Because, say the pluralists, people simply have not organized and put in the time and energy necessary to play the game effectively at the highest levels of politics. In addition, even when people play interest-group politics successfully, they tend not to lump themselves in the same category with the "special interests" who are blamed for the rise of gridlock and the fall of the public interest. Finally, say the pluralists, there is probably no grand governing vision that would satisfy most of the people anyway. Most people are probably getting about all that can be expected from a government that was, after all, never intended to intrude heavily into social life. If people are unhappy with the results, they are victims of their own unreasonable expectations.

WHO IS RIGHT ABOUT THE POWER STRUCTURE?   The debate about "Who governs?" is not just an abstract intellectual question. It is also in many respects the core conflict in American politics. People have argued about the design for power since the Constitutional Convention and will continue to do so. The struggle for power is the struggle for living the kind of life in the kind of society one prefers. Who governs determines in important ways who lives well. The question of who governs does not have a simple answer because the answer changes with the ongoing political struggle over who *should* govern.

The eternal debate about power in America may seem less frustrating if understood as both an academic question and a real political issue with important implications for the kind of government and society we live with. Patterns of power in government and society have changed from one era to the next depending on how political struggles were waged, by whom, and for what ends. Perhaps the power-elite and pluralist views of power reflect different *potentials* or possibilities within our constitutional system for distributing power at different times to different groups under different political conditions.

The Constitutional Power Chart Revisited

As suggested at the opening of this chapter, the Constitution can be viewed as a grand scheme for dividing up power. First, power is *separated* among three branches of government. To further check the abuse of any of the separated powers, specific activities such as presidential approval of legislation and congressional approval of presidential appointments require the involvement of more than one branch. Second, to keep many issues in the realm of local values and grass-roots power, many powers are *divided* between national government and the states. Finally, to guard these arrangements and protect the private lives of individuals, there are numerous powers that are prohibited or *denied* to government altogether, and a list of individual protections against abuses of power is contained in the Bill of Rights.

The Organization of Government Power in England

3.5

Although England is often said to have a political tradition close to that of the United States, the structure of government power is very different. Not only is power not separated among different branches of government, but there are no federal divisions of power between national and state governments. In addition, the concept of independent, protected individual rights expressly guaranteed by law is weaker than in the American system. The core difference is a parliamentary government in which the executive is formed from the legislative branch and is dependent on that branch for its power. The political party with a majority of seats in Parliament chooses the executive (the prime minister and the cabinet officers). However, this executive group can be forced to resign if the legislature rejects its programs, resulting in either the formation of a new executive or, in some circumstances, a call for a new election for the entire Parliament. This means that "gridlock" is less common in British politics because inability to reach agreement either results in re-constituting the executive or in electing a new legislature (which, in turn, creates a new executive).

Does this mean that all parliamentary systems are immune from gridlock? No. For various reasons of culture, institutions, and social power, Italy, for example, seems to exist in a nearly constant state of governmental gridlock. However, England offers a closer comparison with the United States in other ways, suggesting that more centralized institutional power arrangements might be one way of addressing some American complaints about governmental gridlock.

At a minimum, this organization of power is very different from many other democratic nations where power is more concentrated in one or all of three ways:

- in fewer branches of the national government
- by the creation of a unitary (non-federal) government without state divisions of power
- by the absence of strong individual rights protections

See "How We Compare" Box 3.5 for a comparison of the United States' organization of governing power with that of England.

The U.S. Constitution's system of broadly dispersed powers permits many different kinds of challenges to national legislation. This raises the important question of whether periods of gridlock may reflect not only the design of the government but, more fundamentally, a lack of social consensus about in what direction the nation should be moving. When divisions exist in society, the many limits on power written into the Constitution permit people at different levels to block the initiatives of other groups. While this may appear to be gridlock, it also may prevent drastic actions at times when little agreement exists about what should be done to solve pressing national problems. If James Madison could survey the contemporary American scene, he might warn us that until we become more united as a society with more agreement about what we want from government, we should recognize that there are worse things than gridlock. In fact, Madison might well look with satisfaction on a government doing just what is was designed to do when faced with conflicting social pressures.

A final bit of perspective is in order here: What has been described as governmental gridlock in the 1990s may not be a particularly extreme case historically. It simply is not easy to get this government moving rapidly in sweeping directions or to keep up the momentum for long periods, *which is not necessarily a bad thing.* Support for broad political action must come from many levels: the three national branches; the states; parties, interest groups, and elites; and from individual citizens who see personal rights tied up with many of the things the government does socially and economically. Looked at this way, many Americans might agree that these limits on power are *good* things. In fact, as a challenge, try to imagine any sweeping new governmental design that might be even remotely acceptable to the majority of Americans. When people think that gridlock is a problem, they may well have different and quite incompatible ideas about what they would like the government to do. For these reasons, it is helpful for citizens to think about the costs and benefits of a system of broadly dispersed governing powers before leaping to conclusions about supposed problems like "gridlock" or how best to solve them.

A CITIZEN'S QUESTION
The Constitution

Is gridlock a built-in feature of American govern-ment? If gridlock is more the rule than the excep-tion, does this mean adjusting my expectations about government itself? All citizens form expec-tations about the things government should or should not do, particularly as it affects them. An additional question for all citizens to consider is, *How realistic are my expectations?* The discussion of political gridlock throughout this chapter raises the question of whether people who complain about it are likely to agree on what direction the government should take.

The American system may seem overwhelm-ing to some citizens *because* there are so many points of political access within it. There is the added challenge of discovering that just when your concerns seem to be nailed down at one point, they may start coming loose again somewhere else. However, these frustrations have not stopped millions of people from taking the political plunge and discovering that they can get things done.

There are a number of strategies available within the broad constitutional design of power that have worked for average citizens with real-istic expectations and goals. For example, the long history of grass-roots politics and social movements in America makes it clear that money and status are not the only resources that make a difference. For example, the law can be used to block abuses of power and pro-tect weaker individuals who cannot play the in-sider's game. Another strategy for getting the government moving in the right direction is to work to strengthen the political parties. When a political party stands behind a vision that in-spires many people, the wheels of government turn more smoothly. Voters can give a party enough power to convert its ideas into law. Fi-nally, many citizens' campaigns on the environ-ment, tax reduction, election reform, health care, and other basic issues have succeeded in dramatically affecting the lives of the people in-volved and providing models for the rest of the nation to follow.

Politics is a group activity in most nations, but the broad design of power in the United States allows individuals to form many kinds of groups and to play out many different strategies in various political arenas. However, as James Madison told us, groups can seek very different things from government, and competing group demands can contribute to a stalling of move-ment within government. If there is a problem with governmental gridlock, part of it may in-volve people expecting, and often receiving, personal benefits from government while resent-ing the benefits that others are getting for them-selves and their groups. All of this means that joining or forming political groups requires some special considerations. This brings us back to the opening questions about gridlock and the importance of forming realistic expectations about government and how to participate in it: What do I really want from government? What is government capable of delivering? Given the design of this system, what kinds of politics are likely to produce the best results?

Key Terms

constitution

separation of powers (among three branches)

division of powers (between na-tional and state governments)

federalism

expressed powers

denied powers

elastic, or necessary and proper, clause

checks and balances

the legislative branch (primary powers and shared powers)

the executive branch (primary powers and shared powers)

the judiciary (primary powers and shared powers)

judicial review

amending and ratification

the Bill of Rights

reserved powers

Suggested Readings

Bailyn, Bernard, ed. *The Debate on the Constitution: Federalist and Antifederalist Speeches, Articles, and Letters During the Struggle over Ratification* (2 vols.). New York: Library of America, 1993.

Bloom, Allan, ed. *Confronting the Constitution.* Washington, D.C.: The AEI Press, 1990.

Levinson, Sanford. *Constitutional Faith.* Princeton: Princeton University Press, 1988.

Levy, Leonard W. *Original Intent and the Framers' Constitution.* New York: Macmillan, 1988.

Mead, Walter B. *The United States Constitution: Personalities, Principles, and Issues.* Columbia, S. C.: University of South Carolina Press, 1987.

Sundquist, James L. *Constitutional Reform and Effective Government.* Washington, D. C.: The Brookings Institution, 1986.

[Federalism] is not . . . the sexiest of political issues. Nor is
it . . . the ordinary stuff of "table talk."
But it affects the everyday lives of millions, directly or
indirectly. The Founding Fathers thought it involved the very
difference between liberty and tyranny. And it helped provoke
the Civil War, the bloodiest war in American history.
Today federalism, the complex, constantly shifting set of
power relationships between the states and the central
government in Washington, is at the center of a quiet but
intense debate about how the nation is to be governed and
how its citizens are to be served.
—*THE NEW YORK TIMES*

The Politics

of Federalism

- **THE NEWS ABOUT A NEW FEDERALISM**

- **WHY FEDERALISM MATTERS**

- **WHAT IS FEDERALISM? DEFINITIONS AND CONCEPTS**
  Federalism and Big Government: Disarming a Loaded Concept

- **THE CONSTITUTIONAL DEBATE: COMPETING THEORIES OF FEDERAL POWER**
  Victories for the Nation-Centered View
  Victories for the State-Centered View
  The Civil War and the Deadlock of Federalism

- **THREE MODELS OF FEDERALISM**

- **POLITICAL LIFE IN THREE ERAS OF FEDERAL POWER**
  Dual Federalism (1800–1937)
  Cooperative Federalism (1937–1968)
  A New Federalism? (1968–Today)

- **WHY FEDERALISM MATTERS REVISITED**
  State Experimentation
  Local Governments Take the Lead
  The Problem of Growing Inequalities

- **A CITIZEN'S QUESTION: State and National Citizenship**

- **KEY TERMS**

- **SUGGESTED READINGS**

Beginning with the election of Richard Nixon to the presidency in 1968, the idea of a "New Federalism" started making the news. At first, the stories were often quiet ones that busy readers might skip over in the rush to catch up on the latest war, crisis, fashion trend, or sports scores. Yet the New Federalism movement was worth reading about. Mr. Nixon's plans met with stiff resistance in Congress and failed to fulfill many of their promises to restore more power to the states. However, the introduction of these new ideas started many people thinking about how to shrink the size and responsibilities of the national government.

One of those who liked the idea of returning more power to the states was Ronald Reagan, who came to Washington in 1981 with his own version of a New Federalism. The Reagan brand was intended, as the new president put it in his inaugural address, *"to curb the size and influence of the federal establishment and to demand recognition of the distinction between the powers granted to the federal government and those reserved to the states or to the people."*[1]

This time, the idea took hold. Supporters hailed it as a restoration of the proper limits on national power and a return of local control over a host of basic issues such as education, law enforcement, criminal punishment, morality, and religious freedoms. Meanwhile, opponents saw the New Federalism as a threat to a half-century of national gains in areas such as civil rights, safe working conditions, public health, environmental protection, educational opportunity, and protections of political freedoms. With the sides clearly drawn, the battle was on. The term **New Federalism** appeared in the headlines of one leading national newspaper more than forty times in the next two years alone.[2]

The political importance of this latest struggle to redefine the federal divisions of power was captured in a news story (cited at the start of this chapter) with the headline FOR GOVERNORS, FOCUS IS FEDERAL-

ISM. It noted: "Today federalism, the complex, constantly shifting set of power relationships between the states and the central Government in Washington, is at the center of a quiet but intense debate about how the nation is to be governed and how its citizens are to be served."[3]

By the end of the decade, battles were won and lost by both sides, but one thing was clear: Those who thought that "the federal question" had been

President Ronald Reagan, seen here at a 1988 press conference, ardently advocated a "New Federalism"—a doctrine of limiting the national government and increasing state control over many issues—on the premise that, whenever possible, domestic policy decisions are best made "where the people live," according to individual community values and expectations.

settled once and for all had another think coming. The "federal question," put simply, is: *Where does the Constitution fix the national-state division of government power?* The debate over the proper division of federal powers is back on the political agenda once again, as it has been so many times since the founding of the Republic.

The headlines of the 1990s would play out the story. Mr. Reagan was followed in office by George Bush, another president who subscribed to a state-centered constitutional philosophy. However, many state officials charged that instead of more power, they only inherited more responsibilities and regulations to follow, while receiving less money from Washington to pay for it all. A typical news flash read: STATES TAKE UP NEW BURDENS TO PAY FOR NEW FEDERALISM.[4]

When Bill Clinton was elected in 1992, he promised to ease the burden on the states by moving some expensive state programs to Washington and giving states more control of the programs that Washington shipped to the states. One of Clinton's chief advisors on federalism called for giving the national government primary control over programs like national health care, while the states would take more initiative for things like housing, education, and highways. A former Reagan administration official wrote about that idea in a national newspaper claiming that if Mr. Clinton succeeded where so many presidents have failed, he would "qualify for sainthood in the minds of state governors."[5]

Why is it so difficult to streamline the state-national partnership? Political scientists have referred to the mixture of state and national powers in so many areas of our life as like a marble cake of swirling and endlessly varied patterns of power. Each of the last five presidents has tried different strategies to simplify that swirl of power and discovered a host of political obstacles. As a former governor, Bill Clinton knew that many state and city officials welcomed more control over the social programs that served their citizens, but they also demanded more money to go with running those programs. This is what a disgruntled Republican mayor said when he became president of the United States Conference of Mayors: "I don't think there was any New Federalism. I don't think there's been any transfer of power. I think it's gone the other way."[6] Handing out both money and power is a tall order during an era of record budget deficits in Washington.[7]

As these stories suggest, it might make sense to put a question mark after the term *New Federalism* to indicate the serious questions about whether the efforts to unswirl the marble cake of power have in fact produced simpler and better ways of running the national government. Complaints can be heard from citizens and politicians alike about the federal design of programs that many people look to as their most important contacts with government: environmental regulation, health care, child development and family assistance, education, crime control, drug enforcement, disaster relief, and civil rights, among other areas.

Is it true, as many state and local officials contend, present-day federalism has increased federal regulations on states and reduced national funding for state programs? If true, how did this happen? How do today's battles differ from earlier attempts to define state and national powers? To bring these questions home, we return at the end of the chapter to ask what these federal power arrangements mean for individuals, who are citizens of both the United States and the particular state in which they live.

Why Federalism Matters

If we scratch the surface of Washington politics, we quickly find the pull of state power underneath. It has been said that all politics are local. This simply means that one of the things that members of Congress think about when they deliver programs to the executive is how those programs and their enforcement will be received back home.

Working out the state-national partnership is not easy, whether the issue is environmental quality, building new highways, health care, education, or civil rights. As explained in Chapter 3, advocates of states' rights argue that such basic decisions should be made where the people live, according to the local values and political expectations in the states. If people do not like the way things work in their state, they can work to change the system or even move to another state. Advocates of stronger national powers respond to this by saying that the Constitution guarantees the same basic rights to all Americans; if there are no minimum national standards for health, welfare, education, air pollution, or highway safety, then it is hard for them to think of the United States as one nation with a Constitution that protects all citizens equally. These views are sharply in conflict and have led to political fights over many different issues since the founding of the nation.

Both sides have a point. More importantly, as explained in Chapter 3, both sides find support for their points in the Constitution. Supreme Court interpretations of these arguments directly affect some of the most personal areas of our lives, from the legality of abortion, to the quality of the air we breathe, to the safety of the water we drink, to the ways in which businesses operate and make profits. Many of the greatest triumphs and tragedies of American politics can be traced to federal power struggles over different issues. The Civil War was the greatest breakdown of federalism, reflecting a complete failure to resolve the state-national power conflict over slavery. Race in America continues to strain federal politics. The great triumphs of federalism come in areas where states are allowed to experiment with their own solutions for common problems. Many of those experiments have become models for the rest of the nation: California's air quality programs, Minnesota's voter registration system, and Wisconsin's pioneering income tax plans are just three examples among hundreds of innovations that have come from the fifty state laboratories.

What Is Federalism? Definitions and Concepts

There are some basic concepts that are generally agreed upon when it comes to federalism, and they provide useful background for thinking about the politics behind state and national power battles. To begin with, it is clear that the Constitution created a *federal* system, giving broad powers to the states, and not a **unitary system** in which all powers reside in a central government. (See "How We Compare" Box 4.1 for a discussion of federal and unitary governments in the world.) A third basic type of government organization is the *confederation,* in which the subunits retain considerable autonomy by voluntarily granting powers to the central government or holding a veto power over its actions. As described in Chapter 2, the first American government after the Revolution was a confederation of states. You may recall that the states had to authorize requests from the Confederate Congress, and they reserved important veto powers, including the power of any state to veto proposed amendments to the Articles.

The Constitution offers a number of guidelines about how to divide powers. In some areas, those guidelines have been accepted fairly easily, and in other areas, they have been disputed vigorously. For example, there have been few serious disputes over the national government's power to issue patents and copyrights, but bruising battles have been fought over its powers to regulate economic practices and race relations. Even when disputed, the Constitution provides a legal framework for interpreting and ruling on those disputes. As we will see, however, rulings by the Supreme Court have differed dramatically over time, and they have not always settled matters for very long. In the years leading up to the Civil War, opinions of the Court fanned the flames of racial and economic conflicts that ultimately provoked some states to reject the Constitution altogether and secede from the Union.

If only to understand where the nation's political time bombs are buried, it is important to know which powers the Constitution assigned to the national government, which ones went to the states, and which ones were divided both ways. In addition to reviewing these divisions of power, Table 4.1 also notes which divisions of power have generally been accepted as clear, and which divisions have been disputed.

HOW WE COMPARE

Federal and Unitary Systems of Government

4.1

*F*ederal systems of government are those in which various powers are *divided* between a national government and states (also commonly called provinces). In *unitary* governments, by contrast, all powers reside in the central government, and the various state, county, or local governments operate as extensions of that central authority. Thus, *unitary* governments may delegate varying degrees of authority to governors, mayors, tax collectors, police commissions, or school boards, but ultimate powers over these functions reside with the national government itself.

There are many different ways of dividing federal authority between state and national governments. Sometimes the lines are not well drawn or well enforced, as in Mexico, a federal system with a history of weak state governments. The existence of even weaker federal systems than Mexico's leads some analysts to disagree about whether to classify some countries as truly federal or unitary.

Although some nations arc hard to classify as federal or unitary systems, it is generally agreed that there are about twenty federal governments in the more than two hundred nations in the world. Since many of the larger countries have adopted federal systems, roughly 40 percent of the world's population live with some form of federalism. The connection between size and type of government is not a rule, however, as the case of China (a unitary system) indicates.

Examples

Federal	*Unitary*
Argentina	Chile
Australia	China
Brazil	England
Canada	France
Germany	Japan
India	New Zealand
Malaysia	Portugal
Mexico	Saudi Arabia
United States	Sweden
Switzerland	Zaire

SOURCE: Daniel J. Elazar, *Exploring Federalism.* Tuscaloosa: University of Alabama Press, 1987.

Federalism and Big Government: Disarming a Loaded Concept

A final clarification of federalism may be helpful before plunging into the constitutional issues and political realities. Over the years, many Americans have associated the government in Washington with "big government." Politicians stir up crowds with promises to discipline the national government and return power to the states and localities. The news and political campaigns are filled with vows to slay the big government dragon and restore power where it properly belongs: to the governments of the states and localities in which the people live.

The struggle against big government is a story that will be retold a thousand times around a thousand different issues. However, easy political attacks blur serious questions. Here are some serious questions about federalism: Should the states or the national government decide whether local hospitals and health clinics can perform abortions? Should school boards or the Supreme Court decide about saluting the flag and praying in school? Should the national government impose plans on local communities to integrate schools and monitor hiring and promotion in the workplace? These are not so much "big government" issues as political disagreements about where important government decisions will be made. Yet it is easy for politicians to fire up voters by asking

"We'd better get re-elected. It would be hard to make it in the business world after the legislation we've passed."

TABLE 4.1

The Federal Divisions of Powers

EXAMPLES OF POWERS CLEARLY GRANTED BY THE CONSTITUTION			EXAMPLES OF CONSTITUTIONAL POWERS VAGUELY DEFINED OR HISTORICALLY DISPUTED
TO THE STATES	TO THE NATIONAL GOVERNMENT	TO BOTH	
Regulate internal commerce.	Coin money and regulate its value.	Borrow money and pay debts (within their separate spheres of power).	Civil rights (equal access to voting, employment, education, transportation, public places, and so on).
Set up local governments.	Issue patents and copyrights.	Create courts (within separate spheres).	Regulating the economy (manufacturing standards, product safety, workplace safety, pollution, health protection, labor organization and disputes with management, and so on).
All other powers not specifically granted to the national government or specifically denied the states*: —organize elections —most criminal laws —education codes —morality —health, safety —business and professions	Regulate commerce between states and with other nations. Organize the military and make war. Negotiate treaties. All other powers necessary to carry out the specified powers.**	Taxation (within separate spheres). Legislation and law enforcement (within separate spheres).	

*See the Constitution, Article I, Section 10 for powers denied the states.
**The Constitution also denies specific powers to the national government. See Article I, Section 9.

when the government in Washington is going to stop running our lives. It is easy to slip back and forth between difficult questions of how to divide federal powers, and easy but misleading questions about when the national government will finally be made to keep its nose out of everyone else's business. Figure 4.1 illustrates the increasing concerns expressed in opinion polls that the state–national power balance has shifted too far in the national direction.

Today's skepticism toward big government taps into a long cultural tradition that goes back to the debates over the Constitution and even the American Revolution itself. The very first federal government was feared by many as too big, even though it was microscopic by today's standards. The Constitutional Convention was tied in knots about how to limit the powers of a government that had, at birth, a paltry budget, few specific duties, and only three cabinet departments: War, Treasury, and State. Generations of politicians ever since then have accused their opponents of being "big-spending insiders." Every successful presidential candidate since 1968 has campaigned against big

FIGURE 4.1
Public Opinion About State and National Government, 1941–1993

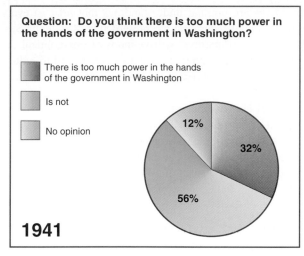

Question: Do you think there is too much power in the hands of the government in Washington?

■ There is too much power in the hands of the government in Washington

■ Is not

□ No opinion

12%
32%
56%

1941

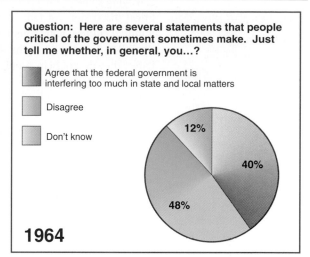

Question: Here are several statements that people critical of the government sometimes make. Just tell me whether, in general, you…?

■ Agree that the federal government is interfering too much in state and local matters

■ Disagree

□ Don't know

12%
40%
48%

1964

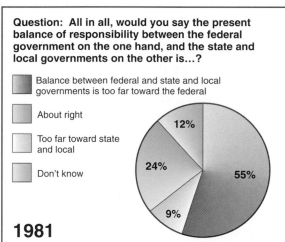

Question: All in all, would you say the present balance of responsibility between the federal government on the one hand, and the state and local governments on the other is…?

■ Balance between federal and state and local governments is too far toward the federal

■ About right

□ Too far toward state and local

■ Don't know

12%
24%
55%
9%

1981

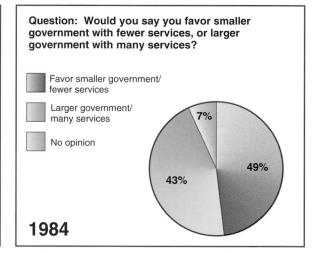

Question: Would you say you favor smaller government with fewer services, or larger government with many services?

■ Favor smaller government/ fewer services

□ Larger government/ many services

□ No opinion

7%
49%
43%

1984

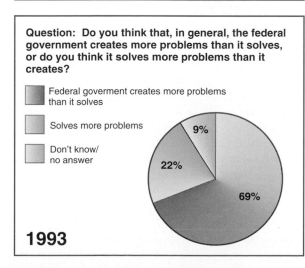

Question: Do you think that, in general, the federal government creates more problems than it solves, or do you think it solves more problems than it creates?

■ Federal goverment creates more problems than it solves

■ Solves more problems

□ Don't know/ no answer

9%
22%
69%

1993

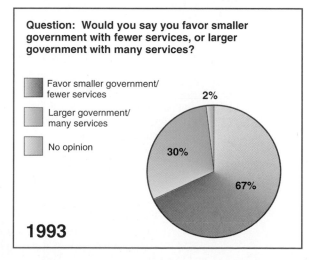

Question: Would you say you favor smaller government with fewer services, or larger government with many services?

■ Favor smaller government/ fewer services

□ Larger government/ many services

□ No opinion

2%
30%
67%

1993

SOURCE: *The Public Perspective*, March/April 1993, Vol. 4, No. 3, pp. 87–90.

government. Bill Clinton in 1992 did his best to dodge the "big government" and "tax-and-spend" charges made by his opponents. Learning about federalism is easier after clarifying some of the political myths about big government that can influence public political discussions of federalism. Myths are popular understandings that arise in every *political culture.* Four common myths about federalism are presented in "Inside the System" Box 4.2. While myths about big government may drive many of our political debates, they do not help people understand that the reality of federalism is hard to reduce to a simple question of shrinking the national government. Just what would it mean to "shrink" the government?

Looking beyond the general fears of big government, we find more answerable questions about what *specific* government powers should be divided in what *particular* ways. The reality of federalism is that no single division of powers will satisfy most of the people on all of the issues. There will always be debate about the eternal American question: *Which level of government should have the power to decide what fundamental social and economic issues?*

The Constitutional Debate: Competing Theories of Federal Power

The easy stereotype about federalism is that conservative Republicans favor states' rights, while liberal Democrats back stronger national government. While containing the usual grain of truth, this stereotype often fails to capture the political realities on either side. As noted in the opening example, Democrat Bill Clinton favored streamlining federal powers to give states more control over particular social programs. By contrast, Republican Ronald Reagan made considerable headway toward a New Federalism, but like many politicians he did not hesitate to reach into traditional domains of state powers on issues he felt strongly about. For example, he threatened to withhold a portion of federal highway monies from states that refused to go along with his goal of raising the national minimum drinking age to twenty-one. Drinking ages clearly fall within the constitutional area of state powers. In addition, Mr. Reagan followed the precedent of that earlier New Federalist, Richard Nixon, in making national highway money conditional upon lowering state speed limits to 55 miles per hour. Speed limits, like drinking ages, would seem to be things that states' rights advocates would leave alone.

Needless to say, many states objected to the national government meddling in areas like drinking ages and speed laws which fell squarely within the powers of states. A journal for state government officials reacted to President Nixon's earlier intrusion into the domain of state speed laws with an article titled "Federal Supersession: The Road to Domination."[8] It turns out that speed laws are among the many areas of local life over which the national government has no constitutional power. But Congress and the president do hand out huge sums of money to build and maintain highways, and many other things, giving them considerable leverage in state life if they want it. While some states resisted, the majority quickly fell in line and raised the drinking age. On the speed limit issue, the majority of states once again yielded to national pressure, but a few defended their sovereignty by lowering the posted speed limit to 55 MPH and then selling booklets of coupons to motorists, who could pay a fine of around $5 on the spot if caught speeding.

There are two morals to the federalism story. Not surprisingly, both involve politics. First, even in areas where the Constitution appears clear about which level of government has power over what specific aspects of social life, struggles over the actual divisions of those powers can and do go on. Second, even when politicians say they are strong advocates of a national or a state-centered view of constitutional powers, they often make exceptions when pursuing specific political goals. A brief look at the history

Political Culture and Big Government: Clarifying Some Myths About American Federalism

4.2

Myth #1: The growth of big government in Washington automatically means shrinking the power of states.

Political power is not fixed in volume like liquid in a sealed system. In some areas, it is true that granting the national government a power (e.g., the power to protect voting rights) takes a similar power away from the states (e.g., the power to deny the vote to particular individuals or groups). However, in many areas, this give-and-take does not apply, as when national powers to regulate the economy increased greatly between 1937–1968 without measurably shrinking state sovereignty in many other areas.

Myth #2: Cutting back the government in Washington automatically increases the powers of state and local governments.

This is not necessarily so, for the same reasons given above. In many, and perhaps most cases, programs and services cut in Washington will not be replaced at state and local levels because they are too costly or complex to run. In addition, some states exercise their own initiatives (e.g., California's pioneering environmental laws) no matter what Washington does.

Myth #3: *Federalism* refers to the national government in Washington.

No, the national government is just one (the largest one) of more than 83,000 units of government that make up the federal system today. Other units in the federal government that have some autonomous powers include states (50), counties (3000+), municipalities (19,000+), towns (16,000+), school districts (14,000+), and special districts for water, power, and transportation (29,000+).

Myth #4: Government is growing all the time.

This statement is broad and somewhat misleading. Between 1940 and 1965, for example, the number of governmental units in the U.S. actually dropped from more than 150,000 to just over 81,000 (due for the most part to the consolidation of school districts). However, about 2,000 units have in fact been added since 1970, mainly to coordinate power, water, and other life-support systems in complex metropolitan areas and interstate "regions." National government employment has grown since the 1950s from just over 2 million to just under 3 million. The major growth has been at state and local levels, which grew from around 5 million employees in the 1950s to roughly 11 million today.

SOURCES: Richard Leach, *American Federalism (New York: Norton, 1970);* U.S. Advisory Commission on Intergovernmental Relations; U.S. Census Bureau.

---

of federalism suggests that the two grand constitutional philosophies have been applied very selectively to promote very specific political goals.

Victories for the Nation-Centered View

What do Alexander Hamilton, Chief Justice John Marshall, Abraham Lincoln, Theodore Roosevelt, Franklin Roosevelt, John Kennedy, and Lyndon Johnson all have in common? Despite enormous differences in party affiliations, ideologies, and political agendas, they all promoted their causes through a nation-centered view of federalism. When such a diverse group can embrace a common constitutional principle, it pays to look at what they were doing with it politically. A good place to begin is with the first great nation-centered victory for federalism. Recall from the previous chapter the Supreme Court ruling in the case of **McCulloch v. Maryland** (1819). Chief Justice Marshall wrote the court's majority opinion that the state of Maryland did not have the power to tax national government property, namely, the Baltimore branch of the Bank of the United States. In that ruling, Marshall affirmed that the *supremacy clause* (Article VI) was central to the meaning of the Constitution. He also proposed a flexible interpretation of the *elastic clause* by stating that while Congress was not empowered specifically to set up a national bank, that power was *implied* by the provision authorizing Congress "to make all laws which shall be **necessary and proper**" for carrying out other powers (regarding taxes, money, and commerce) that *were* specified in the document.[9]

Marshall reinforced and expanded the *supremacy* of the national government a few years later in another landmark ruling: **Gibbons v. Ogden** (1824). The state of New York had granted an exclusive license to steamboat entrepreneur Robert Fulton to operate an interstate service between New York and New Jersey. Fulton then sold a license to Mr. Ogden. Meanwhile, a former partner of Ogden's named Gibbons went to court asking that he also be allowed to compete in this commerce between states. When the case finally reached the Supreme Court, Chief Justice Marshall opined that the state of New York had never possessed the power to regulate commerce between states. Therefore, Gibbons could not be prevented by the state from operating his shipping business. Thus, *Gibbons v. Ogden* established the precedent for granting the national government broad powers over *interstate commerce.*[10]

It is important to put these and many other nationalist victories in perspective: *Even the strongest claims to national powers have often been very limited in their actual political application.* In the century after *Gibbons v. Ogden,* for example, *national supremacy* in interstate commerce was limited to developing a national economic infrastructure of railroads, shipping, pipelines, and communications. At the same time, the domain of national economic supremacy was strictly limited by the high Court. The Court overruled many attempts by Congress to regulate manufacturers and businesses that took refuge behind state protections.

For example, Congress passed a variety of laws in the late 1880s (the "Gilded Age" of industrial expansion) aimed at restricting the interstate sale or transportation of various goods made in factories where employees suffered "inhuman" working conditions. Factory life during this period was often a nightmare of child labor, "slave wages," endless workdays, unsafe equipment, and other dangerous practices like locking workers inside firetrap factories. Time and again, however, the Court struck down national laws aimed at getting these abuses under control. The reasoning was guided as much by politics and

Photographer Lewis Hine encountered these children working at midnight in an Indiana glass factory in 1908. Clashing interpretations of the Constitution's division of national and state powers have shaped governmental attempts to regulate such social concerns as child labor, business-union relations, food and drug safety, and industrial monopolies.

an ideology of nonintervention in economic matters (called **laissez-faire**) as by legal principle. (The idea of *laissez-faire,* which literally means "to let do" or "to let alone" in French, is that government should intervene in the private sector only to the degree necessary to preserve property rights and civil order.) Taking strict definitions of both "interstate" and "commerce," the courts reasoned that while goods produced in unsafe factories often entered into interstate trade, the production of those goods had to do with manufacturing, not commerce. And manufacturing, along with most other business practices, were matters the Court left to the states.

In limiting the application of the *national supremacy* principle to a narrow set of economic matters, the courts, in effect, took a middle course that kept national and state powers fairly neatly divided into *dual* federal layers: Congress was allowed to build a national system of trade, transportation, and communications, while states and local industries were allowed a large amount of *laissez-faire* economic freedom, which some abused. For more than a century following the first nationalist victories, the Court intruded into state economies only occasionally to control life-threatening or socially disastrous situations such as the shipment of poisoned food or the labor market in kidnapped children.

It was not until the New Deal social and economic reforms of the 1930s that a willing Congress and president (Franklin Roosevelt) were finally united with a Supreme Court that was also willing to push the nationalist definition of federalism farther into areas of state power. The expansion of national powers was aimed at correcting the abuses of *laissez-faire* that helped create the Great Depression. And so, after 1937, the national government *gradually* became involved in regulating what individual states were doing (or allowing to happen) to their citizens as workers, business owners, consumers, investors, students, bus riders, restaurant patrons, and voters.

When nationalist interpretations of the Constitution were driven by these more activist political and economic goals, a much different system of federal powers emerged. The *dual* or layered federal divisions were replaced by more intertwined or *cooperative* power relations, creating that "marble cake" swirl of power between national and state governments. The differences between *dual* and *cooperative* federalism will be explored in a later section. For now, we turn to the politics behind state-centered interpretations of constitutional powers.

Victories for the State-Centered View

What do Thomas Paine, Benjamin Franklin, Thomas Jefferson, John C. Calhoun, Chief Justice Roger Taney, Ronald Reagan, George Bush, and Chief Justice William Rehnquist have in common? Seeking to advance quite different political goals, they all subscribed to more state-centered definitions of constitutional powers. *States' rights* advocates generally say that the Constitution amounts to a contract between states and a national government, not between individuals and that government. First of all, individuals are better off negotiating their "social contracts" directly with their own states. Second, it was the states, after all, that sent delegations to Philadelphia in 1787 to work out a plan for giving *limited* powers to a national government. If the national government claims that it can bypass the states and impose its powers directly on individuals, the whole spirit of the constitutional contract (along with the concept of people having access to power close to home) is broken. Jefferson first offered this line of reasoning when threatening state resistance to early Federalist efforts to limit freedom of political speech in the Alien and Sedition Acts passed by Congress in 1798.

In his ruling in *McCulloch v. Maryland,* Chief Justice Marshall infuriated many states' rights advocates by explaining one simple reason why states could not overrule the national government: The people, not the states, ratified the Constitution. A major challenge to the idea of the Constitution as a direct contract between people and a national government came several decades later when southern states began to attack national tariff laws. Elites in the southern states felt disadvantaged by these trading regulations that favored the industrialized North over the cotton-exporting, agricultural economy of the South. Lurking in the background was the fear that northern abolitionists and business interests might gradually eliminate the practice of slavery altogether. The state most deeply indentured to the idea and the economics of the plantation was South Carolina, which was also the home of the South's most brilliant politician, John C. Calhoun.

The Civil War and the Deadlock of Federalism

To defend the state-centered view of the Constitution, Calhoun derived *the doctrine of* **nullification.** The idea was simple: *If the national government passed laws that violated its obligation to respect state powers, the states had the right to reject (or "nullify") those national laws.* And so, South Carolina became the first state to formally nullify a national law (a federal tariff act in 1832). The crisis was worsened when President Andrew Jackson charged South Carolina with threatening the Union, a charge that became loaded when Congress authorized the use of military force to make the state obey. This dress rehearsal for the Civil War was finally called off when Congress backed down and amended its law, and South Carolina retracted its nullification. Both sides declared victory for their respective readings of the Constitution, however.

The claims for state-centered interpretations of the Constitution became even stronger in the years following this standoff, particularly in the most stubborn battlefield: race relations. The position of the states' rights advocates was strengthened in 1835 when Chief Justice Marshall left the scene. He was replaced by Roger B. Taney, a proponent of the state-centered view, who issued a series of rulings that kept the national government out of state affairs, particularly in the regulation of race relations and the definition of citizenship itself. The landmark decision that finally angered the nation-centered forces beyond the point of tolerance was the Court's ruling in the case of a slave named Dred Scott in 1857 (**Dred Scott v. Sanford**).[11]

More than thirty years earlier, Congress had tried to finesse the problem of slavery by passing the Missouri Compromise of 1820, which, among other things, made slavery illegal in states and territories that came into the Union as nonslave or "free." *Dred Scott*

Dred Scott in a contemporary engraving. Scott, a slave, sued unsuccessfully for his liberty after he was taken into a "free" territory. The Supreme Court ruled that the national government had no constitutional authority to release him. (Soon after the decision, however, Scott and his family were emancipated by a new master, and he lived out the rest of his life a free man.) The state-centered concept of the Constitution extends to many areas beyond racial matters; but for a century after the 1857 Dred Scott v. Sanford *ruling, the public often associated the term* states' rights *with reactionary attitudes on race and segregation.*

raised a tricky legal question that exposed a whole century of contradictions, compromises, and prejudices involving slavery and race in America. With the help of a sympathetic owner, Scott sued for his freedom on the grounds that one of his owners had taken him out of Missouri (a slave state) and into the "free soil" of Illinois and the Wisconsin territory. Although a sympathetic jury ruled in Scott's favor, their verdict was overturned when the Missouri State Court ruled that he remained a slave under state law. When the appeal reached the Supreme Court, Chief Justice Taney used the Scott case to avoid greater national involvement in the explosive "citizenship" questions pertaining to slavery. He argued for a majority of the Court that there was no national remedy for Scott, who, like all slaves, was "never thought of or spoken of" in the Constitution "except as property."[12]

To add to the impact of the ruling, the Court went on to review the Missouri Compromise itself and declared it unconstitutional on grounds that Congress had no power to decide the "slave or free" status of new states and territories coming into the Union. Backed by a state-power president, James Buchanan, the decision was seen as appeasing the angry southern states. However, the effect of the ruling in much of the North was inflammatory. The Court's ruling underscored the problem of racism in the American democracy by including the opinion that slaves were, after all, "beings of an inferior order."[13]

At one stroke, the state-centered view of the Constitution had won a major victory. However, Abraham Lincoln's condemnation of the ruling and promise to gradually abolish slavery won him a slim 40 percent victory in the presidential election of 1860 (a divisive four-candidate race). Lincoln not only favored a nation-centered definition of federal power, but specifically rejected the idea of the Union as a limited contract between states and a national government. When the electoral college vote cast Lincoln as the winner in 1860, the state of South Carolina saw the (constitutional) writing on the wall and reacted accordingly. This time, South Carolina, in effect, nullified the entire Constitution by seceding from the Union. Ten more states that would shortly form the southern Confederacy followed suit. True to their state-power principles, these eleven joined in a weak central government reminiscent of the first national *confederation* under the Articles.

Meanwhile, Abraham Lincoln wasted no time raising his nationalist banner. In the inaugural address of 1861, he explained that the point of the Philadelphia Convention and the government it produced was "to form a more perfect Union." Lincoln argued that "more perfect" meant the Union already existed at the time of the Convention, and the Constitution therefore could not be regarded as a contract with the states creating a union from scratch. This gap between states' rights and nationalist forces was now too wide to bridge with court rulings about the meaning of words on paper. The Civil War was on. The Confederacy fought fiercely but ultimately proved no match for the industrialized and more unified (federal) forces of the North, and the world's bloodiest battle over the definition of federalism ended in military defeat for the state-centered forces.

Surely the outcome of the Civil War meant that the nation-centered view of government powers had finally won over the state-centered view? Although this is a common interpretation of the Civil War and its legacy in American politics, it is not that simple. In fact, it was fully seventy years after the Civil War before the national government was involved in enough areas of state life to make a convincing case that the balance of power finally tilted toward a predominantly nation-centered view of constitutional powers. Even at the dawn of the era of national dominance in the 1930s, the states still retained most of their powers involving race, citizenship, and civil rights—despite a Civil War and three constitutional amendments (Thirteenth, Fourteenth, and Fifteenth) aimed at establishing national dominance on these very issues.

The ruins of Richmond, Virginia, in the aftermath of the Civil War (1861–1865). In addition to vanquishing slavery, the North's victory began the gradual ascendancy of the national government over those of the individual states, an outcome which even some northerners viewed with misgivings. Herman Melville (a New Yorker and Union supporter) predicted in an 1866 poem, "The Iron Dome [of the Capitol], / Stronger for stress and strain, / Shall fling her huge shadow athwart the main; / But the Founders' dream shall flee."

So divisive was the war and its bitter legacy that the national government often lacked the unity, and the states the willingness, to expand national powers in many areas. In addition, the *laissez-faire* economic philosophy of limited government further restricted the application of national powers into many areas of state life. The eventual expansion of national powers was stimulated by the Great Depression of the 1930s, with its many social and economic crises crying for quick and sweeping national political action. Even after many spheres of social and economic life were opened to federal "cooperation," the areas of race and rights lagged far behind. Once again, the moral of the story is that the division of constitutional powers depends not just on the words in the Constitution, but on the political applications of those words by the government.

While the Civil War and the enduring American struggle over race and civil rights is an extreme case, many other nations with federal governments have experienced conflicts over how to divide their governing powers. Canada, for example, has struggled with defining the rights and powers of a French-speaking minority who live primarily in the province of Quebec. In order to avert the secession of Quebec from the government, repeated efforts have been made to rewrite the Canadian Constitution to satisfy both the French-speaking citizens of Quebec and the other English-speaking provinces. See "How We Compare" Box 4.3.

Three Models of Federalism

As noted earlier, the idea of states' rights evokes a model of clearly divided, or layered, *dual* powers. By contrast, nation-centered views of the Constitution see power as mixed or spread through these layers of state and national government in *cooperation* or partnership. One of the great scholars of federalism, Morton Grodzins, once described the old era of **dual federalism** with its relatively clear separation of powers as a layer cake, in which the national government filled in one layer of powers and the states filled in another. (Perhaps we should add that business, blessed with so many *laissez-faire* freedoms, became the icing between the layers.) With the increased mixing of powers in the *cooperative era,* following the Great Depression of the 1930s, the layers began to run together, like a marble cake in which vanilla and chocolate fillings swirl around in often convoluted ways.[14]

Canadian Federalism

Canada is a federal system that has experienced great struggles and conflicts. Although the Canadian Union was not shattered by civil war, it has been threatened repeatedly by a number of serious conflicts between the national government and the subnational units called provinces.

Most familiar to Americans is the long-standing issue of Quebec separatism, raising the possibility that a geographically and economically central province will withdraw from the union, with dire consequences for the nation. The separatist movement in Quebec won great provincial autonomy over the years, and Canada is officially a bilingual nation, recognizing the French-speaking Quebeçois population.

There are also other sources of tension in Canadian federalism: strong provincial political parties, great provincial control over natural resources, claims by native peoples for autonomy and control of their lands, and relatively weak spending powers at the national level. (The Canadian national government accounts for a smaller portion of total government spending than in any other federal government.) These strains led one observer to describe national policy-making in Canada as a "federal-provincial diplomacy" that sometimes resembles international relations.*

The strains in Canadian federalism have led to important battles over the Constitution itself. A proposed major reform of the Constitution failed to win approval in all the provinces in 1990, sending negotiators back to work on a new attempt that met with another divisive vote in 1992. The constitutional reform crises led one observer to pronounce Canadian federalism "clinically dead."** However, Canada's decentralized power system may have helped avoid a permanent breakup through so many serious conflicts.

Although Canada's system is much different from the United States model of federalism, there is one important similarity: Both American and Canadian federalism demonstrate that divisions of power between the units of government are rarely settled once and for all.

*Thomas O. Hueglin, "Federalism in Comparative Perspective," R.D. Olling and M.W. Westmacott, eds., *Perspectives on Canadian Federalism.* Scarborough, Ontario: Prentice-Hall Canada, 1988, p. 20.
**Ronald L. Watts, "Canadian Federalism in the 1990s: Once More in Question," *Publius* 21 (3), p. 171.

The cake metaphor helps to simplify what has always been a more complex picture. It can be argued, for example, that the early practice of giving national land to states for school campuses (a practice that dates to before the Constitution—to the Land Ordinance of 1785 under the Articles of Confederation government) was a mixing of national powers into the layer of state powers. However, as a generalization, it is safe to say that the United States operated under a relatively *dual* (or "layered") power system for much of its first hundred and fifty years, and then developed a much more *cooperative* (or "marbled") system for thirty years after that, and has been going through another period of change in the last thirty or so years.

The current debates over a New Federalism are too far from being resolved to predict just how the marble cake swirl of cooperative powers might be changed. Thus, the somewhat generic term *New Federalism* reminds us that efforts have been under way for more than two decades to change the divisions of federal power. One change worth noting is the increasing involvement of state governments in Washington politics. By one count, California has opened up over seventy branch offices in Washington and hired some twenty lobbyists to represent state interests.[15] Students of federalism refer to this increased state involvement in national policy-making as adding a *horizontal* power dimension to federalism, in which states increasingly join forces with or against one another in their battles involving the national government. The definitions of dual and **cooperative**

federalism, by contrast, primarily involve vertical power relations between a central national government and individual states. Table 4.2 illustrates some of the subnational government-interest organizations that put pressure on the national government.

This *horizontal* action at the state level suggests yet another cake metaphor. We might think of a two-layered checkerboard cake, with chocolate and vanilla squares representing power linkages; some squares run up and down between states and national government, other squares operate fairly independently of the others, and still other squares connect the states to one another in horizontal power arrangements through lobbying, sponsoring legislation, or trying to block other state initiatives. For those who do not mind mixing their metaphors, another image attached to this new feature of federalism is that of a "picket fence" in which the vertical slats continue to reflect one-on-one power relations between state and national governments, and the horizontal slats represent states organizing their own national political agendas. In Chapter 15, we will explore the case of a group of states that joined in suing the national government to get it to write the state regulations needed in a national clean air law so those states could get on with the business of obeying the law. Each of these broad patterns of federal power reflects the political forces operating in different periods in American history. A look at the politics of each era shows how different federal power arrangements are possible under the Constitution, and how they affect the lives of citizens.

Political Life in Three Eras of Federal Power

As noted earlier, most intrusions of national powers into state life before the 1930s were fairly minor, creating a long period of *dual federalism* that ended when the Supreme Court changed key interpretations of the Constitution. From roughly the late 1930s until the late 1960s, state and national powers were increasingly mixed through *cooperative* arrangements in many areas, including environmental regulation, economic and labor relations, social welfare, health care, and some of the most basic questions of citizenship, civil rights, and political participation. Since the late 1960s, efforts have been made at the national level, assisted by the Court, to "unmix" some of these powers. The jury is still out, however, on just what lasting effects will come of these efforts to define the hazy concept of a New Federalism.

Dual Federalism (1800–1937)

The government in Washington expanded its powers cautiously in its first century and a half, asserting its supremacy primarily in *interstate* disputes over trade, transportation, and communication. It left the states and businesses to work out most of their own internal arrangements. Some people who visited different parts of the country were often struck by enough diversity to question whether they could all be part of the same nation. States differed profoundly on almost every basic measure of life quality: health, sanitation, education, salaries and wages, working conditions, housing, public health and safety, and the relations among various racial, ethnic, and income groups. In some regions (primarily the Midwest and West), state governments provided fairly well for most citizens. In other areas (primarily the South and the industrial North), life conditions often reflected little government intervention on behalf of poor people, workers, immigrants, and blacks.

It would be too simple to ascribe the political results of dual federalism to a passive Court and willful states alone. When some states attempted bold economic and social reforms for their citizens, those reforms were often overturned by the same Supreme

TABLE 4.2

The Big Seven: Major State and Local Interest Groups

ORGANIZATION	HEADQUARTERS	NUMBER OF MEMBERS	DISTINCTIVE TRAITS	LOBBIES?
National Conference of State Legislatures (NCSL)	Denver (research) Washington (lobbying) (formed in 1975)	50 state legislatures, including legislators and staff	Union of three formerly competing legislative organizations; emphasizes policy development across states	Yes
National Governors' Association (NGA)	Washington (since 1958)	50 governors	Created "Hall of States" where many state and local groups are housed	Yes
National Association of Counties (NACo)	Washington (since 1958)	2,100 counties	Large and effective interest group for county governments	Yes
National League of Cities (NLC)	Washington (since 1954)	1,175 small-to-medium cities	Highly developed research and professional staff	Yes
U.S. Conference of Mayors (USCM)	Washington (since 1932)	Mayors of 600 larger cities	Represents "big-city" interest; relies on direct lobbying by mayors	Yes
International City Management Association (ICMA)	Washington (since 1967)	7,000 city administrators	Professional organization for city managers	No
Council of State Governments (CSG)	Lexington, Ky. (Washington office since 1983)	50 states plus territories	Six regional offices; has many affiliate organizations, such as associations of chief justices, attorneys general	No

SOURCE: Charles H. Levine and James A. Thurber, "Reagan and the Intergovernmental Lobby," in Allan J. Cigler and Burdett A. Loomis, eds., *Interest Group Politics*. Washington, D.C.: CQ Inc., 1986, p. 202.

Court that claimed to respect the rights of states to run their own affairs in other areas. The politics behind the uses of constitutional powers during this era can only be explained by bringing another actor into the political scene: big business. Business never was, and surely never will be, a passive player in American politics. However, since the Constitution does not assign business its own branch of government, it is often left out of many textbook explanations of politics. After the Civil War came a period of rapid industrial expansion, encouraged by national politicians and business elites who shared a vision of the United States' becoming a great world power. This expansion was aided by Court decisions which, as noted above, did not always fit neatly into either a state-centered or a nation-centered philosophy of the Constitution. The Court's decisions instead often related to the economic and political philosophy of *laissez-faire*.

A SHORT LESSON IN POLITICAL ECONOMY: *LAISSEZ-FAIRE*.   If anything could have brought the national government rushing into the political lives of states, it was the Fourteenth Amendment (ratified 1868) to the Constitution. Among the "operative" passages in this amendment is this one:

> No State shall . . . deprive any person of life, liberty, or property, without due process of law; nor deny to any person within its jurisdiction the equal protection of the laws.

Although the intent of these words may seem clear, the political uses to which they were put until 1955 were anything but consistent with that intent. Consider, for example, the case of Mr. Homer Plessy, who in 1892 had the nerve to sit in a "whites only" train car in New Orleans. Mr. Plessy was arrested, prosecuted, and convicted of violating the racial separation laws of the state of Louisiana. (Plessy protested that he was seven-eights white by ancestry, but Louisiana law at the time defined a Negro as anyone having one sixteenth nonwhite ancestry, or one great-grandparent who was black.) What was unusual was that Homer Plessy appealed the state decision all the way to the U.S. Supreme Court, where he was told, in what became a landmark ruling, that separate public facilities for whites and blacks, were not necessarily unequal, and therefore did not violate the Fourteenth Amendment.

What is the point here about economics? Even though the Fourteenth Amendment was intended to promote civil rights for blacks after the Civil War, the Court ignored these intentions of the Constitution for almost a century, leaving state governments to order their own societies. But this does not mean that the Fourteenth Amendment was sitting idle during all these years of dual federalism. The Court used that same amendment to protect the so-called Robber Barons, who were being told by some of the more progressive states to clean up their unsavory business practices. "Inside the System" Box 4.4 puts the focus on how business ran important areas of American political life during this era.

The philosophy of *laissez-faire* was easy to justify on states' rights grounds when the Supreme Court had regulatory laws from Congress to strike down. However, finding legal arguments was more difficult when states themselves began regulating the businesses within their borders. That was when business owners and their lawyers hit upon the idea of trying to use the Fourteenth Amendment to protect businesses from the states. After all, the amendment did specifically prohibit states from depriving people of things like property, and the amendment did not specifically refer just to black people.

If the Supreme Court could be persuaded to look beyond the historical intent of the amendment's authors and think of businesses as being entities like people, the case could be made. The first time this argument reached the Supreme Court (1873) was too close to the actual passage of the Fourteenth Amendment to stretch the legal imagination that far, and the argument was rejected. However, as time passed and state efforts to control businesses increased, the Court became more sympathetic to the argument. During the 1890s the Court struck down state laws limiting hours of work and other exploitative practices on grounds that they deprived the owners of businesses of "life, liberty, or property" (depending on the law). On into the 1900s, the Court blocked state laws protecting workers' rights to unionize by ruling that they violated owners' rights to deal individually with workers in contract matters.

During the same period, Congress was blocked in numerous efforts to regulate business practices. As early as 1890, for example, Congress had passed the Sherman Antitrust Act in an effort to break up the huge "trusts," or business monopolies, that controlled entire markets in key products, including many manufactured goods, foods, and oil. (The giant Standard Oil monopoly, for example, had swallowed up all the nation's major oil refineries.) Although the executive branch was able to use the Sherman Act once to reduce the size of the huge American Sugar Refining Company (which had

Social Power in One Era of Federalism
Elite Rule and Dual Federalism

4.4

Limiting the economic powers of government under the doctrine of *laissez-faire* created a power vacuum—one that big business was only too happy to fill. By the end of the "Gilded Age" (late 1800s), the so-called Robber Barons of banking and industry wielded enormous influence over American life. This influence was not felt just in the workplace, but in the political parties, through legislation and appointments to the courts, through influence in many state and local governments, and by encouraging American military and economic expansion abroad.

Charles Adams, an astute observer of this age, once claimed that the industrial giants "declared war, negotiated peace, reduced courts, legislatures and sovereign states to an unqualified obedience to their will, disturbed trade, agitated the currency, imposed taxes and boldly setting both law and public opinion at defiance, have freely exercised many other attributes of sovereignty." *

And no less a political authority than President Grover Cleveland declared in his Inaugural Address of 1888: "We discover the existence of trusts, combinations, and monopolies, while the citizen is struggling far in the rear or is trampled to death behind an iron heel. Corporations, which should be carefully restrained creatures of the law and servants of the people, are fast becoming the people's masters." **

After the Great Depression of the 1930s, even many business leaders began calling for government regulations. Government regulation of business, banking, investment, labor relations, and many manufacturing practices became an important feature of the era of "cooperative federalism." In this respect, the shift to cooperative federalism helped balance social power between elites and other groups in society.

*From Richard Leach, *American Federalism,* New York: Norton, 1970, p. 54.
**Ibid.

"DANCE, YER LITTLE RUNT! DANCE!"

In this Puck *cartoon, the common citizen appears to be the helpless prey of Big Business (the "Coal Trust") on one side and Big Labor (the "Miners' Union") on the other. Looking on with seeming glee (at center) is a rowdy cowboy resembling President Teddy Roosevelt. Roosevelt in fact set an important milestone when the national government intervened in a 1902 coal strike, acting as a mediator. He also helped to bring about the Pure Food and Drug Act and the Meat Inspection Act—actions contrary to a rigid laissez-faire approach. TR called his program "the Square Deal."*

absorbed forty other sugar companies), the Supreme Court quickly put a stop to any similar moves in other industries. Beginning in 1895, a series of rulings removed manufacturing from the definition of national interstate commerce powers, implying that it was one of the areas reserved to the states under the Tenth Amendment. Yet in most cases where states tried to regulate manufacturing they were told that their efforts violated the Fourteenth Amendment rights of business owners and corporations.

THE GREAT CRASH OF DUAL FEDERALISM.   The general result of this nearly constant green light for economic elites was, of course, a heyday for business. The stock market boomed, profits soared, unions were broken, consumers were at times sold faulty goods, and governments in Washington and in many states eventually gave up much hope of bringing the system under control. The bubble finally burst in 1929 with a stock market crash. Businesses failed. Banks that had loaned out depositors' money on get-rich-quick fantasies went bankrupt. Tens of millions of American workers and their families were left with nothing. No jobs. No savings. No houses. No farms. Worst of all, people had nowhere to turn. The government in Washington, and particularly the Court, continued to claim that neither it nor the states had the power to do anything about the situation. This quickly became an unpopular view of federalism.

People demanded action, ranging from the regulation of industries to banking practices. Workers demanded the right to form unions and to have government insurance against major economic hardships, including simply becoming too old to earn a livable wage (the origin of the Social Security program). By the early 1930s even big business was joining the bandwagon for federal regulation. Many owners recognized that the business climate had been poisoned by the excesses of *laissez-faire*.[16] In light of this broad social pressure for the redefinition of government powers, you might say that a political force no smaller than the *majority of the American people* brought an end to the era of dual federalism.

On March 10, 1933—less than a week after taking office—Franklin Roosevelt signs a bank reform bill as Treasury secretary William Woodin looks on. Roosevelt's campaign slogan had promised "a New Deal," but many of his attempts to vastly expand national governmental powers and programs were declared unconstitutional. Not until Roosevelt's second term did the Supreme Court, under the enormous political pressure of the Great Depression, begin to uphold the constitutionality of such unprecedented measures as the Social Security Act and the National Labor Relations Act.

Laborers paint a theater marquee as part of a WPA (Works Progress Administration) project. The WPA aimed to give dignity to the jobless by serving as a public-works program rather than simply passing out financial aid; the WPA's Federal Arts Project in particular employed many muralists, sculptors, and graphic artists. While serving as morale boosters, such programs yielded only sporadic relief, and only the approaching world war brought sustained economic recovery to the nation.

Cooperative Federalism (1937–1968)

Franklin Delano Roosevelt led the Democratic party to landslide victories in national and state elections throughout the Great Depression. The Democrats first captured the White House in 1932, and by 1934 they had enough strength in Congress to write sweeping legislation based on their campaign promise of a "New Deal" (FDR's campaign slogan) for the protection of the people. These ideas were nothing short of radical, considering Supreme Court rulings up to that point in history.

The scope of change was too much for most of the justices on the Court to accept, and for the first term of Roosevelt's presidency the Court stuck to its dual federalism and *laissez-faire* views. As a result, much of the New Deal legislative package was stalled by constitutional disputes. In the election of 1936, however, *the power of the majority* was stepped up as another Democratic landslide returned Roosevelt and the New Deal coalition to public office throughout the land. Meanwhile, the Depression worsened and unemployment deepened. Angry citizens marched on Washington and state capitals. Others who were homeless set up poor people's camps around the country. (The Democrats called the camps "Hoovervilles" after the previous president.) Roosevelt even tried (unsuccessfully) to add additional justices onto the Court in a "court-packing" scheme to break the hold of the old *laissez-faire* bloc.

A combination of these social and economic pressures finally broke through the psychological wall of lifetime tenure established by the founders to protect justices on the Supreme Court from the tides and passions of day-to-day politics. The pace of change was also increased greatly by the departure of four justices from the court over a short period. The remaining conservative justices joined the new Roosevelt appointees in rethinking the last century of constitutional interpretations that had created the system of dual federalism. Beginning in 1937, *dual federalism* finally started to collapse when enough justices began voting to uphold the constitutionality of New Deal legislation.

After 1937 came a series of rulings that did the once unthinkable: They permitted the national government to regulate the economy. The constitutional principle that made all of this possible was the same interstate commerce clause that had been used for more than a century to *limit* national intervention in the state economies! Reinterpreting that clause was suddenly thinkable once the political pressures from *voting majorities, interest groups,* and *economic elites* all demanded it. The Court redefined commerce to include things like manufacturing and labor relations, and what many refer to as a "revolutionary" new era of federalism was launched. In 1937 alone, the Court reversed its long-held views of dual power and upheld

- The long-denied rights of workers to unionize and bargain collectively with owners over wages and working conditions (rights specifically defined by Congress in the Wagner Act and upheld in the Court's ruling in the case of *National Labor Relations Board v. Jones & Laughlin Steel*).[17]
- The formerly denied rights of states to set minimum wages for workers (*West Coast Hotel Company v. Parrish*).[18]
- The power of the national government to set up a social security program for workers (*Stewart Machine Company v. Davis*).[19]

Once these and other precedents were established, the national government became involved in many areas of social, economic, and political life. Congress created *regulatory agencies and commissions* to protect workers from unsafe working conditions; to regulate banks and lending practices; to watch over the stock markets for the protection of investors; to regulate the production of food on farms; to test the quality of meats, medicines, and other consumer products; and (in later years) to prevent businesses from discriminating against employees because of race or gender.

All aspects of the political system became involved in bringing about these changes, from *cultural attitudes about the role of government,* to the relations between *the three branches of government,* to the interplay of *all forms of power in society.*

Cultural factors: A depression that threw millions out of work, and robbed the savings of millions more, broke down some of the cultural taboos against a strong, activist central government. Many people became receptive for the first time to national government solutions to local social and economic problems. These new attitudes became the core of an ideology known as New Deal liberalism.

Institutional factors: Even though the Democratic party won landslide victories for the White House, Congress, and many of the state governments, the Supreme Court remained committed to its *laissez-faire* pro-business philosophy for nearly the first decade of the Depression. The gridlock was finally broken by a combination of (unsuccessful) presidential threats to try to expand the number of justices on the Court, four justices leaving the Court, new liberal appointees who were sympathetic to the political goals of the New Deal, and tremendous public pressure for reform. With a new constitutional philosophy emerging in the Court, many new national programs were eventually introduced into state life.

Social power: The power of business *elites* who dominated much of the era of dual federalism was weakened by the effects of the Depression and by the blame they received for it. In addition, the Depression created new opportunities and powerful motives for grass-roots organizations of workers, farmers, and unemployed people to rise up and apply pressure on their own. Many reforms were aided by this rise of *pluralist* power from grass-roots groups in society. Finally, the pressure for change was kept up by *majoritarian* power in the form of voters who returned the Democratic party to control of both Congress and the White House from 1932 until after World War II, including electing Franklin Roosevelt an unprecedented four times as president.

THE POLITICS OF COOPERATION.   The national government began taking on new responsibilities and assuming new powers, but many of these required partnership arrangements with the states to get the job done. Here is one example: Suppose that a natural disaster strikes a state—a river floods, a volcano erupts, or a hurricane strikes, causing damage far greater than the state can handle on its own. The state governor asks the national government for help, and the state is declared a "disaster area," which qualifies it to receive federal relief money. Delivering this money requires a cooperative effort between the national government and the state. The national government determines the amount of relief and the conditions for giving it out, but the state estimates the size of its need and provides most of the actual personnel and bureaucratic organization to deliver the aid to its people. It is hard to find a clear separation of powers anywhere in this process. The very nature of such activities requires cooperation to get them done.

Consider another example: the protection of the environment. In the simpler and less regulated days of dual federalism, not much was done about the environment in many states. There were, of course, a few states that had active environmental programs, and now continue to set higher standards than national laws require. However, the years of neglect in many states left a legacy of severe contamination of air and water supplies. Yet national environmental programs could not just set up huge bureaucracies within state borders. The cost and inefficiency of duplicated efforts would not permit it. Nor would states be happy with armies of federal bureaucrats running around trying to figure out what their state needs were and upsetting business elites who might threaten to go elsewhere. The cooperative solution was to create the national Environmental Protection Agency (EPA) to coordinate national laws and regulations with state agencies that retain many local enforcement powers and work directly with polluters. Many of these federal arrangements are held together by the promise of national money if states cooperate, and the threat of losing money when states fail to cooperate.

THE POLITICAL ECONOMY OF CARROT-AND-STICK COOPERATION. Beginning with the Great Depression, the national government faced two big challenges: implementing dozens of large-scale social and economic programs, and getting all the states on board in more or less the same way. The strategy employed by Congress (again, with the approval of the executive and the support of the Court) was to offer lumps of money to the states, provided they use that money for very specific kinds, or *categories,* of action. For example, New Deal legislation offered *categorical grants* to the states for public-jobs programs, meaning that recipients had to be put to work in public (not private) services. State legislators were eager to appease angry voters who had been thrown out of work by the Depression, and so they snapped up the money. As a result, many colleges, universities, parks, dams, bridges, and public buildings still in use were built by state jobs programs funded and supervised by the national Works Progress Administration (WPA) during the Great Depression. If you check around your town or state—perhaps even on your own campus, if it is a fairly old state school—you will find some of these great monuments to cooperative federalism.

In the decade following World War II, long after the country as a whole had been returned to prosperity by the war boom, some of the politicians who had been influenced by New Deal ideology began to argue that for many Americans the Depression had never ended. At the close of the 1950s perhaps as many as 20 percent of Americans continued to live in poverty. In the 1960s President John Kennedy declared "war on poverty," and

Lyndon Johnson followed him with the promise of a "Great Society." Their weapon, as in the New Deal, was the **categorical grant.**

Where the New Deal had focused more on cooperative economic development between states and the national government, the War on Poverty and Great Society programs emphasized cooperative efforts to develop human potential through nutrition, job training, day care for working mothers, health clinics, educational programs, treatment for alcohol and drug problems, and intervention in dozens of other areas. The Great Society also offered states categorical grants to beautify their highways by planting roadside areas and cleaning up trash. Parks were built in the inner-city neighborhoods so that poor children would have places to play. All in all, it was a grand vision. By the mid-1960s there were nearly four hundred major categories of grant programs operating just to build the "Great Society." There were many notable achievements. For example, the percentage of American children living in poverty was cut in half between 1959 and 1969.[20] Parks and green spaces began to pop up in urban neighborhoods. Anti-litter campaigns and rest stops began to change the landscape of the nation's highways.

But many of the core problems in society did not disappear. Progress seemed slow, not just to weary taxpayers but to many recipients of the programs as well. Perhaps problems of race and poverty had been neglected too long. Perhaps America was not rich enough to wage a war on poverty at home and a war against communism in Vietnam. Some critics charged that there were too many layers of bureaucracy to make many programs workable, no matter how well-meaning they may have been.

THE FALL OF COOPERATIVE FEDERALISM.   By the late 1960s the country was in turmoil, and not just over the war in Vietnam. In city after city, ghetto residents took to the streets in fiery riots that left their neighborhoods in ashes and faith in the Great Society badly shaken. Both middle-class taxpayers and the recipients of many federal programs themselves began to question the whole approach to this brand of cooperative federalism.

The lesson drawn by most voters and politicians about the failures of cooperative federalism was in keeping with traditional cultural concerns about big government: The national government forced so many rules, regulations, and bureaucrats onto the states that nothing could possibly work. In short, people concluded that the real trouble with cooperative federalism was that government had simply grown far too BIG.

The news of the 1970s and 1980s was filled with "fed up on federalism" stories. People were tired of tax dollars that brought little social relief, and tired of having Washington tell them how to run their lives. In a popular 1976 movie, *Network,* a television newscaster led the nation in an angry chant of "I'm mad as hell, and I'm not going to take it any more!" During the 1970s, 1980s, and 1990s, many politicians attracted votes with that oldest political promise of all: to get big government off the people's backs. And what would replace the federalism of the cooperative era?

A New Federalism? (1968–Today)

Enter President Richard Nixon. After a narrow victory over one of the last of the New Dealers (Hubert Humphrey) in 1968, Nixon piled up a landslide in 1972 over George McGovern, an advocate of expanding the Great Society programs. Sensing that the times and the voting public were ripe for change, Nixon looked around for a weapon to use in his personal war against the old power system of cooperative federalism. Just as the New Dealers and Great Society builders had found their tools already lying around in the form of categorical grants, Nixon spotted another type of existing federal grant that suited his purposes.

A lone soldier patrols a Washington, D.C. street, enforcing a curfew imposed to halt rioting that followed the assassination of civil rights leader Rev. Martin Luther King, Jr., on April 4, 1968. By the close of the 1960s, many people across the political spectrum had lost faith in the ability of the national government, despite its many programs, to respond competently to the needs of society.

Block grants had been around for a half-dozen years, but they were not used prominently until Nixon pushed his New Federalism in 1972. A *block grant,* as the name implies, is less specific than a *categorical grant* because it gives states a "block" of money for solving a "block" of problems in a broad area. States are left more latitude to define problems and work out solutions more to their liking. For example, under *categorical grants,* federal jobs programs laid down strict guidelines about who should receive money and what kinds of jobs they should be given. *Block grants,* by contrast, gave states more leeway in selecting recipients and creating job descriptions. With less national supervision, it is not surprising that some states abused their powers to decide who needed jobs, and for this and other reasons, many jobs and other block grant programs were eventually terminated by Ronald Reagan.

Another innovation of Richard Nixon's New Federalism was an even less restricted no-strings approach to giving money to the states called **revenue sharing,** which involved giving lumps of federal tax money back to the states to do with as they pleased. Revenue sharing placed further limits on state and national cooperation by giving states even more independence than they had with the block grants. However, Congress was reluctant to give up the design of federal programs, and, more importantly, the national budget crisis of the 1980s eventually squeezed surplus money for revenue sharing out of the budget altogether.

The results of Mr. Nixon's approach to creating a new federalism were mixed. Although states gained more control over programs, Congress continued to pull many strings, and the amount of federal spending continued to increase. The next president elected, Jimmy Carter (1976–1980), was a Southern Democrat who also ran against big government. He continued using block grants and even began slowing the rate at which federal aid flowed to the states. When Ronald Reagan became president in 1981, he decided that the sheer amount of money itself was corrupting the state governments, leaving them dependent on the central government and encouraging bureaucrats to do things their own citizens in fact did not want or need. If the people really wanted all those programs, Reagan and the other advocates of New Federalism reasoned, let them create and pay for them at the state level.

Determined to cut back on the amount of spending *and* to continue using block grants to distribute what was left, President Reagan launched a major offensive against cooperative federalism. Using his skills as a "great communicator," he fired up popular support for federal reforms with statements like these: "We are turning America away from yesterday's policies of Big Brother government. We are determined to restore power and authority to states and localities."[21] It is interesting that Franklin Roosevelt had used similar communication techniques (but different rhetoric) in directly addressing the people when he launched the era of cooperative federalism a half-century before.

These efforts to create a new federal power arrangement once again involve every aspect of the political system: *cultural attitudes about the role of government,* political battles among *the institutions of the national government,* and the mobilization of *elite, group, and majority power in society.* "Inside the System" Box 4.5 describes some of the key political factors at work in attempts to build a different kind of federalism.

WHY A NEW FEDERALISM IS HARD TO BUILD.   It has turned out to be easier to weaken cooperative federalism than to replace it with something completely different. By the time Ronald Reagan became president, both Congress and many interest groups had become committed to hundreds of cooperative federal programs. Presidential power alone, even when wielded by a popular president, could not simply sweep the old federalism and its entrenched programs away. However, by using a combination of budget cuts and orders to his own administration, Mr. Reagan began to dismantle as much of the old cooperative system as he could. He instructed his top appointees to ease up on the enforcement of many rules and regulations.

Efforts to reduce federal environmental regulation illustrate the general approach of the Reagan years. The budget of the Environmental Protection Agency (EPA) was cut by 10 percent and its staff reduced by 20 percent.[22] Anne Gorsuch Burford, director of the EPA, relaxed supervision and enforcement of existing air, water, and toxic waste regulations. As a result, many states chose to stop their environmental programs almost entirely, and some industries took advantage of the situation to turn local property into toxic-waste storage sites.

Among the other executive branch regulatory cutbacks during the Reagan years were these:[23]

- The Interior Department reduced enforcement of strip mining regulations by nearly 60 percent.
- The Occupational Safety and Health Administration cut four hundred inspectors and reduced the number of citations issued by one-half.
- The National Highway Traffic Safety Administration trimmed 22 percent of its budget and cut the number of investigations into possible auto defects by over half.
- The Food and Drug Administration issued three times the number of emergency exemptions for new pesticides (some of which later proved harmful).

While these moves clearly weakened cooperative federalism in many areas, the state-national partnership was by no means dead. Many states were not eager to lose what they regarded as beneficial programs. Other state officials complained that their new freedoms meant very little because budget cuts restricted what they could do. The politics of budgeting quickly became another battleground. Using the promise (popular among many state governors and legislatures) to turn more categorical grants into block grants, Ronald Reagan persuaded Congress to merge over seventy major categorical programs into fewer than ten big block grants. At the same time, however, he cut the total amount of money in those grants; states got more control, but over less money. Many former supporters then turned angry, complaining that it was not fair to take money away.

The Political Struggle for a New Federalism

4.5

The decline of cooperative federalism and the uneven development of a New Federalism to take its place can be traced to a combination of *cultural, institutional,* and *social power* factors operating inside the system.

Cultural factors: Fueled by the political upheavals of the 1950s and 1960s, racial tensions, tax burdens, and signs of a weakening economy, many middle-class voters and politicians returned to a familiar cultural vision of small government, lower taxes, and more individual responsibility for social problems.

Institutional factors: Athough the Reagan and Bush administrations appointed a number of conservative justices to the Supreme Court, the proponents of the New Federalism never

secured control of Congress, meaning that many initiatives for more dramatic cuts in social programs and more restoration of state powers were not fully realized. As a result, the New Federalism became a curious patchwork of less national regulation in some areas of state life and more in other areas.

Social power: Majoritarian aspects of the New Federalism are evident in strong voter support for Ronald Reagan in 1980 and 1984, and George Bush in 1988. However, many voters also split their tickets, electing Democrats to Congress, and signalling that they wanted some level of continued national partnership in social and economic programs. At the same time, intense interest-group activity saw *pluralist* forces defend many programs in the national budget that the new federalists wanted to cut. This

prevented a more complete break with the old federal power system and its political agenda. In addition, economic *elites* who financed political parties and candidates secured a great deal of favorable legislation in Congress and deregulation by the executive branch. The stamp of elite power in the struggle over a New Federalism can be seen in the economic spheres of trade legislation, tax and banking laws, and other areas.

With the return of the Democrats to the White House in 1993, the uncertain path of a New Federalism took yet another turn. Bill Clinton promised more state power and more money to run programs. Opponents argued immediately that the national budget crisis would not make that path of federalism possible. And so, the struggle to define a New Federalism goes on.

Congress virtually halted the merging of categorical grants into block grants after that. Still, the number of categorical grants had been reduced from a 1960s high of over seven hundred to slightly over four hundred following the Nixon and Reagan years.

Running into resistance from Congress on converting more categorical grants into block grants, President Reagan attempted to eliminate wasteful and troublesome bureaucracies entirely. The comparatively new departments of Energy and Education (created in 1977 and 1979 under President Carter) were targeted for liquidation. It turned out to be impossible to just lay off tens of thousands of career civil servants whose jobs are secured through lifetime employment contracts. Neither Congress nor the bureaucrats cooperated politically with this idea. For a time it appeared that Mr. Reagan and his vision of a New Federalism might be on the ropes.

In one of the most clever rounds of the fight, the team in the Reagan corner came up with the idea of a trade. The national government would send a whole bundle of social welfare programs to the states C.O.D., meaning the states could do whatever they wanted with them, including paying all costs. In exchange, the national government would take over the costs of medical care for the poor and the elderly. It was to be a clean separation, with the national government running one set of programs, and the state governments another. However, many state governments and members of Congress were now wary of the idea of trading more political control for less money. What, they asked, if some state governments just stopped funding their social welfare programs entirely? The idea was rejected, and Mr. Reagan's vision of a New Federalism was blocked again.

So much for attempts at fancy footwork to eliminate bureaucrats and clever combinations of block grants and program swaps. The Reagan team, and later the Bush administration, returned to slow and steady cuts each year in the growth rate of the national budget for state programs. Table 4.3 illustrates some of the shifts in budgeting that took place between the first budget that Ronald Reagan inherited in 1981 and the budget proposed by the Bush administration ten years later, in 1991.

The New Federalists reasoned that state governments would *have* to become more independent if they received less money from Washington. Many members of Congress found this reasoning flawed, because many states had become so dependent on federal funds that they faced bankruptcy without national funding for many programs. However, the national government also faced a grim budget problem, and the national debt was soaring. An easy place to cut was aid to the states. The result was that Congress went along with many of the proposed cuts, resulting in a dramatic change in the politics and economics of the nation's social policies.

When Bill Clinton came to Washington in 1993, many of his proposals sounded like earlier plans to trade programs between state and national governments in order to simplify the lines of governmental control. However, Clinton promised to send money to the states along with the programs they inherited. A New Federalism that would give state governments both power and money appealed to many state officials, but left economists (and taxpayers) wondering where the money would come from.

THE NEW POLITICAL ECONOMY OF FEDERALISM.   In the early years of New Federalism, the implications of combining block grants with large spending cuts were not clear. People on all sides began playing politics with the national budget. The amount of federal aid to states actually increased somewhat from 1980–1990, leading supporters of Reagan's New Federalism to minimize the economic hardship on the states. However, the *growth rate* of federal aid to states slowed dramatically, as shown in Table 4.4. The picture becomes even sharper when we control for inflation during those

TABLE 4.3

The Evolution of New Federalism: The Critical Decade (1980–1990)— The Changing Philosophy of Federal Spending

FEDERAL PROGRAM	1981[*]	1991[**]
Community Development block grants	$5.7 billion	$2.7 billion
Urban mass transit	$5.4 billion	$2.5 billion
Employment and training	$8.4 billion	$3.75 billion
Economic Development Administration	$570 million	$0
Clean water construction grants	$5.4 billion	$1.6 billion

*Budget inherited by Ronald Reagan from the Carter administration.
**Budget proposed by the Bush administration.
SOURCE: United States Conference of Mayors, Advisory Council Report, 1990.

In this 1982 photograph, workers check the contents of storage drums that have accumulated over the past decade at a Chem-Dyne hazardous-waste storage site in Ohio. Among the most hotly debated issues of federalism is which government—national or state—bears responsibility for managing "cooperative" programs and enforcing regulations. When in the 1980s, as part of the New Federalism, the Reagan administration tried to shift the focus of federal power, some states used the opportunity to relax or curb their individual programs.

TABLE 4.4

Evolution of the New Federalism: Federal Aid to State Governments, 1950–1990

YEAR	BILLIONS OF DOLLARS	GROWTH RATE (%)
1950	2.3	
1960	7.0	200
1970	24.0	242
1980	91.5	281
1990	122.0	33[*]

[*]Represents a 13 percent decrease after inflation.

SOURCE: Advisory Commission on Intergovernmental Relations, *Significant Features of Fiscal Federalism*, Vol. II, 1991. *Historical Tables, Budget of the United States Government, Fiscal Year 1992*, U.S. Office of Management and Budget.

years, and see that federal funding to state programs in effect fell by 13 percent.[24] There were sharp decreases in both the percentage of the federal budget spent on grants to the states and the percentage of state budget money funneled from the national government.[25] These trends are shown in Figure 4.2.

All of these changes hit state governments at a time of economic recession in the late 1980s and early 1990s, meaning that state revenues from sales taxes and business taxes were also declining. More than half the state governments faced financial emergencies. Budget shortfalls had to be made up through either higher taxes (which angered voters and caused further recession), or drastic budget cuts (which reduced the availability of state services in such areas as health, education, and welfare). These economics set in motion a scramble at the state level to try to restore programs through national funding. State governments increasingly became active with and against each other in the *horizontal* power pattern described earlier as a checkerboard cake or picket fence.

The open question for the 1990s remains how states can manage complex problems with less money, in the face of a national government with a paralyzing budget crisis. Another serious unresolved issue is that, despite the rhetoric of greater state power and less national government regulation, there was little or no decrease in the number of regulations imposed on the states. How was this possible? The answer is that the national government has turned out to be very selective in its deregulation, aiming mainly at economic targets and cutting particular budget categories. Strange as it sounds, at the same time that economic regulations were suspended, and particular budgets were being cut, many other kinds of federal regulations binding states to national guidelines actually increased. Figure 4.3 shows the general increase in national laws superseding state authority, with only a modest decline in the key decade of the 1980s.

FIGURE 4.2

Evolution of the New Federalism: The Critical Decade (1980–1990)— Federal Aid to the States

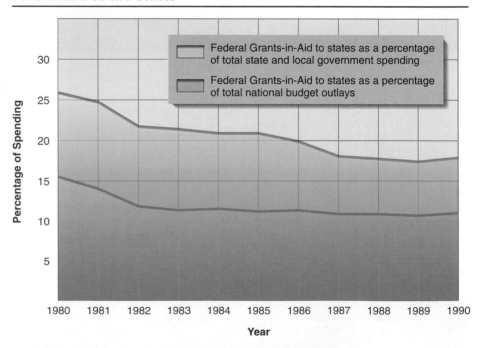

SOURCE: U.S. Advisory Commission on Intergovernmental Relations.

FIGURE 4.3

Where the National Government Overrides or Mandates State Authority

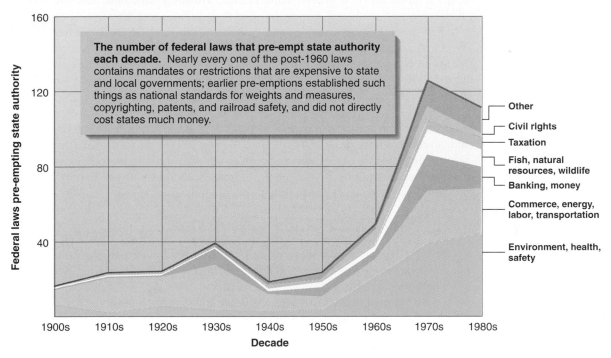

The number of federal laws that pre-empt state authority each decade. Nearly every one of the post-1960 laws contains mandates or restrictions that are expensive to state and local governments; earlier pre-emptions established such things as national standards for weights and measures, copyrighting, patents, and railroad safety, and did not directly cost states much money.

Legend (top to bottom): Other; Civil rights; Taxation; Fish, natural resources, wildlife; Banking, money; Commerce, energy, labor, transportation; Environment, health, safety

Y-axis: Federal laws pre-empting state authority. X-axis: Decade (1900s–1980s)

SOURCE: U.S. Advisory Commission on Intergovernmental Relations–1992 estimate. Reprinted in *The New York Times,* March 24, 1992.

THE NEW REGULATION GAME.   Congress and the executive branch have many ways of reaching into state governments to prevent, adjust, or otherwise force particular kinds of behaviors. For example, states can be *ordered* to do things like not dump sewage into oceans. Then, again, states can be *required* to do things (like not discriminate) if they want to participate in other federal programs and receive the related money. Thus, states that discriminate in school admissions or give more money to men's than women's athletic programs may find themselves threatened with being cut out of other federal programs. And when the national government really decides to play rough, it can effectively blackmail states by threatening to withhold money for one thing unless they do something else in return. The bureaucratic term for this is a *crossover sanction.* A textbook case was provided by the earlier example of Ronald Reagan's threat to withhold highway funds from states unless they raised the minimum drinking age to 21 years.

Trying to regulate the drinking age through national authority illustrates what is perhaps the main confusion associated with the evolution of a New Federalism. On the one hand, states have been encouraged to do more with less, and dramatic levels of deregulation occurred in selected social and economic programs. On the other hand, interest groups and national politicians promoting specific causes (such as reducing drunk driving), have all learned how to pull regulatory strings in Congress and the bureaucracy to impose their will on the states. (Chapter 15 explores the politics within the bureaucracy further.) At the same time that many politicians are talking about restoring states' rights and powers, they may be quietly pushing new regulatory statutes on already hard-pressed states.

Another favorite national power tool involved in this struggle is a regulatory statute called a **preemption.** Preemptive statutes simply instruct states to carry out federal wishes by prohibiting (or preempting) existing state practices that go against the federal goals. It turns out that **orders, requirements, crossover sanctions,** and *preemptive statutes* were on the rise all during the years that cutbacks and "creative deregulation" captured the headlines in news stories like those mentioned at the beginning of this chapter. According to one study, a total of 354 preemptive statutes were written during the entire two hundred years from 1789 to 1989 (the end of Ronald Reagan's presidency). Fully 95 of those came during the Reagan years, and more than half of all the preemptive statutes in history came after Richard Nixon heralded the era of New Federalism in 1972.[26]

It appears that as the old system of cooperative power began to decay, interest groups and government factions began to rush into the new power vacuums to save or promote favorite programs. In other cases, political leaders who were determined to shrink the national government may have taken the dubious method of lifting regulatory burdens off the federal bureaucracy and putting them onto the states.

Why Federalism Matters Revisited

The future of federalism will affect not only how society's complex problems are solved, but how well those solutions work. The reasons for creating a state-centered New Federalism have been consistent since the days of Richard Nixon and Ronald Reagan. George Bush, who followed in their footsteps, explained it this way: "It moves power and decision-making closer to the people. And it reinforces a theme of this administration: appreciation and encouragement of the innovative power of 'States as Laboratories'."[27]

State officials often applaud these ideals, but object to the cutting of aid to states and cities that occurred as a result. Democratic mayor Raymond Flynn of Boston denounced New Federalism as "an assault on America's cities."[28] Speaker of the House Thomas Foley (also a Democrat) expressed his own view of the New Federalism: "It's very easy to say that [state governments] are closer to the people. . . . I mean, that's sort of a warm thought, but it isn't our practical experience."[29]

Beyond the lofty arguments about national supremacy and states' rights is a world of politics involving particular groups and very specific issues. However, the broad power arrangements operating between the national and state governments affect how these specific conflicts can be worked out. If Bill Clinton's own promise of a New Federalism succeeds in turning over more responsibilities *and* more money to the states, the best case for the future may be greater experimentation in the fifty state "laboratories." With creative federal funding for the nation's cities, new ideas might spring from the thousands of local governments that often receive considerable license from their states to experiment, as explained below. However, if funding for states and cities remains in jeopardy, the worst-case scenario may be a growing difference in living conditions in the fifty states and thousands of communities across the land.

State Experimentation

The greatest strength of federalism has always been the room it provides for states to experiment and innovate. The most progressive states are often ahead of the national government in creative solutions to common problems. If a New Federalism is to result in a more workable system of federal power, the answers may lie with the states. Among the innovations that seem to be helping states do more with less are the following:

- State lotteries that raise substantial amounts of "nontax" revenue to pay for a variety of programs, from education to the environment.

Whither the Welfare State?

The concept of a federal "safety net" for citizens began with FDR's New Deal, but grew tremendously with Lyndon Johnson's "Great Society" programs. At right, Johnson signs, in 1964, a "War on Poverty" bill that eventually cost some $950 billion. Below, a bureaucrat presents a mother and daughter with newly issued "Medicare" insurance cards. Yet by the 1980s, neoconservative theorists such as Charles Murray (in his book *Losing Ground*) argued that at least some federal programs perpetuated the social ills they were meant to cure. Above, California governor Pete Wilson and Texas governor Ann Richards sit in on a 1991 discussion of innovative health-care ideas at the state level. Recent studies have found that often over half of a typical state budget is set aside for programs required by—but not funded by—the national government.

The Players

New Yorker Pasquale Consalvo talks to the media after winning $30 million in the state lottery in 1986. Critics argue that such lotteries (which are increasingly common throughout the country) act in effect as a regressive tax, exploiting the poor and ill-informed, who play them against staggering odds. Such games are, however, among the many innovative measures state governments have adopted of late to meet budgeting demands.

- State branch offices in foreign countries to attract new international business to the states. (A recent count showed forty-one states with offices in twenty-four countries.)
- More aggressive state environmental programs paid for by polluters.
- Partnerships with private business to build housing for elderly and low-income residents.
- More effective lobbying in Washington to get state views represented. (Recall the seventy-plus branch offices that the state of California maintains in the national capital.)
- Coordinated publicity efforts to get state government views into national news stories.[30] The states are finally beginning to make their own headlines, which should help in defining the national debates over federalism in the future.

Local Governments Take the Lead

Another great strength of American federalism is the tradition of strong local government. The word *tradition* is important here. After reading the Constitution, you may have noticed that *nowhere* does it mention specific powers for any level of government below the states—not for counties, municipalities, school districts, or townships. Indeed, the Constitution gave the states power to *create* local governments. Since cities came before states in the scheme of American development, it was often the case that cities were better developed, richer, and politically more sophisticated than many of the states that legally controlled them. As a result, most states have followed a tradition of **home rule,** in which cities and other units of local government are sometimes granted as much (informal) autonomy by states as states are given formal autonomy by the Constitution. The most positive result of home rule is broad experimentation with many different approaches to solving problems. A tour of America's cities reveals a great diversity of approaches to dealing with problems of drugs, crime, public health, economic development, race relations, environment, education, and even world trade. As many observers have noted, the strength (and wealth) of a nation lies in the strength of its cities. Metropolitan areas are centers of culture, trade, tourism, manufacturing, and learning. The constitutional protection of state powers has allowed states, in turn, to extend many informal powers to their cities.

Many important activities are conducted with considerable autonomy and great diversity at the local level: solving environmental problems, running airports, operating schools, regulating gambling, creating good business environments through enterprise zones, and running health-care systems, among others. Health-care systems in Hawaii and Oregon have stimulated considerable debate as possible national models, as has a city health program in Rochester, New York. What about states and cities opening branch offices in foreign countries? Why not? What level of government is better suited to develop trading relations than the states and cities in which goods are produced and sold? If there is any area in which the cutbacks in cooperative federalism are likely to produce positive results, it is in the increased incentives for states and cities to innovate.[31]

The Problem of Growing Inequalities

In contrast to the best-case scenarios outlined above, there is a more pessimistic possibility that some states will become disadvantaged because they lack both the resources and political leadership to tackle complex problems. The "do more with less" philosophy of a New Federalism may magnify the troubles of already struggling states and cities. Although state-to-state inequalities are less severe today than during most of the dual federalism era, substantial gaps in the quality of public life are pulling at the states and cities at this critical juncture of federalism.

Getting a handle on state-by-state inequalities is not easy, but some features are hard to miss. Consider, for example, the case of Alabama, as described by the author of a history of poverty in that state:

> Almost a fifth of the citizens have no basic health insurance and 4 percent have no running water. Birmingham, home of the state's only medical school and its best hospital, has an infant mortality rate rivaling that of many third world countries. . . Alabama ranks 43rd among the states in per capita income, and 21 percent of its citizens exist below the Federal poverty level of $12,700 for a family of four.[32]

What was the response to these statistics from the governor of Alabama at the time? Newspaper accounts quoted him as saying: "What we need to remember, in many countries that would be called a rich life."[33]

Conditions like those noted above exist in a number of states and localities, and they often reflect political choices on the part of elected officials. Consider, for example, two facts about how the state of Alabama raises revenues. Poor people in Alabama pay more in taxes relative to what they get in public services than residents of any other state in the Union. Meanwhile, companies and wealthy individuals pay lower taxes in Alabama than just about anywhere else in the nation. For example, the Kimberly-Clark company owns a large tract of timberland that runs across the Alabama-Georgia border. On the Georgia side, the company pays over $4 an acre in state taxes. On the Alabama side, the state tax bill per acre is less than $1.[34]

The national government cannot do much to order states to set up more equitable tax systems, nor can it affect most decisions about how a state government spends the money of its citizens. Indeed, many states' rights advocates argue vehemently that the national government should not worry about life inside the states. However, there may be something to worry about if states that were barely meeting the basic needs of many

A CITIZEN'S QUESTION
State and National Citizenship

What does it mean to be a citizen of a particular state? Every American is both a citizen of the United States and of the state in which he or she lives. Think about how many aspects of your legal identity and responsibility are wrapped up in state citizenship. The average person has many forms of identification: a driver's license, a voter registration card, a Social Security card, and a birth certificate, among others. The most important of these proofs of legal identity are state documents. Citizenship is more than just a matter of identification, of course. Indeed, many of the activities of everyday life are governed by state laws. It might be useful to make a list of the areas of personal life that are affected primarily by state citizenship, primarily by national citizenship, and those where both state (and local) and national authority come into play.

In addition to defining various state and national obligations of citizenship, federalism also defines where the government becomes involved in many very personal decisions. Many struggles over federal powers have involved issues that directly affect individual life quality: the chances for getting a good education, the quality of health care, treatment on the job, basic freedoms of political expression, and even the age at which people can drink and the speeds at which they can drive. Pick an area that matters to you personally, and see if you can locate the parts of the national, state, and local governments involved in making the laws and regulations that affect you. Is your state following national guidelines, resisting them, or setting the national pace with creative solutions to the problem?

How can you become more involved in this issue? Understanding how the federal division of power works in this case is a good place to start. State and city governments are often the most accessible places for citizens to make their concerns heard. It is possible to go to a city council session, a neighborhood development meeting, or an environmental committee hearing at the state capital, and become a part of the action. State and local politics are generally open to people with a little time, a good idea, and the political insight about how to promote it. Where would you go to promote your ideas?

---

citizens during the era of cooperative federalism inherit even more responsibilities under new federal arrangements. Political scientists who study federalism suggest that the best hope for the future is to find ways to divide basic responsibilities more cleanly between states and the national government and to make sure states have the money to carry out their part of the bargain.[35] Which future will it be? This is the political challenge ahead for the New Federalism

Key Terms

federalism, federal system

unitary system

McCulloch v. Maryland

Dred Scott v. Sanford

Gibbons v. Ogden

state-centered view of constitutional powers

nation-centered view of constitutional powers

nullification

laissez-faire

dual federalism

cooperative federalism

New Federalism

block grant

categorical grant

revenue sharing

sanctions—orders—requirements—preemptions

home rule

states and cities as experimental laboratories

Suggested Readings

Anton, Thomas J. *American Federalism and Public Policy,* Philadelphia: Temple University Press, 1989.

Grodzins, Morton. *The American System,* Chicago: Rand McNally, 1974.

Leach, Richard H. *American Federalism,* New York: Norton, 1970.

Nathan, Richard P. and Fred C. Doolittle, *Reagan and the States,* Princeton: Princeton University Press, 1987.

Peterson, Paul E., Barry G. Rabe, and Kenneth K. Wong, *When Federalism Works,* Washington D.C.: Brookings Institution, 1986.

• • •

"I am sick and tired of marijuana-planting, dope-smoking hippies burning the American flag."
—JAMES DAVID CAIN, LOUISIANA STATE REPRESENTATIVE

• • •

"It's tough being black in America. I'm at the top, but not a day goes by without somebody reminding me in some way that I am black."
—JOHN H. JOHNSON, OWNER OF *Ebony* AND *Jet* MAGAZINES

• • •

"I do not believe that the meaning of the Constitution was forever 'fixed' at the Philadelphia Convention. Nor do I find the wisdom, foresight, and sense of justice exhibited by the Framers particularly profound. . . . When contemporary Americans cite 'The Constitution,' they invoke a concept that is vastly different from what the Framers barely began to construct two centuries ago."
—THURGOOD MARSHALL

• • •

"Liberty is the right to do what the laws permit."
—MONTESQUIEU

• • •

The Personal Constitution: Civil Liberties and Civil Rights

- **THE NEWS ABOUT HARASSMENT**
- **THE POLITICS OF RIGHTS**
  How Americans Think About Rights
  A Political Culture Based on Rights
- **CLARIFYING THE CONCEPTS: CIVIL LIBERTIES AND CIVIL RIGHTS**
  The American Rights Tradition
  A Working Definition of Liberties and Rights
- **CIVIL LIBERTIES**
  Dual Citizenship
  Freedom of Speech and the First Amendment
  Freedom of Religion
  Freedom from Injustice
  The Right to Privacy
  The Civil Liberties Scorecard
- **CIVIL RIGHTS**
  A Second American Revolution
  The Civil Rights Movement
  Expanding the Definition of Civil Rights
  The Difficulty of Righting Social Wrongs
- **THE POLITICS OF RIGHTS REVISITED**
- **A CITIZEN'S QUESTION: Rights**
- **KEY TERMS**
- **SUGGESTED READINGS**

The News About Harassment

It has become increasingly common to hear about the problem of harassment: women being harassed on the job by male co-workers and bosses; female students harassed by their male teachers; Navy women at an aviators' convention being attacked and humiliated by male pilots, and black students on a number of college campuses subjected to degrading treatment by white students. Such incidents are not new, but their increasing appearance in the news suggests that society has become more aware of them, and people are more willing to explore their political significance.

Probably the most dramatic—and controversial—of these stories was the Senate testimony in the autumn of 1991 by Anita Hill, a law professor at the University of Oklahoma. Professor Hill made headlines when she testified at the Senate hearings on the nomination of Judge Clarence Thomas to the Supreme Court. She alleged that when she had worked for Thomas in two government posts a decade earlier in their careers, he had made sexual advances and used language that made her uncomfortable to the point of having to take time off work and worry about her job—a claim which Judge Thomas flatly denied. Thomas was confirmed by the Senate, but the general topic of sexual harassment continued to make the news. As the story worked its way through society from talk shows to dinner-table conversations, people began to express greater concern about the problem. Some observers said that, whatever the facts were in the Hill-Thomas case, it helped to launch the so-called "Year of the Woman" in American politics, which saw many women candidates compete for and win public office in 1992.[1]

What makes these news stories worth following and the political questions worth talking and voting about is the growing recognition that fundamental individual rights are at stake. Few things are more important to people than their sense of what kind of treatment they are entitled to in society. The harassment question signals an impor-

tant social change, as people who have long experienced treatment they regard as degrading and uncomfortable begin to assert their feelings politically.

As with many sensitive areas of social life, from the protection of private property to freedom of

In October 1991, only days before the Senate was set to vote on Supreme Court nominee Clarence Thomas, Anita Hill appeared before its Judiciary Committee and alleged that Thomas had sexually harassed her a decade earlier. After investigating the claim—which the judge flatly denied—the Senate confirmed Thomas's appointment by a 52–48 vote. However, Hill's accusation did raise in the public mind the broader question of harassment as a civil-rights issue.

speech, political concerns about harassment often take the form of claims that people have certain *rights*. Freedom from harassment involves the right not to be treated in coercive, humiliating, or degrading ways. On the other side of the conflict are those who argue that their words or behaviors were not intimidating and that complaints about "harassment" deprive people of their own fundamental right to free expression.

Where should the line be drawn? What constitutes a right for one person, and when does that right begin to take away the rights of someone else? How are these issues worked out in the political system? These are some of the questions discussed in this chapter. Consider just two typical cases that have made the news and that illustrate why these conflicts over rights are difficult to work out both socially and constitutionally.

A headline proclaimed: U.S. JUDGE UPHOLDS SPEECH ON CAMPUS.[2] The case involved a decision by the administration of George Mason University in Fairfax, Virginia, to suspend a fraternity that staged an "ugly woman" contest which included one mock contestant who was a white man in drag wearing blackface. Although potentially offensive to various groups, the contest drew a letter of complaint to the university president from a group of minority students who were in the school cafeteria when the unflattering racial portrayal was, in their view, inflicted upon them.

Racial tensions on campus increased even though the fraternity apologized, and the president finally suspended members of the fraternity from participating officially in campus activities for two years. The fraternity convinced a lawyer from the Northern Virginia chapter of the American Civil Liberties Union to represent them in a civil suit in federal court to overturn the suspension as a violation of their First Amendment free speech rights. Although the lawyer also found the contest offensive and inappropriate, he argued that the freedom of speech issue was more important. Federal Judge Claude M. Hilton of the U.S. District Court for the Eastern District of Virginia agreed with him, issuing a ruling that said "The skit contained more than a kernel of expression, therefore the activity demands First Amendment protection." That ruling was upheld on appeal. What do you think? Should someone's "right" to be "protected" from offensive speech be as strong as other individuals' rights to act and speak? If this question does not seem challenging enough, consider another case that divided even the lawyers of the American Civil Liberties Union.

The headline read: HARASSMENT, FREE SPEECH COLLIDE IN FLORIDA.[3] The story describes a conflict between male and female workers at a Florida shipyard. Women objected to working in an environment that included pinup calendars and nude photos, and in which men routinely used sexual language in the presence of women employees, making statements like "I'd like to get in bed with that," and "Hey, pussycat, come here." One woman, represented by the National Organization for Women's Legal Defense Fund, argued in federal court that these aspects of life at the shipyard violated a federal law against

harassment. In the case of *Robinson v. Jacksonville Shipyards*, U.S. Judge Howell Melton ruled that the men's behavior violated Title VII of the U.S. Civil Rights Act, a law that, among other things, permits the government to "punish or ban speech that creates 'a hostile environment' for women at work."[4] The judge ordered the shipyard to make its employees take down the pictures and stop using offensive speech.

The case did not stop there, however, as the shipyard and some of its male workers appealed on grounds that the ruling, along with the law in question, violated First Amendment guarantees of free speech. As the appeal worked its way toward the Supreme Court, even the American Civil Liberties Union became divided on the question of which principle of rights (free speech or freedom from harassment) should be more dominant in the situation. The national office of the ACLU agreed with the argument of the National Organization of Women that all speech (blackmail and extortion, for example) is not protected by the First Amendment, and the male workers' behavior should not be protected either. Meanwhile, the executive director of the Florida chapter of the ACLU, Robyn Blumner, called the federal court ruling "a flagrant violation of the First Amendment. Just because an employee is offended by a message doesn't mean it is illegal."[5]

This case raised the possibility that if the appeal reached the Supreme Court, different branches of the ACLU might write briefs for the opposing sides, illustrating the difficult problem of resolving rights in conflict.

These examples suggest a useful perspective for learning the material in this chapter. It is clear that rights are often in conflict in society, and those conflicts can create serious legal problems as they move from social settings into the court system. Do not assume that there are clear, easy answers to questions about rights just waiting in the Constitution to be discovered. Instead of expecting to find prepackaged constitutional answers, think of the Constitution and the legal methods for answering questions about rights as parts of an ongoing process of political conflict and change.

It is also important to remember that the idea of rights is applied to very personal issues and conflicts. When it comes to civil liberties and civil rights, the Constitution is the individual citizen's most personal political resource. This personal approach also helps to keep the focus on the practical uses of rights, as discussed at the end of this chapter. Learning how other people have used claims about rights to change their lives in society is the best way to figure out how to do the same.

The Politics of Rights

The idea of rights makes the Constitution a personal document—one that gives individuals a meaningful everyday source of political power. Laws and the rulings of courts affect people directly and indirectly from the bedroom to the boardroom. Public opinion is often divided over questions involving the rights of homosexuals, the right to develop private property in "environmentally sensitive" areas, and the right to speak freely about religion or politics at work.

The law and public opinion are not always in agreement, of course, nor would we always want them to be. However, because of public debates and conflicts, many rights that were barely imaginable in earlier times are considered fundamental today. The point is that rights evolve and change. The changes are guided by laws and a constitutional framework. Political conflicts over rights touch many people deeply, making Americans able to talk about and claim their rights in often inventive ways.

How Americans Think About Rights

It may be tempting to think of Americans as only dimly aware of their rights. Polls cited frequently in the news seem to indicate shocking ignorance. For example, an American Bar Association poll in 1991 found that only 33 percent of the respondents in a national survey correctly identified the Bill of Rights as the first ten amendments to the

For many, the Bill of Rights (especially in its guarantee of the four freedoms of speech, worship, assembly, and the press) is a uniquely American cultural ideal. This 1941 drawing celebrated the Bill's hundred-and-fiftieth anniversary at a moment when, as President Franklin Roosevelt observed, the United States was faced on one side with "Nazi tyranny" and on the other with "the Soviet Union . . . a dictatorship as absolute as any other dictatorship in the world." Ironically, those wartime threats led, for a time, to laws restricting political speech at home.

Constitution. The same survey also found that only 54 percent of the respondents opposed searching a drug suspect's home without a search warrant, suggesting a fairly high level of disagreement with an established (Fourth Amendment) provision of the Bill of Rights.[6] What should we make of these poll results?

It would be preferable, of course, for more citizens to have a better factual grasp of their government and to be able to correctly identify the Bill of Rights. However, what about those who support police searches without warrants? Are they wrong in the same factual sense as those who could not pass an easy identification question on an "Introduction to Government" test? Before making an easy judgment about this, remember that political controversy has created turmoil around the application of various provisions of the Bill of Rights throughout our history, including disagreements among politicians, legislators, and judges who know the law inside and out. Members of the current Supreme Court have even disagreed recently about some aspects of police searches and the rules for obtaining evidence.

Although they are not legal scholars, many average citizens do struggle with problems of how to define and apply these rights. Allowing for differences in language and legal reasoning, many of the issues that divide the general public are similar to those that divide lawyers and politicians.

Consider, in this regard, a study by political scientist John Gilliom who surveyed members of a large industrial union who faced the issue of mandatory, or involuntary, drug testing in their workplaces. The reactions of these workers suggested that ideas about rights figured in their thinking about whether employers or the government should be able to demand that workers be tested for drugs on the job. Many of those among the 819 workers surveyed opposed drug testing primarily on grounds that their rights to privacy and protections against unwarranted search and seizure were more important than any other consideration. Even those who favored drug testing often took these rights into account, weighing them against what they considered to be larger social values such as safety in the workplace and the need to do more to control the national drug crisis.[7]

A Political Culture Based on Rights

In establishing their rights, people are struggling over such basic cultural values as freedom, equality, and social order. The politics of rights can touch virtually every area of life that matters to people: religion, political beliefs, protection from government intimidation, protection of personal property, and sexual practices, just to name a few. People express their demands about these rights by using virtually every core theme of the political culture outlined in Chapter 1: liberty, equality, patriotism, limiting the powers of government, and the need to preserve social order.

For example, the harassment cases described earlier involve the enduring cultural tension over how much individual *freedom* of expression can be tolerated before damaging the rights of others to receive *equality* of treatment in society. In the above study of workers' attitudes about drug testing, we see people making difficult cultural choices among *individual freedom*, *protection from government* intrusion in their lives, and the need to maintain *social order*, beginning with safety in the workplace. The cultural themes expressed by those workers in thinking about their rights are illustrated in "Inside the System" Box 5.1.

Considering how deeply conflicts over rights can touch the everyday lives of individuals and how often they trigger explosive divisions in the political culture, it is not surprising that the politics of rights is often intense. What may be more surprising is that over the last seventy-five years there have been so many relatively enduring agreements reached about how to define and protect various rights and liberties. The rest of this chapter explores these evolving political definitions of liberties and rights.

Clarifying the Concepts: Civil Liberties and Civil Rights

As should be clear by now, the creation of rights is an evolving political process.[8] Before they become written into law, claims about rights begin as moral and philosophical arguments. The Founders adopted ideas of such European philosophers as Locke who discussed **natural rights** of individual freedom and the protection of private property. Those were nothing short of revolutionary ideas in an earlier age shaped by philosophies of *divine* rights, meaning that monarchs claimed God-given rights that were superior to those of all other people.

In recent years, there has been a worldwide movement for "human rights" based on another broad natural rights claim: all people have the basic right to be free from the oppression and torture inflicted upon them by brutal governments of any ideological type. In most countries, these claims about rights are staked as moral arguments without formal legal backing. However, political pressures behind those claims can get oppressive governments to change. In most nations, the struggle for rights has been long and painful because every protection sought by one group in society may be resisted as a loss of power or privilege by another.

Cultural Themes and Personal Views of Rights

Americans may not always recognize the formal legal basis of rights and liberties, but they understand the cultural values and conflicts that underlie many disputes over rights. The trade-offs between the cultural themes of *freedom* and *order*, for example, are evident in the responses of 819 workers asked about their attitudes towards mandatory drug testing on the job. For those who opposed testing (roughly 44 percent), the dominant reason given was the preservation of constitutionally protected *freedoms*, broadly defined to include privacy and protection from false legal charges. Here are some typical responses:

"This is America! *The* country where a person is innocent until proven guilty in a court of law only after charges are filed. What happened to due process?"

"I strongly oppose drug testing because it invades my privacy."

"It is an invasion of privacy, unconstitutional and an o.k. to open the door to true programming of people and their private lives."

"My urine is my biz."

For those (roughly 45 percent) who were in favor of testing, there were frequent mentions of freedoms and rights, but the balance came down on the side of *social order*, often in the form of concerns about safety on the job, or the need to control the larger drug problem in society. Similar trade-offs often appear in court opinions about civil liberties:

"I know mandatory testing would violate my civil rights. Yet as dangerous as this trade can be, can we afford to let alcohol and drug abusers work side by side with us?"

"I have some real reservations about drug testing on constitutional grounds. I also have an awareness of the seriousness of the drug problem in the U.S.A."

"I do not feel like being killed by some doper."

"I feel that drugs are undermining the United States. I feel that people buying drugs should be dealt with just like the pushers. I feel that drug testing will keep people from using drugs. If you don't have a job you can't buy drugs."

SOURCE: John Gilliom, Ohio University, with permission. See also, Gilliom, "Rights and Discipline," *Polity*, Summer 1992.

The American Rights Tradition

In the American tradition, rights are central to the political culture and the daily politics of the nation. Both the language and the politics of rights in this country can be traced to a larger Anglo-American tradition of written rights that began with Magna Carta, protecting English nobles from arbitrary taxation by the king. (Recall the discussion from Chapter 2.) This tradition is now almost eight hundred years old. From that beginning, the sphere of rights slowly expanded far beyond the landed nobility. As more people demanded and won *the rights of citizenship*, the areas of protected freedom grew to include the freedom of speech, religion, assembly, press, bearing arms, and protection for households against unwarranted searches and the quartering of troops, among others. These lists of protections and freedoms evolved through a succession of formal documents, including the Bill of Rights and subsequent amendments to the Constitution. The constitutions of a number of states, along with many statutes (laws) written by the states and Congress, are also part of this tradition of rights.

The American tradition has carried the *written* constitutional protection of rights farther than England. As noted in Chapter 3, England does not have a formal written constitution. Although there is a strong tradition of rights for English citizens, the absence of a written constitution with a Bill of Rights attached means that the government can pass laws that would strike many Americans as violations of their basic rights. (See "How We Compare" Box 5.2.)

A Working Definition of Liberties and Rights

In the early days, rights were used mainly to limit or restrain governments from acting in ways that interfered with individual freedoms or liberties. *Thus, what we commonly call* **civil liberties** *are spheres of personal freedom protected by (rights claims aimed at) restraining the government.* The idea is that a *limited government* is the best guarantee of individual freedom. This traditional definition of government restraint has been used successfully to create basic spheres of freedom for speech, religion, press, assembly, fairness in criminal justice procedures, and the emerging area of individual privacy.

As society became more diverse and new groups were given equal rights of citizenship (under the Fourteenth Amendment), it began to be argued that the traditional idea of "passive government" was often not enough to make people full and equal citizens. The last few decades have witnessed the development of the notion of requiring the government to take actions to "correct" threats to freedom and equality that do not go away on their own.

For example, when blacks and women were granted equal citizenship by amending the Constitution (see the Thirteenth, Fourteenth, Fifteenth, and Nineteenth Amendments), many of them discovered that society was still discriminating against them. A passive "civil liberties" role of government did little or nothing to immediately change the way in which existing social institutions continued to ignore constitutional guarantees. As a result, a broad movement to expand the political definition of "civil rights" took root in America during the last half of the twentieth century. *In recent years, it has become common to use the term* **civil rights** *to refer to claims calling for government intervention to stop discrimination and secure equal protection under the law for citizens.*

In the discussion that follows, this distinction is generally maintained between civil rights and civil liberties: *"Civil liberties" refers primarily to constitutional freedoms secured by restraining the government. By contrast, "civil rights" refers to constitutional guarantees for all citizens to have equal protection under the law—which often implies government-imposed intervention or sanctions to stop discrimination.*

This convenient distinction between "civil liberties" and "civil rights" can be a bit confusing because most of what we call liberties are contained in a document called the **Bill of Rights**. Indeed, most legal scholars define rights simply as legal claims people make about citizenship guarantees of freedom *or* equality, whether those guarantees are secured through government restraint or government action. However, the strong historical association of the "civil rights" movement with questions of *equality* before the law has made it common for the media and people who are not legal experts to draw the above distinction. The following discussion adopts this popular distinction because it helps to simplify things, but bear in mind that legal scholars might not draw the distinction as clearly.

Civil Liberties

Few things are more central to the American political culture than individual freedom. *Liberty* was the grand inspiration of the Revolution and remains a guiding ideal to this day. Yet few aspects of the Constitution took so long to be put into use as the various provisions in the Bill of Rights. Many states always respected specific rights and liberties of their citizens and wrote bills of rights into state constitutions. However, other states

HOW WE COMPARE

American Civil Liberties: A Comparative Luxury

5.2

Because rights and liberties are such a familiar part of political life, Americans may assume that all or even most other democracies have the same kinds of individual protections. Some democracies do, of course, have an equivalent to the United States Bill of Rights, but may lack an independent judiciary branch or a supreme court to interpret those rights. In those systems, the same parliament or legislature that makes the law also decides on its constitutionality. In the British system, as noted in Chapter 3, there is no formally written constitution and no modern bill of rights.

The long tradition of British *common law* offers citizens some protections in the courts, but those protections do not prevent Parliament from passing specific laws against particular kinds of speech or press activity. In addition, there is no guarantee of rights to prevent the legal system from holding certain prisoners without trial. As one student of British government described this system:

"One could search the Statute Book in vain for acts conferring upon citizens the rights of free speech, freedom of association, or freedom of movement. These rights rest simply on the age-old assumption by British courts that a citizen is free to do as he likes provided he does not commit any specific breach of the law."[*]

What is to hold such laws in check? Strictly speaking, nothing save tradition. However, British courts have protected rights and liberties in cases where legal restrictions on speech and the press seemed too severe.

[*]Anthony H. Birch, *The British System of Government,* London: George Allen & Unwin, 1980, p. 236.

did not have such strong traditions and simply ignored the national Bill of Rights after it was ratified.

The basic obstacle to adopting national standards for civil liberties can be traced to a core aspect of federalism explained in the last chapter: the tremendous independence given to states by the Constitution. As explained in Chapter 4, this has created an historic struggle to get state governments to do things they do not want to do. Perhaps it would have been easier to make wayward states join the civil liberties program if James Madison had been successful in adding language to the Bill of Rights requiring the states to honor its provisions. However, Madison lost that fight when the Bill of Rights was debated in Congress. Some opponents said that the Constitution already contained the necessary language in Article IV, Section 2 granting the citizens of each state the "Privileges and Immunities" of citizens in the other states. As it turned out, however, this **privileges and immunities** clause was not (and never has been) used by the Supreme Court to subordinate state citizenship to national citizenship. The Bill of Rights was left hanging as a somewhat rootless set of protections against *national* abuses of freedoms. States won the most intimate powers to define and regulate the lives of their citizens. And the states have guarded those powers throughout much of American history.

At this point, return briefly to Chapter 3 and read the Bill of Rights again, paying special attention to the language. Notice that the First Amendment opens with the clear signal: "*Congress* shall make no law. . ." It does not say that states cannot violate the freedoms of their citizens. The plot thickens over the next seven amendments outlining the rest of America's basic liberties. They are all written in the passive voice. It does not say who "shall not" violate these freedoms. Perhaps Madison took advantage of poetic license in writing the document to leave a tiny bit of doubt about whether these amendments applied to the states or only to citizens' more distant relationships to the national government. If there was any doubt in the beginning, however, the Supreme Court quickly removed it with constitutional rulings that set up a system of **dual citizenship** to go along with the dual federalism described in Chapter 4. As a result, average people made little headway in their attempts to use the Bill of Rights for well over the first hundred years of the nation's history.

Dual Citizenship

The idea of dual federalism discussed in the last chapter also applied to citizenship. Being cautious not to intrude in state politics, the Supreme Court also avoided applying the Bill of Rights to matters involving citizens and state law until well into the twentieth century. The case of **Barron v. Baltimore** was pivotal in the history of civil liberties because of the precedent it created for establishing a system of dual citizenship. The Supreme Court ruling in *Barron* clarified the responsibility of states to uphold the Bill of Rights: they had none! Mr. Barron sued the city of Baltimore because its street crews dumped material into the water near his dock, making it impossible to use the dock. Barron argued that the city of Baltimore had violated one of his Fifth Amendment rights by depriving him of property without just compensation. When the case reached the Supreme Court in 1833, Chief Justice John Marshall said, in effect, that these questions were matters to be decided by state constitutions and that "the fifth amendment must be understood as restraining the power of the general government, not as applicable to the States."[9]

Following the Civil War, the Fourteenth Amendment granted all citizens equal treatment under the law. Many people thought that this simple addition to the Constitution would remove any doubt about how to apply the Bill of Rights. However, just passing a clarifying amendment to the Constitution was not enough to bring the list of national rights into everyday life in the states. While the Fourteenth Amendment eventually turned out to be the method used to *incorporate* provisions of the Bill of Rights into state life, it took a long time for this to happen.

In 1873, with the intent of the Fourteenth Amendment fresh in mind, the Court heard what were called **The Slaughterhouse Cases**. In something of a replay of *Barron v. Baltimore*, the owners of slaughterhouses in New Orleans complained that a state government monopoly granted to a single slaughterhouse had put all the rest of them out of business, depriving them of their Fifth Amendment rights to property and "just compensation" for being deprived of that property. The slaughterhouse owners argued that the Fourteenth Amendment clearly brought the Bill of Rights into state life. Not so, said the Court, which reasoned that the Fourteenth Amendment was written to protect blacks and thus could not be used to bring a blanket redefinition of state powers to deal with their own citizens.[10] However, you may recall from the last chapter on federalism that the Court later refused to apply the Fourteenth Amendment to protect the rights of blacks. The point is that the politics of the times favored states retaining the basic powers to define relations with their citizens.

Following the Court's decision in *The Slaughterhouse Cases*, the federal courts resisted granting Bill of Rights protections for personal freedom and equality issues for another fifty years. During this time, political pressures built up in society for the Court to begin protecting the freedoms of individuals, particularly the political freedom of speech. At last, beginning in the 1920s, the process of **incorporating** the Bill of Rights into the lives of the states moved slowly forward. The Fourteenth Amendment was ultimately used as intended, to enable various provisions of the Bill of Rights to be brought into state life. The process used by the Court has been called **selective incorporation** because various provisions of the Bill of Rights have been taken up one at a time, and some provisions have not been incorporated at all into our lives. This process of selective incorporation of particular rights is described in more detail in "Inside the System" Box

Incorporating Civil Liberties and Civil Rights into National Life, Selectively

5.3

The Fourteenth Amendment was added to the Constitution to make the laws and protections of that document available to all citizens of the United States, including blacks freed from slavery. However, a strong states' rights view of the Constitution prevailed on the Supreme Court for more than fifty years after the Fourteenth Amendment was ratified. During this time, the amendment was not used as its original supporters intended. Finally, in the 1920s, the Supreme Court began to hear conflicts over free speech as involving provisions in the Bill of Rights that the Fourteenth Amendment justified applying to citizens of the states.

Free speech and other key civil liberties provisions of the Constitution were *incorporated* into state life by using the *due process clause* of the Fourteenth Amendment which says that no state shall "deprive any person of life, liberty, or property without due process of law." Later on, many civil rights guarantees were incorporated through the *equal protection clause* of the same amendment, which says that no state shall deny to any person "within its jurisdiction the equal protection of the laws."

It is said that this incorporation process has been *selective,* meaning that the Court has never felt an obligation to incorporate the entire Bill of Rights into everyday national life. The guideline used to decide what to incorporate in civil liberties cases was developed early in the process by Justice Benjamin Cardozo. In the case of *Palko v. Connecticut* (1937) Cardozo proposed the "test" of *ordered liberty,* which is aimed at selecting only those rights that are so important that "neither liberty nor justice would exist if they were sacrificed." This turns out to be a fairly tough test to pass, as poor Mr. Palko found out. Palko was tried on a first degree murder charge in Connecticut but only con-

victed of second degree murder. The state of Connecticut appealed and tried him again, this time succeeding in getting a first degree conviction. Palko appealed all the way to the Supreme Court on grounds that the second trial violated his Fifth Amendment rights not to be put twice in jeopardy for the same offense. The court agreed that it was a clear case of double jeopardy, but not important enough to warrant activating the Bill of Rights on his behalf. Put simply, the majority of the justices agreed that double jeopardy for Mr. Palko did not shake the foundations of "liberty and justice that lie at the base of our civil and political institutions."[*] And so, Palko was executed. The right to be protected against double jeopardy was eventually incorporated much later in the case of *Benton v. Maryland* (1969).

[*] *Palko v. Connecticut,* 302 U.S. 319 (1937).

5.3. The first provisions of the Bill of Rights to become incorporated involved freedom of speech.

Freedom of Speech and the First Amendment

The United States experienced its first "Red scare" after the Bolsheviks overthrew the Russian provisional government in October 1917. In response, the government in Washington passed the Espionage Act of 1917 and the Sedition Act of 1918 (reminiscent of 1798, when the Alien and Sedition Acts followed the "French scare" of that era). The Sedition Act made it illegal to "attempt to cause insubordination. . . in the military. . . or willfully obstruct the recruiting or enlistment service of the United States."[11]

Charles Schenck was arrested during World War I for handing out pamphlets that encouraged draft resistance. The Supreme Court heard his appeal for protection under the free speech provision of the First Amendment. Since the law involved was a national law, the case did not raise the complicated question of state powers that would come up

Following the Bolshevik coup in Russia in late 1917, many Americans looked with alarm upon a new government that promoted, in the words of the Communist Manifesto, *"forcible overthrow of all existing social conditions." Political activity by U.S. followers of the communist agenda quickly led to a cultural conflict pitting free speech against concerns about social order and national security. Following the arrest, prosecution, and sometimes deportation of thousands of communists, socialists, and labor organizers, the Supreme Court began tilting the cultural balance back toward freedom by extending First Amendment protections.*

later. However, the case did produce an important rule about free speech that would become central to many later cases. The Court was conflicted about the issues raised in the Schenck case. Some justices felt that it was time to do something about the serious government and individual attacks against political speech. Most were concerned about how much free speech could be tolerated when the country was at war.

As often happens under challenging circumstances, a clever justice developed a guideline that has endured to this day in free speech cases. Justice Oliver Wendell Holmes developed the **clear and present danger** test. In the ruling in **Schenck v. United States** (1919), Holmes opined that in normal times what Schenck did could be protected as free speech, but in time of war, those words in those pamphlets created a "clear and present danger" that Congress had the right to prevent. The famous analogy that Holmes offered to illustrate "dangerous" speech was falsely shouting "fire" in a crowded theater and causing people to harm themselves in the resulting stampede.

Although the *clear and present danger test* would eventually allow a broad range of speech to become protected under the First Amendment, the Court's rejection of Schenck's appeal was taken by many in society as authorization to declare open season on radicals. A series of government attacks on dissidents followed shortly thereafter. Union members were arrested, held without charges, and in many cases deported. Under the cover of the war panic, these attacks on unions and other political groups went on for two years.

A chance to begin restoring the *cultural balance* of personal freedom against what many saw as too much political order finally arrived before the court in 1925 with the case of *Gitlow v. New York*. Benjamin Gitlow advocated nothing short of another American revolution and was promptly arrested by the police in New York state. Although the Court once again sacrificed the individual involved (Gitlow's conviction was upheld),

Why Civil Liberties Matter: The Case of John Henry Faulk

5.4

The onset of the Cold War in the late 1940s elevated cultural concerns about patriotism and national security over the value of freedom of expression for many Americans. This political climate was abused by the demagogic senator Joseph McCarthy (1908–1957), who launched a campaign of unproven accusations against numerous individuals, charging them with subversive activities. McCarthy was ultimately censured by his Senate colleagues, who by 1954 came to view his reckless behavior as a blot on the anti-Communist cause. For several years before that, however, mistrust pervaded the political climate. One person who spoke out against it was John Henry Faulk, who might have

become to the 1950s what Will Rogers was to the 1930s: a folksy, down-home comedian who offered homespun political opinions through stories about people he met in his native South. The difference was that Faulk launched his career at the height of the anti-Communist feelings of the 1950s. After Faulk's CBS Radio program "Johnny's Front Porch" achieved national popularity, he made the mistake of running (and being elected) for office in the American Federation of Television and Radio Artists. He openly opposed the networks yielding to pressures from an "anti-communist" group called Aware, whose actions resulted in many people being fired from their jobs in the entertainment industry. Faulk in turn was blacklisted after being named in

an Aware publication as a suspected communist; sponsors withdrew their support for his program, and CBS fired him. Unable to get work anywhere in the industry, he returned to Texas, where he ran a small advertising business. Years later, he won a suit against Aware, but the organization could not pay the damages the jury awarded him. After his name was cleared, Faulk became the subject of a TV "docudrama," and found work on a national television show. But his stand on principle during a period of "hard times" for freedom of speech cost him ten years of hardship and a prominent career.

SOURCE: *The New York Times* article commemorating Faulk's death, April 11, 1990, p. A 17.

---

the majority opinion paved the way for **incorporating** First Amendment protections in future cases involving state laws. At last the Court acknowledged the importance of the Fourteenth Amendment as a bridge between the Bill of Rights and the *states*:

> Freedom of speech and of the press—which are protected by the First Amendment . . . are among the fundamental personal rights and "liberties" protected by the due process clause of the Fourteenth Amendment from impairment by the states.[12]

A few years later, in 1931, the *freedom of the press* provision of the First Amendment was formally incorporated in the case of *Near v. Minnesota*. Mr. Near published a small paper that specialized in anti-Jewish provocations and attacks on politicians. The state government shut it down. When the Supreme Court took the case, it ruled against the idea that states could exercise **prior restraint** of the press through forms of censorship such as shutting down papers. Later court rulings incorporated the freedom of assembly (*DeJonge v. Oregon*, 1937 and *Hague v. CIO*, 1939) and freedom of religion (*Cantwell v. Connecticut*, 1940). The struggles and legal decisions involved in defining freedom of religion are reviewed separately in a later section.

THE CONTINUING STRUGGLE OVER FREE SPEECH.   With the onset of World War II, national security concerns were back. Congress passed another law (the Smith Act) against advocating the overthrow of the government or associating with people who did. After the war, another wave of anti-Communist crackdowns went on, costing hundreds of Americans their jobs, reputations, and freedoms. (See Box 5.4 above.)

During the Vietnam War, the Nixon administration used the Espionage Act of 1918 to order *The New York Times* to stop publishing legally classified documents that raised serious questions about government Vietnam policy and public officials. The *Times* received the classified documents that became known as the "Pentagon Papers" from a source whose security clearance prevented him from making the documents public directly. However, both the source and the newspaper felt that the information contained in those papers revealed that the government had misled the American public about the war. Should government secrecy and security laws protect such deception? The Court eventually ruled that the government did not show that publication of the "Pentagon Papers" was damaging enough to national security to warrant "prior restraint" of publication.

The more recent battles over flag burning illustrate another dimension of the ongoing struggle to define and practice free speech. Those who burn and otherwise desecrate the American flag have always been an unpopular minority in American society, opposed by legislatures and law enforcement officials in many ways. Yet those who burn or desecrate the flag claim that free speech means little if the ultimate symbol of the nation and its politics is off limits to their activities.

During his term in office (1989–1993), President Bush repeatedly called for a constitutional amendment making it illegal to desecrate the chief national symbol. Amending the Constitution is not something that Congress is eager to do, however, for reasons discussed in Chapter 3. At the same time, many members of Congress sensed strong public support for protecting the flag and passed a law called the Flag Protection Act of 1989.

The flag protection law quickly triggered another round of flag-burning protests around the country, many of which resulted in arrests. Courts in Seattle and the state of Washington were the first to rule that the law should not be enforced because it violated the First Amendment rights of the flag burners. The Supreme Court finally overturned the national statute in *United States v. Eichman* (1990). Although the Eichman ruling was a close decision, its tone was very clear: It is a "bedrock principle underlying the First Amendment . . . that the government may not prohibit the expression of an idea simply because society finds the idea offensive or disagreeable."[13] (See "Inside the System" Box 5.5 for an historical look at conflicts over the chief national symbol.)

The politically incendiary act of flag-burning provokes many Americans, who fail to see it as a defensible exercise of freedom of expression. Disputes over such deeply cherished cultural emblems as the flag (and the pledge of allegiance to it) played a major role in the 1988 presidential election, and the "proper" limits of the First Amendment continue to be debated today at virtually all levels of government.

INSIDE
THE SYSTEM

U.S. Flag: Tussle Over the National Icon

5.5

By E.J. Dionne Jr.
Washington Post Service

To foreigners, there is something downright peculiar about the deep reverence Americans show for their flag, a reverence that has burst into the realm of politics in the battle over a proposed constitutional amendment to ban flag burning.

"At the foreigner's first glance, the steamy and conflicting emotions of the American public and the tortured posturing of politicans over the issue of banning the burning of the Stars and Stripes seemed ludicrously exaggerated," Ian Smiley wrote in The Sunday Telegraph of London. "Worse things have been done" he said, to the Union Jack, "with barely a whimper of outrage in the Commons."

But as Mr. Smiley conceded, and as historians and students of popular culture testify, there really is something special about America's relationship to its flag, which is why conservatives believe they have much to gain from making an issue of flag "desecration."

That very term—rooted in the word "sacred"—endows a thoroughly secular object with near-religious meaning, and America's flag, say the historians, carries cultural and emotional burdens that in most societies are spread among various other symbols and rituals. As a country that is not based on a single ethnic group or race or religion, the United States has to anchor its unity in ideas—and in humanly created symbols.

"America invented itself in a way that England, France and Russia did not," said the Rev-

erend Richard John Neuhaus, the author of "The Naked Public Square," a book that traces a decline in national consensus around ethical and religious values. "The flag is coterminous with our national existence. Most other nations had flags, plural."

The Stars and Stripes were decreed by the Second Continental Congress in June 1777, less than a year after the Declaration of Independence. Many have the notion that the flag has been there from the beginning.

"What other national symbol is there really?" asked Peter Marzio, a historian who directs the Museum of Fine Arts, Houston, and is a student of American popular art. "You don't have royalty. You never had an established church in the European sense. So the flag is almost isolated. There's nothing else. It has no competition."

And in a nation that so often finds itself divided over fundamental values, said Amitai Etzioni, a sociologist at George Washington University, the flag has an additional virtue. "Nothing's written on it," he said. "So we can all project on it what we want. Some people project free speech."

That, of course, goes to the heart of the debate over the constitutional amendment to ban flag burning. "The flag has played a dual role," said Benjamin Barber, a political science professor at Rutgers University. "It's the symbol of the Consitution and the Bill of Rights and tolerance and diversity, but it has always been a symbol of the American nation. Those who want to ban flag burning are playing to the symbol of the nation. But as they do so, they're

rubbing against the very symbols of tolerance and diversity that the flag stands for."

What strikes Alan Brinkley, a historian at the City of University of New York Graduate School, is how much more important the flag became in the 20th century—partly in reaction against the diversity that some see the flag as representing.

Mr. Brinkley says that the flag became a central element in popular campaigns to "Americanize" the waves of immigrants who arrived in America between 1870 and 1920. The flag also was used as a symbol in the drive against radicals after World War I, since many saw radicalism as an "un-American" import, brought by the new immigrant groups. Those campaigns led to the adoption of "The Star Spangled Banner" as the national anthem in 1931.

The flag's identification with opposition to radicalism—and with the prosecution of the Cold War after World War II—made it all the more attractive a target for opponents of the Vietnam War. Flag burnings, Mr. Brinkley said, became an important part of New Left "iconography," and so opposition to flag burning became increasingly important to the New Left's opponents.

Mr. Neuhaus recalled that at least one person on the left who understood the power of the flag as symbol was the late Socialist leader, Norman Thomas. He suggested not mass flag burnings, but mass flag washings. "He said our purpose should be not to burn the flag but to cleanse it," Mr. Neuhaus said.

Some relgious traditionalists like Mr. Neuhaus are uncomfortable with attributing sacred qualities to a secular object.

"The use of the language of holiness with respect to a national symbol raises serious questions for Christians, Jews, Muslims and others who have a keen awareness of the dangers of idolatry," he said. "It's a kind of ersatz sanctification of a national symbol."

"You can burn a cross and no one will put you in jail," said Robert Bellah, a sociologist at the University of California at Berkeley. "You can burn a Star of David and no one will put you in jail." To then ban flag burning, he said, seems odd. "In a nation where we claim to believe that God is higher than the nation, that's bizarre," he said.

SOURCE: *International Herald Tribune*, Friday, June 22, 1990, p. 3.

Following the Eichman ruling, the call went up once more for a constitutional amendment or some other political solution to protect the flag from objectionable symbolic uses. While the White House renewed the pressure for an amendment, grass-roots groups went back to work in state legislatures around the country. Federalism is both a national safety valve and an engine of creative political solutions. Sometimes those "solutions" end up recycling old political conflicts. Perhaps the most creative political alternative was a bill passed by the Louisiana House of Representatives. As described in the news account that went out over the United Press International news wires, the legislation was intended to "dramatically lessen the penalties for a person convicted of assaulting someone who desecrates the U.S. flag."[14] Under Louisiana law, the existing maximum penalty for assault was a $500 fine and six months in jail; the *proposed* maximum punishment for attacking a flag burner was to be lowered to a $25 fine and no jail time. One suspects that a lot of red-blooded Americans would line up and pay $25 to take a crack at a flag burner.

Passed in an emotional session on Memorial Day, the bill triggered the strong feelings on both sides that often go along with civil liberties conflicts. One opponent in the legislature (a Vietnam veteran) condemned the bill as "vigilante government." Another suggested that if the bill became a law, it would place "every freedom, every privilege guaranteed to us and embodied in our Constitution at risk for $25." The author of the legislation, Representative James David Cain, replied: "I am sick and tired of marijuana-planting, dope-smoking hippies burning the American flag. Not a one of us in this room has not lost an ancestor at some time defending the American flag." One legislator went on record saying that the proposed law did not go far enough, adding that "anybody who destroys or burns the flag ought to be automatically deported."[15]

Although the bill did not become state law, it reflects the kind of legal solutions that are possible within the federal framework when one side or the other sees the political tide running against their favored issue. The rapid response of a state legislature to a Supreme Court ruling also suggests how questions of rights and liberties run up and down the federal power structure, letting off emotional steam along the way, but keeping this most personal set of political conflicts going in the process.

What good are civil liberties if they can be attacked again even after they appear to have been established clearly by the Supreme Court? As the case of the "Pentagon Papers" shows, having a history of constitutional precedents (tests, guidelines, and rulings) makes it easier for people (and newspapers, churches, and other groups) to effectively defend their liberties when they are threatened. *The battle over where to draw the lines of freedom and order will never stop, but the ability to cite strong legal precedents greatly strengthens the power of individuals to protect their liberties.*

Freedom of Religion

Reflecting the importance of religious freedom, the First Amendment begins by ordering Congress to make no laws "respecting an establishment of religion, or prohibiting the free exercise thereof." The first clause, known as **the establishment clause**, was intended to keep church and state separate and prevent the establishment or promotion of

The Supreme Court continues with each new session to refine its interpretation of the Constitution's edict against "an establishment of religion, or prohibiting the free exercise thereof." Here students from around the country unite in prayer outside the Supreme Court Building while demonstrating in support of prayer in public schools.

any religions by the government. The **free exercise clause** was intended to protect the diversity of beliefs and social practices found among members of different religions. As with other civil liberties provisions of the Bill of Rights, these two clauses have been incorporated selectively over a long period of time and often with great social protest surrounding the rulings.

The free exercise clause was first incorporated in 1940 in the case of *Cantwell v. Connecticut*, in which the Supreme Court ruled that an individual was entitled "to worship God according to the dictates of his own conscience." The establishment clause began its long process of incorporation in 1947 with the case of *Everson v. Board of Education* which upheld publicly financed transportation of students to parochial schools as an allowable part of a public transportation program. Later cases involving both clauses would add considerable complication to religious liberties, reflecting the considerable conflict surrounding these issues in society.

The most politically explosive case involving *the establishment clause* was the 1962 ruling in *Engel v. Vitale* in which the Court said that the reading of a daily prayer in New York public schools was a case of the state "establishing" religion and therefore had to be stopped.[16] Later rulings stopped the practice of school prayer in other states, creating protests to this day.

As with many other areas of civil liberties, the Court has developed a test that has been used in various establishment cases. The so-called "Lemon test" was outlined in the 1971 case of *Lemon v. Kurtzman* involving state funding to hire teachers in nonreligious subjects in parochial schools.[17]   In order not to violate the establishment clause, the Court said that links between government and religion *must have specifically secular purposes, could not be aimed at promoting one religion or damaging another*, and *could not involve government excessively in religious affairs*. The specific school program challenged in *Lemon* failed on the third test of too much involvement of government in religious activities. Several later cases were put to this test, with the Court ruling in favor of some and against others. Among those *passing* the Lemon test was a case of a local government using public funds to set up a Nativity scene at Christmas.

State legislatures have attempted many times since to find passable wording for laws permitting some form of religious observance in schools. The case of *Wallace v. Jaffree* (1985) is an interesting ruling because it reflected an opening in the Court's thinking about the establishment clause and the separation of government and religion. The majority opinion overturned Alabama laws requiring public school teachers to observe a moment of silence for meditation or prayer. However, the Court's objection was specifically to the word "prayer," leaving open the possibility that new language could be introduced in future state laws enabling them to legislate a moment of silence that might pass the religion test. In addition, a dissenting opinion from Chief Justice William Rehnquist declared that "nothing in the Establishment Clause requires government to be strictly neutral between religion and irreligion."[18]

The free expression clause has generated an equally rich and interesting history of civil liberties politics, from questions of being forced to salute the flag when it is forbidden by one's religion to being required to work during a day of worship on which work is forbidden by one's religion. One of the most interesting cases involved a member of a church who was fired from his job and denied unemployment benefits for using the drug peyote as part of his religion.

Alfred Smith, a member of the Native American Church, used peyote as part of a church religious ceremony. He was fired from his job and denied state unemployment benefits because his firing was considered "work-related misconduct." (Smith worked at a drug rehabilitation clinic.) The Oregon Supreme Court eventually ruled that the state law against the use of peyote did not make an exception for religious use and was, therefore, an unconstitutional violation of Mr. Smith's freedom of religious expression. The Employment Division of the Oregon State Department of Human Resources appealed to the Supreme Court of the United States.

Although the majority of the Court ruled against Mr. Smith and in favor of the Oregon law, the ruling illustrates the difficult issues in free expression conflicts. In an opinion for the majority in *Employment Division v. Smith* (1990), Justice Antonin Scalia said that since Oregon's law was not intended to restrict a practice that *only* members of a particular religion engaged in, it was not an abridgment of religious freedom. This ruling clearly struck the political balance between individual freedom and social order on the side of order, favoring the need of society to control the use of drugs and showing apprehension that granting this exemption would open up endless other exemptions to drug statutes and other laws.[19]

However, Mr. Smith's argument won some support. At the core of his case was the claim that if the state of Oregon could criminalize his religious activities, he and other members of the church would be forced to go somewhere else to practice their religion safely—a gross restriction of free expression. In support of the argument, Smith's lawyers cited twenty-three other states that had granted exemptions from laws against peyote use to members of the Native American Church. This argument was persuasive to Justice Blackmun, who objected to the majority opinion, saying that this interpretation of the First Amendment offered "to Native Americans merely an unfulfilled and hollow promise."[20]

In between these opinions was Justice Sandra Day O'Connor, who said that the First Amendment probably did protect religious practices of the sort involved in this case and that the majority decision probably created a severe burden for Mr. Smith and others in his situation. However, in striking a balance among the political values in conflict, the state's "significant interest" in the uniform application of drug laws overrode the "severe burden" that those laws placed on the exercise of Native American religion.[21]

While the cases reviewed above may make it seem that there is a clean separation between issues involving the establishment of religion and the protection of free religious expression, the two sets of issues often come up together in specific cases. For example, should public money be spent on military chaplains? In his dissent in the case of *School District v. Schempp* (1963), Justice Potter Stewart noted the tangle between the two clauses. On the one hand, paying a chaplain's salary with government money appears to some people to violate the establishment clause. On the other hand, sending soldiers to remote locations and not offering them religious counsel can be seen as denying them freedom to exercise their religion, which would violate the free expression clause. [22]

What about state laws that require businesses to close on Sundays? Do these laws favor religions that worship on Sundays and at the same time interfere with the religious expression of people who have to work on Saturday even though their religion observes it as their day of worship? Through the course of a long series of rulings, the Court has evolved what constitutional law scholar Laurence Tribe calls a basic test: If the government action in question is compelled by the free exercise clause, then it cannot be a violation of the establishment clause. [23] This rule has guided a number of different Court decisions, including ruling in favor of the government paying military chaplains; deciding against giving release time for prayer on school premises; upholding release time for prayer *off* school premises; overturning a state law requiring accountants to swear an oath that they believed in God; and ruling against mandatory time for silent prayer in public schools. (This last case is *Wallace v. Jaffree,* mentioned above.)

Freedom from Injustice

Another major group of civil liberties "incorporated" by Supreme Court rulings since the 1930s involves protections for individuals in their dealings with the criminal justice system. One of the worst nightmares a citizen can face is to become caught up in an uncaring police system: wrongly accused, held without charges or bail, denied access to a lawyer, forced to sign a false confession, or made to provide self-incriminating evidence. These are the recurring plots of suspense novels and movie thrillers, perhaps because they were also the real-life fates of many victimized by law enforcement authorities before the Supreme Court began restraining police and courts with civil liberties rulings based on provisions of the Fourth, Fifth, Sixth and Eighth Amendments.

At first it appeared that the Supreme Court might incorporate provisions of the criminal justice amendments as rapidly as it began incorporating provisions of the First Amendment. As early as 1932, for example, the Court heard the appeal of a defendant who was convicted of rape in Scottsboro, Alabama. Two white girls charged that they were raped by a group of blacks. The defendants were denied legal counsel, and quickly convicted by a white court while a white mob surrounded the courthouse. In its ruling in *Powell v. Alabama* (1932), the Court opined that in such consequential cases (rape in Alabama carried a possible death sentence), defendants were entitled to legal counsel at state expense if they could not afford lawyers' fees. Following this narrow incorporation of the Sixth Amendment, the defendants were retried, this time with the benefit of legal counsel. Although their cases dragged on for a decade of convictions and appeals, the defendants were eventually freed, and evidence demonstrated they were innocent. Without a timely ruling and volunteer lawyers, the young men would probably have been executed. The constitutional door was now open for protecting future individuals against runaway justice proceedings.

However, the Court did not open the justice door very wide for several more decades. The decision (described in Box 5.3) not to grant Palko's double jeopardy (Fifth Amendment) claim in 1937 signalled that the Court was not going to intrude boldly into state domains of law enforcement. Over the next quarter century, the Court issued only modest restraints involving Fourth Amendment "search and seizure" provisions and Sixth Amendment "public trial" rights. Beginning in the 1960s, however, landmark rulings began to radically redefine the citizen's relationship to the law. Today persons suspected of criminal activity have substantial rights that must be protected by states and law enforcement officials. Indeed, many Americans now feel that the rights of suspects are protected too much, and at the expense of crime victims, hampering the efforts of police and the courts to put criminals behind bars.

On the other side of a tough "law and order" stance, however, are wrongly arrested citizens whose "presumed innocence" was not taken seriously by police and courts, who denied them the basic protection necessary for fair trials. Beginning in the 1960s, the Supreme Court issued a series of landmark rulings that tipped the balance of justice more in favor of the individual and against the chance that innocent people might be railroaded by the system:

In 1961, the ruling in the case of **Mapp v. Ohio** incorporated *Fourth Amendment protections against "unreasonable searches and seizures."* This ruling limits the powers of police to gather evidence without a proper search warrant. In particular, illegally obtained evidence cannot be used in a trial as a basis for convicting a defendant. The case involved a search of the house of Dollree Mapp. Police were looking for evidence related to the bombing of the house of Don King, who later became a famed boxing promoter. What the police found, instead, was pornographic material which they seized and used in successfully prosecuting Mapp. The Supreme Court ruling *excluding the use of this illegally obtained evidence* against Mapp has become known as the **exclusionary rule**. Many battles have been fought over how to apply this rule to decide what kinds of evidence can be legally introduced against defendants in trials and what kinds of evidence must be ignored or excluded from the cases against them.

In 1963, the case of **Gideon v. Wainwright** extended *the right of legal counsel* to all criminal (felony) cases. When he was finally given an attorney, Clarence Earl Gideon was acquitted after the lawyer proved that he could not have committed the crime. This decision has been celebrated in a book (and movie) titled *Gideon's Trumpet*.[24] Today, it has become routine to assign "court-appointed" lawyers to defend people who cannot afford the costs of legal counsel. In this and other rulings, several key provisions of the *Sixth Amendment* have been incorporated.

In 1964, the Court decided that Chicago police violated Danny Escobedo's rights when they refused his demands for a lawyer and extracted a confession under pressure. The ruling in **Escobedo v. Illinois** overturned his conviction based on that confession, while incorporating *Fifth Amendment rights against self-incrimination*. This has imposed restraints on police temptations to use physical force or other pressure to make people confess.

The rights against self-incrimination from Escobedo were strengthened in the 1966 decison of **Miranda v. Arizona**. The logic of this ruling is that defendants are better able to decide whether to talk to the police if they are specifically informed of their *Sixth Amendment rights to remain silent until after seeing a lawyer*. Miranda was later retried and convicted of kidnapping and rape based on the testimony of his common-law wife.

As every television and movie fan knows, police today must inform suspects of their *Miranda* rights: "You have the right to remain silent. Any statement you make may be used as evidence against you in court. You have the right to an attorney. If you cannot afford a lawyer, one will be appointed for you. Do you understand each of the rights that I have just stated?"

Some law enforcement officials welcomed the above rulings. However, others joined citizens and politicians in worrying that criminals were getting too much of a break. As a result, political battles have been waged over the years to relax these restraints. Politicians have won more than a few elections campaigning on promises to pass tougher criminal laws and appoint judges less sympathetic to the rights of criminals and more worried about the safety of citizens. As political "law and order" politicians stay in office long enough to appoint like-minded judges, we can see how *majority power* in society enters into the political struggle to define and limit rights. One major struggle has been waged over the exclusionary rule (mentioned above). The requirement to exclude evidence not obtained through legal procedures such as search warrants has been relaxed in several important cases.

Another area of considerable interest has been the death penalty and other issues that touch on the "cruel and unusual punishment" and "excessive bail and fine" prohibitions of the Eighth Amendment. Federal courts and the Supreme Court have considered the "cruel and unusual punishment" clause in ruling on various prison practices, from overcrowding of jails to the beating of prisoners. The Supreme Court has based several rulings in death penalty cases on interpretations of the Eighth Amendment. For example, in *Woodson v. North Carolina* (1976) and *Furman v. Georgia* (1976), the Court objected to the ways in which state death penalty statutes were written. In *Woodson*, the Court said that a mandatory imposition of the death penalty for particular crimes deprived specific defendants of justice based on their personal situations. In *Furman*, the Court objected to a state death penalty law that contained no direction to the jury about how it should be applied.[25] These rulings resulted in a moratorium on executions while death penalty states rewrote their sentencing laws.

The Right to Privacy

Those who wrote and debated the Bill of Rights were unwilling to close the door for all time on new rights claims. For this reason, the Ninth Amendment leaves open the possibility that other rights beyond the ones specified in the first eight amendments might be "retained by the people." You may have noticed that privacy is not mentioned specifically in the Bill of Rights. Although several amendments seem to hint at the idea of privacy, none states it explicitly. Privacy has become recognized by the Court as a new right consistent with the expansion of rights allowed by the Ninth Amendment.

In light of their slow and cautious approach to selective incorporation, the early Supreme Courts were reluctant to take on the problem of defining new rights. However, an important trend appeared in the Court of the 1950s and 1960s under Chief Justice Earl Warren and the Court of the 1970s under Chief Justice Warren Burger.[26] *The expansion of civil liberties protections over the years seemed to be moving toward something greater than a mere collection of isolated Bill of Rights provisions.* In the opinions of many justices, granting people greater freedom of speech, assembly, and security from police surveillance and self-incrimination added up to a metaphorical "umbrella" granting them more *privacy*.

As was true for all the earlier liberties, the right to privacy evolved from very limited beginnings—specifically, as a protection against governments demanding to know whose names appeared on the membership lists of political and social organizations.[27] Later on, when privacy became linked to protecting the sanctity of the bedroom, it was on its way toward becoming a much more universal and volatile civil liberty with implications for all Americans. This expansion of the idea of privacy occurred in a case involving the sensitive issue of birth control.

Police in Connecticut arrested Estelle Griswold, director of the state chapter of the Planned Parenthood League. Her crime: providing information about birth control to married couples. When the Court heard the case of **Griswold v. Connecticut** in 1965, Justice William O. Douglas opined that the modern history of civil liberties added up to the right of privacy. After all, he reasoned, what was the central intent of protecting individual speech, freedom of association, religion, and personal security against invasions by law enforcement authorities? Justice Douglas' answer was that civil liberties, taken as a whole, created a "zone of privacy" around the individual. The idea of police searching the bedrooms of married couples for evidence that they were using contraceptives was, in his opinion for the majority, "repulsive to the notions of privacy surrounding the marriage relationship."[28] Later, in 1972, the Court reaffirmed this privacy right by overturning a Massachusetts law against contraceptive use by unmarried individuals.[29]

The right to use contraceptives was one thing, but the Court stirred up an enduring national controversy when it extended its reasoning the next year to protect a woman's decision to terminate pregnancy. The landmark case of **Roe v. Wade** (1973) continues to rock American politics. While its supporters claim that no decision is more private or personal than the *right to choose* to have an abortion, its opponents respond that no right is any higher in the scale of liberties and moral values than the *right to life* of the unborn child.

Since 1973 the news has been filled with thousands of headlines and dramatic pictures of marches, protests, and new court challenges. Elections have been won and lost on the issue, and public opinion has been divided and re-divided depending on how the question is asked. Seldom have grass-roots organizations been so mobilized, so intensely, for so long on a single political issue. With both *majoritarian* and *pluralistic power* pressing on institutions, it is hardly surprising that so many laws have been written at so many levels of the federal system, or that so many challenges have reached the courts.

The abortion struggle reminds us that liberties and rights are not just won or lost in abstract legal cases argued in distant courts. Important political struggles for rights are typically waged on many fronts. Whether the struggle is over abortion or school desegregation, it is common to find politics going on at the following levels:

Politics Involving Different Kinds of Power in Society

Majority Power:

- voting for politicians who will write or enforce the laws
- voting for politicians who will appoint judges

Group Power (pluralism):

- joining and supporting interest organizations that apply group pressure

Individual Power (available to both elites and ordinary individuals):

- individuals making personal claims about their rights
- going to court to press those claims

Political Conflicts Between State and National Institutions

- executive decisions to enforce or not enforce laws
- executive appointment of court judges and justices
- legislative activity/writing laws and penalties
- courts interpreting laws and ordering remedies

Without all of these different political levels engaged, conflicts over rights would be far less democratic and personally meaningful. Because people can affect the outcomes of conflicts over rights by voting and by joining groups, both majoritarian and pluralist forms of power often operate behind the scenes of specific civil liberties and civil rights conflicts. When combined with the opportunity for individuals to take their complaints directly to courts, the politics of rights offers more individual power to ordinary people than any other area of government. (See Box 5.6, p. 177.)

On the twentieth anniversary of the 1973 Roe v. Wade *decision, pro-life demonstrators gather outside the Supreme Court. Recent Supreme Court decisions make it appear unlikely that* Roe *will be overturned, but the Court has in recent sessions found some legal limits on abortion to be constitutional.*

After the decision in *Roe*, Supreme Court members continued to affirm that a privacy right protects a woman's abortion decision. However, more conservative justices appointed by presidents Reagan and Bush moved the Court in the direction of allowing states some control over the abortion process. In 1989, the Supreme Court, with William Rehnquist as Chief Justice, supported a Missouri law that denied women the right to have abortions in *public* (government) health clinics. Although neither the general privacy right nor the legality of abortions was reversed by this case (*Webster v. Reproductive Health Services*, 1989), the Court upheld the right of Missouri to prohibit public employees and facilities from performing abortions unless the life of the mother was threatened. Moreover, doctors could be ordered to test the viability of fetuses to see if they could survive outside the womb. The signal in the *Webster* ruling to the states was clear: the Court was willing to hear creative state measures to limit abortions. However, the justices were anything but united about what kinds of restrictions were allowable.

In 1992, the Court ruled on *Planned Parenthood of Southeastern Pennsylvania v. Casey*. Many abortion supporters feared that *Casey* might overturn *Roe* and redefine the sphere of constitutionally protected privacy. The majority opinion did uphold a number of restrictions that Pennsylvania law had placed on abortions. The majority of the justices approved of an "informed consent clause" requiring doctors and clinics to issue a state-prepared information packet on abortion and impose a 24-hour waiting period. Also upheld was a requirement that females under the age of of eighteen years obtain consent from one parent or a judge before having an abortion. In the opinion of the Court, these restrictions did not fundamentally interfere with the abortion right itself.

While recognizing the right of states to impose such restrictions, the *Casey* opinion did not come close to overturning the core of the *Roe* decision. To the contrary, the majority opinion in *Casey* affirmed at some length the "personal liberty" principles on which the *Roe* decision was based. In a remarkable statement demonstrating how the Court understands the social impact of its decisions, the opinion written by Justices O'Connor, Kennedy, and Souter said this about the importance of the *Roe* decision:

> For two decades of economic and social development, people have organized intimate relationships and made choices that define their views of themselves and their places in society, in reliance on the availability of abortion in the event that contraception should fail. The ability of women to participate equally in the economic and social life of the nation has been facilitated by their ability to control their reproductive lives. The Constitution serves human values, and while the effect of reliance on *Roe* cannot be exactly measured, neither can the certain cost of overruling *Roe* for people who have ordered their thinking and living around that case be dimissed.[30]

Sweeping reversals of the privacy ruling on abortion did not come as quickly as some court-watchers predicted. In other areas, however, the more conservative Court of the 1980s and 1990s took a narrower view of privacy. For example, in the important ruling in *Bowers v. Hardwick* (1986), a narrow majority upheld Georgia's sodomy law, citing the state's right to protect long-standing social traditions. This decision signalled that the definition of privacy would be subject to more political struggles in the years ahead.

The Civil Liberties Scorecard

As a result of the gradual evolution of civil liberties based on the idea of "ordered liberty" (liberties so important that social and constitutional orders depend on them), many of the civil liberties that Americans hold dear have been brought into everyday life roughly in the sequence noted in Table 5.1. As the ongoing conflicts in society indicate, some of those liberties could be redefined and even reversed in the future.

In addition, it is important to note that some provisions of the Bill of Rights have not been, and probably will never be, considered by the courts. The Second Amendment concerning the right to bear arms is an interesting example. Many Americans feel that this amendment protects their cherished right to own guns. However, a clause in the Second Amendment refers to the maintenance of militias and "the security of a free state" as the reason for bearing arms. Since today's debates over such issues as the rights of hunters or collectors to own assault weapons do not address the spirit of the Second Amendment, it may never be used in deciding the boundaries of modern-day gun rights. In addition, the Third Amendment has never been taken up by the courts since soldiers have not been quartered involuntarily in private homes since the adoption of the Constitution. (However, Justice William O. Douglas did cite the Third Amendment as evidence that privacy is central to the Bill of Rights.) The Seventh Amendment granting the right to jury trials in "common law" simply does not apply to our legal system as it has evolved since the founding of the nation. In addition, the Tenth Amendment is not a civil liberties amendment, but refers to the reserved powers of the states. All of this means that the liberties that have come into play through the courts are based primarily on interpretations of the First, Fourth, Fifth, Sixth, Eighth, and Ninth Amendments.

Civil Rights

As noted earlier, it has become common to draw the popular distinction between *civil rights* as having to do with issues of equality and discrimination, and *civil liberties* having more to do with matters of individual freedom. The following discussion adopts this convenient distinction to explore the idea of rights that go beyond the protection of personal freedoms to the correction of social inequalities created by discrimination.

A Second American Revolution

Just as the original idea of restraining the government from interfering with private life was radical a few hundred years ago, the idea of bringing in governmental force to define and correct discrimination seems radical today to some Americans. To others, government intervention is a tool for creating a livable society for all people. What prompted this redefinition of rights from a restraint of government to a broader political tool involving active government protections and remedies?

THE PROBLEM OF DISCRIMINATION.   Justice Thurgood Marshall was fond of telling audiences that the men who drafted the Constitution may have been radical, even revolutionary, in their time, but times have changed. Many of the Founders, after

TABLE 5.1

Order of Incorporation of Key Civil Liberties Provisions of the Bill of Rights

AMENDMENT	LIBERTY	YEARS OF INCORPORATION
I	Free speech	1925
I	Free press	1931
I	Freedom of assembly	1937, 1939
I	Freedom of religion	1940, 1947
IV	Protection against unreasonable search and seizure	1949, 1961
V	Right to avoid self-incrimination	1964
V	Protection from double jeopardy	1969
VI	Fair trial and counsel (capital punishment case)	1932
VI	Right to counsel (all felony cases)	1963
VI	Right to remain silent	1966
VIII	Cruel and unusual punishment	1962
I, III, IV, V, IX	Right to privacy*	1965, 1973

*The right to privacy is not specifically mentioned anywhere in the Bill of Rights. It is a right that the Supreme Court has *constructed* from other rulings involving the amendments noted.

all, accepted the idea of slavery, and generally imagined a world in which liberties would be granted to a fairly homogenous society.

The rosy vision of a neatly bounded society came to an end in the bloody Civil War. After that came more bloody battles of working people to organize unions and bargain as a group against owners of businesses. Then came the struggle of women and blacks to gain access to the full range of social and economic life. After securing the right to vote, many people found that this political power did not help them get jobs or advance within the bastions of business and government. It turned out that as legal barriers to full citizenship based on property, race, and gender fell down, many people felt that they encountered equally effective barriers against entry into the mainstream of social life itself. What good is citizenship, asked these groups, if there is no society to belong to as equals? *Thus, the notion of equality became increasingly a theme and a source of tension in the political culture.*

On the other side are many citizens who feel that after legal obstacles are removed, the state has done all it needs to for individuals to compete on their own. The conservative view is that all people should have the *opportunity* to compete equally for positions in society—thus emphasizing *freedom* over regulated equality. Not surprisingly, the problem of discrimination remains one of America's most difficult problems. Consider, for example, the responses of whites and blacks to the question: *Do you think the United States currently has enough federal laws and regulations aimed at reducing race, religion, and sex discrimination, or does Congress need to pass additional laws and regulations aimed at reducing this type of discrimination?*[31]

	HAS ENOUGH	NEEDS MORE	NO OPINION
Whites	58%	34%	8%
Blacks	30%	62%	8%

After laws are passed and courts declare specific forms of discrimination illegal, what should be done if many institutions in society continue to discriminate as if nothing had changed? Without *active* government intervention, argue civil rights advocates, citizenship in the United States would be awarded in two classes: first would come those born into the right social circles with the power and connections to live the "first-class" life, and then would come those permanenlty assigned at birth to a second-class existence. In response, federal and state governments began to impose sanctions and remedies on institutions that seemed unable and unwilling to change on their own. Although this helped in some areas, it turned out that there was an even deeper problem.

THE PROBLEM OF PAST DISCRIMINATION.   Even after being ordered to stop "active" discrimination, many institutions seemed resistant to change. "Too few" women and minorities were hired, and they often received less pay for the same jobs performed by whites and men. The great political challenge in correcting the problem of discrimination was that it had gone on for so long that fixing the imbalances of race and gender would require something of a social revolution. Explosive political conflicts developed over giving actual *preferences* in training, hiring, and promotion to women and minorities (and later, to people with disabilities and other "disadvantaged" groups). Ideological battles raged. Liberals saw these remedies as necessary for correcting historical injustices that were not going away on their own. Conservatives saw affirmative action programs and other government attempts to impose equality as direct attacks on cherished cultural ideals of individual freedom and competition.

Many people felt that they should not have to pay for the sins of their ancestors, while many others felt that unless the injustices of the past were remedied, society would never have places for them as equals. Thus, an additional point of friction was created by trying to correct the results of past discrimination. The troublesome political question in this area became: What does it mean to be free or to have equal opportunities if privileged groups were given a two-hundred-year head start to design a society and lay claim to its top positions? Guided by this question, advocates began expanding their political definitions of rights to claim that the government should create—or require schools, businesses, and other organizations to create—programs to remedy the unjust legacy of the past. Many schools were ordered by courts to come up with plans to change their racial composition, and many private and public institutions were forced to come up with plans to create a balance of race and gender among their employees. In recent years, women have fought new civil rights battles on the grounds that all employees should receive comparable pay for performing comparable jobs (an issue that has become known as determining **comparable worth**).

The struggle to create a better social balance in workplaces and to define comparable worth guidelines for employee salaries has moved the boundaries of civil rights even farther into the area of equality. Will this evolution of rights from *individual freedoms* to *equal opportunities* continue toward some sort of equality based on the *social results* (for instance, jobs, salaries, school admissions) obtained by various groups? The answer depends ultimately on how people conduct their politics. Indeed, the politics of one of the nation's most impressive social movements explains a great deal about how the definition of rights has evolved to its present state.

The Civil Rights Movement

For nearly a century after the Civil War and the ratification of the Fourteenth Amendment, *the equal protection of the laws* was denied in many states to the very group that most clearly inspired that clause in the amendment. The political struggle of blacks for equal treatment under the law continued throughout this time. Without the protection of the national government and the Supreme Court, the fight for and against civil rights was often nasty and bloody. Intimidation, illiteracy, harassment, and lynching were common means of keeping the aspirations of African Americans in check.

As noted in the last chapter, early efforts to get the federal government to enforce its own constitutional mandate were in vain. Recall from Chapter 4 the landmark Supreme Court ruling in **Plessy v. Ferguson** in 1896. In this opinion that relied on racism as its guide, the Court ruled that separate social facilities (in this case, railroad coaches) were equal for racial purposes, inasmuch as true equality between superior and inferior races could not be created by social conditions.[32] This ruling endorsed a system of legalized segregation throughout much of the United States—a system that became rooted in neighborhoods, schools, workplaces, and public facilities.

By the 1940s America had become two separate and unequal societies, one black, the other white. In many places blacks could not ride in the same sections of public transportation with whites, go into white restaurants, use the same restrooms, or drink from the same water fountains, much less attend the same schools, compete for the same jobs,

The "colored entrance" to a Pensacola, Florida movie theatre, circa 1938. In its 1896 Plessy v. Ferguson *decision the Supreme Court had found "separate but equal" facilities for blacks and whites to be constitutionally defensible; but in practice the separation of races did not mean equal treatment for black Americans. Following World War II, however, the civil rights movement helped to bring about a reinterpretation of the Constitution (in 1954–55) that opened a new door to social change.*

or hope to receive the same degree of respect in public encounters. The most popular black entertainers were refused rooms at the same hotels where they played to packed white audiences. Talented black athletes were forced to play for little pay and recognition in the "Negro leagues." Two justice systems existed, offering blacks little in the way of due process of the law or legal representation. And even though the Fifteenth Amendment (also passed after the Civil War) guaranteed blacks the right to vote, legal evasions in Southern states, and elsewhere, kept blacks from being registered in substantial numbers until the late 1960s.

What happened between the 1940s and today? Do the notable changes in some areas of society (like integrated public facilities, black voter registration, highly respected and well-paid black professionals, and increasing numbers of black elected officials) translate into a general closing of the social divide created by so many years of legalized discrimination? The first question turns out to be easier to answer than the second.

The period from 1930–1950 saw great social changes sweep the nation. The upheaval of the Great Depression threw millions of people onto the streets, giving them a bitter taste of the lifestyles of the poor and unfortunate. More importantly, the New Deal promised by Democratic President Franklin Roosevelt cast government in the role of social problem solver for the first time in history. Although blacks were given little specific help as a group during the Depression, they began to organize during the 1940s and made their demands known to both the government and the Democratic party after the Second World War.

World War II contributed to the developing civil rights movement. Blacks and other minorities fought bravely and died alongside white soldiers, only to return to a society that continued to turn its back on them and their families. The internment of Japanese Americans during the war also raised questions about how white society should treat minority citizens. In addition, many women held jobs in defense plants and other key industries only to be pushed back into the home when the men returned from the war—a development that would later become significant in the history of the women's movement.

The war also created an unprecedented economic change, with the United States emerging as the greatest global economic power, consuming nearly half the planet's harvested raw materials in a wave of domestic prosperity and international growth. Black leaders saw the moment as one they could not miss if they ever hoped to achieve social equality. Meanwhile more whites began to feel less threatened by admitting blacks into the competition for what then seemed to be endlessly expanding economic opportunities. At the same time, millions of blacks left the South, moving to the North, Midwest, and West, where they encountered racism that was not "supposed" to exist outside the South.[33] In one historical moment, the racial struggle had become nationalized, and the quest for social justice had taken on an important economic dimension.

Meanwhile, government policy makers and their academic advisors began to see racial conflict as the major burden on an otherwise free and enviable society. The great Swedish economist Gunnar Myrdal published a book on race relations in America called, appropriately enough, *An American Dilemma*.[34] This book, among others, argued that *stable democracy was impossible when a substantial group of citizens was denied the rights and opportunities enjoyed by the rest*. Many Americans recognized for the first time that the eyes of the world were watching to see if the emerging superpower and world leader in the struggle between democracy and its enemies would offer the promise of democracy to all of its own citizens.

Blacks from all walks of life organized and pressed for changes where they lived, worked, went to school, rode public transportation, ate meals, gathered in public places, and sought political representation. Dedicated black lawyers like Thurgood Marshall (who argued the Supreme Court case in **Brown v. Board of Education** and was later appointed to the Supreme Court) pressed their demands in court. Young leaders like the

Parties in the Struggle

The civil-rights movement of the 1950s and 1960s was advanced by resolute individuals, by groups united in their aspirations—and by officials who often faced violent reprisals for their efforts. The arrest of Rosa Parks (*above,* with attorney Charles Langford), for refusing to give up her bus seat, sparked a massive, well-organized boycott in Montgomery, Alabama. Below, Clifford Vaughs of the Student Nonviolent Coordinating Committee is seized by National Guard troops during a 1964 demonstration in Maryland. The battle took place less dramatically but with equal impact in the courtroom. Federal District Judge Frank M. Johnson (*right*), a solidly Republican magistrate appointed by Dwight Eisenhower, fostered civil rights from the bench. His reward was to live with constant threats, harassment, and, on one occasion, a household bombing.

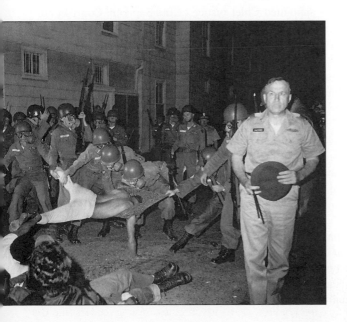

The Players

The Reverend Martin Luther King, Jr., spiritual leader of the civil-rights movement addresses a Montgomery, Alabama crowd in 1965. Marches and demonstrations were one aspect of a struggle for equal rights that was also carried on less visibly but with equal effect in courtrooms.

Reverend Martin Luther King, Jr., inspired courage and commitment to continue to press for what was right inside the institutions of our society. Established organizations such as the National Association for the Advancement of Colored People (NAACP) were joined by such new organizations as the Southern Christian Leadership Conference. The SCLC was organized by Dr. King and others as part of a broad effort to apply grass-roots pressure to society and political institutions, while legal pressure was applied through the courts. At an important early juncture in this struggle, a loud and positive signal was sent from the national government.

THE SUPREME COURT ANSWERS THE CALL.   Through the window of opportunity opened by that vast social movement entered an unlikely hero and an important legal case. Earl Warren was appointed Chief Justice of the Supreme Court by Republican President Dwight Eisenhower. There was little to suggest that Warren would be the person to engineer one of the most radical rulings in constitutional history. (See Chapter 16.) However, the case of *Brown v. the Board of Education of Topeka, Kansas* (1954) turned Warren's attention back to *Plessy v. Ferguson* and led him to question the whole assumption that "separate" could possibly be "equal."[35]

The case was brought to the Court through the legal activism of the National Association for the Advancement of Colored People (NAACP) on behalf of Mr. Brown who questioned the legality of being forced to send his daughter to a school across town because she was denied admission to a "whites only" school much closer to home. The key to the decision was Warren's belief that beyond all the legal technicalities, segregation was simply wrong, and that the legal reasoning in *Plessy* that set so much discrimination in motion was driven by the fundamentally racist assumption that blacks were inferior to whites and therefore had no claim to an equal place in white society. Where other, more legalistic approaches might have produced a mixed and ambiguous ruling from the Court, Warren's insistence upon confronting the legalized mask of racism in America pressured the other eight justices to sign on with his decisive rejection of the separate but equal ruling of *Plessy*.[36] The legal process through which this opinion was created is discussed in considerable detail in Chapter 16. For now, the important point is that with this landmark ruling, the equal protection clause of the Fourteenth Amendment was finally—nearly a century later—recognized by the Supreme Court as a mandate to provide blacks the same protections and opportunities available to whites in society. It had taken one hundred years of political struggle, including a Civil War and a vast social movement to put the simple idea of equal protection under the Fourteenth Amendment into practice.

The dilemma, of course, was that a ruling on a piece of paper in 1954 was inherently no more powerful than the words of the original Fourteenth Amendment that the ruling revived. The important question was how many people in society would take those words seriously and do something about them this time around. Rather than settling the civil rights struggle in America, the *Brown* ruling effectively opened it up and gave black groups an important political arena denied them for so long: the courtroom. It was clear, however, that no matter how many victories were won in court, courts had little power to force people and social institutions to change. At best, attempts by courts to work out plans to integrate school systems and workplaces were slow. At many steps along the way, there was resistance, fueled by charges that federal courts were overstepping their constitutional limits by taking legislative and executive actions all in one institution.[37] On the other side were people who demanded even more rapid change.

LAW AND THE POLITICS OF SOCIAL PROTEST.   The struggle for rights continued with ever-greater intensity in the streets. The resistance of white society often resulted in violence against civil rights activists. Federal troops were sent to quell riots and confrontations. FBI agents were dispatched to investigate incidents including conspiracies to obstruct justice involving local officials. Yet the civil rights movement grew and held firm to its tactics of *civil disobedience. Civil disobedience refers to disrupting society by using the nonviolent methods of protests, sit-ins, and boycotts as weapons.*

Civil-rights lawyers George Hayes, Thurgood Marshall, and James Nabrit shortly after their landmark victory against segregation in Brown v. Board of Education *(1954). Marshall would subsequently become, with President Lyndon Johnson's nomination, the first black Supreme Court justice. Marshall dedicated his career as a lawyer and a Supreme Court justice to making the Constitution serve the aspirations of all Americans.*

Ordinary citizens like Rosa Parks became courageous leaders who inspired others to change the society around them. (See "Inside the System" Box 5.6, opposite.)

The tradition of individual action has kept the civil rights movement going to this day and made ordinary people like Rosa Parks as important to the history of civil rights as the more famous individuals who have also participated. The actor Denzel Washington remarked, after playing black leader Malcolm X in the 1993 movie by that name, that he realized that even the choices he made about movie roles were important personal contributions to the cause: "unless we make a stand individually to make a difference, then there will be no difference made. And that means swimming upstream in this society, because it's coming downstream on us. Hard!"[38]

In the early years of the movement while the pressures of civil disobedience were applied at street level, the growing network of civil rights lobbying groups pressured Congress to pass laws specifying the forms of illegal discrimination in more detail and making the penalties more persuasive. The first sign of progress came with the Civil Rights Act of 1957, the first national antidiscrimination law since the Reconstruction period following the Civil War. This pioneering law made it illegal to prevent people from voting in federal elections and authorized the executive branch (through the Attorney General) to bring suit when voting rights were violated by states or local voting officials.

Following this first law, there have been many others aimed at specific forms of discrimination that deprive citizens of their social, political, and economic opportunities. Important to this day is the Civil Rights Act of 1964, which outlawed discrimination in employment, in public accommodations, and in federally funded programs (for example,

TABLE 5.2

A Selection of Important Civil Rights Laws

Civil Rights Act of 1957	Made it a federal crime to prevent people from voting in federal elections. Executive branch (Attorney General) authorized to bring suit against states, localities, and officials who deprive citizens of their voting rights.
Civil Rights Act of 1964	Outlawed discrimination in employment, public accommodations, and federally funded programs based on race, gender, religious preference, or national origin. Equal Employment Opportunity Commission established to create guidelines and review complaints. In 1988, the law was expanded to include entire institutions if any of their programs received federal funding.
Voting Rights Act of 1965	Authorized the executive branch to appoint federal officers (examiners) to register voters in areas practicing discrimination. Increased penalties for noncompliance.
Age Discrimination Employment Acts of 1967, 1975, 1986	Outlawed employer discrimination against older workers. Later acts made mandatory retirement policies more difficult for companies to implement.
Fair Housing Acts of 1968, 1988	Outlawed discrimination in sale or rental of housing. Later law increased executive branch (Department of Housing and Urban Development) enforcement powers, and included provisions for the handicapped and families with children.
Americans with Disabilities Act of 1990	Extended Civil Rights Act of 1964 to specifically include rights of disabled citizens to have access to employment, transportation, public accommodations, and communication services. Also broadened the provisions of the *Rehabilitation Act of 1973* to provide disabled access to public offices and businesses, whether or not they receive federal funds.

The Power of Ordinary People: Rosa Parks

5.6

The power of groups and majorities is often engaged by civic rights issues as they move through legislatures and come into play in elections. However, the personal focus of rights gives ordinary individuals important roles in some of the most heated conflicts in American politics. Individuals are not only the sources of political complaints in society, but their complaints are the subjects of the cases that move through legal institutions. Civil rights activist Rosa Parks stands as a reminder of the importance of individual power in this unique area of the American system.

On December 1, 1955, a tired Rosa Parks simply "had had enough" and refused to move from her seat in the front of a bus in Montgomery, Alabama. Mrs. Parks had long fought for civil rights, serving as a secretary for the local and state chapters of the NAACP (see text), and she had organized local actions which included encouraging young people to try to borrow books from white libraries.

Before the day of her arrest, Mrs. Parks had refused on several occasions to give up her seat on buses and had been ejected once before by the same driver who called for her arrest on that December day. As she described it, "My resistance to being mistreated in the buses and anywhere was just a regular thing with me and not just that day."*

After Mrs. Parks' arrest for sitting in the front of the bus, she was supported by members of the local NAACP chapter who posted her bail and joined in using her case to challenge so-called "Jim Crow" laws which regulated virtually all aspects of relations in public between blacks and whites in much of the South. For example, in Montgomery, it was a law that blacks had to stand in the back of a bus when seats in the front were empty. In addition, blacks had to pay at the front of the bus and then step down and walk to the rear door to get on board.

Inspired by Rosa Parks' act of civil disobedience (see text) the local NAACP and the Women's Political Council (another activist group in town) organized a boycott of city buses. The Reverend Martin Luther King, Jr., became a leader in the Montgomery protest, as did other black clergymen. The broad support for the boycott in the black community inspired other communities to take action to correct social injustice. Thus, Rosa Parks and the activities of the local civil rights organizations became models for civil disobedience in a rapidly growing social movement.

The success of Rosa Parks' leadership has been attributed to two factors: that "not only was she a quiet, dignified woman of high morals, but also [because] she was an integral member of those organizational forces capable of mobilizing a social movement."*

*Quotes are from Aldon D. Morris, *The Origins of the Civil Rights Movement,* New York: The Free Press, 1984, pp. 51–52.

education) on the basis of race, gender, religion, or national origin. Equally pathbreaking was the Voting Rights Act of 1965 which appointed federal officers to help register voters turned away illegally by local registrars and raised the penalties from the 1957 law for denying citizens the right to vote. Table 5.2 reviews some important advances in civil rights laws. The struggle for civil rights continues, with new laws aimed at new forms of discrimination.

Expanding the Definition of Civil Rights

As the examples of civil rights laws in Table 5.2 make clear, the scope of civil rights is broad, now including older persons, women, religious believers, Native Americans, immigrant groups, families with children, disabled persons and, more recently, the homeless and people with catastrophic diseases such as AIDS. Although each group has waged its own struggle, the general strategy of legal activism is common to all. Activist groups often pursue political strategies involving all the branches of government to advance

Black students make their first attempts to integrate a public high school in Little Rock, Arkansas—with the help of U.S. Army troops sent by President Dwight Eisenhower. The conflict over integration further aggravated national-state government relations, as some state governors, under the banner of states' rights, attempted to obstruct desegregation.

their particular causes. On a national level, winning legal rights in Court, lobbying for legislation from Congress, and pressing for law enforcement from the executive branch seem to be the most effective political methods to open society's doors to those who have been shut out.

Many groups have been successful in expanding the definition of civil rights. Women have made progress in defining and drawing attention to various forms of sexism, often seeking compensation for a range of harms from inadequate pay to the psychological stresses of sexual harassment. Older citizens have won the right to continue working when employers wanted to exchange them for younger, less expensive, or more "attractive" workers. Handicapped people have made gains in both the workplace and the marketplace by getting buildings and public spaces re-engineered to suit at least some of their special needs.

Rights are more secure when they do not sonstantly require lawyers and police agencies to enforce them. Indeed, the most secure rights are those that have passed through the day-to-day struggle for law enforcement and entered into the consciousness and traditions of society. To some extent, as society changes, people's attitudes follow. Often, however, groups must wage equally fierce public education campaigns to bring their difficulties to the attention of larger and sometimes insensitive publics.

A constant problem for securing rights is that one person's right may be another's wrong. While much of the politics of the civil rights struggle has been waged by groups using *pluralist* and *majoritarian* forms of power to force institutional change, the specific court rulings that facilitated the evolution of specific rights were granted to individuals. When those rulings require institutions in society to change their ways, other individuals often protest that the remedies deprive them of their rights.

The Difficulty of Righting Social Wrongs

The idea that rights belong to individuals, not to groups, becomes the most troublesome in the area of how to remedy past discrimination. The agonizing struggle over decades of **affirmative action** in America suggests that for nearly every case where attempts are made to right past wrongs against individual members of one group, individuals in another group may see that remedy as taking away their rights. It is this second dimension of civil rights, the problem of remedies or correcting injustices, where the political conflicts become most intense and hard to reconcile.

To bring all of this home, consider a case that occurred in the Birmingham, Alabama Fire Department during the 1980s. For background, it is useful to know that the Birmingham fire department did not hire its first black fireman until 1968. A second black was not hired until 1974, the year a lawsuit was brought against the city to open its employment doors more widely to blacks. It was not until 1979, the year Birmingham elected its first black mayor, that the city finally agreed to stop fighting the legal action and to begin matching every white hired or promoted with a black person hired or promoted. Even with this compromise affirmative action plan, it would take decades before the fire department came close to the same racial composition as the population of taxpayers who paid its salaries. Even though it seemed rather modest, the compromise plan drew immediate objections from a white fireman named James Henson.

Henson and a black fireman named Carl Cook both took the test for lieutenant and passed, but Henson scored higher than Cook. However, under the affirmative action plan adopted by the city, Cook was promoted and Henson was not. Henson and other whites began challenging the affirmative action plan, using all the methods that blacks had used to create it in the first place. Today, race divides Birmingham both in terms of competition for city jobs and in politics at all levels. Both sides see their conflicting rights claims clearly. Here is what the two people involved in the original Birmingham fire department case say:[39]

> *Cook:* Say your father robs a bank, takes the money and buys his daughter a Mercedes, and then buys his son a Porsche and his wife a home in the high rent district. Then they discover he has embezzled the money. He has to give the cars and house back. And the family starts to cry: "We didn't do anything." The same thing applies to what the whites have to say. The fact is, sometimes you have to pay up. If a wrong has been committed, you have to right that wrong.

> *Henson:* I can understand that blacks had been historically discriminated against. I can also understand why people would want to be punitive in correcting it. But they want me to pay for it, and I didn't have anything to do with it.

What would you do? Right a wrong done to a group in the historical past, or honor the claim of an individual with a higher test score in the present? Since the Court adheres to the constitutional tradition that rights belong to (often competing) individuals, legal rulings on affirmative action cases have become very complicated. Deciding what kinds of remedies institutions should employ has become more challenging. Two important rulings illustrate these problems of finding remedies that are fair to all.

The most famous case is *University of California Regents v. Bakke* (1978).[40] Allan Bakke had a strong academic record when he applied to medical school at the University of California at Davis. The school admitted one hundred new students each year, and saved sixteen of those slots for minorities under an affirmative action plan designed to open up admission to groups that had been excluded in the past. Allan Bakke was rejected while students from the targeted groups were admitted with lower scores on various admissions criteria. (In fact, Bakke's test scores were higher than the average of *all* those admitted to the affirmative program in general.) After being rejected two years in a row, Bakke brought suit in federal court claiming that his civil rights had been violated under the Civil Rights Act of 1964 and the equal protection clause of the Fourteenth Amendment of the Constitution. The Supreme Court issued a complicated ruling that found the U.C. Davis affirmative action plan unconstitutional, but upheld the constitutionality of other approaches to affirmative action programs that considered race as one factor balanced against others in attempts to create more socially representative student bodies. The reasoning specified that institutions could not create categories (popularly called "quotas" today) that excluded whites in favor of other groups.

Although the Court has upheld a number of other affirmative action plans over the years since Bakke, a more recent ruling has rejected another common affirmative action remedy: the set-aside program. In *Richmond v. Corson* (1989), the court ruled against a city program requiring nonminority contractors working for the city to hire minority subcontractors to do at least 30 percent of the value of the work on city contracts.[41] In the aftermath of this ruling, the burden of affirmative action has been put squarely on Congress, calling attention to the provision of the Fourteenth Amendment empowering Congress to do what is necessary to create equal protection of the laws. The recent mandate to Congress, however, has been to come up with tests of discrimination in specific situations and to design equally precise laws to fit those specific cases. Even in cases where Congress has attempted to do so, as in the employment discrimination bills passed in 1990 and 1991, opponents including then President Bush have objected that the new laws still called for illegal quotas and set-aside programs that would cause reverse discrimination.

The problem of how to create better racial balances in society strikes at the heart of individualism in the American political culture. Nothing is more sacred than the idea that rights are vested in individuals, *not* groups, and that government remedies cannot deprive one individual of rights to satisfy another. Yet without some sort of social adjust-

Bill Clinton, during the 1992 election season, visits the charred sites of the 1991 Los Angeles riots with U.S. Representative Maxine Waters. The longer-term consequences of the riots suggest some of the complex cultural conflicts among elites, pluralities, and majorities: While California went solidly Democratic in 1992 national elections, the following year Los Angeles elected as its new mayor a conservative Republican businessman, Richard Riordan, who had campaigned on the themes of individual responsibility and social order.

ments, the progress of more balanced racial representation in society is likely to be very slow indeed. Without some sort of remedy, some argue, the important cultural ideal of equality is threatened.

The Politics of Rights Revisited

The American rights tradition is different from that of many other societies. The most obvious difference is the extent to which rights in this society are written down. Both the national government and many of the state governments have put important rights in writing as part of formal constitutional agreements. The American tradition is also interesting because rights are continually undergoing conflict and change in this political system. Written contracts between individuals and governments are important political resources for people, enabling them to claim specific *legal rights*.

At the same time, this formal legal tradition can be frustrating. People may develop a false sense of security that a favorable court ruling establishes a right for all time, and there is no need for further political action to protect it. In reality, before rights were written into law, they were first imagined, argued, and often demanded with considerable force. And after they become written into law, rights must still be argued and reclaimed, or they remain little more than words on paper.

When we stand back from the political fray, we can see important long-term gains from the struggles over rights and liberties. Although fights still go on over free speech, religion, and the rights of those accused of crimes, there are many more protections for individuals today than there were fifty years ago. Americans do not always understand or agree with all of those protections, but people have learned how to defend their freedoms. For all of the political conflicts involved, the American tradition of civil liberties is arguably the strongest in the world.

Evaluating the gains of the civil rights era is a bit more difficult. By some measures, most of the groups that have waged the struggle for civil rights have made important gains. Women have closed some of the salary gap separating them from men (although women still earn an average of only 70 percent of men's salaries). Homosexuals have drawn attention to social prejudices that cost them jobs, and result in degradation and physical harm because of their sexual preferences. Many blacks joined the ranks of the middle class in the 1980s while contributing to mainstream popular culture in literature, arts, film, sports, and music among other categories. The disabled have transformed the public landscape to make it possible for them to use public facilities and gain mainstream jobs. Yet for all these groups, two facts mark their gains with reason for caution. Prejudice still lurks under the surface of humanity, and sometimes out in the open in social relations. In addition, most of the top jobs in business, industry, and government continue to go to white, Protestant, able-bodied men. It is obvious that Americans no longer live in a society filled with signs directing people to "whites only" and "negroes only" facilities. Perhaps more importantly, tremendous gains have been made in the numbers of blacks registered to vote, which nearly doubled between 1970 and 1990. These gains translate into even greater increases in the numbers of black elected officials, a number that grew more than six-fold in some categories (such as mayors) over the same period. In fact, blacks have done much better than women, for example, in getting elected to public offices.

Just how much (or little) blacks have gained economically is a matter of some dispute among scholars. Among those who take a pessimistic view, there is still talk of "two nations" unchanged in the most important aspects of economic status and social dignity over the last fifty years. For example, Andrew Hacker, in his book *Two Nations*, claims that blacks today receive only 7.8 percent of the national income despite representing over 12 percent of the population. Even with comparable education, blacks earn only $798 for every $1,000 earned by whites. And the future looks anything but bright for nearly half the black children who are growing up in poverty (compared to 16 percent of white children). Looking at the big picture over time, Hacker notes that unemployment among blacks has stayed about twice that of whites, no matter how well the economy was doing. Factoring unemployment and underemployment into the racial equation means that the median income for blacks between the ages of twenty-five and thirty is roughly $14,000 compared to more than $20,000 for whites in the same age group, a factor that Hacker argues pushes many black men toward crime, resulting in 20 percent of them having spent some time in jail.[42]

Although a majority of whites and near-majority of blacks believe that progress has been made in the last twenty-five years, large majorities of both groups still think that race relations are best characterized as "bad." Figure 5.1 illustrates public opinion on various aspects of the racial struggle in the United States. Note, among other things, the large differences between white and black respondents on the issue of giving blacks preference in hiring in order to correct historical discrimination. The difference in how the races see the proper political balance between law and protests is also important to note.

Not all analyses are as pessimistic as Hacker's. For example, Thomas and Mary Edsall note that some blacks have made *considerable* gains, resulting in "a striking expansion of the black middle class, and a powerful contribution from blacks to the mainstream culture."[43] Supporting this claim, they note that in 1940s America virtually the only middle-class jobs open to blacks were those of being preachers and teachers in all-black churches and schools. Today, by contrast, there has been a tenfold increase in the numbers holding all manner of professional jobs. Although the black population only doubled from 1940 to 1990, the number of blacks in white-collar occupations increased more than nine times.

However, Edsall and Edsall also agree that while more blacks have joined the institutions and careers of white society, many more seem to have become stuck in a permanent dead end of low-paying jobs, second-class education, unemployment, or welfare. If anything, the fact that blacks have made it in white society has weakened the organized civil rights movement, and made many whites (and some blacks) less sympathetic to demands by those on the bottom. As a result, neither political party is willing to push civil rights aggressively for fear of losing middle-of-the-road voters who increasingly wonder: "If some blacks have entered middle-class society, what's wrong with those who remain behind?" and "Why should remedies be handed out to people who have not taken advantage of the opportunities that have opened up in the last few decades?" All of this suggests that the United States may be facing its most challenging period of racial politics in the years ahead.

As noted earlier, struggles over civil liberties and civil rights awaken the most intense values and the deepest divisions in the political culture. *These continuing conflicts suggest that civil rights, like civil liberties, are not things that are won (or lost) once and for all. Rights and liberties are continually asserted, defined, and promoted through all manner of political action, from simple insistence on respect and fair treatment in everyday life to passing laws that can punish those who do not "do the right thing" in those everyday encounters.*[44] Not surprisingly, this expanding struggle for civil rights has been joined by many different groups over the years and surely will expand to new groups making further demands in the future.

FIGURE 5.1

Views on Race: Progress Made, Needed

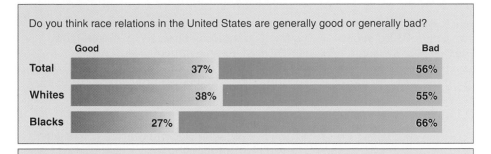

Do you think race relations in the United States are generally good or generally bad?

	Good	Bad
Total	37%	56%
Whites	38%	55%
Blacks	27%	66%

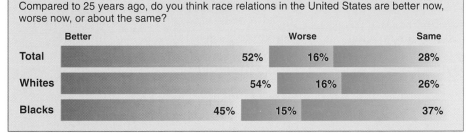

Compared to 25 years ago, do you think race relations in the United States are better now, worse now, or about the same?

	Better	Worse	Same
Total	52%	16%	28%
Whites	54%	16%	26%
Blacks	45%	15%	37%

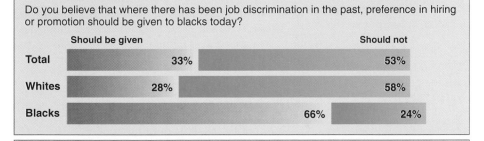

Do you believe that where there has been job discrimination in the past, preference in hiring or promotion should be given to blacks today?

	Should be given	Should not
Total	33%	53%
Whites	28%	58%
Blacks	66%	24%

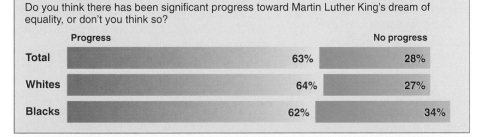

Do you think there has been significant progress toward Martin Luther King's dream of equality, or don't you think so?

	Progress	No progress
Total	63%	28%
Whites	64%	27%
Blacks	62%	34%

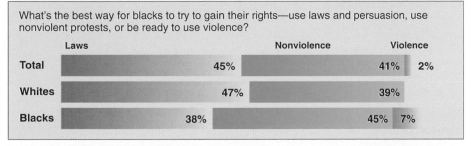

What's the best way for blacks to try to gain their rights—use laws and persuasion, use nonviolent protests, or be ready to use violence?

	Laws	Nonviolence	Violence
Total	45%	41%	2%
Whites	47%	39%	
Blacks	38%	45%	7%

Source: The New York Times/CBS News Poll. From *The New York Times,* April 4, 1993, p. 12.

A CITIZEN'S QUESTION Rights

What are my rights? How can I best protect them? These questions can be asked about many situations in daily life. Most of the great political struggles described in this chapter began with these questions in the minds of ordinary individuals. As the examples in this chapter indicate, rights are not won just in court but through struggles on many fronts: in daily life situations, by electing politicians, lobbying legislatures, and, of course, seeking relief from courts.

Think of a right that feels threatened in some area of your life that really matters. What kind of case can you make for claiming to have a particular right in this situation? What is the best way to advance that claim politically? By now, you should realize that there are many resources available to people who want to protect particular rights or liberties that seem threatened.

Let's start close to home, in the state where you live. Does your state have a bill of rights? You already know from reading this chapter, along with Chapter 4 on federalism, that Americans are both citizens of the United States and of the state in which they live. Many states have strong rights traditions, including bills of rights written into state constitutions. These state protections of rights can be even more immediate and politically accessible than national provisions. For example, the state constitution in Michigan has an explicit provision against the death penalty. This means that even if the United States Supreme Court says that it is permissible for states to execute persons convicted of particular crimes, Michigan cannot do so without first amending its constitution. Florida has a constitutional right to privacy which the state supreme court has interpreted to include abortion, meaning that even if the United States Supreme Court overturns *Roe v. Wade*, the Florida protections stand independently. Is your right already protected by your state constitution? If not, how would you go about promoting your right in your state?

States can also protect their citizens' rights through statutes (ordinary laws passed by legislatures). In addition, states that permit voter initiatives on the ballot even make it possible to protect (or weaken) rights legally

through grass-roots voter actions. In 1990, for example, a majority of voters in Washington state feared greater Supreme Court revisions of the *Roe* decision and passed a ballot initiative requiring the state to adopt the provisions of the *Roe* decision as state law.

Last, but by no means least, there is, of course, the avenue of the federal court system itself. (You will learn more about how it works in Chapter 16.) It may seem overwhelming to think about a lone individual taking a complaint into the legal system. Remember, however, that most of the great advances in liberties and rights described in this chapter were the results of ordinary and often very poor individuals, who simply valued their rights and liberties enough to protect them. As many of these cases also make clear, people seldom do this alone. There are many national organizations that exist to help individuals decide if their rights or liberties have been violated and whether they have a sound case on which to base legal action. Such organizations as the National Association for the Advancement of Colored People and the American Civil Liberties Union, among others, have state and local offices where citizens can come to discuss issues concerning their personal freedom and equality. In addition, many schools and companies have ombudsmen and civil rights officers who can be approached for similar consultations. You, too, can contact these organizations and officials.

Perhaps the most important step a citizen can take, however, is to start developing a personal sense of how he or she expects to be treated and what kind of society he or she wants to live in. Formation of these expectations can be guided by the examples of others who have defended their rights in the past. To return to a point from the very opening of the chapter, the key to rights is claiming them and acting personally to keep them alive. This is the idea of the personal Constitution. Developing a personal view of the Constitution may be the most vital aspect of American democracy because we all can use rights to make an important difference in our lives.

Key Terms

natural rights, divine rights

Bill of Rights

civil liberties

civil rights

dual citizenship

Barron v. Baltimore

The Slaughterhouse Cases

clear and present danger test

Schenck v. United States

due process clause

equal protection clause

incorporation

the establishment clause; free expression clause

the exclusionary rule

Mapp v. Ohio

Miranda v. Arizona

Griswald v. Connecticut

Roe v. Wade

Plessy v. Ferguson

Brown v. Board of Education

affirmative action

comparable worth

the problems of discrimination and past discrimination

the problem of remedies

civil rights laws enacted by Congress

state protections of civil rights

Suggested Readings

Abraham, Henry J. *Freedom and the Court: Civil Rights and Liberties in the United States*, 4th ed. Oxford: Oxford University Press, 1982.

Brigham, John. *Civil Liberties and American Democracy*. Washington, D.C.: Congressional Quarterly Press, 1984.

Epstein, Richard A. *Forbidden Grounds: The Case Against Employment Discrimination Laws*. Cambridge: Harvard University Press, 1992.

Hacker, Andrew. *Two Nations: Black and White, Separate, Hostile, Unequal*. New York: Scribner, 1992.

Henthoff, Nat. *The First Freedom: The Tumultuous History of Free Speech in America*. New York: Delacorte, 1980.

_____. *Free Speech For Me But Not For Thee*. New York: HarperCollins, 1993.

Irons, Peter, and Stephanie Guitton, eds. *May It Please the Court. . .: Historic Oral Arguments Before the United States Supreme Court* (book/tape set). New York: New Press/Norton, 1993.

Lewis, Anthony. *Gideon's Trumpet*. New York: Vintage, 1964.

Nedelsky, Jennifer. *Private Property and the Limits of American Constitutionalism*. Chicago: University of Chicago Press, 1990.

Powlege, Fred. *Free at Last? The Civil Rights Movement and the People Who Made It*. Boston: Little, Brown, 1990.

Siegan, Bernard H. *Economic Liberties and the Constitution*. Chicago: University of Chicago Press, 1983.

Walker, Samuel. *In Defense of American Liberties*. New York: Oxford University Press, 1990.

Part III

THE CIVIC CULTURE
PARTICIPATION AND POWER

CHAPTER 6

Public Opinion: Culture, Society, and the Individual

CHAPTER 7

Participation: The Forms of Political Action

CHAPTER 8

Interest-Group Politics

CHAPTER 9

Political Parties: Engines of Government

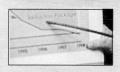

CHAPTER 10

Campaigns and Elections: The Political Guidance System

CHAPTER 11

Mass Mediated Democracy

Polls are the obsession of every modern White House and every political professional, Republican and Democratic, I know. In every political meeting I have ever been to, if there was a pollster there his words carried the most weight because he is the only one with hard data, with actual numbers on actual paper. . . .

There is nothing wrong with taking the temperature of the electorate in order to know how the people of a vast nation feel about an issue. Lincoln himself said, "Public opinion is everything," and he might have appreciated having such a sophisticated tool to help guide him in how to achieve an objective. But we would like to think—in fact, we know—that he would not have used polls to tell him whether to pursue the objective, or whether it was worth pursuing. . . .

One of the reasons Lincoln was great is that he would have looked at the data presented by his pollster and said something like, "I see they're against the war, so I guess I'll have to communicate the argument for keeping the Union together better than I have." He would not have said, "Gee, they're against it—guess I'd better not spend my capital on a losing game just to help the Negroes!"

—*PEGGY NOONAN*

Public Opinion: Culture, Society, and the Individual

- **OPINION POLLS IN THE NEWS**
- **OPINION, POWER, AND DEMOCRACY**
  Defining Public Opinion
  Opinion and Democracy
  The Power of Opinion
  The Politics of Public Opinion
- **OPINION FORMATION AND CHANGE**
  Socialization and Political Learning
  Social Characteristics and Opinion
  How Opinions Change
- **POLITICAL CULTURE AND IDEOLOGY**
  Ideology
  American Pragmatism
- **THE BATTLE FOR PUBLIC OPINION**
  Climates of Opinion
  The Uses of Political Symbols
  The Media
- **DESCRIBING AND MEASURING OPINION**
  Describing Opinion Formations
  Opinion Measurement
- **OPINION, POWER, AND DEMOCRACY REVISITED**
- **A CITIZEN'S QUESTION: Forming More Effective Opinions**
- **KEY TERMS**
- **SUGGESTED READINGS**

Although there are many forms of public opinion that appear in the news, polls are probably the most easily recognized. Opinion polls are cited regularly in news reports on many aspects of American politics. However, polls can be challenging to interpret. The opinion reported in them can change rapidly, sometimes because people do not have much information to anchor their thinking, and sometimes because they are responding to important and dramatic changes in political reality. The examples below illustrate why news reports about polls are easier to interpret with some basic understanding of what public opinion is, why it changes, and how it can affect politicians and their actions.

When large numbers of people react similarly to a situation like a war or an economic recession, reporters and pollsters may talk about a national mood or climate of opinion. For example, during and shortly after the Persian Gulf War against Iraq in 1991, Americans were overwhelmingly enthusiastic about the leadership of President George Bush. His presidential "approval" levels of 88 percent were the highest ever recorded in the history of polling. A year later, however, the glow of the war had faded, and Mr. Bush faced approval ratings in the low 30 percent range, and eventually lost the 1992 election despite predictions just a year earlier that he was unbeatable. Opinion about Mr. Bush's record on specific domestic problems eventually undermined his general approval ratings.[1] Poll-watchers and media experts agreed that the president had to do something bold to regain public favor and save his presidency. However, in the end, he did not introduce such programs into his election campaign. On the eve of his defeat to Bill Clinton, he even canceled his daily poll briefings. (See Chapter 10.) He seemed unwilling to adjust politically to being an "opinion object"—a sort of moving symbolic target onto which people project their feelings about changing life circumstances.

Opinion swings often reflect public (and media) attention shifting from one topic to another. Overwhelming media attention to a victorious war leads people to different thoughts and feelings than when a struggling economy is the main topic in the daily news, creating a source of worry for individuals trying to earn a living. For example, just three months before the Persian Gulf War broke out, a struggling economy and a budget deadlock in Washington competed with the crisis in the Persian Gulf for national attention. Only 19 percent of those surveyed in a Washington Post/ABC News poll said the country was on the "right track." A few months later, in March of 1991 after the public had rallied in support of a victorious war effort, a majority of 58 percent

President Bush welcomes home veterans of the 1991 Persian Gulf War. In the wake of Operation Desert Storm, Bush's approval ratings hit nearly ninety percent; yet on November 3, 1992 he would lose his bid for re-election, receiving only thirty-eight percent of the vote. Theorists debate whether such a rollercoaster ride in public standing reflects an officeholder's job performance or instead reveals the instability of popular sentiment.

said the country was on the right track. Only a month later, when the glow of victory began to fade and economic problems began creeping back into the news, the number who felt that the country was on the right track dropped to 42 percent, and continued dropping after that. These dramatic public opinion swings were analyzed in a news story with the headline: POSTWAR GLOW HAS FADED, POLL FINDS.[2] As pollster Linda DiVall said of the shift in opinion about the direction of the country after the end of the Persian Gulf War: "It's not surprising. Now it appears the country is focussing on the next problem and . . . it's the economy more than anything."[3]

Consider another example of how opinion can change in response to changing political situations. As you may recall from Chapter 1, a defining characteristic of American political culture is a relatively high level of public opposition to government solutions for such social problems as poverty, homelessness, or unemployment. In a fairly typical poll result, a 1988 survey showed that only 35 percent felt that the government was spending "too little" to improve the conditions of black Americans. Just four years later, in 1992, rioting broke out among thousands of residents in Los Angeles following the acquittal of several police officers who had been accused of beating a black motorist. In the wake of the great devastation and days of frightening television coverage of those riots, a national poll recorded fully 61 percent saying that the government spent "too little" on improving the conditions of black Americans. One reason why public concern for the problems of

blacks rose so sharply was suggested in the headline of a news story: LOS ANGELES RIOTS ARE A WARNING, AMERICANS FEAR.[4]

These examples suggest that opinion can be shaped by many factors, both short- and long-term. Short-term factors include fears and emotional states, shifting media attention patterns, the persuasion techniques used by political players, and the climate of surrounding opinion. These short-term, situational factors are filtered through more enduring individual attitudes based on social characteristics such as gender, race, or religion, along with ideology and political party affiliation. These shifting forces behind opinions present challenges both for citizens trying to work out their own views in a changing world, as well as for officials trying to decide what the public wants. What is the "real" opinion about government programs to help blacks and other groups suffering poverty and other inequalities, 35 percent or 61 percent? Should officials listen more seriously to opinion expressed in the abstract (when no particular situation or crisis grabs public interest and attention), or should they pay more attention to opinion that arises in response to actual political situations, even if those situations inject dramatic and emotional elements into the thinking of individuals? These and other questions make it challenging to interpret public opinion.

The problem of how to interpret public opinion is not restricted just to the opinion expressed in polls. In fact, some observers discount the polls as artificial expressions of opinion.[5] After all, the people whose

Dramatic events, such as the riots that devastated south-central Los Angeles in April 1992, often cause brief spikes in public awareness and concern—but the effect tends to be short-lived. By the time general elections were held in November of that year, most voter attention had turned from urban and racial problems to topics such as the federal deficit, a flat economy, and the tantalizing possibility (raised during the campaign) of a middle-class tax cut.

opinions are reported in surveys do not form coherent social groups as the idea of a "public" might imply, and they are often asked about issues that hold little importance for them before the pollster called. Other analysts criticize polls because they may draw out the least stable and knowledgeable opinions in society:

> Do we or don't we have a citizenry whose views are worth soliciting? Does polling give real answers to trivial questions and trivial answers to real questions? In other words, does grass roots democracy work, or are people barely knowledgeable enough to elect better-informed citizens to represent them?[6]

Despite reservations about placing so much importance on polls, news organizations and politicians alike continue to use them as a simple way of representing "public opinion." Polls are compelling because they are based on scientific methods, and they provide estimates of the ways in which large populations of individuals think and feel about many different issues and leaders. As long as they are not taken as the only form of public opinion expression, the polls reported in the news can contribute to the richness of our national political communication. Whatever one thinks about their qualities as "public opinion," polls will remain an important feature of our democratic process, and it is therefore a good idea to know how to interpret them.

Whether we are trying to understand opinion reported in polls, or as it comes at us in other forms, it is helpful to think about these larger questions that frame the discussion in this chapter: What is public opinion? When is it (and when should it be) taken seriously by leaders in making decisions? Why does public opinion change? How do pollsters measure opinion and describe its changes? How do politicians react to changing opinion, including attempts to control it? In addition to helping students understand the role of opinion in democratic government, this chapter also suggests why citizens might want to think about their own opinions. Learning how opinions translate into power is also useful for thinking about how to make your own views more effective as they join the chorus of public opinion.

Opinion, Power, and Democracy

Beyond the familiar form of opinion polls, it is important not to forget that public opinion comes in many other forms, ranging from the messages promoted by interest organizations to the angry sentiments expressed in protests and demonstrations. Before looking at how various forms of opinion enter into politics and how they are created in the first place, a simple definition of the concept may be useful.

Defining Public Opinion

An **opinion** *is simply a personal evaluation of something in the outside world.* Psychologists refer to the people (Bill Clinton), places (China), things (the American flag), and actions (raising taxes) that people evaluate in their opinions as **opinion objects**. Forming an opinion involves a) deciding what the object is, and b) how one feels about it. For example, if the issue is taxes, one person may link taxes with economic enterprise, while another may connect taxes more with balancing the budget. If the first person believes that raising taxes is a sure way to kill economic incentive, his or her opinion on tax increases will be different from the person who believes that raising taxes is the only way to reduce the national debt. These differences of opinion can be described in terms of their **direction**, meaning that one is positive and the other negative. Sometimes people feel neutral about something, either because they really don't have an opinion, or because their opinion is conflicted, having both positive and negative aspects to it. For example, someone who believes that taxes are bad for the economy, but also necessary to reduce the national debt, might express a more neutral opinion because of this conflict. Depending on how important an issue is and how much conflict a person experiences in thinking about it, opinions also have an **intensity**. An opinion's intensity reflects the strength of feeling behind it, ranging from a *strong* negative or positive reaction to only a *weak* feeling in one direction or the other.

Opinion becomes public when numbers of individuals express their views about the same object. As noted above, there are many ways in which public opinion can be expressed, including: responding to opinion polls; calling talk shows; voting; interest group activities; displaying bumper stickers, pins, and decals; and joining demonstrations and protests. Most social scientists who study opinion think of society as having many potential publics that form and dissolve in response to changing social, economic, and political conditions. This is precisely what makes democracy such a surprising and often volatile form of government. Opinion is the foundation from which the various patterns of power and participation in American politics develop.

Opinion and Democracy

What does it mean when a thousand or a few hundred thousand individuals out of a population of millions care enough to demonstrate for a particular cause? How much more seriously should their feelings be taken simply because they care intensely about something? For that matter, how seriously should majority opinion be taken by government officials, recalling from the opening examples how fluid those opinion formations can be? These are fundamental questions about democracy because the basis of democratic legitimacy is popular sovereignty.

The questions of who the government should respond to, and how it should respond are the most sensitive questions of democracy. When people feel that they are being neglected, they often find ways of expressing their opinions more forcefully. Recall from Chapter 2, the debates at the time of the Constitutional Convention about how to deal with unruly outbursts of public opinion like the rebellions in Massachusetts and elsewhere. Even though direct links between opinion and specific governmental decisions were discouraged in the constitutional design of American government, it is clear that the founders understood that public opinion would be a major force. The major question in 1787 was: How *should* public opinion enter into the process of governing? A major question for political scientists ever since is: How *does* opinion enter into the decisions of government?

A study of polls and policy over the last fifty years conducted by political scientists Benjamin Page and Robert Shapiro suggests that there has been a strong relationship between what the majority wants and what the government does in most areas of domestic and foreign policy.[7] What is far less clear, however, is whether the broad relationship between majority opinion and government policies is because leaders generally follow the will of the people, or because they have learned how to drum up public support for their policies. Each of the models of social power introduced in Chapter 1 is helpful for sorting out these questions about how opinion is formed and what its political effects really are.

The Power of Opinion

How might a **majoritarian** view of power lead us to think about opinion? To begin with, we immediately think of elections in which majorities express their opinions of candidates. Through the vote, majorities have a direct say in who wins and loses public office. It is also clear that on a few issues that really matter to large numbers of people, representatives are more likely to think of themselves as *delegates* of the publics who voted for them rather than as independent-minded *trustees* of the public interest. Thus, the majoritarian model of power in the American democracy helps to explain at least two important roles of opinion in government:

- majorities express their views about national priorities by electing leaders who support those views

- in-between elections, important issues and problems can arouse strong majority opinion that may pressure government representatives into action

The **pluralist** view of power explains how relatively small publics can exert enough pressure on government officials to get their issues on the agenda and influence government actions. For example, groups of AIDS activists have shaped government policies in important ways, using a variety of political tactics to make their opinions heard: enlisting experts to give their opinions credibility; recruiting celebrities such as Elizabeth Taylor, Michael Jackson, and "Magic" Johnson to publicize their cause; and staging demonstrations to indicate frustration with slow government responses. Over the years, both government officials and members of the general public became more aware that AIDS was not just a problem for homosexuals, or that in any event it deserved a higher government priority. Pluralist perspectives remind us that:

- groups far smaller than majorities can express their views effectively and get their issues on the government agenda

- by using public information campaigns, the endorsements of respected personalities, and public protests, minority opinion can sometimes be expressed effectively enough to change majority opinion

An interesting example of small but intense groups affecting majority opinion involves homosexuals struggling for acceptance or toleration in mainstream society. Figure 6.1 shows that majorities have gradually come to accept hiring homosexuals in many walks of economic life. However, the support of majorities can erode quickly when leaders, who provide cues for public opinion, take political positions opposed to the

Film star Elizabeth Taylor addresses a press briefing at an international conference on AIDS held in Amsterdam, July 1992. In a society as hyperconscious of the media as is the United States, celebrities often seem to influence opinion powerfully. The images of prominent people, whether celebrities or politicians, serve as cues for many individuals trying to simplify complex issues.

FIGURE 6.1

Patterns of Majority Opinion on a Minority Issue

Question: Do you think homosexuals should or should not be hired for each of the following occupations?

Homosexuals should be hired for...

Armed forces

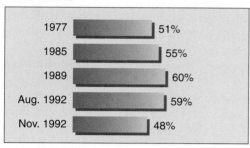

President's cabinet

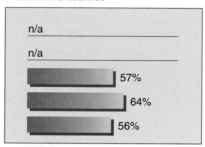

Salespersons

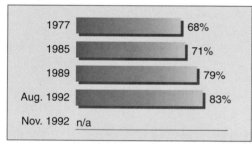

Doctors

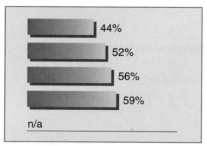

High school teachers

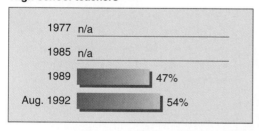

Elementary school teachers

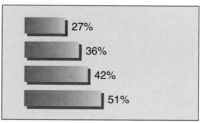

Clergy

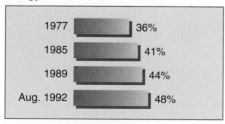

Note: n/a–not asked.

Source: Surveys by the Gallup Organization. Reprinted from *The Public Perspective*, March/April 1993, Vol. 4, No. 3, p. 84.

demands of such organizations. Figure 6.1 also shows the erosion of public support for admitting overt homosexuals into the military after a number of prominent politicians and military officers spoke out against President Clinton's proposal to lift the Pentagon ban on homosexuals in the armed forces.

The **elitist** view of power reminds us of important limits in both the majoritarian and the pluralist models. Sometimes government responds to a few prominent insiders who have personal access to politicians. For example, it is common for the heads of major business companies to meet personally with members of Congress, cabinet officers, and even presidents. This personal access can make elite opinions heard more clearly at times than those of less powerful interest groups or even majorities. In at least one well-documented case, business owners and Wall Street insiders convinced President Eisenhower (through his Secretary of State and CIA director, who were former Wall Street insiders) to support the overthrow of an elected government in Guatemala in 1954. That government was threatening to tighten up on special deals given to American companies. Public relations experts were also hired to present the coup to the American public as a restoration (rather than an overthrow) of Guatamalan democracy.[8] This suggests that even when larger publics agree with elite opinions and the government acts that flow from them, their opinion may be shaped by public information campaigns sponsored by elites. Political scientists such as Murray Edelman argue that the use of emotional symbols and propaganda by elites to define issues can have important effects on how people

In the view of some elite theorists, political insiders generally exercise power while either operating entirely outside the venue of public opinion or else steering it along desirable paths. During the 1950s, for example, the Dulles brothers wielded enormous authority in government posts with little direct public accountability; both men had risen to power through diplomatic and appointive roles. Here, at Washington National Airport in 1956, John Foster Dulles (left), Secretary of State under Dwight Eisenhower, speaks with his brother Allen, long-time head of the Central Intelligence Agency. However, even such positions may not be wholly secure from majority restraints: Allen Dulles resigned amid the public reaction to the abortive 1961 Bay of Pigs operation, in which CIA-backed Cuban exiles made a disastrous military foray against the Castro regime.

Opinion and Power in Environmental Politics

6.1

Conflicts over how to conserve the environment often involve all three forms of power (majoritarian, pluralist, and elitist) as opinion enters the resolution of those conflicts.

Many environmental disputes begin with environmental interest groups like the Sierra Club, Friends of the Earth, or Greenpeace, who object to the ways in which natural resources are being used or harvested. Typical of *pluralist* patterns of power, these groups often find ways to mobilize their members by alerting them to a particular case of environmental damage and publicizing information to dramatize the situation. Small but intense expressions of opinion become directed at key pressure points in government.

Larger publics may also become involved when these environmental "crisis" situations are publicized through news and public affairs programs, or through national information and advertising campaigns sponsored by the groups. Majority opinion may be stirred by photographs and video images of ghastly oil spills, clear-cut forests, the bloody bodies of seal pups, endangered spotted owls, or porpoises dying in tuna fishing nets. When *majorities* become more concerned about protecting the environment, as they have over the years, politicians may fear voter reprisals and worry about being associated with unpopular policies. As a result, laws and regulations may become more environmentally sensitive.

In order to preserve their economic practices, *elite* groups of industry owners may hire advertising and marketing firms to create more positive images of their activities and counterattack with powerful symbols of their own. Arousing fears about losing jobs can limit the willingness of majorities to support wholesale environmental regulation. Keeping environmental issues from becoming too volatile makes it easier to reach political compromises between government regulators, economic elites, and environmental groups.

Without public opinion operating at all three levels of power, environmental politics in America would be much different than it is. Can you think of an opinion-power balance that would lead to greater environmental protection? Less protection?

---

think.[9] The elite view of opinion and democracy also contributes two important factors to round out the political picture of public opinion:

- because elites have special access to politicians, their opinions may be heard more clearly than other opinion

- elites can afford to hire opinion and public relations experts to generate broader public support for their opinions and the government policies that flow from them

Sometimes all three patterns of opinion and power come into play as a political situation unfolds. For example, political conflicts may develop through the activities of small publics (pluralism in action) who eventually attract the attention and support of larger majorities (majoritarianism comes into play), magnifying public demands for political action. When those demands get the attention of government officials, elites (elitism is engaged) who are concerned about losing their grip on an issue may launch persuasion campaigns aimed at changing public opinion. This scenario often develops in conflicts over the protection of the environment, as illustrated in "Inside the System" Box 6.1.

The Politics of Public Opinion

The interplay of power and opinion in actual political situations reminds us that it is too simple to think that opinions spring independently into the minds of individuals and then become expressed in ways that pressure decision makers to act according to the will of the people. Rather, it makes sense to think of opinion as a political force that changes as political situations develop and different political players try to win public support for their positions. As the tides of opinion change, power in a situation may flow from one side to another. An economic downturn can turn a supportive majority against a president and his policies. An interest group can strengthen its political position by educating the majority about its cause. Elites can try to represent their activities as being in the broad public interest. Here is how political scientist Benjamin Ginsberg suggests thinking about the politics of public opinion:

> It can be misleading to ascribe to [public opinion] a causal role in the political process. Opinion is not like the weather on election day—a . . . force that affects politics but is not affected by it. Instead, public opinion is itself a result of political struggles and conflicts. To assert that a particular decision or policy was caused by public opinion is often misleading because it ignores the underlying reality of groups, forces, and interests that struggle to influence both opinions and policies. . . . The popular attitudes that [are often presumed] to be the determinants of political outcomes and policies are often in fact the results of efforts by competing political forces to shape opinion precisely in order to enhance their ability to influence policy.[10]

When thinking about where opinion comes from and what it does, it helps to keep an open mind about the broad range of different political situations. Political scientists use concepts and theories to analyze opinion in actual situations. The next sections illustrate how public opinion can be shaped by different political forces.

Opinion Formation and Change

To expand upon our earlier definition, recall that an opinion is an evaluation or judgment about some external object. This means that opinions are the product of interactions between possibly short-term properties of situations and more enduring orientations of individuals. In this section, we explore the ways in which individuals acquire and change their orientations to politics. The core elements of a political orientation are beliefs and values. This means that underlying *an opinion is a belief component that tells people what something is and how it fits into their reality, and a value component that affects how they feel about it.* Our basic beliefs and values are acquired through a process called *political socialization.*

Socialization and Political Learning

The things that people learn about politics in childhood can affect their political thinking throughout life. This idea of some lasting effects from early political socialization has been called the **primacy principle**, referring to the idea that things learned early in life can remain in an adult's political orientation. Although it is clear that children pick up many political ideas from their parents, peers, and teachers, those early learning experiences can fade when people change their social environments, move away from home, take new jobs, go to college, make new friends, or live through life-changing experiences like unemployment, divisive wars, or periods of social upheaval. Some researchers find a carryover of early childhood learning into adult life in areas like party identification and racial prejudice. However, when early socialization is so persistent, it also tends to be accompanied by little change in social surroundings later on as people move through the stages of their adult lives.

Most political scientists see socialization as a lifelong process in which people continue to learn new ideas and develop new patterns of behavior and party affiliation as long as their environments continue to change.[11] The idea that socialization is an ongoing process of adaptation and learning helps explain changing patterns of public opinion in a diverse society in which people move, experience dislocation, and confront new problems, all within a flexible culture that permits relatively easy shifts among political values and beliefs. People are influenced in this ongoing process of social and political adaptation by family, friends, teachers, work associates, the media, and by inspiring political leaders who influence the individual's political outlook. Social scientists refer to these sources that shape an individual's political orientations as **agents of socialization**.

FAMILY.   The family, of course, is the place where political education starts. Children are sensitive to what their parents approve and disapprove of. Long before children understand what a political party is or what it does, they may know which one they belong to. By the age of ten, fully half of all children claim some sort of political party affiliation. A few decades ago, when party loyalty was stronger than it is today among adults, it was stronger among children, too. In recent years, more children have followed their parents by claiming to be political "independents." The important lesson about family is that children tend to start their political lives with outlooks similar to those of their parents. Figure 6.2 shows how often children follow the party identification of their parents.

FIGURE 6.2

*Children Following Their Parents in Party Identification
(During an Earlier Era of Stronger Democratic Identification)*

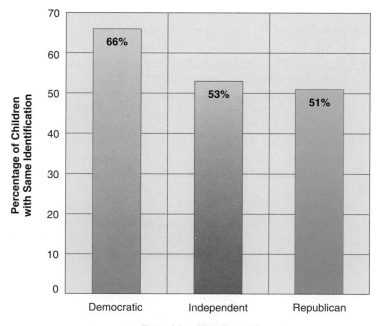

Party Identification of Parents

Source: M. Kent Jennings and Richard G. Niemi, *The Political Character of Adolescence: The Influence of Families and Schools.* Princeton: Princeton University Press, 1974, p. 41. Note that this study was done at a time when parental Democratic identification was strong; current polling would therefore reveal identification in line with prevailing trends.

Parental and family views of politics are often decisive factors for many people in forming their own political opinions. Above, a family in Centralia, Illinois, waves at the passing of the Clinton–Gore campaign bus in 1992.

Note that this study was done in the 1970s, when more of those parents were Democrats than Republicans, meaning that the surrounding society was more supportive of children who became Democrats, too. This explains the higher percentage of children from Democratic families who adopted the family party identification. Today we would expect Independent and Republican family socialization effects to be higher, since those family patterns are more reinforced in the surrounding society. Studies have shown that the impact of family begins to weaken somewhat in the late teen years as young adults encounter other powerful agents of socialization such as schools and peer groups.[12]

SCHOOL.   The school is a force that can rival the family in forming our political orientations. For this reason, many parents and religious groups become involved with school board politics and try to shape the content of the public school curriculum. It is not surprising that fierce political battles are fought over how much explicit political and religious indoctrination should go on in the schools. Not surprisingly, most public schools tend to play it safe, presenting a generally positive and patriotic view of American politics. Until they enter college, many students experience school as a patriotic environment with flag displays and national anthems at sporting events. Civics courses tend to promote positive views of American democracy, and history books emphasize popular myths over critical perspectives and minority viewpoints. As a result, many students (and their parents) are shocked later on if the college curriculum contains other, more critical perspectives. College instructors often encourage the clash of perspectives in the classroom as a way to motivate students to think analytically about the political differences in society.

Beyond the political content of the curriculum, an equally important point about schools is that students encounter there new agents of socialization who may compete with their parents. Teachers may provoke new ways of thinking about politics, and new circles of friends can provide different ideas about society and authority. Throughout life, from school to the job, the peer group remains an important agent of socialization.

PEER GROUPS.   The peer group is the third pillar of political socialization. Most of us would acknowledge that outside of family and school, our views of the world are shaped most importantly by our friends and associates. When friends, classmates, fraternity brothers, or sorority sisters feel strongly about something, it can be hard to resist the pressure to "join the crowd." This point was illustrated dramatically in one of the classic studies in the history of the social sciences. During the Depression years of the 1930s, a psychologist named Theodore Newcomb studied the political cross-pressures experienced by students at Bennington College in Vermont. In those years, Bennington was an

Peer groups and scholastic influences (frequently working in tandem) continue the shaping of political views begun by the family. Thus participants in academic battles over "multicultural education" and "political correctness" often view their skirmishes as part of a broader struggle over society's vision of the national culture itself.

exclusive women's college that catered to the daughters of some of the wealthiest families in America. These families were predominantly Republican and opposed to the social policies of Franklin Roosevelt. This Democratic leader was elected in 1932 by a popular landslide to implement his "New Deal" package of social reforms to ease the suffering brought on by the Depression. As the Depression deepened, social passions ran high. Many of the faculty at Bennington were liberal Democrats who made persuasive arguments for the Democratic programs. Away from the influences of family, many students adopted the new views, creating a strong climate of *peer group pressure* in the school. The results of this combination of faculty and peer pressure were striking. Whereas the majority of students declared themselves Republicans when they entered the college, the majority were Democrats by the time they graduated. Moreover, many of those who resisted the pressures to change reported to school counselors that they often felt like outcasts, and some suffered severe psychological problems as a result.[13]

Newcomb later followed up to see what happened to these women later in life. The pattern that emerged twenty-five years later was equally fascinating. Those who moved to liberal communities and joined liberal peer groups after college tended to maintain their Democratic party allegiance and hold more liberal opinions about social issues. On the other hand, those who moved to more conservative communities and joined more conservative peer groups became Republicans and adopted more conservative political views.[14] These studies illustrate the idea that socialization is a lifelong political learning process. To the extent that our socialization experiences change later in life, the foundations of our opinions may well change along with them. What will become of today's more independent students if there is a strong shift in social attitudes about parties? Be prepared for new socialization experiences ahead!

THE MEDIA.   Families, schools, and peer groups are generally regarded as *primary* **agents of socialization** because they have the most important effects on individuals' political outlooks. *Secondary* agents of socialization refer to a variety of less powerful but commonly encountered sources of political learning. The media promote many important political ideas that can help fill in an individual's political thinking. Demands by women and minorities for removal of stereotypes in television entertainment programming have begun to introduce more realistic social issues and characters in the nation's most popular medium. How people see others like themselves portrayed in the media can affect their self-image and their sense of *political efficacy,* or their confidence that they can act politically in ways that make a difference.

POLITICAL LEADERS AS ROLE MODELS.   People also learn things from their political leaders. Inspiring leaders can encourage people to participate in politics and have the confidence to express their opinions forcefully. Leaders can make isolated individuals aware that other people share the same frustrations and bring people together to do something about them. When people lack inspiring leadership they can draw the conclusion that nobody cares about their opinions. The political world can seem distant and hostile. Popular leaders, by contrast, are like political teachers, helping people to understand their problems and showing them how to express their opinions effectively. Over the years, whole generations of Americans have been inspired personally by great political leaders. Can you think of a leader, either national or local, who has made a difference in your thinking about politics?

Social Characteristics and Opinion

The socialization experience is very personal. No two individuals pick up quite the same mix of values and beliefs. However, many people do share some similar social experiences because they have some social characteristics in common, such as being male or female; rich or poor; black, white, Latino, or Native American; Protestant, Catholic, Jewish, or Buddhist. While not all boys or girls, black or white children are raised in the same way, it is clear that some experiences are fairly common. Boys tend to be encouraged to be competitive and aggressive. Whites generally experience authorities as more supportive than minorities do. With greater education, people learn to be more tolerant of different viewpoints. Social differences do not enter into our thinking about everything, but they can have dramatic effects on public opinion about many topics.

Social differences have not had much effect on public opinion about legalization of drugs. It appears that drugs are associated with problems for almost every group in society. For some time, the vast majority of Americans have opposed the legalization of drugs, no matter what their race, religion, education, income, or political party affiliation. One national survey on drug policies broke the respondents down into twenty-four different social categories, only to find that the differences across most of those groups were very slight, with opposition to legalizing drugs running in the mid-70 percent range in most groups. The only slight exceptions were the 80 percent of nonwhites who opposed legalizing drugs, and a low of 67 percent opposition among residents of the western states.[15]

On some political issues, by contrast, many different social characteristics enter into the formation of opinion. For example, opinion about the causes of poverty is affected by no fewer than eight social categories, including gender, age, region, race, education, political party affiliation, ideological self-definition, and income. Of the nine social categories measured in one survey on the causes of poverty, only religion had little effect on the opinions of those who responded. See Table 6.1 for an illustration of how different social experience categories affected thinking about the causes of poverty in that survey.

RACE.   As noted in previous chapters, race is one of the most serious points of conflict and tension in American society. On average, members of racial minority groups

TABLE 6.1

Social Differences Affecting Opinions About Why People Are Poor

Survey Question: Which is more often to blame if a person is poor—
lack of effort on his or her part, or circumstances beyond his or her control?

RESPONSES SAYING POVERTY IS DUE TO A LACK OF EFFORT

ENTIRE SURVEY		35 %
SEX	Male	41
	Female	31
AGE	18–29	39
	50 and older	31
REGION	South	42
	East	29
RACE	White	37
	Black	22
EDUCATION	At least some college	40
	High school incomplete	26
POLITICS	Republicans	46
	Independents	35
	Democrats	27
IDEOLOGY	Conservative	45
	Moderate	38
	Liberal	28
INCOME (ANNUAL)	Over $50,000	46
	Under $20,000	27
RELIGION	Protestant	36
	Catholic	39

SOURCE: Adapted from Gallup Survey conducted May 17–20, 1990. Survey GO 922010, Q's 29, 31. *The Gallup Monthly,* July 1990, p. 35.

receive less income, education, health care, and other measures of life quality than do white persons born in America. Not surprisingly, the life experiences of racial minorities and white persons create some striking differences in the opinions that members of racial minorities and majorities express on particular issues. For example, Chapter 5 noted much higher levels of support for expanded civil rights legislation among blacks than whites. In addition, blacks are more likely than whites to describe themselves as liberals and to support the Democratic party.

Race also affects how people think about many economic issues. A question often asked by pollsters is whether the government should do something to reduce income differences between the rich and the poor. Figure 6.3 shows the results of a series of surveys conducted between 1978 and 1989 on this question, illustrating steady differences of opinion between different racial groups on this issue.

FIGURE 6.3

Racial Differences of Opinion About
Government Policies to Reduce Income Differences

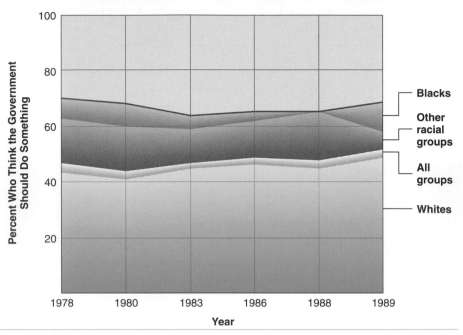

Source: Adapted from National Opinion Research Center surveys, reported in Floris W. Wood, ed., *An American Profile—Opinions and Behavior, 1972–1989.* Gale Research Inc., 1990, pp. 570–572.

As with all social effects on opinion, the differences shown in Figure 6.3 reflect general tendencies, or averages. Enduring social differences (also called cleavages) are generally not so large as to cause a complete alienation between members of different groups, although they may be great enough to cause considerable social tension and conflict. A balance between group differences and overlaps in society means that for most people, no single social trait dominates the entire social experience. People are not just black or white, they are also men or women, young or old, and rich or poor. Thus, taking different combinations of social characteristics into account often changes the patterns of opinion that emerge. Surveys of black Americans reveal substantial differences of opinion within the black population on many subjects. For example, 73 percent of blacks surveyed in a 1992 poll said they identified with the Democratic party, but the percentage of black Democrats dropped to just 62 percent in the age group under thirty-five years old, reflecting the different social experiences and views of younger people.[16]

CLASS.   Income is another major social division that affects opinion on many issues. Most Americans think of themselves as middle class, but important differences in social experience may separate those at the low-income and high-income ends of the spectrum. Life is simply easier for those with more money. Not surprisingly, their political concerns tend to be different. These income differences often show up on opinion questions having to do with freedom and equality. In general, people earning higher incomes are more likely to favor ideas and policies that expand personal freedoms, while those in the lower income brackets are more supportive of equality-oriented ideas such as jobs programs, health care, public housing, and higher wages and better benefits. These differences of opinion underscore how dramatically a social difference such as the size of a paycheck and the lifestyle it buys can structure our public debates about welfare policies and other public issues. In such European societies as Germany, the Netherlands, and Sweden there is a tendency for upper-income groups to be less resistant to policies that redistribute the wealth. Recall this discussion of different political cultures from Chapter 1.

GENDER.   Gender is another category through which differences in social experience are often reflected in public opinion formations. Although the socialization of men and women may not be as different as it was in an earlier era of traditional sex roles, it is clear that women continue to be encouraged to play less aggressive, peacemaker roles in the family and in society. Later in life, women often experience much greater levels of financial hardship than men. These experiences clearly enter into the political outlook of many women, creating a "gender gap" in opinion on many issues. For example, many polls show that women have been significantly more opposed than men to American involvement in wars ever since the Vietnam era of the 1960s. In other areas, women tend to be more supportive of funding for social programs, reducing the defense budget, controlling the sale of firearms, and pursuing diplomacy over military solutions in international relations. On the issue of government action to reduce poverty, women are slightly more supportive than men, but more opposed to such government action than members of racial minority groups.[17] Can you think of some of the differences in sex roles that might account for men being more opposed to welfare programs, gun control, closing the poverty gap, and reducing the defense budget?

RELIGION.   Religion is so central to the lives of many Americans that it also affects their political thinking on many issues. For example, members of fundamentalist Christian churches have pressed for a political agenda of moral legislation that includes outlawing abortion and legalizing prayer in schools. Such groups have been very effective in

Despite the formal separation of church and state that marks the Constitution, religious values clearly shape the political views of many Americans. Here, while their rabbi lights a menorah (as if in a common spirit with the Statue of Liberty), young boys of the Lubavitch Youth Organization gather on Liberty Island during a Hanukkah observance. Indeed, the Jewish writer Will Herberg termed the modernist vision of a wholly secular society "a cut-flower culture"—arguing that any society lacking roots in some spiritual source must inevitably wither.

mobilizing their supporters to lobby politicians, elect candidates, and use the media to publicize their causes. These political successes illustrate the capacity of political minorities to express their opinions effectively, offering a good example of the pluralist model of opinion in action. This illustrates the important link between public opinion and political action which will be explored further in the next chapter.

Beyond the impact of religion on specific issues, the more general importance of religion in American politics is simply due to the fact that so many Americans hold strong religious beliefs. This creates a greater public acceptance for religious imagery and references to God in speeches, public ceremonies, and other areas of political life than is common in many other countries. "How We Compare" Box 6.2 shows different levels of religious belief in the United States as compared to selected European nations.

Among the many other social divisions that can enter into the formation of public opinion are age, education, and the region of the country in which people live. Astrological signs, by contrast, do not have any measured effect on public opinion.[18] No matter how avidly millions of people may read their astrological forecasts in newspapers and magazines each day, they do not organize their social worlds and political beliefs around this experience, as they do around experiences related to their race, gender, class, education, age, or religion.

How Opinions Change

Social experiences also explain a great deal about when and why people change their opinions. Perhaps you have witnessed a dramatic political conversion in yourself or in a friend. Or maybe you have been surprised at how quickly public opinion can shift, as when George Bush went from the heights of public approval in 1991 to the depths of public disapproval in 1992. As noted at the beginning of the chapter, Mr. Bush rode a public opinion roller coaster that began with predictions that he could not lose his bid for reelection and ended with his decisive electoral defeat by Bill Clinton. In thinking about how opinions change, it is helpful to consider two kinds of changes—**long-term changes** in individual experience, and **short-term changes** in political situations that affect the thinking of individuals in more volatile ways.

There are many enduring changes that individuals go through in life: leaving home, going to college, moving to another city, getting married, growing older, and becoming richer or poorer, just to name a few. For the reasons outlined above, these social experiences can lead people to react differently to the political world around them. Long-term changes in political thinking are particularly likely to occur if, as his or her social conditions change, the individual also forms new peer groups and becomes *socialized* in new ways of thinking about those life conditions. Long-term social changes can affect what people pay attention to, how they filter information, and how they make their political judgments.

Opinions can also change dramatically in the short term even if individual lives are relatively stable. Dramatic events or effective persuasion campaigns can grab the attention of individuals, creating changes in opinion that people would not have come to on their own. In the opening example of public reactions to the Los Angeles riots in 1992, levels of popular support for improving the conditions of blacks living in poverty leaped more than 25 points during the week following the riots. It is also typical for such short-term opinion formations to collapse after the triggering events fade from the news or from memory. However, extended periods of social upheaval can have more lasting effects, often polarizing people, as happened during the Great Depression of the 1930s, and the long years of social struggle over the Vietnam War during the 1960s and 1970s. In fact, a prolonged social crisis such as a war or a depression can be classified as a socialization experience that may leave its mark on the political thinking of a whole generation.

The Importance of Religion in Five Democracies

6.2

Percent who agree with the following statements:

"I never doubt the existence of God."

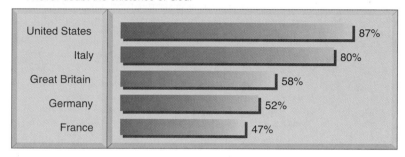

United States	87%
Italy	80%
Great Britain	58%
Germany	52%
France	47%

"There are clear guidelines about what is good and evil."

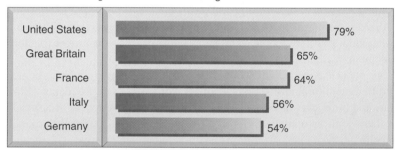

United States	79%
Great Britain	65%
France	64%
Italy	56%
Germany	54%

SOURCE: Times Mirror Center for the People and the Press. Interviews with 13,000 people across Europe. Adapted from *The Public Perspective,* December 1991, p. 8.

Loggers in the state of Washington take a break from their labors. While the public is overwhelmingly supportive of conservation and wildlife-protection measures, those feelings erode sharply—particularly among middle-class and blue-collar families— when strict environmental regulations are seen to threaten existing jobs. For this reason, environmentalist groups and businesses wage public-relations battles for the support of the broader public.

Many opinion shifts reflect a combination of long-term and short-term factors. For example, more Americans have become concerned about the environment over the last twenty years as a result of such long-term factors as environmental education in schools and coverage of environmental problems in the media. However, opinion on a particular environmental issue can change dramatically if people see economic threats attached to environmental protection. Many environmental conflicts become reduced to symbolic exchanges of heart-rending pictures of endangered species countered with the most powerful economic symbol, "jobs."

How do we explain that many enduring views of society and politics sit comfortably alongside changing reactions to everyday social and political issues? Psychologists refer to more stable judgments about abstract issues as *attitudes*, to distinguish them from *opinions,* which are shorter-term judgments affected by specific situations. Research shows that even the most stable political attitudes can bend under the social pressures and value conflicts that arise in specific situations. Because of these shifting patterns of political judgment, the role played by ideology in American politics is different from that found in many other nations.

Political Culture and Ideology

As people develop their political outlooks, their personal views are often inspired by the dominant themes of the political culture. In Chapter 1, some of those core cultural themes were introduced: *liberty or freedom* (including popular ideas about individualism, competitiveness, and respect for private property), creating *social order* through the rule of law, *limiting the power of government*, using *government as a social problem solver*, and providing *equality of opportunity* and *equal treatment under the law* for all citizens. These themes are not all perfectly compatible. Indeed, they reflect historical struggles over what kind of society people want, and what they see as the proper role for government in maintaining that society.

As a result of personal experiences involving these values in society, individuals come to identify with different cultural ideals. Some people favor freedom over equality. Others emphasize law and order over individual freedoms. Some see government as a social activist, while others want to minimize this role. These patterns of political thinking often become labelled in such ideological terms as **liberal** and **conservative**. The meaning of these terms often becomes confused in everyday conversation, as well as in news reports and analyses of opinion polls. It is important to define and use these terms carefully.

Ideology

An **ideology** refers to a well-organized, strongly held set of beliefs and values that a person uses to form very consistent and usually very intense opinions. If by ideology we mean this ability to apply a set of political principles consistently to political issues and situations, only a tiny percentage of Americans (probably less than 10 percent) can be called ideologues.[19] Some political scientists have constructed ideology tests that are easier to pass, requiring only that people identify themselves somewhere along a left-to-right range from liberal to moderate to conservative.[20] Not surprisingly, many more people qualify as having an ideology by these measures.

Although the concept of ideology may not help us understand how most individuals actually think, many people do use ideological references to identify themselves. Ideological terms become symbols that help people identify with and against others in society. When people are asked to place themselves along a scale ranging from extremely liberal to extremely conservative, with moderate in the middle, nearly everyone is able to do this task. More than a decade of national surveys using this self-placement method reveal that only 4–5 percent typically say they do not know where they fit or cannot place themselves on such a scale. When people are pushed to choose which way they "lean" politically, roughly 40 percent say they are moderates, slightly more than 30 percent fall into the conservative range, and around 25 percent claim they are liberal to some degree.[21] When people are not encouraged to say whether they lean in liberal or conservative directions, nearly *half* of the American public are content to call themselves moderates. Figure 6.4 shows the trends in ideological self-placement over the last two decades. These data are drawn from poll questions that do not "push" respondents to say whether they are more liberal or conservative. Figure 6.5, on page 210, shows the levels of ideological self-placement among college freshmen. The even higher levels of political moderation in this group reflect a combination of less clearly developed political orientations among younger people and a slightly different survey instrument in these polls that combines the categories of conservative with far right, and liberal with far left. As we will see in the later section on polling techniques, differences in question wording and response options often produce different results.

Beyond their value as a handy social membership statement, it is not clear exactly what these self-descriptions mean or whether they mean very much. In one study that asked people whether they had thought much about their ideological leanings, more than

FIGURE 6.4

Ideological Self-Placement of the General Public
(Based on Poll Questions that Do Not Push for Liberal or Conservative Leanings)

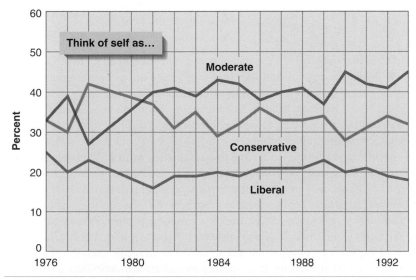

Question: How would you describe your views on most political matters? Generally, do you think of yourself as liberal, moderate, or conservative?

	Lib.	Mod.	Con.
*1976	25%	33%	33%
1977	20	39	30
1978	23	27	42
1981	16	40	37
1982	19	41	31
1983	19	39	35
1984	20	43	29
1985	19	42	32
1986	21	38	36
1987	21	40	33
1988	21	41	33
1989	23	37	34
1990	20	45	28
1991	21	42	31
1992	19	41	34
1993	18	45	32

Note: First asking of each year shown.

Source: Surveys by CBS News/*New York Times,* latest that of January 12–14, 1993. Reprinted from *The Public Perspective,* March/April 1993, Vol. 4, No. 3, p. 84.

FIGURE 6.5

Ideological Self-Placement of College Freshmen

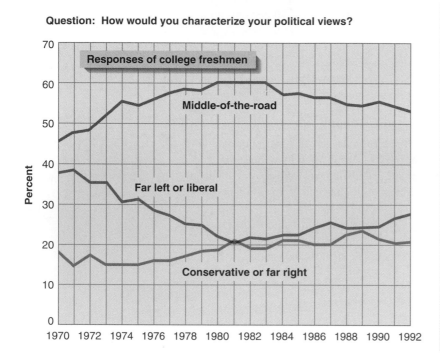

Question: How would you characterize your political views?

Responses of college freshmen

Middle-of-the-road

Far left or liberal

Conservative or far right

	Lib.	Mod.	Con.
1970	37%	45%	18%
1971	38	47	15
1972	35	48	17
1973	35	51	15
1974	30	55	15
1975	31	54	15
1976	28	56	16
1977	27	57	16
1978	25	58	17
1979	25	58	18
1980	22	60	18
1981	20	60	21
1982	21	60	19
1983	21	60	19
1984	22	57	21
1985	22	57	21
1986	24	56	20
1987	25	56	20
1988	24	54	22
1989	24	54	23
1990	24	55	21
1991	26	54	20
1992	27	53	20

Source: *The American Freshman* (1970–92). American Council on Education, University of California, Los Angeles. Reprinted from *The Public Perspective,* March/April 1993, Vol. 4, No. 3, p. 85.

one quarter replied that they had not thought very much about it at all.[22] To make a long story short, the debate among political scientists over how many people are really ideologues has generated many different definitions of ideology without really clearing up very much about how Americans think.[23] Therefore, identifying someone as a liberal or a conservative does not always lead to an easy prediction about how they will react to particular issues, candidates, or situations.

All of this said, there remains an undeniable fascination with how people identify themselves ideologically. Since the terms "liberal" and "conservative" seem to have taken on a life of their own, you will encounter them in the press, in political discussions, and in debates between candidates during election campaigns. As an aid to thinking critically about what these terms really mean, there are a few careful generalizations we can make about them. To begin with, "How We Compare" Box 6.3 shows where Americans line up compared to the populations of other nations when asked to locate themselves along a left to right scale of political thinking. In a limited sense, these self-definition approaches to ideology may shed some light on why citizens in some countries support more equality-oriented social programs in areas such as health care, education, housing, and welfare, while citizens in other countries are more likely to let individuals fend for themselves in these areas.

Ranking of Different Nations: How Citizens Place Themselves Ideologically

6.3

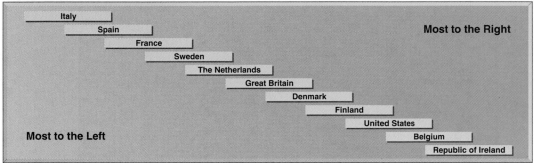

SOURCE: Adapted from Russell J. Dalton, *Citizen Politics in Western Democracies.* Chatham House Publishers, 1988, p. 123.

In addition, our national political debates are often framed sharply in the media by politicians and talk-show personalities who are ideologues, and whose views may influence the opinions of general publics looking for cues to direct their own thinking about issues. For example, such *conservatives* as television host Rush Limbaugh or prominent Republican leader Jack Kemp display the defining characteristics of favoring individual freedom over forced social equality, government restraint over interventionism, and law and moral order over limitless civil liberties. Liberal opinion leaders such as economist John Kenneth Galbraith or New York governor Mario Cuomo may favor social equality and equality of opportunity even if it sometimes means encroaching on individual freedoms (as in affirmative action programs). Since leaders of the two major political parties also divide along liberal and conservative lines on many issues, national politics often becomes more ideological than we might predict from just looking at the thinking of average individuals. When issues heat up in government, members of the public often take their opinion cues from national political leaders, giving particular conflicts some ideological coherence. In these ways, ideologies can become politically influential beyond the often-small numbers of people who adhere strictly to them.

In addition to liberalism and conservatism, many Americans are also familiar with libertarianism, socialism, and populism. *Libertarianism,* as noted in Chapter 1, is based on a strong commitment to the value of individual freedom. Libertarians differ from conservatives primarily in opposing government attempts to enforce morality in society through legal means. (For example, libertarians often favor legalization of prostitution and drug use, considering them "victimless crimes.") At another extreme is *socialism,* which applies the value of social equality to almost all social issues, even when individual freedoms may be sacrificed. Socialists go beyond liberals (who favor equality of opportunity for people to compete in society) to advocate government programs that would forcibly level social conditions among all citizens. *Populists* are an interesting breed who have rallied around Ross Perot's themes of economic protectionism and social opportunity (sounding a little like liberals), and greater government concern with social order and morality (sounding a little like conservatives), all wrapped around a cultural core of patriotism. In 1992, as a presidential candidate, Perot demonstrated that there is still a strong populist streak in American culture. Nearly 19 percent of the public voted for him.

American Pragmatism

Because these ideologies incorporate familiar ideals from the political culture, people may become drawn to them from time to time. However, most Americans are not committed ideologues in the sense that they strive for or achieve strict consistency in their opinions. Most Americans are **pragmatic**, meaning they are willing to borrow and combine ideas that make sense in a particular situation or during a particular time in their lives.

This ideological pragmatism means that compared to citizens in many other societies where political parties are more ideological and social-class divisions are sharper, American political thinking tends to be more fluid and more likely to permit individuals to change their opinions as they move from issue to issue and situation to situation. This flexibility in the political culture helps to explain why so many conflicts in American politics boil down to battles over public opinion, with each side trying to win the short-term support of larger publics. Winning public support can make a difference in how the government responds to a situation.

The Battle for Public Opinion

If opinions were formed solely on the basis of socialization and shared social experiences, politics would be a simple matter of presenting issues, candidates, or ideas to people who deliver predictable judgments about them. In reality, much of the fire and fury of politics involves the struggle to create public support for different causes. Among the factors that most affect opinion formations are the surrounding **climates of opinion** in society, *the uses of persuasive symbols to define issues,* and *the uses of the media* to advertise points of view and plant political ideas in the news.

Climates of Opinion

Although they can be hard to measure, public moods can be difficult for individuals to ignore. Sometimes the mood is pessimistic, and sometimes it feels optimistic. Dramatic events can stir up intense expressions of patriotism or fear. These public moods or *climates of opinion* can be so strong that they override existing divisions of opinion in society. For example, during the months before Allied bombing began, women opposed going to war against Iraq in 1991 by a margin of 25 percent over men. However, after the war started, the nation was swept by a great wave of patriotism, with people wearing yellow ribbons and displaying American flags to show their support for the national cause. In this climate of patriotism, most women modified their opposition to war, and the opinion gap closed to just 7 percent more women opposing the war than men.[24]

Opinion analysts warn that these public moods can sometimes be artificial or inflated. When the voices of factions or minorities are raised so loud that they appear to be a majority, other individuals may be intimidated into keeping their opinions to themselves, which only adds to the spiraling impression that those who do voice their opinions speak for the majority. An example of this so-called *spiral of silence* occurred during the years of Nazi domination in Germany in the 1930s and 1940s. Some sociologists and historians have argued that many, and perhaps a majority of, Germans did not personally support the Nazi cause, but were afraid to express their opposition in a climate dominated by public rallies, hatred for nonbelievers, intense displays of national patriotism, and the constant threat of police repression.[25]

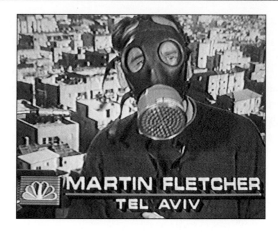

A Division of Supporters

After diplomacy failed to reverse Iraq's August 1990 invasion of Kuwait, a United Nations coalition initiated air strikes in January 1991. American animosity was heightened by Iraq's bombing of Israel (a traditional U.S. ally), vividly conveyed by the media *(above)*. While some isolationist and anti-war sentiment emerged *(below)*, intervention aroused broad support. Kuwait was liberated after only 100 hours of ground fighting. However, as public attention to Iraq slowly lessened, it turned toward domestic issues such as a flat economy; and President Bush's approval ratings declined steadily. In November 1992—after enjoying numerous foreign-policy triumphs that had once made him appear invincible as an incumbent—President Bush was unseated in his bid for reelection.

The Players

Less extreme examples also suggest that climates of opinion do not always arise spontaneously, but can be created through strategic media use and public relations campaigns. During the later years (1970–1972) of the Vietnam War, for example, President Nixon argued that the antiwar protesters were an irresponsible minority who created a climate of opinion in America that was helping the enemy. (During Lyndon Johnson's presidency, one popular antiwar chant had been "Hey, hey, LBJ,/How many kids did you kill today?") Nixon also said that the war was supported by a great "silent majority" who had been intimidated into silence by a noisy minority and a liberal media that amplified the voices of the protesters. The Nixon administration launched a campaign of rallies and attacks on the media aimed at countering the voice of the opposition and building a climate of opinion more supportive of the policies of the administration. Did the "silent majority" exist? The true answer is hard to determine. The more important factor for public opinion is that many people thought it did.

The Uses of Political Symbols

Whether they are reacting to images of publics, or to images of specific issues or politicians, people are sensitive to the **political symbolism** used in mass communications. Political scientist Murray Edelman has pointed out the important ways in which leaders and groups use symbolism to define political situations.[26] Selecting the right symbols to define a situation can make a big difference in winning public support or arousing opposition to a proposed policy or action. In recent years, for example, many states, cities, and private companies have restricted smoking. The movement to restrict smoking worried the tobacco companies, who saw a threat to sales and profits. In a number of places where antismoking ordinances and initiatives appeared on ballots, tobacco companies rallied the opinion and votes of smokers by running advertising campaigns equating smoking with personal freedom. Smokers were more likely to defend their embattled and increasingly unpopular habit if they had a positive concept such as *freedom of choice* to defend their views. Many battles for public opinion are waged around powerful symbols that are planted politically for people to use in thinking about what is at stake in a situation. The symbols that attract the most public attention reach people through the mass media.

Mr. John Butts takes a drag while attending a 1989 "Smokers' Rights" group meeting in Quincy, Massachusetts. Issues viewed with apathy or even hostility by the majority (such as health habits and sexual topics) may gain a more positive image if their proponents can manage to recast public debate in terms of popular political symbols and cultural themes.

The Media

Political advertising has become a big business in America. Candidates and interest groups find advertising and public relations techniques effective in selling citizens on candidates and issues, just as companies find them effective in selling consumers on their products. The use of television, radio, and print media to create political images is now a standard feature of American politics and is rapidly gaining acceptance in other nations as well.

In addition to being shaped by advertising and information campaigns, public opinion is also affected by the ways in which political situations are presented in the news. Techniques of news management have taught politicians how to get their ideas across, using quick verbal messages (called "sound bites") backed up with dramatic settings that attract journalists and draw media attention to a political message. Many public opinion campaigns use advertising and news events together to reinforce a political message and give it greater credibility. Journalists such as Walter Lippmann and such political scientists as Shanto Iyengar and Donald Kinder have demonstrated the importance of the news in the formation of opinion.[27] The stories that receive the most coverage affect *what people think about* and regard as politically important. In addition, the ways in which people and problems are symbolized or represented in the news can affect *what people think* and shape the opinions they form.[28] These political uses of the media will be explored in greater detail in Chapters 8, 10, and 11 on interest groups, elections, and the news media, respectively.

Describing and Measuring Opinion

Because opinion formations can change in important ways, the people who study public opinion have developed a special vocabulary to describe and keep track of them. Some of these terms such as *direction* and *intensity* were introduced earlier in the chapter. (See page 192.) The vocabulary used for describing public opinion can be applied to different forms of opinion expression, from polls to demonstrations. However, this special language for describing opinion is applied most often to the opinions expressed in polls because their scientific methods invite more precise description.

Describing Opinion Formations

As noted earlier, the most basic term used to describe opinion is its *direction*. An expression of agreement or support is described as an opinion with a positive direction, and an expression of opposition or disagreement has a negative direction. Just knowing the direction of an opinion does not tell us how strongly people feel. The term *intensity* is used to describe the strength of feeling. Strong opinions are said to be intense. A third descriptive term is required to fill out the picture of opinion: **stability**. It can be very hard to "read" opinion if people express opinions in one direction only to change their minds and express opinions of a different direction or intensity a short time later. Opinions that display a constant direction and intensity over time are described as *stable*. Change in the direction or intensity of opinion over time is called *instability*.

Since many different individual opinions make up the opinion of a group or a public, this complicates the description just a bit. For example, we might discover that the majority opinion on abortion favors the right of women to have an abortion, but their opinions are less intense than a sizable minority that is strongly opposed to abortion. In addition, the intense minority may be very stable in its opposition to abortion under most circumstances, whereas members of the less intense majority are more willing to change their opinions to go along with certain restrictions on abortions, such as requiring minors to obtain the permission of a parent. When intense and stable minorities compete with less intense and less stable majorities, they may succeed in winning more than their share of political battles, as abortion fights in many states have shown over the years. Figure 6.6 illustrates a hypothetical distribution of opinion about abortion at two different points in time, before and after a pro-life interest-group media campaign; the figure shows majority opinion as somewhat less intense and less stable than the opinion of a strong minority. This formation represents a classic problem of democracy: What to do when a substantial minority feels very strongly about something? The issue of abortion suggests that when this pattern persists over time, so do political conflicts.

Representing the opinion of large numbers of people as pictured in Figure 6.6 is called a **distribution**, simply because it shows how opinions about something are distributed in a particular population. The distribution in Figure 6.6 is called a **bimodal distribution** because there are two dominant clusters or *modes* of opinion, each with a different direction. A **unimodal distribution** means that opinion is distributed around a single dominant response. If that dominant response is decidedly positive or negative, the distribution is said to be *skewed* in a positive or negative direction. For example, when polls ask people to express their opinion about whether to permit abortions in extreme cases of rape, incest, or when the life of the mother is in danger, many more people support abortion, skewing the distribution of opinion in a positive direction, as shown in Figure 6.7.

Other distributions of opinion are described as *normal* if the modal (most frequent) response is around the middle point of the opinion scale, and the rest of the opinions are distributed evenly in both positive and negative directions from that middle point. Volatile issues like abortions almost never have normal distributions. Normal distribu-

FIGURE 6.6

Distributions of Opinion on Freedom to Have an Abortion Before and After a Strong Pro-Life Information Campaign (HYPOTHETICAL)

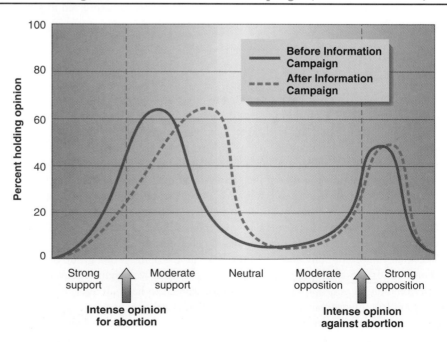

tions better describe such issues as ideological self-identification or party affiliation, in which large numbers of people are moderate or independent in their thinking, and the responses of the rest fall fairly evenly on both sides. An example of a normal distribution is shown in Figure 6.8.

FIGURE 6.7

Distribution of Opinion on Freedom to Have an Abortion Only in Case of Rape, Incest, or Danger to Mother's Life (HYPOTHETICAL)

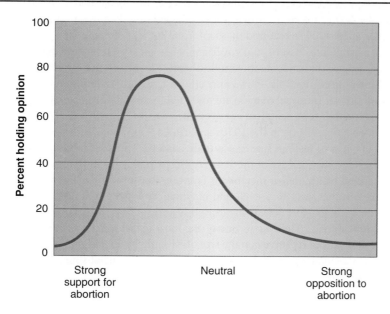

FIGURE 6.8

Distribution of Opinion Typically Found on Support for Political Parties and Ideological Self-Placement (HYPOTHETICAL)

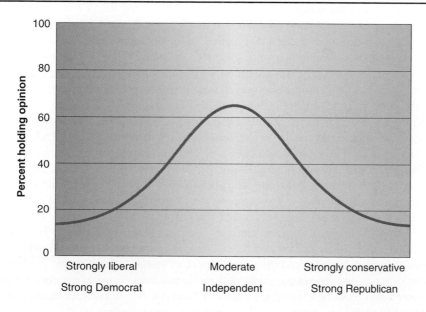

Opinion Measurement

It can be dangerous to try to guess the direction, intensity, or **distribution of opinion** of such large groups as the citizens of a state or an entire nation. Estimating the opinion of large populations has become a more precise science over the last fifty years through the methodology of opinion polling. Politicians now use opinion polling routinely to keep in touch with the people and to decide how to present their ideas most effectively in public.

POLLING TECHNIQUES.   Americans have always been fond of hearing what others think by taking informal "straw polls" of opinion. Nineteenth and early twentieth century newspapers often featured these informal surveys of reader and local community reactions to candidates, issues, and government activities.[29] Television news programs in many cities today still conduct straw polls of their viewers on the big news stories of the day. Radio and television talk shows also offer a fascinating glimpse into the views and concerns of others. Informal opinion surveys and discussion forums may be provocative, but they are neither representative nor accurate.

Some pioneering efforts in the 1930s and 1940s to promote informal polls as reliable estimates of national feelings turned out to be fiascoes. The most legendary of these early polling disasters was the case of the *Literary Digest* poll in 1936 that predicted Republican Alf Landon would defeat incumbent Franklin Roosevelt by a landslide in the presidential election that year. Roosevelt and his large New Deal coalition of voters handed Landon one of the biggest defeats in election history.

What went wrong? The *Digest,* one of the most respected magazines in the country, staked the accuracy of its survey on the size of its sample (the number of people to whom it mailed questionnaires). Indeed, it was an impressive sample of some ten million Americans, of whom more then two million returned responses. The majority leaned heavily in Landon's direction. The trouble was, the magazine collected the addresses for all those people from telephone books and motor vehicle bureaus around the country. What was wrong with that method of polling? During the Great Depression of the 1930s the only people who could afford the luxuries of telephones and cars tended to be wealthy. The vast majority of poor people who supported Roosevelt were never given the chance to register their opinions because the **biased** *sampling procedure* used by the *Digest* excluded them from the survey.

The moral of this opinion-polling story is that it is not the size of the sample so much as the way it is drawn or selected that matters most. **Unbiased samples** give everyone in the population whose opinion is being estimated an equal chance or probability of registering his or her views. The most common form of unbiased sampling (also called probability sampling) is the **random sample**, in which every member of the target population has the same (random) chance of being included in the survey.

Common sense might tell you that the whole population should be questioned in order to get an accurate reading of opinion. In theory, if you could find all adults in the country on a given day, you would have a perfectly accurate survey. In practice, this is impossible, not to mention prohibitively expensive. Even the U.S. Census Bureau conducts this kind of survey only every ten years, always at huge expense, and often with limited success in rounding everyone up. In the 1990 census, many big-city mayors and governors of large states complained that the census failed to find many members of such groups as migrant workers, the homeless, and illegal immigrants. These errors would hurt their states and cities when it came to getting enough federal aid for programs that those people need. Since an important feature of the census is to deliver updated population figures for states and residential areas (population changes affect representation in Congress and allocation of federal money), the Census Bureau will continue to attempt to count the entire population every ten years.

Scientific probability sampling makes it unnecessary to include everyone in the general population in a typical survey. Most of the national polls conducted in America currently are based on the responses of between 1,000 and 1,500 people. If the sample is carefully selected from housing units drawn randomly from census data or from random telephone dialing (more households have telephones today than a half century ago), the results will be very close in approximating the opinions of the population as a whole.

How good are the estimates based on unbiased samples? For a random sample of 1,000, the error rate will be 3 percent on either side of the average response, 95 percent of the time. What does this mean? Suppose that we want to follow voter attitudes in a presidential campaign. Based on a sample of 1,000, our first poll shows that 52 percent of those sampled favor candidate Jones over candidate Smith. Since we only sampled 1,000 people, however, we have to live with an error rate of 3 percent around this figure, meaning that the "real" level of support for candidate Jones in the larger population we are trying to estimate is somewhere between 49 percent and 55 percent, and we can be confident of this estimate in 95 polls out of 100, which is to say, fairly confident. How well did the polls do in predicting the 1992 election? In fact, all of the major polls taken within the final week did quite well. The only surprise was the tendency to underestimate the Perot vote, which may mean that some of those voters remained undecided until the last minute.

One of the great problems with polling is that opinions change according to how the questions are worded and how responses are recorded. If a question concerns solving a particular social problem, responses will vary depending on how the problem is described and whether the government in Washington is mentioned as the problem solver. (Some people may want a problem solved, but oppose solutions from Washington no matter what.) Just as symbols affect opinions in the real world, the words used in questionnaires affect responses in surveys. This means that pollsters must be cautious in interpreting their results, especially when different polls show different outcomes on the same issue. Those differences may simply reflect the ways in which the questions were worded.[30] In Figure 6.9, for example, an ideological self-definition question did not

FIGURE 6.9

What Happens When an Ideological Self-Definition Question Excludes "Moderates" as an Option

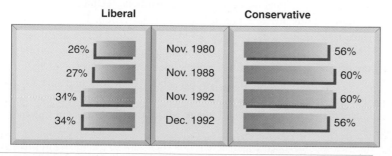

Question: In politics today, do you consider yourself to be a liberal or a conservative on most issues?

Consider self to be a...

Liberal		Conservative
26%	Nov. 1980	56%
27%	Nov. 1988	60%
34%	Nov. 1992	60%
34%	Dec. 1992	56%

Source: *The Public Perspective*, March/April 1993, Vol. 4, No. 3, p. 85.

invite people to say if they were moderates. The result was a series of polls showing a very high percentage of conservatives in the population.

With the development of such a powerful way of "reading the public mind," it is not surprising that politicians routinely call upon pollsters to help them develop better public relations. For some of those politicians it becomes irresistible to see if there aren't some areas of public concern, fear, or compelling symbolism they can attach themselves to. Many techniques of image making were developed originally by commercial advertisers in search of emotional appeals and images they could use to sell products. Today, similar techniques are used by candidates, elected officials, interest groups, and even foreign governments who want to improve relations with the American people.

Polls are often too expensive and crude to use to explore how people feel in much depth. In-depth understanding of how people think can be gained from using a technique known as **focus groups**. Focus groups enable opinion researchers to identify the precise words, slogans, or images that capture popular concerns and that can be used to turn public opinion to the advantage of a candidate or a political cause.

Focus groups can be as small as fifteen or twenty individuals who represent the kind of people whose support is most important to a politician or an interest group. They are invited to come together to talk informally with a "facilitator" whose job is to introduce topics, encourage discussions, and draw out the symbols, feelings, buzzwords, images, and themes that capture interest and attention in the group. From these beginnings, rough slogans, issue definitions, political ad images, or lines for political speeches may be constructed and shown to other groups for their reaction. In larger settings audience members are often given devices called "people meters," "vox boxes," or "perception analyzers" to electronically record their feelings about the ideas and images being presented. When political advertisements are tested in this way, people can record their emotional responses to every scene and image before the final ad is put together and run on television or radio.

Once the message has been constructed, it is then sent to the media in press releases, commercials, or news events intended (but not always successful, of course) to get that

Focus Groups: A Power Tool for Opinion Management

6.4

The scene: a focus group of thirty voters from the Chicago suburbs in 1992. They were not just any voters. These people had voted for President Bush in 1988, but were undecided about 1992. They watched the president's last State of the Union address. Each held a "perception analyzer," a dial numbered 0–100 and wired to a computer programmed to summarize the reactions of the group at any moment or phrase in the speech. Although the speech was a preview of the president's coming campaign, little of it moved these voters. Only in the closing minutes did the dials crank up to the 90s when the president said: "The government is too big and spends too much." The Bush campaign produced a series of commercials around this theme.

The scene: another focus group several months earlier in New Hampshire. Bill Clinton was fighting for a victory in the primary, but something was wrong with his message on welfare reform, a theme that normally played well in that state. The focus group revealed that because of tough economic times, potential Clinton voters were more likely to relate to people receiving government assistance. The Clinton campaign quickly and quietly dropped the themes of welfare abuse and welfare reform from its speeches and advertisements.

Focus groups have become a core element of elections and issue information campaigns, providing information to political managers about what images and symbols move the audiences that their campaigns are trying to reach. Focus groups revealed that the Democrats were losing support in the 1980s among white middle-class voters because of their policies on civil rights and social programs. Republican candidates waged successful campaigns around racial themes and the image of Democrats as big-spending liberals.

These themes may have become less effective as middle-class families hit harder economic times in the 1990s.

Using focus groups to pitch political issues and candidates to the short-term feelings of selected or *targeted* groups of citizens has been criticized as short-circuiting the public opinion process by telling people what they want to hear, rather than stimulating critical public debate and reasoned opinion. However, practitioners often defend focus groups as a way of raising democracy to a science, allowing public opinion to drive public debates. Political consultant Roger Ailes, one of the pioneers in using focus groups to design election and information campaigns, once joked, "When I die, I want to come back with real power. I want to come back as a member of a focus group."

SOURCE: Elizabeth Kolbert, "Test-Marketing a President," *The New York Times Magazine,* Aug. 30, 1992, pp. 19–22.

---

message across effectively. Polling comes back into the picture at this point, as the political management team looks for signs that their persuasion campaign is working. Favorable polls can, in turn, be promoted in the media to create a "groundswell" or "bandwagon effect" intended to bring undecided people on board. If the polls show no signs of public relations success, they can be downplayed and quietly discounted as "just polls." During his losing presidential campaign in 1992, George Bush encouraged voters to ignore the "crazy pollsters" whose surveys showed him losing the election. Meanwhile, behind the scenes, the public relations experts went back to the drawing boards, studying new polls and assembling more focus groups. "Inside the System" Box 6.4 illustrates some uses of focus group techniques in election campaigns.

Opinion, Power, and Democracy Revisited

In the opening of this chapter it was suggested that it is too simple to say that opinion is strictly an input that drives the democratic process. Nor is opinion merely an output that is driven by leaders, propaganda, and social moods. Far from being a simple or constant force in government, opinion takes many forms and is shaped by different political and social conditions. However, the recent rise of opinion management technologies linked to polling and focus groups warrants a special look at how efforts to construct opinion politically might affect the role of the people in American democracy.

Public opinion has probably always been somewhat vulnerable to the sway of grand symbols, the deception of demagogues, and the turbulent emotions of individuals looking for the promise of a better deal from government. For example, a respected social critic of one hundred years ago bemoaned the way the public of that era was railroaded into supporting a war against Spain (in Cuba and the Philippines) by a band of self-interested newspaper publishers and politicians:

> We boast that we are a self-governing people. . . . [Yet] the war with Spain was precipitated upon us headlong, without reflection or deliberation, and without any due formation of public opinion. Whenever a voice was raised in behalf of deliberation . . . it was howled down. . . .
>
> Everything was done to make us throw away sobriety of thought and calmness of judgment.[31]

While publics may always be vulnerable to emotions and manipulation, they have never been polled, test-marketed, and manipulated with the routine intensity that they are today. Many experts in the political management field claim that their techniques take democracy to its highest level, by giving people exactly what they want, as reflected in Roger Ailes' statement at the end of Box 6.4. However, some political scientists are not so sure that democracy is served by finding out what moves people emotionally and then feeding it back to them with clever images that have little relationship to actual issues, candidates, and situations. Many students of public opinion are concerned that opinion has increasingly become a product of politicians and public relations consultants seeking public support for policies and their political careers.[32]

Also noted at the beginning of this chapter, studies over the years show fairly strong correlations between opinion (measured by polls) and government policies in many areas. However, the key question for democracy remains "What does this mean?"[33] Is public support for many of the specific actions of government a product of enlightened debate, the exchange of ideas, and reasoned consensus, as an idealized picture of democracy would have? Or, as critics have suggested, is support for leaders and the legitimation of policies more often constructed through the work of elites and government officials using public relations techniques to "prepare" public opinion to accept the policies they are planning?

Political scientist Benjamin Ginsberg has described the modern citizenry as a "captive public" continually being studied, polled, and persuaded.[34] Publics are probed for a willingness to buy candidates and ideas that, like many consumer products, they do not necessarily need. Also as in consumer marketing, the political products being promoted often fail to live up to the wishes and fantasies aroused by the advertising. Citizens, like wary consumers, may grow increasingly cynical about appeals for their support. In this image, the public is not so much a sovereign, or even a collection of citizens whose views count equally, but a market to be exploited for votes and short-term political support. When "the public" is a force to be constructed and reconstructed from one political situation to the next, it is not surprising that public opinion can change so dramatically from one situation to the next.

If this idea of a public held captive by the media, polls, and political advertising is at all accurate, it may spell great changes for our democratic traditions. Consider just one of these changes. In the traditional theory of democracy, all people are supposed to count equally and have an equal chance to stand up and be heard. The irony is that nothing seems better suited to this principle than opinion polling with its capacity to accurately estimate opinion on almost any issue. Yet when citizens are thought of as markets and political consumers, democracy suddenly becomes a different game. For one thing, it is not necessary to sell everyone on an idea, or even to try. All that is needed is to sell just enough voters on a candidate or an issue to win the election. Public relations experts may aim at shifting just enough opinions to claim a majority in the polls while their client's issue passes through Congress. Building stable majorities of active and informed citizens is not a goal of this kind of politics. In fact, it may not even be desirable.

In a shocking statement about the "brave new world" of political marketing, one of the gurus of the business remarked, "I don't want everyone to vote. Our leverage in the election quite candidly goes up as the voting population goes down."[35] The "issues" in elections are increasingly constructed to appeal to targeted groups of "swing voters" in the political middle whose opinions could decide the outcome. As a result, great efforts are made to take the pulse of and design political images for small and selected segments of the public. Not surprisingly, polls in recent years show that many Americans have become turned off to politicians, campaign practices, and in many cases, to politics in general. In light of the growing citizen awareness of the methods used to shape public opinion, this may be one issue on which the public knows what it is talking about. The question is, what, if anything, can citizens do about it?

Key Terms

opinion

opinion object

majoritarian, pluralist, and elitist models of opinion and power

socialization

agents of socialization (family, school, peer group, media, leaders)

primacy principle

social characteristics and opinion (race, gender, class, religion)

opinion change processes, long- and short-term

culture and opinion

beliefs and values

problems with liberal and conservative labels

American pragmatism

the politics behind opinion formations

climates of opinion
political symbolism
the media

terms for describing opinion

direction, intensity, stability, opinion distributions

opinion measurement

polling techniques, sampling

biased vs. unbiased samples

margin of error

random samples

focus groups

A CITIZEN'S QUESTION

Forming More Effective Opinions

How can I make my opinions count? The next several chapters contain citizens' questions about voting, election reforms, choosing interest groups, and, more generally, finding effective ways of participating in politics. However, all of these forms of participation rest on a foundation of opinion. If people form shallow opinions and respond to the emotional appeal of the moment, the rest of the civic culture from voting and elections to the agendas of parties and interest groups will suffer. The discussions about opinion in this chapter contain useful information for thinking about developing your own personal opinions.

A good place for people to start examining their opinions is to think about the larger society around them. As noted in the discussions of socialization and the social characteristics of opinion, we are influenced both by our immediate circles of friends and associates and by the experiences attached to our social identities (gender, age, religion, race, education, and so on). These social influences are perfectly normal. However, it helps to think about the political realities of others in society beyond our immediate experiences. Society becomes a more livable place when people try to be more tolerant in their views. Among other things, tolerance means adjusting personal opinions to try to recognize and appreciate the concerns of others. This is not to say that people should give up their self-interest or put themselves at odds with their family and friends. However, recognizing that we have personal choices about what we value and who we identify with is not a bad idea. The perceptive French observer Alexis de Tocqueville, who visited America in the early years of the Republic, noted that American culture contained a delicate balance between self-interest and altruism (caring about the welfare of others). He expressed the worry that if self-interest alone drove the judgments of too many individuals, American society would end up being a less caring and less livable place for all. Many Americans feel that this has happened in recent years. Do you?

Another important lesson about forming more effective opinions is to think critically about the information you use in judging specific candidates, issues, or ideas. It is easy to let existing beliefs and prejudices act as screening devices that let in only the information that supports what we already believe. This makes propaganda and public relations campaigns all the more effective. Learning to engage critically with new information is a difficult but useful thing to do. If the opinions we hold are worth anything, they should stand up to an occasional test or challenge.

After thinking about what others in society are saying and looking carefully at the information you accept, the next step in the opinion process is to decide how to express your views most effectively. People who sound like they know what they are talking about are more likely to persuade others. Your arguments should be adjusted according to who you are trying to convince, and what kind of government action you are recommending to promote your cause. The way an opinion is expressed should change depending on whether you are convincing someone to vote for a particular candidate, lobbying a representative to support a new law, or thinking about how to take a case to court. Getting people to vote for a candidate may mean linking their concerns about a specific issue such as environmental protection, for example, to something you know about the environmental record of your candidate. To cite another example, feeling that abortion is right or wrong may not be enough to convince anyone that your case would hold up in the Supreme Court where opinions on abortion must be backed by arguments about constitutional precedents, rights, and legal principles. In the final analysis, the effective expression of an opinion requires understanding how to tailor it to a particular audience and to convince them that your views have some realistic chance of prevailing in government.

Suggested Readings

Asher, Herbert. *Polling and the Public.* Washington, D.C.: Congressional Quarterly Press, 1988.

Edelman, Murray. *Constructing the Political Spectacle.* Chicago: University of Chicago Press, 1987.

Ginsberg, Benjamin. *The Captive Public.* New York: Basic Books, 1986.

Hartz, Louis, *The Liberal Tradition in America.* New York: Harcourt, Brace, 1953.

Key, V.O., *Public Opinion and Democracy.* New York: Knopf, 1961.

Kirk, Russell. *The Conservative Mind: From Burke to Eliot*, 7th ed. Washington, D.C.: Regnery Gateway, 1986.

Lippmann, Walter. *Public Opinion.* New York: The Free Press, 1922.

Margolis, Michael, and Gary Mauser, eds. *Manipulating Public Opinion.* Belmont, Calif. Brooks/Cole, 1989.

Neuman, W. Russell. *The Paradox of Mass Politics: Knowledge and Opinion in the American Electorate.* Cambridge: Harvard University Press, 1986.

Page, Benjamin, and Robert Shapiro. *The Rational Public.* Chicago: University of Chicago Press, 1992.

Tocqueville, Alexis de. *Democracy in America.* (Originally published in two volumes, 1835–1840; available in various editions.)

• • •

Most [citizens] are not interested in most public issues most of the time. In a society like ours, it apparently is quite possible to live comfortably without being politically concerned. Political activity is costly and eats up time and energy at an astounding rate. . . . One must attend meetings, listen to or participate in discussions, write letters, attempt to persuade or be persuaded by others, and engage in other time-consuming labor. This means foregoing other activities, like devoting extra time to the job, playing with the children, and watching TV.
—*NELSON POLSBY AND AARON WILDAVSKY,*
POLITICAL SCIENTISTS, ON CONTEMPORARY AMERICA

• • •

The political activity that pervades the United States must be seen in order to be understood. No sooner do you set foot upon American ground than you are stunned by a kind of tumult. . . . To take a hand in the regulation of society, and to discuss it, is his biggest concern, and, so to speak, the only pleasure an American knows.
—*ALEXIS DE TOCQUEVILLE, FRENCH OBSERVER,*
ON AMERICA IN THE 1830S

• • •

Participation:
The Forms of
Political Action

- **GOOD NEWS AND BAD NEWS ABOUT VOTING**

- **VARIETIES OF PARTICIPATION AND THE NEEDS OF DEMOCRACY**
  Participation and Personal Commitment
  Conventional and Unconventional Participation

- **VOTING**
  The Psychological Basis of Voting
  The Social Basis of Voting
  Election Laws and Procedures
  How Does It All Add Up?

- **JOINING GROUPS**

- **PARTICIPATING IN SOCIAL MOVEMENT ACTIVITIES**
  Making a Commitment to Unconventional Participation
  Mobilizing People: What It Takes
  Movements and Elections

- **NONPARTICIPATION**

- **VARIETIES OF PARTICIPATION AND THE NEEDS OF DEMOCRACY REVISITED**

- **A CITIZEN'S QUESTION: Getting Involved**

- **KEY TERMS**

- **SUGGESTED READINGS**

Most observers agree that voting is the core act of political participation. Voting and elections set the political system in motion, selecting candidates, electing representatives, empowering parties, and more generally, providing a way for large numbers of people to participate in the democratic experience. Yet the news has told a tangled tale about this basic form of participation: The voters are angry, cynical, turned off, ready for change, withdrawn from politics, and, perhaps, showing new signs of life. Consider some of the news about the American voter that came from the 1992 election.

VOTING: NOT THEIR PRIMARY THING, *Area Students Show Little Enthusiasm.*[1] The reporter went to a college near the nation's capital and interviewed students, including nineteen-year-old Craig Phelps who explained why he was not registered and probably would not vote: "Personally, I just really don't want to vote. It's so screwed up. They always say they're going to pull it together and do something and they don't. It's just a bunch of lies to get into office. I don't trust any of them." The article then pointed to a trend behind these sentiments. In 1972, the first presidential election after the voting age was lowered from twenty-one to eighteen years, 42 percent of eligible eighteen- to twenty-four-year-olds voted. In 1988, only slightly more than 36 percent in that age group voted. What would 1992 bring?

Early in 1992, few observers expected much change in the low participation trends either among young people or in the general population. Another article echoed this early pessimism about the 1992 youth vote: MAYBE IF THEY TELEVISED IT ON MTV? YOUNGER VOTERS HAVE TUNED OUT POLITICS.[2] The story opened with a joke about the low level of interest in politics among younger people, finding significance in the fact that the closest thing to a political statement in the popular 1992 movie *Wayne's World* was a comment by Wayne's friend Garth about an attractive woman: "If she were a president, she would be Babe-raham Lincoln." Political scientist Gregory Marcus was also quoted, pointing out that *registration* to vote in the eighteen to twenty-four age group had dropped from 59 percent in 1972 to 44 percent at the beginning of the 1992 campaign. Marcus also chided the political outlooks of young Americans, pointing out that democracy is not like a shopping mall; it requires the participation of all citizens if it is to endure. Perhaps, the article implied, democracy would be healthier if MTV, *Wayne's World,* and other purveyors of youth culture took it more seriously, as well.

It turned out that MTV had been running a voter registration and turnout campaign called "Rock the Vote" since the 1988 election. During the 1992 campaign, MTV news carried regular reports from the conventions and the campaign trail. The candidates all appeared on the cable channel in one way or another, although losing candidate George Bush declined an early invitation to appear on an open forum program to take questions from a live audience, saying that MTV was a "teeny-bopper" network. It is hard to know how much influence MTV had in 1992, but by election day there were signs of stirring among the electorate, particularly among younger voters.

The entry of a third candidate, Ross Perot, in the 1992 race also brought new interest to the election among young voters and other low-participation groups. There was talk of change from the candidates and the media. Never before had candidates relied so heavily on such TV talk shows as *Larry King Live* and the morning breakfast programs to get their message across in such a personal way to voters. These developments in campaigning will be explored further in Chapter 10. For now, the question is whether they affect how people become involved and participate in politics.

Presidential candidate Bill Clinton, in Hollywood, appears on MTV's Choose or Lose, *answering questions from an audience of eighteen- to twenty-four-year-olds. Voter turnout among this age bracket in 1992 increased twenty percent over that in the 1988 election.*

As the election neared, the headlines began to indicate signs of a stirring in the electorate. Less than a month before election day, the front page of a leading national paper ran this story: AMERICANS SIGN UP IN RECORD NUMBERS TO CAST A BALLOT: 20 YEAR DECLINE IS REVERSED AS VOTERS CITE A FEELING THAT THERE'S A REAL CHOICE.[3] Indeed, when election day arrived, the overall turnout was up over past years to around 54 percent, from a modern era low of just over 50 percent in 1988. The biggest increase was in the voting rate of young people in the eighteen to twenty-nine age group which recorded a 20 percent gain in turnout over 1988.[4]

MTV, which did televise the election, ran a national ad congratulating the new voters and inviting them to think of MTV as "the community of the future," an idea that would unsettle most political scientists. The stirring of the electorate in 1992 was still puzzling, however. Was the vote a sign of a turnaround in a long decline in political participation, particularly among younger citizens? The overall jump to a 54 percent turnout, while an improvement, was still not a landslide vote.

What did it all mean? In an era of political cynicism and citizen pessimism, many observers tried to

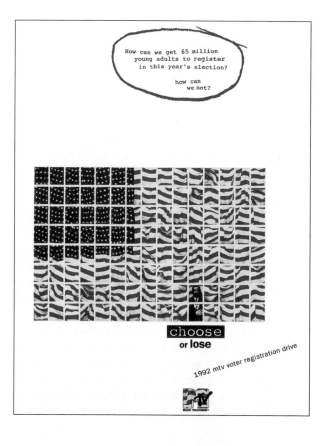

How can we get 65 million young adults to register in this year's election?

how can we not?

choose or lose

1992 mtv voter registration drive

put a positive spin on the results. Most attributed the rise in turnout to the third candidate, billionaire populist Ross Perot, who won 19 percent of the popular votes cast. Although it might seem reasonable to expect even higher participation in a three-way race fueled by high levels of voter discontent, most of the news coverage, and most of the academic experts in the news, took a tone of cautious optimism, as reflected in this headline after the election: VOTING RATE REVERSES 30-YEAR DECLINE.[5]

Perhaps the best interpretation of the 1992 vote was that it showed that voters were ready for change, but that other conditions were required for major upswings in participation to follow. *Elections and voting, like other forms of participation discussed in this chapter, occur within the context of a larger political system.* Voters do not just vote for candidates, they also vote for ideas and for parties that demonstrate more or less commitment to turning those ideas into policies. Surrounding the voting act are other forms of participation ranging from the volume of discussion in society (from the dialogue in movies to the family dinner table) to levels of political activity generated by social movements. When these vast popular movements sweep the nation, they can lead to important changes in civil rights, improving women's status in society, protecting the environment, promoting Christian values, or reforming the government itself.

Looking at these broader patterns of political involvement makes it easier to decide what the smaller parts of the picture (like voting turnouts) really mean. In this chapter and the next one on interest groups, we will see that Americans have many different forms of participation available to them. It may help to start thinking of participation as a personal creative process of turning values and opinions into effective forms of political pressure. This chapter explores what motivates people to participate in particular ways or not to participate in politics at all. We will also consider how different kinds of participation affect the way government responds to people in society.

Varieties of Participation and the Needs of Democracy

Participation involves the ways in which people turn their private opinions about issues they care about into actions aimed at accomplishing a goal. Sometimes those actions simply involve letting others know how we feel. The most common form of political participation is just talking about politics. Although it is easy to take for granted, Americans have fought long and hard for the simple right to talk freely about what matters to them politically. (Recall the discussions of civil liberties from Chapter 5.)

Not only do many people express themselves politically to their friends and associates, but radio and television talk shows have become national forums for getting issues on the public agenda. Politicians have learned how to use these talk-show formats to publicize policies, build political support, and run election campaigns. Many people seem to be discovering that the boundaries between talking to friends, calling talk shows, and directly contacting politicians are easy enough to cross. In the early weeks of his presidency, Bill Clinton made two controversial moves, one involving his nominee for attorney general and the other announcing his intention to drop the military ban on homosexuals. In the first week of the 1993 congressional session, the Capitol Hill switchboard received 1,650,143 calls mainly on those issues, compared to just 710,465 calls registering opinions on a variety of issues during the opening week of the 1992 session. Many government offices reported huge loads of calls, faxes, and letters, as well. A news story discussing this trend proclaimed: THE PEOPLE FIND THEIR VOICE: *Washington Is Bombarded with Phone Calls and Faxes.*[6]

Participation in these national political discussions may make a difference. In the case of Clinton's first nominee for Attorney General, Zoe Baird, some members of Congress

Bill Clinton, campaigning for the presidency in 1992, addresses a "town-hall" meeting broadcast from Chillicothe, Ohio. Critics argue that such "soft" formats simply allow candidates to circumvent reporters; thus artful politicians can avoid tough questioning by skilled journalists, and instead offer rehearsed responses to the more tentative efforts of voters. Others argue that this format does at least make individual voters feel like active, important participants in the electoral process.

confessed that they did not think at first that there was a problem with her having hired illegal aliens to work in her home. When the switchboards lit up, however, grass-roots participation turned the issue into a problem big enough to force her to withdraw from consideration.

It appears that communicating with each other and with government officials is a form of participation that more Americans are taking seriously and doing more effectively. There are even commercial fax services that will send faxes on particular topics to targeted officials. All that is required is to call a phone number, leave instructions, and a modest charge is added to one's credit card or phone bill. One citizen interviewed in a news story about this participation trend even bought a fax machine. As Patty Woodard of Flagstaff, Arizona explained, "I spent $500 on a fax machine just so I could make my feelings known with a little more alacrity and speed."[7]

There are many forms of participation beyond talking, letter-writing, and faxing. Some are relatively easy, while others require greater commitments of time and personal resources. People make these commitments for a variety of reasons: the personal satisfaction of just getting an opinion off one's chest; voting for a candidate or party that promises to govern differently; or joining a social movement that promises to change some aspect of culture, institutions, or power inside the political system.

Participation and Personal Commitment

Different forms of participation can be compared according to *how much effort or commitment they require from people.* The easiest form of participation is simply *talking about politics* with friends, family, and associates. As noted above, and in Chapter 6, climates of opinion can be created when large numbers of people either express concerns about particular problems or withdraw from political discussion altogether. A bit more commitment is required to *write letters, make phone calls, or communicate in other ways with representatives* to register opinions on issues. *Voting* is also a bit demanding because it requires a three-step effort of registering, making decisions, and going out to cast a ballot. Even more demanding are various kinds of *organizational activities* like *working on political campaigns* or *working on behalf of community or interest-group causes.* These latter kinds of group and campaign-related activities are cited by only 15–30 percent of people when asked if they have *ever* done them.[8] Still more demanding are such activities as *joining social movements* and *engaging in protest activities* (for instance, demonstrations, or boycotting products) aimed at changing society and government. At the extreme end of the commitment scale is running for office or becoming a leader in a social movement.

Students of participation often look at the whole picture of activism in a society when evaluating the health of a civic culture. For example, political scientists Carole Pateman and Benjamin Barber stress the importance of participating in decisions in many areas of life beyond formal government, including in the family, on the job, and in the community. Barber says that citizens need to see the importance of many kinds of participation to build a "strong democracy."[9] Other observers emphasize the importance of participation in building public support, or **legitimacy** for what the government does. For others, participation is the only way for people to develop political *power* in the system. Even many observers who believe that *elites* have more power in the system than *majorities* or *pluralities* of people argue that the best way to strike a better power balance in society is by encouraging more grass-roots participation.[10] Some of these consequences of participation are pictured in Figure 7.1.

Conventional and Unconventional Participation

Among the most difficult commitments people make are decisions to engage in unconventional forms of political participation. As the name implies, **unconventional participation** refers to doing things that others regard as deviant, challenging to authority, or generally *outside the normal channels of government and electoral participation.* By contrast, **conventional participation** refers to such actions as talking in familiar terms about

FIGURE 7.1

The Importance of Political Participation in a Democratic System

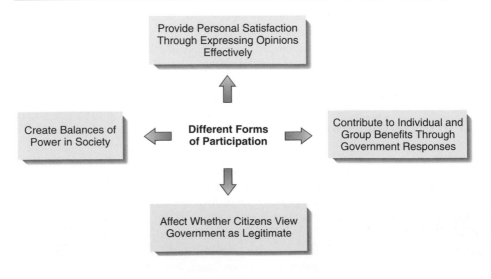

issues, writing letters, voting, campaigning, and interest-group activity, that fit *within the normal channels of government and electoral participation.* Table 7.1 shows what most political scientists consider to be the main forms of conventional participation. Note that these data were gathered during an earlier era of higher participation. In addition, voting estimates in this table are inflated because some people tell researchers that they voted simply because they feel pressure to say they did. The important thing to remember about this table is the different kinds of conventional activities and the *relative* differences in the numbers of people engaging in them.

Many of the historic moments and great changes in American politics have resulted from people acting against government and established authority by devising methods of

TABLE 7.1

Twelve Acts of Conventional Political Participation

TYPE OF PARTICIPATION	PERCENTAGE
1. Report regularly voting in Presidential elections*	72(%)
2. Report always voting in local elections	47
3. Active in at least one organization involved in community problems	32
4. Have worked with others in trying to solve some community problems	30
5. Have attempted to persuade others to vote as they were	28
6. Have ever actively worked for a party or candidates during an election	26
7. Have ever contacted a local government official about some issue or problem	20
8. Have attended at least one political meeting or rally in last three years	19
9. Have ever contacted a state or national government official about some issue or problem	18
10. Have ever formed a group or organization to attempt to solve some local community problem	14
11. Have ever given money to a party or candidate during an election campaign	13
12. Presently a member of a political club or organization	8

Number of Cases: weighted   3,095; unweighted   2,549

*Composite variable created from reports of voting in 1960 and 1964 presidential elections. The percentage is equal to those who report they voted in both elections.
Note: Reports of individuals' voting levels (Items 1 and 2) tend to be exaggerated, due to a sense of obligation to vote felt even among those who have not done so. (See text.)
SOURCE: Sidney Verba and Norman H. Nie, *Participation in America.* New York: Harper & Row, 1972, p. 31.

unconventional participation. Shays' Rebellion (recall Chapter 2) involved the unconventional activity of seizing courthouses so that judges could not repossess the land of poor farmers who were unable to pay debts and taxes. Women won the right to vote by marching, protesting, and eventually pressuring legislatures to ratify a voting rights amendment to the Constitution. The long struggle for civil rights involved unconventional tactics, including marches, sit-ins, hunger strikes, and bus boycotts to get government and society to respond to the demands of blacks. Most people stick to the course of playing inside the system by adopting a range of conventional politics to achieve their goals. However, when people are convinced that the system is not working or has no room for them, they too may contemplate unconventional forms of participation.

Some forms of unconventional politics have taken people so far beyond the bounds of social and legal acceptance that they have ended up in jail, or worse, with little to show for their causes. Many members of the communist and socialist movements during the 1920s and later in the 1940s and 1950s were arrested, jailed, or ostracized professionally for activities deemed too threatening for government and society to tolerate. The causes of communists never gained the popular acceptance or political success in the United States that they did in European industrial democracies at the time.

The risks of unconventional participation are greater, of course, the more opposed the activists are to the foundations of the political system itself. For example, many members of the communist and socialist movements expressed fundamental opposition to many basic values in the American *culture:* They valued and promoted a welfare state, government ownership of industries, and radical economic equality, among other things. Many also favored radical changes in the governing *institutions.* Most advocated the overthrow or levelling of powerful economic elites to give *social power* to the "working class." These political goals were not well received by authorities, who, with considerable public support, suppressed many forms of communist and socialist activities.

When groups take political aim at less radical adjustments in culture, institutions, and power, their unconventional activities are likely to be better received. (However, unconventional politics almost always carries a price in terms of social and government resistance.) For example, women were marching and demanding the vote around the same time that communists and socialists were opposing U.S. involvement in World War I and the Allies' subsequent efforts to overthrow the Bolshevik government of Russia. However, the women's suffrage movement called for an adjustment in the existing system to allow women to compete in public life, not for a radical transformation of the whole political system and its values. Women were seeking not to overturn institutions, but to reform them so that they could participate under the same rules offered to men. Table 7.2 illustrates some of the issues and activities that are likely to fall within the range of unconventional participation that most citizens and authorities find tolerable. As these examples indicate, unconventional participation can be very creative. Jeffrey Berry, the political scientist who compiled this sample of unconventional politics, called these protest activities forms of political "theater."

Decisions about how to participate are also statements about how people see themselves fitting into the political system itself. For the most part, people operate within the bounds of the system, as shown in "Inside the System" Box 7.1. The forms of unconventional politics, by contrast, are often aimed at making changes in the system, as shown by the table at the end of Box 7.1.

It is interesting that most conventional activists and many unconventional activists see voting as a central form of political action. The socialists and communists ran candidates for president. Women and blacks waged unconventional politics to win the right to vote. This is not because voting is the only or always the most effective form of citizen

TABLE 7.2

Varieties of Unconventional Political Participation

GROUP	ISSUE	ACTIVITY
Cattlemen	High cost of producing beef	"Beef-in": Brought 47 steers and calves to Washington and put in pens on the Washington Mall
Motorcyclists	Laws requiring cyclists to wear helmets	Bike-in at the Mall
"Massachusetts People's Bicentennial Commission"	"Tyranny" of big business	Dumped 100-pound sugar bags (actually filled with leaves) into Boston Harbor
Alaska Anti-Abortionists	Legalized abortion	Chained themselves to a procedure table
American Agriculture Movement	Shrinking profits	Tractorcade into Washington
Greenpeace	Proposal to open one billion acres offshore for oil and gas exploration	Dumped marbles in Interior Department's lobby because Secretary Watt "lost his marbles" in making the proposal

SOURCE: Jeffrey M. Berry, *The Interest Group Society.* Boston: Little, Brown, 1984, p. 150.

INSIDE THE SYSTEM

Participation and Political Change

7.1

People tend to choose unconventional forms of participation when they believe changes are needed in the political system itself. Unconventional politics may seem necessary to them when they feel that the public and government officials need to be made aware of new values or ideas in the cultural realm, needed changes in existing institutions, or gross inequities in social power that cannot be corrected through established politics. Participation is thus also a statement about how people see themselves fitting into the political system. Some distinctions between conventional and unconventional forms of participation are offered below.

Here is a portrait of a conventional activist that reveals the pursuit of traditional political values through mainstream activities. A team of sociologists interviewed Mary Taylor (a fictional name). Taylor had been named to a citizen's position on the California Coastal Commission, a governmental panel responsible for protecting the shoreline environment. Her political profile was described like this:

"A housewife married to a literature professor, Mary became involved in politics by volunteering in the League of Women Voters and has since moved on to work in a number of organizations concerned with a broad range of environmental issues in California, particularly Friends of the Earth. . . . Mary lays great stress on the need to tolerate the fact that different individuals have very different interests and viewpoints, and she stresses the need to establish fair procedural rules within which such individuals can negotiate their differences. 'It's very important to realize that other people have other values, but they are to be respected. That is what freedom is all about.'"*

The Reverend Martin Luther King, Jr., was one of the nation's most famous activists and an advocate of unconventional forms of participation in cases where the government was unresponsive to demands expressed through more conventional means. King was arrested during protests in Birmingham, Alabama in 1963. When he learned that a group of fellow clergy had condemned his political tactics, he wrote about his rea-

sons for resorting to unconventional politics:

"You deplore the demonstrations taking place in Birmingham. But your statement, I am sorry to say, fails to express a similar concern for the conditions that brought about the demonstrations. . . . It is unfortunate that demonstrations are taking place in Birmingham, but it is even more unfortunate that the city's white power structure left the Negro community with no alternative.

"Birmingham is probably the most thoroughly segregated city in the United States. Its ugly record of brutality is widely known. Negroes have experienced grossly unjust treatment in the courts. There have been more unsolved bombings of Negro homes and churches in Birmingham than any other city in the nation. These are the hard, brutal facts of the case. On the basis of these conditions, Negro leaders sought to negotiate with

the city fathers. But the latter consistently refused to engage in good faith negotiations. . . .

". . . Nonviolent direct action seeks to create such a crisis and foster such a tension that a community which has constantly refused to negotiate is forced to confront the issue.

". . . Lamentably, it is an historical fact that privileged groups seldom give up their privileges voluntarily."**

*From Robert N. Bellah, Richard Madsen, William M. Sullivan, Ann Swidler, and Steven M. Tipton, *Habits of the Heart.* New York: Harper & Row, 1985, p. 192.

**From Martin Luther King, Jr. "Letter From Birmingham Jail," reprinted in William F. Grover and Joseph G. Peschek, eds., *Voices of Dissent.* New York: HarperCollins, 1993, p. 251.

Participation and the Political System: An Overview

CONVENTIONAL *PARTICIPATION*	ASPECTS OF THE *POLITICAL SYSTEM*	UNCONVENTIONAL *PARTICIPATION*
People are comfortable using traditional values and ideological terms to make their demands.	Culture	People introduce new ideas, new symbols, or radical ideologies that challenge conventional wisdom.
People regard existing procedures, rules, and methods as adequate to make decisions and resolve demands.	Institutions	People demand new rules of the game, requiring constitutional amendments or other reforms in government institutions.
Normal power resources appear adequate. People vote, organize interest groups, contact representatives and contribute money as usual.	Power	People see their lack of power as part of the problem and resort to social disruption as a way to pressure those with power to change the system.

action, but because voting is the core form of democratic participation in this system. Voting literally creates governments by electing the representatives who are empowered to act for the people. Because of this governing importance of elections, other forms of participation tend to play into or against voting patterns either directly or indirectly. For example, people who feel that electoral majorities do not represent their interests may join interest groups to lobby elected officials on particular issues. Social movement activities may try to mobilize people to vote as part of a broader strategy of political and social change. In these and other senses, the many forms of political action tend to orbit, sometimes distantly, and sometimes more closely, around voting.

Voting

The low voting turnouts of recent decades fueled talk about a participation crisis in modern American democracy. As Figure 7.2 shows, the trends since the late 1960s in American voting have generally not been encouraging.

The challenging question is: *What do these trends mean?* If we compare American voting levels to those of almost any European nation, they appear very low, as indicated

FIGURE 7.2

Trends in American Voting 1790–1992: Percentages of Eligible Voters Who Voted

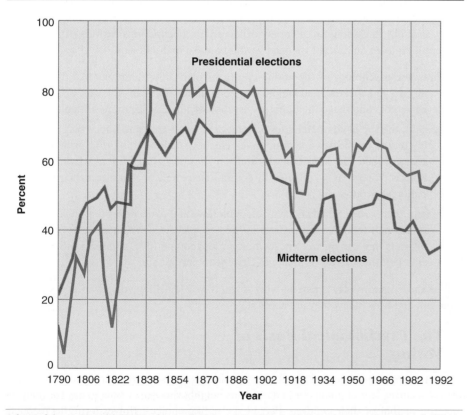

Adapted from: Harold W. Stanley and Richard G. Niemi, *Vital Statistics on American Politics.* Washington, D.C.: CQ Press, 1992, p. 85.

in "How We Compare" Box 7.2, which shows recent voting levels in other nations. Among the industrial democracies in the modern era, only Switzerland has a record of lower electoral participation than the United States. Is it fair to compare the U.S. to other democracies? In some ways it may not be, caution political scientists such as Raymond Wolfinger. Americans are called on to vote in more elections and make more complicated choices among candidates and ballot issues. Most parliamentary systems have fewer elections, and the choices are usually simpler to make (often just selecting a party list of candidates for different offices). In addition, registration is virtually automatic in many other nations, and voting is mandatory in some. These and other factors would suggest that American electoral participation is reduced to some extent by complicated choices and election procedures.

Just looking at American participation on its own in the period from the early 1970s to the early 1990s, there still appear to be reasons to think that there has been something of a voting problem. On the surface, a steady 70–80 percent (depending on the election) still said they were interested in election campaigns. However, what they saw and heard in campaigns by the late 1980s often left people distressed. The 1988 election, for example, was commonly criticized by some voters and by the media as the most dissatisfying in memory for its negative campaigning and the perceived lack of meaningful choice between candidates. In 1992 there was still a healthy share of negativity and name-calling, but voters rated it an improvement over previous years. Perhaps due to the novelty of and controversy surrounding independent candidate Ross Perot, 60 percent of voters reported that they felt there was more discussion of the issues in 1992 than in 1988, and 70 percent reported that the debates among the candidates helped in making their choices (compared to the less than half who found the debates helpful in 1988).[11] As changing voter reactions indicate, people make their choices (including whether to participate at all) in response to a variety of factors in their political worlds. At least three different kinds of factors are weighed as voters make their choices.

First, the **psychology of the voting choice** involves considerations like party loyalty, issue concerns, and candidate personalities that can motivate or discourage voters and make their choices psychologically easy or more difficult.

Second, the **social characteristics of voters** can come into and out of play depending on the candidates and issues in an election, making things like gender, race, or age a factor in some contests and not in others. In addition, whole generations of voters can be affected by common experiences that affect their participation as groups.

Finally, there are national and state **election laws and procedures** that make it easy or difficult for voters to register in the first place, create boundaries of voting districts that can make contests more or less competitive, and exert other influences on the interest or ability of citizens to participate.

All of these factors play a part in who votes, how often they vote, who and what they vote for, and how happy they are about it.

The Psychological Basis of Voting

Voters may be concerned about many problems or issues in their lives: jobs, health, world security, fear of going out in dangerous neighborhoods, or how to pay for their education or that of their children. Part of the voting choice involves trying to reconcile those personal feelings with what the candidates are saying and doing. People tend to use

Voter Turnout in Eight Industrial Democracies

7.2

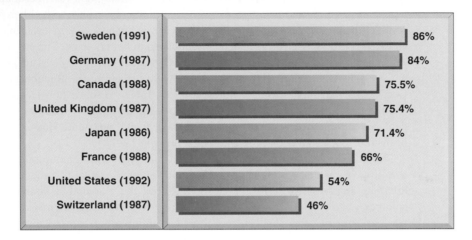

Sweden (1991)	86%
Germany (1987)	84%
Canada (1988)	75.5%
United Kingdom (1987)	75.4%
Japan (1986)	71.4%
France (1988)	66%
United States (1992)	54%
Switzerland (1987)	46%

SOURCES: Thomas T. Mackie and Richard Rose, eds., *The International Almanac of Electoral History,* 3rd ed. London: Macmillan, 1991; Swedish Institute of North American Studies, Uppsala University.

three broad frames of reference to "screen" or simplify the mass of information they encounter in an election:

- How the individual feels about the political parties. This is called **party identification**.
- The **issues** being debated in the contest, and whether they matter to the voter or appear to be things the candidates really take seriously.
- The evaluation of **candidate character** *or personality*. Voters pay a lot of attention to whether candidates seem trustworthy, able to hold up under pressure, and willing to fight for what they promise to do in office.

PARTY IDENTIFICATION. American party loyalties have had important effects on participation patterns and election results. For example, the rise of the Democratic party with its New Deal program in the 1930s brought a wave of voter loyalty that kept the Democrats in power for much of the period until 1968. For reasons to be discussed in Chapter 9, the party system became disrupted during the late 1960s and 1970s. The main result of those changes was a substantial loss of support for the Democrats, which translated into some gains for the Republicans, and more importantly, *large increases in the category of independent voters* who are more likely to vote for individual candidates and issues than to support one party consistently over the other. Figure 7.3. illustrates long-term trends in party identification.

The big news about party identification is that more voters have become independent in recent decades. In addition, Democrats have been increasingly willing to shift their votes to Republicans, particularly in presidential elections. These important *swing voters* have played an important part in recent elections. For example, the success of the Republicans at the presidential level in 1980, 1984, and 1988 depended on picking up a majority of independent voters and a large minority of Democratic voters. In 1992, a slow economy hit many conservative Democrats personally, and Ross Perot appealed to independent voters and many people who identified only weakly with either party. As a result of these factors, Republican candidate George Bush picked up fewer independents and Democratic *swing* voters than any Republican in twenty years. The election of 1992 even disrupted Republican voting patterns. Ordinarily the most loyal of party voters, with party voting in the high 80 percent to low 90 percent range, Republicans voted for George Bush at "only" a 73 percent rate in 1992. Table 7.3 shows how Democratic party identifiers voted in the elections from 1976 to 1992, and Table 7.4 shows how independents voted in those years. These swing voters delivered the White House to the Republicans in 1980, 1984, and 1988, and took it away in 1992.

Although the patterns that held in the 1980s for Republican, independent, and Democratic swing voters were disrupted in 1992, it would be wrong to conclude that new political loyalties resulted from that election. Rather, the safe analysis is that it has been common since 1968 for many voters to split their votes, or hedge their electoral bets as it were, and in 1992, they simply placed those bets differently. Chapter 9 discusses the con-

FIGURE 7.3

Trends in Political Party Identification 1952–1992

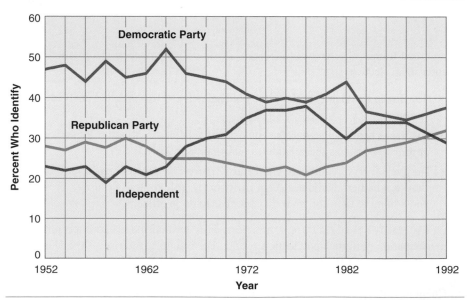

Source: National Election Studies, 1952–1988. 1992 data are from voter exit polls conducted by Voter Research and Surveys, sponsored by a consortium of television networks on election day, 1992. Note: the 1992 figures may be affected somewhat by being gathered on election day immediately after voting.

TABLE 7.3

How Self-Identified Democrats Voted in Five Presidential Elections, 1976–1992

	PERCENTAGE OF DEMOCRATS WHO VOTED FOR:		
YEAR	DEMOCRATIC CANDIDATE	REPUBLICAN CANDIDATE	INDEPENDENT CANDIDATE
1976	77%	22%	—
1980	67	26	6*
1984	74	25	—
1988	82	17	—
1992	77	10	13**

*John Anderson
**Ross Perot
SOURCE: Various exit polls sponsored by television news organizations, reported in *The New York Times,* November 5, 1992.

ditions necessary to create the more significant and enduring shifts in party loyalty that political scientists refer to as political party *realignments.*

For all of its fickleness, party identification remains the single best predictor of a person's vote. Democrats have voted for their party's candidates 70 to 80 percent of the time over the last thirty years, and even with the slight dip in 1992, Republican tendencies to vote for their party's candidate have averaged in the mid-80 percent range over

TABLE 7.4

How Self-Identified Independents Voted in Five Presidential Elections, 1976–1992

	PERCENTAGE OF INDEPENDENTS WHO VOTED FOR:		
YEAR	DEMOCRATIC CANDIDATE	REPUBLICAN CANDIDATE	INDEPENDENT CANDIDATE
1976	43%	54%	—
1980	30	55	12*
1984	36	63	—
1988	43	55	—
1992	38	32	30**

*John Anderson
**Ross Perot
SOURCE: Various exit polls sponsored by television news organizations, reported in *The New York Times,* November 5, 1992.

the same extended period. This suggests that political party still means something to people. For some, party affiliation is the symbol that best expresses the political membership they share with family, friends, or fellow workers. It is a sort of social membership badge, something people would change only at risk of being criticized or rejected by others. For other people, parties stand for policies and social programs they agree with, based on identifying Republicans as pro-business, Democrats as pro-labor, Republicans as the party of lower taxes, and the Democrats as favoring more government spending on social programs, and so forth.

ISSUE VOTING.   Most people say that issues are the most important part of the voting decision for them. In many recent elections, they also have said that they have been disappointed by the way candidates have addressed (or failed to address) the issues they cared about.[12] Candidates often discover they are on safer ground if they stick to what have been called **valence issues**, involving ideas or promises that tap into intense voter opinions on which large majorities line up in one direction, either positive or negative (the direction of an opinion is also called its valence). It is common to hear candidates line up behind patriotism, God, family values, peace, prosperity, and other abstractions that make people feel good or that stimulate positive fantasies. On the negative side, candidates often compete to see who can be tougher against crime and for controlling budget deficits, reducing taxes, or protecting us from the enemies that most voters hate.

The uses of empty promises, emotional symbols, and appeals to the core symbols of the *political culture* (freedom, patriotism, opportunity, and so on) led one pollster to warn that just because candidates claim they have something to say about "the issues," voters may decide that those pronouncements are not serious issues at all.[13] However, if all the voters are offered are appeals to their emotions, they will probably take them into account to some degree.[14] In 1988, for example, many voters reported that crime, patriotism, and Republican candidate George Bush's pledge of "no new taxes" were important in their decisions. One study of the 1988 election found that, as the campaign progressed, more time was devoted to these symbolic issues and less to hard policy options. Not surprisingly, press coverage of the issues declined, and the news focused on how the campaigns were trying to use the media to manipulate voters.[15] Meanwhile, voters expressed growing disapproval of the choices they were being offered. The moral of the 1988 campaign seemed to be that if unconvincing issues are all the voters get, they will make the best use they can of them, but they do not have to like it.

Enlivened by Ross Perot and fired by voter concern about economic stagnation, the 1992 race offered more credible issues, in the eyes of most voters. A New York Times/CBS news poll taken shortly after both the party conventions were over in August found that more than 90 percent of voters wanted to hear about the candidates' plans to improve the nation's economy. More than 86 percent wanted to hear about plans for improving health care. Upwards of 40 percent wanted more discussion about family values, and over 20 percent were concerned about the issue of legal rights for homosexuals.[16]

By election day, the top issues remained the economy (broken into separate issues of jobs and the budget deficit), health care, and family values. Table 7.5 shows the results of interviews with a large national sample of voters as they left voting places. Although George Bush backed the most popular positions on several issues (including such valence issues as patriotism and family values), those were not the issues that mattered most to the voters. By contrast, Bill Clinton won the support of larger numbers of voters who were more concerend about the top issues of jobs, the deficit, and health care. Ross Perot won most of his support from voters who were most concerned about the national budget deficit. The moral of the 1992 election seems to be that having distinctive and popular positions on issues really helps *if* they are the issues that people care most about.

In 1992, as noted above, there were special circumstances driving the issue debates, including a sluggish economy and a third candidate challenger who forced a more open

TABLE 7.5

*The Issues of 1992 Mentioned as Important by People
Voting for Different Candidates*

PERCENTAGE OF VOTERS WHO SAID THE ISSUE WAS IMPORTANT TO THEM

| | | **PREFERENCE OF ISSUE VOTERS** | | |
ISSUE	**ALL VOTERS**	BILL CLINTON	GEORGE BUSH	ROSS PEROT
Economy (Jobs)	43%	52	24	24
Budget Deficit	21	36	26	38
Health Care	19	67	19	14
Family Values	15	23	65	11
Taxes	14	26	57	17
Abortion	13	37	55	8
Education	13	60	25	15

SOURCE: Voter Research and Surveys national exit poll of 15,490 voters leaving 300 polling places on election day, 1992. Sponsored by a consortium of national television networks. Adapted from *Newsweek*, Special Election Issue, November/December 1992, p. 10.

Where the 1988 presidential election had focused upon symbolic issues, personal character, and broad beliefs, the 1992 election hinged more on specific issue voting. Although polls showed that many voters harbored persistent doubts as to Bill Clinton's character, and often agreed with the "values" theme voiced by incumbent George Bush (left) and the Republican party, their concern over the federal deficit and a flat economy outweighed their misgivings. Many who were particularly worried about the deficit turned to Ross Perot, which some observers feel helped to throw the election to Bill Clinton with a plurality of 43 percent.

discussion of economic issues and the budget problem in Washington. In most elections, it is more difficult for candidates to stake out serious issue positions. When there are only two candidates or parties in the race, it is tempting for both candidates to look over their shoulders. If the opponent's issue position is more popular, the tendency is to inch toward that position, until both candidates end up sounding pretty much the same on most of the major policy issues that interest the voters. As political scientist Benjamin Page has described it, this tendency to head for the middle of the road in most elections leaves voters without much in the way of meaningful issue differences to consider.[17]

When party or issue choices do not offer solid prospects for betting on the future, the most reliable form of issue voting is to see in *retrospect* how well a particular party or candidate has performed. Originally introduced by political scientist V. O. Key, and developed more fully by Morris Fiorina, the term *retrospective voting* applies when voters cannot trust the promises of candidates, but can judge whether candidates or parties have done a good job in the past.[18] One of the things people can see most clearly in retrospect is how well the economy has performed under a president or a party.

Ronald Reagan rose to power in 1980 on the tide of retrospective voting when he invited voters to "Ask yourself if you are better off today than you were four years ago." At the time, the country was in the midst of a severe economic slump, and enough voters answered "no" to the above question to stick incumbent Jimmy Carter with the blame. Not only is the state of the economy important to people, but it is often the only solid issue for people to evaluate. As a result, elections (particularly presidential elections) often boil down to a national thumbs up or thumbs down on the state of the economy. George Bush fared poorly in 1992 as voters looked retrospectively at his economic record.

CANDIDATE CHARACTER. Bill Clinton's victory in 1992 might have been much easier if the issue of his character had not played such an important role in the campaign. During the primaries in the spring of 1992, accusations surfaced that Clinton had engaged in an extramarital affair. After months of trying to put that problem behind him, he then admitted to smoking marijuana once, adding that he did not inhale. No sooner had the marijuana issue blown over, so to speak, than it came out that Mr. Clinton had opposed the Vietnam War when he was in college and attended protests against the war while he attended Oxford University in England. From the beginning of the campaign to the end, the most effective attack against Bill Clinton was against his character. Since George Bush had few issues that were helping him in the polls, he tried unsuccessfully to make character and trust the main issues in the campaign.

Americans place more emphasis on the character of their leaders than is common in most other political systems. This is partly because voters in most other democracies vote for ideological parties, not individual candidates. Making a choice based on personalities may be appropriate in American politics for other reasons, as well, particularly at the presidential level. The presidency is a pressure cooker of stress and responsibility. It makes sense for people to consider carefully the character defects and strengths of people who want to put themselves to that test.[19] Moreover, as we will see in Chapter 14, much of the power of the president depends on the "power to persuade" the public, the Congress, and sometimes the bureaucracy itself of the proper course of political action. In short, character has a lot to do with presidential success, and voters may have reason to be concerned with the personality of anyone who wants to fill the office.

Not surprisingly, character is a major focus of campaign media coverage. In one study of news coverage of the 1992 election, stories about candidate character appeared as often as coverage of specific candidate issues and policy proposals. Both issues and character received about 13 percent of the space in the nation's leading newspapers, with coverage of campaign strategies, poll results, "horse race" stories filling in the background with a combined news share of around 40 percent.[20]

In 1988, when Democratic candidate Michael Dukakis tried to sell his dull, buttoned-down persona to the voters as "personal competence," they weren't buying it. The presidency, many felt, required more than that. By the end of the campaign, George Bush won the personality contest between the two candidates hands down, being voted in the polls as the person people would most like to have as a next-door neighbor, invite over to dinner, and put in charge of a crisis situation.[21] In 1992, however, Mr. Bush was perceived as out of touch with ordinary people and not sufficiently concerned about their problems.

With so much riding on how they come across to the voters, it is not surprising that candidates have become increasingly image-conscious over the years. Many politicians take lessons in how to act in front of the cameras, how to deliver speeches, how to answer questions, how to move their hands, and even what to say. Hired pollsters and media consultants are always looking for weaknesses in the candidate and creating issues, performances, and commercials designed to overcome them. According to his market researchers in 1988, George Bush was, in the minds of some voters, indecisive and a bit of a whiner. These political character problems soon came to be termed by the media as the "wimp factor." Media advisers came to the rescue. Candidate Bush was outfitted with a tougher personality, given to attacking his opponent and quoting lines from Clint Eastwood movies in his speeches. Was he comfortable with the new style? Not really. In fact, according to the report of Bush's top media guru, Roger Ailes: "He hates it, but he knows we'd be getting killed if we didn't go negative."[22] In 1992, the Bush character strategy called for a balance between tough attacks on challenger Clinton and more compassion toward average Americans suffering from economic hard times. In the eyes of many voters, neither dimension of Mr. Bush's character came across convincingly. All of this raises the serious problem of how much the voters can trust the candidate images they encounter in campaigns.

The Social Basis of Voting

Voting can be thought of as a particular way of expressing a complex opinion. It is an opinion because the vote expresses a feeling or a judgment about the choices in an election. It is a complex opinion because the vote sums up a whole collection of judgments about candidate, party, issues, the opponent, the state of the economy, and the quality of life lately, all weighed and condensed into one behavioral statement. Part of this weighing and condensing is, like the formation of any opinion, a private psychological act, influenced by the kinds of considerations discussed in the last section. Like most opinions, voting is also affected by the experiences associated with who we are socially. As discussed in Chapter 6, social characteristics can affect how people are socialized, how they think and feel politically, and in this case, how they vote.

GENDER.   Women are more likely to experience poverty than men and more likely to have to both work and find ways to take care of their children. These experiences make women more supportive of government social programs and more likely to vote for Democrats. While 47 percent of women in 1992 and 49 percent in 1988 voted Democratic, only 41 percent of men in both years voted for Democratic presidential candidates.[23]

The media labeled 1992 the "Year of the Woman" in American electoral politics for the large number of women who ran, the increase in those who voted, and the substantial increase in women who were elected to public office. Exit polls in 1992 suggested that women voted more than men (54 percent to 46 percent) and that working women were a substantial 31 percent of the electorate. This does not mean that all women's experiences are the same, of course. Chapter 6 explained how different kinds of experience can affect political thought and action. For example, *working women* in 1992 voted Democratic over Republican by a margin of 46 percent to 36 percent, while women who described themselves as *homemakers* voted in just the opposite pattern, supporting

Republican George Bush at a 45-percent rate over Bill Clinton's 36-percent vote in that group.[24] It is clear that candidates and parties must be careful about how to define themselves to different types of women in the future.

RACE.   Race is another important element in the voting equation. One of the major participation decisions that people make based on racial experience is party identification. While 95 percent of Republicans are white, only 72 percent of Democrats are white, and fully 18 percent are black. To put the black support of Democrats in perspective, over the last five elections, the percentage of blacks who voted for Democratic presidential candidates was:[25]

1976: 83%

1980: 85%

1984: 90%

1988: 86%

1992: 82%

Latino voters are also predominantly Democratic, but less so than blacks, as reflected in the following patterns of Democratic presidential voting over the same elections:[26]

1976: 76%

1980: 59%

1984: 62%

1988: 69%

1992: 62%

Like gender, race also interacts with other factors in affecting voting choices. For example, the region of the country in which people live has figured importantly into racial voting patterns. After the Civil War, northern blacks voted mainly for the Republicans as the party that abolished slavery, while southern whites backed the Democrats as the party that fought the Republicans. Beginning with the social programs of the 1930s and continuing through the 1960s, however, the national Democratic party was transformed by an alliance of blue-collar workers, poor people, and minorities. Something of a *wedge* was driven into the Democratic party support base with the passage of the Civil Rights Act of 1964 and the Voting Rights Act of 1965 which identified the Democrats squarely as the party of civil rights. When he signed the voting bill into law, President Lyndon Johnson remarked to an aide, "I think we just delivered the south to the Republican party for a long time to come."[27] His prophecy turned out to be right. White southerners abandoned the Democrats by wide margins in every presidential contest after the first national voting law was passed, with the exception of 1976 when the white southern vote split fairly evenly with Georgian Jimmy Carter winning the presidency. Even in 1992, a three-way race with a southern Democratic ticket of Bill Clinton (Arkansas) and Al Gore (Tennessee), the white southern vote still went to Republican George Bush by a margin of 48 percent over Clinton's 34 percent and Perot's 18 percent.[28]

Since the national Democratic party became identified with the issue of civil rights, there has been a low-level but intense competition between the parties in national elections over the race issue, with the Democrats trying to keep it low key, and the Republicans succeeding in various ways in highlighting it. Race has become what is known as a *wedge issue* in American politics because, by driving a wedge into the vote, it splits traditional blocs of party support. Because of this wedge in the white vote, Democratic campaign strategy has been, in recent years, to downplay the support of such black leaders as Jesse Jackson. Party pollsters say that showcasing Jackson or addressing black issues would alienate many white *swing* voters and drive them to the Republicans. Most blacks, the pollsters said, would vote for the Democrats anyway.

However, the Republicans have not been content to let their opponents downplay the race issue. In 1988, for example, the Republicans ran an effective media campaign labelling Democratic candidate Dukakis a liberal on all counts, including patriotism, abortion, religion, and civil rights. Probably the most devastating appeal to those white swing voters was an independent political group's commercial about a black prisoner named Willie Horton, who was released onto the streets in Governor Dukakis' state through a "prison furlough" program. Horton went on a crime spree that included raping a white woman. Market research using focus groups (see Chapter 6) showed that this image was very effective in dismaying many white Democrats. (In fact, the issue of the "furlough" program had first been raised in the Democratic primaries by one of Dukakis' opponents, Al Gore.) Lee Atwater, the Bush campaign manager, reportedly claimed that Horton had in effect become Mr. Dukakis' running mate.[29] Two years after the Bush election victory, as Mr. Atwater was dying of a brain tumor, he apologized for capitalizing politically on the racial tensions conveyed to some by Horton's vicious crimes.

In 1992, the pollster for the Clinton campaign, Stan Greenberg, reminded his employers that the race issue continued to drive a wedge between the party and its potential white suburban middle-class supporters, and the national Democratic campaign minimized national appeals to black voters once again. Blacks tend to vote in lower numbers than other groups to begin with, largely because many are poor, and poor people vote less often. (The reasons for this are discussed later in this chapter.) In 1992, black turnout was even lower than usual, at around 8 percent of the total national vote, compared to an estimated 10 percent in 1988, and in both cases, below the black proportion (12 percent) of the total national population.[30] Although it had a different look, racial imagery came into American living rooms again in 1992 and can be counted on to do so as long as campaigns are run as marketing operations and the pollsters advise their clients that race sells.

AGE. As noted in the opening section of this chapter, young people have been less likely to vote than older people. Why? Perhaps because they are busier getting their lives started, have not figured out a personal connection between politics and life-quality issues, and because they move around too much going to school and finding work to keep registered and follow politics. As noted in the opening section, voting turnout among those under twenty-four dropped steadily from 1972 until the upswing in 1992. Over the same period from 1972 to 1992, the political leanings of younger voters changed dramatically as well.

Two generations ago, the youth vote was predominantly liberal and Democratic. In the 1980s, people under thirty began edging toward the Republicans, and by 1984 gave Ronald Reagan a whopping 59-percent to 40-percent edge over Democratic opponent Walter Mondale. Since then, however, the youth advantage has edged back toward the Democrats. In 1992, voters under thirty delivered Democrat Bill Clinton 44 percent of their vote, with 34 percent going to George Bush and 22 percent to Ross Perot.[31]

What accounts for the shift in party identification among young people? If we simplify a complicated story, the answer lies in a change in values. Children of the 1960s and 1970s grew up in a society shaped by the values of the civil rights movement, the "War on Poverty," and such leaders as John Kennedy, who challenged them with the statement: "Ask not what your country can do for you, ask what you can do for your country." Children of the 1980s grew up in an era of conservative "family values," evangelistic religious movements, an emphasis on economic success and hard work, and leaders such as Ronald Reagan, who pointed to government as a cause of many national problems.

Where young people in the 1970s told pollsters that "making a contribution to society" was their most important goal or value, the 1980s generation placed less value on contributing to "society" and emphasized personal success as their most important goal. The generation who came of voting age in the 1990s was given a cold political awakening by learning that the economic glory days of the 1980s were over. Jobs would be harder to find, salaries would be lower, and the task ahead was to put the national economy back in order. These changing patterns of *political socialization* illustrate some of the lessons from Chapter 6 about how different social experiences affect patterns of political participation.

CLASS.   The wealthy vote more often than the poor for a variety of reasons, including better education, more time and information, and a sense that they get more from the system. People in the top 20 percent of the income ladder vote at nearly twice the rate as those at the bottom, and they also vote more Republican. In 1992, Americans earning over $75,000 delivered a healthy advantage to George Bush—48 percent (compared to 36 percent for Bill Clinton and 16 percent for Ross Perot). This group had delivered even larger advantages to the Republicans in earlier elections going back to 1976.[32]

In 1992 a major shift came in the next two income groups of voters earning $50,000–75,000, and $30,000–50,000. These two groups split their votes evenly between Bill Clinton and George Bush, in sharp contrast to the heavy Republican landslides delivered by these same groups during all three presidential elections of the 1980s. These all-important middle-class and upper-middle-class independent voters swung their support away from the Republican administration that seemed to offer little substance for fixing an ailing economy. It probably did not hurt that Democratic campaign promises in 1992 were aimed squarely at the middle class and its concerns.

OTHER SOCIAL FACTORS.   Social characteristics are important bases of individuals' voting decisions. As people experience changes or personal strains involving race, gender, class, education, religion, and other aspects of their social identity, these factors may enter into their patterns of political participation. How much effect a particular characteristic has depends on how it shapes the lives of individuals, and how election campaigns get those individuals thinking about their lives.

Election Laws and Procedures

The laws and procedures regulating voting can have big effects on who votes and who does not. The most unfortunate examples occurred in the South after the Civil War when a variety of restrictions were placed on black participation. These so-called **Jim Crow laws** ("Jim Crow" was a white slang term for a black person) made it virtually impossible for blacks to use their Fifteenth Amendment rights to vote. Many voting districts imposed a **poll tax,** which most blacks could not afford to pay. It was also common to restrict Democratic party primaries (the state Democratic parties controlled most of Southern state politics after 1865) to white voters only. To make it even more difficult to participate, **literacy tests** were used to further discriminate against blacks, who often were not provided with public education. Since some white people were also illiterate, "grandfather clauses" were added to the literacy laws, making it possible for illiterate people to vote if their grandfathers had voted before the end of the Civil War. Since no black people voted in the south before the Civil War, the grandfather clauses effectively imposed the literacy requirements only on blacks.

The burden of winning the right to vote under the Fifteenth Amendment was placed on individuals, who had to prove that their rights had been violated. Although the grandfather clause was declared unconstitutional in 1915, other legal restrictions on black participation were not defeated in court cases until the 1940s and 1950s. As noted in Chapter 5, some obstacles to black voting were not cleared away until Congress passed national voting rights legislation in 1965. Although the system of legalized restrictions on voting was finally eliminated, there remain many features in the American electoral system that continue to limit participation by some groups, as we will explain.

Black Americans attempting to vote often met with overt intimidation, as well as incomprehensible requirements, literacy tests, poll taxes, and other legal roadblocks, hindering them from even the most basic participation in the political system. Here black Mississippians undertake a registration drive in 1966.

VOTER REGISTRATION.   It is more difficult to vote in the United States than in any other industrial democracy. The fact that American turnout in presidential elections is hovering in the low 50 percent range compared with an average of more than 80 percent over the past decade in the twenty other major industrial democracies[33] can be attributed, at least in part, to **strict registration procedures** that make it difficult for many people to vote simply because they are not registered.

Through most of the first hundred years of the Republic, registration and voting were easy—perhaps too easy. During the years of highest election turnout in the 1870s and 1880s (when more than 80 percent of eligible voters cast ballots), there were also notoriously corrupt practices that may have artificially boosted the levels of participation. You may have heard of the famous "voting graveyards" of Chicago. In Chicago and other cities run by "machine" politics, it was not uncommon for loyal followers of a party to keep voting long after they had died. And before the secret ballot came to America (from Australia), parties used to print their own ballots with lists of candidates already checked off to make things easier for the voter. Many local party bosses simply bought votes. In some areas the prices paid for voting were published, and occasional price wars made voting a fairly profitable thing to do.

Angered by the corruption in party politics, a social reform movement swept the land in the early 1900s calling for "progressive" reforms in elections and other areas of public life. One of the first reforms won by the Progressives was the secret ballot, which made vote-buying less sure (people could take the money and then enter the privacy of the voting booth and vote their own way). Next came voter registration reforms, which created lists of eligible voters who had to vote in a particular locale, or *precinct*. This made it more difficult to truck bands of voters around from one polling place to another so they could vote repeatedly. Having a list of names with the dates on which people last voted made it possible to trim "dead wood" from the rolls when voters died or moved. These reforms undoubtedly cut down on the degree of fraud in elections, but they also made it difficult for some people to vote, either because the process of registration was cumbersome or because they moved to a new district too late to register for the next election.

Although the Voting Rights Act of 1965 outlawed overt discrimination, states still retained considerable control over many voting procedures, including registration. States that simplified registration had the highest turnout rates, led by Minnesota (66 percent in 1988, 71 percent in 1992), Maine (62 percent in 1988, 72 percent in 1992) and Wisconsin (62 percent in 1988, 69 percent in 1992).[34] In states that still required long application forms and waiting periods (often thirty days) prior to an election, voting rates were lower. Ruy Teixeira, a political scientist who studies voting patterns, estimated that making registration easier could boost actual voting rates by around 8 percent, a big gain that would help bridge the participation gap between the United States and most other industrial democracies.[35] After several efforts in Congress to pass national registration laws, a bill to make registration available in state motor vehicle bureaus and other government offices was passed by Congress in 1993 and signed by President Clinton.

CREATIVE REDISTRICTING.   Every ten years, state legislatures engage in a round of political wheeling and dealing, redrawing the boundaries of state voting districts. As you know, population is the basis of representation in the U.S. House of Representatives and various state elective offices. Every ten years the census tells us how much the population has changed, and the political scramble begins to draw new boundary lines on the political map. The parties in power in the state legislatures may try to employ the ancient techniques of **gerrymandering** to cram as many opponents as possible into the smallest number of districts. Another strategy is to scatter potentially unfriendly voters over a large number of districts where they will be condemned to be minorities. When *gerrymandering* occurs, limits are placed on the number of legislative seats a party

Gerrymandering: A Way of Making Votes Count Unequally

7.3

In addition to more obvious legal and procedural limits on voting participation, the ways in which voting districts are drawn can pack certain groups of voters (for instance, Republicans, Democrats, blacks, whites, and others) into a small number of districts or scatter them across a large number of districts, giving people unequal chances for representation, and possibly discouraging them from participating. In modern times, court cases commonly challenge these practices as unconstitutional, and extreme cases of gerrymandering are generally detected and corrected by federal court order. However, each time a new census is taken (every decade), political parties in the states seek to redraw district lines to gain advantages by minimizing the impact of opposing voters.

The term *gerrymandering* originated in early Massachusetts politics in 1812, when the state legislature drew up a voting district that had a dragon-like shape *(left)*. The painter Gilbert Stuart recognized the form and added a head, wings, and feet, calling it a "salamander." Editor Benjamin Russell renamed it a "gerrymander" for the state governor Elbridge Gerry.

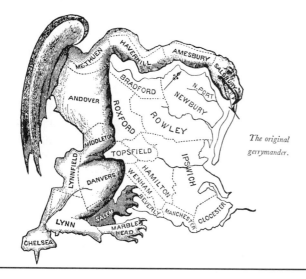

The original gerrymander.

can win, often quite out of keeping with its numbers of potential voting supporters. Living in a gerrymandered district can be discouraging for all concerned. Voters who have been stacked on the winning side feel that their candidates will win whether or not they participate in the election. And voters on the losing side of the political deal know that their numbers will never be great enough to turn the tide. "Inside the System" Box 7.3 describes the history of the term *gerrymander,* and explains why the practice continues to create political conflict inside the system.

Big political fights often break out while drawing the legal boundaries around voting districts. Following the 1990 census, for example, the U.S. Justice Department threatened to sue the state governments of Mississippi and Louisiana for drawing district boundaries that allegedly discriminated against the equal representation chances of blacks, in violation of the federal Voting Rights Act of 1965. According to the Justice Department case, these state legislatures used population shifts in the 1990 census as an excuse to create new political maps that "packed" blacks into some districts and split black population clusters up in others. The results would have made it impossible for black voters to gain representation in state or national offices in proportion to their numbers—a factor also likely to discourage participation in the affected districts. Under the threat of legal action, the Mississippi state legislature agreed to redraw 29 of its 122 state House districts and 12 of 52 state Senate boundaries. There were no changes called for in the U.S. Congress map.[36]

COMPLEX ELECTIONS. Perhaps the most easily overlooked factor that depresses American voting rates is the sheer number of elections that Americans have to vote in. The complex federal system was designed to keep as much power as possible at the grass roots, which results in a large number of elections for state, local, and national office, along with special elections for county posts, school boards, and metropolitan area governing bodies. In addition, many states have extended the idea of electoral democracy into direct forms like the *initiative,* in which voters can put legislative ideas directly on the ballot, and the *referendum,* in which laws are submitted directly to the voters for approval. When you add up all of these chances to vote, and factor in the relative lack of party guidance about how to vote, many citizens may become overwhelmed. It is worth considering that the only other democracy that has consistently had lower voting rates than ours is Switzerland, which is also probably the only country that provides more voting opportunities to its citizens.

How Does It All Add Up?

Given the number of considerations people must keep track of, deciding whether to vote, and how to vote are fairly complex decisions. Although people do not agonize over voting the way they think about buying a house or a car, most people do spend some time thinking about their options. Political scientist Samuel Popkin has described the voting act as "low information rationality":

> Voters actually do reason about parties, candidates, and issues. . . . They think about who and what political parties stand for; they think about the meaning of political endorsements; they think about what government can and should do. . . .
>
> The term *low information rationality*—popularly known as "gut" reasoning—best describes the kind of practical thinking about government and politics in which people actually engage.[37]

Political scientists follow the voting *trends,* or evolving patterns of electoral participation. These trends can shift with the candidates, issues, and voter moods from election to election, often changing the composition of the government in the process. The results of five presidential elections are shown in Figure 7.4.

FIGURE 7.4

Voting Patterns in Five Presidential Elections, 1976–1992

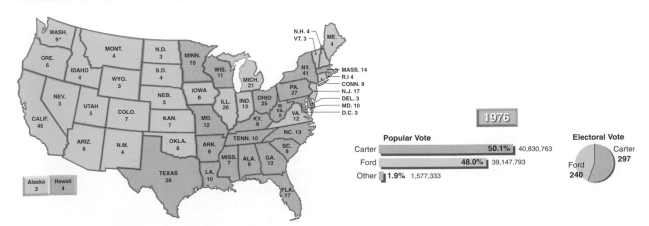

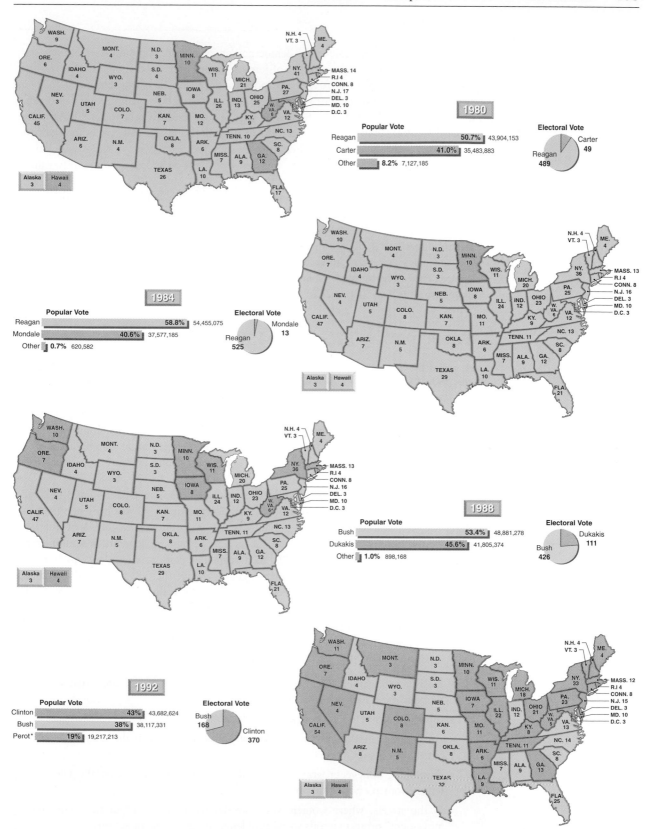

1980

Popular Vote
Reagan 50.7% 43,904,153
Carter 41.0% 35,483,883
Other 8.2% 7,127,185

Electoral Vote
Carter 49
Reagan 489

1984

Popular Vote
Reagan 58.8% 54,455,075
Mondale 40.6% 37,577,185
Other 0.7% 620,582

Electoral Vote
Mondale 13
Reagan 525

1988

Popular Vote
Bush 53.4% 48,881,278
Dukakis 45.6% 41,805,374
Other 1.0% 898,168

Electoral Vote
Dukakis 111
Bush 426

1992

Popular Vote
Clinton 43% 43,682,624
Bush 38% 38,117,331
Perot* 19% 19,217,213

Electoral Vote
Bush 168
Clinton 370

Joining Groups

Although voting is the basic act of democracy, an even more common form of civic participation is probably the simple act of joining groups and associations that serve some community, patriotic, or more explicitly political purpose. The overwhelming majority of people (more than 90 percent) report belonging or having belonged to groups as diverse as the YMCA or YWCA, Boy Scouts or Girl Scouts, Sierra Club, Rotary, fraternities, sororities, sports clubs, charities, unions, or neighborhood associations. About half the population report belonging to three or more such groups.[38] Most of these associations exist for reasons other than politics, but many of them do promote community values, and some support political lobbying activities.

During the same period in which voting declined in the 1970s and 1980s, the explosion of interest groups and their lobbying branches in Washington was most dramatic. After the passage of laws in the 1970s making it easy for organized interests to contribute directly to political campaigns, the whole electoral process became tilted, in the view of many observers, toward representing organized interests as well as individual voters. The interest-group system in America is important enough to warrant an entire chapter of this book (Chapter 8).

Participating in Social Movement Activities

A **social movement** is *an enduring collection of large numbers of individuals who see themselves as identified with common goals and values, and who engage in a variety of political activities to promote their politics.* Recall that one of the themes of this chapter is that different forms of participation often combine and play off of one another to create and change balances of power in society. Social movements often combine *unconventional political activities* such as protests and rallies, with more *conventional forms of participation* such as voting, legal action, or interest-group pressure to advance their causes.

It can take years of activism just to get the attention of fellow citizens and public officials, and some movements have resorted to violence and civil disobedience to do it. After the attention of publics and public officials has been won, voting, lobbying, and other conventional activities can be useful for advancing a movement's case. For example, delivering large numbers of voters to a particular party or candidate can help persuade politicians to support a movement's goals. One of the first goals of the women's movement early in this century, for example, was to gain voting rights. After winning the vote, many women unionized, joined professional associations, and created national women's organizations to push for other political reforms to improve the lives of women in society. Today, the political struggle over women's issues has many political fronts, both conventional and unconventional:

- elections (remember the "gender gap" from Chapter 6, and the "Year of the Woman" from earlier in this chapter)
- lobbying efforts in Congress and state legislatures
- court cases (another important form of political activism is the lawsuit, as discussed in Chapter 5)
- developing college programs in Women's Studies and changing the ways in which women's issues are presented in academia
- in the streets, where women who consider themselves part of the "women's movement" protest various social problems and government actions.

One form of unconventional political participation that reached a peak in the 1960s was demonstrating in the streets and thus (through the media) in the public eye. This tactic has since been adopted by social movements of the "New Right" as well as the "New Left"—as may be seen in the protests and abortion-clinic blockades of Operation Rescue during the 1990s. Here, New York protesters rally against America's involvement in Vietnam in September 1969.

The aims of social movements involve *broad changes in the life conditions of large numbers of people.* These kinds of changes may require reforming aspects of the political system itself, as explained in Box 7.1. Fundamental political change is often hard to accomplish through conventional political means of voting and interest-group activities alone. You can tell that a social movement is at work when large numbers of people become politically active for long periods of time, often resorting to unconventional activities to change the way other citizens think about particular problems, and to bring about new government solutions for the social problems in question.

Movements know few social or ideological boundaries. In the past two generations Americans have been caught up in movements called the "New Left" and the "New Right." Movements have mobilized behind religious values, as well as behind the freedom to reject religion. Membership in movements has known no limits of color, wealth, education, or gender. Movement goals have ranged from promoting values marginal to the political culture (white supremacy) to extending core cultural values to marginalized social groups (civil rights for blacks and women). A list of some of the social movements that have been active in contemporary American politics is provided in "Inside the System" Box 7.4.

Some of the Social Movements in Contemporary America

7.4

Because social movements are so much a part of the political landscape, it is easy to take them for granted. Yet at any point in history, there may be dozens of important grass-roots movements at work pressing their values at all levels of government and society. Here are just a few examples of the movements operating in contemporary America:

Pro-choice and anti-abortion movements. Large coalitions of opposing groups, pitting the rights of women against the rights of the unborn. Large numbers of grass-roots groups using tactics from protests to lobbying and voting.

American Indian movement. Tribal and interest groups pushing for more favorable treaty relations with the U. S. government, and public recognition of poverty and social conditions among Native Americans.

Christian right. Broad coalition of evangelical and fundamentalist churches and conservative political activists with effective fundraising organizations and strong representation in Republican party politics.

Civil rights movement. Historically a black-led movement based in churches, legal-action groups, lobbying and social improvement organizations. Broadened in recent years to include more feminist issues, and rights for the disabled and for homosexuals.

Environmental movement. Dozens of lobbying groups, wildlife preservation societies, and activist organizations aimed at promoting conservation of world resources, reducing pollution, saving endangered species, and raising consciousness about living in harmony with nature.

Homosexual rights movement. Homosexuals have organized a grass-roots network of activists to change social attitudes about their sexual behaviors and lifestyles. The movement is concerned with a range of basic issues, including safety from violence, preventing discrimination in jobs and other areas, and better medical care for AIDS patients.

Human rights. A coalition of international groups promoting respect for human dignity and political freedom. Has become a strong lobbying force encouraging American foreign policy that avoids supporting governments that kill and jail their citizens for political activities.

Senior citizens. Networks of interest groups using newsletters, community organizations, and direct mail campaigns to mobilize tens of millions of senior citizens to act in various ways on issues of concern to them. In addition to such specific issues as health, retirement, and social security benefits, seniors have raised social awareness of their needs and problems.

White supremacists. Secretive network of groups advocating a segregated society with whites in power. Often use terror tactics against nonwhite "enemy" groups. Targets also include gays, Jewish people, and public officials who try to enforce civil rights laws. Occasional efforts have been made to run members for state and local office.

Feminist movement. Large coalition of groups and publications aimed at securing equal status and power for women. Recent successes include victories in lawsuits securing equal pay for the same jobs performed by men. Also concerned with basic social problems of violence toward women, rape, and sexual harassment. Forms of political action span the range of "consciousness raising" and education, battered women's support groups, rape counseling, legislative lobbying, legal action in courts, and election campaigning.

American Indians have organized to draw attention to their ancestors' unique historical role in U.S. society, as this demonstrator attests. Groups such as the Navajo Code Talkers Association celebrate their illustrious deeds, and in 1992 Colorado elected the first American Indian U. S. senator, Ben Nighthorse Campbell.

Making a Commitment to Unconventional Participation

People join social movements when they feel that broad changes are needed in their lives and that conventional forms of political participation are not working. They see the advantages of joining with others to find creative ways of making their political demands more effective. In the process, people are generally attracted to the sense of community and belonging they get from finding others who share their problems and have the strength to do something about them. Engaging in unconventional politics often puts social activists at odds with the society around them and so social movements must spend a great deal of energy keeping up the commitment of their members.

Even though many Americans say they disapprove of the unconventional tactics used by some social movements to get attention and promote change, movements tend to attract more followers in the United States than in many other democracies.[39] Polls show that solid majorities of Americans (from 70–98 percent) say they are opposed to such activities as tax resistance, disrupting traffic, rioting, and damaging property. However, substantial numbers are willing to support other common forms of social movement action such as petition drives (58 percent support), boycotts (40 percent) and demonstrations (24 percent).[40] Differences of opinion about appropriate forms of political participation are often reflected within movements as well. It is common for the same social movement to have different "wings" that advocate more conventional and more unconventional forms of political action. The choice of political tactics is important to movements because they have to strike a fine balance between keeping public attention focused on their problems and the danger of alienating the public.

The news brings us numerous stories about social movements and their tactics. Protesters write in blood on the walls of abortion clinics. Silent vigils are held for world peace. "Hunger banquets" appear at Thanksgiving to raise consciousness about the plight of the world's starving masses. Crosses are burned on the lawn of a black family who broke the color barrier in a white neighborhood. Homosexuals march to proclaim their rights in public. These and other dramatic stories probably would never reach us as "news" if the social movements behind them did not resort to unusual methods to get their messages across.

Mobilizing People: What It Takes

People do not just automatically come together in large numbers every time they have a problem. History tells many tales of people who suffered similar plights for years, sometimes generations, before something sparked them to take collective action to change history. What is it? What is that spark that gets people to see they have some fundamental issue in common and that they can do something about it? There are, of course, many things that must occur for people to: a) recognize a shared problem, b) conclude that something can be done to change it, and c) do it (these being the steps of political mobilization).

LEADERSHIP AND INDIVIDUAL EMPOWERMENT. People may be aware that something is wrong in their lives but unsure whether others feel the same way or unclear about what to do about it. Sometimes it takes a leader to get people moving by expressing exactly how they feel, convincing them that others feel the same way, firing up their motivation to change things, and presenting their case in public.

A strong movement depends on many leaders to sustain it. The long political struggle of African Americans has been advanced by thousands of strong leaders who pursued different courses of action: Frederick Douglass, Harriet Tubman, George Washington Carver, W. E. B. Du Bois, Booker T. Washington, Malcolm X, Martin Luther King, Jr., Barbara Jordan, and Sojourner Truth, to name just a few. Many gave their lives to the cause and inspired others to take their places. In addition to those recorded in history books, there have been thousands of less well-known leaders at local levels who inspired friends and neighbors to take action and keep the faith that their struggle would result in change. Leadership can be based on many different qualities, including:

- **charisma**, or the embodiment of personal qualities that people admire;

- **organizational abilities** that enable some people to bring groups together and get things accomplished;

- *knowledge or* **information** about law, history, group traditions, or political strategies that makes certain people a resource for others to turn to;

- **communication skills** that can be used to project a social vision and to rally people when support for that vision needs to be reinforced.

Great leaders often combine all of these leadership qualities. However, most movements depend on many leaders, great and small, with different skills to keep people involved. Some leadership acts become models of courage for others, as when Rosa Parks launched a drive to integrate public transportation in the South by refusing to yield her seat to a white person on a Montgomery, Alabama bus. Other deeds open paths of legal action, as when Thurgood Marshall argued the historic Supreme Court case for the National Association for the Advancement of Colored People in *Brown v. The Board of Education of Topeka, Kansas.* Marshall later went on to serve as a justice on the Supreme Court. Each leader brings a skill, a style, and a group of followers to the larger movement. Great leaders convince ordinary people that they can become leaders, too.

ORGANIZATION AND POLITICAL COMMUNITY.   Social movements adopt many different organizational forms depending on who is involved and what their goals are. For the most part, movements that are large, well established, and dedicated to long-term changes in society tend to be *decentralized* in their organization. This means that they operate through many different organizations at many levels, with local, state, and national chapters. For example, the women's movement consists of hundreds of organizations with different specific goals. Common understandings and support networks enable the decentralized groups to join forces.

Specific organizations within a movement (like the National Organization for Women or the National Abortion Rights League) may be more *centralized,* with national officers, boards of directors, state and local branch offices, and committees to handle various organizational tasks. However, because of their grass-roots focus, few movements are driven by single organizations. Decentralized movements are more flexible and open to decision making by ordinary people at local levels. When coordination is required for larger political activities, different groups join together through loose confederations called *councils, networks,* and *alliances.*

The great challenge in many movements is for people to find each other in the first place and stay in contact long enough to become organized into a more enduring movement. Because of the very social problems they suffer, people may be isolated from each other and discouraged from undertaking political actions. Governments and communities opposed to social movements have tried to use tactics ranging from police surveillance to laws against loitering and public meetings to prevent people from coming together to discuss politics.

Most groups find creative ways to get around restrictions placed on their efforts to communicate and plan activities. Songs sung by slaves on plantations often contained

Unconventional Means. . .

While delegates of the two major political parties regularly unite in conventions, other players in the political game choose unconventional means. Such participants are often concerned with a single overriding issue. Above, nuclear-disarmament proponents march on the nation's capital in 1986; below, homosexual-rights advocates parade in Cambridge, Massachusetts. Supporters of the 1992 presidential candidacy of populist billionaire Ross Perot (*at right,* a June rally in Hartford, Connecticut) were commonly troubled by the growth of the federal deficit or related economic topics. Such unconventional political participants rarely elect candidates, but can push the major parties in certain ideological directions.

The Players

powerful political messages and themes of solidarity and resistance. An impressive communication network existed among enslaved peoples on plantations throughout the South. Word of rebellions such as the one led by Nat Turner in 1831 spread rapidly among black people on plantations and the network of freed slaves and white support groups in the North.[41] The black church has been an important political meeting place to this day, and many preachers from Martin Luther King, Jr., to Jesse Jackson have become leaders in the civil rights movement.

Women, too, have used everyday social settings to build community and communication networks. With the admission of women to more colleges in the last half of the nineteenth century, a public space was created to explore women's issues. Before that, women came together in forums ranging from "sewing circles" to literary societies to discuss shared life experiences. In recent years, the women's movement has made use of the media to communicate about issues through talk shows, movies, books, magazines, and in news events.

The mass media have opened the frontiers of social movements beyond anything that was possible even a few decades ago. The rise of the religious broadcasting networks, for example, has connected millions of people in local communities and local churches into a powerful movement still capable (despite the scandals of the 1980s) of generating large sums of money and grass-roots political pressure. The religious right remains a powerful force shaping the moral agenda of the nation. One of its key communication tools is the television church.

USING THE MASS MEDIA.   In addition to using the media to hold meetings (television church) and communicate ideas (documentaries and paid informational programs), many movements have discovered the importance of getting their causes into the news. The value of the news in keeping public attention on a group and its demands is obvious. The problem is how to get the message across in a sympathetic way without appearing too disruptive or deviant. Protests, demonstrations, and other unconventional acts are dramatic events that make for good news stories. However, groups have learned the hard way that the media often film an activity from afar, and then invite unsympathetic public authorities to do the scripting and narration. Needless to say, the authorities who are being protested against do not usually give a sympathetic presentation of the group's demands and motives.

Over the years, social movements have learned how to improve the coverage they get in the news by using a variety of techniques designed to appeal to news production values. For example, the radical environmental group Greenpeace softened the image of its "commando ship" by painting it in vibrant colors and naming it the *Rainbow Warrior*. The ship was often used to stage news events such as cutting the nets of fishing boats to free trapped dolphins.

The dilemma, of course, is that even when using the media effectively, a movement's message is just one bit of information in a crowded and often changing news picture. Even if Greenpeace is identified in the minds of many viewers as being on the side of helpless dolphins, what is the end result? When the news story contains a rebuttal from a well-prepared spokesperson for the fishing industry who talks about their efforts to solve the problem of killing dolphins and about the people who will lose their jobs if net fishing is made illegal, what are viewers to conclude? Both sides have a point. And who can be trusted? After all, both sides are using the media to their political advantage.

Movements have learned to combine their news appearances with public relations campaigns that may include advertising and direct mail information packages. In addition, spokespeople go on the talk-show circuit to try to put the best possible media "spin" on the issues that their movement is concerned with. Movements know that the

Increasingly, media-wise political groups have adopted unconventional tactics as a way to achieve not only their primary goals but other, less obvious, objectives as well. For example, the Greenpeace organization's Rainbow Warrior II, *christened in 1989 in Hamburg, West Germany, has starred in many unconventional activities, such as rescuing dolphins ensnared in tuna-fishing nets. The ship also functions as tasty media bait, aiming to lure in the TV viewer's fancy with its colorful looks and thus net future members and their contributions.*

media battle for the hearts and minds of the public is endless and must be a source of continuous planning. At the same time, movements realize that their own members also follow the news, watch informational programs, and tune in to talk shows. It is important not to confuse or water down the goals and objectives that are important to maintaining the loyalty of movement activists in the process of trying to improve relations with broader publics.

DEFINING GOALS AND KEEPING PEOPLE MOTIVATED. Out of leadership and communication come a sense of what is possible and how to go about attaining goals. Movements that endure are those capable of instilling a sense of purpose in their members and updating those purposes as history moves ahead. One of the reasons why the antiwar movement of the 1960s fell apart in the 1970s was the inability of the dozens of groups making up the movement to agree on specific goals. Was it just a movement to stop a war, or was it a large force for social change? Doubts and disagreements played up in the media clouded this question in the minds of many supporters.[42] When the government suddenly ended the military draft, one of the most personal issues for many young men involved was suddenly removed, and it became even less clear what they wanted out of the movement.

The evangelical Christian movement in recent times has been successful in keeping certain issues (abortion, prayer in schools, family values) on the national agenda. Members are reminded of the importance of those issues through a variety of communications methods from church sermons to direct-mail political appeals to the television programs of public figures such as Pat Robertson, and through conservative allies such as syndicated columnist Cal Thomas.

PROMOTING ACCEPTANCE OF UNCONVENTIONAL POLITICS.   Most people who join social movements eventually face tough questions about what they are willing to do for the cause:

- Go to meetings that may be watched by law enforcement agencies or terrorist organizations.
- Attend public meetings or demonstrations that may brand one as a misfit and cause trouble at work, with neighbors, and even with family members.
- Spend long hours on picket lines, doing mailings, gathering signatures on petitions, or trying to get press coverage for the cause.

For many who join them, social movements present moments of truth for their political convictions, raising questions about whether one wants to live with a problem or endure the social resistance against trying to change it.

While most social movements use both conventional and unconventional methods to press for social change, it is often the unconventional that make the greatest impression. As a result, many groups engage in activities that result in their members being arrested or bring on the risk of physical abuse from authorities or fellow citizens. Burning the flag, trespassing at a nuclear power plant, reciting a prayer in a public school classroom, or blocking the entrance to an abortion clinic are good ways to get some sort of reaction from authorities, onlookers, and neighbors. Groups often provide important networks of social support for members who find themselves at odds with their communities. In addition, some groups train their members in the methods of nonviolent protest to prevent confrontations with authorities from getting out of hand.

Movements and Elections

Although movements employ a range of activities to bring their issues to public attention, the bottom line often involves using the methods of conventional participation to get their goals turned into policies. Even small and isolated movements such as the white supremacists have supported candidates for office, as in the unsuccessful gubernatorial candidacy of David Duke in Louisiana in 1991.

Few groups have been as successful in converting a social movement into electoral power as the religious right. In the 1970s and 1980s more and more Americans felt the country had lost sight of traditional values of hard work, small government, and basic religious beliefs. By the millions, people were born again as Christians. Church attendance boomed, and television programs with religious themes attracted huge audiences. Television preachers and travelling evangelists built great media empires with large followings. Talk began to turn to finding political outlets for the values of this vast movement. Political marketing firms sprang up and tapped the financial potential of this "Religious Right" and put the money to work lobbying Congress and state legislatures, and electing candidates around a whole agenda of issues that have by now become familiar ones: prayer in public schools, anti-abortion legislation, cutting back social programs, and spreading the word of God and American democracy throughout the land and around the world. This movement found a spokesman for many of its causes in Ronald Reagan, the man who would later become president and open the doors of the Republican party to the ranks of the New Right. The movement has continued to get its issues onto the national party platform, as illustrated by the strong anti-abortion plank and the family values theme in the 1992 election.

In the 1990s, the Christian right put the focus on local politics and began organizing campaigns for state legislatures, city councils, and school boards. One news report on the 1992 elections summarized the success of those electoral efforts as follows:

> In a nationwide push for power at the state and local levels, conservative Christian candidates won hundreds of races on Election Day, establishing themselves as a grass roots political force and giving them a base from which to push for control of the Republican party.
>
> The liberal lobbying group People for the American Way, which has led the fight against the religious right around the country, said fundamentalist Christian candidates had won about 40% of the 500 races it monitored nationwide. The fiercest battleground was California, but the movement has also scored successes in states like Iowa, Kansas, Florida, Texas, and Oregon. . . .
>
> [According to the president of People for the American Way] the religious right was already gearing up for the mid-term elections of 1994, when lower voter turnout and lighter press scrutiny are likely to help Christian candidates, who often succeed by keeping a low profile and getting their committed minority constituency to the polls.[43]

It should be clear by now why it is important to understand how the different forms of political participation are used together as ways for people to adjust the balances of power in society. Without seeing the relationships among forms of political action such as voting, interest groups, and social movements, it might be easy to conclude that participation was some sort of duty or a mere civic obligation. For millions of people, participation involves making creative political decisions about how to improve their lives.

Nonparticipation

Despite all the forms of participation available to people, there are still many citizens who do not take an active part in the system. It is too easy to conclude that nonparticipation is the result of increasing alienation or cynicism about politics. **Alienation** refers to the feeling that social norms and institutions do not represent one's values or needs, and **cynicism** is the matching feeling that institutions are actively representing other groups to the exclusion of your own. It is true that both alienation and cynicism have been on the rise in America since the 1960s. For example, the Harris Poll has measured alienation over this period and found that in 1966 only 29 percent scored as alienated, while in 1991 the percentage had reached an all-time high of 66 percent (with some notable ups and downs in the years in between).[44]

Alienation and cynicism are not desirable among such large numbers of citizens, but it is dangerous to conclude that people participate less because they are alienated or cynical. It turns out that alienation and cynicism have grown fairly equally among those who participate and those who do not. For example, a 1992 survey found that 75 percent of those who vote agreed that the government can be trusted to do what is right only some of the time or never. In the same study, 72 percent of the nonvoters felt the same way.[45]

Many studies of voting behavior find that there are relatively few differences between voters and nonvoters that can be explained by cynicism, alienation, or many other common-sense psychological explanations.[46] There are, however, some obvious social differences between voters and nonvoters, with age, income, education, and gender all figuring into the equation (nonvoters are younger, poorer, male, and less educated). Some experts argue that for many people, these **social differences** are not such serious barriers to participation. After dismissing nine commonly heard "myths" about nonparticipation, political scientist Ruy Teixeira suggests that the gulf between participants and nonparticipants in American politics is really fairly shallow, which is pretty good news. What mainly separates voters from nonvoters, according to Teixeira, is that people who vote feel connected to politics and nonvoters do not. The key to more participation in this view is simple motivation and minimal involvement:

> Even a very low level of campaign involvement—perhaps just reading an article or two in the newspaper—or of knowledge about the candidates and issues or of faith the government is paying attention may be enough to turn a nonvoter into a voter. The key is breaking through the extraordinary **detachment** that many citizens have developed from the political process, so that they are connected, in even a minimal way, to the world of politics.
>
> There are no sure remedies here, but a lot of plausible ones. They range from campaign finance reform to regulating television commercials to issues-based media coverage of campaigns. The idea is to make the campaign process easier to get involved in, more informative, and less susceptible to political manipulation. We have good reasons to believe that if this goal can be accomplished, more citizens would step forward and participate. It does not take, after all, a great deal of motivation to vote, so even small gains in voter involvement and understanding could pay large dividends on election day.[47]

Chapters 9 and 10 explore some of these aspects of political parties and election campaigns that may encourage or discourage broader citizen participation. In the remainder of this chapter, we turn to the things that citizens can do now to better connect themselves to the system.

Varieties of Participation and the Needs of Democracy Revisited

As the discussion has made clear, people have a variety of participation options available to them in the American system. There are no guarantees that people will pick the right or even the most effective ones. What motivates people to participate, and how they participate depends on the life experiences of each individual: how people are socialized into politics, how their adult lives develop, and the people, candidates, parties, and other opportunities they encounter along the way. All of this makes participation a rich and often surprising set of activities that form the creative links between people and government.

Whoever the actors are, and whatever methods they choose, the ultimate goal is to turn participation into government action. In recent years, there has been a deluge of talk about how government has grown unresponsive to the demands of many different kinds of people. Consider, for example, responses over a thirty-year period to a poll question asking people if they think the government is run primarily for the benefit of a few big interests. At the beginning of the 1960s, only 25 percent of those surveyed agreed with the *elitist* thesis that government mainly represented a few big interests. In 1970, the number rose to 50 percent. By 1980, fully 70 percent agreed that the government was run for the benefit of big interests. At the outset of the 1990s, the percentage in agreement with this view of government had hit 77 percent.[48] Also at the beginning of the 1990s, roughly 80 percent of the public expressed concern that the nation was in se-

Political participation can take many forms. One common sign of voter discontent is the periodic drive to simply jettison incumbent officials (regardless of their past achievements or current performance) for outsiders (regardless of their qualifications), on the premise that "a new broom sweeps clean." However, for some, "RE-ELECT NOBODY" serves as an excuse not to vote at all.

rious trouble.[49] The drop in trust in government was about the same for voters and non-voters alike, so do not jump to the conclusion that this psychology of pessimism caused the decline in voting discussed earlier.

Despite the slump in voting and the pessimism about politics, few political scientists would advise pronouncing either political participation or democracy dead. Remember that there are many ways to participate, and that the various forms of citizen power are always changing in response to conditions in society and government. If participation is part of a system, people find ways to become involved. For example, voting levels may fall while other ways of exercising citizen influence are on the rise. In the next chapter, for example, we will see that the very period of greatest decline in voting was also the period of the greatest rise in interest-group activity in modern American politics.

Even in the area of elections, the only form of political action that fell off dramatically was voting itself. Surveys during the 1970s and 1980s recorded stable patterns or slight increases in other election-related activities, even as voting declined. For example, data gathered in the National Election Studies conducted by the University of Michigan showed that all of the following types of electoral participation either held steady or increased during the period in which voting declined (percentages indicate the range of responses in each category from 1960–1988):

- attend party meetings/work on campaigns (5–10 percent)
- try to persuade others about how to vote (30–35 percent)
- interest in following political campaigns (70–80 percent)

The main point is that different forms of participation may rise and fall as people react to their life experiences and find new ways of expressing their political concerns. These patterns of participation can change rapidly, as a trip back into American history suggests. Anyone looking at the first elections in America could have drawn a pretty gloomy forecast about the prospects for democracy. In the first congressional elections, for example, perhaps as few as 10 percent of the eligible voters participated, yet by the 1820s voting rates were much higher than they are today. (Look again at Figure 7.2, and trace the upswings and downswings in voting from the early 1800s.) Similarly, turnouts ran embarrassingly small in the first presidential contests (less than 20 percent). Yet by the end of the Jacksonian era (1840), upwards of three-fourths of the eligible white males were voting.[50] When the French observer Alexis de Tocqueville arrived on the scene, he witnessed the height of this participation boom. Not surprisingly, he pronounced the American system something of a democratic miracle. You might reread Tocqueville's observation at the opening of the chapter. What might his reaction have been had he visited the country twenty years earlier or arrived on our shores today?

One hundred years after Tocqueville came to America, the 1930s ushered in another period of great political changes. (Recall the discussion from Chapter 4 on the Great Depression and the rise of the era of cooperative federalism.) It may be surprising to discover from Figure 7.2 that voting was not much higher in the elections of that turbulent era than in recent years. Yet other forms of citizen action were in high gear during that period. Vast social movements stirred the people. Workers joined the labor-union movement and participated in strikes and marches and voted for Democratic party candidates who promised new labor laws. Farmers protested low prices for their crops and won programs to help stabilize the farm economy. Across the land, an explosion of groups and interest organizations magnified the impact of voting and other forms of participation.

History suggests that the nation has faced periods of citizen discontent in the past and that people have expressed that discontent in different ways. What scenario will play out

A CITIZEN'S QUESTION · Getting Involved

What can I do to make a difference? How can I act more effectively? The opening discussion in this chapter raised questions about why younger people participate less. For many, nonparticipation is based on a sense of social *detachment:* not being married or having children or a stable career or owning property, and the other things that connect people to the institutions of society and government. Feeling more connected to politics is a process that grows with age. As people acquire jobs, property, and stable places in communities, they become more connected to society through a broader set of interests, and those interests are affected by government actions.

Another part of the participation dilemma experienced by many young people may simply result from not knowing how to express personal concerns in political ways. Most of us have concerns about larger issues that never get to the action stage. Frustrations about the environment, or homelessness, or increases in college tuition may simply be carried around as low-level anger or annoyance. It is not a bad idea to take a *personal inventory* from time to time to think clearly about what in the world may be arousing personal interest and concern. Just defining your political interests and frustrations more clearly is a step toward participation. Next, it is easy to begin asking friends or teachers if they know any groups at the local level

that are doing something about your concerns. In most cases, it will be surprising to discover how many people are active in most of the issues that come to mind. Some local groups may provide opportunities to study or learn more about problems, while others may have fully developed programs of action to which you may want to devote some free time. Many colleges and universities even have internship programs that enable students to combine some forms of political participation with their studies.

If you are already engaged in politics, perhaps the connections among different forms of participation pointed out in this chapter will provide some ideas about how to promote your interests in other and possibly more effective ways. Can you think of a new avenue of participation to promote some cause you are already involved with? Perhaps you have decided that increasing voting participation among students is an important political goal, worthy of your time and energy. You might want to think about participating in a voter registration effort on campus. If there is not already a registration drive at your school, you can find out how to start one by writing to:

Student Campaign for Voter Registration
215 Pennsylvania Ave., S.E.
Washington, D.C. 20003
202-546-9707

in the 1990s? Will new social movements emerge to change the course of history? Will the political parties become rebuilt around new ideas and attract new coalitions of voters at election time? If history and political culture are reliable guides, it is reasonable to predict that new patterns of participation and power will emerge as citizen discontent finds effective ways of being expressed.

This does not mean that cynicism about politics or declines in voting or other forms of participation should be taken lightly. There are surely problems of participation that can cause serious harm to democracy or, at the very least, result in periods of disastrous government. However, before pronouncing the body politic dead, it is a good idea to make sure that all of its life support systems really have stopped functioning. A good place to begin evaluating the quality of citizen action in contemporary American politics is to recognize some of the different forms of participation available to citizens and to think personally about why participation matters in a democracy.

Key Terms

participation and democracy

 legitimacy

conventional and unconventional
 forms of participation

psychological bases of the
 voting choice

 party identification
 issues
 valence issues
 candidate character

social bases of voting (gender,
 race, class, age, education)

election laws (effects on political
 participation)

 Jim Crow laws
 white primaries
 poll taxes
 literacy tests
 registration requirements
 gerrymandering voting districts
 complexity of elections

social movements

 defining characteristics
 how people are mobilized
 leadership (charisma, organizational skills, information,
   communication skills)
 organization and networking
 political tactics
 role of the media

explanations for nonparticipation

 alienation, cynicism
 social factors
 detachment from politics

Suggested Readings

Conway, Margaret M. *Political Participation in the United States,* 2nd ed. Washington, D.C.: Congressional Quarterly Press, 1991.

Cronin, Thomas E. *Direct Democracy: The Politics of the Initiative, Referendum, and Recall.* Cambridge: Harvard University Press, 1989.

Dalton, Russell J. *Citizen Politics in Western Democracies,* Chatham, N. J.: Chatham House, 1988.

Evans, Sarah H. *Born for Liberty: A History of Women in America.* New York: The Free Press, 1988.

Morris, Aldon. *The Origins of the Civil Rights Movement: Black Communities Organizing for Change.* New York: The Free Press, 1985.

Popkin, Samuel L. *The Reasoning Voter: Communication and Persuasion in Presidential Campaigns.* Chicago: University of Chicago Press, 1991.

Teixeira, Ruy A. *Why Americans Don't Vote: Turnout Decline in the United States 1960–1984.* New York: Greenwood Press, 1987.

If public opinion was the decider in this country you'd have gun control and prayer in the schools. In fact, public policy is driven by small, highly motivated groups of activists who focus their political energies on these questions.
—PAUL WEYRICH, CONSERVATIVE ACTIVIST

8

Interest-Group

Politics

- **WINNING AND LOSING: THE INTEREST-GROUP STORY**
- **DEMOCRACY AND INTEREST-GROUP POLITICS**
  The Turbulent History of Organized Interests
  The Dilemmas of Interest-Group Democracy
- **WHO ARE THE INTERESTS?**
  How Many Are There?
  Reasons for the Growth of Groups
  How Groups Keep Their Members
- **HOW INTEREST GROUPS OPERATE POLITICALLY**
  Lobbying
  Campaign Contributions
  Litigation
  Mobilizing Public Opinion
  Mixed Strategies: The Auto Lobby and Fuel Economy Laws
- **GROUP ORGANIZATION AND RESOURCES**
- **DEMOCRACY AND INTEREST-GROUP
  POLITICS REVISITED**
  The Future of Interests
  The Public Interest
- **A CITIZEN'S QUESTION: Joining Interest Groups**
- **KEY TERMS**
- **SUGGESTED READINGS**

The headline introduced a tale of political victory: WINNING STRATEGY ON TAXES: REAL ESTATE INTERESTS PREVAIL AS WASHINGTON SEEKS TO STIMULATE THE ECONOMY.[1] According to the story, a group of top real-estate executives and lobbyists convinced the president that their industry was in trouble and that fixing it would be good for the economy in general. Similar meetings took place in Congress, backed up by more than $11 million in contributions to individual campaign funds and to the Republican and Democratic party organizations. Large contributions were also made to the president's re-election campaign. The legislative and executive branches agreed to support tax breaks designed to stimulate home sales and real-estate investments. Critics charged that the tax benefits were driven mainly by lobbying pressure and political contributions. Supporters defended the actions as good for an ailing economy. Industry representatives claimed victory for their cause and credited lobbying with bringing important problems to the attention of leaders and for helping them to work out creative solutions.

Another headline told a tale of political defeat: INTEREST GROUPS GEAR UP FOR NEW SPATE OF LOBBYING.[2] The issue, again, was taxes. Small-airplane owners and manufacturers were sure they had convinced leaders of the House and Senate budget committees to kill a luxury tax on small planes. The Aircraft Owners and Pilots Association sent out a news release proclaiming victory and heralding the economic benefits for small-aircraft manufacturers and buyers. It turned out that the declaration of victory was a bit premature. Pressures for budget-balancing increased the pressure for new taxes, which triggered fierce lobbying from different groups to keep those taxes from affecting their industries. The small-plane lobby was up against alcohol and tobacco companies, automobile dealers and manufacturers, and the nation's truckers, to name just a few of the interests that wanted to keep new taxes away from their products and businesses. In a last flurry of negotiating and adjusting budget figures, many members of Congress felt that restoring the luxury tax on planes was better (or at least less painful) than some of the alternatives. To the horror of the plane lobby, Congress voted down what had been celebrated as a "done deal." The president of the owners and pilots association admitted, "We obviously screwed up."[3] The tired lobbyists could do little else but shrug off the loss as part of the game and gear up for another round of lobbying to win back what they had just lost.

Win or lose, interest organizations are usually in the political game for the long haul. They learn to publicize their current situation in the media with an eye to the next round of the battle. Thus, at the same time that critics deliver somber warnings about the evils of "special interest" politics, the victorious groups proclaim their gains as beneficial to the public. And so the battle of the interests continues to go around and around.

Interest-group politics is not the exclusive domain of elites and industries. Many grass-roots groups attract members from diverse segments of society, among them senior citizens, workers, people interested in children's welfare, Mothers Against Drunk Driving, and environmentalists. Despite the diversity of groups, important questions about their impact on democracy continue to be debated:

- Is power wielded disproportionately by groups with more money and insider access? *or*

- Do non-elite groups have their own political advantages, including large numbers of members

Interest groups are not necessarily the tools of the rich and powerful alone. The organization Mothers Against Drunk Driving (MADD), for example, has operated as a nationally recognized grassroots lobby for over a decade. Here relatives of the casualties of drunk drivers look over a "victim board" (displaying photographs of killed family members), erected outside the Washington, D.C. Capitol building.

and supporters who can pressure representatives through elections and in other ways?

- Do too many interests fighting over small issues bog the government down, leaving it unable to deal with broader social and economic concerns? *or*

- Are interest groups the main salvation of a system that is unwieldy (and, some would say, unworkable) by design?

These and other key questions are discussed in this chapter. Some observers defend interest-group politics in America, while others condemn this system, warning the public against the evils of this or that "special" interest. Such terms as "special" are loaded politically and may not be very helpful in understanding how, and how well, the interest-group system works. There are many aspects of interest-group politics worth considering before you decide

how you feel about that next news story on the proverbial wheeling and dealing between government and some collection of interests. We will return later in the chapter to reconsider the pros and cons of interest-group politics as debated among political scientists.

It is also important to remember, when thinking about interest groups, that most of us are affected by the things they do. Most people are represented in one way or another by interest organizations, either as formal members or simply as people whose interests in some area are affected. Citizens should become aware of the interest organizations that concern them. Which interest groups promote values you care about? How can you join them? What is the participatory experience like in different interest organizations? This chapter will help you to evaluate joining a group and show you how to find the kind of group that best represents your interests.

Democracy and Interest-Group Politics

Interest groups *are organizations that seek to influence government policy.* Although interest groups may support particular political parties and help to get their candidates elected, they are generally concerned about a much narrower range of issues than are parties, and often cultivate support from *both* major parties as a way to promote their causes. Interest groups often begin as informal associations of people who have some interest in common. From these informal beginnings, formal organizations develop and become important parts of the legislative and governing process. The influence that formal interest groups "peddle" is regulated by laws that affect how they raise and spend money,

TABLE 8.1 *Selected Interest Groups and Their Political Activities*

Interest Group	Estimated Number of Members	Campaign Contributions	Lobbying	Media Outreach	Initiative/ Referendum Campaigns	Litigation	Grass-roots Organizing	Polling	TV/Radio Production	Voter Registration	1990 Budget (millions)
Nat'l Abortion Rights Action League (NARAL)	450,000	X	X	X	X	X	X	X			$9.3
Nat'l Right to Life Committee	Not available	X	X	X	X	X	X	X			$10.9
Nat'l Rifle Assn. (NRA)	2.65 million	X	X	X	X	X	X	X	X	X	$86.9
U.S. Chamber of Commerce	180,000 companies, 2,800 state/local chambers*		X	X	X	X	X	X	X		$70.0
Nat'l Fed. of Ind. Business	560,000	X	X	X			X				$50.0
Nat'l Taxpayers Union	200,000		X		X		X				(1989) $3.0
Amer. Assn. of Retired Persons (AARP)	32 million		X	X			X				Not available
Amer. Civil Liberties Union (ACLU)	280,000		X	X	X	X	X	X	X		$18.7
Nat'l Assn. for the Advancement of Colored People (NAACP)	345,000		X	X	X	X	X	X	X	X	$12.0
Nat'l Organization for Women (NOW)	250,000	X	X	X	X	X	X			X	$7.0
Nat'l Gay & Lesbian Task Force	17,000 100 organizations		X	X	X	X	X				$1.0
Mothers Against Drunk Driving (MADD)	2.95 million		X	X	X	X	X	X	X		$43.5
The Conservative Caucus	660,000		X			X	X		X		Not available
People for the American Way	290,000			X			X	X			$7.3
Consumer Alert	6,800		X	X		X		X			(1990-91) $.357
Sierra Club	650,000	X	X	X	X	X	X	X	X		$35.0
In Defense of Animals	55,000 400 organizations		X	X	X	X	X				(1989) $.655
Amer. Israel Public Affairs Committee (AIPAC)	55,000		X				X				(1991) $12.0
SANE/FREEZE: Campaign for Global Security	170,000	X	X	X	X		X			X	$2.5
The United States Conference of Mayors	Approx. 800 mayors of cities over 30,000 population										Not available
Nat'l Conference of Catholic Bishops/U.S. Catholic Conference	300 U.S. Catholic Bishops		X	X			X		X		$31.0
League of Conservation Voters	60,000	X	X			X	X			X	$1.3

* plus 1,300 trade & professional associations and 60 American Chambers of Commerce abroad.

SOURCE: Foundation for Public Affairs, *Public Interest Profiles* (Washington, DC: Congressional Quarterly Inc., 1992), pp. (in order of listing) 137, 181, 173, 54, 48, 51, 75, 81, 141, 169, 255, 718, 195, 321, 579, 507, 605, 645, 755, 822, 541.

contact government officials, and report their activities. Table 8.1 illustrates some of the different interest organizations in the United States and describes their political operations.

Interest groups engage in activities that involve them in all levels and branches of government. It is probably not too much of an exaggeration to say that almost any activity of government has interest groups monitoring, promoting, or opposing it behind the scenes. Here are some of the common government activities that involve interest groups:

- providing lawmakers with information about problems and getting particular issues on the agendas of state and national government
- suggesting ways of writing laws by offering technical expertise and legal input into the legislative process
- working with state and national bureaucrats who put the laws into effect and write the rules and regulations that connect government with the people
- organizing legal actions to defend helpful legislation or to attack laws passed by opponents.

In a government with so many separate parts that must be connected in order to get things done, if interest groups did not exist, they would probably have to be invented. Some observers credit interest groups with being essential to the very functioning of government. They get issues onto the government agenda and bring the key players together to act on those issues. Important national accomplishments in highway and automobile safety, environmental quality, and many other areas are due to the efforts of interest groups. Even many critics agree that interest groups have accomplished important things, but they say that the focus of interest-group politics is so narrow that the overall direction of government ends up being uncoordinated. Many social problems never get solved, either because interest groups are not strong enough in those areas or because competing groups block effective action. A brief review of the history of this debate reveals why interest groups have become both such an indispensable and such a controversial part of American politics.

The Turbulent History of Organized Interests

Despite being an important part of the governing process in the United States, interests have been viewed warily since the beginning of the nation. In his farewell address upon leaving the presidency, George Washington warned the country of entering into foreign entanglements inspired by the motives of political "factions," as groups with enduring interests were commonly called. In the 1830s, Andrew Jackson fired up public anger against wealthy bankers who had convinced Congress to charter a national bank, giving them a monopoly over the nation's money supply. In 1860, Abraham Lincoln waged a divisive election campaign, followed by an even more divisive war, against the interests of slaveowners who had managed to get the institution of slavery written into the Constitution itself.

In 1888, Grover Cleveland warned the nation that "the citizen is struggling far in the rear" in the battle for political power, losing ground to well-organized "corporations, which should be carefully restrained creatures of law and servants of the people [but] are fast becoming the people's masters."[4] Franklin Roosevelt rode the crest of public anger at "Big Business" during the Great Depression to champion the interests of farmers and the unemployed. As discussed in Chapter 4, Roosevelt called his program a New Deal that made it easier for grass-roots interests to organize and find an ally in government.

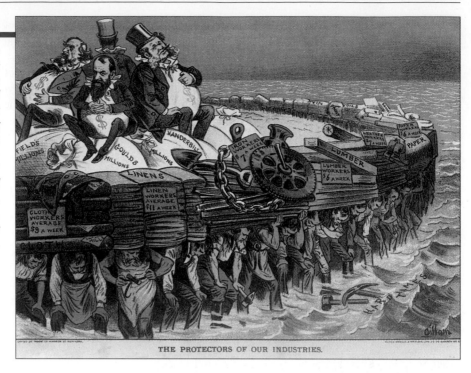

Skepticism toward big business lobbies and their goals is almost as old as the republic itself. This 1883 car-toon, from the satirical magazine Puck, *suggests that as "Hard Times" (the engulfing tide) wore away the common workers, the supposed "protectors of [American] industries" (millionaire financiers and capitalists such as Cyrus Field, Jay Gould, Cornelius Vanderbilt, and Russell Sage) did little except add to their misery.*

World War II hero Dwight Eisenhower left the presidency in 1961 after a chilling warning to beware "the military-industrial complex" that was setting the nation's industrial priorities at home and charting the course of foreign policy abroad while eating the lion's share of the national budget. These words came home decades later in the 1990s, as the national government struggled to reduce a vast defense establishment and shift the focus of the economy after the end of the Cold War and the collapse of the Soviet Union.

In the 1980s, Ronald Reagan condemned the Democrats as the party of special interests for platforms that favored the agendas of labor unions, feminist groups, civil-liberties organizations, entrenched bureaucracies, and entitlement programs. Meanwhile, the Democrats accused the Republicans under Reagan and Bush of handing out special favors to big corporations and the rich in the form of tax breaks, investment incentives, government subsidies, and reduced regulation of businesses. As for the public who followed all this finger-pointing, the majority told pollsters at the beginning of the 1990s that they were more convinced than ever that the government was being run for the benefit of special interests, not average citizens. (Recall the poll data from the discussion of the participation crisis in Chapter 7.)

In many ways the greatest political challenge facing Bill Clinton at the start of his presidency in 1993 was how to persuade thousands of conflicting interests to join together around broad reform programs in health, education, defense, energy policy, transportation, urban revitalization, industrial retooling, and job training—all in a time of serious budgetary limitations. In his campaign to sell his program to the people, Clinton called for putting narrow interests aside and recognizing the sacrifices that all groups would have to make for the national good.

It is not surprising that key questions about power and progress in American politics often involve interest groups. It is ironic that the government designed in the Constitution was *intended* to limit the ability of any particular group to take over the government. The result was a constitutional design that created many arenas of power, in which many groups could compete.

WHEN IT'S BUDGET CUTTING TIME, THEY ALWAYS START WITH THE EASIEST TARGETS.

Children can't stand up for themselves. Which makes them an easy mark for politicians when they're cutting back. Give children a voice. Yours. Kids can't vote, but you can. **THE CHILDREN'S DEFENSE FUND**

The Children's Defense Fund is a comparatively new interest organization which asserts that it speaks on behalf of a previously voiceless group. This advertisement suggests that children are "targets" for spending cutbacks because they have little power— hence the need for a lobby that will protect children against politicians "when they're cutting back." However, satisfying the thousands of groups demanding their share of a tight federal budget will be a significant political challenge throughout the 1990s.

The Dilemmas of Interest-Group Democracy

Perhaps the biggest news about interests in American politics was first published in that series of essays we now collectively call *The Federalist*. As explained in Chapter 2, these essays, widely published in newspapers, helped persuade various factions to accept the Constitution. The arguments in *The Federalist* returned time and again to the problem that may be called "the passions and the interests." To put it simply, as Madison did in *Federalist* No. 10, society is always divided by factions who are passionately stirred up by the things that matter most to them. If left unchecked, factions would try to impose their will on others, and, in the worst case, capture the institutions of government to do their bidding.

Factions form around all manner of concerns, from international relations to religion. But the issue that Madison regarded as the "most common and durable" source of faction was the "unequal distribution of property" in society. Most of the designers of the United States' government regarded some inequality as inevitable. The question was how to create a government that would not be torn apart by class or other factional conflict. As the Civil War illustrates, this was no small challenge, and the nation continues to this day to wrestle with a number of clashing interests.

One solution, of course, would be to outlaw organized interests. However, Madison saw that this would also snuff out freedom and individual initiative, the very driving forces of democracy. The chosen solution was to create a government with so many separated powers among the institutions and so many divisions among federal units that it would be hard to mobilize the whole government around the interests of any one faction. In addition, public officials were protected from direct pressures by a system of electoral representation. At least that was the theory that Madison, Hamilton, and Jay brought to the attention of the reading public in the various essays of *The Federalist*. (See, in particular, Nos. 10 and 51.)

The system that they advocated was eventually put in practice with the ratification of the Constitution, and to a remarkable degree it did just what it was advertised to do. Not only was direct involvement of the people in most government decisions limited, but with a little help from the Supreme Court (recall the discussions from Chapters 4 and 5), the interests of those with property were largely protected from the complaints of those without it. *Perhaps most importantly, a variety of organized interests have had considerable success ever since in linking up the separated power centers required to get the government to act.*

The political initiative in this system went to those interests capable of organizing themselves and then influencing the required units of government. This explains why interests are centrally involved with so many functions of government listed earlier. In many respects, this system of interest-group politics is unique to the United States. All political systems, of course, experience the pressures of interest groups and develop ways of dealing with those pressures. "How We Compare" Box 8.1 discusses a more common form of interest-group politics called *corporatism* that is found in many other democracies.

This discussion suggests two major issues for American democracy in interest-group politics: 1) the possible inequalities of group power, and 2) the potential inefficiencies and chaos of group-driven politics. The first issue of whether interest competition has been fair and open to all groups has been debated throughout our history. This is, of course, the classic question that has divided *pluralists* and *elitists* since the beginning of the nation. The second question, increasingly asked in modern times, is whether the proliferation of groups has created too much strain and gridlock in government.

As far as the first issue goes, if the battles are evenly waged and everyone's interests fairly represented, there is a strong case for saying that the political system is competitive and healthy. You should remember by now that one of the leading theories of American democracy is called *pluralism*, for the idea that many (plural) groups compete openly and fairly equally in the political arena. This image of pluralist democracy is too idealistic, say its critics: The trouble with interest-group politics is that victory often goes to the groups with the most money and the best political connections. One of the early

Corporatism: Another Kind of Interest System

8.1

The interest group system in the United States has several distinguishing features: competition among many groups, the frequent inability of groups even in the same interest area to cooperate with each other, and the lack of much government control over groups and their political agendas. A much different system exists in various European democracies. **Corporatism** refers to more coordinated relations between groups in similar interest areas and between those more tightly incorporated groups and the government. In corporatist societies like those of France, Austria, and Sweden, the interest system has the following important differences from more pluralistic societies like that of the United States:

1. Each broad interest area in society (labor, business, agriculture, professions, and so on) has a strong central organization that all smaller organizations join and through which they forge common political positions. In some corporatist countries, membership in the broad interest organization is a legal requirement.

2. Government decisions that affect one or another of these political sectors are made through consultations with the leaders of the sector who represent the interests of the members.

3. Interest organizations become a formal part of the governing process, acting as representative bodies, and often forming close alliances with parties. In the give and take of corporatist power, both the interests and the government may compromise in reaching agreements.

In contrast to the patterns of winning and losing that mark the fortunes of American groups, corporatist groups are more likely to compromise and modify their interest demands.

Some students of corporatism point out that the creation of powerful interest organizations sets up a competing center of power that can weaken the representation of political parties. Others say that corporate interest arrangements simply add another dimension of representation to democracy.

For additional discussion, see Gerhard Lembruch and Philippe Schmitter, eds., *Patterns of Corporate Policy-Making* (Beverly Hills: Sage Publications, 1982, pp. 16–20).

observers of the interest-group system argued that the trouble "in pluralist heaven is that the heavenly chorus sings with a strong upper class accent. Probably about 90 percent of the people cannot get into the pressure system."[5] The explosion of interest-group activity in recent years has surely brought more than 10 percent of the public into the pressure system, but the patterns of power and representation remain uneven, in the view of many elite theorists.

With the growth of interest-group membership and support, the second issue (interest-group gridlock) becomes all the more relevant. It may be true that the American government could not operate without interest groups bringing pressure to bear at key decision points, but the impact of so many groups exerting pressure in so many directions at once may make it difficult for broad and coordinated social policies to be debated, enacted, and then sustained. Given the design of the government, however, it is hard to imagine an alternative to the driving force provided by interest groups.

In thinking about these political issues, it helps to see them as logical developments of the more basic patterns of American culture, institutions, and power introduced in

Chapter 1. "Inside the System" Box 8.2 explains why interest groups have become such an integral part of the American political system and offers an evaluation of interest-group politics by two experts in the field. In forming your own views about interest-group politics, the next step is to understand what kinds of groups are out there and how they operate.

Who Are the Interests?

Most interest groups emerge from existing occupational, business, or professional communities. Political scientist Jack Walker estimated that as many as 80 percent of interest groups evolve from the concerns among people in everyday social and economic activities: manufacturers producing similar products; workers in particular industries; professionals in medicine, social work, education, and other fields. Most of these groups tend to pursue **"inside" political strategies,** relying on money or professional expertise to meet directly with legislators and bureaucrats whose decisions affect their interests. The other 20 percent of groups, according to Walker's estimates, are more generally open to public membership and evolve from broader social-movement concerns such as women's rights and protecting the environment. These groups are more likely to use **"outside" political strategies** that involve the media and grass-roots opinion to pressure government officials.[6] Such groups as labor unions which combine existing occupational concerns with large memberships can employ a combination of inside and outside strategies to pressure government.

Most interest groups are known as **voluntary associations,** meaning that members join them voluntarily to promote some cause. In recent years, other types of interest organizations have appeared on the scene. Political scientist Robert Salisbury has identified three additional types of organizations at play in Washington and in the larger federal power game:[7]

Institutions are defined by Salisbury as "individual corporations, universities, state and local governments, and religious denominations [which are] active on their own behalf as well as often belonging to voluntary associations" of similar organizations.[8]

Think tanks are organizations dedicated to researching and promoting social and economic policy agendas. These policy factories, which employ academics and out-of-office politicians, include the American Enterprise Institute, the Heritage Foundation, the Brookings Institution, and the Institute for Policy Analysis, among many others.

Agencies for hire work for various clients and causes, providing legal services, contacts, and public relations services. A number of Washington law firms and public relations companies (for example, Hill & Knowlton) have become powerful centers of influence in their own right, even though they do not represent any particular organization or cause.

How Many Are There?

It is hard to come up with a precise count of interest groups because many social, business, and community organizations apply pressure to government from time to time without really considering themselves interest organizations. In addition, the rise of

What Shapes the American Interest-Group System and How Well Does It Work?

8.2

A combination of cultural, institutional, and social power factors creates an active and competitive interest-group system that plays an important part in the governmental process in the United States:

- CULTURAL FACTORS: Concerns about *limiting the central power of government* and *preventing the dominance of single groups or factions* have promoted broad competition among groups.
- INSTITUTIONAL FACTORS: *Separating the powers of the national institutions* and *dividing federal powers* make it necessary for groups to apply pressure to different branches and levels of government if they want action on their concerns. Groups become key links in an otherwise fragmented system of government power.
- SOCIAL BASES OF POWER: Different groups have been successful in using different kinds of power. Many groups depend on the activism of large numbers of dedicated citizens, creating a broad base of *pluralism* in many interest areas such as environmental protection, consumer protection, and professional associations. Other groups rely on greater wealth and better connections inside the corridors of power, forming networks of *elite* influence in areas like banking, heavy industry, and real estate development. Some groups combine pluralist organization (many organizations in the same area) with the ability to mobilize larger publics in actions like voting and social

movements. Although interest groups may not reflect majority opinion, they can mobilize enough public pressure to make a difference. For example, politicians know that their actions in areas of interest-group concern can be turned into campaign issues in close elections, giving interest groups the capacity to tip the majority balance. This form of *majoritarian power* particularly at state and local level, has been important in the successes of groups interested in civil rights, women's issues, labor, and environmental protection.

Without these cultural, institutional, and power factors, the American interest-group system would be much different, perhaps more centralized and less chaotic, but also probably involving fewer people personally.

The fact that the U.S. political system encourages so much interest-group activity has generated considerable controversy among political scientists about whether this is an effective way to conduct politics. One view is that government would not work at all without interest groups. This may be true, say the critics, but it does not work very well with them, either. The core of the debate about interests is summarized by political scientists Burdett A. Loomis and Allan J. Cigler:

The ultimate consequences of the growing number of groups . . . remains unclear. From one perspective, such changes have made politics more representative than ever before. . .

From another perspective, more interest groups and more

openness do not necessarily mean better policies or ones that genuinely represent the national interest. . . . [M]ore participants may generate greater complexity and too many demands for decision makers to process effectively. . . . [E]lected leaders may find it practically impossible to build the kinds of political coalitions necessary to govern effectively, especially in an era of divided government.

This second perspective suggests that the American constitutional system is extraordinarily susceptible to the excesses of minority factions. . . .Decentralized government. . . provides no adequate controls over the excessive demands of special interest politics. . . .

In sum, the problem of contemporary interest group politics is one of representation. For particular interests, especially those that are well defined and adequately funded, the government is responsive to the issues of their greatest concern. But representation is not just a matter of responding to specific interests or citizens; the government also must respond to the collective needs of a society. . . . The very vibrancy and success of contemporary groups help contribute to a society that finds it increasingly difficult to formulate solutions to complex policy questions.*

*Burdett A. Loomis and Allan J. Cigler, "The Changing Nature of Interest Group Politics," in Allan J. Cigler and Burdett A. Loomis, eds., *American Politics: Classic and Contemporary Readings*. Boston: Houghton Mifflin, 1992, pp. 333–334.

agencies and think tanks promoting many different causes blurs the traditional social-group basis of interest activities. Even if we draw the line at more formal political activities such as lobbying Congress, the numbers are hard to estimate. Technically speaking, federal law requires any group contacting government employees with the aim of influencing policy to register with the branch of government involved and report expenses. Although upwards of 6,000 lobbyists have registered with the U.S. House of Representatives and the U.S. Senate in recent years, there are surely many more than this engaged in some sort of lobbying activity.[9] If we count just the number of "associations" with Washington headquarters, the figure is around 3,200, with a total payroll of over 80,000 workers, which according to one source makes them the third largest industry in the nation's capital, behind government and tourism.

What is an **association?** A network of related businesses, professions, or other interest organizations that occasionally join ranks to magnify their impact. Who are these mysterious associations? The National Association of Margarine Manufacturers, the American Hot Dip Galvanizers Association, the National Association of Governors' Highway Safety Representatives, and the American Association of Sex Educators, Counselors, and Therapists, among 3,197 others.[10]

This tally of Washington-based associations does not begin to include the even larger numbers of private businesses, professional groups, grass-roots activists, and cultural organizations that do not rent Washington addresses, but keep some sort of hand in government policies. In addition, as noted above, state, local, and regional governments

BY LUCKOVICH FOR THE ATLANTA CONSTITUTION

have expanded their spheres of political operation to make their needs known to the national government. Even if the federal law had stricter registration and enforcement procedures, the number of groups is so large that it would be difficult to keep track of them all.

Another way of estimating the size of the pressure system is to start from the other end and see how many people make a living representing groups to the government. At the beginning of the 1990s, the publication *Washington Representatives* listed over 11,000 people involved in lobbying the government. The number of lobbyists had nearly doubled during the decade of the 1980s.[11] This figure of 11,000 is somewhere between estimates provided by a recent director of the American League of Lobbyists (5,500) and by another former director of the same organization (20,000).[12] According to the current executive director of the American League of Lobbyists (ALL), Patti Jo Baber, one reason it is difficult to get a precise estimate of the number of lobbyists is that some organizations count all their employees, including secretaries and office staff, as being involved in lobbying activities, while other organizations count only those employees making direct contact with members of government.

Even lobbyists have organizations to look out for their interests. ALL was founded in 1979 to improve communication among professional lobbyists. ALL publishes a newsletter for members and has developed guidelines for professional conduct among lobbyists. The organization's activities range from monthly luncheons with speakers from Congress to public information services explaining the role of lobbyists in the American governmental process. In addition, ALL develops positions on issues affecting the lobbying profession, and has sent representatives to testify before Congress on lobby reform legislation.

Reasons for the Growth of Groups

It is safe to say that the number of groups pressing their demands on government has more than doubled in the last several decades. Some estimates put the growth rate even higher. A number of changes have occurred in national politics over this span of time to stimulate the growth of interest organizations.

First, the major political parties may have weakened as ideological organizations capable of mobilizing majoritarian support for broad political platforms. The reasons for these changes will be discussed in the next chapter. For now, the important point is that groups have increasingly organized and gone to government directly to promote their own interests.

Second, a series of major government reforms made it easier for groups to be heard in Washington. During the 1970s, for example, Congress reformed itself, largely in response to pressures from junior legislators for a greater piece of the political action. One result was to create more committees and subcommittees, which spread control over legislation to more lawmakers, and created many more points of pressure in the system. These reforms will be discussed in Chapters 12 and 13.

Also during the 1970s, a series of scandals involving election practices and campaign financing led to important reforms in the way parties and candidates raise money. One of the ironic outcomes of election finance reform was to make it easier for businesses and other interest organizations to form *political action committees,* or *PACs,* to channel money directly to candidates and parties. A **PAC** is a legally chartered branch of an association, business, or other type of interest group that raises money from members to give to parties and politicians for their campaigns. (The origins and workings of PACs are covered in Chapter 10.) Making direct cash contributions may not overtly buy the support of lawmakers, but it surely helps to get their attention. When many PACs get together to spread money around Congress, the sums can be quite impressive, and legislative action often seems to follow the trail of the money. The rapid growth of PACs during the late 1970s and the 1980s is illustrated in Figure 8.1.

Finally, the explosion of sophisticated marketing and mass communication technologies has made it easier for people with shared interests to find one another and form groups even though they may never meet in person. America has become thoroughly mapped and marketed by direct-mail companies that specialize in assembling lists of people whose lifestyles and known group memberships make them likely joiners and contributors to various causes. As sophisticated marketing techniques make it easier to find and motivate these potential group members, the numbers and sizes of interest groups naturally increase. The biggest challenge for an interest group, after recruiting enough members to be viable, is figuring out how to keep them.

How Groups Keep Their Members

For a corporation or an industry, hiring a lobbyist or forming a PAC is often simple business sense. Corporations can see a direct return on their investment in lobbying. When new tax laws, trade regulations, or environmental regulations threaten to change the way they do business, they had better be there with a strong argument—and an open checkbook to make that argument heard.

FIGURE 8.1

The Rise of Political Action Committees

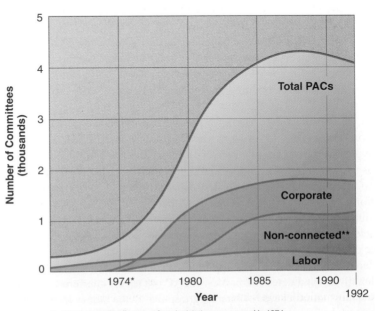

* Major campaign finance reform legislation was passed in 1974.
** *Non-connected* refers mainly to ideological and single-issue oriented
   organizations not directly connected to corporations or labor unions.

"Sex education classes in our public schools are promoting incest."

America has always been blessed with characters who claim to have all the answers.

The problem is, they don't always practice what they preach. And hypocrisy can be extremely harmful.

Take leading "pro-lifers," for example. They want the government to outlaw abortion for every woman, even in the case of rape or incest.

Yet prohibition has never stopped abortion. It has only made terminating a pregnancy dangerous for the poor. And more expensive for the better-off.

"Pro-lifer" leaders claim they're ready to stop abortion by any means necessary. Yet they violently oppose proven ways

to avert abortion, like effective family planning programs and sex education that addresses young people's real-life problems and concerns.

According to Jimmy Swaggart, "Sex education classes in our public schools are promoting incest." While according to Phyllis Schlafly, "Sex education is a principal cause of teenage pregnancy."

Of course, enforcing ignorance and preventing young people from making safe, responsible decisions will only result in more unintended pregnancies and more abortions.

In fact, the "pro-lifers" couldn't do more to increase the number of abortions if they tried – while they push for measures

that actually threaten women's lives.

Make time to save your right to choose. Before the "pro-lifers" start making your choices for you.

Take action! To join Planned Parenthood's Campaign to Keep Abortion Safe and Legal, please mail this coupon to: PPFA, 810 Seventh Ave., New York, NY 10019-5818.

NAME

ADDRESS

CITY   STATE   ZIP

Don't wait until women are dying again. Planned Parenthood® Federation of America

Grass-roots interest groups, lacking the steady financial backing common to business associations, sometimes seek to stimulate membership interest through highly emotional appeals. This Planned Parenthood Federation of America advertisement suggests that, without the reader's help, "violent" pro-life "characters" are ready to pass laws that "threaten women's lives."

It is more challenging to hold together large, public-based groups interested in, for example, the environment, civil rights, or stricter laws against drunken driving. The members of such groups may have other causes that call upon their time and money. Their participation is also limited by the demands of their lives. Some members will drop out because they feel their direct participation is unnecessary. They assume they will reap the benefits without having to pay dues, write letters, or otherwise share the costs of membership.

This last circumstance has been called the **free rider problem** by political economist Mancur Olson.[13] This is particularly troublesome in cases where the benefits provided by a group are *collective*—such things as clean air, higher social security payments for everyone over 65, or higher government subsidies for all farmers who grow rice. When all members of a group share a government benefit, there is a temptation for potential group members to sit back and enjoy the free ride provided by those who actually join the group and do the work. This free rider problem is so common that it has been termed part of the **logic of collective action.** It is a serious dilemma for groups that cannot divide or restrict what they get from government just for their active members.

With the advent of direct-mail marketing techniques, many groups have been able to keep their memberships together by finding out about members' lifestyles and personal needs, and offering **special benefits to members** that are more divisible and tangible than the general mission of the group itself. One of the great interest-group success stories is that of the American Association of Retired Persons (AARP), a group dedicated to protecting and promoting the government programs available to senior citizens. The AARP has become the nation's largest interest group, now numbering over 30 million, by offering its members a low annual fee along with a large package of special membership benefits, including a magazine, discount travel rates, and a low-priced mail order pharmacy service. Various members' benefits, as listed by the managers of different kinds of interest groups, are shown in Table 8.2.

Other groups have found more questionable ways of building their memberships. Take the case of another senior citizens' organization, the National Committee to Preserve Social Security and Medicare. Using letters that closely resemble official government documents, this group raised more than $90 million by warning people about sinister plots to do away with their Social Security and Medicare benefits. One mailing even implied that the Social Security fund would run out of money unless people made contributions to the Committee.[14] Although the National Committee has come under sharp criticism (and even a congressional investigation) for its tactics, it is by no means alone in using scare tactics and emotional appeals to keep its members paying their dues. Anti-abortionists have circulated pictures of aborted fetuses; environmentalists, photos of bloody little seal pups slaughtered for their fur; a civil rights organization, pictures of a young black man hanging from a tree after a Ku Klux Klan lynching. With so many causes to support, and the ever-present tendency of people to "let someone else do it," groups often rely on a combination of *special benefits* and **psychological appeals** to attract and keep members.

How Interest Groups Operate Politically

The pressure applied by interest groups in pursuit of their goals can take many forms. Whether groups rely more on lobbying, lawsuits, campaign contributions, or letter-writing campaigns depends on the kinds of resources the group has to work with and the kinds of response it seeks from government. Below are the main strategies commonly employed in interest-group politics.

Lobbying

The stereotype of the Washington lobbyist is a back-slapping, cigar-smoking, joke-telling "good old boy" with plenty of cash on hand and enough connections to do special favors for his friends in Congress and the bureaucracy. Indeed, much **lobbying** does involve entertaining public officials, offering transportation on company jets, invitations to

Lobbyists socialize outside a meeting of the U.S. House Ways and Means Commitee. Not only have they burgeoned in sheer numbers, but lobbyists have also become silent partners in the legislative process by supplying research data, technical information, and even drafts of proposed laws and regulations.

TABLE 8.2

Percentage of Groups Providing Various Member Benefits (by Group Type)*

BENEFIT	PROFIT	NONPROFIT	CITIZEN
PROFESSIONAL BENEFITS			
Conferences	99%	97%	92%
Professional contacts	98	97	79
Training	91	92	86
PURPOSIVE BENEFITS			
Advocacy	96	96	97
Representation before government	93	88	92
Participation in public affairs	86	82	91
SOLIDARY BENEFIT			
Friendship	97	94	92
PERSONAL MATERIAL BENEFITS			
Trips, tours	41	40	36
Insurance	36	37	22
Discount on consumer goods	15	18	18
OTHER BENEFITS AND SERVICES			
Publications	98	98	99
Coordination among organizations	93	89	88
Research	76	77	81
Legal help	51	33	28
Maintain professional codes	40	41	13
Collective bargaining	14	11	9

* *Profit:* primarily corporate and trade associations; *Nonprofit:* nonbusiness organizations that restrict membership by professional or insitutional affiliation; *Citizen:* nonbusiness organizations open to all citizens.

SOURCE: Jack L. Walker, Jr., *Mobilizing Interest Groups in America.* Ann Arbor: University of Michigan Press, 1991, p. 86. Based on that author's survey of 892 interest organizations.

golf weekends in sunny climes, and special help with business deals, personal finances, and housing. One successful lobbyist said, "Golf is a great game for lobbyists. I can't think of a better way to spend a morning with somebody than riding around a golf course, letting 'em win. But I think you should always do a little bit of business. Let 'em know you're not just fluff, that you have some concerns, knock a few ideas around. And you ought to do that on the front nine."[15]

The number of scandals involving lobbyists has led the state and national governments to impose stricter standards of conduct on both lobbyists and public officials. And the press has been increasingly watchful of shady goings-on, as when one-time White House chief of staff John Sununu flew on private corporate jets to attend to both personal and political business. After Bill Clinton nominated Democratic Party chairman Ron Brown to become U.S. Secretary of Commerce, questions were raised about Brown's days as an influential Washington lobbyist. Brown was confirmed to the post, but a party in his honor was abruptly cancelled after news coverage revealed that the planned celebration was sponsored and paid for by a number of Brown's former lobbying clients. Despite the tougher ethics standards and press monitoring, the relations between lobbyists and public officials remain grey areas. Much of the lobbyist's job is to win access to decision makers so the client's position can be heard. In the battle to win access, connections and favors remain powerful tactics.

Who is to say that a congressional staffer should not have dinner with a representative from the Sierra Club, or that a senator should be prevented from playing golf with an old friend (who happens to be a high-powered Washington lawyer representing a major corporation with business coming up before the senator's committee)? The lines separating ethical from unethical influence in Washington are hard to draw, especially when the people drawing them are public officials themselves. There are laws requiring *public disclosure* of lobbying activities, but they have not been aggressively enforced, as noted in "Inside the System" Box 8.3. In the end, there is no doubt that lobbying is an insider's game. The most successful and highly paid lobbyists are often former members of Congress, congressional staffers, bureaucrats, and White House advisers. As the saying in Washington goes, "They came to govern and stayed to lobby."

Press coverage of lobbying tends to stress the more dramatic aspects of "influence peddling." It is now a familiar news image to see lines of lobbyists in the corridors of Congress trying to grab a key representative or staff member to press for last-minute changes in legislation. However, there is another side of lobbying that people hear less about. **Lobbyists** are important sources of technical information on legislative and regulatory issues. One thing that interest groups generally do is research the issues they care about, often gathering the best collections of data on their own subjects. Once trust and personal rapport have been built, the delivery of fast answers and technical assistance is welcomed by busy congressional staffers and bureaucrats. At this point, lobbyists become, in effect, silent members of congressional committees and executive agencies. It is not unusual to find lobbyists assisting congressional staff in drafting legislation and then going across town to help write up executive branch procedures, rules, and regulations.

Not only do private groups lobby the government, but branches of the government often lobby one another. The classic case is the Pentagon, which depends on congressional approval to keep its budgets funded each year. Defense Department "information officers" work the halls of Congress, compile reports, and deliver briefings to convince legislators of the need for maintaining existing defense programs or building new ones. Key members of Congress on the defense appropriations and armed services committees, along with their staffs, are routinely flown at Pentagon expense on junkets around the world to tour bases, watch military maneuvers, and witness tests of new equipment. As with private lobbying, the idea is to build personal bonds and to cultivate loyalties to military programs, while delivering small favors in the form of working vacations, rides on aircraft carriers, and flight jackets for the children.

Even presidents use lobbyists to win support for legislative programs or to get high-level nominees approved in the Senate. After watching Ronald Reagan lose a bitter battle trying to get Robert H. Bork confirmed to the Supreme Court in 1987, President Bush called on lobbyists to manage his nominees. For example, the Supreme Court nomination of Federal Court Judge Clarence Thomas in 1991 was farmed out to Kenneth M. Duberstein, a former high-ranking White House official. Working together with chief White House congressional liaison Frederick McClure, Duberstein began by working the offices of the Senate Judiciary Committee, which holds the hearings on Supreme Court nominees. The lobbying strategy included briefing members of the committee, preparing answers to challenging questions, orchestrating media appearances for Judge Thomas's supporters, and organizing the White House staff to write a "blizzard" of op-ed page articles supporting the nomination in the nation's newspapers. In addition, Judge Thomas

Regulating the Lobbyists

8.3

By its very nature, the influence business walks a fine line between providing useful information and undermining good judgment with favors and financial contributions. There has been a "disclosure law" on the federal books since 1946 requiring lobbyists on Capitol Hill to register with the House and the Senate, and to disclose the money they receive from clients and the money they spend on winning the support of lawmakers. The official disclosure form asks for information on gifts, food, travel, and operating expenses. A separate law and reporting procedure exists for the campaign contributions of PACs, which are supposed to be independent of lobbying operations.

Critics charge that the disclosure law imposes little discipline on lobbyists or their activities. One investigation showed that in the past fifteen years only five complaints of lobbying abuses had been registered with the Justice Department (responsible for enforcing the law) and that none of those cases was prosecuted. In addition, lobbying may represent only the tip of the pressure system, particularly in the elite circles where major corporations operate. Most large companies may hire lobbyists who are registered and disclose expenditures. However, the same companies may spend even more money on political initiatives of their own that are not reported. Most corporations follow the legal rule of thumb that individual lobbyists, not their corporate sponsors, are governed by the law, meaning that none of the ten largest American corporations (including Mobil Oil, General Motors, AT&T, or Exxon) is registered or held up to much public accountability for their behind-the-scenes pressure activities.

Many registered organizations probably do not disclose their activities fully. For example, the National Rifle Association reported expenditures of $1.1 million in a recent year, but its annual operating budget was in the neighborhood of $60 million, with $11 million of that being spent on its Institute for Legislative Action. Tightening the disclosure requirements and reforming ethics standards are on the agendas of public-interest groups like Common Cause (discussed later in this chapter).

In 1993, Congress addressed lobbying reform once again, trying to find ways of tightening up on the registration of lobbyists and the reporting of activities in both Congress and the executive branch. Among the most conspicuous people testifying at the legislative hearing were lobbyists themselves.

SOURCE: Richard Cowan, "None Dare Call It Lobbying," *Common Cause Magazine,* March/April, 1989, pp. 13–16.

---

was coached in media relations and told to reveal as little as possible about his judicial philosophy, particularly on sensitive matters such as abortion.[16]

Despite the best-laid plans, the Thomas nomination (like that of Bork) ran into opposition from liberal interest groups who feared that Thomas's judicial conservatism would spill over into such political issues as civil rights and abortion, tilting an already conservative Supreme Court farther away from their views for a long time to come. The political balance became even more precarious when two reporters were leaked confidential FBI reports that Thomas had allegedly sexually harassed a former assistant, Anita Hill. (Recall the discussion of this in Chapter 5.) Women's groups and Democratic women members of the House stepped up their own lobbying efforts, accusing the all-male committee of not taking the charges seriously, reflecting the "men's club" atmosphere in the Senate. The interests on both sides of the Thomas nomination launched an ugly battle that filled the nation's TV screens and newspapers. Although the Thomas forces eventually prevailed in a close Senate vote of 52–48, the news and talk shows continued to discuss the possibility that the procedure for appointing justices to the nation's most august court had been captured by "special interests." Perhaps this is simply how American politics is designed to work. As the Senate Majority Leader, George Mitchell, noted in a speech just before the Senate vote, Supreme Court nominations in past eras had been challenged politically by interest groups.

Most lobbying is about more mundane issues than who sits on the Supreme Court. It is important to understand what the routine lobbying situation looks like. Consider, for example, a very ordinary case of lobbying.

A DAY IN THE LIFE OF A JUNK FOOD LOBBYIST.   Meet Steve Eure. As lobbyist for the Snack Food Association, he was described by journalist Peter Carlson as "the man paid to keep America safe for snack foods."[17] Head of the Snack Food Association, he coordinated and managed the interests of some "140 manufacturers of potato chips, nacho chips, tortilla chips, popcorn, pretzels, and pork rinds, among other delicacies."[18] Among his many duties:

- publishing the Snack Food Association newsletter
- writing a column in the association magazine, *Snack World*
- running the association's political action committee, the Snack PAC (what else?)
- playing Santa Claus on Capitol Hill, giving away bags of chips
- lobbying, of course.

Where did Steve Eure lobby? Wherever duty called: "In congressional offices, in committee hearing rooms, in Capitol Hill restaurants, on the fairway at the Congressional Country Club, wherever he's called to defend the fragile chip from the iron heel of Big Government."[19]

One morning he received a call at home from a friendly congressional staffer. (Steve began his Washington career as a staffer.) The friendly caller tipped Steve that a bill he had been fighting was scheduled to be "marked up" in the House subcommittee. The "mark-up" is where a committee makes its final changes on a bill before the legislation is sent to the House floor for approval. The bill, HR 2148, would require foods containing palm oil, coconut oil, or palm kernel oil to carry the label "Saturated Fat." For many member companies of the Snack Food Association, the label would be a kiss of death to label-savvy buyers, forcing manufacturers to lose customers or find other oils for their foods. The industry was unwilling to change ingredients, both out of fear of altering the tastes of products like Fritos, Cheetos, and Doritos, and out of concern about the costs and availability of alternative oils. Most of the preferred oils in junk foods are bought cheaply from third-world countries—which, it turns out, is where the plot thickens in our little story. So grab a bag of chips, and read on.

The master lobbyist's first move was to rally the allies at other associations and call snack-food companies with their own lobbyists to help out. He alerted the National Food Processors' Association, the National Confectioners' Association, the American Frozen-Food Institute, and lobbyists working for Frito-Lay, Kraft, Kellogg, Procter & Gamble, and General Mills. He even alerted agents at the PR firms representing countries, such as the Philippines and Indonesia, that produce the embattled oils.

Then he was off to visit key members of the subcommittee that would decide the fate of the bill. He tried first to persuade an aide to the representative co-sponsoring the bill not to buy the arguments of health lobbyists that the legislation, if enacted, would be an important step toward eliminating unhealthy fat in the national diet. Claiming that only 5 percent of the bad fats consumed by Americans came from snack foods, Steve Eure argued that the legislation would do little for the public's health. Eure claimed that this was really a sneaky trade bill in disguise, a move for protection by those crafty soybean farmers of America who hoped to sell more soybean oil. His arguments had little effect;

Steve Eure, formerly a Washington-based lobbyist for the Snack Food Association. For Eure, junk food was manna from heaven.

it seemed that minds were made up. It did not help that one key committee member was suffering from heart disease and not feeling particularly charitable toward junk foods.

Just when things looked darkest, another friendly staffer offered the tip that a liberal member of the committee who would ordinarily vote against snack-food interests was wavering. That representative was not interested in health or domestic trade, but his interests in foreign policy led him to worry about the negative effects the legislation might have on the economies of struggling countries such as Indonesia that produce snack oils. At the last minute, the sponsors of the bill tabled HR 2148 until they could respond to those foreign policy questions.

With sweet victory seized miraculously, even if temporarily, from the jaws of defeat, Steve Eure went off to celebrate with his colleagues from the other associations. Reflecting on the victory, and looking ahead to the next battle in the endless snack-food war, he said, "Never in a million years would I have guessed that a liberal representative. . . would be opposed to this bill because of his concern with the Philippines. Never in a million years. That's why you never give up. You keep fighting every step of the way."[20]

However such battles come out, and no matter which side wins, interest-group politics are often described in terms of delicate balances, fragile alliances, timing, tenacity, and luck. As it is guided by interest groups across the crowded floors of Congress, the legislative process has been called "the dance of legislation." In this dance, one thing that helps in lining up regular partners is money.

Campaign Contributions

As noted earlier, the election reforms of the 1970s opened the way for businesses and other interest organizations to form PACs (a tool that labor had used for years) to contribute to political campaigns. Suddenly, the stakes in the lobbying game went up. In 1990, for example, PACs contributed upwards of $150 million to congressional campaigns, most of that money going to incumbents. The figures in 1992 were even higher. The next two chapters explore the workings of PACs in parties and elections more fully, but for now, suffice it to say that all of those campaign contributions add up.

Who are some of the high rollers in the PAC game? A number of PACs pour more than $1 million into every national election. Here are a few members of the million-and-up club: the American Medical Association, the National Association of Realtors, the International Association of Machinists and Aerospace Workers, the Association of Trial Lawyers of America, the International Brotherhood of Teamsters, and the American Federation of State, County, and Municipal Employees.[21]

Although PACs are limited to $5,000 per candidate during an election cycle, they often contribute much larger sums to party organizations and voter mobilization efforts that benefit a candidate's election chances. Even the smaller direct-to-candidate contributions add up, however. The costs of getting elected have soared in recent times, requiring the average senator, for example, to raise thousands of dollars *each day* of his or her six-year term to be ready to run again. To make this continuous fund-raising bearable, it is important to be able to count on a long list of regular contributors. PACs magnify their influence by joining together with other PACs in the same category to target large sums of money to the key players in a particular legislative area—all the members of defense-related congressional committees, or banking committees, or agriculture committees, for example.

While no one would (or legally, could) admit that this campaign money actually buys votes on legislation, most observers admit that **campaign contributions** are effective ways of buying goodwill and gaining a hearing from busy legislators who would rather spend their time talking about legislation than raising money.[22] As one congressman put it, "My door is always open, but for you folks (who gave money), it will be open just a little wider."[23] PACs and lobbyists thus provide corporations and other interest groups with a one-two punch. PACS open doors for the lobbyists, and the lobbyists sharpen their requests with reminders of past and future funding. As suggested above, however, the real secret to their success is that groups of PACs with related interests can band together and make multiple contributions to groups of key members of Congress. The "multiplier effect" of PACs representing an entire industry can put a lot of money in election bank accounts year in and year out. And, as the history of the defense industry suggests, it can produce dramatic results.

HEAVY WEAPONS: THE DEFENSE PACS. According to research by Common Cause (a public-interest group to be discussed later in this chapter), when corporations band together and concentrate their PAC contributions to members of Congress on key military defense committees, they often reap big rewards in government weapons contracts. For example, when California governor Pete Wilson was in the Senate, he received nearly $400,000 in PAC contributions prior to the election of 1988 from California defense contractors including McDonnell Douglas, Lockheed, General Motors, Rockwell, and General Dynamics. These defense giants also donated to other California politicians serving on the armed services and defense appropriations committees. The contributions were large, but the return on the money was even larger. While the political contributions to the California delegation amounted to about a million dollars, Congress authorized more than $10 billion in defense contracts for those companies.[24]

An even more ambitious investigation by UPI reporter Greg Gordon found that for the year 1987, 82 percent of military contracts (amounting to $230 billion) went to one-third of the states—those with senators serving on the Senate Armed Services Committee and the Senate Defense Appropriations Subcommittee. The wealth was spread out a bit more in the House, although states with members on the key defense committees were still twice as likely to receive defense contracts as states without defense committee membership. The members of those committees also received the lion's share of defense PAC money.[25] Given the tendencies of Congress to favor home districts through "pork barrel" politics, defense contracts would probably go to home states of committee members with or without the financial incentive of PAC contributions. However, the PAC pressures may reinforce another dimension of interest-group power known as the iron triangle.

IRON TRIANGLES.   **Iron triangles** (a term coined by President Dwight Eisenhower) refer to strong influence ties between interest groups, key congressional committees, and executive offices or agencies that implement programs (for example, buying weapons) important to the interest groups. Iron triangles, viewed positively, are ways for interest groups to bring separated governing institutions together and keep those institutions moving in a particular direction. However, the lobbying pressures on Congress and the executive can create unnecessary programs or continue them after their usefulness has ended. The authors of the Common Cause study cited above concluded that PACs not only strengthened the lobbying positions of various defense interests, but hardened, as well, the iron triangles that unite interest groups, Congress, and the bureaucracy as inseparable elements of the governing process:

> Money has become the glue that cements what's become known as a classic example of the "Iron Triangle," uniting Congress, the Pentagon and the defense industry. This relationship makes it possible for defense contractors to get the business they want, the Pentagon to get the weapons it wants, and members of Congress to get the jobs and federal money they want back home.[26]

Once created, iron triangles are difficult to break down. Even when one side of the iron triangle gives way, the other two may hold firm, creating considerable pressure from the two remaining sides to restore the old political structure by shoring up the weak side. For example, when the Pentagon or Congress decides to eliminate a major weapons program or close a base, there is an onslaught of lobbying from the industries, workers, and communities affected. Unless both Congress and the Defense Department stand firm with the decision, the lobbying may lead one government side of the triangle to bring pressure on the other, often with the result of overturning, or at least softening, the decision. A classic case is the Osprey, an expensive Marine Corps transport plane with vertical landing and takeoff capability. Pressed to shrink the defense budget to match a new era of reduced world tensions, the Pentagon decided to terminate the program. However, the aircraft manufacturers put together a powerful lobbying coalition of industries, workers, and politicians from communities where the planes were being built. Leaders of the interest coalition met regularly with members of Congress from the affected districts to plot strategy to restore the program. On the following page, "Inside the System" Box 8.4 reveals some of the details of the campaign to save the Osprey.

This sort of lobbying can be expected from weapons manufacturers and powerful members of Congress all the way down the line as pressures mount to trim military spending in the post-Cold War era. There will, of course, be program cuts, but many iron triangles will hold, particularly if military boosters can convince the public that a dangerous new enemy has replaced the Communists. Drug lords? Terrorists? Heavily armed

Saving the Osprey: An Endangered Species?

8.4

The Cold War is over, and military programs are on the chopping block. Does this mean the defense lobby is on the run? To the contrary, the defense PACs are hungrier and more aggressive than ever. The one hundred registered lobbyists for the big ten defense contractors are, in the words of one lobbyist, "trying to influence more members of Congress than ever before." A popular tactic is to redefine the uses of military equipment from combating Communist enemies to countering terrorism or drug traffickers. The strengths of iron triangles are being tested all around Washington.

Case in point: a campaign in 1990 to save the Osprey, an expensive vertical-takeoff transport plane ordered by the Marine Corps, but cancelled at higher levels of the Pentagon as unnecessary and too expensive. The other sides of this iron triangle proved too strong for the military bureaucracy. The interest-group side was represented by the aerospace companies (led by Boeing) and unions (led by United Auto Workers) that produced the plane. They mobilized a national network of workers and supplier companies with a toll-free hotline to Congress, and a national "Tilt Rotor Appreciation Day" capped off by a flight demonstration in Washington. Members of Congress whose districts would lose jobs and money were brought on board. Several members began weekly strategy sessions with lobbyists, and one representative hosted a cocktail party that drew 200 lobbyists and industry officials, checkbooks at the ready. Defense PACs vowed to step up contributions to members of key congressional committees who had already received $2 million the year before. And the bureaucratic side of the triangle, working inside the Pentagon, was the Marine Corps, which wanted its program back.

Efforts like this do not save every endangered weapons species, but they do protect some, raising the question of how much the defense budget might have been cut without all those iron triangles to protect it. Despite another attempt to cut the Osprey in 1992 (boosted by an embarrassing crash of a test model), a wave of election-year spending saved it once again.

SOURCE: Richard L. Berke, "Lobbying Steps Up on Military Buying as Budget Shrinks," *The New York Times,* April 9, 1990, p. 13–16.

---

third-world nations with nuclear capabilities? Here is how one observer has described the scramble to keep the new world order from dismantling the neatly ordered iron triangles:

> Lobbyists for military contractors have gone into overdrive, refining their pitches and plying their pressure tactics on research groups and Administration officials and the general public through commercials and advertisements.
>
> They concede the possibility that Congress will scuttle a major hardware program. Yet the lobbyists make a new pitch to Congressional offices. They argue that their aircraft systems or helicopter programs are still indispensable, perhaps for more popular programs like detecting drug traffickers.[27]

As one lobbyist for a military contractor put it, the threat of world peace sent the defense industry into a lobbying frenzy: "We are all trying to influence more members of Congress than ever before. Each of us knows that some program somewhere will be cut. We all work to make sure that our most important program is not cut." We will return to look at iron triangles as they operate in Congress (Chapters 12 and 13) and the bureaucracy (Chapter 15).

Litigation

Sometimes groups lack the resources to lobby effectively or spend large sums of money on political campaigns. Sometimes they simply see their lobbying efforts losing politically to competing groups. In these circumstances, it may be to the advantage of a group to go to court to seek a more favorable ruling.

Although the crowded court system gives the appearance that anyone can sue anybody for practically any reason, that is not quite the case. Individuals and representatives of corporations must show that they have *standing to sue,* which means showing that they are directly affected by a law and its possible violation. However, even without standing to sue, groups can use a number of indirect legal strategies to help advance their interests. One route is to provide financial assistance or free legal services to those who do have a legal case. This tactic has been pioneered by the American Civil Liberties Union (ACLU), a group discussed in Chapter 5. The ACLU defines its mission as preserving Bill of Rights freedoms for Americans who lack the resources to have their day in court without ACLU assistance. The ACLU has a paid membership estimated at more than 250,000 people and a $25 million annual budget to run offices in all fifty states with a paid staff of 300, and thousands more who volunteer their legal and administrative services. The ACLU provides services in more than 6,000 legal cases a year.[28]

Probably the heaviest users of **litigation** are businesses that retain lawyers to fight through rules and regulations that affect their operations. Although business leaders often complain about being strangled by regulations, they are the first to lobby for rules that will give them an edge or lead to an increase in their profit margin. The trouble is that other businesses and groups are also pushing for rules and regulations that serve their interests. Thus, the world of regulatory politics is a tangled and constantly changing one, often requiring legal action to chart the course.

Whether in business or social areas, a legal strategy is a two-edged sword, sometimes advancing the cause of one side, and sometimes aiding the other. Probably no case better illustrates the ups and downs of litigation as an interest-group strategy than the prolonged and bitter fight over abortion.

THE ENDLESS ABORTION BATTLE.   Of all the areas of social life affected by the legal strategies of interest groups, abortion is one of the most dramatic and endlessly contested. Opponents and supporters of abortion have made use of the whole range of interest-group strategies, from lobbying to campaign contributions, and mobilizing large numbers of people to participate in demonstrations, rallies, and marches in Washington and numerous state capitals. But the most dramatic and decisive episodes in the fight over abortion involve court cases. Does a woman have a right to terminate her own pregnancy? If so, are there limits to that right? Do states have jurisdiction over this issue, or is it a constitutional question involving the Bill of Rights? Can federal funds be withheld from health organizations that perform abortions or counsel women on how to obtain them? Can clinics, doctors, and hospitals receiving federal money be ordered not to offer abortion-related services? These are just some of the thorny legal questions that have engaged abortion groups in legal battles all the way to the Supreme Court.

The legal path that led to the first landmark ruling on abortion began with interest groups concerned primarily with family counselling and birth control. The issue was privacy. Namely, did the Constitution provide people with the right of privacy to discuss birth control with counselors (such as Estelle Griswold of the Connecticut chapter of Planned Parenthood), and did that right of privacy also give married couples the right to use birth control methods in the privacy of their own bedrooms? Recall from the discussion in Chapter 5 that the opinion of the Court in the case of *Griswold v. Connecticut*

The pro-life/pro-choice battle over abortion limits has proven to be one of the most intractable issues in American public life. Both sides have used the full range of lobbying techniques, including backing legislation and involvement in court cases. In the more than twenty years since Roe v. Wade, *a clear public consensus has yet to emerge on this fractious topic.*

was yes on both counts. Next came cases that extended these rights to unmarried people. The big legal leap on the abortion question came in a case supported by a variety of feminist, civil-liberties, and family-planning groups, *Roe v. Wade* in 1973, in which the Court ruled that the right of privacy also protected a woman's right to have an abortion. As explained in Chapter 5, the legal battles have gone back and forth ever since.

Some critics say that groups are mistaken if they think they can promote their interests through legal activism alone. Abortion is a good example. Legal scholar Gerald Rosenberg argues that many pro-choice activists thought they had won their battle definitively with the *Roe* decision in 1973.[29] However, they failed to understand that court decisions on civil rights and civil liberties are inherently weak and must be protected by creating a broad base of social support for them, if possible. Rosenberg claims that after the *Roe* decision, abortion activists should have stepped up other related interest-group activities. Instead, many of the pro-choice activists went on to different issues just at the time there was a backlash against the *Roe* decision. Abortion opponents pursued a whole range of interest-group strategies to pass new state legislation, and used churches and other social institutions to launch a broader anti-abortion movement that eventually tilted the *majoritarian* power balance in many elections during the 1980s. The moral of the abortion story (and of many other civil-rights issues), according to Rosenberg, is that legal strategies alone do not work unless combined with other interest-group strategies, the most important of which is mobilizing public opinion through grass-roots activism. As of the mid-1990s, the struggle over abortion does indeed appear to be shifting from the national level and the judiciary to the state level and the arena of public opinion.

Mobilizing Public Opinion

In this age of media and marketing, many groups pursue so-called "outside strategies" by publicizing their causes. Appealing to the broader public beyond the membership of the interest group itself can be done by running ad campaigns, staging media events to dramatize the cause, or interesting journalists in investigating the problems they care about. In addition to media campaigns, other **opinion-mobilizing techniques** are available. *As with all interest-group politics, the size, resources, and goals of the group affect the selection of the most practical and effective political strategies.*

Some interest groups have large memberships to begin with. As the case of the American Association of Retired People (detailed below) indicates, 30 million people can stir up quite a ruckus with letters, phone calls, and most frightening of all, votes on election day. But even groups with small memberships can mobilize public opinion. As the case of the Osprey (Box 8.4) illustrates, companies may call out their workers or enlist the help of unions when government actions threaten projects or jobs. And businesses or small organizations with enough money can "create" publics by running information (or propaganda) campaigns to stir up concern about their issues.

Groups employ a variety of marketing, advertising, and public relations techniques to take their concerns public. Hundreds of direct-mail marketing companies have popped up in recent years—companies that hire out primarily to political groups and deliver mailing lists of people likely to be sympathetic to particular kinds of causes. These companies get the word out on short notice and ask supporters for various responses: sending money, returning reply cards to members of Congress, making phone calls to

No network of back-slapping "good old boys," the new breed of Washington lobbyist forges group links to government officials by employing a panoply of marketing, publicity, and fund-raising strategies—from phone banks to direct mail, from media advertising to one-on-one "get out the vote" drives.

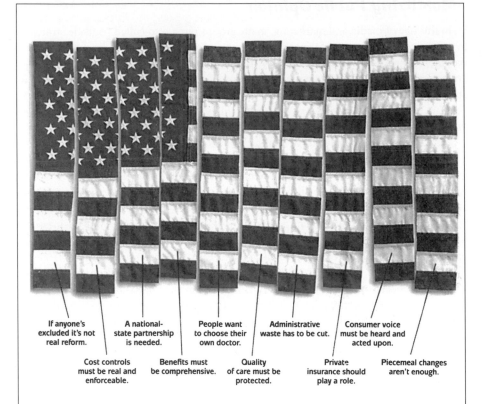

If anyone's excluded it's not real reform.

A national-state partnership is needed.

People want to choose their own doctor.

Administrative waste has to be cut.

Consumer voice must be heard and acted upon.

Cost controls must be real and enforceable.

Benefits must be comprehensive.

Quality of care must be protected.

Private insurance should play a role.

Piecemeal changes aren't enough.

Without each of these principles, health care reform in America just won't fly.

America's had enough piecemeal solutions. It's time for a program that makes health care reform a practical, legislatively-passable reality.

The Health Security Partnership does just that. Rooted in efforts begun by the Committee for National Health Insurance in 1968, this is the only plan created by respected health experts, after years of careful work.

Unlike other plans, the Health Security Partnership tackles the *entire* problem—organization, access, delivery, quality and cost. So not only is it comprehensive and accessible to all, its *achievable*—through pragmatic, enforceable cost constraints.

Today, the Health Security Partnership gives America a unique chance to do the right thing. To replace

our failing patchwork system with major reform, not major trade-offs.

Write Congress and let them know you support that reform with the Health Security Partnership. And for complete details, contact the Committee for National Health Insurance. It's the totality and reality America's been waiting for.

The Committee for National Health Insurance. Where reform meets reality.

1757 N Street, N.W., Washington, D.C. 20036 (202) 223-9685 **Douglas Fraser**, Chairman, Committee for National Health Insurance and former President, United Automobile Workers; **Melvin Glasser**, Director, Committee for National Health Insurance; **Rashi Fein**, PhD, Chairman, Technical Committee CNHI and Professor, Harvard Medical School.

Public information campaigns seek to influence both general opinion and legislation by communicating broad declarations of positions and beliefs (often under the banner of an anonymous but official-sounding "committee") and urging readers in agreement to write, telephone, or fax their elected officials.

politicians, calling friends, or all of these. The direct-marketing technologies available today can literally create publics where none existed (at least with enough organization to make a political impact).

Equally impressive are the Madison Avenue **public information campaigns** designed by advertising and public relations firms to influence opinion or improve the public image of a client's issue. If coordinated with direct mail or other marketing efforts, public information campaigns can channel public pressure directly to targeted politicians. Making a lot of noise in the media may help lobbyists on the inside convince decision makers that a sensitive issue really has some popular support out there. Not only do groups and corporations hire PR firms to market images for their causes, but foreign governments do it, too. One of the first things that the royal family of Kuwait did after being driven into exile by Saddam Hussein's invasion in 1990 was to hire the giant Washington PR firm of Hill & Knowlton to present their cause to Congress, the media, and the American public.

In general, small, exclusive interests must create public followings using advertising and marketing techniques, while mass membership organizations can mobilize their own members into action. When large coalitions of groups become involved in an issue, officials take notice as switchboards light up, mail trucks pull in, and heads roll on election day.

CALLING ALL SENIOR CITIZENS. As noted earlier, the largest interest group in the country is the American Association of Retired Persons (AARP), boasting a membership of over 30 million Americans. AARP places its membership on alert whenever the government takes up an issue of concern to senior citizens. The organization communicates with its members through a monthly magazine, *Modern Maturity,* as well as through special mailings, polls to gauge members' interests, and the formation of local chapters to recruit new members.

Although much of the work of AARP is standard lobbying, every once in a while an issue comes up that may be too big for the lobbyists to handle alone. Then it's time to call out the membership. That is what happened during the Reagan administration when the newly elected president began to carry out some of his campaign promises to cut government spending. Although there was considerable public support for cutting big government down to size (including support among senior citizens, who voted for Reagan in large numbers), many of them apparently never imagined that those cuts would include their own Social Security checks and medical benefits.

When President Reagan announced that he intended to trim benefits to the nation's seniors, he found himself in the midst of an uproar created largely by the ability of AARP and other interest groups to mobilize millions of their members. Eventually the president backed down, and extracted his cuts in other areas of the budget, most notably from welfare, education, and children's programs where there were few powerful interest groups to cause trouble. More than a decade later, another new president, Bill Clinton, searched for ways to balance the budget. He also suggested trimming Social Security. Switchboards lit up all over Capitol Hill, leading key members of Congress to quickly dismiss the idea as politically impossible. President Clinton also abandoned the idea.

Why do presidents back down in the face of pressure from the nation's elders? Those millions of letters, postcards, and phone calls that arrive on Capitol Hill and at the White House promise revenge at the next election—not just against the president, but against members of Congress who stand with him. A president might survive some loss of support from senior citizens in a general election, but many members of Congress come from districts where seniors are a powerful voting force. Considering the political revenge of 30 million voters, it is clear why Washington is careful when it comes to the idea of saving money at the expense of retired folks.

Mixed Strategies: The Auto Lobby and Fuel Economy Laws

As the above examples indicate, there are many ways for groups to promote their interests. Table 8.3 shows the percentage of groups using different political strategies. Organizations often resort to mixed strategies when they can. A classic case is the twenty-year battle between the auto industry and environmental groups over fuel-efficient automobiles. Detroit has had trouble competing with the Japanese in producing reliable, fuel-efficient autos. So, for better or worse, American car companies have tried to hold onto a segment of the market abandoned by producers in countries with higher gas taxes: the big, beefy, gas-guzzling, performance car. In addition, the profit margins on big cars are simply much larger. For example, Ford can make $10,000 on each $30,000 Lincoln it sells, compared to $1,000 on every $10,000 Escort.[30]

The political situation first began to change in 1973, when OPEC (the Organization of Petroleum-Exporting Countries) raised the price of crude oil, sending gasoline prices soaring at the pump and forcing American drivers to wait for hours at gas stations and to endure rationing programs. With a crisis around them, and spurred on by demands from consumers and environmentalists to do something, members of Congress eventually passed the Corporate Average Fuel Economy (CAFE) law in 1975. CAFE required auto makers to begin producing fleets of cars that had better gas mileage, aiming at a target of 27.5 miles per gallon by 1985. Companies could still produce gas guzzlers, but they had to produce enough fuel-efficient cars to make the average of all models meet the law.

Table 8.3

Percentage of Interest Organizations Using Various Political Strategies

1. Testifying at hearings	99 %
2. Contacting government officials directly to present point of view	98
3. Engaging in informal contacts with officials—at conventions, over lunch, and so on	95
4. Presenting research results or technical information	92
5. Sending letters to members of organization to inform them about activities	92
6. Entering into coalitions with other organizations	90
7. Attempting to shape the implementation of policies	89
8. Talking with people from the media	86
9. Consulting with government officials to plan legislative strategy	85
10. Helping to draft legislation	85
11. Inspiring letter-writing or telegram campaigns	84
12. Shaping the government's agenda by raising new issues and calling attention to previously ignored problems	84
13. Mounting grass-roots lobbying efforts	80
14. Having influential constituents contact their congressional representative's office	80
15. Helping to draft regulations, rules, or guidelines	78
16. Serving on advisory commissions and boards	76
17. Alerting congressional representatives to the effects of a bill on their districts	75
18. Filing suit or otherwise engaging in litigation	72
19. Making financial contributions to electoral campaigns	58
20. Doing favors for officials who need assistance	56
21. Attempting to influence appointments to public office	53
22. Publicizing candidates' voting records	44
23. Engaging in direct-mail fundraising for organization	44
24. Running advertisements in the media about position on issues	31
25. Contributing work or personnel to electoral campaigns	24
26. Making public endorsements of candidates for office	22
27. Engaging in protests or demonstrations	20

SOURCE: Kay Lehman Schlozman and John T. Tierney, *Organized Interests and American Democracy*. New York: Harper & Row, 1986, p. 150. Based on a study by the authors of the Washington representatives of 175 nationwide interest organizations. Note that the figures for use of litigation and protest activities are higher in this study than figures reported in Walker's study of a larger sample of organizations. (See Jack L. Walker, Jr., *Mobilizing Interest Groups in America*. Ann Arbor: University of Michigan Press, 1991, p.109.)

Under legal obligation to comply, Detroit began building more economy cars and doing research on fuel-efficient engineering. According to one supporter of the law, "The fuel economy law passed in 1975 has been one of the most effective conservation measures ever undertaken," saving about 1.8 million barrels of oil each day, and reducing annual gasoline consumption from 785 gallons per car in 1972 to 507 gallons in 1988.[31]

However, Detroit never took its eyes off the profit advantages of big cars and never stopped fighting the CAFE law. Since there was little hope of overturning the law or wiggling out of it through litigation, the car makers turned to intense lobbying and found a sympathetic ear in President Ronald Reagan, who promised to make American business competitive again by freeing up government regulations. In 1986, the chief executive ordered his bureaucrats to relax their monitoring of car companies, citing the "hardships" that such regulations caused businesses. From the auto industry's point of view, these hardships included expensive car redesign, massive retooling of factories, and direct competition with more advanced, fuel-efficient imports from Japan and Germany.

Meanwhile, back in Congress, some of the sponsors of the original CAFE legislation viewed Detroit's backsliding with alarm. New legislation was introduced whose goals were the antithesis of the Reagan administration's—to make CAFE laws *more* stringent. Environmentalists and consumer groups once again joined the fight and began to bombard Congress with facts and figures such as these:

- With only 5 percent of the world's population, Americans consume more than 25 percent of the world's oil.

- The country is more dependent on imported oil than ever before, with nearly half the oil used every year coming from abroad.

- Oil imports represent a big part of our trade deficit.

- Over 40 percent of oil is burned in cars.

- Americans use twice as much gas, per person, as the next country (Sweden).

- With little public transportation and few incentives to save fuel, Americans drive about 1.4 trillion miles a year—or more than 7,000 trips to the sun and back.[32]

The car makers did not take all this lying down. One congressional source revealed that the industry spent some $8 million in efforts to block newly proposed changes in the CAFE law in 1990 and 1991.[33] What did this money buy? A lot of lobbying, a lot of campaign contributions, and an expensive stable of public relations firms trying to mobilize public opinion. It also enlisted an ally in Reagan's successor, George Bush, who campaigned in 1992 against stiffer CAFE laws as bad for the economy. According to a Common Cause study, the effort to block new legislation included the following tactics.

LOBBYING.   When the Senate showed signs of moving on new legislation, the chiefs of General Motors, Chrysler, and Ford asked for and received a meeting with President Bush at the White House. Invitations were also extended to key members of Congress to come to Detroit at industry expense, for a tour giving the auto makers' side of the issues. The chairman of the Ford board of directors met personally with a number of senators. As a result, a fuel economy amendment was dropped from the Clean Air Act of 1990, and the car companies turned their full attention back to defeating the new CAFE legislation.[34]

The lobbying effort included an information deluge on economic problems in the industry. As a bureaucrat involved with administration energy policy put it, "When you talk to environment groups, they don't have a big staff, so they tend to give you broad, somewhat nebulous arguments. When you talk to the car people, they give you hundreds of pages of printouts and test results. Anything that you could possibly ask for that you've ever thought of, they'll have their specialist in Dearborn call you up to tell you the results."[35]

CAMPAIGN CONTRIBUTIONS.   The industry pulled out all the stops, beginning with members of the Michigan congressional delegation. Michigan Democrat Don Riegle, who led the anti-CAFE fight in the Senate, received more than $38,000 in campaign gifts from auto PACs between 1983 and 1990. Chrysler Corporation chairman Lee Iacocca personally hosted a fundraiser for Michigan's junior senator, Carl Levin, also a Democrat. Other powerful allies were also recruited with PAC money. The highest-ranking Republican member on the Senate energy conservation subcommittee received more than $37,000 in PAC money between 1983 and 1990. Even the sponsor of the new CAFE legislation received over $8,000 from the car companies. When it came time to call in the favors, this high finance did not hurt. Supporters of the car companies held a filibuster (see Chapter 13) to keep the legislation from moving onto the Senate floor.

The Faces of Influence

Interest groups represent far more than stereotyped "Big Business" elites. They span the ideological range from the liberal feminist group NOW (the National Organization for Women, below) to the American Conservative Union. Some lobbyists represent one government body to another; Kenneth Duberstein, a top Reagan White House official (above left, with then-Defense Secretary Frank Carlucci), later lobbied the Senate on behalf of the Bush administration to confirm Supreme Court nominee Clarence Thomas. Though not often thought of as a lobbyist, "consumer advocate" Ralph Nader (right) became a father of the public-interest group movement through his 1960s research into the safety standards of American automobiles.

The Players

• • •

If I could not go to heaven but with a party, I would not go there at all.
—*THOMAS JEFFERSON*

• • •

The political parties of the United States are unique. They seldom perform the function that parties traditionally perform in other countries, the function of gathering together diverse strands of power and welding them into one. . . . The American parties rarely coalesce power at all. Characteristically, they do the reverse, serving as a canopy under which special and local interests are represented.
—*MARTIN GRODZINS*

• • •

The evidence is now overwhelming that government without parties does not work. There is no accountability; therefore, no responsibility; therefore, no incentives for presidents or legislatures to make the hard choices.
—*DAVID BRODER*

• • •

Political Parties:

Engines of

Government

- **HEARD THE NEWS? THE PARTY'S OVER**

- **A DEFINITION OF PARTIES**

- **PARTIES ON TRIAL: THE CHARGES**

- **A BRIEF HISTORY OF PARTIES**
  Controlling Parties by Constitutional Design
  The Two-Party System
  Third-Party Politics

- **THE POLITICS BEHIND THE TWO-PARTY SYSTEM**
  Strong Culture, Weak Parties
  The Institutional Basis of Two-Party Democracy
  Social Power and the Party System

- **WHAT THE PARTIES DO AND HOW THEY DO IT**
  The Functions of Political Parties
  Choices and Channels for Political Demands
  Developing Leaders, Nominating Candidates
  Governing

- **POLITICAL CRISIS, VOTER ALIGNMENTS, AND PARTY GOVERNMENT**
  The Parties and Political Change
  The Party System Today

- **THE CHARGES AGAINST THE PARTIES REVISITED**

- **A CITIZEN'S QUESTION: Party Activism**

- **KEY TERMS**

- **SUGGESTED READINGS**

Heard the News? The Party's Over

The political parties have come under fire in the press in recent years. To many journalists and more than a few political scientists, these centers of political power seem to have lost their vision. They have been faulted with poor organization and lack of political will. The news and editorial pages have carried warnings about the decline of parties. Columnists and television pundits have urged party leaders and voters alike to tune up these engines of government to achieve better performance or risk losing the capacity to govern effectively.

A sure sign that these concerns are not just the usual political finger-pointing is that political publications and opinionated columnists are criticizing their own parties. Liberal *Harper's* magazine reported on a meeting of concerned Democratic intellectuals in an article titled "What's Wrong with the Democrats?"[1] Charles Krauthammer, a conservative columnist, became so frustrated at the GOP's lack of an agenda that he wrote a column with the title "The Republican Party Ought to Declare Bankruptcy."[2] And Republican strategist-turned-journalist Kevin Phillips surveyed a national political scene in which neither party could inspire voters with a governing program: "From the White House to Capitol Hill, the critical weakness of American politics and governance is becoming woefully apparent: a frightening inability to define and debate emerging problems. For the moment, the political culture appears to be brain-dead."[3]

Some said the parties were weakened by interest-group pressures (described in Chapter 8). In the view of these critics, candidates have grown too loyal to their campaign contributors and have lost their allegiance to the party organizations that actually get things done. Others point to the loss of voter loyalty described in Chapter 7, raising the chicken-or-egg problem of whether voters abandoned the parties or the parties let down the voters first. With the exceptions of 1976 and 1992, the voters had developed the habit of sending one party to Congress and another to the White House, in what seemed to some observers a kind of curse on both the political houses. In this view, the split-ticket voters were sending something of a wake-up call to the parties: If neither party could inspire loyalty and trust among the voters, then neither would have full governing power. In this view, 1992 represented a cautious experiment to see if one party (in this case, the Democrats) could be trusted with the reins of government. But instead of quickly launching new political programs, the Democrats in Congress (along with the Republicans) soon put up resistance to the new president.

It had been so long since Americans lived with single-party government that entire generations came of age under the split-party model. The last time that a single party controlled the White House and both chambers of Congress for more than a single presidential term was from 1961–1968, when the Democrats were in power. Are Americans in danger of forgetting the importance of parties? In 1992 when Ross Perot threatened to shake up the system with his independent presidential bid, political scientist Theodore Lowi published a prominent national editorial reminding Mr. Perot that he forgot to throw a party for his candidacy. Under the headline MR. PEROT, FORM A PARTY, Lowi delivered an impassioned reminder about the importance of parties:

> You must use your mass support in 1992 to build a new political party for 1996 and beyond. Judging from your public discourse, I think you would agree that America's real political problem is the party system.
>
> . . . Each [party] has held power too long. We should have a third party to oppose both. Since you can't govern without a party, and the two are unavailable and undesirable, form your own.

Presidential hopeful Ross Perot appears at a Washington state rally in early July 1992. Perot criticized both parties as agents of the status quo, but two weeks later he dropped out of the race. He reentered the campaign in October, ultimately pulling some nineteen million votes. The devotion shown by Perot's followers led critics to term them "Perotistas." However, they faced the challenge of sustaining their movement after the election.

. . . The last opportunity like yours came in 1856. Instead of an independent running against the corrupt Democrats and Whigs, the Republican Party was formed. It elected Lincoln four years later.[4]

Ross Perot attempting to play Abraham Lincoln to usher in the twenty-first century? Even if the parallel seems far-fetched, there is more than a grain of truth in Lowi's reminder that Mr. Perot did not explain how he planned to govern if he made it to Washington. He simply promised to go up there and "fix it," referring to the mess in government, beginning with the budget deficit. When asked by reporters just how he would do that, he said that he would just have to "hold their hands" until they could agree, referring to the hands of squabbling party leaders who were allegedly so divided by special interests that they lost

their grip on the national interest. While that plan of action may have amused many voters, one suspects that the party leaders in question found the idea a bit naive, if not deliberately disingenuous.

Before giving up on the party system, it is worth remembering that parties and elections have gone through high times and low for nearly two hundred years. Periods of visionary leaders and committed voters have been followed by times of upheaval and breakdown resulting in such catastrophes as the Civil War that make the current era of electoral decline seem mild by comparison. Through it all, there have been energizing bursts of reform aimed at putting an often unwieldy system back on track again.

The discontent with parties that opened the 1990s turns out to be similar to other periods in history. Political frustrations in America have often been expressed through third parties, political reform movements, and changes in voter support for the major parties themselves. Through it all, parties have been criticized and often supplemented by other methods of organizing political power, but they have never been abandoned. Parties are engines of power, and the question is: Who will drive them?

Perhaps the most useful aspect of the contemporary media focus on parties is reminding both voters and politicians to think about what parties are there for. In a book titled (appropriately enough) *The Party's Over*, columnist David Broder put it like this:

We have been spinning our wheels for a long, long time; and . . . we are going to dig ourselves deeper into trouble unless we find a way to develop some political traction and move again. I believe we can get that traction, we can make government responsible and responsive again, only when we begin to use the political parties as they are meant to be used.[5]

Just how are the parties meant to be used? What role have they played in American politics in the past? Is the current state of party politics all that unusual? What would it take to turn up the power on the party engine of government and deal with national problems in ways that might satisfy more people? How are parties organized to carry out their political roles? These are some of the questions that will be addressed in this chapter. They are worth thinking about before deciding if the party is over in American politics.

A Definition of Parties

Parties are the most broad and durable links between society and government. They are organized to recruit candidates, promote policies, and connect state and local branches nationally. If these organizations are working, they channel political demands into government institutions, work out compromises, and offer programs (called platforms) that promise what they would do if elected to run the government. This process of joining society and government in broad programs of political action requires that parties:

- recruit candidates and party leaders
- nominate and run candidates for office
- assign people to specific tasks and positions in government after they are elected
- carry on internal dialogues (through party councils, committees, caucuses, and conventions at local, state, and national levels) about how to govern
- provide a national organization to coordinate all these functions.

Parties differ from social movements and interest groups in important ways. Parties appeal to much broader slices of society and promote many more issues than interest groups. Parties offer the inside connections to government institutions that social movements, by definition, generally lack. For these reasons, interest groups alone would not produce very coherent or popular government, and social movements alone do not have the access to government institutions to promote their visions of society.

Viewed from the smallest unit of political power—the individual—it is not clear what would guide elected representatives after they took their places in government if most individuals voted completely without regard to party. Even the founders of the nation quickly abandoned the romantic notion that representatives would be guided by an enlightened sense of their responsibility to the public interest. Parties were the first major additions to American government, despite the nearly universal dislike for the idea among those who founded them.

Senate Majority Leader George Mitchell poses with fellow Democrats and incoming freshman senators Barbara Boxer and Dianne Feinstein of California, and Carol Moseley Braun of Illinois, at right, days after their November 1992 election. The so-called "Year of the Woman" favored the Democratic party in 1992, but increased political activism among women promised to bring new talent into both major parties.

Parties on Trial: The Charges

Critics have charged that parties no longer serve the grand coordinating and governing functions outlined above. Has the decline of parties left national politics in the sway of interests, social movements, and increasingly isolated voters, none of which offers much hope for coherent government? The charges against parties in the modern era are serious ones that should be considered by every student of politics. This chapter provides the information necessary to weigh the charges and draw your own conclusions.

Charge Number 1: Neither party has a clear vision or broadly appealing choices to offer voters. Some critics say this is because powerful minorities have forced party organizations to adopt positions that frighten large numbers of voters: against abortion for the Republicans, pro-affirmative action for the Democrats, for social spending for the Democrats, against business regulation for the Republicans. Others charge that because of these divisive issues, party visions about how to build a more liveable society have become poorly defined.[6] The problems of blurred vision and poor choices are compounded by voters who have grown increasingly wary of parties and candidates, as explained in Chapter 7. Many people have come to regard voting independently as a good thing rather than as a sign of something gone seriously wrong with the party system.

Charge Number 2: Party platforms and campaign promises are aimed more at getting elected than at governing afterwards. Whether because voters abandoned the parties or parties let down the voters, government has been damaged because candidates and parties do whatever it takes to get elected, even if that compromises their ability to govern when they win office. It is commonly charged that candidates have abandoned party platforms and turned to marketing experts and image consultants (see Chapter 6) to cover their lack of governing ideas.[7] After elections, the image consultants follow their clients into office to help them invent governing images, much as they helped create the appearance of leadership during the campaign.[8] Parties, not image consultants, are supposed to be the source of ideas about what to do once elected.

Charge Number 3: Parties have been corrupted and weakened by money from interest groups. Whether interest groups have corrupted politicians, or politicians simply needed more money to chase more fickle voters, the result, say critics, is that the parties have become corrupted. In the view of political scientist Theodore Lowi, when parties become money machines for careerist politicians, this is precisely what it means to say that "power corrupts."[9] Some critics charge that professional politicians, instead of being members of party teams, have become renegades—political entrepreneurs looking out for their own personal fortunes rather than for the good of the party and its supporters.

Charge Number 4: The breakdown in party discipline and loyalty has changed the nature of political leadership and weakened government in America. Here is an illustrative story from the bad old days of "machine politics," an era when parties were too tightly organized and corrupted in other ways: An idealistic young man showed up to work on a Chicago campaign. The party campaign chief asked for a letter of introduction from the party captain in the voting precinct where the young man lived. Upon being informed that nobody sent the young man, that he just came to volunteer on his own, the party boss sent him away with the admonition: "We don't want nobody that nobody sent." The author of a book about today's fragmented parties says that the current problem may be just the opposite, but no less serious: "Who sent these candidates we see nowadays?" Alan Ehrenhalt, the author of *The United States of Ambition,* explains the modern party dilemma this way:

> The skills that work in American politics at this point in history are those of entrepreneurship. . . . People nominate themselves. . . . Candidates do not win because they have party support. They do not win because they have business or labor support. They win because they are motivated to set out on their own and find the votes.[10]

Commenting on this charge, columnist David Broder noted that none of the Democratic party candidates for president in 1992 was "sent" to the people by the party. To the contrary, "They nominated themselves for the honor of running. . . . Every one of them is in the race primarily because of his own ambition."[11] This kind of outside-the-party-politics made presidents out of Jimmy Carter in 1976 and Bill Clinton in 1992, but it can leave such successful political entrepreneurs with an insufficient party power base to use in governing after they are elected. Even though Bill Clinton had a majority of his own party in both houses of Congress, he was forced to take to the road and the airwaves immediately after becoming president in an attempt to drum up public support for his programs. Equally importantly, says Broder, the weakening of ties between elected officials and parties has changed the nature of politics itself:

> In this kind of politics, traits that once were important—experience, credentials, loyalty to the party or the cause, the ability to work with others—count for very little. Independence is an asset. So is articulateness, because you have to convince people of your own merits.[12]

The problem, say these critics, is that after candidates have convinced enough voters to get themselves elected, how are they going to convince legislatures full of renegades like themselves to do anything together? Parties, not single-minded individuals, make the government go. The following information about parties in American politics is intended to help evaluate these charges.

A Brief History of Parties

In evaluating the above charges, it is useful to begin with a brief historical overview. Some of these charges may ignore historical limitations in the American party system. In addition, as the age of machine politics indicates, simply having stronger parties may not lead to any better or more public-spirited government. While some contemporary problems are unique to today's society and politics, other patterns reflect more enduring patterns, in culture, institutions, and social power.

Controlling Parties by Constitutional Design

As noted in Chapters 1 and 2, the founders had strong reactions against any concentrations of power in government. Beyond the cultural fear of tyranny, there seemed to be a genuine idealism about the possibility of elected representatives making independent and enlightened choices in the interests of all the people. Both the idealism and the suspicions of the founders were probably revealed most clearly in their hostility toward parties. Although Madison was as hostile toward parties as any of the early leaders, he also recognized that they were probably inevitable. In *Federalist* No. 10, for example, he put it bluntly: "In every political society, parties are unavoidable. A difference of interests . . . is the most natural and fruitful source of them."[13] *In what remains a key to understanding the American parties, Madison then went on to promote the Constitution as a way of weakening parties through a combination of separate branches of government (which parties would have trouble controlling all at once) and federal divisions in which many state power centers would weaken the rise of national parties. Many (but not all) of the things that critics still find lacking in the American parties can be traced to these constitutional design features of the government itself.*

Madison's prediction soon came true. Conflicts in government over economic development, trade policies, and foreign relations soon had national leaders competing for political power and, even more distressing to elitists such as Hamilton, reaching out for support from the voters themselves. With the rise of party politics, Hamilton lamented that "we must renounce our principles . . . and unite in corrupting public opinion."[14] The first party was no more than a caucus of elites who formed around Hamilton and called themselves Federalists. They promoted the interests of northern business and trading companies and advocated a foreign policy allied with England. Opponents who favored farmers, small business interests, and an alliance with France, drifted toward Jefferson and took the then-revolutionary name *Democratic-Republican.*

These first attempts to organize governing power bore little similarity to today's parties. Relatively few people were entitled to vote in those days, and the first parties had no conventions or platforms. In addition, the Federalists were generally opposed to the idea of appealing to "the people" for support, creating a built-in limit on their growth potential. Indeed, the Federalists were all but extinct by 1816. Even the Democratic-Republicans were so weak that Jefferson referred to his party's strength as a "rope of sand."[15] In much of the period following the War of 1812 against England and the early push westward, there was so little conflict and party-building that the period has been called the "Era of Good Feeling."

In the divisive election campaign of 1824, however, the good feelings turned sour. The Federalists had long since disappeared, but the Democratic-Republicans fell apart at the seams, reflecting the lack of party organization and the absence of common interests among the many local factions that had formed the national party. Around the same time, the frontier exploded. Many western residents demanded and won the right to vote without property requirements and other similar restrictions. This created a new era of party-building, in which parties competed *directly* for the support of voters. By the 1830s, parties began holding conventions to select candidates and to write platforms representing their ideals. The first broadly voter-based party emerged as a splinter of the old Jefferson-led Democratic-Republicans. Taking the name *Democrats,* this party supported the successful candidacy of Andrew Jackson for the presidency in 1828 and remains the nation's oldest political party.

The opposition to the Democrats in the early years came from a party called the *Whigs* that also splintered off the old Jeffersonian Democratic-Republicans. Although

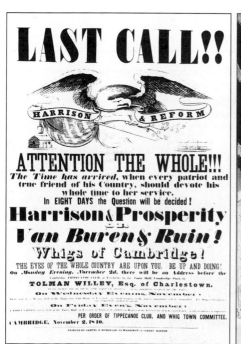

Left: *A campaign poster urges the election of Whig nominee William Henry Harrison, who would become the ninth president in 1840, then die within a month of taking office.*
Right: *A Currier and Ives lithograph of 1844 promotes Henry Clay (without success) as the Whig presidential standard-bearer. The Whigs would elect one subsequent president (Zachary Taylor in 1848), but by the Civil War era, the Whig party was in its death throes, while the modern Republican party was being born.*

led by distinguished politicians such as Henry Clay and Daniel Webster, the Whigs tried to combine too many regional and economic interests in one party, and fell apart by the late 1850s. Madison's prediction held up again: In this case, the federal system with its many state and regional power bases and local issues did in the Whigs.

Conflicts over slavery, economic development, westward expansion, and immigration policy led to another splintering of parties during the 1850s, and to the creation in 1854 of a new party, the Republicans, with an antislavery platform and a pro-northern business philosophy. (Many southerners regarded the Republican opposition to slavery as a northern plot to gain control of the national economy.) In the divisive election of 1860, Republican candidate Abraham Lincoln emerged with less than 40 percent of the popular vote, but took nearly 60 percent of the electoral vote, and the Republicans began their reign as the next-oldest American party.

Since 1860, the United States has alternated between periods of Republican and Democratic rule in a stable two-party system. However, there have been frequent periods of third-party activism, when the two major parties were unable to represent all the interests that emerged in a rapidly changing and complex society. Figure 9.1 traces the rise and fall of the major parties in American history.

The Two-Party System

The two-party tradition is an established feature of American politics. Multiparty systems occur primarily in parliamentary governments where the executive arm of government is constructed from parties that hold a majority of seats in parliament. This arrangement can end up giving small parties a great deal of power if they can join with larger parties to form the majority bloc of votes in the legislature. In most parliamentary systems, small parties get into national legislatures through proportional representation which, you may recall from Chapter 3, is an election and representation system in which parties receive seats in legislatures in rough proportion to the percentage of the total vote they receive in an election. "How We Compare" Box 9.1 illustrates how small parties can thrive under proportional representation in parliamentary systems.

FIGURE 9.1

The Major Parties in American History

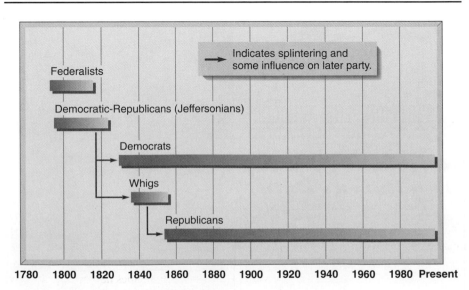

HOW WE COMPARE

Small Parties, Big Power: Why Small Parties Can Thrive with Proportional Representation

9.1

Danish politics in the late 1980s offers one example of how small parties can exercise considerable influence in a multiparty system. In 1987, the Conservative People's Party won only 38, or about 20 percent, of the seats in the Danish parliament, called the *Folketing.* Even if the Conservatives won the support of all the other small parties, they could not control a majority and form a government without the support of the Radical Liberal Party. This made the support of the radical Liberals very valuable indeed, particularly since the Conservatives' opponents, the two Socialist Parties, were also trying to persuade the Radical Liberals to join them in government. Either coalition that won the support of the Radical Liberals could form a government. In the end, the Radical Liberals joined the Conservative coalition, and as their reward they received five positions to fill in the executive (cabinet) of the new government, a great deal of power for such a small party.

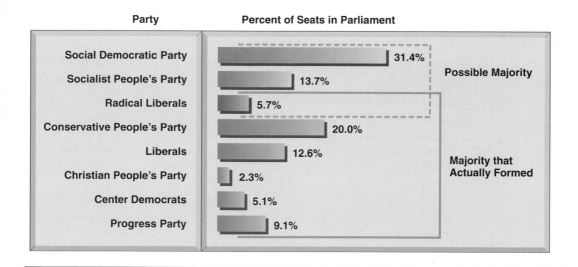

Party   **Percent of Seats in Parliament**

Party	Percent
Social Democratic Party	31.4%
Socialist People's Party	13.7%
Radical Liberals	5.7%
Conservative People's Party	20.0%
Liberals	12.6%
Christian People's Party	2.3%
Center Democrats	5.1%
Progress Party	9.1%

Possible Majority

Majority that Actually Formed

As in most democratic legislatures, representation in the U.S. House of Representatives is based on population, but not in proportion to the number of votes all parties or candidates receive. Each congressional district is represented by a *single member* in Congress. This means that in an election, only one candidate or party wins, severely limiting the chances of small parties gaining power. In addition, the executive in the United States is not drawn from parliament but elected independently, also reinforcing the winner-take-all, two-way competition of the American system. Since most state election systems also favor the major parties, the two-way competition for power has been institutionalized throughout the federal system. All of this raises the question of what Ross Perot might have gained by forming a party in 1992. With or without a party, Perot's 19 percent of the national popular vote would have produced no electoral votes. This winner-take-all adaptation of the electoral system has little to do with what the founders intended: independent voting by electors as a check on popular passions. However, the state-based winner-take-all system increases the importance of state parties, further reinforcing the two-party system. These state and national party politics help to explain why the electoral college system persists to this day (and why few people can explain its survival).

Third-Party Politics

Why do third parties exist in this system? The political origins of the two-party tradition outlined above may mean that specific groups, regions, classes, religions, business interests, or other segments of society feel poorly represented by such broad parties. The greatest irony of the American two-party system may be this: A government designed to limit the power of factions ended up creating two very large ones. *However,* each is so unwieldy and weakened by regional and other social differences that it poses little threat of cutting too far against the social grain. This is essentially what Madison predicted the constitutional design would do. If the major parties are often out of step with substantial minorities in the society, third parties allow people to vent their frustrations, get their positions publicized, and, from time to time, put a scare into the major parties.

The names of American third parties are as rich as the tradition itself: Locofocos, Know-Nothings, Populists, Bull Moose Progressives, Socialists, Communists, Libertarians, Right to Life, Peace and Freedom, Dixiecrats, Anti-Masonic, and hundreds of tiny parties such as Washington state's OWL (Out With Logic) party that ran candidates in state elections. Of all of these small parties, only seven have carried even a single state in a presidential race, and only four have ever drawn as much as 10 percent of the national vote for president:[16]

American Know-Nothing party took 22 percent of the popular vote and eight electoral votes in 1856 on a platform of anti-immigration and restricting the political rights of immigrants.

Bull Moose (Progressive) party won 27 percent of the popular vote and eighty-eight electoral votes behind Teddy Roosevelt in 1912 and shifted the election from the Republicans to the Democrats. (Roosevelt had been president earlier as a Republican.) The platform stressed government reform and regulating big business.

Progressive party won 17 percent of the popular vote and thirteen electoral votes in 1924 under Robert LaFollette. Tax fairness and government reforms were major themes.

Having served as a Republican president, Teddy Roosevelt returned to the political scene in 1912 under the banner of the Progressive ("Bull Moose") party. Running against incumbent Republican president William Howard Taft, Roosevelt split his longtime party so badly that the election went to Democrat Woodrow Wilson. Third parties may not win elections, but can promote their agenda by pushing the major parties in specific directions.

The cover to a piece of sheet music—a quickstep, or marching tune— lauding the "Know-Nothing" party. (Even before today's media-dominated campaigns, elections were still celebrated in campaign songs.) The "Know-Nothings" were actually the American party, a somewhat secretive fraternity whose primary features were anti-Catholicism and nativism (that is, an anti-immigrant agenda). This minor party flourished briefly in the 1850s, but the issue of slavery split its members, and it vanished.

American Independent party took 14 percent of the popular vote and forty-six electoral votes in 1968 behind the presidential candidacy of George Wallace and an appeal based on states' rights to decide racial policies and other issues.

Another important small party in history was the Populist party, which joined ranks with the Democrats in 1896 to fight the Republicans and ran a strong but unsuccessful national campaign behind William Jennings Bryan in an election that divided the nation and the party system for thirty years to come, as we will discuss later. The Populists and the four national parties listed above are among the few exceptions to the rule that small parties have little national influence.

Eugene V. Debs, a union organizer, ran for president on the Socialist ticket five times in the early twentieth century, drawing a small but creditable percentage of the vote at a time when the term social-ism held an idealistic vision for some, but threatened the cultural ideals of many others. During World War I, Debs went to prison under sedition laws, but was ordered released by President Warren G. Harding.

Even if the two-party system means that small parties will be unsuccessful at winning office (much less winning enough offices to run a government), third parties have been effective throughout American history at expressing popular discontent with the major parties. From time to time, enough people have turned to a minor party to deny an election to a major party, as happened when the Bull Moose party under Teddy Roosevelt (a former Republican) attracted enough Republican voters in 1912 to deliver the White House to the Democrats and Woodrow Wilson. The threat of enough voters defecting to minor parties can force the big parties to address neglected issues. Even when minor parties do not threaten the major parties, people may feel that keeping certain ideas alive is important enough to organize parties to promote them. Figure 9.2 illustrates the history of some of the more memorable minor parties in American politics.

Perhaps these reasons explain why political scientist Theodore Lowi advised Ross Perot to form a party. Lowi certainly recognized that in most elections, the goal of small parties is less to defeat the leading parties than to express minority views and popular discontent. When small parties attract large enough followings, they can begin to force

FIGURE 9.2

Minor Parties in American Politics

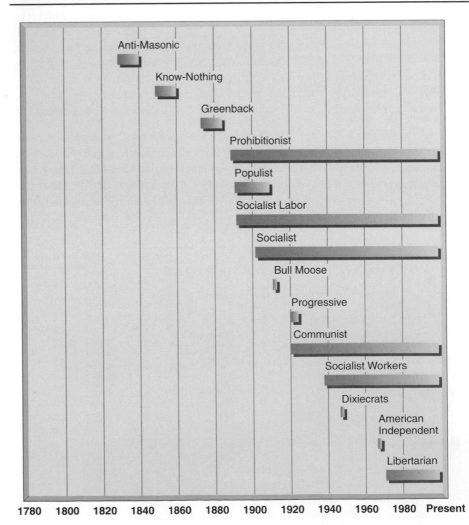

the major parties to address issues that large numbers of voters feel they are ignoring. The major reason offered by Ross Perot for his candidacy was to force the major parties to address economic issues (especially the deficit) that he and his followers felt had been neglected. By the show of voters, Perot succeeded in doing this. If Perot converted his movement into a party, the result might be to keep the heat on the major parties and make sure that his issues of budget-balancing, tax policy, and government-business relations continued to be addressed in the future. Poll results reported in Table 9.1 show that a large majority of Perot voters and substantial numbers of the general population favor the formation of a new political party.

TABLE 9.1

Backing for a New Political Party

PROPOSITION	ALL RESPONDENTS (%)	THOSE LEANING TO PEROT (%)	NEW PARTY VOTERS* (%)
1. Agree: If Democrats and Republicans continue to run things, we'll never get reform.	46%	64%	76%
2. Agree: Need a new political party to reform American politics.	47	67	100
3. Yes, would like to see new national party run candidates.	57	75	100
4. Agree: Neither party can get things going; need new party.	50	72	100
5. Agree: Current incumbents will never reform political process.	69	83	87
6. Yes, angry at both political parties and their candidates.	56	79	84
7. Would switch and vote new party if positions match their own.	65	81	100

*New party voters are those answering "yes" to items 2, 3, 4, and 7.

Questions:
1. The following are some negative things people are saying about state and national politics these days. For each one, please tell me whether you agree or disagree with the statement. . . . If the Democrats and Republicans continue to run things, we'll never get real reform.
2. (Same preface as 1) . . . We need a new political party to reform American politics.
3. Would you like to see a new national political party form, and run candidates for office?
4. Some people are saying that neither the Democrats nor the Republicans are capable any longer of getting this country going in the right direction, and that we need a new national political party. Do you strongly agree, moderately agree, moderately disagree, or strongly disagree?
5. (Same preface as 1) . . . The current incumbents in office will never reform the political process.
6. Some people are angry at both political parties and their candidates. Would you say that describes how you feel right now?
7. Suppose that a new reform-oriented political party is created to run candidates for Congress, the Senate, and even your state legislature. Assuming for a moment that this new party was supporting YOUR positions on many of the issues you care about, would you be MOST likely to vote for the candidates of the new reform party or would you be MOST likely to continue to vote either for the Republican or the Democratic candidates?

SOURCE: Survey by Gordon S. Black Corporation, May 1992. Adapted from *The Public Perspective*, Nov.-Dec. 1992. p. 3.

The Politics Behind the Two-Party System _____

If the rise of a two-party system in the United States cannot be defended as the best way of channeling political demands or as the most effective empowerment of individual voters, how can we explain it? As with so many other features of American government discussed in this book, the answers involve politics inside the system—our familiar framework of **culture, institutions,** and **power.**

Strong Culture, Weak Parties

If Americans today were asked how they would change their parties, they might say they want to reduce the influence of money or restrict interest-group access. However, Americans probably would not agree in large numbers that the parties ought to become more powerful or more centralized. Nor would most Americans favor removing the partitions between the branches of government, or the divisions in state and national power so that parties could control government more centrally. For all the criticism of the parties, the core of cultural resistance to centralized power would undermine many proposals that might strengthen party power and reduce the chaos and conflict within party politics. Thus we still live with the ever-popular Madisonian belief that it is a good idea to limit the power of factions and parties.

Another cultural limitation on the strength of parties is the very relationship between individuals and society in America. More than citizens in most societies, Americans fancy themselves as independent individuals who do not line up easily behind distant groups or parties. The rise of independent voters in recent decades (recall the discussion from Chapter 7) increases the wariness that many individuals have about strong party programs. The American image of society as a place for individuals to coexist makes it challenging for parties to come up with broad social visions that many people want to support, particularly if they have to make personal sacrifices to do so.

The Institutional Basis of Two-Party Democracy

As noted earlier, there are also institutional design features that promote two large and often unwieldy parties in American politics. These institutional factors include:

- single member representation districts that encourage two-way races;
- separate, winner-take-all races for presidents, governors, and other executives that also discourage more than two competing power bases;
- separating the branches of government, which makes it hard for parties to run the whole government even if they could agree on how to run it;
- federal divisions of power that magnify state and regional interests and weaken national party organizations ideologically.

Social Power and the Party System

The creation of a broad, two-party democracy in the United States means that different groups are forced to come together and march somewhat uneasily under the same party banners. Such broad coalition parties may promote compromises among different groups who want to ride the same party into government, but those compromises may leave people unsatisfied with the very party they helped build. As a result, there has been a history of instability in the parties.

Since the parties must try to appeal to so many different consitituencies if they are to be successful, it is not clear how they can truly *represent* those often-fragmented "majorities" of voters. Even if a party wins elections with a group coalition strategy, different groups who contributed to the victory may make competing demands on the elected party officials. Such *pluralistic* power bases may be better suited to interest-group activities where groups can win or lose without such serious compromises in their interests. This means that it may be too simple to say that elections always involve *majority* power, since those majorities can dissolve quickly into incompatible groups.

Whether their voter coalitions are unstable and pluralist or stable and majoritarian, there is another sphere of party life behind the scenes that is often very *elitist*. This elitism operates in the area of party finance. Unlike many systems where public funding is given to parties in proportion to their strength in legislatures, the United States has relied largely on private political financing, which means that while parties are juggling coalitions of voters, they are also juggling coalitions of financiers, along with the often-conflicting demands that people with money can put on them. The costs of elections for local, state, and national offices in the United States during a presidential year are well in excess of two billion dollars, of which only a tiny portion comes from public financing to presidential candidates, as discussed in the next chapter.[17]

Political scientist Thomas Ferguson and sociologist Joel Rogers have studied the history of party finance and conclude that, since the late 1960s, both major parties have been competing increasingly for the same money, particularly from "big business." Ferguson and Rogers agree with the earlier charge that the choices parties offer voters have been narrowed. They argue that this is not because voters have grown more alike in their demands, but because pressure from party contributors has led the Democratic party to take a "right turn" ideologically.[18] Other analysts agree that money affects parties, but instead think that the pull of money is in many different directions. In either case, it is important to recognize that parties are more than just the sum of their pluralities or majorities of voters; they are also made up of the elites who finance them and whose interests may differ considerably from those of average voters. The different forces in the political system that promote a two-party system in American politics are summarized in Table 9.2.

TABLE 9.2   *Factors that Promote a Weak Two-Party System in America*

CULTURAL	INSTITUTIONAL	SOCIAL POWER
Enduring fears of strong parties, factions. Independence of individuals in political thinking and identification. Independence from parties is often viewed as a strength rather than a weakness.	Single-member congressional districts promote two-way races. Separate election of the executive also favors two-way races (magnified by winner-take-all electoral voting in the states). Separation of powers in three branches of government makes party control of government difficult. Divisions of federal powers create fifty state parties within each national party.	*Majority* vote often breaks down into *pluralist* factions within parties, creating strains and making it difficult to find broad majority appeals that are stronger than specific group issues. *Elitist* influences enter parties through campaign funding and other ties between candidates, party leaders, and business elites. Pressures from elites sometimes conflict with demands from voters.

What the Parties Do and How They Do It _____

For all their cultural and institutional peculiarities, American parties continue to do many of the things done by parties elsewhere in the world. This section identifies three ideal functions of political parties and considers how (and how well) the American system carries them out.

The Functions of Political Parties

Simplifying the definition offered earlier in the chapter, we can reduce the ideal functions of political parties to three:

- Offering people choices and providing channels for expressing political demands within the system;
- Recruiting and nominating candidates to support the party program and to run in elections at all levels of government;
- Organizing winning candidates into governing coalitions to implement party programs and promises.

As you might expect, American parties come closer to some of these ideals than to others. The following discussion examines how the major American parties function in the eyes of the political scientists who study them.

Choices and Channels for Political Demands

As explained in Chapter 6, most Americans do not view the political world in consistently ideological ways. Although the two major parties are less ideological than many of their European counterparts, they *do* offer voters some ideological choices having to do with the role of government, economic philosophies, and the need for moral order. Republican platforms tend to advocate limited government, letting the marketplace regulate itself, and protection of traditional values. In contrast to these conservative principles, Democratic platforms tend to favor more liberal positions, including a more interventionist role for government, greater regulation of the economy, and more encouragement for a diversity of social lifestyles.

In part, the ideological patterns in the parties reflect the fact that many activists who shape party ideas and write the platforms are much more ideological than average party supporters (see Table 9.4). Here is how Franklin Roosevelt described the ideological differences between the two parties toward the end of the Great Depression, a time when those differences were probably as great as they have ever been:

> Generally speaking, in a representative form of government there are usually two general schools of political belief—liberal and conservative. . . . The liberal party is a party which believes that, as new conditions and problems arise beyond the power of men and women to meet as individuals, it becomes the duty of the government itself to find new remedies with which to meet them. . . .
>
> The conservative party in government honestly and conscientiously believes the contrary. It believes that there is no necessity for the government to step in, even when new conditions and problems arise. It believes that in the long run, individual initiative and private philanthropy can take care of all situations. . . .
>
> In these later years, at least since 1932, the Democratic party has been the liberal party, and the Republican party has been the conservative party.[19]

Newspaper columnist and political commentator Patrick Buchanan, a former speechwriter for presidents Nixon and Reagan, entered in the 1992 Republican primaries as a way of voicing the dissatisfaction of some GOP conservatives. Buchanan won no primaries, but his persistent take of twenty to thirty percent of the vote caused President Bush considerable discomfort and gained protracted media attention.

In addition to offering these ideological choices, parties may also take opposing stands on specific issues that matter to voters. Recall from Chapter 7, for example, that voters found the issue choices for president more meaningful in 1992 than 1988. The conditions were different in 1992: The economy was stagnant; the incumbent president, George Bush, faced conservative competition from within his own party in the primaries, which in turn pushed several strong issues onto the platform; and an independent candidate, Ross Perot, stimulated issue discussion from both the major parties. "Inside the System" Box 9.2 illustrates how some of these political forces showed up as differences in the 1992 Republican and Democratic party platforms on a variety of issues.

INSIDE THE SYSTEM

The Politics Behind the Differences in the Republican and Democratic Party Platforms 1992

9.2

Party platforms reflect a combination of long-term ideological differences and short-term issue concerns of activist groups who try to take over the parties from within. The enduring liberal–conservative differences between the Democrats and Republicans generally show up most clearly in platform planks on the role of government and the economy. In some years

sharp issue differences also appear in the platforms. In 1992, for example, anti-abortion and "religious right" groups in the Republican party secured major representation on the platform committee. In part, this was because conservative Patrick Buchanan challenged George Bush in several presidential primaries, giving the conservatives a number of delegates at the convention and more political leverage over internal party poli-

tics. On the Democratic side, environmental groups secured strong representation, as did pro-abortion and homosexual rights activists. Neither party offered a strong future vision on foreign policy, reflecting the difficulty of charting a new course in a rapidly changing world. The Republicans emphasized their role in the downfall of communism, but this issue was not all that important in the minds of many voters. Some of these differences in the political choices offered by the parties are illustrated below.

Issue: The Role of Government

Democrats: We believe in an activist government, but it must work in a different, more responsive way. We [respect the marketplace], but economic growth will not come without a national economic strategy.

Republicans: We believe government has a legitimate role to play in our national life, but government must never dominate that life. . . . The Democrats argue that government must . . . override the market. Republicans regard the worst market failure as the failure to have a market.

Issue: The Economy

Democrats: America is on the wrong track. The American people are hurting. The American dream of expanding opportunity has faded. Middle class families are working hard, playing by the rules, but still falling behind. Poverty has exploded.

Republicans: Inflation has fallen. . . . Interest rates dropped. . . . Productivity has sharply risen. Exports are booming. Despite a global economic downturn . . . real economic growth resumed last year. . . .

With low interest rates and low inflation, the American economy is poised for stronger growth through the rest of the 1990s.

Issue: Abortion

Democrats: Democrats stand behind the right of every woman to choose, consistent with *Roe v. Wade.* . . .

Republicans: We believe the unborn child has a fundamental right to life which cannot be abridged.

Issue: Homosexual Rights

Democrats: Democrats will continue to lead the fight to ensure that no Americans suffer discrimination . . . [on the basis of] sexual orientation. . . .

Republicans: We oppose efforts by the Democratic party to include sexual preference as a . . . minority receiving preferential status under civil rights statutes. . . .

Issue: The Environment

Democrats: We will protect our old growth forests, preserve critical habitats. . . . and oppose new offshore oil drilling and mineral exploration and production in our nation's environmentally critical areas. . . .

Republicans: We have taught the world three vital lessons: First, environmental progress is integrally related to economic development. Second, economic

growth generates the capital to pay for environmental gains. Third, private ownership and economic freedom are the best security against environmental degradation.

Issue: Foreign Policy

Democrats: During the past four years, we have seen the corrosive effects of foreign policies that are rooted in the past, divorced from our values, fearful of change. . . . Under President Bush, crises have been managed rather than prevented; dictators like Saddam Hussein have been wooed rather than deterred. . . . human rights abusers have been rewarded, not challenged.

Republicans: Never in this century has the United States enjoyed such security from foreign enemies. With President Bush leading the free world, the Soviet Empire has collapsed. . . . Eastern Europe is liberated, Germany is peacefully united. . . . Israel and all of its Arab neighbors talk face to face for the first time. Nicaragua and Panama celebrate democracy.

Source: Democratic and Republican Party Platforms, 1992.

THE CHOICES FOR THE 1990s.   What choices are likely to divide the parties in the years ahead? According to one Democrat—Stuart Eizenstat, a former adviser to Jimmy Carter—the 1990s could open up broad differences in the following areas:[20]

- *Foreign vs. Domestic Policy*: With the end of the Cold War, traditional Republican advantages in foreign policy may become less important, while concerns about social problems at home may gain an edge. The results of the 1992 election indicate that Mr. Bush's significant accomplishments in foreign policy did not help him much. Look for the Republicans to turn to domestic issues by 1996.

- *Government industrial policy*: Democrats are more likely to propose government involvement in retooling the national economy, with education programs, job training, and research. The Republicans are more likely to take a hands-off position on economic development. This division also appeared in the 1992 race.

- *Tax fairness*: While the Republicans in the 1980s favored a reduced tax burden, the Democrats in the 1990s are talking about higher taxes for the wealthy. Both parties promise tax relief for the middle class.

- *Abortion*: Once regarded as a strong issue for the Republicans, the pro-life forces in the party have alienated some Republican moderates, and turned off voters who are pro-abortion rights. Democrats came out strongly for the right to abortion in 1992. Look for continued division on this issue.

ARE THE PARTY CHANNELS OPEN?   An important question is whether these choices are sweeping enough and credible enough to keep people looking to parties for realistic solutions to their problems. When parties are trusted and followed faithfully, political demands and discontents are kept channeled within the system. When parties are not effective in channeling discontent, society can become more volatile politically, as people look for other ways to express their frustrations.

An interesting comparison of the United States, Norway, and Sweden by political scientists Arthur Miller and Ola Listhaug indicates that while American parties appear to be offering people enough choices (as mentioned above), something is breaking down on the way to government. Americans have much less trust in the parties they vote for than do Swedes or Norwegians. Perhaps most alarming, Americans do not trust the government much more when their own party is in power. This may be an important sign that parties have lost their ability to convert promises into credible policies in the minds of voters. As a result, the American parties may have become poor channels for keeping social discontent within the formal institutions of government.[21]

Developing Leaders, Nominating Candidates

Parties bring young people into politics to work on campaigns, to serve as interns, to work on legislative committees, and eventually, to become leaders, run for office, and promote the interests of the party at higher levels of power and government. The success of a party depends in part on how well it recruits and promotes leaders. The health of a democracy depends on the ability of parties to bring good people into politics.

PARTY ORGANIZATION AND LEADERSHIP.   The activities of recruiting talent, backing candidates, and winning elections are coordinated in both the Democratic and Republican parties by a large internal organization. This organization consists of a system of state and national committees and conventions designed to promote internal dialogue, develop platforms, and nominate candidates at all levels of government. Although the party nominating procedures have grown more democratic, many of the key posts on party committees continue to be won on the basis of old fashioned horse-trading, influence, and power. It would be naive (and, many would argue, a mistake) to expect these most political of organizations to be run in entirely democratic ways. According to students of parties, the most effective organizations tend to be anything but democratic behind the scenes. Many observers think the pressures to make party organizations more democratic has further weakened an already loose party system. The conventional wisdom is that parties should thrive on insider politics behind the scenes, and let democracy begin at the voting booth.[22]

The grand authority in both the parties is the **national convention** that meets every four years to *nominate the presidential and vice presidential candidates.* These conventions also *approve the* **platforms** (written by party platform committees) that tell people what the parties stand for. Conventions also *adopt the official rules* that govern the parties and determine how the conventions themselves work.

Party organizations in the states recruit lower-level candidates, and have considerable control over the timing and procedures of primary elections, caucuses, and other methods used to select delegates to attend the national conventions. State legislatures also draw the boundaries of voting districts (recall the discussion from Chapter 7). National parties spend a great deal of money on state legislature races before a national census to try to improve their power positions in the negotiations over redrawing the national political map every ten years. The Republican party has angrily argued for years that Democratic advantages in state legislatures have resulted in unfair *gerrymandering* (see Chapter 7) which keeps Republicans out of Congress. It is certainly true that the Republicans have held less power in state governments (see Table 9.3), and it is probably true that Republicans get more votes in congressional elections than are reflected in the percentage of seats they get in Congress. However, it is surely a difficult argument to make, as did a member of the Republican National Committee, that "essentially, we have been gerrymandered out of the majority in the House of Representatives."[23]

Although state and local party organizations perform many important tasks, they have become less powerful over the years in choosing national candidates and influencing national party policy. Increasingly important are the **national committees,** which coordinate the state parties, organize national election campaigns, and run the parties in between the national conventions. The committees are large, with memberships running into the hundreds (the Republican National Committee is generally less than two hundred, the Democratic National Committee is generally more). Committee members include party insiders, state party officials, and people loyal to such key members of the party as state governors, powerful members of Congress, and the president. Each *national committee* is run by a full-time chairperson who raises money, coordinates election campaigns, and oversees the spending of election budgets that run into hundreds of millions of dollars. Separate committees exist in Congress (called *congressional election committees*) to run congressional campaigns.

The *party chairman or chairwoman* is generally a shrewd politician selected to fill a particular political need in the organization. For example, before Ron Brown became Secretary of Commerce in the Clinton administration in 1993, he was chairman of the Democratic party. Part of his job was to mend the rift between the party moderates and the more liberal supporters of Jesse Jackson who felt that they were not given enough attention in party platforms or in campaign strategy. After George Bush won the presidency in 1988, he used his influence in the party to appoint his campaign manager, Lee Atwater, as party chairman. This move was designed to keep the same loyal party machinery in place for the next election. However, Mr. Atwater died shortly thereafter, and Mr. Bush fell in public approval, opening the party to a power struggle in 1992 led by political commentator Patrick Buchanan.

With so many different factions and state organizations making up the national party organization, being **party chairman** is not like running most other kinds of organizations. The party chair cannot simply order things done or dictate the ideological tone of the issue agenda of the organization. Rather, the organization of the parties is a highly political affair requiring considerable diplomacy, horse-trading, and conferencing to keep the organizations together from one election to the next.

POWER AND RECRUITMENT INSIDE PARTIES. The main purpose of the party committee system is to build an organization to recruit and assist candidates to win as many public offices as possible. As mentioned above, there has been a breakdown at state and local party levels. Where national leaders in the past often had strong ties to local parties and officials such as mayors and governors who brought them into the political process, today's candidates for national office have much weaker ties at the local level, raising the earlier question of "Who sent them?" One study found that 95 percent of a sample of national congressional candidates had some contact with local parties, but few of those contacts were close enough to be described as having been "recruited" by, or having strong loyalties to, local parties.[24]

While local parties have grown weaker, national parties appear stronger in some areas such as coordinating election campaigns and giving out money to candidates. By 1990,

TABLE 9.3

Party Competition in the States, 1968–1990: Percentage of Republican Wins[a]

0–20%		21–40%	41–60%	61–80%	81–100%
Alabama	Mississippi	Illinois	Alaska	Arizona	Indiana
Arkansas	Missouri	Maine	Delaware	Colorado	New Hampshire
California	Nevada	Michigan	Iowa	Idaho	South Dakota
Connecticut	New Mexico	Montana	Nebraska[b]	Kansas	
Florida	North Carolina	New Jersey	New York	North Dakota	
Georgia	Oklahoma	Oregon	Ohio	Utah	
Hawaii	Rhode Island	Pennsylvania		Vermont	
Kentucky	South Carolina	Washington		Wyoming	
Louisiana	Tennessee	Wisconsin			
Maryland	Texas				
Massachusetts	Virginia				
Minnesota	West Virginia				

[a]The governorship, control of the lower chamber, and control of the upper chamber are figured separately. That is, if in a given year the Republicans won the governorship and control of one chamber, they had 66.7 percent of the wins.
[b]Results are for the governorship only because the legislature is nonpartisan.
SOURCES: 1968–1986: Republican National Committee, *Republican Almanac, 1987: State Political Profiles* (Washington, D.C.: Republican National Committee, 1987); 1987–1990: *Congressional Quarterly Weekly Report* (1988), 3298, (1990), 3840; National Conference of State Legislatures, unpublished data. Reprinted from Harold W. Stanley and Richard G. Niemi, *Vital Statistics on American Politics*, 3rd ed., Washington, D.C.: CQ Press, 1992, p. 138.

79 percent of Democratic and 83 percent of Republican party total resources were collected and given out by national party organizations.[25] At first glance, this might seem good for party unity since centralized parties can reward obedient members and punish disobedient ones. However, national parties themselves are often pulled in different directions by PAC influence and long lists of financial backers.[26] The loss of local recruitment functions and the weakness of national party discipline add to the concerns about how well the parties are providing for America's leadership.

NOMINATION PROCEDURES.   No matter where the recruits come from, parties still organize the procedures for nominating candidates for office. In the old days of party politics, the common image was the smoke-filled room, somewhere behind the scenes at the convention, where deals were made and party nominations were sent down to the voters from on high. A great series of reforms began in the parties after 1968, and the procedures for nominating candidates shifted from the power brokers in the back rooms to the direct democratic selection of delegates through state *primary elections* and *caucuses*. The importance of these changes for the way in which elections are run is discussed in Chapter 10. For now, we will just review the nuts and bolts of the procedures.

Political Pathfinders

When Bill Clinton and Al Gore *(below)* stood on the dais at Madison Square Garden in July 1992, then went on to win the White House, their victory was shared by a horde of volunteers, experts, consultants, and party officials. One such player was David Wilhelm *(right)*, Clinton's campaign director, who piloted the candidate's course along with campaign manager James Carville, pollster Stan Greenberg, and media expert Mandy Grunwald. Wilhelm subsequently became—with Clinton's backing—Democratic party chairman, a common reward for the triumphant politico. At about the same time, Haley Barbour *(above)*, became Republican party chairman after Rich Bond resigned that spot (a common sacrifice for the loser) following President Bush's defeat. Barbour, a Mississippi attorney and long-time party official, was the candidate most acceptable to the various GOP factions maneuvering for power in anticipation of the 1994 and 1996 elections.

The Players

In **caucus** states such as Iowa, Maine, and Washington, registered voters can go to party meetings in their voting precincts and directly select delegates to county and state conventions, from which delegates for national conventions are chosen. More common are **primary elections** which involve voting for competing candidates who seek a party's nomination for an office. Primary votes are actually cast for party delegates who go to national conventions pledged to support a particular candidate.

There are different ways in which primary elections can be organized. The most common model used in a majority of states is the **closed primary** in which voters have to declare their party preference before the election, and they are given that party's list of competing candidates when they go to the voting place. The idea here is to promote party loyalty and keep one party from using the primary as a way to defeat the other party's strongest candidates. The **open primary** allows voters to come to the voting place without declaring a party affiliation and to request one party's ballot or the other on election day. **Blanket primaries** are rare, and allow people to vote for candidates from both parties. Figure 9.3 illustrates the dramatic growth in the number of states that have adopted primaries as the method for choosing most of the delegates to the national party conventions.

Critics say that the move to more democratic nominating procedures was a serious mistake because:[27]

- Parties have become vulnerable to unstable collections of activists who try to take them over to promote particular issues.

- Experienced leaders who once worked their way up the party ranks may be rejected by voters who prefer "outsider" candidates who may have little experience and even less commitment to the party.

- These seemingly democratic nominating procedures really represent a false democracy since so few people participate in them. Turnouts in the primaries often run in the 20 percent range. Caucus and precinct convention attendance is even lower, often including only one or two percent of registered voters. This

FIGURE 9.3

States Using Presidential Primaries to Select Delegates to National Party Conventions

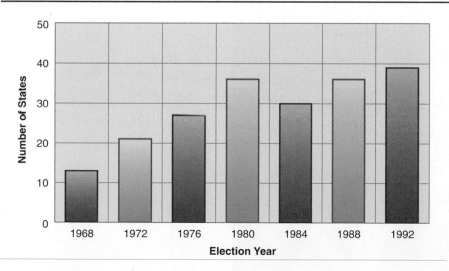

means that people who participate in nominating candidates may be out of step with the larger numbers of voters who turn out in the general elections later on.

PARTY DEMOCRACY.   The controversy over party democracy was taken to new heights by a California Democratic party plan in 1991 to select national convention delegates. The California primary is held late in the spring long after much smaller states such as Iowa, Maine, and New Hampshire have had considerable impact on the fates of candidates simply because they hold earlier caucuses or primaries. The California plan called for a two-stage selection process, beginning with a round of caucuses to select about 30 percent of the party convention delegates early in the election season around the first of March. Then the traditional primary would be held in June to choose the bulk of the remaining delegates. The idea would be to make the candidates come to California early, and make California a player all the way through the Democratic party presidential primary process. Critics from the Democratic National Committee worried that the California caucuses would be "commandeered by pressure groups," spreading the image of "West Coast liberalism" to the entire party, a result that one member of the national party Leadership Council described as a "political death wish by liberal activists."[28] Supporters of the plan disagreed with the assessment of national party insiders. Political historian James MacGregor Burns said: "Caucuses are the best one-word answer we have to big money and media manipulation [because they] attract knowledgeable local activists who evaluate candidates in terms of issues and who cannot be controlled."[29] Kay Lawson, a political scientist and California Democratic party activist, regarded the proposal as a way to restore the legitimacy of parties "so that they are more interesting to the electorate and so that they funnel more money from small contributors to the candidates."[30] A simpler plan was proposed in 1993 to move the primary to March.

None of the lively debate over party democracy implies that party insiders who attended conventions in the old days of smoke-filled rooms were more representative of the general population. As noted earlier, parties in the pre-1968 era made little pretense of internal democracy. Democracy was what took place after the party nominated its candidates. There is little doubt that the new system is more open than the old, but the fact remains that the activists who participate in today's nomination process do not look or think much like the general electorate who shows up on election day to cast a vote. Table 9.4 illustrates some of the differences of opinion between the delegates to the 1992

Patty Murray, freshman U.S. Senator from Washington state. In a year hostile to incumbents, Murray ran her 1992 campaign as "just a mom in tennis shoes," underplaying her credentials as a state senator. One function political parties serve is the recruiting and grooming of potential leaders, but many candidates minimize their party ties when dealing with voters.

TABLE 9.4

Opinions of 1992 Democratic Convention Delegates vs. Those of Democrats in the General Population

POLL QUESTION/ISSUE	CONVENTION DELEGATES (%) AGREEING	DEMOCRATS IN GENERAL* (%) AGREEING
Support more federal education spending	87 %	75 %
Believe too little spent on cities	79	64
Favor government-guaranteed medical care	91	82
Believe gov't should uphold family values	28	51
Believe abortion should be available to all	78	46
Favor economic aid to former Soviet Union	72	48

*Registered Voters
SOURCE: *New York Times* poll, reported July 13, 1992.

Democratic convention and members of the larger voting public who identified themselves as Democrats.

Who is right about the pros and cons of party democracy? Appealing arguments are made by supporters of open parties such as political scientist Leon Epstein who argues that American parties have seldom had strong national organizations, and the current era of party democracy is a healthy sign of adaptation in an age of voter mistrust of government.[31] On the other hand, opponents worry that the takeover of parties by citizen activists may create turmoil at the expense of building stable organizations for recruiting experienced national leaders. Besides, say the critics, whatever the causes of citizen mistrust may be, party democracy has not cured it. Opening up party nominating procedures to popular participation has not inspired greater voter confidence in candidates or in parties. How important do you think it is to have democracy within parties? You may want to add your voice to this important debate about democracy.

Governing

It is clear that today's parties are weakened by the rise of more independent candidates, disloyal incumbents, the single-issue politics of activists, and a decline in the recruitment function at the local level. However, other signs point to greater stability: more national committee control over party resources and more coordinated election campaigns. In Chapters 12 and 13 on Congress, we will also discover that party discipline in legislative voting has actually gone up over the last few decades. How can we evaluate the governing capacity of the parties?

The bottom line of party government is that in order to govern decisively, parties require sustained voter support. It is reasonable to ask whether any sweeping program of party action would be supported by most Americans. Why should we assume that there is some magic governing solution that would immediately win popular favor if only one of the two parties would promote it? If parties get elected by appealing to different groups on different issues, as they often do, they may have trouble maintaining everyone's support when they start doing things in government.

Americans may be eternally conflicted about how much party government they really want. *By party government here, we simply mean sweeping policy programs pushed by party supporters in all three branches of government for extended periods of time.* The relatively few periods in history when large numbers of voters have backed one party for long periods of time tend to have been times of national crisis and great social change. In this unwieldy two-party system, with its cultural and institutional limits, only crisis and social change may be able to override factional squabbles within the parties and weaken cultural taboos against too much centralized government power.

Political Crisis, Voter Alignments, and Party Government

According to one popular theory of elections and parties, the party system behaves closest to the three ideals outlined earlier when forced by crisis to do so. In the view of political scientist Walter Dean Burnham, coherent interest representation is frustrated by a broad two-party system and further weakened by separated institutions and many levels of federal government.[32] The result is that governments often neglect social problems or act ineffectively on them until crisis erupts: depressions, social protest movements, racial conflicts, urban decay, and in one extreme case, civil war.

During periods of national crisis or change, the parties finally begin to react and change because:

- voters threaten to switch their allegiance;
- new groups take over party conventions;
- politicians begin talking about new programs;
- ideas that have been circulating in society finally appear in party platforms and election appeals.

During these periods, parties propose new governing ideas and voters shift their party loyalties, often for long periods of time. A party is given a mandate to make changes and chart a new political course.

The Parties and Political Change

Such a period of electoral upheaval often develops over the course of several elections. This **critical election period** results in a new social power base for one party and a weakened support level for the other. The long-term voter shift is called a **party realignment.** In a realignment, large numbers of voters shift their support to a new party for an extended period of time, sometimes lasting several decades. In the periods following realignments, elections that maintain the party in power, indicating voter approval, are called **maintaining elections.** When the crisis passes, new issues begin to divide the party, resulting in occasional opposition victories that deviate from the current political alignment. These so-called **deviating elections** signal new social strains or discontent among the voters, which can build to another realignment or simply weaken the dominant party's mandate to govern.

This pattern of realignment, maintenance, and deviation has been described as a safety valve or tension management process in a weak or underdeveloped party system. Following from the work of V. O. Key who developed the idea of critical elections and party realignments, Walter Dean Burnham theorized about their significance:

Critical realignment emerges as decisively important in the study of . . . American politics. It is as symptomatic of political nonevolution in this country as are the archaic . . . structures of the political parties themselves. But even more importantly, critical realignment may be defined as the chief tension-management device available to so peculiar a political system. Historically, it has been the chief means through which an underdeveloped political system can be . . . brought once again into some balanced relationship with the changing socioeconomic system, permitting a restabilization of our politics.[33]

Such is the ever-tenuous connection between elections, parties, and government. In this view, the strongest electoral connections are forged through periods of great social tension and upheaval. Burnham has observed five periods of critical realignment in American history:

- the early 1800s, which saw the decline of the Federalists and the emergence of a national party system around the Jefferson-led Democratic-Republicans

- the period of 1828–1832, which drew the rapidly growing frontier society into national politics behind the leadership of Andrew Jackson and the new Democratic party

- the 1856–1860 period, when tension over race and economic development blew the party system apart, leaving Abraham Lincoln to lead the North into Civil War, and the newly formed Republican party to govern afterward on a program of national political and economic reconstruction

- the elections of 1896–1900, when industrialization and depression were squeezing the farmers of the Midwest and the workers in the cities, producing a decisive party split that saw many urban workers cast their political fortunes with the Republicans, who held the reins of government for much of the next thirty years

- the election period of 1932–1934, which registered voter discontent after the economic boom of the 1920s burst, throwing millions of workers out on the street and into the ranks of the Democrats, who dominated the national government for most of the next three decades.

The Party System Today

But something strange has happened in recent years. As noted in the last section, the parties have not done a good job of channeling social demands into government. There has been no new party alignment to adjust the political system to the social strains of the 1970s, 1980s, and early 1990s. Not even the Reagan revolution could be called a realignment. The blue-collar Reagan Democrats who swung their support to Ronald Reagan in the 1980s were still being courted by both parties in the 1990s, and many swung their votes to the Democrats or to Ross Perot in 1992.

More than one analyst suggested that instead of building toward a traditional realignment, what has happened to the American party system in recent years is better described as **dealignment**.[34] Voters were detaching from parties and seemed content to stay that way. Despite the evidence that many strains were building in society, the parties were not addressing them (at least to the satisfaction of voters): failing industry, banking collapse, national debt and budget deficits, chronic poverty, a generation of children growing up poorly prepared to take their places in a prosperous society (see Chapters 17, 18, and 19 for a look at these social problems).

In other words, the nation faced the kind of big-picture problems and issues that only broad party and electoral solutions could hope to address. Yet, as one team of observers

George and Barbara Bush embrace the cheers of delegates to the 1992 Republican convention in Houston. Bush served as the GOP's chairman in 1973–74, a difficult time; he was forced to fight for the party in the midst of the Watergate scandals.

President Ronald Reagan addresses the 1984 Republican convention in Dallas, Texas. Reagan helped to revitalize the Republican party in the mid-1970s, a time when it had been severely damaged by the Watergate affair. That scandal was at least partly the result of a campaign organization, CREEP (Committee to RE-Elect the President), which had run wild after it was allowed to function outside of the political party's control.

saw it, people were abandoning elections and parties as means of governing and turning, instead, to "politics by other means" such as interest groups. As political scientists Benjamin Ginsberg and Martin Shefter put it:[35]

> In the United States today the electoral process seems to be declining in importance. The electoral arena seems to be less decisive than we assume it to be under most democratic theories and less decisive than at any other time in our history. We are entering what could almost be called a post-electoral era in the United States.[36]

As explained in the next chapter, this period of party limbo may have been reinforced by an era of expensive campaigns aimed at marketing individual candidates who place little emphasis on parties as the solution to the nation's problems.[37]

The Charges Against the Parties Revisited

Understanding party politics inside the system helps in evaluating the charges presented at the beginning of this chapter. For example, party traits that are rooted in core aspects of culture and institutions are probably not likely to change. As a result, criticisms about the lack of strong centralized organization and discipline in the parties becomes less interesting simply because there is not a realistic alternative. On the other hand, if we decide that the current campaign financing system is introducing a needless amount of political pressure (or sheer chaos) into party programs and undermining the loyalty of candidates, perhaps there are reform possibilities that do make sense.

Charge Number 1: The parties lack distinctive governing visions and seldom offer clear choices to voters. It should be clear by now that two broad parties are not likely to disagree so sharply that they alienate large numbers of independent voters in the middle. However, ideological and issue choices become sharper when the right election

Candidate Ross Perot presses the flesh at a Kentucky rally shortly before the November 1992 election. Perot qualified for the ballot on all fifty states, but received no electoral votes. After the election, he continued to elude political labels, making his group United We Stand America, Inc. into a carefully formed legal entity.

conditions prevail (economic turmoil, third candidates, and so on). Figure 9.4 illustrates dramatic changes in voter perceptions of the party most likely to keep the country prosperous. The more troublesome problem related to choices seems to be that for some reason, people have lost confidence that the parties will do the right thing after they win power. It is less the choice problem than the channel problem (channeling public demands into government action) that seems worrisome.

Charge Number 2: Party choices (platforms and promises) are aimed more at getting elected than at governing afterwards. This may help explain part of the above "choice vs. channel" dilemma. As Chapter 10 makes clear, many of the issues that appear in elections are the products of marketing research aimed at winning votes. Voters have become increasingly skeptical about how strongly parties and candidates really stand behind those market-driven issues. In addition, when candidates do not stand behind the entire party program, they pick and choose the issues that work for their own elections. Recent elections raise serious questions about just how many Republican and Democratic candidates are willing to go to the voters to stand up for party programs.

FIGURE 9.4

The Party Better Able to Keep the United States Prosperous, 1951–1990

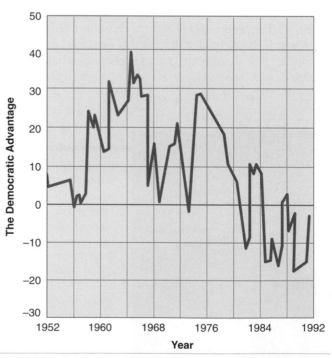

Note: Question: "Which political party—the Republican or the Democratic party—would do a better job of keeping the country prosperous? "Democratic advantage" is the percentage responding Democratic minus the percentage responding Republican.

Sources: The Gallup Report, October 1988, 5; *The Gallup Poll News Service,* vol. 55, no. 18, September 12, 1990, 1; and unpublished data from the Gallup Poll. Adapted from Harold W. Stanley and Richard G. Niemi, *Vital Statistics on American Politics,* 3rd ed. Washington, D.C.: CQ Press, 1992, p. 168.

A CITIZEN'S QUESTION Party Activism

*W*hat can I get out of working for a party? How can I find out how to become involved in party politics? The place to start thinking about your involvement with parties is with your own personal political agenda. If, for example, you are mainly interested in a single issue such as the environment or abortion, a political party may not be the best channel for your participation. Interest groups may offer more effective expression of your concerns. Also, as discussed in this chapter, single-issue activism may further weaken party organizations. In the aftermath of the 1992 election, for example, some Republican party leaders expressed concern that the party platform contained too many narrow issues that offended large numbers of voters, while providing few common themes that a broader majority could agree upon. A headline after the 1992 presidential defeat echoed the news stories discussed at the opening of this chapter: GOP RETHINKING FUNDAMENTALS OF PARTY SPECTRUM.[38] In this article, Republican strategist Vin Weber acknowledged that his party needed the votes of religious conservatives, pro-life activists, and other factions, but argued that the GOP had to be careful not to become identified as a collection of often-divisive issues and factions: "The main thing is we have to have a message that a lot of people will find more powerful than the messages that people disagree with. If that message ceases to exist. . . then the side fights are going to be what defines your party."[39]

*W*hen becoming active in a party, then, think about promoting a larger vision of society. Consider the political reasons why one party or the other might be more effective in bringing your vision to life. For example, many people these days are talking about new economic ideas. Political parties are important forums for debating those ideas and for proposing ways of putting them into practice. Perhaps you are more concerned about broad social concerns such as health, education, and housing.

*I*f you become convinced that neither party is likely to take your social visions seriously, then there is always the third-party alternative.

However, before heading in that direction, try applying some of the lessons from this chapter. When considering a third party, be clear about your (and the party's) goals. If the party aims at bringing neglected ideas to national attention, fine. If the goal is to force the other parties to consider new ideas, fine again. But do not become discouraged when you discover that winning protest votes does not translate into winning elections.

*O*nce your motives for party participation have become clear, it makes sense to get involved where the action is in parties: in the nomination process for candidates likely to support your ideas. Involvement in the candidate selection process can be rewarding in many ways. For example, it may be possible to get inside political primary campaigns because many early candidates have few resources and small organizations. There is always room for volunteers. It is also possible to be selected to go to local and state party conventions where grassroots activists can have considerable impact.

*I*f you want to find out more about party activities near you, the national party committees will help you get in contact with your state party organizations. For the numbers of state Democratic party organizations, call the Association of State Democratic Chairs (an office of the Democratic National Committee in Washington, D.C.). The phone number is:

202-479-5121

*F*or information about state Republican party activities, call the Information Services Department of the Republican National Committee. (You can also request an information packet on the history of the Republican party and what the party stands for). The number is:

202-863-8790

Charge Number 3: Parties have been corrupted and weakened by interest-group money and influence. In part, the problem of candidate loyalty may be a historic dilemma of weak parties in a two-party system. However, it is clear that the party system of a hundred years ago exacted greater loyalty from candidates and members of Congress simply because the party organizations were much more controlling than they are today, punishing members of government who did not follow the party program. Today's incumbents are much more independent of their parties because they have their own funding, meaning that the PAC and interest-group system has probably weakened party loyalty. The greatest single effect of interest-group pressures may simply be in loading the national political agenda up with so many small issues that it becomes difficult for the parties and governments to focus on broader governing programs.

Charge Number 4: Party breakdown has undermined leadership in America. This is a tricky charge to evaluate because leadership in America has often been a very individual process to begin with. Where many other nations look to party organizations for leadership (meaning that individual politicians are not as important), Americans have often rallied around strong or charismatic individuals. Still, there is reason to worry that if individual leaders have less personal loyalty to party organizations, they may not govern as effectively after they win office. In addition, it is clear that parties are not serving as recruitment organizations for new political talent the way they once did.

On balance, some of the problems of American parties stem from enduring cultural and institutional features of the political system. However, other problems reflect recent institutional changes, such as campaign-finance reforms and more open nominating procedures. In addition, changing patterns of power in society, such as social movements and interest-group activity, continue to affect parties, creating hope for a return of stronger party government in the future.

Key Terms

political functions of parties

differences between parties, interest groups, social movements

four commonly expressed criticisms of parties

five major parties in American history

reasons for a two-party system

single-member congressional districts

winner-take-all elections

characteristics of multiparty systems

characteristics of the American party system

cultural

institutional

social power patterns

party organization

national party committee

national convention

platforms

party chair

nominating procedures

primary elections

open primaries/closed primaries/blanket primaries

caucuses

crisis theory of strong party government

party-voter relationships

realignment/critical elections

maintaining elections

deviating elections

dealignment

Suggested Readings

Burnham, Walter Dean. *Critical Elections and the Mainsprings of American Politics.* New York: Norton, 1970.

Epstein, Leon D. *Political Parties in the American Mold.* Madison: University of Wisconsin Press, 1986.

Ferguson, Thomas, and Joel Rogers. *Right Turn: The Decline of the Democrats and the Future of American Politics.* New York: Hill and Wang, 1986.

Kayden, Xandra, and Eddie Mahe, Jr. *The Party Goes On.* New York: Basic Books, 1985.

Sorauf, Frank J., and Paul Allen Beck. *Party Politics in America,* 6th ed. Glenview, Ill.: Scott Foresman, 1988.

Conventions deserve to be sustained—and to be given a fair break on television. Conventions are the [focal points] of the system that for two centuries brought a measure of stability to American politics. The crumbling away of parties would transfer political power to personalist movements, founded not on historic organizations but on compelling personalities, private fortunes, and popular frustrations. Political adventurers would roam the countryside like. . . warlords, building personal armies equipped with electronic technologies. Without the stabilizing influence of parties, American politics would grow angrier, wilder, and more irresponsible. Maybe that is already happening.
—*ARTHUR SCHLESINGER, JR.*

A modern presidential candidate comes close to living in a world where every waking hour is recorded on videotape, and I actually encouraged that as a way of drawing attention to my [1988] campaign [during the Democratic primaries]. I had cameras come into my bedroom while I was still woozy in the morning. I had cameras with me when I went to buy a Christmas tree with my kids. I remember the time a documentary crew. . . filmed an NBC crew. . . filming me. . . as I watched myself in a monitor. The whole scene was in danger of spiraling. . . into infinity.
—*BRUCE BABBITT*

Campaigns and Elections: The Political Guidance System

- **CAMPAIGNS TRY TO BEAT, NOT MEET, THE PRESS**
- **ELECTIONS AND AMERICAN DEMOCRACY**
  Direct vs. Representative Democracy
- **A BRIEF HISTORY OF ELECTIONS**
- **GETTING ELECTED: THE NUTS AND BOLTS**
  The Nomination
  The Convention
  The Campaign
- **GETTING ELECTED: THE POLITICAL REALITY**
  The Great Money Chase
  Marketing the Candidates
  Media Management
- **THE SELLING OF THE PRESIDENT 1988**
- **THE SELLING OF THE PRESIDENT 1992**
- **REFORMING THE SYSTEM**
- **ELECTIONS AND AMERICAN DEMOCRACY REVISITED**
- **A CITIZEN'S QUESTION: Elections Beyond Voting**
- **KEY TERMS**
- **SUGGESTED READINGS**

Campaigns Try to Beat, Not Meet, the Press

The big news about the election of 1992 was that candidates found ways to bypass the press and use television to go directly to the people. Under the headline CAMPAIGNS DO THEIR BEST TO BEAT, NOT MEET, THE PRESS, one story put it this way:

> For under $500,000, a Presidential candidate can now buy his own program. If that is out of reach, he can appear on *Larry King Live* to answer questions from his mom. And if worst comes to worst, he can beat the press with his running mate on *Donahue*.
>
> All season long, the Presidential candidates have been avoiding traditional political programs like CBS's *Face the Nation* or ABC's *This Week* in favor of what might be called less challenging formats.[1]

Independent candidate Ross Perot, an immensely wealthy businessman, spent over $60 million of his own money on the campaign, much of it on producing and airing his own programs—*after* his campaign had first been launched and then boosted by free appearances on CNN's *Larry King Live*. One of Mr. Perot's half-hour talks to the nation received better ratings than the entertainment programs on the other channels, and even outdrew a baseball playoff game that followed it.[2]

A news story titled IF YOU CAN'T BEAT 'EM, BYPASS 'EM quoted academic experts saying that new patterns of power and information were emerging in campaigns. It appeared that voters preferred to listen to candidates directly, via non-news television formats.[3] Did the new campaigning signal a basic change in the way Americans elected their leaders? That was the claim in a story that ran under the headline ELECTION '92: THE YEAR OF THE TRULY WEIRD:

> It's hard to say what it all adds up to. But there is something about seeing the president of the United States . . . Leader of the Free World . . . Most Powerful Man on Earth . . . fielding questions on MTV two days before the election. Something that says: The rules have forever changed.[4]

If the rules for playing the election game have changed, it would not be the first time. In 1860, when Abraham Lincoln's opponent Stephen Douglas went around the country delivering his own speeches, people were scandalized that anyone seeking the nation's highest office would stoop so low as to campaign for himself. Even though Lincoln was one of the nation's most popular speakers, he did the proper thing and stayed home in Illinois, saying not a word in his own behalf, leaving the work of getting himself elected to others. The idea of candidates engaging in the whole range of full-service campaigning—going out on the campaign trail, delivering speeches, showing up at conventions to accept the nomination and rally the party—did not become fully accepted until the 1930s. The scandalous idea of advertising candidates the same way that deodorants, detergents, or automobiles are sold did not become fully accepted until the 1960s. As late as the 1956 election, Democratic challenger Adlai Stevenson spoke harshly against what he regarded as Republican president Dwight Eisenhower's "disgraceful" use of television ads to promote his reelection.

Some critics think the new media formats may be too easy on candidates, allowing them to dodge the tough questions. In an article headlined BYPASSING THE PRESS HELPS CANDIDATES; DOES IT ALSO SERVE THE PUBLIC INTEREST?, media expert Stephen Hess of the Broookings Institution expressed this concern: "We had a talk-show campaign. Will we have a talk-show presidency?"[5] Political scientist Michael Robinson worried that the appeal of the talk show campaign was not healthy for the national interest because it promoted too much selfishness in voters: "There is nothing more self-centered than an audience of untrained voters who ask the same question: [What about] me, me, me [?]" While interesting, these concerns beg the questions of what an audience of "trained" voters would look like, much less, whether they react less selfishly to information from the usual channels of news programs and campaign advertising.

Some observers say that even before the introduction of talk-show campaigning in 1992, campaigns and elections had already become too personalized. Candidates have long used news and advertising to offer easy emotional appeals to voters. By contrast, candidates taking unpopular stands on difficult issues have often felt the sting of opponents and the wrath of voters. For example, Democratic presidential candidate Walter Mondale was destroyed in 1984 for saying, among other things, that the nation *needed* a tax increase to take a responsible approach to the budget. Mondale complained about winning candidates who feed voters "fantasies" with promises of tax cuts while the budget deficit ran out of control: "We've got a kind of politics of irrelevance."[6] Said Republican representative Mickey Edwards of Oklahoma, "We've tended to trivialize issues to the point where meaningful debate has become almost impossible."[7]

For all the concerns that the talk-show format has further trivialized elections, however, voters found the 1992 contest more satisfying than other recent elections in issue content and interest level. Who then is right about the quality of our most important collective political experience? In deciding what kind of campaigning is most "appropriate" and useful, it first helps to decide what an election is all about. What purpose do elections in fact serve? What is at stake? The methods of campaigning cannot be understood or evaluated without a sense of how elections fit into the larger scheme of democracy and government.

This chapter explores the role of elections, with an emphasis on the political factors behind the scenes that affect how (and how well) elections work. It turns out that there are factors that run deeper than talk shows that affect how well elections serve their purpose of addressing and solving national problems—problems that, if left unattended, can divide society and undermine faith in government itself. It is important to consider such factors as party breakdowns and the interest-group financing of campaigns introduced in Chapters 8 and 9. Whether candidates meet the press or beat the press, the more important issue may be whether or not elections provide a forum for realistic explorations of national problems and proposals for solving them. In the pages that follow, we explore the workings of contemporary campaigns with an eye to the political forces inside the system that affect the quality of the national political dialogue. You will also discover how citizens can do more than just vote in elections by joining one of the many citizen efforts to improve the election process.

Ross Perot on Larry King Live. *The billionaire businessman's numerous appearances on the cable-television talk show, which highlighted his folksy persona and cracker-barrel homilies, ultimately served as a springboard for him to enter the 1992 presidential race as an independent candidate, bypassing both political parties and the resulting primary exposure.*

Elections and American Democracy

Elections are the guidance system of the modern democracy, addressing popular concerns in ways that adjust (or fail to adjust) government to the political conflicts and tensions in society. In the process of electing representatives to national office, elections serve at least four broad political functions:

- **The debate function:** Problems are discussed (or not), solutions are proposed (or not), and individual candidates stand behind party programs (or don't).

- **The leadership function:** Voters screen candidates as leaders, and decide who is most likely to represent their interests, handle crises well, and otherwise provide the kind of authority they are looking for.

- **The accountability function:** Whether or not voters *initially* trust parties or candidates to keep their promises, they can vote retrospectively by looking back at the past two or four years to see if a particular candidate or party delivered on the issues that mattered. Without accountability, the idea of representation would mean little, and democracy would lose its meaning as a system defined by popular sovereignty.

- **The participation function:** Elections are the one universal mode of participation in American politics, allowing people to peacefully interact together or against one another in an organized fashion. Without elections, participation could be chaotic and quite possibly destructive.

Direct vs. Representative Democracy

The framers of the Constitution generally opposed granting too much decision power *directly* to the people. The form of democracy they designed was limited in a number of ways. Most importantly, the involvement of people in government decisions was limited to the periodic **election of representatives** who would decide for them. There have been debates ever since over whether citizens should have more direct involvement in government decisions. Over the years since the founding, voters in twenty-one states have secured more **direct democracy** in the form of **initiatives** that enable citizens to propose laws and put them on the ballot by getting the required number of signatures on petitions. In half the states, voters can petition to hold a **referendum,** which puts a particular law passed by the state legislature up for review by the voters.[8]

In 1992, citizens in different states voted on a variety of ballot initiatives. A partial list includes:

- Maryland voters eased restrictions on abortion.
- Arizona voters defeated an initiative that would have increased restrictions on abortion.
- Massachusetts voters defeated an initiative to impose tighter regulations on product packaging.
- California voters defeated a measure that would have required all employers to provide health care to employees.
- Colorado voters passed a measure denying homosexuals special protection against discrimination.
- Oregon voters defeated a move to decrease taxes for renters and increase taxes on some kinds of property.

TABLE 10.1

Support for "Direct Democracy"

PROPOSAL	PERCENTAGE (%) AGREEING
1. Give citizens in your state the right of "initiative."	92%
2. Establish the right of initiative for federal legislation.	85
3. Provide for a referendum on annual state budget.	80
4. Provide for constitutional amendment requiring national referendum on federal tax increases.	72
5. Provide for recall elections of public officials.	84
6. Provide for constitutional amendment requiring balanced budget every year.	84

Questions:
1. There are several other rights that some states give their citizens to provide them with a way of influencing their government. The right of citizens to sign a petition to have a law placed on the ballot for a vote by everyone is called the "initiative." In general, do you favor or oppose giving citizens the initiative in your state?
2. Would you favor or oppose giving citizens the right to petition the federal government to have a law placed on the ballot for national elections?
3. In some states certain proposals must be on the ballot so that everyone has an opportunity to vote on them. This is called a "referendum." In general, do you favor or oppose requiring a referendum on the annual budget of your state?
4. Would you favor or oppose a constitutional amendment to require that any federal tax increase be voted on in a national referendum by the general public?
5. Some states permit citizens to sign petitions asking for a recall election for an elected public official. When enough signatures are obtained, a special election is held where the voters can vote a public official out of office. Would you favor or oppose giving citizens the right to have a recall election where they can vote an elected state or local official out of office?
6. Would you favor or oppose a constitutional amendment that would require Congress and the President to provide a balanced budget every year?

SOURCE: Survey by Gordon S. Black Corporation, May 1992. Adapted from *The Public Perspective,* November/December 1992, p. 5.

- South Dakota voters defeated a proposal to end the state video lottery.
- Fourteen states passed measures to limit the terms that U.S. senators and representatives can serve. (This topic is discussed further in Chapter 13.)

As the poll results shown in Table 10.1 indicate, the idea of expanding the forms of direct democracy is extremely popular. However, observers disagree about how desirable these experiences with direct democracy truly are. One political consultant has called initiatives "a rare and precious flowering of democracy . . . controlled neither by right, left, nor special interests, but by the people." Consultants may, of course, profit from running initiative campaigns. A Maryland state representative took a less flowery view:

Demonstrators hold a candlelight vigil protesting Colorado's "Amendment 2" proposition, an amendment to the state constitution intended to refuse homosexuals special anti-discrimination protection on the basis of sexual preference. A majority of Colorado voters voted for the proposition, but the measure's foes continued to contest its legality.

"Initiatives and referendums are just as vulnerable to special interests and corruption as any other political process." Views among political scientists are also divided. Some agree with Thomas Cronin, who claims: "The initiative and referendum are worthwhile because legislators can be ponderously resistant to innovation and needed change." Others share the view of Eugene Lee who says, "The initiative has become a political monster."[9]

How much direct democracy is a good thing? The answer to this question depends in part on *cultural* attitudes about the desirability of grass-roots participation. In addition, the evolution of direct democracy depends on the *institutional arrangements* that balance the ease and the citizen responsibilities of direct participation. Finally, direct democratic participation may be more or less desirable depending on how political *power* is distributed among voters, interest groups, and elites in society. Political conditions in some societies favor more direct democracy than is practiced in the United States. Some of the strengths and weaknesses of greater direct democracy in Switzerland are noted in "How We Compare" Box 10.1.

In poll after poll (see Table 10.1, for example), Americans report that they favor more chances at the national level to vote directly on the issues that affect them.[10] With the advent of sophisticated electronic communication, there is more talk than ever before of more direct national participation. Will national elections of the future include more in the way of direct democracy? Are the talk-show candidates and electronic "town halls" of 1992 forerunners of things to come? If history is any guide, it would be naive to reject such changes simply because they seem new and startling at the present time. Most of the national election procedures we live with today reflect changes that many people regarded as unlikely or undesirable in times gone by.

A Brief History of Elections

Americans live with one of the most complicated election systems in the world. Like many of the other complications in American politics, the electoral system began with the Constitution. Many state leaders, including a majority of those who came to the

Direct Democracy, Anyone?

10.1

Of all the forms of participation available to Americans, the one that remains the most illusive is direct democracy, the chance to debate and vote on the actual laws and decisions that affect our lives. With the exception of initiatives and referenda, all of the other forms of electoral participation are aimed at influencing the behavior of representatives. Direct voter initiatives and referenda are used in about half the states, and not at all on the national level. Is more direct democracy desirable? That is a good question.

Switzerland is a nation that practices a much greater degree of direct democracy than the U.S. By getting 100,000 signatures on a petition, Swiss citizens can propose and vote on constitutional amendments. What's more, all constitutional amendments have to be submitted to direct vote by the people. Ordinary laws are also voted on in general elections, and many are based on popular initiatives and petition drives. What are the results? Obviously, Switzerland is a stable, well-functioning society where the trains run on time, the roads and trams are in good repair, the public schools are well funded, and people vote themselves a hefty tax bill to pay for it all. This in a society with three official languages, considerable economic diversity, and distinct regional differences.

On the down side, not all is idyllic in this alpine paradise. Chemical companies continue to pollute the rivers and seem to get away with it. Big banks operate in the shadow of the law. The constitution is often cluttered with amendments such as one calling for national hiking trails. And despite support in the national parliament, laws granting the vote to women were defeated by men in national elections until 1971. Participation suffers as well. Partly because of the number of elections being held all the time, national voting rates are even lower than in the U.S. Still, the Swiss system creates a strong sense of public accountability, something that many Americans feel their system lacks these days.

SOURCE: Based in part on Jurg Steiner, *European Democracies.* New York: Longman, 1986, ch. 8.

Philadelphia Convention in 1787, feared letting a democracy run out of control. Attempts to agree on a national election process went through many (at least seven) rounds of revisions at Philadelphia, including two proposals for popular election of the president that were defeated by huge majorities of the delegates.[11] It is impressive that any agreements could be reached at all on such institutions as the Senate (originally elected by state legislatures), the House (elected by direct votes in the states, but with varying state restrictions on voting eligibility), and the president (chosen by electors, who were selected by methods left to state legislatures).

This mix of election procedures, with many of the important details left up to the states, began to change almost as soon as it was put in practice. Over the years, parts have been discarded while new customs and rules have been adopted around the core of the electoral college. As explained in Chapter 3, the electoral college has endured despite having quickly departed from its original function. The role of the electoral college system in today's elections is explained below.

As noted in Chapter 9, political parties quickly entered the national picture, further changing the election system. In the first elections, party caucuses in Congress recommended presidential candidates to state legislatures, who selected members of the electoral college, who voted on the party candidates. This system quickly produced a constitutional crisis (described in Chapter 3), leading to the Twelfth Amendment and another series of changes in election procedures worked out in the states and by the parties. Between the 1830s and 1850s, more practices resembling modern elections began to appear. Parties began to nominate candidates for president and vice president at conventions, where party activists also drafted platforms to explain to the voters what they stood for. For the first time, parties organized voter support through national campaigns and began pledging that their slates of electors in presidential elections would abide by the will of the majority of voters in the states. Parties began competing for supporters by using their power in state legislatures to engineer popular changes in state election laws. For example, by 1832 all but two states had electors chosen directly by voters (though many states continued to limit participation based on income, race, and sex).

As the electorate expanded, election reform movements became stronger. Pressures increased on the parties to open up the process for nominating candidates. By 1916, half the states held presidential primaries for at least one party, and slightly more than half the delegates at the Democratic and Republican party conventions were selected by some sort of direct citizen input. Around this time, women also pressed for and won (in the Nineteenth Amendment, ratified in 1920) the right to vote. In a backlash against these trends, many state parties abandoned primary elections during the period from the mid-1920s through the mid-1960s, restoring much of the power in candidate nomination to party activists.

Another major wave of election reforms followed the social upheavals of the 1960s, beginning with the Voting Rights Act of 1965 (aimed at halting discrimination against blacks). After the riot-scarred Democratic party convention of 1968, both parties expanded the use of primaries and caucuses to increase direct voter input in the nomination process. Since then, the overwhelming majorities of the delegates at both parties' conventions have been sent by voters (the number varies by party and year).

It is natural that changes in election rules and practices that determine who is allowed to participate are accompanied by changes in the methods of campaigning used to win the support of those voters. As noted at the start of this chapter, it was not until 1860 that a major presidential candidate actively campaigned in his own behalf, and not until this century that the custom became established as an unquestioned part of campaigns. Other features of campaigns that we take for granted today were added over the years. Candidates began appearing at conventions in the 1930s to accept their party nomination and rally the troops for the campaign ahead. By the 1950s, commercial advertising techniques were used to sell candidates to voters. Most recently, candidates have begun appearing on talk shows and entertainment programs.

What does today's election and campaign system look like? How does it work? The remainder of the chapter explores these questions with an eye to the impact of today's election process on the ability of the winners to govern.

National Guardsmen halt protesters outside Chicago's Convention Hall during the Democratic National Convention there in the summer of 1968. The party gathering came soon after the assassinations of Senator Robert Kennedy and the Reverend Martin Luther King, Jr., and was disrupted by protests (largely by anti-Vietnam War groups), which in turn met a harsh response from the police force of Chicago's autocratic mayor, Richard Daley. These ugly confrontations led the two major parties— especially the Democrats—to revamp their primary and nomination rules.

Getting Elected: The Nuts and Bolts

Since the politics and procedures for getting elected are in a constant state of evolution, it is less important to remember every detail than to grasp the broad overview of an election. Later in the chapter we talk specifically about campaigns for the House and Senate, but this overview describes a presidential election, beginning with the first step of how candidates win a nomination.

The Nomination

Presidential hopefuls trudge through the snows of Iowa and New Hampshire a full year before the general election; this news image is a reminder of how long the American election runs. The early stories about the Iowa and New Hampshire campaigns also bring to mind the different state and party practices that go into nominating a candidate for president: Iowa is a caucus state, while New Hampshire is a primary state. (Refer back to the discussion of primaries and caucuses in Chapter 9 to refresh your memory about the differences.) There is no simple way to remember which states have primaries and which use caucuses. Since these are processes run by the state political parties, some states may have a primary for one party and a caucus procedure for the other. Even if you remembered all the specifics for one election, there would be some changes by the next one. Tables 10.2 and 10.3 illustrate the caucus and primary states, along with the timing of different state activities for the Democratic and Republican parties during the 1992 presidential nomination season. Out of the different state selection procedures come delegates sent to the national party conventions in the summer, where those delegates cast votes for the party nominees to run in the national presidential election in the fall.

The name of the primary game is to win enough delegates to clinch a majority of (or at least have the most) delegates at the party convention. When races for the nomination are competitive, as they often are, serious candidates must run early and run often. One observer headlined a discussion of nomination strategy simply—THE ONLY STRATEGY: START EARLY. While not quite the whole story, it is clear that candidates cannot afford to be left out of the media race that begins in Iowa and New Hampshire.

Although national parties have tried to limit the media impact of victories in these small states by pressuring state parties to hold their selection procedures closer to the same time, many states continue to set their own schedules because it increases their power and prominence in the presidential process. For example, the Democratic party has officially declared a period from early March until mid-June as the time frame for delegate selection, yet a number of states such as Iowa and New Hampshire violate the request, leaving the national party no choice but to grant them "exceptions."

Even states that stay within the time period may adjust their schedules to create strategic advantages for local or regional interests. In the 1980s, a block of southern states began to hold their primaries simultaneously to compel candidates to pay attention to their interests. The adopted date was the second Tuesday in March, a day that quickly became known as "Super Tuesday." Soon other states began moving into the same time slot, to get their share of the candidates' attention. Many states now crowd the primary calendar in early March, as a quick glance at the tables reveals.

A campaign develops its strategies based on the scheduling of the primaries and the appeals the candidate has in different states and regions. Even candidates who break out of the pack in the early primaries can stumble on Super Tuesday and fall out of the race. At times, candidates who show poorly in the early primaries can focus their efforts on the South and recoup with a good showing in March. For example, the Bush campaign manager in 1988, Lee Atwater, explained how he brilliantly dealt with the likely prospect

TABLE 10.2

The Road to the 1992 Democratic Presidential Nomination

Dates for primaries (P) and caucuses (C) to select delegates to the 1992 Democratic National Convention.
Delegate total is 4,287, including 771 superdelegates certified throughout the process.

DATE		STATE, GROUP, OR TERRITORY	PRIMARY OR CAUCUS	DELEGATES AT STAKE	CUMULATIVE DELEGATE TOTAL	PERCENT OF TOTAL DELEGATES
FEBRUARY	10	Iowa	C	49	49	1.14
	18	New Hampshire	P	18	67	1.56
	23	Maine	C	23	90	2.10
	25	South Dakota	P	15	105	2.45
MARCH	3	American Samoa	C	3	108	2.52
		Colorado	P	47	155	3.62
		Georgia	P	76	231	5.39
		Maryland	P	67	298	6.95
		Minnesota	C	78	376	8.77
		Idaho	C	18	394	9.19
		Utah	P	23	417	9.73
		Washington	C	71	488	11.38
	5–19	North Dakota	C	14	502	11.71
	7–9	Democrats abroad	C	7	509	11.87
	7	Arizona	C	41	550	12.83
		South Carolina	P	43	593	13.83
		Wyoming	C	13	606	14.14
	8	Nevada	C	17	623	14.53
	10	Delaware	C	14	637	14.86
		Florida	P	148	785	18.31
		Hawaii	C	20	805	18.78
		Louisiana	P	60	865	20.18
		Missouri	C	77	942	21.97
		Mississippi	P	39	981	22.88
		Oklahoma	P	45	1,026	23.93
		Rhode Island	P	22	1,048	24.45
		Tennessee	P	68	1,116	26.03
		Texas	P	196	1,312	30.60
		Massachusetts	P	94	1,406	32.80
	17	Illinois	P	164	1,570	36.62
		Michigan	P	131	1,701	39.68
	24	Connecticut	P	53	1,764	40.91
	28	Virgin Islands	C	3	1,767	40.98
	31	Vermont	C	14	1,771	41.31
APRIL	2	Alaska	C	13	1,784	41.61
	5	Puerto Rico	P	51	1,835	42.80
	7	Kansas	P	36	1,871	43.64
		New York	P	244	2,115	49.34
		Wisconsin	P	82	2,197	51.25
	11–13	Virginia	C	78	2,275	53.07
	28	Pennsylvania	P	169	2,444	57.01
MAY	3	Guam	C	3	2,447	57.08
	5	D.C.	P	17	2,464	57.48
		Indiana	P	77	2,541	59.27
		Ohio	P	151	2,692	62.79
		North Carolina	P	84	2,776	64.75
	12	Nebraska	P	25	2,801	65.34
		West Virginia	P	31	2,832	66.06
	19	Oregon	P	47	2,879	67.16
	26	Kentucky	P	52	2,931	68.37
		Arkansas	P	36	2,967	69.21
JUNE	2	Alabama	P	55	3,022	70.49
		California	P	348	3,370	78.61
		New Jersey	P	105	3,475	81.06
		New Mexico	P	25	3,500	81.64
		Montana	P	16	3,516	82.02
"Superdelegates" who can declare their allegiance to a particular candidate at any time				771	4,287	100.00
Needed to nominate					**2,144**	**50.01**

Source: Democratic National Committee

TABLE 10.3

The Road to the 1992 Republican Presidential Nomination

Dates for primaries (P) and caucuses (C) to select delegates to the 1992 Republican National Convention. Delegate total is 2,210. Unlike the Democrats, The Republican party has no "superdelegates"—elected officials and other dignitaries who are automatic delegates by virtue of their status.

DATE	STATE, GROUP, OR TERRITORY	PRIMARY OR CAUCUS	DELEGATES AT STAKE	CUMULATIVE DELEGATE TOTAL	PERCENT OF TOTAL DELEGATES
JANUARY 25–31	Hawaii	C	14	14	0.6
FEBRUARY 10	Iowa	C	23	37	1.6
18	New Hampshire	P	23	60	2.7
25	South Dakota	P	19	79	3.5
6–29	Nevada	C	21	100	4.5
Varying dates	Guam	*	4	104	4.7
	Wyoming	C	20	124	5.6
MARCH 2	Alaska	C	19	143	6.4
3	Colorado	P	37	180	8.1
	Georgia	P	52	232	10.4
	Maryland	P	42	274	12.3
	Minnesota	C	32	306	13.8
	Washington	C	35	341	15.4
7	South Carolina	P	36	377	17.1
10	Florida	P	97	474	21.4
	Louisiana	P	38	512	23.1
	Massachusetts	P	38	550	24.8
	Oklahoma	P	34	584	26.4
	Rhode Island	P	15	599	27.1
	Tennessee	P	45	644	29.1
	Texas	C	121	765	34.6
15	Puerto Rico	P	14	799	36.1
17	Illinois	P	85	864	39.1
	Michigan	P	72	936	42.3
19	American Samoa	*	4	940	42.5
24	Connecticut	P	35	975	44.1
28	Virgin Islands	*	4	979	44.2
31	Vermont	C	19	998	45.1
Varying dates	Maine	C	22	1,020	46.1
APRIL 7	Kansas	P	30	1,050	47.5
	New York	P	100	1,150	52.0
14	Missouri	C	47	1,197	54.1
18	Mississippi	C	34	1,231	54.7
27	Utah	C	27	1,258	56.9
28	Pennsylvania	P	91	1,349	61.0
Varying dates	Delaware	*	19	1,368	61.9
	Virginia	C	55	1,423	64.3
MAY 5	District of Columbia	P	14	1,472	66.6
	Indiana	P	51	1,523	68.9
	North Carolina	P	57	1,580	71.4
	Ohio	P	83	1,663	75.2
10	Arizona	C	37	1,700	76.9
12	Nebraska	P	24	1,724	78.0
	West Virginia	P	18	1,742	78.8
19	Oregon	P	23	1,765	79.8
26	Arkansas	P	27	1,792	81.1
	Idaho	P	22	1,814	82.1
Varying dates	Kentucky	P	35	1,849	83.6
	Wisconsin	C	35	1,884	85.2
JUNE 2	Alabama	P	38	1,887	85.3
	California	P	201	2,088	94.4
	Montana	P	20	2,108	95.3
	New Jersey	P	60	2,168	98.0
6	New Mexico	P	25	2,193	99.2
9	North Dakota	P	17	2,210	100.0
Needed to nominate				**1,106**	**50.04**

* Selected by other methods.

Source: Republican National Committee

of a lackluster showing in Iowa (friendly territory for midwestern contender Bob Dole) and the dangers of Vice President Bush's being portrayed as a loser by the media:

> I didn't see how we could win in Iowa. We decided that we should never say that publicly and that we should fight hard in Iowa but we had to be prepared to lose in Iowa. We thought there would be a very short attention span. In 72 hours, regardless of what happened in Iowa, if we ran a good campaign on the ground, we could prevail in New Hampshire. If we could get South Carolina 72 hours before the rest of Super Tuesday, we could get 8 or 10 points just off a good victory in South Carolina. . .
>
> We also made a decision to really concentrate on three governors that I felt had strong enough organizations in their states—if we could get them lined up early—to bring about a win no matter what else happened. They were John Sununu in New Hampshire, Carroll Campbell in South Carolina, Jim Thompson in Illinois.[12]

By contrast in 1992, Bill Clinton's handlers knew he could not afford a poor showing in the early primaries since he was running against stiff competition and was under attack concerning a number of character issues. He launched a series of television "town hall meetings" to go over the heads of the press. He promised the voters of New Hampshire that if they delivered for him he would never forget their state "until the last dog dies." His second-place showing in New Hampshire (behind Paul Tsongas) kept him in the race and, with clever media and marketing strategies in other states, he went on to win the nomination.

And so each campaign team looks at its strengths and weaknesses, checks the bank account, calculates where its political allies are, and develops a strategy for the primaries. The goal is to stay competitive in the news accounts, and arrive at the party convention with enough delegate support either to win the nomination or become a player in one of the important political games going on behind the scenes.

The Convention

Before the nomination process was opened up through primaries and caucuses, the convention was the center of political action. Nominations often required multiple votes among delegates representing state parties and national power brokers. Politics spilled out frequently onto the convention floor in spirited debates and demonstrations for favorite candidates. A century ago in 1896, for example, candidate William Jennings Bryan delivered his legendary "Cross of Gold" speech that broke a lengthy Democratic convention deadlock and won him the nomination. After the speech, Bryan was hoisted on the shoulders of the crowd and paraded around the hall in a scene that provoked one observer to remark: "For the first time, I can understand the scenes of the French revolution."[13] Today, such popular outbursts are reserved for winning football coaches, while party conventions tend to be relatively uneventful affairs. One observer marked the change in the role of conventions with this conclusion: "the convention, once the central forum for . . . nominating politics, became a fallback mechanism."[14]

Today's candidates are likely to show up at the convention with the nomination already in the bag, or nearly so. Even when fights erupt over issues in party platforms or internal party procedures, parties have learned that they must orchestrate these disputes to minimize the appearance of internal disorder and to highlight the party's most appealing features and personalities for prime-time audiences. The Democratic convention of 1972 was a legendary reminder of the uncontrolled convention; floor fights filled prime-time television and nominee George McGovern was not actually nominated until the wee hours of the morning—long after most people had turned off their television sets and gone to bed.

Today, the demonstrations, banners, and balloons are still there, but they happen on cue, with a soundtrack, and timed to fit with television schedules. In recent years the parties have been so successful in keeping the real politics of conventions hidden and off the floor that the media are increasingly reluctant to spend the money to cover them. There is something of a vicious cycle at work, with the parties spending more to script and stage each convention, and the television networks cutting back on coverage out of a belief that the conventions are dull and staged affairs. In 1988, ABC's executive producer for convention coverage dismissed the party conclaves as political dinosaurs, vowing not to cover another one.[15] In 1992, the three major networks were still there, but on a reduced scale. Even CNN, which covered more of the conventions, went to great lengths to create a sense that something dramatic was going on.[16] The only gavel-to-gavel coverage of the 1992 conventions was found on C-Span, a cable channel run as a public service obligation of the cable companies. (For more about C-Span, see Chapter 12.)

The modern convention still presents the possibility of an open floor fight for the nomination if no candidate gains close to a majority in the primaries. However, the more common scenario is a party lovefest designed to minimize possible media damage to the victorious candidate and the party. With any luck, the convention produces enough in the way of interest to send the candidate out on the campaign trail with a boost in the polls, known as a "convention bounce," to launch the campaign.

The Campaign

Although the press reports national opinion polls frequently for dramatic reasons, the campaign is not waged around winning a majority of the national vote. The name of the game is **playing the electoral vote** to win enough key states to add up to a majority in the electoral college. Voter patterns in those key states must be studied to fashion a candidate's appeal to different groups. It is particularly important to **play the swing voter** properly, as noted in Chapter 7. Running this kind of sophisticated national campaign requires forming a professional **campaign organization**. The sections that follow review campaign strategy and organization.

PLAYING THE ELECTORAL VOTE.   The hardest aspect for most Americans to understand about their elections is what has come to be known as the *electoral college* system, that strange legacy of the Committee for Unfinished Business at the Philadelphia Convention. Although they are seldom sure why, most Americans know that their presidential votes are cast not for candidates but for electors in each state, who then cast their votes for candidates. (As explained in Chapters 2 and 3, the electors were originally intended as something of a buffer to second-guess the wisdom of the voters and in some states to bypass the voters altogether.[17]) As participation expanded and parties competed for the loyalty of voters, the parties staked their reputations (and popularity) on running lists of electors who would honor the wishes of voters. As explained in Chapter 9, it also became accepted among the states to use a winner-take-all rule to deliver the entire state electoral vote to the candidate receiving the most popular votes. This curious system introduces important strategic considerations into running an election campaign.

The common pattern in modern elections has been for the popular-vote winner to actually win an even greater share of electoral votes. This is because a few large states have so much electoral clout (magnified because of the winner-take-all rule) that presidential campaigns focus on the big states, often turning slim popular vote victories in those states (particularly California, New York, Texas, Florida, Illinois, Pennsylvania, Ohio, and Michigan) into bigger electoral vote margins. For example, big states made Ronald Reagan the winner of a landslide 91 percent of the electoral college in 1980, though his

William Jennings Bryan, three-time (unsuccessful) Democratic nominee for the presidency. At the 1896 convention in Chicago, Bryan became at age 36 the youngest major presidential nominee ever, through his electrifying "Cross of Gold" speech, which inspired a gathering that had been deadlocked. Convention stalemates brokered by party bosses in "smoke-filled rooms" were once common occurrences; Bryan's successor, Woodrow Wilson, was nominated only on the forty-sixth balloting of delegates. Today's primary system, however, makes such an event almost impossible.

popular vote margin was simply 51 percent to Jimmy Carter's 41 percent (there was also a third candidate in that election).

In 1968, also with three candidates in the race, Richard Nixon gained only 43 percent of the popular vote, and the election went into the early morning hours with the possibility that no majority would emerge in the electoral college. The media analysts got out their rule books and began bracing viewers for a potentially nasty battle in the House of Representatives. (When no candidate receives a majority of votes in the electoral college, the election is decided in the House of Representatives, with each state delegation casting one vote, a scenario that could produce, and has produced, bizarre results.) Late in the evening, Illinois came in narrowly for Nixon in the popular vote column, giving him all the state's substantial electoral vote and putting him over the top with a 56 percent majority of the electoral vote. The magnifying effect was even more dramatic in 1992, when third candidate Ross Perot won nearly 19 percent of the popular vote, but did not carry a single state, leaving him with no electoral votes. This meant that Bill Clinton, with (like Nixon) only 43 percent of the popular vote (compared to 38 percent for President Bush), ended up with a deceptive 370-to-168 electoral vote victory.

Although many critics condemn the electoral college, its hidden virtue may be to turn close races into comfortable winning mandates, while keeping three-way races from being decided in the House of Representatives. All of this puts a slightly different emphasis on the popular fear that a winner of the majority of the popular vote might lose the electoral vote and the election. Although this scenario is possible, don't hold your breath for it to develop. In only three elections in the history of the Republic (1824, 1876, and 1888) has the candidate winning the most popular votes ended up losing the election.[18]

It is not accidental that the two parties have held on to the electoral college. Figure 10.1 illustrates the modern pattern in which the electoral college distorts the popular vote and explains why most of the campaign dollars are poured into crucial battles in a few large states.

PLAYING THE SWING VOTE.   Recall from Chapter 7 that some voter groups are less committed to party voting than others but can be moved in large numbers by specific issues and appeals. During the dozen years of Republican leadership in the

Supporters of Richard Nixon gather to watch televised returns on election night, 1968. Nixon won the presidency with only a forty-three percent plurality of the popular vote (as would Bill Clinton a quarter-century later); but he (like Clinton) received a majority in the electoral college. Nixon won 301 electoral votes, to 191 for Democrat Hubert Humphrey and 46 votes for third-party candidate George Wallace.

FIGURE 10.1

The Electoral College Magnifying Effect: Popular and Electoral Vote Trends, 1932–1992

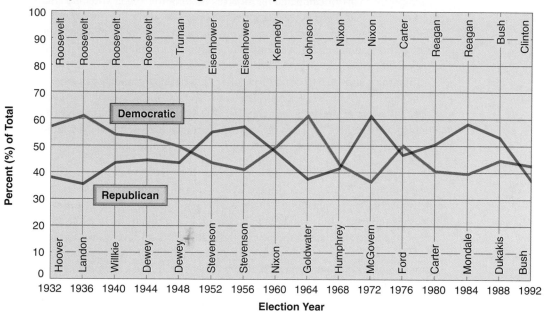

Popular Vote, Excluding Third-Party Candidates

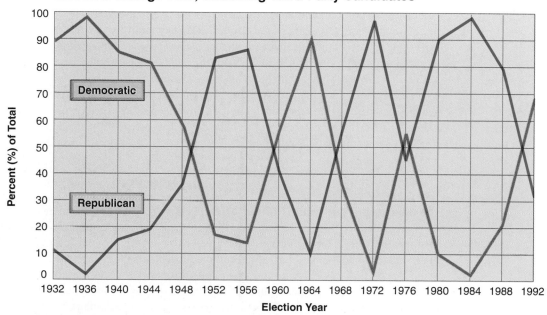

Electoral College Vote, Excluding Third-Party Candidates

Source: Popular vote data from U.S. Census Bureau reports.

White House from 1981 to 1993, for example, many working people who had once identified themselves as Democrats swung their support to the GOP, gaining themselves labels like Blue-Collar Republicans and (in 1980 and 1984) Reagan Democrats. For an even longer period, many middle-class whites have turned away from the Democrats at the presidential level because of the perception that the party unduly favored minorities. An important part of campaigning involves reading the swing vote and finding ways to get key groups in the right (electoral vote) states to swing the right ways. In 1992, the Clinton campaign appealed successfully to blue-collar voters by playing up the economic fears of the nation and by avoiding strong appeals on welfare (another wedge issue) to block the middle-class swing to the Republicans.

Running a state-by-state and group-by-group national campaign involves a number of challenges: designing separate strategies for the key electoral college states; fitting appeals to swing voters into the equation; reassuring party loyalists that the party still stands for them; and, while doing all this, keeping at least some of the candidate's principles intact. These jobs require large staffs of professional campaigners.

THE CAMPAIGN ORGANIZATION.   The campaign organization works for the candidate but must coordinate its activities with the national and state parties. An effective campaign organization usually begins with a strong *director* at the top, someone who has the trust of the candidate and the ability to direct the two-way communication between the candidate and the rest of the staff. The next level down is centered around the *campaign manager* who coordinates the activities of the key strategy people. Surrounding the campaign manager is the campaign brain trust of *chief media advisor, pollster, fundraiser,* and an issue or *policy advisor.*

Working for the campaign manager are deputies or assistants who work with national and state party coordinators to make sure that the candidate's message is echoed as much as possible in the campaigns of other party candidates. Members of this brain trust around the campaign manager also have paid assistants to help implement the campaign strategies. In addition, thousands of volunteer workers are added down to the local level to do everything from polling, voter turnout, and telephoning, to putting up posters and yard signs and decorating the halls for victory parties or wakes on election night.

As the campaign develops, the organization reacts daily to extensive polling and market research. New themes and communications strategies are debated internally, while commercials and lines for speeches are test-marketed with sample audiences. Intelligence is gathered on the other side's strategy, and planning goes into countering the opponent's message and personal image. Above all, the successful campaign is one that learns to react quickly to its own miscalculations and the opponent's successes.

Getting Elected: The Political Reality

The contemporary election is driven by forces that may be transforming its role in democracy itself. If you ask someone on the inside of a campaign what drives his or her business these days, you will hear about three factors (assuming your informant is willing to talk frankly): **money, marketing,** and **media.** These factors have produced a spiral of high-cost, slick campaigning that has made elections less satisfying to many voters. The changes in campaigning, in turn, can be traced to fundamental changes in patterns of participation and power in America that were explained in Chapters 7 and 9: the rise of independent voters, the decline of parties, and the emergence of more independent candidates. These factors that drive campaigns are explained in "Inside the System" Box 10.2.

The result of this cycle of media, money, and marketing is that campaigns are now very cautious affairs, with candidates reluctant to make bold statements, take risks, or

INSIDE THE SYSTEM

The Forces That Shape Campaigning Today

10.2

Increasingly independent voters, weaker parties, and more independent candidates have brought about three great sources of political pressure inside today's campaigns: money, marketing, and media management.

MONEY

The high costs of selling independent candidates to independent and skeptical voters requires large amounts of money in campaigns at almost all levels of government. Pressures from the interests who give this money drive candidates and parties apart and restrict what candidates can say to voters. The restriction of campaign issues requires sophisticated and costly marketing efforts to sell candidates to voters. The 1992 election set new records. According to the Federal Election Commission, House and Senate candidates spent over $500 million getting elected, a new record that topped the old mark set in 1990 by more than $100 million. Each major presidential campaign (including the "soft money" support of the parties) topped $200 million. Independent candidate Ross Perot personally spent more than $60 million. The costs have spiraled at every level, making American elections the most expensive by far in the world.

MARKETING

Image campaigns are designed for candidates much as they are created for commercial products. Appeals are aimed at triggering short-term emotional responses from often narrowly targeted voter groups. Broad public appeals become sacrificed to win the support of key voter groups. This disrupts the potential of elections to be broad forums about national problems. The result is that the media, including news programs, are viewed as part of the candidate marketing effort, not as open, two-way communication channels between voters and future leaders. Techniques for controlling information in the media thus become more important and more sophisticated. The advertising formats are always changing. Negative advertising swept American politics in 1988, and even more negative ads were produced (although fewer may have been run) in 1992. The latest trend is the "infomercial," developed into lengthy program-length formats by Ross Perot in 1992. At a cost of over $35 million, Perot's infomercials made such an impact that *Advertising Age* magazine named him their "Adman of the Year" for 1992. Commercial advertisers began to imitate Perot in ads for their products.

MEDIA MANAGEMENT

Not only are the mass media, particularly television, used to sell candidates, but efforts are made to control interference from the press. Techniques of press control and news management have developed to minimize the potential damage of critical news coverage, and to put the campaign in control as much as possible of the content of the daily news. Bill Clinton learned to go on talk shows and entertainment programs to get around negative press coverage. After the election, Clinton continued to use such techniques to "campaign" for his policies and programs, raising concerns that the line between campaigning and governing may be dissolving.

THE SYSTEM FRAMEWORK

The result of these political pressures is that new balances of *power* enter elections through interest group financing. The bases of participation, loyalty, and party power may also be breaking down as voter coalitions are constructed through marketing. The *institutions* of government may be weakened as individuals continue to use campaign techniques to remain popular while in office, avoiding the political compromise and cooperation required for making tough governing decisions. Even the *political culture* may be strained as popular symbols are used arbitrarily by candidates without much regard for the meaningful connections to a condidate's actual proposals or plans in office.

appeal to one voter group if it may lose other key swing groups in important states. As a result, much of a campaign these days is aimed not at the broad spectrum of all Americans, but at the relatively small percentage of undecided and swing voters in the key states that will make the difference in the outcome of the contest. As the media, money, and marketing forces behind the scenes of the campaign have become driving forces, the

American election may have lost its capacity to be a broad forum of national debate and public accountability, thus diminishing its role in the democratic process as described earlier.

The Great Money Chase

"I've raised millions upon millions for the Democratic Party and I've never seen this happen," said [M. Larry] Lawrence. The 61-year-old chairman of the fashionable Hotel del Coronado in Coronado, California, donated $100,000 of his own to the Democrats in the primaries, and has pledged to raise an additional $1 million for the general election. "We're raising money like it's going out of style. It's beyond comprehension. It's gorgeous. It's so exciting."[19]

In at least one respect, this wealthy businessman and long-time Democratic fundraiser is right: It's beyond comprehension. A presidential election these days costs each candidate upwards of $100 million, and the total cost for the whole presidential race comes in at over $600 million if we add the price of the primaries and conventions and party spending to the total.[20] Figure 10.2 illustrates the spiraling costs of presidential politics.

Although federal funding roughly matches the amounts raised by the candidates in the primaries, they must first raise millions of dollars on their own just to become competitive. Then the race is on for the tens of millions more that must be raised (even with the large federal allotments) to stay competitive in the general election. In addition to competing with one another for voter approval, candidates increasingly compete for the support of a much more select and seldom-recognized group: political campaign contributors. Competition for these huge sums of money is stiff, and the nature of this offstage maneuvering does not often reward those who tackle new issues or come up with innovative policy proposals.

FROM PRESIDENT TO STATE OFFICIALS: THE CHASE IS ON.   The strings manipulated by financial backers can be long ones, reaching far beyond the

FIGURE 10.2

The Cost of Presidential Elections, 1960–1992

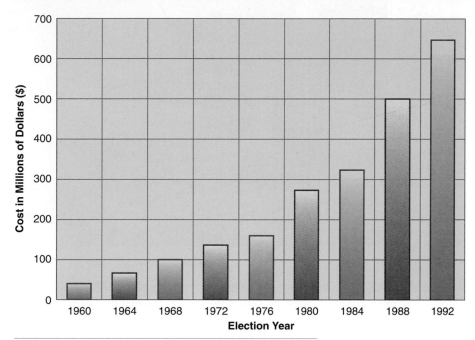

Sum of all expenses for candidates and parties in the nomination process, conventions, and general elections.

Source: Estimates for 1960–1988 are from Herbert Alexander, "Financing the Presidential Elections, 1988," in Wayne and Wilcox, eds. *The Quest for National Office,* 1992, p. 41; 1992 is the author's estimate based on Federal Election Commission spending reports and contributions to parties.

White House and Congress to smaller state and local offices. Even candidates for state and local office have become dependent on big money, often creating strains between political idealism and political necessity. An idealistic politician from California shared with me the hard facts of running for an assembly seat in his state. He lamented that it takes a staggering sum of money, for which the candidate must go to state party leaders. The leaders first size up the candidate, look at track record and marketability factors, and, finally, ask the big question: Are you willing to "get with the program" on the half-dozen or so major issues of interest to the investors who have put their money into the party and its candidates? If the candidate says yes, and the leadership thinks that he or she is electable, the money flows. But, said the young candidate, if you say yes, you have already sold out on the issues that really mattered to you and your constituents in the first place. What are you supposed to go back and talk to the voters about?

In California, candidates for public office spent more than $60 million in 1988, with running for the legislature costing more than two-thirds of that amount. In 1990, the candidates for governor, alone, spent nearly $40 million. To get ready for the 1992 California Senate race, John Seymour was handed the gift of incumbency, being appointed by

The media labelled 1992 "the Year of the Woman" in politics. One sign that women have arrived politically is the election of former San Francisco mayor Dianne Feinstein (right), who won her Senate seat through her own popularity and superior fundraising abilities. Feinstein campaigned frequently as a twosome with U.S. Representative Barbara Boxer, and the "coattail effect" of Feinstein's and Bill Clinton's popularity in California helped Boxer to pull off a much narrower win over conservative challenger Bruce Herschensohn for the state's other Senate seat.

the governor in 1991 to fill a vacant seat. His main job? Raising the $20 million that he estimated he would need to simply be competitive in the election. Critics charged that Seymour may have been appointed in part because he was so well-connected with wealthy backers that he could raise that kind of sum.[21] In the end, Seymour raised "only" about $7 million (according to Federal Election Commission reports) and lost to Dianne Feinstein, who had learned from her $20 million loss in the 1990 governor's race how to conduct a media campaign.

To put all of this in perspective, a British general election is estimated to cost *in total* somewhere between $10 million and $30 million.[22] Thus, the race for Senate or governor in California costs more than all the national races combined in a country with more than twice the population of California. The 1991 general election in Sweden was estimated at $15 million.[23] By contrast, the total cost of running for public office in the United States in presidential years is pushing $3 billion. The average winner in a U.S. Senate campaign spends about $4 million, and the typical cost of a House seat is more than $400,000.[24]

As the costs go up, contests become less competitive simply because challengers cannot raise the amounts of interest group money that well-connected incumbents are able to attract. At the same time, campaign financiers place their bets on incumbents because they are more likely to win, creating a vicious cycle. Figure 10.3 shows the gap between incumbent and challenger spending for House of Representatives elections. In 1988, a new record was achieved when 98 percent of the incumbents seeking reelection in the House and the Senate were returned to office. In 1990, the incumbency advantage was 96 percent, and even with the voter discontent and talk of change in 1992, 90 percent of incumbents in the House and Senate who sought reelection won. Figure 10.4 shows the success rates of incumbents in holding onto their offices.

CAMPAIGN FINANCE AND THE LAW.   At the Congressional level, the major driver behind the political influence of money is the political action committee or PAC system (introduced in chapters 8 and 9). The **PAC system** is just one part of a larger federal effort to try to organize and regulate national election financing. In response to the growing abuses and corruption in the finance practices of parties and candidates, a

FIGURE 10.3

The Spending Gap Between Incumbents and Challengers: Average Spending in House of Representatives Races, 1974–1992

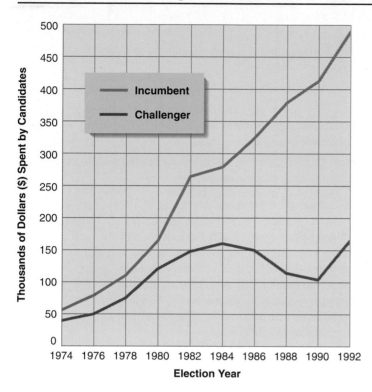

Source: 1974—1990 compiled from FEC Reports by Larry Makinson, in *Open Secrets: The Cash Constituents of Congress,* CQ Press, 1992, p. 3; 1992 based on author's projections from FEC reports. The shift in 1992 reflects the unusually large number of retirements, producing many contested races involving no incumbents.

FIGURE 10.4

The Incumbency Advantage in Congress: Percentage of Incumbents Seeking Reelection Who Won, 1978–1992

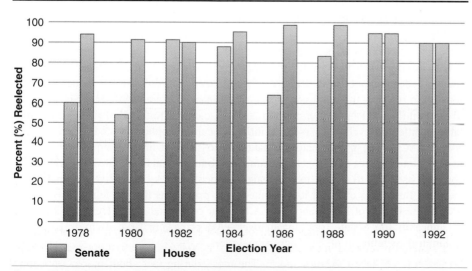

Source: Federal Election Commission, 1992 returns.

major set of revisions were made in the law known as the **Federal Election Campaign Act** of 1974. This law requires:

1. Detailed public reporting of contributions
2. Limits on individual ($1,000) and PAC ($5,000) contributions to candidates for each election
3. Limits on individual contributions to specific candidates or national parties in a given year ($25,000)
4. Federal funds for presidential candidates
5. Limits on how much personal money candidates can spend, and ceilings placed on presidential campaign spending (amended in 1976 to apply only to candidates who voluntarily accept federal funds)
6. Creation of a Federal Election Commission to watch over the system, along with criminal and civil penalties for violations.

This system was adjusted several times more, beginning in 1976 after the Supreme Court ruled in the case of U.S. Senator James Buckley in *Buckley vs. Valeo* that it was unconstitutional on First Amendment/free speech grounds to limit the total amount of personal candidate spending in a campaign. As a result, Congress passed a 1976 amendment to FECA that established the principle of **voluntary spending limits**. This means that presidential candidates who (voluntarily) accept federal funding for their campaigns also must accept the campaign spending limits attached to that funding.[25] This explains how Ross Perot could spend more than $60 million of his own money to run in 1992; he did not seek nor did he qualify for federal campaign monies.

Although a few PACs have existed since the 1940s, there was a huge growth after the mid-1970s when it became clear that they could be used to get around the tighter restrictions on direct corporate, union, and individual contributions written into law by the 1974 revisions in the Federal Election Campaign Act.[26] Corporations, industry associations, interest groups and unions form these "voluntary" action committees among their members to channel limited contributions to particular candidates (up to $5,000) and to national parties (up to $15,000). However, the federal law does not regulate monies donated to state and local parties, and this means that huge amounts of what is known as **soft money** can be given to the parties for state and local activities not specifically aimed at the election of a particular candidate.

With the importance of state campaigns discussed above, and the expense of such key background activities as polling and voter turnout, such money has become a sizeable iceberg lurking under the visible tip of regulated financing. While the **hard money** regulated by federal finance laws is restricted to thousands of dollars, soft money contributions often run into the hundreds of thousands from the same sources.[27] Since there is no limit on the total amount of money that PACs can give to different parties and candidates at different levels, their political influence can be applied throughout the election system. PACs often "bundle" money, making it possible for many groups in a related industry or interest area to channel large amounts to individual candidates. In recent years, Congress has tried to amend the campaign finance laws. A bill was vetoed in 1992 by President Bush who objected to continued PAC provisions that he felt favored Democrats in the House of Representatives. A bill that originated in the House in 1993 met resistance in the Senate, once again over PAC provisions and attempts to impose (voluntary) spending limits in congressional races.

CASHING IN ON CONGRESS. The most glaring fact about money on Capitol Hill is that so much of it began pouring in as politicians and parties learned to use the new election laws. The most visible issue is PAC funding, which escalated from $55 million in 1980 to upwards of $160 million in 1992, with the vast majority each year going to incumbents.[28] The deluge of PAC money allows incumbents to keep their seats by greatly outspending opponents, as noted in Figure 10.3 above.

The average incumbent's political career depends on keeping hundreds of PACs making their contributions each year. Suppose, for example, that Senator Foghorn needs to raise $6 million for the next election. That translates into $1 million a year over the six-year term, or around $3,000 that must be raised *every day* of each of those six years, weekends and holidays included. Suddenly, those "small" PAC donations start to make sense. And just as suddenly, it becomes clear that even if U.S. Representatives cannot promise their votes to PACs in advance, neither can they afford to turn PAC representatives away very often. When many small PACs "bundle" their donations, the concerns of a particular interest group become even more important to the career of a politician.

Now, factor in the power of big PACs that have the resources to shower funds on dozens or even hundreds of representatives each year. Just to cite one example, the American Telephone and Telegraph PAC gave over a million dollars spread broadly over members of both parties in Congress in 1988.[29] With all the key votes wired, so to speak, it becomes easier to secure passage of legislation and, more importantly, regulations affecting an industry. In addition, companies in similar industries can band together and concentrate their collective contributions.

Suggesting such a direct exchange of campaign dollars for national priorities is, of course, scandalous, not to mention illegal. But many members of Congress are coming to conclusions like these:[30]

> "The only reason it isn't considered bribery is that Congress gets to define bribery."

> "If you give a dog a bone, he'll be loyal forever. And if you give a Congressman some money, he may not fetch your slippers for you, but he'll always be there when you need him."

> "I fear we could become a coin-operated Congress. Instead of two bits, you put in $2,500 and pull out a vote."

> "I take money from labor, and I have to think twice in voting against their interest. I shouldn't have to do that."

> "More and more on the floor I hear people say, 'I can't help you. I've gotten $5,000 from this group.'"

The point is not whether budget items are boondoggles, or tobacco subsidies are hazardous to your fiscal health, or junk-food legislation is junk. The question is whether governing can go on when the governors are being pulled from so many sides at once, by so many narrowly defined and often utterly unrelated interests. Perhaps the point was made best by Senator Robert Dole (R–Kansas), who said: "When these political action committees give money, they expect something in return other than good government. It is making it difficult to legislate. We may reach a point where everybody is buying something with PAC money. We cannot get anything done."[31] And yet Senator Dole has been one of the most successful of all in playing the PAC game.[32] And therein lies the essence of the system.

PADDING THE PRESIDENCY.   The point of public funds for presidential campaigns was to equalize the competition and keep spending within reason. Yet according to one expert, the soft money frenzy drove costs of presidential campaigning to $500 million in 1988, up from $325 million in 1984.[33] Then 1992 topped that amount—even without the addition of Ross Perot's expensive candidacy. Sniffing a Democratic victory, the big contributors put so much money behind Bill Clinton and his party that the Republicans finished second in the money race—as they did in the election.

Who were some of the high rollers in the 1992 presidential election game? The soft money for the Democrats rolled in from sources including these: United Steel Workers of America ($386,000); RJR Nabisco ($301,000); the National Education Association lobby ($279,000); and Atlantic Richfield ($247,000), among many others. The Republicans also received money from RJR Nabisco, which hedged its electoral bets ($427,000); as well as Archer-Daniels-Midland ($1,012,000); and Merrill Lynch ($427,000).[34] These and other interests are regular players in the soft money game. The most regular and generous supporters of the Democrats include the Association of Trial Lawyers of America; the United Auto Workers; American Federation of State, County, and Municipal Employees; the American Federation of Teachers; the National Education Association; and the AFL-CIO, among others. The most regular and generous supporters of the Republicans include the Atlantic Richfield Co.; RJR Nabisco; Irvine Company; American Financial Corp.; Archer-Daniels-Midland; and Beatrice Corp., among others.[35]

Nowadays, the money given in federal funding to the candidates during the general election ($110 million in 1992) is not only equalled by candidate fundraising, but exceeded by these largely unregulated party soft money efforts as well. The "limit" on how much the candidates can accept from their own parties (roughly $10 million in 1992) if they "voluntarily" take public funding has become something of a joke. As explained above, the soft money bank accounts can be spent on a wide array of vote-getting activities so long as the candidate's name is not specifically mentioned.

Campaigns end up being planned around how to divide up the hard and soft money expenses. In practice, the "ground war" (registration, get-out-the-vote drives, and so on) in a campaign is waged primarily with soft money—money that otherwise individual campaigns would still need to spend. Diverting most of the soft money to "ground war" activities allows candidates to spend more of their personal campaign accounts on the "air war" of television ads and candidate images. This drives up the budgets for advertising and marketing, and leads candidates to rely increasingly on the "air war" as the heart of the campaign.[36]

The money wars between the parties escalated sharply in the late 1980s when the Democrats learned how to use the finance system as well as the traditionally better-connected Republicans and threatened to beat the GOP in fundraising in 1988. This fact led George Bush's chief fundraiser, Robert A. Mosbacher, Jr. (later Secretary of Commerce) to remark with tongue in cheek: "The Democrats are saying they're going for the big money. And I don't think there's much we can do about it but match them."[37] And Mr. Mosbacher had the plan to do it: Join the "Team 100" club. The membership fee was $100,000 to the Republican National Committee. *Common Cause Magazine* called "Team 100" a veritable Who's Who of American Business:

> The $100,000 contributors include 66 in the investment and banking community, 58 in real estate and construction, another 17 in the oil industry, and 15 from food and agriculture. Team 100 also includes members from the entertainment, cable, insurance, steel, and auto industries.
>
> Almost across the board, Team 100 members or the companies they are associated with want something from the government—whether it's broad policy initiatives like Bush's proposed reduction in the capital gains tax or favors more specific to a company or industry. Many gave their $100,000 at a time when they had significant business or regulatory matters pending with the federal government—or knew they likely would under the Bush administration.[38]

And once these donors were on the team, they kept on giving, to the tune of $25,000 a year between elections, adding up to another $100,000 in 1992, and making each Team 100 member a signer of checks totalling at least $200,000 for the two elections.[39]

Meanwhile, the Democrats weren't doing too badly either. Although slowed somewhat in 1988 by Mr. Dukakis' difficulty in soliciting corporate funds, many Democratic state parties joined the moneyfest on their own. The California Democratic party chairman boasted at one point that the state campaign was being financed by "every big California corporation you can think of."[40]

Running for office, whether executive or legislative, leads candidates into the world of high finance and interest pressures, a world that critics say places money ahead of ideas as the main requirement for national leadership. In this view, the spiral of money and ideas sends increasingly issue-less candidates chasing after the votes of increasingly skeptical and disloyal voters. The improvement in campaign content noted by voters in 1992 can be attributed to two outside factors entering the race: the candidacy of Ross Perot, and the recession and federal deficit problems that made economic worries an issue. Even with these special conditions in 1992, the importance of marketing became more central than ever, led by none other than Ross Perot, as noted in Box 10.2.

Marketing the Candidates

Needless to say, marketing research, polling, and advertising costs are the main items on campaign budgets. Here, for example, is a fairly typical budget for a Senate campaign. This is a look not at an incumbent's campaign, but a challenge by Harriet Woods of Missouri, who raised enough money to put on a credible (but losing) campaign:[41]

SOURCES OF MONEY	EXPENSE BREAKDOWN
Individuals in Missouri $1,150,000	TV time & ad production $2,550,000
Individuals outside Missouri . . . . $ 600,000	Polling . . . .$ 200,000
Direct mail & phone solicitation $1,200,000	Staff and operations . . . . $ 875,000
"Bundling" (outside groups) collecting money) . . . . .$ 300,000	
PACs . . . . $ 800,000	Fundraising
Democratic party funds . . . $ 350,000	cost . . . . $ 775,000
$4,400,000	$4,400,000

Of the $390,000 spent by the average incumbent in House of Representatives races in 1990, only $28,000 was listed in the budget category of "actual campaigning," compared with an average of $87,000 spent in the category of "advertising."[42] Marketing introduces a different logic into electoral politics. Instead of worrying about how to develop *ideas* that might be of use in *governing,* marketers worry about how to win market shares of votes. This does not involve communicating to a broad general public, as democratic logic might have, but to narrow slices or "market segments" of that public. These market segments need not understand the candidate, only vote for him. Thus, people are induced to vote for Candidate A over Candidate B much as soap buyers may favor Brand X over Brand Y without feeling they have established a meaningful relationship with their laundry detergent in the process. This further diminishes the importance of coherent governing programs and the articulation of campaign issues. The premium is on short-term emotions and candidate images.

This sort of fast-sell campaigning offends a lot of people, but the logic of political marketing does not regard voter withdrawal as a bad thing. To the contrary, in a classic commentary on the new political age, a Republican strategist said, "I don't want everyone to vote. Our leverage in the election quite candidly goes up as the voting population goes down."[43] Borrowing this page from the Republican playbook, the Democrats from the mid-1980s into the 1990s began to chase with a vengeance after market segments such as blue-collar Republicans and middle-class white voters, even though this meant affronting traditional constituencies such as blacks, poor people, and liberals. Not surprisingly, the marketing of candidates who compete more for money than votes can leave many voters feeling unrepresented at election time. It is, in short, a long way from the idealism of James Madison to the marketing ideas of Madison Avenue.

MADISON AVENUE DEMOCRACY.   Expressing concern about the way marketing consultants dominate elections, political scientist Mark Petracca said: "The United States faces a monumental challenge to the practice of democratic governance. The challenge stems, in part, from significant changes in the conceptualization and practice of political campaigning and from the revolutionary effects of the technology deployed in contemporary campaigns."[44] Beyond turning the decline of participation from a problem into a virtue, campaign consultants exert a number of other influences on the quality of national political life, not the least of which, Petracca suggests, is turning a tendency toward empty rhetoric in American elections into standard, institutionalized procedure.[45]

What exactly do marketing specialists contribute to a campaign? For starters, they accept the limitations on what candidates are willing to say to voters, while taking up the challenge those limits pose for creating voter enthusiasm. Next, the consultant sizes up the population of people likely to vote and applies basic marketing techniques (polling, focus groups, "people meter" sessions) to evaluate the relative strengths and weaknesses of the client and the opponent. Finally, a marketing strategy is devised to deliver favorable candidate images, unfavorable opponent images, and salient themes to key segments of the voting market. These key voter blocs or "target audiences," are determined by applying four criteria:

- Are they already likely to vote? (There is no point in complicating an already difficult job by stirring up dormant voters.)

- Are they undecided? (It is nearly impossible to get people to change their minds if they are strongly committed to the opposing candidate or party.)

- Is it possible to appeal to these groups without creating a backlash in some other group already likely to vote for us? (This would be a very poor return on the marketing dollar.)

- Which of the "finalist" groups are located in key states in sufficient numbers that winning their support could make a difference in the outcome of the electoral college vote? (There being no point in turning out people whose votes would not tip the final outcome.)

Running the voting population through these screening steps explains why campaigns can seem so out of touch with a candidate or a party's most loyal supporters. In 1988, for example, many Democratic party diehards wondered how nominee Michael Dukakis could shrink from accusations that he was a liberal while apparently selling out the minority vote. On the other side of the fence, many conservatives fretted over George

Bush's softening on defense and the budget, not to mention his pledge to become the "environmental president." In 1992, efforts to shore up conservative support may have cost Republicans some moderate voters, who felt the abortion and family values positions taken by Bush and Quayle were either too extreme or at least irrelevant to their major concerns. On the Democratic side in 1992, Clinton pollster Stanley Greenberg explained the continuing Democratic avoidance of minority group appeals by pointing to evidence from focus groups that white middle-class voters reacted against Democrats who identified themselves with racial groups and civil rights issues.[46]

Contemporary presidential elections can boil down to spending hundreds of millions of dollars to make delicate marketing pitches to groups that may be as small as ten percent of the total electorate. Yet, in the view of consultants, this tiny percentage of the population meets the four criteria on which campaign strategy is based. Thus, a relatively small number of voters becomes the focus of the entire election (raising important questions about what this means for the idea of democracy). In addition to requiring creative use of the media to sell candidates, this style of campaigning requires equally creative techniques for keeping the press from blowing the cover off a delicately crafted candidate image.

Media Management

Members of the press generally regard issues and ideas as the most important grounds for electoral choice. Idealess elections antagonize reporters searching for meaningful differences between the candidates to write home about. An aroused press can be expected to assume an adversarial role, leaping upon inconsistencies, making much of candidate slips and blunders, seizing upon anything inflammatory in the absence of much to say about policy positions. As a result, campaigns tend to isolate their candidates from the press corps and stick to a tightly controlled and carefully scripted daily schedule. This means, in media guru Roger Ailes' words, that reporters are handed a lot of visuals and attacks, while mistakes (and ideas) are held to a minimum. In short, the goal is to make the news fit into the campaign marketing strategy.

MAKING THE NEWS. It is by now widely accepted that good media strategy entails three tactics:

- Keeping the candidate away from spontaneous contact with the press
- Feeding the press a simple political line of the day delivered by the candidate in a telegenic setting
- Making sure the daily news line echoes (*magnifies* may be the better word) the images from campaign ads, thus blurring the distinction between commercials and news "reality."[47]

Candidates and their handlers vary in the ability to keep the press pack at bay, but when they succeed, reporters are left with little but a set of campaign slogans to report. ABC reporter Sam Donaldson said: "When we cover the candidates, we cover their campaigns as they outline them."[48] And so, a willing, if unhappy press becomes a channel for the often impoverished ideas that reflect the interplay of advertising strategy and the concessions made to campaign contributors.

In recent years, the media have showed signs of trying to be more critical of campaigns. Encouraged by a public angry at candidates and politicians (*and* angry at the media), the news contains increased coverage of the illusory world of marketed candidates and media manipulation. During the 1992 campaign, for example, many newspapers and TV news programs ran features calling attention to campaign advertising.

These regular "adwatch" pieces may help consumers think more critically about the advertising they are watching, but they appear to have little effect on the ads themselves. "Inside the System" Box 10.3 illustrates how one national paper covered two campaign ads.

In addition, some of the television networks vowed to try to cover more of what the candidates said in speeches, by lengthening the **sound bites,** or the short actual statements made by the political actors in the news. (One of the sound bites of 1988 was George Bush's "Read my lips: no new taxes.") These sound bites give many newswatchers their only actual taste of the candidates' ideas in TV news coverage of campaigns. However, the length of sound bites had plummeted over the years: from 43.1 seconds in 1968, to 25.2 seconds in 1972, to 18.2 seconds in 1976, to 12.1 seconds in 1980, to 9.9 seconds in 1984, to a record low of 8.9 seconds in 1988.[49] By one calculation, at that rate of decline, the length of a sound bite in 1992 would have been just long enough for a candidate to say "Me President, you voter."[50] CBS News undertook the strongest measures to boost the length of candidate statements by issuing an order to run no sound bites under 30 seconds. The final results did not even come close, however. It seems that candidate speeches these days are written with media sound bites in mind, meaning that reporters and producers could edit 10-second bites much more cleanly into their reports than 30-second quotes.[51]

The Media Cover the Ad Campaigns

10.3

I n the 1990s, many print and television news organizations began regular coverage of the advertising used by candidates. The press responded to concerns from political analysts that the very *institutional* in- tegrity of elections was being undermined by marketing. Democracy requires some degree of responsible debate and reliable information in public communication. Although the media can be faulted for running misleading advertising, they also appear to be concerned with restoring some truth in political advertising.

Here is an example of how *The New York Times* covered Bush and Clinton campaign ads on one day in 1992.

Bush: The Two Faces of Clinton

T he Bush campaign began broadcasting a commercial Thursday that attacks Gov. Bill Clinton for the first time on the draft and other issues. Campaign officials said the 30-second advertisement was placed in several markets around the country but they would not be specific.

ON THE SCREEN

Opens with split screen of two candidates (both in jackets; one with a red tie and the other with a dark blue tie) speaking, gesturing, their faces obscured by gray dots. By the end of the ad, the dots disappear to show that both candidates are Mr. Clinton.

PRODUCER

The November Co.

SCRIPT

Announcer: "The Presidential candidate on the left stood for military action in the Persian Gulf, while the candidate on the right agreed with those who opposed it.

"He says he wouldn't rule out term limits, while he says he's personally opposed to term limits. This candidate was called up for military service, while this one claims he wasn't."

"One of these candidates is Bill Clinton. Unfortunately, so is the other."

Mr. Clinton's booming voice from a speech: "There is a simple explanation for why this happened."

ACCURACY

On the gulf war, Mr. Clinton had said he would vote with the majority in a close vote, but also said he agreed with the argu-

ments of people in the minority. Long after the war, he spoke in stronger terms of his support for United States intervention. Mr. Clinton has long criticized term limits, but he once said he would not rule them out.

As for his draft record, Mr. Clinton said early this year that he had never been called up, saying "it was just a fluke" that he had not been. Later, after press reports revealed that he had received an induction notice in April 1969, he acknowledged that this was so.

SCORECARD

The ad seeks to raise questions about Mr. Clinton's credibility on more than one issue. It tries to portray him as flip-flopping on issues and it also touches on the sensitive questions of whether he dodged the draft and whether he would be a strong Commander in Chief. Bush advisers said the dot was intended to lend humor.

RICHARD L. BERKE

Clinton: Reminding Voters of a Promise

The Clinton campaign released a 30-second commercial yesterday. Campaign officials did not say where or how often it would run.

ON THE SCREEN

Opens with "1988" in black letters on a white background. Cut to Mr. Bush at his 1988 nomination, saying "read my lips." Cut to words parroting the announcer, then to a repeat of Mr. Bush's tax pledge. More screens starkly print the announcer's charges. Final words: "We can't afford four more years."

SCRIPT

Announcer: "1988"
Mr. Bush: "Read my lips. No new taxes."
Announcer: "Then George Bush signed the second-biggest tax increase in American history."
Mr. Bush: "Read my lips."
Announcer: "George Bush increased taxes on the middle class. Bush doubled the beer tax and increased the gas tax by 56 percent. Now George Bush wants to give a $108,000 tax

break to millionaires. $108,000! Guess who's going to pay? We can't afford four more years."

ACCURACY

Mr. Bush did sign a 1990 tax law projected to raise $137 billion in revenue over five years, second to Ronald Reagan's $214 billion tax increase of 1982. The 1990 law included higher rates on beer and gas—the "middle-class" tax increases the ad trumpets. Not mentioned: the 1990 tax law was largely dictated by Congressional Democrats, who at the time hailed it as a working-class victory over the wealthy. Indeed, it sharply raised income taxes on those with adjusted gross income over $200,000 and lowered them on those making less than $20,000.

The claim of a $108,000 tax break for millionaires is a bit strained. The $8,000 relies on an assertion that Mr. Bush supports a 1 percentage-point cut in income-tax rates, a hypothesis mentioned in a Bush speech last month. The remaining $100,000 is tied to Mr. Bush's advocacy of a 12.6 percentage-point cut in capital-gains taxes. It assumes the $40.4 billion

in capital gains reported by all 40,385 millionaires in 1990 is divided equally, as it surely is not. The capital-gains cut also would benefit far more than just millionaires, although the great majority of the break would go to people earning more than $100,000.

SCORECARD

The ad aims to dull Mr. Bush's attacks on Mr. Clinton's record of tax increases by turning the President's fateful "no new taxes" pledge of 1988 against him. It suggests that Mr. Bush is a high-tax President and that his word can't be trusted—the very arguments that Mr. Bush is making against Mr. Clinton.

MICHAEL WINES

SOURCE: *The New York Times*, October 3, 1992, p. 8. See also Elizabeth Kolbert, "Maybe the Media *Did* Treat Bush a Bit Harshly," *The New York Times*, November 22, 1992.

DAMAGE CONTROL.   In the end, a more critical press may only reinforce the determination of campaigns to control relations between the candidates and the media as much as possible, including finding new ways to control the potential damage of more critical news coverage. Indeed, the term **damage control** has taken its place in the language of modern campaigns, referring to strategies used to minimize the impact of negative news coverage. Campaign managers circulate among the press each day on the campaign trail, suggesting alternative interpretations for any candidate statement or slip that might be taken the wrong way. This has become known as putting a **spin** on the news, and campaign staff who are good at spin control are **spin doctors.**

If the marketed candidate is to survive in this volatile atmosphere, the name of the game is to control media damage before it happens by scripting and directing the candidate and the daily campaign appearances as much as possible. As Mark Hertsgaard has noted, contemporary campaigning follows simple media control strategy: "Control your message by keeping reporters and their questions away from a scripted candidate; capture TV's attention with prefabricated, photo-opportunity events that reinforce the campaign's chosen **'line of the day.'**"[52]

When all else fails, as it did for Bill Clinton at several crucial moments in the 1992 campaign, the best strategy appeared to be to bypass the news channels altogether and take the campaign on other televised routes such as live "town hall" meetings, MTV forums, and blowing the saxophone on the *Arsenio Hall* show. Clinton's strategy and his "lines of the day" on policy issues were being drowned out by press stories about an extramarital affair and his activities to evade the draft during the Vietnam War. In a post-election interview (appropriately enough) with *TV Guide,* Clinton explained how he (and his campaign managers) decided to bypass the news in an effort to regain control of the media content of the campaign:

> TV GUIDE: It's been an incredible year for both TV and politics. When did *you* decide you needed to run a radically different kind of campaign?
>
> BILL CLINTON: New Hampshire. During the first primary, in February. I started getting bad press (about infidelities and the draft) and nobody wanted to talk about the issues anymore. I wondered if the voters felt the same. So I started having town hall meetings . . . I noticed there were large crowds at our meetings. So I just took that idea to television.
>
> TVG: (There was) quite a jump—from TV town halls to Arsenio Hall. Was there a particular moment when you and your advisers said "OK, nobody's listening—time for the sax, time for the shades?"
>
> CLINTON: Yes, during the New York primary. Again . . . what I was saying was still not being reported. The media were more interested in the horse race. That's when we decided to go full steam ahead in the new way. When people look back at this year and ask, "What really happened?" I think the two-way communication on TV between the candidate and the people will be the story.[53]

If we put the money chase together with the marketing race and the media strategies, the result is an inside look at the kind of campaign the voters experience at a personal level. Since at least 1968 when a "new and improved" Richard Nixon was presented to the nation's voters, the popular expression for the modern campaign experience has been "the selling of the President."[54] The dominance of media, money, and marketing has never been more evident than in the selling of the presidents in the elections of 1988 and 1992.

The Selling of the President 1988

The key to the Democratic loss in 1988 was the inability of candidate Michael Dukakis' marketing and advertising team to counter the attacks that were launched against him by the Bush team. In addition, the Dukakis campaign played out a kind of "death wish" marketing strategy to the bitter end, trying to get working class, Southern, and morally conservative market segments to buy the contrived image that, beneath his Boston liberal technocratic exterior, he was really just "an average guy, with a 25-year-old snow blower, a modest duplex, a loving family. He was Joe Suburbia ennobled—worthy of the White House."[55] The Dukakis loss in 1988 may be a comforting sign that candidate marketing is not always crafty, manipulative, or successful. There is both good news and bad for democracy here. First, the good news: There are no guarantees that marketing will always work. But before breathing too easily, consider the bad news: Even when one side's marketing strategy is inept, the other side's marketing strategy is winning the day. Whether the strategies are good, bad, or indifferent, one of two marketed candidates wins the election.

George Bush was victorious in 1988 under the masterful direction of James Baker and the master planning of "the Three Marketeers," campaign manager Lee Atwater, chief pollster Robert Teeter, and top media man Roger Ailes (with strong assists from pollster Richard Wirthlin and a public relations wonk named Sig Rogich, who was later rewarded the ambassadorship to Iceland for his impressive ad campaign). This lineup of heavy hitters illustrates campaign consultant Walter de Vries' observation that as consultants hold more sway over campaigns, their roles become more specialized and their ranks more numerous:

> The early consultants—in the campaigns of the 1960's—were generalists. They knew something about every piece of a campaign and advised candidates on everything. What you have now increasingly is more and more specialized consultants who deal only with television production, media buys, fund raising, polling and so on. Today, a campaign can have as many as three, four, or five consultants and I'm not just talking about presidential campaigns; I'm talking about statewide and even lesser campaigns.[56]

Saddled with a candidate who (the marketing research revealed) had an overwhelming image problem of being treated by the media as "a wimp," the Bush team went to work fashioning "tough guy" attacks on the opposition. Bush attacks (on crime, abortion, the ban on school prayer, and Dukakis' stance on the Pledge of Allegiance) weren't pretty, but they were effective. The heart of the Bush strategy was to keep the blue-collar Reaganites in the fold with a host of attacks summarized by conservative columnist George Will as the "Eek!—a liberal!" campaign.[57] *New York Times* reporter Mark Green opined that the Bush strategy was a "slur du jour" approach.[58]

Pollster Teeter, however, argued that "people don't decide [their vote] based on some great revelation. They form their views based on thousands of little bits of information that shake out from television ads and news stories, from pictures of the candidates' wives, kids, dogs, and homes."[59] Knowing how to deliver those bits of information in a range of styles is made easier by working up what Teeter calls a "perceptual map," a psychological model of how people see the candidates and what happens to that perception when this or that bit of information is added or subtracted.[60]

It turned out that adding the charges of being soft on crime, not caring about the flag, and other liberal quagmires both solved the Bush problem and exposed Dukakis' greatest weakness with his target audience, those blue-collar Republican or Reagan Democrat

Of Candidates and Consultants

The links between a candidate and his advisors are complex and often uneasy—especially when the candidate is as uncomfortable campaigning as was George Bush. In 1988, Bush benefited from the experience of media advisor Roger Ailes (*above*) and campaign manager Lee Atwater. When CBS News arranged to broadcast a "campaign profile" and interview with Dan Rather (*right*), Bush expected a routine encounter; Ailes, however, drilled Bush—over his protests—for combat. When Rather's interview turned into a verbal brawl, Bush scored by counter-attacking the journalist. The upshot was, noted Atwater, "a defining event" in the race. By 1992, however, Ailes had moved on to other activities; this loss was compounded by Atwater's untimely death. The patrician Bush appeared in such forums as the popular radio talk-show of Rush Limbaugh (an Ailes protégé, *below*), but his efforts never quite clicked, and he lost vital centrist support to the more media-savvy Bill Clinton and the more populist-minded Ross Perot.

The Players

swing voters who wanted attention paid to their values and problems. Bush consultants worked with focus groups of Reagan Democrats and gradually found what drove them away from Dukakis and toward Bush. The most effective image of all was delivered in the now-famous Willie Horton story about a prison furlough program in Dukakis' home state that released a black convict, jailed for murder, who raped a white woman during his "weekend furlough." The story appalled the targeted blue-collar voters. Whatever its "racial overtones," it was clear that the Willie Horton story strongly evoked the feeling that Dukakis was soft on crime. After observing the effects of the Horton story on focus groups of targeted voters, Atwater is reported to have said, "If I can make Willie Horton a household name, we'll win the election."[61] Horton did become a household name, and Dukakis never recovered from the attacks against him.

To counter the danger that the Bush image would become too tough and mean-spirited, the Dukakis attacks were limited to about fifty percent of the content of the media campaign, while the other half of the messages showed Bush sympathetically: playing with his many grandchildren; promising relief for the poor and the overtaxed; and occasionally pointing out that he personally liked Dukakis, who was a decent human being beneath that regrettable liberal exterior. And so, when Bush was not slashing away at Dukakis, he spoke of a "kinder, gentler nation" illuminated by "a thousand points of light." At first, Bush expressed discomfort with the hard persona fashioned by his consultants. Roger Ailes summarized Bush's early reactions to the negative ads and the "attack days" on the campaign trail by saying, "He hates it, but he knows we'd be getting killed if we didn't go negative."[62] While expressing a distinct preference for "kinder, gentler" ways, Bush acknowledged that the "sweet and sour" persona was having its desired effect on voters. "I like the mix," Bush told *New York Times* reporter Maureen Dowd in a tone that she described "as though he had just sipped a martini or tasted a pasta sauce and found the ingredients perfectly blended."[63]

In this age of the mass-marketed candidate, it no longer matters who is the "real" George Bush, just as it is beside the point to ask what the "real" Michael Dukakis stood for. Candidate marketing shapes a candidate's personality and rhetoric. The key to it all is the ironic human capacity that leads voters to make sense of almost any available information. The hardy souls who stay tuned to the contest must strive to make the whole experience credible. As political scientist Marjorie Hershey put it, these "voters respond to the political stimuli they receive."[64] Thus, in the words of one analysis, "The public's response to symbols—the flag, tanks, liberals, and criminals—dominated the 1988 campaign."[65]

In the opinion of communications scholar Kathleen Jamieson, an expert on political marketing: "Never before in a presidential campaign have televised ads sponsored by a major party candidate lied so blatantly as in the campaign of 1988."[66] The line between illusion and deception is a fine one in political marketing. The Bush campaign of 1988 probably stands as a masterpiece of modern political marketing.

The Selling of the President 1992

Perhaps the biggest surprise of 1992 was that there was a campaign at all. Through early and mid-1991, the time when opponents begin to appear, President Bush was enjoying the highest levels of popularity of any president in modern history. Following the resounding American victory in the Persian Gulf War (discussed in Chapters 6 and 11), Mr. Bush's popularity approached a formidable 90 percent approval level, leading pundits to suggest that he was unbeatable. The only Democrat to declare an early candidacy was Paul Tsongas, a former Massachusetts senator.

For most of 1991, in the victorious aftermath of the Persian Gulf War, President George Bush seemed assured of reelection, and only former Massachusetts senator Paul Tsongas (right) campaigned for the Democratic nomination. As the national economy remained flat into 1992, however, the race was abruptly joined by (from left) former governor Jerry Brown of California, Governor Bill Clinton of Arkansas, Senator Tom Harkin of Iowa, and Senator Bob Kerrey of Nebraska. Tsongas won the influential New Hampshire primary, but Clinton— labelling himself "the Comeback Kid"—went on to gain the nomination and the November election.

Suddenly the climate of public opinion shifted as people felt the sting of economic recession. Bush's approval ratings fell so fast that one headline summed it up this way: HIS POPULARITY IN A "FREE-FALL," BUSH WILL ACCELERATE HIS RE-ELECTION CAMPAIGN.[67] And just as suddenly, the lone Democratic challenger was joined by four more trooping through the snows of Iowa and New Hampshire. With a little help from the media, the Democratic primaries soon turned into an exciting horse race. The media played off Mr. Bush against the field of Democrats, with some polls showing the president finishing in a virtual tie with any unnamed Democrat.[68]

If the story of 1988 was the poor performance of the Democratic campaign team and the brilliance of the Republicans, the plot was reversed in 1992. The old Bush team had scattered with the winds: Lee Atwater had died; James Baker had become Secretary of State; Sig Rogich was Ambassador to Iceland; and Roger Ailes had declined to serve again as chief media guru. Through it all, President Bush appeared not to worry until it was too late. Only after the convention did he recall James Baker and Sig Rogich from diplomatic duties. However, at that point, there was no strategy, no media plan, and few issues in the Republican platform that seemed to interest voters concerned about an economy that Mr. Bush assured them would get better on its own.

What resulted was a replay of the negative campaign of 1988, with Rogich throwing together a batch of attack ads, and Mr. Bush making appearance after appearance in which he offered little economic change, while attacking his opponent much as he had

Michael Dukakis four years earlier. The major theme opening the campaign at the convention was summed up in this headline: REPUBLICANS ASSAIL CLINTON AS RADICAL AND BIG SPENDER AND ASSERT BUSH STRENGTHS.[69] In a further sign that the Bush team had failed to design a new sales effort appropriate to the new conditions of 1992, chief pollster Robert Teeter described the marketing strategy in words he might well have used in 1988 by just changing the name Clinton to Dukakis. Teeter said that the election had become a referendum on Mr. Clinton's character, and that "It is Mr. Bush's job to persuade the public to vote 'no.'"[70]

The problem was that there was no single image to spark the campaign against Clinton. Neither the marriage problems nor the draft record seemed to register with voters who were worried about the economy. The Bush team never produced a convincing economic statement, and its ads instead became more negative as election day drew closer.[71] On the campaign trail, Mr. Bush's attacks on Clinton and Gore ran to these terms, among others:

"The Waffle Man."
"Governor Taxes and the Ozone Man."
"A couple of yuppies dressed as moderates. Watch your wallet."
"Those deadly talking heads."
"Bozos."

When Mr. Bush's daily opinion polls reported that the negativity appeared to be backfiring, he simply cancelled his daily poll briefing. In 1992, it appeared that it was Mr. Bush who inflicted the political "death wish" on his campaign team. The moral of 1992 appears to be that a negative campaign is bound to work better when voters are reasonably satisfied with the state of the economy, as they were in 1988.

The big issue of 1992 was not lost on the Clinton campaign, as indicated by a large sign on the wall of its Little Rock headquarters that read: "The economy, stupid!" The campaign team was reminded every day to keep the media line of the day focused on this issue of greatest concern to their targeted voter groups. Clinton speeches and ads (see Box 10.3) drummed economic fears into the news, advertising, the candidate debates, and other television appearances.

The economy was clearly turned into an even more important issue by the candidacy of Ross Perot, who used the media to put the economic heat on both major party candidates, including unprecedented televised chalk talks that drew remarkably good ratings. As previously noted in Box 10.2, the $35 million that Perot spent on television "infomercials" was regarded as so successful in terms of getting public attention that *Advertising Age* magazine crowned Mr. Perot the "Adman of the Year" for 1992.[72] As explained in Chapter 7, the Clinton and Perot economic positions registered with a majority of voters who said that these were important factors in their voting.

Whenever the press became critical of Clinton, the final stroke of campaign genius was simply to bypass the press by using other television formats, as described earlier. The Clinton campaign also learned from the Dukakis disaster of 1988 to respond to personal attacks immediately, not allowing doubts to grow in the minds of undecided voters. Throughout the campaign, the Clinton team found ways to win back press favor and restore positive news coverage. At several key junctures, Clinton and Gore took to the campaign trail on bus trips that provided the media with great photo opportunities of small-town American life and the illusion that old-fashioned, person-to-person campaigning had been restored. Perhaps there was a return to "retail," or direct campaigning in 1992, but every appearance was staged to be sold "wholesale" to the mass audience watching a carefully scripted drama unfold in their living rooms. Down to the last bus trip, *Al and Bill's Excellent Political Adventure* was carefully contrived for the television audience of targeted voters who had to be sold on Bill Clinton.

Al and Bill's Excellent Political Adventure. *Democratic candidates Al Gore and Bill Clinton engage in a photo-opportunity session with an unidentified worker at an Iowa aluminum plant, during one of their campaign-bus excursions. As is true of much modern campaigning, this seemingly close, "one-on-one" political style was carefully calibrated by campaign experts to reach a mass-media audience.*

Reforming the System

An American election campaign must be hard to grasp for the majority of people in other democracies, where the length of campaigning is much shorter (three weeks in Britain), spending is severely limited (a British member of parliament was limited to raising $15,000 during the 1992 election campaign), political advertising is restricted, all major party candidates generally receive equal amounts of free air time, and the taxpayers provide the bulk of financing to the parties in order to minimize private political influence.[73]

If the American election system is costing huge amounts of money, increasing private political influence in elections, and leaving most voters unsatisfied, why not force the American system more into line with the rest of the democratic world? Part of the reason is that Americans know little about the other world democracies because of cultural feelings of being geographically separate, politically unique, and at times downright superior. However, few observers find today's election system to be working well enough to call it superior. (Unique, perhaps, but not superior.) Among the many reforms that might make a difference in how elections work are the following.

One idea aimed at restoring an electoral system with healthy parties at the center would be to reform the **campaign finance** system: tighten (voluntary) spending limits, re-

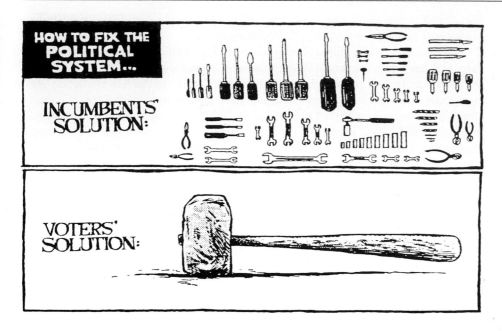

strict or eliminate PACs, publicize lists of contributors, and channel money to parties rather than individual candidates. Strengthening party organizations might encourage campaigns to be built around party programs, rather than fragmented into multiple candidate images and contracted out by individual candidates to marketing and consulting firms. As noted earlier, Congress has grappled with finance reform in recent years, but few observers expect dramatic results even if legislation is passed.

Reforms would have more impact if Congress and the president agreed on the public financing of campaigns for *all* national offices as a way of getting special interest money out of the election process. Even if the costs of public financing campaigns for national office in a presidential year exceed $2 billion (the costs of all offices, both state and national are around $3 billion), that is just about the price of two Stealth bombers. It might not be a bad tradeoff for democracy.

The costs of campaigning could be reduced dramatically, perhaps by as much as half, if the United States adopted the same regulations on political advertising and the uses of the media that we find in most other nations. For starters, Congress and the president could press the Federal Communication Commission (see Chapter 11) to regard election messages as part of broadcasters' public service obligations required as part of the deal for being granted use of the public airwaves. Broadcasters resist such regulation as a violation of free speech, but what they often mean is that it would destroy the income they make selling political ads at election time. Congress and executive branch regulatory agencies have had no qualms about regulating other forms of program and commercial content on the airwaves (pornography, abusive and sexual language, alcohol and tobacco ads, just to name a few). Were it not for the fact that politicians and broadcasters all benefit from the current system, we probably would have more public-spirited political communications codes as well. The federal communication rules could also prescribe longer periods for candidates to appear in their free air time, reducing the use of slick commercials and encouraging longer statements of ideas and policies. Broadcasters themselves could alter the format of candidate debates—as they showed signs of doing in 1992—moving either in the direction of real debates between the candidates, or in the direction of more focused press examination of such campaign issues as defense, the economy, social policies, and the environment. After thirty minutes on a single issue, it might become easier to tell if the candidates had anything to say.

What would it take to bring about such sweeping election campaign reforms? The force that has driven reforms in the past: pressure from the people themselves through social movements and political parties. Women won important changes in election laws by demonstrating and lobbying state and national representatives. Earlier eras of corruption in government were battled by movements such as the Progressives, who organized influential third parties. As the poll data in Figure 10.5 reveals, the public favors sweeping election reforms. It may be time for people to organize at the grass roots and reform the election system in the way most likely to make a difference: by capturing the existing parties or by creating a new one around the issue of reforming elections and campaigns first. After all, the way in which the electoral guidance system works affects all the other issues the government faces.

FIGURE 10.5

Public Support for Reform of the Electoral Process

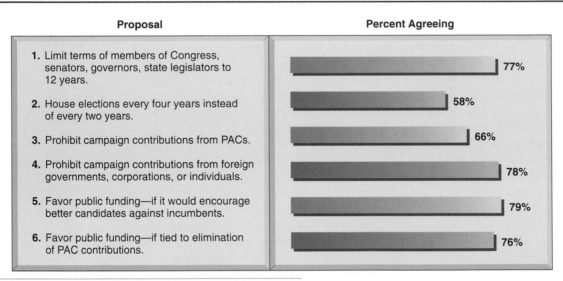

Proposal	Percent Agreeing
1. Limit terms of members of Congress, senators, governors, state legislators to 12 years.	77%
2. House elections every four years instead of every two years.	58%
3. Prohibit campaign contributions from PACs.	66%
4. Prohibit campaign contributions from foreign governments, corporations, or individuals.	78%
5. Favor public funding—if it would encourage better candidates against incumbents.	79%
6. Favor public funding—if tied to elimination of PAC contributions.	76%

Questions:
1. The following are proposed changes in election laws. For each one, please tell me whether you approve or disapprove of the proposal. . . . Limit the terms of office of members of Congress, senators, governors, and state legislators to 12 years.
2. (Same preface as 1) . . . Have members of the House of Representatives run every four years, instead of every two years as the Constitution currently requires.
3. (Same preface as 1) . . . Prohibit campaign contributions from the Political Action Committees.
4. (Same preface as 1) . . . Prohibit campaign contributions from foreign governments, foreign corporations, or foreign individuals.
5. If public funding of campaigns would encourage more good people to run against incumbents, would you favor or oppose public funding of congressional and senatorial candidates?
6. If public funding were tied to the elimination of all special interest campaign contributions, would you favor or oppose public funding?
SOURCE: Survey by Gordon S. Black Corporation, May 1992. Adapted from *The Public Perspective*, November/December, 1992, p. 4.

A CITIZEN'S QUESTION
Elections Beyond Voting

How can I become involved with reforming the election process? As this analysis of elections suggests, the citizen's role in democracy goes well beyond voting. In fact, the problems with elections these days cannot be fixed by simply voting them away. Many citizens have stopped voting, either out of a sense that campaigns are meaningless, or out of a deeper frustration that the candidates are no longer even interested in their vote. While the strategies of modern campaigning suggest that some of these impressions may be reasonable, the solution is not to withdraw from elections. To do so is to give up on the only forum for participation that contains the possibility of addressing and solving the broadest problems faced by the whole society.

What can citizens concerned about the condition of the nation's political guidance system do? It turns out there are a number of citizens' campaigns for election reform already under way. Each takes a slightly different focus and sees the issues a bit differently. Based on the information from this chapter, you are in a position to understand and evaluate the programs of the different groups. For information about some of the citizen action options related to elections, write or call:

Center for Responsive Politics
1320 19th St., N.W. Suite M-1
Washington, D.C. 20036   202-857-0044
(Focus: Congressional campaign finance reform)

Citizens Action Against PACs
2000 P St., N.W. Suite 408
Washington, D.C. 20036   202-463-0465
(Focus: PAC influence in congressional elections)

Honest Ballot Association
272-30 Grand Central Parkway
Floral Park, NY 11005
(Focus: Clean elections through registration and voting procedures. Information center on local election laws)

Initiative Resource Center
235 Douglass St.
San Francisco, CA 94114   415-431-4765
(Focus: Information clearinghouse on initiative and referendum campaigns and procedures)

Elections and American Democracy Revisited _____

The politics behind the scenes in recent national elections explain a great deal about why voters are discouraged, why voting seems to have little connection to party responsiveness, and why parties, in turn, have trouble with coherent governing. These trends are driven by three key forces behind modern election politics: money, media, and marketing. Each of these factors feeds the other, sending elections into ever-more-costly chases by candidates for the hard-to-win support of ever-more-suspicious voters.

Once elected, government officials either discover that they have few ideas to implement or find little support from parties or other politicians for the programs they do have. The cure, once again, is to call on the image consultants to maintain popularity in office, much as it was created on the campaign trail. The addiction of leaders to their public images appears to be turning the national political scene into an endless campaign, in which the goal is to dodge the problems and issues of the day, keep one's image strong, and make it to the next election with a full campaign chest and no mistakes to live down. Even when leaders come to Washington with new ideas, they often must revive campaign-style tactics to put public pressure on their own parties. The challenges of "going public" (as described in Chapter 14) have confronted Republicans and Democrats alike, from Ronald Reagan to Bill Clinton.

These conclusions may sound strong, but they are shared increasingly these days by political scientists, the public, and even elected officials. These concerns about problems inside the election system explain many expressions of voter discontent, ranging from the popularity of Ross Perot to the numerous proposals for election reforms. The more controversial question is how to reform the electoral system in ways that promote the health of democracy.

Key Terms

functions of elections in democracy
  debate/leadership/accountability/
    participation

direct vs. indirect democracy
  elections for representatives
  initiative and referendum

getting elected, the nuts and bolts
  the nomination
  the convention
  the campaign
    playing the electoral vote
    playing the swing vote
    campaign organizations

getting elected, the politics
  media/money/marketing

campaign finance
  Federal Election Campaign Act
  campaign contributions
  hard money/soft money

candidate spending limits
  voluntary limits
PACs and how they work
  impact on parties, party cohesion

marketing strategies
  advertising and the uses of
    television
  impact on candidate relations
    with parties
  implications for democracy

media campaign strategy
  line of the day
  sound bites
  damage control
  spin/spin doctors

reform possibilities
  campaign finance
  television content guidelines
    and advertising reforms

Suggested Readings

Alexander, Herbert E. *Financing Politics: Money, Elections and Political Reform.* Washington: Congressional Quarterly Press, 1984.

Asher, Herbert B. *Presidential Elections and American Politics,* 4th ed. Chicago: Dorsey Press, 1988.

Bennett, W. Lance. *The Governing Crisis: Media, Money and Marketing in American Politics.* New York: St. Martin's Press, 1992.

Cramer, Richard Ben. *What It Takes: The Way to the White House* (updated ed.). New York: Vintage, 1993.

Germond, Jack W. and Jules Witcover. *Mad as Hell: Revolt at the Ballot Box, 1992.* New York: Warner Books, 1993.

Jackson, Brooks. *Honest Graft: Big Money and the American Political Process,* rev. ed. Washington, D.C.: Farragut, 1990.

Magelby, David B. and Candice J. Nelson, *The Money Chase: Congressional Campaign Finance Reform,* Washington: Brookings Institution, 1990.

Owen, Diana. *Media Messages in American Presidential Elections.* New York: Greenwood Press, 1991.

Sabato, Larry J. *PAC Power.* New York: Norton, 1985.

Simon, Roger. *Road Show: In America, Anyone Can Become President.* New York: Farrar, Straus & Giroux, 1990.

Wayne, Stephen J. *The Road to the White House 1992.* New York: St. Martin's Press, 1992.

Wayne, Stephen J. and Clyde Wilcox, eds. *The Quest for National Office.* New York: St. Martin's Press, 1992.

• • •

[A president's relationship with the media] truly is a
damned-if-you-do, damned-if-you-don't proposition. If you try
to manipulate the press, you'll be accused of manipulation. If
you don't, you'll be accused of incompetence.
—*GERALD F. SEIB, WHITE HOUSE CORRESPONDENT*

• • •

The American electorate is astride an inescapable fault line
that divides those who grew up on TV . . . and those who
didn't. Neither side fully understands the other or speaks the
same language or sees quite the same reality in their perceptions
of the world. The older half still generally control things . . .
But the younger half is . . . replacing them. . . . The future of
democracy—if it has a future—inevitably belongs to those
who can watch MTV without feeling crazy.
—*WILLIAM GREIDER*

• • •

We are no longer obsessed with television, we are addicted to
it (half the people in the stadium watch the game on the
monitors, half the people at the convention watch the
demonstrations on the monitors), and we are not only
addicted, we are saturated (the monitors are all over). It isn't
enough that they're experiencing it; it isn't real unless it's
ratified, and television is the ratifier.
—*PEGGY NOONAN*

• • •

Mass Mediated Democracy

- **THE MEDIA GO TO WAR**

- **INFORMATION, POWER, AND DEMOCRACY**
  What's News?
  The Medium and the Message
  Information Characteristics of Mass Media News

- **THE PRESS AND THE GOVERNMENT**
  Government Regulation of the Press
  Truth and the First Amendment

- **MAKING THE NEWS**
  The Working Relations Between Press and Politicians
  How to Make the News
  How Do Outsiders Make the News?

- **PUBLIC OPINION AND THE NEWS**
  The Battle for Public Opinion
  Setting the Agenda

- **INSIDE THE NEWS ORGANIZATION: THE ECONOMICS OF INFORMATION**
  A Social and Economic History of the American Press
  How Journalists Work
  Routine News: Deadlines, Beats, and Packs
  Popular Tastes and News

- **INFORMATION, POWER, AND DEMOCRACY REVISITED**

- **A CITIZEN'S QUESTION: Political Information**

- **KEY TERMS**

- **SUGGESTED READINGS**

The Media Go to War

In January of 1991, the United States launched a massive military offensive against Iraq in retaliation for Iraq's invasion of neighboring Kuwait some six months earlier. Before the final decision to attack, there were serious divisions in public opinion between those who wanted to allow more time for economic sanctions to force Iraq from Kuwait, and those who felt that retaliation had become the only realistic solution. A congressional debate granted the president (by a vote of 250–183 in the House and 52–47 in the Senate) authority to participate in a United Nations military action.

The war scenario was cast with the help of important political images operating through the news. For example, Iraqi dictator Saddam Hussein was equated with Hitler in hundreds of news accounts. How would the public have reacted if they had known that Hitler was the name that scared people the most in test-marketing research with focus groups (recall Chapter 6) conducted by a Washington public relations firm, Hill & Knowlton? Would Americans have been any less sympathetic to the plight of the Kuwaiti people had they known at the time that the government of Kuwait and its royal family paid Hill & Knowlton to conduct a campaign to strengthen American support to liberate their tiny nation?[1]

As the important congressional debate drew near, another major news-making effort was mounted by Hill & Knowlton. A young Kuwaiti girl named Nayirah appeared before Congress, testifying that as a hospital worker in Kuwait she saw Iraqi soldiers throwing Kuwaiti babies out of incubators and onto the hospital floor to die. Not until a year later, long after the war was over, was it revealed that the girl who worked in a hospital was also the daughter of Kuwait's ambassador to the United States, and her testimony was part of a public information campaign organized by Hill & Knowlton.[2] At the time, Nayirah's congressional testimony became big news, in part because Hill & Knowlton produced what is known as a Video News Release (VNR), suitable for showing as a television news story. Not only did the VNR appear on NBC's *Nightly News,* but it was distributed to some 700 TV stations and ended up broadcast to an estimated audience of 35 million Americans.

By the time of the January 12 congressional vote to approve military action, estimates in the press and in Congress ran as high as 312 "documented" incubator deaths at the hands of Iraqi soldiers, a factor cited by many members of Congress in deciding their vote.[3] After the war was over, ABC News sent a reporter to the hospital where the atrocities were alleged, and learned from doctors there that babies

Saddam Hussein's media skills in late 1990 were, on the whole, as blunt as his military subjugation of Kuwait: He alternately posed for photographs while smiling at small children, announced that foreign hostages were being held as "human shields" at Iraqi military bases, and, in this videotaped September address, warned Americans that they faced "a war more terrible than Vietnam." Western authorities proved somewhat more subtle in presenting their case to the press.

had in fact died in the chaos and shortage of nurses resulting from the invasion, but nobody could remember seeing any thrown from their incubators. Nayirah later said that she personally saw only one infant thrown from its incubator. Although the facts were finally corrected in several places,[4] this story-behind-the story never became big news. By the time the politics behind the news came to light, the war was long over, and the attention of press and public were on other things.

The war was a relatively short and one-sided affair. As one commentator put it, Iraq was bombed back into the previous century. Millions of Americans watched this live, prime-time war on television. TV screens filled with video-game images. Bird's-eye pictures relayed from cameras inside of bombs and missiles took living-room audiences along on trips to the targets. News briefings were delivered by the military commanders themselves. Local television news crews were flown to Saudi Arabia, often at Pentagon expense, to do stories on troops from hometown bases. Pre-war divisions of opinion quickly turned into an overwhelming rally of support in the polls, including record levels of approval (near 90 percent) for President Bush.

Not only did the war effort become popular, but the ratings of many news programs were among the highest ever recorded. Local stations and national networks alike displayed special sets, including war game boards that were used to chart the military maneuvers. Advertising spots and logos gave viewers a sense of identification with news programs, as did theme music with driving beats. In the view of many media critics and scholars, these media formats blurred the line between entertainment and information that once defined news itself. A new word, **infotainment,** suggests that the distinction between fact and fantasy may be of diminishing importance to producers and consumers of news in this age of "teledemocracy."

Infotainment thrives on the drama of news reports that may later turn out to be wrong or misleading. For example, in the early days of the war, the news was filled with glowing stories about the American arsenal of high-tech weapons. A missile named the Patriot was championed by headlines like this one in a major national paper: BATTLE-NEW PATRIOT MISSILE SOARS TO STARDOM. In the story, the Patriot was heralded for shooting down an enemy missile to which the Pentagon gave the unheroic name of Scud. More than a year and a half later, however, the same newspaper ran a much different headline about that same incident from the beginning of the war: THE BULLS-EYE THAT NEVER HAPPENED: THAT FIRST PATRIOT DIDN'T NAIL A SCUD.[5] It seemed that the Pentagon had misrepresented that first deployment (and many later ones) of Patriots that never hit their targets.

Managing news images in time of war is a difficult issue—one that touches the very heart of democracy. Does the public have a right to know exactly how the nation's military power is being used, against whom,

General Colin Powell, then chairman of the Joint Chiefs of Staff, briefs reporters on the destruction of Iraqi radar capabilities by massive coalition aircraft bombing in January 1991. By the start of the 1990s, military officials—many of whom felt the press had trampled on their objectives during the Vietnam War—had become almost as adept at media tactics as military tactics.

with what effects, and for what reasons? And if the tides of battle run against the American side, should "the people" be told about it, and have the right to step in and stop the conflict? All of those questions haunted the nation after the war in Vietnam. In the minds of some Americans, the reasons for that divisive conflict were never explained adequately, and the military's poor performance was hidden from the press for years. A different point of view, however, was shared by the military and others, who attributed the American defeat to hostile media coverage of battle scenes, combined with sympathetic treatment of the antiwar movement at home. Vietnam was, in this view, not so much a military defeat as a media-led national loss of will.

Vietnam taught the generals not to trust media relations to the politicians who seemed easily caught up in the whims of public opinion. After the relatively open access enjoyed by the press in Vietnam, latter-day journalists gradually became conditioned to spoon-fed news handouts. As the Chairman of the Joint Chiefs of Staff, Colin Powell, put it before the U.S. intervention in Panama in 1989, "Once you've got all the forces moving and everything's being taken care of by the commanders, turn your attention to television because you can win the battle or lose the war if you don't handle the story right."[6] And handle it, they did, both in Panama and even more impressively in the war against Iraq. In the words of Michael Deaver, who ran press management in the Reagan White House, "If you were going to hire a public relations firm to do the media relations for an international event, it couldn't be done any better than this."[7] Or, in the words of Hodding Carter, a press officer from the Carter administration, "If I were the government, I'd be paying the press for the kind of coverage it is getting right now."[8]

Many journalists were resentful of their position. As one correspondent saw it, "We have sort of become adjuncts of the government. The line between me and a government contractor is pretty thin."[9] Another complained that "Each pool member is an unpaid employee of the Department of Defense, on whose behalf he or she prepares the news of the war for the outer world."[10] ("Pools" refer to groups of journalists escorted by military personnel to selected locations. Their coverage was then shared with the rest of the press corps.) Despite the presence of more than a thousand U.S. news people at various times and places throughout the Persian Gulf region (most in Saudi Arabia, the center of military operations), one observer concluded that "To get at the real story in the gulf, reporters did not have to travel to the front. They did not even have to travel to Saudi Arabia. Most of the information they needed was available in Washington."[11]

Despite grumbling off-camera about the loss of press freedom, reporters on the air showed numerous signs of jumping willingly on the bandwagon. Bombing missions were reported with assessments like "It was spectacular news. We've lost only one casualty." Another spoke of "almost picture-perfect assaults." A network anchor congratulated a general for "a job wonderfully done." Many news accounts adopted a we–they, us–them vocabulary, as in "We knocked one of their Scuds [missiles] out of the sky." U.S. bombers taking off were described in one report as a "sweet beautiful sight." Enemy missiles were not described by their Soviet-made military designation, SS-1s, but by the Pentagon's designation of "Scud." Reporters described the Scud as "a horrifying killer," and "a quarter ton of concentrated hatred," in contrast to the Patriot, which one news account described as "three inches longer than a Cadillac Sedan de Ville." What's more, "our side" had "smart bombs" applauded by one network anchor as the "brilliance of laser-guided bombs," while the other side's airborne threat was termed "an evil weapon, but not an accurate weapon."[12]

The question here is not whether the war against Iraq was a good idea, but whether the American people received the kind of information they needed to

U.S. Admiral Eugene Carroll (retired) of the Center for Defense Information deadpanned to the press during the Persian Gulf War: "B-52 bombing from thirty thousand to forty thousand feet is very accurate. They hit the ground every time."

decide that question in a critical way. The quality of political information, and the atmosphere in which it is presented and debated, are among the key factors in evaluating the relations among the press, the government, and the people in a democracy. How people think about and debate important issues facing the nation is affected by how the press covers those issues. Press coverage, in turn, is affected by how governments and other political actors (such as the Kuwaiti government with its public-relations outreach campaign) try to manage the information that goes to the press.

The Persian Gulf War is not typical of most news coverage. The public has been treated to open and sustained debates in the media about health care, world trade policy, the environment, abortion, and other issues. However, many of the factors that affected press coverage of the Persian Gulf War are present in less extreme forms in many political situations. *The political battle to shape public opinion and participation through the news is always under way.* Sometimes political factions compete effectively to get diverse messages and images into the mainstream national media, and sometimes the flow of information is much more restricted. Either way, information about politics in the news is itself very political. This chapter explores the political relations among the press, the government, and the public. In addition to introducing academic views about the role of the press in a democracy, ideas about how citizens can use the news more critically are developed throughout the chapter.

Information, Power, and Democracy

The big question about government control of public information, whether in war or peace, is this: Who in a democracy should be responsible for deciding the political truth: the government, the press, or the individual citizen? In reality, all three are involved in the struggle over information, and it is important to understand how each plays its part. From the first American government to the latest, people have known that governments cannot always be trusted to tell the people everything about their activities. Without some independent check on the information provided by governments, the people are left powerless in the most fundamental sense of not knowing what their representatives are really doing or why. A free and independent press is a rallying symbol of the political culture, representing the enduring importance of monitoring government activities and stimulating debate.

The news of two hundred, one hundred, or even fifty years ago had little resemblance to that of today. Town meetings, speeches in public squares, travelers, troubadours, and small, often very political, presses served the information needs in the last century. Citizens today depend almost entirely on the mass media. However, the basic importance of information for democracy remains much the same as always:

> Freedom of expression is not only an individual but also a social good. . . . [T]he soundest and most rational judgment is arrived at by considering all facts and arguments which can be put forth in behalf of or against any proposition. Human judgment is a frail thing. It may err in being subject to emotion, prejudice or personal interest. It suffers from lack of information and insight or inadequate thinking. . . . Hence an individual who seeks knowledge or truth must hear all sides of the question, especially as presented by those who feel strongly and argue militantly for a different view.[13]

The values of competing information and different points of view, along with holding government accountable to the people, keep the idea of a free press at the center of the political culture. Thomas Jefferson once quipped that if forced to choose between a government without a free press or a press without a government, he would take the latter.

These cultural ideals are often tarnished by the realities of politics. Jefferson became one of the most vocal critics of the press after he was elected president. Sometimes the heat of political battle or the belief in the importance of one's own interests leads politicians and average citizens alike to settle for less quality in the information exchange than the ideals of the political culture might recommend.

What's News?

Most scholars agree that the information in the news is affected by a combination of: *public tastes* (what people already believe and want to hear); *institutional control* (government institutions produce official information and directly regulate aspects of communication); *power and political interests* (some groups and politicians are more successful in getting their views into the news); and *the economics of the news media* (the kinds of information that sell and that can be produced profitably). If the first three factors sound related to our organizing framework of *culture, institutions,* and *power,* they are. And each of these three factors connects with the fourth information force—the economics of the news business—in important ways.

Culture, of course, is a foundation of popular taste; what people believe about politics is anchored in culture. Not surprisingly, most of the plots in news stories revolve around familiar cultural themes: the story of individual freedom, the ideals of American democracy, the struggles of people to win their day in court or to tame big government, the fight of the United States against forces of evil in the world, and the triumphs of the free enterprise system, among others.[14] Playing to these cultural themes also helps news organizations maintain their audiences by selling them a familiar product. It is important to recognize that the cultural ideal of a free flow of information may come into conflict with popular beliefs and tastes in ways that limit what people care to think about.

Government institutions affect the news indirectly by passing laws that keep some government information secret (discussed below and in Chapter 20). Other laws, also noted below, tell news organizations what they can report without being sued for libel. Institutions also produce the information and reports that tell the official story about what the government is doing in its various activities. In addition, the offices and departments of government provide news information services such as briefings, press conferences, and press releases that serve as the basis for a great deal of the news about government. Finally, government institutions regulate how broadcast licenses are given out and decide what kinds of public information responsibilities the companies who hold those licenses have.

Power in society affects which groups and officials get their messages into the news and how they do it. The president, as the most powerful and prominent political actor, is covered more than any other news source. Sometimes presidents receive far more media attention than they want, but the constant presence of so many journalists around the president also gives him an advantage for getting his point of view into the news. Groups with other power bases, from money to large memberships, can find other ways to make the news: hiring public relations firms, staging demonstrations, publicizing the results of research about their causes, and training their leaders in how to relate to the press. Like government actors, nongovernment newsmakers also learn to schedule events, hold press conferences, deliver press releases to news rooms, and do other things that attract journalists.

These political system factors help in thinking about what the news is and is not. It is tempting to think that the news is (or should be) Truth, or Objective Fact, or Reality itself. These images may be comforting, but they are also misleading. The news is a valued political prize for the competing groups trying to make it, meaning that it almost always has political points of view embedded within it. Reporters generally try to be fair

Anchoring the Ship of State

The media have been called the fourth branch of government. If so, its top legislators may be network television's evening news-program anchors, including NBC's Tom Brokaw; CBS's Dan Rather and Connie Chung; and ABC's Peter Jennings *(below)*. Reaching millions daily (and earning millions yearly), these journalists have huge public recognition. Watched by a smaller but perhaps more informed, activist audience is PBS's *MacNeil/Lehrer News Hour* (with Robert MacNeil and Jim Lehrer, *right*), which features issue analysis, panel discussions, and extended interviews with newsmakers. A growing competitor to the networks is Atlanta's CNN (Cable News Network), featuring Bernard Shaw *(above)*. While they may not legislate, TV news anchors and their teams can strongly influence the public agenda.

The Players

and impartial in gathering information about a situation, but they are always faced with the above political forces that shape and limit what becomes news.

Political scientist Doris Graber suggests that news is not just any information, or even the most important information about the world; rather, the news tends to contain information that is *timely;* often *sensational* (scandals, violence, and human drama make the news); and *familiar* (drawing on familiar people or life experiences that give even distant events a close-to-home feeling).[15] These characteristics remind us that the news is not reality; it is what news organizations report about reality. In other words, the news is not a mirror, or an all-seeing eyewitness account; it is a representation. Like all representations, from paintings to photographs to the stories we tell about things that happen to us, some details are included while others are left out.

Unlike many representations, however, news is deceptively "realistic" because it is so standardized. The way in which mass media news is produced, distributed, and consumed makes it regular and predictable, with substantial overlaps in content no matter what mass media news source one turns to. In addition, mass media news about politics is realistic because so many of the sources that journalists use are government officials who are, after all, called "authorities."

FIGURE 11.1

Where Americans Get Most of Their News

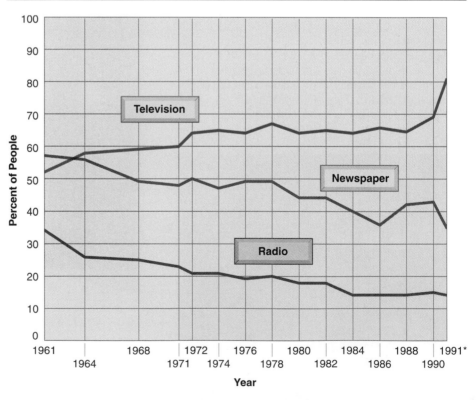

Note: Some people rely on multiple news sources, making the totals add up to more than 100 percent.

*The figures for 1991 are inflated by the Gulf War against Iraq. This shows how people turn to television even more during crises.

Source: *America's Watching: Public Attitudes Toward Television.* National Association of Broadcasters, 1991, p. 21.

The Medium and the Message

Research shows that people do not retain much information from the news about politics, and what they do remember tends to be more about personalities than about issues or power.[16] The focus on personalities (and the inability to recall other information) is even stronger for the majority of Americans who get most of their information from television.[17] Some observers trace a general decline in knowledge about politics over the last several decades to the rise of television as the main national information source over the same period.[18] Others point out that the very nature of information itself may have been changed by television, which means that people may receive important understanding from television news, but the information is coded visually. Factual information, such as the name of one's congressional representative, is stored by people in ways that can be measured by paper-and-pencil testing, whereas visual information may not be measured as easily.[19]

Whether or not television is providing people with poorer information or simply a different kind of information, it has become the information medium of choice for a majority of Americans. Figure 11.1 shows the changes over three decades in the use of television, radio, newspapers, and magazines. Not surprisingly, people find the medium they use most to be the most believable. Perhaps in the case of television, as the saying goes, "seeing is believing." Figure 11.2 illustrates the changes in the credibility of different information media in the minds of Americans over three decades.

FIGURE 11.2 *What News Source Is Most Believable?*

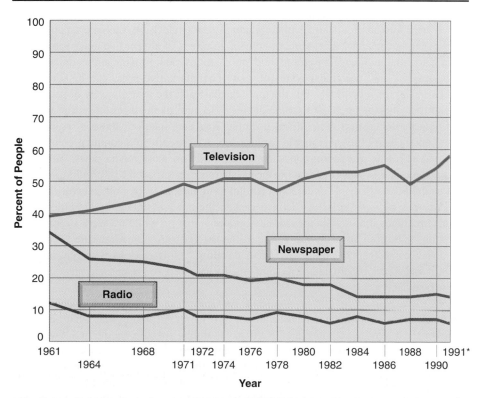

*The figures for 1991 are inflated slightly by the Gulf War against Iraq, showing that people found television crisis coverage very credible in this case.

Source: *America's Watching: Public Attitudes Toward Television.* National Association of Broadcasters, 1991, p. 21.

Just how much TV do people watch? Figure 11.3 shows that the average family has a television set turned on approximately seven hours each day, a pattern that has held relatively stable since 1980. (It is not clear how much more TV people could "watch," if the remainder of a typical day includes eight hours of work and eight hours of sleep.) Figure 11.3 illustrates the saturation of the television culture in American society.

Television seems to have become the main information source for politics all the way down to the local level, where it has recently displaced newspapers as the main source of information about local elections. It is reassuring to note that other people also remain a source of information about elections. Friends and associates also provide sounding boards when people try to fit the pieces of the daily news together in what Doris Graber has called "taming the information tide."[20]

The dominance of television becomes even more pronounced when a major event or crisis breaks in the news. For example, a survey taken a month before the outbreak of the Persian Gulf War recorded 69 percent who said that television was their main source of information. During the next two months while the war was on, that figure jumped to 82 percent.[21] Although people watch news programs more intently when a crisis or scandal is brewing, on a typical news day over 80 percent of the adult population reports hearing some news from some source. Only about half of that number supplement their daily source with some national magazine or television interview program that provides background information on the stories.[22]

Information Characteristics of Mass Media News

Most of the discussion in this chapter refers to **mass media news,** meaning the most widely used information sources of commercial radio, television, daily newspapers, and weekly news magazines. There are, of course, hundreds of **alternative news sources,** referring to small-audience programs and publications that provide more detailed and often more explicitly political points of view. The alternative press can be stimulating and enriching for individuals, but the mass media reach the vast majority of people and set the tone and the agenda of public debates. Because of this **agenda-setting function** (defining the issues and the political positions that dominate our national political debates) and because the mass media connect most Americans in a common communication network, this discussion concentrates primarily on mass media news. Most mass media sources, whether broadcast or print, share three important information patterns that can affect how people understand (or fail to understand) the political world.[23]

The news is fragmented. As defined earlier, the news is timely. By definition, news events are things that just happened: late-breaking; just in; while we were sleeping. The questions that often go unanswered due to the emphasis on immediacy are "Where did this event come from?" and "How did it develop?" Only citizens who rely on many sources and who look outside of the mass media are likely to grasp the origins of events in the headlines.

The news is dramatic and personalized. As Graber noted above, sensationalism and familiarity are defining characteristics of news. It is not surprising that what people remember most are the activities and events surrounding specific people in a news story. Part of the explanation here is that journalists are, after all, telling us stories. The classic news formula is the human interest story. Putting the news focus on political personalities sells because it is interesting, but it often fails to inform or educate because it leaves out important background information about how institutions work, how power is used, and how those dramatic personalities at center stage are working out their conflicts behind the scenes. Political information in the news becomes easier to understand after

FIGURE 11.3

The Saturation of Television in American Society

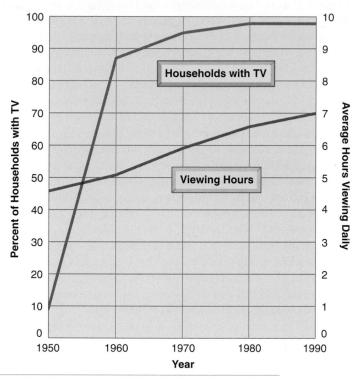

Source: Harold W. Stanley and Richard G. Niemi, *Vital Statistics on American Politics*. Washington, D.C.: Congressional Quarterly Press, 1992, p. 53.

taking a college course like this one which provides the background information needed to interpret the fragments and personalities in the news.

The news is officialized. Most of the news about politics is about what government officials are saying and doing. This is reasonable in many cases. After all, who should have more say in the news than officials who are elected by the people to run the government? The trouble is that when officials make bad judgments or mistakes, they may avoid telling the whole story. Some students of the news and American democracy think the press should play an even more critical "watchdog" role.

The Persian Gulf War stories discussed at the beginning of this chapter illustrate these basic characteristics of news information. As the earlier examples make clear, the Persian Gulf War coverage was highly *dramatized.* Viewers were treated to a TV miniseries drama that the Pentagon code-named "Operation Desert Storm." It was complete with heroes (George Bush and his generals), villains (the evil Saddam), a cast of millions (two huge armies and the peoples of the region), and a dazzling array of special effects, including pictures of smart bombs dropping down the air shafts of targeted buildings. Over the phone wires came breathless, crackling accounts from correspondents in Baghdad describing cruise missiles as if they were flying at 500 miles per hour down streets outside their hotels, turning left at the corner and screaming on to their targets. News magazines included pullout maps that resembled the playing boards of war games.

Generals became personable and lovable heroes. "Stormin' Norman" Schwarzkopf was mentioned as a presidential candidate. Americans confessed to pollsters they were unable to tear themselves away from the news.

The vast majority of the war news also emphasized the *official* version of events. Most of the Gulf War reports were written around statements by White House and Pentagon officials, or they were the products of escorted press pool coverage. Even the majority of independent experts used by news organizations were former military officers or government officials. When CNN correspondent Peter Arnett covered the allied bombing of Baghdad from inside the city, his reports were greeted with charges of disloyalty from prominent members of Congress as well as other news organizations.

The resulting news information was *fragmented*. Absent, or nearly so, from mass media coverage were discussions of issues such as these: Why was the United States there, and what did our government mean to accomplish? Did military victory translate into any larger foreign policy goals? In light of all those loose ends, Secretary of Defense Dick Cheney is reported to have said: "If we had lost, boy, would *we* be in trouble."[24] Instead of addressing the big-picture questions, the mass media overwhelmingly reported the (sometimes inaccurate) information offered up by official news sources, leading one media critic to conclude that "This, perhaps, is the most significant, most troublesome aspect of television's first 'real-time' war: the uneasy blend of instant, immediate, round-the-world, round-the-clock access to information that is inherently incomplete, fragmentary or downright wrong."[25] The same critic observed, "News gathering is an inherently messy business. It's been said that no one who loves laws or sausages should ever watch either one being made, and the same can be said of journalism."[26]

A disturbing study by a team of University of Massachusetts researchers found that "the more people watched TV during the Gulf Crisis, the less they knew about the underlying issues, and the more likely they were to support the war."[27] Most people surveyed had trouble answering basic questions about the problems in the Middle East or United States foreign policy, but 81 percent of those interviewed knew that the name of the U.S. missile used to shoot down Iraqi Scuds was the Patriot. All of this suggests a troublesome question: Are people confused about politics because they do not pay enough attention to the news, or because they pay too much attention to news images

Cable News Network reporter Peter Arnett continued to broadcast from Baghdad—with the okay of Iraqi authorities—even after UN coalition forces began fighting their way into Kuwait City, prompting a number of furious Americans (such as Senator Alan K. Simpson, Republican of Wyoming) to reproach him as a willing dupe of Saddam Hussein. Arnett responded, in an interview with Newsweek *magazine, "It's sort of a game. What is manipulation? I covered the White House in the Reagan era for six months."*

Peter Arnett
Baghdad, Iraq

CNN

CHAPTER 11 – Mass Mediated Democracy **399**

which drum up political support rather than create public understanding? The researchers who studied reactions to Persian Gulf War news concluded, for their part, that the public had been *"selectively misinformed."*[28]

What conditions can turn the press from a channel of government-approved views into a forum capable of challenging policies, as happened during the Vietnam War? In the early years of the Vietnam conflict, the press tended to report the official line. What caused the change to a more critical press during Vietnam? Most researchers agree that when doubts about the war began to appear in statements by government *officials,* presidential candidates, and other prominent politicians, the press also became much more hostile and opened up the debate.[29]

Understanding the American press system requires understanding how different mixtures of culture, institutions, and power operating behind the scenes in political situations shape the quality of public debate in ways ranging from open and critical to relatively closed and uninformative. The remainder of this chapter explores how these factors work. In the balance between a press that is openly adversarial and one that is not critical enough rests the quality of public information and the possibility of informed citizen input in a democracy.

The Press and the Government

The information quality of the news is shaped in a number of ways—through broad **government regulation** of the communications industry and through court rulings about free speech, truth, and libel; in the daily *working relations between press and politicians;* and in the ways in which *popular tastes shape public information.* (It is important to consider, for example, that a majority of the public *supported* military restrictions on press coverage during the Persian Gulf War.) These and other factors affecting the quality of political information are discussed in the remainder of the chapter, beginning here with formal government regulation of the press.

Government Regulation of the Press

Until the advent of broadcasting in the 1920s, there was little explicit government regulation of the media. With the rise of radio came a number of problems calling for government solutions: how to keep competing broadcasters from drowning out one another's signals; how to divide up the airwaves to assure clear signals; how to hand out the "scarce" number of broadcasting bands or wavelengths in a fair, or at least organized, manner; how to make sure the public would receive a broad range of political views after all the precious air space had been allocated; and how to limit the danger of a small number of owners monopolizing those airwaves.

Most of these tasks fell to a government commission, the Federal Communications Commission **(FCC),** created by Congress in 1934. Appointed by the president and guided by legislation from Congress, the FCC continues to work out regulatory solutions for the sensitive and always changing problems of broadcasting. Once a simple matter of giving out licenses and setting technical (electronic) standards for public and private radio corporations, the scope of broadcast regulation now includes television and cable operators, questions of fairness and equal time for political views, the delicate problem of what content is suitable for children, and what to do about giant corporations, including foreign media giants, who want to buy up American airspace and production facilities.

American broadcast media are far less regulated than in most other nations. Many countries have placed much of their radio and television production and programming under public broadcasting systems as described in "How We Compare" Box 11.1. Yet even in the largely private United States system, there are many hotly contested struggles between government and broadcasters over political communications issues. For example, broadcasters have applied pressure for years to get the FCC to lift its requirement that they charge their lowest commercial rates for campaign advertising. When the FCC held firm on its ruling in 1992, a number of stations simply refused to air any election advertising, raising the question of whether a new regulatory strategy is needed.

Based on the idea that the airwaves belong to the public, the FCC is required to consider the public interest in regulating the political content of broadcasting. Perhaps least controversial is the **equal time provision** of the broadcast law requiring stations that either sell time (for example, to political candidates) or give free access (for example, to interest advocates) to provide equal time to opponents. A much trickier issue has been the FCC's own 1949 ruling that broadcasters must adhere to a so-called **fairness doctrine** offering (non-news) program time to explore competing views on important public issues.

Who could condemn the idea that broadcasters lucky enough to own a precious band of public airspace should provide "reasonable opportunities for the expression of opposing views on controversial issues of public importance?" However reasonable the fairness doctrine seems *in the abstract,* the problem of what is "reasonable," politically speaking, has bothered broadcasters and politicians since the doctrine first appeared in 1949. In the 1980s, the FCC was staffed with appointees of conservative President Ronald Reagan, who felt that free speech came before the abstruse issue of political "fairness." Sensing that the doctrine was threatened, some members of Congress tried to turn it into law, but the bill was vetoed by Reagan. Lacking sufficient support to override the veto, advocates of "fairness" watched the FCC officially drop the doctrine in 1987. This is an important example of how Congress, the president, and commission members all have different institutional input into the regulatory process.

During the 1980s, the FCC also eased its regulations on ownership of media outlets. For example, the FCC allowed existing owners to buy more AM, FM, and TV stations. At the same time, the FCC eased regulations on the sale of stations and the valuable broadcast licenses that go with them. As a result, the late 1980s and early 1990s saw an explosion in the sale and consolidated ownership of stations—often to large conglomerates with little background in the media or commitment to public affairs.

Although the government does not regulate newspapers in the same way as broadcast stations, restrictions have been eased in the application of trade and monopoly rules in the newspaper industry. The result is that the press is becoming owned by a smaller number of large companies. In America today, only a tiny percentage of cities (about 2 percent) have competing daily papers, and most daily newspaper circulation is no longer owned by local interests. Add to this the broadcast trend of more stations owned by fewer big corporations, and some critics argue that the United States may be suffering what one analyst has called a **media monopoly.** Ben Bagdikian, a former dean of the school of journalism at the University of California, Berkeley, has published research showing that the majority (measured by audience share) of American media outlets were in the hands of over fifty companies before the deregulation period of the 1980s. The number of corporate owners dropped to fewer than twenty-five going into the 1990s.[30] Bagdikian argues that this consolidation of the mass communications industry has made news and public affairs divisions cut back and generate profits like any business. These days, the news is produced and marketed much like other products, with the result that its content becomes more standardized and its sales depend more on things like packaging and theme music than on inherent quality. In this environment, more news outlets may mean "less information diversity." These trends may well lead to new political conflicts over regulatory policies in the future.

HOW WE COMPARE

Public and Private Broadcasting Systems in Other Nations

11.1

M ost European nations have adopted a very different kind of broadcasting system than the United States. While the U.S. has promoted private ownership and management of radio and TV, and allowed only a very small public broadcasting system, most European nations have emphasized public broadcasting, with a minor role for commercial ownership, advertising, and programming. Newspapers in Europe are privately operated, although many of them have clear affiliations with political parties and place explicit ideological interpretations on the news. Europeans commonly read different papers for different points of view.

The philosophy behind public communications systems is that the government should regulate broadcasting in the public interest, just as health, food, sanitation, power, and water should be public functions. The concern is that commercial and consumer forces may not result in the highest quality or the most diversity in entertainment and information programming.

Most nations using the public broadcasting model tax the owners of television sets through a license fee to pay for the costs of producing and airing programming. Germany has allowed advertising during prime evening hours to provide additional income, and Spain has always relied heavily on advertising to fund public television.

To keep public broadcasting from being a propaganda outlet for the party in power, the management of most European systems is placed in the hands of commissions on which the major political parties are represented, along with representatives from churches, unions, and other social institutions. Sweden, for example, has a broadcasting commission with broad social group representation.

In recent years, public radio and television have faced competition from commercial broadcasting in many nations. Following a decade of conservative governments and pressures from business interests, Great Britain has opened its system to both public television (funded by license fees) and commercial television (funded by advertising). The British Broadcasting Corporation (a public, government-run corporation) faces increasing competition from expanding commercial broadcasters and continuing opposition from the conservative (Tory) party in government.

SOURCE: Jay G. Blumler and Wolfgang Hoffman-Riem, "New Roles for Public Television in Western Europe: Challenges and Prospects," *Journal of Communication,* Vol. 42, 1992, pp. 20–35.

Nicholas J. Nicholas and Richard Munro, then president and chairman (respectively) of Time, Inc., discuss a possible merger with Warner Communications, headed by chairman Steven Ross (now deceased). Critics viewed the 1990 union, which created the multimedia giant Time Warner, Inc., as characteristic of a broader shakedown in the media industry—a trend that they say pushes financial gain above professional standards.

Truth and the First Amendment

Long before the invention of formal government regulatory procedures, the political struggle over truth vs. **libel** (defamation of character) pitted journalists, public figures, and the courts against one another. The legendary trial of printer Peter Zenger before the American Revolution established the principle that the truth cannot be libelous no matter how much it may damage a public reputation. However, the question of what is truth has not always been easy to answer, keeping the libel issue alive over the centuries. In the 1964 landmark case of *The New York Times Company v. Sullivan,* the Supreme Court made it difficult for politicians to suppress their media critics. The *Sullivan* ruling required offended public figures to show that journalists intended to do them harm (malice) by actively disregarding the truth.[31]

Malice is hard to prove, but that does not stop some hard-pressed public figures from trying. In the most famous case since the *Sullivan* ruling, U.S. commander in Vietnam General William Westmoreland sued CBS News over a documentary that suggested he misled both the public and his own superiors about the strength of the enemy in order to influence the course of the war. CBS eventually agreed to settle the suit out of court. However, the costs of the lengthy legal defense were considerable, as, perhaps, was the damage to the reputation of the network. In 1993, NBC News publicly apologized (forestalling a lawsuit) after it was proven that its filmed "test crash" of an allegedly unsafe model of truck had been deliberately rigged to force the vehicle to explode.

In addition to the threat of libel suits, journalists can face other legal pressures in their decisions to publish dangerous or sensitive "truths." Most investigative reporting, for example, depends on sources who are willing to leak important information to the press, but who may fear losing their jobs or damaging their own reputations. As a result, key informants often do not want to be identified as the source of troublesome news. Although about half of the states have so-called **shield laws** protecting reporters from being forced to reveal their sources, neither the Supreme Court nor Congress has made such protection a national policy.

Beyond the occasional incident of government intimidation of the press, many areas of government activity are formally protected from press scrutiny by law. Beginning with the **National Security Acts** of 1947, the federal government has claimed a right to legal secrecy surrounding many of its activities. The reasoning is that we live in a dangerous world filled with enemies, and the public's right to know certain things (for instance, about state-of-the-art weapons, political deals with governments, or espionage activities) is outweighed by the value that information would have to enemies of our nation.

The trouble with legal secrecy arises if government officials use it to deceive the public. One of the most controversial incidents involved media suspicions of official deception (the so-called credibility gap) during the Vietnam War. *The New York Times* made a fateful decision to document those suspicions by publishing a series of secret war documents that were leaked to it by a government employee named Daniel Ellsberg. That decision landed the newspaper in a legal battle with no less formidable an opponent than the United States government (*The New York Times v. United States,* 1971).[32] This popularly named "Pentagon Papers" case was eventually decided in favor of the press. The Supreme Court ruled that the press and the public's First Amendment right to decide the truth was greater, in that particular case, than the government's right to keep legal secrets.[33] In the end, however, it was a battle won by the paper only at great expense and against considerable pressure.

What is the net result of these legal pressures on the press? There are signs that the willingness of news organizations to gather and distribute critical information has de-

General William Westmoreland (at right, flanked by an attorney) sued CBS after a documentary alleged that he had deliberately misled both his civilian superiors and the public while commanding U.S. forces in Vietnam during the 1960s. The network ultimately settled the case out of court.

clined from the "crusading" days of Vietnam and Watergate in the 1960s and 1970s. According to one study, the number of TV news documentaries has dropped by half from the mid-1970s to the 1990s.[34] Investigative reporting is the exception rather than the routine in contemporary journalism.[35] The grumbling acceptance of Pentagon news control during the Persian Gulf War might be taken as another sign of the times. All of this suggests that the content of the daily news is a reflection of the political relations between the press and politicians. Formal government regulations and laws are just small aspects of a larger set of press–government relations that shape the news, as described in the next section.

Making the News

The news is an uneasy production. Many politicians and journalists would describe their mutual relations as adversarial, wary, and even aggressive and nasty at times. Politicians often feel misunderstood because their world of pressure and compromise contains few easy answers to the kinds of questions that journalists ask. More than a few political careers have been ruined by revelations in the media. For their part, journalists often develop a healthy mistrust of politicians who keep them at arm's length, feed them carefully prepared press releases, and seldom engage in serious debates with the cameras rolling and notebooks open. Members of the press are often painfully aware that politicians use them, when they can, as channels for sending their views to the public. This frustration may send the press into a "feeding frenzy" when there is a chance to dramatize a scandal or play up a politician's blunder.[36] The fear of an aroused press pack, in turn, explains why politicians tend to keep reporters at a distance.

The news produced from these uneasy relations is more likely to focus on scandals and personalities than on questions of power and the inner workings of institutions. In part, the guarded attitudes of politicians mean that disclosures to the press seldom contain much spontaneity, depth, or explanatory value.[37] For their part, journalists keep coming back to the same sources for most of the daily news, limiting the amount of investigative reporting that might fill in the larger political picture. Each side depends on the other to get its job done, and each holds a certain power that the other cannot ignore.

The Working Relations Between Press and Politicians

Political officials control a large and steady supply of information that fills up most of the daily "news hole" of papers and TV programs. Without the official supply of news handouts (briefings, press releases, photo opportunities and other news events), the press would face serious dilemmas. Who would they turn to for a predictable supply of daily news, if not government officials? How would journalists fill their news demands cheaply and efficiently if they had to figure out what mattered in the world every day, and who (besides government officials) had something important to say about it?

The fact that government officials figure prominently in most of the news content is due in large part to the assumption that since the government is elected to represent the people in their political affairs, government officials *ought* to be the most visible newsmakers in the land. Yet there are other reasons equally worth considering. For one thing, U.S. news organizations are set up largely on the basis of "beats," within which reporters cover the doings of officials in Congress, the State Department, the White House, and other prominent locations around Washington. Since most of the nation's reporting talent is standing by at these places, it is hardly surprising that most of the news is reported from them. The inner workings of news organizations will be further discussed later in the chapter. For now, consider the results of this reporting system.

A classic study by political scientist Leon Sigal found that government officials dominated the political stories in two of the nation's leading papers, *The New York Times* and *The Washington Post*. Fully 46.5 percent of the stories originated with U.S. government

Dee Dee Myers was one of the few members of the White House press office who survived the early days of the Clinton administration. One imbroglio arose when the White House called in an FBI spokesman to publicly justify scrutiny of some longtime members of the White House travel staff for possible malfeasance. Critics suggested the FBI was being used for political purposes. Myers continued in her post, but soon thereafter communications director George Stephanopoulos was shifted to an advisory job.

officials. Another 26.5 percent originated with foreign government officials. Including the 4 percent of the national news that came from state and local officials, a total of more than 75 percent of political news stories came from government officials.[38] More recent studies confirm the same pattern—with a slight drop in government officials being offset by a slight increase in the representatives of groups and interest organizations.[39] Television news displays much the same source pattern as print media. A major study of weekday network evening news programs during the 1980s found that "some 72 percent of all sources were officials of government or politics or groups and institutions, and another 2.7 percent were former officials commenting on their areas of official status."[40]

How to Make the News

If political actors (and this applies equally to government officials and other newsmakers) are to make the most of their moments in the press, they must learn how to shape the news to their advantage. Managing the media has become an essential part of successful governing and politics. Increasingly this is true for all levels of politics from city hall to the White House, and from grass-roots social movements to big-budget interest organizations.

Nowhere is the newsmaking game played with more intensity and for higher stakes than in the White House. In the case of the president, the sheer growth of the national mass media in the last half of this century *requires* considerable daily management. When Harry Truman ordered atomic bombs dropped on Japan in 1945, he personally broke the news to a White House press corps that numbered twenty-five reporters. Today, more than 1,700 reporters cover the White House, and a total of 2,800 people (including television producers, technicians, and other crew members) are allowed to pass through the press entrance of the president's residence these days.[41] It is hard to imagine anyone interacting with such a crowd without considerable staging, planning, and scripting.

White House press secretaries from six administrations gather for a 1990 symposium. In the front row (from left) *sit Larry Speakes (of the Reagan administration); Pierre Salinger (Kennedy era); newsman John Chancellor, the symposium moderator; George Christian (Johnson era); and James Brady (Reagan era). Standing in the second row are* (from left) *Jerald ter-Horst (Ford era); Jody Powell (Carter era); Ron Nessen (Ford era); Bill Moyers (Johnson era); Ron Ziegler (Nixon era); and George Reedy (Johnson era).*

President Richard Nixon created the White House Office of Communications with the aim of controlling the flow of information out of the entire executive branch and "going over the heads of the press" to communicate directly with the people. These goals were disrupted when the Watergate affair and a series of congressional investigations aroused a press pack that followed a trail of scandal leading eventually to the Oval Office.

Elected on a promise to restore trust in government, Jimmy Carter neglected news management with a possibly foolish determination to run a White House that was open to the press. With plot assists from a struggling economy, opponents in Congress, and an embarrassing 444 days of news about Americans being held hostage in Iran, the media sent Carter out of Washington with unpopularity levels approaching those suffered in the polls by Richard Nixon after Watergate. It was not until the Reagan presidency that the White House Communications Office was finally developed into a finely tuned machine that helped turn President Reagan into the "Great Communicator."

THE TEXTBOOK CASE OF NEWS MANAGEMENT.   The textbook on how to manage the media was written during the Reagan administration. It is an open book available for others to follow, although few politicians may attempt to manage the press as well as the Reagan communications staff did. What does the textbook say about media management for politicians? The first step is to adopt the proper frame of mind. In the words of Reagan White House communications director David Gergen (who later became counsellor to the president in the Clinton White House, helping to revamp *its* troubled media relations): "To govern successfully, the government has to set the agenda; it cannot let the press set the agenda for it."[42] How did Mr. Gergen put this goal into action during the Reagan years?[43]

> Step 1. Weekly, long-term strategy meetings of policy officers and press handlers to plan the future news agenda and assess the results of ongoing media control efforts.

> Step 2. Daily meetings of the White House communications group to decide, as one member put it, "What do we want the press to cover today, and how?"[44] According to Michael Deaver, one of the masterminds of the press operation in the Reagan years: "We would take a theme, which we usually worked on for six weeks—say, the economy. The President would say the same thing, but we had a different visual for every one of [the regularly scheduled media events]."[45]

> Step 3. As Step no. 2 indicates, *repetition* is the key. Feed the press the same message with a new (and therefore "newsworthy") visual setting to satisfy the media need for changing video footage and new photo opportunities. As Deaver recalled, "It used to drive the President crazy because the repetition was so important. He'd get on that airplane and look at that speech and say, 'Mike, I'm not going to give this same speech on education again, am I?' I said, 'Yeah, trust me, it's going to work.' And it did."[46]

> Step 4. Put out the "line of the day" to all the other potential newsmakers in the executive branch to "make sure we're all saying the same thing" to the press.[47] During the Reagan years, the "line of the day" was sent out over a computer network to all the offices in the administration. All that any official had to do was call it up on his or her screen before meeting with reporters.

> Step 5. Coordinate the day's news via conference calls to top administration officials to make sure they understand the line of the day and to orchestrate which officials will say something, when they will say it, and who will keep their mouths shut, as in "Look, the President's got a statement tomorrow, so shut up today, just shut up, don't pre-empt the President, (we'll) cut your ——— off if you leak anything out on this one."[48]

The political desire to influence media coverage transcends partisan boundaries. During their first few months in office, Democrats Bill Clinton and Al Gore (left, at a March 1993 press briefing) encountered increasing media skepticism and criticism over what was seen as the White House's cool attitude to the press and scattershot approach to policy-making. By the end of May 1993, Clinton felt compelled to enlist the help of David Gergen (right, at podium), a magazine editor and PBS television commentator who had previously served on the staffs of presidents Nixon, Ford, and Reagan—all Republicans.

Step 6. Working the press. Calling reporters and their bosses to see if they understood the story correctly. This has become known as "spin control." During the Reagan years the White House made it a regular practice to call the national TV network executives just prior to their nightly newscasts to check on what they were running and to offer additional clarification on the stories.

Step 7. Weekly seminars held for the spokespeople of the various federal bureaucracies to educate them on how to present the administration to the press.

Step 8. A heavy volume of opinion polling and marketing research to see what was on the public mind and how the president could tap into it through the news. The White House conducted its own marketing research on the public images of news people like (anchor) Peter Jennings, (columnist) George Will, (reporter) Sam Donaldson, and a host of others in order to decide who to give scoops, who to give interviews, and who to treat more or less deferentially. In assessing marketing chief Richard Wirthlin's award-winning performance, one observer concluded that the mapmaker of the public mind "probed just about every aspect of public affairs on a scale unmatched in U.S. history."[49]

Follow these eight steps, set the media stage, introduce a president who is comfortable with the TV lights and cameras, and you have the Great Communicator. The Reagan press management plan was so effective that Richard Wirthlin was named Advertising Man of the Year in 1989 for his accomplishments as Director of Consumer Research for Ronald Reagan.[50] Another measure of the success of the Reagan press program is that even when the press attempted to be critical, the efforts seldom produced results that stuck to the so-called "teflon" coating that seemed to protect the president from the press.

The classic case of neutralizing the critical press was an incident involving CBS correspondent Lesley Stahl, who put together a long report claiming to show the gaps between Ronald Reagan's news images and his policies. Stahl was nervous about the piece because of its critical tone and the practice of the White House Communications Office to call reporters and their employers about negative coverage. The phone rang after the report was aired, and it was "a senior White House official." Stahl prepared herself for the worst. In her own words, here is what happened:

> "And the voice said, 'Great piece.'
>
> "I said, 'What?'
>
> "And he said, *'Great piece!'*
>
> "I said, 'Did you listen to what I said?'
>
> "He said, 'Lesley, when you're showing four and a half minutes of great pictures of Ronald Reagan, no one listens to what you say. Don't you know that the pictures are overriding your message because they conflict with your message? The public sees those pictures and they block your message. They didn't even hear what you said. So, in our minds, it was a four-and-a-half-minute free ad for the Ronald Reagan campaign for reelection.'
>
> "I sat there numb. I began to feel dumb 'cause I'd covered him four years and I hadn't figured it out. Somebody had to explain it to me. Well none of us had figured it out. I called the executive producer of the Evening News . . . and he went dead on the phone. And he said, 'Oh, my God.'"[51]

The textbook news management system worked even with adversarial reporters. TV is the medium through which most people get their news. When politicians and their handlers are careful to stage their public appearances to convey the right images, reporters are denied the visual "evidence" they want to back up a hard-hitting attack. As one of the Reagan news officials put it, "What are you going to believe, the facts or your eyes?"[52]

George Bush's White House clearly did not set out to manage the media as completely as the communications group did during the Reagan era. Even Lesley Stahl could be heard complaining about the "night and day" difference in the Bush administration: "This White House doesn't care if the president gets on the evening news or not."[53] Another reporter elaborated on Stahl's comment: "That's not an impeachable offense—yet—but it does raise some interesting questions. Not least for the White House press corps, which seems to be looking back on the slick, well-packaged Reagan presidency with a touch of—can it be?—nostalgia."[54]

Despite Mr. Bush's decision to spend less time managing the press, the media criticism became too much to tolerate, and the White House soon brought in the media team that got him elected (recall the discussion in Chapter 10). For example, former public relations executive Sig Rogich, who had produced several campaign commercials in 1988, came to the White House as Special Assistant to the President for Activities and Initiatives.[55] Rogich was rewarded for helping to restore the Bush reputation by being named ambassador to Iceland. In 1992 Mr. Bush once again forgot the lessons of news and image management, and Mr. Rogich was recalled to produce Bush campaign commercials. However, Rogich and the other image doctors arrived too late to save the election.

What about the Clinton White House? During the 1992 campaign, news management was one of the strengths of the Clinton political organization; indeed, it had to be, considering that the press looked into his draft record and his sex life. As noted in Chapter 10, when the press became concerned with Clinton's character problems, the candidate went over the heads of serious journalists, resorting to appearances on MTV and the *Arsenio Hall Show,* media outlets with important audiences among both younger and baby-boomer voters. When his media image improved, the Clinton news team staged such events as the bus tours that sparked considerable positive coverage from the media.

Bill Clinton found media management simpler on the campaign trail than in office. As a presidential candidate, Clinton gained favor with a large portion of the public by blowing a saxophone chorus of "Heartbreak Hotel" on late-night television's popular Arsenio Hall talk show. More conventional methods proved less effective when trying, for example, to persuade either Washington insiders or the broader public to embrace his policy agenda.

After the election, it was disclosed that Clinton's political model for presidential communication was not Harry Truman or John Kennedy, but Ronald Reagan.[56] When, as noted earlier, the press turned critical shortly after the inauguration, Clinton hired none other than David Gergen (once President Reagan's communications director), giving him the title of Counsellor to the President, to oversee his press operation.

Given the power of the well-managed media, few politicians at any level of government today can afford to ignore the techniques of public relations and "strategic communications."[57] Although few play the game as well as the Reagan White House did, few are willing to dismiss media management as unnecessary. And so, the press and politicians live in a state of uneasy **mutual dependence.** Each needs the other, yet each is wary and, by definition, adversarial toward the other. When reporters become too aggressive and critical, news management operations often come to the rescue. The world of modern politics has become peopled by various experts in news management: *spokespeople* who explain the politician to the press; **handlers** who escort and coach politicians in their encounters with the press; **spin doctors** who talk to reporters and suggest favorable interpretations (called putting a **"spin"** on events); and behind the scenes, the ranks of *pollsters, public relations experts,* and **image consultants** who plan what politicians do and measure the results.

How Do Outsiders Make the News?

Public officials often have the experience and the resources to produce high quality, big-budget news events. However, all political players in society who want their issues on the political agenda must think about how to make the news. Many interest groups and social movements have been very effective in getting the attention of the press. Although grass-roots groups lack some of the advantages of prominent government officials (who have reporters waiting for news handouts each day) or well-financed interest groups (who can hire public relations firms and pollsters), they often find ways of making the news. For example, political groups can:

- Schedule visually dramatic events like demonstrations or protests at times that are convenient for reporters to cover them and file stories.
- Make sure their political messages are visually communicated through signs and banners in case the press does not report what speakers for the group say.
- Train spokespeople in press relations so that press conferences will be conducted in an organized way, press handouts will be available, and statements will contain tight **sound bites** (10–20 seconds) likely to make the television news.
- Keep their issues alive by planning activities to keep repeating their message in the news.

Outsider groups that learn how to follow these rules can have considerable news-making success. For example, the environmental group Greenpeace has been successful in staging media events ranging from protests at nuclear plants to high-seas raids in small speedboats. The high-seas adventures have brought media attention to protests against fishing practices that endanger dolphins and against nations that practice nuclear testing in the ocean, among other issues on the organization's agenda. Greenpeace has been so effective that companies and nations targeted by some of their news protests have plotted counter-strategies to minimize the damage of unfavorable news. For example, in 1993, Greenpeace planned a worldwide news event campaign to alert people to the alleged dangers of chlorine, a chemical commonly found in laundry products. A public relations firm employed by the Clorox Corporation (a major manufacturer of chlorine products) anticipated how to handle possible news events surrounding the Greenpeace campaign, as described in "Inside the System" Box 11.2.

Public Opinion and the News

Long ago, a highly respected journalist named Walter Lippmann observed that political reality is something that most people experience vicariously through the news.[58] What disturbed Lippmann, and several generations of media watchers since, is the way in which "news realities" are constructed by politicians and journalists. Although the images in the news are often misleading and incomplete (or, to use the terms introduced earlier, fragmented, dramatized, and officialized), that same news shapes public opinion, with real and important political results.

The Battle for Public Opinion

Because the news is often so *realistic,* people can be moved to support government actions that may not be well represented in the news. Widespread disillusionment can result when policies fail, or when people conclude that politicians have used the media to deceive them. Political scientist Murray Edelman has described the emotional cycles of arousal (fear, enthusiasm, patriotism), reassurance (leaders taking charge), and periodic disillusionment as the core of the political experience for most people in modern society.[59] Opinion can be aroused simply because political actors roll out the symbols of the political culture, defining issues and promises around images of freedom, individual choice, patriotism, economic enterprise, and other cultural themes that people care about. In the world of mediated politics, people often have to base their judgments on whether politicians give a credible performance based on familiar cultural scripts.

INSIDE THE SYSTEM

Outsiders and Insiders Battle for Public Opinion Through News Coverage

11.2

The power struggles among interest groups often spill into the news in efforts to sway public opinion. For example, big corporations worry when the environmental group Greenpeace organizes media campaigns to alert people to the "dangers" of company activities. When Greenpeace expressed concern about the chemical chlorine, a leading maker of chlorine-based cleaning products, the Clorox Company, was alarmed. Ketchum Communications, a public relations firm hired by Clorox, drew up a list of possible "crisis scenarios," anticipating how Greenpeace might stage news events that could damage their client's image, and, in turn, hurt its product sales. Here is one of the scenarios developed by the PR firm:

CRISIS SCENARIO #1: CHLORINE FREE BY '93

The Issue: Greenpeace has announced a worldwide effort to rid the world of chlorine by 1993. . . . In Europe [the campaign has already been working, and the public has] decreased use of household chlorine bleach in some areas.

Worst-Case Event: Greenpeace activists arrive at Clorox corporate headquarters [in Oakland, California] with signs, banners, bullhorns, and several local television crews and proceed to launch a rally. . . . They release the results of a new "study" linking chlorine exposure to cancer. [The story is picked up by the national media.] Clorox Corporate Communications receives several calls from local and national press seeking comments.

Recommended Response: Make sure this is a one-day media event, with no follow-up stories, that results in no long-term damage to Clorox's reputation and market position.

Strategy: Crisis team announces that the company will seek an independent . . . review of the Greenpeace study and promises to report back to the media. . . . Names of independent scientists who will talk about chlorine are given to the media. (A list of these scientists should be kept on file.) A research firm [conducts a poll] to assess the impact of the event. Based on the results (available the next morning at 9:00 AM), team will decide on further steps.

SOURCE: *Harper's Magazine,* August 1991, p. 24.

Edelman has called politics in the media age a "spectacle," complete with heroes, villains, grand leaders, despicable enemies, domestic and foreign crusades, and all of it just out of reach in the news.[60] There is even a role for the citizen to play in the spectacle, but it is seldom a direct or powerful one. The average citizen is the spectator—the public is a political audience. If the news spectacle is well staged, people may feel that they have had some sort of democratic experience. The trouble is that it is often a passive or *quiescent* experience, creating a vicarious democracy rather than an actively participatory one—a democracy of smoke and mirrors, of media events and videotapes.

There are, of course, important ways in which opinion remains an active force in the system, from voting to joining interest groups to punishing politicians with low approval ratings. The good news is that it is not always easy to manipulate public opinion. It is clear that different people watching the same news event can get different messages out of it.[61] However, it is also clear that the techniques of opinion research and image management described throughout the last five chapters become ever more sophisticated.

The battle for public opinion is continuous, not only because different groups and actors compete for public attention, but because the media are not always cooperative with those trying to get their messages across. Political scientist Anthony Downs describes an *issue attention cycle* in the news, in which the press initially gives a new issue intense coverage, but then slackens suddenly in that coverage as new or easy angles on the story become harder to find, or when audiences appear to be getting tired of the topic.[62] Getting an issue or a point of view into the news is one challenge—keeping it there is another.

People are often aware that their attention is an important prize in the news, and they often resent the efforts made to politicize the news. It may not be entirely fair to blame the media for the political messages that go into the news, but public confidence in the press has been low for most of the last twenty years. Figure 11.4 compares levels of public confidence in the press and other public institutions over the last two decades. While the public has placed the blame on both press and politicians for various national problems, it is clear that many people think the fault for political information defects in the news largely belongs to the press, as shown in Table 11.1.

Whether or not people have placed the blame fairly for defects in the nation's information system, they seem to understand that what ends up in the news does affect how they think about politics. Walter Lippmann ushered in the dawn of the modern media age in the 1920s with the warning that the news may not tell us what to think, but it tells us what to think about. A series of experimental studies by political scientists Shanto Iyengar and Donald Kinder have confirmed that when a topic appears in the news, people are likely to think that it is important.[63] A subsequent run of experiments by Iyengar

FIGURE 11.4

Public Confidence in Different Institutions: Big Business, Congress, the Military, Newspapers

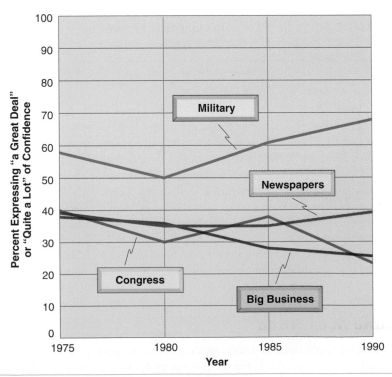

Source: *The Gallup Poll* (Wilmington, Del.: Scholarly Resources, Inc., 1992, pp. 212–215).

TABLE 11.1

What's Wrong with the Press

QUESTION: In presenting the news dealing with political and social issues, do you think that news organizations deal fairly with all sides, or do they tend to favor one side?

RESPONSE	PERCENTAGE (%) AGREEING
A. Deal fairly with all sides	28%
B. Tend to favor one side	68
C. Don't know	4

QUESTION: In general, do you think news organizations are pretty independent, or are they often influenced by powerful people and organizations?

RESPONSE	PERCENTAGE (%) AGREEING
A. Pretty independent	33%
B. Influenced by powerful organizations	62
C. Don't know	5

QUESTION: In general, do you think that news organizations get the facts straight, or do you think that their stories and reports are often inaccurate?

RESPONSE	PERCENTAGE (%) AGREEING
A. Get the facts straight	54%
B. Inaccurate	44
C. Don't know	2

SOURCE: Adapted from *Columbia Journalism Review*, February 1992, p. 15. Based on Times/Mirror and Gallup Polls.

also suggests that the way news events are "framed" around familiar symbols, characters, and plots affects how people think about the political issues in them.[64] Iyengar found that the emphasis on drama and personality in news stories makes it difficult for people to grasp how political issues may be shaped by power, economics, or the workings of political institutions. All of this suggests why the battle for public opinion through the news can be so intense: the issues that make the news set the agenda of national politics to an important degree.

Setting the Agenda

Imagine the chaotic world of events and people clamoring for attention just beyond our immediate lives. What we find in the news each day is just a small sample of all the important things that might be going on in the world. Journalists are responsible for *opening the information gates* and letting a select few of these events and viewpoints inside for our attention. This image has led to a popular saying that journalists are the **gatekeepers** of society. Does this mean that the press independently sets the political agenda?

In recent years there has been considerable debate about whether a biased press has used its gatekeeping power to actively *set the agenda* of our national political priorities.[65] Like many complex questions, a simple answer is hard to pin down, for reasons already suggested in this chapter. The news is constructed out of the political relations between politicians and journalists. Thus, news organizations may promote their own issue agendas some of the time, but often they respond to the agendas of the government officials, politicians, and groups that play the newsmaking game effectively. We will return to look at how various political players try to use the media to set the agenda in the public policy process described in Chapter 17.

Understanding how news organizations work fills in our political picture of the news: what is reported, what might be missing, why politicians' newsmaking strategies work, and why the news is often fragmented, dramatized, and officialized. The news picture becomes even sharper by understanding the business end of the mass media. The next section explores the economic and bureaucratic aspects of the organizations that gather and sell news.

Inside the News Organization: The Economics of Information

It helps to remember that what we think of as news is always changing. News is a product of the society that produces and consumes it at a particular time. At the time of the American Revolution, for example, the news and its manner of production were very different than they are today. To begin with, there were no national news organizations. The few daily newspapers that existed were relatively chaotic mixtures of essays, opinions, shipping schedules, and personal announcements. The idea of daily news gathered by regular reporters and edited into organized categories of events is something that has developed fairly recently in history. Since the way in which news is gathered, produced, and sold has a lot to do with its contents and effects, a brief history of the press in America is a good place to start.

A Social and Economic History of the American Press

In the early years of the American republic, what became printed up as news often originated with private parties who were fired up enough to hire a printer to publicize something they cared about. In place of regular newspapers, people encountered leaflets, "broadsides," or handbills distributed or posted around town. Printers themselves often promoted their views on issues that concerned their businesses, such as the hated tax stamps that cut into their livelihoods before the Revolution. Since "news" of this sort was distributed by interested parties to make a political point, the news of yesterday was steeply slanted. A classic case is *The Federalist,* those political arguments designed to sell the Constitution to influential citizens of the various states. That series of short political arguments was paid for and distributed at private expense by a very partisan group: supporters of the Constitution. The key issues of the Philadelphia Convention were presented in anything but an objective or impartial manner. To the contrary, *The Federalist* stands as perhaps the greatest example of persuasive political argument or *rhetoric* in American history.

The twentieth-century idea of an objective (and more recently, a fair) press evolved slowly, influenced by changes in communication technologies, business opportunities, and public tastes. The introduction of the telegraph in the mid-1800s probably pushed the news in its current direction more than any other single factor. When the nation was "wired" from eastern seaboard to the western frontier, it became possible to communicate rapidly about national events. However, the wires permitted only the simplest exchanges of what came to be called "telegraphic" communication: the *who, what, when, where, and how* of events. Thus was born the skeletal outline of the news *story,* an information form that owes as much to the technology and economics of communication as to any superior information value it may have.

As manufacturing grew, immigration increased and people became concentrated in cities, a large market was created for selling this news. William Randolph Hearst and other barons of the "yellow presses" competed in newspaper wars to sell their products to the newly arriving urban masses. (The term *yellow press* began with the *World,* a New York newspaper that ran a popular color cartoon called "The Yellow Kid" on its front page.) What sold best to a poorly educated and barely literate audience was scandal, crisis, human interest stories, and tall tales of war and adventure.

The association of yellow journalism with political and industrial corruption grated uneasily on a newly emerging middle class of educated professional people who became the managers of business and civic life after the turn of the century. As this middle-class market for more responsible journalism grew, so did the number of papers willing to supply the product. By the 1920s, journalists began to adopt a professional code of fairness, responsibility, and objectivity outlined by the newly formed American Society of Newspaper Editors. Once again, the characteristics of news information were driven by social and economic factors.

Next came the broadcast age. Radio carried Franklin Roosevelt's famous fireside chats with their reassuring words about hope in a depression and victory in war into millions of American homes. The Second World War further established a national broadcast media with crackling reports of far-off battles. The war correspondents became the first television news personalities of the fifties. Television news programs became badges of prestige for networks on which such programs as *I Love Lucy* were busily selling coffee, soap flakes, and cigarettes to a prosperous national media audience.

The television medium soon became America's preferred means of getting the daily news. Quick, dramatic, and realistic, TV offered people a window on the world that made them feel somehow closer to events. By the end of the 1980s, newspapers had become a weak link in the news system, changing into forums for news of entertainment, fashion, and sports at the local level, while a few prestigious national papers such as *The New York Times* and the *Wall Street Journal* remained information sources for leaders, opinion-makers, and perhaps most importantly, other journalists, who also need sources of ideas about what in the world matters.

With the advent of cable, satellites, and live broadcast technologies, there is the potential for more diversity and competition of information than ever before. In the coming years, the TV network news programs may become dinosaurs from the past. Local stations can assemble their own national news from satellite feeds and a growing industry of video image wholesalers. At the same time, however, new information formats appear to be replacing the telegraphic communications of the last century, challenging the journalistic ideals of fairness and objectivity from the recent era. What, say many media executives, is wrong with *infotainment,* if, indeed, that is what people want? After all, what sells best to a poorly educated and barely literate audience is scandal, crisis, human interest stories, and tales of crime, sex, and violence.

As for the news of the future, CNN along with an emerging network of world cable organizations and video wholesale services are rapidly creating an international news system. Will this produce more diversity of information, or will the information of the future be shaped by business decisions aimed at producing a saleable generic news product with low cost and mass appeal? Whatever the future of news may hold, the social and economic forces that shape it will be most visible in the ways in which journalists and news organizations work to gather and re-present information.

How Journalists Work

It should be clear by now that news does not emerge from the vapors of truth swirling around society. News is assigned, gathered, written, selected, rewritten, displayed, packaged, and distributed by people doing their jobs within organizations. With the possible exception of the few remaining small-town newspapers, most news organizations adopt the bureaucratic aims of making the news a routine and efficient daily product. These news organizations compete with each other to get reporters to the scene first, file the first story, shoot the most dramatic pictures, and win the professional prizes. Yet with the exception of occasional investigative reports that bring a scandal or social problem to our attention, most of the competitive energy in the news business ends up creating a strange result: The news is remarkably the same whether we watch NBC or CNN, whether we read *The New York Times, The Chicago Tribune,* or *The Altanta Constitution.* True, a paper like *USA Today* comes out of a vending machine that resembles a TV set, and the paper itself is something like a morning television talk show in print. But sprinkled around all those color graphics, people pictures, full-page weather charts, and gossipy features are the same basic political news stories that appear in all the other mass media outlets on a given day. News junkies will find more stories and more details in *The New York Times,* but the big stories of the day and the range of political views reported in them is much the same no matter where in the mass media one turns for information.

Photojournalists in Little Rock, Arkansas, interview Socks, the Clinton family cat, shortly after the November 1992 election. President-elect Clinton was finally compelled to scold members of the media over such harassment, which continued long after it became apparent that Socks had little of substance to contribute to policy discussions. Freedom of the press, it seems, does not necessarily ensure a high level of public discourse.

The reasons for the standardization of the news are important to grasp. Most of today's mass media news organizations:

- Use roughly the same set of norms or professional standards to guide their thinking about what is newsworthy and how to cover it.

- Buy their raw product from much the same wholesale suppliers (for example, the wire services, and the video news services).

- Send their reporters out to cover the same big events, go to much the same (official) sources for information about those events, digest the same press handouts prepared by those sources, and then look over their shoulders to see if they got the story right.

Not that the editors at *The New York Times* read *USA Today* each morning, but it is a safe bet that editors at *USA Today* read the *Times*. And the staffs of both publications read the same wire service feeds. Meanwhile, the people producing radio and television news begin their days reading the wires and *The New York Times*. And everybody in the media tunes into CNN to keep on top of a breaking event such as the crash of a space shuttle, the assassination of a leader, or the progress of the latest war.

As a result, mass media news is a remarkably standardized product behind cosmetic differences such as theme music, anchor personalities, the use of color photos, the layout of articles, and other stylistic differences designed to market much the same news product to varying consumer tastes. Underneath it all, this information production system displays a flair for the *dramatic,* a preference for *official* views, and a "here today, gone tomorrow" *fragmentation* of events as the press and the camera's eye follow the latest stories around the world. This information packaging (television news pieces are called "packages") begins with bureaucratic routines inside media organizations.

Routine News: Deadlines, Beats, and Packs

Rather than wondering each day where to look for news, reporters are sent to places where they are likely to find it. Thus, from local to national media, most journalists work specific **news beats.** Local reporters may be assigned to such beats as the city hall, police or crime, schools or education, business and commerce, and so on. One local newspaper in southern California, *The Orange County Register,* has kept pace with the suburban lifestyle by assigning reporters to cover traffic and shopping-mall beats. At the national level, the most common news beats are the White House, Congress, the Supreme Court, the State Department, and the Pentagon. Gaps in this system are filled in by giving some reporters "at large" or "roving" assignments such as "national affairs correspondent" or "science and technology correspondent."

At the same time, large organizations maintain branch offices called "news bureaus" in different places. Needless to say, no organization can be in all places at once, so the number of bureaus is limited. With the exception of CNN, the budget cuts at the major television networks have resulted in a shrinking bureau system. Most television news organizations today rely heavily on generic video produced by news wholesalers who often save expenses by sending "smart camera crews" (in other words, without reporters) to shoot footage.

Beats, bureaus, and other bureaucratic conventions of the news business shape the picture we get of the political world in important respects. So many reporters are assigned to cover the president compared to Congress and the Court that one could easily get the impression that most of what the government does emanates from the Oval

Office. Indeed, the president's health, dietary habits, recreational trips, and helicopter flights loom larger on the news screen most days than the legal reasoning of the Supreme Court or the daily lawmaking activities of Congress. If news audiences took these coverage patterns to reflect the distribution of power in American politics, their image of the political system might look something like that shown in Figure 11.5.

The news image of where important things are happening around the United States is also shaped by where journalists are stationed. Thus, Washington, D.C. dominates the news scene, followed by New York (almost entirely represented by New York City), California (dominated by Los Angeles), Chicago (surrounded by a nebulous place called Illinois), Houston, Boston, and on down the line. Who knows? Important things may be going on in Alabama or Montana, but there is nobody there to report them most of the time. When a disaster or unusual event occurs, the press pack will descend and offer a fragmentary glimpse of life out of balance in those other places. For the most part, however, the news map of the United States looks something like that shown in Figure 11.6.

Now, let's zoom out to the news view of the world. The first thing we notice is that the United States dwarfs the rest of the news globe. Europe is at least ten times its geographical or population size. South America is microscopic, except when coups, scandals, or a burning jungle bring the news cameras into the region. Africa is almost nonexistent except for the occasional famine, war, or apartheid-related violent incident in South Africa, which barely keep the huge continent on the news map. Israel is the size of the rest of the Middle East combined. And where is Asia outside of China, Japan, and the occasional student riot in Korea? Well, there just isn't much room.

Now all of this is as it should be, some might say. The president *is* more important in the political scheme than Congress or the Court. Europe *is* more important than Africa. Israel *is* worth the same attention devoted to the rest of the countries in the region com-

FIGURE 11.5

Images of Government Based on News Coverage

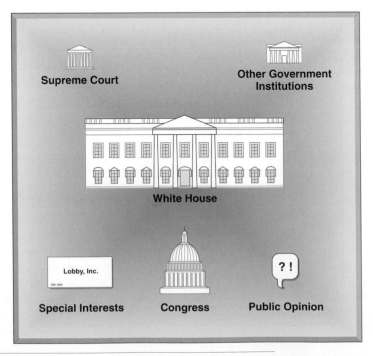

Source: Author's estimates based on studies of coverage of various political issues.

FIGURE 11.6

News Map of the United States: Ratio of Populations of States and Regions to News Coverage They Receive

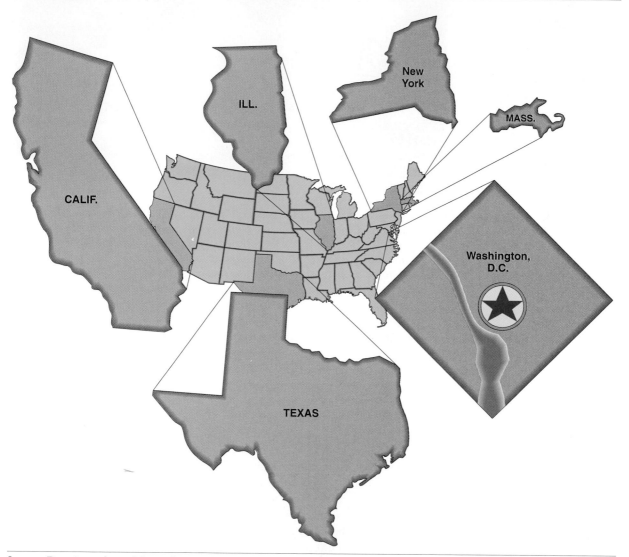

Source: Drawing adapted from data gathered by D. Charles Whitney, et al., "Geographic and Source Biases in Network Television News," *Journal of Broadcasting and Electronic Media,* Vol. 33, 1989, pp. 159–174.

bined. Perhaps. But is this because of some intrinsic property of these frequently covered news subjects? Or, is it because appearing in the news enhances the visibility, concern, and importance that human beings attribute to the things that populate their worlds?[66]

Due to the beat system and the conformity-producing competition to get the same story, reporters keep turning up in the same places to cover the same stories. The common way of putting it is that journalists travel in *packs:* on the trail of the same government official, stalking the same story, bedding down in the same hotels, hanging out in

CBS television anchorman Dan Rather (at left) *speaks with a soldier in the field after President Bush sent troops into famine- and violence-wracked Somalia in "Operation Restore Hope," begun during the closing days of his administration. At right, members of an eager press pack dog the footsteps of servicemen landing on Somali beaches. "Feeding frenzies" such as this—more often focusing on domestic scandals or crises—are a hallmark of the American media as reporters compete furiously for the hottest, latest news stories.*

the same briefing rooms and bars, being fed the same press releases and speeches.[67] It is not surprising that different news organizations end up discovering the same news. In fact, the dynamics of the pack inevitably lead journalists to compare notes and discuss how to play a story. Moreover, if a reporter or news crew on the scene produces a story different from the one running in the other media, editors and producers back at the home office may well want to know why their representative missed *the* story.[68]

As noted earlier, the pack can also turn vicious, looking for signs of weakness in its political prey, leaping upon the official who stumbles and falls in a public performance, sniffing out a scandal in the making. When the pack is off and running, the political prey may be cornered, and a political career ruined. What does this really accomplish? Exposing corrupt politicians rather than the system that encouraged their corruption may discourage the public about leadership and the chances for serious reforms.[69] Many media executives respond to these charges by saying that they are simply providing the kind of coverage that people want. People may not like all the scandals and the crises, but they watch them. More important, relatively few people watch public television or read alternative news magazines from which they might get a better picture of the politics behind the scenes. The news, it is often said, is simply a reflection of popular tastes.

Popular Tastes and News

There is an important truth to what journalists say about the public getting the kind of news it wants. An election night draws far fewer viewers than a superbowl these days. (See Figure 11.7.) The war against Iraq was nearly as well-staged as a TV drama, and it topped the ratings charts. When the military landed in Somalia in 1992 to deliver food in a famine, the landing was complicated by the reporters and photographers who had already taken up positions on the beach to record their landing. Although the press was clearly authorized by the Pentagon to get the most dramatic coverage, the press pack ran out of control, as one journalist put it, "driven by an entertainment desire."[70] At one

Dish-raising at Mogadishu.

This 1992 cartoon echoes, ironically, a celebrated World War II photograph of U.S. servicemen raising the American flag on Iwo Jima in 1945, following a terrible battle with Japanese forces for control of the island. Here the one-time onlookers have displaced the battle-weary heroes in the public eye; and their "banner," the satellite dish, has supplanted the very Stars and Stripes itself.

FIGURE 11.7 *The Political Ratings Are Falling*

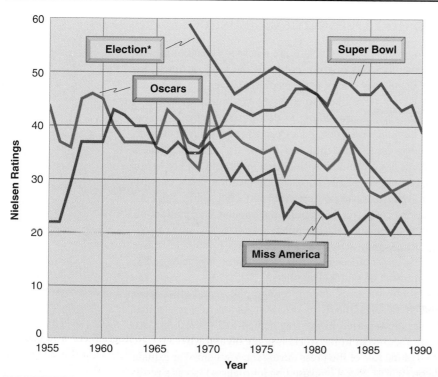

Source: *The New York Times,* March 26, 1990, p. A10.

point, Navy SEALs forced some reporters to turn out the television lights and clear the area to make it easier to secure the beach. The balance between information and info-tainment is a delicate one, indeed.

What is the obligation of the press to communicate information that people may not want to hear, read, or see? Imagine, for a moment, that you are an editor for a news or-ganization covering the Persian Gulf War. Should your paper or magazine publish a grisly photo showing the charred remains of an Iraqi soldier who was killed in battle while trying to escape his burning vehicle? Such a photo was run in leading English and French newspapers on the grounds that it brought home the fact that at least 100,000 Iraqis died in the war, and people should be forced to consider the consequences of the Persian Gulf War. In the United States, that photo was not even sent out over the wire services, meaning that most newspaper editors did not even get to look at it.

The editor of the Associated Press wire service explained that he did not buy and dis-tribute the photo because he already knew what the reaction of newspaper editors would be: "Newspapers will tell us, 'We can't present pictures like that for people to look at over breakfast.'"[71] The picture editor at *Time* magazine said this about the picture: "It's dramatic. It's horrific. It says it all about war." However, he admitted that even if he had seen it in time, *Time* probably would not have printed it because, "Whenever we run a picture like that, we're heavily criticized. We get a lot of reader mail."[72] What do you think? Should such images be part of the news? Are they worse than images commonly shown in movies? How should the news limit its representations of reality? Should peo-ple in a country going to war rest comfortably with images of war as they prefer to think about it, or should they be stimulated, even shocked, into thinking about the conse-quences of their political decision? If driven primarily by organizational efficiencies inside the business and public tastes in the marketplace, the news may not serve the in-formation needs of democracy.

Information, Power, and Democracy Revisited

The working relations between journalists and politicians are a nervous blend of mutual dependence and antagonism. Sometimes this mixture produces the kind of timely, in-depth, critical information that democracy needs if the representatives are to be ac-countable to the citizens. When is such news likely to emerge? *News debates are most open and informative when public officials are willing to debate issues openly for ex-tended periods and invite citizen participation in the policy process as it evolves.* In such cases, the news organizations cover issues in depth and follow the political process through the halls and hearing rooms of government with citizen in-put in tow. For better or worse, we see this kind of open, often volatile mass communication going on with many of the moral issues that enliven American politics. Abortion, civil rights, gun con-trol, flag burning, and other enduring controversies capture the popular imagination, pit politicians and parties against each other, and take the public on extended tours of gov-ernment institutions at work. Citizens may actually see in the news how issues move from elections to legislatures to executive offices to courts to regulatory agencies and at times spill over into the streets in sustained political conflicts.

At other times, complex issues of economics, energy, foreign policy, and other areas of elite power politics are handled more guardedly by officials. As a result, issues that are important to America's future are reported in the fragmented and officialized lan-guage that keeps people guessing about what in the world is going on and why.

As noted earlier, some studies of the role of the press during the Vietnam War explain critical press coverage less as a product of liberal or crusading journalists than as a result of news organizations becoming more hostile toward government policies *after* those policies came under attack by powerful figures in Washington and by presidential candidates.[73] In the case of the Persian Gulf War, most members of Congress were cautious in expressing their views about going to war before the bombing started, and the majority of Washington elites quickly joined the rallying public after the fighting broke out. As a result, the media paid little attention to opposition views or even to unpleasant reminders of the realities of the war such as the photo discussed previously. Even though there were numerous national demonstrations against going to war, television news ran a mere twenty-nine minutes of protests out of a total of 2,855 minutes of war coverage by the three major TV networks.[74] To put this in perspective, about the same amount of airtime was given to protesters as to interviews with tourists and business people about how the war affected their travel plans.[75] The emerging conclusion about mass mediated democracy is that news debates tend to be more open and informative when the government itself is already functioning ideally: that is, when government officials are openly debating and investigating public policies in front of the news cameras. On the other hand, when elites are not debating policy options in public, the media tend to shut the news gates and turn to other agenda items.

Political scientist Robert Entman argues that our mass mediated democracy is in danger of becoming a *democracy without citizens,* since most news coverage is driven by forces that involve people more as passive consumers than active citizens.[76] For both politicians and journalists, the public has become more of a market to be tested, persuaded, and sold than an equal partner in communications and government. Political reality for many people is anchored in electronic images that move them psychologically in private ways that are detached from society and from face-to-face politics.[77]

The irony in all this is that the technology exists to communicate more information, farther, faster, from more sources to more people than ever before. At the same time, the political (news management) and business pressures operating behind the news may end up creating just the opposite results. Perhaps the electronic age would not be so worrisome if politicians and the press used the potential of today's electronic technology to communicate critical ideas to people. It is clear that visual communication *can* be both moving and insightful. The question is how to move politicians and the media away from the paths of least political and economic resistance in their communications strategies. In the end, the big question about the future of news is this one: Should the press be required to keep debates or issues alive when leaders and publics prefer to ignore them? That is the question that gets at the heart of the responsibilities of the press in a democracy. What do you think?

Key Terms

infotainment

information and democracy

information sources used by most
   Americans

mass media vs. alternative media

government regulation
   equal time provision
   fairness doctrine

the politics of newsmaking
news management techniques
   sound bite
   spin
   handlers, spin doctors, image
     consultants

agenda setting
   journalists as gatekeepers

A CITIZEN'S QUESTION

Political Information

*H*ow can I get more out of the news? Understanding how the news system works is a big help for learning how to use news information more effectively. There is nothing wrong with being entertained by news dramas, but the information in news stories is not very useful unless an effort is made to extract and organize it meaningfully. When news stories seem confusing, think of them as being written in a political code, and your job is to crack that code to get more information out of them. Here are some helpful hints for decoding the news:

*R*emember that news information tends to be *fragmented, dramatized, and officialized.* This means that decoding the news requires some work. For example, the immediacy of news means that we cannot look to the daily headline news for in-depth analysis or history lessons. In part, the gaps can be filled in by reading magazines with different viewpoints, Sunday newspaper "perspective" articles and opinion pieces, and an occasional book. More to the point of this course, the events that pop in and out of the headlines are often recognizable as enduring issues in the political system itself: civil rights, abortion, prayer in the schools, gun control, flag burning, taxation, foreign alliances, and hundreds more. If you apply ideas from this class to understand why these issues are so enduring, how power and participation keep them going, and how the government responds to them, their periodic appearances in the news will make more sense. Finally, remember that government officials shape much of the news. Think about why officials may or may not be addressing particular issues. Some issues may not be in the news simply because officials are avoiding them, not because they are unimportant. When following the news, remember that politicians tend to speak in "political code" when the press is around.

*U*se what you know about culture, institutions, and power to interpret news stories. If stories contain familiar *cultural* symbols such as freedom, democracy, or the flag, think for a moment whether you are responding more to those symbols, or to the issues and events that are wrapped up in those symbols. Since the news may not provide much detail about how the *institutions* of government are working behind the scenes of stories, always try to apply information learned from this course to fill in missing details. Practiced news watchers learn to make educated guesses about what political players are doing, and what institutional factors may be helping or hindering them in achieving their goals. Finally, remember that newsmakers use their *power* (offices, money, connections, large numbers of supporters) to shape news coverage of their activities. Knowing how people (including journalists) try to get their messages into the news makes it easier to decide what the political bias of those messages might be. Some viewpoints may be left out of the news, or just not emphasized, simply because some groups were not as effective as others in using their political resources to manage the news.

FCC

laws affecting political information
    libel
    national security acts
    shield laws

mutual dependence of press and
    politicians

how news organizations work
    beats, news routines
    business profits and news
     products
    citizens as markets
    media monopoly

Suggested Readings

Bagdikian, Ben H. *The Media Monopoly,* 2nd ed. Boston: Beacon Press, 1988.

Bennett, W. Lance. *News: The Politics of Illusion,* 2nd ed. White Plains, N.Y.: Longman, 1988.

Emerson, Thomas. *Toward a General Theory of the First Amendment.* New York: Vintage, 1966.

Entman, Robert. *Democracy Without Citizens.* New York: Oxford University Press, 1989.

Garment, Suzanne. *Scandal: The Culture of Mistrust in American Politics.* New York: Random House, 1991.

Graber, Doris. *Mass Media and American Politics,* 3rd ed. Washington, D.C.: Congressional Quarterly Press, 1989.

Greider, William. *Who Will Tell the People? The Betrayal of American Democracy.* New York: Simon and Schuster, 1992.

Hallin, Daniel C. *The "Uncensored War": The Media and Vietnam.* Berkeley: University of California Press, 1989.

Kowet, Don. *A Matter of Honor: General William C. Westmoreland versus CBS.* New York: Macmillan, 1984.

Lippmann, Walter. *Public Opinion.* New Brunswick, N.J.: Transaction Publishers, 1990 (originally published in 1922).

Powe, Lucas A., Jr. *The Fourth Estate and the Constitution: Freedom of the Press in America.* Berkeley: University of California Press, 1991.

Sabato, Larry. *Feeding Frenzy: How Attack Journalism Has Transformed American Politics.* New York: The Free Press, 1991.

Smith, Hedrick. *The Power Game: How Washington Works.* New York: Ballantine, 1989.

Part IV

INSTITUTIONS AT WORK

CHAPTER 12

Congress: The Legislative Process

CHAPTER 13

Congress: Power and Organization

CHAPTER 14

The Executive: Presidential Power and National Leadership

CHAPTER 15

The Executive: Managing the Bureaucracy

CHAPTER 16

The Judiciary: Courts, Law, and Justice

The framers of the Constitution expected. . . that Congress
should be the dominant branch of the Federal Government.
They sought to establish a strong Executive but, reasoning
from past experience in America, they assumed the supremacy
of the legislature. They put it first in order in the Constitution,
the Executive second, and the Judiciary third. They vested in
Congress immense legislative powers. They gave it the power
of the purse and the power of the sword—the two primary
engines of government. They authorized Congress to
determine the structure of the executive department, the
powers of all administrative officers, the number of justices in
the Supreme Court, the appellate jurisdiction of that Court,
and the form and jurisdiction of inferior federal courts.
And, what is highly important, though usually forgotten, they
left Congress free to determine the nature and form of its
relations to the President and its subordinates. If Congress has
largely failed to develop this phase of its responsibility and has
allowed the President to assume a dominant position, the fault
lies with Congress, not with the Constitution.
—*CHARLES A. BEARD*

Congress: The Legislative Process

- **AN END TO GRIDLOCK? MORE OF THE STORY**
- **LAWS, LEGISLATURES, AND REPRESENTATION**
  Constitutional Design: Legislation and Representation
  A Brief History of Legislatures
  The Logic Behind the American Legislature
  Congress Then and Now
  Representation Revisited
- **CONGRESS, SOCIETY, AND PUBLIC OPINION**
  The Social Composition of Congress
- **HOW CONGRESS USES ITS POWERS**
  Making Laws
  Overseeing the Executive
  The Politics of Pork
  Delivering Services (From Our House to Yours)
  Getting Reelected, of Course
- **LAWS, LEGISLATURES, AND REPRESENTATION REVISITED**
- **A CITIZEN'S QUESTION: Evaluating Congress**
- **KEY TERMS**
- **SUGGESTED READINGS**

An End to Gridlock? More of the Story

The 1992 election marked the first time since 1980 that the same party controlled the White House and a majority of seats in both chambers of Congress. In addition, a large number of retirements from Congress made for more competitive races in both the House and the Senate, resulting in the biggest freshman class on Capitol Hill since 1948. Would all of this end the "gridlock"? The news suggested that gridlock might, indeed, be over. Headlines such as these sounded a note of cautious optimism: ON THE HILL, TRAFFIC MIGHT START MOVING AGAIN,[1] THERE'LL BE SOME CHANGES IN CONGRESS,[2] and THE OLD ORDER CHANGES IN CONGRESS—A LITTLE.[3] At the same time, such qualifiers as *might* and *a little* raised questions about just how much change to expect when an election moves a new president and a slightly different congressional lineup into place on both ends of Pennsylvania Avenue, that corridor of power connecting the White House and the Capitol Building.

As the discussion of gridlock in Chapter 3 indicated, having the same party in both the executive and legislative branches can reduce the friction in the legislative process. However, even under this best-case scenario, political pressures are present at every step of the legislative process, creating divisions or weakening consensus on what government should do and how to do it. In addition to the political importance of parties, elections, and interests already discussed in earlier chapters, we will see in Chapter 14 that presidents are key legislative players, bringing public pressure to bear on Congress. In addition, presidents must personally convince powerful members of Congress to join in forging broad programs of legislation.

This presidential leadership of Congress is most effective when presidents bring together congressional power brokers from both parties to participate in discussions of the legislative agenda. One headline described how newly elected President Bill Clinton

intended to approach the leadership issue: AVOIDING GRIDLOCK BY WOOING BOTH SIDES OF AISLE.[4] The point of the story was simple: The newly elected president would have to do more than just remind Congress that the American public had voted to

President Bill Clinton makes his first address to a joint session of Congress in February of 1993, promoting his budget proposal. A compromise version of the budget bill would not emerge from the legislative process until several months later; when it did, it would pass by the narrowest margin possible—a single vote—in both the House and Senate, even though the Democratic party held a majority in the two chambers. Senate passage of the reconciliation package required a tie-breaking vote by Vice President Al Gore.

end gridlock. Mr. Clinton would have to work on the Republican leadership as well as his fellow Democrats to convince them of the merits of his programs.[5] The new president soon discovered, however, that powerful leaders in Congress play hardball. Feeling ignored by the administration, Senate Republicans soon rallied under minority leader Bob Dole and managed to stall some new expenditures by means of filibusters, lengthy floor debates, and amendments. When members of the president's own party became worried that voters might join the rebellion against "tax-and-spend" Democrats, Clinton battled gridlock within his own party. He discovered the hard lesson that party loyalty is not automatic in a system laboring under many competing pressures.

Presidents such as Lyndon Johnson and Ronald Reagan made considerable efforts to court the opposition party and to mobilize their own party's leadership. As noted in the previous chapter, the Reagan administration also used the news media to mobilize public pressure on Congress. By contrast, Jimmy Carter sent a broad legislative agenda to Capitol Hill from 1977–1980 but had little success in organizing either public pressure or political support on "The Hill." His programs met with resistance from both parties, resulting in an earlier episode of governmental gridlock. Part of Carter's problem was that recently enacted congressional reforms weakened the control of party leaders, as described in Chapter 13. To a large extent, however, Carter failed to sell his programs to either party in Congress. Aware that he would be compared to Carter, Bill Clinton brought congressional Democratic leaders squarely into the governing picture, as indicated by the opening lines of this news story:

> President-elect Bill Clinton gathered Democratic leaders around him today to pronounce an end to the "cold war" between Congress and the White House. But Mr. Clinton quickly confronted the degree to which his campaign pledges strain the [legislative] coalition he will need to enact his programs.[6]

In this chapter and the next, we will look at the important mix of politics and power from outside Congress (party control of the White House, presidential leadership, public pressure) and inside Congress (party unity, committee power, campaign finance, and individual members' needs for reelection) that go into the legislative process. This chapter explores the constitutional design of the national legislature, along with the various powers wielded by Congress. Chapter 13 takes a look at the internal system of committees and subcommittees responsible for different kinds of legislation. Along the way we will explore a number of political factors: the power of individual senators and representatives who chair the committees; the iron triangles that create independent spheres of power among committees, interest groups, and bureaucracies (recall Chapter 8); and the various campaign financing and voter pressures that affect the calculations of individual members of Congress who must get reelected.

At stake is not just how many bills become law, but which ones do, which ones do not, and how they add up. The popular view in the media is that gridlock happens when Congress is paralyzed by interest-group politics compounded by pressures to deliver government services to individual constituencies. It is often assumed that gridlock will break up when Congress and the president are pushed by voters to recover party unity around a common set of social and economic goals. These broad generalizations may be reasonable starting points for thinking about Congress in its larger political context, but you will quickly learn that an important degree of friction is built into the design of the institution itself. Moreover, there is a strong base of cultural support for keeping Congress from having too much power. Finally, voters often have personal political agendas. While they may get upset at *other* representatives giving their districts expensive projects and services, they tend to like it when *their own* representatives bring home similar "pork barrel" projects. (The *pork barrel* image refers to members of Congress, who, like hungry people on southern plantations, rushed to the pork barrel when it was time to eat.) With this attitude, voters, too, play a part in creating gridlock. All of these factors are useful for understanding how Congress works and for deciding how well it works.

Laws, Legislatures, and Representation

Congress is among the world's most independent and, on paper at least, most powerful legislatures. Yet, as the discussion above suggests, few Americans probably think of it that way. Perhaps the greatest aid to understanding the American legislature is to see the logic behind the constitutional design of Congress. Both the design of representation and the procedures of lawmaking were aimed at reducing the threat of any political group or class dominating the others. The net result may have been to structure legislative power so that it is difficult for lawmakers to engage in broad-based debates on national priorities, much less to reach consensus on those priorities. "Inside the System" Box 12.1 suggests that our thematic framework is again helpful for understanding the politics inside the legislative branch.

Constitutional Design: Legislation and Representation

The two most important checks on Congress are the **limits on legislative power** itself and the creation of a complicated system of **representation** that introduces different ways of thinking about the very role of the institution. The limits on legislative power should already be familiar. As you know by now, the legislative powers specified in the Constitution were checked first by giving each of the three national institutions some share in lawmaking. Congress was given the additional internal check of requiring the same bills to pass both the Senate and the House. Finally, different areas of law were divided—not all that cleanly—between the national and the state governments. This legislative obstacle course suggests that so-called gridlock may be the rule rather than the exception in American government.

The second design feature, *representation*, is a bit trickier to grasp. The basic question of representation is simple: *How should voters' demands on elected representatives translate into laws?* There are two broadly different views of this, and, for better or worse, they were both built into the American legislative system. As discussed briefly in Chapter 3, the two chambers of Congress were designed to provide very different kinds of deliberation and representation:

- *In the House of Representatives*, representation was based on population and smaller districts with a short (two-year) election cycle, creating more of a **delegate** chamber. In the *delegate* view of representation, the representative is responsive to the will of the people and held directly accountable through frequent elections.

- *In the Senate*, election was originally by state legislatures, not by popular vote, and senators were given a longer election cycle of six years, creating more of a deliberative and debating chamber, an independent **trustee** of the public interest. The *trustee* view of representation is that lawmakers should not be bound by the whims, passions, and ignorance of the people, but be somewhat free to decide what is in the nation's best interest.

These differences in representation probably never emerged in the two chambers as clearly as some of the Founders envisioned. Distinctions in representation became blurred even further with the direct election of the Senate. However, important differences in representation styles have been detected by students of the modern Congress and will be discussed in more detail below. For now, consider the possibility that differences in the design of the two chambers can affect how their members think about the problems of their own voters (called constituents) and about the larger national interest.

Are these problems of power and representation common to all legislatures? The short answer is *no*. A few other national legislatures resemble the American Congress in some ways, but the United States is probably unique in the degree to which legislative power is checked, and the degree to which very different kinds of representation are tol-

The Enduring Limits on the Powers of Congress

12.1

Although the politics of parties, interests, and voters can greatly affect how Congress performs, many of the problems that worry critics in fact reflect enduring features of the American political system: *cultural resistance* to an overly powerful central government, a resulting *institutional design* that discourages hasty legislative agreement, and the often conflicting pressures of many centers of *power in society*.

Although the Founders recognized the legislature as the central institution of government, they also expressed fundamental cultural concerns about holding government in check and keeping factions in society at bay. The response to this enduring cultural orientation to government was to design a two-chamber legislature, with each chamber as unlike the other as possible. (Recall Madison's justification for this in Chapters 2 and 3.) This institutional design created a built-in check on sweeping government action by guaranteeing that only measures agreed on by two very different chambers (and, after that, by the executive) could become law. While this greatly reduced the chances of any major faction holding permanent government power, it also created a system of conflicting social powers competing for the attention of national representatives:

• Voters (reflecting majority power) often hold important sway with representatives.
• Competing interests (pluralism) have organized effectively to work the legislative process around their often narrow concerns.
• Powerful elites (elitism) often gain individual access to members of Congress through their political support back home, or by providing favors while in Washington.

Competing social powers may discourage the dominance of any particular group or interest in government, but they can make sweeping legislative programs difficult to pass. It is possible that the Founders did not foresee the growth of such a complex power system or imagine the strain on a legislative institution already designed to make political consensus difficult.

---

erated within the same system. A look at the origins of different legislative systems illustrates why the U.S. Congress is so distinctive.

A Brief History of Legislatures

The legislature in modern history had a noble beginning—literally. Beginning in the thirteenth century, groups of nobles were called together by the kings of England to encourage broader support for tax policies. With the historic rallying cry of "No taxation without representation" echoing around the world since that time, the general trend over six hundred years has been toward broad representation in all democracies on a wide range of political decisions. However, the route to representation taken in the United States has resulted in a pattern of legislative power different from most other democracies. As Robert Axelrod put it:

Legislatures were originally developed in Britain, and later in France, because the kings constantly found themselves short of money. After trying many methods of raising money by command, they eventually realized that they would have to attain the support of broader and broader segments of society. The representatives of society, once called together, decided that they would only agree to provide tax money if they had a

The Right Honourable (now Baroness) Margaret Thatcher, the celebrated "Iron Lady" who served as Britain's prime minister for an extraordinary three consecutive terms (May 1979 to November 1990). Under the parliamentary system, Thatcher and her Cabinet members were actually members of the legislature (the House of Commons); and her ruling power derived from her position as leader of the Conservative party. The closing of Thatcher's reign came not through a general election, but from a party vote.

say in how it was spent. So the long process of development of the relationship between the executive and the legislature began as a struggle to control taxes and budgets. Over time, the entire range of political issues became included in the legislative process.

As the power of royalty declined, the executive authority of the state was increasingly placed in a powerful bureaucracy led by executive officers who were responsible to the citizens. The relationship between the executive and the legislature has evolved in two quite different directions in the west. The most common method is the parliamentary system, whereby the executive is answerable to the legislature. The method used in the United States is the presidential system, in which the leader of the executive branch of government is directly elected by the public independently of the elections for the legislature.[7]

Many of the world's legislative bodies are **unicameral,** meaning that they have one chamber. And many that are **bicameral,** having two chambers, grant one chamber dominance over the other: The British House of Commons overshadows the House of Lords, and the German Bundestag overshadows the Bundesrat. The United States, however, has a bicameral legislature in which each chamber has (nearly) equal powers.

Recall the discussion from Chapter 9 about the governing arrangements in a typical **parliamentary system.** The executive (usually called the prime minister) and the cabinet are drawn from the legislature. This means that governing powers are by no means separated and that the government can be dominated by a small number of party leaders able to make broad decisions. Not surprisingly, voters in the industrialized parliamentary democracies (where much power can be concentrated in one institution or party) tend to watch politics closely, be informed, vote fairly often, and belong to party-related organizations such as labor unions, business associations, and even recreational clubs that have party ties. In the American system, the institutions check each other in ways that limit broad swings of government action following elections, which may help explain why Americans feel freer to go their individual ways, participate less, and follow politics less closely than citizens in other countries. The next section explores how this system came to be.

The Logic Behind the American Legislature

Perhaps the most fateful decision of the Constitutional Convention was to adopt a bicameral model from England—surely not to reproduce the conflict between the "common" citizens (House of Commons) and the nobility (House of Lords), but to divide legislative powers into two bodies as different in size, composition, and term of service as imaginable. To make matters more complicated, the Constitution not only sent lawmakers to separate chambers but granted them considerable freedom to decide how they would conduct business within those chambers. As a result, there are important differences in the procedures through which a bill passes in the Senate and the House.

These differences were championed as great virtues by the supporters of the Constitution. What today are regarded by some as sources of confusion (such as the ambiguity of "delegate" vs. "trustee" models of representation) were advertised in *The Federalist* as innovative ideas. Consider, for example, some of the arguments for designing the House along a delegate model of representation and the Senate as the trustee of a higher public interest.

Here is what *Federalist* No. 57 says about the House as delegate of the people:

> The House of Representatives is so constituted as to support in the members an habitual recollection of their dependence on the people. Before the sentiments impressed on their minds by the mode of their elevation can be effaced by the exercise of power, they will be compelled to anticipate the moment when their power is to cease, when their exercise of it is to be reviewed, and when they must descend to the level from which they were raised; there for ever to remain unless a faithful discharge of their trust shall have established their title to a renewal of it.

Translation: The House was designed to constantly remind its members of their accountability to the people. Terms in office were made short so that before members could be corrupted by power, they would come up for review by the people. If they had not used their power well, they would be removed from office. (That, at least, was the theory.)

Here is what *Federalist* No. 62 says about the Senate as trustee of the people:

> The qualifications proposed for senators, as distinguished from those of representatives, consist in a more advanced age and a longer period of citizenship. A senator must be thirty years of age at least; as a representative must be twenty-five. And the former must have been a citizen nine years; as seven years are required for the latter. The propriety of these distinctions is explained by the nature of the senatorial *trust* . . . requiring greater extent of information and stability of character. . . . [T]he senator should have reached a period of life most likely to supply these advantages.

> The necessity of a senate is [to counter] the propensity of all single and numerous assemblies, to yield to the impulse of sudden and violent passions. . . . [A] body which is to correct this infirmity ought itself to be free from it, and consequently ought to be less numerous. It ought, moreover, to possess great firmness, and consequently ought to hold its authority by a tenure of considerable duration.

Translation: Because senators are intended to sit back and reflect upon the wisdom of laws, they should be more mature. In addition, large, single-chambered legislatures are prone to be carried away by passions. A second, smaller chamber with longer terms in office should check the passions of the "people's chamber" and be more able to stick to its principles. But what if paralysis resulted from two different chambers, with different political calculations, having to agree on the same legislation to make it law? This was also held to be a virtue, as these words from *Federalist* No. 63 indicate:

> So there are regular moments in public affairs, when the people, stimulated by some irregular passion . . . or misled by the artful misrepresentations of interested men, may call for measures which they themselves will afterwards be the most ready to lament and condemn. In these critical moments, how salutary will be the interference of some temperate and respectable body . . . to check . . . the blow mediated by the people against themselves, until reason, justice and truth can regain their authority over the public mind?

Translation: There are any number of ways that people may be misled, and it is important to have some independent chamber of the legislature keeping the nation's longer-term interests in mind until an impassioned public regains its senses. In these cases, legislative "interference" is a good thing. However, it is difficult to design a system in which this "interference" is switched on only against corruption and deception and switched off again when good ideas come along. Thus, some of the features that are today sources of complaint against Congress were its greatest selling factors in 1787.

Congress Then and Now

Channeling the nation's political demands through this complex two-chambered process is a formula sure to produce a degree of commotion at the center of government. And commotion is just what resulted from the very beginning. Scuffles and fist fights were fairly common inside the Capitol. Some members took to attending sessions armed, and duels were fought in the woods outside the building. Since the members were left to work out their own rules, the result was a code of conduct that favored freedom of personal expression. As a result, much was debated and little resolved.

One account from the early 1800s described the life of Congress like this: "Political hostilities are waged with great vigor, yet both in attack and defence there is evidently an entire want both of discipline and organization. There is no concert, no division of duties, no compromise of opinion. . . . Any general system of effective co-operation is impossible."[8] Based on other similar accounts, it seems safe to say that in many ways Congress was more of a public spectacle in the early years than it is today. In those early days, however, there were no television cameras to broadcast the spectacle daily.

Life inside today's Congress may not be as turbulent, but it is anything but calm. An internal study by the House Commission on Administrative Review found that in a typical twelve-hour workday, the average member could find only twelve minutes to write laws or speeches and another eleven minutes for reading.[9] The rest was hearings, floor votes, staff meetings, committee meetings, subcommittee meetings, meetings with other legislators, meetings with constituents, meetings with lobbyists, meetings with contributors, and, perhaps, an occasional meeting with the family.

Out of all this activity, many things do, of course, get done. In some ways, particularly in writing regulatory legislation and monitoring the executive branch, Congress has been very active in recent times. In other areas, such as seizing the legislative initiative from the president and waging great partisan debates, Congress was probably in its prime during the late 1800s. However, people in that era complained of too much power being concentrated in the hands of party leaders in Congress.

It is possible that Congress ends up on the hot seat no matter which way it moves; both a strongly focused Congress and a divided and paralyzed one trigger public disapproval for different reasons. But one conclusion seems safe: Through most of its history,

Home Style Representation

12.2

How legislatures work depends heavily on the type of representation created both through institutional design and political tradition. Balancing the roles of "delegate" and "trustee" may be the most difficult part of a U.S. representative's job. Even when it seems safe to exercise personal judgment on an issue, a member may be called on every two years to explain his or her position to voters back home. At these moments, representatives hope they have built up enough trust either to make their explanations stick or to weather unpopular actions. According to political scientist Richard Fenno,

such trust is built up slowly as representatives present themselves to their constituents in the course of hundreds of pilgrimages back home to attend events, make speeches, meet with voter and business groups, and stand for reelection.

If the representative "presents" himself or herself credibly, the move from delegate to trustee roles is smoother, giving the lawmaker more leeway and the voters greater confidence in their representative. Developing an effective "home style" helps representatives avoid being judged on one or two volatile issues, because it encourages voters to think about them as human beings, leaders, and trusted friends. The failure to develop an effective home style,

or neglecting to go home and cultivate it after many terms in office, can result in surprising defeats when opponents or the media seize upon a volatile issue, and voters are no longer willing to give the incumbent's explanation a charitable hearing. While home style representation helps to balance the conflicting representation pressures on members, the result is often a very personalized political process in which local ties weaken party loyalty. As former House Speaker Tip O'Neill once said, "All politics is local."

SOURCE: Richard F. Fenno, Jr., *Home Style: House Members in Their Districts*, Boston: Little, Brown, 1978.

with the exception of the strong Congresses after the Civil War and during the Great Depression, the American legislature has done pretty much what its designers intended it to do—minimize sweeping legislative change, and grind potentially large and volatile factions into smaller and gentler ones.

Representation Revisited

As noted earlier, the neat division between the Senate as *trustee* chamber and the House as *delegate* chamber never materialized as clearly as the Founders intended. However, some signs of this division have been observed in studies of the House and Senate by political scientist Richard Fenno. Many members of Congress agree that constituency pressures are greater in the House, requiring members to develop a more intimate and voter-sensitive "**home style**" of politics (see "Inside the System" Box 12.2) to communicate with voters back in the district.[10] By contrast, senators are more removed from short-term voter pressure. As one senator put it, a six-year term offers more "squirming room," which can produce different votes in the two chambers, even when personal opinion may be similar among senators and representatives.[11]

An issue fresh in the minds of members during Fenno's study was the Senate debate and approval of a treaty with Panama to give back control of the Panama Canal in the year 2000. Public opinion was sharply divided on the issue, but the Senate supported the president's treaty. Although the House does not vote on treaties, many observers doubted that the majority of representatives in the House would have held firm against negative public opinion. Perhaps this is precisely what the founders had in mind when the Constitution gave the Senate the exclusive power to approve treaties, without any input from the House.

Despite these signs that the institutional design of Congress does affect representation, Fenno argues that it would be far too simple to say that the House is a delegate body and the Senate a trustee institution. These are very rough characterizations that miss the subtle politics of Congress. In his study of House members, for example, Fenno found that personal philosophies of representatives also shape the style of representation, with many adopting the delegate model and many acting as trustees. For example, one "delegate" said: "I'm not going to vote my own convictions. I'm here to represent my people." Explaining why he voted against his own beliefs on a bill, another "delegate" put it like this: "I rationalize it by saying that I owe it to my constituents if they feel strongly about it." The "trustees," on the other hand see their roles differently, sometimes even telling their constituents: "If I were sitting where you are, I think that I would want to elect a man to Congress who will exercise his best judgment on the facts when he has them all." Another "trustee" imagined how he would respond to a petition from a majority of his constituents:

> It's hard for me to imagine a majority of my constituents agreeing on anything. But if it did happen, then no, I would not vote for it [for that reason alone]. I would still have to use my own judgment. . . . You can express opinions. I have to make the decision. If you disagree with my decisions, you have the power every two years to vote me out of office. I listen to you, believe me. But, in the end, I have to use my judgment as to what is in your best interests.[12]

Which brings us back to the importance of developing a "home style" or a personal relationship with constituents. More important than a precise formula of representation is the member's ability to explain his or her actions when questioned about them back home. As Fenno put it:

> The ability to get explanations accepted at home is, then, the essential underpinning of a member's voting leeway in Washington.
>
> So the question arises: How can representatives increase the likelihood that their explanations will be accepted at home? And the answer that House members give is: They can win and hold constituent trust. The more your various constituencies trust you, members reason, the less likely they are to require an explanation of your votes and the more likely they are to accept your explanation when they do ask for it.[13]

Which means that a member's home style is not necessarily based exclusively upon one model of representation or another, but gives the member flexibility to alternate to suit the situation.

A similar pattern seems to prevail in the Senate. In his classic study of that chamber, political scientist Donald Matthews found some greater tendencies toward a trustee model of representation, but also concluded that the key was the senator's relationship with constituents. Matthews noted an ironic pattern in which senators spent early years building "a larger circle of friends" back home, and later years wielding greater power in Washington, only to discover that their relations back home were strained, often resulting in electoral "defeat suffered at the peak of careers . . . a cruel reminder of the constituents' power."[14]

Not only do lawmakers try to build trust and a personal style of communication, but, as we will see later in this chapter, they get a lot of mileage (particularly in the House) out of providing special services such as finding lost social security checks and keeping their office doors open to influential groups in their districts. This begins to explain why most voters like their own representatives but hate Congress. For this and other reasons, most incumbents who seek reelection win. The numbers tell a dramatic tale: Since 1980, roughly 80 percent of the senators and 95 percent of the representatives seeking reelection have won, and most have done so by wide margins.[15] Even in the much-heralded "change" election of 1992, 90 percent of incumbents seeking reelection won.

Congress, Society, and Public Opinion

As explained in Chapter 6, studies show that there are strong correlations between public opinion and congressional decisions.[16] It is difficult to answer precisely why. Is it because members of Congress practice electoral "defense," playing it safe and leaning in the direction of their supporters on many issues to prevent voter uprisings at the next election? Or is it because media-savvy organizations like the Pentagon, the White House, and interest groups bombard Congress and public alike with information campaigns on key issues to create a broad consensus of opinion that paves the way to the desired political results?[17] If it is the former, the delegate method of representation is working more smoothly (in other words, without the need of electoral punishment) than even the designers of the system anticipated. If it is the latter, we need to rethink our models of representation altogether, updating James Madison by bringing in the modern influence of Madison Avenue in shaping public opinion. Modern theories of representation would also do well to address the impact of national interest groups that have little connection to a representative's home territory other than sending checks to a campaign bank account.[18]

The Social Composition of Congress

Another link between Congress and society is the fit between the social composition of Congress and the social or **demographic** composition of society. Some critics claim that members of Congress cannot grasp certain social problems unless they belong to the particular group (ethnic, racial, religious, sexual, or other) that experiences those problems.

For example, the discussion of sexual harassment in Chapter 5 noted assertions by feminist organizations that an all-male Senate committee had little understanding of the

Senator Russell Long (D–Louisiana) debates a 1986 tax measure on the Senate floor. Members of Congress commonly fit in with the political culture of their states. Long, who retired in 1987 after nearly forty years in office, was probably the most restrained offspring of the colorful Long family dynasty. His father was Huey "Kingfish" Long, a Depression-era politician whose meteoric and highly controversial career ended in his assassination; Huey's brother Earl subsequently served three times as governor. Russell Long brought to the national arena a more subdued form of Louisiana's colorful political style.

FIGURE 12.1

Percentage of Women and Minorities in the U.S. House, 1971–1994

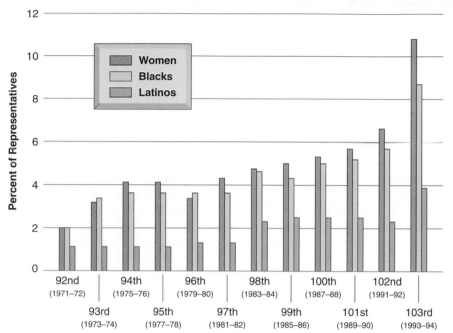

Source: Harold W. Stanley and Richard G. Nieme, *Vital Statistics on American Politics*. Washington, D.C.: Congressional Quarterly Press, 1992, p. 201, updated with 1992 election results.

FIGURE 12.2

Percentage of Women and Minorities in the U.S. Senate, 1971–1994

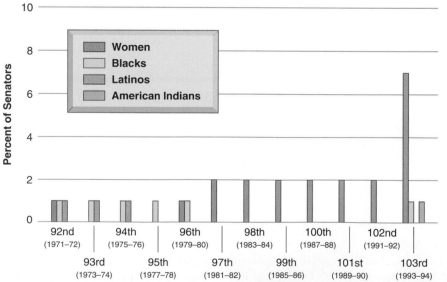

Source: Harold W. Stanley and Richard G. Niemi, *Vital Statistics on American Politics*. Washington, D.C.: Congressional Quarterly Press, 1992, p. 201, updated with 1992 election results. In a 1993 special election, Kay Bailey Hutchison (R–Texas) was elected to fill the Senate seat vacated by Lloyd Bentsen.

HOW WE COMPARE

Percentage of Women in the Legislatures of Twenty-five Democratic Nations

12.3

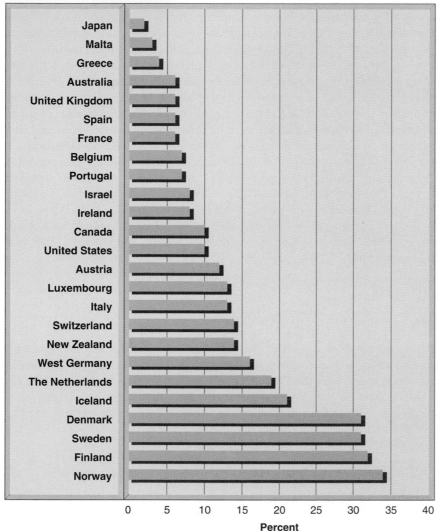

SOURCE: International Centre for Parliamentary Documentation, *Distribution of Seats between Men and Women in National Assemblies* (Geneva, Switzerland: 1987). USA figures reflect 1992

importance or the nature of the harassment allegations that Anita Hill made against Supreme Court nominee Clarence Thomas. Perhaps as an indirect result of this furor, the 1992 election resulted in a sizeable increase in women (and minority) representatives in the House and Senate. Figure 12.1 illustrates the changes in race and gender demographics in the House from 1971 to 1994, and Figure 12.2 illustrates trends in the Senate. With these increases, the United States ranks midway on a list of nations in its percentage of women in the legislature, as noted in "How We Compare" Box 12.3.

Although the 1992 election showed some signs of change, Congress differs from the general population in categories of race (a higher percentage of whites), in age (it is much older), in gender (there are more males), in income (much wealthier), in occupation (many more lawyers, bankers, and business executives), and in education (more college and advanced degrees). Studies show that similar differences have always characterized Congress.[19] Do these differences matter?

Some say "yes," *demographic representation* matters, because the people best able to represent our interests are those most like us in social terms. Such critics argue that until more women, minorities, and "ordinary working people" gain power, Congress will be slow to grasp some basic social and economic problems.[20] Their argument for demographic representation is this: "Women and minorities will more often express their concerns on the floor of Congress without going through the filter of white men."[21]

One argument against sheerly demographic representation is that the legislative agendas of congressional committees may already be influenced by interest groups representing feminist, ethnic, and other "group" views. Another view argues that demographic representation is a simplistic and divisive way of viewing the complexities of government; and that politicians should be judged by their philosophies, programs, and deeds rather than categories such as race, gender, income bracket, or religious affiliation.

It remains to be seen what will become of California senator Dianne Feinstein's 1992 campaign slogan, "The status quo has got to go."[22] Nonetheless, it cannot be denied that many voters believe "people like them" are better able to represent them. In analyzing the 1992 vote, Democratic party pollster Celinda Lake noted that both parties picked up large (6–8 percent) vote gains when they had women candidates running for Congress: "Opinion polls showed that voters overwhelmingly believed that women were in touch with their concerns."[23]

How Congress Uses Its Powers

Journalists assume, as do most Americans, that making law is the most important function of Congress. This is not an unreasonable assumption. After all, the Constitution says that Congress is empowered to "make all laws . . . necessary and proper." When Congress does not act on some problem that the media or public thinks is important, the easy conclusion is that the institution has failed again, and gridlock has returned to Capitol Hill. In fact, Congress is doing lots of things all the time, and making laws is just one of them. The basic activities of Congress are these:

- Making laws (technically, passing bills for the president to sign into law)
- Overseeing the executive
- Delivering a share of the national budget back to states and home districts through "pork barrel" projects
- Delivering services and doing favors for constituents
- Getting reelected.

Making Laws

Like most congressional activities, legislation has gone through historic changes, from the simple days of the early 1800s when scarcely more than two hundred bills were introduced in a typical session, and half of them passed, to the modern era—in which the number of bills and resolutions has topped 10,000, with only a few hundred of them being passed by both chambers. Today's Congress is neither highest nor lowest in the numbers of bills and resolutions introduced (the period from 1895–1911 saw an escalation from 12,000 to 44,000 measures introduced). However, the *percentage* of measures actually passed in recent years is near the all-time low. In recent sessions, only 3–5 percent of measures introduced have been passed, compared to 10–20 percent at the turn of the century. Figure 12.3 shows the volume of measures (bills and resolutions) introduced in the modern era, and Figure 12.4 illustrates the proportion of measures passed from the earliest congressional sessions to the recent period.

FIGURE 12.3

*Measures Introduced and Measures Enacted**
U.S. Congress, 1947–1990

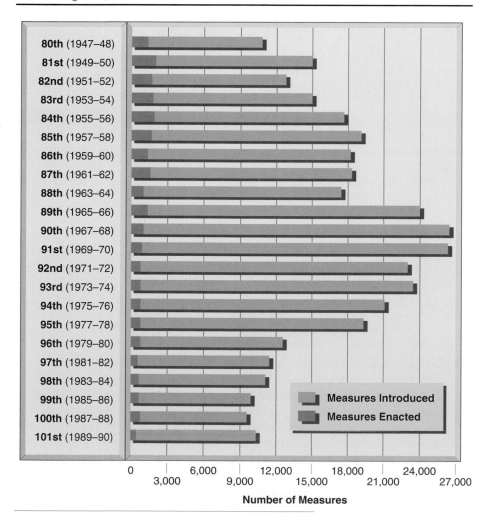

Number of Measures

*Measures include bills and joint resolutions of Congress. Bills make up more than 90 percent of these totals. Excludes simple and concurrent resolutions.

Source: Harold W. Stanley and Richard G. Niemi, *Vital Statistics on American Politics*. Washington, D.C.: C Q Press, 1992. p. 201.

FIGURE 12.4

Percentage of Measures Introduced in the U.S. Congress That Were Passed, 1789–1990

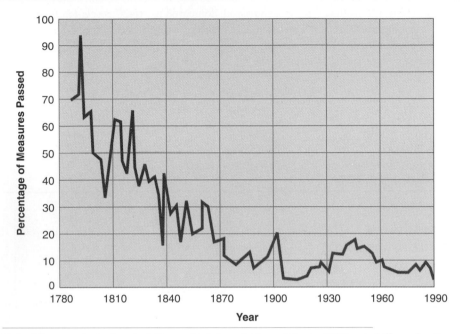

Note: Measures include acts, bills, and joint resolutions. Prior to 1824 only bills and acts are included. Figures are for each Congress.

Source: Harold W. Stanley and Richard G. Niemi, *Vital Statistics on American Politics.* Washington, D.C.: Congressional Quarterly Press, 1992, p. 217.

A rough generalization is that Congress in recent years has been working more and producing less than at almost any time in its history. Yet there is more to the story than this simplification. Here are several reasons why the number of pieces of legislation have increased while the number passed has declined:

- *Society is more complex today* than ever before, with many more demands for government action than can be met.

- *The rise of self-contained congressional careers* (related to the breakdown in party discipline) makes it easy for individual members of Congress to introduce personal or "vanity" legislation, often with little expectation of getting it passed. Lawmakers learn that they get good publicity out of sponsoring legislation that sends "positive signals" to constituents. The worst cases are the thousands of vanity bills introduced each year to honor members' home states, prominent industries, and important constituents. While there is little chance that Congress will pass a proposal for a National Bee-Keepers' Day, or a public holiday to honor John P. Contributor, there is little to stop legislators from introducing such measures.

- *The breakdown of political parties* (see Chapter 9) and of the old party machine systems has left congressional leaders unable to weed out "vanity" legislation that has little chance of passing, while making it difficult to line up support for solid legislation that interest groups or rival party leaders oppose. Students of Congress point out that party solidarity is actually up in recent years over the stunning lows recorded in the early 1970s. However, current legislative voting patterns show that half (or more) of the Democrats in the House are opposed by half (or more) of the Republicans only about half of the time. By contrast, in the early 1900s, 90 percent of the members of each party opposed a like number of their opponents over 60 percent of the time. The historic party voting trends shown in Figure 12.5 suggest that levels of current party solidarity are not strong enough to sustain a broad legislative agenda from either party.

- *The rise of interest groups* (see Chapter 8) has compounded the breakdown of parties because interests can gain direct access to powerful individual members and committee chairs. Many groups come to The Hill with legislation already written (making it easy for members of Congress to introduce) but without the political support necessary to pass it.

- *The divided government* has seen different parties in the White House and Congress for much of the era of low productivity. As noted above, the test of the Democrats in the 1992–1996 period is whether they can overcome the above factors to introduce greater political focus to the legislative process.

FIGURE 12.5

Party Votes in the House, 1887–1990

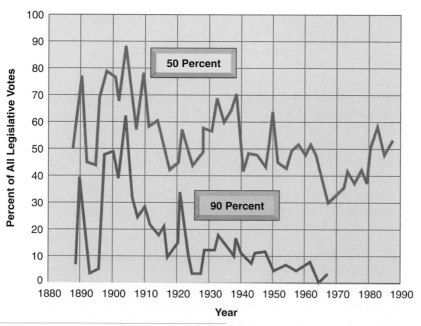

Note: Figures shown by Congress. A party vote occurs when the specified percentage (or more) of one party votes against the specified percentage (or more) of the other party. Figures for 90 percent party votes are generally unavailable after 1970. In 1987–1988 the proportion of 90 percent party votes was 7 percent.

Source: Harold W. Stanley and Richard G. Niemi, *Vital Statistics on American Politics*, 3rd ed. Washington, D.C.: CQ Press, 1992, p. 213.

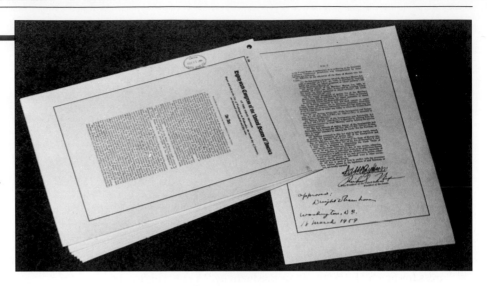

The official copy of the bill that made Hawaii into America's fiftieth state, bearing the signatures of House Speaker Sam Rayburn, Vice President Richard Nixon, and President Dwight Eisenhower. Eric Redman, a legislative staffer turned author, characterized the complex choreography of political forces required to enact new laws (whether major or minor) as "the dance of legislation."

HOW A BILL BECOMES A LAW: THE PROCEDURES. Put aside all the confusing diagrams and drawings from your high school civics book. The basic process of legislation is very simple. The same legislation must pass both chambers of Congress (with a simple majority—50 percent+—of votes) and then be signed by the president to become law. If the president vetoes a bill, it is returned to both chambers where it must pass again, this time by two-thirds majorities, to become law. For the most part, the procedures in the House and Senate are similar (with one notable difference), as a bill works its way toward the president's desk. Here are the high points.

Step 1: The bill is introduced.

To begin with, a bill must have a sponsoring member or a group of co-sponsors in each chamber to *introduce* a rough draft of the bill. In the House, proposed laws are dropped in a box near the Speaker's desk. In the Senate, they are either handed to a clerk or announced for the record from the Senate floor. The House and Senate versions are assigned numbers corresponding to the order of their introduction in a legislative session, as in S24 or H.R.537. Sometimes the proposed legislation starts out the same in both chambers, and sometimes there are differences in the House and Senate versions, but *the legislation must become the same in both chambers by the time it is passed and sent to the president*. The way in which any differences in the House and Senate versions of a bill are resolved is explained below.

Step 2: The bill is assigned to a committee.

After it is introduced into the chamber, a bill is assigned to the **standing committee** having (or claiming) the most obvious jurisdiction over the subject. It is important to understand that the work of legislation is done by committees and subcommittees that claim special knowledge and jurisdiction (authority) over different areas of legislation. Committees, and their specialized subcommittees, hold the hearings at which problems are defined, solutions proposed, and expert witnesses provide guidance about how to draft legislation. (The committee system is explained in more detail in the next chapter.)

Most committee assignments are routine, but some are not: A bill asking for higher government subsidies for corn farmers will go to the Agriculture Committee, and a bill increasing foreign aid for democratizing nations will go to Foreign Relations—but a bill proposing to let banks sell insurance may set off a fight between the Banking Committee and the Energy and Commerce Committee, as in fact happened in the House during a battle over new banking laws in the 102nd Congress (1991–1992). The Speaker of the House is responsible for assigning bills to committee, and his power over legislation can be enhanced when he has to choose which committee will get a contested bill. Under House rules, the Speaker is also permitted to send a bill to more than one committee, a practice known as multiple referral. The leader of the majority party in the Senate (called the *majority leader*) generally resolves any disputes over which committee should review and develop a piece of proposed legislation.

Each committee screens the large number of bills it gets each session and decides which ones are the most well developed, politically important, and otherwise worthy of consideration. Standing committees can exercise power over legislation in several ways: by never assigning bills to a subcommittee for deliberation (this happens in the Senate only); by holding more hearings or changing a bill after it has come back from a subcommittee; and, less often, by refusing to "report" a bill that has passed subcommittee screening back to the full chamber for debate and voting. In the House, the death of bills usually occurs in subcommittee, since House rules require committees to refer bills to subcommittees within fourteen days of receiving them. Between committee and subcommittee actions, 95 percent of all bills are killed before reaching a debate in the entire chamber.

Step 3: The bill is drafted in subcommittee.

Most of the work of legislation is done in the **subcommittees** that specialize in the area of a proposed bill. Subcommittees evaluate the merits of the proposal, call for more research, and give political interests a say in the process by holding hearings. Following the hearing and information stage, the subcommittee holds a "**markup session**" in which, as the name implies, changes are made in the proposal based on input from hearings, staff research, and members. The bill is then returned to the full committee for another, usually shorter, round of discussion, perhaps another hearing, and a *final markup*. At this stage, opponents on the full committee may kill a bill by voting not to report it, but this does not happen often and reflects poor politicking by the bill's supporters and poor relations on a committee. If the bill's supporters have done their political homework and enlisted the support of the committee chair, the committee normally *reports* the bill to the full House or Senate for debate and a vote.

Step 4: The bill is reported for House or Senate action.

At the reporting stage, there is a difference between procedure in the House and Senate: a bill takes a slight detour on its way to the House floor, passing through the **Rules Committee,** where rules are attached determining how the bill will be debated. In general, supporters of the bill lobby their colleagues on the Rules Committee for a "**closed rule,**" placing limits on debate and preventing amendments from being introduced on the floor. Opponents, by contrast, go to allies on the Rules Committee with suggestions for an "**open rule,**" permitting extended debate and amendments. In the Senate, the bill is reported directly to the floor for debate and amending.

Step 5: Floor debate and vote.

In the House, the rules assigned by the Rules Committee govern the length and kind of debate that goes on. In the Senate, debates are governed by rules that permit much more open debate. In rare cases, a Senate **floor debate** can threaten to go on without end, as long as the bill's opponents can continue talking and there are not enough supporters to vote to end the debate. *This possibility of "talking a bill to death" is called a* **filibuster** and will be discussed further in the next chapter on the internal organization of Congress. (The term *filibuster* originally referred to lone soldiers of fortune—called *filibusteros* in Spanish—who raided nations, disrupted trade, and even set up their own governments in Latin America during the 1800s.) After the debates are over in both chambers, the bills, possibly *amended*, are finally *voted* upon. Even if majorities support the bill in both chambers of Congress, the chances are that, after going through this arduous process, the final versions are no longer identical even if they started out that way.

Step 6: Conference committee (if necessary).

If there are differences in the House and Senate versions of a bill, they are worked out in a temporary committee called a **conference committee,** composed of key senators and representatives involved with the legislation. A bill is "sent to conference" for differences to be resolved, and a single version of the bill is returned to each chamber for another vote. If "changes in conference" sour the original support for the legislation, the bill may not pass and must be returned to conference for more changes.

Step 7: Presidential action.

When both chambers are satisfied enough with a common version of the bill to pass it, the legislation then goes to the president who has ten days either to *sign* or *veto* the bill. If the president does nothing, *unsigned bills* become law after ten days, *unless* it is the end of a session and Congress is adjourning before the ten days are up. In this scenario, called a *pocket veto*, a president can decide not to sign a law, but due to the adjournment, the ten-day period is never fulfilled, and the bill dies. In recent years, many congressional sessions have run until the end of the year, and few pocket vetoes have been possible. Most of the time, the president either signs a bill into law or vetoes it and sends it back as a challenge for Congress to raise the often difficult two-thirds majority required to override a veto.

As the summary in Figure 12.6 indicates, this process is really not so complicated. It may seem more confusing in the news because reports often focus in on the fragment of

The full body of Congress— along with cabinet officials, the Joint Chiefs of Staff, the diplomatic community, and other dignitaries—meets for President George Bush's 1990 State of the Union Address. The president sways Congress through fellow party members; through leadership, intimidation, and deal-making; and through veto power; during his term in office, Bush vetoed 41 bills from Congress, and his veto was overridden only 2 times.

FIGURE 12.6

How a Bill Becomes a Law (A Simplified View)

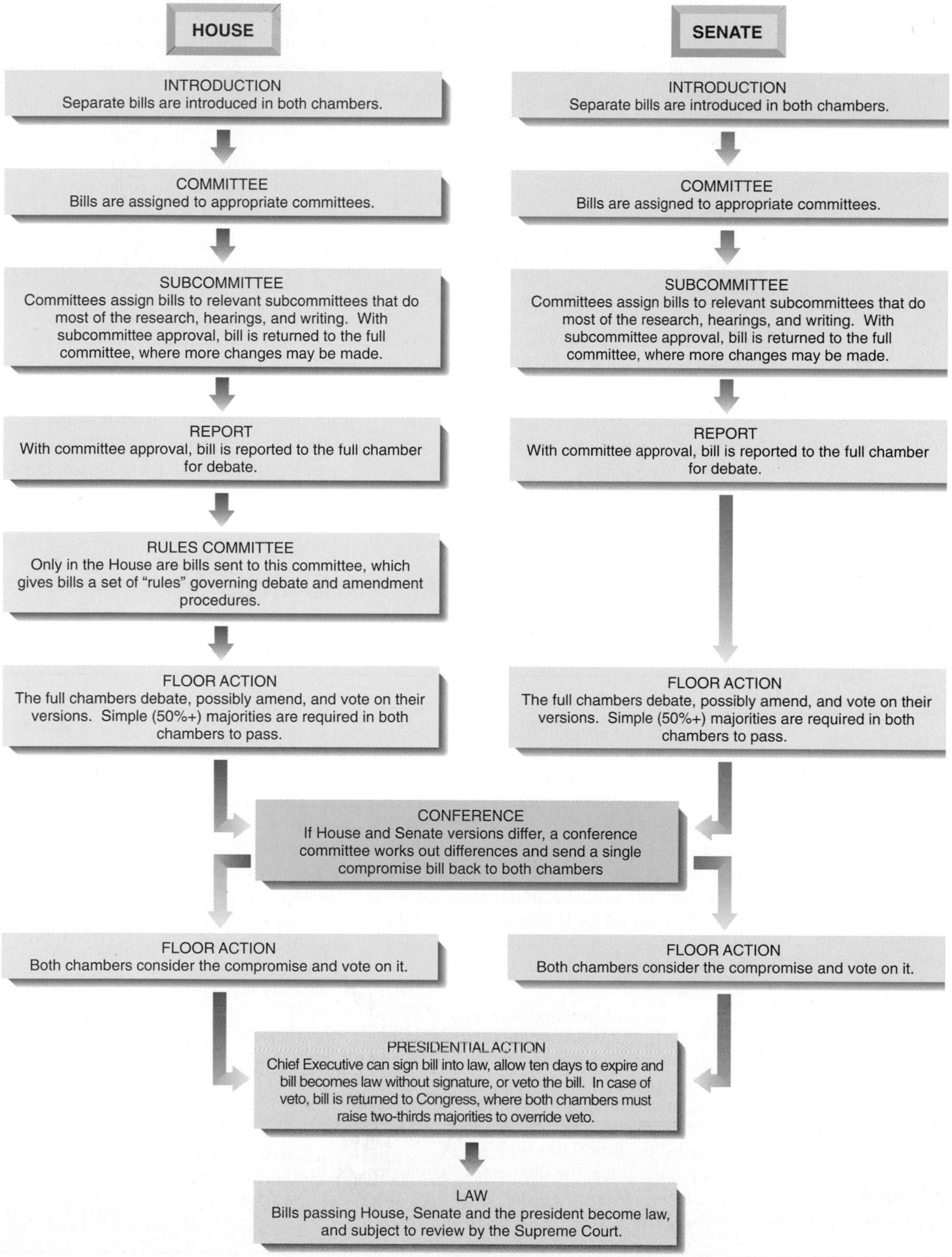

HOUSE

SENATE

INTRODUCTION
Separate bills are introduced in both chambers.

INTRODUCTION
Separate bills are introduced in both chambers.

COMMITTEE
Bills are assigned to appropriate committees.

COMMITTEE
Bills are assigned to appropriate committees.

SUBCOMMITTEE
Committees assign bills to relevant subcommittees that do most of the research, hearings, and writing. With subcommittee approval, bill is returned to the full committee, where more changes may be made.

SUBCOMMITTEE
Committees assign bills to relevant subcommittees that do most of the research, hearings, and writing. With subcommittee approval, bill is returned to the full committee, where more changes may be made.

REPORT
With committee approval, bill is reported to the full chamber for debate.

REPORT
With committee approval, bill is reported to the full chamber for debate.

RULES COMMITTEE
Only in the House are bills sent to this committee, which gives bills a set of "rules" governing debate and amendment procedures.

FLOOR ACTION
The full chambers debate, possibly amend, and vote on their versions. Simple (50%+) majorities are required in both chambers to pass.

FLOOR ACTION
The full chambers debate, possibly amend, and vote on their versions. Simple (50%+) majorities are required in both chambers to pass.

CONFERENCE
If House and Senate versions differ, a conference committee works out differences and send a single compromise bill back to both chambers

FLOOR ACTION
Both chambers consider the compromise and vote on it.

FLOOR ACTION
Both chambers consider the compromise and vote on it.

PRESIDENTIAL ACTION
Chief Executive can sign bill into law, allow ten days to expire and bill becomes law without signature, or veto the bill. In case of veto, bill is returned to Congress, where both chambers must raise two-thirds majorities to override veto.

LAW
Bills passing House, Senate and the president become law, and subject to review by the Supreme Court.

the process where trouble is occurring. Today the president vetoes a bill. Last week, the TV lights were turned up in a hearing chamber. Tomorrow, the headlines tell of a conference committee working late into the night, unable to agree on a budget bill. News reports almost never cover the process from beginning to end; only fragments are highlighted—usually a different fragment each time. But surrounding each news slice, the rest of this process is in motion. As we also learn from the news, politics goes on at every turn. Indeed, the politics behind the procedures can greatly complicate the lawmaking process and often bring parts of it into the headlines.

HOW A BILL BECOMES A LAW: THE POLITICS.   If ten thousand bills are reduced each session to a few hundred laws, there must be some powerful force at work behind the scenes. There is: politics. Many good books on the legislative process have followed a single bill through Congress with the pace and tone of a thriller.[24] It is typical for bills to be introduced in session after session until they win enough support to pass. Many never do. The ones that finally make it into law often display a common set of political characteristics, including:

- **Leadership.** Sponsors of legislation enlist the support of leaders who know how to work the institution to collect votes. In the 1950s, Senator Lyndon Johnson was famous for giving his colleagues "the treatment," a combination of charm, persuasion, intimidation, and trading votes for favors. Modern legislative powerhouses are fewer in number, but there are still some on the scene with enough clout to make or break a piece of legislation. See, for example, the profile of John Dingell in "Inside the System" Box 12.4.

INSIDE THE SYSTEM

Some Power Brokers Still Remain: John (The Truck) Dingell

12.4

Power inside Congress involves learning to use the committee system and other resources of the institution to become a key player in the legislative process. One of the legislative leaders on Capitol Hill is Representative John Dingell (D–Michigan), who has honed his closed-door negotiating skills and developed the powers of his committee to a degree unusual in this day of independent subcommittee and weak committee chairs. His secrets?

Staff: Hires aggressive, competent staff people to push legislation and get the jump on other committees.

Mastery of rules and proce-dures: Able to redefine problems to fit his committee's jurisdiction, use oversight procedures to control bureaucrats, and other tactics.

Committee politics: Adept at delivering cooperation from his subcommittee chairs to political allies. Develops support by giving junior members of committee responsibility. Forms coalitions across party lines.

Moving and shaking: Rewards friends, punishes enemies. Reputation for being aggressive, pushing well-defined agenda, timing his moves, staying behind the scenes, and avoiding floor fights where his enemies can settle old scores.

Close relations with the party leadership: Voted with party leadership recommendations 99 percent of time in one congressional term and was rewarded with appointment to the Democratic Steering and Policy Committee, enabling him to hand out favors and make key appointments to his own committee.

Powerful backers and a safe district: Auto industry and union backing, along with help from the state legislature, which moved his district out of Detroit to the suburbs where he has a safe margin of support to protect his nearly forty years' seniority.

SOURCE: Rochelle L. Stanfield, "Plotting Every Move," *National Journal*, March 26, 1988, pp. 792–797.

Commanders within Congress

Just as Congress is split into two chambers, so primary authority within it is divided among several institutional and party leaders. As minority leader in the Senate, combative Republican Bob Dole *(above)* serves as the *de facto* head of the loyal opposition in Washington. Dole's counterpart in the House, Rep. Bob Michel, *(right),* has been criticized by some junior GOP members for a supposedly defeatist view. Heading up the Democrats in Congress are *(below)* Senate majority leader George Mitchell, House majority leader Dick Gephardt, and Speaker of the House Tom Foley. These men may arouse little enthusiasm or allegiance among most voters (*New York Times* columnist Walter Goodman called Foley "an ineffably colorless and creaky Washington artifact"), but their power among their colleagues is considerable.

The Players

One aspect of the constitutional checks-and-balances system can be seen in Congress's task of executive oversight—the monitoring of executive-branch operations. Here a Senate committee holds hearings on the so-called "Iran-contra" affair that blemished the Reagan White House. Ironically, these televised proceedings, combined with the granting of immunity to some witnesses, appeared to boomerang on the Senate. A special prosecutor found his work muddied by Senate actions, and spent several years and some $40 million on the task with few results. Marine colonel Oliver North even became a hero in certain quarters for his unfriendly testimony; within a few years he was contemplating his own career in politics.

Congress—is not the typical mode of executive oversight, the Constitution specifically empowers Congress to investigate and judge the president and other federal officials on charges of treason or other "high crimes and misdemeanors" committed against the office and its duties.) Relations between Congress and the president in the 1980s will be remembered, among other things, because a few key Reagan administration officials ignored congressional restrictions on their efforts to overthrow the pro-Communist *Sandinista* government of Nicaragua. Congress held the "Iran-*contra*" hearings in 1987 to explore covert arms sales to Iran and the channeling of the resulting profits to support the Nicaraguan resistance, known as the *contras*.

Grand spectacles like Army–McCarthy, Watergate, and the Iran-*contra* hearings are rare. However, every year brings routine oversight operations such as the annual budget hearings, in which legions of bureaucrats troop to the Hill to tell the committees appropriating their funds what a great job they have been doing. Although the bureaucrats often have the upper hand in these hearings, sharp subcommittee heads frequently gather independent information about failed programs, mismanagement, and corruption, providing fireworks for the TV cameras, and with any luck, a change in wayward bureaucratic habits.

MONITORING BUREAUCRATIC RULE-MAKING.   Perhaps the most challenging problem of oversight is simply figuring out what the executive was supposed to be doing in a particular area in the first place. As explained in Chapter 8, Congress leaves many of the fine points of **rule-making** to executive agencies. Administrative *rules* translate general laws into specific government practices. Because of the *iron triangles* (also described in Chapter 8), these rules often end up being worked out between executive agencies and the interest groups or organizations being regulated.

Critics call for Congress to gain more control of this important rule-making process where law and government action meet, but members of Congress say they lack the time and the expertise to write all or even most of the rules that guide bureaucrats in implementing the law. A clever substitute was the use of what became known as the **legislative veto,** which authorized the executive branch to act but reserved to Congress the right to cancel the authorization if it didn't like the results. A Supreme Court ruling in 1983 prohibited this means of executive oversight on grounds that it really was a method of changing or repealing laws without the president's signature. However, Congress has continued to use the legislative veto, often with the silent approval of presidents willing to gamble that writing rules would increase executive control of programs.

Despite the combination of congressional information-gathering, hearings, and legislative vetoes, the media often tell tales of executive branch failings: federal housing money for the poor that went to friends of the bureaucrats in charge; a savings-and-loan industry that collapsed under the noses of federal banking regulators and congressional committees; and oil spills that polluted vast stretches of wilderness despite reassurances by Congress and executive agencies that careful monitoring was taking place. To many Americans, the blame for these and other failings goes largely to Congress. The vast bureaucracy remains complex and unfathomable, but Congress created it, and is seen to have let it get out of control. Perhaps there is more that Congress could do with oversight, but most members claim they have "better" things to do. Many spend their spare time back home, shrugging their shoulders along with the voters and disowning the mess in Washington. The same members may soothe angry constituents by announcing the delivery of a new dam, highway, or other local program that will require an executive agency to administer and somebody in Congress to watch. Which brings us to . . .

The Politics of Pork

Among the time-honored traditions of Congress is throwing a little fat into the budget for those legendary "pork barrel" projects back home. As defined earlier in the chapter, **pork barrel politics** refers to the use of personal power and influence to "feed" special projects back to the home district or state. The stereotype goes something like this: Senator Foghorn—who chairs the Wheat, Corn, and Soybean Subcommittee of the Senate Agriculture Committee—amends a farm bill so as to fund a new center for research on corn crop diseases at Our State University. Meanwhile, Senator Bill Barnacle, the other esteemed Senator from Our State (and chairman of the Agriculture Appropriations Subcommittee of the Senate Appropriations Committee), finds enough support on his committee to pledge $10 million in taxpayer money for the project. Both senators attend the ribbon-cutting ceremony five years later when the new Foghorn-Barnacle Corn Research Laboratory is finally opened. Governor Airbag, along with Dr. Kornsmutt, the university's Nobel Prize-winning expert on plant diseases, shows up to praise the work of the two distinguished senators from Our State and to remind voters that clout like this will be lost if they pass a term-limit law in the upcoming election. Charges that the nation already has three similar pork barrel research centers in other states were not reported in the local press, where editorial pages spoke of the great economic benefits and prestige the new facility would bring to the people of Our State.

Political pork is nice to give and receive, for the local folks and politicians. And what should representatives do, if not benefit their states? And how can they better repay favors to colleagues who have helped them in the past? Or as Vic Fazio, chair of the Legislative Appropriations Subcommittee in the House, put it: "What else could anyone do if they wanted to say thank you to Vic Fazio? Help me, help my district. I don't have any way of quantifying it, but most of the reasonable things I've asked for, eventually I've gotten."[25] What do people have to thank Vic Fazio for? Representative Fazio's subcommittee hands out money for running the House itself, including sensitive matters such as pay raise legislation. Known alternately as "the mayor of Capitol Hill," "the shop steward of the House," and "Prince of Perks," Fazio can make friends with his use of the House budget. In appreciation, colleagues on other appropriations committees can return favors to Mr. Fazio's district.

The traditional complaint, of course, is that the sum of all pork does not add to the national welfare. In fact, the popular definition of "pork" is an *inefficient* use of national

resources and taxpayer money to pay for local boondoggles. The leading academic definition goes like this: "The pork barrel consists of inefficient projects—those for which benefits do not exceed costs."[26] The main problem with both the popular and the academic definitions of pork is they do not always explain what is and what is not the most efficient way to spend public money. Contrary to the stereotype that Congress seldom weighs the public value of its pork, research by political scientist John Hird suggests that pork is carved up with some consideration of its utility beyond the sheer value to the politicians and the home districts involved.[27]

The Army Corps of Engineers was the subject of Hird's study. When not building military bases or war zones, the Corps is often commandeered by Congress to build domestic projects such as dams, bridges, roads, and other large-scale "public works." As a result, the Corps is a prime target of pork barrel requests from Congress. Hird concluded that, while a great deal could be explained about Corps projects simply by looking at who sits on the Armed Services and Military Appropriations committees that oversee and fund Army operations, considerable committee attention is also paid to issues of efficiency and cost-benefit calculations. However, Hird stopped short of saying that pork makes as much sense as legislation based on the broader input of many members of Congress with less personal interest at stake.[28]

Unless evidence of pork's positive benefits becomes stronger, the image of congressional waste and abuse of personal power will prevail. In addition, pork barrel politics reinforces the tendency of constituents to hate Congress but love their own representatives. This love-hate relationship between the public and Congress is further reinforced by another major use of congressional power, particularly in the House of Representatives: delivering individualized **services to constituents** back home.

Delivering Services (from Our House to Yours)

According to studies by a number of political scientists, the motto of the modern Congress ought to be "We Deliver." Political scientist Morris Fiorina, one of the leading students of Congress, lists the three main activities of the institution as "lawmaking, pork barreling, and casework."[29] Congress, and particularly the House of Representatives where members face election every two years, has learned the advantages of helping individual constituents with problems: lost Social Security checks, medical benefits that have been screwed up by an incompetent or seemingly heartless bureaucracy, the child of a prominent supporter seeking entry to one of the military academies, or a group back home angry about some government policy and wanting a sympathetic ear. These and other forms of congressional **casework** pay dividends—so much so that members have assigned increasing numbers of their staff to home district offices over the years in order to devote more time and resources to handling personal requests from voters. People remember when their representative helps them, and they tell their friends. Over the years, service delivery and casework can build up a solid base of voter loyalty that can matter more at election time than whether the representative sponsored much legislation or voted the right way on all the key bills. Thus, casework has become a major part of what Congress, particularly the House, does with its powers.

The trouble with casework is that it may be too rewarding for lawmakers, who create *more* federal programs that deliver *more* benefits to individuals, which, in turn, lead to *more* casework. As Firoina put it:

> The nature of the Washington system is now quite clear. Congressmen (typically the majority Democrats) earn electoral credits by establishing various federal programs (the minority Republicans typically earn credits by fighting the good fight). The legislation is drafted in general terms, so some agency. . . must translate a vague policy mandate into a functioning program, a process that necessitates . . . numerous rules and regulations and, incidentally, the trampling of numerous toes. At the next stage, aggrieved and/or hopeful constituents petition their congressman to intervene in the complex (or at least obscure) decision process of the bureaucracy. The cycle closes when the congressman lends a sympathetic ear, piously denounces the evils of bureaucracy, intervenes in the latter's decisions, and rides a grateful electorate to ever more impressive electoral showings. Congressmen take credit coming and going. . . .
>
> The popular frustration with [the bureaucracy] is partly justified, but to a considerable degree it is misplaced resentment. *Congress is the lynchpin of the Washington establishment.* The bureaucracy serves as a convenient lightning rod for public frustration and a convenient whipping boy for congressmen. But so long as the bureaucracy accommodates congressmen, the latter will oblige with ever larger budgets and grants of authority. Congress does not just react to big government—it creates it. All of Washington prospers. More and more bureaucrats promulgate more and more regulations and dispense more and more money. Fewer and fewer congressmen suffer electoral defeat. Elements of the electorate benefit from government programs. . . . But the general, long term welfare of the United States is no more than an incidental byproduct of the system.[30]

What, then is the principal product of this system? According to some observers, it is *getting reelected*. Doing things that help lawmakers stay in office may be among the most common uses for the powers of Congress. Isn't this natural? That depends on how you look at it.

Getting Reelected, of Course

There are two ways of thinking about the uses of institutional powers such as pork barreling and casework to get reelected:

- Of course representatives must be concerned with getting elected; the rest of the job would not exist without efforts on this front.

- If the main purpose of lawmakers has become getting reelected, the rest of the job has become secondary.

The second perspective has been developed into an entire theory of congressional behavior by political scientist David Mayhew:

> I shall conjure up a vision of the United States congressmen as single-minded seekers of reelection, see what kinds of activity that goal implies, and then speculate about how congressmen so motivated are likely to go about building and sustaining legislative institutions and making policy. . . .
>
> Whether they are safe or marginal, cautious or audacious, congressmen must constantly engage in activities related to reelection.[31]

According to Mayhew, these activities are of three types: *advertising*, or using the advantages of incumbency to become well known by voters; *credit claiming*, or taking credit for pork barrel projects, casework, and passing or defeating laws that might please constituents; and *position taking*, or using the media, newsletters, and local supporters to get the word to voters that the member of Congress stands for the same things they do. These election-related activities provide a neat way of explaining why and how lawmakers do what they do, from passing the pork to finding lost Social Security checks to voting on laws and being conveniently out of Washington when a difficult bill comes to the floor.

Critics argue that reducing lawmakers to vote-getting animals is too simple and plays into popular stereotypes rather than explores the other motives that make Congress tick. Yet the power of this simple theory is that it not only summarizes much of what representatives do, but members of Congress admit the overwhelming pressures of elections even as they condemn the effects of those pressures on the institution and its output. As one member of the House of Representatives, Edward Markey of Massachusetts (who is one of the leading opponents of PACs), put it:

> The first time a guy runs for Congress, he puts his own home on the line, his friends and family come up with whatever they can, and it's always the biggest political miracle in the district's history. Then he discovers he has to raise another $200,000 for the next time. He can do it night after night with ten-dollar, twenty-dollar, fifty-dollar fundraisers. Or he can go meet ten PAC guys, pick up five grand each, and he's done for half a year.[32]

This **electoral connection,** with its special appeals to local voters and bargains struck with special interests, may simply be the final element that bends congressional power to the pursuit of narrow issues, reducing the chances that the considerable powers of the institution will be directed toward larger goals. As one senator confided to a journalist, his reelection costs were so high that he spent 80 percent of his time travelling around the country to raise money, being distracted from serious issues, and having to walk a fine line with all the pressure groups that pay his bills. He summed it up with the plea "What do I need this for?"[33]

Like it or not, the senator may "need" to do these frustrating things as long as maintaining the careers of individual lawmakers remains a principle focus of Congress, competing in importance with the concerns of parties and governing programs. We will return in the next chapter to the impact of these individual political calculations on the internal political organization of Congress that affects how the institution works. For now, let's return to our opening question of how the various limits on congressional power and representation affect what the institution does.

Laws, Legislatures, and Representation Revisited ___

To overcome the temptation of reducing the workings of Congress to any single factor such as parties, interests, or PACs, it was suggested at the opening of this chapter how to fit Congress into the thematic framework of this book: *culture, institutions,* and *power.* It is clear, for example, that the institutional powers of Congress were limited from the outset due to broad *cultural concerns* about big government and the fear of centralized power. The resulting *institutional design* was complex: two chambers, each with different election rules and requirements for officeholders, and both sharing legislative powers with the executive. Such institutional complexity requires the right configuration of *power* to make it work. Because of so many institutional pressure points, Congress responds to a complex combination of *majority power* through voter pressures and party promises, *pluralist power* through interest groups lobbying key legislative committees, and *elite* influence through financial contributions to campaigns and contacts between individual members of Congress and powerful heads of industry and local communities back home.

It is easy to see how these different power points can drive Congress in different directions, fragmenting the law against different power centers (powerful individuals and committees) inside the institution. It is also easy to see from this picture of power how the convergence of special political conditions is needed to create a coherent legislative agenda: the leadership of presidents and powerful members of Congress, the ability of parties to discipline members, strong public opinion formations combined with voting pressure, and the willingness of interest groups and individual citizens alike to sacrifice narrow legislation and congressional services for a broader public interest agenda.

In light of these system factors, it is clear that the cure for gridlock is more than just having the same party dominating both ends of Pennsylvania Avenue, although *this may be a necessary first step* to begin breaking legislative gridlock. Without the convergence of a larger set of political pressures, parties alone cannot forge a government. As we learned from Chapter 9, the two major American parties often lack the ideological vision and internal unity to agree on a governing program even when they control the government. The deeper roots of gridlock are suggested by Bill Clinton's trials in trying to gain his own party's support to pass a deficit-reduction package during his first year in office.

In the end the people themselves may be an important obstacle to the kind of sweeping legislative programs that many journalists and citizens seem to expect from government: programs aimed at retooling the economy, retraining the work force, or creating a more liveable society for all. Recall from Chapter 6 how continuing cultural resistance to a strong central government makes citizens and voters reluctant to authorize government to go too far, too fast in any particular direction. These cultural limits may be compounded by the equally strong cultural principle of self-interest that enables people to expect their representatives to bring home the pork and deliver casework services even when they know these things may defeat the larger national interest.

As a provocative conclusion to this chapter, consider the possibility that the moral of the American political story and the secret to understanding "gridlock" are much the same. The entire political system operates broadly to limit centralized government action, particularly when that action might interfere with the basic values at the core of the political culture: protection of free enterprise and private property, promotion of individual freedom and initiative, and limits on government interference with these guiding values. Only serious efforts by citizens at all levels of power should make this system move in a different direction.

A CITIZEN'S QUESTION

Evaluating Congress

*W*hat kind of performance should I expect from Congress? One possibility for citizens to contemplate when judging Congress is that it may be too simple to single out Congress for blame when so many outside factors affect what Congress does. To begin with, citizens themselves may expect their representatives to do special favors for them and their districts. This means that the very things that many people dislike most about the institution may be what they expect (or at least forgive) in their own representatives. This suggests that thinking about Congress begins at home: If, as the polls suggest, Americans are concerned about truly nationwide problems of education, economic growth, competitiveness, job security, and health care, then people should try to send their representatives signals that these are the issues that should occupy their time—not delivering pork barrel projects and personal constituent services for the folks back home. Is it reasonable to expect individuals to look beyond their immediate self-interest? Perhaps not, but this issue should be considered in the process of evaluating Congress in particular and the government in general.

*A*t the same time, citizens may want to hold their representatives accountable if they pass laws that conflict with clear and stable majorities of the public. Just how can individuals find out what Congress is doing in various areas? There are few nations in which it is easier to follow the action in the national legislature. More than 60 percent of American households have cable television, and most of them receive the channel called C-Span, a public service information link between Congress and the people. C-Span covers the world of committee and subcommittee hearings, showing who is up to what inside the Capitol. In addition, the broader Washington power scene is covered to provide a sense of how Congress fits into the surrounding government. Spending a bit of time every week watching C-Span provides a sense of how the Washington game works.

*W*ith a little information about the issues before Congress, it is easy to begin pressing for the kind of laws you want passed. It turns out that public opinion and voter threats are among the political forces to which members of Congress respond. Are you too busy to write a letter to your representative or to the key committee members and legislative leaders who are considering legislation on an issue you care about? Why not just call the U.S. Capitol switchboard and ask to be connected with the message lines for the members you want to reach? The number of the U.S. Capitol is

202/224-3121.

Key Terms

constitutional limits on legislative
   power
shared powers
bicameral: two chambers with
   (nearly) equal powers
federalism and lawmaking

bicameral vs. unicameral
   legislatures

parliamentary system

representation (types of)
   trustee
   delegate
   demographic

home style

the legislative process
   committees and subcommittees
   standing committees
   conference committees
   subcommittee role

House Rules Committee
open rules/closed rules
hearings
markup session
floor debates/floor votes
filibuster

the politics of legislation
logrolling
issue networks
leadership
interest groups

executive oversight role of
    Congress
    Government Accounting Office
    informational hearing
    rule-making
    legislative veto

pork barrel legislation

casework and constituent services

the electoral connection

Suggested Readings

Cain, Bruce, John Ferejohn, and Morris Fiorina. *The Personal Vote*. Cambridge: Harvard University Press, 1987.

Fenno, Richard F., Jr. *Home Style*. Boston: Little, Brown, 1978.

Fiorina, Morris. *Congress: Keystone of the Washington Establishment*. New Haven: Yale University Press, 1977.

Mayhew, David R. *Congress: The Electoral Connection*. New Haven: Yale University Press, 1974.

Oleszek, Walter J. *Congressional Procedures and the Policy Process*, 3rd. ed. Washington, D.C.: Congressional Quarterly Press, 1989.

Ripley, Randall. *Congress: Process and Policy*. New York: Norton, 1988.

• • •

The House has as many leaders as there are subjects of legislation. . . . It is this multiplicity of leaders, this many-headed leadership, which makes the organization of the House too complex to afford . . . any easy clue to its methods of rule. [The Senate] has those same radical defects of organization which weaken the House.
—*WOODROW WILSON*

• • •

The U.S. Congress has a persistent image problem. The other branches of government have nothing quite comparable to the comic-strip figure of Senator Snort, the overblown and incompetent windbag. Pundits and humorists find Congress an inexhaustible source of raw material. Seemingly, the public shares this disdain. . . .
The view of Congress held by serious commentators—seasoned journalists and scholars—is often scarcely more flattering than the public image of Congress. The currently fashionable textbook portrait . . . is a collection of politicians obsessed by reelection fears and surrounded with staff and facilities for constituency errand running (not a wholly erroneous picture, to be sure, but a caricature nonetheless).
—*ROGER H. DAVIDSON*

• • •

13

Congress: Power and Organization

- **NO NEWS IS GOOD NEWS: WHY CONGRESS HAS AN IMAGE PROBLEM**
- **SOME GOOD REASONS WHY CONGRESS LOOKS BAD**
- **THE POWER STRUCTURE OF CONGRESS**
- **THE INDIVIDUAL VERSUS THE ORGANIZATION**
  The Career Management System
  Congress in the Media Age
- **TWO CULTURES: NORMS AND RULES IN THE HOUSE AND SENATE**
  The Senate Club
  The House Fraternity
  Fighting Styles: The Rules for Debates
  The Breakdown in Tradition
- **POWER IN COMMITTEES**
  A Map of the Committee World
  Power to the Subcommittees
  Pros and Cons of the Committee System
- **PARTY POLITICS AND CONGRESSIONAL LEADERSHIP**
  The Problem of Party Loyalty
  How the Parties Govern Congress
- **REFORMING CONGRESS**
  Reforming the Party Machine
  Reforming the Staff
  Reforming the Committee System
  Reforming Campaign Finance
  The Results of a Hundred Years of Reform
  Term Limits: Reform from the Outside
- **THE POWER STRUCTURE OF CONGRESS REVISITED**
- **A CITIZEN'S QUESTION: Term Limits and Other Reforms**
- **KEY TERMS**
- **SUGGESTED READINGS**

No News Is Good News: Why Congress Has an Image Problem

The "gridlock" stories and the hopeful "end of grid-lock" stories described in the previous chapter appear in the news whenever Congress is attending to its business of making law. At other times, media messengers bring word of Congress's scandals, ethical breakdowns, interest-group friends, midnight pay raises, overflowing campaign chests, Caribbean junkets, and pork barrel projects. And all of it presided over by 535 preening egoists, well-schooled in the art of passing blame and smiling sincerely while looking into the TV camera. Or so a widely shared public impression has it.

During a particularly unfortunate period that ushered in the anti-Congress mood of the 1990s, the headlines told of disguised salary increases, taxpayer subsidies for bargain haircuts at Capitol barbershops, and a wild check-bouncing spree at the lawmakers' private bank. These stories came on the heels of several years of ethics scandals involving no-interest loans, free condominiums, bogus book sales, expensive "breakfast clubs" where lobbyists paid heavily for the company of powerful lawmakers, and an assortment of sexual improprieties. Typical of this run of bad news was a report from Ralph Nader's watchdog group Public Citizen titled "They Love to Fly, and It Shows." With a title like that, the report easily made the nightly news, publicizing the details of nearly 4,000 trips taken by members of the House of Representatives during the 101st Congress (1989–1991)—trips paid for by lobbyists, corporations, trade associations, and other special interests. A spokesperson for the Public Citizen group delivered a newsworthy sound bite that played to prevailing public suspicions about Congress: "Business wouldn't invest this kind of money and time . . . if they didn't think they were getting something out of it. All of this allows wealthy special interests privileged access to Congress."[1]

Objecting to the charge that they took "lobbyist-funded vacations," sensitive legislators reacted angrily, fueling the personal drama of the news coverage. Speaker of the House Tom Foley called the

Howell Heflin (D–Alabama, left) and Malcolm Wallop (R–Wyoming, right) of the Senate Ethics Committee talk to the media following a May 1981 closed-door session on fellow senator Harrison Williams (D–New Jersey), who had been convicted in court the previous week on bribery and conspiracy charges. Public anger over congressional sleaze is heightened by the seeming reluctance of even honorable legislators to discipline their colleagues over unethical acts.

trips "within the law and appropriate practice," and cited the unfriendly report as one of the reasons why the Nader group had "lost influence with Congress." Representative Pat Schroeder, chairwoman of the Select Committee on Children, Youth, and Families, said the report made her "very angry" and that she had made most of her 98 trips to talk about problems related to her committee's mandate. The press secretary for House Ways and Means chairman Dan Rostenkowski dismissed the report as "stupid," and went on to call Rostentowski's frequent travels "an exercise in good government."[2]

Such reactions did not elicit sympathy from an angry and alienated public. The decade opened with a New York Times/CBS News poll showing that 40 percent of the public believed a majority of lawmakers were financially corrupt. One Gallup poll recorded an approval rating of Congress below 20 percent.[3] Congressional approval hit bottom at 17 percent in 1992 after the check-bouncing scandal, as reported in a story headlined PUBLIC BELIEVES WORST ON BANK SCANDAL.[4] The trouble with Congress became such a hot media topic that *Business Week* turned temporarily from financial news to put Congress on its cover with the headline CONGRESS: IT DOESN'T WORK, LET'S FIX IT.[5] Legislators themselves are often the first to chide the institution. Indeed, with so much public anger at The Hill, incumbents have learned that a good election strategy is to run against Congress.

One headline on the future of Congress proclaimed CONGRESS AT THE CROSSROADS. The article opened with a joke said to be circulating on The Hill: "There was this congressman who asked a group of visiting Cub Scouts if they could explain the difference between the United States Congress and the Cub Scouts. A few seconds of uneasy silence ensued before one piped up, 'We have adult supervision.'"[6]

Such public disapproval took its toll. So many members became fed up that the 1992 election was preceded by one of the largest voluntary exits from the ranks of Congress in modern times. Headlines like this one told the tale: CITING RISE IN FRUSTRATION, DOZENS OF LAWMAKERS QUIT.[7] Many who fled the Congress of 1992 were the best and the brightest of the younger generation, fed up with what was termed the "Congress from Hell" by House Speaker Thomas Foley.[8] The news told of the frustrations of young idealists such as Senator Kent Conrad, who had promised the voters of North Dakota that he would either get the budget mess in Washington under control or get out. Playing on the image of *Mr. Smith Goes to Washington,* the classic 1939 Frank Capra film about an idealistic young leader who found himself in over his head in Washington, a prominent story on Mr. Conrad ran the headline MR. SMITH LEAVES WASHINGTON.[9] One of the Senate's rising stars, Tim Wirth of Colorado, explained why he could no longer live with the chaos in Congress in an article called "Diary of a Dropout." Wirth said: "I am leaving the Senate now because I have become frustrated with the posturing and paralysis of Congress. I even fear that the political process has made me a person I don't like."[10]

It is no wonder that the popular conclusion is that Congress is broken and someone ought to fix it. But fixing it requires understanding how Congress actually works on the inside. Voters in many states have adopted the increasingly popular remedy of passing term limits, designed to force lawmakers out of office after they have served a maximum specified number of years. However, it is not clear that term limits are the best cure if some of the best lawmakers are already leaving voluntarily. After an inside look at how Congress works and why it sometimes doesn't, we will return to the issue of how to reform Congress.

Some Good Reasons Why Congress Looks Bad

Consider why it may be easier for the media to deliver (and for citizens to believe) bad news about Congress than good. Political scientists Roger Davidson and Walter Oleszek have offered several reasons why Congress has been a "traditional whipping boy of the press and the public." Here are some factors they cite for the "poor public image of Congress":[11]

- *Uneven press coverage.* Much of what Congress does is not covered at all. Even when journalists are on the scene, they often focus on personal squabbles, foibles, and mistakes. In other words, the news about Congress may be even more dramatized, personalized, and fragmented than news about other branches of government, and members of Congress are seldom able to manage the news in ways that make both themselves and the institution look good at the same time. Presidents, by contrast, have been more successful at manipulating the media to their advantage while laying the blame for domestic failures on Congress. (Recall these aspects of the news from Chapter 11.)

- *Uneven public expectations* about the proper role of Congress. Should it be a rubber stamp for the president, or a critic? Should it deliberate and explore issues or act decisively with one voice? Should it represent national or local interests? Should representatives act as delegates or trustees?

- *Internal political disorganization* in Congress. The political parties are not disciplined or united enough to provide leadership or clear ideas about solving national problems. The result is fragmentation and infighting. Moreover, individual members of Congress are among the loudest critics of their own institution. With so many voices addressing different audiences and issues, Congress lacks the clarity and leadership of a president who can command great media attention and present a unified vision.

- *The complexity of the legislative process* makes routine activities of Congress hard for the press to report and difficult for people to understand. The hearing process often appears (and sometimes is) more political than informational. Obscure features such as the Senate filibuster and the legendary politics of the House Rules Committee further damage the public image of the legislative process.

Many of these problems are of Congress's own making, reflecting the will to power of individual members and the internal power structure of Congress itself. Public demands for reform have grown in recent years as confidence in the institution has eroded. Figure 13.1 presents an historical overview of opinion about Congress.

The Power Structure of Congress

The previous chapter examined the ways in which constitutional constraints on lawmaking (along with the cultural, political, and institutional factors that move the process from the outside) make coherent legislative efforts difficult. This chapter explains why the internal power structure imposes additional *institutional* limits on what Congress can do. This power structure consists of:

- **The individual political calculations of members** of Congress, which create many centers of personal power that can work against political unity

- **Political norms and rules in each chamber** that create the internal cultures of Congress, providing political guidance to members but also making change difficult

- **The network of committees and subcommittees,** which makes the legislative process go but also creates many pockets of power that may make it go in different directions

- **The party organizations** that assign individuals to committees and try to promote discipline in the ranks, creating yet another power base within Congress.

FIGURE **13.1**   *The Public's Opinion of Congress, 1937–1992*

A Joint Committee on the Organization of Congress has worked on recommendations designed to rebuild public confidence in the institution. The committee was modeled after the reorganization efforts in 1946 and 1970 and ordered to report by December 1993. The data below show how confidence in Congress has eroded.

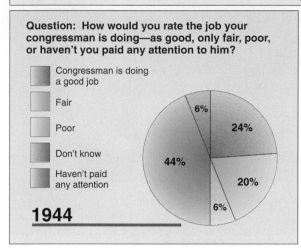

Question: How would you rate the job your congressman is doing—as good, only fair, poor, or haven't you paid any attention to him?

- Congressman is doing a good job
- Fair
- Poor
- Don't know
- Haven't paid any attention

1944

6%
24%
44%
20%
6%

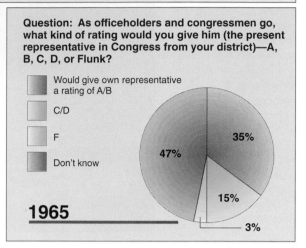

Question: As officeholders and congressmen go, what kind of rating would you give him (the present representative in Congress from your district)—A, B, C, D, or Flunk?

- Would give own representative a rating of A/B
- C/D
- F
- Don't know

1965

35%
47%
15%
3%

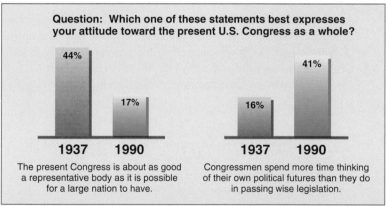

Question: Which one of these statements best expresses your attitude toward the present U.S. Congress as a whole?

44%   17%
1937   **1990**
The present Congress is about as good a representative body as it is possible for a large nation to have.

16%   41%
1937   **1990**
Congressmen spend more time thinking of their own political futures than they do in passing wise legislation.

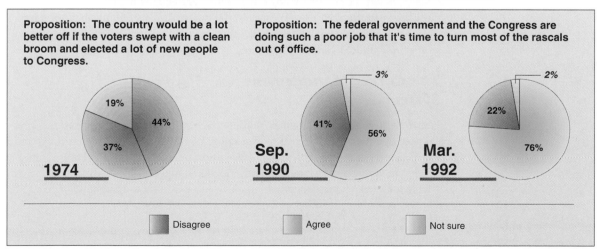

Proposition: The country would be a lot better off if the voters swept with a clean broom and elected a lot of new people to Congress.

19%
37%
44%
1974

Proposition: The federal government and the Congress are doing such a poor job that it's time to turn most of the rascals out of office.

3%
41%
56%
Sep. 1990

2%
22%
76%
Mar. 1992

■ Disagree   ■ Agree   ■ Not sure

Source: *The American Enterprise: Public Opinion and Demographic Report,* November/December 1992, p. 82.

Democratic members of the House confer in July 1993 over a compromise budget bill. The power structure of Congress is increasingly complicated by its fragmentation into specialized subcommittees, a breakdown in party discipline, and personal career concerns. Left to right: Butler Derrick (of South Carolina), Speaker Thomas Foley (Washington), David Bonior (Michigan), and Vic Fazio (California). Later that year Bonior would challenge his own party's leader, Bill Clinton, over a major free-trade agreement.

After explaining how these internal power centers work, we will consider how attempts at congressional reform have worked in the past, and how they might work in the future. How did Congress become so internally complex, with so many spheres of power working against legislative unity? "Inside the System" Box 13.1 suggests ways in which the organization of Congress reflects the workings of the larger political system on the outside.

The Individual Versus the Organization

Chapter 12 explored the idea of an "electoral connection"—that congressional activities are motivated by the desire of individual members to be reelected.[12] Critics respond that this charge is too simple, that many other factors are equally important for understanding how the institution works.[13] We need not try to explain *everything* about Congress as the product of individual political motives, but it would be a mistake to ignore the political impact of hundreds of individual careers on the whole institution.

The Career Management System

Far from its origins as a citizen legislature, today's Congress reflects the rise of professional politicians who have mastered the consummate professional skill: getting reelected. The cost of the professional legislature, one member of the House told a reporter, is "an absence of risk-taking, both individual and collective. Risks become a detour from a nice, safe, permanent job. . . . This job is getting to the point where you feel as if we're incapable of making serious public policy decisions."[14]

The conflict between individual careers and legislative unity may explain why so many members have left Congress in recent years. In an article titled "Why I'm Quitting the Senate," former senator Dan Evans lamented that recent elections may be remembered "not so much for those candidates who ran, as for those who chose not to run. Seldom have so many senators in mid-career chosen to call it quits."[15] Although many

How Outside Political Forces Affect Politics Inside the Congress

The many divisions of power inside Congress reflect the long tradition of senators and representatives setting their own procedures. However, these divisions also reflect how pressures from the surrounding political system have shaped the inner workings of the institution.

As noted in Chapter 12, *cultural concerns* about limiting the powers of government, and particularly the legislative branch, led to the creation of two chambers as different from each other as possible. Since there was little interest in making the two halves of the legislature fit together, the Framers further left the internal organization of each chamber to the members themselves. The Constitution is silent on how the House and Senate should go about their day-to-day business. The result has been two separate sets of *institutional traditions and customs*, with different ideas about debate, committees, decorum, and the spreading of power among members. The freedom to organize the politics within the chambers of Congress has greatly affected the *institutional process* of legislation.

The many different forms of outside *social power* that converge on Congress (see "Inside the System" Box 12.1) also reinforce fragmentation of power. For example, the challenges of reelection have led to the adoption of many organizational features that promote the career interests of individual members. The weakness of national parties and importance of state politics in the reelection of members creates a constant strain with internal party organization in both chambers. In addition, interest groups and wealthy elites can give individual members further independence from party organizations. The drive for personal power increases the importance of getting good committee assignments and becoming committee chairs. From such powerful positions, members can attract the support of interest groups and elites while repaying political favors from those backers. In short, the social forces that pull the legislative process in so many directions from the outside have these effects in large part because they influence the ways in which members of Congress have organized their political affairs inside the institution.

---

voters and members of Congress might regard independence and individual power as good things in representatives, Evans finds fault with earlier reforms of Congress that gave more power to individuals:

> Perhaps the current crisis can be traced to the coming of the large new Congressional class during the mid-1970s. The power of the leadership began to crumble in both houses; authority became atomized. Today there are 100 power centers in the Senate, and each member is as quick to speak out on almost any issue as he or she is slow to agree to a compromise.[16]

Independence may be good for careers but bad for legislation. Research on the last forty years of congressional careers by political scientist John Hibbing confirms that jobs are more secure and positions of committee power easier to attain than in the past, but these career gains have not helped in getting legislation introduced and passed. To the contrary, says Hibbing, "the gap between senior and junior members in this area has, if anything, widened in recent years."[17]

Still, it is no doubt comforting for junior legislators not to be under the thumb of old committee barons such as Carl Vinson, who chaired the House Armed Services Committee for years during the 1950s and 1960s. The regime that such chairmen once imposed on junior members has been described as an **apprenticeship system** in which newcomers followed the orders of senior committee chairs, much as workers learning a trade serve as assistants and underlings to craftsmen. Working on a committee under the iron rule of chairs like Vinson was described as follows by a former representative who had to endure it: "When I came to Congress in 1960, Carl Vinson had a rule that first term committee members were permitted one question in all the deliberations that took place during that term; that's it—one question in an entire term; they were permitted two questions in their second term; three in their third; and so on."[18] While such indignities no longer face new members of Congress, they now find themselves confronted with the frustration of being unable to drum up the interest or support of colleagues in passing legislation to go along with their greater freedoms. They learn the hard way, as Hibbing put it, that "a subcommittee chair does not a legislator make."[19]

What today's aspiring lawmaker finds waiting in Washington instead of the *apprenticeship system* of the old days is a **career management system,** designed to keep the legislator in office even if he or she is not doing much legislating. Indeed, Hibbing concludes that this career management system may be the biggest change in Congress in the last forty years from the standpoint of individual members:

> Newly elected members of Congress are today presented with a battery of seminars, workshops, retreats, lectures, and publications, all designed to teach them how to organize a congressional office, how to utilize congressional procedures to generate publicity, and (more generally) how to get reelected. We know that advisors, pollsters, interest groups, and political parties are there with advice about the district and the process. We know that there is a more egalitarian ethos in Congress than existed 30 years ago and that there are more opportunities for junior members than there used to be. We know that representatives are watched more carefully than they ever have been. . . . Every contribution received, every junket taken, every vote missed . . . every piece of franked mail sent, every joke told, . . . every bill introduced, every trip not taken home all now have the potential to be major issues in the next campaign, or the next, or the next. Why venture off the well-trod path in such a climate?
>
> As a result, it seems that members are constantly working at putting themselves "on display" and that little time is left for real legislative growth.[20]

Being on display means, among other things, creating the appearance of being involved in the legislative process, the next best thing to real involvement. And the best way to create such an appearance is through managing the news media and developing other means of communicating with constituents back home (like franking privileges, the heavy use of taxpayer-subsidized mail to send "updates" to voters and ask them to fill out opinion surveys stating their legislative preferences). But learning to use the media may have become the key to the modern career.

Congress in the Media Age

Research by political scientist Timothy Cook shows that members spend considerable time staking out legislative issues that are newsworthy and learning how to stage media events to link themselves to those issues in the news. In part, this might be viewed as a cynical ploy to get the public to see lawmakers as concerned about such popular issues as gun control, health care, budget-balancing, and world peace, even when Congress as a whole is either unable or unwilling to do much about those things. Few Capitol Hill events are more likely to draw the television cameras than a dozen blow-dried senators, sound bites at the ready, holding a committee hearing on drugs, terrorism, or a juicy corruption scandal. In fairness, as Cook points out, the media have also become increasingly important consensus builders and agenda setters in American politics, particularly in the

Incoming freshman members of the 103rd Congress smile for the camera before assuming their seats in January of 1993. With the breakdown of the apprentice system and weakening of party discipline, junior legislators are attempting to exert a stronger influence in their chambers—while protecting their own careers.

absence of internal coherence in Congress. Many members of Congress seem to feel that they are more effective as lawmakers when they go outside the institution to help bring public pressure on the institution to do something.[21]

Whether or not they drum up enough public pressure to affect legislation, congressional media strategies may help with other aspects of career management. As political scientist Stephen Hess has noted, it is hard to tell whether committees are powerful in and of themselves or if particular committees merely seem powerful because they have more television cameras covering them. Hess produced a "camera count" of various Senate committees, and found that Foreign Relations led the press pack with 522 cameras counted in one year, while Indian Affairs attracted not a single television news crew.[22] As Hess put it, "When I asked Joseph Biden [who once aspired to be president] what he felt accounted for his newsworthiness, he replied without hesitation. 'It's the committees, of course.'"[23] With the end of the Cold War, and a public mood to put domestic problems ahead of world issues, the careerists in the 1990s are turning away from such committees as Foreign Affairs and Armed Services and toward "hot" committees such as

Ways and Means or Appropriations that decide how to raise the money and how much to spend on the (newsworthy) domestic priorities of health care and education. Figure 13.2 illustrates the issues that lawmakers in the 103rd Congress (1993–1994) cited as most important to them.

It is hard to sustain media interest in any issue long enough to generate useful public pressure. As former senator Tim Wirth put it in his "Diary of a Dropout," the media spend more time chasing scandals than trying to cover "real issues." As if that were not

FIGURE 13.2

Legislative Priorities of the 103rd Congress, 1993–1994

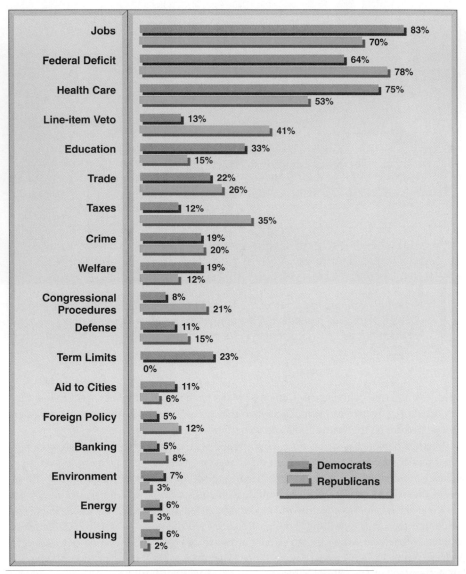

Based on Gallup Survey of 100 returning members and 49 new representatives and senators. Margin of error: ±8 percentage points. Adapted from graphic in *The Washington Post National Weekly Edition*, December 14–20, 1992, p. 36.

enough, "scandalized" members of Congress then have to run the media gauntlet in their election campaigns:

> With the news media all too ready to treat rumor as news and . . . accusations as truth, I knew I would be subjected to unending . . . attacks [in the 1992 election]. I would have to counterattack. . . . I believed I could win that kind of campaign, but in tearing down my opponent, wouldn't I inevitably end up diminishing myself?[24]

Where is the incentive to take risks in this sort of environment? But why stay if nothing gets done? That, in oversimplified form, is one of the dilemmas of the modern congressional career. How would you reform Congress if you were one of the new members of the large class of '92? Would you, as a junior member of Congress, want to go back to the old days of power brokers and party machines, with junior members speaking only when spoken to? Is there another alternative? Consider some of the other aspects of political life on The Hill before deciding.

Two Cultures: Norms and Rules in the House and Senate

The differences between the Senate and the House become apparent just by looking at their organization charts (see Figure 13.3 on following page). As discussed in Chapter 3, the Constitution gives the two chambers the power to organize themselves. Since the intent of the framers was to create fundamentally different organizations, it is not surprising that the differences over the centuries have become much deeper than their organization charts.

Most of the procedures employed by Congress grew out of years of tradition and just plain muddling through the legislative process. No matter how idiosyncratic the customs of Congress may be, tradition is hard to throw off. The House and the Senate have been described as having their own internal cultures, each affecting the behaviors of individual members and the fate of legislation itself. Although the rise of careerist politicians has created strains in some of the old ways of Congress, the traditions inside the chambers still explain a great deal about how things get done.

The Senate Club

Important traditions of the Senate can be traced back to its origins as a smaller, elite body given to debate and deliberation. Such beginnings leave their marks on an institution. As political scientist Donald Matthews has observed, the Senate has a number of *folkways, referring to the unwritten rules and customs that guide relations among members.* Because the *folkways of the Senate* affect almost every aspect of how members relate to one another, they also shape the way power is exercised in the chamber.[25] More than the larger, busier, less prestigious House, the Senate resembles something of an elite club, in which members generally show mutual respect, honor traditions, protect the privileges of membership, and respect the seniority of elder members. (Some recent exceptions are noted below.)

The overall tone of the Senate club is set by the **reciprocity** norm. To put it simply, members exchange many favors, ranging from small social courtesies to trading votes on legislation (called *logrolling*, as discussed in Chapter 12). Underlying this norm of reciprocity is the assumption that the favor will be returned when it is called in. (A similar reciprocity norm is also one of the most basic and enduring traditions in the House.)

FIGURE 13.3   *The Formal Organization of the Senate and the House*

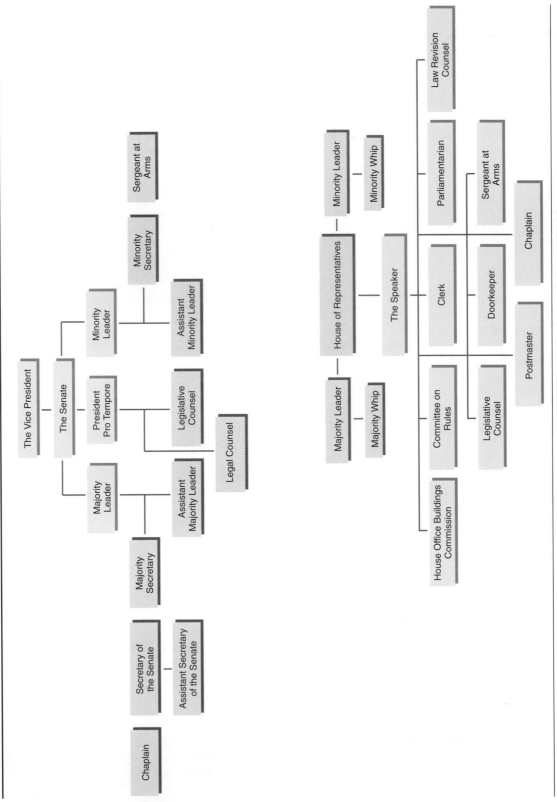

Source: *U.S. Government Organization Manual*, Washington, D.C.: U.S. Government Printing Office, 1991–92, pp. 26–27.

Another important Senate custom is the important tradition of **respect** for colleagues. Listen to a debate on the Senate floor or in committee and you will often hear bitter opponents address each other as "my distinguished colleague," "my learned opponent," or "the esteemed senator from Nebraska." Perhaps because of the growing independence of the careers and the intrusion of the media into the chamber, there are signs in recent times that the civility may be wearing thin, as in the harsh personal attacks between North Carolina conservative Jesse Helms and Massachusetts liberal Ted Kennedy. The bitter confirmation hearings of Supreme Court Justice Clarence Thomas in 1991 captured rare instances of rudeness between senators on television.

Still, the norm of respect is important in keeping the chamber close-knit, and the elite tone of the Senate tends to show in more flowery displays of praise and deference than in the House. While still in the Senate, Tim Wirth summed up the importance of the personal relations and the club atmosphere for being politically effective inside the Senate:

> One of the things that's so impressive about this place is the personal relationships that exist. . . . Because of the filibuster and the fact that so much gets done by unanimous consent . . . what grows up is a great deal of personal rapport among members of the Senate that is real.
>
> People talk about this place being a club. It has to be a club in order to get unanimous consent. But beneath that grow up very strong, very real relationships. It takes a while to develop those relationships so that people know your style and approach enough to trust you and take you seriously.[26]

The House Fraternity

If the Senate balances the sensitive power relations among its one hundred often-egoistic members by adopting the respectful atmosphere of an elite club, the House is a

Patricia Schroeder of Colorado's First Congressional District, a twenty-year veteran of the House. An advocate of feminist and family-oriented causes (she authored a 1989 book boldly titled Champion of the Great American Family*), Schroeder has developed considerable prominence in Congress despite the so-called "old boy" networks that still dominate the institution.*

The Breakdown in Tradition

While some of the customs of Congress have held firm over the years, others have changed in recent times. As noted above, for example, it was once customary for new members to go through a period of apprenticeship to the great political barons who chaired the committees and held the leadership posts. Today's Congress has little of the old apprenticeship path left. Members come in and begin to make speeches, schedule press conferences, talk to the media, and take their seats as subcommittee chairs. The apprenticeship system was once even stronger in the House than in the Senate because power had to be distributed among more members, meaning that more had to wait their turn. Today, the House apprenticeship has crumbled even more dramatically with the growth of subcommittees enabling new members to rise to chair positions relatively quickly.

Although some aspects of congressional custom have weakened in recent years, others remain at the center of political life in Congress. For example, the traditions of debate are still important in understanding how bills pass the two chambers. In addition, the norms of reciprocity and respect are important for understanding how political deals are made, how new members are socialized, and why some individuals can attain great powers in the institution simply by playing by the rules. For a summary of similarities and differences in the norms that representatives and senators live by, see "Inside the System" Box 13.2.

Power in Committees

The next organizational structure that helps explain the patterns of congressional power is the committee system. In the early years of Congress, both chambers tried to make most of their decisions in open debate. At the close of debate, a temporary group called a **select committee** was appointed just for the time required to write up into formal law the agreement that had been reached. Needless to say, few agreements were reached, debates were chaotic, and it often proved difficult to summarize the results in an agreeable fashion. While Congress still appoints *select committees* from time to time, they now serve primarily to investigate emergency or crisis situations (such as the improprieties committed by the White House in the Watergate scandal of the 1970s), or to recommend legislative action in new or complex areas that don't fit well with current legislative committees (such as how to handle international narcotics trafficking or how to monitor the vast intelligence and espionage operations that the executive branch carries on in secret).

Since those first experiments with collective legislation failed, the bulk of the work of Congress has been done in permanent or **standing committees.** Instead of having the whole body debate an issue and try to reach consensus on a law, it was better to appoint standing committees that specialized in different areas of legislation, and let those committees work out the details of proposed legislation (through different subcommittees) and bring a well-developed proposal to the full body for debate and action. This system, with some modifications over the years, has done the work of making laws ever since.

A Map of the Committee World

Committees in Congress work much the way committees operate in other organizations: they *divide the labor* so that people can concentrate on specific tasks and not have to worry about everything. Committees focus on broad subjects of legislation: banking,

The Political World of Congress: Norms and Customs

13.2

I nstitutions cannot be understood just by looking at their formal rules and constitutional descriptions. They are also defined by years of political tradition. Congress has the power to organize most of its own procedures, meaning that many of the powers of the institution are based on unwritten traditions. Some are common to both chambers, while others are unique to the House or the Senate. And, as with all tradition, some have endured while others have faded. Here are some of the similarities and differences, along with some of the changes in the customs of Congress.

Enduring Similarities Between House and Senate
RECIPROCITY: Keeping promises, repaying favors, trust.

SPECIALIZATION: Becoming an expert, wielding power in that area.
OLD BOY NETWORK: Men's club/fraternity atmosphere.
RESPECT: Deference and courtesy even among opponents.

Enduring Differences Between House and Senate
STYLES OF DEBATE: Senate acts as a debating society with (nearly) unlimited debate, reflected in the filibuster. House has more bureaucratic approach to legislation, limited debate, reflected in House Rules Committee.
STAR SYSTEM: Senators, because of their smaller numbers, have relatively more power, draw more media attention, and play greater national political roles than the more numerous, less powerful, less visible House members.

Key Changes
APPRENTICESHIP: New members rise more quickly to become subcommittee chairs, spend less time in the shadows of senior members. Most dramatic change in the House.
POWER OF LEADERSHIP: Party leaders and standing committee chairs have less control over junior members and party legislative agendas.

labor, foreign affairs, education, agriculture, and how to pay for it all. Committees come in different forms, beginning with the *standing committees* (described above) that deal with recurring issues that face the nation: defense, agriculture, transportation, banking, and education, among many others. As the nation has become more complex, the work in these broad legislative areas has been handled primarily by *subcommittees* where the focus is narrower and the actual details of legislation are worked out. (Members of subcommittees also sit on the parent or standing committee.)

As members gain experience with legislation, they become experts in an area of subcommittee concern, such as naval defense strategies, primary education policies, or corn farming problems. The subcommittee system develops special knowledge and expertise among the members of Congress and allows the organization to handle a huge range of complex problems without requiring all members to try to understand all the issues facing the nation.

When new problems arise, each chamber can create new committees to investigate them. These new committees generally begin as temporary or *select committees* which may be dissolved when the problem they were created for is resolved, or they may evolve into standing committees if the issue persists in society. One of the most famous select committees in history was the Senate select committee that investigated charges against

Cardinals of Capitol Hill

Within their respective domains, congressional committee heads wield great influence in passing or killing legislation. The three Democrats seen here—diverse in their geographic, political, and philosophical backgrounds—have all played key roles in the nation's affairs in the early 1990s. As chairman of the Senate Armed Services Committee, Sam Nunn of Georgia *(above)* effectively blocked Bill Clinton's proposal to change military policy toward homosexuals. Patrick Moynihan of New York *(below),* chairman of the Senate Finance Committee, is renowned as an academic heavyweight; he helped to pass Clinton's first budget package by working closely with the head of the House Ways and Means Committee, Dan Rostentowski *(right),* a longtime Chicago "machine" politician who was the subject of corruption charges in late 1993.

The Players

the Nixon administration during the Watergate scandal. In recent years select committees have come and gone to deal with issues that include hunger, aging, narcotics, and ethics (see Table 13.1).

Each chamber maintains its own, and rather different, set of *standing committees*, each with various *subcommittees* to handle the work of legislation. (The majority party names these committees and controls a majority of seats on them.) After a bill has been

TABLE 13.1

The Committees of Congress

THE HOUSE OF REPRESENTATIVES	THE SENATE
STANDING COMMITTEES	STANDING COMMITTEES
Agriculture	Agriculture, Nutrition, and Forestry
Armed Services	Appropriations
Banking, Finance, and Urban Affairs	Armed Services
Budget	Banking, Housing, and Urban Affairs
District of Columbia	Budget
Education and Labor	Commerce, Science, and Transportation
Energy and Commerce	Energy and Natural Resources
Foreign Affairs	Environment and Public Works
Government Operations	Finance
House Administration	Foreign Relations
Interior and Insular Affairs	Government Affairs
Judiciary	Judiciary
Merchant Marine and Fisheries	Labor and Human Resources
Post Office	Rules and Administration
Public Works and Transportation	Small Business
Rules	Veterans' Affairs
Science, Space, and Technology	
Small Business	SELECT COMMITTEES
Standards of Official Conduct	
Veterans' Affairs	Aging
Ways and Means	Ethics
	Intelligence
SELECT COMMITTEES	Indian Affairs
Aging	
Children, Youth, and Families	
Hunger	NOTE: Based on committees of the 102nd Congress (1991–1992).
Intelligence	
Narcotics and Abuse Control	

developed by committees in each chamber and approved by a majority of the full chamber, any differences in the language are ironed out by appointing a **conference committee** which, as the name implies, is a temporary committee that enables key legislators involved in the original deliberations in the House and Senate to get together and work out their differences.

A conference committee is a special type of **joint committee,** referring to any committee with members drawn from both chambers. In addition to the temporary conference committees appointed to deal with specific bills, there are a few permanent joint committees organized to deal with issues that require ongoing cooperation. For example, the Joint Economic Committee of Congress studies and recommends legislation on broad economic policy matters. For the most part, however, the work of Congress is organized differently in the House and the Senate according to the standing (relatively permanent) and select (more temporary, problem-oriented) committees that the parties in each chamber regard as necessary to handle the nation's legislative business or to investigate new problems. (See Table 13.1 for a recent listing of the committees of the House and Senate.)

Despite the obvious differences between the two chambers, the committee system is not as complex as it may seem. If you look closely at the lists in Table 13.1, you will see that there is some overlap in the titles of the House and Senate committees, reflecting the fact that some of the ways in which the two chambers approach their work are fairly similar, as in the areas of Armed Services, Foreign Affairs, and Small Business legislation, for example. In other areas, each chamber has organized the legislative process very differently. For example, the House has a Committee on Energy and Commerce, while the Senate distributes energy and commerce activities over no fewer than three different committees.

All modern legislatures use committee systems to do the basic work of legislation, but some, such as France's, have much more centralized and less independent committee systems, while others, such as Germany's, have committees that are more independent than the French, but less powerful than the American model. American legislative committees are among the most independent and powerful in the world, which adds to the reasons why coordinated legislative programs are difficult to achieve in American politics. For a contrast with the French model of weak legislative committees, see "How We Compare" Box 13.3.

Power to the Subcommittees

Today, most of the work of Congress is done in subcommittees, hundreds of them. For example, the foreign policy committees of the House and Senate have subcommittees that handle different regions of the world, along with special topics such as human rights and disarmament. And the House Appropriations Committee has thirteen subcommittees to decide how to fund programs in the bureaucratic departments of defense, education, agriculture, transportation, and so on. The heads of the appropriations subcommittees are so powerful that they are known as the "College of Cardinals," after the highest committee of the Catholic Church.

Reformers who want to shrink the number of subcommittees meet resistance from junior lawmakers whose subcommittee roles give them great freedom from the chairs of the standing committees. Younger members of the House and Senate rise to positions of political prominence more quickly than in the past. A joke on Capitol Hill is that if you cannot remember the name of a colleague, it is probably a safe bet to address him as "Mr. Chairman," or in a few cases, "Ms. Chairwoman." More than half of the Democrats (the majority party) in the House serve as heads of committees or subcommittees, and a much larger percentage of Democrats (the majority party) in the Senate chair one or

HOW WE COMPARE

Committees in the French National Assembly

13.3

The committee system of the French National Assembly was once as powerful and independent as that of the U.S. Congress. Today, the power of committees has been greatly reduced, but, unlike the American trend, control over legislation has become more centralized. The number of standing committees has been reduced from nineteen to six in each chamber of the French Assembly: constitutional laws, legislation, and administration; cultural, social, and family affairs; finance; foreign affairs; national defense; and production and trade. These committees are huge, with from 60-120 members representing the different parties in the legislature. Moreover, the committees cannot amend or bring bills to the floor without approval from the executive. Further reducing the independence of the legislature is the fact that French Cabinet ministers must resign their seats in the legislature (if they are members of the Assembly) when they join the administration, a requirement that strengthens their loyalty to the president and reduces their independent legislative power bases. One scholar observed that "French ministers, including the Prime Minister, have been reduced to messenger boys for the President."* The reforms in legislative power in France have tightened the working relations between executive and legislature but caused complaint about too much centralized power.

*Quote from Michael G. Roskin, *Countries and Concepts*, 2nd ed. Englewood Cliffs, N.J.; Prentice-Hall, 1986, p. 93.
SOURCE: Henry W. Ehrman and Martin A. Schain, *Politics in France*, 5th ed. New York: HarperCollins, 1992.

A 1993 gathering of L'Assemblée Nationale *in Paris.*

more committees or subcommittees. As noted later in this chapter, reform efforts have reduced the number of subcommittees from their historic peak in the mid-1970s.

The movement from government by committee to government by subcommittee has done little to ease the complaints about Congress. The overall efficiency of Congress may have suffered due to squabbles about which subcommittee should take responsibility for what bills, how many staff positions should go to which subcommittees, and how to schedule the many legislative activities going on at once. In addition, by making the legislative process more specialized, the access of interest groups may have increased. These complaints aside, it is hard to imagine running Congress in a complex society without many committees and subcommittees.

Pros and Cons of the Committee System

For all its political twists and turns, the committee system has at least three strengths and three related shortcomings:

PRO: *The committee and subcommittee system simplifies screening* the thousands of legislative proposals that come forward each session of Congress. In most cases, bills are sent routinely to the committees best equipped to think about them.

CON: *The law is carved up* into bureaucratic categories. Broader programs of legislation that might tackle complex and related social problems are difficult to navigate through this system.

PRO: *The committee and subcommittee system efficiently divides up the labor of Congress*, spreading the huge workload around, and allocating such resources as offices, rooms, and staff positions (at least somewhat equitably) on the basis of committee workloads.

CON: *This gives too much power and independence* to the powerful individuals who chair the committees and who can dominate national policy in important areas such as agriculture, banking, or energy.

PRO: *The committee and subcommittee system allows legislators and staff members to become experts* in particular areas, with the result of improving the quality of legislation.

CON: *Specialized committees are vulnerable to interest groups* who can lobby a small number of individual members and often help write the laws in the bargain.

Whether the balance tips in the pro or the con direction depends to an important degree on whether the political parties have enough influence to bring different committee chairs and members together around a coherent legislative agenda. Thus the workings of the political parties inside the institution must be figured into any understanding of how Congress has developed its internal powers.

Party Politics and Congressional Leadership

The heyday of strong congressional parties was probably the turn of the century (1880–1910) when committees were run by iron-fisted potentates, and leaders of the parties controlled the political fates of junior members. In those days, according to the data

In 1992, congressional Democrats sat on their hands while their Republican colleagues rose to applaud President George Bush's proposals during his State of the Union address (above); *a year later, the situation was reversed. Despite declines from earlier times, party loyalty is still important in the internal organization of Congress.*

in Figure 12.5, fully 60 percent of the votes in Congress were strong "party votes," with as many as 90 percent of the Republicans opposing 90 percent of the Democrats. The age of party conflict was replaced by a long period of decline in party discipline.

As noted in Chapter 12, some observers see a return to party voting in recent times. However, levels of party strength these days do not come close to the earlier age of strong party government. It remains to be seen what the future holds either in the way of bipartisan cooperation or more effective partisan conflicts.

The Problem of Party Loyalty

Despite the weakness of parties as ideological or legislative organizations, there is one important way in which parties do stick together: as organizations dedicated to maintaining the personal power of their members. In recent years, only one successful candidate for Congress (Bernie Sanders, from Vermont) has declared an independent affiliation outside the two major parties. Is this continuing affiliation with weak political organizations merely out of habit or nostalgia? Far from it. It turns out that the parties remain very important to the political life inside Congress.

What do the parties do for their members? First, they are paths of recruitment into Congress. Although this function is weakening, as noted in Chapter 9, most members of Congress still begin their careers in party politics back in their states. Second, parties help members after they are elected with a variety of services designed to get them reelected in the future: the career management package described earlier. Finally, and, perhaps most importantly, parties determine who sits on which committees and who holds the leadership positions in each chamber. This last role of parties may be the most important. To put it bluntly, without parties to organize Congress, the power of individuals would be destroyed. Parties assign members to the committees of Congress, elect the leaders of Congress, and, from time to time, depose them. Without party solidarity in the all-important matter of filling the committee and leadership slots, Congress would explode in short order, and the precious shares of political turf staked out by individuals would be endlessly contested.

How the Parties Govern Congress

The single most important bit of information about the internal workings of Congress is that the parties organize themselves to run the institution. This means, among other things, that the majority party in each chamber exercises a substantial margin of control over the legislative process. Consider, for example, the post of Speaker of the House, the position second in line to the presidency after the vice president, and the person responsible for assigning bills to committees, handling floor debates, and generally representing the House in delicate negotiations with the Senate and the president. In theory, the speaker is elected by a majority vote of the entire House. In practice, the majority party always elects the speaker. Why? Because the parties meet in what are called *caucuses* (by House Democrats) or *conferences* (the name preferred by the House Republicans and the members of both parties in the Senate) to agree on leadership positions and vote as a party on candidates. Since the Democrats hold a majority of seats in the House, and have for all but two terms since 1930, the Democrats have elected all but two Speakers of the House in modern times. Given the great power that Speakers and other congressional officers can wield, it would be foolish for the parties to fail to organize themselves politically. Thus, while party solidarity can be weak in ideological terms, it remains strong in terms of controlling political power and positions within the Congress.

PARTY LEADERSHIP. The powerful position of House Speaker is one of the major differences (along with the House Rules Committee) in the organization of House and Senate. The chief officer of the Senate, as prescribed by the Constitution, is the vice president of the United States. Except for casting an occasional vote to break a tie in a

Senate Minority Leader Bob Dole (at podium), *backed by fellow Republican senators (including newly elected Sen. Paul Coverdell of Georgia, at the easel) reviews Bill Clinton's first hundred days in office. Outnumbered in both chambers of Congress, GOP legislators have been forced to rely on guerrilla warfare in the media, occasional filibustering (in the Senate), and alliances with conservative Democrats to achieve even modest goals.*

House Speaker Sam Rayburn of Texas (1882–1961), one of the last great eminences of the pre-television era in Congress. A U. S. representative for nearly half a century, Rayburn's work was vital in achieving congressional passage of FDR's "New Deal" programs. Aside from the enormous authority he wielded during some sixteen years as Speaker of the House, Rayburn also served as mentor and advisor to such powerful figures as Lyndon Johnson.

floor vote on a bill, being the president of the Senate is not much of a job. Since the vice president does not spend much time presiding at the Capitol, the Senate selects from its own ranks a *president pro tempore,* a temporary or stand-in presiding officer. Like the Speaker of the House, the "president pro tem" is elected by the majority party, but unlike the Speaker of the House, the president pro tem of the Senate has little power and often delegates the tedious job of sitting in the high chair above the Senate floor to junior members of the party. The real power struggles in the Senate, like those in the House, are for the leadership posts of the parties and the chairs of the powerful committees.

The *majority parties in each chamber (acting as a caucus or conference)* elect *majority leaders* who head their party in the Senate and are second in command (after the Speaker) in the House. The minority parties, in turn, elect *minority leaders* who head their parties in both chambers. The leaders of the parties are "power brokers" who line up votes on key bills, work out problems for members, and help them win the committee assignments that they seek. In the cases of prized committees, the help of the party leadership is often repaid later on with loyalty on legislation or internal party decisions (as when, for example, the party leader is challenged by another contender for the job). As this sketch of party power suggests, there is a whole lot of politicking going on behind the scenes in Congress: politicking over leadership posts in the parties, committee assignments, office spaces, campaign money, and, of course, legislation. In day-to-day matters, this politicking is carried out through party officers appropriately called *whips,* who are appointed by the party leaders to whip up support for party positions and bring back word of problems with members whose support is soft. The job of the whip is to stay in close communication with the rank-and-file members of the party, acting as intermediaries between the leadership and the troops.

As we move down the list of committees, away from the "glamour appointments," most committee assignments are made routinely. The Republican party in both House and Senate make committee assignments through a *committee on committees.* In the Senate, the Democrats have separate committees for making committee assignments (called the Steering Committee) and working out a legislative agenda (called the Policy Committee). In the House, the Democrats have a combined Steering and Policy Committee to handle both committee assignments and the legislative agenda. Both parties also have their own campaign committees built right into the leadership and governance system of each chamber. The party organization of the House is illustrated in Figure 13.4, and the party system that runs the Senate is shown in Figure 13.5.

SENIORITY. Once senators or representatives are appointed to committees, they usually remain at their own pleasure until they move to a better committee, die, retire, or are defeated in an election. In rare cases, senior committee or subcommittee chairs may be removed by a vote from the party conference or caucus, which may be spearheaded by a rebellion from unhappy committee members. As old members leave, however, it is still customary (although not as automatic as it once was) for committee members to rise through the seniority ranks (measured by length of service on a particular committee) to become chair if they are from the majority party, or ranking minority member if they are from the minority party. In 1993, for example, 82-year-old Jamie Whitten of Mississippi, the ranking Democratic member of the House Appropriations Committee, was moved out as committee chair in favor of the next ranking Democrat on the committee, William Natcher of Kentucky, who at 83 was actually older than Whitten.

Although seniority still rules in the committee world, the growth of subcommittees headed by more junior legislators means that committee chairs simply do not wield the power they once did in Congress. Thus, the seniority principle was never really done away with, only spread out by creating many more subcommittees, thereby giving more members the chance to become "senior." As one student of congressional reforms put it, "Seniority, like monarchy, may be preserved by being deprived of most of its power."[29]

STATE POLITICS AND REAPPORTIONMENT. Party unity also operates at the state government level in ways that have important consequences for Congress. An important link between party organizations at the national and state levels is the fact that the national political maps are drawn by state legislatures, as discussed in Chapter 9. Every ten years, the U.S. Census Bureau registers changes in where people live. When substantial shifts occur, some states gain seats in the House of Representatives and others lose. Moving seats from state to state in the House of Representatives to adjust representation is called *reapportionment*. The process that determines the boundaries, and

Strom Thurmond, U. S. Senator from South Carolina since 1955. Thurmond's enduring political clout at the age of 90–plus years is a vivid testimonial to not only his own stamina but the continuing influence of seniority in the Senate.

FIGURE 13.4

The Party System in Congress: Internal Government of the U.S. House of Representatives

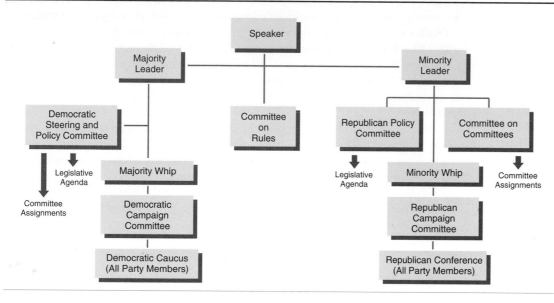

FIGURE 13.5

The Party System in Congress: Internal Government of the U.S. Senate

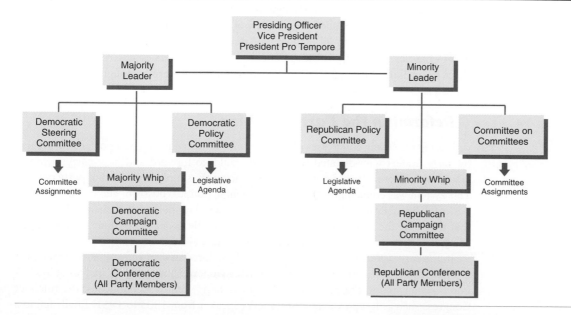

more importantly, the social and political composition of the new districts of members of the House of Representatives is called **redistricting.**[30] State legislatures and governors bargain over this process, making the party that controls the state legislature and the governor's mansion the party with an edge in securing more safe seats for its members in the U.S. Congress. Recall, from Chapter 9, that the art of drawing politically advantageous lines is known as **gerrymandering.** Like it or not, the gerrymander has endured. One of the designers of the Congress of the 1990s, Representative Vic Fazio of California, put it this way: "I don't think gerrymandering is something easily defined by courts or anybody else. It's a political process. It's like obscenity. Some people see it and some people don't."

Like party loyalty inside Congress, the discipline between state and national parties often ends with working out political arrangements that benefit individual members. There is often no love lost between state and national party chapters when it comes to volatile issues such as school prayer, welfare, abortion, or taxation. In fact, many state parties are as divided internally on these issues as are the national parties in Congress. But foolishness when it comes to self-interest is not a political survival trait, and so the parties often bury their substantive differences long enough to organize themselves politically.

Reforming Congress

Much of the fragmentation in Congress described above can be explained by tracing the hundred-year history of reform movements aimed at breaking up centralized power within the institution. In many ways these reforms have "democratized" the institution by broadening the base of individual power within parties. The important political result has been to reduce the capacity of the parties to act together politically. There is some irony in the idea that the more democratic a party becomes on the inside, the less unified and effective it becomes in its actions in the outside political world. More than an irony, this principle has been called an iron law by the great observer of European political parties, Roberto Michels, who concluded that no matter how democratic the voter support for a political party, its power in a legislature depends on tight, centralized control by a handful of party bosses. Called the **iron law of oligarchy,** this idea points to a fundamental dilemma for parties in all democratic systems. The idea of centralized, oligarchical parties has never set well in U.S. politics, either with voters or enterprising politicians eager to break into the inner circle of power before they grow enough grey hair to become leaders themselves.

Reforming the Party Machine

During the strong congresses around the turn of the century, great power was wielded by party leaders who dictated which bills would go forward and how party members would vote. Those who did not toe the party line were simply frozen out of party politics. This system was condemned by critics as machine politics, bossism, and corruption. The powerful Republicans who ran the House in those days defended their rule by arguing that they were the majority party, elected by the people to get things done, and enforcing party discipline was the only way to do it.

In the early 1900s the country was swept by a "progressive" reform movement aimed at doing away with party machines and bosses wherever they existed, including in Congress. Hammered in the press as well as by unhappy fellow Republicans, the rulers of Congress such as Joseph Cannon of Illinois (Speaker from 1903 to 1911) finally fell to a revolt by their own lieutenants, and power flowed out a bit more broadly to the chairs of the standing committees. The oligarchy was not so much ended as merely expanded to include more feudal lords.

Reforming the Staff

The next wave of reforms came in the 1940s, culminating in the Legislative Reorganization Act of 1946, intended to streamline the legislative process by reducing the number of committees and increasing the number of *staff* members (both for members and committees) to assist lawmakers in drafting ever-more-complex and technical laws. As a result of that reform, the level of technical assistance has grown enormously over the years, with more than 10,000 professional staff now serving in the 535 offices of members, and an additional 4,000 staff assigned to the 300 or so committees and subcommittees of Congress.[31] This reform cemented the committee system as the power structure of Congress by giving committees the help they needed to research and write legislation. It also opened up 14,000 lines of access to interest groups and lobbyists who often make their most important contacts with the staff who do most of the work of committees and have the attention of legislators. Figure 13.6 shows the enormous growth of congressional staff over the past century.

The reforms of the 1940s fueled new complaints about the power of committee chairmen, who now had armies of lawyers and researchers to do their bidding. In the post-1946 era, it is fair to say that many key staff members and aides probably had more

FIGURE 13.6

Staff of Members and of Committees in Congress, 1891–1989

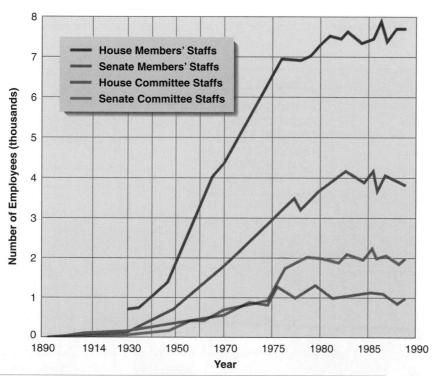

Source: Norman J. Ornstein, Thomas E. Mann, and Michael J. Malbin, *Vital Statistics on Congress*. Washington, D.C.: CQ Press, 1992, p. 127.

power than junior members of Congress who spent years as "apprentices" on committees. Public discontent peaked in the 1960s and 1970s with calls for congressional reform spurred by both the scandals that racked the Republicans and complaints about the entrenched power of the Democrats, who have controlled Congress for most of the time since the 1930s.

Reforming the Committee System

The mid-1970s saw the election of many new faces to Congress who came to Washington as rebels, intent on changing things and getting into the legislative game without having to endure the long apprenticeships. The first target of committee reforms was the Democratic party system in the House, the hard core of congressional power. The House Democratic Caucus voted changes in the procedures for selecting speakers, leaders, and committee chairs. (In what amounted to a palace coup, the entering class of 1975 showed its newfound muscle by ousting three standing committee chairmen.) Senate Democrats followed suit, making substantial changes in committee organization and leading an effort to loosen up the rules for ending filibusters. The Republicans in both chambers also moved down the path of party reform, but with less at stake, since the Democrats controlled both chambers and therefore had more power up for grabs and more control over the reform process itself.[32]

When the dust had settled, Congress was more democratic than ever before. And there were more subcommittees than ever before. And more members had committee and subcommittee chairs than ever before. And there were more staff positions than ever before. And there was a new Congressional Budget Office to provide research and independent economic forecasts as an important check against optimistic White House budget analyses. The explosion of subcommittees proved unwieldy, however, and was eventually cut back—dramatically in the Senate and slightly in the House, as shown in Figure 13.7.

FIGURE 13.7

Development of the Congressional Committee Systems: Number of Standing Subcommittees of House and Senate Standing Committees (80th to 101st Congress)

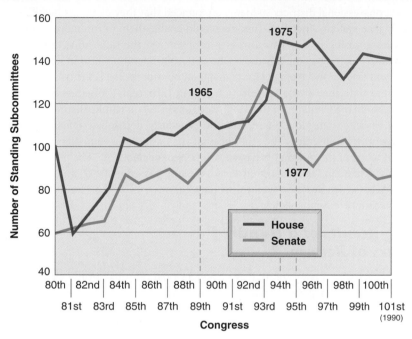

Source: Sula P. Richardson and Susan Schjelderup, "Standing Committee Structure and Assignments: House and Senate" (Congressional Research Service, March 12, 1982). Updated by and reprinted from Steven S. Smith and Christopher J. Deering, *Committees in Congress.* Washington, D.C.: Congressional Quarterly Press, 1990, p. 43.

Reforming Campaign Finance

Campaign finance reform from the mid- to late 1970s made it possible to channel interest-group money directly into individual campaign accounts, further weakening the leverage of parties over members. Since these reforms have already been discussed in Chapters 8 and 9, the main point here is that Congress created a system of campaign finance that enabled careerist politicians to raise large amounts of money on their own and gain even more independence from party organizations. Later reforms restored a bit of party control over the campaign purse by allowing big spenders to give large amounts of "soft money" directly to the parties.

In response to voter pressure and the threat of a grass-roots term limit movement (below), Congress tackled campaign finance reform again in the early 1990s. A spending limit bill was passed in 1992 and sent to President Bush, who vetoed it. Many of those who voted for the bill *knew* that the president would veto it and that there was not enough support to override. According to one investigative journalist: "Numerous congressional sources say that the only reason the bill got through was that everyone understood that Bush would veto it and that there weren't enough votes in either chamber to overturn the veto."[33] Despite Democratic party promises to send the same bill back to

Bill Clinton in 1993, and a large number of new legislators who were elected on a promise to clean up the mess in Washington, campaign finance was not one of the top priorities of the new 103rd Congress (1993–1994). In fact, a meeting between House Democratic leaders and sixty-three freshman Democrats produced a surprising response to President Clinton's renewed call for finance reform. Some of the members from the poorest congressional districts suddenly announced that they were less hostile to the existing finance system, since PAC funding would enable them to run more securely in districts where raising money was always a problem. At the same time, senior members from wealthy districts complained that the $600,000 spending limit in the proposed legislation was fine for the average House member, but not for the seventy-one of them who spent more than that in the last election to win their seats (nineteen House members spent more than $1 million in the 1992 elections).[34] As a result, there was much quiet political resistance inside Congress to the popularly demanded reforms, leading the above reporter to observe: "The real question isn't whether a campaign finance bill will pass, but whether the one that is passed will be real or phony."[35] The bill that eventually passed the Senate in 1993 looked little like the one passed in 1992, and its tougher limits on PACs (which are more central to political survival in the House) brought sharp criticisms from House members.

The Results of a Hundred Years of Reform

What was the net result of all these congressional reforms? In the view of many observers, the national legislative agenda has become more fragmented, while party control of the process was further weakened, and interest groups have gained more points of access to Congress than ever before.[36] Those who feel that machines and political bosses are inherently bad—as did the authors of *The Federalist* so long ago, and most Americans ever since—can rejoice that the subcommittee and party reforms probably put an end to the tradition of grand Capitol Hill power brokers such as legendary Speaker of the House Sam Rayburn, or his student, Senate Majority Leader Lyndon Johnson (who may have suffered a power cut when he became president). But for those who like the idea of strong political parties and coherent programs of public policy, the reforms of Congress have reduced the chances of those as well. Voters seem to like the idea of more independent representatives and more democracy within parties, yet few seem to like the results. The latest congressional reform idea is one being imposed from the outside by the voters themselves.

Term Limits: Reform from the Outside

As explained in Chapter 10, many states permit voter initiatives on the ballot. In more and more of those states, voters have expressed their conflicting feelings about Congress by going to the ballot box and dropping in a vote for their favorite representative, along with a vote to limit the term in office for that same representative. Speaker of the House Thomas Foley rushed back to his home state of Washington to help defeat a term limit initiative in 1991, but failed to stop another initiative that passed in 1992. Foley's argument against term limits was simple: "I have to face the electorate every two years. If people want to force me out of office, they can do it, by vote."[37]

Discontent with Congress runs deep when loyal supporters talk about sacrificing—for the good of the system—a powerful representative like Foley, who had served his district for over a quarter century. That was the talk inside the Two Geezers' Deli in Spokane, Washington, in the heart of Foley's district. Said Stephen Portch, one of the owners of Two Geezers: "I cast my first vote ever for Tom Foley and he's been just a great, a fantastic congressman. But I'm going to vote for term limits. If that means losing the clout that Tom Foley has given us, so be it. Clout isn't everything."[38] A Spokane barber named Bob Moore added this opinion: "I think it would be very foolish for us to lose Tom Foley, but something needs to be done. [Referring to televised hearings of the Judiciary Committee] When I saw Senator Kennedy and that old gentleman from the South—what's his name? Senator Thurmond—I said, 'My God we've got to get those people out of there.'"[39]

In 1992, Washington voters joined voters in thirteen other states (representing 35 percent of the electorate) in passing limits of different sorts: Arizona, Arkansas, California, Florida, Michigan, Missouri, Nebraska, North Dakota, Ohio, Oregon, South Dakota, and Wyoming. The most common limits were twelve years for senators and anywhere from six to twelve years for representatives. In earlier elections in 1990, voters in Colorado set the national term limit precedent in motion. A previous California initiative applied to state legislators and cleared the first of many legal hurdles when the state Supreme Court voted to accept it as "reasonable" protection from an "entrenched, dynastic" legislature.[40] It remains to be seen how the Supreme Court will finally interpret the constitutionality of states setting limits on national offices when different senators and representatives file suits as they hit their limits.

Are term limits a good idea? Many voters clearly think so, but they might change their minds after reading this chapter. If members of Congress and the public have become discouraged with Congress because of too much independence and too little internal discipline, term limits seem tailormade to increase these problems. A more principled objection to term limits has been raised by nationally syndicated columnist David Broder, who contends that if democracy means anything, it must involve accountability: Citizens have to think about their leaders, evaluate them, and make hard decisions in each case. Term limits are, in effect, a "no-brainer" for democracy, a sort of automatic pilot which allows the citizen to avoid hard choices, while sending a bad signal to officials that they will not be rewarded even if they do a good job. Says Broder:

> The Founders believed that elections were the proper device for the discharge of these mutual responsibilities. By introducing an alternative, effortless way of changing officeholders, term limits kill an incentive for officials to serve well. They also tell citizens that they can have the benefits of democracy without any exercise of vigilance over their elected officials. Term limits promise an effortless republic—democracy without active citizenship. That promise is dangerously false.[41]

The problem may be that Americans have grown up with a system designed to run on automatic pilot perhaps more than any other in the world. Add to this the strong cultural belief in limiting the power of institutions under almost any conditions, and it is easy to see the appeal of term limits, even if they end up accomplishing just the opposite of their intent. Perhaps the greatest recommendation for term limits is that even if they are ineffective, they send a clear and scary signal to Congress that something had better be done to change the way it works. Another round of internal reforms is on the horizon.

The Power Structure of Congress Revisited

The result of one hundred years of reforms is far greater democracy and political independence *inside* the American legislature, which may have lessened the chances of Congress passing broad, sustained, and coherent legislative programs. And so, we come full circle, returning to the image of an individualistic, fragmented institution which many Americans condemn for failing to address a broad social and economic agenda. Yet we return to this point with a much better understanding of how all of this came about, and why it works the way it does.

As explained in the opening of the chapter, the easy media story on Congress is the story of scandal and corruption. For reasons that you learned in Chapter 11, it is easier for the media to tell the story of corruption than the more complex story of how power works inside Congress. Not surprisingly, most people see the problem with Congress as involving some vague sort of corruption, when the more important problem may be a power outage (more like a brown-out) inside the institution.

Consider a provocative and slightly disturbing possibility. The media and public preoccupation with corruption aside, this may be the cleanest Congress has ever been. Going back to the Continental Congress before the Constitution, members made profits from selling arms to George Washington's army and financing the deals at public expense. In the late 1800s, the Robber Barons bought and sold members of Congress as if they represented shares on some sort of political stock market. In the 1920s through the 1940s, it was accepted practice for representatives and senators to endorse commercial products such as automobile tires and cigarettes. In the age of such great power brokers as Lyndon Johnson and Sam Rayburn, after World War II, cash contributions from lobbyists were collected in plain envelopes and handed out to cooperative team players. And some of the most powerful figures in Congress in the 1970s suffered alcoholic blackouts, cavorted in public with strippers, and hired sexual companions on the public payroll. In the words of the journalist who compiled this history of corruption, "In truth . . . most close observers agree that Washington is probably cleaner than ever."[42] The trouble is that Congress may also be less able than ever to get things done, thus calling greater public attention to its shortcomings—shortcomings that are also more likely to be covered in the press than ever before.

Like it or not, the series of reforms to clean up Congress may have succeeded all too well, creating as a by-product 535 individualistic representatives with little allegiance to any particular party or program. Not surprisingly, the care and feeding of individual lawmakers has become the principle focus of Congress, above parties, programs, ideological blocs, or broad efforts to win public favor. Political scientist Richard Fenno has noticed this tendency for almost all of the organizational structures of Congress to promote highly individualized uses of institutional power:

> Neither body is organized in hierarchical—or even well coordinated—patterns of decisionmaking. Agreements are reached by some fairly subtle forms of mutual adjustment—by negotiation, bargaining, and compromise. And interpersonal relations—of respect, confidence, trust—are crucial building blocks. The members of Congress, in pursuit of their individual desires, have thus created an institution that is internally quite complex. Its structure and processes are, therefore, very difficult to grasp from the outside.[43]

The overall shift from centralized to decentralized power in Congress becomes easier to grasp if we summarize the factors discussed in this chapter. It turns out that every major area of power inside Congress has shifted politically in the direction of more individual power and less central control and coordination of the legislative process:

- THE CAREER SYSTEM: Members of Congress are more independent, with their own means of supporting careers (media skills, campaign finance, personal relations with voters). The career system is so established that even the parties offer services that promote individual careers (public relations workshops, television production assistance, pollsters, election campaign seminars).

- CRUMBLING TRADITIONS: The apprentice system that built strong committees and parties is all but dead. Other traditions that still thrive (such as reciprocity and debating rules) do not promote unity in the same way.

- THE PROLIFERATION OF SUBCOMMITTEES: More subcommittees mean more specialized legislation and less central coordination. Although the number of subcommittees has declined from the peak of the mid-1970s, roughly half the members of the House and 90 percent of the Senate chair one or more committees or subcommittees.

- PARTY DISCIPLINE: More independent subcommittees, weaker committees, and more participation in selecting internal party leadership means less discipline and more individual independence.

- CONGRESSIONAL REFORMS: Reforms of party machines, internal party government, committee and subcommittee selection and procedures, staff, campaign financing, and term limits all reinforce the above tendencies.

Our political system framework of *culture*, *institutions*, and *power* simplifies these political forces operating inside Congress. Perhaps Americans find the idea of more independent representatives and less powerful institutions comfortable *culturally*, but it is worth considering that an *institution* like Congress that is already limited by constitutional design (as noted in Chapter 12) may require greater concentration of power *within the institution* to make it work. The question, of course, is what kind of *power* is most desirable? If voters and parties could agree to sacrifice some of the pork barreling and service delivery and avoid some of the narrower interest-group pressures, a basis for *majoritarian* politics organized around a broader social agenda might emerge. Otherwise, the future will look much like the present, with unstable voter-party coalitions sending few clear signals to Congress from the outside, leaving politics inside Congress to be driven by a combination of *pluralist* (interest group) and *elitist* (business and high-level lobbying) forces. Armed with these insights about why Congress is organizationally weak, readers of this book may now be able to think differently about current citizen pressures for more reforms.

Key Terms

individual career calculations

the old apprenticeship system

the new career management
system

individual sources of power in
Congress

media, importance of in modern
careers

norms and customs in Congress

similarities and differences in
House and Senate norms

reciprocity

respect

rules for debates

filibuster

House Rules Committee

committees, appointment to and
organization of

types of committees: standing/select/joint/conference

election of committee chairs

how committee assignments are
made

majority and minority party
membership on committees

party organization in the House
and Senate

party discipline, methods of, and
obstacles to

role of parties in the legislative
process

A CITIZEN'S QUESTION

Term Limits and Other Reforms

Can Congress be made more responsive through term limits or other reforms? Although term limits appear to be the most popular citizens' response to reforming Congress, there are reasons to be skeptical that they will solve the institution's internal political problems. In addition to the arguments above, citizens might consider that term limit initiatives have been fueled by national interest organizations with large bank accounts. Businesses, trade associations, and other interests are betting they will have even more clout in a Congress of novices who are even more desperate for campaign money than before.[44]

But what other way do citizens have to get Congress to change? One reform that might open the door to others is to press for campaign finance reform. Breaking the ties between PACs and incumbents and increasing the levels of public funding for all national offices might be a better way to stimulate the competitiveness in elections that supporters of term limits seek. In addition, shutting off the flow of PAC money to individual politicians might restore closer ties between legislators and their parties, which would be the natural organizations to receive and distribute the public campaign financing, as they do in most other countries.

Both parties claim to support campaign finance reform. As explained earlier, the Democratic party passed a bill during the 102nd (1991–1992) Congress that was vetoed by President Bush as being too carefully designed to the political needs of the Democrats. Bill Clinton promised to sign that legislation if the 103rd Congress (1993–1994) sent it back, but the realistic expectation of passage led both chambers of Congress to redraft their bills, including in them more self-interested provisions. Whatever the outcome of the latest round of reform, citizens will do well to think independently about any campaign finance package (and, for that matter, any other internal congressional reform) passed. Since there are internal political pressures in Congress that work against serious finance reforms, citizens must think critically about reform efforts and keep the pressure on.

At the same time, citizens need to be realistic about politicians' needs to finance their campaigns. A newspaper editorial framed the reform issues like this:

> The need to restore integrity to political life is obvious. And the best way to begin is at the top, with a massive overhaul of Congress's odious system of campaign financing. . . .
>
> Greed is one enemy of reform. Some members balk at even a modest limit on contributions from special interest political-action committees. Fear is another. Some members are too cowardly to vote for tax dollars for public financing.
>
> Sure, a lot of Americans don't like the idea of using tax dollars for politicians' campaigns. But it is the only practical way to reduce reliance on favor-seekers; and so far, House Speaker Thomas Foley has not tried very hard to persuade the public that it is the right course.
>
> If the polls are right, the public would welcome almost any reasonable alternative to business as usual. If congressmen genuinely care about their institution, and not just themselves, they have no choice but serious reform.[45]

Do you agree with this approach? Perhaps you want to aim your reform thinking at slightly different, more concrete targets such as the career system, the parties, the committee system inside Congress, or other power centers inside the institution described in this chapter. There are many ways in which the individualized power system of Congress might be reformed. At this point you can probably imagine different reform strategies and think about how to promote them. When you come up with a plan, see if there are public interest groups (Chapter 8) you can join who are thinking along similar lines. Or, simply pick up the phone and dial the number at the end of Chapter 12.

majority and minority party
  membership on committees

party organization in the House
  and Senate

party discipline, methods of, and
  obstacles to

role of parties in the legislative
  process

role of parties on committees

party leadership

redistricting and gerrymandering

reforms of Congress

  the iron law of oligarchy

  reforming the party machine

  reforms in the committee system

  staff reform

  campaign finance

  term limits

  reasons why these reforms
    increased individual rather
    than institutional power

Suggested Readings

Cook, Timothy. *Making Laws and Making News: Media Strategies in the U.S. House of Representatives.* Washington, D.C.: Brookings Institution, 1989.

Fiorina, Morris. *Congress: Keystone of the Washington Establishment.* New Haven: Yale University Press, 1977.

Hibbing, John R. *Congressional Careers: Contours of Life in the U.S. House of Representatives.* Chapel Hill: University of North Carolina Press, 1991.

Munson, Richard. *The Cardinals of Capitol Hill: The Men and Women Who Control Government Spending.* New York: Grove Press, 1993.

Rieselbach, Leroy. *Congressional Reform.* Washington, D.C.: Congressional Quarterly Press, 1986.

Sinclair, Barbara. *Majority Leadership in the U.S. House.* Baltimore: Johns Hopkins University Press, 1983.

Will, George. *Restoration: Congress, Term Limits, and the Recovery of Deliberative Democracy.* New York: The Free Press/Macmillan, 1992.

• • •

Stripped to its essentials, the Presidency requires two cardinal political skills: the ability to appeal directly to mass publics, at home and abroad, and the ability to negotiate with rival leaders holding independent bases of power.
—*JAMES MACGREGOR BURNS*

• • •

What it takes to become President has nothing to do with what it takes to be President.
—*RICHARD ROSE*

• • •

My country has in its wisdom contrived for me the most insignificant office that ever the invention of man contrived or his imagination conceived.
—*JOHN ADAMS* (*upon becoming vice president*)

• • •

The Executive:

Presidential Power and

National Leadership

- **THE GREATEST POLITICAL JUGGLING ACT**
- **PRESIDENTS, PUBLICS, AND POWER**
  The Opinion Rally
  Presidential Approval
- **TOO MANY RESPONSIBILITIES, TOO LITTLE POWER?**
- **THE HISTORY OF AN OFFICE**
  Going Public
- **THE VICE PRESIDENT**
- **WHAT PRESIDENTS DO: THE CONSTITUTIONAL JOB DESCRIPTION**
  The Powers of Office
- **THE REST OF THE JOB: TRADITIONAL PRESIDENTIAL ROLES**
  Chief National Symbol
  Party Leader
- **THE PRESIDENT IN ACTION: FORMAL POWERS VS. INSIDE POLITICS**
  The Executive Arena
  The Legislative Arena
  The Military and Foreign Policy Arena
- **THE SECRET OF SUCCESS: THE POWER TO PERSUADE**
  The Media Spotlight
- **THE PRESIDENTIAL CHARACTER**
  Searching for the Ideal Presidential Personality
- **TOO MANY RESPONSIBILITIES, TOO LITTLE POWER, REVISITED**
- **A CITIZEN'S QUESTION: Presidential Performance**
- **KEY TERMS**
- **SUGGESTED READINGS**

The roles of the president are many: party leader, chief national politician, the nation's representative abroad, legislative promoter, chief economic power broker, manager of the world's biggest budget, and chief of the federal bureaucracy, among others. The president is also a barometer of the national mood, as the polls record public approval and disapproval of how all of these jobs are being handled. As discussed in Chapter 11, the president is the most covered individual politician in the country, by far. Not only are more reporters assigned to the president than to probably any other individual in the world, but presidents quickly learn that success in office requires constant attention to using the news media to advance political goals and to avoid looking like a failure.

Many presidents have not succeeded in handling all of their many tasks to the satisfaction of the press and the public. Following Bill Clinton's election in 1992, the news contained a great deal of advice from members of past administrations about how not to be president. One story ran under the headline HOW NOT TO BE PRESIDENT: CLINTON HOPES TO LEARN FROM CARTER'S BLUNDERS.[1]

Jimmy Carter was the last Democrat in the White House before Bill Clinton. It is generally agreed among pundits that Carter ran a politically smart election campaign in 1976, using many of the techniques of media management and political marketing discussed in Chapter 10, but dropped the political football once in power. President Carter rejected many of his advisers' suggestions about continuing to rally public support for his programs. Even more damaging was Carter's failure to develop solid political relations with leaders in Congress before sending his legislative wish list to Capitol Hill. A complex energy package became bogged down almost immediately. From there, things got worse. Relations between the Oval Office and the bureaucracy soured as many cabinet officers and their deputies

went off on their own agendas with little loyalty to the man who had appointed them. Things fell apart during a frustrating foreign policy debacle in which the American embassy in Iran was raided, and hostages were held by the revolutionary government there for 444 days, during which Carter's unsuccessful efforts to gain their release were examined daily in the news. By the end of his term, Jimmy Carter appeared to be something of a hostage, trapped inside the Oval Office by events beyond his control. His public approval ratings plunged, leading to his defeat by Ronald Reagan in 1980.

How did the Clinton team attempt to launch a more successful administration? They interviewed dozens of top Carter administration officials and asked them what they would do if they could do it all over again. They studied the record of the Carter administration and searched for points where things went off track. Then they put together a simple political game plan that was described like this in "How Not to Be President":

> From the conversations with Carter's advisers and from their own analysis of how the early days of the Carter administration worked, they have distilled the lessons learned to a succinct list: Keep the campaign alive to maintain support for the president's agenda; concentrate on a few big things but don't overreach; work with Congress; don't roll over when challenged; and confront the establishment but don't just bash it. . . .
>
> "The most important lesson we take is that it's important not to let your political apparatus become disengaged from the governing apparatus," says George Stephanopoulos, Clinton's communications director.[2]

As it turned out, Stephanopoulos did not last long as communications director. While he was undoubtedly right that presidential success is more than just giving orders and expecting them to be carried out,

the lessons of the Carter years still did not seem to sink in. To be sure, getting the job done as president involves using many of the political skills required to get elected: generating favorable news coverage, maintaining support among many voter groups, and sustaining the image of being a capable leader. However, the demands of the job go far beyond running an "endless campaign," Clinton discovered. The new president quickly found himself floundering in the complex power game of Washington.

In addition to keeping up their base of public support, presidents must work out good relations with Congress and find ways of keeping the bureaucracy in line. All of which explains why the job is so challenging and why so few presidents leave office with their popularity intact. This chapter explores what makes the presidency such a difficult job and suggests ways in which citizens can think about judging presidential performance.

Presidents, Publics, and Power

The modern presidential power game involves coordinating public opinion campaigns with shrewd but discreet political maneuvering with Congress and the bureaucracy. When presidents are popular, their ability to pressure other powerful Washington players goes up. At the same time, failure to make the right overtures behind the scenes can alienate powerful members of Congress or bureaucratic chiefs. When the Washington elite turns against the president, so does the press, making it more difficult to court public approval. In his early days in office, Bill Clinton neglected to cultivate key Washington players on matters from homosexuals in the military to tax policy. As a result, he began to lose political battles. He soon lost favor with the media and began to plummet in the polls. What this means is that while presidents can use their office as a "bully pulpit," in the words of Theodore Roosevelt, to rally public support and promote their ideas and programs, they also risk losing popular support while they fight a daily battle with the press and Washington power brokers to rescue their political agendas. The modern presidency has become an edgy game of press management, public relations, dealmaking, and opinion polling that few presidents have mastered successfully. As Bill Clinton learned, even an elaborate public relations strategy can flop if it is not paired with smooth back room politics in Washington.

Ronald Reagan, with his skilled communications team, was the modern master of public relations (recall the discussion in Chapter 11 of communications strategies in the Reagan White House). Yet Reagan barely rescued his presidency from criticism of his "hands-off" management style following the Iran-*contra* affair, leaving town with an approval rating just above 50 percent. We have to go back to Dwight Eisenhower, president from 1953 to 1961, to find a president who left office with a public support level above 60 percent. Lyndon Johnson (1963–1969) absorbed the shocks of the Vietnam War and massive social unrest and saw his ratings plunge from over 70 percent to below 40 percent at the time he decided not to run for another term in 1968. After a generally successful first term as president, Richard Nixon (1969–1974) fell from public grace and resigned from office during the Watergate scandal with barely 25 percent of the public supporting him.

Jimmy Carter enjoyed the approval of well over 60 percent of the public during the **honeymoon period** in which people rally around their new leader and give him the benefit of the doubt. Like every president, Carter's honeymoon eventually ended, but he did little to stop his public ratings from crashing afterwards. His popularity plunged steadily into the 30-percent range over the course of four years. Carter practiced poor public relations, failed to cultivate relations with Congress, let his own cabinet get out of control, and endured the media spectacle of 444 days in which the public was reminded that he had failed to win the release of American citizens in Iran.

President John F. Kennedy addresses the nation via television and radio on October 22, 1962, announcing that he has ordered a naval blockade (which he delicately termed a "quarantine") of Castro's Cuba, following the discovery (by reconnaissance airplane flights) of Soviet-made nuclear missiles there. A surge of presidential support usually meets such a crisis. The Cuban Missile Crisis—which many believe to be the closest the world has ever come to an all-out nuclear war—led to a rally of opinion for Kennedy that lasted well over six months after Soviet ruler Nikita Khrushchev agreed to withdraw the weapons.

Probably no president has felt both the elation of public support and the sting of disapproval more than George Bush.[3] The honeymoon between Mr. Bush and the public was a long one, sustained by the end of the Cold War, a breathless year of world travel and arms-cutback summits. His approval ratings were above 75 percent and still rising well into the first year, long after the honeymoon is over for most presidents. Just as grumblings were beginning to be heard about a flat economy, Mr. Bush invaded Panama to oust the drug-running dictator Manuel Noriega and benefited from a public opinion *rally,* the term used to describe the boost of public support that often follows dramatic presidential actions and responses to crises.

The Opinion Rally

Each of the last ten presidents has experienced the surge of public support surrounding a crisis event—something that researchers call an opinion rally.[4] When George Bush ordered the bombing of Iraq in 1991, his surge of 18 points was one of the largest rallies ever recorded. Jimmy Carter initially received a 19-point boost in the polls after American hostages were seized in Teheran in 1979. Many of these rallies last for long periods of time: thirty weeks for Franklin Roosevelt after the bombing of Pearl Harbor; thirty-one weeks for John Kennedy after the announcement that Soviet nuclear missiles were aimed at the United States from the island of Cuba in 1962, and thirty weeks following the hostage crisis that occupied the Carter administration in 1979. However, as many presidents have also discovered, rallies can turn sour, and public support can shift into hostility and criticism very quickly. After more than a year of frustration in failing to gain the release of the hostages, Mr. Carter fell to near-record lows in the public approval column. After being pronounced unbeatable for reelection after the Persian Gulf War in 1991, George Bush received intense criticism from political opponents on his domestic policies and watched his approval ratings plummet into the 30-percent range during the primary election campaign of 1992. Rallies and dips in presidential approval suggest that high public expectations and emotional reactions surround the situations in which presidents act. As explained in Chapter 6, large opinion-support levels can crash in the face of criticism from opponents.

"It's Bill Clinton . . . He wants to know how he's doing."

The advent of "snap polls" and high-tech surveying techniques has led to an almost constant taking of the emotional temperature of the American public. Yet much of the modern presidency's power derives less from an institutional base than from the president's ability to bring public pressure to bear on senators, representatives, and other elected officials.

Presidential Approval

The political importance of public approval and the difficulty of maintaining it help explain why Bill Clinton's staff immediately went to work on a game plan to keep their boss on top of the polls, while staying in tune with Congress and his own bureaucracy. Yet after six months in office, Clinton had a lower approval rating than any other modern president at the six-month mark—including Gerald Ford after he pardoned Richard Nixon in the aftermath of the Watergate scandal. The great presidential juggling act involves so many responsibilities, all conducted with such intense media scrutiny, that many students of the modern presidency have concluded that being a successful president is a nearly impossible task. When presidents begin the slide into unpopularity, their leverage over Congress and ability to promote their policies usually falls off as well. Figure 14.1 illustrates the trends in presidential approval since the beginning of regular polling in the 1930s. (These trends are yearly averages, and therefore do not reflect the very highest and lowest points different presidents reached in particular polls.)

The fact that presidential approval is so changeable suggests that it is a dangerous basis for power and influence. Yet much of what modern presidents do depends on persuading people to follow them, rallying support for their programs, and using that

FIGURE 14.1

Trends in Public Approval for the Presidents, 1938–1993

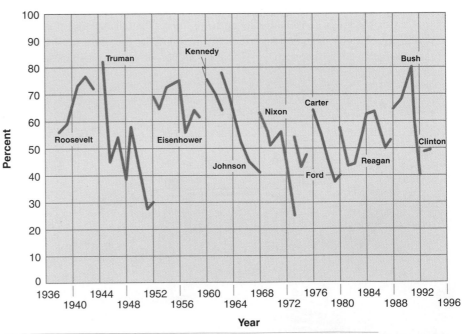

Note: Averaged by year. The 1993 figure reflects the starting point for Bill Clinton in 1993. Based on Gallup polls asking the question: "Do you approve or disapprove of the way (*president's name*) is handling his job as president?"

Adapted from Harold W. Stanley and Richard G. Niemi, *Vital Statistics on American Politics.* Washington, D.C.: CQ Press, 1992, p. 278.

The President as Focal Point of the System

14.1

From the early days of the republic, the president has been the chief national symbol, an emotional focus for both the ideals and the conflicts within the *political culture*. People expect presidents to be all things, from heroes to representatives of often competing national values. One of the great ironies of the American system is that precisely because of the singular visibility of this office, the founders placed severe *institutional limits* on its powers. The Constitution gives the president significant powers in military decision-making and foreign relations, but little leverage beyond the veto in the central legislative process of government. In parliamentary systems, by contrast, the chief executive generally heads the majority party in the legislature and draws a cabinet from key legislative players.

As a result of this curious combination of grand public expectations and serious institutional constraints in the American system, presidents must engage with virtually every level of *power in society* to be effective:

• Continual efforts must be made to maintain *majority approval,* both to create the appearance of success and to maintain the threat of voter punishment against opponents.
• Cultivation of interest groups is important. As the core of *pluralist power* in the system, groups can organize to promote or block legislative programs. As the power of groups has increased in the system, so have efforts by presidents to cultivate their support.
• The support of powerful business *elites* is crucial. The leaders of industry, banking and trade are important for the all-important confidence of the business community on which markets and public support ultimately depend. In addition, elites often provide useful connections with power brokers in Congress and interest associations.

With these political constraints inside the system operating on the presidency, it is not surprising that many presidents have left office without fulfilling the great expectations placed on them when elected. More than any other political actor, the president must engage creatively and effectively with a broad range of cultural, institutional, and social power factors.

support to pressure Congress to go along. The problem, as illustrated in the previous section, is that the foundation of presidential support is often very weak, leaving room for opponents to attack presidents, for Congress to work out its own agenda, and for the media to turn yesterday's heroic leader into tomorrow's scapegoat. All of which suggests that being the nation's most powerful symbol and most visible figure has its limits, limits that may create problems for strong and long-lasting initiatives from any president. As explained in "Inside the System" Box 14.1, these limits on presidential politics are rooted in key features of the political system itself.

Too Many Responsibilities, Too Little Power?

In the pages that follow, we see that the constitutional powers of the president are not as extensive or well defined as those of Congress. Yet over the years, the executive branch has become the center of government—partly because of the growth of the bureaucracy that runs so many programs under the president's command, and partly because presidents have become full partners with Congress in many areas of national policy. With so much public and media attention focused on them, presidents often become the national lightning rods for successes and failures in many areas of politics. As noted in Box 14.1, however, the constitutional design of the office creates unique limits on presidential power that are not placed on chief executives (presidents or prime ministers) in most other political systems. In France, for example, the design of government gives the president much greater input into the legislative process, as described in "How We Compare" Box 14.2

Presidential scholars worry that the president has too many roles to play and too little formal power to carry them out, while being too dependent on the shifting tides of public approval to guarantee success in any of them. Even presidents who run away from the confusion and conflicts of domestic politics and into the realm of world affairs find that the area of foreign policy does not offer automatic congressional approval or easy public recognition. The national fetish with presidential popularity may even spell dangerous changes in the nature of democracy itself, as Benjamin Barber warns ominously that "democratic politics thus becomes a matter of what leaders do, something that citizens watch rather than something [citizens] do."[5]

Is presidential popularity too elusive and shifting to be taken as seriously as we do? Does the president have too many roles and too little real power to carry them out consistently or effectively? Have the media created a presidential spectacle that leads to unrealistic expectations on the part of passive citizen-spectators? These are some of the big questions that surround the modern presidency and, according to some observers, signal a new era of change in the role of the executive branch.

The History of an Office

As noted in Box 14.1, the institutional design of the presidency has created a great deal of tension within the political system. The Founders never intended the president to be at the center of power in government. Most of the time at the Constitutional Convention was spent designing a Congress, which, as the lawmaking branch and the most broadly representative institution, was regarded as the proper center of political power. The common assumption was that the president would be something of a spiritual leader who would carry out the will of Congress, represent the nation abroad, and keep peace among the political factions. Although periods of crisis and change elevated a few of the early presidents such as Andrew Jackson and Abraham Lincoln to positions of important national leadership, Congress was firmly in command of the national destiny, for better or worse, until the twentieth century. Many observers mark the emergence of the modern presidency in the 1930s with Franklin Roosevelt, who governed the country through the Great Depression and during the Second World War. (Some argue that Woodrow Wilson was the first modern president because of his leadership in World War I and his work to rally public opinion for the League of Nations.)

For most of the period of congressional dominance, the office of the president and the executive bureaucracy were relatively small, with few employees and resources to do the president's bidding until after the 1930s. Recall from Chapter 4 that the era of dual federalism with its greater state powers left the executive with relatively few national programs to manage. The rise of cooperative federalism during the Great Depression of the 1930s required more centralized executive branch control over more national programs. On the international scene, the rise of the United States as a world power began at the turn of the twentieth century and did not fully develop the foreign policy role of the president until World War II and the Cold War that followed. In short, the presidency has changed dramatically in the last half century. As with most change, the grand forces of history and society are responsible. A combination of social upheaval at home and world wars abroad forced presidents to the center of the political stage in the 1930s and have kept them there ever since.

The Presidency in France

14.2

France has developed an interesting combination of parliamentary and presidential democracy. The president of France is elected directly by the voters, unlike most parliamentary systems in which the chief executive (called the prime minister) is the leader of the party coalition in parliament that has enough seats to organize a government. The balance of power in the French system is tipped in favor of the president by giving this elected leader the power to appoint the cabinet (including a chief minister called the premier). Cabinet members often come from the parliament, called the French National Assembly, but they must give up their legislative seats, which gives the president even more influence over them. Finally, French presidents have a number of other formal powers that give them a political edge in governing:

- The power to organize the bureaucracy and the cabinet to best suit the president's political agenda and administrative style
- The power to call a national referendum on issues
- The power to declare a state of emergency which suspends the power of the National Assembly to veto presidential decisions

To keep some balance of power in this system, the National Assembly can force the cabinet to resign. The President, in turn, can dissolve the Assembly and call for new national elections as a means of overcoming governmental gridlock.

SOURCE: Michael G. Roskin, *Countries and Concepts*, 2nd ed. Englewood Cliffs, N.J.: Prentice-Hall, 1986, pp. 92–93.

The hallmark of the modern era is the activist president. As noted above, the demands to protect people from the Great Depression were addressed by Franklin D. Roosevelt, who seized the opportunity to become the first activist president, going directly to the public to rally support for programs that would eventually make the federal government a partner in many areas of state life. As political scientist Fred Greenstein described it, "FDR . . . established the practice of advocating, backing, and engaging in the politics of winning support for legislation. By the end of his long tenure, presidential activism had come to be taken for granted, if not universally approved."[6]

Going Public

The idea of presidents appealing directly to the people for support with their political agendas has been called going public. As explained above, going public is a late development in the evolution of the presidency.[7] Franklin Roosevelt with his frequent radio "fireside chats" was the first president to go over the heads of Congress and the Court and rally public opinion directly on a regular basis—something that has become an important part of the contemporary presidency. In fact, Roosevelt became the first to show up at a party convention (in 1932) to accept the nomination in person and rally his political party for the fight ahead. For much of the nation's history before that, it was regarded as unseemly for the chief executive to beg for public support or become personally soiled in the grimy business of party politics. As discussed in Chapter 10, few candidates in the first hundred years of presidential elections did any campaigning on their own behalf, and only in the last fifty years has it become customary for candidates and presidents to sharpen their rhetoric and go after each other and their political opponents directly.[8]

During the evolution of this activist phase of the presidency, the use of conventional communication channels such as press conferences has actually declined, as illustrated

TABLE 14.1

Presidential News Conferences with White House Correspondents, 1929–1991

PRESIDENT	AVERAGE NUMBER OF PRESS CONFERENCES PER MONTH	TOTAL NUMBER OF PRESS CONFERENCES
Herbert Hoover (1929-1933)	5.6	268
Franklin Roosevelt (1933-1945)	6.9	998
Harry Truman (1945-1953)	3.6	334
Dwight Eisenhower (1953-1961)	2.0	193
John Kennedy (1961-1963)	1.9	65
Lyndon Johnson (1963-1969)	2.2	135
Richard Nixon (1969-1974)	0.6	39
Gerald Ford (1974-1977)	1.3	39
Jimmy Carter (1977-1981)	1.2	59
Ronald Reagan (1981-1989)	0.6	53
George Bush (1989-1991)* *As of June 15, 1991.	1.5	45

SOURCES: Hoover and Truman through Carter: compiled by the editors from *Public Papers of the President* (Washington, D.C.: U.S. Government Printing Office); Roosevelt: Elizabeth Denier, comp., "List of FDR Press Conferences" (Hyde Park, N.Y.: Franklin Delano Roosevelt Library, n.d. [1991]); Reagan and Bush: compiled by the editors from *Congressional Quarterly Weekly Report*. Reprinted from Harold W. Stanley and Richard G. Niemi, *Vital Statistics on American Politics*, 3rd ed. Washington, D.C.: CQ Press, 1992, p. 59.

FIGURE 14.2

Public Appearances by Presidents, 1929–1990
(Yearly Averages for First Three Years of First Term)

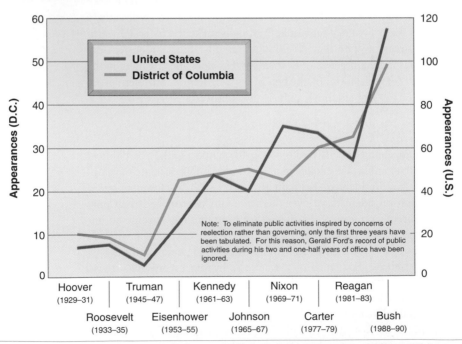

SOURCES: Data for Hoover, Roosevelt, Truman, Eisenhower, Nixon, and Carter are from William W. Lammers, "Presidential Attention-Focusing Activities," in *The President and the American Public*, ed. Doris A. Graber (Philadelphia: Institute for the Study of Human Issues, 1982), Tables 6-2 and 6-3, 154-156. Data for Kennedy, Johnson, Reagan, and Bush are from *Public Papers of the Presidents* series. Reprinted from Samuel Kernell, *Going Public*. Washington, D.C.: CQ Press, 1993, p. 98.

in Table 14.1. At the same time, the numbers of public appearances by presidents have increased (see Figure 14.2), as have the numbers of presidential addresses on minor topics and to more selected audiences (as shown in Figure 14.3). These trends clearly show that presidents increasingly prefer to go over the heads of the press directly to the people, often designing their public appearances as media events that use the press as a passive channel to reach larger publics.

Among recent presidents, Ronald Reagan took the art of going public to new heights, resulting in great success in reaching the people, but only mixed success in getting his agenda through Congress. "Inside the System" Box 14.3, on page 512, discusses the increasing tendency to "go public," which many scholars see as the greatest change in the modern era of the presidency.

The turbulent history of George Bush's public approval record suggests that Mr. Bush could have paid more attention to going public at important moments when his popularity suffered. As explained in Chapters 10 and 11, neither his 1992 election campaign nor his press relations while in office were geared to managing his public image as effectively

FIGURE 14.3

Presidential Addresses, 1929–1990
(Yearly Averages for First Three Years of First Term)

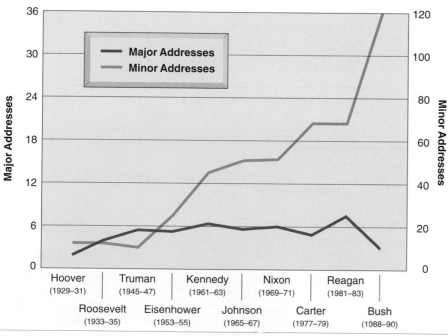

Note: To eliminate public activities inspired by concerns of reelection rather than governing, only the first three years have been tabulated. For this reason, Gerald Ford's record of public activities during his two and one-half years of office have been ignored.

*The Reagan entry includes only television addresses. With radio included, Reagan averaged 24 addresses a year.

SOURCES: Data for Hoover, Roosevelt, Truman, Eisenhower, Nixon and Carter are from William W. Lammers, "Presidential Attention-Focusing Activities," in *The President and the American Public*, ed. Doris A. Graber (Philadelphia: Institute for the Study of Human Issues, 1982), Table 6-1, 152. Data for Kennedy, Johnson, Reagan, and Bush are from *Public Papers of the Presidents* series. Reprinted from Samuel Kernell, *Going Public*. Washington, D.C.: CQ Press, 1993, p. 94.

Going Public: A Way of Expanding Weak Institutional Powers

14.3

Many presidential scholars believe that the constitutional limits on executive powers leave presidents with too little power to do the many jobs that the public and the political demands on the modern office require. In the modern era since Roosevelt (some would cite Woodrow Wilson), presidents have found ways of creating more power by mobilizing majority opinion in support of their programs. The public has become a major (but not always reliable) ally in pressuring Congress to cooperate with the executive agenda. Few have been more successful than Franklin Roosevelt and Ronald Reagan in going public. Although from different parties and different eras, Roosevelt and Reagan understood the ingredients of effective communication with the people. Both talked personally with the public through the media, Roosevelt using radio "chats" on a regular basis, and Reagan all the mass media, particularly television.

By going public, a president invites the people inside the political process to help do battle with political opponents, including Congress. Reagan, for example, objected strenuously when Congress attempted to exercise its role in foreign policy during arms control negotiations between himself and Mikhail Gorbachev. The president called on the public to pressure Congress to stop limiting his options. In a national radio address reminiscent of the old Roosevelt fireside chats, Reagan urged Americans to retaliate against members of Congress who "trifle with our national security." He threatened lawmakers with public retaliation: "The members of Congress should know that as I said at the beginning, the people are the experts in any democracy, and you will hold accountable those who, for the sake of partisan advantage, trifle with our national security and the chances for peace and freedom."*

*The New York Times, October 5, 1986, p. A 1.

President Bush takes a breather at his Kennebunkport, Maine, summer home during the August 1990 deployment of U.S. military forces to Saudi Arabia following Iraq's invasion of Kuwait. After serving two terms in Congress, Bush rose to national prominence largely through a series of appointive positions (including stints as director of the CIA, U.S. ambassador to the United Nations, chairman of the Republican National Committee, and U.S. liaison to China); and he often seemed more at ease with the governing side of the presidency (especially in foreign affairs) than with its public-relations side. Slighting domestic issues and his own public relations, however, helped to cost him the 1992 election.

as possible. The contrast with Bill Clinton could not be sharper. Clinton saved his election campaign by finding ways to go public with electronic town halls, bus trips, and talk show appearances, as described in Chapter 10. Clinton also vowed to keep up those practices as an important part of his political style as president. Once in office, however, Clinton failed to lay the necessary political groundwork behind the scenes in Washington to secure key supporters and neutralize key opponents. This, combined with a number of media blunders (such as obstructing a major airport to get an expensive haircut on board Air Force One), gave the press plenty of material for negative coverage. As a result, attempts to go public were constantly self-sabotaged, leaving Mr. Clinton with what may go down as the shortest honeymoon in modern presidential history, and requiring a concerted political effort in his first year to save his presidency.

The Vice President

Through much of American history, the office of the vice president was a relatively powerless and poorly defined political outpost. Vice presidents seldom attained much prominence while in office, and they were even more likely to suffer historical neglect. As stand-ins for the president, most attempted to look busy by making occasional speeches, attending cabinet meetings, showing up on Capitol Hill in rare cameo appearances as president of the Senate, and representing the boss at funerals and political events that require high-level recognition but are not important enough for the busy president to attend.

Although the vice president might seem a natural launching point for a presidential bid, that has not been the pattern. Vice presidents are more likely to get the top job due to the death of the president than because people feel strongly enough about their record in office to elect them. In the period since 1940, Harry Truman and Lyndon Johnson made it to the top because of the deaths of their presidents, and then they went on to win elections on their own. When Richard Nixon tried to succeed Dwight Eisenhower through election in 1960, he lost and did not become president until eight years later. In the recent period, only George Bush in 1988 was able to use his vice presidency as a springboard to winning election for the next term in office.

Two major problems have darkened the political potential of the office. First, the vice president has no important constitutional powers or duties as long as the president is alive and capable of making decisions. Second, the main job requirement is not to upstage the president. Despite these obstacles to using the office to build a strong leadership image, recent vice presidents have developed greater areas of personal responsibility in office. The modern vice presidency probably began with Walter Mondale, who served as Jimmy Carter's vice president (1977–1981). Mondale was an experienced legislator and a respected Democratic party leader upon whom Carter relied for political advice and for delegation of many responsibilities. Mondale used his public visibility and party connections to run for president (unsuccessfully) in 1984.

George Bush was another active vice president. He was not given much of a public role, as the national stage was reserved for his popular boss, Ronald Reagan. However, Bush used his background as a former CIA director to become involved in intelligence issues and foreign policy. He also cultivated ties in the Republican party (he had been its national chairman), and ran successfully for president in 1988. Candidate Bush surprised many people by picking a relatively unknown senator, Dan Quayle, to be his running mate. Although Quayle had a tough time with the media and committed a number of memorable slips in public (including the misspelling of "potatoe" at a school spelling bee), he became an active member of the Bush administration and a key advisor on domestic policy. Quayle served as the presidential liaison with the national space program

In September 1992, Vice President Dan Quayle (center) *and wife Marilyn* (at right) *watch the television situation-comedy* Murphy Brown *at the home of Washington, D.C., friends. Quayle—a magnet for (often hostile) media attention from the moment he was nominated for the vice-presidency in 1988—was an earnest if somewhat inept promoter of conservative issues such as family values, and drew a firestorm of liberal criticism for suggesting that one of the TV show's plotlines glamorized illegitimacy.*

and ran the Competitiveness Council, which screened government regulations to make sure they were not placing undue burdens on business (see Chapter 15). In addition to these activities, Mr. Quayle became an assertive speaker for conservative causes, perhaps gaining widest notice when he denounced the TV show *Murphy Brown* after its title character gave birth to a child out of wedlock, a storyline he saw as glamorizing illegitimacy and thus detrimental to family values. Throughout his years as vice president, Quayle, despite hostile media coverage, positioned himself to win support from the conservative wing of the Republican party in hopes of making a presidential bid in 1996.

Al Gore positioned himself during the campaign of 1992 as a close adviser to his running mate Bill Clinton and promised to take a leading role in administration environmental policy. When Bill Clinton went public to sell the nation on his economic recovery program in 1993, he took Al Gore with him for many town hall meetings and other appearances. Later, Gore was put in charge of a major review of government spending, given the optimistic designation of "Reinventing Government." Gore also appeared likely to use the vice presidency to launch a future presidential bid—something he had tried as a U.S. senator in 1988 and failed. Dan Quayle in 1996? Al Gore in 2000? Perhaps, but the jury is still out on whether being vice president offers great advantage for those who want to be elected president someday.

What Presidents Do: The Constitutional Job Description

Despite the above concerns about too many constitutional limits, the office still has a good deal of clout to go with its duties. In fact, many of the delegates at the Constitutional Convention in Philadelphia worried that the executive was too strong, although others such as Alexander Hamilton (who personally favored an executive who would serve for a life term) convinced the majority that the lack of a strong executive was one of the main things that doomed the government under the Articles of Confederation. Most were relieved when George Washington became the first president, believing that the great commander of the Revolution would set the right tone for the nation's highest office.

The Powers of Office

The Constitution that was ratified after the Philadelphia Convention gave the president in Article II a long list of **formal** or **enumerated powers.** In the years since, presidents have expanded those powers by claiming that the spirit of the Constitution also gives them a number of implied or inherent powers necessary to getting the job done. The enumerated powers of the president include:

- executing the laws of Congress
- commanding the military
- recommending needed legislation to Congress
- vetoing legislation
- appointing judges, ambassadors, cabinet officers and others (often subject to confirmation by the Senate)
- negotiating treaties (with Senate confirmation)
- granting pardons
- calling Congress into special session to consider emergency problems.

These and other enumerated powers may seem sufficient to accomplish the job. However, many issues have come up over the years that fall outside these powers, and presidents have acted on them anyway. Recall from Chapter 3 that Congress has relied on the so-called elastic clause of the Constitution to pass laws deemed necessary and proper to do things not formally specified in the Constitution. Although there is no such clause for the executive, presidents have claimed that they have **implied** or **inherent powers** which, although not formally enumerated, are necessary for them to carry out their job. Chief among the inherent powers that have expanded the activities of the office are:

- **proclamations,** in which presidents simply proclaim the policy of the government
- **executive orders,** in which bureaucratic activities are initiated without specific legal authorization from Congress
- **executive agreements,** negotiated with foreign governments, can be as binding as **treaties,** even though presidents do not call them that or submit them for Senate approval.

The precedent for simply proclaiming government policy was set by George Washington who proclaimed the United States neutral during the war between England and France, despite strong voices on both sides who wanted formal alliances with one country or the other. Abraham Lincoln proclaimed that slaves would be freed. Lincoln also used executive orders to gain control of the national crisis surrounding the Civil War. For example, he issued an order increasing the army beyond the size legally authorized by Congress. Even when legal challenges have been raised against executive proclamations, orders, and agreements, the Supreme Court has often ruled in favor of these inherent powers of the president, giving those powers an implicit, or, as the name implies, inherent constitutional standing. In Chapter 17 we will discuss the politics behind Bill

A Presence on the World Stage

Among the most important and visible duties of the presidency are negotiating treaties and conferring with other heads of state on world affairs. *Above,* Ronald Reagan and Mikhail Gorbachev meet at a 1985 Geneva summit conference that paved the way for major nuclear-arms reduction treaties. *Below,* George Bush confers with Pope John Paul II. Full U.S.–Vatican relations were restored only in 1984, after a lapse of over a century. *At right,* Bill Clinton greets British prime minister and Conservative party leader John Major in 1993. Clinton had been elected out of voter concern over domestic issues, but was promptly confronted by crises in Russia, Iraq, and Somalia; a problematic conflict between Bosnia and Serbia; and the challenge of a major Israeli–Palestinian peace iniative.

The Players

Clinton's attempt to issue an executive order to change military policies banning homosexuals from the armed forces.

The Rest of the Job: Traditional Presidential Roles ___

In addition to the formal executive, military, and legislative responsibilities of the president, other responsibilities have evolved more out of tradition than legal requirement. However, these traditional requirements of the job can be just as important as the constitutional requirements of office. The major traditional duties of the president include being the symbolic leader of the nation and the political party leader.

Chief National Symbol

Representing the nation at state functions and playing ceremonial head or chief symbol have been traditional duties since the American Revolution broke with the idea of monarchy. Many countries still have monarchs to play this ceremonial role: England, Sweden, Belgium, and Spain, among others. Others such as Germany and Italy have largely ceremonial presidents to play head of the national family and to represent the nation in ceremonial affairs. The American president must be everything to all citizens, at once national figurehead and partisan politician. The president welcomes foreign dignitaries, presides at important dinners and ceremonies, and becomes the source of gossip and human interest by providing a surrogate "royal family" for the populace to adopt.

President Lyndon Johnson frolics on the White House lawn with his pet beagles in May of 1964. Johnson served during an era when traditional political skills such as (literally) pressing the flesh and forceful, one-on-one politicking behind the scenes were giving ground to the "cooler" skills of media manipulation. Some found LBJ's Texas drawl, homely looks, and unrefined style ill-befitting for America's head of state. New York intellectual Susan Sontag, for example, called him "the man in the White House who paws people and scratches [himself] in public," adding that "today's America, with [Governor] Ronald Reagan the new daddy of California and John Wayne chawing spare ribs in the White House, is pretty much. . . Yahooland."

When Bill and Hillary Clinton decided to send their daughter Chelsea to an elite private school, the nation buzzed with discussion of what sort of example this was from a president who had promised to revitalize the nation's public schools. Even the president's pets have become the focus of attention. Lyndon Johnson received criticism for pulling the ears of his pet dog, and the Bush family spaniel "wrote" a best-selling autobiography, *Millie's Book* (with a little help from First Lady Barbara Bush, who donated the royalties to a literacy foundation).

As government has grown in response to society's needs, the growth of new ceremonial demands on the office has been enormous: making state visits, receiving foreign dignitaries, inviting sports champions to the White House, putting in a word for charity, being patron of the arts, and being careful not to violate any important national traditions. These symbolic roles have grown in importance due to media coverage, opinion polling, and the visible world leadership role of the United States.

Party Leader

The American president must balance the role of figurehead with hard-nosed party politician—often a tough balancing act, indeed. With the decline of party platforms and the rise of congressional candidates who have their own war chests, the job of rallying parties around a presidential program has become all the more difficult. The task is further complicated by the modern party nomination system described in Chapter 9. Since candidates for the high office are selected by a primary election system, there is a greater chance that party outsiders (like Jimmy Carter in 1976) will make it into the White House without the strong support or loyalty of power brokers in their own party. This makes party leadership challenging, to say the least. Even Ronald Reagan, who rallied the Republican party around his ideas during his rise to power, had trouble lining up the troops on some key issues such as tax reform and budgets.

Presidents often employ a combination of threats and rewards to line up party support for their ideas. For example, popular presidents will campaign for loyal members of Congress and try to funnel party resources to those who cooperate. Ronald Reagan often campaigned for Republican members of Congress, and for his own ideas at the same time, during the elections of the 1980s. Early in his term, Bill Clinton was unable to save incumbent Democratic senators Wyche Fowler (of Georgia) and Bob Kreuger (of Texas), Governor Jim Florio (of New Jersey) or Mayor David Dinkins (of New York).

Success in the job can depend on how well an individual masters both the ceremonial and party leadership duties of the presidency. Jimmy Carter and George Bush were not particularly charismatic at either of these roles, and their ability to get things done may have suffered for it. By contrast, Franklin Roosevelt and Ronald Reagan were both masters of symbolism and strong party leaders who left a mark in the formal channels of presidential power as well. From his campaign to the early days in office, Bill Clinton worked at party unity, trying to keep the many Democratic factions together within his administration. However, in his first major legislative test, Clinton had to send vice president Al Gore to preside over the Senate and to cast tie-breaking votes on the 1993 budget bill due to defections from the Democratic majority.

The President in Action: Formal Powers vs. Inside Politics

Although many observers claim that the executive has become the most powerful branch of government through the expansion of informal duties and the uses of inherent powers, this very growth of responsibilities also means that people may expect more than any individual politician can deliver. Successful presidents are those who master the politics behind the scenes. Behind the scenes of each area of presidential action (executive, legislative, foreign, and military), there is often an intricate maze of politics that must be navigated. In the following sections, the formal powers are contrasted with the politics behind the scenes that can make or break a presidency.

The Executive Arena

The most important formal or enumerated power, of course, is to enforce the laws of Congress. To support this task, the Constitution grants presidents specific powers to appoint (and remove) all top administration officers who are in charge of the various cabinet departments and executive agencies. The appointment powers also extend to federal judges and foreign ambassadors. Most presidents have assumed that this formal command of the bureaucracy implies that they can give orders to the departments and agencies.

In addition, assumptions about the implied or **inherent powers** of the Constitution have created an active tradition of presidents issuing **executive orders** directing departments, agencies, and sometimes the entire federal bureaucracy to do something at the president's bidding. For example, Lyndon Johnson issued an executive order prohibiting discrimination in the offices of the federal bureaucracy. Ronald Reagan used an executive order to stop economic trade with Nicaragua's revolutionary Sandinista regime in the early 1980s. Reagan also issued a so-called "gag" order to prevent pro-abortion counseling in hospitals and clinics receiving federal money. Prior to the 1992 election, George Bush issued an executive order declaring a moratorium on new bureaucratic regulations that might restrict business growth.

As you might imagine, presidents sometimes resist carrying out particular laws. One tactic that presidents have used for this purpose is the **impoundment** of funds appropriated by Congress for specific programs. Impoundment simply means setting aside and not spending money authorized by Congress for a program the president does not like. Needless to say, this can set the sparks flying between the White House and Capitol Hill, but that has not prevented presidents over the years from such actions as stopping shipbuilding, welfare programs, pork barrel projects, and arts funding. In 1974, Congress passed the Budget and Impoundment Control Act which placed limits on the length of time the president can avoid spending money without specifically informing Congress of the programs involved and the reasons for not executing them. Even with the limits of the 1974 law, presidents have continued to use impoundment as one of the tools to keep their own bureaucracy in line and occasionally to resist carrying out the orders of Congress.

POLITICS BEHIND THE BUREAUCRATIC SCENES.   Being the chief executive officer of the bureaucracy would seem to be a source of instant power and gratification. Yet it is not always the case that when the president barks an order, the bureaucratic ranks carry it out. Civil servants are, after all, lifetime employees who are obligated to carry out the laws of Congress and who must explain any failure to do so at the annual budget hearings on Capitol Hill. The appearance of bureaucratic resistance to Congress can change the future of an agency and break a rising bureaucratic career. Presidents who become great bureaucratic leaders must make careful appointments to the top executive offices (cabinet officers and heads of executive agencies), protect agency heads in their budget conflicts with Congress, and rally the morale of the rank-and-file bureaucrats who may grow weary of new administrations trying to turn everything upside down.

Presidents have vastly different political management styles befitting their personalities and the scope of their agendas. Ronald Reagan, for example, had an ambitious vision to roll back federal regulation and cut through the red tape slowing down businesses and weakening the country. However, he was a hands-off administrator who preferred to give his lieutenants wide powers to carry out his will. As a result, many of his most far-reaching political initiatives, from foreign policy to environmental deregulation to easing regulations on the nation's savings banks, were left to highly zealous (and in a few cases, downright corrupt) subordinates. When the dust settled after Reagan's eight years in office, either ethics complaints or legal charges had been filed against more than two hundred appointed officials. Many loyalists left the Reagan Revolution wondering who had been overseeing it.[9]

At the other extreme was Jimmy Carter, who came to Washington as a hands-on manager who seemed to review every proposal and program personally, right down to scheduling the use of the White House tennis court. A former Carter appointee in the Energy Department told this author about a report on his agency's activities which he had prepared at the request of a congressional committee. As a formality, he sent a copy to the White House; to his surprise, it was returned some time later with detailed comments and suggestions scribbled in the margins. What surprised him even more was the handwriting—that of President Carter himself. Many critics of the Carter administration feel that too much time was lost in such superfluous fine-tuning of particular policies, while little attention was paid to building political support in Congress, among the bureaucrats, and with the public to get things moving. As a politician, Carter seemed to have trouble seeing the forest for the trees. To make matters worse, many of his appointees displayed little loyalty to the administration and let its programs drift off course.

The Clinton administration vowed to delegate authority to the political appointees in charge of the various departments and agencies, while looking carefully at the political loyalty of the people appointed. During the transition period between the election and the inauguration, Washington was buzzing about which F.O.B. (Friend Of Bill) was headed for what bureaucratic post. At the same time, Democratic leaders were encouraged to consider themselves part of the new administration, in an effort to keep the bureaucracy from being pulled in different political directions from the White House and Capitol Hill. However, relations with Congress soon became rocky, and Clinton soon revealed a Carter-like penchant for micro-managing too many items on his agenda.

To coordinate the political efforts required to keep the White House, the bureaucracy, and Congress moving in the same direction, President Clinton appointed Thomas F. "Mack" McLarty to be his chief of staff. The chief of staff is the political coordinator inside the White House and the main gatekeeper between the president and the numbers of people who want to get his attention. Clinton and McLarty had been close friends since kindergarten. Although hardly a Washington insider, McLarty was a millionaire businessman and had been a key advisor to prominent Arkansas politicians. As McLarty put it: "I am not a Washington insider. . . . But through my experience as a citizen, as a businessman, as a former state legislator, and as a former state party chair, I know Washington well and I know how to make organizations work."[10] Even with all of those efforts, managing government activities proved difficult, and the media told of bungled decisions and strained relations with Congress. Soon, Washington insider David Gergen was added to the White House political team to smooth relations with the press and to offer advice on moving within the power circles around town.

The Legislative Arena

The formal legislative powers of the president as specified in the Constitution are fairly narrow: veto power, informing Congress on the State of the Union, and permission to ask for laws "necessary and expedient" to the welfare of the nation.

Veto power is the best known of the legislative powers of the executive. There are two forms of veto. The standard veto involves the executive returning a rejected bill to Congress (to the chamber that originated the bill) along with a formal explanation of his objections. If Congress decides not to revise the legislation along lines suggested by the White House, the members can *override* the veto (make the bill become law anyway) by taking another vote in which two-thirds of each chamber supports overriding the veto.

A second form of veto is know as a *pocket veto*. The Constitution specifies that if the president does not sign a bill within ten days of receiving it from Congress, it automatically becomes law. However, if a bill arrives at 1600 Pennsylvania Avenue when there are fewer than ten days left in the legislative session, the president has the option to simply "pocket" or not sign the bill. Under these conditions, the legislation suffers a sure, if technical, death simply because time runs out on the session. With the growing length of congressional sessions in recent years, there have been fewer chances for presidents to use this maneuver. Table 14.2 shows the veto records of the presidents, along with the numbers overridden by Congress.

It is important to remember that even when legislation has been vetoed, the same bill can be introduced again in the next legislative session, sometimes with better results if the political climate has changed. In the session following Bill Clinton's election, for example, many bills that had been vetoed successfully by President Bush were reintroduced and sent to the White House again, giving the early days of the Clinton administration at least the appearance of considerable activity.

In addition to the formal veto powers, there are implied or informal powers that also bring the president into the legislative arena. For example, **the uses of executive orders** described above can bring presidents very close to intruding on the legislative powers of Congress. Given the separation of powers, it is hardly surprising that there is a grey area between where the legislative initiative of Congress stops and where the administrative power of the executive begins. In fact, Congress often writes laws that are so vague in their specifics that the executive agencies that carry them out effectively take over the lawmaking process.

Congress has even attempted to introduce something called a *legislative veto*. Recall the discussion from Chapter 12 explaining how Congress has been criticized for passing vague laws that presidents are invited to make more detailed by issuing executive orders or writing regulations. However, Congress has asserted the right to review these executive actions to see if they conform to the spirit of the original law. Although the Supreme Court has declared this legislative veto practice unconstitutional, both sides have continued to use variations on it to fine-tune their powers. (This "dance of legislation" between Congress and the executive will surely bring the Court into their affairs in the future, as more questions are raised about the fine line between making and implementing the law.) When the legislative process comes down to a duel over vetoes, something has gone astray in the politics between the institutions at opposite ends of Pennsylvania Avenue.

THE POLITICS BEHIND THE LEGISLATIVE SCENES. The Constitution invites a subtle, two-way legislative relationship between president and Congress. Article II, Section 3 says that "from time to time," the executive shall give Congress a report on the State of the Union and recommend needed legislation. Over the years, the "State of the Union" address has become an annual event, delivered in a speech directly to the joint assembly of Congress. Similarly, the legislative proposals of the executive have become both regular and numerous, with the White House often drafting laws that it wants passed and lobbying vigorously for and against different legislative initiatives going forward on Capitol Hill. In recent times, presidents have begun to put together legislative packages, often tied to budget requests, and delivered to the lawmakers through a

TABLE 14.2

Presidential Vetoes, 1789–1993

YEARS	PRESIDENT	REGULAR VETOES	VETOES OVERRIDDEN	POCKET VETOES	TOTAL VETOES
1789–1797	Washington	2	0	0	2
1797–1801	Adams	0	0	0	0
1801–1809	Jefferson	0	0	0	0
1809–1817	Madison	5	0	2	7
1817–1825	Monroe	1	0	0	1
1825–1829	J. Q. Adams	0	0	0	0
1829–1837	Jackson	5	0	7	12
1837–1841	Van Buren	0	0	1	1
1841–1841	Harrison	0	0	0	0
1841–1845	Tyler	6	1	4	10
1845–1849	Polk	2	0	1	3
1849–1850	Taylor	0	0	0	0
1850–1853	Fillmore	0	0	0	0
1853–1857	Pierce	9	5	0	9
1857–1861	Buchanan	4	0	3	7
1861–1865	Lincoln	2	0	5	7
1865–1869	A. Johnson	21	15	8	29
1869–1877	Grant	45	4	48	93
1877–1881	Hayes	12	1	1	13
1881–1881	Garfield	0	0	0	0
1881–1885	Arthur	4	1	8	12
1885–1889	Cleveland	304	2	110	414
1889–1893	Harrison	19	1	25	44
1893–1897	Cleveland	42	5	128	170
1897–1901	McKinley	6	0	36	42
1901–1909	T. Roosevelt	42	1	40	82
1909–1913	Taft	30	1	9	39
1913–1921	Wilson	33	6	11	44
1921–1923	Harding	5	0	1	6
1923–1929	Coolidge	20	4	30	50
1929–1933	Hoover	21	3	16	37
1933–1945	F. Roosevelt	372	9	263	635
1945–1953	Truman	180	12	70	250
1953–1961	Eisenhower	73	2	108	181
1961–1963	Kennedy	12	0	9	21
1963–1969	L. Johnson	16	0	14	30
1969–1974	Nixon	26[*]	7	17	43
1974–1977	Ford	48	12	18	66
1977–1981	Carter	13	2	18	31
1981–1989	Reagan	39	9	39	78
1989–1993	Bush	37	2	4	41
Total		1,431	103	1,054	2,485

[*]Two pocket vetoes, overruled in the courts, are counted here as regular vetoes.

Sources: *Congressional Quarterly Weekly Report* (1989), 7, (1990). Adapted from Harold W. Stanley and Richard G. Niemi, *Vital Statistics on American Politics*, 3rd ed. Washington, D.C.: CQ Press, 1992, p. 276.

combination of White House legislative aides, cabinet officers, and personal briefing sessions from the president.

The power to request legislation from Congress becomes even stronger when presidents play up the politics behind their status as national symbols and go public to apply pressure on Congress. Recall from Chapter 1, for example, Bill Clinton's efforts to sell his economic program as a "patriotic" issue. If the nation is faced with serious problems or crises (drug abuse, education, economic decline, and others) and a president has the approval of many voters for new ideas or solutions, then asking Congress to deliver on the legislation can become an important symbolic move that often gets results. After all, the executive is at once inviting Congress to share his popularity, and threatening to point the finger of blame at them during the next election if they refuse his requests. Thus, a weak constitutional power can become a much stronger legislative force in the hands of a persuasive leader. Figure 14.4 illustrates the intensity of legislative politics between presidents and Congress measured in terms of presidential success in getting Congress to support their legislative requests.

Many administrations have failed to play the politics of legislation skillfully, often relying more on the veto power to prevent things they don't want, than succeeding in convincing the lawmakers to deliver the things they promised to the voters. It has become common for Congress and the president to blame each other for lack of progress on national priorities. With the same party in control of both the White House and Congress during the Clinton administration, it became more difficult to point the finger of blame.

Bill Clinton looks into a TelePrompTer while addressing Congress on health-care issues in early 1993. Democratic Party control of both the executive and legislative branches in 1993–94 made Clinton's success or failure at legislative politics a paramount concern.

FIGURE 14.4

Presidential Victories on Votes in Congress, 1953–1990

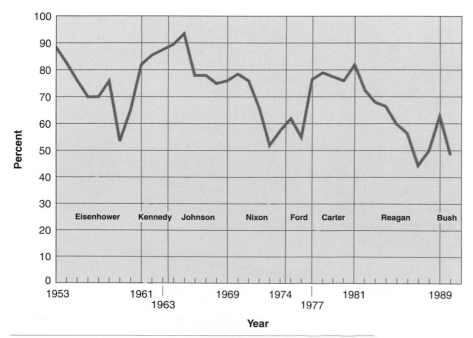

*Percentages indicate number of congressional votes supporting the president divided by the total number of votes on which the president has taken a position.

SOURCE: Norman J. Ornstein, Thomas E. Mann, and Michael J. Malbin, *Vital Statistics on Congress.* Washington, D.C.: CQ Press, 1992, p. 195.

When the same party controls both branches of government, legislative failures are more likely to be blamed on external factors such as special interests and budget deficits.

The Military and Foreign Policy Arena

The Constitution grants specific authority to the president to appoint ambassadors, negotiate treaties (which must be approved by the Senate), and command the armed forces. Treaties, for example, are formally defined in the Constitution, and they often receive prominent coverage in the press, complete with regal signing ceremonies and sometimes windy Senate debates. However, a far more common practice has been for presidents to simply enter into executive agreements with the heads of other governments. As defined above, **executive agreements** are in the grey area of constitutional powers. They have been upheld by the Court as not requiring the same approval of the Senate that is necessary in formal treaties, but for that reason, they can trigger turf battles with Congress over where the line separating the powers of the two branches should be drawn. In deciding when to sign an executive agreement and when to make a formal treaty, presidents often make political calculations such as how much political support and blame-sharing they will take on such volatile issues as trade policies or control of U.S. assets abroad. For example, leases on military bases are usually handled as agreements, while the return of control over the Panama Canal to Panama was handled in a pair of treaties concluded in 1978, returning ownership and control of the Canal to Panama in the year 2000. As shown in Table 14.3, the use of treaties is generally down, while the use of executive agreements has soared.

What seems to be the most straightforward power of the Constitution is the designation of the president as Commander in Chief of the armed forces. The ability to order the military might of the nation into action is awesome in its implications. Although Congress was constitutionally given the balancing power of declaring war, many large-scale military actions are possible (including the most likely scenario for nuclear holocaust) without ever having a formal declaration of war.

Over the years, many large-scale "wars" have been fought largely on the initiative of the executive with no **formal declaration of war** from Congress. A few examples of **undeclared** wars include the capture of Panamanian dictator Manuel Noriega and the military action to repulse Iraq's invasion of Kuwait, during the Bush administration; the invasion of Grenada and the resulting expulsion of Cuban troops from that island, during the Reagan administration; and, of course, the conflict in Vietnam, which spanned the Kennedy, Johnson, and Nixon administrations. In many of these cases, Congress assisted the executive by passing resolutions of support (for example, during Vietnam and the more recent "Persian Gulf War" against Iraq) and by authorizing increases in military spending and operations.

In addition to using the military as a leading arm of foreign policy, presidents have also sent troops into American cities and states over the years to protect citizens during natural disasters, restore order in riots, or enforce laws, as when Republican president Dwight Eisenhower sent paratroopers to Little Rock, Arkansas in 1957 to protect black students who had been legally empowered by a court order to enroll in a formerly all-white high school. The fact that the governor of Arkansas at the time, Orval Faubus, had ordered the state's National Guard to block the students raised a direct challenge to the president's constitutional power to enforce the laws of the land. When it comes to the ultimate in law enforcement agencies, there are few to compare with having the United States Army at your disposal.

TABLE 14.3

Treaties and Executive Agreements Concluded by the United States, 1789–1990

YEAR	NUMBER OF TREATIES*	NUMBER OF EXECUTIVE AGREEMENTS
1789–1839	60	27
1839–1889	215	238
1889–1929	382	763
1930–1932	49	41
1933–1944 (F. Roosevelt)	131	369
1945–1952 (Truman)	132	1,324
1953–1960 (Eisenhower)	89	1,834
1961–1963 (Kennedy)	36	813
1964–1968 (L. Johnson)	67	1,083
1969–1974 (Nixon)	93	1,317
1975–1976 (Ford)	26	666
1977–1980 (Carter)	79	1,476
1981–1988 (Reagan)	117	2,837
1989–1990 (Bush)	34	757

Number of treaties includes those concluded during the indicated span of years. Some of these treaties did not receive the consent of the U.S. Senate. Varying definitions of what constitutes an executive agreement and its entry-into-force date make the above numbers approximate.

SOURCES: 1789–1980: Congressional Quarterly, *Congressional Quarterly's Guide to Congress*, 3rd ed. (Washington, D.C.: Congressional Quarterly, 1982), 291; 1981–1990: Office of the Assistant Legal Adviser for Treaty Affairs, U.S. Department of State. Reprinted from Harold W. Stanley and Richard G. Niemi, *Vital Statistics on American Politics*, 3rd ed. Washington, D.C.: CQ Press, 1992, p. 278.

The crisis in Little Rock was complicated because a state governor took full command of the state's National Guard. In reality, the National Guard is a joint command between state governors and the president, a complex organization that one observer described as "a hydra-headed, mind boggling, bureaucratic monster."[11] Almost entirely funded by the Pentagon budget, the Guard is over a half million troops that, when fully mobilized, would rank as one of the largest armies in the world (actually, the eleventh largest army but the third largest air force).[12] The executive branch decides where Guard units are stationed and what military standards they must meet. However, state governors appoint the commanders of the Guard and can order the Guard to duty. Because of the federal chain of command, however, authorization to arm the troops and move them out of their armories must come from Washington. Over the years, the

Guard has been used for natural disaster relief, crowd control at sporting events, and to control riots such as the Los Angeles riots in the spring of 1992.

Critics said the Guard was slow to respond to the crisis in Los Angeles, but the reasons were unclear. State officials claimed federal authorizations were slow in coming, but Pentagon officials responded that permission to move California Guard units into Los Angeles had been granted almost immediately. In fact, many observers suspected that political considerations operated behind the scenes in making a potentially volatile decision to send troops to quell a domestic disturbance in which angry protestors commingled with armed looters and violent assailants.

THE POLITICS OF MILITARY AND FOREIGN POLICY DECISIONS.

Although the military command powers of the president may seem the most straightforward of all, there are political considerations at work behind many orders to use military force. It turns out that one does not simply order the army to go to war; it is best to consult first with the generals and to seek their advice. For example, when George Bush explored the military options following Iraq's invasion of Kuwait, he is reported to have discovered that his commanders were not eager to fight a large war in a distant desert region under difficult conditions. Not only did the commanders take some persuading, but they insisted on substantial control over their own public relations activities, and military regulation of the press as part of the deal.[13] Likewise, the military initially resisted efforts to be deployed in drug wars against international narcotics traffickers. However, pressure from the Bush White House and Congress eventually persuaded the top brass

President Bush disembarks from Air Force One during an overseas visit in 1992. Like his recent Republican Party predecessors (especially Richard Nixon), Bush excelled in foreign-policy issues. Earlier presidents may well have dreamed of partaking in all that transpired during his term in office—a period marked by such momentous events as the Persian Gulf War; the liberation of Eastern Europe from Soviet domination; the subsequent collapse of the Soviet Union; and, subsequently, the signing of an historic nuclear-disarmament treaty with Russian president Boris Yeltsin. Domestic concerns, however, proved to be Bush's electoral undoing.

that their peacetime images, as well as their budgets, might be improved by fighting the drug lords of South America and by patrolling the shipping lanes of the Caribbean.

With the end of the Cold War and the reduced threat from the former Soviet Union, the politics behind nonmilitary aspects of foreign policy has become trickier as well. When the United States emerged as the leading superpower after World War II, that position was quickly challenged by the military and ideological threat of the Soviet Union. The dangers and split-second timing of superpower confrontations led Congress to defer to the president on many foreign policy decisions. In addition, the sharp ideological division of the world of the 1950s and 1960s created something of a political consensus in Washington about the general goals and policies in foreign affairs.

All of these factors made the politics of running the foreign policy show somewhat easier for presidents. For a time, it was popular to think there was a great political divide between the domestic and foreign policy roles of the president. Political scientist Aaron Wildavsky even talked about "two presidencies." One was a foreign policy president with nearly imperial powers to command the armed forces, strike deals at the summit, and operate as national ambassador to the world. The other was a domestic policy president with increasing responsibility for thousands of vital national issues, each with the potential to drag him into losing battles with states, Congress, the Court, and interest groups. No wonder the president was often seen cheerfully boarding Air Force One and heading off to a summit in some exotic spot, leaving the political dangers of Washington politics far behind.

This view of two presidencies, however, may have oversimplified the politics behind foreign policy, particularly in recent years, as its author now admits.[14] If the "two presidencies" image ever offered a good description of the divisions of presidential politics, it was during the peak years of the Cold War in the late 1950s and early 1960s when an *establishment* of Eastern bankers, brokers, corporate heads, and Ivy League intellectuals advised the leaders of both parties on world affairs, and there was more agreement on viewing the world in black-and-white terms. In later years, the world order has developed many more shades of grey. The foreign policy establishment crumbled with the collapse of Communism, and domestic political divisions began to break out in many areas of foreign policy from trade to military strength.

Still, given the challenges of domestic politics, it is understandable why many modern presidents have continued to take refuge in foreign policy. It must be appealing for presidents embattled at home to look at a Constitution which gives them wide authority to negotiate treaties, appoint ambassadors, command the military, and generally represent the country abroad. Time after time, however, these same presidents have gotten themselves into politically fatal situations. Every president from Lyndon Johnson in the late 1960s until George Bush (the history book is still open on Bill Clinton) has suffered some sort of foreign policy damage, often on the heels of some great foreign policy triumph.

The foreign policy roller coaster must have seemed particularly rough to George Bush, who scaled the political heights with his military victory over Iraq in 1991. According to presidential pollster and campaign manager Robert Teeter, compared to other aspects of the Bush political record, foreign policy was "the ace in the hole" going into the 1992 election. "Voters view national security as the single most important quality in a president, and they have always been unwilling to take risks with it."[15] Those turned out to be famous last words in an era where even a highly praised foreign policy had suddenly become a hard sell to voters more worried about problems on the homefront than conditions abroad. It appears that even presidents like Mr. Bush, who do well at foreign affairs, may not always reap the benefits of their successes. Despite what many regarded as a foreign policy triumph in the war against Iraq, Mr. Bush was judged guilty in the voting booth of spending too much time on world affairs at the expense of domestic policy.

The Secret of Success: The Power to Persuade

As noted at the opening of the chapter, the game plan for the Clinton presidency was to act in office much as he campaigned, going directly to the people, keeping the focus on domestic issues, and never forgetting that sign on the wall of his 1992 campaign head-quarters: THE ECONOMY, STUPID. These plans addressed the part of the presidency that must *go public*, but the rest of the job requires persuading powerful members of Congress and bureaucrats to join the political team. It is in the difficulties of building the Washington coalition where presidential politics often falls apart. When powerful Washington insiders begin criticizing presidents in the press, as happened early on to Bill Clinton, levels of public support usually decline as well.

The secret to success in both going public and building a political coalition is something that is not given to presidents in the Constitution, nor is it a political skill easily learned. It is the **power to persuade** others to follow them: to persuade members of Congress to support legislation, to persuade members of one's party to stand together behind programs, to persuade bureaucrats to play as a loyal team, and, all the while, to persuade the public to support presidential initiatives and bring pressure to bear on Congress to do the same.

The author of this idea is political scientist Richard Neustadt, who observed that the formal powers of the office do not explain why some presidents are more successful and become stronger leaders than others.[16] Indeed, Neustadt has argued that the formal powers of the presidency are not clear and focused enough to handle all the responsibilities that have developed over the years. What the creative leader must do is invent a leadership style that works to persuade various groups in Congress, the public, the bureaucracy, and the interest sectors to follow his lead.

Behind the constitutional powers and the responsibilities of the office, then, are many political calculations. Chief among these calculations is the daily political question of how to persuade whom, for what political ends. "Inside the System" Box 14.4 explores persuasion styles of two different presidents, Franklin Roosevelt and Bill Clinton.

Many aspects of presidential persuasion occur in private, from meetings with legislative leaders to cabinet sessions. However, the increasing importance of going public means that much of the persuasion that presidents do these days is in public, in front of the television cameras.

The Media Spotlight

Much of the political drama of the modern presidency is brought to us on television each day. With rising national expectations and the public opinion focus on the president, the media cover the president and White House politics more closely than any other aspect of national life. TV crews keep a so-called "body watch" on the occupant of 1600 Pennsylvania Avenue and follow his every move, whether across the Rose Garden or across the ocean, whether going fishing or signing an agreement about fishing rights on the high seas. Presidents quickly learn that a casual remark made on the golf course or walking across the lawn to board a helicopter can have positive or negative effects on their public image.

Saturation news coverage is at once an opportunity for presidents to use their powers to persuade, and a potential political minefield that they must negotiate each day. Every time a president succeeds in raising his level of public support, he also raises the political stakes of public expectations. As one author put it:

> Initially, the national media coverage generates expectations of quick results from a newly elected President. During the postinaugural honeymoon, the President is invariably pictured as about to embark on a new era, aided by an energetic new cabinet and

Contrasting the Persuasion Styles of Franklin Roosevelt and Bill Clinton

14.4

As noted throughout this chapter, presidential politics is complicated by a number of related institutional limits:

- The Constitution limits the power of the office.
- Yet the expectations on the office have expanded greatly over the years, requiring constant efforts to build support in Congress, with bureaucrats, among interest groups, with the party, and with the public.
- However, presidents cannot simply *order* any of these groups to follow them.

Success in office requires *persuading* others to follow the presidential lead. The techniques of persuasion are different depending on whether the audience is the general public (see Box 14.3) or the leaders of Congress. In addition to using public relations and media skills, presidential persuasion also includes displays of character, from charm to intimidation, and setting personal examples that inspire trust and confidence.

Powerful government officials can require considerable personal attention before offering their support to a president. During the Great Depression of the 1930s, Franklin Roosevelt often failed in his efforts to win personal support from key congressional opponents. To get what he wanted from Congress, he frequently used the veto, while "going public" to mobilize public opinion pressure on Congress. However, when Japan attacked Pearl Harbor on December 7, 1941, Roosevelt understood that he had to convince powerful opponents in Congress to support him and give him added powers that he would need to conduct the upcoming war. One of the first congressional leaders that Roosevelt called to the White House on the day of the Japanese attack was House Republican Minority Leader Joseph W. Martin of Massachusetts, who emerged from the private session to announce: "In the hour of danger there is no partisanship. In that hour we all stand as one people in support of America."* During the next several years, congressional opponents responded to the personal requests of the president by reluctantly giving him great power over setting national wages, prices, and consumption patterns. Despite his often-rocky relations with Congress, Roosevelt used the great crisis facing the nation to apply considerable personal pressure on opponents, changing the face of the presidency forever.

Bill Clinton also attempted to rally public opinion to his causes, but tried to develop a personal rapport with members of Congress more along the models of Lyndon Johnson and Ronald Reagan. Although Clinton's style of insider persuasion surprised some, fellow Arkansas politician Dale Bumpers said that Clinton was "a very persuasive lobbyist" as governor of Arkansas, so much so that "legislators used to hide from him because they thought he was going to talk them into doing something they didn't want to do."**

When seeking support in Congress for his economic recovery plan, Clinton met with many legislators. He even put out the word that he wanted more congressional jogging partners. As one journalist put it: "for Mr. Clinton, the massaging of congressional egos is virtually nonstop. He invites even Republicans to travel with him aboard Air Force One. During an unusual visit to Capitol Hill to meet just with Republicans . . . Mr. Clinton called many of them by their first names." The lawmakers clearly got something out of the personal treatment too. After newly elected Representative Eric D. Fingerhut of Ohio had his moment with the president, he issued a press release aimed at the folks back home with the title "Fingerhut meets with President at the White House." One prominent Washington lobbyist observed: "There is an intimacy between the president and Congress that we have not seen in some time."

Despite these efforts, Mr. Clinton soon earned the antagonism of some powerful members of his own party in Congress (notably senators Sam Nunn and David Boren) by failing to meaningfully confer with them in private on issues ranging from allowing homosexuals in the military to increasing taxes on energy. Sensing a political opening, Republicans quickly joined ranks against early presidential initiatives, putting the new president's persuasion powers to a stiff test.

*Cited in David Brinkley, *Washington Goes to War.* New York: Knopf, 1988, p. 200.
**All Clinton quotes are from Richard L. Berke, "Looking for Alliance, Clinton Courts the Congress Nonstop," *The New York Times,* March 8, 1993, p. 1, p. 8.

staff. But then reality sets in. Innovation in our system of limited government and checks and balances is never easy, especially if it involves domestic legislation.[17]

As students of the media have long pointed out, the news, particularly television, has trouble telling complicated stories about power, and the reasons why things are or are not happening in Washington.[18] When presidents cannot win real victories in Congress, their media managers can try to create the illusion of winning in the news, or at least they can avoid the appearance of having lost.[19] All of which explains why cultivating a positive public image is essential to the modern presidency, but successful image management does not always guarantee success in governing the nation.

Persuasiveness in the modern presidency involves many things: media management, theatrical skills, a passing command of language and rhetoric, and intimate knowledge of how to push the political buttons of powerful politicians. To an important degree, however, the persuasiveness of the great presidents is also a matter of character. Character can be displayed on television, of course, in ways that voters try to assess and media consultants try to manufacture. But character can also come across in one-on-one sessions of the sort that Lyndon Johnson was famous for having with members of Congress when he solicited their support for his programs. Few who received the Johnson "treatment" were able to say no to his requests. And many who said no later regretted it. Thus, persuasiveness comes in many forms, both public and private, and in an important way it reflects a president's character.

The Presidential Character

The many responsibilities of the office may add up to more than any mortal can handle for very long. Watch any president go through the routine crises and conflicts of the job: The face ages dramatically under the glare of the TV lights, health problems begin to pop up, and moments of irritability with the press are often recorded by the television cameras for future replay. Insider reports tell stories about personal responses to the strain. Richard Nixon seemed to his closest associates ready to crack under the strain of the Watergate crisis.[20] In the final years of his tenure, Ronald Reagan appeared to some critics

Jimmy Carter was strongly criticized as president for his obsessive attention to detail. Among his other activities, Carter personally oversaw the booking of the White House tennis courts. Yet Carter went on to become one of the most active and popular modern ex-presidents.

to grow distant from what was going on around him, leaving his top speechwriter to put together his arguments.[21]

Even under the best of circumstances, the job may have become too big and too stressful. Presidential observers such as Bruce Buchanan advocate reducing the responsibilities of the job and bringing public expectations back within reason.[22] The reality, of course, is that without such drastic reform as restoring strong party government or changing the balance of power in the Constitution, the nation will continue to cry out for strong leadership and a symbolic focus for our national aspirations. Perhaps the most amazing fact is that people of considerable ambition continue to compete for what looks to be an impossible, not to mention dangerous, job. Table 14.4 reviews just one of the stressful aspects of the job: living with the constant possibility of being assassinated.

Long ago, during the age of strong parties and machine politics, the British observer Lord Bryce included a chapter titled "Why Great Men Are Not Chosen President" in his classic text on American government. He referred to the old-style bargaining among machine factions that often eliminated strong candidates who promised to be great leaders and who might tip the power balance among the party factions. Today's much more open selection process may produce much the same results for different reasons. Today's candidates are screened for the slightest personal flaws by the media and then limited to a few seconds in which to express their most profound solutions for national problems. Scholar Steven Hess argues that no screening process could more assure that people of sensitivity, eloquence, and vision would be well advised not to run.[23]

Indeed, the person motivated to run for the top political prize may be driven more by ambition and power than genius. Says Hugh Sidey, who has reported on presidential elections since the 1950s, "If you look at the current crop [of presidential candidates], you see that the profile of their lives is just grubbing for power."[24] Other correspondents worry that these most ambitious politicians "live in a tunnel" and "get their entertainment from riding an exercycle in front of television news shows," channeling "all their

TABLE 14.4

A Dangerous Job: Presidential Assassinations and Attempted Assassinations

PRESIDENTS KILLED IN OFFICE	PRESIDENTS ATTACKED OR PLOTTED AGAINST BUT NOT KILLED	PRESIDENTIAL CANDIDATES TARGETED FOR ASSASSINATION
Abraham Lincoln, 1865	Andrew Jackson, 1835	Theodore Roosevelt, 1912 (not killed)
James A. Garfield, 1881	Franklin D. Roosevelt (as president-elect), 1933	Robert Kennedy, 1968 (killed)
William McKinley, 1901	Harry Truman, 1950	George Wallace, 1972 (permanently disabled)
John Kennedy, 1963	Richard Nixon, 1974	
	Gerald Ford, twice in 1975	
	Ronald Reagan, 1981	
	George Bush (after leaving office), 1993	

mental capacities in the pursuit of political ends."[25] One losing presidential candidate even slammed his peers by challenging reporters to ask this question during a presidential debate: "Do you know the price of a loaf of bread or a dozen eggs?"[26]

While it is nice to think about simplifying the job and finding well-rounded and thoughtful people to fill it, the reality is that the leader of the world's most powerful state will face a daily stress-test, and only the most ambitious politicians are likely to apply for the job. Within these limits, however, there are many different character types who will respond differently to the task. Political scientist James David Barber has long argued that some of those types are better suited to the stresses and the constant political give-and-take than others.

Searching for the Ideal Presidential Personality

Professor Barber proposes that we consider two important dimensions of the character of people who want the nation's top job: how actively they are inclined to pursue goals and engage in the struggle of politics, and how positively they approach their job and the life of a public personality. There are, in this scheme of **character types,** four broad classifications:[27]

- *The active-positive type* who relishes the give-and-take, and the promise of accomplishment, while genuinely enjoying the job and its often demanding public

Political scholar James David Barber characterized President Franklin Roosevelt (photo at left) *and his successor, Harry Truman* (center of right-hand photo, sitting with wife Bess), *as "active-positive" presidents—leaders enjoying both the give-and-take of daily governing and the ceremonial aspects of the presidency. Roosevelt (shown with Nationalist Chinese leader Chiang Kai–Shek during a World War II parley), visibly relished his job, and was often caricatured as grinning ear-to-ear while a trademark cigarette-holder dangled at a jaunty angle from his lips. Truman (seen here during a 1957 visit to Disneyland, after his retirement from office) was cheered for his feisty ways, later celebrated in such entertainments as the film* Give 'Em Hell, Harry! *and Merle Miller's "oral memoir,"* Plain Speaking.

aspects. Franklin Roosevelt, Harry Truman, John Kennedy, Gerald Ford, and George Bush are among the presidents deemed by Barber to be best suited for the demands of high office.

- *The active-negative* enjoys the political battle but not the heat of publicity or the risks of public disapproval. This type may get involved in ambitious activities but not respond well to crisis. Cases in point: Richard Nixon, Lyndon Johnson.

- *The passive-positive* president avoids personal involvement in daily politics and conflicts but enjoys the public ceremonies and the limelight. This is a prescription for either little accomplishment or for ambitious appointees who operate with little supervision: Warren Harding, Ronald Reagan.

- *The passive-negative* is a reluctant president who answered the call of party or public without really wanting either the publicity or the responsibility of office: Dwight Eisenhower, Calvin Coolidge.

Some scholars disagree with how Barber has categorized particular presidents, but it is clear that personalities do play an important role both with voters during campaigns and in response to the demands of office. Yet even if accurate character information is available to voters, some may still prefer personality styles other than the active-positive one that Barber himself deems best suited for the strains of office. For example, Ronald Reagan held considerable appeal precisely *because* he wanted government to do less, and he set a personal example along those lines, taking naps, enjoying trips to his ranch, and leaving the details of administration to his appointees.

For all the elusiveness of the concept, many observers have recognized the importance of character, arguing that personal styles may account for more of presidential accomplishment than strict analysis of power or institutional limits.[28] And one of the long-standing insights about the presidency is that formal powers are so limited that the real difference between one administration and the other boils down to an individual leader's strength of character and "power to persuade" others to follow.

Too Many Responsibilities, Too Little Power Revisited

Today's students of the presidency see anything but a simple picture. Far from two presidencies, there appear to be many, and there is not enough power to sustain them. Although the office has attracted much more responsibility than the founders probably could have imagined, the formal powers are still limited much as the original Constitution prescribed. To handle all the demands and expectations, presidents usually try to mobilize their parties in Congress as Franklin Roosevelt did in his initial attempt to become an activist president. However, American parties have never been disciplined or easy to lead, especially from the great constitutional distance of the White House. According to many scholars, the inevitable temptation is for presidents to appeal directly to the voters for support. This results in even higher expectations placed on the lone incumbent of the Oval Office, often without generating much more party support in Congress or any greater obedience from the ranks of bureaucrats who look to Congress for their money each year.

As the government grew during the decades between Franklin Roosevelt and today, Congress yielded more and more responsibilities to the executive out of sheer necessity. Relatively small and understaffed, Congress could not hope to write in detail all of the laws creating all of the programs being managed in the executive branch. The political problem is that for all the responsibility that Congress ceded to the White House, it gave up relatively little power to get those jobs done. At every turn, the executive branch must

A CITIZEN'S QUESTION · Presidential Performance

*D*o I expect too much from presidents, considering the institutional limits on their powers? As the above discussion suggests, many of the forces swirling around the modern presidency invite citizens to participate in a national "thumbs up" or "thumbs down" on almost any political issue simply by evaluating the president. Citizens cannot be blamed for reacting in often volatile ways to the president when the national political drama in the news is centered around presidential politics and when pollsters take presidential approval polls so often. Indeed, presidents themselves invite strong public reaction by going public in efforts to gain political strength.

However, it might be a good idea for citizens to think twice before paying so much attention to just one actor in a complex government. It may feel good to have a simple, moving target onto which many feelings about the state of the nation can be projected. However, the results may not be good either for government or for citizen attitudes in the long run. To begin with, presidents who must spend a great deal of time shoring up their public images may not be devoting enough energy to other important political tasks. At the same time, the unrealistic assumption that the executive is most responsible for what the government does may not point public pressure to the place in the government where actual breakdowns are occurring. Finally, the "personal presidency" may be satisfying psychologically, but it ignores the importance of more active citizen involvement in national politics. It is possible that even with a strong leader in the White House, only the actions citizens are willing to push for will be accomplished by government.

If Americans want more responsiveness from government, the alternatives seem to be two very different ones: more citizen activism in party politics or political movements, or else a constitutional reform aimed at giving the president more powers to go along with the responsibilities of office. These alternatives are radically different in their visions of democracy. Which makes the most sense to you?

---

answer to Congress: to gain approval on the budget to run programs, to get new laws passed, and to gain agreement on just what the laws mean in the first place.

All the while, the public watches, granting and withdrawing its approval for presidential moves as it might follow a sports match on television. The worry is that this citizen response to the president is passive rather than active and based on unrealistic expectations. One political scientist talks about "hero worshipping" and how it leads to the "decline of [active] citizenship":

> No modern president can expect to succeed without the support of the public. Yet this support must be grounded in a firm rejection of the unrealistic textbook presidency notion of presidential power. Citizens who respond to the presidency in a highly personalized and reverential manner are likely to be disappointed by presidential performance and are also likely to embrace political passivity.[29]

Theodore Lowi describes the modern office as a "**personal presidency**" in which the chief executive becomes the subject of a nonstop plebiscite for all national concerns. (A *plebiscite* is simply a national poll of approval or disapproval for government policies or for the leaders in power.) According to Lowi, we have come to the worst of all possibilities, what he calls the "plebiscitary presidency," in which the president is unduly influenced by polls about his actions on all national issues.[30] Lowi stresses that the American people need to recognize more clearly that Congress, the courts, and the political parties actually share the power required to get anything done.[31] All of which suggests why many students of the presidency these days are concerned about an office burdened with too many unrelated expectations and too little clearly focused power in either domestic or international affairs.[32] While the United States does not have the only presidential system with important responsibilities shared by different branches of government, it may have the only one in which no branch has a clear power advantage over the others.

To make matters worse, since presidents cannot really escape the expectations of the public, they often end up playing to them, making promises and constantly rallying support. Presidents become perennial candidates for their own office, doing and saying things to keep their approval ratings up in the short run. In the long run, however, public moods often sour when presidential promises are dashed against the harsh realities of governing. As Richard Rose and others have pointed out, the things that get presidents elected and keep them popular while in office may not help much at all when it actually comes to the task of governing.[33]

Key Terms

honeymoon period

opinion rally

going public

enumerated powers

   executive, legislative, military, and foreign policy powers

inherent powers

   proclamations, executive orders, impoundment

traditional presidential roles

   national symbolic leader, party leader

executive politics

appointing bureaucratic managers

the uses of executive orders, impoundment

legislative politics

   veto, building legislative support

military and foreign policy politics

   undeclared wars

   executive agreements, treaties

   domestic risks of foreign policy

the power to persuade

presidential character types

the personal presidency

Suggested Readings

Berman, Larry. *The New American Presidency*. Boston: Little, Brown, 1987.

Cronin, Thomas E., ed. *Inventing the American Presidency*. Lawrence: University of Kansas Press, 1989.

Kernell, Samuel. *Going Public: New Strategies of Presidential Leadership*, second edition. Washington, D.C.: Congressional Quarterly Press, 1993.

Lowi, Theodore J. *The Personal President: Power Invested, Promise Unfulfilled*. Ithaca: Cornell University Press, 1985.

Neustadt, Richard. *Presidential Power and the Modern Presidents*. New York: The Free Press, 1990.

• • •

To understand practically anything about American society today, it's necessary to understand the dynamics and incentives that exist in the large institutions that dominate our lives. In government and out, bureaucratic behavior strongly influences the way the country works.
—*CHARLES PETERS AND NICHOLAS LEMANN*

• • •

Newton Minow [one-time Federal Communications Commission chairman] tells of an encounter with House Speaker Sam Rayburn soon after being appointed. Rayburn, exuding friendship, put his arm around Minow and said, "Just remember one thing, son. Your agency is an arm of Congress, you belong to us. Remember that and you'll be all right." Rayburn then warned Minow to expect a lot of pressure from outsiders. In retrospect, Minow said, "What he didn't tell me was that most of the pressure would come from Congress itself."
—*THOMAS REDBURN*

• • •

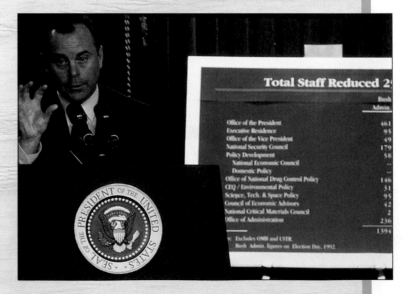

The Executive: Managing the Bureaucracy

- **OLD NEWS: CONTROLLING THE BUREAUCRACY IS HARD TO DO**

- **A POLITICAL HOTBED**
  Bureaucratic Politics: The Case of Environmental Regulation

- **IMPLEMENTING THE LAW: THE BUREAUCRATIC MISSION**

- **BUREAUCRATIC ORGANIZATION**
  Decoding the Alphabet Soup
  The Command System

- **HISTORICAL CHANGES IN BUREAUCRATIC POLITICS**
  The Spoils System
  The Rise of a Professional Civil Service
  The Rise of an Activist Bureaucracy
  The Rise of the Bureaucratic State

- **THE POLITICS OF BUREAUCRATIC INTERESTS**
  Iron Triangles Revisited

- **POLITICS IN THE DEPARTMENTS AND THE CABINET**

- **THE EXECUTIVE OFFICE OF THE PRESIDENT**
  A Secret Government?
  Shrinking the White House Establishment

- **THE PRESIDENT'S PERSONAL STAFF**

- **THE POLITICAL HOTBED REVISITED**

- **A CITIZEN'S QUESTION: Bureaucratic Politics**

- **KEY TERMS**

- **SUGGESTED READINGS**

When Bill Clinton began appointing the people who would run the major departments and councils of government, the news spotlight was turned on the glamour appointments. Secretary of Defense Les Aspin, a former congressman with experience in overseeing military affairs, was said to be a good political bridge between Congress and the defense establishment in an era of changing military roles. Secretary of Treasury Lloyd Bentsen, former chairman of the Senate Finance Committee, was declared another shrewd political appointment, welcomed by Congress and Wall Street alike. Carol Browner as head of the Environmental Protection Agency stirred a bit more controversy, but drew cheers from environmentalist groups. Some industries, seeing the costs of tougher environmental protection as a threat to keeping company ledgers in the black, warned that a weak economy could not afford more environmental regulation. In her Senate confirmation hearings, Browner called herself a "pro-business

As Vice President Al Gore looks on, Bill Clinton—flanked by Treasury secretary Lloyd Bentsen (left) and Commerce secretary Ron Brown (right)—prepares in January 1993 to sign a directive creating a national economic council. Clinton soon found that creating new government bodies often proves easier than controlling the existing ones.

environmentalist" and was careful to reassure Senator John Warner (R–Virginia) that she wanted to improve relations between the EPA and the business community, and would not be driven by "alarmists."[1]

Each of these and other appointments reflected political calculations about how to handle the forces that clash in bureaucratic politics: congressional power and conflicting interests. Presidents also must be careful in their approach to large organizations such as the Defense Department that have their own power base and a sense of their mission. Reviewing the Clinton cabinet appointments, one journalist saw an effort to balance competing political forces: CLINTON'S CABINET CHOICES PUT HIM AT CENTER, BALANCING COMPETING POLITICAL FACTIONS.[2]

Yet no matter how presidents choose their top administrators, the bureaucracy remains hard to manage. Many of the biggest news stories from past administrations have been about the bureaucracy: from corruption scandals to the inability to get programs (in health, the environment, education, and so forth) running smoothly. High-level administrators often fail to win the support of the civil-service bureaucrats who supposedly work for them. And the news tells of wrangling among the White House, Congress, and interest groups over how to interpret and implement the laws.

Although news coverage concentrates on the top administrators appointed to run the bureaucracy, most chief executives in the modern era have turned to a shadow command system inside the White House to make sure the job is getting done. Surrounding the president are two inside layers of management that often prove more important than the cabinet in running the government: the Executive Office of the President, and the White House staff. The **Executive Office of the President** includes a number of councils of advisors who keep the president posted on defense, foreign policy, economic and trade relations, and the budget, among many other policy areas. Even closer to the president is the White House staff, consisting of the president's personal advisors, communications team, speechwriters, and strategists, all managed by a chief of staff. The chief of staff wields considerable political power simply by controlling who gets to see the president and what information reaches the Oval Office desk. In some administrations the chief of staff and the top staff advisors have consolidated enough power in the White House to bypass the bureaucracy on important issues.

As noted in Chapter 14, Bill Clinton appointed one of his oldest personal friends as White House chief of staff. This headline told most of the story: CLINTON GOES WAY BACK TO FILL A KEY WHITE HOUSE JOB, "MACK" McLARTY, AS THE OLDEST "FRIEND OF BILL," WON'T BE AN INSULATOR.[3] "Friend of Bill" was the term that captured Washington's imaginations to describe the large network of friends that the Clintons called into the new administration. McLarty was the oldest "F.O.B.," going back to kindergarten in Hope, Arkansas. His selection as the gatekeeper who controls the flow of people and ideas reflected Clinton's concern about having a trusted friend who would keep any secret, not impose his own political agenda, and help to

tame that vast network of councils, offices, and departments stretching out from the White House and into every state in the nation. Effective management of the bureaucracy means many things, from simply getting things done efficiently to promoting the goals that got the president elected in the first place. As noted in Chapter 14, the Washington power game gave McLarty and Clinton headaches as they tried to get the new administration moving. Developing a management style that uses the staff, the Executive Office councils, and Cabinet officers and other administrators to act as a team is perhaps the most challenging task any president faces.

People generally view the bureaucracy as a faceless, soulless machine. Nonetheless, in the offices and agencies of the executive branch laws are turned into the social realities of health care, roads, retirement funds, power plants, missiles, agriculture research, and technological development. This chapter explores bureaucracy as a political flashpoint where many forces of government and politics come together. It is important for citizens to consider the political importance of what bureaucracy does. Perhaps the most important lesson about bureaucracy is that much perceived red tape, regulation, and bungling is the result of conflicting political forces.

A Political Hotbed

As explained in the previous chapter, the president cannot simply command the bureaucracy into action and expect results. Bureaucracy is hard to move for a number of reasons. First, the thousands of programs make it hard to simply keep track of what is going on in all the agencies and offices where the real activities of government take place. In addition, Congress commands a good deal of bureaucratic loyalty because programs are authorized by Capitol Hill, and the taxpayer money to keep them going must be approved from year to year in budget hearings. Finally, many interest groups work the halls of the bureaucracy almost as actively as they work the halls of Congress. The bureaucratic stage of writing rules and regulations can be as crucial as the original legislative process was in the first place. Looking down on all of this must seem dizzying for presidents, who are charged with the task of managing it in some coherent way. The bureaucracy is at the center of a political tug-of-war in which Congress, interest groups, and the president may all pull for different interpretations and priorities in the law. Presidents try to pick their openings and enter the fray at crucial points, telling bureaucrats what their priorities should be, issuing executive orders that affect how laws are implemented, or reviewing rules and regulations inside Executive Office councils where programs may be delayed or given a new emphasis. All of this makes bureaucratic politics among the most interesting of Washington spectator sports. The average taxpaying voter, however, is seldom amused by bureaucratic gamesmanship, exerting added political pressure on the government as explained in "Inside the System" Box 15.1.

Bureaucratic Politics: The Case of Environmental Regulation

Consider an example of how high-level political infighting can affect the implementation of programs. Here is how Henry A. Waxman, a Democratic member of Congress, viewed the Bush administration's enforcement of the Clean Air Act of 1990: "In less than a year and a half, his Administration has broken the law 35 times in failing to issue regulations needed to carry out the act."[4] Waxman even accused the administration of failing to implement provisions of the law in an effort to grant favors to political supporters. Campaigning during the election of 1992, the president promised power plant operators in Texas he would not control nitrous oxide emissions. Speaking to auto executives in Michigan, he promised to exempt domestic automobiles from certain emissions standards. Were these cases of lawbreaking? Or political favoritism? The administration denied the Democratic charges, saying that the spirit of the law was to balance environmental values with free-market protection so that regulations would not damage economic growth. In other words, the president said he was simply living up to the spirit of compromise that went into passing the original law.

The order to be less rigid in enforcing regulations was sent by the Competitiveness Council (inside the Executive Office of the president) to the Environmental Protection Agency (EPA), the bureaucratic unit responsible for implementing the Clean Air Act. The EPA's own legal council decided that it could not independently grant higher emission levels without holding a public hearing. As a result, William Reilly, President Bush's appointed head of the EPA, told the White House that his agency could not act as instructed. At this point the president became involved personally, ordering his EPA administrator to issue a formal rule permitting the emission increases. Again, the EPA chief refused, but he tried to appease his boss by saying he would go along if the president

At left, President Bush signs the Clean Air Act of 1990 as EPA chief William K. Reilly (left) and Department of Energy secretary James Watkins (right) look on. At right, Carol Browner—who succeeded Reilly at the EPA when Bill Clinton became president—testifies at a 1993 House hearing. Clinton had mocked Bush's 1988 pledge to become "the environmental president," but soon found his own environmental agenda was not easy to implement.

Why Americans Hate Bureaucracy

15.1

The creation of a vast federal bureaucracy during the era of cooperative federalism triggered a later backlash of public demands to cut big government and trim the fat from the bureaucracy. Yet, although there is bound to be inefficiency in any large organization, polls also show that most Americans object to cutting programs that benefit them, and that many favor the addition of new programs. What accounts for these contradictory political reactions? Once again, we turn to features of the system that affect the politics surrounding the federal bureaucracy.

Cultural resistance to big government plays an obvious role here; an even deeper factor may be cultural concerns about the anonymity and permanence of bureaucratic institutions. The American *political culture* continues to deeply value personal-ized government, with officials being held accountable to citizens. Bureaucracy may appear out of control because career officials seem less accountable to the public than the term *public servant* implies. (Indeed, bureaucrats may arguably turn their "double accountability"— to both the elective executive and the legislature—to their own advantage, by playing one branch against the other.) In addition, our individualistic political culture leads many citizens to evaluate government in terms of what it offers them personally rather than what it contributes to the quality of society as a whole. Compared to many other nations, citizens of the United States seem to have greater difficulty placing a value on the quality of public services (consisting largely of the programs run by bureaucratic agencies).

Finally, an *institutional design* that holds bureaucracies accountable to both the legislatures that create and fund them and the executives who manage them, makes political control difficult. This encourages interest groups to work their way into bureaucratic politics, further weakening clear lines of political control.

Because many points of *power in society* focus on bureaucratic politics, the aims of majorities, interest groups, and elites may often conflict. *Majorities* often demand sweeping bureaucratic cutbacks at election time, yet individuals in those majorities may support *interest group efforts* to save pet bureaucratic programs ranging from trade subsidies to senior citizens' benefits. All the while, influential *elites* may be operating behind the scenes to sustain programs that hold little interest for support from either majorities or pluralities of the public. These competing pressures on bureaucracy can make coherent bureaucratic action and reform difficult to achieve. All of this may reinforce the deeply rooted cultural outlook about bureaucracy's inefficiency and lack of public accountability.

could convince the attorney general (the government's top lawyer) to state in writing that such a ruling was legal. The attorney general wrote a memo saying that such increases could be granted under some circumstances, and the EPA eventually issued a rule to that effect. Is the refusal of an agency head to obey a presidential order insubordination to the president? Or is it simply a case of a cross-pressured bureaucrat attempting to carry out the will of Congress? These are common tensions in the political forces that affect bureaucratic action.

Although the above rule allowing for pollution *increases* was written by the EPA, other rules called for in the law were *not* being written. Angry critics demanded that something had to be done to put the law into effect. At this point, another force came into play in another political arena. Some states began suing the EPA directly to enforce the law. In a federal suit brought to the district court in Albany in 1992, nine states argued that the bureaucratic failure to write rules covering many provisions of the law put the states themselves in danger of violating the law.[5] While the states were required by the Clean Air Act to regulate polluters by issuing permits and monitoring the outputs of factories and automobiles, the lack of rules made it impossible to carry out these tasks. Not only did some states want to apply the law within their borders, but the failure to do so might cost them certain funds—such as federal highway construction money that the Clean Air Act offered to states that successfully implemented the pollution rules. If the states won the case, the federal courts could compel the EPA to act independently of the orders of the president. As it turned out, however, President Bush lost the 1992 election, and these became dead issues because the Clinton administration promised to implement the law according to the wishes of Congress.

However, the arrival of a new administration did not mean that political pressures would be lifted from the EPA. At her Senate confirmation hearings, Carol Browner, Clinton's EPA nominee, signalled the intention of the new administration to adopt a tougher line on enforcing pollution standards; yet she also promised that there would be limits on how aggressive the new regime would be. One of those limits was to stop short of creating economic hardships for businesses. And so the bureaucratic battle goes 'round and 'round.

Implementing the Law: The Bureaucratic Mission ___

To such administrative agencies as the EPA in the above example belongs the task of writing the hundreds of rules and regulations that bring the force of law into action. In the case of air pollution, this means establishing the levels of allowable pollution, developing procedures for monitoring emissions, dividing enforcement responsibilities between state agencies and federal regulators, and setting up the procedures and penalties for enforcement. In light of such powers, it is not surprising that bureaucratic agencies become centers of political action, watched by Congress, lobbied by interest groups, and pressured by the White House to move in particular directions. Figure 15.1 illustrates the pattern of bureaucratic rules and regulations over the years, as measured indirectly by the number of pages in the *Federal Register* that publishes rules, regulations, executive orders, and proclamations, among other documents.

When a president signs a bill, as President Bush signed the Clean Air Act of 1990, there are often political pressures involved and political compromises made. Presidents may try to recover lost political ground during implementation. In this sense, the politics of legislation can live forever through the politics of implementation.

Regulatory issues, which make up much of the task of bureaucracy, offer different administrations considerable room for political maneuvering. Consider, for example, the politics surrounding the regulation of toxic substances in the workplace, one small part of the Occupational Safety and Health Act of 1970. Deciding what toxic substances to regulate and how to do it is a political struggle that has been going on since the passage of the act. The players include various committees of Congress, offices within the Department of Labor, offices in the Executive Office of the President, and the millions of American workers affected. One of those workers was Homar Stull, who died in the National Beef Packing plant in Liberal, Kansas, along with two other workers who tried to rescue him. All were overcome by concentrations of deadly fumes given off by a vat of animal blood. Family members charged that these workers might have lived if regulations governing safety in confined spaces had not been stalled for over two decades after passage of the OSHA act.[6] The responsible regulatory body, the Occupational Safety and Health Administration, was frustrated by a combination of many different workplaces to regulate, conflicting pressures from manufacturers' groups and associations, and lack of enthusiasm from politicians concerned about stymying business growth. The Clinton administration vowed to restore workplace safety as a top priority, but—as with its

FIGURE 15.1

The Growth of Bureaucratic Regulations

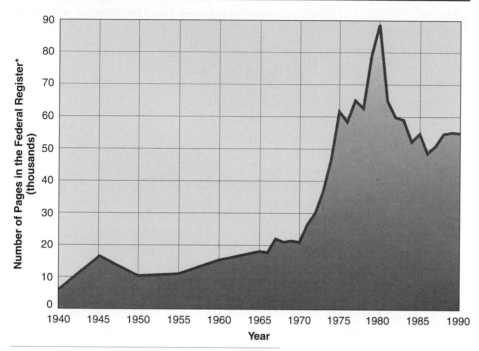

*In addition to rules and regulations, the *Federal Register* also contains executive orders, proclamations, and reorganization plans. Thus, these estimates of rules and regulations are only approximations.

Source: *Federal Register*, 1940–1990, U.S. Government Printing Office. Adapted from Harold W. Stanley and Richard G. Niemi, *Vital Statistics on American Politics*, 3rd ed., Washington, D.C.: CQ Press, 1992, p. 271.

environmental regulation policy—also promised not to create hardships for businesses. Once again, the story of bureaucracy was a political one: in this case, striking the balance between saving jobs and saving workers' lives—values that are very hard to compare. Remembering such instances of bureaucratic politics may enliven the seemingly dull subject of bureaucratic organization.

Bureaucratic Organization

The idea of bureaucracy is very old and nearly universal. Long before nations existed in Europe, the empires of Asia stretched over vast territories thanks to bureaucratic organizations that provided the links between central leaders and the local administrators who did their bidding. In its simplest sense, *bureaucracy refers to a hierarchical chain of command within an organization in which each office, or bureau, has specific duties and responsibilities and a clear set of authority relations with offices above and below*. The defining characteristics of bureaucracy include:

- *Specialization of tasks*: Offices have well-defined responsibilities, and workers have special skills needed to perform particular duties.
- *Hierarchy*: A clear chain of command and responsibility exists.

In addition to these defining characteristics of all bureaucracies, we add two special characteristics of the American federal bureaucracy in the modern period. Although our system allows for political appointments at the top of organizations to implement the policies of particular administrations, the ranks of those who actually do the work of bureaucracy have been isolated from politics in two ways:

- *Career employment*: In the modern era since the passage of the 1883 Pendleton Act (to be discussed at length later in this chapter), civil service bureaucracies generally involve regular advancement, long-term tenure or seniority protection for workers, and employee benefits such as retirement security.

- *A professional commitment to political neutrality:* In another modern innovation, career civil servants are impartial, independent of party or partisan loyalty, and obligated to carry out the orders of new political superiors when administrations change. This commitment to nonpartisanship and impartiality came about with the enactment of the 1939 Hatch Act, which aimed (among other provisions) to prevent members of political organizations from pressuring government employees into making political contributions or otherwise coercing them (by threatening job security or possible promotions, demotions, or reassignments) into participating in partisan activities or campaigns. However, in 1993 both chambers of Congress took steps to weaken the Hatch Act, making some previously off-limits political activity permissible. Conservative opponents vigorously fought the move, arguing that, for example, the IRS official who audits your taxes should not be able to visit you that same evening kindly requesting a donation to a political campaign. Bill Clinton, urged on by federal and postal union PACs, expressed his support for softening Hatch Act checks on partisanship.

Today in the United States, the basic units of bureaucracy go by many names: *bureaus*, *agencies*, *offices*, *boards*, *commissions*, *federal corporations*, and *services*, among others. Some of these units are housed within larger **departments** that coordinate such broad areas as education or defense and report to the president through departmental secretaries of the Cabinet. Other units are independent of the department structure and report directly to the president or to the Executive Office of the President. Still other branches of the bureaucracy are insulated against political intervention by the executive. What may be most confusing is not just the number of different units in the federal bureaucracy, but that they go by so many different names, making a regular alphabet soup of government.

Decoding the Alphabet Soup

It is easy to become confused about bureaucracy because of the hundreds—if not thousands—of technical names that pass through the news from time to time with little explanation. All those governmental acronyms (DOD, FDIC, FDA, NASA, OSHA, EPA, ATF, NSA, and so forth) are where laws become public policy that directly affects the way we live.

Many bureaucratic terms—*offices*, *administrations*, or *bureaus*—can refer to units fairly similar in their missions and makeup. Yet there are some distinctive terms that signal something special about the organization and help bring some order to the bureaucratic alphabet. Some organizations are huge conglomerates called **executive departments,** which are made up of many smaller offices, bureaus, and administrations dedicated to a common general purpose. The largest of these is the Department of Defense (DOD), with over 900,000 employees, not counting the fighting forces. DOD is an *executive department*, often known as a *cabinet department* because the heads or secretaries of departments belong to the president's Cabinet of formal advisors. Table 15.1 shows the growth of Cabinet departments since 1789.

Within the executive departments, the alphabet soup becomes even thicker, as bureaus, offices, administrations, and corporations have been created over the years to perform specific tasks. For example, the Occupational Safety and Health Administration (OSHA) is inside of the larger Department of Labor and is charged with turning the

TABLE 15.1

The Growth of Cabinet Departments

CABINET OFFICE	YEAR ESTABLISHED	NUMBER OF PAID CIVILIAN EMPLOYEES	
		1980	1991
State	1789	23,644	25,479
Treasury	1789	123,754	159,785
War*	1789		
Navy*	1798		
Interior	1849	79,505	71,290
Justice	1870	56,426	84,867
Post Office*	1872		
Agriculture	1889	122,839	108,935
Commerce and Labor*	1903		
Commerce	1913	46,189	45,013
Labor	1913	23,717	17,337
Defense	1947	972,999	1,014,212
Health, Education and Welfare*	1953		
Health and Human Services	1979	158,644	123,348
Housing and Urban Development	1965	16,890	13,211
Transportation	1966	72,066	66,688
Energy	1977	21,729	17,900
Education	1979	7,370	4,676
Veterans Affairs	1989	235,501**	249,957

*Asterisks denote departments later reconfigured or split into separate departments. The Post Office, formerly a cabinet-level department, is now the U.S. Postal Service, an independent government entity.

** Includes nationwide Veterans Affairs hospital staff and related personnel.

workplace safety laws of Congress into regulations affecting workers whether they go down into the mines or stare at computer screens. The FDA, or Food and Drug Administration, is a branch of the Department of Health and Human Services that brings food and drug purity laws to reality by sending inspectors into packing houses, food plants, and drug companies to make sure they are following the rules.

Other bureaucratic units are called **independent agencies,** which function a bit like departments, but do not have cabinet rank, usually because their tasks are not deemed as important or complex as those of the departments. For example, *EPA* refers to the Environmental Protection Agency which is an independent agency (meaning that it is not inside a larger department), and its director (like cabinet officers, a political appointee) answers directly to the White House. Bill Clinton announced his intention to elevate the EPA to cabinet rank because of the importance he attributed to its functions. Presidents may invite administrators who are not department heads to attend cabinet meetings simply because they are regarded as important players in the administration game plan.

Another type of executive branch organization is the **independent regulatory commission,** set up by Congress and run by a board of commissioners who serve terms fixed by law. Although commissioners are nominated by the president and confirmed by Congress (the Senate), their mandate is to be bipartisan, and their fixed term in office means that they cannot be removed when the president does not like their political decisions. As these special considerations suggest, the independent regulatory commissions are charged with overseeing and investigating the workings of important and sensitive areas of national life such as broadcasting (FCC, or Federal Communications Commission), labor relations (National Labor Relations Board, or NLRB), and trading practices in the stock markets (Securities and Exchange Commission, or SEC), among others.

There are also government chartered and supervised corporations known as **public corporations** that operate in some ways like private corporations, from selling insurance (Federal Deposit Insurance Corporation, or FDIC) to selling electricity (the Tennessee Valley Authority, or TVA). Like the regulatory agencies, some of the public corporations are housed within larger departments, and others are independent. For example, the

Internal Revenue Service (IRS) employees sort income-tax forms in a Georgia office that serves the southeastern United States. The IRS remains one of the less popular federal bureaucracies, but its activities help to make all those other government programs possible.

Federal Crop Insurance Corporation is run out of the Department of Agriculture. The FDIC is an independent public corporation set up by Congress to insure the nation's savings accounts and monitor banks and savings institutions that participate in those programs. Could private insurance corporations provide similar services? Yes, but the failure of many banks and insurance companies during the Great Depression convinced Congress that a government corporation would be more reliable. When large numbers of savings banks went bankrupt during the 1980s, the FDIC reserves were too small to cover the losses, but its status as a public corporation made it easier for Congress and the executive to funnel public money into the lost accounts and to coordinate the national bailout without creating a financial panic.

Some organizations have unique political heritages that make them hard to classify. For example, the U.S. Postal Service looks in many ways like a public corporation, but it was not created like most others, according to the guidelines of the Government Corporation Control Act. The Postal Service has its own personnel system that is not run according to civil service guidelines. Before becoming the largest independent bureaucratic entity, the Postal Service was an executive department whose chief, the Postmaster General, was a member of the president's cabinet as recently as 1970.

As the above examples suggest, some clues about an executive branch organization may be revealed by its title, but many names in the alphabet soup are arbitrary inventions of the congressional committees that create most of the bureaucracy. As in many other things in Washington, there can be political considerations behind the decision to call something an office or a bureau and whether to house it within a department or to give it independent standing. Political calculations thus enter into the design and even the naming of different branches of the bureaucracy.

The Command System

The federal bureaucracy spreads out broadly around the president. Some units are shielded from direct Oval Office management (the Postal Service and the independent commissions, for example). Others, such as the departments and independent agencies, come directly under the command of presidential appointees, yet they can resist taking orders because of their sheer size, complexity, and accountability to Congress. Still other units, such as the councils and offices in the Executive Office of the President, are political creations of the chief executive and generally respond quickly to commands.

The challenge of bureaucratic management from the Oval Office is to mobilize three million civil servants on behalf of the president's agenda without getting them into too

FIGURE 15.2   *The National Government: Executive Branch in Relation to Other Branches*

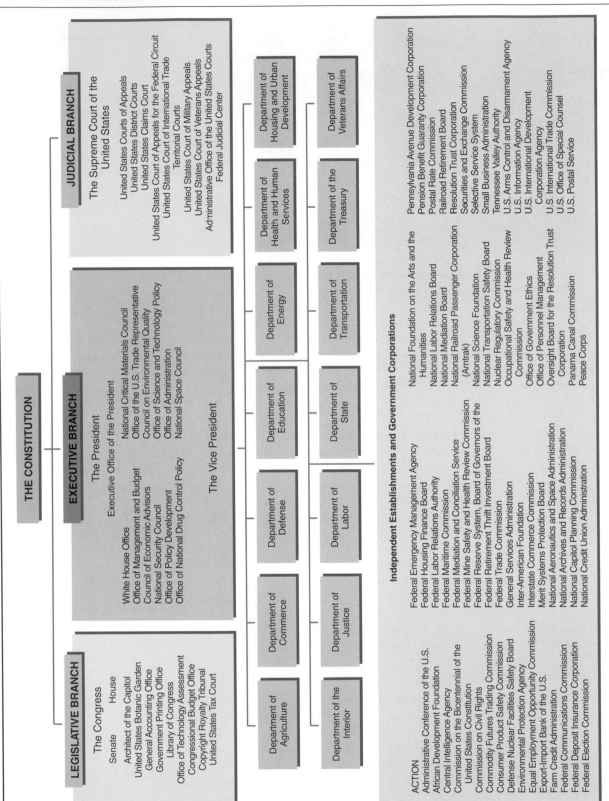

Source: *U.S. Government Manual*, 1991–1992, p. 21.

much trouble with Congress in areas where the president and Congress disagree. The hottest political conflicts in Washington occur deep in the bureaucratic maze where the directives of the president may come squarely up against a congressional committee charged with overseeing a particular program. While the bureaucracy has always been a place of political conflict, the nature of politics inside the bureaucracy has changed greatly over the years as both the organization of the executive branch and the roles of government have changed.

Historical Changes in Bureaucratic Politics

Bureaucratic politics have changed considerably as the institutions that regulate our society have shifted over time. In the first administration, there were just three departments in the executive branch: State, War, and Treasury. (The first State Department had ten employees, including the Secretary!) Today there are fourteen departments and some sixty independent regulatory commissions and agencies (such as the Environmental Protection Agency) employing nearly three million people. Over 900,000 of these (not including soldiers in uniform) are in the Department of Defense, and roughly 800,000 are in the U.S. Postal Service. By comparison, the legislative branch employs some 38,000 people; the judicial branch is smaller, at around 26,000. Figure 15.2 illustrates the organization of the federal government with the executive bureaucracy at its core, and Figure 15.3 illustrates the relative size of the three branches in terms of numbers of employees.

FIGURE 15.3

Civilian Employees in the Three Branches of Government

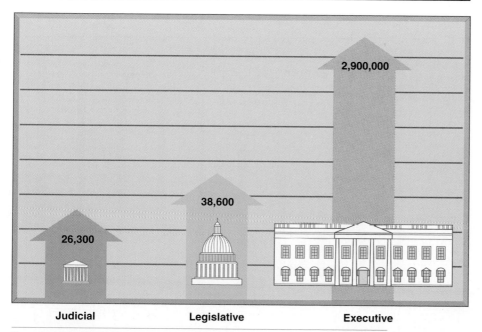

Source: U. S. Department of Labor, Bureau of Labor Statistics, *Employment and Earnings Supplement, 1992*, p. 206.

Many people oversimplify the problems of government by pointing to the growth of bureaucracy in Washington. In fact, national government employment has grown at a comparatively slow rate since the end of World War II. The size of the national government is not only smaller than the total of the states and the total of all local governments, but has grown at a slower rate than either of these two, as shown in Figure 15.4. The number of independent agencies (shown in the large box at the bottom of Figure 15.2) increased from fewer than ten at the turn of the last century to more than sixty by 1980. However, the number of agencies and commissions actually shrank due to government reorganizations during the Reagan and Bush administrations in the 1980s and had stabilized at around sixty at the start of the 1990s. More important than the growth of agencies or numbers of employees are fundamental historical changes in the political roles of the bureaucracy itself.

The Spoils System

The first century of federal (and state) bureaucracy was heavily politicized, making today's bureaucratic politics seem tame. Most government jobs were awarded by parties as patronage appointments to reward their supporters. This so-called spoils system proved effective in building party machines and motivating party workers to campaign and turn out voters. This system was corrupt and bureaucracies were often staffed by people with few qualifications for their jobs. Although many countries have eliminated the spoils system because of its corruption and inefficiency, some nations have adapted to highly political bureaucracies, usually as a means of maintaining support for dominant

FIGURE 15.4

Civilian Employment in National, State, and Local Government, 1950–1992

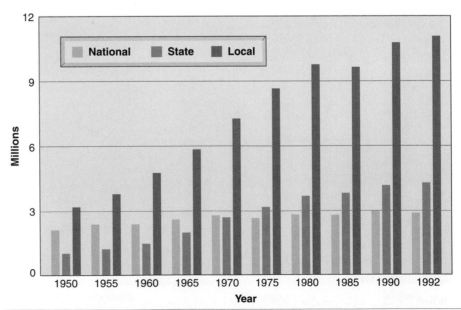

Source: U.S. Department of Labor, Bureau of Labor Statistics, *Employment and Earnings Supplement, 1992,* pp. 206–207; *Employment and Earnings, 1991,* pp. 874–882.

The Political Bureaucracy in Mexico

15.2

I n the United States, the term *civil service* describes the ranks of independent, nonpartisan bureaucrats. Mexicans refer to their administration as a "political bureaucracy." For most of the twentieth century, it has been difficult to separate the activities of the bureaucracy from the interests of the political party that has dominated Mexican politics. The PRI, or the Party of the Institutionalized Revolution, rose to power in 1929. It has not lost a single presidential election since that time.

Since the Mexican bureaucracy is so political, it has considerable power to develop and implement party policies. The line of command is fairly simple, with the president of Mexico controlling the bureaucracy on behalf of the party, and the various bureaucratic organizations doling out services and programs with an eye to rewarding local areas and politicians who have been party supporters.

This system has a strong element of "spoils" in it, with government jobs being awarded to helpful politicians and their friends and family. Good political careers are made by rising through the bureaucracy. Along the way, workers make contacts with clients in various public and private sectors who can do favors for bureaucrats and be offered favors, in turn, by the party. This large machine organization obviously protects the interests of rich and powerful groups, but Mexico has developed a strong network of local support down to the village level.

Critics charge that the main purpose of the government has been to keep the PRI and its associates in power. New parties have challenged PRI rule from both the left and the right with some success in state-level elections, but the PRI holds on firmly to the national government, thanks largely to its bureaucracy.

SOURCES: Robert E. Gamer, *The Developing Nations: A Comparative Perspective.* Boston: Allyn and Bacon, 1982; and John J. Bailey, *Governing Mexico: The Statecraft of Crisis Management.* New York: St. Martin's Press, 1988.

---

political parties. The example of a political bureaucracy in contemporary Mexico is discussed in "How We Compare" Box 15.2.

The Rise of a Professional Civil Service

In 1883, Congress passed the **Pendleton Act,** creating a professional *civil service,* meaning that *jobs would be filled by people who had to pass qualifying examinations,* and *careers could not be terminated for political reasons.* (It came about only after President James Garfield was killed by a disgruntled office-seeker.) The idea of a professional bureaucracy was slow to take hold, however. At first, the Pendleton Act was applied to only a small percentage of government jobs. During the early decades of the century, state and national politicians calling themselves "progressives" pushed for cleaning up the bureaucracy by expanding the ranks of the civil service. By the end of the 1920s, the vast majority of federal employees were hired under the guidelines of the civil service laws.

The Rise of an Activist Bureaucracy

When the Great Depression created broad public demand for solutions to people's economic woes, the number of government offices, bureaus, and agencies grew enormously. Following the shift to cooperative federalism during this period, the federal bureaucracy acquired the power to impose its standards on states, individuals, and businesses. A leading theory of the modern bureaucracy is that of political scientist James Q. Wilson, who argues that its size is not the real issue at all. Rather, the political struggle surrounding the bureaucracy results from the evolution of an increasingly *activist bureaucracy* in which programs intervene directly in almost every area of life—programs that create strong interest-group support and make offices and agencies active political players in the tug of war between Congress, the president, and political interests.[7] Today's bureaucrats are often *permanently* situated in the middle of conflicts between states, interest groups, lawmakers, and even their boss, the president. Wilson calls this phenomenon **the rise of the bureaucratic state.**[8]

The Rise of the Bureaucratic State

As bureaucratic tasks have moved more into the center of society, some of the greatest political conflicts in government descend upon the bureaucracy and must become resolved there. Even the impartiality of the career civil service cannot save bureaucrats and their departments from becoming politicized. This political mobilization of the bureaucracy is not like the sort that characterized the old spoils system, where parties forged direct links with government employees. Rather, it is more subtle, and in many ways more worrisome. Bureaucrats often develop political sympathies for their *clients,* the groups they regulate or provide services to. Those clients, in turn, belong to interest groups that pressure Congress to maintain favored bureaucratic programs. Over time, these relations between bureaucratic organizations, the interests they serve, and the influence of those same interests in Congress can become very entrenched, as explained in the discussions of *iron triangles* in Chapter 8 on interest groups and Chapter 12 on Congress. We will explore the third side of iron triangles in their bureaucratic context in the next section.

The Politics of Bureaucratic Interests

When bureaucracies become too tightly connected to the clients they serve, there is a problem of accountability. Are bureaucrats accountable to Congress or the president—or to the very interests they are supposed to be regulating? *In the bureaucratic state, interests become the organizing force of power, even though they have very little accountability to the people—and no direct accountability through elections.* "Inside the System" Box 15.3 illustrates this power behind the scenes in the bureaucratic state.

Consider the bureaucratic politics behind a situation in which the Air Force convinced the Secretary of Defense that it needed a new high-tech bomber with "stealth" capabilities to evade radar detection. The potential for profits building the plane motivated a defense contractor to "sell" a design to the Pentagon more elaborate than the design originally envisioned. Inside the Pentagon, the plane represented a prominent role in war and defense planning which was good for the Air Force as an organization, providing for bigger budgets and more numerous and prestigious career opportunities for officers and civil service employees alike.

What happened when Air Force procurement and planning specialists learned that the plane had a design defect and would cost far more than estimated? What happened when that "bad news" was compounded by the end of the Cold War and the reduced military threat of the former Soviet Union, all of which, according to military experts, reduced the need for expensive, high-tech weapons such as the new bomber? What should the Pentagon and Congress do?

Power in the Bureaucratic State

15.3

I nterest groups can establish direct political links with members of Congress, with presidents, and with the bureaucrats who run programs. Even if one side of an iron triangle is broken, the others often hold strong, keeping programs alive. As the bureaucracy has become more the center of political struggle, the line between the legislative and executive functions has become less clear, and bureaucracy often writes many of the details of laws through the rule and regulation process.

As a result of their independent ties with the interest groups they serve or regulate, and their increased control over the laws they implement, bureaucratic departments cannot simply be commanded by Congress or the president to do things. The bureaucracy increasingly has its own sphere of power and its own political relations with client groups in society. The dilemma of power in this bureaucratic state is that *the framers of the Constitution did not envision the rise of this large and semiautonomous part of the government.*

There is some accountability for bureaucratic power through the public hearing process, in which interest groups (such as environmentalists and loggers) may offer their views on issues (from monitoring endangered species to managing national forest lands). Workers and employers may have direct input into rules about safety in the workplace. Doctors, drug companies, and patient groups may all testify at hearings about the release of new medications for public use. However, with the exception of the few presidential appointments at the top, bureaucrats are not replaced by election, which means that the major channel of *majoritarian power* is not very effective in controlling the bureaucratic state. All of this adds to the public concerns about bureaucracy discussed in Box 15.1 (page 541).

Iron Triangles Revisited

The above scenario describes what in fact did happen with the B-2 bomber, a plane that cost about $2 billion each and became threatened by a combination of design problems, federal budget strains, and a sudden outbreak of world peace. Yet the Air Force announced that the difficulty in achieving stealth capability was not really a problem, particularly since wars of the future might not be against such high-tech opponents as the former Soviet Union. Meanwhile, threats from Congress to cut massive projects from a strained budget were silenced at the last minute when the builders of the plane, along with defense interests working to save other threatened weapons programs, put on a huge lobbying blitz before the 1992 election. At stake, said the contractors, were jobs in an already sluggish economy. (Also at stake were fat campaign contributions and votes in an election year.) In a last-minute rush to pass a budget and go home with some good news for their districts to kick off the campaign, committees of Congress approved funding for more B-2 bombers, along with a number of other threatened programs.

The ability of the players in this iron triangle to protect their interests gave each what it wanted: The Air Force held its budget and protected the careers of the people connected with the program; defense contractors kept their contracts and saved jobs; and members of Congress received valuable electoral support—while avoiding the difficult issue of how to revitalize a sluggish economy that has become heavily dependent on government spending. But—whether the marginal program involves defense or housing or agricultural subsidies—are the *interests of the nation* best served by such arrangements?

Such bureaucratic patterns are hard for the chief executive to disrupt. Whatever the political agenda of a president may be, there are several ways in which the struggle to control the bureaucracy is played out:

- Appointing loyal cabinet officers and top administrators to try to control the departments and agencies of government
- Using the resources of the Executive Office of the President to monitor operations and, in many cases, make policy directly from the top, and
- Organizing a loyal and efficient personal staff to bring as much information and as many policy decisions to the president's attention as possible.

Understanding the politics in each of these areas may help us see how the bureaucracy works and why it sometimes does not.

Politics in the Departments and the Cabinet

Broadly related functions and categories of activities are often lumped together in the *departments*. Figure 15.5 shows how the State Department is organized. Notice that there are offices for various parts of the world, for ocean and environmental policies, for fighting narcotics trafficking, for human rights monitoring, for information gathering, and for relations with Congress, among others. The State Department's organization reflects not only its broad mission of foreign relations, but various hot topics in world affairs and the importance of its political link with Congress. Figure 15.6 shows the Department of Health and Human Services, which is organized around its primary activities of family policy, health care, public health, and social security.

To help control these complex bureaucratic departments, presidents nominate (and the Senate approves) the heads or *secretaries* of the departments, along with a number of deputies and assistants who help to manage the departments. (See the fourteen departments under the president in Figure 15.1.) The secretaries of the departments sit in the president's *cabinet*. Also attending cabinet meetings are people the president regards as crucial for coordinating national policy at the highest level. For example, the vice president commonly attends cabinet meetings, along with the director of the Office of Management and Budget (OMB), who writes up the president's proposal to fund executive programs each year. The cabinet is a council of advisors who meet regularly to report to the chief executive, discuss important policy issues, and report the wishes of the boss back to their departments. At least that is how the cabinet is *supposed* to work.

In practice, the cabinet seldom turns out to be a unified team capable of providing focused advice. The cabinet is a large group with different interests and loyalties and a high turnover rate. In developing the political game plan of the administration, most presidents rely on a "kitchen cabinet," an informal group that may consist of some trusted members of the cabinet, key advisers on the personal staff, and even close friends or family members with no official role in the administration. As a result of the diminished planning role of the cabinet, most presidents use cabinet meetings to inform top administrators of plans already made inside the White House and to gain their cooperation.

A variety of factors have made the cabinet system a weak method for controlling the bureaucracy. Among the problems that have confronted presidents over the years are two in particular:

- *Cabinet officers may not be sufficiently loyal to the president.* Often presidents cannot find close associates with the skills to handle demanding posts such as

FIGURE 15.5   *The Organization of the State Department*

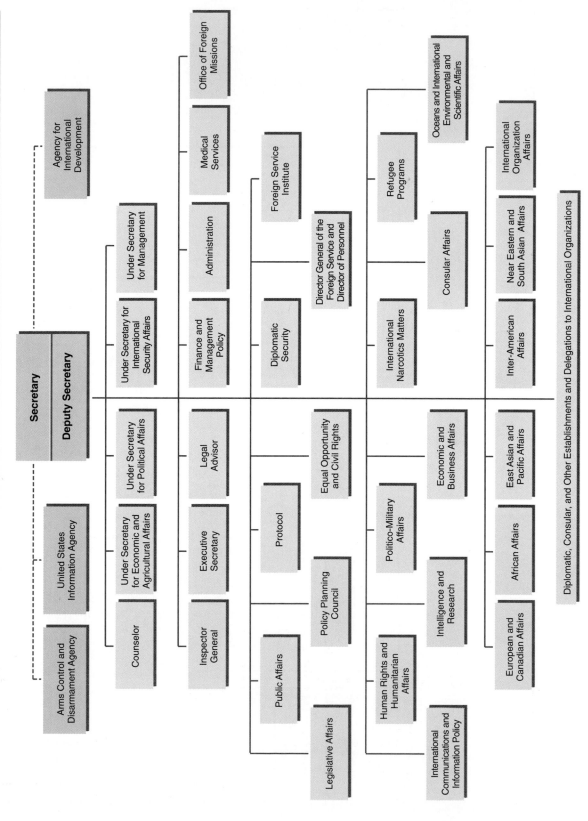

Source: *U.S. Government Organization Manual*, 1991/1992. U.S. Government Printing Office, p. 439.

FIGURE 15.6   *The Organization of the Department of Health and Human Services*

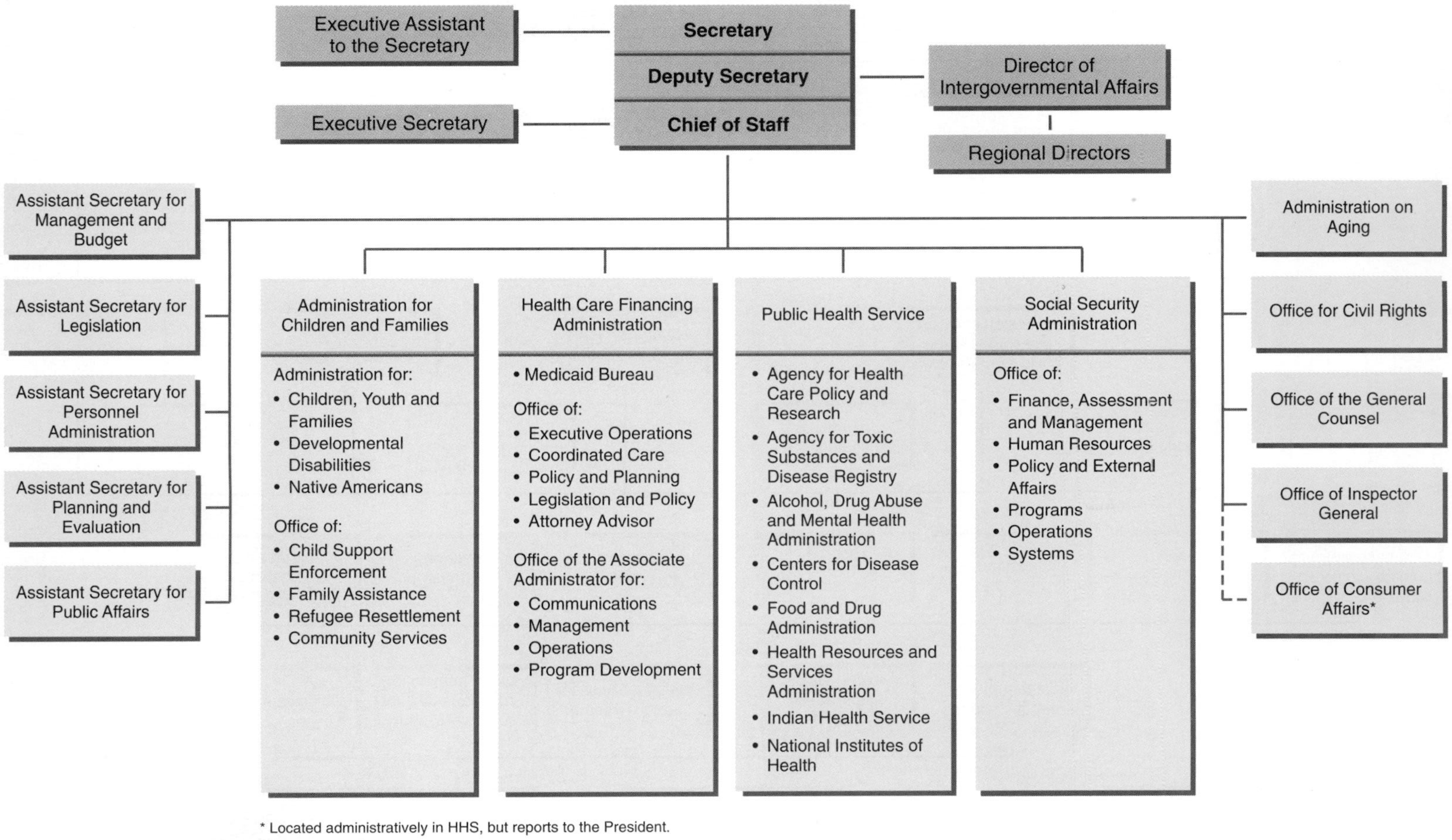

* Located administratively in HHS, but reports to the President.

*Located administratively in HHS, but reports to the president.
Source: *U.S. Government Organization Manual,* 1991/1992. U.S. Government Printing Office, p. 303.

A Diverse Cabinet?

As president-elect, Bill Clinton promised that his cabinet would be a diverse one. Whatever his success, he did draw on both insiders and new faces. Lloyd Bentsen (*right*), a moderate Texas Democrat with twenty years' Senate experience, left the chairmanship of its Finance Committee to become Secretary of the Treasury. Attorney General Janet Reno, however, had been virtually unknown. The third choice for the post (after nominations for Zoë Baird and Kimba Wood fell apart), the former Miami prosecutor (*above*) nonetheless soon proved herself a popular figure. Taking the oath of office from Chief Justice William Rehnquist (*below, with back to camera*) are (*from far left*) Donna Shalala, Robert Reich, Ron Brown, Mike Espy, Bruce Babbitt, Les Aspin, Bentsen, and Henry Cisneros. Clinton's diversity pledge was belied in one sense: Most of his cabinet picks were—lawyers.

The Players

Bill Clinton, flanked by Secretary of State Warren Christopher (left) *and Secretary of Defense Les Aspin* (right), *begins his first cabinet meeting in early 1993. While bringing some new players into government, Clinton relied heavily on Democratic insiders for key posts. Christopher had been a sub-cabinet level figure during the Carter years; Aspin had established his defense record during a twenty-year career in the House that included a stint as chairman of the Armed Services Committee.*

secretary of defense or secretary of state. In these cases, presidents often tap into "the establishment" in their parties to find people with the experience to do these jobs. While these secretaries may be competent, they also may have their own ideas about how to run their departments. In some cases, they even "go native," coming to identify with the values and views already established within the bureaucracy and protecting existing programs from White House interference.

- *Cabinet officers may not be respected by the bureaucrats below them.* Some of the political appointees who head departments are being rewarded for helping the president win the election and may not know much about the areas of government they have been assigned to run. Experienced civil servants often disregard inept bosses and try to make the best of leaderless situations. One result is that relations between the White House and the bureaucratic ranks can become strained.

Either way, whether cabinet officers are inept or simply too independent, it becomes hard for presidents to gain control of the departments. As a result, presidents with an interest in controlling the bureaucracy try to do it through other means. One common strategy is to use the Executive Office of the President either to get around unhelpful cabinet officers or in some cases to get around entire recalcitrant departments.

The Executive Office of the President

What is the Executive Office of the President? It is a collection of offices and councils that serves as a central command for gathering information and developing policy around the president's agenda. There are offices for economic planning, budget writing, security monitoring, trade relations, science and technology, and other activities that presidents have felt personal concerns about. Increasingly, this cluster of offices has become the eyes and ears of the chief executive.

Some presidents have even used the resources of the Executive Office to create a shadow bureaucracy to take over many of the functions of the cabinet and the bureaucratic departments. This was not the intent when Franklin Roosevelt created the Executive Office in 1939 by issuing an executive order stating explicitly that "in no event shall the Administrative Assistants to the President be interposed between the President and the head of any department or agency."[9] While the intent of the Executive Office may have been to monitor and coordinate activities in a growing bureaucracy, the size of the Executive Office has grown over the years, as have its political activities.

A Secret Government?

At times, the activities of the Executive Office are much more aggressive than just monitoring and coordinating policies. Many presidents have used the Executive Office to preempt the normal functions of the departments and agencies. For example, the National Security Council (NSC) is set up in the Executive Office to gather and analyze information from the many intelligence agencies in the government and to brief the president on world events that affect U.S. interests. The meetings of the NSC generally include members of the cabinet (for example, secretary of state and secretary of defense) and intelligence agency heads (for instance, director of the Central Intelligence Agency), along with members of the NSC staff. However, the daily work of this council is done by a full-time Executive Office staff headed by the assistant to the president for national security affairs. The occupant of this position holds considerable influence both as the central link in the intelligence community and as coordinator of sensitive national security policies.

It has been tempting for presidents and national security advisors who share a vision of foreign and military policy to carry out many initiatives directly from the White House, bypassing normal channels in the State Department and the Defense Department. These **back-channel operations,** as they are known, can result in a dangerous combination of concentrated power and little accountability. For example, when Henry Kissinger was the national security advisor to Richard Nixon, many international initiatives were run directly from the Executive Office, bypassing the departments and selectively involving such organizations as the CIA. One such activity was backing a military coup in Chile that overthrew Salvador Allende and installed Augusto Pinochet.[10] Mr. Kissinger eventually became secretary of state, and he began making foreign policy through more traditional bureaucratic channels.

During the Reagan administration, the National Security Council became the center of planning covert support for Nicaraguan rebels. The operations were run by members

The National Security Council (NSC) meets in March 1993. From left are NSC chairman Anthony Lake, Al Gore, Lloyd Bentsen, White House Chief of Staff Thomas "Mack" McLarty; Leon Panetta of the Office of Management and Budget, General Colin Powell of the Joint Chiefs of Staff, Warren Christopher, Clinton, Les Aspin, and CIA head James Woolsey.

of Mr. Reagan's NSC staff, despite opposition from Congress and words of caution from his own secretary of state. Although Congress had specifically forbidden many of the activities coordinated by National Security Advisor John Poindexter and his assistant, Oliver North, those activities went forward in secret. Congress was kept in the dark by North and others when they were called to Capitol Hill to testify about their activities. It ultimately turned out that North and Poindexter had effected a scheme to sell arms to Iran to generate money to help the *contras*—Nicaraguan counterrevolutionaries waging war against the revolutionary Sandinista regime.

This "secret government" operating out of the White House basement is the stuff of spy novels and movies. Indeed, North played out his role in the spirit of high drama, flying a secret mission to Iran to the intrigue. When the congressional investigations finally pieced the story together, it became clear the *entire operation had been conducted out of sight even from formal National Security Council operations,* since such members of the council as the secretary of state (George Shultz) and the vice president (George Bush) stated they were left "out of the loop"—not knowing about or authorizing North and Poindexter to proceed with the plan. President Ronald Reagan also testified he had known nothing of the illegal activities. The problem with moving the policy process inside the Executive Office of the President is that it can easily become hidden within the maze of backchannel operations, and bypass normal bureaucratic channels with their established accountability and oversight relations to Congress.

Shrinking the White House Establishment

Presidents who become frustrated with unwieldy departments have been tempted to expand their personalized bureaucracy in the Executive Office to get things done more to their liking. Critics, of course, point to this as a violation of constitutional checks on presidential power. Because of the controversy surrounding the uses and size of the Executive Office of the President, every president since Richard Nixon has promised to reduce it and curtail its activities. Jimmy Carter responded to the Nixon years by promising to cut the executive staff dramatically if he became president. After his first year in office, however, Carter realized that the bureaucracy was more a creature of Congress than his own domain. Even worse, he failed to command the loyalty of many of his own cabinet officers, whom he proceeded to fire. In the end, his own aides and assistants were given great powers, and the executive staff actually grew slightly over those of the previous administrations.

During the Reagan years, the size of the staff was reduced, but power was concentrated even further, with great responsibilities being delegated to members of the president's personal staff. *The president's staff consists of the personal appointees who are the innermost circle around the president. Some members of the staff may run the offices and councils of the Executive Office.* The presidential staff members of the Reagan years were often accused of running the executive offices as their personal political domains.

The Bush administration concentrated even more power in the Executive Office. Such top presidential advisors as John Sununu (who stepped down over charges of abuse of privilege) and Richard Darman (who headed the OMB) ran much of the domestic policy show, to the great dismay of many cabinet officers and bureaucrats alike, who felt excluded from the administration. After making a campaign promise to cut the White House staff, Bill Clinton faced the same dilemma of how to get control of the bureaucracy without an aggressive personal staff. Clinton did reduce the size of the lower-level Executive Office staff, but other political activities were stepped up inside the White House to coordinate policy initiatives. Figure 15.7 compares the sizes of the president's personal bureaucracy from the Nixon to the Clinton administrations.

FIGURE 15.7

White House Staffs from Nixon to Clinton

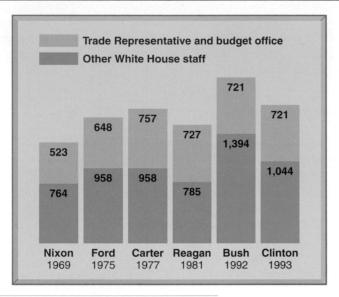

*The office of the Trade Representative and the budget office are part of the President's Executive Office staff, but were exempt from President Clinton's cuts.

Source: Office of Management and Budget. Adapted from *The New York Times,* February 10, 1993, p. A 8.

John Sununu, President Bush's first chief of staff, quietly surveys the scene at a 1989 presidental press conference. A former governor of New Hampshire, Sununu had played a key role in Bush's election by helping him to win that state's 1988 Republican primary. Once in the White House, however, Sununu developed a mixed reputation as a shrewd and capable administrator afflicted with an abrasive, arrogant personality. Chiefs of staff commonly act as "lightning rods," taking criticism that might otherwise hurt their bosses; Sununu ultimately resigned after accusations of misusing government transportation for personal business began to damage Bush politically.

The continuing political advantages of direct Executive Office intervention in bureaucratic affairs create a great dilemma. As political scientist Thomas Cronin put it:

> Plainly, the cabinet has lost power and the Executive Office has grown in status, in size, and in powers. In light of experience, should Roosevelt's promise [not to "interpose" staff between president and cabinet] be revised? Can the performance of the Executive Office be made to conform to Roosevelt's promise? Can the presidential establishment really be cut back?[11]

The President's Personal Staff

Much of the success or failure of an administration often depends on the **management style** developed within the president's staff. For example, President Eisenhower ran a hierarchical political operation learned from his days as Commander of the Army. His chief of staff screened all access to the boss and imposed a clear chain of command within the White House offices and the cabinet. Eisenhower delegated considerable responsibility and relied on department heads to do their own jobs, but he kept close supervision of the whole operation through his staff. Ronald Reagan also employed a hierarchical staff system in which he was separated from much of the mundane daily routine. Unlike Eisenhower, however, Reagan only loosely monitored the operations of his chief aides, resulting in periods of conflict inside the White House and in little supervision of cabinet officers and top administrators.

In contrast to the hierarchical staff systems favored by Eisenhower and Reagan, John Kennedy put himself at the center of a wheel, with spokes going directly out to his kitchen cabinet. Kennedy met regularly with working groups and encouraged debate and input in those meetings. The model favored to date by Bill Clinton is Kennedyesque: a hub-and-spokes approach with an open chief of staff permitting considerable access to the president, with certain cabinet officers and top administrators given political initiative as long as they stay on the team.

Clinton Chief of Staff Thomas "Mack" McLarty discusses White House staff cuts at a 1993 press briefing. Critics suggested McLarty had in fact achieved the reductions largely through a smoke-and-mirrors approach—transferring some personnel to other areas, redefining job titles, and making significant cuts only in lower-level clerical positions that had little impact on the scope or cost of White House operations.

A CITIZEN'S QUESTION   Bureaucratic Politics

*D*o *we have too much bureaucracy?* The rise of the bureaucratic state reflects the demands of different groups to influence the society they live in. When thinking about the reasons for so much bureaucracy in our lives, it is easy to condemn other people's programs while assuming that the ones that benefit us are not part of the problem. As a challenge to evaluating bureaucratic intervention in society, think of five government programs that some groups in society regard in a positive way. Decide which two of them you would cut to shrink the government, eliminate bureaucratic red tape, or reduce the budget deficit.

*F*or example, suppose you named programs in food quality inspection, agricultural subsidies, student loans, national park services, and the administration of Social Security retirement benefits. All of those programs have been subjected to or considered for budget cuts in recent years. How does each program affect you directly? If it does not affect you right now, will it become more important to you in the future? Are there free-market, nongovernmental alternatives to these programs, or alternate ways of funding them? After thinking about these questions, you may continue to think that there is too much government regulation and that particular programs should be eliminated or cut back; however, you may now be better able to make that judgment with a clearer vision of the kind of society that might exist without those bureaucratic programs.

*A*s a second-thought experiment, consider the possibility that much of the reason for the bureaucratic inefficiency and turmoil that we read about in the news is that bureaucracy has become central to so many of our national political conflicts. Congress, the president, and interest groups battle for power inside the bureaucracy as actively as they fight for legislation and as strongly as they argue for interpretations of law in the courts. It may not be the inherent size or inefficiency of bureaucracy that antagonizes so many citizens. Rather, the real problem may be that the Constitution's framers never envisioned that bureaucracies would become so involved in political conflicts. Therefore, the Constitution offers little help in solving or even debating bureaucratic problems. If we begin thinking of bureaucracy less in terms of images (too big, impersonal, inefficient), and more as a hotbed of political conflicts, perhaps it becomes easier to understand its role in government and figure out how to make that role manageable. How would you propose getting control of the forces that shape bureaucratic politics?

No matter what model a president employs, at the first sign of political crisis there is a tendency to retreat into the privacy of the innermost circle of trusted advisors. When this happens, administrations become embattled and important units of the bureaucracy may come into conflict with the White House. This is why the calls for reforming the Executive Office of the President and shrinking the staff are seldom realized.

The Political Hotbed Revisited

The political turf battles between Congress, presidents, interests, and bureaucrats have grown more complex over time. At stake is control over the activities of government that are increasingly concentrated within the federal bureaucracy. To stay equal in the struggle to control the bureaucracy, the Executive Office and personal staff of the president grew in size and importance, making the White House a bureaucratic power center of its own, often competing with departments and agencies in interpreting law and making policy.

For example, the decisions of the Bush administration to hold off on writing many bureaucratic rules for the Clean Air Act of 1990 originated inside the Executive Office, in the Council on Competitiveness headed by Vice President Quayle. The council was authorized by Bush to review and, if necessary, block bureaucratic regulations that might, in Quayle's words, keep U.S. business from being "number one in the global market."[12]

Is this kind of second-guessing a back-door intrusion of special interests in government, or a much-needed streamlining of the bureaucratic morass created by lawmaking in today's complex society? Perhaps it is a bit of both. On the one hand, the directives handed down from the council to the EPA may seem to resemble political favors to businesses who felt they did not fare well enough in their previous lobbying. Yet, on the other hand, the Clean Air Act of 1990 is typical of much recent legislation in that it imposes a dizzying set of rules and regulations on federal bureaucrats, states, and businesses alike. For example, the pioneering Clean Air Act of 1970 was a mere 68 pages long compared to the 778 pages of the 1990 law, and those nearly 800 pages are just the tip of the bureaucratic iceberg. If all the rules and regulations called for in the law are ever written, the number of pages could easily top 10,000.[13] Does all of this mean, as discussed in Chapter 12 on Congress, that the bureaucracy has been wrongly entrusted to carry out too much of the legislative process? Has the center of government passed from lawmaking to bureaucratic rule making, as many critics of the bureaucratic state contend? These are the tough questions facing today's bureaucracy.

The actions of the Competitiveness Council so annoyed the Democrats who controlled Congress that the House of Representatives ultimately voted to suspend its funding. In the end, only the 1992 election resolved this particular political battle. However, the political agenda of the Clinton administration created other bureaucratic battles. And so the war for control of the bureaucracy goes on, with the centers of conflict changing as presidents and their agendas come and go.

Key Terms

defining characteristics of bureaucratic organization

sources of political pressure on the bureaucracy
Congress/the president/interests

layers of presidential control of the bureaucracy
administrative appointments (cabinet and agency posts)
Executive Office of the President
presidential staff and advisors

bureaucratic units
executive departments
independent agencies
independent regulatory commissions
public corporations

evolution of the U.S. bureaucratic system
the spoils system
the rise of a professional civil service
Pendleton Act
the rise of an activist bureaucracy
the rise of the bureaucratic state

clients

Executive Office of the President
back-channel operations

the presidential staff system
management style

Suggested Readings

Downs, Anthony. *Inside Bureaucracy.* Boston: Little, Brown, 1966.

Fisher, Louis. *The Politics of Shared Power: Congress and the Executive.* Washington, D.C.: Congressional Quarterly Press, 1987.

Heclo, Hugh. *A Government of Strangers.* Washington, D.C.: Brookings Institution, 1977.

Morone, James A. *The Democratic Wish: Popular Participation and the Limits of American Government.* New York: Basic Books, 1990.

Rourke, Francis E. *Bureaucracy, Politics, and Public Policy.* Boston: Little, Brown, 1984.

Wilson, James Q. *Bureaucracy: What Government Agencies Do and Why They Do It.* New York: Basic Books, 1991.

The Constitution . . . is a mere thing of wax in the hands of
the judiciary, which they may twist and shape into any form
they please.
—*THOMAS JEFFERSON*

• • •

Scarcely any political question arises in the United States that
is not resolved sooner or later into a judicial question.
—*ALEXIS DE TOCQUEVILLE*

• • •

The Court . . . has improperly set itself up as . . . a super-
legislature . . . reading into the Constitution words and
implications which are not there, and which were never
intended to be there. . . . We want a Supreme Court which
will do justice under the Constitution—not over it.
—*FRANKLIN ROOSEVELT*

• • •

To consider the Supreme Court of the United States strictly
as a legal institution is to underestimate its significance in the
American political system. For it is also a political institution,
an institution, that is to say, for arriving at decisions on
controversial questions of national policy.
—*ROBERT DAHL*

• • •

The Judiciary:

Courts, Law, and

Justice

- **A DAY IN COURT: A STORY FOR ALL CITIZENS**
- **LAW AND SOCIETY**
  Types of Law
  Jurisdiction
- **LAW AND POLITICS**
  Judicial Review
  Separation of Powers Cases
- **LAW AND PROCEDURE IN THE FEDERAL COURTS**
  Cases, Trials, and Procedures
  The Basis of Legal Judgment
  Courtroom Ritual
- **CONGRESS AND THE ORGANIZATION OF THE FEDERAL COURTS**
  The Politics of Judicial Organization
- **HOW THE SUPREME COURT WORKS**
  Jurisdiction and Paths to the Court
  Case Selection
  Judicial Philosophy: Activism vs. Self-Restraint
  The Endless Debate: What the Framers Intended
  Deciding Cases and Writing Opinions
  Inside the Court
  The Politics of Nominations
- **LAW AND SOCIETY REVISITED**
- **A CITIZEN'S QUESTION: Justice**
- **KEY TERMS**
- **SUGGESTED READINGS**

A Day in Court: A Story for All Citizens

Among the unique and most personal features of American government is the court system. Yet headlines like this one raise doubts about how well this personalized system of justice is really working: SO MANY DEFENDANTS, SO LITTLE TIME.[1] People have been bombarded with news and television dramas about a court system that is overcrowded. "Plea bargain" has become a household term, widely understood as a form of cut-rate justice to avoid lengthy trials. The public has grown frustrated by rising crime and revolving-door prison policies. Fueled by law-and-order politicians, many citizens have adopted a "lock them up and throw away the key" philosophy of justice.

Whether the problem is the numbers of criminal defendants or the waves of disputed economic regulations that clog the courts, the solutions to legal gridlock are not simple because the judicial system reflects enduring tensions in both the political culture and the design of the government itself. Consider, for example, the current controversy over an issue that was originally settled some thirty years ago: the right of poor people to legal representation when they are accused of crimes. In marking the thirtieth anniversary of the landmark Supreme Court case on this issue, a news story explored ONE POOR MAN'S LEGACY.[2] The headline referred to Clarence Earl Gideon, who won the right to legal counsel in a Supreme Court ruling in 1963. His legacy, according to the story, is that the right of poor people to legal assistance is now regarded around the world as a hallmark of American courts. That

Gregory Kingsley, a minor, sued for "divorce" from his biological parents in a landmark 1992 court case. The American populace, marked by the greatest concentration of lawyers of any society in the world, seems ever more eager to decide social issues through litigation.

The modern Supreme Court Building was begun only in 1932, and completed three years later. Said Chief Justice Charles Evans Hughes at the laying of the cornerstone, "The Republic endures, and this is the symbol of its faith." The portico bears the idealistic motto EQUAL JUSTICE UNDER LAW.

was the good news. The bad news is that cities, counties, and states are going broke trying to provide justice for all. There are roughly 13 million criminal charges filed in this country each year, and eight out of ten defendants qualify for publicly funded legal assistance. In even the best of circumstances, public defense lawyers seldom have the time or investigative resources to do justice to their clients.

Although law and order advocates arouse voters with charges that the system is too soft on crime and the people accused of committing crimes, it is unlikely that the Supreme Court will reverse its landmark ruling (*Gideon v. Wainwright,* 1963) extending the Sixth Amendment to include the right of indigents to legal representation in all felony cases.[3]

When Gideon finally received the legal representation granted him by the Court's ruling, new evidence was introduced on his behalf, and he was found innocent of the charges that earlier sent him to jail.[4]

In this era of taxpayer revolt, however, voters seem unwilling to pay for more legal services for the poor. Today's news tells the tale of a justice system straining under the weight of too many cases and too few resources to handle them. New Orleans was the subject of the report in SO MANY DEFENDANTS, SO LITTLE TIME. A typical public defender there may represent five hundred people accused of crimes each year, which means trying to deal with two or more trials going on every day and finding the time to interview clients sitting in jail waiting for their cases to come up. Rick Tessier, a lawyer in the New Orleans Public Defender's Office, petitioned a judge to relieve him of all cases until the injustices of the system were corrected. Judge Calvin Johnson went a step further and declared the mess in the public defender system unconstitutional, citing a later (1984) Supreme Court ruling that it was not enough merely to have a lawyer present if that lawyer was not providing adequate representation. The judge ordered the state to spend the money required to provide meaningful legal representation to accused persons.

The state appealed the ruling to the Louisiana Supreme Court, where Tessier's original complaint was joined by the Louisiana Association of Criminal Defense Lawyers. A lawyer who filed a brief for the Association on behalf of Tessier's case said that the current system was far from the spirit of the original Gideon ruling: "There you go, you've got an attorney, but you don't have an attorney who can research the facts of your case or the law on the case, or talk to you adequately about the case and find out what's happening and put on a defense."[5]

Characteristic of many landmark rulings, the aftershocks of Gideon are still reverberating within the justice system and society many years later. One moral of the story is that an individual's day in court can end up affecting social institutions that touch people all the way down to the grass roots. When people at the grass roots disagree with how their lives have been affected by the highest law of the land, the political shock waves often travel back up the court system once again. As new political and legal initiatives develop, new rulings of law can help society to adjust. This possibility of social and political change through legal action exists because the courts, society, and the law are constantly interacting. In this chapter we will explore the workings of the court system in the United States with an eye to understanding how cases move through this system in response to changing political pressures and legal philosophies. In the process, you will be better able to decide what kind of justice this system produces.

Law and Society

The Supreme Court was described by the great Justice Oliver Wendell Holmes, Jr., as a "storm center," quiet in its internal movements, but often surrounded by great tumult and disturbance.[6] Considering how personally and how often the law affects each member of society, it is hardly surprising that interpretations and applications of law stir up storms of political reaction. In reading this chapter, it is important to keep in mind that the courts in the United States are centers of political conflict more than in most other nations. In part, this is because individuals can take personal disputes to court fairly easily and seek constitutional protections. In addition, the review powers of the federal courts (recall the discussion from Chapter 3) leave both state and national laws open to political challenges.

Recall from Chapter 4 that the courts played a major role in changing the structure of national power in this century. During the period of rapid industrial expansion in the United States (1880–1930), the court used a *laissez-faire* economic philosophy to overturn a number of laws aimed at regulating business practices. With the advent of the Great Depression, under enormous political pressure from Congress, the president, and the public, the Supreme Court eventually changed its philosophy in the late 1930s and allowed the economy to increasingly come under the rule of law. (This has become known among legal wits as "the switch in time that saved nine.") Following this period, the

FIGURE 16.1

Economic and Civil Liberties Laws Overturned by the Supreme Court in the Twentieth Century

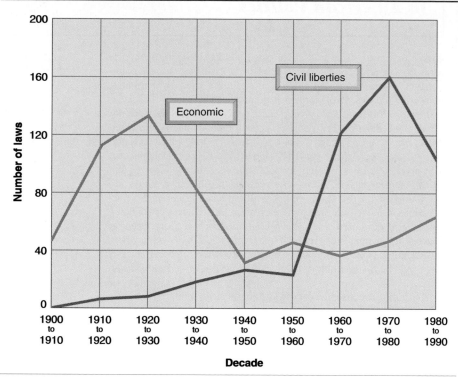

Note: Civil liberties category does not include laws supportive of civil liberties. Laws include federal, state, and local.

Source: Lawrence Baum, *The Supreme Court*, 4th ed. Washington, D.C.: CQ Press, 1992. Adapted from Harold W. Stanley and Richard G. Niemi, *Vital Statistics on American Politics*, 3rd ed. Washington, D.C.: CQ Press, 1992, p. 307.

Court turned from striking down economic legislation to overturning (primarily state) laws that infringed on civil rights. This shift in political emphasis resulted in the incorporation of many provisions of the Bill of Rights into social life, as noted in Chapter 5. The dramatic shift in the political focus of the Court in this period is illustrated in Figure 16.1.

The grand political shift shown in Figure 16.1 was like an earthquake, altering both the economic and social foundations of everyday life. The most fundamental issues in our lives, including economic protections, religious beliefs, how we are personally treated by others, and even our freedom of sexual expression are all affected by the activities of the courts. Many Americans take the court system for granted, yet it is among the most personally accessible, politically contested, and institutionally powerful in the world. The political role of the federal court system is simplified by our political system framework, as indicated in "Inside the System" Box 16.1.

572   PART IV – Institutions at Work

INSIDE
THE SYSTEM

Why the Judicial Branch Is So Important in American Politics

16.1

The federal courts are important in part because a government that has so many separations and divisions of power requires an elaborate mechanism for resolving disputes and adjusting power relations. Because of this complex institutional design, each distinct unit of government is a potential source of conflict that may require legal remedies.

In addition, there are some personal reasons why the courts are so important. The struggle for individual protection against the abuse of government power began with the American War of Independence and continues to this day. Although most people might not be able to offer precise definitions for such legal concepts as *due process,* or *equal protection under the law,* they understand that they are entitled to their day in court and to the same judicial treatment as anyone else. These are core features of the *political culture.*

This combination of complex governmental design and cultural concerns about access to personal justice have left their marks on the *design of judicial institutions* themselves, giving the United States more courts with more jurisdictions (see below) than any other nation. The amazing volume of activity in this system has led some to pronounce it on the verge of a breakdown. Indeed, as the examples at the start of this chapter suggest, the demands of processing criminal defendants alone have reached something of a crisis.

The political consequences of this judicial system are important to understand, particularly as they affect the balances of *power in society.* Although there are complaints about the wealthy receiving a higher quality of justice than the poor, it would be a mistake to underestimate the ways in which different groups can utilize judicial institutions. True, *elites* may use the court system to their advantage, protecting personal or corporate interests by hiring expensive legal talent. However, the courts have increasingly become a political resource used by feminists, minorities, religious believers, and others who feel they are not getting their demands addressed satisfactorily by elected representatives. This important aspect of *pluralism* in the legal system reflects the fact that courts are both numerous and relatively accessible. Moreover, even when a case is lost in one court, a similar case may be won somewhere else, keeping political causes alive that might be blocked in a more centralized system. Although these patterns of elite and pluralistic power would not seem to allow room for *majoritarian power* in the courts, rulings in particular cases can provoke broad political reactions that are expressed both through public opinion and elections. In this way, the court system accommodates different forms of power while remaining central to both the political culture and the workings of the other institutions of government.

Many of the core features of the American judiciary are not at all like the judicial systems operating in other nations. "How We Compare" Box 16.2 shows how the courts in three other democracies differ politically.

Types of Law

The U.S. judicial system has its own institutions and rules, but the law itself is guided by a broad philosophy that flows from the English **common law** tradition. In the communities of medieval England, people organized their lives around social customs that provided a fairly predictable order. When that order broke down, judges attempted to find a commonly acceptable justice principle that applied to the case. These principles became known as the common law. Many common law principles later became written into law codes passed by legislatures in the United States. These laws enacted by legisla-

The Judiciary in Denmark, Canada, and Germany

16.2

In contrast to the United States, the judicial branch in Denmark is very nearly apolitical. It "has no tradition of making political judgments or resolving political problems." Denmark's 1849 and 1953 constitutions grant no express power to the judiciary to judge the constitutionality of the laws; the only explicit power of this sort that the courts exercise is the right to strike down legislation or "ministerial orders" "if they do not conform to enabling legislation." Though some judges have opined that they do possess the authority to engage in judicial review, the Danish courts have actively avoided conflict with both the legislature (*Folketing*) and the executive and have generally declined to declare any laws unconstitutional.*

Somewhere in between the political extremes of Denmark and the United States lies Canada. The Canadian Supreme Court was not included in Canada's original constitution. Through a series of constitutional reforms, the Canadian Supreme Court became the highest court in Canada and was granted substantial control over its own jurisdiction and agenda. Finally, in the 1980s, it was raised to a level of equality with the Canadian legislature and executive—a true separate branch. The Canadian Supreme Court now has the constitutional power of judicial review and can "overrule legislation and executive acts of government not only on the grounds that they violate the federal division of powers, but also on the grounds that they violate fundamental rights and freedoms of citizens." Despite these powers, the Canadian court has been cautious because of the relative weakness of the national government.**

Germany is one of the few countries, along with the United States, with a judicial branch explicitly (constitutionally) possessing powers equal to the legislative and executive through the right of judicial review. (This equally empowered judiciary was insisted upon by the United States after World War II, as it was believed that it could halt the rise of any new Hitlers waiting in the wings.) The German Federal Constitutional Court has played a decisive role in German politics; for example, declaring certain radical parties of both left and right illegal, declaring unconstitutional a 1974 abortion rights law, and holding that Chancellor Helmut Kohl did not violate the constitution ("Basic Law") when in 1983 he arranged to lose a legislative vote of confidence in order to hold early elections. However, since German law is founded upon the more rigid system of Roman law, the Constitutional Court does not have the same ability to affect national politics that the U.S. Supreme Court does. In the U.S. system, the decisions of the Supreme Court are literally the law of the land.***

* John Fitzmaurice, *Politics in Denmark*. London: C. Hurst, 1981, pp. 71–74.
** Robert J. Jackson and Doreen Jackson, *Politics in Canada*. Scarsborough, Ont.: Prentice-Hall Canada, 1990, pp. 197–201.
*** Michael G. Roskin, *Countries and Concepts*, 2nd ed. Englewood Cliffs, N.J.: Prentice-Hall, 1986, pp. 165–166.

---

tive bodies (Congress, state legislatures, and city councils) are known as **statutory law.** Today, most of the laws that guide the rulings of courts are statutory laws.

Laws regulate the relations among individuals, government, and such social institutions as corporations. The two grand categories of law are criminal and civil. *Criminal laws* define offenses that are considered to be antisocial or dangerous to the very survival of society itself. This is why in all **criminal law** cases, the government *prosecutes* the case, which simply means that some public official called a prosecutor accuses a **defendant** of committing a crime against society. These cases are recognizable in court records by names like *The People of the State of California v. Oilspill Industries, Inc.,* or *The People of the United States v. John B. Mafia.* The most serious crimes, such as murder, rape, robbery, narcotics trafficking, and kidnapping, are classified as **felonies** and have more severe penalties attached. **Misdemeanors** are less serious offenses and their punishments are milder. However, what is considered a misdemeanor in one state may be a felony in another. In fact, something that might not even be a crime in one area can be heavily punished in another. These are characteristics of a common-law tradition in which the customs of a community remain the basis for statutory law.

The other general legal category, *civil law,* pertains to areas of rights, contracts, conditions of property ownership, and other matters that are generally not seen as threatening to public safety. Any individual who feels wronged under civil statutes can bring a civil suit. In place of a government prosecutor, civil suits are initiated by a **plaintiff** who seeks some sort of compensation or payment of damages from the defendant who caused the harm. States often have separate courts for criminal and civil law, but the federal court system hears both types of law. The line between civil and criminal law can be hazy. For example, a traffic accident with injuries may end up in a civil trial if the issue is to decide on medical costs and damages. However, a driver might also face criminal charges if there is evidence of criminal misconduct such as drinking and driving. Thus, many areas of life are regulated by both criminal and civil statutes, giving both government authorities and victims options in deciding how to pursue justice.

Jurisdiction

Jurisdiction refers to *the authority of a particular court or law enforcement agency to handle a case.* There is a strong sentiment in the political culture that favors local rule in many areas of social life. As explained in Chapter 4, this cultural tradition has always been in political conflict with one of the core issues of federalism: How can the problem of dual citizenship be worked out so that people live comfortably as both citizens of their states and of a united nation? This political tension creates many interesting challenges for *legal jurisdictions.*

As any TV or movie crime buff knows, jurisdiction is not just a matter of territory, but also the wording of the legal statute that empowers particular courts and law enforcement agents to become involved with particular kinds of crimes and civil disputes. A much-used plot in crime dramas is the frustration of the savvy cop who knows just how to handle a case, but must give up control to a squad of clueless federal agents who have the jurisdiction (or vice versa). Jurisdiction also explains which courts will hear the evidence gathered by those agents. In some cases, just deciding the jurisdiction becomes a politically challenging issue that can end up going all the way to the Supreme Court, as happened in the divorce case described in "Inside the System" Box 16.3.

After these basic questions of procedure have been agreed upon, the next challenge becomes how to interpret the law in a given case. Questions of *legal substance* can be even trickier than *legal procedures.* Laws are often ambiguous because they can't anticipate all the details of human behavior. Many laws are unclear simply because they reflect political disagreements among the lawmakers. The difficulties of legal interpretation become politically volatile in the federal judiciary where the courts must review laws of both Congress and the states, decide appeals from lower courts, and judge these interpretations in terms of a two-century-old Constitution that must be applied to the realities of today's society.

Law and Politics

There are two important kinds of political tangles in which the Court can find itself in the middle:

One Legal System or Many? Why Jurisdiction Can Be Complicated

16.3

On the surface, it seemed like a trivial case. A man from New Jersey was visiting California. He dropped in on his estranged wife, who lived there. She surprised him with divorce papers. He appealed all the way to the Supreme Court on the grounds that his stay in California was too short to bring him under jurisdiction of that state's courts and divorce laws. In *Burnham v. Superior Court of California*, the Supreme Court ruled 9–0 against his claim, and the California divorce was allowed to go ahead. However, there was considerable disagreement among the justices as to the reason for the ruling. For example, Antonin Scalia argued that legal tradition alone justified California's jurisdiction in the case, basically saying that it had always been that way, and that was enough. At another extreme, William J. Brennan, Jr.,

argued that "All rules of jurisdiction, even ancient ones, must satisfy contemporary notions of due process." Justice Brennan worried that contemporary standards of fairness and due process must be part of decisions about jurisdiction and other procedural questions, or else threaten the "evolution of our legal system." Thus, even when the Court reaches a common decision, there may be important disagreement on what it means legally.*

These and other problems in deciding cases in the courts can be traced to the unique mix of *culture* and *institutions* that defines the legal system. To begin with, the cultural legacy of common law remains strong. People often believe that they should be judged by the standards of the community where they live, not where they happen to be passing through as strangers. Federalism reinforces this legal mosaic by granting considerable constitu-

tional powers to states to make their own laws. At the same time, the Constitution also implies that the Supreme Court will make sure that citizens living in these various states and localities receive equal treatment under the law with fair procedures of justice applied to their cases. The difficulty of maintaining these separate legal systems while applying constitutional standards fairly to all citizens can result in confusion about how to handle some cases upon procedural grounds alone. Should a person living in New Jersey be subject to California divorce law? In this case, the Supreme Court agreed unanimously that he should, but the justices had a bit of trouble in explaining why.

* Linda Greenhouse, "High Court Still Groping to Define Due Process," *The New York Times*, May 31, 1990, p. A 16.

- *conflicts between laws,* either involving state and federal statutes, or between any of those statutes and the Supreme Court's current view of the Constitution

- *separation of powers cases,* in which one branch of government challenges an activity of another as overstepping its constitutional authority, and the Court is drawn in to decide the issue.

The first political minefield awaits the Court when it exercises its power of *judicial review,* while the second comes up in a special category known as *separation of powers decisions.* In addition, the Supreme Court can stir up a storm of controversy by issuing a new interpretation of the Constitution in a so-called **landmark ruling**, or by *overturning* a landmark ruling issued by a previous court.

Judicial Review

Political storms like the one that has surrounded abortion for decades often result from the federal courts doing their most important, but routine job of judicial review.

The federal courts review the laws of states to make sure they are consistent with federal law, and they review both state and congressional statutes to make sure they conform to the Constitution. Recall from Chapter 3 that the power of judicial review was first exercised in the famous case of *Marbury v. Madison* (1803) in a clever opinion written by Chief Justice John Marshall. Since then the Court has routinely reviewed laws to make sure they agree with the evolved Supreme Court interpretations of the Constitution. Figure 16.2 shows how often the Courts of different eras have overturned state and federal laws.

We will return later in the chapter to explain how the legal mechanics of the review process work, but for now, the focus is on politics. There are several scenarios for the political battles that swirl around judicial review, but the most common pattern looks like this:

- An individual (often with the help of concerned lawyers or interest groups) challenges a state or federal law as unconstitutional.

- The challenge works its way through lower courts in either the state or the federal system (depending on the original jurisdiction for the legal issues involved), and the Supreme Court decides to hear the case on appeal.

- The Court rules that the law in question or some part of it is unconstitutional. Sometimes a new interpretation of the Constitution is issued at the same time, making the case a *landmark* that will be cited in many future rulings.

- Groups who supported the old law, or who disagree with the new interpretation of the Constitution (or both), begin lobbying state legislatures or Congress to pass a new version of the old law, either to test for weaknesses in the ruling or to find a creative way to get around the ruling entirely.

- Meanwhile, there is constant *interest-group pressure* for (or against) the appointment of judges at all levels who support certain interpretations of the law. These interest groups can trigger intense political battles, such as the one over George Bush's appointment of Judge Clarence Thomas to the Supreme Court in 1991.

- In extreme cases, when attempts to write new legislation fail, or new laws are overturned in subsequent court cases, political activists may begin talking about amending the Constitution itself. In most instances society is so divided over the issue in conflict that amendments fail to pass either in Congress or in state legislatures.

Both opponents and supporters of the *Roe v. Wade* abortion ruling discussed in Chapter 5 have fought on all of the above battlefronts for decades, marching in the streets, struggling at the doors of abortion clinics, organizing voters, electing candidates for state legislatures or Congress who will support laws favoring one view or the other, lobbying for pro-choice or anti-abortion judges to be appointed (or elected) to courts at all levels, and threatening from time to time to draft a constitutional amendment. What is important to understand is that the procedures and the precise legal issues involved in channeling these conflicts through the court system constantly limit, contain, and change the course of the conflict itself. A good case in point is a Supreme Court decision in the 1989 case of *Webster v. Reproductive Health Services* upholding provisions in a Missouri law that placed serious restrictions on abortion.[7] Although the legal ruling in the case stopped short of overturning the *Roe* decision, there were signals in the justices' opinions that would guide another round of more creative state lawmaking. For example, Justice Sandra Day O'Connor indicated in her *concurring opinion* on Webster that the

FIGURE 16.2

Judicial Review in Action:
Laws Declared Unconstitutional by the Supreme Court

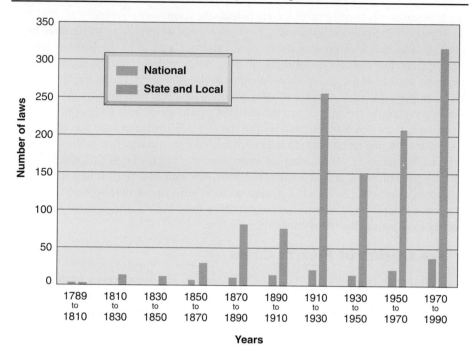

NOTE: During its first decade in existence, from 1789 to 1799, the Court did not declare any laws to be unconstitutional. Over the total period covered, the Court declared 126 national laws, and 1,151 state and local laws, unconstitutional.

Source: Lawrence Baum, *The Supreme Court,* 4th ed. Washington, D.C.: CQ Press, 1992. Adapted from Harold W. Stanley and Richard G. Niemi, *Vital Statistics on American Politics,* 3rd ed. Washington, D.C.: CQ Press, 1992. p. 306.

constitutional support for the right to an abortion could not be withdrawn until a case came before the Court raising the same constitutional issues that were involved in the *Roe* decision.[8] (A **concurring opinion** means that a justice agrees with the general decision of the majority in a case, but not with the specific legal reasoning of the other justices in the majority.) In her *concurring opinion* in the *Webster* decision, Justice O'Connor agreed with the other four justices to uphold the specific restrictions in the Missouri abortion law, but she disagreed that the case involved the right constitutional issues necessary for overturning the original *Roe* decision. By contrast, at least one other justice was clearly ready to use *Webster* as a basis for overturning *Roe*. Antonin Scalia wrote an opinion criticizing his colleagues in the majority for not acting more boldly, saying that: "It thus appears that the mansion of constitutionalized abortion law, constructed overnight in *Roe,* must be dismantled door jam by door jam, and never entirely brought down, no matter how wrong it may be."[9]

It is hardly surprising that legal rulings and political conflicts in society adjust and adapt slowly to each other. At the time of the *Webster* decision, for example, public opinion polls indicated considerable disagreement about how abortion should be handled in our society. As Table 16.1 shows, different ways of defining the abortion issue in poll questions produced radically different public responses to what social policy should be. (Recall how public opinion changes in response to different definitions of an issue, as explained in Chapter 6.) The apparent caution of legal rulings often reflects the volatility of the political conflicts going on in society outside the courtroom.

Typical of the political adjustment to court rulings, several state legislatures began drafting laws that incorporated the limits on abortion upheld in the *Webster* opinion. Anticipating the possible overturning of *Roe,* states with strong pro-abortion forces began to draft laws protecting abortion rights at the state level. For example, Washington state passed a ballot measure in 1991 adopting language directly from the *Roe* opinion as state law. In the span of two decades, the pendulum of legal and political conflict had swung from one extreme back toward the other. Washington state was one of only four states offering its citizens virtually unrestricted rights to abortion at the time of the original *Roe* decision. Recall from the more extensive discussion in Chapter 5 that another round of political and legal adjustment followed the 1992 ruling in *Casey v. Planned Parenthood.* Perhaps the greatest political influence of the Supreme Court (and the entire federal court system) lies in containing the often volatile political conflicts in society by adjusting the limits imposed by the law.

Separation of Powers Cases

Even though "the judiciary is not the ideal place to resolve interbranch conflicts," as one observer has noted, "increasingly, the administration, Congress and private individuals, with the help of astute lawyers, have turned political fights into legal ones, arguing that an action by one branch transgresses on the power of the other and therefore is invalid."[10] One of the classic examples of an interbranch political conflict being turned into a legal challenge was the case of the *United States v. Nixon* in 1974.[11] The Senate did not trust the attorney general to conduct an impartial investigation of his boss, President Nixon, and Nixon's possible involvement in the break-in at the Democratic party headquarters in the Watergate office complex. The Senate appointed a special prosecutor, Archibald Cox, to conduct its investigation. The evidence developed by the Senate investigation and hearings eventually led the House Judiciary Committee to consider impeaching the president.

One of the biggest surprises in the Senate hearings was the disclosure that President Nixon used a secret taping system to record his conversations in the Oval Office. The special prosecutor requested some of the tapes to see if Nixon personally participated in the cover-up of the break-in. Nixon claimed that this request stepped over the line that separated the powers of Congress and the executive. He claimed that the president had a constitutional executive privilege to keep matters of state security confidential, and that Congress had no right to listen to his Oval Office conversations. The case went to the federal district court of John Sirica in Washington who had jurisdiction in the original trial of the Watergate burglars (who were convicted). President Nixon refused Judge Sirica's order to turn over the tapes.

Pursuing the ladder of appeal, Cox took his case to the next highest court with jurisdiction, the Court of Appeals for the District of Columbia Circuit. The Court of Appeals also ordered Mr. Nixon to hand over the tapes, but the president again refused. Cox rejected an offer of summaries of the tapes, and Nixon ordered him fired. Both the attorney general and his deputy resigned rather than carry out the order. Finally, the next in command at the Justice Department, Solicitor General Robert Bork (who more than a decade later was turned down by the Senate for a Supreme Court position) agreed to fire Mr. Cox. A new special prosecutor, Leon Jaworski, was named and the president refused another court order, provoking the special prosecutor to appeal directly to the Supreme

TABLE 16.1

Public Opinion on Various Legal Questions Related to Abortion

PERCENT (%) FAVORING LEGALIZED ABORTION . . .	UNDER THE FOLLOWING CONDITIONS
88 %	The woman's health is endangered
82	The pregnancy results from rape
70	The baby may have a birth defect
58	The woman's doctor agrees
49	The family can't afford the child
48	The woman doesn't want to marry
47	A pregnant teen would leave school
34	A woman would interrupt career
6	When it is primary birth control

SOURCE: CBS News/*New York Times* Poll, September 17–20, 1989. Adapted from analysis by Carl Everett Ladd, "Abortion: The Nation Responds," *The Ladd Report #8*. New York: Norton, 1990, pp. 21–22.

Court on grounds that questions of constitutional powers were at stake. The Supreme Court agreed to hear the case of *United States v. Nixon.*

The president added to the fears of a constitutional crisis by suggesting that he might not obey the Supreme Court unless he regarded its ruling as definitive, whatever that meant. The Court heard the arguments of both sides. The attorney for the president, James St. Clair, reiterated the White House claim of executive privilege and argued that turning over the tapes would violate the separation of powers in the Constitution. Jaworski said that to apply executive privilege in this case would place the president above the law and allow him to interpret the Constitution as it suited his political needs.

The justices retired to chambers and began their deliberations. The questions of constitutional power were so delicate, and a presidential refusal to obey a Supreme Court ruling would have been so unsettling, that the fine details of the opinion took two weeks of negotiating among the justices to work out. Chief Justice Burger's first draft went all the way back to *Marbury v. Madison* to justify the Court's review powers. Justice White objected to the chief justice's suggestion that the Court somehow "created" its review power with the clever *Marbury* ruling. Like many constitutional experts, he believed that the review power was clearly implied in the Constitution from the beginning.[12] White threatened to write a separate opinion unless Burger toughened his position. The chief justice went back to the drawing board since a unanimous opinion was highly desirable in such an important case. On July 24, 1974, the chief justice handed down the Court's unanimous opinion to the president. While recognizing that executive privilege was necessary for the president in some matters, the justices strongly rejected the specific claim of executive privilege in the case at hand.

In a move timed to give the president little room to maneuver, the House Judiciary Committee opened debate on charges of impeaching the president the same day the

Archibald Cox (left), *the special prosecutor appointed to investigate the Watergate scandals, addresses the media in late 1973. Fired by President Richard Nixon in the so-called "Saturday Night Massacre" (which also included the angry resignations of Nixon's own Attorney General, Elliott Richardson, and his assistant, William Ruckelshaus), Cox was succeeded by distinguished Texas lawyer Leon Jaworski, a one-time prosecutor of Nazi war criminals at Nuremberg. Jaworski promptly resumed inquiries where Cox had left off, and White House audiotapes ultimately revealed that President Nixon had indeed sought to protect aides enmeshed in the scandals. On August 9, 1974, Nixon resigned* (right), *avoiding almost certain impeachment.*

Court issued its ruling. President Nixon resigned from office within two weeks, leaving historians to guess what might have happened if he refused the Supreme Court, and what would have happened if the impeachment trial had gone forward. The case of the *United States v. Nixon* did not fully resolve the president's responsibilities to deliver evidence to congressional investigations. Nor did the case settle for all time the larger separation of powers issues between Congress and the executive.

Some scholars see no problem with the branches testing each other and the Court at the same time. Separation of powers cases may be necessary if the government is going to come up with "novel approaches to deal with significant problems," as one observer put it.[13] However, others see wrangling over constitutional power as accomplishing little, because, as one observer put it, "The Supreme Court does not think of itself as writing mega-theory on separation of powers."[14] This is another way of saying that few of these cases resolve general issues clearly enough to prevent future disputes between the branches.

In the area of foreign policy, the Court has steered clear of most separation of powers cases. The standard reason given is that they are "nonjusticiable," or beyond the scope of court action because they involve political, not legal, questions. This **political question**

doctrine was articulated long ago by Chief Justice Marshall as part of his influential opinion in *Marbury v. Madison*. He stated that the role of the Court was "solely to decide on the rights of individuals, not to inquire how . . . executive officers perform duties in which they have a discretion. Questions in their nature political . . . can never be made in this court."[15] This simply means that the Court tries to avoid cases where one branch does not like how another has used its powers, which is different from deciding where those powers begin and end.

Law and Procedure in the Federal Courts ⸻⸻⸻⸻

Some of the pressure may be taken out of political conflicts if adversaries feel that impartial judges using impartial procedures offer some hope for satisfactory solutions to their problems. In other words, the idea of a day in court contains, for many people at least, a predictable set of procedures associated with fairness and justice.

Cases, Trials, and Procedures

The basic procedural assumption in the justice system is that the two sides, whether prosecutor and defendant in criminal cases or plaintiff and defendant in civil cases, will be **adversaries**. This means that there must be some disputed legal issue between the parties. The issue in legal dispute becomes the basis of the case. An adversarial system of justice also means that both sides will be treated as equals. In criminal cases, the defendant is presumed innocent until proven guilty.

FEDERAL CRIMINAL PROCEDURE.   *Criminal cases* at the federal level begin when a government officer (usually the attorney general or one of many deputies) brings *charges* against someone for violating a federal criminal statute. A *warrant* is issued to arrest the accused, and if the arrest is made, the defendant is brought before a *magistrate* (a hearing officer) of the federal court with *jurisdiction* in the matter. The magistrate hearing the case decides if evidence is sufficient to go to trial and, if so, whether the defendant should be allowed to go free on *bail*. If the evidence is deemed sufficient, the defendant is **indicted** (*charged*) with a crime and brought to an **arraignment**, *a hearing where the indictment or charges are formally read.* Evidence leading to an indictment may be gathered and evaluated by a *grand jury, a special body empowered to assist a federal investigation by calling witnesses, requesting documents, and evaluating gathered evidence.*

After hearing the charges at an arraignment, the defendant enters a *plea*. In the case of a not guilty plea, the lawyers and judge meet to discuss motions to dismiss charges, to consider *changing the venue* (the location of the court where a trial will be held) or whether the defendant will *waive the right to a jury trial*. If the case goes to trial, there are standard procedures for selecting a jury, for admitting and excluding evidence, for calling and examining witnesses, and for instructing the jury members on the law pertaining to their verdict.

If a criminal trial results in a guilty *verdict*, the defendant can *appeal*, usually from the Federal District Court to the next level, the U.S. (Circuit) Court of Appeals, and possibly on to the Supreme Court. Appeals are granted when the next higher court issues what is called a **writ of certiorari**, *which is a formal request for the record of the trial from the lower court*. With so many layers of procedures, the right to have a lawyer can make all the difference between a day in court that seems fair and one that is a confusing ordeal of injustice. This is why the case of Clarence Earl Gideon remains so important today, and

"If at first you don't succeed, appeal to a higher court."

why the problem of overloaded courts may represent a crisis for the American justice system.

FEDERAL CIVIL PROCEDURE.   *Civil cases* require that plaintiffs can demonstrate **standing to sue**, which means that an individual must *"show injury to a legally protected interest or right and demonstrate that other opportunities for defending that claim* (before an administrative tribunal or a lower court) *have been exhausted.* The claim of an injury 'must be of a personal and not official nature' and 'of some specialized interest [of the individual's] own' to vindicate, apart from political concerns which belong to it."[16] This definition of standing to sue illustrates the basic assumption in the American system that justice is a personal, individual matter involving some sort of wrong that has a legal remedy. While the political concerns of groups may lurk behind a legal complaint, they cannot be the basis of a complaint. Thus, for example, civil rights disputes that may affect a whole community are fought as legal battles by individuals who have standing to sue. Even the ideas of "public interest," "consumer protection," and "class action" law are rooted in the principle of individual standing to sue.

Legal standing is not always easy to establish, as when the Burger Court denied a Sierra Club challenge to the government issuing a permit to build a ski resort in a national park. Yet the same court granted standing to a group of law students who fought an increase in railroad freight charges that made recycling unprofitable. The students claimed that this damaged the environment and, thereby, caused direct personal harm to them as plaintiffs. In *United States v. Students Challenging Regulatory Agency Procedures* (1973), the Court agreed, saying that just because "particular environmental interests are shared by the many rather than the few does not make them less deserving of legal protection through the judicial process."[17]

If standing is established, the plaintiff files a *complaint* in federal court, asking that a *summons* be served. *A summons is a court order calling the defendant to appear in court and respond to the charges.* Both parties enter their *pleadings* (the charges and the response to them) into the record as the basis of the trial. If a *settlement* cannot be reached, and a jury trial is requested, the jury may not always contain twelve people; many civil suits are heard by juries of six people. If the decision is for the plaintiff, a secondary decision may award an amount of damages.

The Basis of Legal Judgment

The judgment of cases relies heavily on establishing **precedent**, that is, *finding legal rulings that have applied to similar cases in the past, and that fit the current case better than any other.* This reasoning from precedent is known in the legal trade as **stare decisis** (Latin for "let the prior decision stand") and is an important check on inconsistency and whim in the legal process. As any law student knows, however, many cases are ambiguous enough to support different theories about what legal precedent best applies. The process of legal judgment will be explored in detail later in the chapter in describing how the Supreme Court works.

Courtroom Ritual

Each court has additional procedures involving etiquette, formal patterns of speech, legal language, and deference to judges. These ceremonial aspects of justice remind people of the respect required for the law to be taken seriously. In case you think that small symbols surrounding the judicial ceremony aren't an important part of the procedure, consider what happened to two lawyers arguing a case before the Supreme Court. Everything seemed under control until one lawyer referred to Chief Justice Rehnquist as "justice," upon which, the top justice retorted "I am the *Chief* Justice." The other lawyer then made the mistake of calling him "judge," unleashing the same scolding and causing the lawyer considerable embarrassment: "Rehnquist's face seemed very, very red. I thought his head was going to explode." One reporter covering the Court averred that the lawyers meant no disrespect: "It's not as if he is being addressed as 'Bill' or 'Yo.'"[18] Still, the formality of the Court prevails in all public ceremonies, and the titles used to refer to the people wearing the robes matter as much as the robes themselves.

Many Americans are upset with lawyers for making it nearly impossible for ordinary people to understand the legal process. Yet the law persists with its specialized jargon. Like the language of church, economics, or medicine, the language of law helps establish its own authority. Below are some examples of "legalese" translated into everyday English:

- *Legal Language*: "The dicta, however, is clearly inapposite."

  Standard English Translation: You cited the wrong thing.

- *Legal Language*: "Unilateral nullification of the terms and conditions of the expiring agreement absent bona fide impasse is prohibited."

  Standard English Translation: One party cannot leave the contract early without a good reason.

- *Legal Language*: "Matters should be held in abeyance pending the meeting in order to determine whether the facts there adduced will warrant a further extension."

- *Standard English Translation*: We should wait until we see what happens at our next meeting, where we might decide to put it off again.[19]

The rituals of the courts also remind judges and lawyers that they have a responsibility that overrides their personal feelings about a case. As the eminent Supreme Court Justice Frankfurter once said (at a time before many women served on the bench): "One of the things that laymen, even lawyers, do not always understand is indicated by the question you hear so often: 'Does a man become any different when he puts on a gown?' I say, 'If he is any good, he does.'"[20]

The court system in which all these procedures and principles are applied is constantly growing and changing. The framers of the Constitution had the good sense to see that they could not anticipate all the justice needs of the future and left to Congress the basic organization of the federal court system, down to the number of justices sitting on the Supreme Court, which has varied over the years from five to ten!

Congress and the Organization of the Federal Courts

Article III of the Constitution clearly specifies particular jurisdictions for the Supreme Court (known as original jurisdiction and discussed in the next section). However, much of the design and purpose of the federal judiciary was left up to Congress to decide. The very first Congress set the foundation of the federal judiciary with the Judiciary Act of 1789 which created the district court and the circuit (appeals) court systems. Today, the trial court or district court system has grown to ninety-four districts, with one or more in each state, one for the District of Columbia, and one for the territorial possessions of the United States. The **district courts** are *the trial courts of the federal judiciary*, handling both civil and criminal cases. In 1789, Congress also created the first court of appeals to take the pressure off the Supreme Court in hearing appeals. The number of **U.S. Court of Appeals circuits** has grown to thirteen. The name "circuit" court is still used to describe the appeals courts, referring to the days when judges rode from courthouse to courthouse along a circuit to hear appeals. Figure 16.3 illustrates the map of federal district and circuit (appeals) courts.

In addition to the district and circuit courts, Congress has created several special courts under the guidelines of Article III of the Constitution to handle cases that do not fall within the jurisdictions of the district courts. The Court of Claims has jurisdiction over claims to receive compensation from the federal government. The Customs Court deals with tariff and import disputes. The Court of Customs and Patent Appeals handles appeals cases from the Customs Court and also hears appeals of decisions made by the patent office. The basic organization of the federal court system is shown in Figure 16.4. In addition to the "constitutional" courts set up under the guidelines of Article III, Congress has also created a group of courts known as "legislative" courts. They have been designed specifically to handle special justice problems, including appeals from the military justice system and tax disputes involving taxpayers and the Internal Revenue Service. However, with the exception of the military appeals court, these special courts have jurisdictional overlaps with the other courts in the system that make it hard to draw a clear line between "constitutional" and "legislative" courts.

FIGURE 16.3

Federal District Courts and U.S. Court of Appeals Circuits

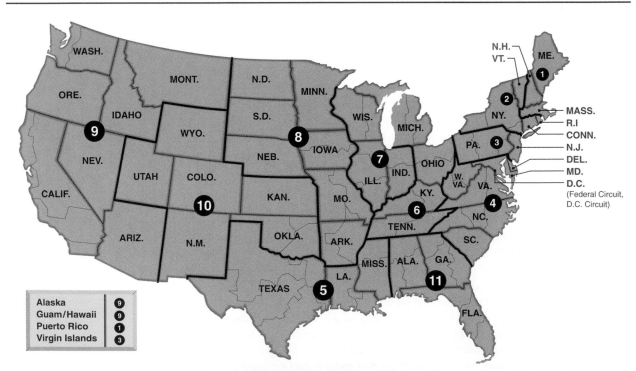

Number and composition of circuits set forth by 28 U.S.C. §41

Source: Administrative Office of the United States Courts. Adapted from Harold W. Stanley and Richard G. Niemi, *Vital Statistics on American Politics*, 3rd ed. Washington, D.C.: CQ Press, 1992, p. 286.

FIGURE 16.4

Organization of the Federal Judiciary

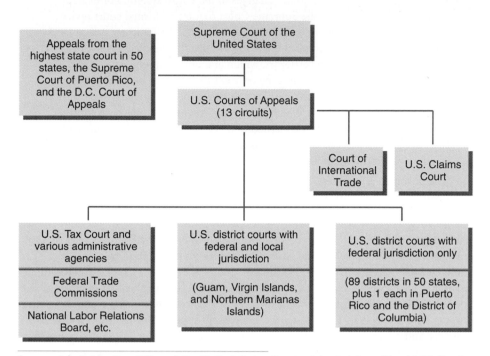

Source: Administrative Office of the United States Courts. Adapted from Harold W. Stanley and Richard G. Niemi, *Vital Statistics on American Politics*, 3rd ed. Washington, D.C.: CQ Press, 1992, p. 285.

The numbers of judges sitting on the federal courts varies according to the judgment of Congress about what each jurisdiction requires. For example, the circuit courts of appeals have from four to more than twenty-five judges. At the present time, the Supreme Court has nine justices. In the famous court-packing controversy of 1937, President Franklin Roosevelt wanted Congress to increase the number of justices on the court so he could appoint people more sympathetic to his New Deal programs than the existing justices. Congress was reluctant to play politics with the size of the court on that occasion, but political considerations can enter the relationship between Congress and the federal courts.

The Politics of Judicial Organization

There are four basic ways in which Congress can regulate the activities of the federal courts:

- When Congress sets up a court, it also specifies many matters of procedure, staff, and jurisdiction.
- Particular laws passed by Congress may specify what courts have jurisdiction, and how the appeal process can go forward. In the Flag Protection Act of 1989,

for example, the law permitted appeals directly to the Supreme Court from district courts without having to go through the normal circuit court of appeals in between.

- Congress can legislate procedural changes in the entire system. For example, prior to 1925, appeals to the Supreme Court required a formal court review, creating an enormous workload on the High Court. The Judiciary Act of 1925 reformed this process by replacing the direct appeal in many cases with something called a **petition for certiorari,** which amounts to a request for the Court to review a case. The Court can deny or grant this petition without going through a full review of each case. This change of procedure gave the Court a great deal of discretion over which cases it will review. Before this reform, 80 percent of the court's docket consisted of direct appeals that the Court had to review. Now, 95 percent of the appeals docket is on *certiorari*, giving the court freedom to choose a smaller number of cases more selectively.

- The power to reject presidential judicial appointments gives Congress some control over the political and legal philosophies of the judges who sit on the federal courts.

In recent years the nation has become fascinated by the televised spectacles as Congress and the president have battled over nominations to the Supreme Court. (Recall the nomination of Clarence Thomas discussed in Chapters 5 and 8.) The fact that nomination fights have become common again, as they were during the first century of the republic, reflects the importance of the courts in balancing executive and legislative powers. As explained in Chapter 8, the increasing involvement of interest groups in screening and promoting judicial nominees introduces a broader base of citizen power into the workings of the judicial branch than at any time in the past. The next section examines the Supreme Court in detail and returns to take another view of the political fights over presidential nominations.

How the Supreme Court Works

The Supreme Court differs in several important respects from other courts. To begin with, even if a case falls in its jurisdiction, the Court is not always obligated to hear it. Over the years the Court has been given considerable discretion over its case selection. In addition, some decisions of the Court become landmark rulings, setting new precedents for all lower courts to follow. While the rulings of lower courts also may set precedents, the Supreme Court has the last word on legal standards. The unusual discretion and influence of the Court make it the subject of intense study by scholars.

Jurisdiction and Paths to the Court

All legal cases go first to the court that has original jurisdiction. The Constitution gives the Court original jurisdiction over cases "affecting ambassadors, other public ministers and consuls, and those in which a state shall be party." The Constitution goes on to say that in all other cases, the Supreme Court "shall have appellate jurisdiction . . . under such regulations as the Congress shall make." This means that, aside from the limited areas in which the Court has original jurisdiction, its primary responsibility is to review appeals. The *appellate jurisdiction* of the Supreme Court is thus its most important jurisdiction for several reasons:

- More than 95 percent of the cases heard by the Supreme Court come through appeals.

- These appeals cases generally contain the most important questions of individual rights and the constitutionality of laws, giving the judicial review power its greatest social impact.

- The Court sends many cases that fall under its original jurisdiction (for instance, disputes between states or between states and out-of-state corporations) down to district courts for trial. Thus, the Court's narrowing view of its original jurisdiction has further emphasized its appellate role.[21]

Aside from the small number of cases each term (often as few as fifteen) that come under original jurisdiction, the most important paths to the Supreme Court are appeals from the state court systems, representing about 35 percent of the appeals case load, and from the lower federal courts which provide about 65 percent of the Court's appeals docket. In addition to the roughly 2,500 cases that reach the Court through these channels, another 3,000 or so cases are sent by people in jail who are too poor to hire legal counsel. They exercise their right to personally take their cases directly to the Supreme Court. This is how Clarence Earl Gideon got the attention of the Court in the example that opened this chapter. Gideon was fortunate because the issue he raised was one that the Court was looking for a case to act on. The overwhelming majority (95 percent) of these "pauper" cases are dismissed or denied without formal explanation. Although the Court has tried to limit the incoming flow of cases in various ways, the overall trend has been toward a staggering increase in caseload, as shown in Figure 16.5.

FIGURE 16.5

Caseload of the U.S. Supreme Court, 1938–1990

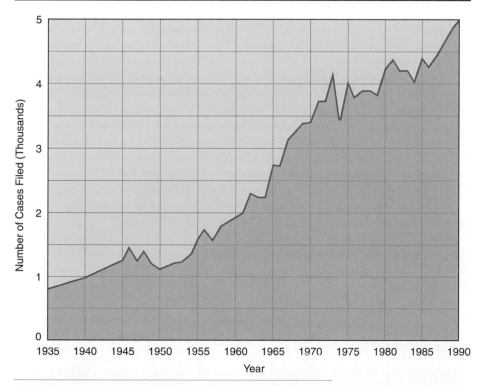

Source: Harold W. Stanley and Richard G. Niemi, *Vital Statistics on American Politics,* 3rd ed. Washington, D.C.: CQ Press, 1992, p. 301.

Supreme Court justices chat during an informal conference. From right: David Souter, Antonin Scalia, Clarence Thomas (writing at desk), Sandra Day O'Connor, John Paul Stevens, Byron White (now retired and succeeded by Ruth Bader Ginsburg), Chief Justice William Rehnquist, and Anthony Kennedy. The Court usually keeps well out of the public eye; in 1993, the release by the Library of Congress of some of Justice Thurgood Marshall's private notes caused considerable uproar.

As noted on page 586, the Judiciary Act of 1925 (sometimes called the Judges Bill) enabled the Court to select cases by reviewing a *petition of certiorari* which is not a formal legal appeal, but a *request* for the Court to review a case because it contains important legal issues. If the Court agrees, it can look at the records of the case by issuing a *writ of certiorari*. This means, as explained earlier, that the Court can simply *request the records of a case* without explaining why or without committing itself to a full review. This gives the Court much more freedom "to pick and choose the cases it would hear."[22] Most of the cases heard by today's Court come through the *certiorari* process. However, formal appeals are still made in a number of cases. Since the late 1920s, the Court has required those bringing a formal appeal to provide a *jurisdictional statement* explaining why the case belongs before the Court. The key to these statements is the argument about why the case presents a "substantial" legal question in federal cases, and a "substantial federal question" in cases coming from state courts.[23] In practice, the Court evaluates these much the way it considers the reasons given in a *certiorari* petition.

In the view of political scientist Stephen Wasby, the increasing selectivity of the Court has effectively split the federal judiciary into very different roles for the Supreme Court and the circuit appeals courts: "The Supreme Court is a 'policy court' primarily pursuing constitutional issues; the courts of appeals, without discretionary jurisdiction, are engaged far more in 'statutory interpretation, administrative review, and error correction in masses of routine adjudication.'"[24] This is the key to the federal judiciary in its current state of political evolution: Congress has invited the Supreme Court to focus on legal resolutions for the nation's political flashpoints. The Court has responded by picking and choosing its openings, while leaving most routine matters of law to be decided by the lower courts. It is important to understand how the Court chooses its cases and what factors affect its opinions.

Case Selection

Deciding what to decide takes a large amount of the Court's time. The price of so much political discretion is screening thousands of cases on the dockets each year to find the few that seem important to the justices. (The **dockets** are simply the lists of cases that have reached the Court through various channels.) As recently as a few decades ago, the justices attempted to personally screen all the cases, meaning that the Clerk of the Court's Legal Office had to track down the justices over the summer to prepare for the work of the new term beginning in October. In the past, this meant that "bags of petitions and appeals were sent out by the Clerk throughout the summer to the justices wherever they were vacationing; this was done when Hughes spent his summers in Jasper Park, Canada, Stone retreated to the Isle du Haute, and Douglas made his annual trek to Goose Prairie, in the Pacific Northwest."[25]

In recent years, the justices have turned over much of the screening to their personal law clerks who write memos to their bosses about the merits of various cases on the docket. Critics have raised questions about whether such important judgments should be left to junior assistants. As long as the case load remains high (over 5,000) and the number heard is small (below 200), there is little alternative but to turn much of the screening over to the law clerks. To help make these decisions, the Court staff has grown over the years, and the number of clerks assisting each justice has increased.

By tradition, the Court grants *certiorari* (issues requests to lower courts for case records) by the vote of four justices. However, the Court can decline to hear the case if the records are not found to contain the "substantial" questions promised in the petition.[26] Although most of the cases on the docket have been screened when the term begins in October, new cases continue to arrive during the year, and they may either be added to the current term's docket or moved to the next term as the workload dictates. The Court holds weekly conferences during its regular session from October until June to discuss the cases coming up for argument and to decide what to do about new cases that continue to arrive.

Many justices accept that the Supreme Court is at the center of national controversy and push for selection of only the high-impact cases. For example, Justice Vinson offered one of the early arguments for the Court becoming a political activist:

> If we took every case in which . . . our prima facie impression is that the decision below is erroneous, we could not fulfill the Constitutional and statutory responsibilities placed upon the Court. To remain effective, the Supreme Court must continue to decide only those cases which present questions whose resolution will have immediate importance beyond the particular facts and parties involved.[27]

Not all justices share this view, with some being much less "activist" than others. As political scientist Doris Marie Provine has observed, the balance between law and politics varies with different courts at different times: "Political scientists who have done so much to put the 'political' in 'political jurisprudence' need to emphasize that it is still 'jurisprudence.' It is judging in a political context, but it is still judging."[28] As Provine concluded, the balances between the political and legal roles "are essentially the only limits upon judicial discretion in case selection."[29] This freedom of the top Court to decide its role explains why battles over appointments to the Court can become so heated and why the focus of the Senate hearings is on the judicial philosophy of the nominees.

Judicial Philosophy: Activism vs. Self-Restraint

When presidents nominate candidates for an opening in the Supreme Court, news stories typically talk about whether the nominee is liberal or conservative on abortion, law and order issues, free speech, affirmative action, or other civil liberties and civil rights questions. Legal scholars are more likely to ask whether he or she practices legal activism or self-restraint. The reason why standard liberal or conservative labels do not fit neatly with legal scholars' debates is that in some periods liberals have favored an activist role for the Court, and at other times political conservatives have been the activists. In the modern (post-1937) era, liberals have favored an activist role for the Court in striking down laws that restricted civil rights. Before that, the conservatives tended to be activists on economic issues, overturning many laws of states and Congress that limited business activities. (Recall these patterns from Figure 16.1.)

What this boils down to is the fact that the two greatest periods of judicial activism in American history—(roughly, 1910–1937 and 1953–1973)—were produced by courts that would be labeled extremely conservative, in the first case, and extremely liberal, in the second. The willingness or reluctance to use the power of the Court to intervene in state and federal conflicts is more basic than political ideology. For example, what a justice may believe about abortion matters little if he or she follows the principle of self-restraint and refrains from intervening in the rights of states to write their own laws on the subject. Some of the great justices have made an effort to separate law and personal politics by placing their judicial philosophies first. A classic case in point is Felix Frankfurter, who came to the court branded as a political liberal and one of the architects of the Roosevelt administration's New Deal economic policies. Yet Frankfurter was one of the greatest practitioners of judicial self-restraint, as that philosophy was outlined by the great legal theorist and Supreme Court Justice Oliver Wendell Holmes, Jr. Holmes' recommendation that the law, not social beliefs, should guide the thinking of judges was something that Frankfurter took seriously.

Restraint from the Court was all that Roosevelt and the economic liberals were asking to give their economic policies a chance, and so, Frankfurter's judicial philosophy was perfectly suited to the economic liberalism of the later Roosevelt years. However, Frankfurter was still a member of the Court when Earl Warren became Chief Justice in 1953. Although Frankfurter was persuaded to go along with the landmark ruling in *Brown v. Board of Education*, he objected to many of the activist civil rights opinions of the Warren Court. Until Frankfurter's retirement, the Supreme Court was split between an activist majority and a vocal minority led by Frankfurter who preached self-restraint in sometimes unrestrained ways. In one conference session, Frankfurter reportedly snapped at Warren: "You're the worst Chief Justice this country has ever had."[30] On another occasion, he admonished Warren to "Be a judge, god damn it, be a judge!" Frankfurter even wrote in a letter that Warren's "crude, heavy-handed repetitive moralizing makes me feel like eating rancid butter."[31] It would appear that legal minds can get every bit as upset about judicial philosophy as everyday citizens do about politics and ideology.

The Endless Debate: What the Framers Intended

Jurisprudence refers to the process of legal interpretation. For example, those who practice self-restraint are more likely to stick close to legal texts, looking for narrowly legal issues rather than more broadly political ones. By contrast, activists take the view that all law arises from social and political contexts, and therefore, the political context of a case should enter a legal decision. The first philosophy of legal interpretation is known as **strict constructionism** in popular terms, or **legal formalism** among scholars, for its tendency to construct legal opinions that look strictly to legal precedent for guidance in a case. The **broad constructionist** approach, also known as **legal realism** among scholars, advocates adapting and changing the law to fit the needs of society. It is easy to see why advocates of judicial self-restraint tend to favor strict constructionism, while judicial activists recommend a broader approach. Legal scholar Walter Berns explains strict constructionism as the method behind judicial self-restraint:

> Issues of the "public good" can "be decided legitimately only with the consent of the governed." Judges have no legitimate say about these issues. Their business is to address issues of private rights, that is, "to decide whether the right exists—in the Constitution or in a statute—and, if so, what it is; but at that point inquiry ceases."
>
> The judge may not use "discretion in the weighing of consequences" to arrive at his decisions and he may not create new rights. There must be no judicial creativity or "policy-making."[32]

Since the Constitution is a short and simple document, its words alone cannot instruct judges how to rule on *particular* cases. Strict constructionists therefore try to decide how the Framers of the Constitution would have applied it to particular issues. Consider the case of *Wallace v. Jaffree* discussed in Chapter 5. You may recall that this case involved a state statute permitting a moment of silence for prayer in public schools. A federal district court judge applied a strict construction to the Constitution and concluded that the Framers never intended the First Amendment to forbid prayer in schools. A circuit appeals court reversed the district court ruling, citing Supreme Court precedent. Although the Supreme Court upheld the circuit court decision, Chief Justice William Rehnquist wrote a dissenting opinion based on strict constructionist reasoning. He cited writings of James Madison (a principal author of the Bill of Rights) to support a conclusion that religion was so basic to the thinking of the Framers that a moment for silent prayer in schools could not be construed as violating the freedoms of nonbelievers. (Rehnquist did not draw upon the thinking of the somewhat more liberal Thomas Jefferson, who was not a delegate at the Constitutional Convention.[33])

Legal scholar and judge Richard Posner, a legal realist, argues that strict constructionists are unrealistic: "There has never been a time when the courts of the United States, state or federal, behaved consistently in accordance with this idea."[34] Legal realists argue that questions of original legal intent cannot be separated from the politics surrounding a current case. The best principles of law, claim the realists, are those that look to guidance from past legal precedent while advancing new opinions to keep the law in tune with social change. Moreover, say realists such as Posner, the Constitution was hotly debated in its day, and it is a stretch of the imagination to think that the Framers all left Philadelphia in perfect agreement about the document they had just signed. In conclusion, says Posner, "The Constitution does not say, 'Read me broadly,' or 'Read me narrowly.' That decision must be made as a matter of political theory."[35]

In a book on the subject of the intent of the Founders, legal scholar Leonard Levy concluded that if there was a clear intent, it was to set in motion a living document that was vague enough to invite the interpretations of future ages.[36] As evidence for this somewhat heretical view, Levy noted that no record was kept of the thinking behind the debates and decisions in Philadelphia that summer of 1787. What group concerned with preserving its original intent would have been so "careless," he argues, as to bar a stenographer from its proceedings, assuring that no record was kept? Only James Madison took notes, and he refused to have them published during his lifetime. Levy argues that the idea of finding some presumed original intent of the Framers is a mythology used by conservatives to cloak their own brand of political activism with high purpose.

While debates over judicial philosophy go on in law schools and in judicial nomination hearings, the philosophies themselves continue to be put into practice in the courts. As the advocates for each view rightly suggest, being a legal realist or a legal formalist (strict constructionist) does make a difference. Those differences can be seen in the opinions written by the courts.

Deciding Cases and Writing Opinions

After the Court has decided to hear a case, the clerk of the Court notifies the lawyers for both sides. They are requested to submit briefs informing the justices of their arguments and the legal basis for a recommended decision. The briefs are circulated among the justices, and a date is set for the two sides to present oral arguments before the Court. In times past, the oral arguments could consume a week. Today, they are generally limited to an hour or two, with justices often asking pointed questions to clarify their thinking about the case. After hearing the arguments, the justices employ their own brands of legal reasoning (as outlined above) to reach their decisions.

Decisions on cases are made at **conferences** attended only by the justices. The tradition once was for junior justices to cast their votes before the senior ones so that, as one justice put it, "the juniors are not influenced by the vote of their elders."[37] Today, there is no tradition of voting up the ranks. Justice Blackmun observed that if there has been a pattern in recent years, it is just the opposite: "we vote by seniority, as you know, despite [the fact] that some texts say we vote by juniority."[38]

In an important or divisive case, intense discussion may occur before voting. Conferences may turn into real debate sessions with justices trying to convince one another of their reasoning. The Court buzzes with discussion, memo writing, and informal politicking in efforts to build strong majorities around a single opinion. In the landmark case of *Brown v. Board of Education*, for example, final agreement on the two opinions issued in the case took years to produce, and the lobbying among the justices required to achieve unanimity was intense. However, a typical conference involves little more than a brief statement by each justice explaining his or her vote. Either the chief justice or, more often, a justice designated by the chief justice keeps a tally of the votes and reports them to the clerk.

When a clear majority exists, and he is in it, the chief justice decides who will write the opinion for the majority. In some cases the chief writes the opinion. When the chief is not in the majority, the senior justice in the majority assigns the opinion. The opinion is drafted and circulated to others in the majority for comments and changes. If agreement is reached, the majority sign the opinion, and it is "handed down" to the parties in dispute. When a majority votes for the same decision but their reasoning differs, justices in the majority may choose to write a *concurring opinion*. *A concurring opinion agrees with the decision but disagrees with the legal reasoning of others in the majority*. Justices who find themselves in the minority and disagree strongly with the reasoning behind a decision have the option of writing a **dissenting opinion** to promote a different line of thinking about future cases. When a case seems of little importance or the Court is unable to reach agreement on the legal basis for an opinion, *a decision may be handed down without an opinion attached*. This is known as a **per curiam opinion**.

Clarity and agreement in opinions on major cases are important because, as Justice Potter Stewart once said, "The business of the Court is to give institutional opinions for its decisions." Elaborating on this idea, law scholar David O'Brien noted that too much disagreement weakens an opinion, robbing it of authority as well as making it difficult to use as precedent for deciding future cases:

> The Court's opinion serves to communicate an institutional decision. It should also convey the politically symbolic values of certainty, stability, and impartiality in the law. In most cases, justices try to persuade as many others as possible to join an opinion.[39]

While crafting clear, unanimous opinions may be a noble goal, many justices are cautious about joining strong opinions that might change the course of future law. The history of abortion cases after *Roe* indicates that the Courts of the 1980s and early 1990s

Judging the Constitution

In its own restrained fashion, the Supreme Court has
regularly played a pivotal role in shaping America's
history. At times it has been graced with particularly
august jurists. Among the most celebrated was Oliver
Wendell Holmes (*right;* served 1902–1932). Called
"The Great Dissenter," Holmes was known for his deep
skepticism and detachment in interpreting the law, on
one occasion writing a friend: "If my fellow citizens
want to go to Hell I will help them. It's my job." The
renowned Felix Frankfurter (*above;* served 1939–1962)
similarly wrote: "One's own opinion about the wisdom
or evil of a law should be excluded altogether when
one is doing one's duty on the bench." Below, the Court
at the time of Ruth Bader Ginsburg's appointment:
(*from front row, left*) John Paul Stevens, Byron White
(*retired*), Chief Justice William Rehnquist, Harry
Blackmun, Sandra Day O'Connor; (*back row*)
David Souter, Antonin Scalia, Anthony Kennedy,
Clarence Thomas.

The Players

disagreed increasingly with the earlier landmark decision but refrained from rushing to issue a strong opinion to overturn it. At the other extreme are the majority of cases in which the legal and political issues are simply not monumental. The quality of routine opinions often reflects the hectic pace of an overworked Court rushing through as many cases as possible each term. As Justice Blackmun once observed about the rush to produce opinions in order to adjourn for the summer: "I think we do our cruddiest, our shoddiest work in April, May and June."[40] As this remark indicates, the Court consists of nine human beings who are capable of brilliance and sloppiness, of bending to political motives and pursuing the highest purpose. Understanding the workings of the Court requires being realistic about this blending of law and human relations.

Inside the Court

Much of the authority of the Court is the ability to speak with an institutional voice rather than convey the impression that each opinion is simply the product of haggling among nine fallible humans. For years, the mystique of rituals, legal language, and robes was enhanced by a cult of silence among members of the Court who seldom, if ever, revealed the nature of their personal relations or their political deliberations. The world was finally given a look behind the scenes of the Supreme Court with a book called *The Brethren,* a journalistic account of the politics and personalities of the Court.[41]

It should not be surprising that the justices often lobby each other for support, or that they sometimes fall prey to the human foibles of jealousy, pettiness, and personality conflicts. Nor should it shock anyone to discover that an occasional justice who postpones retirement too long may be affected by senility. And who should expect all appointees to the Court to be equally brilliant legal minds? Yet the people were scandalized when one of the justices reportedly referred to former Chief Justice Warren Burger as a "dummy." The book also revealed that the other justices began working as a team of eight after the refusal of William O. Douglas to retire following a stroke that left him incapacitated and an embarrassment to the Court.[42] Some scholars take issue with the accuracy of *The Brethren*, and others question how much emphasis should be given to the personal dimension of the Court.[43] However, even critics agree that the opinions of the Court must be understood in the context of the personal and political relations among the justices:

> The decision process in the Court is essentially a political process (in the nonpejorative use of that word). Yet all the 'lobbying' and efforts at persuasion that go on—the sometimes petty infighting, the drafts and memoranda going back and forth among the Justices, the changes made in opinions as part of the bargaining process—all this is done for the purpose of reaching what the individual justice considers the best result. There is, to be sure, politicking, compromises, and horsetrading in the often complex negotiations and compromises needed to attain a working majority, yet all for the purpose of advancing not the Justices themselves but the judicial doctrines in which they believe.[44]

How do the justices regard each other? Here are some of Justice Harry Blackmun's insights about his colleagues from the Rehnquist Court:

- Chief Justice William H. Rehnquist: "The chief in conference is a splendid administrator. He gets through the agenda in a hurry. . . . If there is anything to be criticized about it, he gets through in too much of a hurry at times."

- Sandra Day O'Connor: "Sandra's tough, she's conservative, she's a states' righter, she wants the states to decide things . . . But . . . the . . . soft spots in her armor . . . are children and are women."

- Antonin Scalia: "Nino is and always will be the professor at work. . . . He asks far too many questions. . . . Even Sandra, who asks a lot of questions, a couple of times gets exasperated when Nino interrupts her line of inquiry and goes off on his own. She throws her pencil down and 'umh, umh'. . . . He analyzes very finely, very carefully. I think some of his opinions are very difficult to read, but they generally, they make sense."

- Anthony M. Kennedy: "He's settled right in. He's able, articulate, doesn't ask too many questions, takes a positive position and doesn't equivocate in any way."[45]

It is common to refer to Courts in different periods by the names of their chief justices, as in the Warren Court, the Burger Court, and the Rehnquist Court, to name the most recent three. This is because the chief justice brings a particular leadership style to the job of running conferences, organizing majorities, and assigning opinions. Observers note, for example, that Earl Warren brought a strong political lobbying style to the Court. With his growing commitment to judicial activism in civil rights cases, he pushed the Court toward much bolder rulings than it might have issued in his absence. In the case of *Brown*, Warren came to a Court that was divided on the race question. The previous chief justice, Fred Vinson, feared that overturning the "separate but equal" ruling that had governed civil rights law since 1896 (*Plessy v. Ferguson*) would result in the "complete abolition of the public school system in the South."[46] (Recall the discussion of these cases from Chapter 5.) The Court was so divided that the case was delayed for more argument the next term. Chief Justice Vinson died in the interim, an event that prompted the ever-acerbic Justice Frankfurter to remark that "This is the first indication that I have ever had that there is a God."[47] Warren arrived and patiently lobbied his new colleagues to come around to his view that the separate but equal doctrine had little basis in the Constitution and rested almost entirely on a foundation of racism in society. He continued to develop the legal argument to support his brand of realism while meeting individually with the other justices. When he had convinced all but one justice, Warren confronted the lone Justice Reed: "Stan, you're all by yourself in this now. You've got to decide whether it's really the best thing for the country."[48] Reed finally agreed to join the rest, and a final conference was held to explore the terms of their agreement. At the end of this lengthy process, Warren drafted the unanimous opinion for the Court.

What difference can a chief justice make? According to Frankfurter's analysis, if *Brown* and other segregation cases had been pushed to decision a year earlier under Chief Justice Vinson, "there would have been four dissenters . . . and certainly several opinions for the majority view. That would have been catastrophic."[49] Justice Burton wrote in his diary that "It looks like a unanimous opinion—a major accomplishment for his leadership."[50] When agreement was finally reached on *Brown*, Justice Burton wrote a note of congratulations to the chief justice, saying, "To you goes the credit for the character of the opinions which produced the all important unanimity."[51]

Here is the core of Warren's *Brown* opinion as expressed in a memo that he circulated to other justices as part of the process of drafting the final opinion:

> Does segregation of school children solely on the basis of color, even though the physical facilities may be equal, deprive the minority group of equal opportunities in the educational system? We believe that it does. We believe that it applies particularly to children of tender age, and that the reasons stated for striking down segregation in the college cases apply with added force to children in the grade and high schools. To separate them from others of their age in school solely because of their color puts the mark of inferiority not only upon their status in the community but also upon their little hearts and minds in a form that is unlikely ever to be erased. We believe that it has

many other divisive results not necessary to enumerate here but which, in aggregate, make the doctrine of "separate but equal" inapplicable to education.[52]

The tone of the Court changed with Earl Warren's departure and the appointment of Warren Burger as chief justice. Although Burger inherited a Court that was more conservative due to retirements and appointments made by President Nixon, Burger was not the assertive leader that Warren had been. Some accused him of being less bright, less committed to an agenda, and more interested in the pomp and prestige of his position. In some areas, the Burger Court outraged conservatives, as with its ruling in *Roe*. Yet the same Court withdrew some of the protections granted by the Warren Court in such areas as criminal justice and pornography.

When William Rehnquist became chief justice in 1986, the Court was still divided between veterans of the Warren and Burger eras and newer appointees who subscribed more openly to doctrines of legal formalism (strict constructionism). Rehnquist was not the assertive leader to forge a stable coalition in this group. Although a conservative and a strict constructionist, Justice Rehnquist occasionally surprised his critics. For example, he wrote the majority opinion overturning a $200,000 jury award to evangelist Jerry Falwell. The money was awarded when Falwell won a suit against *Hustler* magazine for "intentional infliction of emotional distress" resulting from a parody of Mr. Falwell published by the magazine. The Rehnquist opinion surprised conservatives with its emphasis on the importance of giving "adequate 'breathing space' to the freedoms protected by the First Amendment."[53] Still, critics charged that Rehnquist preferred the path of least resistance, allowing the majority of the moment to guide the Court, while he concentrated more on "getting things out and doing it fast so that he can keep his tennis schedule and recess for the summer by July 4."[54] A more impartial assessment is that Rehnquist, like Burger, played a low-key strategy to keep from dividing a polarized Court, often aligning himself with the majority so he could steer the opinion.[55]

Whether due to laziness or caution or both, Rehnquist's style may have eased the shock of transition as the last justices of the Warren era Court were replaced by Reagan and Bush appointees who preached philosophies of restraint and formalism: O'Connor

William Rehnquist, appointed to the Supreme Court as an associate justice by President Richard Nixon in 1972, succeeded Warren Burger as Chief Justice upon Burger's retirement in 1986. A consensus-building judicial conservative, Rehnquist has also written a widely praised popular history of the Court, titled The Supreme Court: How It Was, How It Is.

INSIDE THE SYSTEM

The Politics of the Rehnquist Court as the Sum of Individual Legal Philosophies

16.4

Most law scholars agree that the Supreme Court was not given a strong leader when Ronald Reagan appointed Associate Justice William H. Rehnquist to be chief justice in 1986. The Court was divided on many cases, and even the conservative majority could not reach agreement on the reasoning behind many civil liberties decisions. However, the appointment of five justices by Republican presidents during the 1980s and early 1990s resulted in a voting majority on the Court whose decisions aroused political opposition from liberal civil liberties activists, particularly in the area of criminal justice procedures. These cases, among others, illustrate how even without a strong chief justice, the political impact of the institution can be considerable. Here is a partial list of key rulings of the Rehnquist Court in the area of the rights of suspects and convicts:

• *McCleskey v. Zant*: Raised nearly insurmountable barriers to the ability of a convicted person to file second or successive petitions of *habeas corpus*.

Judges must dismiss them as an "abuse of the writ" except in unusual circumstances. (*Habeas corpus* petitions are requests for a court review of the legality of a person's detainment. This is the most common form of the "pauper's petition" of the sort filed by Gideon that resulted in the 1963 landmark ruling.)

• *Coleman v. Thompson*: Held that prisoners forfeit their right to file even initial writs of *habeas corpus* if, through a procedural or lawyer error, they fail to present their appeal properly in the state courts.

• *Arizona v. Fulminante*: Held that coerced confessions may be considered only a "harmless error" and not invalidated as evidence if other evidence presented at trial is adequate to sustain a guilty verdict.

• *Wilson v. Seider*: Held that difficult prison conditions do not violate prisoners' Eighth Amendment rights against cruel and unusual punishment unless prisoners can show that prison officials acted with "deliberate indifference."

• *Harmelin v. Michigan*: Upheld a Michigan law requiring a mandatory life sentence for non-violent first offenders convicted

of possession of more than 1.5 pounds of cocaine.

• *California v. Hodari D.*: Held that drugs or other evidence discarded by a person fleeing the police are admissible evidence regardless of whether or not the police had reason to suspect the person of a crime when they began the chase; since such persons have not been "seized," the Court reasoned, their Fourth Amendment rights cannot have been violated.

• *California v. Acevedo*: Held that police can search closed containers in automobiles without a search warrant as long as they have probable cause to suspect the presence of drugs or other contraband.

• *Georgia v. McCollum*: Completed the Court's redefinition of lawyers' rights to remove jurors by barring defense lawyers from disqualifying jurors on the basis of race (a 1986 decision had done the same for prosecutors).

• *Keeny v. Tamayo–Reyes*: Further limited prisoners' ability to file writs of habeas corpus.

SOURCE: *The New York Times*: June 30, 1991, Sec. 4, p. 3; and July 5, 1992, Sec. 4, p. 1.

(1981), Scalia (1986), Kennedy (1988), Souter (1990), and Thomas (1991). By the time President Bush left office, the Court had taken on the qualities long feared by liberal legal activists: an institution pursuing a conservative agenda through a language of legal formalism (strict constructionism). Even without a strong-willed leader as chief justice, the Rehnquist Court clearly changed the law, particularly on civil liberties issues affecting people (such as Clarence Earl Gideon) charged with or convicted of crimes. "Inside the System" Box 16.4 illustrates some of the key rulings of the Rehnquist Court that affect the rights of citizens in their dealings with law enforcement agencies. Perhaps the conservative activism of the Court in these and other areas of civil liberties law had swung as far as it would go when Justice Byron White announced his retirement in 1993.

White's retirement gave Bill Clinton his first chance to begin putting his political and legal stamp on the Court with the nomination of Ruth Bader Ginsburg.

The Politics of Nominations

Battles over appointments to the Court have been big news in recent years. Television screens have been filled with images of senators leaning over their microphones, taking off their glasses, and asking nominees how they would vote on sensitive issues such as civil rights and abortion. Although Sandra Day O'Connor admitted to the Senate panel in 1981 that she felt abortion law should be left to legislatures to write, she refused to say how she would rule in abortion cases. Few nominees since have been willing to offer even that much of a preview of their judicial behavior in substantive areas of law. Antonin Scalia played it so cagey with the senators in 1986 that he declined to share his views even on the case of *Marbury v. Madison!*

Both O'Connor (99–0) and Scalia (98–0) were confirmed by unanimous votes in the Senate. Robert Bork was not so lucky in 1987 when he engaged in acrimonious disputes with liberal senators over how his strict constructionist philosophy of "original understanding" would apply the values of the framers to the legal disputes of modern times. Many liberal senators regarded Bork as an ideological conservative who would become a judicial activist hiding behind an obscure legal philosophy. His nomination was rejected in a Senate vote of 42 in favor and 58 opposed. Paying attention to the Bork disaster, the next nominees were carefully coached. They scripted their remarks at the hearings and refused to engage in much discussion about specific cases or general principles of law. This recent pattern of avoiding political controversy has led one observer to call contemporary confirmation hearings the "stealth" confirmations.[56]

The stealth approach worked for Anthony Kennedy and David Souter, but nearly backfired on Clarence Thomas, who was nominated by George Bush in 1991. Thomas, a black man with a conservative reputation on civil rights, stirred up great opposition among liberal interest groups and Democrats in the Senate. Although Thomas was carefully coached to avoid substantive debates with the senators, the interest group campaign against him drew national attention to the hearings. Just when it appeared that Thomas was on the brink of confirmation, two reporters were given leaked records indicating that one woman interviewed about Thomas alleged that he had harassed her sexually when she worked for him in two different jobs a decade earlier. A storm of protest once again surged around the nominee, and the nation turned to the television sets in even greater numbers.

Campaigns of support were drummed up both for Thomas and for Anita Hill, the University of Oklahoma law professor who accused him of harassment. Debates raged on talk shows about whether such matters were appropriate for confirming a Supreme Court justice. Those who felt they were relevant pointed out that character was extremely important for one of the highest justice officials in the land, and, in addition, Thomas's personal views might enter his opinions on cases involving sexual discrimination. Anita Hill's character was attacked with equal intensity, while Thomas's supporters called the whole affair a desperation move by angry liberals who were losing their grip on the Court. As the TV melodrama unfolded, public opinion polls revealed shifting divisions of support between Professor Hill and Judge Thomas. Thomas denied the charges and compared the second round of hearings to a "high-tech lynching." In the end, Thomas was confirmed by the margin of 52 to 48.

What do we make of the recent battles over Court appointments? The troubles encountered by Presidents Nixon (who lost battles over Clement Haynsworth and G. Harrold Carswell), Reagan (who lost the fight for Robert Bork and withdrew the nomination

Judge Ruth Bader Ginsburg (right), *nominated to the Supreme Court in June 1993 by Bill Clinton, was confirmed without incident several weeks later. Ginsburg's tranquil confirmation was in jarring contrast to the one endured by Judge Clarence Thomas (left, with President George Bush, wife Virginia Thomas, and Justice Byron White). Thomas joined the Court in October 1991 only after grueling Senate hearings that ran throughout the summer. These hearings were capped by last-minute accusations from a former employee, Anita Hill, that Thomas had sexually harassed her a decade earlier, when she worked for him in two government positions. Thomas flatly denied the allegations, terming the second round of hearings "a high-tech lynching for uppity blacks." The Senate gave Thomas the benefit of a doubt, confirming him by a 52–48 vote. One investigative reporter, David Brock, later called into question Hill's veracity; and Ginsburg may have benefited from the public dismay that attended her colleague's highly politicized hearings.*

of Douglas Ginsburg) and Bush (who narrowly won the Thomas nomination) all involved political struggles between Democratic Congresses and Republican presidents. Moreover, with the entry of interest groups in the confirmation process, senators are put on the hot seat back home at election time if they fail to please voters that the interest groups can mobilize. Once again, the point is that politics plays an important role in the life of the Court, from nominating justices to deciding cases.

Law and Society Revisited

What links the federal court system so personally to society and politics? By now it should be clear that many connections exist, from the political power of Congress to design courts, screen judicial appointments, and establish jurisdictions to the power of individuals to have their day in court. In fact, what may be unique about the federal courts of the United States is the multitude of connections they have to the nation's politics: from the everyday disputes among individuals to the power struggles between national governing institutions. Equally impressive about the politics of the American justice system is the involvement of citizens, both as television audiences and through interest groups, in screening and debating the legal philosophies of judges.

The relationship between politics and judicial philosophy is likely to remain an uneasy one. Perhaps that is the only way it can be. The law, after all, is a reminder about cultural standards from the past, and, at the same time, it must be relevant in order to be

A CITIZEN'S QUESTION Justice

When do the political aspects of the legal system produce unjust results? One of the main themes of this chapter is that citizens often use the law to advance their political goals. Yet the law has an image of being above politics, offering a higher resolution for political dispute. How can law and politics exist comfortably together in the same system? Often they do not, as reflected in the frequent battles people have over court decisions and the appointment of judges.

Rather than becoming discouraged by the political uses of the law, it may help to see the legal system as one of the major safety valves that takes pressure out of volatile political conflicts in at least two ways: by offering opportunities for appeals that can be used to challenge outcomes that seem unfair, and by providing laws and procedures that should be applied equally in all cases. In addition, challenging laws on political grounds can be thought of as a way of keeping the justice system in tune with society. Does this mean that the results of legal contests will be regarded as fair by all of the people involved? Obviously not. The more appropriate question is whether the courts handle the issues before them in ways that generally seem fair to most of the people most of the time.

Think about the social impact of court rulings on an issue you care about (abortion, affirmative action, prayer in school, the rights of criminal defendants). Now ask yourself two simple questions: How much of my feeling about the fairness of these rulings is based on my personal feelings about how this issue should be decided? How much of my reaction is based on a realistic analysis of the political conflict in society surrounding this issue, recognizing the impossibility that any solution will satisfy everyone? Should our sense of justice be based on our personal wishes or a sense of balancing society's conflicts?

accepted and obeyed. It is hard to imagine keeping politics out of the courts, as roughly 90 percent of presidential appointments to the Supreme Court have come from the President's political party. Yet political ideology does not translate directly into legal opinions; the judicial philosophy of a particular justice may produce surprising results on the bench. Surely Felix Frankfurter's personal views were more liberal than many of the legal opinions guided by his sense of judicial self-restraint. And when Dwight Eisenhower nominated Earl Warren to the post of chief justice, he surely thought he was getting a conservative on civil rights and social policy issues. Yet Warren's conversion to judicial activism and legal realism led Eisenhower to lament the Warren appointment as the "biggest damn fool mistake I ever made."

The debates in society and the media about judicial philosophy are healthy signs. Neither side will convince the other of its correctness, but that may not be the point. Perhaps the justice system requires both sides to keep it balanced. The advocates of self-restraint and formalism remind us that *the law reflects a tradition of logic, precedent, and intent* that cannot be taken lightly, while the activists remind us that the surest way to bring on the downfall of that legal tradition is to be "unrealistic" in its application. Since the courts attract political disputes that threaten social order, there is no guarantee that their resolutions will settle issues permanently. However, given the number of points of access and the opportunities for appeal, conflicts are tempered with the hope that justice will be done. Perhaps that is the best one can hope for in politics.

Key Terms

common law

statutory law

docket

prosecutor, defendant, criminal law

plaintiff, defendant, civil law

felony, misdemeanor

jurisdiction

landmark ruling

political question doctrine

adversarial procedure

petition for certiorari

writ of certiorari

indict

arraign

standing to sue

U.S. District Court, district courts

U.S. Court of Appeals, circuit courts

judicial activism

judicial restraint

strict constructionism, legal formalism

broad constructionism, legal realism

concurring opinion, dissenting opinion, per curiam opinion

legal reasoning from precedent (stare decisis)

conferences

nomination politics

Suggested Readings

Abraham, Henry J. *Justices and Presidents: A Political History of Appointments to the Supreme Court*, 2nd ed. New York: Oxford University Press, 1985.

Baum, Lawrence. *American Courts: Process and Policy*, 2nd ed. Boston: Houghton Mifflin, 1990.

Corwin, Edwin S. *Court Over Constitution: A Study of the Judicial as an Instrument of Popular Government*. Magnolia, Mass.: Peter Smith, 1990. (Originally published in 1938.)

Levy, Leonard W. *Original Intent and the Framers' Constitution*. New York: Macmillan, 1987.

O'Brien, David M. *Storm Center: The Supreme Court in American Politics*. New York: Norton, 1986.

Schwartz, Bernard. *A History of the Supreme Court*. Cambridge, Mass.: Oxford University Press, 1993.

Tribe, Laurence H. *American Constitutional Law*, 2nd ed. Mineola, N.Y.: The Foundation Press, 1988.

Wasby, Stephen L. *The Supreme Court in the Federal Judicial System*, 3rd ed. Chicago: Nelson-Hall, 1988.

Woodward, Bob and Scott Armstrong. *The Brethren: Inside the Supreme Court*. New York: Simon and Schuster, 1979.

Part V

POLICY
THE SUM OF THE PARTS

CHAPTER 17

The Policy Process

CHAPTER 18

Social Policy: Managing the Quality of Life

CHAPTER 19

Economic Policy: Paying for It All

CHAPTER 20

Foreign and Defense Policy: National Security and World Power

Here are the political players and procedures mentioned in a single news story about efforts to work out a policy for logging old-growth forests in the Northwest:

Congress
The U.S. senators from Oregon
The House of Representatives
Militant demonstrators, both loggers and environmentalists
Arthur Johnson, citizen activist
Timber workers
Court injunctions and appeals
Administrative appeals
Preservationists/conservationists/environmentalists
James Geisinger, president, Northwest Forestry Assoc.
Public opinion polls
Portland Oregonian newspaper
The governor of Oregon

Environmental leaders meeting with the governor
Timber industry leaders meeting with the governor
John Hampton, president, Hampton Lumber Sales
Seattle Audubon Society
Sierra Club Legal Defense Fund
U.S. Forest Service officials
Federal courts
Oregon voters backing ballot proposition halting the overseas shipment of raw logs
Doug Stout, vice president, Bohemia Lumber Company
2,000 pairs of spotted owls, the last in existence

Policy analysis is like a hot dog—its contents are both variable and suspect.
—*JOSEPH STEWART, JR.*

17

The Policy Process

- **NEWS FEATURE: THE AMERICAN AGENDA**
- **THE MANY PATHS TO POLICY**
  Policy and Politics
  The Politics of Compromise
- **POLICY INSIDE THE SYSTEM**
  Power and Policy
  Culture and Symbolic Politics
  Constitutional Design: Institutions and Federalism
- **BUILDING THE POLICY AGENDA**
  The Bottom-Up Path to Policy
  The Top-Down Path to Policy
  Case: Getting Health Care on the Agenda Again
- **THE REST OF THE PROCESS: FROM GOVERNMENT TO SOCIETY**
  The Decision Process
  Policy Logjams
  Looking for Windows of Opportunity
  Implementation and Evaluation
- **THE MANY PATHS TO POLICY REVISITED**
- **A CITIZEN'S QUESTION: Policy**
- **KEY TERMS**
- **SUGGESTED READINGS**

As explained in Chapter 11, the news continues to place its emphasis on the political battles in government. However, the increasing appearance of *political agenda* features in the media is drawing more public attention to important problems that have been neglected in the normal course of government and news reporting. In Seattle, the major daily newspaper, *The Seattle Times,* has adopted an editorial policy of highlighting regional political needs through special reports. The national paper *USA Today* runs regular editorial-page debates on national issues and often leads its front page with a feature story on the same topic. One of the most widely watched "agenda" features is ABC News' "American Agenda" segment, which airs regularly on the *World News Tonight* program anchored by Peter Jennings.

The ABC format consists of a series of reports on such issues as health care, education, drugs, race relations, or the quality of children's lives. One report addressed the problem of American companies moving their factories across the border into Mexico to use cheap labor and avoid pollution laws. In addition to the problems created on the Mexican side, toxic wastes were coming back across the border into the drinking water of such towns as Brownsville, Texas, where serious birth defects and other health problems were on the increase.[1] The reports combine human-interest angles, facts, figures, and a discussion of what can be done. A notable feature of the ABC approach is to keep the issue on the agenda by following up to see if anything has been done or to ask whether any of the remedies tried have had an effect.

One important series of ABC reports focused on children. The angle was simple: Children are the nation's future, and that future may not be bright. It was reported that growing numbers of children live in poverty, suffer ill health, and grow up in drug-plagued environments. Many of tomorrow's citizens

are sleepwalking through failing schools and developing emotional scars from growing up in difficult circumstances. As adults, many will face poor job prospects and continued personal hardships.

These ABC reports pointed to the work of a National Commission on Children, staffed by prominent politicians and experts on children's issues. Its task was to suggest broad policy guidelines for the government to strengthen families and help children develop into solid citizens. ABC reported that the commission was holding hearings around the country, interviewing experts, and conducting national opinion surveys of families on their problems. Some findings of the polls were positive: 70 percent of families eat together, and 60 percent worship together. But there were also many dark clouds: 53 percent of parents worry about having enough money to give their children what they need; 23 percent of single parents earn less than $10,000 a year; 42 percent of parents in poor urban environments worry that their children will drop out of school; and 40 percent of the urban poor fear that their children may be shot.[2]

One follow-up to the initial story looked at the recommendations of the National Commission on Children. Its chairman, Senator Jay Rockefeller (R–West Virginia), outlined a legislative package that he planned to introduce on behalf of the Commission. The plan called for measures including a government subsidy of $1,000 per child, reduced taxes for poor families, stronger enforcement of child support laws, and government health care for children and pregnant women. It was, Rockefeller admitted, a tall order, but one designed to test the commitment of politicians who get a lot of political mileage out of using the family as a symbol.

The Los Angeles Times also ran a series of policy stories on the nation's children. The *Times* took a provocative look at the interest-group system (see Chapter 8) that shapes government policy in many

A mother and her children enjoy the sun from the porch of their Mississippi home. While media "exposés" often paint dramatic pictures of social issues such as domestic poverty, crime, drug abuse, and the like, such stories rarely leave their audiences with much understanding of the complex causes underlying these problems—or the full range of policies conceivable for solving them. However, "news-agenda" features may be raising the value of policy coverage.

areas, and concluded that there is not much of a children's lobby. One headline proclaimed: CHILDREN'S LACK OF POLITICAL VOICE LEAVES NEEDS UNMET. The reports looked at national children's lobby groups such as the Children's Defense Fund and KIDPAC and their involvement in developing policy guidelines. Also introduced was the House Select Committee on Children, Youth, and Families. A staff member of that committee unfavorably compared U.S. policies for children with those of European governments that take more responsibility for child welfare.[3]

Adding to this flurry of media interest, a piece in *The New York Times* delivered the stunning conclusion of a report issued by a joint Commission of the American Medical Association and the National Association of State Boards of Education: "Never before has one generation of American teenagers been less healthy, less cared for or less prepared for life than their parents were at the same age."[4] Such news is shocking, but it may provide a beginning point for people and their governors to begin addressing national problems.

These modifications of the usual sixty-seconds-and-a-soundbite news format are something of a risk for the media. For years, academics and politicians have debated whether the media do, and whether they should, *set the political agenda.* By covering particular issues and topics, are the media telling the public what matters and what needs to be done? Recall from Chapter 11 that political scientists Shanto Iyengar and Donald Kinder concluded that when the media focus on an issue, viewers are more likely to think the issue matters.[5] In later research, Iyengar showed that the way a story is told influences *how* people think about the political issues involved.[6] The human-interest angles of most political news stories leave people with little understanding of underlying issues.

Intense news coverage is one of several factors that affect whether social problems become part of the **public agenda**: the list of problems that citizens think are important enough for the government to attempt to solve. When public pressure is brought to bear on government officials, those problems may then move onto the **government agenda**: the list of problems that the institutions of government are actively trying to solve. When the institutions dealing with a particular problem begin to develop broad guidelines about how to deal with it, those guidelines are called policies. This chapter explores how these processes of *agenda-building* and *policy-making* work.

The tools that you have acquired so far in reading this book will help you to simplify the world of government policy-making. For example, the movement of issues onto the government agenda reflects different types of *power in society,* from the pressure of majorities, to manipulation of the media by interest groups, to inside maneuvering among elites. Once on the agenda, policy problems are complicated by the different *institutions* of national government and levels of the *federal system* that must be engaged. Finally, basic values and conflicts in the *political culture* shape how problems are defined and what solutions are acceptable. The "simple" solution for poverty, for example, might be to guarantee everyone a minimum income or standard of living, but this solution would be, to many people, inconsistent with American values. The policy process thus reflects all of the parts of the political system in action. Your knowledge of the system in action will enable you to see how you personally fit into the policy picture on different issues.

The Many Paths to Policy

Policy *consists of a general agreement among government officials about the nature of a political problem and the general approaches that government should take toward it.* Policy is thus a broad pattern of government response to a problem. Policies often involve many government activities working together to tackle complex problems. For example, executive orders, legislation, and court rulings have all become important parts of government civil-rights policies. Beyond the responses of government institutions, various forms of public pressure, from interest-group action to individual lawsuits, may also contribute to keeping a policy on course, or changing a policy that has fallen out of favor.

What aspects of the political system become engaged in making a policy depend on what political issues are involved. The specifics of policy-making depend on whether we are talking about buying lunches for hungry children or building new bombers for the Air Force. Understanding the differences and the many political paths involved may help you to follow the next news report about the next pressing issue on the national agenda.

Policy and Politics

There is more agreement in some areas of policy than in others. Even when government programs appear fairly well defined by laws, there may not be strong agreement among officials about just how to apply them. Recall, for example, the battle over the Clean Air Act discussed in Chapter 15. The Bush administration decided not to implement certain parts of the act, perceiving them as damaging to economic growth. The Clinton administration, by contrast, promised a more aggressive *policy* of using the same laws and regulations to police polluters. *These different responses to the same law suggest that no matter how clearly government responses to problems are defined by laws and bureaucratic regulations, an important part of policy is also defined by the political judgments of those enforcing the laws and regulations.*

The distinction between laws and policies may appear tricky at first, but it is important to grasp. Policies are broader *political guidelines* within which laws or other procedures evolve and are enforced or not. After Bill Clinton named lawyer Zoë Baird as his first nominee for Attorney General, it was revealed that she had hired illegal aliens to work in her home. As head of the Justice Department, she would have been in charge of enforcing the laws regarding illegal aliens and their employment. Clinton withdrew her nomination after people protested that she, too, should have obeyed those laws. In her defense, Baird said that she understood that Justice Department *policy* was not to enforce such laws in cases involving domestic employment. The public was not sympathetic to this argument in which policy and the law were at odds. You can probably find

Marion Wright Edelman, head of the Children's Defense Fund, a social-policy lobbying group. A Yale-educated attorney well known on the Washington, D.C., political scene since the 1960s, Edelman is also a longtime confidant of fellow Yale Law alumna Hillary Clinton. Soon after Bill Clinton assumed the presidency, Edelman became a member of the First Lady's health-care task force.

areas in which you agree or disagree with government policies of strict or lax enforcement of laws. Should government be more or less strict in policies regarding speeding? Drunken driving? Sexual harassment? Pollution control? Sexual relations among consenting adults? Arresting those who do not repay their student loans?

The Politics of Compromise

There is a long tradition of political compromise in the United States, beginning with the compromises in the Constitution that created the national government itself. In a system with so many divisions of government decision-making, so many kinds of power available to different players in society, and so much conflict among such fundamental values as freedom and equality, it is hardly surprising that policies seldom deliver everything that any one group or faction wants. The ability to balance the demands of factions was James Madison's boast in *Federalist* No. 10 about the strength of the design of American government.

It is not surprising that policies are where compromises often show up most clearly. In defense-budget politics, for example, each branch of the military usually receives less than it requests, yet the unified military command of the Joint Chiefs of Staff must work out a broad set of defense policies to fit the resources they are given. Thus budget cuts affect broad policy calculations, such as how many wars of what type the military is prepared to fight. Even these policy compromises often come under fire from opponents (in Congress and interest groups) who say that military spending is still far more than is necessary to defend the nation. In this give-and-take, the compromises go on, and policies change gradually.

Students gather around a statue of Theodore Roosevelt outside New York's Museum of Natural History to celebrate "Earth Day" in April 1990. Roosevelt, an energetic outdoorsman and explorer, added millions of acres to the national park system, and considered his conservation policies to be the major domestic legacy of his years as president.

Similar stories can be told involving other players and other institutions. "Inside the System" Box 17.1 looks at the politics of compromise involved in trying to coordinate environmental protection policies with energy policies. The players from energy industries (coal, oil, nuclear, and gas) and environmental organizations often see one another's goals as unacceptable. Making policy in one of these complex areas would be challenging enough, but trying to coordinate them requires that tough compromises be hammered out by state and national institutions. Although it may be tempting to dismiss compromise as unsatisfying because it does not deliver everything your side asked for, first think about what it would be like to live with policies that delivered everything one of the

The Politics of Policy Compromise: Energy vs. the Environment vs. the Economy

17.1

Think about the complexity of energy policy. How should we conserve energy? How should we create it efficiently? Both of these questions touch on dozens of other areas of policy, from economic productivity to environmental quality. If we burn coal and other fossil fuels in homes and factories, the emissions create air pollution, along with acid rain that destroys lakes and forests. The carbon dioxide given off contributes to global warming, which may threaten life quality and survival in other ways. On the other hand, reducing national dependence on fossil fuel energy may drive up the costs of industrial production, damaging the economy and eliminating jobs. The need to balance economic considerations with environmental concerns brings energy policy directly into conflict with (at least) these two other major policy spheres.

This complexity is mirrored in virtually every energy policy question, form what to burn in factories to where to build dams and how to design automobiles. Cars turn out to be a major part of the American energy picture. One conservation option is to raise fuel economy standards for new cars, as discussed in Chapter 8. However, auto makers have resisted government efforts to force them to produce more fuel-efficient cars, arguing that it will increase costs and curtail production. On the other side, environmental critics cite government estimates that more than 40 percent of our oil currently comes from the unpredictable Middle East, and could rise to as much as 75 percent dependence on foreign oil if current trends continue over the next twenty years.* Oil companies have proposed legislation to open up more domestic and wilderness areas for drilling. These moves have been resisted strongly by environmentalists on grounds that they would destroy the environment without solving the energy problem in the long run. Once again, policy in one area runs against policy in the others.

At every turn, the interests battle one another, forcing state, national, and regional governments to try to work out compromises. The resulting policies strike often precarious balances among environmental, economic, and social needs. Policy advocates in each area claim that their goals are impeded by the gains of opponents. For example, environmentalists say that energy policies are so aligned with economic interests that the environment is essentially neglected while the government orders new studies and delays costly conservation programs. Corporations say they cannot compete in a tough world market if environmental policies drive up costs and alienate consumers. In a sense, the charges and countercharges may all be true. In many policy areas, tradeoffs between issues leave all sides unhappy. Because of the politics of compromise, policies may not be very stable. Yet the politics of compromise is an inevitable feature of a system in which competing interests try to use their power to find allies in government.

*Department of Energy figures, 1991.

other sides asked for. Compromise gave birth to this system, and compromise is what the government was designed to produce in divisive policy struggles.

Most nations rely on compromise to resolve difficult political conflicts, but the procedures are often quite different. For example, many European nations try to promote dialogues among opposing groups with the goal of reducing the kind of protracted policy conflicts common in the United States. For example, many European interest-group systems are organized around high-level bargaining conducted out of public view between groups in conflict and the political parties in power. This kind of behind-the-scenes dialogue is easier in parliamentary systems with more centralized decision-making. By contrast, politics in the more decentralized U.S. system more often involves lobbying, passing laws, and writing regulations, all of which give a legalistic tone to many policies.

Making Environmental Policy in France

17.2

Forging national policies on most domestic issues in France is dramatically different than in the United States. In the area of environmental policy, for example, the French process has traditionally been: a) highly centralized, with little chance for local governments to participate, b) run by powerful administrators (often called "commissars") with great authority to make deals with various interests, and c) less adversarial and more stable, because centralized bargaining encourages opposing groups to agree to political compromises that are not likely to be changed by the party in power. (Recall the discussion of "corporatist" interest systems from Chapter 8.)

There have been some changes in these procedures in recent years as critics charged that such centralized policy-making often left government policies out of touch with local politics and needs. Reforms have been introduced to give communities affected by policies a greater say in formulating them. For example, in environmental policy-making, local governments now have permission to review applications for new industries and to add environmental standards to zoning regulations. However, the behind-the-scenes bargaining among various groups remains a feature of the French system. This maintains a more centralized and less adversarial aspect to the process than is typical of environmental politics in the United States. Students of comparative public policy describe most European nations as having policy processes based more on political dialogue and agreement among the players than is common in the United States. Because of the adversarial nature of policy fights in such areas as the environment in the American system, resulting policies are much more legalistic, rule-based, and formal than is common in most European systems.

SOURCE: David Lewis Feldman, "France," in Frederic N. Bolotin, ed. *International Public Policy Sourcebook*, Vol. 2 (New York: Greenwood Press, 1989), pp. 235–273; and David Vogel, "The Comparative Study of Environmental Policy," in Meinhoff Dierkes, Hans Weiler, and Ariane Bertholin, eds. *Comparative Policy Research* (Berlin: WZB Publications, 1987), pp. 99–170.

As noted earlier, however, even the most detailed U.S. laws and regulations may be adjusted considerably by (policy) decisions on how to enforce them. "How We Compare" Box 17.2 illustrates environmental policy in France.

Policy Inside the System

In this and the coming chapters, we will see that there are great differences in how and how well government responds to different national problems. For example, making foreign policy to guide American relations with other countries is so different from such domestic matters as taxation, abortion, the environment, welfare, or education, that it requires a separate framework (see Chapter 20) to explain. Within the broad range of domestic issues, there are also important political differences, reflecting the different kinds of power, institutional arrangements, and cultural themes that come into play politically. Because there are so many different kinds of policies coming from government, it helps to simplify the policy picture by asking three broad "system" questions:

- Has a policy problem reached the government agenda more through the pressures of majorities, interest groups, or elites wielding different kinds of **power**?
- How are **cultural themes** and political symbols used by these various players in defining the problem and proposing solutions?

- How is the developing policy shaped by the **institutional design** of the national government and by the **federal** arrangements involved in working out compromises?

Power and Policy

Different *patterns of power* inside the system offer insights about how policies are made in different areas. For example, issues do not always reach the government agenda because they are pushed by broad public discussion and media attention, as was the case with the child welfare problems discussed at the opening of this chapter. Many, and probably most, policy problems reach the government agenda through the less visible efforts of interest groups quietly promoting their particular causes. Policies involving agricultural subsidies or the regulation of airlines may be hammered out inside Congress and the bureaucracy through well-organized interest group networks of consumers and industries. Still other policies are forged through the pressure of influential insiders wielding power even farther from public view. Some policy analysts argue, for example, that national security and military defense policies are often based on the influence of a small number of prominent elites who have inside access to presidents and important members of Congress. Changes in these power relations can mean important changes in government policy. In Chapter 20, for example, we will discover signs that both defense and foreign policy have been affected in recent years by interest-group politics in much the same manner as domestic policy.

Culture and Symbolic Politics

Recall from Chapters 1 and 6 that American public opinion, unlike that in many other democracies, does not readily support government intervention in society's problems. Even if our problems and conflicts were simpler, many Americans would resist the efforts of government to get involved. For example, most Americans regret that any of their fellow citizens live in poverty, and that many children have difficult starts in life. However, even if easy solutions were workable (such as simply giving poor people money), large numbers of the public would find such policies unacceptable.

In most European societies welfare is more likely to be seen—even by many people who are not on the political left—as a necessary ingredient of a livable, harmonious society. By contrast, the term *welfare* is widely stigmatized in the United States. While most Americans talk about giving others a hand, they are generally opposed to giving them a government "handout." Most Americans have trouble with government policies that promote economic equality, generally drawing the line at *equality of opportunity*, which means favoring policies that give people a chance to compete. These and other cultural orientations can be heard loudly in debates about many areas of government social policy discussed in Chapter 18.

What these cultural limits on acceptable policy solutions mean is that the players in the policy game cannot just ask for anything from government. They must be sensitive to how their demands will play symbolically if and when political conflicts come to the attention of the general public. Even when people convince the government to do something bold and innovative, they may have to explain it using familiar political symbols aimed at winning broad social acceptance. These observations about the importance of culture and symbolism in policy-making come from political scientist Murray Edelman, who tells us, for example, that economic policies of benefit to a particular industry become easier to sell to the public if they are explained in the language of free enterprise. Policies aimed at reducing job discrimination may be easier to sell if they are not presented as favoring minorities, but as providing equal opportunity for all people, in keeping with more general cultural values.[7]

A 1987 display of the "AIDS Quilt" in Washington, D. C. Lobbying groups often try to affect government social policy by using symbols that draw on cultural themes that touch public emotions. The quilt, each panel of which is embroidered with the name of someone who died of AIDS, subsequently went on a nationwide tour, promoted with the slogan: "You don't have to have AIDS to feel the power of the Quilt. . . You just have to have a heart." Tour organizers touted the quilt as "a powerful symbol of grief, caring, and love."

One thing that politicians and political activists have learned, particularly in this age of sophisticated polling, marketing, and public relations techniques, is that symbols and images matter. The political uses of symbolism help tip the balance of public support and opposition in many policy areas. The enduring battle over abortion reflects what can happen when parties in conflict are well organized, similarly powerful, and armed with important **cultural symbols** (the right to life *vs.* the right to choose) for their preferred policies.

The most powerful political concepts, such as freedom and self-reliance, among others, appeal to basic themes that unite and divide groups in the culture. In the view of some analysts, these symbols of politics are as close as many people ever get to policy.[8] This explains why the leaders of government and interest groups are so careful about how they present their policy ideas to the public. Does a new civil rights bill provide needed protection for workers who are being discriminated against? Or is it really a liberal plot to make employers use quotas for hiring women and minorities? One definition or the other may give one side or the other needed public support and political maneuvering room. For example, President Bush viewed a civil rights act passed by Congress in 1991 as a "quota bill" and threatened to veto it. Its Democratic backers and civil rights groups claimed that Mr. Bush was hostile to civil rights and had a habit of using phrases like "racial quotas" to stir up the public. In the end, the president decided that his opponents' charges of stirring up racial tensions were hurting him, and decided to sign the bill, making a little symbolic capital in the process by proclaiming it a victory in the American struggle for fairness and civil rights for all.

Constitutional Design: Institutions and Federalism

Making policies fit somewhere in the range of accepted values and beliefs of the culture (or at least appear to do so) is by no means the last obstacle in getting the government to act on an issue. Some observers say the biggest "obstacle" of all is the governmental structure created by the Constitution. In the view of political scientists David

Robertson and Dennis Judd, for example, policy reforms in areas as diverse as civil rights, economic regulation, and the environment have been delayed or weakened by the many divisions of power and authority in the American system:

> America's policymaking structure divides responsibilities among several institutions at the national level, and the same fragmentation exists in the states. In addition, most policies are decentralized through the federal system. This structure impedes efforts to secure . . . policy objectives equitably and efficiently across the nation. The fragmentation of decisionmaking authority that characterizes the American political system has, over the long run, become a vehicle for frustrating policy reforms.[9]

As noted in the earlier discussion of compromise, defenders argue that compromise and slowness are the genius of a system designed to restrain government in a diverse society. Other policy analysts favor more uniform national standards in such areas as health care, environmental regulation, education, and social welfare. In this view, the constitutional provisions that allow policies to be filtered through separate branches of government and state politics are serious obstacles to the creation of coherent national responses to society's problems.

Sorting out this debate can be challenging because the Constitution is, in many ways, the chief symbol of our political culture, embodying many other national values within it. History and civics courses often idealize the constitutional order as our highest national achievement. Without taking anything away from the genius of the political compromises that created the Constitution, it is important to be realistic about the policy implications of that design, as Robertson and Judd note:

> American history and civics texts never fail to recount the advantages of the government plan that the founders produced. There were checks and balances among the several branches of government. . . .
>
> The founders were also politically shrewd enough to design a *federal* republic, and they could scarcely have done otherwise: the Constitution would not have been ratified without agreement by the states. . . .
>
> This fragmented political structure has continued to regulate and channel social and political change. In many areas . . . government efforts can be so diverse and uncoordinated that experts question whether welfare, health, civil rights or other "policy" exists at all. Most of the time, American policy seems very *incoherent*—that is, it lacks national consistency, order, and uniformity.[10]

This does not mean that the separate national institutions and the federal divisions of power have always been obstacles to policy. Recall from the discussion in Chapter 4 on federalism that very different kinds of national politics have occurred within the boundaries of the Constitution. During the period of "dual federalism," for example, the states were left to make their own policies in many areas. From the period of "cooperative federalism" in the 1930s to the continuing efforts to define a "New Federalism," the national government has taken a much more active role in trying to create national policies. However, as the history of federalism indicates, the periods of strongest, most coordinated national policy-making were defined by broad concentrations of majoritarian power, uniting voters and parties at both state and national levels.

In recent decades, majority power has become more fragmented, parties have become weaker, and interest-group conflicts more pronounced, making it difficult to mobilize parties and elections as engines guiding broad national policies in many areas. As opposing groups become more adept at using different institutional and federal paths to block and outmaneuver one another, policy battles spill from one institution to another and go from states to the national capital and back again. It is common for one institution to move government in one direction at the same time another institution is pulling in another.

The result: In many policy areas, there exist few truly national standards imposed uniformly throughout the land. In some cases, states write their own laws to adopt stricter standards than the national norm. In other cases, states block national programs and relax their standards. Thus, some states have "progressive" records in civil rights while others tolerate discrimination in education, housing, jobs, and public services. Some states and localities have taken bold steps to clean up their air and water, while others continue to dump raw sewerage and tolerate industrial pollution. These generalizations seem to apply whether the issues are complex, technology-related problems such as energy and environmental policy (described in Box 17.1) or moral and civil rights concerns.

Even matters that seem to be fairly straightforward decisions of one branch of the national government can end up involving other branches using their shared powers under the system of checks and balances described in Chapter 3. For example, what may appear to be a simple issue that can be resolved by executive order can turn into a struggle with each branch of the government pulling the president's policy goals in a different direction. These complications of the constitutional design are illustrated by the case of Bill Clinton's attempts to change military policy on homosexuals in the armed services, as described in "Inside the System" Box 17.3.

Building the Policy Agenda

It is tempting to simply say that policy is the sum total of the political system acting on a problem to produce some sort of government response. However, this does not explain very much. Many political scientists who study how policies are made (and why they are sometimes not made very smoothly) talk about a general process of agenda-building. The idea is simple. Government institutions and decisionmakers are limited in time and resources and cannot deal with everything at once. Therefore, the single most important act may be just getting a problem onto the agenda of an appropriate institution (or set of institutions). **Agenda-building** has been defined this way: "The process by which demands of various groups in the population are translated into items vying for the attention of public officials."[11]

Political scientists Roger Cobb and Charles Elder explain that a common first step toward the government agenda is to get the attention of the general public. Many issues

After being discharged from the Navy for declaring his homosexuality on nationwide TV, Petty Officer Keith Meinhold won reinstatement under the Fourteenth Amendment's citizenship guarantees; a federal judge granted his petition in late 1992. (The pennant opposite the American flag behind Meinhold is a "Gay Pride" banner.)

INSIDE THE SYSTEM

Why Simple Policy Questions Can Become Complex: The Case of Military Policy on Homosexuals

17.3

The Constitution says that the president is Commander-in-Chief of the military. When Bill Clinton became president, he thought it would be a simple matter to issue an executive order to keep his campaign promise to end the military policy of banning homosexuals. Clinton seemed to be on safe legal ground after a federal judge ruled that it was unconstitutional for the Navy to dismiss an officer because he had acknowledged on television that he was gay. Judge Terry Hatter, Jr., of the Ninth U.S. Circuit Court of Appeals ruled that Petty Officer Keith Meinhold was "a dedicated and disciplined sailor" who was entitled to protection under the equal protection clause of the Fourteenth Amendment (see Chapter 5), *unless* the Navy could prove that being homosexual had negatively affected Meinhold's performance of expected duties. Saying that the Navy had not demonstrated any job-related misconduct on Meinhold's part, the judge ruled that "the Department of Defense's justifications for banning gays and lesbians are based on cultural myths and false stereotypes. These justifications are baseless and very similar to the reasons offered to keep the military racially segregated in the 1940s."

Bill Clinton optimistically said that the judge's ruling "strengthens my hand," and announced that he would issue an executive order forbidding discrimination based on sexual preference. Suddenly phone calls began lighting up switchboards on Capitol Hill and the White House. Citizens and activist groups registered their objection to the order. General Colin Powell, Chairman of the Joint Chiefs of Staff, expressed the reservations of his colleagues in the military command. He suggested that the president should not just issue orders without discussing the matter first with the top brass. Soon the news showed pictures of a formal meeting between President Clinton and Vice President Gore and their aides sitting on one side of a long table, facing the generals and admirals and their aides on the other side. The picture resembled a summit conference or a peace treaty negotiation more than a comfortable working session between the military commanders and the White House.

To make matters even more complicated, a powerful voice in Congress also weighed into the controversy. Sam Nunn, (D–Georgia) Chairman of the Senate Armed Services Committee (which oversees many areas of military policy), announced that the checks and balances of the Constitution gave Congress a voice in such matters. Specifically, he suggested that an executive order could be reversed through legislation specifically prohibiting homosexuals from serving in the military. This would throw the issue back into the courts, keeping the policy clouded well into the future. Nunn suggested that the president would be well advised to hold up any executive orders until the committee held hearings on the matter.

Not wanting to appear to lose his first policy initiative after becoming president, Clinton chose the course of compromise and issued an ambiguous "suspension" of the military ban for a six-month period while a more workable policy could be coordinated among the many players who demanded a voice in the process. The eventual result was the much-discussed "Don't ask, don't tell" policy.

SOURCE: All quotes are from Don Phillips, "Judges Are Having Their Say on Gays in the Military," *The Washington Post National Weekly Edition,* February 8–14, 1993, p. 32.

---

begin their "policy lives" as part of what Cobb and Elder called a broader systemic agenda, which later analysts have termed **the public agenda.** This consists of issues discussed in the media and by community leaders as important public problems that the government ought to solve. When enough public pressure reaches elected officials, problems may move from this public agenda to the institutional or **government agenda** where they can become resolved.[12]

Operation Policy Storm

During his first days in office, Bill Clinton attempted to lift a ban on open homosexuals in the military. The Senate Armed Services Committee (*below*), led by Sam Nunn (D–Georgia; *above right*, on a fact-finding tour), held hearings on the topic. Opponents of the proposal, such as Gen. Norman Schwarzkopf (*right*), cited the themes of Samuel Huntington's *The Soldier and the State: The Theory and Politics of Civil–Military Relations*, which depicts the military as not a microcosm of society but rather a "community of structured purpose" whose "sense of organic unity and consciousness" sanctions special requirements of its members. Strong resistance to Clinton's bid ultimately led to a compromise policy that left few players entirely satisfied. Our government's institutional design allows many factions to play the policy game; a common result is ongoing compromise and change.

The Players

For many such issues as civil rights or the environment, the path to the government agenda begins with the public agenda as grass-roots groups and even majorities make their views known through elections, opinion polls, contacting government officials, and dialing talk shows. However, this simple "people-to-government" model of policy may not explain what goes on in other areas. On such issues as space or military defense policy, the public agenda may be more restricted due to the technical nature of issues or to the efforts of elites to keep issues out of broad public discussion for one reason or another.

This suggests that there are two broad **paths to policy.** One moves **from the bottom up**, with the public and interest groups mobilizing social concern to get issues on the public agenda on the way to making the government agenda. The other is a **top-down** path with government officials taking the initiative from the inside to solve problems. Some of these "inside initiatives" occur because certain problems are too technical to interest the public or to be trusted to public debate. Other issues get on government agendas from the inside because government officials are in contact with business elites who can effectively bypass the public agenda to get government attention. In some cases, government officials come already equipped with their own agendas they want to enact while in government.

The Bottom-Up Path to Policy

Many descriptions of the bottom-up path to the government agenda derive from the work of political scientist Richard Hofferbert.[13] He points to a foundation of history and social conditions as the origins of many policies. Out of these life conditions come public demands for government action. The public agenda can be shaped by public opinion, voting, protests, social movements, and riots, among the many means that people can use to make their concerns heard by officials. (Recall the range of conventional and unconventional participation discussed in Chapter 7.)

Sometimes the connection between the public agenda and the government agenda is direct, as when elections throw one party out of office and install another cast of players committed to a new agenda. Sometimes the link is less direct, as when media coverage dramatizes neglected social problems and calls for more attention from government officials. Many bottom-up views add the media to the equation as an important link between the public and government.[14] In the case of child and family policy (mentioned at the

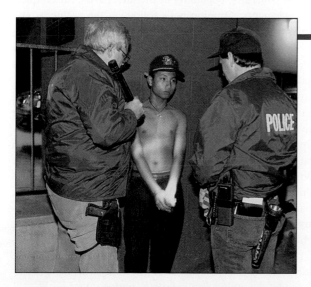

Los Angeles police officers check an arrested Vietnamese-American youth for telltale tattoos indicating gang membership. Public demand for strict law enforcement and the preservation of social order helped to elect Republican Richard Riordan as mayor of Los Angeles following catastrophic rioting and looting there. Such majoritarian action is characteristic of the "bottom-up" path in policy-making.

opening of this chapter), news coverage gave an important boost to the efforts of small interest groups to get onto the government agenda.

At the next stage, if government institutions are engaged with enough political pressure in the right places, key decisionmakers may work out a government response. This response is a policy. Policies, in turn, can feed back into every level of the process: reforming the government itself, satisfying or angering new groups in the public, and sometimes even changing the course of history or the structure of society. Thus, any particular policy can be thought of as one round in an ongoing, larger political process. Figure 17.1 illustrates a typical bottom-up model of government policy-making.

The bottom-up path provides a fairly good description of many kinds of policy. For example, the passage of civil rights laws in the 1960s can be traced to such historical conditions as slavery and the pressures of the lingering social conditions of poverty and discrimination. These conditions, when ignored long enough by government, finally motivated massive grass-roots actions of boycotts, sit-ins, marches, and demonstrations. The activities of this social movement engaged government institutions and decision makers at a number of points, both indirectly and directly. Indirect influence included disturbing media images showing rioters setting cities in flames, bombings of black homes and churches, and black students escorted into white schools and universities by federal marshals. At the same time, more direct links between the public and government agendas were forged by pushing legal actions all the way to the Supreme Court.

The Top-Down Path to Policy

Other areas of policy are harder to fit into a bottom-up scheme. Some issues are too complex or obscure to generate much public interest or action. Other policy problems are managed by elites and political insiders with an eye to keeping them from becoming volatile, bottom-up issues.

Nuclear energy policy is one good example of an area in which both technical issues and elite interests have kept policy debates off the public agenda at key decision points. Decisions in the 1950s and 1960s to invest in nuclear facilities for both military and commercial uses were made by relatively small numbers of industry elites and government officials. Decisions to build nuclear power plants were often passed along to the public after the fact and presented as symbols of national progress that offered solutions for the nation's energy problems. Large numbers of people and the media became involved only after accidents and cost overruns, beginning in the late 1970s, raised questions about earlier official pronouncements. Opinion polls following the accidents and scandals showed strong opposition to nuclear energy and support for development of large-scale solar- and wind-power systems. However, the government spent little money developing these alternatives, creating new openings to revive nuclear energy policies when the next national energy crisis comes along.

Similar patterns in defense spending, telecommunications development, science and technology policy, and other areas have led many analysts to a top-down explanation for some kinds of government activity. These observers see the shortest route to the government agenda as that taken by elites who have inside connections to party leaders in Congress and to top bureaucrats in the executive branch. Recall from Chapter 3, for example, that sociologist C. Wright Mills proposed that many key national decisions were made by networks of business elites and government officials who circulated back and forth between corporate boards and top government posts.[15] More recently, sociologist G. William Domhoff has argued that looking at policy from the top down does not imply any sort of conspiracy behind elite rule. In fact, elites often have conflicting interests and competing bases of power. Far from admitting a neat policy conspiracy, Domhoff argues that elite agenda-building makes for a chaotic system of insider government prone to inefficiency and scandal, lessening public faith in national leaders.[16]

FIGURE 17.1

The Bottom-Up Path to Policy: A Simplified View

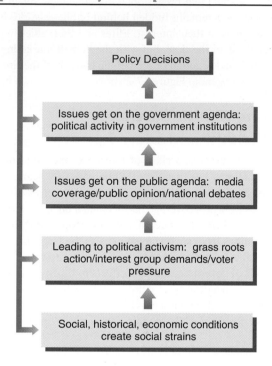

A few top-down perspectives take the conservative view that the public is simply not interested or qualified enough to get involved in making policy. As developed by such political scientists as Thomas Dye and Harmon Ziegler, this perspective differs from more leftist analyses by claiming that no matter how the system was designed or how power was originally distributed, elites would end up making key decisions simply because of public ignorance and apathy. Like the elite theorists of the left, however, the conservatives also worry that too much insider politics has undermined the coherence of government policy in many areas.[17]

What many of these views fail to explain is how so much insider politics can go on in a system that advertises itself as dedicated to the majority of people and their interests. According to political scientist Murray Edelman, the answer has to do with how issues are dressed up symbolically, as noted earlier.[18] Elites and government leaders maintain power by offering ready-made, ideologically familiar definitions of public problems, persuading publics to accept their proposed solutions. Thus, publics do not so much initiate policy as they play a role in *legitimizing* or accepting it.

True, politicians may be thrown out of office from time to time by angry voters who feel cheated, but the same elites are waiting to greet the newly elected replacements when they arrive in Washington. Public anger may keep particular issues off the agenda for a time, but after public attention has died down, a new crisis and the right set of symbols can restore the same old solutions, even though they did not work the last time around. This kind of image of government is similar to the view offered by Ross Perot in the 1992 presidential election, suggesting that this situation angers many voters on both the left and the right. (However, critics remarked that Perot has used personal connections in the past to promote his own interests in government.)

When the policy process works top-down, symbols and political rhetoric are as close as most people get to understanding decisions or the reasons for them. With the exception of the occasional scandal that breaks open in public view, much of the wheeling and dealing in the policy process remains hidden behind public-relations efforts to sell the results to the public as being in their interest. Elites and their allies in government cannot convince all the people all of the time, but with the help of marketing experts and media managers, they can persuade enough of the people enough of the time to keep their concerns on the government agenda. Figure 17.2 shows this top-down model.

Case: Getting Health Care on the Agenda Again

Health care politics illustrates a clash of top-down and bottom-up forces that have frustrated coherent national health policy for the past fifty years. In recent years, it is clear that politicians have begun to hear the (bottom-up) voices of the nearly 40 million Americans whose lack of health coverage has become a big news story. At the same time, government decision makers continue to feel the (top-down) pressure of campaign money and insider politics from such elite sources as the large insurance companies and the American Medical Association (AMA) that have contributed millions of dollars to politicians at all levels of government in past efforts to block government reforms. Some proposals for a national health care system offend doctors because they would reduce the fees they can charge for their services. Other plans would force insurance companies to provide lower cost coverage while spending more money policing hospital and doctor costs.

With so much resistance, it is easy to see why the problem of national health care moved on and off the government agenda without much success since 1948 when Harry Truman first promised to get a plan through Congress. During the 1960s, national and state programs were created for senior citizens and certain categories of poor families with dependent children. However, the large category of low-income working Americans was never included in the health safety net. Since health care is an issue that concerns us all, these repeated failures to make national policy had to be explained to the public. Looked at from the top down, it was relatively easy in the past for elites and government officials to convince average Americans that government involvement with national health care would only add more bureaucracy, increasing the costs and reducing the quality of health care for those already receiving good treatment. For years, opponents of a national health plan also used the powerful symbol of "socialized medicine" to discourage public support. In the past, those explanations seemed to satisfy a majority of Americans who share a cultural skepticism about government solutions to many public problems. For example, in a survey taken during the early 1980s, only 42 percent of Americans favored government solutions for health care, compared to 74 percent of those surveyed in Britain.[19] That survey reflected attitudes at a time before health care began its latest move onto the policy agenda of the 1990s, and long before the media had declared the nation in a health care crisis. Later polls at the end of the 1980s and early 1990s showed large majorities of Americans suddenly favoring government action on health care.[20] What had happened? How did health care reform return as one of the most important issues on the government agenda in the 1990s?

Part of the explanation here is that the national doctors' lobby, the American Medical Association, began to soften its opposition. The private health care system turned out to be inefficient in many ways, with local hospitals competing with one another to buy expensive equipment and medical costs rising above what insurance companies would pay. Doctors, hospitals, and insurance companies all began to think about changing a poorly functioning system. In short, several sources of top-down resistance began to crumble.

FIGURE 17.2

The Top-Down Path to Policy: A Simplified View

Meanwhile, back on the bottom-up side of the equation, even members of the public with private health insurance began feeling the pinch of health costs and a decline in the quality of services. One result was that public tolerance for rich doctors began to fade. This further provoked elite players to rethink their opposition stance. At the same time, small networks of health care advocates, with the support of research foundations, had been doing their homework. Study after study showed that America was paying more for health care and getting less than any other industrial democracy. Advocates of health care reform got their word out by using political rhetoric that fit health care reform into the mainstream culture. They talked about the inefficiency and unfairness of a system that resulted in a shocking lack of medical attention for so many people in the world's richest society.

These themes quickly became the focus of news reports, documentaries, and countless agenda features in the media, with the result that health care moved near the top of both the public agenda and the government policy agenda during the 1990s. Making the agenda, of course, did not guarantee that new policy would emerge. Health care had been there before. Even with Bill Clinton backing health care as one of his top priorities, and appointing First Lady Hillary Rodham Clinton to coordinate the many players in the policy process, skeptics argued that there were too many conflicting demands both from above and below in the power ladder to give much hope of sweeping national reform. We will pick up the story of health care again in the next chapter, and look at these political forces in more detail. For now, the point is that while making the government agenda is probably the most crucial step in the policy process, there are several steps to go after that.

The Rest of the Process: From Government to Society _____

After finally making the government agenda, policies pass through three other stages, in which: a) decisions are made, b) those decisions are put into practice, and c) policies are evaluated to see how well they are working. Beginning with the agenda-building (also called agenda-setting) stage, **the four stages of the policy process** have been summarized by political scientist Paul Sabatier as follows:[21]

> *AGENDA SETTING*: An issue gets the attention of government decision makers who begin to think about it seriously. They explore options and test the political waters with the public and the media.
>
> *FORMULATION AND ADOPTION*: Decisions are made. (Congress passes a law, courts issue rulings, bureaucrats make rules, other government actions are ordered.) This stage usually involves negotiations and political compromises.
>
> *IMPLEMENTATION*: The action is carried out. (Laws are enforced, rules applied, court orders delivered.) This stage usually involves further negotiations and coordination among different units of government and groups affected by the policy.
>
> *EVALUATION*: Studies are done to see if the policy is working as intended. Where are the successes and failures? What can be done to improve results?

The Decision Process

As you can imagine, policy-making can involve many players in different institutions and levels of government. It is difficult to track all of the key decisions along the way, and policy analysts tend to take many different paths in their efforts to understand how particular kinds of policies emerge. Some policy analysts keep the focus on how *individual decision makers* respond to various kinds of pressures from inside and outside their institutions. What this approach offers is an understanding of how people behave in different organizations under different political pressures. It is clear that the way a decision process is organized (for instance, its procedures, communication channels, accountability) affects what decision makers end up doing.[22] This focus on individuals within institutions is useful for thinking about key points in a decision process and how to improve the quality and coordination of results. However, most policies involve so many different decision makers that it is difficult to use this approach to connect them all and explain the whole process.

A broader view is provided by looking at **policy networks**. A network is made up of the key players inside and outside of government who join together to stake out a common position to guide policy as it flows from society to government and on through the decision, implementation, and evaluation stages. Depending on the issues involved, a network may include grass-roots citizen activists, coalitions of interest groups, educators, researchers and experts, business elites, government bureaucrats, and legislators who all work together to keep an issue alive and coordinate solutions between different institutions and levels of government.

The network approach is useful for explaining how momentum for various policies is built and how political pressure is applied at different levels of the system. "Networking" can make the difference between the issues that rise to the top of government and media agendas and the ones that do not.[23] For example, the push for national health care in the 1990s involved broad networks of experts, private research foundations, state governments straining under the burden of existing limited federal health programs, and many small interest groups all working together. Different members of such a network will take the lead in educating the public, finding ways to keep the issue in the news, lobbying politicians, and providing plans for decision makers to evaluate. However, even the full force of a network may not be enough to get new policy made on complex and conflicted issues. With so many institutions and people involved in deciding policy questions, there are plenty of **logjams** that can slow progress.

Policy Logjams

Just because issues are on the government agenda, they do not always result in anything that could be described as clear new policies. The separation of government powers provides advocates of old policies many avenues for blocking initiatives for change. As Bill Clinton found out (Box 17.3), he could not change military policies on homosexuals simply by issuing an executive order, even though he was commander-in-chief. In another area of military policy, Mr. Clinton had similar trouble introducing his ideas about cutting the military budget.

During his campaign for president, Clinton promised to cut large amounts from military budgets—at least larger amounts than promised by his predecessor, George Bush. When he took office, Clinton put the issue on the government agenda and suggested that the kinds of cuts he had in mind would require a restructuring of the military itself, calling for new thinking about the role of the national defense force in the post-Cold-War world. Only with a reorganization aimed at combining some functions and eliminating duplication could large savings on the order of Clinton's proposed $60 billion be achieved.

What Mr. Clinton quickly found out was that the military commands a considerable government power base of its own. As explained in Chapter 15, bureaucratic departments can resist the president with the support of powerful allies in Congress, which in

Haitian "boat people," attempting to enter U.S. waters illegally, are halted by a Coast Guard vessel in November 1991. During the 1992 presidential election campaign, Bill Clinton strongly criticized President Bush's Haitian policy, calling it "immoral." Once in office, however, Clinton found himself instituting an only slightly modified version of the Bush policy. The feasible options for dealing responsibly with a potential deluge of refugees proved to be far more limited than Clinton had believed—a not uncommon policy logjam.

this case included many members of Clinton's own Democratic party. In an opening shot, signalling that major budget cutting would be difficult, the Pentagon issued a routine "roles and missions" report, projecting no major restructuring of the armed services and proposing budget cuts of only a few hundred million dollars. The report was issued in the first month of the Clinton presidency, before the new president had a chance to announce his own budget priorities. As Colin Powell, then chairman of the Joint Chiefs of Staff, explained, "If we proceed too quickly, or impose changes so large they cannot be absorbed, the risk is that we may destroy the basic fabric of our fighting force." He said that the proposed smaller cuts "may be nibbling at the edges to some, but to others this is significant change."[24]

The Clinton administration was clearly left in the awkward position of having to come up with its own military organization plan without the help of those who really understood the organization of the armed services best. At the same time, the Pentagon served its budget position up to Congress with the hope that its supporters on Capitol Hill would also favor smaller cuts and avoid the major reorganization required by Mr. Clinton's plan. Without Pentagon movement in the direction of a new military policy, the largest available area for cutting the national budget would be lost, and the new administration would end up looking much like the old, walking down the path of more deficits and more governmental gridlock.

Looking for Windows of Opportunity

As the above examples indicate, top-down and bottom-up models help explain how issues get on public and government agendas, but they do not always explain which issues develop into new government policies and which ones do not. We need to understand how logjams are overcome in some issues and not in others. At these key decision points in the policy process, many observers see clashing and chaotic political forces coming into play. One description of the policy decision and implementation process is even called the garbage can model![25]

One popular view is that coherent policies depend on a convergence of favorable political conditions that help an issue pass from the government agenda into a new government policy. The convergence of these favorable political factors has been called a **window of opportunity** by political scientist John Kingdon.[26] The history of many policy reforms in the United States shows that windows of opportunity may come in the following forms:

- In some cases, a crisis shakes popular faith in existing government solutions, or a focusing event draws attention to the need to solve a problem.
- At other times, powerful opponents are defeated economically or politically, opening the way for agreement among government officials.
- New leadership may emerge with strong party and voter support to create changes.
- Perhaps new information reaches the public through the media to arouse enough public concern to pressure warring decision makers into a compromise.

Implementation and Evaluation

The basic idea here is that there may be political activity going on in lots of policy areas at the same time, but only once in a while can we expect to find a convergence of the right political conditions to create or change policy. Even when the various players in the policy game announce agreement on general guidelines, they must still agree on how

Policies not only have to be formulated, they must then be implemented as well; and implementation can prove difficult when public resistance is strong. Widespread military and civilian opposition met Bill Clinton's campaign promise to permit avowed homosexuals into the armed forces; the ultimate result was a compromise among the various policy players known as "Don't ask, don't tell."

to implement and evaluate the policy. There are politics involved in these stages also. For example, a policy banning discrimination against homosexuals in the military is only as good as its implementation. If military officials find covert ways of discouraging the recruitment of homosexuals, it would counteract a publicly declared policy of a military open to gays and lesbians. In a similar scenario of "policy making through implementation," many states continued to discriminate against black voters even after the federal government adopted (through laws, court actions, and investigations) a policy of enforcing voting rights. No matter how clear they may be at the decision stage, policies can be changed dramatically as they are implemented. In addition, the policy continues to evolve through the evaluation stage. To return to the example of homosexuals in the armed forces, if resistant military commanders can find evidence that seems to show homosexuals failing in some important area of military duty, the policy may be challenged politically once again at the evaluation stage. With politics entering at so many points in the policy process, it may be easier to understand why the paths to government action on national issues can be so numerous and the results so surprising.

The Many Paths to Policy Revisited

Because policy can be made in so many ways involving so many different players, general theories do not come easily. However, you now have a set of simple tools to use in thinking about different policy situations:

- how players with different kinds of social power can get their issues on the government policy agenda;
- how political symbols and themes from the political culture become important in defining public problems and limiting the acceptable solutions;
- how the institutional design of the government itself complicates the coordination of the many political players who must become involved.

We have also introduced a simple set of stages through which many issues pass on their way to policy: bottom-up or top-down agenda setting, formulation and adoption, implementation, and evaluation. These stages of the policy process can be used to keep track of issues as you follow them through the system. At the time you read this, is health care still on the public agenda? The government agenda? Have policy decisions been

A CITIZEN'S QUESTION
Policy

Can I become involved in making government policy on some problem that I care about? A good place for students to receive "on-the-job training" inside the policy process is to consider an internship experience with an interest group or a government agency that is trying to work out policy in an area of personal interest.

A government internship offers a chance to look at the policy process from the inside. There are internships available at every level of government: in the offices of national or state legislators, state governors, city planning offices, and hundreds of state and national executive agencies that deal with everything from consumer protection to health care and transportation.

An internship in a nongovernmental organization offers a look at the bottom-up politics that get issues on the government agenda. There are many internships available with organizations such as Citizens for Participation in Political Action, the National Civic League, the Center for Environmental Information, and the American Civil Liberties Union, just to name a few. These volunteer positions often provide a view of how political strategies are formulated, along with hands-on experience in putting those strategies into action.

One national program that offers internships in both government and nongovernment organizations in Washington, D.C. is called The Washington Center. This program combines career-oriented internships with academic seminars and credit. Washington Center internships cover a broad range of political experiences from the Senate and the House of Representatives to Ketchum Public Relations, *Larry King Live,* the Small Business Administration, and the American Federation of Teachers. Some scholarships are available in cases of financial need. For more information, contact:

The Washington Center
750 First Street, N.E.
Suite 650
Washington, D.C. 20002
202-336-7600

For information on other internships, you can consult several sources, beginning with your own school. Most colleges and universities have offices that help students find internships. Ask a teacher or an adviser to direct you to the one on your campus. It may be called the Placement Office, Career Office, Internship Office, or the Advising Office. The contact person will help you write an effective application and suggest ways in which you might be able to obtain academic credit for your experience. If your campus does not have a service like this, ask a reference librarian for books or directories on internship opportunities. For example, your library probably has a book called *The National Directory of Internships*, which explains different programs and how to apply for them. An internship can be a first step toward a career in government or public service. In addition, internships open windows of opportunity for more effective citizen participation.

---

made? What steps have been taken to implement those decisions? If there has been some sort of change in national health care policy, what is being done to evaluate it to see if it is really working as intended?

Policies move through the various stages when windows of opportunity open to bring different political forces, institutions, and key players together. If it is unsettling to think that the difference between policy success and failure often hinges on something as fragile as political opportunity, remember that the government was designed to disperse political power, not to concentrate it. As one student of the policy process put it:

> While political decision-making has become increasingly complex all over the world, there is only one country of economic, political and military importance today which affords itself the luxury of a highly divisive decision-making system—the United States.[27]

Key Terms

policy

political system factors in
  policy-making
    power/cultural themes/institu-
      tional and federal design

cultural symbols in the policy
  process

the public agenda

the government agenda

stages of the policy process
  agenda building
  decision or formulation
  implementation
  evaluation

the bottom-up path to policy

the top-down path to policy

policy networks

logjams

window of opportunity

Suggested Readings

Dye, Thomas R. *Understanding Public Policy*, 7th ed. Englewood Cliffs, N.J.: Prentice-Hall, 1992.

Hofferbert, Richard. *The Study of Public Policy*. Indianapolis: Bobbs-Merrill, 1974.

Jenkins-Smith, Hank. *Democratic Politics and Policy Analysis*. Pacific Grove, Calif.: Brooks/Cole, 1990.

Kingdon, John. *Agendas, Alternatives, and Public Policies*. Boston: Little, Brown, 1984.

Robertson, David B., and Dennis R. Judd. *The Development of American Public Policy: The Structure of Policy Restraint*. Glenview, Ill.: Scott Foresman/Little, Brown, 1989.

Sabatier, Paul A., ed. "Toward Better Theories of the Policy Process," special section of *P.S.: Political Science and Politics*, Vol. 24, No. 2, June 1991, pp. 144–173.

• • •

Our families will never be secure, our businesses will never be strong, and our government will never again be fully solvent until we tackle the health care crisis.
—BILL CLINTON

• • •

In a very fundamental sense, there is no education policy in the United States.
—JAMES D. SLACK

• • •

The growth of income inequality in the United States since the 1970s is hardly an inconspicuous part of the economic landscape. On the contrary, it is apparent in virtually every economic statistic, and colors nearly everything about our national life.
—PAUL R. KRUGMAN

Social Policy: Managing the Quality of Life

- **A STORY OF NATIONAL RENEWAL**
- **POLITICS AND SOCIAL POLICIES**
  The Problems, The Politics, The Proposals
- **MEDICAL ALERT: THE NATIONAL HEALTH CARE CRISIS**
  The Problem: Soaring Costs, Human Needs
  The Politics: The Power of Interests
  The Proposals: Who Pays, Who Regulates
- **EDUCATING THE NATION: KEEPING UP WITH THE COMPETITION**
  The Problem: Preparing People for Life
  The Politics: Maximum Federalism
  The Proposals: Getting Around Federal Obstacles
- **FULL SYSTEM ALERT: POVERTY, WELFARE, AND SOCIETY**
  The Problem: Is Poverty Political?
  The Politics: A Deep Cultural Divide
  The Proposals: Crossing the Cultural Divide
- **POLITICS AND SOCIAL POLICIES REVISITED**
- **A CITIZEN'S QUESTION: Social Responsibility**
- **KEY TERMS**
- **SUGGESTED READINGS**

A Story of National Renewal

The news told a sobering tale about the political reality confronting the nation in the 1990s. It seemed that everything needed fixing at once. Schools were failing. Roads, bridges, communications systems, and airports needed upgrading. Poverty was on the rise. The nation's health care system was in critical condition. The budget crisis in Washington made it unclear how to pay for these and other high-ticket items even if the political forces involved could agree on what needed to be done. The headlines were often alarming: AMERICA: WHAT WENT WRONG?[1] MANY NATIONS, UNDER GOD, WITH LIBERTY AND JUSTICE FOR SOME.[2]

The polls and the talk shows confirmed that Americans wanted relief from economic and social problems in many areas of their lives. The news was filled with stories using data from the 1990 census to paint a dramatic picture of American society:[3]

- The middle class was shrinking. In 1990, fully 42 percent of households lived on less than $25,000 compared to just 31 percent below that level a decade earlier. Only 55 percent of Americans fell in the "extended" middle income range ($15,000–75,000) in 1990 compared to just over 70 percent in 1970, adjusting for inflation.
- Poverty was rising: More than 20 percent of the nation's children were growing up in poverty. In all, 36 million Americans lived in poverty at the opening of the decade. Income disparities were increasing in other ways, too. For example, the median household income in Mississippi was just half that of Connecticut. (The median is the figure that half the population falls above and below.)
- America was becoming more of a multicultural society, with nearly 20 million foreign-born residents and 32 million people speaking a language other than English at home. This created unusual challenges for education and employment policies.
- The education picture was clouded by poor student performance, high dropout rates, and illiteracy.
- There was a sharp rise in the numbers of working mothers and single women with children living in poverty. Fully 60 percent of all women with children under the age of six were in the work force, compared to just 46 percent in 1980.
- Nearly 40 million people had no health protection, a problem compounded by soaring health care costs for those with medical insurance.

Voices in the media began calling for programs of national renewal to keep society together. One article even outlined a sweeping social policy agenda under the headline of THE NEXT NEW DEAL. The authors argued that despite huge amounts spent on social welfare, the overall result was an uneven set of policies that failed to address many important needs:

> Consider how little we as a nation are getting back for the money we are spending: no national health insurance plan, no maternity benefits or family allowances such as are available in Germany and France, no guarantee against falling into poverty or even becoming homeless—in old age or at any other time of life.[4]

In the 1992 election, political candidates debated proposals for getting government to provide for the needs of more people in more efficient ways. Bill Clinton was elected in 1992 on promises to reform health care, education, and welfare policies, while straightening out the national budget at the same time. Conservative opponents charged that all this could not be done without more taxing and spending, which would only worsen the national economic picture. Besides, said these critics, the government should not try to manage social needs because the best solutions to society's problems are those worked out by the people involved.

Social problems such as health, education, and poverty present considerable political challenges. In this chapter we will consider, among other things:

- the large number of competing interests with different bases of power that complicate health care policy as it moves through Congress and the executive branch;

- the complex federal power structure involved in education;

- the enduring cultural resistance to government welfare solutions for people who live in poverty.

If these sound like parts of our framework of culture, institutions, and power, they are. What you have learned throughout the book will come into play in understanding these issues.

The discussions of health, education, and poverty are presented in ways to help you compare them. First, *the nature of the problem* in each area will be explained. Next, we turn to *the politics* surrounding each set of policy conflicts, identifying the key players and the aspects of the political system most rele-

A street corner in the south Bronx, New York. Years of social programs seem to have had little impact on much of poor America, leading some critics to ask whether new strategies—beyond traditional liberal and conservative approaches—are required.

vant to understanding how those conflicts are played out. Finally, we will explore the major *policy proposals* in each problem area with an eye to understanding what has been tried in the past and what the future may hold. The aim of the chapter is to illuminate the politics going on inside three challenging areas of social policy and to stimulate thinking about how (and whether) government should become involved in managing basic aspects of life quality.

Politics and Social Policies

The social policy areas compared in this chapter are health, education, and poverty. Other social problems could be covered in equal detail: drugs; moral issues, such as prayer in school or regulating the expression of sexual preference; civil rights problems such as affirmative action or sexual harassment; or how to best provide for the needs of senior citizens, a growing segment of the population. However, health, education, and poverty are good ways to begin exploring social policy for several reasons:

- each raises different but very important questions about the responsibilities of government for building a liveable society for all citizens;

- each affects people differently and stirs up different kinds of ideological responses, illustrating why intense political conflicts often develop around social problems and their solutions;

- each illustrates different ways in which the political system engages with complex policy problems.

In addition, each of these problems is sure to be on the government agenda for years to come. Failures or political setbacks may cause these issues to drop out of the political fray from time to time, but their importance ensures that they will be back the next time a window of opportunity opens. The simple framework of problems, politics, and proposals will help to simplify these complex issues the next time you encounter them in the news.

The Problems, The Politics, The Proposals

As explained in the last chapter, there are many ways for policy issues to get on the government agenda. Once on that agenda, many things can happen to affect the kinds of policies that result. Health, education, and poverty each have different political profiles. However, there are some unifying questions that help in thinking about all three areas.

WHAT IS A POLICY PROBLEM?   Many social conditions can create difficulties for the people who live with them. Large cities are crowded with too many cars and people, making daily life a noisy, jostling, sometimes nerve-racking experience. However, the population density of cities is not always seen as a problem. Some people celebrate the high-energy existence of living in a city like New York or Chicago. The point is that many troublesome social conditions are not necessarily defined as *problems*.

Other social conditions become problems when many people begin to tell each other that something ought to be done about them. These issues may even become topics on talk shows and in the media. For example, many Americans complain about the stresses of everyday life in a complex society in which they have to work hard, raise children, struggle to make ends meet, and try to squeeze in a bit of fun. There is a huge supply of self-help books and stress-reduction programs to help people cope with this broad social problem. Although stress is widely seen as a **social problem**, it is not considered a **political problem** because most people do not call for government action to reduce everyday stress in society.

According to political scientist John Kingdon, problems become *political problems* when large numbers of people think that the government should do something about them.[5] Intense conflicts can break out over the very question of what is a political problem, meaning that some issues (poverty, for example) may sit on the agenda of public discussion for long periods of time, but have trouble winning the public and government support required for new policies to emerge. As we will see below, many conservatives think that poverty is not a problem that the government can or should solve. This does not mean that they are always insensitive to the social problems associated with poverty, but they do not see appropriate government solutions for those problems.

On other issues, there may be agreement that government action is appropriate, but little consensus about what that action should be. These political problems can appear and reappear in Congress, the courts, bureaucratic agencies, and state governments without resulting in clear policy. The example of health care is an interesting case because different groups finally became willing in recent years to stop blocking government action on the problem. However, the policy process was complicated by radically different views of what national **health policy** should look like. The point is that even after a problem has been accepted as a political problem and won a spot on the government agenda, the divisions among the political players involved can complicate and in some cases prevent coherent policy from being made.

WHY ARE SOME POLICY PROBLEMS SO POLITICALLY VOLATILE?
As noted in Chapters 6 and 17, those who lead national debates about the nation's political problems often see the world ideologically. If government becomes involved in

providing for every need, the principles of individual competition and freedom become compromised, say the conservatives. Liberals respond that if large numbers of people lack the minimal conditions of decent housing, enough to eat, and a good education, they will become disillusioned and drop out of society and politics. This would destroy the ideals of popular participation that define democracy itself, while increasing crime and social disintegration. These deep cultural responses to social problems mean that many policy debates fall into familiar patterns of argument and conflict.

Consider just a small part of the enduring political debate over government solutions for problems related to poverty. Those on the left firmly believe that too much economic inequality is a threat to democracy simply because the power gap between rich and poor undermines the possibility for political equality. To put it bluntly, rich people end up having too much political power, while poor people have too little. Political theorist John Schaar put it like this:

> A democratic conception of equality. . . stresses the greatest possible participation in and sharing of the common life and culture while striving to assure that no person shall determine or define the being of any other.[6]

On the other hand, influential opinion leaders on the right argue that another defining feature of our democracy is protecting the freedoms of individuals, particularly when it comes to their freedom to acquire and use wealth. Conservative columnist George Will put it this way:

> A just society is not one in which the allocation of wealth, opportunity, authority, and status is equal. Rather, it is one in which the inequalities are reasonably related to reasonable social goals.[7]

Since the freedom to acquire wealth and use it to promote political interests are reasonable social goals in the conservative view, inequalities are at least tolerable, if not inevitable, features of society.

A group of homeless people rally in Washington, D. C. Despite the marchers' signs, government-guaranteed housing has not been traditionally considered a right in the American political culture. Attempts to modify or even redefine traditional rights are at the core of many current American cultural conflicts.

Needless to say, these opposing political philosophies fuel many national debates over what to do about poverty, tax policies, health care, education, and the distribution of other public goods, and services. When these issues get on the government agenda, the opposing sides often try to fire up public opinion in support of their views. Since many members of the public can be persuaded of both sides of an issue under the right conditions, roaring battles for public opinion characterize many policy debates. Recall the discussion of these battles for public opinion in Chapter 6.

Conflicting inputs from public opinion, interest groups, and elites can put considerable pressure on decision makers, with the result that the laws and regulations at the core of many government policies reflect the tension and disagreement of the decision process itself. When courts try to decide what the laws mean, they often have trouble untangling the political knots that made policy guidelines hard to apply in the first place. In such areas as civil rights and affirmative action policy, the courts have issued policy guidelines through their rulings, creating additional conflicts over whether the judicial branch should be a passive referee in government or an active player in the policy game.

HOW CAN COMPETING PROPOSALS BE JUDGED? When you follow the news about a policy problem on the government agenda, you will hear different proposals put forward. How to judge which solution would really work? Which solution would be best for society? A starting point is to recognize that each proposal reflects different political interests and quite possibly competing ideological views of government and society. A health care proposal supported by doctors who want to remain well paid will look much different from a proposal sponsored by interest groups promoting medical care for everyone, even if that means putting government price controls on what doctors and hospitals can charge for their services.

You may end up deciding that it is more important for doctors to set their own prices than for everyone to have health care. However, in reaching that decision, it helps to recognize that the players in the process may be trying to sway your judgment with powerful symbols. For example, if doctors promote scary images of government red tape or loss of free choice in medical care, opinion may respond to these symbols rather than to the actual proposals. Likewise, groups that publicize heart-rending stories of people whose lives have been ruined by expensive medical problems are not really helping to explain how their proposals will solve the problem. The first steps in evaluating competing policy proposals are to:

- recognize the political interests behind the proposals, and decide how various plans would promote those interests, and yours;
- look beyond the symbols used and think about how the plan would actually work and whether it seems to be realistic.

Medical Alert: The National Health Care Crisis _____

Recall from the last chapter that the issue of national health care has been moving on and off the public and government agendas for nearly fifty years. In the 1990s, however, different pockets of political resistance to health care reform began to crumble. A new window of opportunity opened in the 1990s, particularly after the issue received a major commitment from President Clinton to propose a workable government policy. Opening a window of opportunity does not mean that new policy will pass through it, but it is important to understand how the conditions required for new policy can develop.

The Problem: Soaring Costs, Human Needs

One sign that political conditions were ripe to try health care reform again in the 1990s was the changing public perception of the problem. A huge majority of the nation began to see medical care as a *social problem*, as reflected in the opening line of a prominent newspaper editorial: "Nine out of ten Americans believe the nation's health care system should be fundamentally changed or completely rebuilt."[8] As noted in the previous chapter, the most significant development was a stable pattern in the polls indicating that a majority also regarded the health care crisis as a *political problem* requiring government solutions. Recall that in the past, majorities had opposed government involvement in the issue.

One reason for the changing public perception of the problem was the sheer personal cost of medical care. By 1991, the average family was paying nearly 12 percent of its income for medical insurance and services. The burden was expected to rise to over 16 percent by the year 2000.[9] Where would families get the nearly $10,000 per year they would need just to stay healthy? That personal question was enough to get the attention of many people who had not been much concerned about the problem even a few years before.

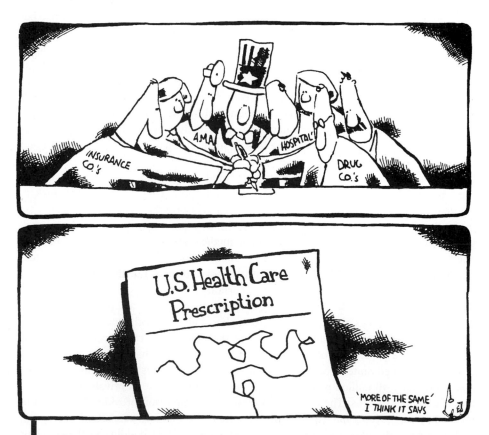

Although public health care is often viewed caustically as being in "gridlock," such a state may be inevitable as long as political solutions are to be achieved through compromise and consensus rather than by governmental fiat. The sheer complexity of a broad social issue such as health care, and the numerous conflicting interest groups involved, renders it—like a perplexing illness—intractable to any simplistic, "cure-all" approach.

What kept the problem on the public agenda long enough for political candidates and government officials to become interested in addressing it? In addition to the growing impact on individuals in society, interest groups launched public information campaigns, and the media adopted the issue as an agenda item (see Chapter 17). The news dramatized the plight of tens of millions of Americans:

> Every day millions of people fail to receive the medical treatment they need.
>
> For many, the reason is lack of health insurance, a fact of life that crosses geographic, economic, and racial boundaries.
>
> At best, the uninsured live with a source of constant worry: A working mother, raising her daughter by herself in Texas, wonders who will pay the bills if she or her child gets sick. A Nebraska farmer hopes he will not be injured in his fields.
>
> . . . At worst, they are forced to make hard choices, day by day, dollar by dollar: . . . A Minnesota woman about to give birth, decides to bypass nearby hospitals and try to get to one 84 miles away where she will not be charged.[10]

An important feature of this news coverage was its balance of human interest drama and hard information to help people think about the problem. Public information campaigns fed news organizations with critical information provided by researchers within health policy networks (recall the discussion of networks from Chapter 17). For example, a study by the Employee Benefit Research Institute received wide news coverage because it showed that the largest number of people without health protection were not the poor or the unemployed, but working families earning between $10,000 and $30,000 a year.[11] These statistics were dramatized by the steady stream of human interest stories about people whose lives had been ruined for lack of health care: a family that went $600,000 in debt because their medical costs exceeded what their insurance would pay;[12] or the tragic story of the mother mentioned above who drove over 80 miles to get to a hospital where she would not have to pay for delivering her baby. The child was born en route, with complications. The lack of medical attention left little David brain damaged, blind, and deaf.[13]

By the beginning of the 1990s, most people could either identify with the statistics, or they identified themselves as one of the statistics. Both citizens and policy makers learned, among other things, that counting government programs and private insurance, the United States spent more per person on health care than any other nation, yet a staggering number of people received no regular medical attention, and many more were poorly covered. Life expectancy is shorter in America than in fifteen other countries, and twenty-two have lower rates of infant death.[14] (Some studies put the rankings slightly higher, at sixteenth or seventeenth in infant mortality.)

Comparisons of health care spending in different countries are provided in Table 18.1. Notice two things about this table. First, almost all of the other nations listed guarantee some level of public health care for all of their citizens, yet none comes even close to spending the percentage of the nation's economic output that goes to cover health costs in the United States. For all the expense, the United States was not providing coverage for nearly 40 million people. Second, we spend far more on private health insurance than other nations. The average nation in this comparison provides 75 percent of medical care at government expense, while we funded around 40 percent.

In the brief discussion of health care to illustrate agenda building in the previous chapter, recall that there are both top-down and bottom-up forces operating in health politics. Without a change in the pattern of top-down resistance by powerful interests, the chances for reform would not have improved so dramatically in the 1990s. Why did so many players who formerly tried to keep the issue off the government agenda now agree that it was a political problem that government should try to do something about?

TABLE 18.1

Spending on Health Care in Different Nations

NATION	PERCENT OF GROSS DOMESTIC ECONOMIC PRODUCT SPENT ON HEALTH CARE	PERCENT OF HEALTH CARE PROVIDED BY GOV'T
Australia	7.7%	69%
Austria	8.4	67
Belgium	7.5	82
Canada	9.0	75
Denmark	6.3	82
France	8.9	74
Germany	8.1	73
Greece	5.5	76
Ireland	7.5	73
Italy	7.7	65
Japan	6.5	71
Netherlands	8.0	73
Norway	7.4	95
Portugal	6.7	61
Spain	6.6	79
Sweden	8.8	90
Turkey	4.0	35
United Kingdom	6.2	84
United States	12.4	42

SOURCE: OECD Observer, June/July 1992, Supplement #176. Figures are for 1990. U.S. 1992 = 14%.

Health care costs were driving hospitals and insurance companies out of business. Doctors who owned shares in hospitals and depended on insurance payments for much of their incomes also began to feel the pinch of soaring health costs. As powerful interests and elites in the insurance industry and medical profession began to see health care as a political problem, the window of opportunity for reform opened even wider. In addition, business leaders who often oppose government spending on costly social programs began to say "ouch" as skyrocketing insurance costs took a big bite out of profits. In the 1960s, for example, businesses spent in the range of 4–8 cents of every profit dollar on employee health benefits. By 1990, the standard cost was in the range of 25–50 cents out of every profit dollar, depending on the industry.[15] Labor groups also turned up the political heat on businesses. When employers cut back on health policies, workers found themselves with unattractive options: weaker coverage, paying a bigger share of the costs, or no coverage at all. According to one union source, as many as 78 percent of all strikes in the late 1980s involved health care issues.[16]

Many politicians who sided with medical and business interests in the past to block government reforms also began to understand the problem in different terms. Even though government programs were limited, payments for hospital and health care soared during the decade of the 1980s and continued to rise in the 1990s, all at a time of serious budget deficits. The states were even more seriously affected than the national government. And public officials were hard pressed to explain how so much money could be spent while so many people received little or no coverage. As President Clinton explained in the quote at the opening of the chapter, if the sheer human need were not enough reason to reform the system, the prospects for bankrupting the government through rising costs required action. Figure 18.1 illustrates the rise in health costs in the United States compared to other nations and shows where costs would be in the year 2000 without reforms.

The Politics: The Power of Interests

Consider just a few of the heated political issues that entered health reform politics. A major political sticking point was that if the government became the main health insurance provider for the nation (described in more detail as the "single payer" proposal in

FIGURE 18.1

Increases in Health Care Costs:
The United States Compared to Other Nations

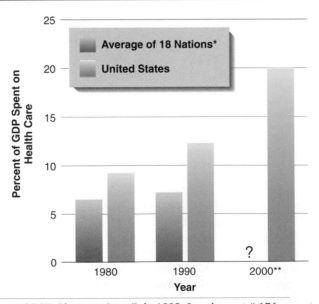

Source: OECD Observer, June/July 1992, Supplement # 176.

*Average of the 18 nations listed in Table 18.1.

**U.S. projection for the year 2000 based on Office of Management and Budget Estimates, 1992, assuming past policies.

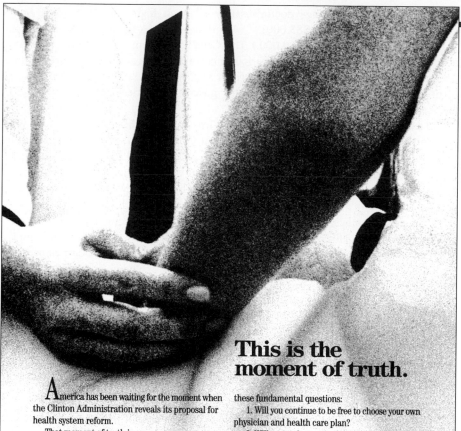

This is the moment of truth.

America has been waiting for the moment when the Clinton Administration reveals its proposal for health system reform.

That moment of truth is upon us.

Soon, the legislative debate will begin. Debate that will produce laws which will affect your relationship with your doctor.

During the long months leading up to this moment, America's health care system has already begun to change. Insurance companies and hospital networks are forming giant alliances that are altering the way health care is being delivered in your community — often without any input from physicians who deliver the care.

Our fear is that doctors' hands — hands that have always provided the human touch — may be tied by large companies whose primary focus is on profits.

We hope that the Clinton Administration's proposal will put you first. And we ask you to consider these fundamental questions:

1. Will you continue to be free to choose your own physician and health care plan?

2. Will you and your physician be free to make medical decisions that are in your best interest — without interference from government bureaucrats, insurance companies or your employer?

3. Will health plan administrators assume the physicians' responsibility for establishing medical treatment policies and standards of care?

Talk to your doctor about health system reform. We also invite you to call **800 348-3047**, Dept. 89, for our booklet *How Will the Clinton Health Reform Proposal Affect You and Your Family?*

The call will only take a moment.

American Medical Association
Physicians dedicated to the health of America

Professional organizations such as the American Medical Association have long been extremely wary of government attempts to formulate public health care policy. Physicians note that where doctors in the past frequently made their medical practice a lifelong calling, today a large number simply retire early rather than struggle with the burdensome levels of paperwork and bureaucracy already in place. Any "reform" that further exacerbates this situation would, ironically, worsen the health care crisis itself. However, some critics charge that what doctors really fear is any reform that would cut into their income.

the next section), insurance companies would lose a huge chunk of their business. Thus, one model commonly used in other nations faced built-in resistance from one of the most powerful groups involved in the issue: the insurance industry, with its well-financed PACs and elite executives who maintain inside contacts with politicians.

Another factor commonly cited in driving up health care costs is that the vast majority of American doctors go into high-paying specialty fields, meaning that Americans who receive medical attention are more likely to get more costly, high technology treatment than they may really need. For example, in Canada, only 48 percent of physicians are specialists in particular fields of medicine, with the majority being trained as general practitioners. In the United States, by contrast, 87 percent of doctors train to be specialists, leaving only 13 percent who become general practitioners offering lower cost care.

Not surprisingly, the average doctor's salary is much higher in the United States ($172,000) than in Canada ($83,000).[17] (According to AMA figures, doctors in private practice average more than $190,000.) The Canadian system also involves provincial governments negotiating the costs of various medical services, a factor that further limits doctor salaries. Needless to say, the American Medical Association objected to government regulation of physician training and government price controls for medical services.

No plan could succeed politically unless at least some of the opposing groups were brought on board before it got to Congress. Bill Clinton put the interests on warning when he announced the high priority that health reform would have in his administration. He also appointed First Lady Hillary Rodham Clinton to coordinate the proposal that he would send to Congress. She established a White House working group that consulted with more than four hundred experts from various health policy networks. This White House group held hearings around the country to expand the input from experts and average citizens alike. Some of the input came from policy networks that included influential doctors and insurance executives. A key political decision point came when the powerful American Medical Association asked to be included in the White House planning operation. As noted earlier, the AMA had changed its political stance in announcing that it would try to be more cooperative. A spokesperson for the AMA explained it this way:

> The AMA's old style was to react and be against things. But there has been a philosophical change in our house of delegates [the group's policy-making body]. We will be out front where the action is. We'll stop being just selfish and only thinking of our own welfare.[18]

But could the AMA be trusted with a position inside the administration planning operation? What was the best political strategy here? On the one hand, if the AMA actually endorsed a Clinton plan, that would be a tremendous benefit when it came to introducing that plan to Congress. On the other hand, the AMA might use its inside position to block some aspects of the plan and then turn around and push Congress to weaken anything that it could not obtain from the inside. The political strategy finally adopted by the White House was to exclude the AMA and other powerful interests from the President's Task Force on National Health Care Reform, as the group headed by Hillary Clinton was called. The reason given was to prevent the same kind of divisive interest group pressures that had paralyzed so many past efforts at reform.

Most of the core policy group invited to the White House were researchers from universities and health care policy networks who did not have specific business or professional interests at stake in the reforms. The grand political strategy was to use public opinion and well-organized policy networks as the power base to promote the administration plan. If the doctors, insurance companies, and hospital groups objected to the plan, they would be denounced as "special interests," and the public would be encouraged to turn the pressure of majority opinion on Congress to remind the lawmakers how the people felt about the influence of "special interests" in Washington. Here is how one news account described the political strategy behind excluding the most powerful interests from the White House task force:

> The political benefit for the administration is that the President and Mrs. Clinton will be free to denounce doctors, hospital lobbyists and anyone else who criticized their plan. . .
>
> Mrs. Clinton said today that it would "take a lot of public support to beat back the powerful lobbies and special interests that are already lining up to defeat any plan we develop."[19]

Some Health(y) Policy Debate

In early 1993, Bill Clinton told Congress he wanted major health care legislation passed "this year—not next year, not five years from now." He named First Lady Hillary Clinton (*right*) to head the 12-member President's Task Force on National Health Care Reform, aided by over 500 staffers. Despite Clinton's desires, however, the task proved as tough as Washington insiders had predicted. Among those wary of the repercussions of change were Dr. John Clowe, chief of the American Medical Association (*above*). Small business owners also worried about the potential burdens to them. Said one, "We want. . . reform, but we want to make sure that the medicine. . . doesn't kill the patient." However, support came from policy networks such as the "Jackson Hole Group" (*below*), a group of major corporate players including figures from the insurance, drug, and hospital industries.

The Players

Thus, the politics of promoting the administration plan began before the plan itself had been developed and sent to Congress.

The Proposals: Who Pays, Who Regulates

Even if they did not agree on what to do, it had become clear to many players that the existing national health system had to be changed. The two major programs already in place were not working:

- The **Medicare** program was established in 1965 to provide health services for the retired and disabled. Paid for by employee and employer payroll taxes, this program turned into a major national tax burden. The growing costs of Medicare made it one of the largest items on a strained national budget (recall the quote from Bill Clinton at the opening of the chapter).

- The other major government health program is called **Medicaid**, which has evolved as part of the nation's poverty policy to provide health care for poor people who qualify for state public assistance. The national government matches state funding for this program. However, states exercise considerable control over who qualifies and what will be paid for medical treatments. As a result, the quality of care varies widely from state to state, and substantial numbers of poor people (35–40 percent) receive no coverage because of state restrictions. In many states, doctors resist taking Medicaid patients because state payments are so low. States that try to offer decent care for all poor people face severe financial crises.

Problems in these existing government programs alone convinced many politicians that reform was essential. But what should a new policy look like?

Where do policy proposals come from? Competing groups generally introduce proposals which are political blueprints designed to promote their goals and interests. However, some proposals draw upon what is learned from past government policies, as well as from the policy experiences of state governments and other nations. As discussed in Chapter 4, the states and cities serve as "political laboratories" in the American federal system. For example, one health plan that received considerable national attention was a system developed by the city of Rochester, New York. Rochester's plan resulted in care for fully 94 percent of the city's residents at almost half the cost of the New York state average, and a third less than the national average for insurance rates. How? Almost all of the city's businesses subscribed to the same Blue Cross medical plan, including such large employers as Kodak and Xerox that often run their own corporate health plans. This large volume of subscribers to the same plan drove down the costs of insurance, particularly for small businesses that often cannot afford to pay higher premiums. For its part, the insurance company agreed to offer a standard rate to most residents in the community so that people in higher-risk health categories did not face prohibitive insurance costs. Their risks were absorbed through slightly higher rates for everyone. Yet the premium rate was still far lower than the national average because of the volume of coverage and efficiency measures at the hospitals. (To keep costs low and provide efficient services, the area hospitals established a research and planning group called the Rochester Area Hospitals Corporation to coordinate ways of reducing expensive overlap in equipment and services in hospitals serving the same community.) This plan received considerable attention in efforts to develop national models.

Many nations also provided useful policy models from which to learn. A key feature of the Canadian system, as noted above, is the power of provincial governments (where health care plans are run) to negotiate prices with health care providers so that costs and government budgets can be kept balanced. As mentioned above, this and other features

What Can We Learn from German Health Care?

18.1

As noted in Table 18.1, Germany spends less of its national income on health care than the United States. Germany has also controlled the increase in medical costs, with a smaller percentage of national income going to health expenses today than a decade ago. Figure 18.1 contrasts this with the steep rise in the United States. How does the German system work? How well does it work?

The German government set up a system of private, nonprofit "sickness funds" to which roughly 90 percent of the population belong. All employees and businesses contribute to the funds, and the government pays for retirees and poor people. This means that wage earners, businesses, and government all have political interests in keeping down the costs of care. Doctors complain that they are not paid enough for their services, but with an average salary of more than $95,000 (compared to far more for American doctors), they remain near the top of all income groups in the country. Doctors participate in negotiations with the directors of the funds to work out fee schedules and prices for treatments.

How does the system work? People are free to choose their own private doctors and hospitals, and they pay almost no medical bills. Their sickness funds are billed directly for services. Costs are kept down by prescribing generic drugs wherever possible and by distributing expensive medical technologies to the nation's elite university teaching hospitals so that community hospitals do not have to invest in so much equipment. Patients in need of special care are referred to the hospital best equipped for their needs. To discourage hospitals from keeping patients longer than necessary, negotiations will begin soon on a fee system that will pay for the kind of treatment a person receives, not the length of stay.

Germans who earn more than $40,000 per year are not required to join a fund if they purchase private insurance, but most citizens of all income groups join the funds. Regular policy negotiations between doctors, hospitals, the government, and the managers of the sickness funds have kept the quality of service high and minimized delays in treatment that have led to complaints about other national health plans, most notably the British.

SOURCES: OECD Figures (see Table 18.1 and Figure 18.1). Also, Craig R. Whitney, "Medical Care in Germany: With Choices, and For All," *The New York Times*, January 23, 1993, p. 1.

of the Canadian plan have drawn fire from doctors and hospital associations, but the Canadian idea of "managed competition" entered the U.S. health policy debate. Government management is justified by proponents who point to the race among hospitals to acquire expensive, high-technology equipment that has pushed many to the brink of bankruptcy and created a vast imbalance of medical resources in the American system. According to health policy experts Philip Lee and Richard Lamm, the United States has half the world's CAT scan machines and two-thirds of the MRI or magnetic resonance imaging machines, which are the state of the art in taking pictures of brains and other hard-to-diagnose organs. California, alone, has 400 MRI machines, compared to just 20 in all of Canada. Does this mean that Californians receive much better health care than Canadians? On average, no, say Lee and Lamm. There is no need for so many expensive machines in the United States, and the temptation to use them in order to pay for them drives up the cost of many health problems. Besides, the vast majority of Americans cannot afford the benefits of such expensive technology. In Canada and most of Europe, advanced technologies are available to more citizens, but patients must pass stricter screening to get access to them.[20] To cite just one more example, "How We Compare" Box 18.1 explains how German national health policy offers ideas for the United States to spend less and get more health care for its citizens.

Aspects of existing systems are modified to fit the objectives of the political players who produce competing policy proposals. Theodore Marmor and David Boyum, two leading health policy researchers, say that most proposals fall into one of three categories:

- **Pay or play** plans require employers to provide health plans. If they choose not to "play" the insurance game, they must pay into a government fund that would provide insurance to those not covered. Under play or pay schemes, retired people and others without jobs would be covered under other government programs.

- **Single payer** proposals call for the government to take over most of the health care responsibility. Different models, such as the Canadian, German, or Swedish, could be adapted to the social and political realities of the United States. The key to single payer plans is for the government to manage competition, negotiate costs, regulate the access to high-technology care, and make sure the supply of doctors and specialized training fits the health needs of the population.

- **Procompetitive** proposals reject government regulation of competition and suggest, instead, stimulating the health care market to improve competition and expand coverage. The most common proposal is to issue tax credits and vouchers to those without insurance, and allow them to create new consumer demands that will be satisfied by insurers and health providers.

Needless to say, each of these proposals is tailored to some political interests more than others. The single payer idea draws heated opposition from the insurance industry because it would put many companies out of the health insurance business. Doctors and insurers like the tax and voucher plans in the "procompetitive" category because they minimize government disruption of the medical marketplace. However, many government officials worry that, without regulation of costs and competition, the biggest problems cannot be solved. Many health researchers claim that successful policies in other countries involve some government regulation of the medical industry.

Because the proposals are so different, and the interests so divided, many experts doubted that any proposal from the Clinton administration could succeed at all. Even if the Clinton plan made some compromises among the three broad types of proposals outlined above, powerful interests would still demand more compromises. The pessimists predicted that no matter how much public pressure could be generated, powerful insurers, doctors, and businesses would still have their way with Congress. In the end, too much compromise would result in policy that would simply not work.

The fate of the Clinton health plan was not decided by the time this book went to press. However, one thing was clear: with so many of the opposing players recognizing that the old system was not working well for their interests, the window of opportunity for new health care policy was open as wide as it had ever been. By the time you read this, you will know (or be able to find out) the details of the Clinton health proposal, and what happened to it in Congress. How effective was Clinton's strategy of mobilizing majority opinion to keep the pressure on Congress and to keep the most powerful interests on the run? You now have the background to explain what happened to the rest of this policy story.

Educating the Nation: Keeping Up With the Competition

For years, people have heard about falling test scores, crowded classrooms, and alarming national dropout rates. Was the nation in an education crisis? Many politicians and education experts said so. Yet the extremely decentralized political structure of American education made it difficult to do anything even if people agreed on the nature of the problem. Recall the opening quote by policy analyst James Slack who said that there is no education policy in the United States. With 14,000 school districts acting as centers of policy activity, education presents an extreme case of how federalism can create political challenges for coherent national efforts to solve problems.

The Problem: Preparing People for Life

On the surface, it may seem obvious what the education problem is: students are not learning! You are probably familiar with shocking statistics like these that appear regularly in the media:

- In geography tests given to 18- to 24-year-olds in nine countries, Americans came in last.

- In tests of 12th graders in twelve industrial countries, American students ranked 9th in physics, 11th in chemistry and math, and 12th in biology,

- A national study in 1990 found that only 12 percent of American 17-year-olds could read well enough to understand a 12th-grade history book.[21]

The problem deepens when we add the fact that only 75 percent of Americans take their first full-time job with a high school diploma in hand. The figure in Japan is 96 percent.[22] Combined with the poor performance of many of those who do finish school, this means that a substantial number of citizens start life lacking the most basic communication and learning skills. A book called *Illiterate America* proclaimed on its cover that "One out of three Americans can't read this book."[23] The author, Jonathan Kozol, said that his figure of 60 million adults with reading problems was a conservative one and that estimates were even higher in some government and research circles.

Aside from what it means to individuals to live without developing the full range of their communication skills and intellectual abilities, the nation cannot compete economically with other countries unless its workers and managers can think and communicate effectively. Education is a problem that the heads of American industry are increasingly concerned about because it affects the very ability of their businesses to compete in the world market. Figure 18.2 illustrates the unemployment pattern for people with different education levels.

While there is considerable agreement that the condition of national education is a problem, there is less agreement about the causes of the problem. Has education failed simply because the United States does not spend enough money on it? Critics charge that America is the only industrial nation in the world that spends less on education than on defense.[24] Compared to spending in other nations, the United States is about the middle of the pack, at around $3,500 per pupil per year spent in public school. Japan spends about $5,000, Germany around $4,000, France about $3,000 and Britain just over $1,000.[25] Although spending may not be comparable with top nations, money alone does not reveal the whole problem: the performance of American students is even lower than in nations that spend far less on their students. In a recent test of math and science skills among public school students in nine nations, American students scored last in math and next to last in science in comparison to much poorer countries such as Russia, Hungary, Ireland, and Spain.[26]

Many experts define the problem less in terms of money and teaching methods and more in terms of the social and economic experiences of children outside of the school. Many American children may fail in the educational system simply because they come from poverty backgrounds, which can present such basic obstacles as poor nutrition.

FIGURE 18.2

Unemployment Rates for People with Different Education Levels

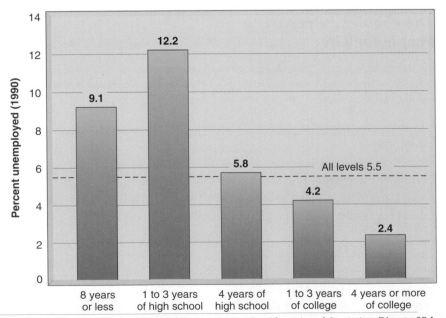

Source: Department of Education, National Center for Educational Statistics, *Digest of Educational Statistics*, 1991, p. 373. (Based on U.S. Department of Labor Research.)

Policy experts view education as a crucial social concern not only for its own sake but because it touches upon so many facets of the broader society. Jobs, the economy, living standards, crime, illegal drug use, sex education, race relations, the instilling of moral values—all these issues are implicit in any broad discussion of education policy.

Looking at the social-economic issues behind national education problems may result in broader social policies with educational payoffs. According to Ernest Boyer, president of the Carnegie Foundation on Teaching:

> Th[e] report card [on American education] is terribly flawed because it fails to take seriously the most important goal. Unless we get our policy toward mother and babies straight, we're never going to have better schools.[27]

Addressing the social problems behind educational performance may be easier for the national government than doing things that directly affect what goes on inside of local school classrooms. Even if the schools are part of the problem, the peculiar federal structure of American education presents greater political obstacles to national policy in this area than in probably any other social policy domain.

The Politics: Maximum Federalism

Not only does the federal government play a role in education policy, but so do the fifty states and more than 14,000 school districts. There is probably no other area of social policy that involves more governmental units. To complicate things further, there are often extreme political tensions pulling against coordinating these many governmental units and levels. People simply have very different ideas about how their children should be educated, and they often resent government at any level coming between them and their local school boards. In many places, even school boards have been criticized as too distant and unrepresentative. Parents and community leaders have demanded and won

How Federalism Affects National Education Policy

18.2

I t is not too much of an exaggeration to say that there is no national education policy in the United States simply because so many decisions are made at state and local levels. The extreme concentration of policy decisions at the local level makes it difficult for the government in Washington, D.C. to impose national standards and coordinate programs in the fifty states and thousands of local districts. As noted in the text, the tradition of local control of schools is a long one that most communities would resist giving up to accept national regulation of what they teach their children. However, the sheer complexity of school governance would make national policy difficult even if localities were interested in receiving more direction from Washington. The methods used to finance schools and make education decisions are so different from state to state and across the school districts inside many states that national coordination becomes virtually impossible. It

is even difficult for many states to work out coherent education policies.

At the local level, school boards exercise great control over education policy decisions and are accountable more to voters than to national (and in many cases, state) education officials. (The major exception has been forcing localities to try to integrate schools and obey national civil rights laws.) In addition to this fragmentation of policy decision making, coherent education policy is further complicated by the arrangements for funding education. A large part of local school funding comes from local property taxes. In communities where incomes and property values are high, school districts receive more in tax revenues and can offer students more expensive facilities, more current materials, and better-paid teachers.

At the state level, another layer of decision making and financing creates additional problems for national education policies. Each state sets up the supervision of local school systems differently. For example,

Texas uses an elected state commission to coordinate education policy. Ohio has a state education department, the head of which is appointed by the governor and serves in the cabinet. Wyoming exercises little state control, leaving policy primarily up to each school district. In addition, state contributions to local education budgets vary enormously, with some states, such as Texas, evening out the differences between rich and poor districts, and other states, such as Alabama, not doing much to minimize local differences. Funding per pupil varies widely from state to state, with Utah contributing $2,500 per pupil and Alaska contributing $9,000. The resulting patchwork of politics and economics makes education policy one of the most complicated areas of social policy and perhaps the most resistant to national reforms.

SOURCE: James D. Slack, "United States," in Frederic N. Bolotin, ed. *International Public Policy Sourcebook*, Vol. 2. New York: Greenwood Press, 1989, pp. 159–186.

large measures of control over managing the schools in their neighborhoods. "Inside The System" Box 18.2 describes some of the political complications introduced by the extremely decentralized pattern of federalism that has emerged in American education.

Trying to convince Americans that more centralization of educational policy might produce better education is further complicated by cultural resistance to giving up local control over what children are taught and what they learn to value. As explained in Chapter 6, the schools are powerful agents of political socialization, and many people want that socialization to be conducted according to local community values. If Americans are resistant to an activist national government in many areas of social life, they are even more resistant to central government control of education policy.

Richard Riley, Secretary of Education in the Clinton cabinet, talks with fellow cabinet member Robert Reich, Secretary of Labor, at an April 1993 conference. Education became the sole focus of a cabinet-level department only in 1979 under President Jimmy Carter (it had previously been handled at the national level within the Department of Health, Education, and Welfare). Even today the prevailing public sentiment seems to be to keep education primarily a concern of state and local governments, where parents and taxpayers feel they can retain more control over it.

A major aim of national policy in modern times has been just to provide equal access to education for all children. This has created intense political fights in many school districts over desegregation. In some cases, courts have ordered resources to be distributed more evenly among schools attended by white and minority, wealthy and poor students within the same district. However, even these efforts to promote equal access have had mixed results. Policy analysts on both the left and the right have suggested that it is time to rethink the role of the national government in educational policy.

The Proposals: Getting Around Federal Obstacles

The national government tried to take an activist role in education policy during the 1960s and 1970s, particularly in efforts to provide equal access to education for all people. One policy strategy was to attach education provisions to the sweeping **Civil Rights Act of 1964**. In news accounts, you will still find references to Title IV or Title IX of that law being used by executive branch agencies or the courts to make states and school districts comply with equal education goals. For example, Title IV of the Civil Rights Act prohibits the national government from giving money to local school districts that are segregated and that have not developed effective plans to become integrated. Another strategy aimed at equality of educational opportunity resulted in the *Elementary and Secondary Education Act of 1965*, which gave districts money to help poor children prepare for entering school and to receive extra help in the classroom after they were enrolled.

During this activist period of cooperative federalism (recall the discussion from Chapter 4), over thirty programs increased the role of the national government in educational policy making at the local level.[28] During the 1980s, by contrast, Republican administrations engaged in a broad attempt to define a new federalism, which included rethinking the national government's role in education as well as in many other social policy areas. Ronald Reagan even tried unsuccessfully to abolish the Department of Education. However, President Reagan did succeed in passing the Education Consolidation and Improvement Act of 1982 that gave states more control over national education money by consolidating more than twenty-five categorical education grants into one educational block grant (recall the discussion of these kinds of grant programs from Chapter 4).

Looking back, it is not clear that either the activist period of the 1960s and 1970s or the restrained approach of the 1980s was greatly effective in improving education. Supporters say that the activist programs of the earlier era improved high school graduation rates and test scores. However, critics charge that they did not improve performance in many of the poor and urban areas that they were specifically designed for. In addition, intense efforts to integrate schools and level out quality differences among schools have had only minimal effects in many cities because the population attending public schools is largely composed of poor and minority students, due to the pattern of white flight to the suburbs and the decisions of many affluent parents to enroll their children in private schools.

As for the attempts in the 1980s to give states more control over national funds for education, opponents charge that there was so little accountability or quality control that no measurable improvement in educational performance resulted. In the view of one expert, the national government has failed to develop coherent education policy whether guided by principles of liberal activism or conservative restraint. The complex politics of educational federalism assure that no matter what the national strategy, "The presence of the federal government will be felt only at the periphery of the education policy arena."[29]

Most of the new proposals and initiatives in education policy recognize these limits of federalism. Recent proposals have encouraged innovation at the local level, both in curriculum and in the management of individual schools. One of the programs promoted by the Bush administration, Education 2000, targeted the development of experimental schools and new teaching methods in each state. The local management of schools has also encouraged new ideas. Many school systems have long experimented with bringing parents directly into management and curriculum development in the schools. In such cities as New York, these experiments with community schools have created conflicts between teachers' unions, parents, and school boards. However, more recent experiments with *school-based management* in Chicago have given individual schools greater autonomy, with some encouraging signs that parent involvement and student performance may be improving. In the future, the most important role of the federal government may be to provide research and share information about what kinds of school experimentation seem most effective. The Clinton approach to education policy acknowledged the obstacles of the federal power structure in education, while emphasizing the national governmental role in encouraging innovation, providing information on successful models, and conducting research on what makes schools effective and what makes students succeed.

Full System Alert: Poverty, Welfare, and Society

A typical news article on poverty in America in the early 1990s began like this:

> WASHINGTON—The United States has more poverty and is less able to cope with it than any of the major industrialized democracies of the Western world, according to a two-year international study released Wednesday.
>
> Compared with Canada and six Western European nations, the study found poverty in the United States is more widespread and more severe; poor families stay poor longer; and government programs of assistance in the United States are the least able to lift families with children out of poverty.[30]

A homeless shelter in Harlem, New York. Once considered the domain of charitable religious and civic-minded benefactors, poverty has now become a routine concern of an activist government.

Government economic reports revealed a shrinking middle class and a polarized income structure with a fairly small number of the "super rich" earning as much in total as the fifty million people living near or below the poverty level. The shifting income patterns illustrated in Figure 18.3 began to alarm government officials. According to figures released by the Congressional Budget Office and the House Ways and Means Committee, the real incomes of the bottom 20 percent of American families dropped 13 percent between 1977 and 1988, while the income of the top 20 percent jumped 35 percent in

FIGURE 18.3

Changing Income Distributions in the United States

Toward a two-class society? The wage and salary structure of American business, encouraged by federal tax policies, may be pulling the nation toward a two-class society.

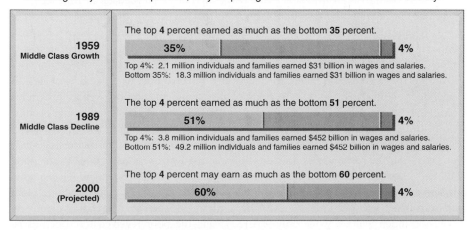

Source: *Seattle Post–Intelligencer*, April 14, 1992.

the same period.[31] And the top 1 percent of the population nearly doubled their average incomes during the 1980s. What did all of this mean? What could the government do about it?

The Problem: Is Poverty Political?

What does it mean to be poor? On the surface, it means not having money, of course. And that means doing without things. Some of those things may be luxuries, like a new car, or vacations, or dinners out. But many of the things missing from the lives of the poor are what most people would regard as necessities. Enough food to feed the family. Enough money to pay the rent, the heat bill, the doctor. It adds up to a life of struggle. When the last window of opportunity opened on government poverty policy in the 1960s, an influential book by Michael Harrington described those in poverty as living in *The Other America*:

> To be sure, the other America is not impoverished in the same sense as [the poorest nations]. . . . The country has escaped such extremes. That does not change the fact that tens of millions of Americans are, at this very moment, maimed in body and spirit, existing at levels beneath those necessary for human decency. If these people are not starving, they are hungry, and sometimes fat with hunger, for that is what cheap foods do. They are without adequate housing, and education and medical care.
>
> The government has documented what this does to the bodies of the poor. . . . But even more basic, this poverty twists and deforms the spirit. The American poor are pessimistic and defeated, and they are victimized by mental suffering to a degree unknown in suburbia. . . .
>
> And finally, the poor are politically invisible. It is one of the cruelest ironies of social life in advanced countries that the dispossessed at the bottom of society are unable to speak for themselves. The people of the other America do not, by far and large, belong to unions, to fraternal organizations, or to political parties. They are without lobbies of their own; they put forward no legislative program. As a group, they are atomized, they have no face; they have no voice.[32]

THE CULTURAL RESISTANCE TO WELFARE.   While many Americans agree that poverty is a terrible *social problem*, many have been reluctant to define it as a *political problem* that government should take major responsibility for solving. Conservatives have long argued that there is not much the government can or *should* do to level the incomes of individual Americans. Imposing high taxes on the rich to transfer more wealth to the poor undermines the very incentives on which the capitalist system is based. By contrast, liberal critics argue that government economic policies on taxes, labor, and industrial growth created the poverty gap in the first place, and that new government policies should try to close it.

Among the greatest obstacles to addressing poverty and its related problems is tremendous cultural resistance to the traditional government solution: welfare programs. (Recall the discussions of this in Chapters 1 and 6.) The very idea of welfare has become such a loaded concept that it may be an obstacle to understanding and thinking creatively about poverty as a social problem. Consider the results of an interesting study that asked half the respondents how they felt about government *assistance* to the poor, while the other half were asked about *welfare*. In the first group, 68 percent felt that government assistance to the poor was too little, compared to only 24 percent who felt that welfare support was too little. At the other extreme, 45 percent felt that the poor received too much welfare while only 9 percent said the poor received too much assistance.[33] Thus the compounding effects of politics and culture have complicated national understandings of the problem.

Food stamps from a 1961 test program, implemented in poverty-stricken West Virginia. Attempts such as this to deal with the immediate symptoms of poverty have failed to address its broader and longer-term aspects, such as helping poor people (through job-training, for example) to escape—and stay out of—poverty through their own individual efforts.

OLD POVERTY, NEW POVERTY. Over the last few decades enough has changed about the patterns of poverty in America to offer new hope that people will think about it differently. Changes in the profile of poverty were dramatic enough for Michael Harrington to look at the situation again in the 1980s and write another book titled *The New American Poverty*.[34] He argued that the problem of the old poverty in the 1960s was viewed by many experts as involving isolated pockets of poor people who simply needed to be trained for jobs and become integrated into a healthy expanding economy. Beginning in the late 1970s, however, the economy seemed to develop new patterns that produced fewer high-paying jobs and more erratic growth. Harrington and other analysts defined the new poverty as the result of a "structural economic crisis" involving declining industrial production and manufacturing jobs moving away from our country. These structural problems in the economy challenge the old assumptions that the nation's industries can absorb poor people if only they are trained for jobs and given better educations.[35]

These changes in the economy itself became recognized by more politicians as a key issue for new poverty policy to address.[36] In 1992, for example, populist presidential candidate Ross Perot appealed to many voters by saying that the government should try to stop the flow of manufacturing jobs to other countries, while promoting the development of more competitive industries at home. Bill Clinton's answer to the declining income problem was also a promise of "better jobs" combined with work programs designed to get people off welfare. Clinton presents himself as one of a new generation of politicians who want to move beyond welfare solutions to the problems of poverty.

Policy experts say that the problems of the new poverty require even more than economic restructuring to fix. For example, the burden of poverty has shifted increasingly to the groups with the least political clout. Children are the greatest victims of poverty in the 1990s, with roughly 25 percent of children under the age of six living in poverty.[37] In addition, women are poorer than men, and African Americans, Latinos, and Native Americans are poorer than whites. Poverty thus becomes an added handicap for groups

FIGURE 18.4

The Growth of Poverty in the United States 1970–1990

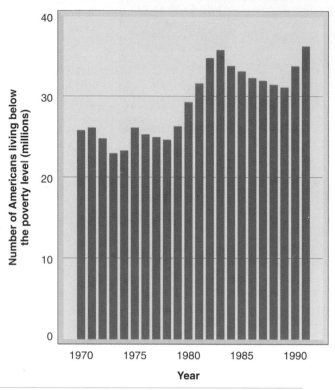

Source: U.S. Census Bureau figures, adapted from *The New York Times*, September 4, 1992, p. 1.

already struggling on the low-power end of the political system. Figure 18.4 illustrates the growth of poverty from 1970–1990, and Figure 18.5 shows how different groups in the population are affected by poverty. For some experts, poverty policy also must involve a broad social vision of providing such resources as health and child care to families, preparing children for school and work, and guarding against the creation of a permanent underclass of people at the bottom who feel excluded from mainstream society.

The Politics: A Deep Cultural Divide

Although new conditions may encourage new ways of thinking about poverty, ideology and culture continue to swirl around debates about poverty policy. Perhaps only an agreement among liberals and conservatives to move beyond the welfare policies of the past will offer hope for new political solutions. As long as traditional welfare programs continue to dominate government poverty policy, ideological battles will be fought right down to the statistical definition of poverty itself. Some policy analysts think the official government poverty levels ($10,500 for a family of three and $12,600 for a family of four at the beginning of the decade) are too high, while others think they are too low.

FIGURE 18.5

How Poverty Affects Different Groups in the Population

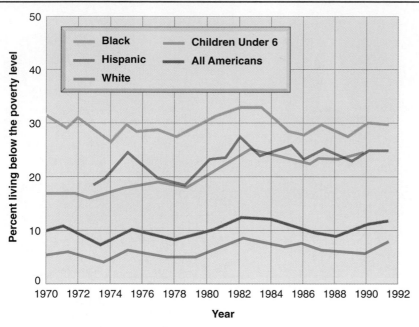

Source: Census Bureau figures reported in *The New York Times*, April 16, 1990, and September 4, 1992.

One expert who advocates reducing poverty by simply revising the official statistical definition is Robert Rector, who works for the Heritage Foundation, a conservative policy "think tank" in Washington. (Recall from Chapter 8 that a think tank is a research center where people study policy problems, propose solutions, and provide expert analysis to the media and government.) He argues that many people underreport their actual incomes. Others are only temporarily underemployed while owning such valuable assets as houses and cars. Another sizable group in the current government poverty category receive value from government welfare benefits such as food stamps and medical care that are not figured into their income levels. For good measure, Rector adds that many "poor" families hardly seem to be living in poverty, with 22,000 poor households listing swimming pools or Jacuzzis, 62 percent with a car, and 31 percent owning microwave ovens.[38]

On the other side of the ideological divide are liberal policy experts who favor raising the statistical definition of poverty. For example, Patricia Ruggles is an economist for the Joint Economic Committee of Congress. She points out that the definition of "needs" the government uses to calculate average family living costs dates from the late 1950s and early 1960s and has changed mainly through adjustments for inflation each year. Ruggles and other critics say that basic family expense patterns have changed in the last thirty years, with people now paying a higher portion of their budgets for housing and utilities. What counts as a necessity has changed too. Since more children live with single working parents today, the cost of day care amounts to a basic necessity for many families, but

Senate Minority Leader Bob Dole (R–Kansas) chats with First Lady Hillary Clinton at the Capitol in February 1993. President Clinton had just named his wife to head a task force on national health care policy. Inter-party attempts to address domestic social problems often founder on the very definition of the issues. Viewed from strongly differing cultural perspectives, policies often break down over the proper roles of various private and governmental institutions in easing the human suffering involved.

day care is not part of the government's "basic need" equation. By some estimates, families now spend about five times the cost of food on basic household necessities, meaning that the poverty level (calculated at three times the cost of food) may be set far too low.[39] By her calculations, Ruggles would raise the poverty level as much as 20 percent to provide more government assistance for millions of struggling Americans who are not currently classified as in poverty at all. Among those who would benefit from raising the statistical definition of poverty is the woman featured in the following news account:

WASHINGTON—Caroline Carter, a 30-year-old Milwaukee widow with two teenage children, earns about $13,800 a year. Is she poor?

The government says no. Her income puts her well above the official poverty line of $10,560 for a family of three. She does not qualify for food stamps, Medicaid, or a variety of other programs. In addition, she lives in an apartment subsidized by the county and receives medical insurance at work—benefits that if assigned a dollar value would raise her income. . . .

Though Ms. Carter thinks the answer is clear—"I am poor," she said, without reservation—her situation illustrates some of the problems with the nation's method of calculating poverty. The method is widely considered outdated, and in recent months Congress and the administration have begun steps that could lead to its revision. . . .

Ms. Carter . . . finds the definition of poverty less complex than the experts. She said that after paying for rent, groceries, utilities, a student loan, and bus fare each month she has about $60 left. With this, she tries to buy clothes, medicine, and entertainment for her children.

At the end of August, she was waiting for a paycheck in order to fill prescriptions for her son's eye infection. "Even if the prescription just cost a dollar," she said, "I don't have the money."[40]

Whether the number of poor Americans is 25 million, as conservatives claim, or 40 million, as liberals claim, many politicians favor redefining the political issue itself. To many leaders, the smoke from decades of battles over welfare had obscured the fact that a sizable number of people had become stuck at the bottom of society, creating a somewhat bigger and different set of political problems. Conservatives such as Jack Kemp (a member of the Bush cabinet) and liberals such as New York senator Daniel Patrick Moynihan began to talk about the emergence of a permanent *underclass* of people who were disconnected from the institutions that define society itself: schools, government, business, and social organizations.

Polls indicated that the emergence of an underclass was, indeed, something that many Americans were beginning to worry about. The friction between mainstream society and growing numbers of angry outcasts fueled calls for action on drugs, violent crime, racial tensions, unemployment, and homelessness. These and other signs of social fracture began to rise on the public agenda of issues people wanted government to tackle. In 1991, a coalition of 180 religious, environmental, civil rights, and labor organizations staged a massive "Solidarity Day" protest in Washington. Addressing a crowd estimated at 250,000 people, Lane Kirkland, the president of the AFL-CIO labor organization, said:

> We're here to insist that democratic government—the White House, the Congress, and the courts—must assure fair play for all, not just those with the most money, the most luck, or the strongest bootstraps. We're here to remind our elected representatives that they were put there to serve, not the faceless market place, but the aspirations of real people.[41]

With these signs of social movement activity, the politics of poverty policy began to heat up. However, an important political difference was that politicians began hearing demands not for more welfare, but for broader policies of social renewal aimed at getting people back to work and participating in the institutions of society once more. Even more important politically, these demands came from many different political and economic sources. For example, here is what Felix Rohatyn, one of the wealthiest investment bankers in New York, told the graduating class of the Wharton School of Business: "Neglect of our internal needs is undermining our future. The role of government and the behavior of a great, modern world power consists of more than just presiding over deficit reduction. It consists in investing for the future to be competitive and to provide opportunity for all its citizens."[42] Talking about an underclass might once have been more common among liberals, but this time around, the possibility was also being headlined in such conservative business publications as *Forbes* magazine.[43]

The Proposals: Crossing the Cultural Divide

The vision of social disintegration surrounding the problem of poverty began to strike many as too big for existing policy approaches to solve. For example, the nation's crime and drug problems (that overwhelmingly afflict the poor) seemed beyond anything that increases in jail cells or police forces could control. Although the United States prison population had doubled in the decade of the 1980s, the rise in violent crime continued to increase even more sharply in many categories, making America the most violent place to live among the world's industrial democratic nations. As noted above, the most promising political breakthrough in recent debates on poverty is the tendency for people on both sides of the ideological divide to begin seeing the issue in broader social terms, and to move beyond the old cultural sticking point of welfare.

THE OLD: THE WELFARE SYSTEM AND ITS TROUBLES.   For many Americans, the word *welfare* is synonymous with government handouts for poor people. *Although experts understand welfare to include a broad range of government social programs, from Social Security for retired people to food stamps for the poor, part of the trouble with the American social service system is precisely that many citizens do not see it that way.* The roughly 40 million people receiving $250 billion per year from Social Security far outweigh the federal revenues channeled to poor people, yet many Americans do not consider Social Security to be welfare, while assistance to poor families has been widely labelled with that loaded political term.

If we add up the public funds to subsidize farmers for the food they grow, provide loans and grants to college students, health services for senior citizens, education benefits and loans for military veterans, and housing assistance for different groups including senior citizens and the disabled, the total comes to roughly half the national budget, and well over $600 billion.[44] If people did not receive those social benefit programs that they resist defining as "welfare," many would find themselves in poverty also. In this context, the numbers of people receiving poverty assistance and the amount of money they get are relatively small. Yet it is the cluster of poverty programs that are generally referred to in negative tones as *welfare.* Why?

People do not see many government support programs in the United States as welfare in part because they are set up as *social insurance programs* into which people pay premiums (such as Social Security deductions from paychecks), and thereby become eligible to collect government benefits (such as Social Security payments) when they retire or become sick or disabled. In contrast to insurance programs are assistance programs aimed at people who cannot provide for their own needs. These are generally referred to as **means-tested programs** because governments (state and national) define what it takes to qualify for assistance. A program called **Aid to Families with Dependent Children** described below is typical of means-tested programs because people must meet certain social criteria (for example, single women with dependent children frequently qualify) and demonstrate particular levels of poverty (little or no income or property) to receive assistance. Table 18.2 identifies the major **means-tested** and **non-means-tested** (primarily insurance programs) offered by the government and shows how much money they consume.

Although means-tested programs such as Aid to Families with Dependent Children and non-means-tested programs such as Social Security Insurance both originated in the Great Depression of the 1930s and came from the same social security legislation in 1935, they have generally not been seen as part of the same kind of government policy by most Americans. Organized interest groups of senior citizens have effectively defended their programs as obligations of the government, while poor people have not had the political organization or the cultural support to make a similar case.

Most non-means-tested social insurance programs and many means-tested assistance programs are mandated by law as long-term programs. These so-called *entitlements* (listed as "entitlements and other mandatory spending" on federal budgets) consume a large share of the national budget. However, the weaker political support for poverty assistance invited greater budget tightening in poor people's programs than in Social Security and other insurance programs. For example, while Social Security has consumed an expanding share of government spending, the percentage of the federal budget spent on Aid to Families with Dependent Children fell steadily from around 6 percent in the early 1970s to around 2 percent today.

Other poverty programs have fared even more poorly than the means-tested entitlements because they are classified as *discretionary spending,* meaning that the

TABLE 18.2

Spending in Billions of Dollars for Means-Tested and Non-Means-Tested Social Programs (1991–1996 Figures Are Congressional Budget Office Projections)

CATEGORY	ACTUAL 1990	1991	1992	1993	1994	1995	1996
Means-Tested Programs							
Medicaid	$41	$49	$57	$64	$72	$80	$90
Food Stamps[a]	16	19	21	21	22	23	23
Supplemental Security Income	11	15	16	17	19	19	19
Family Support	13	15	16	16	17	18	18
Veterans' Pensions	4	4	4	4	4	4	3
Child Nutrition	5	5	6	6	7	7	7
Earned Income Tax Credit	4	5	6	7	8	10	11
Student Loans[b, c]	4	5	6	6	5	4	4
Other	2	3	3	3	3	4	5
Total, Means-Tested Programs	100	120	135	144	157	169	180
Non-Means-Tested Programs							
Social Security	246	266	284	301	318	335	353
Medicare	107	114	127	140	156	173	194
Subtotal	354	379	411	440	473	508	547
Other Retirement and Disability							
Federal civilian[d]	34	36	39	41	44	46	52
Military	22	23	25	26	27	29	30
Other	5	5	5	5	5	5	5
Subtotal	60	64	68	72	76	80	87
Unemployment Compensation	17	23	20	20	21	21	21
Other Programs							
Veterans' benefits[c, e]	13	15	16	17	18	18	17
Farm price supports[c]	6	11	12	10	9	9	8
Social services	5	6	6	6	5	5	5
Credit reform liquidating accounts[c]	0	0	6	5	4	3	1
Other	6	16	14	16	12	12	14
Subtotal	31	47	54	54	49	46	46
Total, Non-Means-Tested Programs	462	513	553	587	619	656	701
Total							
All Entitlements and Other Mandatory Spending, Excluding Deposit Insurance	$562	$632	$687	$731	$776	$824	$881

SOURCE: Congressional Budget Office.

Note: Spending for major benefit programs shown in this table includes benefits only. Outlays for administrative costs of most benefit programs are classified as nondefense discretionary spending, and Medicare premium collections as offsetting receipts.

[a.] Includes nutritional assistance to Puerto Rico.

[b.] Formerly known as guaranteed student loans.

[c.] Program affected by credit reform.

[d.] Includes Civil Service, Foreign Service, Coast Guard, and other retirement programs, and annuitants' health benefits.

[e.] Includes veterans' compensation, readjustment benefits, life insurance, and housing programs.

SOURCE: *Congressional Budget Office Outlook*, 1991, p. 91.

government does not have a legal obligation to continue them on a long-term basis. According to estimates by consumer advocate Ralph Nader and former New York City Commissioner of Consumer Affairs Mark Green, for example, the Reagan administration cut government subsidies for low-income housing by 82 percent. According to the Nader-Green estimates, funding for all *discretionary* low-income programs (meaning those not regarded as entitlements) fell by 55 percent after inflation from 1981 to 1989.[45] They claim that these welfare cuts alone are responsible for three million additional Americans falling into poverty during that time. Meanwhile, critics of welfare continue calling for even more cuts.

If anything suggests that conditions are ripe for considering new proposals, it is that existing welfare programs not only continue to be politically embattled, but are failing badly in financial terms as well. Consider three examples of programs that reflect the traditional policy of trying to ease the burden of poverty without going so far as to actually pull people out of poverty.

The *Medicaid* provisions of the Social Security Act were added originally in 1965 as a means-tested program to provide medical care for certain categories of poor people. Medicaid now provides upwards of $110 billion, a figure that includes amounts provided by the states. States have great control over what services are provided, how much doctors and clinics are paid, and which doctors and hospitals clients can visit. Since state allocations depend on their willingness to match federal funds, benefits vary greatly from state to state. Not surprisingly, the health care crisis is far worse in states that choose not to participate aggressively in Medicaid, and the budget crisis is worse in states that fund their programs adequately. Both the stigma of welfare and the economic burden on the states may be lifted if Medicaid becomes reformed as part of a national health policy rather than continuing to struggle along as an underfunded poverty program.

Aid to Families with Dependent Children is, as noted above, another state-federal partnership aimed primarily at cash payments for child support in families unable to provide proper clothing, housing, and nutrition on their own. As with Medicaid, state contributions vary widely, meaning that families in California receive average monthly payments of over $600, while monthly support levels in Mississippi are closer to $100. Although eligibility requirements in most states were tightened to fit the budget cuts of the Reagan years, the number of AFDC-eligible clients actually increased 20 percent at the beginning of the 1990s, reflecting the disproportionate increase of the number of families with children living in poverty. The average yearly benefits for families enrolled was less than $5,000 a year as of 1991.[46] This program pays out less than $20 billion per year in benefits, which is smaller than 10 percent of the amount paid to Social Security recipients. Many state governors say that figure is far too low to meet basic needs, but most states have not been able to keep pace with increased demands because their budgets are in serious trouble.

The Food Stamp Act of 1964 created a federal family nutrition program run by the U.S. Department of Agriculture to provide food coupons redeemable in grocery stores for basic nutrition items. According to Agriculture Department figures, roughly one American in ten receives food stamps.[47] This represented an increase of 25 percent in the early 1990s and signalled trouble for trying to hold a food stamp budget of $16 billion in check.

Clearly the poverty programs were straining at the seams in the 1990s, and the struggling economy only added to the problem by throwing more people into poverty and generating smaller government revenues to bail them out. All in all, traditional poverty policies appeared to be breaking down. A gradual movement away from stop-gap welfare programs and toward broader social policies aimed at strengthening families, children, and communities offered new proposals for dealing with poverty in the future.

THE NEW: NEW POVERTY, NEW POLICIES?   The idea that the new poverty in America is structurally different from the old is beginning to catch on among poverty experts and government policy makers. For example, one widely reported study by Northwestern University economist Rebecca Blank looked at poverty trends during the two longest periods of economic growth in modern American history, 1961–1970, and 1983–1989. In the earlier period, the economy was able (with the help of government policies) to absorb much of the poverty through jobs, reducing the poverty level nearly 10 percent by the end of the growth period. In the more recent growth period, however, the expansion of good jobs and incomes went mainly to the top, with the result that economic growth only eased poverty about 2.5 percent at the bottom.[48] This means, among other things, that conservative recommendations to shut off the welfare payments so that people will be forced to get a job, and liberal solutions to train people for entry-level jobs, are likely to be equally ineffective methods of addressing poverty in the 1990s.

Perhaps the answer lies in different kinds of social policies. After all, other nations experienced similar economic patterns in the 1980s and came out in the 1990s with much lower poverty rates. For example, in a comparison study of Canada, economist Blank found that although economic trends were even more extreme in Canada during the 1980s (growth of wealth at the top and low-paying jobs at the bottom), the Canadian poverty rate entering the 1990s was lower than here. By her estimates, market forces alone would have resulted in a 17.5 percent poverty rate in Canada, but Canadian poverty policies reduced the rate to 11.5 percent. By contrast, the natural forces of the American economy were somewhat gentler, leaving about 15.5 percent in poverty before welfare came into play, but poverty programs were less kind, cutting that rate only a couple of points to about 13.6 percent in the early 1990s. Which means that our poverty programs began with a less severe situation and did far less than in Canada.[49]

The minimal effects of old policies on the new poverty should not be surprising since most of those policies were developed during the period from 1935 to 1970. Our policies have approached poverty and welfare much differently than most other industrial democracies do, beginning with the political and symbolic separation of poverty programs from other social benefits programs. A new direction for policy would be to distribute a different package of social benefits more broadly to all citizens, while avoiding singling out particular groups to receive "welfare."

Welfare policies in most other industrial democracies include helping families with children, subsidizing health, education, and housing, and providing income assistance to citizens in need. In many countries, poverty is less often a volatile political issue because the welfare system offers something to almost everyone. As a result, taxpayers see themselves as getting something for their tax dollar, or, more properly, for their deutschmark, guilder, kroner, schilling, or franc. By contrast, the traditional American approach of aiming welfare policies directly at the poor sets up an immediately uncharitable situation by taking taxes from one group and giving to another—a situation complicated by the fact that the amount spent does not seem to reduce the level of the poverty problem much at all.

There are signs that policy thinking is changing here. Recall from the discussion in Chapter 17, the National Commission on Children that was formed to develop national family policy with the emphasis on child development. Commission chair Senator John D. Rockefeller IV, along with other members, has promoted a wide range of proposals that might benefit more than just poor families. Using other nations' models of welfare as a guide, Rockefeller said: "The United States is the only Western industrialized nation without a child allowance policy. And it shows."[50] Recognizing the symbolic potential in family policy, Rockefeller has presented the new policy focus as a challenge to conservative politicians who champion family values while condemning welfare: "While everyone wraps themselves in the flag and the family, we will see what is actually done to relieve financial pressures, provide family leave and make neighborhoods safer."[51] The interest in family policies by the Clinton administration gave these ideas a political boost.

Business leaders and politicians are also beginning to hear arguments like those of former Harvard political economist and Clinton Secretary of Labor Robert Reich who says that no matter how many new jobs are created at the bottom of the income ladder, poverty will only grow worse. The answer is to direct resources to the family, invest money in research and industrial development, and rebuild transportation, communications, and other basic systems:

> Global capital will create high wage jobs in the U.S. only if we can offer skilled workers and a first class infrastructure. . . .
>
> We still underfinance Head Start, child nutrition and other pre-school programs; our per pupil spending on kindergarten through grade 12 lags behind that of five other industrialized nations; Federal outlays for worker training have been slashed by 50 percent since 1980, and federal grants and loans for college students have been cut 13 percent over the decade.
>
> Meanwhile, our spending on infrastructure has fallen by almost a third, resulting in collapsing bridges, crumbling highways, dilapidated subways, overflowing sewers and rush hour traffic jams extending for miles. Hard pressed states and localities can't begin to make up the difference.[52]

Corporations that want to stay in their communities are beginning to recognize that the whole poverty picture from education to health quality will leave them without qualified workers in the future. While the government deliberates, some companies are taking direct action, both to create models for policy and to dramatize the issues. For example, the Honeywell corporation of Minneapolis has set up a public school inside its company headquarters. The New Vistas school holds classes in rooms just off the lobby of the headquarters building. All of the students come from poor families, and most are young single mothers who might not attend school otherwise because of lack of care for their children. At New Vistas, public school system buses bring mothers and their children to the facility where the day begins with breakfast together, after which the children are dropped off at a day care center next to the classrooms. Visionary? Unrealistically charitable? Nonsense, says Honeywell chief executive officer James J. Renier. "It's one of the most self serving things in the world for a corporation."[53] The corporation's motives, he says, are purely economic, with welfare being expensive and wasteful for businesses and other taxpayers. According to Honeywell calculations, every dollar invested in child care and education saves taxpayers six. Welfare policy as an investment in society rather than a controversial handout for the poor? Perhaps that is the direction of the future if the right political factors converge in the coming years. Whatever the policy outcomes, these background understandings should help you follow the stories in the news and participate in the debates when the issue moves onto the public and government agendas.

Politics and Social Policies Revisited

Almost every social policy hits people where they live and work. They involve the whole political spectrum: cultural images of society and government, institutional decision-making arrangements and federalism, and different kinds of power in society. Because

A CITIZEN'S QUESTION **Social Responsibility**

*W*hat should I do about social problems that do not directly affect me? One of the most difficult issues facing any society is getting citizens who do not suffer a particular problem to think about how to help those who do. Social policy problems often raise the question of how individuals should value the overall quality of society. Do we get something out of programs that improve the lives of others even if we do not share the particular benefits involved? What do people get from paying for the education of other people's children? What is the benefit in paying for the health care of others? Should those who have succeeded economically pay to protect others from poverty and social ills?

*O*ne of the themes that runs through all of the policy issues in this chapter is that people tend to become more concerned when they see a direct personal problem or benefit. Public opinion on health care reform shifted dramatically as people felt the pinch of soaring costs and declining protection. Education reform efforts were boosted as business interests sounded the alarm about staying competitive in the global economy. Poverty came up for rethinking as government officials struggled with unworkable programs, and as the public grew more alarmed about the problems of crime, drugs, homelessness, and a social values breakdown that all seemed to have the same roots.

*Y*ou now have some helpful guidelines for sharpening your thinking about social policy. For example, you can debate whether or not European approaches to welfare may overcome selfish human tendencies because the benefits are distributed more evenly to more members of society. Do ideological and cultural obstacles stand in the way of new solutions for many of society's troublesome problems? Can you think about new ways of getting around the federal policy maze in education to improve national performance in that area?

*T*hinking about policy problems also means thinking about your place in society and the kind of society you want to live in. Your image of society, in turn, will affect how you think about policy problems. Understanding the politics of different policy problems will help you share your ideas more persuasively with others. It can be helpful to follow the debates about social policies that go on in national magazines. For example, a few magazines that cover a broad spectrum of thinking about the politics of social issues include *Mother Jones* and *The Nation* on the left, *The New Republic* more or less in the middle, and *The American Spectator* and *National Review* on the right. Reading different points of view is a way to challenge your thinking about society, its problems, and your own political responsibilities.

---

social policies can involve so many aspects of the political system, creative politics is often required to solve complex problems. Sometimes, as in the case of education, creativity begins by recognizing and finding ways of working within the political limits created by peculiar federal arrangements. In other cases, political creativity may involve recognizing the entrenched cultural resistance to labels such as *welfare* and finding more acceptable political symbols such as "society," "family," and "children" around which to build poverty policy. In some cases, making creative policy involves the leadership required to bring different powerful interests together in support of proposals that compromise their interests. For example, the challenge of health care policy is keeping powerful members of an unwieldy coalition from blocking new policy initiatives.

Whether opened by crisis or through the work of policy networks, parties, or national leaders, the windows of opportunity for programs of social renewal in health, education, and poverty are there, and they will be open again in the future. As society changes, problems come back onto the government agenda, and political forces create new opportunities for acting on those problems. In the 1980s leaders who talked about problems in America were often condemned as being un-American, and voters were persuaded to go with the tried and true. A decade later, leaders in government and business were beginning to embrace the need for change. Groups that were contented in the 1980s expressed discontent in the 1990s. New alliances were formed. New information reached the public and decision makers. The climate of opinion became more supportive for policy change in many areas.

Because they affect people so directly, social policy questions tend to involve more majoritarian and pluralist participation in society than such other areas as economic or defense policies. Social policy issues run through election campaigns, mobilize social movements, galvanize the memberships of interest groups, and get people in everyday life talking about politics and sharing their ideas on how to solve tough social problems. The levels of participation surrounding these issues is healthy for democracy. However, because these issues can be so volatile politically, workable policies are hard to produce. Before plunging into the political fray, it is a good idea for citizens to think about how they can most effectively address the needs of society.

Key Terms

social problems vs. political
  problems

health policy
  changing definitions of the
    problem
  interest group politics
  key political players
  existing programs
    Medicare
    Medicaid
  new proposals
    play or pay
    single payer
    pro-competitive

education
  federalism as an obstacle to
    national policies
  key players
  existing government policies
    equal opportunity provisions of
      the Civil Rights Act of 1964

family policies
  work-related experience

poverty
  ideological and cultural obstacles
  the problems of welfare policies
  existing programs
    means-tested/non-means-tested
    Aid to Families with
      Dependent Children
    food stamps
  the new poverty vs. the old
    poverty
  models from European welfare
    systems
  family and child policies

Suggested Readings

Galbraith, John Kenneth. *The New Industrial State*. Boston: Houghton Mifflin, 1978.

Gilder, George. *Wealth and Poverty*. New York: Basic Books, 1981.

Harrington, Michael. *The New American Poverty*. New York: Holt, Rinehart and Winston, 1984.

Lieberman, Myron. *Public Education: An Autopsy*. Cambridge, Mass.: Harvard University Press, 1993.

Olasky, Marvin. *The Tragedy of American Compassion*. Washington, D.C.: Regnery Gateway, 1992.

Phillips, Kevin. *The Politics of Rich and Poor*. New York: Random House, 1990.

Reich, Robert B. *The Work of Nations: Preparing Ourselves for 21st Century Capitalism*. New York: Knopf, 1991.

Starr, Paul. *The Logic of Health Care Reform*. Tennessee: Whittle Books, 1992.

• • •

[T]here are ready-made needs for schools, hospitals, slum clearance and urban redevelopment, sanitation, parks, playgrounds, police and a thousand other things. . . . [But] the economy is geared to the least urgent set of human [consumer] values. It would be far more secure if it were based on the whole range of need.
—JOHN KENNETH GALBRAITH

• • •

Economic freedom is the essential requisite of political freedom. . . . [Yet] the government has increasingly undertaken the task of taking from some to give to others in the name of security and equality. . . . Sooner or later . . . an ever bigger government would destroy the prosperity that we owe to the free market and the human freedom proclaimed so eloquently in the Declaration of Independence.
—MILTON FRIEDMAN

• • •

19

Economic Policy:

Paying for It All

- **THIS NEWS STORY JUST COST YOU $5,000**
- **ECONOMY, GOVERNMENT, AND SOCIETY**
  Economic Policy: What's Similar, What's Different?
- **A SHORT LESSON IN POLITICAL ECONOMY**
  From Laissez-Faire to Government Activism
  The Economy Defies the Theories
  Contemporary Economic Theory
- **POLITICS AND ECONOMIC POLICIES**
- **THE LEVERS OF ECONOMIC POLICY**
  Fiscal Policy
  Monetary Policy
  Regulatory Policy
- **ECONOMY, GOVERNMENT, AND SOCIETY REVISITED**
  New Economic Ideas
- **A CITIZEN'S QUESTION: Economic Involvement**
- **KEY TERMS**
- **SUGGESTED READINGS**

This News Story Just Cost You $5,000

During the 1980s more than 40 percent of America's savings banks fell into or near bankruptcy. During the 1990s politicians talked nervously about how to bail out the mess. The bottom line may well exceed five hundred billion dollars, which is a lot of money when the national budget is already tilted dangerously into the red. In short, the S&L disaster was a very big event—one that will end up costing more than the entire Vietnam War. There has been plenty of news coverage, much of it spiced with dramatic accounts of scoundrels, thieves, and corrupt or at least "unethical" politicians. Beyond the political drama, there was another reason for all the news coverage: it touches on very personal economic issues. This is a story that will cost your and every other taxpaying American family $5,000. It is a story that you will keep running across in the news for the next forty years, the length of time the government estimates it will take taxpayers to pay for all the lost savings accounts.

While this Great Savings and Loan Disaster was happening, however, the news story was scattered over ten years, and often placed on the business pages where it was told in terms of isolated bankruptcies, scandals, and frauds. As explained in Chapter 11, the news about daily events often comes to us as fragments—tiny pieces of the whole picture. First one bank failed, and then another. Then came the parade of fraud cases and "unethical" politicians. Even when chain reactions brought down financial houses throughout a state or a region, the national media generally played it as a local story. Thus, when S&Ls collapsed all over Texas, it was a Texas story, full of dramatic moments, to be sure. There were fast operators, Texas-size swindles, ten-gallon hats, Cadillacs, and dry oil wells. But few national reports raised the possibility that all those no-collateral loans on phony oil drilling operations might be part of a bigger national problem: *the abuse of a new government policy of relaxed supervision for the entire savings industry.* In news about the savings and loan case, it was easy to become distracted by the pure drama of stories such as these:

- S&L executives bought expensive works of art with company funds and took them home for "safekeeping."

- Owners and directors of many savings banks received no-repayment personal "loans" from loan applicants, who, in turn, received billions in official loans that were never repaid. (One of those stories involved Neil Bush, the president's son.)

- Corporate dining rooms were outfitted with antiques, Baccarat crystal, and lavish wine cellars, all at depositors' expense.

- One S&L owner flew topless dancers on the company jet from Dallas to Miami for a yacht party with the Texas savings and loan commissioner. The headline read: *He Had Money, Women, an S&L. Now Don Dixon Has Jail.*

- The wife of the above owner used the company jet to fly her girlfriends to Europe for "brunch and shopping," as one news account put it.

- Five prominent U.S. senators, both Democrats and Republicans, were accused of using their power to stall a government investigation of a failing S&L while its owner—who just happened to be a big campaign contributor—looted most of what was left in the till, costing taxpayers an additional billion or two.

- A forward-looking S&L set aside financing for branch offices on the moon.

The unanswered question in these and other dramatic stories was "How did all of this happen?" Because the news coverage was so fragmented and dramatized, and, in addition, complicated by the economic issues involved, many people to this day remain confused about who stole the nation's savings and how it happened. The failure of news organizations to analyze the situation was even cited by journalists trying to explain, as one newspaper article put it, WHY THE PRESS BLEW THE S&L STORY.[1]

Another factor affecting news coverage was that few politicians were willing to step forward and talk about it in public. Recall another important idea from Chapter 11: news stories are developed more fully when prominent government officials are willing to give reporters differing opinions and explanations. In this case, leaders of both parties were involved in making questionable policies. In addition, top executive and legislative branch officials passed the laws and wrote the federal regulations authorizing the risky lending practices that ultimately broke the banks. As a result, few politicians were eager to step forward and explain how it all happened. This created big gaps in news stories written by reporters who depend on official pronouncements for much of their content.

It was not until the disaster had happened and Congress finally began official investigations that news stories started to put the pieces of the political puzzle together. For example, nearly a decade after the first political warning signs appeared in the press, *Newsweek* was typical of other news outlets in running a five-page article followed by a three-page analysis piece titled, "How Did It Happen? Some Lessons from 'The Single Greatest Regulatory Lapse of This Century.'"[2] Political clues about the causes of the policy fiasco finally began to appear in the news:

- The Democrats were in political trouble in the early 1980s. In danger of losing control of Congress, they were looking for campaign money and community support.

- Savings and loans (S&Ls) were in trouble, too, because existing laws stuck them with low interest rates and low-yielding home mortgage investments. As as result, they were unable to compete with banks and brokerage houses which were allowed by law to pay higher interest on deposits and cover those rates with riskier, higher-yielding investments.

- A popular Republican president promised to reduce government regulations and make it easier for banks and other businesses to "do business."

This turned out to be a convergence of political forces made for disaster. The owners of savings banks came to Washington looking like the kinds of community leaders that both parties wanted to attract. Even more tempting, these bankers had lots of campaign contributions to pass out to politicians in both parties. All they asked was to be able to pay higher rates of interest to attract more deposits. Done, said Congress and the president, and new laws were passed. Next, they asked permission to invest their depositors' money in riskier, but higher-yielding schemes in order to pay the high interest rates they were advertising. Done, said Congress and the president, passing laws waiving the requirements that savings and loans invest their money in long-term, low-yielding home mortgages. Finally, said the bank owners, it would give us a competitive edge if we could offer our depositors a little more security than they can get investing in stocks or money markets. Done, said Congress and the president, and laws were passed raising the federal insurance on savings accounts to $100,000.

With a few strokes of legislation, a banker's and big investor's paradise was created where once stood humble but reliable "mom and pop" savings banks. The banker's risk was taken out of high-risk investments by insuring them at taxpayer's expense. Now, add the president's promise to order his banking regulators in the bureaucracy to look the other way, and many bank operators felt they have been given what amounted to a license to steal. Which is exactly what they did. The story that finally emerged goes something like this:

It was a dark and stormy era for savings banks. Caught between stiff competition for depositor's money and restrictions on how they could invest it, many faced a slow death. The savings bank industry organized a lobbying effort at what turned out to be a good time politically. Although the Democrats who controlled Congress were regarded as the tougher party on banking regulation, they were also a party in trouble—trouble attracting campaign money, that is. Staring at the growing Republican strength that eventually brought Ronald Reagan to power in 1980, the party was vulnerable. The S&Ls channeled a lot of funds into Democratic war chests (and Republican coffers, too, of course). It would be indelicate to say that money buys votes, but it does get attention, and the lobbying effort convinced political leaders to relax the laws affecting how S&Ls operate. This in turn gave the green light to a president who promised his supporters to "get the regulators off the backs" of American business. With two green lights ahead of

Depositors line up to recover their money from a failed savings-and-loan bank. Many blame the "Great S&L Bust" on cozy alliances between the nation's business and government elites, who continued to shield one another even after the magnitude of the scandal became apparent. Of the U.S. senators involved in the so-called "Keating Five" affair, for example, only Alan Cranston (D–California) was reprimanded by the full Senate; he had already announced plans to retire from office for health reasons. However, majoritarian politics came into play against Dennis DeConcini (D–Arizona) and Donald Riegle (D–Michigan), who chose not to run again rather than face angry voters in 1994.

them, and spurred by a business boom motivated more by greed than by sound economics, many S&L operators fell first into risky investments and then into outright fraud. The savings accounts of millions of Americans were squandered in the process. In the 1990s, the big political story was how to control the damager, pay for the losses, and restore public confidence in politicians and business leaders in the process.

The trouble is that few Americans realized what was going on until it was too late. Only after the bank vaults were empty did the news media begin to make connections among the scattered clues. Some of those clues were available in the news *much* earlier, but they were not told as part of the savings and loan story. For example, it was known in the early 1980s that the Democrats were in trouble financially as well as politically. It was also known that Ronald Reagan was in favor of reducing the government regulation of businesses of all sorts, including, as it turned out, savings banks. However, it would have required a course in American government and some good detective work to put the pieces together before the policy failure occurred.

Sorting out the politics of the savings and loan disaster and reading between the lines of the news is much easier with concepts from various chapters in this book. This savings and loan deregulation policy involved things that you have already learned about: Congress (Chapters 12 and 13), which passed the laws permitting new financial activities at savings banks; the executive branch (Chapters 14 and 15), where new regulatory standards were applied to the industry; interest groups (Chapter 8), which lob-

bied both Congress and the executive branch for changes in laws and regulations; parties and election-financing procedures (Chapters 9 and 10) that gave the savings industry a broad base of support among powerful politicians, Republicans and Democrats alike; and the news media (Chapter 11), which had trouble reporting such a complex story until it was too late for people to do anything to stop the collapse of the industry.

There is still good reason to understand these various political forces operating behind banking policy. Another round of major banking reforms came before Congress in the early 1990s as a result of reports that many of the major banks in the nation were on the verge of bankruptcy.[3] In 1993, President Clinton announced that he favored loosening the restrictions on the lending and credit standards that the government requires banks to observe. Would these policy makers learn from the mistakes of the savings and loan experience, or was another great banking disaster in the future? You can follow the story with a bit of knowledge about how economic policy is made. It pays to understand something about economic policy because, after all, it is your money that the government is playing with.

This chapter explores the complex world of economic policy with an eye to simplifying questions about how the government regulates the economy, not just in the important areas of banking, but in other areas as well. Government economic policies affect a number of ways in which the economy and society fit together, from raising taxes to pay for government programs to controlling the supply of money and credit that businesses and ordinary individuals need to conduct their daily affairs.

In this chapter, we will see how these policies are made and examine the politics involved. We will discover that some areas of government economic policy (such as the savings and loan example) involve familiar patterns of domestic politics: interests, parties, congressional committees, and bureaucratic agencies. Other policy areas (such as how the Fed-

eral Reserve System controls the money supply) involve special institutions and economic principles that you will learn about for the first time in this chapter. This introduction to economic policy will enable you to follow the story the next time you hear about taxes, economic regulation, or the money supply in the news.

Economy, Government, and Society

Economic policies can involve a different, more specialized set of institutional arrangements, technical calculations, and abstract economic theories than other policy areas. However, this should not frighten the beginner or create the impression that economics is some foreign territory for students of politics. Many very personal aspects of life are affected by government economic policy, from the security of our jobs to the quality of the food we eat to the safety of the products we use. For example:

- Government economic policies affect how industries operate, from regulating the quality of meat and food to the quality of the investments that banks can make with depositors' money.

- Government economic policies affect how workers and consumers are protected from business owners who might try to pay unliveable wages, provide unsafe work conditions, or produce dangerous products.

- Government economic policies guide the collection of taxes from workers, businesses, and consumers to pay for the whole range of government programs from health care and education discussed in the previous chapter to hiring the tax collectors to make sure tax revenues actually get into the national treasury.

- Government economic policies regulate the supply of money in circulation and affect the value of that currency in terms of what it purchases at home and abroad. Economic policies also affect the wholesale cost of money to banks that belong to the national banking system called the Federal Reserve. Federal Reserve policies affect how easy it is for businesses and individuals to borrow money, which makes a big difference in the growth of the economy all the way down to the activities of individuals who borrow money for homes or student loans.

To start thinking about these different kinds of economic policies, it helps to compare them with the social policies described in Chapter 18, using our political system framework.

Economic Policy: What's Similar, What's Different?

As noted above, even such technical issues as bank regulation can have familiar political and social aspects to them. Here are some beginning generalizations that compare economic policies with the social policy issues described in the previous chapter:

Institutions:

- Many regulatory and tax (fiscal) policies are made through the normal congressional and executive agency procedures.

- However, decisions about the money supply and credit (discussed further under monetary policy below) are made by the Federal Reserve and other special institutions which involve the participation of banks, economists, and independent boards of governors.

Culture:

- Many of the broad ideological conflicts in economic policy are based on familiar liberal and conservative values from the political culture, as illustrated in the opening quotes in this chapter from Milton Friedman (a conservative) and John Kenneth Galbraith (a liberal).

- However, many actual economic policy decisions are driven by technical economic theories that can be hard to reconcile with ideology. These theories often reflect the international forces affecting economies and are aimed at coordinating policies among different nations. For example, the theories of British economist John Maynard Keynes (described in the next section) have guided the economic policies of many industrial democracies for much of this century. Although often criticized ideologically by conservatives for prescribing too much government intervention, they have been adopted by liberals and conservatives alike, prompting Republican Richard Nixon to quip, "We are all Keynesians now." Breakdowns in these economic theories have created new challenges for economic policy in recent years.

Power:

- In some areas, there is intense interest-group political activity, resembling a *pluralist* democracy of business, labor, and consumer groups competing for their preferred policies in industrial regulation, consumer protection, or workplace safety. *Majorities* also enter into economic policy calculations when recessions hit and politicians respond to voter unrest with quick fixes aimed at public satisfaction.

- However, economic policy decisions involve an unusual degree of *elite* access through a variety of channels: bankers sitting on the Federal Reserve Board, special panels and counsels of business elites who meet regularly with government officials, and large campaign contributions linking businesses and wealthy individuals to particular policy initiatives on taxes, trade, and other economic issues.

To return to the savings and loan example, the policies were made through routine legislative and regulatory channels and justified culturally as good for the free competition of business. However, the power balance behind those decisions was tilted heavily in favor of elites who maintained insider connections. The owners of savings banks often entertained members of Congress who sat on the House and Senate banking committees and made huge financial contributions to the campaign funds of key players in both political parties. The elite influence in the savings and loan scandal resembled past cases of bad government economic policy based on insider connections leading to the corruption of the policy process. "Inside the System" Box 19.1 describes the role of elite influence in the greatest financial scandal of the past century.

Not all elite influence results in corrupt policy, of course, but in combination with the complex economic issues involved, and the unique institutions that can come into play, average citizens are often left out of the economic policy picture. A good place to start getting back into the picture is to grasp a few basic principles of political economy.

INSIDE
THE SYSTEM

How Elite Influence Contributed to the Greatest Financial Scandal of the 1800s

19.1

By Roy Hoopes

The S&L crisis has been described again and again as the worst case of business and government corruption since the Crédit Mobilier scandal of the Grant administration, and the similarities extend far beyond the staggering amounts of money involved. In both cases the U.S. government virtually gave the businessmen involved license to loot the Treasury; the looting went on for years, and when it finally came to light, it was apparent that close attention by Congress or the administration could have prevented it.

The story begins with the 1862 legislation chartering the Union Pacific Company to build a transcontinental midway. It authorized the sale of $100 million of stock, promised $16,000 to $48,000 per mile in thirty-year government bonds, to be issued as track was completed, and provided for a two-hundred-foot-wide right of way across the continent. The directors and stockholders of the new company claimed—with some justification—that it would be difficult to get businessmen to invest in a risky transcontinental railroad. And so, with the help of bribes, they persuaded Congress to pass a second transcontinental railroad act in 1864. This allowed the company to sell bonds of its own and back them with the railroad's real estate. In addition, that real estate was doubled and made to include iron and coal rights.

The businessmen behind the venture proceeded in effect to mortgage the land for twenty-seven million dollars, and the

unbuilt road for ten million. And they devised a holding-and-construction company to route profits to themselves; by owning both financial shell and construction firm, they could pay themselves inordinate amounts to erect the railway. They found the perfect structure, the Pennsylvania Fiscal Agency, a trade investment firm that the government had chartered to buy and sell railroad bonds and had empowered "to borrow and loan money without limit upon the resources or without the resources of the company."

In organizing the structure, two often bickering factions emerged. One was headed by George Francis Train, who had built the Atlantic and Great Western Railroad in Ohio, and Thomas C. Durant, a vice president of the Union Pacific who said forthrightly that his goal was to "grab a wad from construction fees—and get out." Train, who had admired new French organizations devised to amass credit, rechristened the agency the Crédit Mobilier of America.

The other faction was headed by two brothers named Oakes and Oliver Ames. Oakes Ames was the perfect man to head Crédit Mobilier, which had decided to place its stock "where it will do most good for us"—he happened to be a Republican member of Congress from Massachusetts.

With Crédit Mobilier using Union Pacific's government-authorized stocks and bonds to pay itself roughly twice the cost of building the road, there was always the danger of congressional investigation, so stock

shares went to approximately twenty congressmen and the Vice President of the United States. Ames assured his fellow congressmen that Crédit Mobilier was a "diamond mine." If they could not afford to buy shares, he simply gave key members the stock, promising to pay for it out of its dividends. In one year Crédit Mobilier paid a dividend of 348 percent; in another, five dividends totaling 805 percent.

By the time of Grant's second presidential campaign, in 1872, the railroad was completed. Union Pacific was bankrupt, stripped of what Congress had intended to be a permanent endowment. Crédit Mobilier was out of business, having made a profit estimated at between thirty-three and fifty million dollars on an original investment of less than one million. Train boasted that he had three generations of his family living off Crédit Mobilier.

The unprecedented dividends had produced rumors of a scandal, but nothing substantial surfaced until the fall of 1872, when a squabble among the factions over the division of the spoils resulted in the publication of some incriminating letters of Oakes Ames's in the New York *Sun*. At a hearing the next year, Ames read the list of men he had sold or given stock to, and they included some big names: the future President, James A. Garfield; Speaker of the House James G. Blaine; and Vice President Schuyler Colfax.

A congressional investigation whitewashed almost everyone except Ames. The committee recommended his expulsion, but the House refused to take action. Ames's defenders argued that he had done nothing wrong except the patriotic act of building a railroad, and everybody built railroads with bribery and corruption (which was probably true).

Grant, with a new running mate, won the election of 1872, but most historians agree that the Crédit Mobilier scandal, the

first of many to be exposed during Grant's second term, played a significant role in bringing on the panic of 1873.

The government eventually took Union Pacific to court for misappropriation of funds, but the Supreme Court ruled that the government could not sue until 1895, when the company's debt matured, and that it had no real cause for complaint anyway.

After all—and herein lies the greatest difference between Crédit Mobilier and the S&L mess—the country had come out of it all with a transcontinental railroad.

SOURCE: "It Was Bad Last Time Too: The Crédit Mobilier Scandal of 1872," *American Heritage*, March 1991, pp. 58–59.

A Short Lesson in Political Economy _____

In the same year that American independence was declared, a Scottish economist named **Adam Smith** published the revolutionary book *The Wealth of Nations* that proclaimed the virtues of free economic relations. Smith argued that people were basically rational when it came to economic interests, and they would not enter into ventures that failed to benefit all parties. Thus, **the best economic regulator was individual self-interest** that acted as an **"invisible hand"** to promote social and economic harmony. Probably nowhere in the world did this idea catch on more strongly than in America. To this day, there are powerful cultural taboos against government intervention in the economy. Yet at the same time, people often call upon government to protect them from economic uncertainty, price-gouging by monopolies, unfair wages and work conditions, pollution from industries, and so on. This tension between free enterprise and government intervention has gone on since the beginning of the Republic.

From Laissez-Faire to Government Activism

Although the 1800s are often regarded as an age of little government action in the economy, there was a great deal of political activity affecting commerce, most of it favorable to business. (Recall Box 19.1.) The government granted transportation licenses, gave land and railroad right-of-ways to train companies, opened forests to timber companies, and generally rejected efforts from workers, farmers, consumers, and small competitors to hold the industrial giants in check. While European countries passed labor laws, health programs and retirement protection, the United States resisted such reform efforts. The result was a combination of federal action to promote business growth while resisting state and grass-roots efforts to regulate business practices and protect workers and employees. At the height of the period after the Civil War and prior to the Great Depression of the 1930s, the policy of government taking a hands-off attitude toward business was even elevated to something of an economic philosophy with the name of *laissez-faire.* You should remember the importance of this philosophy in Supreme Court decisions affecting businesses during the era of dual federalism discussed in Chapter 4.

The depression of the 1930s brought on massive suffering. Millions of hard-working Americans lost their jobs, homes, and life savings, and faced destitution. Businesses and banks were widely blamed for greed and irresponsibility. People began to demand government action. Even business people, who were either wiped out or unable to make

John Maynard Keynes (1883–1946), British economist whose theories enjoyed a vogue in the U.S. from the Roosevelt through the Nixon administrations. Asked about the long-term effects of his theories, Keynes reportedly responded, "In the long run, we are all dead." During his first term in office, Nixon told the press, "We are all Keynesians now." He had second thoughts, however, after encountering such intractable economic problems as stagflation, which proved resistant to government-imposed solutions such as a 1971 wage-and-price freeze.

profits because consumers had no money, became more sympathetic to government economic intervention. With politicians being pressured from below and receiving less resistance from business elites, a window of opportunity opened for a new era of economic policy. But what should that policy be?

Once again, an economist provided the answers. The influential British economist **John Maynard Keynes** convinced many American economists, including the advisers to President Roosevelt, that there were things the government could do to make the marketplace work more smoothly. His ideas, like those of Adam Smith, were also published in a timely book. *The General Theory of Employment, Interest, and Money* appeared in 1936 at the peak of the American depression, when unemployment stood at over 20 percent. Keynes' advice to politicians was simple: spend more money.

The core of the theory was also simple: when economies are stuck, with producers unable to attract consumers, and consumers unable to stimulate production, the obvious way to break the downward spiral into depression was for the government to crank the economy by creating jobs programs, and, more generally, putting money into circulation so people will start buying again. Even in normal times, Keynes argued, the government was the obvious economic intermediary, spending money to warm up chilly economies and pulling back to cool off overheated situations. So important was **government spending**, said the Keynesians, that the government should be willing to go into **debt**. And so, the government borrowed money to spend its way out of the depression by creating social security and relief programs that put money into circulation, while adopting public works policies that hired people to build roads, bridges, dams, schools, and community buildings. In the midst of this already-dramatic policy shift, World War II broke out,

FIGURE 19.1

The National Debt as a Percentage of the Gross National Product 1940–1996

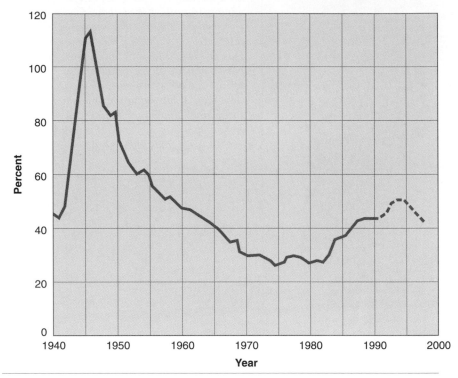

Note: 1991–1996 percentages are estimates. Figures reflect debt held by the public and do not include debt held by the federal government accounts.

Source: Office of Management and Budget, *Budget of the United States, Fiscal Year 1992*, part 7, pp.71–72. Adapted from Harold W. Stanley and Richard G. Niemi, *Vital Statistics on American Politics*. Washington, D.C.: CQ Press, 1992, p. 420.

sanctioning a spending spree that saw the national debt jump from about $43 billion in 1940 to nearly $260 billion in 1945.[4] Figure 19.1 shows modern trends in the national debt as a percentage of the total national economic output. Note that the level of debt during World War II spiraled above the total annual production of the economy.

Economists still debate whether the government's domestic policies helped turn the depression around, or whether it took the massive impact of employment, deficit spending, and new economic opportunities brought on by the war to make the difference. One thing is clear: the United States entered an unprecedented period of economic growth and world economic dominance. The governments of Republicans and Democrats alike adopted Keynesian economic policies, heralding the new political economy as the best defense against economic upheaval. Citizens were reassured that they would never have to look back to economic hard times. Since the Great Depression, the government has become a huge economic engine, spending more, taxing less than it needs to pay the bills, and going further into debt. Figure 19.2 shows the trends in the annual budget deficits and their relation to the national economic output.

FIGURE 19.2

Trends in Annual Budget Deficits in Billions of Dollars (top)
and as Percentage of Gross Domestic Product (bottom)

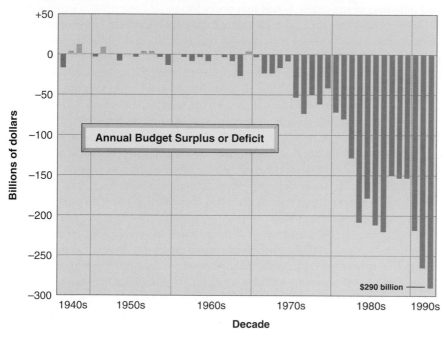

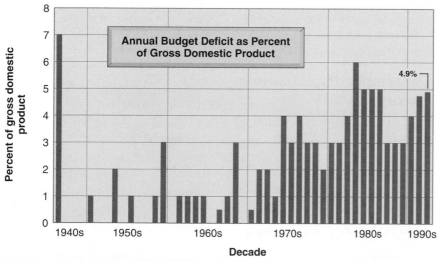

Source: Office of Management and Budget, *Budget of the United States,* adapted from representation in *USA Today,* October 29, 1992, p. 48.

The Economy Defies the Theories

By the 1970s, the debt and the deficits were rising but the economy was not responding to theory. Both the people and the politicians were beginning to look over their shoulders at world economic competitors. Finally, the politicians began to look ahead for new theories about how to make economic policies. Starting in the late 1960s, the economy has developed many strange behaviors that seemed resistant to old Keynesian policy guidelines. Most important to consumers was a troublesome new economic pattern called **inflation**, which simply means that prices increased faster than wages, or the cost of living went up faster than people's ability to pay. Inflation led to other economic disturbances such as demands for higher wages that only increased inflating prices by fueling the demand for goods. When governments took measures to curb inflation (such as slowing spending, or pressuring the Federal Reserve Bank to make money more expensive to borrow), the result was often to throw the economy into **recession**, sometimes without doing much to stop the inflation in the bargain. In simple terms, recession means declining economic growth, usually because of a drop in consumer demand which lowers production, employment, and profits, which in turn further reduces consumer demand. Recession has always been part of the economic picture, but for most of history, recessions held inflation in check. In fact, during much of the past century, the more serious worry was deflation, or declining prices during recessions because of low demand for goods. This puzzling new state of recession and inflation going on at the same time was even given a name, **stagflation**.

Not only were the old Keynesian policies less able to turn around recessions in the new era, but in many cases the government spending hit the streets too late, when the economy was recovering on its own, fueling consumer demands faster than production supplies could be met, sending inflation up again. This lurching between recession and inflation was finally halted in the 1980s, but only at the expense of the greatest government spending spree and debt binge in history, a joint production of a Republican president and a Democratic Congress. In 1980, the national debt was less than a trillion dollars (just over $4,000 per person). By 1990, it had soared to over three trillion (or about $13,000 per person), hit four trillion dollars a few years after that, and showed no sign of levelling off. The economy of the 1990s reeled from the hangover, with a long recession that left economists and politicians more puzzled than ever about what to do.

Contemporary Economic Theory

If history is any guide, grand economic theories that work well enough to guide policy do not come along very often. The present era of economic theory is characterized by many different schools of thought, some still sounding like Keynes, others sounding like a revival of Adam Smith, but few offering tested insights about the proper role of government in managing the economy during the years ahead. Here are the current views that receive most attention from the media and from politicians.

• NEW (NEO) CONSERVATIVISM

Monetarists emphasize monetary policy tools such as adjusting the money supply and controlling interest rates to keep the economy running, but they advise against fiscal policies such as taxing and spending and regard regulation as a disaster. Advocates include Ludwig von Mises, Friedrich Hayek, Wilhelm Roepke, and Nobel-winner Milton Friedman of the University of Chicago.

Supply siders favor fiscal solutions such as tax cuts, particularly for wealthy people who, they say, will invest tax savings back in the economy. The new economic growth is supposed to create more profits to tax, making up for the lower rates. Economists such as Stanford University's Arthur Laffer guided Reagan administration policies with these theories. Reagan's first budget director, David Stockman, said they didn't work, but advocates such as Paul Craig Roberts maintain otherwise.

• TRADITIONAL LIBERALISM

Neo-Keynesians such as Nobel Prize winner Paul Samuelson of M.I.T. still advocate progressive taxation to redistribute wealth downward and government spending as the best cure for recessions.

• NEW (NEO) LIBERALISM

A new **industrial policy** is the key to more effective government spending, say the new liberals. Start with cuts in defense, and shift priorities to new economic growth. Invest in research and development. Build new roads, bridges, airports. Focus welfare spending on education and children and family policies designed to prepare the next generation of workers. Advocates such as Harvard's Robert Reich support these ideas. Reich helped develop Bill Clinton's economic plans and became Secretary of Labor in the Clinton administration.

What does the future hold? To put it bluntly, both the world and domestic economies have changed, and theories are hard pressed to capture the new economic realities. The major changes that have created difficulties for today's economic policy makers are outlined in the next two sections.

THE CHANGING WORLD ECONOMY.   For the first time since World War II, the United States began to face serious industrial competition from European and Asian countries by the mid-1970s. Other nations built newer factories, captured local markets, took advantage of cheaper currencies and lower labor costs. As foreign markets for American goods dried up, less expensive and increasingly higher quality foreign products won our domestic markets. To complicate matters further, the prices of energy and other raw materials were increasingly controlled by foreign cartels. These changes weakened the domestic economy, increased prices, reduced incomes, sent dollars outside the country, reduced government tax revenues, and required more federal borrowing, often from foreign lenders, to run domestic programs. To top it all off, many of the budget dollars spent by the government ended up going to investors in other countries, while federal money thrown at consumers through tax breaks or welfare programs was spent on foreign products that made little impact on jobs and profits in the United States. *In short, direct connections between government spending policies and domestic economic growth became strained.*

THE CHANGING DOMESTIC ECONOMY.   In addition to the spinoffs from world economic change noted above, the focus of economic growth in America also began to change. Industrial production declined, while service activities and financial markets came to dominate, meaning that domestic companies turned to overseas production for cheaper labor, while American labor unions and high-paying manufacturing jobs declined. Although jobs continued to be created, they were lower-paying, with fewer benefits, putting more pressure on government welfare than before, at a time of strained government finances. Although overall economic growth was strong in the 1980s, profits did not trickle down to the majority of people in terms of income increases, as discussed in the section on poverty policy in Chapter 18. All of these structural economic changes further increased the economic pressures on the poor and middle classes. In short, the massive spending of the 1980s did stimulate the economy, but because of the decline in production and domestic industry, the growth in profits was largely at the top, among financial circles and the wealthy. Old Keynesian spending policies resulted in priming a weak and increasingly elite-dominated economy.

David Stockman, one-time director of the Office of Management and Budget (OMB), promotes his memoirs, The Triumph of Politics, *during a 1986 publicity tour. The ambitious Stockman moved from the staff of liberal Rep. John Anderson in the 1970s to the conservative Reagan regime in the 1980s. At the OMB he tried to implement the administration's supply-side doctrines; however, while the desired tax cuts were made, the corresponding budget cuts did not occur. Stockman's misgivings about supply-side theory soon became manifest, and he resigned his post. Enduring advocates of supply-side economics include such figures as Jack Kemp, Jude Wanniski, and George Gilder.*

Politics and Economic Policies

Even though elites dominate the policy scene in most technical areas of economic policy, the public still looms large when it comes to evaluating the overall results. How well is the economy performing as a result of the various policy directions taken by the government? As suggested in Chapters 7 and 11, this question can often come back to haunt elected officials, particularly presidents, at election time. Despite the economic obstacles outlined above, politicians still promise the public **economic policies** that will improve the average citizen's bottom line, and the public still expects them to deliver.

The danger, of course, is that responding to political pressures without reliable economic theories to guide policy can result in actions that either accomplish little, or worse yet, create bigger problems down the line. In retrospect, David Stockman, President Reagan's budget director, admitted that the supply-side economic theories he used to guide economic policy quickly ran aground on political pressures to fix an ailing economy. The pressures made it impossible to cut government spending, which was one of the requirements of supply-side thinking. As a result, the administration's economic experts quietly joined the political spending spree, acting like Keynesians while continuing to use the language of supply-side economic theory to try to convince the people, Congress, and possibly even the president himself that something of an economic revolution was taking place. Behind the rhetorical veils, economic policy was a shambles, at least as Stockman described the "Roaring '80s."[5] The somewhat more contrite '90s still reflect the lack of much consensus in Washington about how to correct the economic situation. Yet the political pressures to do something continue to mount for politicians. Bill Clinton's promise was to increase economically productive government spending (sounding like a Keynesian) and decrease the deficit (sounding like a neo-conservative) at the same time. Economists noted that this had never been tried before, and many were not sure it could be done, but few had better ideas. All of this suggests that the great levers of economic policy remain much the same as they have been over the last fifty years. What tends to vary are the combinations in which politicians push and pull them in response to economic and political pressures.

The Levers of Economic Policy

Since the Keynesian era, there have been three great political levers that politicians could push and pull, expecting some slow changes in the economy to result. They are: **fiscal policy** (taxes, budgeting, and spending), **monetary policy** (raising or lowering the supply and costs of money in circulation), and **regulatory policy** (controlling business, banking, and consumer affairs). In the past, fiscal and monetary policies have been generally relied on to help pull the economy out of recession, as they had relatively rapid effects. Regulatory policies, by contrast, were applied for longer-term adjustments of competition, profits, and risk factors in the economy. Even though much of the fate of the economy is in the hands of private producers and consumers, many economists and politicians in the past believed that important (even if delayed) economic reactions have come from pushing and pulling the great levers of fiscal, monetary, and regulatory policies.

Fiscal Policy

The government spendeth and the government taketh away. The key issues in making fiscal policy are how to raise revenues and how to spend them. Revenues primarily come from taxes on businesses and individuals, but there are also some monies generated by fees for using public facilities and services (for example, people pay entry fees at national parks). Decisions about who to tax and how much to tax them can have big economic effects. For example, raising the taxes on wealthy individuals may generate more revenues,

Negotiating an Economic Policy

Confronting limited options in the face of a large deficit and public hostility toward ever-mounting taxes, U.S. economic policy makers must try to balance national growth against fears of inflation. A leading player in this complex game is Alan Greenspan (*right*), chairman of the Federal Reserve System. Economic policy is complicated by the fragmenting of power involved: "The Fed," for example, was designed to operate autonomously so as to preserve economic stability and avoid the whims of partisan politics.

Bill Clinton's top experts include former UC–Berkeley professor Laura D'Andrea Tyson (*above*), chairwoman of the Council of Economic Advisers, and former investment banker Robert Rubin (*below*), of the National Economic Council. They must work jointly with Congress, the business community, and major players such as Treasury secretary Bentsen and Labor secretary Reich in hopes of fostering a fruitful national economy.

The Players

but some policy makers say that taxing the rich is a sure way to discourage investment, which may have negative effects on economic growth. Other experts favor lowering taxes for the middle and lower income brackets, particularly during recessions, because people with smaller incomes in hard times are likely to spend tax breaks immediately, producing a faster upswing in consumer demand and economic production.

STRATEGIES OF TAXATION.   Some taxes are **progressive**, meaning that the rates get bigger as incomes or profits get larger. The income tax is an example of a progressive tax, because people who make more money pay a larger base rate (percentage) of their income in taxes. Other taxes are **regressive**, meaning that they are the same rate regardless of income, which ends up taking a bigger bite from the poor than the rich. Taxes on gasoline and food, for example, are levied at constant rates for all taxpayers, but create a greater burden for poor people who must spend a higher percentage of their income for basic necessities. Many tax analysts regard property taxes as the fairest of all because they are **proportional**, meaning that the rates are constant like sales taxes, but the tax bill goes up or down with a person's wealth, at least as measured by the value of the property being taxed. Thus, someone with a million-dollar house pays much more in taxes than someone with a hundred-thousand-dollar house.

Deciding who to tax and how to tax them are among the most sensitive policy issues facing governments at all levels. States rely on different mixes of all three types of taxes, with some states putting more emphasis on sales, income, or property, while others have adopted a more even mix. At the extreme, more "progressive" states such as Oregon have traditionally avoided the sales tax entirely, while more "regressive" states such as neighboring Washington have emphasized sales taxes and avoided the income tax. The federal government has resisted most forms of national sales and property taxes (leaving those options primarily to the states), and emphasized income taxes, instead, as the primary national revenue source. "How We Compare" Box 19.2 shows the tax structures of the seven leading industrial nations.

Whatever the form of taxation, there are delicate political calculations and important economic effects wrapped up in every mixture of tax and revenue policies. On the political side, taxing the rich is risky to do because wealthy individuals and corporations make campaign contributions and lobby intensely for favorable tax laws. At the same time, middle-class taxpayers can deliver a lot of votes for or against politicians who please or displease them with tax policies. Polls indicate that the majority of people favor taxing the rich and cutting back on military spending and foreign aid, running against positions that elites and multinational industries have traditionally defended. The result is a complex and sometimes contradictory code of tax laws that reflect the political conflicts between the taxing and spending preferences of different income and interest groups, balanced against the government's needs for money to run programs.

The economic effects of different tax policies also enter into fiscal calculations, further complicating the tax code. Raising taxes too much on the upper-income brackets or for businesses can stifle the incentive to work harder and invest money in new products or ventures. Yet putting too much tax burden on middle-class and working people can discourage consumption and slow down economic growth because of reduced demand. The easy solution would be to lower taxes for all, but the failure to levy enough taxes means that the government has to borrow money to operate. This, in a simplified form, is just what has happened, with the result, as discussed above, that being heavily in debt gives the government less leverage over fiscal options when the economy slows down.

STRATEGIES OF SPENDING.   The old rule of thumb in fiscal policy was that in recessions, the government should spend more than it collected in revenues to fuel the economy. Once the economy was healthy again, increased incomes and profits would generate surplus revenues that could be used to bail the government out of debt, or at

The Tax Structures of the Seven Leading Industrial Nations

19.2

Fiscal policies in the United States turn less of the national economic output into government revenues than any other leading industrialized democratic nation. In the comparisons that follow, note that American income tax rates are the lowest of the seven nations, but the large number of workers in America ends up generating the largest percentage of total government taxes from this source. One way in which the smaller tax bite of the United States shows up is in government spending on public infrastructure (roads, bridges, airports, communication systems) on which the economy depends for transportation and communication. According to data from the Organization for Economic Cooperation and Development, the United States spends only .3 percent of its gross domestic product in this area, compared to an average of 3.5 percent in the other six nations.

SOURCE: Organization for Economic Cooperation and Development. Adapted from *The New York Times,* November 29, 1992, p. 2 E.

Tax Formulas: Where Nations Get Their Money

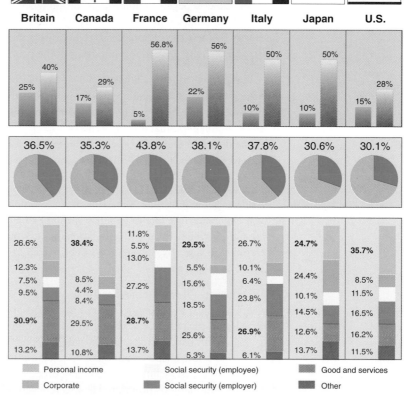

least keep the debt level manageable. At least that was the theory. What has happened, instead, is that governments have spent massively in hard times, without much cutting back or raising revenues in good times. This pattern of high spending and low taxing largely reflects political pressures to keep taxes low. Americans pay less in taxes than citizens of other leading industrial nations, as shown in Box 19.2. At the same time, there are broad political pressures from various interests to keep spending high.

All of which has put the federal government in a fiscal jam. In the best of times, the government does well to stay even and keep existing programs running. In hard times, there is little room for more debt and spending to bail out the economy. Thus, as noted above, fiscal policy has become weaker and weaker as an economic stimulus. To complicate matters further, in hard times, revenues go down because incomes fall and profits drop. This means that government must take one of three desperate remedies: cut programs, shove responsibilities onto the states, or borrow more money. In recent years, fiscal policymakers have resorted to all three. Cutting programs not only lowers the quality of life for people who relied on them, but it further hurts the economy by taking money out of circulation. Shoving responsibilities on the states only adds to state fiscal problems. Many states are already in worse shape than the federal government, for several reasons: national contributions to state budgets have declined, many states depend on regressive taxes (like the sales tax) that decline sharply in hard times, and most states do not have the dubious luxury of simply borrowing their way out of trouble. Which brings us to the last federal resort, borrowing, which only pushes present problems into the future, while compounding them because of the interest that must be paid each year on past debt.

Many experts began to doubt that the sluggish economy of the early 1990s could respond to the usual fiscal remedies, largely because fifty years of pushing and pulling fiscal levers had left the national budget in quite a mess. Two typical newspaper accounts relying on the judgments of economists put the problem like this:

> Usually, when the economy is in a slump the federal government can help end the misery by flexing its fiscal muscle. Franklin Roosevelt's work projects during the depression are an example of how the federal government can help by putting people to work. Nothing like that is going to happen soon: The huge federal budget deficit, which economists said eventually would kill the economy, is killing it now. The government is so far in debt it can't realistically borrow more money to create jobs.[6]

> Ever since World War II, the federal government has employed fiscal and monetary policy to battle recessions. But in the current slump . . . it has been reluctant to resort to fiscal stimulus, by either stepping up spending or cutting taxes. . . .
>
> Anti-recession fiscal policy is becoming less practical. Already, the government's flexibility is severely limited by its debt, which exceeds $3.5 trillion and is growing about $1 billion a day.[7]

Whether or not fiscal remedies are as effective as in the past, presidents continue to try them to adjust the economy. Even a fiscal conservative like George Bush became persuaded that a serious recession in 1989–1991 might be eased by signing a Democratic party-backed transportation bill that would spend $150 billion over six years on road construction and transportation systems, creating many new grass-roots jobs. When he came into office, Bill Clinton immediately proposed an economic stimulus package that included a national jobs program. He also reneged on his campaign promise of a tax cut for the middle class in an effort to control the budget deficit. In other words, Clinton promised to cut the deficit at the same time he wanted to boost particular types of spending in an attempt to stimulate the economy. Economists were reluctant to make predictions about this proposal, since throwing two large fiscal levers in opposite directions had never been tried before. A full test of this plan never developed, as the spending program was killed by Republican opposition in Congress.

One thing that history suggests is that whether conservative or liberal, every president becomes involved in making fiscal decisions aimed at stimulating economic growth. Figure 19.3 shows some of the major fiscal initiatives taken by presidents since 1929. Most of these initiatives were taken in response to recessions or to periods of high unemployment. Note that the extremely high unemployment trends from 1930 to 1940 were due to the Great Depression of that period.

FIGURE 19.3

Fiscal Actions of the Presidents, 1929–1993
in Relation to Unemployment Trends

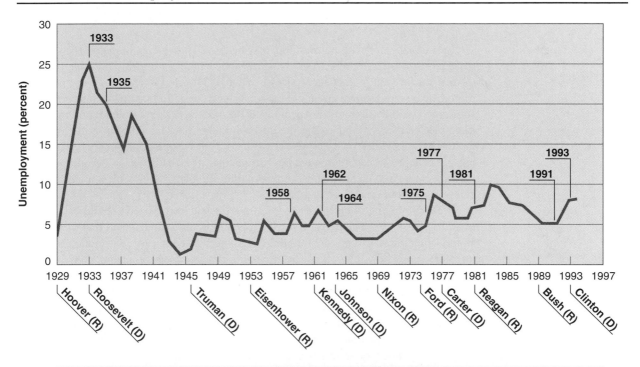

1933 Roosevelt establishes the Federal Emergency Relief Administration; it gives money to the unemployed and finances public works projects.

1935 Roosevelt creates the Works Progress Administration; it employs more than 3 million people in public works projects.

1958 Eisenhower approves a $1.85 billion antirecession act. The money is used to stimulate construction of 200,000 housing units, creating 500,000 jobs.

1962 Kennedy's 7 percent tax credit on industrial equipment purchases becomes law.

1964 Kennedy's personal and corporate income-tax cut proposals are enacted after his assasination.

1975 Ford approves a $4.5 billion emergency stimulus package, including $2.5 billion for state and local governments to hire unemployed workers.

1977 Carter expands the Federal job-creation and training programs.

1981 Reagan pushes through the largest tax cut in American history.

1991 Bush approves an expanded transportation bill calling for spending of $151 billion over six years on roads and mass transit.

1993 Clinton proposes an economic stimulus package that includes $30 million in government jobs and urban programs. The proposal fails in Congress.

Source: Adapted from *The New York Times*, November 24, 1992; 1993 data added by author.

Monetary Policy

As noted earlier, monetary policy has to do with how much money there is in circulation and how easy it is to borrow. The two factors are related, because pumping more money into banks encourages banks to lower interest rates to loan it out. Similarly, lowering the interest rate that banks pay to borrow money from the central banking system (called the **Federal Reserve System**) pushes more money into circulation. As two newspaper accounts put it, when fiscal policies fail, monetary policies should do the trick, but they have not worked according to theory in recent years:

> So that leaves monetary policy—the influence wielded by the Federal Reserve, the nation's central bank, over interest rates and the supply of money in circulation.
> . . . the Fed has been pushing short term interest rates down . . . by pumping money into the nation's banking system [but the economy isn't responding, and] . . . monetary policy is nearly exhausted.[8]

> Monetary policy . . . also has lost some of its punch. The Fed works primarily through the banks, and their economic role is shrinking steadily as they lose business customers.[9]

Even though monetary policies, too, may be less effective than in the past, politicians continue to use them. When the economy stalled midway into his presidential term, George Bush relied on monetary policies aimed at lowering interest rates to encourage more business investment and more consumer borrowing to buy houses and other consumer goods. Bill Clinton also encouraged the Federal Reserve to continue much the same relaxed monetary policies as the Bush administration. However, as both presidents discovered, monetary policy is also a weak tool in a troubled economy. Perhaps the biggest benefit of keeping interest rates lower than they had been in decades was that banks were able to create a higher profit margin on loans, stalling off a major banking collapse that some analysts had predicted.

While presidents often use their powers of persuasion to get the Federal Reserve board to raise or lower the cost of money, it is important to understand that they cannot simply order it done. The Federal Reserve is connected to the executive branch and Congress in various ways, but it functions as an independent decision-making body. Needless to say, it would be dangerous to put the money supply directly in the hands of politicians who might be tempted to use this powerful lever for political purposes with little regard for future consequences. However, there are those who argue that the president's indirect influence over the Federal Reserve may be too great as it is, because of the power to appoint the chairman and vice chairman every four years. Although the chair of "the Fed," as it is called, often resists presidential pressure, there is an uncanny tendency for the central bank to let the money flow at election time if the economy is slipping.

HOW THE FEDERAL RESERVE SYSTEM WORKS.   The Federal Reserve was set up in 1913 as the latest in a long line of experiments with a national banking system. Torn between a central bank with tight control over money and lending, and a loose system of thousands of private banks with great independence, the government settled for the reserve bank system as a compromise. As the name implies, the Federal Reserve is the guardian of the nation's reserve cash supply, making sure there is always enough to cover economic demands, and controlling the flow to banks as economic conditions change. Private banks are not legally required to join this system, but there are considerable advantages for the majority of banks that belong, including the right to participate in the Federal Deposit Insurance program which most depositors regard as a must in the bank where they plan to leave their money. Without this insurance program, the collapse of the savings and loans probably would have triggered a financial panic, not to mention

The Treasury Building in Washington, D.C. The Treasury department is one of the oldest in the government; its first secretary, Alexander Hamilton, was an admirer of England's unified banking and political systems, and sought to fashion the U.S. monetary system in its image.

angry political reprisals from voters. In addition to deposit insurance coverage, member banks also gain access to favorable lending rates when money is borrowed from the federal cash reserve. Member banks also participate in setting national monetary policy. The Federal Reserve System is thus a network for coordinating the nation's banks to prevent such disasters as credit wars or money shortages that might destabilize the nation's economy.

In exchange for joining the reserve system, member banks are required to: follow the rules passed by the board of governors; follow the rules set down by federal banking regulators; and deposit money in the nation's cash reserve by purchasing shares of stock in the system's district bank. There are twelve district banks around the country (Boston, New York, Philadelphia, Cleveland, Richmond, Atlanta, Chicago, St. Louis, Minneapolis, Kansas City [Mo.], Dallas, and San Francisco). In addition to spreading out the banking bureaucracy, each district monitors regional economic conditions and delivers reports to the meetings of the Board of Directors and the Federal Open Market Committee, the two Fed policy bodies. The national banking system, then, consists primarily of four levels:

- *Board of Governors:* Seven members, appointed to fourteen-year terms by the president, confirmed by the Senate (chair serves only four-year term). Makes general policy (decides how much member private banks must deposit on reserve with district reserve banks to secure their loans, and decides on raising or lowering the "discount rate" or the interest on money that member banks borrow from the reserve). Audits banking operations. Admits or denies applications for membership from private banks.
- *Federal Open Market Committee:* All seven members of the Board, plus five members elected by directors of the Federal Reserve Banks. The committee monitors the nation's money supply, and regional economic performance, and recommends changes in interest rates and money in circulation.
- *Federal Reserve Banks:* Twelve district banks hold money from member private banks in reserve and make credit and debt transfers among member banks. They issue the nation's currency (Federal Reserve Notes) with authority of the Treasury Department.
- *Private Member Banks:* The majority of the nation's private commercial banks (over 5,000) buy shares in the reserve system, and use the central banking services to borrow money, retire debts, keep funds on account, and obtain cash.

At the center of the system are the twelve Federal Reserve Banks. Since they are owned by private member banks, they are often called bankers' banks, loaning and depositing money for members. However, the reserve banks are also partly public institutions since they are not allowed to make a profit. Any income above expenses goes into the U.S. Treasury. They must report activities to Congress and the president, and the Board of Governors of the entire system is appointed by the president and confirmed by the Senate. The seven members of the Board serve fourteen-year terms, which means they are not vulnerable to direct political pressures. However, the chair of the Board is appointed or reappointed every four years, usually after consultations with the president and his economic advisers assuring that there is basic agreement with the economic philosophy of the administration.

The system that regulates the nation's money flow is thus both public and private, and subject to influences from member banks, from Congress, the White House, and from the various economic experts who advise the players at every level. Reflecting the public obligation of the Reserve Bank system, the district banks are responsible for putting currency in circulation and keeping track of it. Although the nation's folding money is signed by the Secretary of the Treasury, reflecting the authorization of the executive, the bills themselves are drawn against credits held in reserve, which is the reason why your paper money says Federal Reserve Note on it (and why the Reserve Banks must return any surplus cash and profits to the Treasury account).

DECIDING HOW MUCH MONEY TO CREATE.   The basic policy issue confronting the reserve bankers is how much money to keep in circulation, bearing in mind that it is not so simple as to just start up the printing presses and let the paper fly. In today's world of electronic banking and plastic money, most of the money supply sits in computer disks as electronic debts, credits, and account balances. Because so much money is created through credit transactions, it is not so easy to know what the money supply really is, and economists often disagree about how to calculate it. It is clear, however, that surges in electronic credit and interbank loans can create a surge of money just as fast and as dangerous as turning on the presses. When the money supply expands too fast, consumers can go on a rampage, buying more than manufacturers can produce. This can set price increases in motion based on such factors as hiring new workers, paying more for raw materials made scarce by the demand, and just plain corporate greed. When this happens, more dollars end up buying less, which is another way of saying that inflation happens.

At this point, the Open Market Committee (which includes the Directors of the System) often recommends raising the **discount rate**, which is the fee the reserve banks charge to their best and biggest member banks to borrow money. Member banks in turn pass the increase along to their own customers through higher rates for car loans and credit card debt, and tougher restrictions on getting credit. When the system is working, the result is to slow down spending and decrease the money supply, returning lost value to inflated dollars.

By contrast, when the Open Market Committee notices a slowdown in buying and begins to hear complaints both from member banks and politicians, the policy response is usually to lower the discount rate and let more money flow out. In addition, the central bank may buy back more of the Treasury bonds sold by the government in the past to cover the national debt. This puts money in circulation by transferring government credits into (electronic) cash deposits in commercial bank accounts. Once again, when the economy is working according to traditional monetary theories, this eases the money supply, increases consumer and business borrowing, boosts spending, and helps drive the economy out of recession.

Holiday shoppers at Macy's in New York. Effects of the policies decided upon by the Federal Reserve System, in consultation with various congressional and executive-branch players, are felt here and across the country.

COORDINATING MONETARY AND FISCAL POLICY.   Monetary policy is complex and can interact well or badly with fiscal policy. For example, raising taxes after the Fed has increased the money supply can take surplus dollars out of circulation again, with the result that fiscal policy cancels out monetary policy. Likewise, monetary measures taken to control inflation (like restricting money) can slow the economy and create problems for the government in collecting enough tax dollars to meet its fiscal revenue projections. In a system as dispersed as this economic policy process, a lot of coordination is required among the parts. An important coordinating function is provided by the president's **Council of Economic Advisers**, which includes economists, Treasury officials, and budget officers who meet regularly to survey the economic scene and recommend action directly to the president. Bill Clinton appointed Laura D'Andrea Tyson, an economist from the University of California at Berkeley, to be the chairwoman of the three-member Council of Economic Advisers.

At best, coordinating government economic policy is a tricky business. In recent years, however, it has become even trickier. As noted above, fiscal policy has been blocked by important changes in the economy and by the budget paralysis itself. In addition, both consumers and businesses went on a debt binge in the 1980s. When the recession of the late 1980s and early 1990s came along, the Fed dropped the prime lending rate to a tempting low of less than 5 percent, but many businesses were already so mortgaged that they could not borrow any more money. In addition, changing federal regulations enabled businesses to find other places to get money, such as issuing their own risky, but high-paying instruments that came to be known in the 1980s as junk bonds. In short, the financial system has grown considerably more complex in recent years with the introduction of new sources of money and credit that are less responsive to the monetary policies of the Fed. Which brings us to the deepest and possibly most important level of economic policy, regulatory policy.

This 1921 cartoon shows Wall Street operators fishing for suckers.

Regulatory Policy

If banks are given permission to sell securities (for example, bonds issued by new companies), or to try other methods of making money rather than selling loans, this means that changes have taken place in government regulatory policy. Regulatory policy refers to the rules and regulations governing such matters as how businesses operate, how consumers are protected, and what banks can do to make money. Since these regulations affect such things as consumer confidence and business investment patterns, their impact can be slow to develop. As a result, regulatory policies are seldom used to provide quick fixes in such economic emergencies as recessions. It can take years to determine whether or not the regulatory levers that were pushed or pulled actually worked. The delayed effects of the savings and loan deregulation of the early 1980s did not appear as a major crisis until the late 1980s and early 1990s.

WHAT TO REGULATE? Because of their complexity, their seemingly dull bureaucratic nature, and slowness to take effect, few news stories are written about regulatory policies, yet some of the most important economic changes in history have taken place in the back offices of such bureaucracies as the Treasury Department, the Securities and Exchange Commission, the Comptroller of the Currency, the Federal Home Loan Bank Board, and dozens of other bureaus and offices responsible for regulating the complex economic machinery that can produce so much public security or insecurity.

Prior to the Great Depression of the 1930s, the economy was only loosely regulated, with the result that there was nothing to stop them when bankers and investors plunged into a spiral of debt and shaky investments that made paper fortunes for a few, but eventually wiped out the jobs, savings, and confidence of the many. Following this depression, the government began to regulate many aspects of the economy, including:

- *Commerce:* monitoring prices and competition in different industries;
- *Banking and credit:* requiring banks to maintain cash reserves to back up loans that may go bad, and to observe safe lending practices;
- *Investment:* requiring stock buyers to deposit money with brokers rather than buying on anticipation of future profits; and requiring companies selling stock to the public to disclose financial operations and play by certain business rules;
- *Consumer protection:* making products safe and true to their advertising.

WHAT TO DEREGULATE? When the economy began acting strangely and unresponsively to traditional fiscal and monetary policies in the 1970s and 1980s, many economists and business people charged that the problem was too much **regulation**. There were so many rules and regulations that businesses and markets could no longer adapt or compete. Competition was strangled, new ways of making money were prohibited, limits on prices killed profits, consumer protection was carried to extremes unheard of in other countries. In the late 1970s and on through the 1980s, the regulations began to come off. Airlines were allowed to set their own prices and compete more freely for routes. Banks and securities firms were allowed to create new, higher-yielding kinds of investments including money market funds and junk bonds. Savings and loans were allowed to lend money for items besides houses, while offering more competitive interest rates on larger savings accounts. Businesses once prohibited from merging because of regulations against monopolies or taking on too much debt were bought and sold at a dizzying rate as restrictions were lifted.

While **deregulation** had the undeniable effect of generating huge profits for investors and company executives, the legacy also left many economists worried about the overall health of the economy in the 1990s. Airline bankruptcies (Pan Am, TWA, Continental, Eastern, and others) left a smaller number of huge carriers to consolidate transportation routes and prices. Yet even the remaining large companies such as Delta, United, and American were unable to compete in complex markets with unpredictable consumer patterns at home and with greater foreign competition. Thousands of businesses with huge debts from the corporate buyout frenzy of the 1980s staggered into the recession at the

Pan Am jets sit on a runway at New York's John F. Kennedy Airport in 1991, following Pan Am's shutdown. The deregulation of various industries proved to be a mixed blessing. Its immediate effect seemed to be an epidemic of short-term thinking and greed among some investors, leading to the dissolution of some weaker companies. However, monetarist and neo-conservative analysts argue that industries and consumers alike were ultimately better served in those cases where free-market competition was in fact renewed.

end of the decade. Many were saved from bankruptcy through Federal Reserve low-interest policies that enabled companies to refinance old loans at better rates. As noted earlier, many of the country's savings and loans had to be liquidated, and savings accounts replaced at taxpayer expense, leaving the federal government as the nation's chief property management firm after inheriting all the assets. Meanwhile, the nation's banks were lining up for another round of regulatory relief.

In short, the deregulation binge may have been as paralyzing in the short run as the regulation binge had been before it. Many economic experts worried that the whole economy was leveraged, strained, and distorted beyond any remedy that old theories might prescribe. Still, politicians pressured to perform miracles continued to go through the old fiscal and monetary motions, as if chanting "Keynes is dead; Long live (the) Keynes." Unless something could be done to straighten things out, the biggest casualties of the stalled economy were likely to be the dozens of programs for domestic renewal in the areas of health, education, and child development—programs that might decide the quality of life for the next generation. While the clouds of economic gloom gathered, the media and politicians alike became more receptive at the start of the 1990s to the ideas of economists who advocated taking a new, more integrated look at economic and social policy working together.

Economy, Government, and Society Revisited

The broad levers of government economic policy are known as **fiscal policy**, having to do with taxation and spending, **monetary policy**, having to do with the supply of money and credit, and **regulatory policy**, involving the laws and rules governing banking, trading,

FIGURE 19.4

Public Opinion Trends on Different Fiscal (Taxing and Spending) Options

Views on Paying More...
If taxes had to be raised, would it be acceptable or not acceptable to you to...

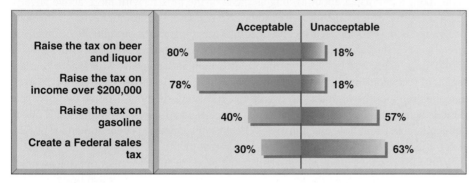

	Acceptable	Unacceptable
Raise the tax on beer and liquor	80%	18%
Raise the tax on income over $200,000	78%	18%
Raise the tax on gasoline	40%	57%
Create a Federal sales tax	30%	63%

...And Accepting Less
If spending had to be cut, would it be acceptable or not acceptable to you to...

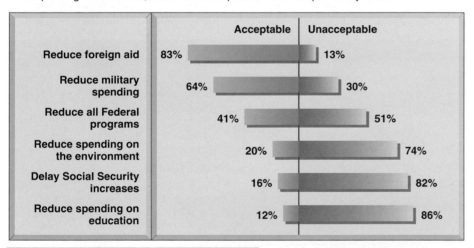

	Acceptable	Unacceptable
Reduce foreign aid	83%	13%
Reduce military spending	64%	30%
Reduce all Federal programs	41%	51%
Reduce spending on the environment	20%	74%
Delay Social Security increases	16%	82%
Reduce spending on education	12%	86%

Based on telephone interviews with 1,140 adults nationwide conducted May 22–24. Those with no opinion are not shown.

Source: New York Times/CBS News Poll, May 1990. Adapted from *The New York Times*, May 27, 1990, p. 13.

and other business practices. These three strategies for controlling the economy have encountered increasing resistance in recent years from changing economic conditions. Also complicating effective economic policy are the often-conflicting political forces involved. While many specific policy decisions are made in response to the inside pressures of banking and business elites, politicians are also sensitive to the political pressures of the general public whose jobs and buying habits are affected by how well all of the smaller decisions have worked. Figure 19.4 illustrates some of the public opinion reactions to different taxing and spending strategies that can complicate the politics of fiscal policy and make it difficult to coordinate with policies in other areas.

More and more economists today are unsure that new economic conditions can be responsive to the old policy levers. Some analysts, including University of California economist Christina Romer, go so far as to doubt that government economic policies *ever* did much good, saying that the recessions of the past century when governments tried to do little about them lasted about as long as those of the present with more active government economic policy. The difference today, Romer says, is that more extensive welfare programs such as Social Security and unemployment insurance put billions of dollars at street level, acting as a *stabilizer* against the worst economic extremes.[10] An opposing viewpoint is expressed by Geoffrey Moore of Columbia University who argues that the length of recessions has been cut by more than half in the last fifty years, lasting an average of eleven months compared to twenty-five to twenty-six months in the two fifty-year periods before this one. However, he says it is unclear how much of this change is due to economic policy and how much involves changes in economic production and the stabilizing effects of greater government spending in general.[11]

While the debate goes on about whether the broad economic policy options do much or whether they even do more harm than good, one thing is certain: when faced with political pressures to do something, politicians will keep pushing and pulling the old policy levers. Until new economic theories come along that clearly work better, it is useful to know about the three basic kinds of economic policy that politicians use to keep the economy moving ahead. You will continue hearing a lot about them in the news.

Robert Reich, Bill Clinton's Secretary of Labor. Reich, a political economist trained (like Clinton) at Yale and Oxford, had a strong academic reputation going into his new job, but soon found that academic theory and political reality sometimes failed to mesh in the halls of government.

New Economic Ideas

As explained in the previous chapter, many politicians and economists are beginning to consider new social policies aimed at family, children, health, and education as acceptable forms of welfare that might have important long-term economic payoffs as well. Even liberal politicians and economists are thinking about welfare policies less in terms of just easing the pain of poverty, and more as part of broad economic policy connecting government, society, and the business sector in new relations to stimulate industrial growth. As noted earlier, there is increasing talk about a new industrial policy that would invest government money in research and development of new products and technologies, while encouraging American corporations to retool plants and halt a flow of jobs to other countries. Part of a new industrial policy would be a new social policy as well, improving basic living conditions so that the next generation of workers will have the skills and motivations to take those new jobs.

In this quest for more integrated social and economic policies, the media play a key role by featuring new proposals on editorial pages and interview programs. For example, one expert who has been in the news with specific ideas is Harvard's Robert Reich, who became Secretary of Labor in the Clinton administration. The core of Reich's analysis was presented in an article that appeared in *The New York Times* prior to the presidential campaign of 1992.[12] He argued that American corporations are still competitive and profitable, but American workers are not and have lost real income and skilled jobs to overseas competition. Corporate investments no longer "trickle down" to workers in our factories, but "trickle out" to workers and factories in other countries, in part, because the government has cut spending on job training, education, and public facilities that might make America a more attractive investment. As a result, the government must invest heavily in the 1990s "to prepare our workforce for the next century." The nation needs a plan for rebuilding America similar to the one directed by General George Marshall to rebuild Europe after World War II. This is where a new economic program would blend with social policies similar to those discussed at the end of Chapter 18.

Where do we get the $2 trillion that Reich estimates that it would cost to rebuild America? Reich's proposals include:

- a 15 percent cut in defense spending, which would yield $450 billion in ten years;

- making the income tax more progressive. Just returning the tax schedule to the way it was in 1978 would generate over $950 billion in revenues from the wealthiest 10 percent of taxpayers over the span of a decade;

- raising Social Security taxes and increasing taxes on Social Security payments to wealthier Americans could generate $600 billion in additional government revenues over a decade.

These proposals are just to open the discussion. Other ideas might make more sense, and there are still great uncertainties about how to renew social and economic institutions in ways that really make a difference. The important thing, however, is that the nation has begun to debate new economic and social policies in election campaigns, within government institutions, in schools, at the family dinner table, and in the office. Without serious national discussions, the temptation for politicians and the public alike will be to continue to play politics with the economic future. What does that future hold? What role can you play in it? Some ideas are offered in the "Citizen's Question: Economic Involvement."

A CITIZEN'S QUESTION   Economic Involvement

*H*ow can I become more involved in the economic decisions that affect the nation's future? The first step toward getting more involved in the national debate over economic policy is to understand how the policy process works and what the economic theories and policy options look like. This chapter is intended to make economic policy easier to understand. When you hear about fiscal, monetary, or regulatory policy in news reports, you will be able to think critically about what is going on. In addition, you will be able to follow debates among neo-conservative, liberal, and neo-liberal economic theorists. Perhaps you will even begin developing theories of your own. While the technical side of economics may require math skills to employ, the theoretical side is not as complicated as many people think. There are clear advantages to joining your interests in political science with your thinking about economics, since government is where the economy and society come together.

*B*eyond becoming informed and feeling more confident in expressing your economic views in public, there are other, more concrete steps that you can take to get involved with economic policy. There are many interest groups that invite citizens to join together to change economic policies. The area of fiscal policy is particularly rich with interest groups, since the questions involved in fiscal policies often affect people directly. For example, the *Encyclopedia of*

Associations (1992 ed.) lists twenty-eight different citizens' organizations concerned with government tax policies. As you can imagine, many of these organizations attract members simply because they advocate lower taxes. However, you might be interested in writing to some of these organizations to find out about their ideas:

Citizens for Tax Justice
1311 L St. N.W., 4th floor
Washington, D.C. 20005
202-626-3780
(Looks for new ways of meeting tax needs of government. Provides technical assistance to local groups.)

National Coalition of IRS Whistleblowers
Box 4283
Pocatello, Idaho 83201
202-546-5345
(Monitors Internal Revenue Service policies and practices with an eye to protecting the privacy of individual taxpayers.)

National Taxpayers Union
325 Pennsylvania Avenue S.E.
Washington, D.C. 20003
202-543-1300
(Tries to reduce government spending and cut taxes. Works to assist citizens' groups at state and national levels.)

Key Terms

Adam Smith
    conservative economic theory
    economic self-interest as best
        market regulator

John Maynard Keynes
    liberal economic theory
    government as best market
        regulator

neo-conservative theories
    monetary theory
    supply-side economics

neo-liberal theories
    industrial policy ideas

inflation

recession

stagflation

economic policy
  fiscal/monetary/regulatory
  similarities to social policy
  differences from social policy

types of taxes
  progressive/proportional/
  regressive

Federal Reserve System
  procedures for managing the
    money supply
  discount rate

Council of Economic Advisors

regulation/deregulation

Suggested Readings

Friedman, Milton. *Capitalism and Freedom*. Chicago: University of Chicago Press, 1962.

Friedman, Milton, and Rose Friedman. *Free to Choose*. New York: Harcourt Brace, 1980.

Galbraith, John Kenneth. *The Great Crash of 1929*. Boston: Houghton Mifflin, 1988.

Gilder, George. *Wealth and Poverty*. New York: Basic Books, 1981.

Hazlitt, Henry. *Economics in One Lesson*. New York: Crown, 1988.

Keynes, John Maynard. *The General Theory of Employment, Interest, and Money*. New York: Harcourt Brace, 1964.

Peters, B. Guy. *The Politics of Taxation: A Comparative Perspective*. Cambridge, Mass.: Blackwell, 1991.

Phillips, Kevin. *The Politics of Rich and Poor*. New York: Random House, 1990.

Reich, Robert B. *The Work of Nations: Preparing Ourselves for 21st Century Capitalism*. New York: Knopf, 1991.

Smith, Adam. *The Wealth of Nations.* (various editions)

• • •

American foreign policy is at sea. With the collapse of
communism and the disintegration of the Soviet Union, the
principles that guided past behavior are gone or are going fast.
Replacements have not yet been discerned and agreed upon.
—C. FRED BERGSTEN

• • •

The urgent questions certain to be asked of mankind in the
next century will be the ones about survival, not security—not
the geopolitical questions about a coup in Panama or a war in
Iran but the geophysical questions about the depletions in the
biosphere and the holes in the ozone, about the disparity of
wealth between the nations of the northern and southern
hemispheres, about famine in Asia and disease in Africa.
—LEWIS H. LAPHAM

• • •

Diplomacy is the police in grand costume.
—NAPOLEON

• • •

Foreign and Defense Policy: National Security and World Power

- **THE NEW WORLD ORDER**
- **THE RISE OF THE UNITED STATES AS A WORLD POWER**
  Culture, Ideology, and History
  Economic Interests and Military Power
- **THE COLD WAR**
  Foreign Policy in the National Security State
  The Great Nuclear Poker Game
- **MAKING FOREIGN POLICY IN THE COLD WAR WORLD**
  Ideological Consensus and Presidential Leadership
  The Foreign Policy Establishment
  Congress, the Interests, and the Public
- **THE DOMESTICATION OF THE FOREIGN POLICY PROCESS**
  Vietnam and the Breakdown of Consensus
  Searching for New Doctrines
  A Policy Breakdown?
- **DEFENSE: A SOLUTION LOOKING FOR A PROBLEM?**
  The Peace Dividend
  The Defense Establishment and the Economy
  New Roles for the Military?
- **THE NEW WORLD ORDER REVISITED**
  Power in a Multipolar World
  Is U.S. Power in Decline?
- **A CITIZEN'S QUESTION: Foreign Policy Participation**
- **KEY TERMS**
- **SUGGESTED READINGS**

The New World Order

The headlines have proclaimed revolutionary changes in the world during the last decade. A "velvet revolution" swept Eastern Europe. Revellers danced atop the Berlin Wall in 1989 as the gates between East and West were opened, ending the political and military division of the city that symbolized the old world order of the Cold War. Soviet leader Mikhail Gorbachev was hailed around the world and received the Nobel Peace Prize for granting unprecedented freedoms to the citizens of the Soviet Communist bloc. Yet with that freedom came the wrenching transition and hardship of political and economic change that would soon topple Gorbachev from power and finish off the Soviet Union itself.

Western leaders took advantage of numerous ceremonial occasions to declare the Cold War over. In 1990, the members of the North Atlantic Treaty Organization, the key Western military alliance, met with leaders of the Warsaw Pact nations, the key Soviet bloc alliance, and signed a treaty that began the demilitarization of Europe and opened the door to an era of superpower cooperation. One headline proclaimed: EAST AND WEST DECLARE THE END OF COLD WAR AT PARIS CONFERENCE.[1] Politicians find it hard to let go of those kinds of headlines, and the declarations of a new era of peace and cooperation continued. By 1992, the Soviet Union was a thing of the past, and a new leader, Boris Yeltsin, had replaced Mikhail Gorbachev as the Russian head of state. Mr. Bush met with Mr. Yeltsin at the presidential retreat in Camp David, and declared world peace once again. As this headline put it: BUSH AND YELTSIN DECLARE FORMAL END TO COLD WAR.[2]

Media pundits joined the news bandwagon, declaring their expert judgments about victory in the Cold War and pronouncing the United States the undisputed leader in the new world order. Some even went so far as to predict that the new world would be a dull and unchallenging place without the great ideological clash between communism and capitalism to give politics meaning.[3] In an act that was defined by President Bush as the proof of world unity around U.S. leadership, American generals led a multinational coalition to war against Saddam Hussein of Iraq in 1991. The reasons for the war against Iraq were not specified clearly enough for some. Protecting U.S. jobs and oil supplies, while fighting aggression against an ally (Kuwait), sounded to them like old motives simply aimed at different targets. According to inside accounts, the very phrase *a new world order* was an invention of the White House press office to keep pesky reporters off their backs while the president and his advisers searched for a guiding theme. When asked how to explain the war against Iraq, National Security Adviser Brent Scowcroft told administration press officers, "Tell them we can't just let Iraq get away with this—there is a new world order developing." Later, when a CNN correspondent wandered into the press office looking for a story, the aide recalled: "We told her it's 'a new world order.' She liked it, and 30 minutes later it was on CNN. So the 'new world order'. . . was really just an accident. The philosophy came later."[4]

Despite the historic foreign events, public support for President Bush's domestic leadership fell. Experts and ordinary people alike raised questions about whether America should continue giving aid to distant nations while its inner cities decayed into increasingly impoverished and unliveable places. In the space of a few short years from the fall of the Berlin Wall to the crash of Mr. Bush's approval rating (recall the discussions from Chapters 6 and 14), many of the old assumptions about U.S. world leadership were challenged. The thrill of victory in the Cold War faded quickly into the past. There were signs that serious problems existed in the new order of things. Velvet revolutions in Eastern Europe gave way to bloodshed as nationalist movements and

In 1987, U. S. President Ronald Reagan stood before the Berlin Wall, since 1961 an instrument and symbol of Cold War tensions, and demanded—in a speech given to West Berliners but heard around the world— "General Secretary Gorbachev, if you seek peace, if you seek prosperity. . . if you seek liberalization. . . Mr. Gorbachev, tear down this wall!" Two years later, in November 1989, an economically broken Soviet Union lost its grip on East Germany, and the Wall came tumbling down. By the following year, East Germany had ceased to exist, and the process of German reunification began. On December 25, 1991, the Soviet Union itself disintegrated with Mikhail Gorbachev's resignation. Today, the United States faces the new challenge of dealing effectively with a post-Cold War world.

opportunistic leaders went to war to control pieces of the former Soviet Empire. Boris Yeltsin, the symbol of Russian democracy in 1992, was under serious challenge from his own parliament by 1993. Former Arkansas governor Bill Clinton faced the unenviable challenge of what to do about it all.

The assumptions underlying foreign policy in the old Cold War world did not apply to the new order. What kind of military policy should the United States adopt? What were the goals of foreign aid? How would power be shared in a world with one superpower (the United States), several economic powers, and no great military enemy? To further challenge basic assumptions, many of the threats to world stability now seemed to be coming from small fragmenting democracies rather than, as in the past, from authoritarian and military regimes. As one respected journalist, Thomas Friedman, put it:

> In the post-cold war era, Washington is going to have to wrestle with the complexities of a world governed increasingly by its own values, or at least imitations of its own values. In such a world, America will increasingly have to acknowledge that elected tyrants . . . are scarcely better than unelected ones, and it will have to choose its allies not by choosing between dictators and democrats, or between friends and foes in a cold war, but between so-called democrats and genuine democrats.[5]

Beyond the economic and military questions then, there was perhaps the most difficult question of all: how to promote democracy in a new world of nations with little or no democratic tradition? These issues were enough to make some observers just a touch nostalgic for the Cold War order, where the military role was clear, the economic relations more balanced, and democratic development was measured primarily by the free election of leaders. What does it all add up to for the future of foreign policy? According to Les Aspin, who became secretary of defense in the Clinton administration after serving as one of the leading experts in Congress on foreign and military policy issues: "The emerging world is likely to lack the clarity of the cold war, and to be a more jungle-like world of multiple dangers, hidden traps, unpleasant surprises and moral ambiguities. The old world was good guys and bad guys. The new world is grey guys."[6]

Important challenges lie ahead for U.S. foreign policy in this changing world: How will the loss of an ideological enemy affect the goals of a new foreign policy? How will the military role change, particularly under pressures to reduce spending? How will the debates at home about domestic priorities and a reduced U.S. world role change the politics behind foreign policy? These are the issues that you will encounter in the media for years to come, and they provide the focus for this chapter.

The Rise of the United States as a World Power

Three factors have driven U.S. policy through the nation's periods of greatest foreign expansion:

- a clear ideological sense of purpose, often brought into focus by enemies standing in the way of U.S. goals and ideals;
- economic motives to control raw materials and expand world markets for U.S. goods;
- using the military to police the world to keep the economic and ideological orders intact.

Culture, Ideology, and History

It would be a mistake to underestimate the importance of ideology behind the rise of the United States as one of the most dominant world powers in history. Appealing to deep cultural themes of American exceptionalism and national destiny, grand visions of American world goals were often manufactured long before the nation had the economic or military strength to carry them out. The earliest and most enduring of these visions was the idea of a so-called **manifest destiny** that guided territorial expansion during the nation's first century. The bloody American Indian wars, the war with Mexico, the acquisitions of the Florida, Louisiana, and Alaska territories from their European owners were all driven by leaders convinced that expansion was the destiny of the new nation, populated by a "chosen" people, and governed by a bold democratic design. Unlike the old regimes of Europe, struggling under aristocratic values and half-hearted democracy, this

MONROE DOCTRINE

CLAIMS

U.S.

REPUBLIC OF SANTO DOMINGO

EUROPE

Dalrymple.

COPYRIGHT 1904 BY JUDGE COMPANY PUBLISHERS, 225 FOURTH AVE, NEW YORK

S-1170

HANDS OFF!

This 1905 lithograph caricatures President Theodore Roosevelt enforcing the Monroe Doctrine by defending Santo Domingo (today the Dominican Republic) from "intruding" European nations. At the same time, however, the United States was careful to act in its own best interests throughout the hemisphere. (U. S. Marines occupied the country from 1916 to 1924; and in 1965 Marines—along with peacekeeping forces from five South American nations—again intervened in a domestic revolt.) Relations between Central and Latin America and the United States have commonly been strained at best. In the 1990s, friction points included despotism in Haiti and Cuba, drug interdiction in Peru and Bolivia, and trade relations with Mexico.

"first new nation" would be the example for the future if only it claimed the land and resources to allow its people to prosper.[7]

This sense of destiny motivated the proclamation of the **Monroe Doctrine** by President James Monroe in 1823, declaring the entire Western Hemisphere to be within the American sphere of influence and subject to economic and political development guided by American values. At the time of this bold proclamation, the United States was hardly in a position militarily or economically to do much about affairs beyond its own rapidly expanding borders. Yet when the former Spanish colonies in Latin America launched their wars of independence, the foreign policy thinkers in Washington served notice to the powers of Europe that they should keep their hands off the new nations that were emerging. The rationale was ideological. Monroe stated plainly that the old world of Europe would not continue to export its systems of aristocracy and oppression to the new world of freedom and democracy that was "essentially different" from Europe.[8]

By the 1850s, U.S. business interests began to develop Latin American investments, get involved in their local politics, and stir up trouble by hiring private armies led by soldiers of fortune called "filibusterers." What the business community started was often finished as official U.S. foreign policy, as the government became more involved, either to bail out influential businessmen who had gotten in too deep, or to keep foreign competition out of the region, or both. To date, over one hundred U.S. military incursions and occupations have occurred in Latin America, often resulting in the installation of dictatorial governments whose main virtues were that they were willing to cooperate with Washington and do business on terms favorable to U.S. companies. In a recent variation on this theme, the United States invaded Panama in 1989 to get rid of drug-trafficking dictator Manuel Noriega, who had been helped to power by earlier military and CIA connections, but who later became too erratic to be tolerated.

The standard reasons offered for repeated interventions in the nation's "back yard" were to stabilize turbulent and ungovernable places and bring the virtues of free enterprise and democracy to their peoples. These explanations often served as public relations gestures to accompany foreign policies that were less than idealistic. Here is how Smedley Butler, a Marine general who led many of the early military interventions, summed up his career when he retired:

> I spent thirty-three years and four months in active service as a member of our country's most agile military force—the Marine corps. I served in all the commissioned ranks from a second lieutenant to a major general. And during that period I spent most of my time being a high class muscle-man for Big Business, for Wall Street, and for the bankers. In short, I was a racketeer for capitalism. . . . Thus I helped make Mexico . . . safe for American oil interests in 1914. I helped make Haiti and Cuba a decent place for the National City Bank to collect revenues in . . . I helped purify Nicaragua for the international banking house of Brown Brothers in 1909–1912. I brought light to the Dominican Republic for American sugar interests in 1916. I helped make Honduras "right" for American fruit companies in 1903.[9]

Although their sincerity may be questioned in light of statements like this, ideological claims about freedom, democracy, and peace have always been an important symbolic part of the policy process to win public acceptance of foreign policies. (Recall the importance of cultural symbolism in the policy process discussed in Chapter 17.) Part of the need for strong ideological arguments about foreign policy is that American culture has always contained an undercurrent of opposition to foreign involvements. From the very beginning of the Republic, there have been elements of *isolationism* in the American political culture opposing the expansionist leanings of the *internationalists*. When the internationalists fail to make a strong ideological case for their policies, the isolationists may succeed in making a case for withdrawing from world entanglements and taking care of problems at home. Recall, for example, George Washington's warning in his farewell address to "steer clear of permanent alliances with any portion of the foreign world."[10] Throughout history, however, internationalists in government and business have pushed for rapid American expansion as a world power. Consider, for example, Secretary of State William Seward who purchased Alaska to the consternation of many who condemned it as "Seward's Folly." Seward was clearly engaged by a vision of global power when he promised in 1846 that "I will engage to give you the possession of the American continent and the control of the world."[11]

To this day, versions of the great ideological debate over **internationalism vs. isolationism** continue to be heard in American politics. The nation became divided during the Vietnam War, for example, between advocates who defended intervention in Vietnam as necessary to check Soviet influence and keep the possibility of democratic development alive in the world, and opponents who saw the alliance with the corrupt government of South Vietnam as anything but democratic. Isolationists of the left called for America to "come home" to attend to its domestic problems. More recently, the voices of isolationism were heard in presidential politics. In the 1992 election, Republican primary oppo-

FIGURE 20.1

Military Spending and Budget Deficits, 1970–1991

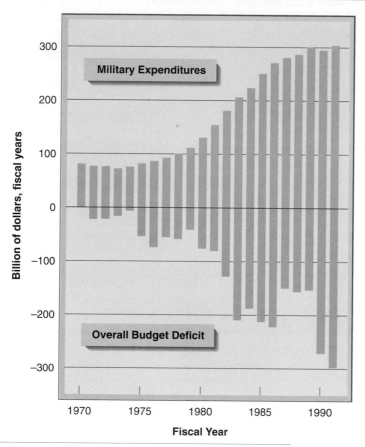

Source: Ruth L. Sivard, *World Military and Social Expenditures, 1991.* Washington, D.C.: World Priorities, 1991, p. 47.

nent Pat Buchanan and independent candidate Ross Perot challenged George Bush's decision to lead a UN coalition against Iraq as a misdirection of national energy and ideals. Perot put the question bluntly: How could the president define a war to liberate what Perot called a "backward monarchy" in Kuwait as a great battle for freedom?

More recent isolationist voices have argued that a military-based foreign policy has become a drag on the national economy. Figure 20.1 illustrates the relationship between military spending and budget deficits in recent years. It is important to remember that increases in military spending do not account for the entire deficit; growth in such entitlements as social security and health care costs (see Chapter 18) have also contributed to budget problems. However, critics cite the high costs of maintaining global military superiority as neither necessary nor practical given today's domestic political needs. Contemporary isolationists also point to economic competitors who are free to invest more of their national wealth in the production of consumer goods, with more positive results for their economies, because of their low military spending. Figure 20.2 shows a

FIGURE 20.2

Military Spending and Manufacturing Productivity:
A Nine-Nation Comparison, 1960–1988

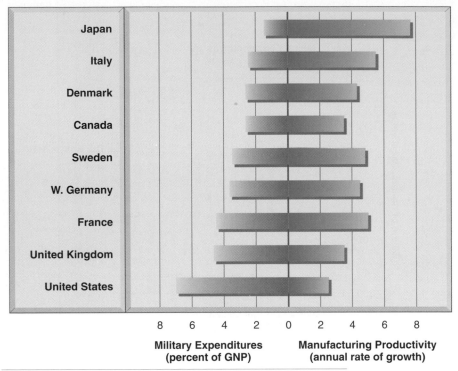

Source: Ruth L Sivard, *World Military and Social Expenditures, 1991.* Washington, D.C.: World Priorities, 1991, p.27.

comparison of military spending and the rate of manufacturing growth in the economies of nine nations.

While it may be more difficult to defend the U.S. military role in the world today as a good economic investment, earlier times saw a clearer connection between military power and economic performance. As is often the case in the life cycle of a great world power, the quest for global military dominance reaped large economic rewards at one time. At the end of this chapter, we will consider a lively academic debate about whether the United States, like many empires before it, is in social and economic decline because of its military burden.

Economic Interests and Military Power

After the territorial push to the Pacific Ocean was completed at the turn of the last century, a great push to step up the global power ladder occurred, launching what historians have called "the American Century." Europe was locked in a massive economic depression, the old colonial powers were losing their grip around the world, and Great Britain was losing its claim as the enforcer of the existing world order. Despite, or perhaps because of, America's own bout with economic depression, leaders in Washington went to war against the weakest of the former European powers, Spain, when an American ship was mysteriously blown up in a Cuban port during Cuba's war for independence from Spanish rule. The Spanish–American War left the United States in possession or control of a string of world ports suitable for expanding its international influence, from Cuba and Puerto Rico in our "back yard" to Hawaii, the Philippines, Wake Island, and Guam across the Pacific. While some historians today see such activities as signs of economic self-interest at work, the national leadership viewed the expansion in terms of an ideological mission to civilize a savage world. Probably the most extreme of the expansionists in Washington was Senator Albert Beveridge, who glorified the Spanish–American War as the destiny of "a conquering race," who must "obey our blood and occupy new markets and if necessary new lands."[12]

Operating behind the scenes at the turn of the century were foreign policy elites like Brooks Adams, advisor to war hero and soon-to-become-president Teddy Roosevelt. Adams saw the chance to take over the world power role of a declining Britain. He proposed a three-step program of laissez-faire industrial growth at home, a new economic ideology of free trade in world markets, and the use of the military as the world's police. Adams' vision came to life in the aggressive Roosevelt, a president who advocated a global police role as an American moral responsibility. Roosevelt sent the American Navy around the world, opening ports to American trade and shipping, while popularizing the new policies at home with such slogans as "walk softly and carry a big stick."[13]

Although the United States stepped forcefully onto the world stage at the turn of the century, several factors stood in the way of economic and military supremacy. To begin with, there was a continuing domestic (isolationist) opposition to becoming a world power. Although isolationist voices are almost always present in U.S. foreign policy debates, they are louder at some times than at others. The toll in lives from American involvement in World War I led to a sobering call to rethink world commitments. In addition, America simply could not dominate a world that still contained a number of rich nations with powerful militaries bent on competing with American markets and alliances. To put it simply, the settlement of World War I was messy, resulting in several antagonistic and uncontrollable power centers: Russia, Germany, and Japan.

This economic and military instability set the stage for what President Franklin Roosevelt would later call the American "rendezvous with destiny"—the refiguring of world power in World War II. The American-led allied victory in World War II was decisive in several ways:

- *On the ideological front*, the victory was over fascist dictators, the kinds of enemies who aroused cultural ideals of freedom and democracy. A figure so evil and easily caricatured as Hitler greatly helped this idealistic cultural definition of the U.S. world mission, and silenced isolationist critics for decades to come. With the onset of the Cold War against the Communists, a new great enemy replaced the old, and critics of American policy were openly persecuted by the government. People often lost their jobs and went to jail for expressing ideological views that did not fit with the nearly religious sense of American destiny to build a world order in the name of freedom and democracy and to defeat the menace of expansionist totalitarian regimes.

- *On the military front*, the second world war accomplished what the first could not: the virtual destruction and demilitarization of America's leading enemies, Germany and Japan, while mobilizing a world network of military alliances strong enough to contain the growth and territorial expansion of the rising new enemy state, the Soviet Union and its satellites.

- Perhaps the greatest breakthrough for world power status came *on the economic front*. The United States emerged from the war as the leading industrial economy, with its factories and farms never touched by war and its business community eager to go out and bind the rest of the globe to American enterprise. The U.S. economy consumed half the planet's raw materials and produced a like proportion of its consumer goods, meaning that the economic dominance of the United States was unchallenged.

Leaving nothing to chance, American foreign policy makers set up a world economic and monetary plan that would rebuild Europe and Japan as the perfect trading partners and establish the U.S. dollar as the world's currency standard for decades to come. American isolationists today still condemn the generosity of the **Marshall Plan** that rebuilt Europe after the war (named for Secretary of State George Marshall of the Truman administration). However, most analysts see that effort, along with the foreign economic and military aid programs since, as policies aimed at creating a world economic order tailored to American interests. The cultural roots of this enduring debate after World War II between the isolationists and the internationalists are described in "Inside the System" Box 20.1.

Despite its economic advantages, the world order that followed World War II was not an easy one. Although the Soviet Union and the United States were allies in defeating Hitler, the alliance fell apart soon after the war, when the two great powers took opposite sides in a fierce battle for world domination. Although the next forty years would see many small wars fought in third-world nations, the superpowers themselves did not go to war, perhaps because the stakes were so high in the age of nuclear weapons. Despite the peace between the superpowers, the tensions ran high, and the brink of war was reached on several occasions. Most of the people on the planet lived with the constant threat of global conflict spurred by ideological, economic, and military differences, thus giving the era its historic name, the **Cold War**.

The Cold War

Although they had been enemies since a Bolshevik coup took Russia out of the capitalist sphere in late 1917, the Soviets and the Americans formed an alliance of convenience to defeat Hitler in World War II. The simple reality when the fighting stopped was that Russian troops occupied huge sections of East and Central Europe, from Poland and eastern Germany through Czechoslovakia to the Baltic states of Latvia, Lithuania, and Estonia. At the historic conference held at Yalta, the spoils of war were divided by the three powers who would soon force Germany's surrender: Stalin represented the Soviet Union, Churchill headed the British delegation, and Roosevelt spoke for the United States. There were promises of free elections, and agreement to create an organization called the United Nations. Yet underneath the appearance of agreement were the hard realities of power: the Soviets controlled great chunks of new territory, and Roosevelt could not accept the idea of starting a new war to push them back to their old borders. Roosevelt and Churchill probably left Yalta knowing that free elections would never be held, and that the hope for a world of peacefully "united nations" was a fleeting dream. Within months of the war's end, Communist governments were installed in the Soviet-occupied lands, and a dangerous civil war erupted in Greece between pro- and anti-Communist forces.[14]

Within a year after the end of the war, Churchill came to the United States to lobby for a more aggressive military response to Soviet expansion. He warned in a speech in Fulton, Missouri, that an "iron curtain" had descended across the world, and that the growth of Communism presented a terrible threat to world peace and the idea of democracy:

INSIDE THE SYSTEM

The Great Cultural Debate: Was Rebuilding the World Economy After World War II Self-Interest or Foolish Generosity?

Isolationists and internationalists continue to debate the wisdom of rebuilding the economies of former enemies such as Germany and Japan after the Second World War. Today, those nations are the chief economic rivals of the United States. However, for decades, American banking and business reaped huge profits from the economic order created by the settlement of the war and by the foreign policy that came afterwards. Isolationists continue to argue that the terms offered to the former enemies were far too generous. However, many internationalists now contend that, if anything, the problem of the post-war economic reconstruction may have been that the world was so geared to American business that decades passed without U.S. industry having to be innovative or highly competitive in order to make profits. Meanwhile, Japan and Germany developed sophisticated products and industries out of the need for sheer survival in a world economy so tailored to U.S. interests.

Many foreign policy experts who look beyond this cultural debate say that the real economic burden attached to the post-war order was the enormous military expense of holding it together. While the American economy became the leading producer of high-tech weapons of war, the demilitarized allies turned to making better toasters, televisions, cars, and VCRs. The ultimate price paid for winning the Cold War may have been an economy geared to produce military products of little value to consumers, at the same time that American workers and consumers were taxed to pay for the world's police force. In this view, the greatest challenge to American power in the new world order is economic stagnation.

Defining a new foreign policy will be politically challenging, particularly if growing numbers of the public and their opinion leaders favor turning inward as a nation. It is significant that conservatives such as Pat Buchanan and populists such as Ross Perot have won large followings with isolationist arguments to withdraw from a world military role and return to more protectionist trade practices. The heated debates on the North American Free Trade Agreement (NAFTA) illustrate the resurgence of cultural conflict between isolationists and internationalists.

Internationalist politicians from both parties have felt the sting of a more inward-oriented public at home. George Bush's considerable foreign policy activities ended up counting for little among voters in the 1992 election. Despite the public resistance, internationalist elites of both liberal and conservative stripes continued to push for something similar to a Marshall Plan to rebuild the former Soviet Empire to fit into the Western economic system. However, Bill Clinton was reluctant to promote that idea over his more popular proposals to rebuild the American economy. All of which suggests that while foreign policy may be driven primarily by *elite* political pressures, it has been historically important to create *majoritarian* support for symbols that overcome the isolationist tendencies in the political culture.

20.1

An iron curtain has descended across the continent. Behind that line lie all the capitals of the ancient states of Central and Eastern Europe . . . [A]ll the famous cities and populations around them lie in the Soviet sphere and are all subject in one form or another, not only to Soviet influence but to a very high and increasing measure of control from Moscow.[15]

Churchill wanted to confront the Soviets militarily, but many in America opposed this course as too risky.

As master of the Soviet Union from 1924 to 1953, Joseph Stalin was the center of an unparalleled "cult of personality" (in Nikita Khrushchev's words) and one of the most brutal despots in world history. During his reign, millions of Stalin's fellow citizens perished in forced-labor camps or starved in famines that had been deliberately induced in an attempt to coerce collectivization, industrialization, and the subordination of various ethnic minorities. The United States formed an uneasy alliance with the Soviet Union against Nazi aggression during World War II, but cessation of those hostilities led immediately into the Cold War, as the Soviet Union's "Iron Curtain" (in Winston Churchill's celebrated phrase) cut off Central European nations from their neighbors. (The portrait above Stalin's head is of Karl Marx.)

In that same year, the State Department's top Soviet expert proposed another course of action that was to become accepted as a doctrine for the next four decades. George F. Kennan sent a famous telegram from Moscow that he later published under the pseudonym "X" as an article in the influential journal *Foreign Affairs*. Kennan's **containment doctrine** advocated matching Soviet expansion with force at every point of weakness. In addition, cultivating friendly governments and leaders would make the Soviet Union's attempts to expand its influence as costly as possible. Out of Kennan's doctrine came a global network of military treaties and alliances (for example, the North Atlantic Treaty Organization, or NATO, and the Southeast Asia Treaty Organization, SEATO) that permitted U.S. military bases to be built around the world, and provided for military responses to Communist aggression.

In 1947, President Harry Truman delivered an historic speech to Congress that translated many of the ideas of containment into specific military and economic policy proposals. Truman proposed a strategy for stopping Communism and advancing the ideological goals of democracy through programs of military and economic assistance to governments such as the one in Greece that was fighting against Communist aggression. This use of military and economic assistance to promote democracy and contain Communism became know as the **Truman Doctrine,** and influenced the policies of every president for the next forty years.

At the same time, Secretary of State George Marshall announced his above-mentioned plan for the economic recovery of Europe. The **Marshall Plan** poured billions of dollars into rebuilding the shattered economies of the continent and integrating former enemy nations into a trading community designed to produce greater interdependence and more open markets. Not only were strong economies regarded as the best defense against Communist advances, but, as noted above, the plan gave the U.S. a strong say in designing the political and economic institutions of the new Europe. Rebuilding Germany and tying it to the world economy was regarded as a necessary step to encourage U.S. business investment abroad. Although the costs of sustaining this order were great, so were the economic benefits in the early years. By the end of the Cold War in the late 1980s, however, the share of world energy and manufacturing exports had declined in relation to the costs of maintaining world military superiority. Figure 20.3 compares the U.S. world position on a number of dimensions at the height of the Cold War in 1960 with the situation near the end of the Cold War in 1988.

The final hallmark of Cold War foreign policy was the creation of a vast bureaucracy, sometimes called the *national security state*, to gather intelligence, develop strategies, and counter enemy initiatives, often with a great deal of secrecy. Although President Truman was personally uncomfortable with the possibility that the Cold War could become a cloak-and-dagger operation in which policies were made and kept secret from the people, he signed the **National Security Act of 1947.** This legislation created the **Central Intelligence Agency** and the **National Security Council** (NSC), in the words of the law, to "advise the President with respect to the integration of domestic, foreign, and military policies relating to the national security."[16]

FIGURE 20.3

The United States in the World Economy, 1960 and 1988

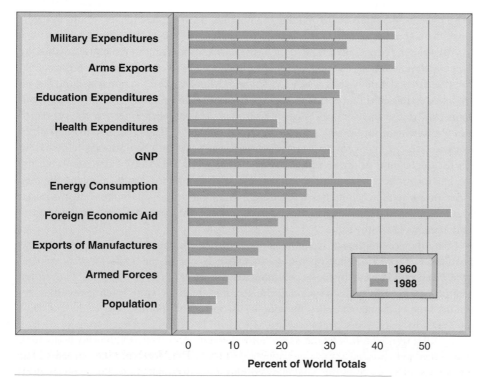

Source: Ruth L. Sivard, *World Military and Social Expenditures, 1991*. Washington, D.C.: World Priorities, 1991, p. 46.

Foreign Policy in the National Security State

The law provided that the regular members of the National Security Council (NSC) would include the president as chair, the vice president, the secretary of state, secretary of defense, the director of the CIA, and the chairman of the Joint Chiefs of Staff. Different presidents have invited other aides to attend meetings, including the attorney general, the secretary of the treasury, the ambassador to the United Nations, and the director of the Agency for International Development, among others. Although the NSC is an advisory body, some presidents have used it as a policy council that often preempted the State Department and other foreign policy bodies, resulting in the making of policy in secret, as described in Chapter 15. Some observers argue that the National Security Act of 1947 (and its various amendments since then) created a secret government with the power to make important foreign policy decisions without the knowledge of the American people or their representatives in Congress.

Congress was intended to be a full constitutional partner in foreign policy. On paper at least, the various National Security Acts passed since 1947 have set up formal procedures to keep Congress informed. However, the small number of people involved with NSC activities and the legal secrecy granted to the intelligence agencies have made it possible for presidents to take many actions without fully informing or consulting Congress.[17] During the early 1980s, for example, President Ronald Reagan authorized the CIA to place mines in the harbors of Nicaragua without fully briefing Congress. Toward the end of the Reagan administration, some members of the NSC staff sold weapons to Iran and used the funds to support a counterrevolutionary or *contra* army fighting a war against the pro-Soviet, Sandinista government of Nicaragua. This so-called Iran-*contra* affair was a serious action because Congress had officially rejected presidential requests for military support to the *contras*. Although no evidence linked the president directly to those policies, the secrecy surrounding the national security state makes it hard to determine just where the authorization (if any) for such acts actually came from.

Although the Senate investigated the Iran-*contra* scandal and found abuses within the Reagan administration, the general conclusion was that it would be hard to reform a national security system based on secrecy. This is how one reporter summarized the Senate (Tower Commission) report that concluded the investigation, "Any attempt to tell Presidents how to use the National Security Council . . . would either destroy the system or lead Presidents to set up new systems to circumvent it."[18] Thus the fundamental problem with secrecy in government remained much the same as when Thomas Jefferson, in his 1801 Inaugural Address, warned against "entangling alliances." No matter what the reasons for it, secrecy contains the potential to subvert democracy by allowing the misuse of power to hide behind possible threats to national security. Despite concerns raised by national leaders following the Iran-*contra* scandal, the basic structure of the security state remains much the same.

Using the dual threats of Communism and nuclear war as their reasons, some presidents moved foreign policy operations increasingly out of the State Department and away from public view. In the Nixon administration, as noted in Chapter 14, even the meetings of the NSC, which included the secretary of state, were often formalities, revealing little of the actual policy thinking of the president and his closest advisers. During the early Nixon years, great power was wielded by Nixon's national security advisor, Henry Kissinger, who functioned as a shadow secretary of state until he eventually took that office and restored somewhat greater visibility to the foreign policy process. The way in which Nixon used the NSC allowed him great personal control over policy decisions, and, as Kissinger himself noted, gave him the power to "bypass the delays and sometimes opposition of the departments."[19] As a result, the Nixon administration was able to back a coup in Chile and conduct secret bombings of Cambodia during the Vietnam War without public debate or approval of those policies.

By contrast, the Bush administration used the NSC more in its original advisory and debate role, while giving considerable foreign policy initiative to Secretary of State James Baker, a trusted friend and political advisor to the president. Although Mr. Bush gained a reputation as a world traveler and foreign policy president, much of the daily business of policy formulation was handled by a team that included the secretary of state and the National Security Council staff.

Whether highly personalized or more bureaucratized, the foreign policy process during much of the Cold War was centered in the national security state with the president as chief policy maker. There were various reasons for granting the president so much power and secrecy. It is clear, however, that the single most important consideration was the constant threat of nuclear war, which provided a strong rationale for the nation to speak with a single voice, to act with a single resolve, and to have just one finger on the nuclear launch button.

The Great Nuclear Poker Game

The great strategic calculation in the Cold War was that the threat of massive nuclear retaliation was the best insurance against the other side starting a war. Both sides adopted this logic and entered a staggering nuclear arms race that cost the economies of the United States and the Soviet Union dearly. In the end, the Soviet economy collapsed, in part due to the insupportable costs of the arms race. For several decades, however, the world sweated under a "balance of terror" engineered by the two great superpowers. The two sides achieved a state of *mutual assured destruction*, with the appropriate acronym MAD, meaning that each could "survive a first strike and still respond with a rain of fire upon the other's great cities."[20]

Many times during this period the world came close to the brink of war, but never closer than during the Cuban missile crisis in 1962 when photos from U.S. spy planes showed that the Soviets were building missile installations aimed at U.S. targets from just ninety miles off the Florida shores. President Kennedy demanded the removal of the missiles. Carefully picking his words, Kennedy used the ambiguous term "quarantine" to describe his policy of sending navy warships to prevent Soviet ships from bringing military supplies to Cuba. A more traditional description of that policy would have been a "naval blockade," something that it is often considered an act of war. The world waited out a tense situation that was later described pithily by Secretary of State Dean Rusk: "We were eyeball to eyeball, and the other fellow just blinked."[21] As this dramatic view suggests, the Soviets at last agreed publicly to withdraw their missiles. In a little-reported behind-the-scenes negotiation, the Americans also agreed privately to withdraw missiles in Turkey that were aimed at Soviet cities from a similarly close range. This sort of brinkmanship inevitably gave Cold War foreign policy the personal signatures of the presidents in charge and led many observers to conclude that foreign policy was fundamentally different in nature from domestic policies.

Making Foreign Policy in the Cold War World _____

The foreign policy of the United States during much of the Cold War was so closely identified with the president that some political scientists not only claimed that there were two presidencies (a foreign policy president and a domestic policy president, as discussed in Chapter 14), but concluded that foreign policy was fundamentally different from domestic decisions in terms of the participants and the distribution of power. While there remains some truth to these generalizations today, many observers say that foreign policies have come more to resemble domestic political battles, full of interest group lobbying, bureaucratic resistance, and congressional partisan politics. Perhaps the place to begin understanding this transformation of foreign policy in recent years is to recognize that the early years of the Cold War were characterized by extremely high levels of consensus among politicians and business elites on what the ideological purpose, the economic goals, and the military objectives of American policy should be.

Ideological Consensus and Presidential Leadership

Despite, or perhaps because of, the hostility between the superpowers during the early decades of the Cold War, there was a strong consensus among powerful elites about the American world role. This does not mean that everyone agreed on every policy. Indeed, there were those who favored more or less aggressive military postures, more or less economic aid to developing countries, and more or less support for undemocratic but friendly regimes. The tendency, however, was for influential members of Congress, the executive branch, and the business community to agree that the broad goals of foreign policy were to develop and deploy a strong military to stop the spread of Communism, while expanding world markets for U.S. business. Consensus on these goals made it easier for presidents to emerge as foreign policy leaders.

Because they presented policies to the nation and represented the country to the world, the focus of political attention, of course, was on the presidents. The press and more than a few scholars even promoted the idea of an "imperial presidency" to explain how presidents were often able to pronounce their own foreign policy doctrines, speak for the entire nation at summit conferences, and sign important executive agreements without the approval of Congress. While presidents in the 1950s and 1960s did make many key decisions and convince others to accept them, the idea of an imperial presidency surely overstated the powers that individual presidents actually wielded. It makes more sense to say that presidential leadership was strengthened in this period because large numbers of influential elites operating behind the scenes agreed on the basic directions of presidential actions. Few presidents dared to act without first consulting the members of this **foreign policy establishment.**

The Foreign Policy Establishment

The circle of experts responsible for developing and carrying out foreign policy was fairly small. These specialists in economic and military affairs were accustomed to crossing each other's paths often as they floated in and out of Washington jobs. Academic experts often became influential because they received the backing of prominent business elites who promoted foreign policies inside the political parties. As both the political parties came to accept the ideology of anticommunism and the economic doctrines of free trade, the level of disagreement in these circles dropped compared to the conflicts often found among experts on domestic policy issues.

Roughly one third of the Cold War policy establishment were career civil servants who moved through the ranks at the State Department or moved from high-level military posts into advisory jobs at the National Security Council. At the highest levels, these officials became authors of memos and analyses that inspired policy doctrines, such as George F. Kennan and his doctrine of containment. The other two thirds of the establishment were from business, banking, law, and academia, with the great majority coming from business and law. They floated in and out of government jobs as administrations changed and presidents called them to serve in important posts. Many of these establishment figures served in more than one top job. For example, before George Bush became

President Richard Nixon with Henry Kissinger, who served first as his national security advisor (1969–1972) and then as Secretary of State (1973–1977) under both Nixon and Gerald Ford. Kissinger was a practitioner of Realpolitik, *the doctrine that a nation's interests are best served not by idealistic pursuits (such as human-rights campaigns) but by the cool calculation of its strategic needs. This doctrine led Nixon, long an ardent anti-Communist, first to a policy of* détente *with the Soviet Union, and then, in February 1972, to an astonishing and historic visit to Beijing, where he met with Chinese Communist party leaders Mao Zedong and Zhou Enlai.*

vice president and eventually president, he was director of the CIA. Before that, he was special presidential envoy to China after Richard Nixon and his Secretary of State Henry Kissinger opened up diplomatic relations to China after decades of Cold War chill. When Ronald Reagan appointed William J. Casey as director of the CIA, he tapped a member of the establishment who had alternated his business and law careers in the private sector with stints as chair of the Securities and Exchange Commission, undersecretary of state for economic affairs, and president of the Export–Import Bank, among other posts.

Prominent business executives made up one of the largest groups in the establishment. A number of secretaries of state were formerly top executives at such corporations as General Motors (Charles Wilson, 1953–1957), Procter & Gamble (Neil McElroy, 1957–1959), Morgan Guaranty Trust (Thomas Gates, 1959–1960), and Ford Motor Company (Robert McNamara, 1961–1967), among others.[22] The other leading group in the establishment came from top New York and Washington law firms specializing in international business, banking, and government dealings. Secretaries of state who came from insider law firms included Dean Acheson (1949–1953), John Foster Dulles (1953–1959), William P. Rogers (1969–1973), and Cyrus Vance (1977–1980).[23]

The remainder of the establishment came primarily from universities and foundations, including such figures as Harvard dean McGeorge Bundy, MIT economic history professor Walt Rostow, Harvard government professor Henry Kissinger, and Columbia government professor Zbigniew Brzezinski, all of whom became national security advisors to different presidents. While such figures had their differences of opinion and sought to leave their individual marks on world affairs, their policies were characterized by much higher levels of agreement than would be the case among domestic policy officials for opposing Democratic and Republican administrations.

Given the importance of this establishment in foreign policy thinking during the Cold War, it is probably an exaggeration to say that presidents forged their own personal foreign policies in an "imperial" manner, and more accurate to say that presidents surrounded themselves with establishment advisors, weighed their inputs, made the final decisions, and stepped forward to represent those policies to the public and the world. Thus, presidential prominence in the Cold War era was important in symbolic and leadership terms, lending credibility and authority to the dominant views of business and academic experts. As one scholar concluded about the policies of presidents Truman, Eisenhower, Kennedy, Johnson, Nixon, Ford, Carter, and Reagan (the Cold War presidents):

> Over the course of forty-three years, none of these presidents ever strayed outside the fairly narrow range that constituted mainstream American foreign policy. . . . Each came to understand, master, and accept the complex but coherent vision of internationalism toward which [American] power was pushing and pulling the world system. Republicans and Democrats, pragmatists, and ideologies . . . for all, continuity rather than discontinuity marked the presidential changings of the guard. And, more than any other variable, it was the presence and power of that foreign policy elite . . . that accounted for that striking stability.[24]

Within the bounds of this elite policy consensus, particular presidents did leave their marks on the world. Eisenhower steered a course through the Korean War and the Suez crisis and left office warning of the "military industrial complex." Kennedy handled the Cuban missile crisis, visited Berlin after the wall was built, and inspired the cry for freedom around the world. Johnson pushed containment to its outer limits with the controversial war in Vietnam. Nixon drove a wedge between former Communist allies China and the Soviet Union when he developed a separate China policy. Carter promoted the idea of worldwide human rights. Reagan and Bush used massive military spending and a series of regional wars to break the Soviet Union's economy and bring its leaders to the negotiating table. Yet all of this leadership occurred within a fairly strong degree of consensus about what the American mission was in the world and what kinds of policies would best advance that mission. This consensus also helps to explain the generally low profile of other players in the Cold War policy processes: Congress, interest groups, and the public.

Congress, the Interests, and the Public

In earlier chapters, the importance of interest groups, public opinion, and congressional power in making policy have all been noted. While these factors have all grown more important in the foreign policy of recent years, the Cold War era was notable for its lack of consistent domestic conflict over foreign policy issues. It was not until the protests and congressional actions involving Vietnam, as discussed below, that foreign policy showed the first signs of becoming more like domestic affairs.

The low profile of players outside the executive branch in Cold War foreign policy must be understood as the result of several factors:

- *Ideological consensus*: At the height of the Cold War, there was substantial agreement about the threat of Communism, and those who challenged U.S. foreign policies often ran the risk of having their patriotism questioned. Citizens found few sources of information in the mainstream press that were critical of establishment views. Members of Congress who challenged establishment policies found little support within the institution or from voters.

- *Domestic benefits of foreign policy*: The first two decades of the Cold War saw unprecedented economic prosperity at home. Interest groups ranging from business and trade associations to labor unions shared in these rewards. Stable world markets for American products meant high corporate profits and high-paying union jobs at home.

- *Key domestic political actors were members of the establishment*. Business and labor leaders were part of the establishment. They were consulted directly in the formation of foreign policy and invited to participate in government programs abroad. Thus, many groups that might be in opposition on domestic issues were invited into the foreign policy process itself, making them political partners in the establishment.

Public opinion was highly supportive of foreign policy activities throughout this period, suggesting that policies were in some sense "representative."[25] However, it is likely that public opinion more often followed than led the consensus of national elites during this period. Politicians and business leaders frequently mobilized information campaigns to sell their policies to a generally uninformed and often frightened public. In one of the classic studies of Cold War policy, political scientist Bernard Cohen interviewed government policy makers who generally said they were not strongly influenced by public opinion. They tended to see their role as educating the public and mobilizing opinion to support their policies.[26] While elites and the national press did their share of propagandizing during the Cold War, public opinion was not entirely plastic and malleable. People responded to events such as the divisive Vietnam War and to such economic changes as the gradual loss of power in the world market. By the mid-1970s, these shifts in public support were not lost on elites, who for reasons of their own were becoming equally troubled and divided by policy failures and economic problems. The elite policy establishment began to fall apart, and changes appeared in the policy process itself.

The Domestication of the Foreign Policy Process

Although the president and the national security agencies remain the key players in making foreign policy, power is more dispersed today than at any time since before World War II. In addition to more actors weighing into the process, there are more disagreements about what the nation's military, economic, and foreign aid policies should be. Increasingly, in the view of many experts, foreign policy is coming to resemble domestic politics, with Congress and the president often in conflict, policy battles reaching the public through media coverage, and the balance on close issues often being tipped by interest groups and public opinion. Signs of the domestication of foreign policy date back to the Vietnam War and grew during the 1970s and 1980s.

Vietnam and the Breakdown of Consensus

Vietnam was a watershed in foreign policy making. Before the domestic upheaval surrounding that war, the division of power in foreign policy was described like this in a popular foreign policy textbook:

> For the first two decades after World War II Congress was largely content to leave the management of foreign relations to the executive branch—thereby providing impetus for the emergence of the imperial presidency; when it did play a significant role in foreign relations, Congress normally supported the diplomatic policies and programs advocated by the White House.[27]

After Vietnam, according to congressional scholar David Rohde, foreign policy became an increasingly partisan affair, beginning with the split within the Democratic party over Vietnam itself and growing into partisan conflicts over many fundamental questions of economic and military policy. Rohde notes, for example, that in 1991 when President Bush asked for congressional support to use force against Iraq following the invasion of Kuwait, he won approval from both chambers, but the measure was challenged by a

In this 1970 photograph, U. S. servicemen patrol a South Vietnamese jungle area only ten miles from the Cambodian border. The Vietnam War, spanning the administrations of U.S. presidents Kennedy, Johnson, and Nixon, proved to be one of the most politically divisive conflicts in American history.

close vote in the Senate and opposed by two-thirds of the Democrats in the House, a far cry from the unanimous House vote of both parties in 1964 authorizing Lyndon Johnson to take action against North Vietnam.[28]

American society was badly divided over the war in Vietnam. Protesters filled the streets and occupied buildings on college campuses. Public opinion became divided between pro and antiwar sentiments. Even the Democratic party, whose leaders presided over the war, was split. The 1968 election saw strong challenges to the incumbent president, Lyndon Johnson, by antiwar candidates Eugene McCarthy and Robert Kennedy. Although Johnson made a dramatic announcement that he would not run again, the Democratic convention in Chicago that summer turned violent. Thousands of protesters demonstrated outside while the party nominated an establishment politician (and Johnson's vice president), Hubert Humphrey, inside. Humphrey was identified with the war, and the antiwar movement expressed outrage over the "undemocratic" methods used to select party candidates. The Chicago police under orders from Mayor Richard Daley attacked the demonstrators and made mass arrests while the nation watched the scenes of violence on their television sets. Such respected news personalities as Walter Cronkite denounced the violence. Meanwhile, the nightly news carried disturbing stories from the war front halfway around the world, suggesting that the battle was going badly and that the troops suffered low morale. Many members of the public began to believe that government officials had been lying to them.

In a rare and unsettling loss of faith in the establishment, the nation was consumed with debate about its foreign policy. For many people, "the establishment" became a dirty word symbolizing what was wrong with American democracy. By the end of the 1960s, Vietnam had raised fundamental questions about the whole framework of U.S. foreign policy and how it was made. As public division grew, and the news media became more critical, Congress became more active in trying to reclaim its lost foreign policy powers.

A series of resolutions and laws were passed in efforts to get the executive to return more of the foreign policy initiative to Congress. In 1969, the National Commitments resolution was passed, urging presidents to tell Congress when they entered into agreements and diplomatic or military arrangements with other nations. This was later formalized as the Case Act in 1972, requiring the executive to notify Congress of all international agreements within sixty days after they had been made. That such an act was required at all suggests the degree to which foreign policy had become removed from Congress.

In 1970, Congress repealed the Gulf of Tonkin resolution that had given the president authorization to expand the Vietnam War in 1964. The War Powers Act of 1973 required presidents to notify Congress of any troop deployment within forty-eight hours, and it placed a sixty-day limit on any presidential commitment of troops to combat without specific authorization from Congress. Since 1973 there have been twenty-five notifications of Congress, but only one case when a president came close to having a military action called back. Ronald Reagan's decision to send a peacekeeping force to Lebanon in 1983 was given an eighteen-month limit by Congress. However, the troops were brought home sooner due to the bombing of a Marine barracks which claimed many lives and raised public doubts about the wisdom of getting involved in Lebanon's civil war.

All of these post-Vietnam legislative actions were aimed at reasserting basic constitutional powers that had been usurped by presidents under the rationales of Cold War consensus, national security, and secrecy. It appeared to many observers that Congress was slowly reasserting the formal divisions of power between the two branches of government that were always clearly spelled out in the Constitution. Table 20.1 reviews the constitutional divisions of power that affect foreign policy decisions.

Searching for New Doctrines

With the rule of the establishment challenged openly and the old Cold War doctrines under fire, foreign policy began to take on a more partisan look. Henry Kissinger came to Washington to become President Nixon's national security advisor and helped formulate a new doctrine of **détente,** a French word meaning "relaxation," as in relaxation of confrontation. Kissinger and Nixon reasoned that it no longer made sense to see the world as a battlefield of good against evil, with Communism as an enemy that had to be defeated at every turn. Other countries, even Communist ones, had a right to exist, *as long as American interests were respected*. This philosophy, termed the **Nixon Doctrine,** guided Nixon administration foreign policy in opening relations with China for the first time since World War II, and it stimulated nuclear arms limitation talks.

Not everyone was enamored of the idea of détente. The "cold warriors" from the old establishment attached themselves to conservative politicians such as Ronald Reagan,

TABLE 20.1

The Formal Foreign Policy Powers According to the Constitution

The President:

1. commands the armed forces
2. makes treaties (with approval of the Senate)
3. appoints ambassadors and other executive branch officials (with approval of the Senate)
4. receives ambassadors from other countries

The Congress:

1. declares war (by a joint action of the House and Senate)
2. the Senate approves treaties, ambassadors, and executive branch appointments
3. funds requests for foreign aid and other international expenses
4. raises, funds, and oversees the military

SOURCE: The U.S. Constitution.

who warned of the dangers of taking Communism too lightly. When Reagan became president in 1981, he talked of an "evil empire," and restored policies of confrontation in various world hot spots while winning unprecedented peacetime increases in military budgets. Following the period of détente in the Nixon and early Carter years, the resumption of old confrontation and containment policies under the **Reagan Doctrine** was labeled Cold War II by some scholars.[29]

Despite voting for his military budgets, Congress challenged Ronald Reagan on several foreign policy initiatives, including the war against the Sandinista government of Nicaragua and support for regimes in El Salvador and Guatemala that abused the human rights of their own people. By contrast, when pre-Vietnam presidents used the CIA to topple unfriendly regimes or support military governments, there had been relatively little opposition from the public, Congress, or the media.

Not only were the military and strategic aims of foreign policy subject to more heated debate and public disagreement, but economic policies began to be questioned as well. For the first time since World War II, U.S. world economic domination was challenged by the growing economies of Europe and Asia. A world oil cartel began setting energy prices in the early 1970s, further disrupting the domestic economy. Long-accepted Keynesian economic theories (explained in Chapter 19) were not adequate for solving economic problems such as simultaneous inflation and lack of growth. For the first time since both political parties became dominated by advocates of free international trade, prominent Democratic and Republican voices argued for protective tariffs and formal agreements with trading partners. Free trade was no longer accepted as economic doctrine by an establishment elite.[30] As political scientist I. M. Destler explains, "Trade politics has become more partisan. The elite has grown less committed to liberal trade. Intellectual challenges to open market policies have grown. Patterns of trade politics have become more complex. All these changes have weakened the old system for . . . managing trade policy pressures."[31] In these important respects, the foreign policy process was coming to look more and more like domestic politics, for better or worse.

A Policy Breakdown?

A sure sign that the politics of foreign policy was changing came when the media, public opinion, and Congress all challenged George Bush's carefully crafted China policy in 1989. Millions of Americans watched as the Chinese army brutally put down a student democracy movement that had created a world television stage in Beijing's Tiananmen Square. The president argued that good relations with China were more important than intruding into that nation's domestic politics. However, public opinion did not respond to the president's arguments, as the media continued to dramatize the death of the Chinese democracy movement. On its own initiative, Congress introduced measures to create trade sanctions against China and to prevent the deportation of Chinese students studying in the United States. Although President Bush eventually regained the initiative on both of those measures (while sending a secret delegation to reassure Chinese leaders), his leadership was challenged openly by partisan opponents and interest groups in ways that probably would not have happened even a decade before.[32]

In almost every area of foreign policy today, observers note the rise of interest groups lobbying for trade restrictions, price subsidies, special sanctions for nations with human rights problems, and many other particular policies. One account laments that the fall of the Cold War establishment left a power vacuum in foreign policy that has been filled by "narrow lobbies and pressure groups rather than an enlightened citizenry. . . . Worse still, these lobbies and pressure groups represent no underlying consensus but only their own separate interests. American foreign policy, once the realm of the Gods, had become the domain of mere influence peddlers."[33]

Domesticating Foreign Policy?

With the Cold War's end, the thrust of 1990s U. S. foreign policy seems to have turned from national security concerns toward economic self-interest. House Majority Leader Dick Gephardt (*above*) broke with President Clinton over the North American Free Trade Agreement (NAFTA), despite its hope for reinforcing open trade and multilateral ties, because of the alleged threat to U.S. unions and low-skill workers. Economic topics also took top priority at a 1993 summit of heads of the major industrialized nations (*below*). Clinton national security advisor Anthony Lake (*right*), a former Kissinger aide and Carter-era official, is known for espousing a non-ideological pragmatism. Yet one hazard of a semi-isolationist, protectionist stance, cautioned the centrist *New Republic* magazine, could be "an America looking inward rather than outward, governed by fear instead of reason."

The Players

Tanks crush the May–June 1989 civilian rebellion (led primarily by students) against the communist rulers of China. Inspired originally by a visit from Soviet leader Mikhail Gorbachev (who was then enacting far-reaching reforms inside his own country), the Chinese people's demonstrations soon turned into pro-democracy rallies attended by hundreds of thousands. On June 3–4, armored personnel carriers attacked participants in Beijing's Tienanmen Square, killing or injuring thousands. U. S. President George Bush—at one time the U. S. liaison to China—was criticized for not taking a strong stand on these events; since then, however, President Clinton has also found it difficult to follow a clear and productive China policy. Beijing's aging communist bureaucracy has historically acted with famously little regard to "outside interference."

Political scientist John Tierney concludes that the growing number of players in the foreign policy game has introduced chaos in many policy outcomes. The future may well see the kind of bargaining and compromising over international issues that characterizes many domestic policy areas. All of which may make the restoration of congressional power in foreign policy a mixed blessing, complicating the daily political lives of members of Congress, and, in the view of one observer, "making them long if not for retirement then at least for a return to the days of the imperial presidency."[34]

In place of an establishment debating and setting the guidelines on foreign policy, the new era finds its intellectuals in rows of Washington think tanks—research institutes set up to develop, publicize, and promote policies of every ideological stripe. The experts in these think tanks make their livings by becoming attached to politicians and identified on television talk shows and news programs with particular policy proposals. Far from consensus among the elites, the new era is more often characterized by intense disagreements among corporate heads, partisan politicians, and the new breed of foreign policy media personalities.[35]

Where does this leave the executive in the foreign policy picture? Still the key player, the president must now steer a more careful course than ever before and build consensus on many issues that would not have been contested at all in previous times. The loss of a clear world enemy means that every situation must be evaluated independently. Decisions to get involved in humanitarian efforts in Africa, or conflicts in the Middle East, or civil wars in the former Soviet bloc all contain personal political risks for presidents who must build coalitions of support for those actions. The political risks may be even greater in areas of trade and economic aid policies because Congress is increasingly moved by pressures from voters who demand attention to problems at home and by organized interests that have agendas of their own. All of these issues are further complicated by short-term political conditions such as presidential popularity, presidential relations with Congress, and presidential leadership within the bureaucracy.[36] After President Bush negotiated a trade agreement with Canada and Mexico, he declined to try to push it through Congress because of his weakened domestic political situation coming into the 1992 election. Bill Clinton also delayed action on the agreement because of his difficulty in lining up the domestic political support. In short, the **domestication of foreign policy** makes it difficult for a president to speak clearly for the nation. Nowhere is this breakdown of policy consensus felt more clearly than in attempts to work out a national defense policy for the new world order.

Defense: A Solution Looking for a Problem? _____

A military map of the world at the end of the Cold War shows a planet bristling with armaments and studded with flashpoints of potential military confrontation around shipping routes, oil fields, resource-rich nations, and borders between Communist and non-Communist powers. In 1990, the United States had more than 300 military installations from radar posts to full-scale air force, navy, and army bases around the world. More than 500,000 military personnel, out of a total of just over two million, were stationed abroad (350,000 in Europe, 150,000 in Asia and the Pacific). With a 600-ship navy, great battle fleets sailed every ocean, participating in military exercises with allies, and reminding foes of the 24-hour-a-day possibility of retaliation if they broke the rules of a world order largely governed by U.S. foreign policies.

The military establishment was the cornerstone of foreign policy, giving diplomatic initiatives credibility in the minds of strategic thinkers. This military profile was presented to the American people and the world as a defensive shield, to deter enemy aggression and to protect democratic freedoms in other nations. Critics often claimed, however, that the military had become too dominant in foreign policy calculations, replacing diplomacy, and offering a blunt but expedient means of whipping wayward countries into shape.

FIGURE 20.4

Defense Spending, 1945–1995

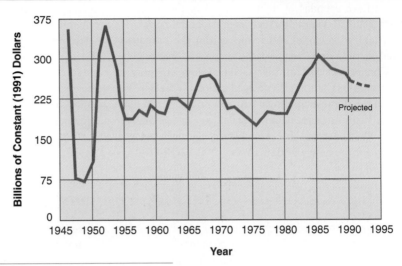

Source: *The Economic and Budget Outlook: Fiscal Years 1992–1996*: Congressional Office, 1991 Annual Report.

As noted earlier, the cost of supporting large high-technology militaries was staggering for both the United States and the Soviet Union. At the end of the 1980s, the Soviet Union spent more for its military than on health and education combined. The United States spent more for defense than for public health (this does not count the considerable sums spent privately on health).[37] The prosperous nations of Europe and Asia boasted higher spending on public services such as health and education than on arms and troops, leading many opponents of U.S. military priorities to argue that the quality of life in the other democracies was higher than in the United States largely because their tax dollars went directly into public services rather than armaments.

The Pentagon eventually responded to political pressure and announced cuts of half a million troops by 1995, proposing a standing force of 1.65 million troops, the smallest force since 1950.[38] Yet investments in expensive weapons systems remained high, and plans to maintain a strong international presence were costly. Projections well into the 1990s showed that the defense budget, despite cuts, would remain substantial, as shown in Figure 20.4.

The Peace Dividend

In the early 1990s, optimists talked of a "peace dividend," implying that money no longer needed for defense could be used to deal with neglected problems at home, improving schools, repairing bridges, building houses, and helping defense industries retool to produce new products. Critics charged that huge outlays for military weapons took money away from research and development that would have greater civilian benefits. "How We Compare" Box 20.2 compares the United States with European nations in relative amounts spent on research and development for military, space, and civilian uses.

HOW WE COMPARE

Government Investments in Research and Development in the United States and Europe

20.2

Because the United States has taken a leading world military role in the modern era, a disproportionate amount of government spending for research and development of new technologies has gone for items such as smart bombs, chemical warfare, nuclear weapons systems, and other battlefield technolo- gies that have little direct civilian payoff. By contrast, member governments in the European community* have spent a dispro- portionate amount of research and development money on such things as high-speed railway sys- tems, automotive safety technol- ogy, health care delivery systems, and passenger aircraft design that have direct civilian payoffs and greater economic stimulus. The figures below compare U.S. and European* spending pat- terns on research and develop- ment for military, space, and civilian uses (1970–1990).

SOURCE: Ruth L. Sivard, *World Military and Social Expenditures, 1991.* Washington, D.C.: World Priorities, 1991, p. 12.

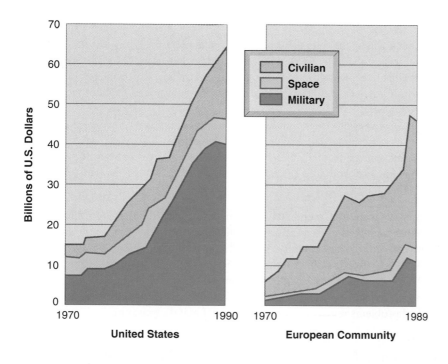

*Belgium, Denmark, France, Greece, Ireland, Italy, Luxembourg, Netherlands, Portugal, Spain, United Kingdom, West Germany.

The "Stealth" bomber. Today U. S. leaders must reconsider the cost and focus of weapons development in a world no longer divided by relatively clear-cut, bipolar conflict.

Unfortunately, the peace dividend did not materialize. The first big blow to a peace dividend was the tough bargain struck between the White House and Congress in 1990 to put a cap on domestic programs and to channel any budget savings to reduce the deficit. Although this arrangement reflected taxpayer concerns about an out-of-control deficit, it ironically offered little incentive to cut defense spending. Although modest reductions were made, many expensive weapons programs were continued, despite the absence of enemies on the planet that were any match for such awesome firepower. The Democrats appeared to be as enthusiastic as the Republicans about funding expensive defense contracts on the eve of the 1992 election. Critics contended that domestic politics played too large a role in making defense policy decisions. One newspaper editorial lashed out at the Democrats for stealing the peace dividend:

> They are providing the votes the Pentagon needs to protect weapons like the Stealth bomber; so what if the trillion-dollar B-2 can't evade radars as well as advertised? The 15 planes already being built aren't enough for key Democrats; they tentatively approved a 16th last year, and now a House subcommittee wants to buy four more—at over $1 billion each.
>
> Even more shamefully, Democrats are trying to restore funds for weapons that even the Pentagon is prepared to cut, like the Seawolf submarine . . .
>
> Proponents contend that the difference between closing down the Seawolf assembly line and building two more subs amounts to "little or no money." Since when is $2 billion little or no money?[39]

All of this suggests that more than foreign policy considerations go into defense spending. What remained in place after the Cold War was a powerful set of political relations between politicians, military bureaucrats, and the defense industry—what Dwight Eisenhower warned about as the "military industrial complex." Consisting of hundreds of *iron triangles* (described in Chapters 8, 12, and 15), this military industrial complex appeared to have a life of its own, continuing to produce military solutions even after potential problems requiring so much military force disappeared.

The Defense Establishment and the Economy

The cornerstone of a military industrial complex consists of the iron triangles between defense contractors, members of Congress, and offices in the Pentagon eager to keep their programs and activities alive. These triangles provide points of continual resistance to cutting military budgets. Members of Congress oppose base closings or defense spending cuts in their districts. Pentagon planners feed information to congressional staffs to defend "go slow" policies in military reductions. Meanwhile, lobbyists for military contractors contribute to congressional campaigns, while developing close ties with Pentagon officials who order new weapons. Many executives and lobbyists in defense industries are former military officers with close Pentagon ties who started lucrative second careers in the private sector.

Once the economy was dependent on defense production, it became hard to break out of the cycle. Even Dwight Eisenhower, who warned of the dependency of the defense establishment, used military spending to help pull the country out of recessions twice during his presidency. When Ronald Reagan took office, he boosted military spending by over $70 billion in three years, putting enormous pressure on the Soviet Union but also ending a recession that plagued his new administration. Lacking an alternative plan to get the industrial economy going in another direction, George Bush had little enthusiasm for severe military cuts, recognizing the economic fallout that would land on his presidency. Yet the reliance on military spending to prime the economic pump reinforces an unproductive economic pattern and drives the government deeper into debt.[40] As explained in Chapter 19, the old Keynesian theories of government spending have not been as effective for stimulating the economy as they once were. This is particularly true of defense spending, where government money does not trickle down to as many people as dollars spent in other ways (Social Security, highway construction, housing construction, and so on). Although jobs in the defense industry are high paying, there are not that many of them, and they have been declining fairly steadily since the 1950s, as shown in Figure 20.5. When defense cuts finally began to hit state economies in California, Maine, Connecticut, and elsewhere, Bill Clinton and other politicians discovered that they had no easy solutions for the economic shock waves.

FIGURE 20.5

The Decline of Jobs in the Military Industrial Complex: 1940–1990
(Military and civilian defense employment
as percentage of all jobs in U.S.)

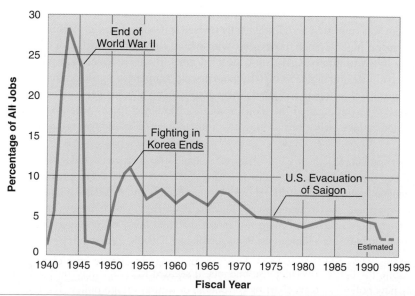

Sources: Defense Budget Project; Office of Management and Budget; Adapted from *The New York Times*, September 13, 1992, p. E 3.

New Roles for the Military?

While Washington continues to struggle to find alternatives to a defense-oriented economy, the Pentagon is at work designing new roles for itself. In the end, the best bureaucratic defense against further military cuts is to remain strategically important. After the end of the Cold War, the military began searching for new world problems that called for military solutions. In the absence of a new doctrine that captured a broad consensus in Washington foreign policy circles, the military began drafting its own reasons for continuing to exist at high levels of strength. The first statement to emerge from these secret policy planning sessions was a 1992 report titled *Defense Planning Guidance for the Fiscal Years 1994–1999*. Although the report was a secret document, not even released to Congress, it was leaked to *The New York Times* by "an official who believes this post-cold-war strategy debate should be carried out in the public domain."[41] The proposal called for the United States to maintain the strength to lead a one-superpower world, using military might to convince competitors and even current allies not to challenge American supremacy. One section of the report outlined the rationale for continuing military solutions to future foreign policy problems:

> While the U.S. cannot become the world's "policeman," by assuming responsibility for righting every wrong, we will retain the preeminent responsibility for addressing selectively those wrongs which threaten not only our interests, but those of our allies or friends, or which could seriously unsettle international relations. Various types of U.S. interests may be involved in such instances: access to vital raw materials, primarily Persian Gulf oil; proliferation of weapons of mass destruction and ballistic missiles, threats to U.S. citizens from terrorism or regional or local conflict, and threats to U.S. society from narcotics trafficking.[42]

The leaked document did, indeed, set off considerable debate, not just at home, but with allies who thought they should remain partners in developing military policies for the new world order. To some allies such as France and Germany, the collapse of Communism presented an opportunity to form a community of more equitable nations operating with a diminished U.S. military presence. In response to these criticisms, the document was rewritten and dramatically revised, provoking new criticisms that neither the Pentagon planners nor the experts with whom they consulted had a clear sense of purpose in world affairs. Criticism continued when it was revealed that proposed military expenditures remained as high in the revised document as in the original draft. Only the language was softened to include more emphasis on alliance partners and diplomatic solutions. One critic called these an incantation designed to say whatever pleased domestic and foreign politicians so long as actual military spending was not affected:

> By speaking the magic word "shazam," a comic strip character could transform himself into [a] superhero. . . . And by rewriting their controversial defense strategy paper, Pentagon leaders have metamorphosed from globocops into milomats, military mavens who appreciate the calming power of diplomatic words. . . .
> Even more magically, Pentagon planners managed these major alterations in doctrine without losing a dime in the Pentagon budget. Double shazam.[43]

Despite the battles over defense budgets, it seemed to critics that there was no compelling new policy doctrine charting the course of future foreign policy. The big question that opened this chapter once again loomed large in the headlines: What was to be the role of the United States in creating a new (post-Cold War) world order?

Russian president Boris Yeltsin welcomes Mikhail Gorbachev back to Moscow following a failed attempt in August 1991 by communist hard-liners to depose the Soviet leader. (Gorbachev had been sequestered by the coup leaders in an isolated dacha.) Although he survived the plot, Gorbachev soon found his authority in a tailspin, even as Yeltsin's popularity soared following his leadership of thousands of Muscovites in defying the coup. By the following year, it was Yeltsin—not Gorbachev—who signed an historic arms-limitation treaty with U.S. President Bush. Yet Yeltsin himself was soon under siege from various factions grasping for power. Instability of this sort poses a major challenge for U.S. foreign policy in the 1990s.

The New World Order Revisited

After the war against Iraq was over in 1991, two other foreign policy crises erupted in the faces of U.S. policy makers. A democratically elected government in Haiti was overthrown by a brutal military coup that sent thousands of Haitians fleeing to the United States, while prompting calls for American assistance to restore the elected government. Meanwhile, in what was once Yugoslavia, ethnic nationalism turned into grisly civil war, filling the nightly news with scenes of human suffering and threatening the stability of neighboring countries. Calls for U.S. military intervention went unanswered, with administration officials deferring to United Nations and European policies.

Despite the rhetoric of world leadership coming from the Bush administration, it was not clear just how and when to exercise that leadership, particularly in situations that might call for military interventions. Although Bill Clinton criticized the lack of a Bush response to Haiti and the former Yugoslavia during the 1992 campaign, his policies were similar to those of his predecessor when he had the opportunity to act as president. The problem was not just with these presidents and their advisors. To the contrary, few presidents had the previous foreign policy experience of George Bush, and his advisors were many of the same policy experts who had counseled earlier presidents. Although not experienced in world affairs, Bill Clinton appointed a veteran staff of foreign policy experts to advise him. What had changed most dramatically was the world itself. As one observer noted, the new world did not fit the much simpler policy postulates of the old Cold War order:

> In some ways, the existence of the Soviet Union made life easy. The Kremlin was the North Star of America's foreign policy. All the policy-makers had to do was take out their compasses, point them at any regional conflict in the world, see which side Moscow was on and immediately decide which side America should take. Virtually every conflict from Namibia to Afghanistan to Nicaragua engaged American interests, and prompted some level of American military involvement, because the Soviets were backing one side or the other.
>
> But with the collapse of the Soviet empire, the old American compass no longer works. As a result, both the "realist" school of American foreign policy and the "idealist" school seem to have lost their way. After all, what does it mean to be a realist when there is no Soviet threat to override human rights considerations? And what does it mean to be an idealist when what is required to preserve human rights in such places as Yugoslavia and Haiti is military intervention?[44]

In the old order, virtually all policy officials agreed on the Soviet threat. The **realists** referred to in the above quote tended to see world power as a hardball game requiring confrontation and, if necessary, supporting undemocratic regimes as long as they were friendly to U.S. interests. **Idealists,** on the other hand, also opposed the Communists but were against supporting regimes that deprived their own people of democracy and basic rights. After the Cold War, it was not clear how to apply either the hardball politics or the democracy and human rights orientation in a much more complicated world. For the realists, there was no great power to confront, leaving each situation to be evaluated on its own often-ambiguous terms. For the idealists, it was not clear what to do with nations that had declared themselves democracies and then elected conservative nationalist leaders who endorsed violence against various minorities. The new world order threatened to degenerate into chaos. Yet without a clear doctrine outlining policy goals and guidelines, the United States could not establish leadership in that world.

Power in a Multipolar World

Political scientist David Deese has noted, "Not since its formative years have the U.S. state and American politics generally been so heavily influenced by the external environment. . . . The result is a more political and less manageable foreign policy process."[45] Building coalitions of nations to agree on trade relations, economic assistance to developing nations, and military interventions are increasingly delicate matters. Nations with the economic clout of Japan are not willing to be told what to do. Indeed, Japanese foreign policy is creating a sphere of influence throughout Asia and around the Pacific rim, using foreign aid programs to create economic alliances that may end up conflicting with American interests in the region. In Europe, part of the push toward political unification involved creating a foreign policy voice capable of asserting regional influence independent of American wishes. Talk about a joint German-French military security pact raised troublesome questions about the NATO military alliance and the continued dominance of the United States in European security matters.

Whether or not European unity becomes fully realized in a federal Europe, it is clear that American leadership will not be granted as easily as when Soviet tank divisions sat poised for attack across the German border. During a heated meeting between French and American diplomats, Bush administration Secretary of State James Baker asked his counterpart, French Foreign Minister Roland Dumas: "Are you for us or against us?" A

A CITIZEN'S QUESTION
Foreign Policy Participation

How can I learn enough about world politics to participate in foreign policy debates? The current world scene is a bit dizzying, with new nations coming into existence, and fights breaking out among people whose cultures and conflicts receive little attention in the press. Even the big powers are in turmoil. How stable is the control over Russia's nuclear arsenal? How will the European allies react to setbacks in the movement toward European unity? Is Japan destined to become more independent in its policies in Asia?

These uncertainties in the world order can baffle the experts. How can a beginning student become involved in thinking about them? Ready or not, Americans have already become more involved in foreign policy debates, as suggested in this chapter. Public opinion has played important roles in the thinking of politicians about trade agreements and involvement in regional conflicts. Rather than hide from challenging questions about the U.S. world role, citizens can steer the course of their nation. This requires thinking clearly about how to balance the needs of defense and economy, along with humanitarian and environmental goals in an unstable world. Just engaging with these issues is a start.

As a next step, you can learn about specific foreign policy issues so that you can contribute informed views to the debates. There are many organizations aimed at educating citizens about foreign policy concerns. A good place to start is to write for information about programs and publications to this broad, nonpartisan educational organization:

The Foreign Policy Association
729 Seventh Avenue
New York, NY 10019

More specialized educational organizations include:

Center for Defense Information
1500 Massachusetts Ave., N.W.
Washington, DC 20005
(Public education on military
and defense issues)

The Center for Strategic
and International Studies
1800 K Street, N.W.
Washington, DC 20006
(Provides information on foreign policy
and international economics)

Foreign Policy Research Institute
3508 Market Street, Suite 350
Philadelphia, Pa. 19104
(Public education and publications
on foreign policy)

When you feel ready to get involved politically, there are many foreign policy interest groups open to grassroots participation. As with most interest groups, they promote specific policy goals and take partisan or ideological positions. A few of these political organizations are listed here:

Peace Action
1819 H Street, Suite 640
Washington, DC 20006
(Arms control and disarmament activism;
reduced military operations)

American Security Council
Washington Communications Center
Boston, Virginia 22713
(Lobbying and citizen organizing for a
strong world military role and
protection of American interests)

Freedom House
120 Wall Street
New York, N.Y. 10005
(Citizen organizing and support for
free institutions abroad and
international human rights)

French official admitted that there was "extreme irritation on both sides," explaining that "We cannot accept that world diplomacy should be a one-man show, while Washington seems convinced that our reflections on the future of Europe are necessarily anti-American."[46]

Is U.S. Power in Decline?

A number of students of world history have noted that great military powers tend to overextend themselves, spending too much money on armies while their domestic economies go into decline. Historical evidence suggests that the collapse of the Soviet Union followed that pattern, as did the declines of all the other great world powers since the 1500s.[47] If the United States follows this pattern of great power decline, argues historian Paul Kennedy, foreign policy makers will cling to military solutions abroad, while domestic politicians will cut social programs to pay the costs of world military commitments. Eventually, the nation will be weakened both internally and externally, subject to social and political unrest at home and unable to meet challenges abroad. Needless to say, such circumstances would place even more extreme limits on foreign policy options than the ones already discussed in this chapter. There are, of course, many who disagree with the decline thesis, at least as it fits the case of the United States. Political scientist Joseph Nye, Jr., argues that the U.S. economy remains strong, and its military is the only force capable of creating world order. Taking a realist's view of a new world order, Nye contends that the United States is the only nation capable of stepping into the power vacuum left with the collapse of the Soviet Union.[48]

Whether U.S. power is in decline or is simply going through an inevitable adjustment to changed world and domestic conditions, only time will tell. As the country moves toward its next rendezvous with destiny, a new opportunity exists for the people and their leaders to discuss foreign policy. Since domestic and international choices are increasingly difficult to separate, and the need for secrecy is less imperative with the collapse of Communism, the stage may be set for more democratic participation in the foreign policy process. One foreign policy analyst called for Bill Clinton to think about a new way of making foreign policy:

> The first task for President Clinton is not to devise a new Truman Doctrine but to construct a new way of making foreign policy—of making a *democratic* foreign policy. The country badly needs a new National Security Act for the post-cold-war era, a law that will include procedures to restore true consultation between the executive and the legislative branches; return secrecy to its proper role; and insure that both branches play a part in any decision to commit Americans to any hostilities abroad.[49]

If foreign policy becomes subject to more open public debate, are you ready to participate?

Key Terms

manifest destiny	**the Truman Doctrine**
Monroe Doctrine	**Central Intelligence Agency**
isolationism	**National Security Act of 1947**
internationalism	**National Security Council**
Cold War	**the Marshall Plan**
containment	**the foreign policy establishment**

détente/the Nixon Doctrine

impact of Vietnam on policy consensus

the Reagan Doctrine

realists, idealists

multipolar world politics

the domestication of foreign policy

Suggested Readings

Kegley, Charles W., Jr. and Eugene R. Wittkopf. *American Foreign Policy: Pattern and Process*, 3rd ed. New York: St. Martin's Press, 1987.

Kennan, George F. *Around the Cragged Hill*. New York: Norton, 1993.

Kennedy, Paul. *The Rise and Fall of the Great Powers*. New York: Random House, 1987.

McCormick, Thomas J. *America's Half Century: United States Foreign Policy in the Cold War*. Baltimore: Johns Hopkins University Press, 1989.

Nye, Joseph S., Jr. *Bound to Lead: The Changing Nature of American Power*. New York: Basic Books, 1990.

Spanier, John. *American Foreign Policy Since World War II*, 12th ed. Washington, D.C.: Congressional Quarterly Press, 1991.

APPENDIX I
THE FEDERALIST PAPERS No. 10 and 51

James Madison

November 22, 1787

TO THE PEOPLE OF THE STATE OF NEW YORK

Among the numerous advantages promised by a well constructed Union, none deserves to be more accurately developed than its tendency to break and control the violence of faction. The friend of popular governments never finds himself so much alarmed for their character and fate, as when he contemplates their propensity to this dangerous vice. He will not fail therefore to set a due value on any plan which, without violating the principles to which he is attached, provides a proper cure for it. The instability, injustice and confusion introduced into the public councils, have in truth been the mortal diseases under which popular governments have every where perished; as they continue to be the favorite and fruitful topics from which the adversaries to liberty derive their most specious declamations. The valuable improvements made by the American Constitutions on the popular models, both ancient and modern, cannot certainly be too much admired; but it would be an unwarrantable partiality, to contend that they have as effectually obviated the danger on this side as was wished and expected. Complaints are every where heard from our most considerate and virtuous citizens, equally the friends of public and private faith, and of public and personal liberty; that our governments are too unstable; that the public good is disregarded in the conflicts of rival parties; and that measures are too often decided, not according to the rules of justice, and the rights of the minor party; but by the superior force of an interested and over-bearing majority. However anxiously we may wish that these complaints had no foundation, the evidence of known facts will not permit us to deny that they are in some degree true. It will be found indeed, on a candid review of our situation, that some of the distresses under which we labor, have been erroneously charged on the operation of our governments; but it will be found, at the same time, that other causes will not alone account for many of our heaviest misfortunes; and particularly, for that prevailing and increasing distrust of public engagements, and alarm for private rights, which are echoed from one end of the continent to the other. These must be chiefly, if not wholly, effects of the unsteadiness and injustice, with which a factious spirit has tainted our public administrations.

By a faction I understand a number of citizens, whether amounting to a majority or minority of the whole, who are united and actuated by some common impulse of passion or of interest, adverse to the rights of other citizens, or to the permanent and aggregate interests of the community.

There are two methods of curing the mischiefs of faction: the one, by removing its causes; the other, by controlling its effects.

There are again two methods of removing the causes of faction: the one by destroying the liberty which is essential to its existence; the other, by giving to every citizen the same opinions, the same passions, and the same interests.

It could never be more truly said than of the first remedy, that it is worse than the disease. Liberty is to faction, what air is to fire, an ailment without which it instantly expires. But it could not be a less folly to abolish liberty, which is essential to political life, because it nourishes faction, than it would be to wish the annihilation of air, which is essential to animal life, because it imparts to fire its destructive agency.

The second expedient is as impracticable, as the first would be unwise. As long as the reason of man continues fallible, and he is at liberty to exercise it, different opinions will be formed. As long as the connection subsists between his reason and his self-love, his opinions and his passions will have a reciprocal influence on each other; and the former will be objects to which the latter will attach themselves. The diversity in the faculties of men from which the rights of property originate, is not less an insuperable obstacle to a uniformity of interests. The protection of these faculties is the first object of Government. From the protection of different and unequal faculties of acquiring property, the possession of different degrees and kinds of property immediately results: and from the influence of these on the sentiments and views of the respective proprietors, ensues a division of the society into different interests and parties.

The latent causes of faction are thus sown in the nature of man; and we see them every where brought into different degrees of activity, according to the different circumstances of civil society. A zeal for different opinions concerning religion, concerning Government and many other points, as well of speculation as of practice; an attachment to different leaders ambitiously contending for pre-eminence and power; or to persons of other descriptions whose fortunes have been interesting to the human passions, have in turn divided mankind into parties, inflamed them with mutual animosity, and rendered them much more disposed to vex and oppress each other, than to co-operate for their common good. So strong is this propensity of mankind to fall into mutual animosities, that where no substantial occasion presents itself, the most frivolous and fanciful distinctions have been sufficient to kindle their unfriendly passions, and excite their most violent conflicts. But the most common and durable source of factions, has been the various and unequal distribution of property. Those who hold, and those who are without property, have ever formed distinct interests in society. Those who are creditors, and those who are debtors, fall under a like discrimination. A landed interest, a manufacturing interest, a mercantile interest, a monied interest, with many lesser interests, grow up of necessity in civilized nations, and divide them into different classes, actuated by different sentiments and views. The regulation of these various and interfering interests forms the principal task of modern Legislation, and involves the spirit of party and faction in the necessary and ordinary operations of Government.

No man is allowed to be a judge in his own cause; because his interest would certainly bias his judgment, and, not improbably, corrupt his integrity. With equal, nay with greater reason, a body of men, are unfit to be both judges and parties, at the same time; yet, what are many of the most important acts of legislation, but so many judicial determinations, not indeed concerning the rights of single persons, but concerning the rights of large bodies of citizens, and what are the different classes of legislators, but advocates and parties to the causes which they determine? Is a law proposed concerning private debts? It is a question to which the creditors are parties on one side, and the debtors on the other. Justice ought to hold the balance between them. Yet the parties are and must be themselves the judges; and the most numerous party, or, in other words, the most powerful faction must be expected to prevail. Shall domestic manufactures be encouraged, and in what degree, by restrictions on foreign manufactures? are questions which would be differently decided by the landed and the manufacturing classes; and probably by neither, with a sole regard to justice and the public good. The apportionment of taxes on the various descriptions of property, is an act which seems to require the most exact impartiality; yet, there is perhaps no legislative act in which greater opportunity and temptation are given to a predominant party, to trample on the rules of justice. Every shilling with which they over-burden the inferior number, is a shilling saved to their own pockets.

It is in vain to say, that enlightened statesmen will be able to adjust these clashing interests, and render them all subservient to the public good. Enlightened statesmen will not always be at the helm: Nor, in many cases, can such an adjustment be made at all, without taking into view indirect and remote considerations, which will rarely prevail over the immediate interest which one party may find in disregarding the rights of another, or the good of the whole.

The inference to which we are brought, is, that the *causes* of faction cannot be removed; and that relief is only to be sought in the means of controlling its *effects*.

If a faction consists of less than a majority, relief is supplied by the republican principle, which enables the majority to defeat its sinister views by regular vote: It may clog the administration, it may convulse the society; but it will be unable to execute and mask its violence under the forms of the Constitution. When a majority is included in a faction, the form of popular government on the other hand enables it to sacrifice to its ruling passion or interest, both the public good and the rights of other citizens. To secure the public good, and private rights, against the danger of such a faction, and at the same time to preserve the spirit and the form of popular government, is then the great object to which our enquiries are directed: Let me add that it is the great desideratum, by which alone this form of government can be rescued from the opprobrium under which it has so long labored, and be recommended to the esteem and adoption of mankind.

By what means is this object attainable? Evidently by one of two only. Either the existence of the same passion or interest in a majority at the same time, must be prevented; or the majority, having such co-existent passion or interest, must be rendered, by their number and local situation, unable to concert and carry into effect schemes of oppression. If the impulse and the opportunity be suffered to coincide, we well know that neither moral nor religious motives can be relied on as an adequate control. They are not found to be such on the injustice and violence of individuals, and lose their efficacy in proportion to the number combined together; that is, in proportion as their efficacy becomes needful.

From this view of the subject, it may be concluded, that a pure Democracy, by which I mean, a Society, consisting of a small number of citizens, who assemble and administer the Government in person, can admit of no cure for the mischiefs of faction. A common passion or interest will, in almost every case, be felt by a majority of the whole; a communication and concert results from the form of Government itself; and there is nothing to check the inducements to sacrifice the weaker party, or an obnoxious individual. Hence it is, that such Democracies have ever been spectacles of turbulence and contention; have ever been found incompatible with personal security, or the rights of property; and have in general been as short in their lives, as they have been violent in their deaths. Theoretic politicians, who have patronized this species of Government, have erroneously supposed, that by reducing mankind to a perfect equality in their political rights, they would, at the same time, be perfectly equalized and assimilated in their possessions, their opinions, and their passions.

A republic, by which I mean a government in which the scheme of representation takes place, opens a different prospect, and promises the cure for which we are seeking. Let us examine the points in which it varies from pure democracy, and we shall comprehend both the nature of the cure and efficacy which it must derive from the union.

The two great points of difference, between a democracy and a republic, are, first, the delegation of the government, in the latter, to a small number of citizens, elected by the rest; secondly, the greater number of citizens, and greater sphere of country, over which the latter may be extended.

The effect of the first difference is, on the one hand, to refine and enlarge the public views, by passing them through the medium of a chosen body of citizens, whose wisdom may best discern the true interest of their country, and whose patriotism and love of justice, will be least likely to sacrifice it to temporary or partial considerations. Under such a regulation, it may well happen, that the public voice, pronounced by the representatives of the people, will be more consonant to the public good, than if pronounced by the people themselves, convened for the purpose. On the other hand the effect may be inverted. Men of factious tempers, of local prejudices, or of sinister designs, may by intrigue, by corruption, or by other means, first obtain the suffrages, and then betray the interest of the people. The question resulting is, whether small or extensive republics are most favorable to the election of proper guardians of the public weal, and it is clearly decided in favor of the latter by two obvious considerations.

In the first place, it is to be remarked that, however small the republic may be, the representatives must be raised to a certain number, in order to guard against the cabals of a few; and that however large it may be, they must be limited to a certain number, in order to guard against the confusion of a multitude. Hence, the number of representatives in the two cases not being in proportion to that of the constituents, and being proportionally greatest in the small republic, it follows, that if the proportion of fit characters be not less in the large than in the small republic, the former will present a greater option, and consequently a greater probability of a fit choice.

In the next place, as each Representative will be chosen by a greater number of citizens in the large than in the small Republic, it will be more difficult for unworthy candidates to practise with success the vicious arts, by which elections are too often carried; and the suffrages of the people being more free, will be more likely to center on men who possess the most attractive merit, and the most diffusive and established characters.

It must be confessed, that in this, as in most other cases, there is a mean, on both sides of which inconveniences will be found to lie. By enlarging too much the number of electors, you render the representative too little acquainted with all their local circumstances and lesser interests; as by reducing it too much, you render him unduly attached to these, and too little fit to comprehend and pursue great and national objects. The Federal Constitution forms a happy combination in this respect; the great and aggregate interests being referred to the national, the local and particular, to the state legislatures.

The other point of difference is, the greater number of citizens and extent of territory which may be brought within the compass of Republican, than of Democratic Government; and it is this circumstance principally which renders factious combinations less to be dreaded in the former, than in the latter. The smaller the society, the fewer probably will be the distinct parties and interests composing it; the fewer the distinct parties and interests, the more frequently will a majority be found of the same party; and the smaller the number of individuals composing a majority, and the smaller the compass within which they are placed, the more easily will they concert and execute their plans of oppression. Extend the sphere, and you take in a greater variety of parties and interests; you make it less probable that a majority of the whole will have a common motive to invade the rights of other citizens; or if such a common motive exists, it will be more difficult for all who feel it to discover their own strength, and to act in unison with each other. Besides other impediments, it may be remarked, that where there is a consciousness of unjust or dishonorable purposes, communication is always checked by distrust, in proportion to the number whose concurrence is necessary.

Hence it clearly appears, that the same advantage, which a Republic has over a Democracy, in controlling the effects of faction, is enjoyed by a large over a small Republic—is enjoyed by the Union over the States composing it. Does this advantage consist in the substitution of Representatives, whose enlightened views and virtuous sentiments render them superior to local prejudices, and to schemes of injustice? It will not be denied, that the Representation of the Union will be most likely to possess these requisite endowments. Does it consist in the greater security afforded by a greater variety of parties, against the event of any one party being able to outnumber and oppress the rest? In an equal degree does the increased variety of parties, comprised within the Union, increase this security? Does it, in fine, consist in the greater obstacles opposed to the concert and accomplishment of the secret wishes of an unjust and interested majority? Here, again, the extent of the Union gives it the most palpable advantage.

The influence of factious leaders may kindle a flame within their particular States, but will be unable to spread a general conflagration through the other States: a religious sect, may degenerate into a political faction in a part of the Confederacy but the variety of sects dispersed over the entire face of it, must secure the national Councils against any danger from that source: a rage for paper money, for an abolition of debts, for an equal division of property, or for any other improper or wicked project, will be less apt to pervade the whole body of the Union, than a particular member of it; in the same porportion as such a malady is more likely to taint a particular county or district, than an entire State.

In the extent and proper structure of the Union, therefore, we behold a Republican remedy for the diseases most incident to Republican Government. And according to the degree of pleasure and pride, we feel in being Republicans, ought to be our zeal in cherishing the spirit, and supporting the character of Federalists.

PUBLIUS

James Madison

February 6, 1788

TO THE PEOPLE OF THE STATE OF NEW YORK

To what expedient then shall we finally resort for maintaining in practice the necessary partition of power among the several departments, as laid down in the constitution? The only answer that can be given is, that as all these exterior provisions are found to be inadequate, the defect must be supplied, by so contriving the interior structure of the government, as that its several constituent parts may, by their mutual relations, be the means of keeping each other in their proper places. Without presuming to undertake a full development of this important idea, I will hazard a few observations, which may perhaps place it in a clearer light, and enable us to form a more correct judgment of the principles and structure of the government planned by the convention.

In order to lay a due foundation for that separate and distinct exercise of the different powers of government, which to a certain extent, is admitted on all hands to be essential to the preservation of liberty, it is evident that each department should have a will of its own; and consequently should be so constituted, that the members of each should have as little agency as possible in the appointment of the members of the others. Were this principle rigorously adhered to, it would require that all the appointments for the supreme executive, legislative, and judiciary magistracies, should be drawn from the same fountain of authority, the people, through channels, having no communication whatever with one another. Perhaps such a plan of constructing the several departments would be less difficult in practice than it may in contemplation appear. Some difficulties however, and some additional expense, would attend the execution of it. Some deviations therefore from the principle must be admitted. In the constitution of the judiciary department in particular, it might be inexpedient to insist rigorously on the principle; first, because peculiar qualifications being essential in the members, the primary consideration ought to be to select that mode of choice, which best secures these qualifications; secondly, because the permanent tenure by which the appointments are held in that department, must soon destroy all sense of dependence on the authority conferring them.

It is equally evident that the members of each department should be as little dependent as possible on those of the others, for the emoluments annexed to their offices. Were the executive magistrate, or the judges, not independent of the legislature in this particular, their independence in every other would be merely nominal.

But the great security against a gradual concentration of the several powers in the same department, consists in giving to those who administer each department, the necessary constitutional means, and personal motives, to resist encroachments of the others. The provision for defense must in this, as in all other cases, be made commensurate to the danger of attack. Ambition must be made to counteract ambition. The interest of the man must be connected with the constitutional right of the place. It may be a reflection on human nature, that such devices should be necessary to control the abuses of government. But what is government itself but the greatest of all reflections on human nature? If men were angels, no government would be necessary. If angels were to govern men, neither external nor internal controls on government would be necessary. In framing a government which is to be administered by men over men, the great difficulty lies in this: You must first enable the government to control the governed; and the next place, oblige it to control itself. A dependence on the people is no doubt the primary control on the government; but experience has taught mankind the necessity of auxiliary precautions.

This policy of supplying by opposite and rival interests, the defect of better motives, might be traced through the whole system of human affairs, private as well as public. We see it particularly displayed in all the subordinate distributions of power; where the constant aim is to divide and arrange the several offices in such a manner as that each may be a check on the other; that the private interest of every individual, may be a sentinel over the public rights. These inventions of prudence cannot be less requisite in the distribution of the supreme powers of the state.

But it is not possible to give each department an equal power of self defense. In republican government the legislative authority, necessarily, predominates. The remedy for this inconveniency is, to divide the legislature into different branches; and to render them by different modes of election, and different principles of action, as little connected with each other, as the nature of their common functions, and their common dependence on the society, will admit. It may even be necessary to guard against dangerous encroachments by still further precautions. As the weight of the legislative authority requires that it should be thus divided, the weakness of the executive may require, on the other hand, that it should be fortified. An absolute negative, on the legislature, appears at first view to be the natural defense with which the executive magistrate should be armed. But perhaps it would be neither altogether safe, nor alone sufficient. On ordinary occasion, it might not be exerted with the requisite firmness; and on extraordinary occasions, it might be prefidiously abused. May not this defect of an absolute negative be supplied, by some qualified connection between this weaker department, and the weaker branch of the stronger department, by which the latter may be led to support the constitutional rights of the former, without being too much detached from the rights of its own department?

If the principles on which these observations are founded be just, as I persuade myself they are, and they be applied as a criterion, to the several state constitutions, and to the federal constitution, it will be found, that if the latter does not perfectly correspond with them, the former are infinitely less able to bear such a test.

There are moreover two considerations particularly applicable to the federal system of America, which place that system in a very interesting point of view.

First. In a single republic, all the power surrendered by the people, is submitted to the administration of a single government; and usurpations are guarded against by a division of the government into distinct and separate departments. In the compound republic of America, the power surrendered by the people, is first divided between two distinct governments, and then the portion allotted to each, subdivided among distinct and separate departments. Hence a double security arises to the rights of the people. The different governments will control each other; at the same time that each will be controlled by itself.

Second. It is of great importance in a republic, not only to guard the society against the oppression of its rulers; but to guard one part of the society against the injustice of the other part. Different interests necessarily exist in different classes of citizens. If a majority be united by a common interest, the rights of the minority will be insecure. There are but two methods of providing against this evil: The one by creating a will in the community independent of the majority, that is, of the society itself, the other by comprehending in the society so many separate descriptions of citizens, as will render an unjust combination of a majority of the whole, very improbable, if not impracticable. The first method prevails in all governments possessing an hereditary or self appointed authority. This at best is but a precarious security; because a power independent of the society may as well espouse the unjust views of the major, as the rightful interests, of the minor party, and may possibly be turned against both parties. The second method will be exemplified in the federal republic of the United States. While all authority in it will be derived from and dependent on the society, the society itself will be broken into so many parts, interests and classes of citizens, that the rights of individuals or of the minority, will be in little danger from interested combinations of the majority. In a free government, the security for civil rights must be the same as for religious rights. It consists in the one case in the multiplicity of interests, and in the other, in the multiplicity of sects. The degree of security in both cases will depend on the number of interests and sects; and this may be presumed to depend on the extent of country and number of people comprehended under the same government. This view of the subject must particularly recommend a proper federal system to all the sincere and considerate friends of republican government: Since it shows that in exact proportion as the territory of the union may be formed into more circumscribed confederacies or states, oppressive combinations of a majority will be facilitated, the best security under the republican form, for the rights of every class of citizens, will be diminished; and consequently, the stability and independence of some member of the government, the only other security, must be proportionally increased. Justice is the end of government. It is the end of civil society. It ever has been, and ever will be pursued, until it be obtained, or until liberty be lost in the pursuit. In a society under the forms of which the stronger faction can readily unite and oppress the weaker, anarchy may as truly be said to reign, as in a state of nature where the weaker individual is not secured against the violence of the stronger: And as in the latter state even the stronger individuals are prompted by the uncertainty of their condition, to submit to a government which may protect the weak as well as themselves: So in the former state, will the more powerful factions or parties be gradually induced by a like motive, to wish for a government which will protect all parties, the weaker as well as the more powerful. It can be little doubted, that if the state of Rhode Island was separated from the confederacy, and left to itself, the insecurity of rights under the popular form of government within such narrow limits, would be displayed by such reiterated oppressions of factious majorities, that some power altogether independent of the people would soon be called for by the voice of the very factions whose misrule had proved the necessity of it. In the extended republic of the United States, and among the great variety of interests, parties and sects which it embraces, a coalition of a majority of the whole society could seldom take place on any other principles that those of justice and the general good; and there being thus less danger to a minor from the will of the major party, there must be less pretext also, to provide for the security of the former, by introducing into the government a will not dependent on the latter; or in other words, a will independent of the society itself. It is no less certain than it is important, notwithstanding the contrary opinions which have been entertained, that the larger the society, provided it lie within a practicable sphere, the more duly capable it will be of self government. And happily for the *republican cause,* the practicable sphere may be carried to a very great extent, by a judicious modification and mixture of the *federal principle.*

PUBLIUS

APPENDIX II
U. S. PRESIDENTS AND VICE PRESIDENTS BY POLITICAL PARTY
AND
MAJORITY PARTY CONTROL OF U. S. HOUSE AND SENATE,
1789–PRESENT

TERM OF OFFICE	PRESIDENT/ VICE PRESIDENT	EXECUTIVE'S POLITICAL PARTY	CONGRESS	MAJORITY PARTY IN CONGRESS: HOUSE	SENATE
1789–1797	**George Washington** John Adams	None	1st 2d 3d 4th	N/A N/A N/A N/A	N/A N/A N/A N/A
1797–1801	**John Adams** Thomas Jefferson	Federalist	5th 6th	N/A Federalist	N/A Federalist
1801–1809	**Thomas Jefferson** Aaron Burr (1801–1805) George Clinton (1805–1809)	Democratic–Republican	7th 8th 9th 10th	Dem–Rep Dem–Rep Dem–Rep Dem–Rep	Dem–Rep Dem–Rep Dem–Rep Dem–Rep
1809–1817	**James Madison** George Clinton (1809–1812)* Elbridge Gerry (1813–1814)*	Democratic–Republican	11th 12th 13th 14th	Dem–Rep Dem–Rep Dem–Rep Dem–Rep	Dem–Rep Dem–Rep Dem–Rep Dem–Rep
1817–1825	**James Monroe** Daniel D. Tompkins	Democratic–Republican	15th 16th 17th 18th	Dem–Rep Dem–Rep Dem–Rep Dem–Rep	Dem–Rep Dem–Rep Dem–Rep Dem–Rep
1825–1829	**John Quincy Adams** John C. Calhoun	National–Republican	19th 20th	National–Rep Jacksonian–Dem	National–Rep Jacksonian–Dem
1829–1837	**Andrew Jackson** John C. Calhoun (1829–1832)† Martin Van Buren (1833–1837)	Democrat	21st 22d 23d 24th	Democrat Dem Dem Dem	Democrat Dem Dem Dem
1837–1841	**Martin Van Buren** Richard M. Johnson	Democrat	25th 26th	Dem Dem	Dem Dem
March–April 1841	**William H. Harrison*** John Tyler (1841)	Whig	N/A	N/A	N/A
1841–1845	**John Tyler** (Vice presidency vacant)	Whig	27th 28th	Whig Dem	Whig Whig
1845–1849	**James K. Polk** George M. Dallas	Democrat	29th 30th	Dem Whig	Dem Dem
1849–1850	**Zachary Taylor*** Millard Fillmore	Whig	31st	Dem	Dem
1850–1853	**Millard Fillmore** (Vice presidency vacant)	Whig	32d	Dem	Dem
1853–1857	**Franklin Pierce** William R.D. King (1853)*	Democrat	33d 34th	Dem Rep	Dem Dem

TERM OF OFFICE	PRESIDENT/ VICE PRESIDENT	EXECUTIVE'S POLITICAL PARTY	CONGRESS	MAJORITY PARTY IN CONGRESS: HOUSE	SENATE
1857–1861	**James Buchanan** John C. Breckinridge	Democrat	35th 36th	Dem Rep	Dem Dem
1861–1865	**Abraham Lincoln*** Hannibal Hamlin (1861–1865) Andrew Johnson (1865)	Republican	37th 38th	Rep Rep	Rep Rep
1865–1869	**Andrew Johnson** (Vice presidency vacant)	Republican	39th 40th	Union Rep	Union Rep
1869–1877	**Ulysses S. Grant** Schuyler Colfax (1869–1873) Henry Wilson (1873–1875)*	Republican	41st 42d 43d 44th	Rep Rep Rep Dem	Rep Rep Rep Rep
1877–1881	**Rutherford B. Hayes** William A. Wheeler	Republican	45th 46th	Dem Dem	Rep Dem
1881	**James A. Garfield*** Chester A. Arthur	Republican	47th	Rep	Rep
1881–1885	**Chester A. Arthur** (Vice presidency vacant)	Republican	48th	Dem	Rep
1885–1889	**Grover Cleveland** Thomas A. Hendricks (1885)*	Democrat	49th 50th	Dem Dem	Rep Rep
1889–1893	**Benjamin Harrison** Levi P. Morton	Republican	51st 52d	Rep Dem	Rep Rep
1893–1897	**Grover Cleveland** Adlai E. Stevenson	Democrat	53d 54th	Dem Rep	Dem Rep
1897–1901	**William McKinley*** Garret A. Hobart (1897–1899)* Theodore Roosevelt (1901)	Republican	55th 56th	Rep Rep	Rep Rep
1901–1909	**Theodore Roosevelt** (Vice presidency vacant 1901–1905) Charles W. Fairbanks (1905–1909)	Republican	57th 58th 59th 60th	Rep Rep Rep Rep	Rep Rep Rep Rep
1909–1913	**William Howard Taft** James S. Sherman (1909–1912)*	Republican	61st 62d	Rep Dem	Rep Rep
1913–1921	**Woodrow Wilson** Thomas R. Marshall	Democrat	63d 64th 65th 66th	Dem Dem Dem Rep	Dem Dem Dem Rep
1921–1923	**Warren G. Harding*** Calvin Coolidge	Republican	67th	Rep	Rep

TERM OF OFFICE	PRESIDENT/ VICE PRESIDENT	EXECUTIVE'S POLITICAL PARTY	CONGRESS	MAJORITY PARTY IN CONGRESS: HOUSE	SENATE
1923–1929	**Calvin Coolidge** (Vice presidency vacant 1923–1925) Charles G. Dawes (1925–1929)	Republican	68th 69th 70th	Rep Rep Rep	Rep Rep Rep
1929–1933	**Herbert Hoover** Charles Curtis	Republican	71st 72d	Rep Dem	Rep Rep
1933–1945	**Franklin D. Roosevelt*** John N. Garner (1933–1941) Henry A. Wallace (1941–1945) Harry Truman (1945)	Democrat	73d 74th 75th 76th 77th 78th	Dem Dem Dem Dem Dem Dem	Dem Dem Dem Dem Dem Dem
1945–1953	**Harry Truman** (Vice presidency vacant 1945–1949) Alben W. Barkley (1949–1953)	Democrat	79th 80th 81st 82d	Dem Rep Dem Dem	Dem Rep Dem Dem
1953–1961	**Dwight D. Eisenhower** Richard M. Nixon	Republican	83d 84th 85th 86th	Rep Dem Dem Dem	Rep Dem Dem Dem
1961–1963	**John F. Kennedy*** Lyndon B. Johnson (1961–1963)	Democrat	87th	Dem	Dem
1963–1969	**Lyndon B. Johnson** (Vice presidency vacant 1963–1965) Hubert H. Humphrey (1965–1969)	Democrat	88th 89th 90th	Dem Dem Dem	Dem Dem Dem
1969–1974	**Richard M. Nixon†** Spiro T. Agnew (1969–1973)† Gerald R. Ford (1973–1974)§	Republican	91st 92d	Dem Dem	Dem Dem
1974–1977	**Gerald R. Ford** Nelson A. Rockefeller§	Republican	93d 94th	Dem Dem	Dem Dem
1977–1981	**Jimmy Carter** Walter Mondale	Democrat	95th 96th	Dem Dem	Dem Dem
1981–1989	**Ronald Reagan** George Bush	Republican	97th 98th 99th 100th	Dem Dem Dem Dem	Rep Rep Rep Dem
1989–1993	**George Bush** Dan Quayle	Republican	101st 102d	Dem Dem	Dem Dem
1993–	**Bill Clinton** Al Gore	Democrat	103d	Dem	Dem

*Died during term of office.
†Resigned from office.
§Appointed to office.

APPENDIX III
TWENTIETH-CENTURY SUPREME COURT JUSTICES

JUSTICE*	DATES SERVED IN OFFICE†	NOMINATED BY PRESIDENT
John Marshall Harlan	1877–1911	Rutherford B. Hayes
Horace Gray	1881–1902	Chester A. Arthur
Melville W. Fuller	**1888–1910**	Grover Cleveland
David J. Brewer	1889–1910	Benjamin Harrison
Henry B. Brown	1890–1906	Benjamin Harrison
Goerge Shiras, Jr.	1892–1903	Benjamin Harrison
Edward D. White	1894–1910	Benjamin Harrison
Rufus W. Peckham	1895–1909	Grover Cleveland
Joseph P. McKenna	1898–1925	William McKinley
Oliver Wendell Holmes, Jr.	1902–1932	Theodore Roosevelt
William R. Day	1903–1922	Theodore Roosevelt
William H. Moody	1906–1910	Theodore Roosevelt
Horace H. Lurton	1910–1914	William Howard Taft
Charles Evans Hughes§	1910–1916§	William Howard Taft
Willis Van Devanter	1911–1937	William Howard Taft
Joseph R. Lamar	1911–1916	William Howard Taft
Edward D. White	**1910–1921**	William Howard Taft
Mahlon Pitney	1912–1922	William Howard Taft
James C. McReynolds	1914–1941	Woodrow Wilson
Louis Brandeis	1916–1939	Woodrow Wilson
John H. Clarke	1916–1922	Woodrow Wilson
William Howard Taft	**1921–1930**	Warren G. Harding
George Sutherland	1922–1938	Warren G. Harding
Pierce Butler	1922–1939	Warren G. Harding
Edward T. Sanford	1923–1930	Warren G. Harding
Harlan F. Stone§	1925–1941	Calvin Coolidge
Charles Evans Hughes§	**1930–1941**	Herbert Hoover
Owen J. Roberts	1930–1945	Herbert Hoover
Benjamin Cardozo	1932–1938	Herbert Hoover
Hugo Black	1937–1971	Franklin Delano Roosevelt
Stanley F. Reed	1938–1957	Franklin Delano Roosevelt
Felix Frankfurter	1939–1962	Franklin Delano Roosevelt
William O. Douglas	1939–1975	Franklin Delano Roosevelt
Frank Murphy	1940–1949	Franklin Delano Roosevelt
Harlan F. Stone§	**1941–1946**	Franklin Delano Roosevelt
James F. Byrnes	1941–1942	Franklin Delano Roosevelt
Robert H. Jackson	1941–1954	Franklin Delano Roosevelt
Wiley B. Rutledge	1943–1949	Franklin Delano Roosevelt
Harold H. Burton	1945–1958	Harry Truman
Fred M. Vinson	**1946–1953**	Harry Truman
Tom C. Clark	1949–1967	Harry Truman
Sherman Minton	1949–1956	Harry Truman
Earl Warren	**1953–1969**	Dwight Eisenhower
John Marshall Harlan	1955–1971	Dwight Eisenhower
William Brennan, Jr.	1956–1990	Dwight Eisenhower
Charles E. Whittaker	1957–1962	Dwight Eisenhower
Potter Stewart	1958–1981	Dwight Eisenhower
Byron R. White	1962–1993	John Kennedy
Arthur J. Goldberg	1962–1965	John Kennedy
Abe Fortas	1965–1969	Lyndon Johnson
Thurgood Marshall	1967–1991	Lyndon Johnson

JUSTICE*	DATES SERVED IN OFFICE†	NOMINATED BY PRESIDENT
Warren Burger	**1969–1986**	Richard Nixon
Harry A. Blackmun	1970–	Richard Nixon
Lewis F. Powell, Jr.	1972–1987	Richard Nixon
William H. Rehnquist§	1972–1986	Richard Nixon
John Paul Stevens	1975–	Gerald Ford
Sandra Day O'Connor	1981–	Ronald Reagan
William H. Rehnquist§	**1986–**	Ronald Reagan
Antonin Scalia	1986–	Ronald Reagan
Anthony M. Kennedy	1988–	Ronald Reagan
David H. Souter	1990–	George Bush
Clarence Thomas	1991–	George Bush
Ruth Bader Ginsburg	1993–	Bill Clinton

*Chief Justices are listed in **boldface** type; other members of the Court are known as associate justices.

†All justices are appointed for life ("hold[ing] their offices during good behavior," in the words of the U. S. Constitution); end dates therefore denote resignation, retirement, or death.

§Charles Evans Hughes, Harlan F. Stone, and William Rehnquist first served as associate justices and were subsequently appointed to the office of Chief Justice by a later president.

GLOSSARY

GLOSSARY

A

accountability function of elections
The evaluation of the parties and their candidates during a campaign to determine whether they deserve the voters' support. (Chapter 10.)

active–negative
Presidential character type who, according to political scientist James David Barber, engages actively in politics but does not enjoy publicity or the risks of public disapproval. Richard Nixon and Lyndon Johnson are examples. (Chapter 14.)

active–positive
Presidential character type who relishes the give-and-take of politics and the promise of accomplishments, while enjoying the job and its demanding public aspects. Franklin Roosevelt and John F. Kennedy are examples cited by political scientist James David Barber. (Chapter 14.)

activist bureaucracy
A bureaucracy that administers programs in almost every area of peoples' lives. (Chapter 15.)

adversarial process
The requirement that there be a disputed issue between the parties in a lawsuit. Also, both sides are to be treated equally. In a criminal case, there is a presumption of the defendant's innocence. (Chapter 16.)

advertising (in Congress)
Congressional member's use of the advantages of incumbency to become well known by the voters. (Chapter 12.)

affirmative action
Plans by governments, private employers, and educational institutions to give preference to protected minorities in employment (hiring and promotion) and admission policies. Called *reverse discrimination* by its critics. (Chapter 5.)

agencies for hire
Organizations that work for various clients and causes, providing legal services, contacts, and public relations services for interest groups. (Chapter 8.)

agenda building (agenda setting) stage
First stage of the policy process, during which an issue gets the attention of government decision makers, who begin to think seriously about the problem, exploring options and testing the political waters with the media and the public. (Chapter 17.)

agenda setting (by the media)
The role of the media in determining what political and social issues are important. (Chapter 11.)

agents of socialization
Sources that shape an individual's political orientations. The agents include the family, schools, peer groups, and the media. (Chapter 6.)

Aid to Families with Dependent Children
Assistance program that uses national and state funds to provide cash payments to support children in low-income families. (Chapter 18.)

alienation
The feeling by an individual that social norms and institutions in society do not represent his or her values. (Chapter 7.)

apprenticeship system
Congressional system that once required junior members of Congress to follow the orders of senior committee chairs, much as workers learning a trade serve as assistants or apprentices to senior craftsmen. (Chapter 13.)

arraign
To formally charge an individual in a criminal case. Arraignments are formal hearings at which the defendant is made aware of the charges and read the indictment. (Chapter 16.)

Articles of Confederation
The "league of friendship" among the original thirteen states that specified the institutions and their powers in America's first national government. The government had extremely limited powers which were concentrated in a unicameral Congress. (Chapter 2.)

association
Group of people united by a common interest. (Chapter 8.)

authority
The right to make decisions. Power considered legitimate. (Chapter 2.)

B

back-channel operations
International operations carried out by the president and the national security advisor directly from the White House, bypassing the normal channels of the State Department and the Defense Department. (Chapter 15.)

Barron v. Baltimore (1833)
Supreme Court case that determined that the protections of the Bill of Rights applied only to restrain the national government, not the state and local governments. (Chapter 5.)

beat
The area of responsibility of a journalist. Examples might include the White House, city hall, schools or education. (Chapter 11.)

biased and unbiased samples
Biased samples are not collected randomly. Unbiased samples give everyone in the population whose opinion is being estimated an equal chance to register his or her opinion by being included in the sample. (Chapter 6.)

bicameralism
A two-chamber legislature, such as the U. S. Congress's division into the Senate and the House of Representatives. (Chapter 12.)

Bill of Rights
The first ten amendments to the Constitution, added in 1791 to protect the fundamental rights of individuals against government infringement. (Chapter 2.)

blanket primary
Form of primary election in which a voter can vote for nominees of any party as long as he or she votes for only one nominee for each office. (Chapter 9.)

block grant
Federal grant provided to state and local governments for a broad group, or block, of problems. (Chapter 4.)

bottom-up path to policy
Direction of policymaking initiated when the public and interest groups mobilize social concern to get issues on the public agenda on the way to the government agenda. (Chapter 17.)

broad construction
Philosophy of legal interpretation that advocates adapting and changing the law to fit the needs of contemporary society. Termed *legal realism* by scholars. (Chapter 16.)

Brown v. Board of Education (1954)
Supreme Court case that established that separate facilities by race in public education could not be equal because of the psychological impact of state-supported segregation. Overturned *Plessy v. Ferguson* (1896). (Chapter 5.)

bureaucracy
Hierarchically structured organization in which each office, or bureau, has specific duties and responsibilities and a clear set of authority relations with the offices above and below. (Chapter 15.)

bureaucratic state
Government sphere of power in which interests have become the organizing force, even though the interests have very little accountability to the people and no accountability through elections. (Chapter 15.)

C

cabinet
The president's formal advisory body, consisting of the secretaries of the fourteen executive departments (and other individuals who have been given special cabinet-level status by the president). Sometimes a president's informal inner circle of advisors is referred to as the *kitchen cabinet*. (Chapter 15.)

campaign contribution
An interest-group tactic to provide financial assistance to candidates for public office who will support the group's interests if elected. See *political action committee (PAC)*. (Chapter 8.)

candidate character
A basis for voting that involves an evaluation of the personal qualities of candidates for public office such as trustworthiness, honesty, integrity, and sincerity. (Chapter 7.)

career management system
Congressional system designed to keep members of Congress in office even if they are not doing much legislating. New members of Congress are taught how to organize their offices, how to publicize their activities, and how to get reelected. (Chapter 13.)

casework
Assistance provided to constituents by members of Congress and their staffs to resolve problems with government. (Chapter 12.)

categorical grant
Federal grant provided to state and local governments for specific kinds, or categories, of activities. (Chapter 4.)

caucuses
Political party meetings at the voting precinct at which participants select delegates to the county or state conventions. (Chapter 9.)

center-of-a-wheel model
The less formal presidential management style that encourages direct access to the president by cabinet members and personal staff. This style facilitates debates and input from working groups and promotes political initiatives by cabinet members. (Chapter 15.)

checks and balances
A system that allows each branch of government to check the powers of the other branches of government. (Chapter 3.)

circuit courts/U.S. Court of Appeals
The United States courts of appellate jurisdiction in most cases, dealing primarily with cases that have been heard by the district courts in the circuit (a geographical area of jurisdiction) or decisions rendered by independent regulatory commissions. (Chapter 16.)

civil law
Those laws that define areas of rights, contracts, conditions of property ownership, and other matters that are not viewed as a threat to public safety but which require protection. (Chapter 16.)

civil liberties
Personal freedoms protected by rights claims aimed at restraining the government. Civil liberties are tied to matters of *individual* freedom. (Chapter 5.)

civil rights
Constitutional guarantees for all citizens to have equal protection under the law. Civil rights are commonly tied to *group* issues of equality and discrimination. (Chapter 5.)

Civil Rights Act, equal opportunity provisions of
The act that attempted to compel states to provide equal education regardless of race, religion, nationality, or gender. (Chapter 18.)

civil rights laws
Laws that have expanded the rights of particular *groups* against discrimination. Examples include the Civil Rights Acts of 1957, 1964, and 1991; the Voting Rights Act of 1965; Fair Housing Acts of 1968 and 1988; and the Americans With Disabilities Act of 1990. (Chapter 5.)

civil service
Government system whereby jobs in the bureaucracy are filled on the basis of merit rather than politics, providing job security for government workers. (Chapter 15.)

clear and present danger
Test used in freedom of speech cases, requiring that the government demonstrate a "clear and present danger" created by an activity. Congress has a right to restrict an individual's freedom of speech only if such a danger can be shown. Established in *Schenck v. United States* (1919). (Chapter 5.)

clients
People or groups served or regulated by the bureaucracy. (Chapter 15.)

closed primary
Form of primary election in which only the voters who indicate their affiliation or allegiance to a political party are allowed to participate in that party's primary. (Chapter 9.)

cloture
Rule for terminating a filibuster in the Senate. Currently, the rule requires a petition signed by sixteen senators followed by a three-fifths vote of the Senate. (Chapter 12.)

Cold War
Ideology-based conflict between the United States and the Soviet Union, sometimes erupting into open combat, and lasting from after World War II to the collapse of the Soviet Union in 1989. (Chapter 20.)

colonialism
System in which one nation exercises economic and political control over another territory, which provides raw materials to the colonial power and markets for the colonial power's products. (Chapter 2.)

committee chairman
That member of the majority party who presides over committee meetings and provides leadership for the committee. See *seniority system.* (Chapter 13.)

common law
"Judge-made" laws that originated when English magistrates applied commonly accepted judicial principles, based on precedent and custom, to situations in which the social structure failed to provide order. (Chapter 16.)

comparable worth
The idea that employees who perform comparable work (based on the social benefit of the work) should receive comparable pay. (Chapter 5.)

complexity of elections
The large number of opportunities for American citizens to vote caused by federalism and attempts to incorporate direct democracy through initiatives and referenda. The effect is to depress voter turnout. (Chapter 7.)

compromise
See *pragmatism.* (Chapter 2.)

compromises on slavery
A number of compromises over slavery were made between northern and southern states before the Civil War. Most important was the "three-fifths compromise," which provided that slaves were to be counted as three-fifths of a person for the purposes of direct taxation and representation. (Chapter 2.)

concurring opinion
Opinion written by a justice or judge who concurs with the *decision* of the majority of the court but who disagrees to some degree with the *legal reasoning* behind that decision. (Chapter 16.)

confederation
A largely voluntary association of sovereign states. In a confederation, the national government is limited to those powers that the states allow the "government to exercise. (Chapter 2.)

conference committee
Congressional committee, composed of both House and Senate members, that reconciles differences in House and Senate versions of the same bill. The Constitution requires that a bill be passed in identical form in the House and Senate to become law. (Chapter 12.)

conferences
Private decision-making meetings of the Supreme Court. The Court currently holds biweekly conferences to decide cases and to set the Court's agenda by issuing writs of certiorari. (Chapter 16.)

Connecticut or Great Compromise
Compromise at the Constitutional Convention of 1787 that settled the issue of representation in Congress by creating a bicameral legislature, in which representation in one chamber (the Senate) was equal among all states, and in the other chamber (the House of Representatives) proportional to each state's population. (Chapter 2.)

conservatism
Ideology that emphasizes individual freedom, respect for tradition, voluntary solutions to economic and social problems, the efficiency of a free-market economy, and government action to uphold social order and defend the state. (Chapter 1.)

constituent service
See *casework.* (Chapter 12.)

Constitution
A fundamental law or document that establishes the institutions of government and their powers. (Chapter 3.)

Constitutional Convention of 1787
Meeting of delegates from twelve of the thirteen American states, called to revise the Articles of Confederation but which instead wrote a new constitution for the United States of America. (Chapter 2.)

containment
The U. S. foreign policy during the Cold War that advocated containing Soviet expansionist tendencies by countering Soviet advances wherever they occurred. (Chapter 20.)

conventional forms of participation
Political actions within the normal channels of government and electoral participation. Examples include voting, writing letters, working in election campaigns. Compare with *unconventional participation.* (Chapter 7.)

cooperative federalism
Form of federalism in which the powers of the national and state governments are mixed so that one cannot readily separate and distinguish each level of government's powers ("marble-cake" federalism). (Chapter 4.)

corporatism
Interest-group system in many European nations that features greater cooperation among groups in similar interest areas and between those groups and the government. (Chapter 8.)

Council of Economic Advisers
A council in the Executive Office of the President that advises the president on economic policy. (Chapter 19.)

credit-claiming
A congressional member's taking credit for pork-barrel projects, casework, and passing or defeating legislation that might please his or her constituents and help his or her reelection. (Chapter 12.)

criminal law
Laws that define offenses considered anti-social or dangerous to the survival of society. (Chapter 16.)

crisis theory of strong party government
Theory that strong political parties exist in the United States only when crises erupt, forcing the parties to propose new governing ideas and chart anew political course. (Chapter 9.)

critical elections
Presidential elections that create a new dominant major party or are the basis for a party realignment. According to this theory, there have been five critical elections in America's history: 1800, 1828, 1860, 1896, and 1932. (Chapter 9.)

cultural themes
Values and beliefs that are most important in the political culture. (Chapter 1.)

culture and opinion
The influence of dominant themes in the political culture on a person's political outlook. Individuals often interpret and share personal experiences using the cultural themes. (Chapter 6.)

cynicism
The feeling by an individual that the social institutions represent other groups to the exclusion of his or her group. (Chapter 7.)

D

damage control
Attempts by a campaign organization to control the negative effects of critical news coverage of its candidate. (Chapter 10.)

dealignment
The continuing detachment of people from the political parties with no indication that a critical election is imminent to reverse the trend, despite strains with the society. (Chapter 9.)

debate function of elections
The discussion of problems, proposal of solutions, and the candidates' adherence to the parties' programs during an election campaign. (Chapter 10.)

decision stage
Stage in the policy process in which policy guidelines are set down. See *formulation and adoption stage.* (Chapter 17.)

defendant
Person accused of violating either criminal or civil law. (Chapter 16.)

delegate representation
The view that elected officials should respond primarily to the views of their constituents rather than rely on their own judgment. Compare *trustee.* (Chapters 1 and 12.)

democracy
System of government in which the people rule, either directly or indirectly through representatives. (Chapter 2.)

demographic representation
The view that Congress should be representative of the population of the United States in terms of social characteristics. The argument is based on the belief that people with shared social characteristics are better able to repre-

sent people with those characteristics because they have shared experiences. (Chapter 12.)

denied powers
Powers that the Constitution specifically declares the national government and/or the state governments *can not* exercise. (Chapter 3.)

departments
Those executive bureaucracies created by Congress and headed by a secretary, who is nominated by the president and confirmed by the Senate. These secretaries make up the president's *cabinet.* Today these departments—fourteen at last count—include Agriculture, Commerce, Defense, Education, Energy, Health and Human Services (HHS), Housing and Urban Development (HUD), Interior, Justice, Labor, State, Transportation, Treasury, and Veterans Affairs (VA). (Chapter 15.)

deregulation
Removal or lessening of government rules and regulations in response to the sense that an industry is suffering from excessive, counter-productive regulation, leading to higher consumer prices and reduced efficiency. Among the first industries to be deregulated was the airline industry. (Chapter 19.)

detachment from politics
The isolation of many people from any involvement with politics, especially campaign politics. Ruy Teixeira's explanation for declining voter turnout. (Chapter 7.)

détente
The lessening of tensions during the Cold War. Détente became a major aspect of President Nixon's foreign policy in response to public divisions over U. S. involvement in Vietnam and changes in the balance of power between America and the Soviet Union. (Chapter 20.)

deviating elections
Presidential elections in which the minority party wins the presidency, indicating social strains or discontent among the electorate. (Chapter 9.)

direct democracy
System whereby the populace rules directly by making decisions that affect them. Direct democracy is fairly difficult to achieve as a regular form of government except in small groups. *Initiatives* and *referenda* allow a degree of direct democracy in many states of the U. S. (Chapter 10.)

direction of opinions
The characteristic of opinions that indicates whether the evaluation is positive or negative. (Chapter 6.)

discount rate
Fee that the reserve banks charge their best and biggest member banks to borrow money. The discount rate affects the interest rates charged to consumers for loans and the ability to get credit. (Chapter 19.)

dissenting opinion
Opinion of a justice or judge who disagrees with the majority opinion. (Chapter 16.)

district courts/U.S. District Courts
The United States trial courts of original jurisdiction in civil and criminal cases. Each state has at least one district court. (Chapter 16.)

divine right
Theory supporting absolute rights of monarchs, based on the divinity of the office. (Chapter 5.)

division of powers
Allocation of powers between the national and state governments. (Chapter 3.)

divisions among the colonies
Differences among the colonies in terms of their economic relations with England, their internal, political, and economic divisions, and the relative satisfaction of the colonial elites. (Chapter 2.)

docket
The list of cases to be decided by a court. The Supreme Court controls its docket through its discretionary power to determine what cases it will hear. See *writ of certiorari*. (Chapter 16.)

domestication of foreign policy
The tendency for foreign policy-making, which had been dominated by the president, to take on the characteristics of domestic policy-making with more players and more conflicts over policy. (Chapter 20.)

Dred Scott v. Sanford (1857)
Supreme Court case that determined that slaves could not become citizens of the United States nor were they entitled to the rights and privileges of citizenship. The Court also declared the Missouri Compromise, which had banned slavery in the territories, unconstitutional. (Chapter 4.)

dual citizenship
National citizenship and state citizenship. A citizen in the United States has rights as a citizen of the nation and as a citizen of the state. (Chapter 5.)

dual federalism
Form of federalism in which the powers of the national government and the state governments are clearly distinguished by the Constitution (layer cake federalism). (Chapter 4.)

due process clause
Clause of the Fourteenth Amendment used by the Supreme Court to make most provisions of the Bill of Rights applicable to the states. (Chapter 5.)

E

economic policy
Government policy concerning the economy. (Chapter 19.)

education policy
Government policy concerning primary and secondary education. (Chapter 18.)

elastic clause
Final clause of Article I, Section 8 of the U. S. Constitution, which states that Congress can make all laws "necessary and proper" to carry out the expressed powers. Termed the "elastic clause" because it has enabled the national government to expand its powers. (Chapter 3.)

election laws
Laws and procedures regulating voting. States control these requirements unless superseded by the national government or a constitutional amendment. (Chapter 7.)

electoral college system
Compromise adopted at the Constitutional Convention of 1787 that provides for the indirect election of the president. Each state receives a number of electoral votes equal to its number of representatives and senators. Each state determines how its electors are selected. In most states, the state's electoral vote is awarded to the presidential candidate who receives the most popular votes in the state in the general election. The electors cast their votes in their state capitals. The electoral votes are counted and the winner is announced at a joint session of Congress in January. A constitutional majority is necessary to win the presidency. If no candidate for president receives a majority of the electoral votes, the House of Representatives, voting by states, elects the president. (Chapters 2 and 10.)

electoral connection
The contention that electoral success is the chief motivation of a congressional member's activities. These activities include advertising, credit claiming, and position taking. (Chapter 12.)

electoral vote
The vote by the presidential electors that determines who wins the presidency. A candidate must receive a constitutional majority to win (currently, 270 of the 538 electoral votes). See *electoral college system*. (Chapter 10.)

Elementary and Secondary Education Act
Act of Congress that included provisions designed to promote equality in education by providing money to school districts to prepare poor children for school and to provide assistance after they entered public schools. (Chapter 18.)

elitism
Theory that power is concentrated in the hands of a small number of very powerful, economically and socially privileged people. (Chapter 1.)

elitist view of the Constitution
Belief that the U. S. Constitution was created by and for people with money, status, and connections. (Chapter 3.)

enumerated powers
Formal powers granted to the president in Article II of the Constitution. (Chapter 14.)

equal protection clause
Clause of the Fourteenth Amendment that has been used to insure that states do not discriminate against their citizens in terms of race, religion, or national origin. (Chapter 5.)

equal time provision
Federal Communications Commission (FCC) rule requiring broadcast stations that sell time or give free access to a candidate for public office to provide "equal time" to his or her opponents for that office. (Chapter 11.)

equality/equality of opportunity
Cultural theme that demands that each individual have an equal chance to pursue his or her goals in life without the imposition of impediments by society. (Chapter 1.)

establishment clause
Clause of the First Amendment that prohibits government from establishing or promoting religion through its activities. (Chapter 5.)

European welfare systems
A broad package of social services provided to all citizens, regardless of income levels. (Chapter 18.)

evaluation stage
The fourth stage in the policy process, during which studies are conducted to determine the effects of the policy, to evaluate the effectiveness of the policy, and to suggest changes to improve the policy. (Chapter 17.)

exclusionary rule
Rule established by the Supreme Court to prevent police officers from conducting "unreasonable" searches and seizures. The rule provides that illegally seized evidence not be admissible in court. (Chapter 5.)

executive agreement
An agreement negotiated by a president that is not subject to congressional approval. Presidents claim an inherent power to make executive agreements. (Chapter 14.)

executive branch
The branch of government responsible for implementing legislation. (Chapter 3.)

Executive Office of the President
A collection of offices and councils that serves as a central command for gathering information and developing policy around the president's agenda. (Chapter 15.)

executive order
A presidential order initiated without specific legal authorization from Congress. Presidents claim an inherent power to issue executive orders. (Chapter 15.)

expressed powers
Specific powers that the Constitution grants to the national government in Article I, Section 8. (Chapter 3.)

F

fairness doctrine
Federal Communications Commission (FCC) rule that required broadcast stations to provide time to competing viewpoints on controversial topics. The requirement was dropped in 1987. (Chapter 11.)

family and child policies
Proposals for public and private programs designed to assist families and children and create an investment in society rather than provide handouts to the poor. (Chapter 18.)

family policies
Policies designed to advance education indirectly by supporting families and encouraging communities to give children "more of what they need" outside the classroom. (Chapter 18.)

Federal Election Campaign Act (FECA)
Law that established the basic rules for contributing, spending, and reporting money and services in federal campaigns. (Chapter 10.)

Federal Reserve System
The equivalent of a national bank. The Federal Reserve System protects the nation's cash reserve by controlling monetary policy through a system of member banks. (Chapter 19.)

federalism/federal system
System in which a constitution divides powers between the national government and state governments so that neither level of government derives its powers from the other level. (Chapter 4.)

Federalist, The ("The Federalist Papers")
A series of more than eighty newspaper articles written by James Madison, Alexander Hamilton, and John Jay to explain the newly written U. S. Constitution and to increase support for its ratification during the debates in the states. (Chapter 2.)

felony
Category of criminal law that includes offenses considered most serious by society and thus are accompanied by more severe penalties. Compare *misdemeanor*. (Chapter 16.)

filibuster
Method of killing a bill by "talking it to death," using the power of unlimited debate granted in the Senate to block its passage. See *cloture*. (Chapter 12.)

fiscal policy
Government levers to affect the economy including taxing and spending policies specified in the government's budget. (Chapter 19.)

floor debate
Discussion of proposed legislation on the floor of the House or Senate. (Chapter 12.)

floor votes
Votes on amendments to bills and on final passage taken on the floor of the House or Senate. (Chapter 12.)

focus groups
Small groups of people chosen by researchers to discover how categories of people feel about certain issues. They usually involve a facilitator, who introduces topics, encourages discussions, and draws out responses. Focus groups provide more in-depth information than do opinion polls. (Chapter 6.)

food stamp program
Assistance program for the poor that provides food coupons redeemable in local grocery stores for basic nutrition items. (Chapter 18.)

foreign policy establishment
A group of career civil servants, businessmen, and academics who advised presidents on foreign policy during the Cold War. (Chapter 20.)

formulation and adoption stage
The second stage in the policy process, during which decisions are made. This stage usually involves negotiations and political compromise. (Chapter 17.)

free exercise/free expression clause
Clause of the First Amendment that protects an individual's right to express his or her religious beliefs without government interference. The protection afforded religious practices by this clause is not absolute; religious practices can be restricted in the interest of the public's health, welfare, and safety. (Chapter 5.)

free rider problem
The problem faced by groups whose benefits are collective, tempting potential members to sit back and enjoy the free ride provided by those who join the group and do the work. (Chapter 8.)

G

gerrymandering
Drawing voting district boundaries so that the composition of the district is favorable to a particular political party or group. (Chapters 7 and 13.)

Gibbons v. Ogden (1824)
Supreme Court case that nullified a state grant giving an exclusive right to use the navigable waters within a state. The decision interpreted the interstate commerce powers of the national government broadly. (Chapter 4.)

going public
The practice of a president's appealing directly to the people for support for his political agenda. (Chapter 14.)

government
The institutions that make law, collect taxes, create public policy, and enforce compliance to laws in a society. (Chapter 1.)

Government Accounting Office (GAO)
The research and investigative arm of Congress. (Chapter 12.)

government agenda
Those issues with which the government is actively attempting to deal. (Chapter 17.)

growth of interest groups
The increase of interest groups in recent decades is considered attributable to the decline of political parties, various government reforms, the creation of PACs, and changing technology. (Chapter 8.)

H

handlers
Experts in media management who escort and coach politicians in their public encounters. (Chapter 11.)

hard money
Contributions that go to candidates for federal office and are limited by the Federal Election Campaign Act (FECA). Compare *soft money*. (Chapter 10.)

health policy
Government policy concerning the medical care of the public. (Chapter 18.)

hearings, congressional
Public meetings of a committee or subcommittee in Congress to gather information from expert witnesses concerning proposed legislation. (Chapter 12.)

hierarchical model
A formal presidential management style that allows the chief of staff to screen access to the president and imposes a clear chain of command within White House offices and the cabinet. (Chapter 15.)

home rule
The ability of local governments to exercise broad governing powers unless the state constitution or state law forbids the action. (Chapter 4.)

home style
The way in which an elected representative, such as a member of Congress, presents himself to his (or her) constituents. (Chapter 12.)

honeymoon
Period of weeks or months following a president's inauguration in which the public usually rallies around its new leader. (Chapter 14.)

House norms
Unwritten rules and customs that guide relations among members. Also referred to as folkways. (Chapter 13.)

House Rules Committee
Standing committee that sets the agenda for the House of Representatives. A rule issued by the committee gives a bill priority over other legislation, establishes the terms under which the bill is debated, and sets a time limit for debate. (Chapter 13.)

I

idealists
Foreign policy officials who opposed Communism but also opposed supporting authoritarian regimes, even if they were anti-communist, that deprived their people of democracy and freedom. (Chapter 20.)

ideology
An individual's set of cultural ideals that are given priority over others and applied consistently when confronting political issues. (Chapter 1.)

image consultants/pollsters/public-relations experts
Specialists in media management who plan what politicians do and/or measure the results. (Chapter 11.)

implementation stage
Third stage in the policy process, during which the action is carried out. This stage usually involves negotiations and coordination among the units of government and the groups affected by the policy. (Chapter 17.)

impoundment
The president's refusal to spend funds appropriated by Congress for a specific program because he does not support the program. (Chapter 14.)

incorporation
Process through which the Supreme Court, on a case-by-case basis, has made most provisions of the Bill of Rights applicable to the states. See *due process clause*. (Chapter 5.)

independent agencies
Bodies created by Congress that are headed by directors and perform functions independently of the executive departments. The Environmental Protection Agency (EPA) is one example. (Chapter 15.)

indict
To bring charges against an individual in a criminal case. Indictments are issued by a grand jury in felonies and indicate that the grand jury, after considering the evidence provided by the prosecutor, decided that sufficient evidence existed to warrant a trial. (Chapter 16.)

indirect democracy
System in which the people rule indirectly through their elected representatives; a *republic*. (Chapter 10.)

industrial policy
Government planning of industrial research and investment, rebuilding of the infrastructure, and designing welfare and education policies. (Chapter 19.)

inflation
Economic condition in which prices increase faster than wages, causing people to demand higher wages. (Chapter 19.)

informational hearing
Public hearing conducted by a congressional committee to investigate an alleged problem in the implementation of a law by the executive branch. (Chapter 12.)

infotainment
Label given to news programs that have taken on the qualities of entertainment programs—hyperbole, re-enactment of events, promotion of news anchors and correspondents as celebrity figures, and so forth—blurring the line between fact and fiction. (Chapter 11.)

inherent powers
Informal or implied powers that presidents claim reside in the spirit of the Constitution to enable them to get the job done. (Chapter 14.)

insider political strategy
Interest-group strategy that relies on money or professional expertise to meet directly with legislators or bureaucrats whose decisions affect their interests. (Chapter 8.)

institutional sharing/separation of powers
The combination of a system of separation of powers with a system of checking and balancing the powers among the branches of government. (Chapter 1.)

institutions
Organizations that include individual corporations, universities, state and local governments, and religious denominations that are active on their own behalf as well as belonging to voluntary associations of similar organizations. (Chapter 8.)

intensity of opinions
The characteristic of opinions that indicates whether the feeling behind the evaluation is strong or weak. (Chapter 6.)

interest group
Organization of persons or corporate members that share a common interest and attempt to influence government policy affecting that interest. (Chapter 8.)

interest-group strategies
Forms of pressure applied by interest groups in pursuit of their goals. The principal strategies include lobbying, campaign contributions, litigation, and mobilizing public opinion. (Chapter 8.)

internationalism
The cultural theme promoting American involvement in global affairs, including those which appear to have no direct bearing on U.S. interests. (Chapter 20.)

iron law of oligarchy
Roberto Michels' observation that all organizations, no matter how democratic their intentions, tend toward oligarchy—rule by the few. (Chapter 13.)

iron triangle
Strong ties of influence between interest groups, key congressional committees, and executive offices and agencies on a particular area of public policy. The triangles promote policies and programs for their own interests rather than the public good. (Chapters 8 and 15.)

isolationism
Element in the American political culture that advocates withdrawal from international commitments and a concentration on domestic problems. (Chapter 20.)

issue networks
Groups of important people linked by interest in a policy area. Typically, they include members of Congress, interest groups, academics, and policy researchers. (Chapter 12.)

issues
Substantive problems debated during a political campaign that affect the voter's choice. (Chapter 7.)

J
Jim Crow laws
Laws enacted in southern states that prevented blacks from exercising their rights under the Fourteenth and Fifteenth Amendments following the Civil War. (Chapter 7.)

joint committees
Temporary or permanent congressional committees that contain members of both chambers, Senate and House. They usually coordinate activities that involve both chambers. (Chapter 13.)

journalists as gatekeepers
The idea that journalists, by deciding to what events and viewpoints the public is exposed, exercise significant control over the issues, events, and viewpoints considered important by society. See *agenda setting*. (Chapter 11.)

judicial activism
Judicial philosophy that advocates an active role for the courts vis-a-vis the other branches of government, arguing that the courts should use judicial review to strike down laws that violate the Constitution or its principles. (Chapter 16.)

judicial restraint
Judicial philosophy that advocates a restrained role for the courts, arguing that the courts should, if at all possible, find the actions of the other branches of government constitutional and permissible. (Chapter 16.)

judicial review
The right of the judiciary to interpret the Constitution and the constitutionality of actions by the branches of government. See *Marbury v. Madison* (1803). (Chapter 3.)

judiciary/judicial branch
The branch of government responsible for interpreting the laws. (Chapter 3.)

jurisdiction
The authority of a particular court or law enforcement agency to handle a case. (Chapter 16.)

jurisprudence
The process of legal interpretation. See *broad constructionism* and *strict constructionism*. (Chapter 16.)

K
Keynes, John Maynard
British economist who advocated government intervention to deal with economic recessions and periods of inflation. His best known book was *The General Theory of Employment, Interest, and Money* (1936).

L

laissez-faire
Economic and, more broadly, political theory that asserts that the government should intervene in public affairs only to the degree necessary to maintain public order and tranquillity. From the French phrase *to let do* or *to let alone*. Libertarians tend to espouse the most doctrinaire *laissez-faire* views.(Chapter 4.)

landmark ruling
Decision by the Supreme Court that establishes a new interpretation of the Constitution, or overturns a previous interpretation by an earlier Court. (Chapter 16

leadership function of elections
The screening of candidates by voters during a campaign to determine which is most likely to represent their interests, handle crises effectively, and otherwise exercise the kind of authority they desire. (Chapter 10.)

legal formalism
See *strict constructionism*. (Chapter 16.)

legal realism
See *broad constructionism*. (Chapter 16.)

legislative branch
The branch of government responsible for lawmaking. (Chapter 3.)

legislative veto
The ability of Congress to figuratively "veto" rules adopted by executive agencies to implement legislation passed by Congress. The legislative veto has been incorporated in hundreds of laws, but the Supreme Court ruled the practice unconstitutional in 1983. (Chapter 12.)

legitimacy
The voluntary acceptance of government powers because people feel that the government has the right to carry out its functions. See *authority*. (Chapters 2 and 7.)

liberalism
Ideology that generally emphasizes social equality over freedom, supports the imposing of government solutions to economic and social problems, and espouses individual liberty in moral and "lifestyle" issues. (Chapter 1.)

libertarian
Ideology that consistently emphasizes individualism, liberty, and freedom over other cultural themes. (Chapter 1.)

liberty–freedom
Culture theme that favors individual freedom from government control. (Chapter 1.)

limited participation
Function of elections providing the opportunity, during a campaign, for people to act together or against each other in a limited or controlled fashion. (Chapter 10.)

line of the day
The political management of media coverage by presenting the candidate in a telegenic setting discussing an issue(the "line") that the campaign organization wants emphasized at that time. (Chapter 10.)

literacy tests
Tests administered as a condition for voting which were used to prevent blacks from the franchise. (Chapter 7.)

litigation
An individual or interest-group tactic that employs lawsuits to further the a particular interest. The NAACP used litigation to promote civil rights when other methods failed. (Chapter 8.)

lobbying
An interest-group tactic to influence public officials toward supporting the group's viewpoint. The principal lobbying activity is providing information. (Chapter 8.)

lobbyist
Person hired by an interest group to present the group's concerns to public officials. (Chapter 8.)

logic of collective action
Theory of political scientist Mancur Olson that it is illogical for a person to join a group if he or she can receive the same benefits without the burdens of membership and participation. See *free rider problem*. (Chapter 8.)

logjams
Impediments to policy-making that slow progress in an area. (Chapter 17.)

logrolling
Favor-exchange system in Congress whereby one member agrees to vote for a bill favored by another in return for a vote on an issue of importance to him or her in the future. (Chapter 12.)

M

maintaining elections
Presidential elections in which the dominant political party wins the presidency, indicating approval of the party's governance. (Chapter 9.)

majoritarianism
Theory that power resides with a majority of the people. (Chapter 1.)

Manifest destiny
Cultural theme that maintained that the United States, populated by a chosen people and governed democratically, had a destiny to expand so that it could serve as an example for entire world and the future. (Chapter 20.)

Mapp v. Ohio (1961)
Supreme Court case that extended the exclusionary rule to state action through the due process clause of the Fourteenth Amendment. (Chapter 5.)

Marbury v. Madison (1803)
Supreme Court case that established the right of judicial review when the Supreme Court ruled that a portion of the Judiciary Act of 1789 was unconstitutional because it attempted to extend the original jurisdiction of the Supreme Court in violation of Article III of the Constitution. (Chapter 3.)

margin of error
The difference in opinion polls between the opinions of the sample and the opinions if everyone in the population had been questioned. Such error usually varies inversely with the sample size. An unbiased sample of 1,000 yields an error of plus or minus 3 percent, 95 percent of the time. (Chapter 6.)

marketing strategies
Techniques of public opinion polling, research activities, and advertising used by campaign organizations to get their candidates elected. (Chapter 10.)

markup sessions
Meetings of subcommittees or committees in which a bill is considered line-by-line, amendments are offered and voted upon, and a final bill is produced, reflecting any changes adopted by the members. (Chapter 12.)

Marshall Plan
Economic program by the United States designed to assist the governments of Europe in recovering from the devastation of World War II. Named after General George C. Marshall, a World War II commander who later served as secretary of state and secretary of defense, receiving the 1953 Nobel peace prize for his work. (Chapter 20.)

McCulloch v. Maryland (1819)
Supreme Court case that involved the interpretation of the *elastic clause* and the *supremacy clause* of the Constitution. The Supreme Court ruled that the national government could create a national bank through its implied powers, and that the state of Maryland could not tax the bank because of the supremacy clause. (Chapter 4.)

means-tested programs
Assistance programs that have qualifications which must be met in order to receive benefits. Medicaid, AFDC, and food stamps are examples. (Chapter 18.)

media campaign strategies
Techniques of campaign organizations to manage the media's coverage of candidates. The techniques include the line of the day, sound bites, damage control, and spin. (Chapter 10.)

media monopoly
The tendency for large corporations to buy news organizations from local or regional owners, resulting in the concentration of the ownership of the news 'media, or a media monopoly. (Chapter 11.)

Medicaid
Government program that provides health care for poor people who qualify for state public assistance. The cost of the program is shared by the national and state governments. (Chapter 18.)

Medicare
Government program established in 1965 to provide health services to retired and disabled persons. (Chapter 18.)

Miranda v. Arizona (1966)
Supreme Court case that established uniform police procedures for conducting interrogations of suspects in criminal cases. (Chapter 5.)

misdemeanor
Category of criminal law that includes offenses considered less serious than others and are accompanied by milder penalties. See *felony*. (Chapter 16.)

mobilizing public opinion
Interest-group tactic that involves activities such as ad campaigns and staged media events, which are used to appeal to the broader public beyond its membership. (Chapter 8.)

monetary policy
Government levers to affect the economy, including the raising and lowering of the supply and cost of money in circulation. (Chapter 19.)

monetary theory
Monetarists maintain that monetary tools such as the money supply and interest rates are more effective than fiscal tools or regulation in maintaining economic growth. (Chapter 19.)

Monroe Doctrine
Presidential proclamation that declared the Western hemisphere to be within the U.S. sphere of influence and therefore subject to economic and political development guided by American rather than European values. (Chapter 20.)

multipolar world politics
An international system in which there are many major powers ("poles") and which is characterized by fluid alliances and requires consummate statesmen to assure that none of the major powers becomes dominant. (Chapter 20.)

Mutual Assured Destruction (MAD)
Politico-military strategy that sought to prevent a nuclear war by ensuring that the United States could survive a Soviet nuclear first strike with sufficient force to retaliate and destroy in turn a significant portion of the Soviet Union's population and industrial capacity. (Chapter 20.)

N

nation-centered view of powers
View that the Constitution was created by the people and that conflicts between the national government and the state governments over powers should be decided in favor of the national government. (Chapter 4.)

national convention
The quadrennial meeting of a political party's delegates from the states and territories, which nominates the party's candidates for president and vice president, adopts the party's platform, and adopts the party's rules. (Chapter 9.)

national party committee
A political party group, composed of members from the fifty states, that runs the party between national conventions, coordinates activities of the state parties, and coordinates national election campaigns. It is headed by a national chairman, formally chosen by the national committee to make the daily decisions necessary for the party to operate. (Chapter 9.)

National Security Act of 1947
Act of Congress that created the Central Intelligence Agency (CIA) and the National Security Council (NSC). (Chapter 20.)

National Security Council
Group based in the Executive Office of the President consisting of statutory members and others whom the president invites. The NSC advises the president on national security affairs and their coordination. (Chapter 20.)

natural rights
The doctrine that human beings have inherent rights to freedom and the protection of property. (Chapter 5.)

necessary and proper clause
See *elastic clause*. (Chapter 3.)

neo-conservative economic theories
Contemporary economic theories advanced by conservatives such as Nobel Prize-winning monetarist Milton Friedman and *supply-side* economist Arthur Laffer. (Chapter 19.)

neo-liberal economic theories
Contemporary economic theories advanced by liberals such as Secretary of Labor Robert Reich. (Chapter 19.)

New Federalism
Attempt to reverse the dominance of the national government over the states by providing the states with greater authority and reallocating national and state powers. (Chapter 4.)

New Jersey Plan
An alternative to the Virginia Plan at the Constitutional Convention of 1787. The plan called or revisions to the Articles of Confederation to strengthen the national government without giving up too many state powers. The plan made the supporters of the Virginia Plan aware of the need for compromise. (Chapter 2.)

new poverty
Form of poverty that results from a "structural economic crisis," involving declining industrial and manufacturing jobs as those jobs are moved to countries where labor costs are lower. This form of poverty challenges the assumption that job training will solve the problem of poverty. (Chapter 18.)

news management techniques
Methods used by politicians to control the coverage that they receive from the media. Experts in news management include spokesmen, handlers, spin doctors, pollsters, public relations experts, and image consultants. (Chapter 11.)

Nixon Doctrine
Presidential proclamation that the United States could not police the world but would provide arms and equipment to nations that wanted to defend themselves against aggression. (Chapter 20.)

nominating politics/federal judges
Process of nominating federal judges and justices, which involves nomination by the president with the advice and consent of the Senate. Recent Supreme Court nominations have involved conflicts exacerbated by partisan conflicts and interest-group influence. (Chapter 16.)

non-means-tested program
Insurance program into which people pay premiums (installments of funds), which make them eligible to collect benefits when they retire or become sick or disabled. Medicare and Social Security are examples. (Chapter 18.)

nullification
Doctrine that the states have a right to reject or nullify national laws that violate the national government's constitutional obligation to respect state powers. (Chapter 4.)

O

old poverty
Form of poverty that involves isolated pockets of poor people who need training for jobs so that they can be integrated into a healthy and expanding economy. (Chapter 18.)

open primary
Form of primary election in which the voter is not required to indicate his or her party affiliation to participate. (Chapter 9.)

opinion change, long-term and short-term
The tendency for a person's opinions to change over time as a result in long-term changes in his or her individual experiences and short-term changes in political situations. (Chapter 6.)

opinion distributions
The direction (positive or negative) and intensity (number of people) of an opinion on an issue. Common distributions are normal, bimodal, and skewed. (Chapter 6.)

opinion measurement
Methods of estimating the opinions of large groups of people, including polling techniques. For more in-depth measurement, *focus groups* are used. (Chapter 6.)

opinion object
People, places, and actions that people evaluate in their opinions. (Chapter 6.)

opinion rally
The surge of public support for a president during a crisis. (Chapter 14.)

order–control
Cultural theme that supports government restrictions on individual actions that harm or offend other people in the society. (Chapter 1.)

orders
Mandates from the national government to the state governments. (Chapter 4.)

outside political strategies
Interest-group strategy that involves the use of the media and grassroots opinion to pressure government officials. (Chapter 8.)

P

packs/pack journalism
Tendency for journalists to turn up in the same places to cover the same stories. Journalists are said to travel in "packs." The result is that different news organizations end up covering the same news—especially domestic scandals or crises—in extraordinary detail, abandoning stories abruptly when public interest appears to be declining. (Chapter 11.)

parliamentary system
System of government in which the legislative and executive branches are closely interrelated. The chief executive (prime minister) is also a member of the legislature (parliament). (Chapter 12.)

party identification
An individual's psychological attachment to a political party. (Chapter 7.)

party leader
Traditional role of the president as political party leader. (Chapter 14.)

party organization
The internal structure of the party consisting of the units of the party organization and the people who occupy positions in those units. See *national convention* and *national party committee*. Party realignment a long-term shift in party identification so that one major party becomes the dominant party and the other major party becomes the minority party in the American two-party system. The shift may occur over several presidential elections but is centered on a critical election. (Chapter 9.)

passive–negative
The presidential character type who is president because of a sense of duty or obligation and does not desire either the publicity or the responsibility of the office. According to political scientist James David Barber, Dwight Eisenhower and Calvin Coolidge are examples. (Chapter 14.)

passive–positive
The presidential character type who avoids personal involvement in the minutiae of daily politics and conflicts, but directs broader policy and enjoys the public ceremonies and limelight. Ronald Reagan and Warren Harding are, according to political scientist James David Barber, examples of this character type. (Chapter 14.)

patriotism–national unity
Cultural theme that encourages pride in one's home country. (Chapter 1.)

Pendleton Act
Law passed by Congress in 1883 that created the professional civil service for the national government. (Chapter 15.)

per curiam opinion
Decision by the Supreme Court that is unaccompanied by a written opinion. Simply put, it is an opinion of the Court. (Chapter 16.)

personal presidency
The contemporary presidency, which is, according to Theodore Lowi, the subject of a nonstop plebiscite for all national concerns. Lowi suggests that Americans have invested too many expectations in their president. (Chapter 14.)

petition for certiorari
Request from the losing party in a case to have his or her case reviewed by a higher court. The petition indicates the basis for the appeal and reasons that the court should review the case. (Chapter 16.)

plaintiff
Person who initiates a suit in a civil case. (Chapter 16.)

platform
Statement adopted by the party's national convention indicating the party's positions on economic, social, and foreign and defense issues. (Chapter 9.)

play or pay
Proposed health care reform that would require employers to provide health insurance for their employees ("play") or put money into a government fund that would provide health insurance for those not covered ("pay"). (Chapter 18.)

Plessy v. Ferguson (1896)
Supreme Court case that established that separate public facilities by race did not violate the "equal protection of the laws" clause of the Fourteenth Amendment. Application of the ruling required that the separate facilities be equal. Subsequently overturned. (Chapter 5.)

pluralism
Theory that power is distributed among diverse social groups and that the competition among those groups explains political decisions. (Chapter 1.)

pluralist view of the Constitution
View that the Constitution was constructed so that various groups within a diverse society could gain access to political decision makers and have an opportunity to influence them. (Chapter 3.)

pocket veto
Presidential veto that occurs if the president refuses to sign or veto a bill, and during the ten days (Sundays excluded) that the president has to consider a bill, the Congress adjourns. If Congress remains in session, the bill becomes law without the president's signature. See *veto, standard*. (Chapter 14.)

policy
A general agreement among government officials about the nature of a political problem and the general approaches that government should take toward it. (Chapter 17.)

policy networks
A group of key players inside and outside government who share an interest in a policy area and have expertise in that area. They typically include grass-roots activists, interest groups, educators, researchers, experts, bureaucrats, and legislators. (Chapter 17.)

political action committee (PAC)
Group formed to solicit funds for and make campaign contributions to candidates for public office. PACs can be independent or created by an existing organization (corporation, labor union, or trade association). Contribution limits for PACs are more generous than for individuals. (Chapter 10.)

political culture
Broadly shared values and beliefs of a society that affect what people want from government and how they express those demands. (Chapter 1.)

political issues leading to the Revolution
A series of actions taken by King George III that precipitated the American Revolution. Those actions included new rules, regulations, and taxes. (Chapter 2.)

political party
An organization that recruits and nominates candidates for public office and tries to get them elected so that the party can form a government and implement its political program. (Chapter 9.)

political question doctrine
Doctrine that the Supreme Court cannot accept cases involving political, rather than legal, questions. Thus,

the Court will refuse to hear a case that involves one branch not liking how another branch has used its power (Chapter 16.)

political socialization
Process through which an individual acquires his or her political beliefs and values. (Chapter 6.)

political system
The mix of culture, institutions, and power relations in a society that determines how political conflicts are resolved. (Chapter 1.)

politics
What people do to get what they want from government. (Chapter 1.)

politics behind opinion formation
The interplay of power and opinion that indicates that opinion is a political force that changes as political situations develop and different political participants try to win public support for their positions. (Chapter 6.)

poll tax
Tax or fee once required for voting in many southern states. Its effect was to disenfranchise blacks and poor whites. (Chapter 7.)

polling techniques
Unscientific (straw polls) and scientific (modern opinion polling) methods of estimating the opinions of large populations by administering questionnaires. (Chapter 6.)

popular sovereignty
Cultural theme that maintains that ultimate political power rests with the people. (Chapter 1.)

pork-barrel legislation
Laws passed by Congress to help a particular member's congressional district. The implication is that the legislation serves no essential purpose and is a poor use of taxpayer money. (Chapter 12.)

position taking
A congressional member's use of the media, newsletters, and local supporters to convince voters that he or she and the constituents agree on political issues. (Chapter 12.)

poverty policy
Government policy related to assisting the poor in society. (Chapter 18.)

power to persuade
The political skill through which the president is able, according to Richard Neustadt, to get others to do what he wants done. (Chapter 14.)

pragmatism
The ability to sacrifice a bit of principle, when that principle is not working, to achieve something that does work. (Chapter 2.)

preemptions
Instructions to states to carry out federal wishes by prohibiting (or preempting) existing state practices that are contrary to federal goals. (Chapter 4.)

presidential character types
Political scientist James David Barber's conception of presidential character, which emphasizes how actively presidents pursue goals and engage in the struggle of politics, and how positively they approach their job

and the life of a public personality. See *active–positive, active–negative, passive–positive, passive–negative*. (Chapter 14.)

presidential management style
The way in which a president deals with the members of his personal staff. See *hierarchical model* and *center-of-a-wheel model*. (Chapter 15.)

presidential staff and advisors
The president's personal appointees who form his innermost circle. See *cabinet*. (Chapter 15.)

primacy principle
The principle that early learning has lasting effects; therefore, the political socialization that occurs early in a child's life can remain in an adult's political orientation. (Chapter 6.)

primary election
Election to decide a political party's nominees for office or, in the case of presidential primaries, to choose delegates to the party's national convention. (Chapter 9.)

problems of discrimination
Problems relating to actions to prevent current, active discrimination by removing the legal and institutional barriers to equality. (Chapter 5.)

problems of past discrimination
Problems relating to actions attempting to make amends for historical discrimination by providing preferences to living members of groups whose ancestors had been discriminated against. (Chapter 5.)

problems of remedies
The problem of correcting injustices to one group without infringing upon the rights of other groups in the process. (Chapter 5.)

proclamation
Presidential statement announcing the government's policy. Presidents claim an inherent power to issue proclamations. (Chapter 14.)

procompetitive
Proposed health care reform that would supposedly stimulate the health care market to improve competition and expand coverage of health care. Proposals suggest issuing tax credits or vouchers to people without insurance and allow them to create a demand that the health care market would meet. (Chapter 18.)

progressive tax
Tax in which rates increase as incomes or profits increase. The graduated income tax is an example. (Chapter 19.)

proportional tax
Tax in which rates are constant. A flat-rate income tax is an example. (Chapter 19.)

prosecutor
Government official who represents "society" and makes the legal case against a person accused of violating a criminal law. (Chapter 16.)

psychological bases of voting
Individual attitudes that influence the voting choice. Examples include party identification, issues, and candidate character or personality. (Chapter 7.)

public agenda
A broad systemic agenda consisting of issues discussed in the media and by community leaders as important public problems that the government "ought" to solve. (Chapter 17.)

public corporation
Government-chartered and supervised entity that may reside within an executive department or be an autonomous unit. Such corporations perform a variety of services from selling electricity (the Tennessee Valley Authority, or TVA) to providing insurance (the Federal Deposit Insurance Corporation, or FDIC). (Chapter 15.)

public information campaign
Interest-group strategy designed by advertising and public relations firms to influence opinion or improve the public image of a client's issue. (Chapter 8.)

public-interest group
Organization that seeks to promote an agenda of issues and broaden the base of citizen participation by promoting what are supposedly the broader concerns of the public. (Chapter 8.)

R
random sample
Polling sample in which every member of the target population has the same (random) chance of being included in the sample. (Chapter 6.)

Reagan Doctrine
Presidential doctrine that resumed the pre-détente policies of confrontation and containment toward expansionist Communist governments, especially Soviet satellites such as Cuba, Angola, and Nicaragua. Culminated in the 1989–1991 collapse of the Soviet Union. (Chapter 20.)

realists
Foreign policy officials who view world power as a "hardball game" that requires confrontation and, if necessary, supporting authoritarian regimes as long as they support United States interests. (Chapter 20.)

recession
Economic condition in which economic growth declines, resulting in less production, more unemployment, lower profits, and a reduction in consumer demand. (Chapter 19.)

reciprocity
House and Senate folkway, or norm, that requires members to exchange favors. (Chapter 13.)

redistricting
Process that determines the geographical boundaries, and consequently the social and political composition, of congressional districts. See *gerrymandering*. (Chapter 13.)

registration requirements
Procedures, set by state governments, for establishing eligibility to vote. Registration procedures usually require that a person prove that they meet the residence requirements of the state—at least 30 days prior to the election—to vote. (Chapter 7.)

regressive tax
Tax in which the taxation rate is constant; yet, because only a certain percentage of income is spent on the products that are taxed, the effect is take a larger percentage of income from poorer people. The sales tax is an example. Lotteries and state-sponsored gambling are often considered *de facto* regressive taxes because poorer people tend to play them much more than the wealthy. (Chapter 19.)

regulation
Rules and restrictions placed on business activities, sometimes affecting the long-term health of the economy. (Chapter 19.)

regulatory commissions
Independent organizations headed by a commission responsive to Congress and to the president. They are created by Congress to oversee and investigate the workings of important and sensitive areas of national life such as broadcasting (the FCC)and the stock market (the SEC). (Chapter 15.)

regulatory policy
Government levers to affect the economy by controlling business, banking, and consumer affairs. (Chapter 19.)

republic
An indirect democracy. (Chapter 1.)

requirements
Actions required of the states by the national government as a condition for receiving federal assistance and participating in federal programs. (Chapter 4.)

requirements for a multiparty system
Procedures that promote a multiparty rather than a two-party system. Proportional representation allocates legislative seats in proportion to the party's vote. For example, a party that receives 20 percent of the popular vote would receive 20 percent of the legislative seats, providing an incentive for even small parties to run candidates for the legislature. (Chapter 9.)

respect
U. S. Senate norm or folkway that requires members to show respect for their colleagues. (Chapter 13.)

revenue sharing
Federal grant of money provided to state and local governments to be used by the recipient government for any legal purpose. (Chapter 4.)

Roe v. Wade (1973)
Supreme Court case that marked the constitutional right of a woman to decide to terminate her pregnancy, by abortion, during the first trimester, and prevented state interference during that period. Subsequent rulings have modified this right. (Chapter 5.)

S
sanction
Threat by the national government to withhold federal funds to the states in one area unless the states do something else in return. (Chapter 4.)

Schenck v. United States (1919)
Supreme Court case that established the "clear and present danger" test for freedom of speech cases. (Chapter 5.)

select committee
Temporary congressional committee that investigates problems and reports its findings. Such a committee cannot legislate but can make recommendations to the appropriate *standing* committee. (Chapter 13.)

Senate norms
Unwritten rules and customs *(folkways)* that guide relations among members. (Chapter 13.)

seniority system
The custom of making that member of the dominant political party who holds the longest continuous service on a committee the chairman of that committee. (Chapter 13.)

separation of powers
System that separates the legislative, executive, and judicial functions among three independent branches. (Chapter 3.)

Shays' Rebellion
A revolt by farmers and veterans in late eighteenth-century Massachusetts, led by Daniel Shays, that protested the government's seizure of their property to pay their debts. (Chapter 2.)

shield laws
State laws that protect media reporters from being compelled to reveal the source of their information. (Chapter 11.)

single-member congressional districts
Each congressional district elects one member to the House of Representatives. (Chapter 9.)

single payer
Proposed health care reform that would have the government assume most of the health care responsibility. The government would manage competition, negotiate costs, regulate access to high-technology care, and attempt to assure an adequate supply of doctors. (Chapter 18.)

Slaughterhouse Cases
Supreme Court cases that interpreted the privileges and immunities clause of the Fourteenth Amendment narrowly, refusing to find a basis for a redefinition of state powers to deal with their own citizens. (Chapter 5.)

Smith, Adam
Scottish economist who proclaimed the virtues of the "invisible hand" of self-interest to regulate the economy and promote social and economic harmony. His best known book, *The Wealth of Nations,* was published in 1776. (Chapter 19.)

social bases of voting
Group or category characteristics that influence the voting choice. Examples include gender, race, class, education, and religion. (Chapter 7.)

social movements
An enduring collection of large numbers of individuals who are identified by common goals and values and who engage in a variety of political activities to promote their politics. (Chapter 7.)

social problems
Difficult social situations that lead many people to resolve that something should be done to improve the problem. Not all unpleasant social conditions, however, are considered social problems. (Chapter 18.)

socialism
Ideology that emphasizes social equality as the dominant cultural theme, and expects government to fulfill most of the needs and wants of individuals. (Chapter 1.)

soft money
Campaign contributions that go to state and local parties for "get out the vote" efforts and other activities that may benefit candidates for federal offices, but which are not regulated by the Federal Election Campaign Act (FECA). (Chapter 10.)

sound bites
Brief statements made by candidates and elected officials and used by the media on news programs. Sound bites may be intentionally devised by candidates, or may be "clipped" from a broader context by the media to fit broadcast time demands (Chapter 10.)

sovereignty
Supreme political power. (Chapter 1.)

special benefits to members
Benefits provided by interest groups which are available only to members, and which are more visible and tangible than the overall mission of the group. (Chapter 8.)

spin
Attempts by campaign organizations to influence the media by interpreting events (such as debates). The term *spin doctor* denotes a news-management expert who performs this function. (Chapters 10 and 11.)

spoils system
Arrangement whereby the winners of elections were able to replace the bureaucrats from the previous administration with their own appointees. Thus the saying, "To the victor go the spoils." See *civil service* and *Pendleton Act.* (Chapter 15.)

spokesman/spokeswoman
News-management expert who explains to the media the positions taken by a politician. (Chapter 11.)

stability of opinions
Characteristic of opinions that indicates whether the evaluations are likely or unlikely to change. (Chapter 6.)

stagflation
Economic condition that involves the simultaneous occurrence of inflation and recession; a portmanteau term combining **stag**nation and in**flation** (Chapter 19.)

standing committee
Any permanent congressional committee that considers proposals for legislation and makes recommendations to the greater chamber. There are 22 standing committees in the House and 16 standing committees in the Senate. Each has jurisdiction over legislation in a particular policy area. (Chapter 12.)

standing to sue
The requirement that a plaintiff in a civil case must show that he or she has suffered an injury to a protected interest or right, and that other opportunities for defending the claim have been exhausted. The plaintiff must have personally experienced the injury. (Chapter 16.)

stare decisis
Literally, "Let the decision stand." Deciding cases on the basis of precedent. If a similar case has been decided, judges will use the applicable legal principle to decide the current case. (Chapter 16.)

state protections of civil rights
Many states, through bills of rights and statutes, have protections that may be more immediate and more accessible than national protections. (Chapter 5.)

state-centered view of powers
The view that the Constitution was created by the states, and that conflicts between the national government and state governments over powers should be decided in favor of the state governments. (Chapter 4.)

statutory law
Legislature-created law that may codify common law principles or deal with situations that are a product of contemporary society. (Chapter 16.)

strict constructionism
Philosophy of legal interpretation that judges should construct legal opinions that look strictly to legal precedent for guidance in a case. Termed *legal formalism* by scholars. (Chapter 16.)

subcommittees
A further specialization within a standing committee. Subcommittees allow the subdivision of each committee's jurisdiction, creating more specialization. (Chapter 12.)

supply-side
Economic theory that favors the use of tax reductions to maintain economic growth. It posits that the money saved by corporations and investors will be "plowed back" into the economy, creating further jobs. (Chapter 19.)

swing vote
Voters who are either weakly attached to or unaffiliated with a political party, and who can be moved in large numbers by similar issues and appeals, thus determining the outcome of an election. (Chapter 10.)

symbolic leader of the nation
Traditional role of the president as ceremonial leader and chief of state. (Chapter 14.)

T
term limits
Reform proposal that seeks to limit the number of times that members of Congress can be re-elected. As of 1993, fifteen states had adopted some form of term limits for members of Congress. (Chapter 13.)

theories of power
Perspectives on how decisions are made in a political system that attempt to explain and/or predict who has the resources to make other people do something that they would not otherwise do. (Chapter 1.)

think tanks
Organizations dedicated to researching and promoting social and economic policy agendas. Examples include the American Enterprise Institute, the Heritage Foundation, and the Brookings Institution. (Chapter 8.)

top-down path to policy
Direction of policymaking initiated when government officials or "insider" elites move to solve problems. (Chapter 17.)

treaty
A formal agreement between the United States and another nations or nations that is negotiated by the president and ratified by two-thirds of the Senate. (Chapter 14.)

Truman Doctrine
Program promoted by President Harry Truman to assist Greece and Turkey in resisting aggression sponsored by forces outside their territory, and a presidential proclamation that the United States would use military and economic assistance to promote democracy and contain communism. (Chapter 20.)

trustee
View of representation that maintains that elected officials should be free to decide what is in their constituents' best interest. (Chapters 1 and 12.)

U
unconventional forms of participation
Forms of political action that challenge government authority and are outside the normal channels of government and electoral participation. Examples include riots, sit-ins, and rebellions. (Chapter 7.)

undeclared war
Military engagements in which the United States is or has been involved without a formal declaration of war by Congress. (Chapter 14.)

unicameralism
A one-chamber legislature. See *bicameralism.* (Chapter 12.)

unifying forces in government
Forces in American politics (political parties, voters, and elections) that have allowed, at critical moments in American history, the separate branches of American government to cooperate and move coherently in the same direction. (Chapter 1.)

unitary system
System in which all powers reside in the national government, and state governments receive their powers from that government. (Chapter 4.)

V
valence issues
Ideas or promises that tap into intense voter opinions on which large majorities line up in one direction, either positive or negative. A candidate's promise to reduce crime would be such an issue. (Chapter 7.)

veto, standard
The rejection of a congressional bill by the president. A president's veto may be overridden by a two-thirds vote of both chambers of Congress. See *pocket veto.* (Chapter 14.)

Vietnam and foreign policy consensus
U. S. involvement in Vietnam was a watershed event that shattered the anticommunist consensus in United States foreign policy, causing splits in the foreign policy

establishment and especially in the Democratic party. (Chapter 20.)

Virginia Plan
The plan at the Constitutional Convention of 1787 that called for the creation of a strong national government consisting of supreme legislative, executive, and judicial branches. The plan was the basis for the Constitution. (Chapter 2.)

voluntary association
An association that members join voluntarily in order to promote a cause. (Chapter 8.)

volunteerism
The cultural theme that promotes individual charity or community-based actions to help people who are in need. (Chapter 1.)

W

white primaries
Democratic party primaries in southern states that were restricted to white citizens only. Since the southern states were one-party Democratic states, the whites-only primary elections effectively disenfranchised black voters. (Chapter 7.)

window of opportunity
The convergence of favorable political conditions that help an issue pass from the government agenda into government policy. John Kingdon identified several forms: crises, defeated opponents, new leadership, and new information. (Chapter 17.)

winner-take-all election
Election in which the candidate receiving the greatest number of votes wins the election. (Chapter 9.)

writ of certiorari
A formal request *(writ)* from a higher court to a lower court to hand over a case for review. In the Supreme Court, a writ of certiorari is issued if four justices vote in conference to issue the writ. (Chapter 16.)

NOTES

CHAPTER 1

[1] *The Seattle Times,* January 31, 1990, p. A 3.

[2] *The New York Times,* January 31, 1990, p. C 18.

[3] *The Washington Post National Weekly Edition,* February 17–23, 1992, p. 23.

[4] Russell Baker, "Budgetary Fables,", *International Herald Tribune,* February 2, 1990, p. 18.

[5] Quoted in the *International Herald Tribune,* July 23, 1990, p. 3.

[6] Harold D. Lasswell, *Politics: Who Gets What, When, How.* New York: McGraw-Hill, 1938.

[7] Byron E. Shafer, "'Exceptionalism' in American Politics," *P.S.: Political Science & Politics,* September 1989, p. 592.

[8] Ibid, p. 592.

[9] See, among others, Alexis de Tocqueville, *Democracy in America.* New York: Anchor-Doubleday, 1969; James Bryce, *The American Commonwealth.* New York: Macmillan, 1960; Louis Hartz, *The Liberal Tradition in America.* New York: Harcourt, Brace, 1955; Seymour Martin Lipset, *The First New Nation.* New York: Basic Books, 1963; Herbert McClosky and John Zaller, *The American Ethos.* Cambridge: Harvard University Press, 1984; and Richard Merelman, *Making Something of Ourselves: On Culture and Politics in the United States.* Berkeley: University of California Press, 1984.

[10] Source: International Monetary Fund, Government Finance Statistics Yearbook, 1991, p. 78.

[11] Source: Edgar R. Feidler, "Till Debt Do Us Part," *Economic Times,* April 1991, p. 6. Also, Knight-Ridder wire service feature by Dan Stets, September 17, 1992.

[12] Source: International Monetary Fund, Government Finance Statistics Yearbook, 1991, p. 74.

[13] See Thomas E. Cronin, *Direct Democracy.* Cambridge: Harvard University Press, 1989.

[14] Byron E. Shafer, "'Exceptionalism' in American Politics?" *P.S.: Political Science & Politics,* September 1989, p. 589.

[15] Richard Morin, "Budget Czars for a Day," *The Washington Post National Weekly Edition,* November 23–29, 1992, p. 36.

[16] Ibid.

[17] Benjamin Page and Robert Shapiro, *The Rational Public.* Chicago: University of Chicago Press, 1992.

[18] Robert Dahl, *Who Governs?* New Haven: Yale University Press, 1961.

[19] See, for example: Theodore Lowi, "The Public Philosophy: Interest Group Liberalism," *American Political Science Review,* Vol. 61, 1967, pp. 5–24; Lowi, *The Politics of Disorder.* New York: Basic Books, 1971; and Benjamin Ginsberg and Martin Shefter, *Politics by Other Means: The Declining Importance of Elections in America.* New York: Basic Books, 1990.

[20] Robert Dahl, *A Preface to Democratic Theory.* Chicago: University of Chicago Press, 1956, p. 151.

[21] Among the classic works in the power elite school are: C. Wright Mills, *The Power Elite.* Oxford: Oxford University Press, 1956; Peter Bachrach, *The Theory of Democratic Elitism.* Boston: Little, Brown, 1967; Thomas Ferguson and Joel Rogers, *Right Turn: The Decline of the Democrats and the Future of American Politics.* New York: Hill and Wang, 1986; and William Domhoff, *The Power Elite and the State: How Policy Is Made in America.* New York: Aldine de Gruyter, 1990.

[22] Charles Beard, *An Economic Interpretation of the Constitution.* New York: Macmillan, 1913.

[23] This view is promoted in a popular American government textbook: Thomas R. Dye and L. Harmon Ziegler, *The Irony of Democracy,* 8th ed., Belmont, Calif.: Wadsworth, 1993.

[24] American Statistical Abstract, 1991, Table # 546, p. 338.

[25] Sources: National Election Studies, University of Michigan. Also, Seymour Martin Lipset and William Schneider, *The Confidence Gap: Business, Labor and Government in the Public Mind.* New York: The Free Press, 1983, p. 17. The 1990 data are from a New York Times/CBS News poll reported in *The New York Times,* November 4, 1990, p. 1.

[26] Sources: Office of Records and Registration, U.S. House of Representatives; Office of Public Records, Secretary of the Senate.

[27] Domhoff, *The Power Elite and the State.*

[28] Ginsberg and Shefter, *Politics by Other Means.*

[29] Figures are from "outlays" and estimates in the Budget of the United States, Fiscal Year 1993, Proposal of the Office of the President, U.S. Government Printing Office, 1992.

CHAPTER 2

[1] See David P. Szatmary, *Shays' Rebellion: The Making of an Agrarian Insurrection.* Amherst, Mass.: University of Massachusetts Press, 1980.

[2] Quoted in Howard Zinn, *A People's History of the United States.* New York: Harper & Row, 1980, p. 91.

[3] Ibid., p. 93.

[4] George B. Tindall and David E. Shi, *America,* brief second edition, New York: Norton, 1989, p. 160. Also Zinn, *A People's History,* 92.

[5] *Massachusetts Centinel,* January 17, 1787, p. 1.

[6] *Massachusetts Centinel,* February 28, 1787, p. 1.

[7] *American Herald,* February 5, 1787, p. 1.

[8] See David P. Szatmary, *Shays' Rebellion: The Making of an Agrarian Insurrection.*

[9] Ibid.

[10] Tindall and Shi, *America,* p. 161.

[11] Zinn, *A People's History,* p. 94.

[12] Tindall and Shi, *America,* p. 161.

[13] Zinn, *A People's History,* p. 95.

[14] Tindall and Shi, *America,* p. 174.

[15] Bernard Bailyn, *The Peopling of British North America.* New York: Vintage, 1986. pp. 9–17.

[16] Quoted in Zinn, *A People's History,* p. 49.

[17] Ibid. p. 40.

[18] Ibid. p. 59.

[19] For an excellent account of the atmosphere of ignorance and mutual distrust among the colonies, see Garry Wills, *Inventing America,* pp. 34–50.

[20] This thesis is proposed, for example, by historian Howard Zinn in *A People's History of the United States.*

[21] Barbara Tuchman, *The March of Folly,* New York: Knopf, 1984, p. 149.

[22] See Wills, *Inventing America.*

[23] See John A. Garraty, *The American Nation.* New York: Harper & Row, 1979.

[24] Walter B. Mead, *The United States Constitution: Personalities, Principles, and Issues.* Columbia, S.C.: University of South Carolina Press, pp. 37–38.

[25] Charles A Beard, *An Economic Interpretation of the Constitution of the United States.* New York: The Free Press, 1986.

[26] See, for example, Charles L. Mee, Jr., *The Genius of the People.* New York: Harper & Row, 1987, pp. 1–4.

[27] These and many other details in this account come primarily from two sources: *1787: The Day-to-Day Story of the Constitutional Convention,* compiled by the historians of the Independence National History Park, New York: Exeter Books, 1987; and Charles L. Mee, Jr., *The Genius of the People.* New York: Harper & Row, 1987.

[28] Mee, p. 168.

[29] *1787,* p. 67.

[30] Mee, p. 276.

[31] Quoted in John K. Alexander, *The Selling of the Constitutional Convention: A History of News Coverage.* Madison, Wis.: Madison House, 1990, p. 9.

CHAPTER 3

[1] Helen Dewar, "The Politics of Gridlock: The Nation's Agenda Is Being Held Hostage to Partisanship," *The Washington Post National Weekly Edition,* August 10–16, 1992, pp. 6–7.

[2] "Capitol Gridlock: Washington's Economic Paralysis Delays Recovery— and Frightens the Public," *Newsweek,* December 9, 1991, pp. 45–46.

[3] Cokie Roberts, "Divided Government Is the Best Revenge," *The New York Times,* August 27, 1992, p. A 19 (Opinion-Editorial page).

[4] "Serious Times, Trivial Politics," *The New York Times,* March 25, 1990, p. E 18. (Editorial)

[5] Quoted from "Capitol Gridlock," p. 45.

[6] Helen Dewar, "The Politics of Gridlock," p. 6.

[7] Cokie Roberts, "Divided Government," p. A 19.

[8] *McCulloch* v. *Maryland,* 4 Wheaton 316 (1819).

[9] Richard E. Neustadt, *Presidential Power,* New York: Wiley, 1960, p. 33.

[10] See Bill McAllister, "It's Never Too Late: In the End James Madison Has His Way," *The Washington Post Weekly Edition,* May 18–24, 1992, p. 34.

[11] E.E. Schattschneider, *The Semi-Sovereign People: A Realist's View of Democracy in America.* New York: Holt, Rinehart and Winston, 1960.

[12] William Riker, *Federalism: Origin, Operation, Significance,* Boston: Little, Brown, 1964.

[13] Edmund S. Morgan, *Inventing the People: The Rise of Popular Sovereignty in England and America,* New York: Norton, 1988.

[14] See Thomas R. Dye and L. Harmon Ziegler, *The Irony of Democracy,* 8th ed., Belmont, Calif.: Wadsworth, 1993.

[15] G. William Domhoff, *The Power Elite and the State: How Policy Is Made in America.* New York: Aldine de Gruyter, 1990.

[16] For a good sampling of the debate about who was favored by the design of the Constitution, see the collections of essays in Leonard W. Levy, ed., *Essays on the Making of the Constitution,* New York: Oxford University Press, 1969.

CHAPTER 4

[1] Reagan Inaugural Address, January 20, 1981.

[2] Based on a search of *The New York Times* in the Nexis-Lexis data base for the years 1981–1983.

[3] William K. Stevens, "For Governors, Focus Is Federalism," *The New York Times,* August 8, 1988, p. 7.

[4] Martin Tolchin, "States Take Up New Burdens to Pay for 'New Federalism,' " *The New York Times,* May 21, 1990, p. 1.

[5] Michael Horowitz, "States of Grace," *The New York Times,* November 24, 1992, p. A 13.

[6] Ibid,. p. A 14.

[7] Martin Tolchin, "States Take Up New Burdens to Pay for 'New Federalism,'"

[8] James B. Croy, "Federal Supersession: The Road to Domination," *State Government,* 48: pp. 32–36, Winter 1975.

[9] *McCulloch* v. *Maryland,* 4 Wheaton 316 (1819).

[10] *Gibbons* v. *Ogden,* 9 Wheaton 1 (1824).

[11] *Dred Scott* v. *Sanford,* 19 Howard 393 (1857).

[12] Ibid.

[13] Ibid.

[14] See Morton Grodzins, "The Federal System," ch. 12 in *Goals for Americans: The Report of the President's Commission on National Goals.* Englewood Cliffs, N.J., Prentice-Hall, 1965.

[15] Tolchin, "States Take Up New Burdens."

[16] For a detailed development of this interesting argument, see Gabriel Kolko, *The Triumph of Conservatism: A Reinterpretation of American History, 1900–1915,* Chicago: Quadrangle Press, 1963.

[17] 301 U.S. 1 (1937).

[18] 301 U.S. 379 (1937).

[19] 301 U.S. 548 (1937).

[20] Source: U.S. House of Representatives, Subcommittee on Public Assistance, Committee on Ways and Means, *Background Material on Poverty.* Government Printing Office, Washington D.C., October 17, 1983.

[21] Source: Advisory Council on Intergovernmental Relations. Reported in *The New York Times,* May 21, 1990, p. 1.

[22] Source: William Greider, *Who Will Tell the People?* New York: Simon and Schuster, 1992, p. 115.

[23] Ibid.

[24] Source: Advisory Council on Intergovernmental Relations. Reported in *The New York Times,* January 20, 1982, p. A 22.

[25] Advisory Council on Intergovernmental Relations study reported in *The New York Times,* May 21, 1990, p. A 14.

[26] National Governors Association report, *The New York Times,* May 21, 1990, p. A 14.

[27] Quoted in Gwen Ifill, "States Nervously Welcome Bush Plan," *The Washington Post,* January 31, 1991, p. A 7.

[28] Quoted in Robert Pear, "Washington's Plan to Funnel Aid Through the States Enrages Mayors, " *The New York Times,* February 10, 1991,p. E 2.

[29] Quoted in Ifill, "States Nervously Welcome" p. A 7.

[30] Many of the facts in the excellent *New York Times* story cited in this section (see footnotes 24–26 above) were provided by research and publicity efforts of the National Governors Association. True, the *Times* could have reported these details of new federalism all during the 1980s, but as we will see later, the media tend not to create issues unless political groups become organized to promote them first. Thus, the governors became more organized, and their views on "new federalism" began to make news.

[31] For an in-depth look at how various states responded to the Reagan "new federalism," see Richard Nathan and Fred Doolittle, *Reagan and the States,* Princeton: Princeton University Press, 1987.

[32] From an address by Wayne Flynt at the Annual Alabama Prayer Luncheon. Reported in Howell Raines, "Alabama Bound," *The New York Times Magazine,* June 3, 1990, p. 42.

[33] Governor Hunt, quoted in Ibid., p. 43.

[34] Ibid.

[35] This is essentially the conclusion reached by Paul Peterson, Barry Rabe, and Kenneth Wong in their assessment of contemporary federalism, *When Federalism Works,* Washington, D.C.: Brookings Institution, 1986.

CHAPTER 5

[1] Michael de Courcy Hinds, "Tempers Flare as Pennsylvania Rivals Debate," *The New York Times,* October 21, 1992, p. A 15.

[2] Anthony de Palma, "U.S. Judge Upholds Speech on Campus," *The New York Times,* August 29, 1991, p. 25.

[3] Dennis Cauchon, "Harassment, Free Speech Collide in Florida," *USA Today,* November 21, 1991, p. 8 A.

[4] Ibid.

[5] Ibid.

[6] Reported on CNN Headline News, December 15, 1991.

[7] John Gilliom, "Rights and Discipline: Competing Modes of Social Control in the Fight Over Employee Drug Testing," *Polity,* Summer 1992, Vol. 24, pp. 591–615.

[8] See, for example, Stuart Scheingold, *The Politics of Rights.* New Haven: Yale University Press, 1971.

[9] *Barron* v. *Baltimore,* 7 Peters 243 (1883).

[10] *The Slaughterhouse Cases,* 16 Wallace 36 (1883).

[11] *Record of the Sixty-fifth Congress,* Session I, Chapter 30, 1917, p. 219.

[12] *Gitlow* v. *New York,* 268 U.S. 652 (1925).

[13] 110 S. Ct. 2404 (1990).

[14] "Vote Is Easy on Flag Burner 'Vigilantes,'" UPI report in the *Seattle Post-Intelligencer,* May 29, 1990, p. A 5.

[15] All quotes from Note 14.

[16] 260 U.S. 421 (1962).

[17] 403 U.S. 602 (1971).

[18] 472 U.S. 38 (1885).

[19] *Employment Division* v. *Smith* 110 S. Ct. 1595 (1990).

[20] Ibid.

[21] *Employment Division* v. *Smith* 110 S. Ct. 1595 (1990). For an extended discussion of this case, see: Geoffrey R. Stone, Louis M. Seidman, Cass R. Sunstein, and Mark V. Tushnet, *Constitutional Law,* 2nd ed. Boston: Little, Brown, 1991, pp. 1519–1534.

[22] *School District of Abington Township* v. *Schempp* (1963).

[23] Laurence Tribe, *American Constitutional Law,* 2nd ed. Minneola, N.Y.: The Foundation Press, 1988, ch. 14.

[24] Anthony Lewis, *Gideon's Trumpet,* New York: Vintage, 1964.

[25] *Furman* v. *Georgia,*

[26] It is worth noting here that the "Warren Court" is often classified as a "liberal" court, while the "Burger Court" has been regarded as more "conservative," but they both participated in the development and "incorporation" of privacy rights.

[27] *NAACP* v. *Alabama,* 357 U.S. 449 (1958).

[28] *Griswold* v. *Connecticut,* 381 U.S. 479 (1965).

[29] *Eisenstadt* v. *Baird,* 405 U.S. 438 (1972).

[30] *Facts on File: World News Digest,* Volume 52, No. 2692, July 2, 1992, p. 480.

[31] *The Gallup Poll: Public Opinion, 1991.* Wilmington, Del.: Scholarly Resources, Inc., 1992, pp. 168–169, poll conducted June 1991.

[32] *Plessy* v. *Ferguson,* 163 U.S. 537 (1896).

[33] See Nicholas Lehman, *The Promised Land: The Great Black Migration and How It Changed America.* New York: Knopf, 1990.

[34] Gunnar Myrdal, *An American Dilemma: The Negro Problem and Modern Democracy.* New York: Harper, 1944.

[35] *Brown* v. *Board of Education,* 349 U.S. 294.

[36] For the politics behind the Warren ruling, see Bernard Schwartz, *Super Chief.* New York: New York University Press, ch. 3.

[37] See Jack W. Peltason, *Fifty-eight Lonely Men: Southern Federal Judges and School Desegregation.* Urbana: University of Illinois Press, 1971.

[38] Lena Williams, "Playing with Fire," *The New York Times Magazine,* October 25, 1992, p. 73.

[39] Quotes are from Thomas B. Edsall and Mary D. Edsall, "Race," *The Atlantic Monthly,* May 1991, p. 70.

[40] 438 U.S. 265 (1978).

[41] *Richmond v. Corson,* 102 L Ed 2d 854, 1989

[42] *Andrew Hacker, Two Nations: Black and White, Separate, Hostile, Unequal.* New York: Scribner, 1992.

[43] Edsall and Edsall, "Race," p. 55.

[44] See Stuart Scheingold, *The Politics of Rights.* New Haven: Yale University Press, 1974.

CHAPTER 6

[1] See, for example, Robin Toner, "Poll Finds Postwar Glow Dimmed by the Economy," *The New York Times,* March 8, 1991, p. A 11.

[2] E. J. Dionne, Jr., and Richard Morin, "Postwar Glow Has Faded, Poll Finds," *The Washington Post,* April 12, 1991, p. 1.

[3] Quoted in Ibid., p. 4.

[4] Reported in Robin Toner, "Los Angeles Riots Are a Warning, Americans Fear," *The New York Times,* May 11, 1992, p. 1.

[5] See, for example, Susan Herbst, *Numbered Voices: How Opinion Polling Has Shaped American Politics.* Chicago: University of Chicago Press, 1993.

[6] Rushworth M. Kidder, "Polls Apart," *The Christian Science Monitor,* July 25, 1988, p. 17.

[7] Benjamin Page and Robert Shapiro, *The Rational Public.* Chicago: University of Chicago Press, 1992.

[8] See the account of Richard Immerman, *The CIA in Guatemala.* Austin: University of Texas Press, 1982.

[9] The classic statement on this is Murray Edelman, *The Symbolic Uses of Politics,* 2nd ed. Urbana: University of Illinois Press, 1985.

[10] Benjamin Ginsberg, "Opinion Mongering," *The Nation,* October 3, 1988, p. 278.

[11] For an excellent review of the history of socialization research, see David O. Sears, "Whither Political Socialization Research? The Question of Persistence," in Orit Ichilov, ed., *Political Socialization, Citizenship Eduction, and Democracy.* New York: Teachers College Press, 1990, pp. 69–97.

[12] See M. Kent Jennings and Richard G. Niemi, *The Political Character of Adolescence.* Princeton: Princeton University Press, 1974.

[13] Theodore Newcomb, *Personality and Social Change.* New York: Dryden Press, 1943.

[14] Theodore Newcomb, K.E. Keoenig, R. Flacks, and D.P. Warwick, *Persistence and Change: Bennington College and Its Students After 25 Years.* New York: Wiley, 1967.

[15] Gallup Survey A1 874 Q. 16c, conducted by telephone July 1–7, 1988.

[16] Survey conducted by Home Box Office and the Joint Center for Political and Economic Studies in 1992, reported in E. J. Dionne, Jr., "Defying Political Stereotypes: Black Americans Can't Be Pigeonholed," *The Washington Post National Weekly Edition,* July 13–19, 1992, p. 37.

[17] NORC surveys reported in Floris W. Wood, ed., *An American Profile: Opinions and Behavior, 1972–1989.* Detroit: Gale Research, 1990, p. 571.

[18] Based on polls conducted by the National Opinion Research Center in 1981, 1982, 1983, and 1984, and reported in *Public Opinion,* August/September, 1984, p. 40.

[19] See, among others: Angus Campbell, Philip Converse, Warren Miller, and Donald Stokes, *The American Voter.* New York: Wiley, 1960; Philip E. Converse, "The Nature of Belief Systems in Mass Publics, in David E. Apter, ed., *Ideology and Discontent,* pp. 206–261. New York: The Free Press, 1964; and Eric R.A.N. Smith, *The Unchanging American Voter.* Berkeley: University of California Press, 1989.

[20] Russell J. Dalton, *Citizen Politics in Western Democracies.* Chatham, N.J.: Chatham House, 1988.

[21] Source: Richard G. Niemi, John Mueller, and Tom W. Smith, *Trends in Public Opinion.* New York: Greenwood Press, 1989, p. 19.

[22] National Election Study of 1988, Conducted by the University of Michigan.

[23] See Russell Neuman, *The Paradox of Mass Politics: Knowledge and Opinion in the American Electorate.* Cambridge: Harvard University Press, 1986.

[24] Prewar polls analyzed by Louis Harris, "A Different Gap This Time," *The International Herald Tribune,* December 8, 1990, p. 6. A New York Times/CBS News poll showing the shrinking gender gap after fighting broke out was reported in *The New York Times,* March 8, 1991, p. A 11.

[25] See Elizabeth Noelle-Neumann, *The Spiral of Silence.* Chicago: University of Chicago Press, 1984.

[26] See Murray Edelman, *The Symbolic Uses of Politics.* (originally published, 1964) New edition. Urbana: University of Illinois Press, 1985; and Edelman, *Constructing the Political Spectacle.* Chicago: University of Chicago Press, 1987.

[27] See: Walter Lippmann, *Public Opinion.* New York: The Free Press, 1922; Shanto Iyengar and Donald Kinder, *News That Matters.* Chicago: University of Chicago Press, 1988.

[28] Shanto Iyengar, *Is Anyone Responsible?* Chicago: University of Chicago Press, 1992.

[29] See Susan Herbst, *Numbered Voices.*

[30] See Howard Schuman and Stanley Presser, *Questions and Answers in Attitude Surveys: Experiments on Question Form, Wording, and Context.* New York: Academic Press, 1981.

[31] William Graham Sumner, from a statement against the Spanish-American War written in 1898. Reprinted in *The International Herald Tribune,* June 11, 1991, p. 7.

[32] See, for example, the collection of studies in Michael Margolis and Gary Mauser, eds., *Manipulating Public Opinion: Essays on Public Opinion as a Dependent Variable.* Pacific Grove, Calif.: Brooks/Cole, 1989.

[33] See, for example, Benjamin I. Page and Robert Y. Shapiro, "Effects of Public Opinion on Policy," *American Political Science Review, 77,* March 1983, pp. 175–190.

[34] Benjamin Ginsberg, *The Captive Public,* New York: Basic Books, 1986.

[35] Paul Weyrich, quoted in Thomas Ferguson and Joel Rogers, "The Reagan Victory: Corporate Coalitions in the 1980 Campaign," in Ferguson and Rogers, eds., *The Hidden Election: Politics and Economics in the 1980 Presidential Campaign.* New York: Pantheon, 1981, p. 4.

CHAPTER 7

[1] Roxanne Roberts, "Voting: Not Their Primary Thing, Area Students Show Little Enthusiasm," *The Washington Post,* March 3, 1992, p. B 1.

[2] Richard Morin, "Maybe If They Televised It on MTV? Younger Voters Have Tuned Out Politics." *The Washington Post National Weekly Edition,* March 23–29, 1992, p. 37.

[3] Jeffrey Schmalz, "Americans Sign Up in Record Numbers. Big Gains For Democrats. 20 Year Decline Is Reversed as Voters Cite a Feeling That There's a Real Choice." *The New York Times,* October 19, 1992, p. 1.

[4] Elizabeth Kolbert, "Bypassing the Press Helps Candidates; Does It Also Serve the Public Interest?" *The New York Times,* November 8, 1992, p. E 2.

[5] Robert Pear, "Voting Rate Reverses 30-Year Decline," *The New York Times,* November 5, 1992, p. B 4.

[6] Story by Kevin Merida and Helen Dewar, *The Washington Post National Weekly Edition,* February 8–14, 1993, p. 6.

[7] Ibid.

[8] See, for example, Sidney Verba and Norman Nie, *Participation in America.* New York: Harper & Row, 1972, p. 31.

[9] Benjamin Barber, *Strong Democracy: Participatory Politics for a New Age.* Berkeley: University of California Press, 1984. Also Carole Pateman, *Participation and Democratic Theory.* Cambridge, England: Cambridge University Press, 1970.

[10] Frances Fox Piven and Richard Cloward, *Why Americans Don't Vote.* New York: Pantheon, 1988.

[11] Survey by the Times Mirror Center for the People, the Press, and Politics, reported on National Public Radio News, November 15, 1992.

[12] For voter issue reactions in the 1988 and 1990 elections, see W. Lance Bennett, *The Governing Crisis* (New York: St. Martin's, 1992), Chapters 1 and 7.

[13] See Everett Carl Ladd, "Campaign '88: What Are the 'Issues'?" *Christian Science Monitor,* June 3, 1988, p. 14.

[14] See Barbara G. Farah and Ethel Klein, "Public Opinion Trends," in Gerald Pomper, ed., *The Election of 1988.* Chatham, N.J.: Chatham House, 1989.

[15] Marjorie Randon Hershey, "The Campaign and the Media," in Gerald M. Pomper, ed., *The Election of 1988.*

[16] New York Times/CBS News Poll, reported August 26, 1992.

[17] See Benjamin Page, *Choices and Echoes in Presidential Elections.* Chicago: University of Chicago Press, 1978.

[18] Morris P. Fiorina, *Retrospective Voting in American National Elections.* New Haven: Yale University Press, 1981.

[19] See James David Barber, *The Presidential Character: Predicting Performance in the White House,* 3rd ed. Englewood Cliffs, N.J.: Prentice-Hall, 1985; and Bruce Buchanan, "Sizing Up Candidates," *P.S.: Political Science and Politics,* Spring 1988, pp. 250–256.

[20] A study of *The New York Times, The Washington Post,* and *The Los Angeles Times* conducted by Fairness and Accuracy in Reporting, reported in *Extra!,* June 1992, pp. 10–11.

[21] Robin Toner, "Dukakis Works at Warmth, But Keeps His Sleeves Down," *The New York Times,* August 8, 1988, p. 1. See poll data in Donald L. Rheem, "Bush Called Strong, Effective," *Christian Science Monitor,* November 1, 1988, p. 3.

[22] Quoted in Maureen Dowd, "For Bush on the Campaign Trail, the Style is First Sour, Then Sweet," *The New York Times,* October 12, 1988, p. 10.

[23] 1988 figures are from CBS News exit poll results, and 1992 figures are from exit polls jointly sponsored by all the television networks reported in *Time,* November 16, 1992, p. 47.

[24] The vote of working women is from *Newsweek,* special election issue of November/December 1992, p. 10, and the vote of homemakers was reported in *The New York Times,* November 5, 1992, p. B 9.

[25] *The New York Times,* November 5, 1992, p. B 9.

[26] Ibid.

[27] Quoted in Michael Oreskes, "The Civil Rights Act 25 Years Later: A Law that Shaped a Realignment," *The New York Times,* July 2, 1989, p. A 16.

[28] Based on voter exit polls reported in *The New York Times,* November 5, 1992, p. B 9.

[29] Eric Altermen, "Playing Hardball," *The New York Times Magazine,* April 30, 1989, p. 70.

[30] 1992 figures are from *The New York Times,* November 5, 1992, p. B 9. The 1988 figures are from *The New York Times,* November 10, 1988, p. 18.

[31] The 1990 Congressional figures are from exit polls reported in *The New York Times* on November 1ᵺ, 1988. All other figures are from a five-election exit poll summary reported in *The New York Times,* November 5, 1992, p. B 9.

[32] *The New York Times,* November 5, 1992, p. B 9.

[33] The top three countries are Australia, Austria, and Belgium, all at over 90 percent turnouts. The only nation close to the United States is Switzerland at around 49 percent. The others are all over 70 percent. For country by country figures, see *Congressional Quarterly Weekly Report,* April 2, 1988, p. 863.

[34] These figures are from Robert Pear, "55% Voting Rate Reverses 30-Year Decline," *The New York Times,* November 5, 1992, p. B4.

[35] Ruy A Teixeira, "Voter Turnout in America: Ten Myths," *The Brookings Review,* Fall 1992, p. 31.

[36] Robert Pear, "U.S. Finds Bias, Rebuffs 2 States on Voting Districts," *International Herald Tribune,* July 4, 1991, p. 3. (Reprinted from *The New York Times.*)

[37] Samuel L. Popkin, *The Reasoning Voter: Communication and Persuasion in Presidential Campaigns.* Chicago: University of Chicago Press, 1991, p. 7.

[38] Jack Walker, *Mobilizing Interest Groups in America,* Ann Arbor: University of Michigan Press, 1991.

[39] See Russell J. Dalton, *Citizen Politics in Western Democracies.* Chatham, N.J.: Chatham House, 1988.

[40] See Samuel H. Barnes and Max Kaase, eds., *Political Action: Mass Participation in Five Western Democracies.* Beverly Hills, Calif.: Sage, 1979, p. 545.

[41] See Eugene Genovese, *Roll, Jordan, Roll: The World the Slaves Made.* New York: Vintage, 1972.

[42] See Todd Gitlin, *The Whole World Is Watching.* Berkeley: University of California Press, 1980.

[43] Seth Mydans, "Christian Conservatives Counting Hundreds of Gains in Local Votes," *The New York Times,* November 21, 1992, pp. 1 and 8.

[44] The Harris Poll report of February 2, 1992, p. 2.

[45] New York Times/CBS News Poll reported in *The New York Times,* November 7, 1990, p. A 16.

[46] See, for example, Stephen Earl Bennett and David Resnick, "The Implications of Nonvoting for Democracy in the United States," *American Journal of Political Science,* Vol. 34, No. 3, August 1990, pp. 771–802.

[47] Ruy A. Teixeira, "Voter Turnout in America: Ten Myths," p. 31.

[48] The data on 1960, 1970, and 1980 are reported in Seymour Martin Lipset and William Schneider, *The Confidence Gap: Business, Labor, and Government in the Public Mind.* New York: The Free Press, 1983. The 1990 figure is from a New York Times/CBS News Poll reported in the *International Herald Tribune,* November 5, 1990, p. 1.

[49] Washington Post/ABC News Poll, reported on the Associated Press Wire, October 17, 1990.

[50] See William Chambers, *Political Parties in the New Nation.* New York: Oxford University Press, 1963.

CHAPTER 8

[1] Sara Pritz, James Risen, and Dwight Morris, "Winning Strategy on Taxes: Real Estate Interests Prevail as Washington Seeks to Stimulate the Economy," *Los Angeles Times,* March 15, 1992, p. 1.

[2] Timothy Noah, "Interest Groups Gear Up for New Spate of Lobbying," *The Wall Street Journal,* October 8, 1990, p. A4.

[3] Ibid.

[4] Quoted in Richard H. Leach, *American Federalism,* New York: Norton, 1970, p. 54.

[5] E. E. Schattschneider, *The Semi-Sovereign People,* New York: Holt, 1960, p. 55.

[6] See Jack L. Walker, Jr., *Mobilizing Interest Groups in America.* Ann Arbor: University of Michigan Press, 1991, pp. 9–15.

[7] See Robert H. Salisbury, "The Paradox of Interest Groups in Washington—More Groups, Less Clout," in Anthony King, ed., *The New American Political System.* Washington, D.C.: The A.E.I. Press, 1990, pp. 203–229.

[8] Ibid., p. 205.

[9] Source: Senate Public Records Office, and Office of the Clerk, U.S. House of Representatives. House records showed 6,104 lobbyists or organizations registered in 1992.

[10] Peter Carlson, "Leader of the Snack PAC," *The Washington Post Magazine,* November 13, 1988, p. 28.

[11] See Salisbury, "The Paradox of Interest Groups in Washington."

[12] Peter Carlson, "Leader of the Snack PAC," p. 28.

[13] Mancur Olson, Jr., *The Logic of Collective Action,* Cambridge: Harvard University Press, 1965.

[14] See Rita McWilliams, "The Best and Worst of Public Interest Groups," *The Washington Monthly,* March, 1988, pp. 19–27.

[15] Peter Carlson, "Leader of the Snack PAC," p. 29.

[16] Ruth Marcus and Ann Devroy, "A Scripted Affair: Thomas Strategists Court Key Support," *International Herald Tribune,* July 20–21, 1991, p. 3.

[17] This account and all of the quotations in it are from Peter Carlson, "Leader of the Snack PAC," *The Washington Post Magazine,* November 13, 1988, pp. 27–29.

[18] Ibid., p. 28.

[19] Ibid., p. 28.

[20] Ibid., p. 29.

[21] Source: *The New York Times,* June 5, 1989, p. A13. Report based on Federal Election Commission data.

[22] See W. Lance Bennett, *The Governing Crisis: Media, Money, and Marketing in American Elections,* New York: St. Martin's Press, 1992, esp. chs. 2 and 4.

[23] Quoted in Craig Humphries, ""Corporations, PACs and the Strategic Link Between Contributions and Lobbying Activities," *Western Political Quarterly,* Vol. 44, No. 2, June 1991, p. 363.

[24] See Jean Cobb, "Top Brass," *Common Cause Magazine,* May/June 1989, pp. 23–27.

[25] Ibid., p. 23.

[26] Ibid., p. 23.

[27] Richard L. Berke, "Lobbying Steps Up on Military Buying as Budget Shrinks," *The New York Times,* April 9, 1990, p. A12.

[28] Jeffrey T. Leeds, "Impeccable Judgment or Tainted Politics," *The New York Times Magazine,* September 3, 1989, pp. 72–78.

[29] Gerald N. Rosenberg, *The Hollow Hope.* Chicago: University of Chicago Press, 1991, esp. pp. 339–340.

[30] According to an investment analyst reported in Jeffrey Denny, "King of the Road," *Common Cause Magazine,* May/June 1991, p. 20.

[31] Ibid., p. 19.

[32] Ibid., pp. 19–20.

[33] Ibid., p. 20.

[34] Jill Abramson, "Auto Makers Lobbied Hard Against Stricter Fuel Rules," *The Wall Street Journal,* April 4, 1990, p. A15.

[35] Denny, "King of the Road," p. 21.

[36] Ibid., p. 22.

[37] Ibid., p. 22.

[38] Earl Latham, "Interest Groups in the American Political System," in Stephen K. Bailey, ed., *American Politics and Government: Essays in Essentials,* New York: Basic Books, 1965, p. 153.

[39] Probably the most distinguished advocate of this position is David B. Truman, *The Governmental Process,* New York: Knopf, 1971.

[40] See, for example, Grant McConnell, *Private Power and American Democracy,* New York: Knopf, 1966.

[41] See, for an elaboration of this argument, Richard Leach, *American Federalism,* pp. 74–75.

[42] Theodore J. Lowi, *The End of Liberalism,* 2nd ed., New York: Norton, 1979.

[43] Dave Barry, "Name a National Gnat," *International Herald Tribune,* October 6–7, 1990, p. 24.

[44] Benjamin Ginsberg and Martin Shefter, *Politics by Others Means,* New York: Basic Books, 1990.

[45] See the discussion in Mark P. Petracca, "Politics Beyond the End of Liberalism," *P.S.: Political Science and Politics,* Vol. 23, No. 4, December 1990, p. 567.

[46] See Benjamin Ginsberg and Elizabeth Sanders, "Theodore J. Lowi and Juridical Democracy," *P.S.: Political Science and Politics,* Vol. 23, No. 4, December 1990, p. 565.

[47] James Q. Wilson, "Juridical Democracy versus American Democracy," *P.S.: Political Science and Politics,* Vol. 23, No. 4, December 1990, p. 571.

[48] James Q. Wilson, *Bureaucracy: What Government Agencies Do and Why They Do It,* New York: Basic Books, 1989.

[49] Robert H. Salisbury, "The Paradox of Interest Groups in Washington."

[50] Paul E. Peterson, "The Rise and Fall of the Special Interest Politics," *Political Science Quarterly,* Vol. 105, No. 4, 1990–1991, pp. 540–541.

[51] For an overview of the growth of public interest groups, see Jeffrey M. Berry, *Lobbying for the People: The Political Behavior of Public Interest Groups,* Princeton: Princeton University Press, 1977.

[52] Chuck Alston, "Common Cause: A Watchdog that Barks at Its Friends," *Congressional Quarterly,* August 26, 1989, p. 2205.

[53] Michael McCann, *Taking Reform Seriously,* Ithaca: Cornell University Press, 1986, p. 180.

[54] Ibid., p. 179.

CHAPTER 9

[1] "What's Wrong with the Democrats?" *Harper's,* January 1990, pp. 45–55.

[2] Reprinted from *The Washington Post* in *The International Herald Tribune,* November 13–14, 1990, p. 8.

[3] Kevin Phillips, "America, 1989: Brain-Dead Politics in a Transition," from *The Washington Post,* reprinted in *The International Herald Tribune,* November 4, 1989, p. 8.

[4] Theodore J. Lowi, "Mr. Perot, Form a Party," *The New York Times,* April 26, 1992, p. A 17.

[5] David Broder, *The Party's Over.* This excerpt from Ann G. Serow, W. Wayne Shannon, and Everett C. Ladd, *The American Polity Reader.* New York: Norton, 1990, p. 508.

[6] See, for example, Howard Reiter, *Parties and Elections in Corporate America.* New York: St. Martin's Press, 1987.

[7] See, for example, Marjorie Randon Hershey, "The Campaign and the Media," in Gerald M. Pomper, ed. *The Election of 1988.* Chatham, N.J.: Chatham House, p. 97.

[8] See W. Lance Bennett, *The Governing Crisis: Media, Money, and Marketing in American Elections.* New York: St. Martin's Press, 1992, ch. 4.

[9] See, for example, Lowi, "Mr. Perot, Form a Party."

[10] Quoted in David S. Broder, "So What Ever Happened to Credentials?" *The International Herald Tribune,* October 2, 1991, p. 9.

[11] Ibid.

[12] Ibid.

[13] Quoted in Howard Reiter, *Parties and Elections in Corporate America.* New York: St. Martin's Press, 1987, p. 77.

[14] Ibid.

[15] Ibid., p. 79.

[16] See Frank J. Sorauf and Paul Allen Peck, *Party Politics in America,* 6th ed. Glenview, Ill.: Scott Foresman, 1988, p. 50.

[17] See Bennett, *The Governing Crisis,* chapter 4.

[18] Thomas Ferguson and Joel Rogers, *Right Turn: The Decline of the Democrats and the Future of American Politics.* New York: Hill and Wang, 1986.

[19] Quoted in David Green, *Shaping Political Consciousness.* Ithaca: Cornell University Press, 1987, p. 119.

[20] From Paul Taylor, "For Democrats, A Greater Voice?" *The International Herald Tribune,* January 30, 1990, p. 7.

[21] Arthur H. Miller and Ola Listhaug, "Political Parties and Confidence in Government: A Comparison of Norway, Sweden, and the United States," *British Journal of Political Science,* Vol. 29, 1990, pp. 357–386.

[22] For a summary of the arguments, see Austin Ranney, *Curing the Mischiefs of Faction.* Berkeley: The University of California Press, 1975.

[23] From Steven V. Roberts, "2 Parties Spend Heavily in States, with an Eye to 1991 Redistricting," *The New York Times,* October 29, 1988, p. 9.

[24] Thomas A. Kazee and Mary C. Thornberry, "Where's the Party? Congressional Candidate Recruitment and American Party Organizations," *Western Political Quarterly,* Vol. 43, 1990, pp. 61–80.

[25] Timothy Conlan, "Politics and Governance: Conflicting Trends in the 1990s?" *Annals of the American Academy of Political and Social Science,* Vol. 509, 1990, pp. 128–138.

[26] See Ibid., and Kevin M. Leyden and Steven Borrelli, "Party Contributions and Party Unity: Can Loyalty Be Bought?" *Western Political Quarterly,* Vol. 43, 1990, pp. 343–365.

[27] For a review of criticisms about various party reforms, see: Nelson W. Polsby, *Consequences of Party Reform.* New York: Oxford University Press, 1983.

[28] Quotes from Katherine Bishop, "California Democrats Adopt Early Caucus System" *The New York Times,* March 10, 1991, p. 15.

[29] Ibid.

[30] Ibid.

[31] Leon D. Epstein, *Political Parties in the American Mold.* Madison: University of Wisconsin Press, 1986.

[32] See, for example, Walter Dean Burnham, *Critical Elections and the Mainsprings of American Politics.* New York: Norton, 1970.

[33] Ibid. This quote is excerpted in Ann G. Serow, W. Wayne Shannon, and Everett C. Ladd, eds. *The American Polity Reader.* New York: Norton, 1990, p. 506.

[34] See, among others, Everett C. Ladd, "The Uselessness of Realignment for Understanding Change in Contemporary American Politics," in Wayne and Wilcox, eds. *The Quest for National Office,* New York: St. Martin's Press, 1992, pp. 79–92.

[35] Benjamin Ginsberg and Martin Shefter, *Politics by Other Means: The Declining Importance of Elections in America.* New York: Basic Books, 1990.

[36] Benjamin Ginsberg, "A Post Election Era?" *P.S.: Political Science and Politics,* March 1989, p. 19.

[37] For a much more detailed development of this argument, see Bennett, *The Governing Crisis,* chs. 2, 3, and 4.

[38] Charles M. Madigan, "GOP Rethinking Fundamentals of Party Spectrum" *Chicago Tribune,* November 29, 1992, p. 4–1.

[39] Ibid., pp. 4–6.

CHAPTER 10

[1] Elizabeth Kolbert, "Campaigns Do Their Best to Beat, Not Meet, the Press," *The New York Times,* October 8, 1992, p. A 14.

[2] Ibid.

[3] Don Balz, "In Media Res: If You Can't Beat 'Em, Bypass 'Em," *The Washington Post National Weekly Edition,* May 25–31, 1992, p. 12.

[4] David Van Drehle, "Election '92: The Year of the Truly Weird," *The Washington Post National Weekly Edition,* November 9–15, 1992, p. 10.

[5] Elizabeth Kolbert, "Bypassing the Press Helps Candidates; Does It Also Serve the Public Interest?" *The New York Times,* November 8, 1992, p. E 2.

[6] Michael Oreskes, "American's Politics Loses Way as Its Vision Changes World," *The New York Times,* March 18, 1990, p. 1.

[7] Ibid.

[8] See David Magleby, "Taking the Initiative: Direct Legislation and Direct Democracy in the 1980s," *P.S.: Political Science and Politics,* Summer 1988, pp. 602–610.

[9] All quotes are from Patrick Cox, "Growth of Initiatives Is Democracy at Work," *USA Today,* October 31, 1990, p. 6 A.

[10] See the extended discussion of public support for initiatives in Thomas E. Cronin, *Direct Democracy: The Politics of the Initiative, Referendum, and Recall.* Cambridge: Harvard University Press, 1989.

[11] Ibid., pp. 4–5.

[12] Ibid., p. 131.

[13] From Paul F. Boller, Jr., *Presidential Campaigns.* New York: Oxford University Press, 1985, p. 168.

[14] Byron Schafer, "The Convention and a Changing American Politics," in Stephen J. Wayne and Clyde Wilcox, eds. *The Quest for National Office.* New York: St. Martin's Press, 1992, p. 149.

[15] Jeremy Gerard, "Convention Coverage: Endangered Species?" *The New York Times,* July 23, 1988, Sec. 1, p. 9.

[16] See, for example, Richard L. Berke, "Milking Drama at a Dry Convention," *The New York Times,* July 15, 1992, p. A 8.

[17] A. James Reichley, "The Electoral System" in Wayne and Wilcox, eds. *The Quest for National Office.* P. 6.

[18] See Stephen J. Wayne, *The Road to the White House 1992.* New York: St. Martin's Press, 1992, pp. 18–19.

[19] Quoted in Richard L. Berke, "Big Money's Election Year Comeback," *The New York Times,* August 7, 1988, p. E 5.

[20] Herbert E. Alexander, "Financing the Presidential Elections, 1988," in Wayne and Wilcox, eds. *The Quest for National Office.* P. 41.

[21] Richard L. Berke, "Enter Senate, Begin Chasing Money," *The New York Times,* June 3, 1991, p. A 8.

[22] The low estimate is for the mid-1980s and comes from Lewis Lipsitz and David M. Speak, *American Democracy,* 2nd ed. New York: St. Martin's Press, 1989, p. 259. The higher figure is the author's estimate of current costs.

[23] *Nytt om Media,* No. 8, 1991, p. 15.

[24] Larry Makinson, *Open Secrets: The Cash Constituents of Congress.* Washington, D.C.: Congressional Quarterly Press, 1992, pp. 2–3.

[25] Wayne, *The Road to the White House,* p. 34.

[26] For a more extensive discussion of PACs, see Larry J. Sabato, *PAC Power: Inside the World of Political Action Committees.* New York: Norton, 1985.

[27] Makinson, *Open Secrets,* p. 17.

[28] Source: Congressional Research Service and Federal Election Commission reports.

[29] Federal Election Commission figures, 1988.

[30] The first four quotes are from Rep. Andrew Jacobs of Indiana, Rep. Dan Glickman of Kansas, Rep. Barbara Mikulski of Maryland, and Rep. Richard Ottinger of New York, all reported in Larry Sabato, *PAC Power,* pp. 126–127. The last quote is from a "Democrat from the West" who preferred anonymity in a news story by Tom Kenworthy, "U.S. House Democrats Struggling with Principles vs. PACs" *International Herald Tribune,* October 31, 1989, p. 2. (From *The Washington Post*)

[31] Quoted in Sabato, *PAC Power,* p. xii.

[32] As with all players, the small donations are as welcome as the large. In a typical year after this statement was made, Senator Dole accepted speaking fees as small as $1,000 and $2,000 from dozens of organizations, including the American Dental Association, the American Pharmaceutical Association, the American Stock Exchange, and the American Academy of Dermatology. Source: *New York Times* data reported in the *Seattle Weekly,* December 27, 1989, p. 19.

[33] Herbert Alexander, "Financing the Presidential Elections, 1988, p. 41.

[34] Stephen Laboton, "Democrats Awash in Money While GOP Coffers Suffer," *The New York Times,* September 15, 1992, p. 17.

[35] Makinson, *Open Secrets,* p. 17.

[36] Jean Cobb, Jeff Denny, Vicki Kemper, and Viveca Novak, "All the President's Donors," *Common Cause Magazine,* March/April 1990, p. 22.

[37] Herbert E. Alexander, "Financing the Presidential Elections, 1988, p. 41.

[38] Jean Cobb, et al., "All the President's Donors," p. 23.

[39] Ibid., p. 23.

[40] Brooks Jackson, "Democrats Outflanked in Previous Elections, Rival GOP in Financing of Presidential Race," *The Wall Street Journal,* October 3, 1988, p. A 22.

[41] This was for a Senate race in 1986! Reported by Richard L. Berke, "Senate Campaign Reform vs. A Senate Campaign," *The New York Times,* May 13, 1990, p. E 4.

[42] Sara Fritz and Dwight Morris, *Handbook of Campaign Spending.* Washington, D.C.: Congressional Quarterly Press, 1992, p. 5.

[43] Paul Weyrich quoted in Thomas Ferguson and Joel Rogers, "The Reagan Victory: Corporate Coalitions in the 1980 Campaign," in Ferguson and Rogers, eds. *The Hidden Election: Politics and Economics in the 1980 Presidential Campaign.* New York: Pantheon, 1981, p. 4.

[44] Mark Petracca, "Political Consultants and Democratic Governance," in *P.S.: Political Science and Politics,* March, 1989, p. 11.

[45] Ibid., p. 13.

[46] See Elizabeth Kolbert, "Test-Marketing a President," *The New York Times Magazine,* August 30, 1992, p. 21.

[47] See, for example, Mark Hertsgaard, *On Bended Knee: The Press and the Reagan Presidency.* New York: Farrar, Straus and Giroux, 1988.

[48] "This Week with David Brinkley," ABC, November 6, 1988.

[49] Dan Hallin, "Sound Bite News: Television Coverage of Elections, 1968–1988," Woodrow Wilson Center paper, 1991.

[50] John Tierney, "Sound Bites Become Smaller Mouthfuls," *The New York Times,* January 23, 1992, p. 1.

[51] Richard L. Berke, "Mixed Results for CBS Rule on Sound Bite," *New York Times,* July 11, 1992, p. 7.

[52] Mark Hertsgaard, "Electoral Journalism: Not Yellow, But Yellow-Bellied," *The New York Times,* September 21, 1988, p. A 15.

[53] *TV Guide,* November 21–27, 1992, pp. 14–15.

[54] See Joe McGinniss, *The Selling of the President, 1968.* New York: Trident Press, 1968.

[55] Robin Toner, "Dukakis Works at Warmth But Keeps His Sleeves Down," *New York Times,* August 8, 1988, p. 1.

[56] Walter de Vries, "American Campaign Consulting: Trends and Concerns," *P.S.: Political Science and Politics,* March 1989, p. 21.

[57] The credit for digging up this gem goes to Marjorie Random Hershey, "The Campaign and the Media," in Gerald Pomper, ed. *The Election of 1988,* p. 83.

[58] Ibid., p. 87.

[59] Maureen Dowd, "Bush's Top Strategists: Smooth Poll-Taker and Hard-Driving Manager," *New York Times,* May 30, 1988, p. 11.

[60] Ibid.

[61] Eric Alternam, "Playing Hardball," *New York Times Magazine,* April 30, 1989, p. 70.

[62] Maureen Dowd, "For Bush on the Campaign Trail, The Style Is First Sour, Then Sweet," *The New York Times,* October 12, 1988, p. 10.

[63] Ibid., p. 1.

[64] Hershey, "The Campaign and the Media," p. 81.

[65] Barbara G. Farah and Ethel Klein, "Public Opinion Trends," in Gerald M. Pomper, ed. *The Election of 1988,* p. 103.

[66] Kathleen Hall Jamieson, "For Televised Mendacity, This Year Is the Worst Ever," in Wayne and Wilcox, eds. *The Quest for National Office,* p. 239.

[67] *Washington Post,* reprinted in the *International Herald Tribune,* November 18, 1991.

[68] See, for example, *USA Today,* December 13, 1991, p. 4 A.

[69] *The New York Times,* August 19, 1992, p. 1.

[70] Maureen Dowd, "On the Trail, the Contradictory Sides of Bush," *The New York Times,* November 2, 1992, p. 1.

[71] Richard L. Berke, "In Late Onslaught, Nastiest of Politics Rules Radio Waves," *The New York Times,* November 2, 1992, p. 1.

[72] *USA Today,* December 28, 1992, p. 5 B.

[73] See, for example, Dudley Fishburn, "British Campaigning—How Civilized!" *The New York Times,* March 14, 1992, p. 15.

CHAPTER 11

[1] See Jarol B. Manheim, "All for a Good Cause: Managing Kuwait's Image During the Gulf Conflict," in W. Lance Bennett and David L. Paletz, eds. *The Press, Politics, and Foreign Policy: The Case of the Gulf War.* Chicago: University of Chicago Press, forthcoming.

[2] Arthur W. Rowse, "How to Build Support for War," *Columbia Journalism Review,* September/October 1992, pp. 28–29.

[3] Ibid.

[4] John MacArthur, *Second Front.* New York: Hill and Wang, 1992.

[5] Both headlines are from *The Washington Post* and are discussed in Ben Sherwood, "The Bulls-Eye That Never Happened: That First Patriot Didn't Nail a Scud," *The Washington Post National Weekly Edition,* September 28–October 4, 1992, p. 24.

[6] Quoted in Bob Woodward, *The Commanders.* New York: Simon and Schuster, 1991, p. 155.

[7] Quoted in *The New York Times,* February 15, 1991, p. A 9.

[8] Quoted in an interview on C-Span cable network, February 23, 1991.

[9] Quoted in *Extra!,* May 1991, p. 3.

[10] Quoted in Michael Massing, "Debriefings: What We Saw, What We Learned," *Columbia Journalism Review,* May/June 1991, p. 23.

[11] Ibid., p. 24.

[12] Ibid., pp. 3–5

[13] Thomas Emerson, *Toward a General Theory of the First Amendment.* New York: Vintage, 1966, p. 7.

[14] See Herbert Gans, *Deciding What's News.* New York: Pantheon, 1979, ch. 2.

[15] Doris Graver, *Mass Media and American Politics,* 3rd ed. Washington, D.C.: Congressional Quarterly Press, 1989.

[16] Doris Graber, *Processing the News: How People Tame the Information Tide,* 2nd ed. New York: Longman, 1988, p. 166ff.

[17] Ibid., pp. 168–169.

[18] Stephen E. Bennett, "Trends in Americans' Political Information, 1967–1987," *American Politics Quarterly,* Vol. 17, 1989, pp. 422–435.

[19] This possibility is developed in Graver, *Processing the News.*

[20] Ibid.

[21] *America's Watching: Public Attitudes Toward Television,* National Association of Broadcasters Report, 1991, pp. 21–23.

[22] Reports from surveys conducted by The Times Mirror Center for the People and the Press, June 1990.

[23] These information qualities are expanded and explained in more detail in W. Lance Bennett, *News: The Politics of Illusion,* 2nd ed. New York: Longman, 1988.

[24] Reported in *Newsweek* (International Ed.), May 13, 1991, p. 14.

[25] Jeff Greenfield, "American Rallies 'Round the TV Set," *TV Guide,* February 16, 1991, p. 6.

[26] Ibid., p. 7.

[27] Reported in *Extra!,* May, 1991, p. 11.

[28] Ibid.

[29] See, for example, Daniel C. Hallin, *The Uncensored War: The Media and Vietnam.* Berkeley: University of California Press, 1986.

[30] Ben H. Bagdikian, *The Media Monopoly,* 2nd ed. Boston: Beacon Press, 1988.

[31] 376 U.S. 254. For an interesting discussion of this case, see: Roger Simpson, "Freedom of the Press: The Press and the Court Write a New First Amendment," in Michael W. McCann and Gerald Houseman, eds. *Judging the Constitution.* Boston: Little, Brown, 1989.

[32] 403 U.S. 317, 1971.

[33] For more about the Pentagon Papers case, see: Sanford J. Ungar, *The Papers and the Papers,* 2nd ed. New York: Columbia University Press, 1989.

[34] On the trends in news documentaries, see Bagdikian, *The Media Monopoly.*

[35] See, for example, Ibid.

[36] Larry Sabato, *Feeding Frenzy.* New York: The Free Press, 1992

[37] For elaborations on this point, see: W. Lance Bennett, *News: The Politics of Illusion,* 2nd ed. New York: Longman, 1988; and Robert Entman, *Democracy Without Citizens.* New York: Oxford University Press, 1989.

[38] Leon Sigal, *Reporters and Officials: The Organization and Politics of News Reporting.* Lexington, Mass.: D.C. Heath, 1973, p. 124.

[39] Jane Delano Brown, Carl R. Bybee, Stanley T. Wearden, and Dulcie Murdock Straughan, "Invisible Power: Newspaper Sources and the Limits of Diversity" *Journalism Quarterly,* Vol. 64, 1987, pp. 45–54.

[40] D. Charles Whitney, Marilyn Fritzler, Steven Jones, Sharon Mazzarella, and Lana Rankow, "Geographic and Source Bias in Television Network News: 1982–1984," *Broadcasting and Electronic Media,* Vol. 33, 1989, p. 170.

[41] Source: Office of the Press Secretary for the President, 1992.

[42] See Larry Sabato, "Political Influence, The News Media, and Campaign Consultants," *P.S.: Political Science and Politics,* March 1989, pp. 15–16.

[43] Quoted in Mark Hertzgaard, *On Bended Knee: The Press and the Reagan Presidency.* New York: Farrar, Straus and Giroux, 1988, p. 33.

[44] The following overview is organized along the lines suggested by Steven Livingston of George Washington University.

[45] Hertzgaard, *On Bended Knee,* p. 35.

[46] Ibid., p. 48.

[47] Ibid., p. 49.

[48] Ibid., p. 36.

[49] Ibid., p. 36

[50] Source: Hedrick Smith, *The Power Game: How Washington Works.* New York: Ballantine Books, 1989.

[51] From Jack Honomichl, "Richard Wirthlin, Advertising Man of the Year," *Advertising Age,* January 23, 1989.

[52] From Hedrick Smith, *The Power Game: How Washington Works,* p. 409.

[53] Ibid., p. 407.

[54] Quoted in David Ignatius, "The Press and the President," *The Seattle Times* (from *The Washington Post*), May 28, 1989, p. A 16.

[55] See Jack Honomichl, "Richard Wirthlin, Advertising Man of the Year."

[56] Ann Devroy and Ruth Marcus, "Guess Who Clinton's Picked to Be His Presidential Role Model," *The Washington Post Weekly Edition,* November 23–29, 1992, p. 14.

[57] Jarol B. Manheim, *All of the People, All the Time: Strategic Communication and American Politics,* Armonk, N.Y.: M.E. Sharpe, 1991.

[58] Walter Lippmann, *Public Opinion.* New York: The Free Press, 1922.

[59] Murray Edelman, *The Symbolic Uses of Politics.* Urbana: University of Illinois Press, 1964.

[60] Murrary Edelman, *Constructing the Political Spectacle.* Chicago: University of Chicago Press, 1990.

[61] See, for example, Michael X. Delli Carpini and Bruce Williams, "Television and Political Discourse: Toward a New Agenda," paper delivered at the International Communication Association Meetings, San Francisco, May 25–29, 1989.

[62] Anthony Downs, "Up and Down with Ecology: The Issue Attention Cycle," *The Public Interest,* Vol. 28, 1972, pp. 38–50.

[63] Shanto Iyengar and Donald Kinder, *News That Matters.* Chicago: University of Chicago Press, 1990.

[64] Shanto Iyengar, *Is Anyone Responsible? How Television Frames Political Issues.* Chicago: University of Chicago Press, 1992.

[65] For a good summary of the agenda-setting debate, see Terence H. Qualter, "The Role of the Mass Media in Limiting the Public Agenda," in Michael Margolis and Gary Mauser, eds. *Manipulating Public Opinion.* Pacific Grove, Calif.: Brooks/Cole, 1989.

[66] This question has been raised provocatively in a classic work on news organizations that emphasizes the impact of bureaucratic routines such as beats, bureaus, and assignments on what we call news: Edward Jay Epstein, *News from Nowhere.* New York: Random House, 1973.

[67] The classic work on the press pack is Timothy Crouse, *The Boys on the Bus.* New York: Free Press, 1978.

[68] This is discussed in Ibid. Also see Mark Fishman, *Manufacturing the News.* Austin: University of Texas Press, 1980.

[69] For a more developed version of these arguments, see David Paletz and Robert Entman, *Media Power Politics.* New York: The Free Press, 1981. Also, Bennett, *News: The Politics of Illusion.*

[70] Director of the Nieman fellowship program interviewed on "Talk of the Nation," National Public Radio, December 9, 1992.

[71] Quoted in David Walker, "The War Photo That Nobody Wanted to See," *Photo District News,* August 1991, p. 16.

[72] Ibid.

[73] See, for example, Dan Hallin, *The Uncensored War.* Berkeley: University of California Press, 1989; and W. Lance Bennett, "Toward a Theory of Press–State Relations in the United States," *Journal of Communication,* Vol. 40, No. 2, 1990, pp. 103–127.

[74] *Extra!,* May 1991, p. 19.

[75] Ibid., p. 5.

[76] Robert M. Entman, *Democracy Without Citizens: Media and the Decay of American Politics.* New York: Oxford University Press, 1989.

[77] Dan Nimmo and James E. Coombs, *Mediated Political Realities,* 2nd ed. New York: Longman, 1989.

CHAPTER 12

[1] Eric Pianin and Guy Gugliotta, "On the Hill, Traffic May Start Moving Again," *The Washington Post National Weekly Edition,* November 16–22, 1992, p. 11.

[2] Helen Dewer and Kenneth J. Cooper, "There'll Be Some Changes in Congress," *The Washington Post National Weekly Edition,* October 19–25, 1992, p. 10.

[3] Clifford Krauss, "The Old Order Changes in Congress—a Little," *The New York Times,* November 8, 1992, p. E 3.

[4] Adam Clymer, "Avoiding Gridlock by Wooing Both Sides of Aisle," *The New York Times,* November 17, 1992, p. A 12.

[5] Ibid.

[6] Thomas L. Friedman, "Clinton and Top Legislators Pledge Amity on Economy," *The New York Times,* November 17, 1992, p. A 12.

[7] Robert Axelrod, "Building a Strong Legislature: The Western Experience," *P.S.: Political Science and Politics,* September 1991, p. 474.

[8] From James Young, *The Washington Community: 1800–1828,* reprinted in Serow, et al., *The American Polity Reader.* New York: Norton, 1990,

[9] Reported in Roger Davidson, "The Two Congresses and How They Are Changing," in Norman Ornstein, ed. *The Role of the Legislature in Western Democracies.* Washington, D.C.: American Enterprise Institute, 1981, p. 16.

[10] Richard F. Fenno, Jr., *Home Style: House Members in Their Districts.* Boston: Little, Brown, 1978.

[11] Richard F. Fenno, Jr., *The United States Senate: A Bicameral Perspective,* Washington, D.C.: American Enterprise Institute, 1982, p. 37.

[12] Fenno, *Home Style.* Above quotes reprinted in Serow, et al., *The American Polity Reader,* p. 193.

[13] Ibid., p. 194

[14] Donald R. Matthews, *U.S. Senators and Their World,* Chapel Hill: University of North Carolina Press, 1960, pp. 241–242.

[15] Larry M. Bartels, "Constituency Opinion and Congressional Policy Making: The Reagan Defense Buildup, *American Political Science Review,* Vol. 85, No. 2, June 1991, p. 471 (fn. 2).

[16] Ibid., pp. 462, 465–67; also see Benjamin I. Page and Robert Y. Shapiro, "Effects of Public Opinion on Policy," *American Political Science Review,* Vol. 77, No. 2, March 1983, pp. 175–190.

[17] For various views on this possibility, see the essays in Michael Margolis and Gary Mauser, eds. *Manipulating Public Opinion,* New York: Dorsey, 1989.

[18] For an excellent discussion of the changing nature of public opinion with the advent of modern polling, marketing, and persuasion techniques, see Benjamin Ginsberg, *The Captive Public: How Mass Opinion Promotes State Power.* New York: Basic B ooks, 1986.

[19] See, for example, Donald Matthews, *The Social Backgrounds of Political Decision Makers.* New York: Doubleday, 1954; and Allan G. Bogue, Jerome M. Clubb, Carroll R. McKibbin, and Santa A. Traugott, "Members of the House of Representatives and the Process of Modernization: 1789–1960," *Journal of American History,* Vol. 63, 1976, pp. 275–302.

[20] See, for example, William Domhoff, *The Power Elite and the State: How Policy Is Made In America.* New York: Aldine de Gruyter, 1990.

[21] Clifford Krauss, "The Old Order Changes in Congress—a Little," p. E 3.

[22] Ibid.

[23] Celinda Lake "Women Won on the Merits," *The New York Times,* November 7, 1992, p. 15.

[24] One of the best is Erik Redman's *The Dance of Legislation,* New York: Simon and Schuster, 1973.

[25] From Robin Toner, "The House Democrat His Colleagues Lean on," *The New York Times,* May 9, 1990 p. A 14.

[26] Kenneth A. Shepsle and Barry R. Weingast, "Political Preferences for the Pork Barrel," *American Journal of Political Science,* Vol. 25, 1981, p. 107.

[27] John A. Hird, "The Political Economy of Pork," *American Political Science Review,* Vol. 85, No. 2, June 1991, p. 430.

[28] Ibid., pp. 436–450.

[29] Morris Fiorina, "The Rise of the Washington Establishment," in Peter Woll, ed. *American Government,* p. 477. Excerpted from *Congress: Keystone of the Washington Establishment.* New Haven: Yale University Press, 1977.

[30] Ibid., p. 483.

[31] David Mayhew, "The Electoral Incentive," in Serow, et al., *The American Polity Reader,* pp. 186–187. Excerpted from Mayhew, *Congress: The Electoral Connection.* New Haven: Yale University Press, 1974.

[32] In Hendrik Hertzberg, "The Education of Mr. Smith," *Esquire,* February, 1986, p. 38.

[33] From an editorial in the *New York Times,* reprinted in the *International Herald Tribune,* October 29, 1991, p. 4.

CHAPTER 13

[1] Quoted in Karen De Witt, "Consumer Group Criticizes Travel by House Members," *The New York Times,* September 13, 1991, p. A 9.

[2] All reactions are from Ibid.

[3] The New York Times/CBS Poll was reported in Robin Toner, "The House Democrat His Colleagues Lean On," *The New York Times,* May 9, 1990, p. A 14. The Gallup poll was reported in Timothy Egan, "U.S. House Speaker in Race with Time," a *New York Times* story reprinted in the *International Herald Tribune,* November 5, 1991, p. 3.

[4] Adam Clymer, "Public Believes Worst on Bank Scandal," *The New York Times,* April 2, 1992, p. A 17.

[5] See Toner, "The House Democrat His Colleagues Lean On."

[6] Reported in Peter Osterlund, "Congress at a Crossroads," *The Christian Science Monitor,* June 17, 1988, p. 3.

[7] Adam Clymer, "Citing Rise in Frustration, Dozens of Lawmakers Quit," *The New York Times,* April 5, 1992, p. 1.

[8] Eleanor Clift, "Revels with a Cause, *Newsweek,* Special Election Issue, November-December, 1992, p. 16.

[9] Lloyd Grove, "Mr. Smith Leaves Washington," *The Washington Post National Weekly Edition,* May 25–31, 1992, p. 10.

[10] Tim Worth, "Diary of a Dropout," *The New York Times Magazine,* August 9, 1992, p. 16.

[11] Adapted from Roger H. Davidson and Walter J. Oleszek, *Congress Against Itself.* The full list of reasons why Congress looks bad have been reprinted in Ann G. Serow, W. Wayne Shannon, and Everett C. Ladd, eds., *The American Polity Reader.* New York: Norton, 1990, pp. 178–186.

[12] David Mayhew, *Congress: The Electoral Connection,* New Haven: Yale University Press, 1974.

[13] See Lawrence C. Dodd, "Congress and the Quest for Power," in Lawrence C. Dodd and Bruce Oppenheimer, eds. *Congress Reconsidered.* New York: Praeger, 1977, pp. 269–283.

[14] Representative Dan Glickman of Kansas quoted in John M. Berry, "Games Congressmen Play," *The New York Times Magazine,* May 13, 1990, p. 87.

[15] Daniel J. Evans, "Why I'm Quitting the Senate," *The New York Times Magazine,* April 17, 1988, p. 48.

[16] Ibid., p. 50.

[17] John R. Hibbing, "Contours of the Modern Congressional Career," *American Political Science Review,* Vol. 85, No. 2, June 1991, p. 418.

[18] Ibid., p. 416.

[19] Ibid., p. 425.

[20] Ibid., p. 425.

[21] See Timothy Cook, *Making Laws and Making News: Media Strategies in the U.S. House of Representatives,* Washington, D.C.: Brookings Institution, 1989.

[22] Stephen Hess, "Live from Capitol Hill It's . . . Picking Committees in the Blow-Dried Age," in Serow, et al., *The American Polity Reader,* p. 201.

[23] Ibid.

[24] Wirth, "Diary of a Dropout," p. 16.

[25] Donald R. Matthews, *U.S. Senators and Their World,* Chapel Hill: University of North Carolina Press, 1960.

[26] Quoted in Ross K. Baker, *House and Senate,* New York: Norton, 1989, p. 183.

[27] Ibid.

[28] John Dingell quoted in John M. Barry, "Games Congressmen Play," *The New York Times Magazine,* May 13, 1990, p. 84.

[29] H. Douglas Price, "Congress and the Evolution of Legislative 'Professionalism,'" in Norman J. Ornstein, ed. *Congress in Change.* New York: Praeger, 1975, p. 19.

[30] See Bruce Cain, *The Reapportionment Puzzle,* Berkeley: University of California Press, 1984.

[31] Peter Woll, ed. *American Government.* Glenview, Ill.: Scott Foresman/Little, Brown, 1990, pp. 510–511.

[32] For a year-by-year list of reforms during the 1970s, see Charles O. Jones, "Can Our Parties Survive Our Politics?" in Norman J. Ornstein, ed., *The Role of the Legislature in Western Democracies,* pp. 24–25.

[33] Elizabeth Drew, "Watch 'em Squirm," *The New York Times Magazine,* March 14, 1993, p. 50.

[34] Ibid.

[35] Ibid.

[36] See, for example, Morris P. Fiorina, *Congress: Keystone of the Washington Establishment.* New Haven: Yale University Press, 1977.

[37] Quoted in Timothy Egan, "U.S. House Speaker in Race with Time," *International Herald Tribune,* November 5, 1991, p. 3.

[38] Ibid.

[39] Ibid.

[40] From David S. Broder, "Term Limits Are Dangerous Medicine," *International Herald Tribune,* October 16, 1991, p. 8. Reprinted from *The Washington Post.*

[41] Ibid.

[42] See Larry Martz, "Congress Gropes to Reform," *Newsweek,* June 12, 1989, pp. 19–21.

[43] Richard F. Fenno, "If, As Ralph Nader Says, Congress Is 'The Broken Branch,' How Come We Love Our Congressmen So Much?", in Peter Woll, ed. *American Government.* pp. 525–526.

[44] Report on the Washington state election campaign by Deborah Potter, aired on CNN, November 3, 1991.

[45] "If Congressmen Care," a *New York Times* editorial in the *International Herald Tribune,* October 29, 1991, p. 4.

CHAPTER 14

[1] Dan Balz, "How Not to Be President: Clinton Hopes to Learn From Carter's Blunders," *The Washington Post National Weekly Edition,* December 7–13, 1992, p. 11.

[2] Ibid.

[3] Poll data reported in the analysis of Bush popularity come from monthly polls taken by *The New York Times* and CBS News between 1989 and 1992, reported by Robin Toner in "Bush and the Economy: Americans Losing Confidence," *International Herald Tribune,* November 27, 1991,
p. 1, and in subsequent reporting in *The New York Times.*

[4] John Mueller, *War, Presidents, and Public Opinion.* New York: John Wiley, 1973. Richard Brody and Catherine Shapiro, "A Reconsideration of the Rally Phenomenon in Public Opinion," *Political Behavior,* Vol. 11, 1989, pp. 353–369.

[5] Benjamin Barber, "Neither Leaders Nor Followers: Citizenship Under Strong Democracy," in Michael Beschloss and Thomas Cronin, eds., *Essays in Honor of James MacGregor Burns,* Englewood Cliffs, N.J.: Prentice-Hall, 1989, p. 121.

[6] Fred I. Greenstein, "Nine Presidents in Search of a Modern Presidency," in Fred Greenstein, ed. *Leadership in the Modern Presidency.* Cambridge: Harvard University Press, 1988, p. 298.

[7] See Samuel M. Kernell, *Going Public: New Strategies of Presidential Leadership.* New York: Cornell University Press, 1985.

[8] Jeffrey Tulis, *The Rhetorical Presidency.* Princeton: Princeton University Press, 1987.

[9] See, for example, the reflections of Reagan speechwriter Peggy Noonan in *What I Saw at the Revolution.* New York: Ivy Books, 1990.

[10] Al Kamen, "Clinton Goes Way Back to Fill a Key White House Job," *The Washington Post National Weekly Edition,* December 21–27, 1992, p. 13.

[11] Bill McAllister, "The Citizen Militia that Has 'Two Masters and Three Leaders,'" *The Washington Post National Weekly Edition,* May 18–24, 1992, p. 32.

[12] Ibid.

[13] See Bob Woodward, *The Commanders.* New York: Simon and Schuster, 1991.

[14] Duane M. Oldfield and Aaron Wildavsky, "Reconsidering the Two Presidencies," *Society,* Vol. 26. No. 5, July/August 1989, pp. 54–59.

[15] R.W. Apple, Jr., "A Short, Persuasive Lesson in Warfare," *The New York Times,* March 3, 1991, p. 2 E.

[16] Richard Neustadt, *Presidential Power and the Modern President: The Politics of Leadership from Roosevelt to Reagan.* New York: The Free Press, 1990.

[17] James W. Davis, *The American Presidency: A New Perspective.* New York: Harper & Row, 1987, p. 130.

[18] See, for example, David L. Paletz and Robert M. Entman, *Media Power Politics.* New York: The Free Press, 1981.

[19] For a look at the masterful public relations efforts and press management strategies of the Reagan White House, see Mark Hertsgaard, *On Bended Knee: The Press and the Reagan Presidency.* New York: Farrar, Straus and Giroux, 1988.

[20] Seymour M. Hersch, *The Price of Power: Kissinger in the Nixon White House.* New York: Summit Books, 1983.

[21] Noonan, *What I Saw at the Revolution.*

[22] Bruce Buchanan, *The Citizen's Presidency.* Washington D.C.: Congressional Quarterly Press, 1986.

[23] Stephen Hess, "Why Great Men Are Not Chosen Presidents," *Society,* Vol. 25, No. 5, July/August 1988, pp. 46–52.

[24] Quoted in Christopher Swan and Amy Brooke Baker, "Politics and the Lost Art of Art," *Christian Science Monitor,* April 1, 1988, p. 16.

[25] Ibid.

[26] Ibid.

[27] James David Barber, *The Presidential Character,* 3rd ed. Englewood Cliffs, N.J.: Prentice-Hall, 1985.

[28] See, for example, Barbara Hinckley, *Problems of the Presidency.* Glenview, Ill.: Scott, Foresman, 1986.

[29] Craig A. Rimmerman, "Teaching the Modern Presidency," *The Political Science Teacher,* Vol. 2, No. 3, Summer 1989, p. 9.

[30] Theodore J. Lowi, "An Aligning Election: A Presidential Plebiscite," in Michael Nelson, ed. *The Election of 1984.* Washington, D.C.: Congressional Quarterly Press, 1985.

[31] Theodore J. Lowi, *The Personal President: Power Invested, Promise Unfulfilled.* Ithaca: Cornell University Press, 1985.

[32] In addition to Richard Rose, *The Postmodern President,* see also, Ryan J. Barrileaux, *The Post-Modern Presidency.* New York: Praeger, 1988.

[33] Richard Rose, *The Postmodern President: The White House Meets the World.* Chatham. N.J.: Chatham House, 1989, p. 6; also, Lester G. Seligman and Cary R. Covington, *The Coalitional Presidency.* Chicago: Irwin, 1989.

CHAPTER 15

[1] National Public Radio, *All Things Considered,* January 11, 1993.

[2] Thomas L. Friedman, "Clinton's Cabinet Choices Put Him at Center, Balancing Competing Political Factions," *The New York Times,* December 27, 1992, p. 12.

[3] Al Kamen, "Clinton Goes Way Back to Fill a Key White House Job: 'Mack' McLarty, as the Oldest 'Friend of Bill,' Won't Be an Insulator," *The Washington Post National Weekly Edition,* December 21–27, 1992, p. 13.

[4] Henry A. Waxman, "The Environmental Pollution President," *The New York Times,* April 29, 1992, p. A 17.

[5] Matthew L. Wald, "Clean-Air Battle: Unusual Cast of Courtroom Foes," *The New York Times,* April 25, 1992, p. 6.

[6] See Karen De Witt, "Senate Panel Hears of Human Toll in Workplace," *The New York Times,* May 7, 1992, p. A 16.

[7] James Q. Wilson, "The Rise of the Bureaucratic State," in Peter Woll, ed., *American Government: Readings and Cases.* Glenview, Ill.: Scott Foresman, 1990, p. 432.

[8] Ibid.

[9] Quoted in Thomas E. Cronin "The Swelling of the Presidency: Can Anyone Reverse the Tide?," in Peter Woll, ed., *American Government,* p. 380.

[10] Seymour M. Hirsch, *The Price of Power: Kissinger in the Nixon White House.* New York: Summit Books, 1983, chs. 21–22.

[11] Cronin, "The Swelling of the Presidency," p. 380.

[12] "Dan Quayle, Regulation Terminator," *Business Week,* November 4, 1991, p. 31.

[13] Cronin, "The Swelling of the Presidency," p. 380.

CHAPTER 16

[1] Ruth Marcus, "So Many Defendants, So Little Time," *The Washington Post National Weekly Edition,* March 16–22, 1992, p. 33.

[2] Ted Gest, "One Poor Man's Legacy," *U.S. News & World Report,* March 22, 1993, p. 19.

[3] 372 U.S. 335 (1963)

[4] See Anthony Lewis, *Gideon's Trumpet.* New York: Random House, 1964.

[5] John Holdridge, quoted in Gest, "One Poor Man's Legacy," p. 19.

[6] See David O'Brien, *Storm Center: The Supreme Court in American Politics.* New York: Norton, 1986, ch. 1.

[7] 492 U.S. 990.

[8] Tamar Lewin, "States Testing the Limits on Abortion," *The New York Times,* April 2, 1990, p. A 10.

[9] Quoted in "Abortion: The Nation Responds," *The Ladd Report #8.* New York: Norton, 1990, p. 7.

[10] Nadine Cohodas, "Courts Play Larger Role as Interbranch Referee," *Congressional Quarterly,* January 7, 1989, p. 13.

[11] 418 U.S. 683.

[12] See O'Brien, *Storm Center,* p. 221.

[13] House legal counsel Steven R. Ross quoted in Cohodas, "Courts Play Larger Role. . .," p. 13.

[14] Law Professor Peter Shane quoted in Ibid., p. 13.

[15] 1 Cranch 137 (1803).

[16] O'Brien, *Storm Center,* p. 166.

[17] Ibid., pp. 167–168.

[18] David Margolick, "Here Comes the Chief Justice (Please Don't Call Him Judge)," *The New York Times,* April 26, 1991, p. B 1.

[19] Maria Odum, "If It Talks Like a Lawyer, There May Be a Cure," *The New York Times,* June 5, 1992, p. B 9.

[20] Quoted in Bernard Schwartz, *The Unpublished Opinions of the Warren Court.* New York: Oxford University Press, 1985, p. 11.

[21] See Stephen L. Wasby, *The Supreme Court in the Federal Judicial System,* 2nd ed. New York: Holt, Rinehart and Winston, 1984, pp. 56–57.

[22] Ibid., p. 57.

[23] Ibid., p. 154.

[24] Ibid., p. 155.

[25] O'Brien, *Storm Center,* p. 183.

[26] Wasby, *The Supreme Court in the Federal Judicial System* p. 159.

[27] Quoted in Doris Marie Provine, *Case Selection in the United States Supreme Court.* Chicago: University of Chicago Press, 1980, pp. 105–106.

[28] Quoted in Ibid., p. 175.

[29] Ibid., p. 175.

[30] Quoted in Schwartz, *The Unpublished Opinions of the Warren Court,* p. 11.

[31] Ibid., p. 12.

[32] From Richard Posner, "What Am I? A Potted Plant?," *The New Republic,* September 28, 1987, p. 23.

[33] Laurence H. Tribe, *American Constitutional Law,* 2nd ed. Mineola, N.Y.: The Foundation Press, 1988, pp. 1162–3.

[34] Ibid., p. 23.

[35] Ibid., p. 25.

[36] Leonard W. Levy, *Original Intent and the Framers' Constitution.* New York: Macmillan, 1987.

[37] O'Brien, *Storm Center,* p. 189.

[38] Ibid.

[39] Ibid., p. 214.

[40] Quoted in Stewart Taylor, Jr., "Blackmun Provides a Peek at the People Under Those Robes," *The New York Times,* July 25, 1988, p. 12.

[41] Bob Woodward and Scott Armstrong, *The Brethren: Inside the Supreme Court.* New York: Simon and Schuster, 1979.

[42] See also, Terry Eastland, "While Justice Sleeps," *National Review,* April 29, 1989, p. 24.

[43] See, for example, Schwartz, *The Unpublished Opinions of the Warren Court,* ch. 1.

[44] Ibid., p. 19.

[45] Stewart Taylor, Jr., "Blackmun Provides a Peek at the People Under Those Robes," *The New York Times,* July 25, 1988, p. 12.

[46] Ibid., p. 445.

[47] Ibid., p. 446.

[48] Ibid., p. 447.

[49] Ibid., p. 446.

[50] Ibid., p. 446.

[51] Ibid., p. 446.

[52] Bernard Schwartz, *The Unpublished Opinions of the Warren Court.* New York: Oxford University Press, 1985, p. 455.

[53] Stewart Taylor, Jr., "Rehnquist"s Court: Turning Out the White House," *The New York Times Magazine,* September 11, 1988, p. 94.

[54] Ibid., p. 94.

[55] Ibid., p. 94.

[56] See Timothy M. Phelps, *Capital Games: Clarence Thomas, Anita Hill, and the Story of a Supreme Court Nomination.* New York: Hyperion, 1992.

CHAPTER 17

[1] "American Agenda," ABC World News Tonight, November 27, 1991.

[2] "American Agenda," a follow-up on "The State of the Nation"s Children," *ABC World News Tonight,* November 21, 1991.

[3] Ron Harris, "Children's Lack of Political Voice Leaves Needs Unmet," *Los Angeles Times,* May 16, 1991, p. 1.

[4] Reported by Anthony Lewis, in an opinion piece in *The New York Times,* July 6, 1990, p. A 25.

[5] Shanto Iyengar and Donald Kinder, *News That Matters.* Chicago: University of Chicago Press, 1990.

[6] Shanto Iyengar, *Is Anyone Responsible?* Chicago: University of Chicago Press, 1992.

[7] See, for example, Murray Edelman, *The Symbolic Uses of Politics.* Urbana: University of Illinois Press, 1964.

[8] Ibid.

[9] Ibid., p. 3.

[10] Ibid., pp. 3–4.

[11] Roger W. Cobb, Jennie-Keith Ross, and Marc Howard Ross, "Agenda-Building as a Comparative Political Process," *American Political Science Review,* March 1976, p. 126.

[12] Roger W. Cobb and Charles D. Elder, *Participation in American Politics.* 2nd ed. Baltimore: Johns Hopkins University Press, 1983.

[13] Richard Hofferbert, *The Study of Public Policy.* Indianapolis: Bobbs Merrill, 1974.

[14] See, for example, Cobb and Elder, *Participation in American Politics.*

[15] C. Wright Mills, *The Power Elite.* New York: Oxford University Press, 1959.

[16] G. William Domhoff, *The Power Elite and the State: How Policy Is Made in America.* New York: Aldine de Gruyter, 1990.

[17] Thomas R. Dye and L. Harmon Ziegler, *The Irony of Democracy,* 9th ed. Belmont, Calif.: Wadsworth, 1993.

[18] See, for example, Murray Edelman, *The Symbolic Uses of Politics.* Urbana: University of Illinois Press, 1964. Also, *Political Language: Words that Succeed and Policies that Fail.* San Diego: Academia Press, 1977.

[19] Russell J. Dalton, *Citizen Politics in Western Democracies,* Chatham, N.J.: Chatham House, 1988, p. 100.

[20] See, for example, the discussion in David B. Robertson and Dennis R. Judd, *The Development of American Public Policy: The Structure of Policy Restraint,* Glenview, Ill.: Scott Foresman/Little, Brown, 1989, p. 2.

[21] Paul A. Sabatier, "Political Science and Public Policy," *P.S.: Political Science and Politics,* Vol. 24, No. 2, June 1991, p. 145.

[22] See, for example, Elinor Ostrom, *Governing the Commons.* Cambridge, England: Cambridge University Press, 1992.

[23] See, for example, Paul A. Sabatier, "An Advocacy Coaliton Framework of Policy Change and the Role of Policy-Oriented Learning Therein," *Policy Sciences,* Vol. 21, Fall 1988, pp. 129–168.

[24] Quoted in David Evans, "Powell's Diet Plan for Armed Forces Steers Clear of Heavyweight Issues," *Tacoma News Tribune,* February 13, 1993, p. 1.

[25] Michael Cohen, James March, and Johann Olsen, "A Garbage Can Model of Organizational Choice," *Administrative Science Quarterly,* Vol. 17, March 1972, pp. 1–25.

[26] John Kingdon, *Agendas, Alternatives, and Public Policies.* Boston: Little, Brown, 1984.

[27] Stephan Gotz Richter, "Climbing Down from the Hill: The Decline of America and the National Crisis in Economic Policy-Making," *P.S.: Political Science and Politics,* September 1989, p. 600.

CHAPTER 18

[1] A nine-part series by Donald Bartlett and James Steele, published in *The Philadelphia Inquirer,* October 20–28, 1991.

[2] Barbara Vobejda, *The Washington Post National Weekly Edition,* June 8–14, 1992, p. 31.

[3] Ibid. Also, the series by Bartlett and Steele.

[4] Neil Howe and Phillip Longman, "The Next New Deal," *The Atlantic Monthly,* April 1992, p. 93.

[5] John W. Kingdon, *Agendas, Alternatives, and Public Policies.* New York: Harper Collins, 1984, p. 116.

[6] John H. Schaar, "Equality of Opportunity and Beyond," in J. Roland Pennock and John W. Chapman, eds. *Equality.* New York: Atherton Press, 1967, p. 248.

[7] George Will, "In Defense of the Welfare State," *The New Republic,* May 9, 1983, p. 25.

[8] "The Wrong Medicine," *The New York Times* editorial, May 26, 1991, p. 10 E.

[9] Data released by Families, USA, a health care interest group, December 1991.

[10] Allan R. Gold, "The Struggle to Make Do Without Health Insurance," *The New York Times,* July 30, 1989, p. 1.

[11] Ibid.

[12] Philip J. Hilts, "Demands to Fix U.S. Health Care Reach a Crescendo." *The New York Times,* May 19, 1991, sec. 4, p. 1.

[13] Gold, "The Struggle to Make Do . . . ," p. 11.

[14] Philip J. Hilts, "Demands to Fix U.S. Health Care Reach a Crescendo," sec. 4, p. 1.

[15] Ibid.

[16] Ibid.

[17] Statistics from: National Center for Health Statistics, U.S. General Accounting Office, and the Canadian Ministry of Health, reported in *USA Today,* November 12, 1991, p. 8 B.

[18] Hilts, "Demands to Fix . . . ", sec. 4, p. 1.

[19] Robert Pear, "White House Shuns Bigger A.M.A. Voice in Health Changes, *The New York Times,* March 5, 1993, p. A 8.

[20] Philip R. Lee and Richard D. Lamm, "Europe's Medical Model," *The New York Times,* March 1, 1993, p. A 15.

[21] Ruth Sivard, *World Military and Social Expenditures 1991.* Washington, D.C.: World Priorities, 1991, p. 48.

[22] *Los Angeles Times,* May 11, 1990, p. 1.

[23] Marc Cooper, "The Dumbing of America," *Utne Reader,* December 1985/January 1986, p. 90.

[24] Sivard, *World Military and Social Expenditures 1991,* p. 48.

[25] *Newsweek,* International Edition, November 26, 1990, p. 3.

[26] Based on a report by the Educational Testing Service, in Keren DeWitt, "Education Panel Sees Modest Gains," *The New York Times,* October 1, 1991, p. A 10.

[27] Ibid.

[28] See James D. Slack, "United States," in Frederic N. Bolotin, ed. *International Public Policy Sourcebook,* Vol. 2. New York: Greenwood Press, 1989, p. 177.

[29] Ibid., p. 170.

[30] Arch Persons, "U.S. Fails Its Poor, Global Study Says," *Tacoma Morning News Tribune,* September 19, 1991, p. A 4. From *The Baltimore Sun.*

[31] See Jason DeParle, "Richer Rich, Poorer Poor, and a Fatter Green Book," *The New York Times,* May 26, 1991, p. E 2. Also, Thomas Byrne Edsall, "The Return of Inequality," *The Atlantic Monthly,* June 1988, pp. 89–94.

[32] Michael Harrington, *The Other America.* Reprinted in Ann G. Serow, W. Wayne Shannon, and Everett C. Ladd, eds. *The American Policy Reader.* New York: Norton, 1990, pp. 650–651.

[33] National Opinion Research Center, 1989 General Social Survey, University of Chicago.

[34] Michael Harrington, *The New American Poverty.* New York: Holt, Rinehart and Winston, 1984.

[35] Ibid., p. 656.

[36] See, for example, Robert B. Reich, "Why the Rich Are Getting Richer and the Poor Poorer," *The Utne Reader,* January/February 1990, pp. 42–49.

[37] J.C. Barden, "Poverty Rate Is Up Sharply for Very Young, Study Says," *The New York Times,* April 16, 1990, p. A 7.

[38] Robert Rector, "Poverty in U.S. Is Exaggerated By Census," *The Wall Street Journal,* September 26, 1990, p. 6.

[39] Ibid.

[40] Jason DeParle, "In U.S., What Does It Take to Be Poor?" *The International Herald Tribune,* September 1, 1990, p. 5.

[41] Quoted in Jeff Gerth, "Thousands Rally in Washington Calling for Action on Social Issues," *The New York Times,* September 1, 1991, p. 18.

[42] Charlotte Saikowski, "Strengthening the Social Fabric," *The Christian Science Monitor,* November 15, 1988, p. 16.

[43] Myron Magnet, "America's Underclass: What to Do?" *Forbes,* May 11, 1987, pp. 130–150.

[44] Based on fiscal year 1991 figures reported in the *Budget of the U.S. Government,* U.S. Office of Management and Budget, Government Printing Office, 1991.

[45] Ralph Nader and Mark Green, "Passing on the Legacy of Shame," *The Nation,* April 2, 1991, p. 444.

[46] Cited in a *Washington Post* editorial, "One American in Ten," reprinted in the *International Herald Tribune,* November 6, 1991, p. 3.

[47] Ibid.

[48] Ibid.

[49] Ibid.

[50] Ibid.

[51] Quoted in Tim Friend, "Parents Lack Enough Time, Money for Kids," *USA Today,* November 22, 1991, p. 9 A.

[52] Robert B. Reich, "Who Champions the Working Class?" *The New York Times,* May 26, 1991, p. E 11.

[53] From Peter T. Kilborn, "School (Inc) for Young Moms," *International Herald Tribune,* December 2, 1991, p. 5.

CHAPTER 19

[1] See Ellen Hume, "Why the Press Blew the S&L Scandal," *The New York Times,* May 24, 1990, p. A 24.

[2] *Newsweek,* May 21, 1990, pp. 34–41.

[3] See John Steel Gordon, "Understanding the S&L Mess," *American Heritage,* February/March 1991, pp. 49–68. Also, Ron Chernow, "Sources of the U.S. Bank Crisis," *The Wall Street Journal,* November 1, 1990, p. 10.

[4] Source: *Historical Statistics of the U.S.: Colonial Times to 1970.* Washington, D.C.: Bureau of the Census, pp. 1117–1118.

[5] David Stockman, *The Triumph of Politics.* New York: Harper and Row, 1986.

[6] Mark Memmot, "Government's Hands Tied on Economy," *USA Today,* November 21, 1991, p. 2 A.

[7] "Back to the Future? Revisiting an Old U.S.," *The Wall Street Journal,* December 9, 1991, p. 1.

[8] Memmott, "Government's Hands Tied . . ." p. 2 A.

[9] "Back to the Future? . . .", p. 1.

[10] Discussed in "Back to the Future? Revisiting an Old U.S."

[11] Ibid.

[12] Robert B. Reich, "Who Champions the Working Class?" *The New York Times,* May 26, 1991, p. E 11.

CHAPTER 20

[1] *International Herald Tribune,* November 20, 1990, p. 1.

[2] *The New York Times,* February 2, 1991, p. 1.

[3] See, for example, Frances Fukuyama, *The End of History and the Last Man.* New York: The Free Press, 1992.

[4] Quoted in Thomas L. Friedman, "Bush's Role on World Stage: Triumphs, But Troubles, Too," *The New York Times,* June 26, 1992, p. A 12.

[5] Thomas L. Friedman, "A New U.S. Problem: Freely Elected Tyrants," *The New York Times,* January 12, 1992, p. E 3.

[6] Quoted in Ibid.

[7] See Seymour Martin Lipset, *The First New Nation.* New York: Basic Books, 1963.

[8] John Spanier, *American Foreign Policy Since World War II,* 12th ed. Washington, D.C.: Congressional Quarterly, 1991, pp. 6–8.

[9] From Peter Rosset and John Vandermeer, eds., *The Nicaragua Reader.* New York: Grove Press, 1983, p. 107.

[10] See Charles W. Kegley, Jr., and Eugene R. Wittkopf, *American Foreign Policy: Pattern and Process,* 3rd ed. New York: St. Martin's Press, 1987, pp. 36–40.

[11] Quoted in Ibid., p. 38.

[12] Ibid.

[13] See Thomas J. McCormick, *America's Half Century: United States Foreign Policy in the Cold War.* Baltimore: Johns Hopkins University Press, 1989, ch. 2.

[14] Ibid., pp. 36–42.

[15] Spanier, *American Foreign Policy Since World War II,* pp. 32–33.

[16] Kegley and Wittkopf, *American Foreign Policy,* p. 345.

[17] See Bill Moyers, *The Secret Government,* PBS series.

[18] R.W. Apple, Jr., "Changing the Guard," *The New York Times,* March 1, 1987, p. E 1.

[19] Quoted in Kegley and Wittkopf, p. 351.

[20] McCormick, *America's Half Century,* p. 170.

[21] Quoted in Spanier, p. 130.

[22] McCormick, p. 13.

[23] Ibid., p. 14.

[24] Ibid., p. 15.

[25] Robert Y. Shapiro and Benjamin I. Page, "Foreign Policy and Public Opinion in a Transformed World," paper presented at the Thomas P. O'Neill, Jr., Symposium in American Politics, Boston College, April 3–4, 1992.

[26] Bernard C. Cohen, *The Public's Impact on Foreign Policy,* Boston: Little, Brown, 1973, p. 206.

[27] Cecil V. Crabb, Jr., and Pat M. Holt, *Invitation to Struggle: Congress, the President and Foreign Policy,* 2nd ed. Washington, D.C.: CQ Press, 1984, p. 58.

[28] David W. Rhode, "Partisanship and Congressional Assertiveness in Foreign and Defense Policy," paper presented at the Thomas P. O'Neill, Jr., Symposium in American Politics, Boston College, April 3–4, 1992, pp. 34–37.

[29] Spanier, chs. 11–12.

[30] Clyde V. Prestowitz, Jr., "Beyond Laissez-Faire," *Foreign Policy,* No. 87, Summer 1992, p. 68.

[31] I.M. Destler, *American Trade Politics,* Washington, D.C.: Institute for International Economics, 1986, p. 163.

[32] Ibid., p. 38.

[33] John B. Judis, "Twilight of the Gods," *Wilson Quarterly,* Autumn 1991, p. 55.

[34] John Tierney, "Congress and the Changing Foreign Policy Community," paper presented at the Thomas P. O'Neill, Jr., Symposium in American Politics, Boston College, April 3–4, 1992, p. 29.

[35] Ibid., p. 30.

[36] Bert A. Rockman, "The Outside Game: Presidents, Opinion, and Institutional Leadership," paper presented at the Thomas P. O'Neill, Jr., Symposium in American Politics, Boston College, April 3–4, 1992.

[37] See Ruth Sivard, *World Military and Social Expenditures.* Washington, D.C.: World Priorities, 1985.

[38] Barton Gilman, "Less Bang, Fewer Bucks: U.S. Military Begins One of its Most Dramatic Retreats," *International Herald Tribune,* December 9, 1991, p. 1.

[39] *The New York Times,* editorial, May 13, 1992, p. A 14.

[40] See Bernard D. Nossiter, "Don't Expect a Peace Dividend from the Military Keynesians," *International Herald Tribune,* May 29, 1990, p. 8.

[41] Patrick E. Tyler, "U.S. Strategy Plan Calls for Ensuring No Rivals Develop," *The New York Times,* March 8, 1992, p. 1.

[42] Ibid., p. 4.

[43] Leslie Gelb, "Shazam Defense," *The New York Times,* May 25, 1992, p. 17.

[44] Thomas L. Friedman, "It's Harder Now to Figure Out Compelling National Interests," *The New York Times,* May 31, 1992, p. E 5.

[45] David A. Deese, "The American State Under Pressure: Interdependence, Transnational Ties, and Domestic Fragmentation," paper presented at the Thomas P. O'Neill, Jr., Symposium in American Politics, Boston College, April 3–4, 1992.

[46] Quotes are from Roger Cohen, "U.S.-French Relations Turn Icy After Cold War," *The New York Times,* July 2, 1991, p. A 5.

[47] See Paul Kennedy, *The Rise and Fall of the Great Powers.* New York: Random House, 1987.

[48] Joseph S. Nye, Jr. *Bound to Lead.* New York: Basic Books, 1990.

[49] Mark Danner, "How the Foreign Policy Machine Broke Down," *The New York Times Magazine,* March 7, 1993, p. 34.

REFERENCE
INDEX

Abraham, Henry J., 185, 601
Abrams, Elliott, 77
Adams, Brooks, 709
Adams, Charles, 125
Ailes, Roger, 245
Alexander, Herbert E., 363, 384
Alexrod, Robert, 433–434
Anton, Thomas J., 143
Armstrong, Scott, 601
Asher, Herbert B., 223, 384

Bagdikian, Ben H., 400, 425
Bailey, John J., 551
Bailyn, Bernard, 104–105
Barber, Benjamin, 159, 232, 508
Barber, James David, 532–533, *532*
Barry, Dave, 304
Baum, Lawrence, 571, 577, 601
Beard, Charles A., 21, 54, 69, 428
Beck, Paul Allen, 343
Bellah, Robert N., 160, 236
Bennett, W. Lance, 384, 425
Berke, Richard L., 292, 373, 529n
Berman, Larry, 535
Berns, Walter, 591
Berry, Jeffrey, M., 235, 309
Birch, Anthony H., 153
Birnbaum, Jeffrey H., 309
Blank, Rebecca, 663
Bloom, Allan, 104–105
Blumler, Jay G., 401
Bolotin, Frederic N., 612, 650
Boyer, Ernest, 649
Boyum, David, 646
Brigham, John, 185
Brinkley, Alan, 159
Brinkley, David, 529
Brock, David, 599
Broder, David, 313, 316, 495
Brown, Robert E., 55
Bryce, James, Lord, 531
Brzezinski, Zbigniew, 717
Buchanan, Bruce, 531
Bundy, McGeorge, 717
Burnham, Walter Dean, 336–337, 343
Burns, James MacGregor, 334

Cain, Bruce, 461
Caplan, Marc, 308
Cigler, Allan J., 123, 279, 309
Cobb, Roger, 616
Cohen, Bernard, 719
Conway, Margaret M., 267
Cook, Timothy, 470, 499
Corwin, Edwin S., 601
Cowan, Richard, 287
Cramer, Richard Ben, 384

Cronin, Thomas E., 267, 350, 535, 562

Dahl, Robert A., 21, 29, 55
Dalton, Russell J., 211, 267
Davidson, Roger, 465
Deering, Christopher J., 493
Deese, David, 732
Destler, I. M., 722
De Vries, Walter, 375
Dierkes, Meinhoff, 612
DiVall, Linda, 191
Domhoff, William, 24, 29, 101, 620
Doolittle, Fred C., 143
Dowd, Maureen, 377
Downs, Anthony, 412, 565
Draper, Theodore, 77
Dye, Thomas R., 621, 629

Edelman, Murray, 196, 214, 223, 410–411, 613, 621
Edsall, Mary, 182
Edsall, Thomas, 182
Ehrenhalt, Alan, 315
Ehrman, Henry W., 483
Eizenstat, Stuart, 328
Elazar, Daniel J., 111
Elden, Charles, 616
Emerson, Thomas, 425
Entman, Robert, 423, 425
Epstein, Leon D., 335, 343
Epstein, Richard A., 185
Etzioni, Amitai, 159
Evans, Dan, 468–469
Evans, Sarah H., 267

Feldman, David Lewis, 612
Fenno, Richard F., Jr., 437–438, 461, 496
Ferejohn, John, 461
Ferguson, Thomas, 325, 343
Fiorina, Morris, 244, 456, 457, 461, 499
Fisher, Louis, 565
Fitzmaurice, John, 573
Friedman, Milton, 674, 680, 699
Friedman, Rose, 699
Friedman, Thomas, 704

Galbraith, John Kenneth, 667, 674, 699
Gardner, John, 307
Garment, Suzanne, 425
Garner, Robert E., 551
Germond, Jack, 385
Gilder, George, 667, 699
Gilliom, John, 149, 151
Ginsberg, Benjamin, 21, 24, 29, 198, 222, 225, 305, 339
Graber, Doris A., 394, 396, 425, 510, 511

Green, Mark, 662
Greenhouse, Linda, 575
Greider, William, 425
Grodzins, Morton, 120, 143
Grover, William F., 236
Guitton, Stephanie, 185

Hacker, Andrew, 181–182, 185
Hallin, Daniel C., 425
Hamilton, Alexander, 69
Harrington, Michael, 654, 655, 667
Hartz, Louis, 225
Hazlitt, Henry, 699
Heclo, Hugh, 565
Henthoff, Nat, 185
Hershey, Marjorie, 377
Hertsgaard, Mark, 374
Herberg, Will, *205*
Hess, Stephen, 471, 531
Hibbing, John R., 469, 470, 499
Hird, John, 456
Hobbes, Thomas, 39
Hofferbert, Richard, 619, 629
Hoffman–Riem, Wolfgang, 401
Holmes, Oliver Wendell, Jr., 570, 590
Hueglin, Thomas O., 121
Huntington, Samuel P., 618
Hyneman, Charles S., 69

Irons, Peter, 185
Iyengar, Shanto, 215, 412–413, 607

Jackson, Brooks, 384
Jackson, Doreen, 573
Jackson, Robert J., 573
Jamieson, Kathleen, 377
Jay, John, 69
Jenkins–Smith, Hank, 629
Jennings, M. Kent, 199
Judd, Dennis R., 615, 629

Kayden, Xandra, 343
Kegley, Charles W., Jr., 735
Kenier, Elizabeth, 510
Kennan, George F., 712, 735
Kennedy, Paul, 734, 735
Kernell, Samuel, 510, 511, 535
Key, V. O., 225, 244
Keynes, John Maynard, 674, 677–678, 699
Kinder, Donald, 215, 412, 607
King, Martin Luther, Jr., 236
Kingdon, John, 626, 629, 634
Kirk, Russell, 225
Kissinger, Henry, 717
Kolbert, Elizabeth, 221
Kozol, Jonathan, 647

Ladd, Carl Everett, 579
Laffer, Arthur, 680
Lamm, Richard, 645
Lammers, William W., 510, 511
Lasswell, Harold D., 6, 29
Latham, Earl, 304
Lawson, Kay, 334
Leach, Richard H., 115, 125, 143
Lee, Philip, 645
Lembruch, Gerhard, 277
Levine, Charles H., 123
Levinson, Sanford, 105
Levy, Leonard W., 69, 105, 591, 601
Lewis, Anthony, 185
Lieberman, Myron, 667
Lippmann, Walter, 215, 225, 410, 412,
    425
Lipset, Seymour M., 69
Listhaug, Ola, 329
Locke, John, 39
Loomis, Burdett A., 123, 279, 309
Lowi, Theodore J., 21, 304, 305, 306,
    309, 312–313, 315, 322, 534–535
Lutz, Donald S., 69

Mackie, Thomas T., 239
Madison, James, 69
Madsen, Richard, 236
Magelby, David B., 385
Mahe, Eddie, Jr., 343
Makinson, Larry, 365
Malbin, Michael J., 491, 523
Mann, Thomas E., 491, 523
Marcus, Gregory, 228
Margolis, Michael, 225
Marmor, Theodore, 646
Marzio, Peter, 159
Matthews, Donald, 438, 473
Mauser, Gary, 225
Mayhew, David R., 458, 461
McBride, Ann, 307
McCann, Michael, 307–309
McClosky, Herbert, 29
McCormick, Thomas J., 735
McDonald, Forrest, 55, 69
Mead, Walter B., 105
Mee, Charles L., Jr., 69
Michels, Roberto, 490
Miller, Arthur, 329
Miller, Merle, *532*
Miss, C. Wright, 620
Mises, Ludwig von, 691
Montesquieu, Baron (Charles–Louis
    de Secondat), 55, 75
Moore, Geoffrey, 696
Morgan, Edmund S., 69, 100
Morris, Aldon D., 177, 267
Munson, Richard, 499
Myrdal, Gunnar, 172

Nader, Ralph, 306, 662
Nathan, Richard P., 143
Nathanson, Stephen, 69
Nedelsky, Jennifer, 185
Nelson, Candice J., 385
Neuhaus, Richard John, 159
Neuman, W. Russell, 225
Neustadt, Richard, 76, 528, 535
Newcomb, Theodore, 200–201
Nie, Norman H., 233
Niemi, Richard G., 96, 199, 237, 331,
    340, 397, 440, 443, 444, 445, 506,
    510, 522, 525, 543, 571, 577, 584,
    585, 587, 678
Nye, Joseph S., Jr., 734, 735

O'Brien, David M., 592, 601
Olasky, Marvin, 667
Oleszek, Walter J., 461, 465
Olling, R. D., 121
Olson, Mancur, Jr., 283, 309
Ornstein, Norman J., 491, 523
Owen, Diana, 385

Page, Benjamin, 193, 225, 244
Pateman, Carole, 232
Peschek, Joseph G., 236
Peters, B. Guy, 699
Peterson, Paul E., 143, 306
Petracca, Mark, 370
Phillips, Don, 617
Phillips, Kevin, 667, 699
Polsby, Nelson, 226
Popkin, Samuel L., 252, 267
Posner, Richard, 591
Powe, Lucas A., Jr., 425
Powlege, Fred, 185
Provine, Doris Marie, 589

Rabe, Barry G., 143
Rector, Robert, 657
Redman, Eric, *446*
Rehnquist, William, *596*
Reich, Robert B., 664, 667, 681, *696*,
    697, 699
Richardson, Sula P., 493
Rieselbach, Leroy, 499
Ripley, Randall, 461
Robertson, David B., 614–615, 629
Robinson, Michael, 346–347
Roepke, Wilhelm, 680
Rogers, Joel, 325, 343
Rohatyn, Felix, 659
Rohde, David, 719
Romer, Christina, 696
Rose, Richard, 239, 535
Rosenberg, Gerald, 294
Roskin, Michael G., 483, 509, 573
Rostow, Walt, 717

Rourke, Francis E., 565
Rousseau, Jean–Jacques, 39
Ruggles, Patricia, 657, 658

Sabatier, Paul A., 624, 629
Sabato, Larry, 385, 425
Salisbury, Robert, 278, 306
Samuelson, Paul, 681
Schain, Martin A., 483
Schattschneider, E. E., 304, 309
Schjelderup, Susan, 493
Schlesinger, Arthur, Jr., 344
Schlozman, Kay Lehman, 299, 303, 309
Schmitter, Philippe, 277
Schwartz, Bernard, 601
Seredich, John, 308
Shafer, Byron, 7, 15
Shapiro, Robert, 193, 225
Shefter, Martin, 21, 24, 29, 305, 339
Sidey, Hugh, 531
Siegan, Bernard H., 185
Sigal, Leon, 404
Simon, Roger, 385
Sinclair, Barbara, 499
Sivard, Ruth L., 707, 708, 713, 727
Slack, James, 647, 650
Smith, Adam, 676, 699
Smith, Hedrick, 29, 425
Smith, Steven S., 493
Sontag, Susan, *517*
Sorauf, Frank J., 343
Spanier, John, 735
Stanfield, Rochelle L., 450
Stanley, Harold W., 96, 237, 331, 340,
    397, 440, 443, 444, 445, 506, 510, 522,
    525, 543, 571, 577, 584, 585, 587, 678
Starr, Paul, 667
Steiner, Jurg, 351
Stockman, David, *682*
Sullivan, William M., 236
Sundquist, James L., 105
Swidler, Ann, 236

Teixeira, Ruy A., 250, 264, 267
Thurber, James A., 123
Tierney, John T., 299, 303, 309, 724
Tipton, Steven M., 236
Tocqueville, Alexis de, 225, 226, 265
Tribe, Laurence H., 163, 601
Tyson, Laura D'Andrea, 691

Verba, Sidney, 233
Vogel, David, 612

Walker, Jack L., Jr., 285, 299, 309
Walker, Samuel, 185
Wasby, Stephen, 588, 601
Wayne, Stephen J., 363, 385
Whitney, Craig R., 645

Whitney, D. Charles, 419
Wilcox, Clyde, 363, 385
Wildavsky, Aaron, 226, 527
Will, George, 499, 635
Wills, Garry, 69
Wilson, James Q., 305, 306, 309, 552, 565

Wines, Michael, 373
Witcover, Jules, 385
Wittkopf, Eugene R., 735
Wolfinger, Raymond, 238
Wong, Kenneth K., 143
Wood, Floris W., 204

Wood, Gordon S., 69
Woodward, Bob, 601

Zaller, John, 29
Ziegler, Harmon, 621
Zinn, Howard, 54

SUBJECT AND NAME
INDEX

A

AARP. *See* American Association of Retired Persons
Abortion
litigation over, 293–294, *294*
public opinion about, 579
Supreme Court and, 576–578
women's rights and, 166–167
Accountability, elections and, 348
ACLU. *See* American Civil Liberties Union
Action, political, 227–267
Activism, *19. See also* Social movements
Adams, Abigail, 37
Adams, Brooks, 709
Adams, Charles, 125
Adams, John, 2, 41, *48*, 500
and Constitution, *53*
Adams, Samuel, 35
Administrations. *See* Bureaucracy
Adversaries, 581
Advertising, *295*
AFDC. *See* Aid to Families with Dependent Children
Affirmative action, 178–180
African Americans. *See* Black Americans
Age, voting and, 247–248. *See also* Senior Citizens
Age Discrimination Employment Acts (1967, 1975, 1986), 176
Agencies, reduction of, 132–134. *See also* Bureaucracy
Agencies for hire, interest groups and, 278
Agenda. *See* Policy; Political agenda
Agenda–building, 616
Agents of socialization, 199
primary, 199–201
secondary, 201–202
AIDS
activists and, *19*
public opinion and, 194, *194*
quilt display, *614*
Aid to Families with Dependent Children (AFDC), 660, 662
Ailes, Roger, 245, 375, *376*, 377
Air Force, as interest group, 552–553
Airline industry, deregulation and, 693–694, *694*
Alcohol. *See* Prohibition
Alien and Sedition Acts (1798), 155
Alienation, 263
Allende, Salvador, 559
AMA. *See* American Medical Association

Amending bills, 448
Amendments. *See also* specific amendments
Article V and, 60
Bill of Rights and, 64–66, 85–91
Civil War and, 119
criminal justice, 163–165
interval between congressional approval and state ratification of, 96
listing of, 92–95
process of, 91–98
Reconstruction (Thirteenth, Fourteenth, Fifteenth), *99*, 100
American Association of Retired Persons (AARP), 283–284, 295, 297
American Civil Liberties Union (ACLU), 147, 293
American Dilemma, An, 172
American Independent party, 321
American Indians
American Indian movement and, 256, *256*
peyote and, 162
poverty and, 655
American Know-Nothing party, 320, *321*
American League of Lobbyists (ALL), 281
American Medical Association (AMA), health care reform and, 622, 641, 642
American Sugar Refining Company monopoly, 124–126
Americans with Disabilities Act (1990), 176
Ames, Oakes and Oliver, 675
Anderson, John, *682*
Anti-abortion movement, 256
Anti-Federalists, 65
Bill of Rights and, 66
Appeals courts, 583–584
Apprenticeship system, 469–470, 479
Aristocratic systems, 62
Aristotle, 2
Arizona v. Fulminante, 597
Arms race, 715
end of Cold War and, 725–726
Army–McCarthy hearings, 453
Arnett, Peter, *398*
Arraignment, 581
Articles, of Constitution, 60
Article I (legislature), 78–79
Article II (executive), 80–81, 521
Article III (judiciary), 60, 81–83,

583, 584
Article IV (interstate relations), 60, 85
Article V, 91
Article VI (supremacy clause), 85
denied powers in, 85
Articles of Confederation, 35, 51–52
Constitutional Convention and, 55
and New Jersey Plan, 56–57
Virginia Plan and, 56
Aspin, Les, 538, *558*, 704
Assassinations, *352*
presidents and, 531
Assembly, freedom of, 157
Associations, 280
campaign financing and, 368
Attucks, Crispus, *48*
Atwater, Lee, 247, 330, 353–356, 375, *376*, 377
Authority, resistance to, 68
Automobile industry, as interest group, 298–302
AWARE (anticommunist group), 157

B

Babbitt, Bruce, 344
Baber, Patti Jo, 281
Back-channel operations, 559
Bacon, Nathaniel, 40
Baird, Zoë, 230–231, 608
Baker, James, 375, 715, 732
Baker, Russell, 4
Bakke, Allan, 179–180
Balanced budget, 18
Balance of power
among branches, 75–77
Iran-*contra* affair and, 76, 77
Ballot. *See* Elections
Bank failures, 126
Banking, savings and loan disaster and, 671
Bank of the United States, 115–116
Bank reform bill, *126*
Bankruptcy, 670
Barber, Benjamin, 159
Barbour, Haley, *332*
Barron v. Baltimore, 154
Barry, Dave, 304–305
Beard, Charles, 428
Behavior, voter, 17
Bellah, Robert, 160
Benefits, of interest-group membership, 283–284
Bennington College, Vermont, political socialization at, 200–201
Benton v. Maryland (1969), 155

Bentsen, Lloyd, 440, 538
Bergsten, C. Fred, 700
Berke, Richard L., 373
Berlin Wall, *703*
Bicameral legislature, 56, **434**, 435
Biden, Joseph, 471
Big Business, 124–126
    failures of, 126
    lobbying and, *274*
Big government, 111–114
    federal myths and, 115
Bill(s). *See also* Law(s)
    politics to become law, 450–452
    procedure to become law, 446–450
Bill of Rights, 64–66, 74, 85–91,
    148–149, *149*
    incorporation of civil liberties in,
      169
    privileges, immunities, and,
      153–154
    Supreme Court and, 571
    written, 152
Birmingham, Ala., Fire Department
    affirmative action and, 179
Black Americans
    affirmative action and, 179–180
    current status of, 181–182
    Fourteenth Amendment and, 155
    Jim Crow laws and, 249
    leaders of, 257–258
    poverty and, 655
    Reconstruction amendments and,
      99, 100
    separate but equal facilities and,
      171–172
    voting and, *90*, 246
Blacklisting, 157
Blackmun, Harry, 162 , 592, 594
    view of Court by, 594–595
Blaine, James G., 676
Blanket primaries, 333
Block grants, **131**
Blummer, Robyn, 148
Board of Governors, of Federal Reserve
    System, 689
"Boat people," Haitian, *625*
Bolshevik coup (1917), 155, *156*
Bonior, David, *468*
Boren, David, 529
Bork, Robert, 286, 578, 598, 599
Boston Massacre (1770), *48*
Boston Tea Party (1773), 35, 45
Bottom-up path, to government
    agenda, **619**–620, 621
Bowdoin, James, 35
Bowers v. Hardwick (1986), 168
Boxer, Barbara, *314*, *364*
Branches of government, 75–83
    lobbying by, 286
Brennan, William J., Jr., 575
Brethren, The, 594

Brinkley, Alan, 159
Britain, *42*
    civil liberties in, 1 53
    parliamentary system in, *434*
    power organization in, 103
    unwritten constitution in, 48, 49
Broadcast media
    in other nations, 401
    regulation of, 399–400
Broad constructionist, **590**
Brock, David, *599*
Broder, David, 310, 313, 316, 495
Brown, Jerry, *378*
Brown, Ron, *19*, *285*–286, 330, *538*
Brown v. Board of Education, 172, 174,
    175, *175*, 590, 592, 595–596
Browner, Carol, 538, 542
Bryan, William Jennings, 356, *357*
Buchanan, Bruce, 531
Buchanan, James, as state–centered
    president, 119
Buchanan, Patrick, 327, *327*, 707
Budget
    balanced, 18
    Clinton and, 4, 134
    elitist view of, 25–26
    majoritarian view of, 24
    national, 4–6
    pluralist view of, 25
    Reagan, Bush, and, 132–134
Budget deficits
    and gross domestic product, 679
    military spending and, 707
"Bull Moose" (Progressive) party, 320,
    322
Bumpers, Dale, 529
Bureaucracy
    activist, 551–552
    command system of, 547–549
    executive management of,
      537–565
    historical changes in politics,
      549–552
    implementation of laws by,
      542–543
    interest groups in, 552–554
    in Mexico, 551
    organization of, 543–549
    politics and, 539–542, 552–554
    public attitudes toward, 541
    regulation and, 543
    rise of, 552
    units of, 544
Bureaus. *See* Bureaucracy
Burger, Warren, 165, 579, 594, 596,
    596
Burke, Edmund, 50
Burnham v. Superior Court of California,
    575
Burns, James MacGregor, 500
Burr, Aaron, election of 1800 and, 60

Bush, Barbara, *338*
Bush, George, *338*, 505
    CAFE laws and, 300
    campaign finance reform and,
      493, 498
    character of, 245
    China policy of, 72
    defense spending of, 729
    educational policy of, 652
    environmental regulation and,
      540, *540*
    Executive Office of, 560, 564
    fiscal policy of, 686
    flag desecration and, 158
    focus groups and, 221
    foreign policy and, 527, 712
    issue voting and, *243*
    media campaign of, 372–373
    media management and, 408
    military and, 526, *526*
    monetary policy of, 688
    New Federalism and, 109, 133
    1988 campaign and, 375–377, *376*
    1992 campaign and, *376*,
      377–379, *378*
    nomination and, 355–356
    NSC (National Security Council)
      and, 560
    public opinion and, 190–191, *190*,
      206, *512*
    vetoes by, *448*
    as vice president, 513
Business, *125*
    campaign financing by, 367–369
    foreign policy impact of, 717–718
    interest groups and, 274
    lobbies of, *274*
    "Robber Barons" and, 124, 125
    use of Fourteenth Amendment by,
      124
Butler, Smedley, 706

C
Cabinet, *557*, *558*
    politics in, 554–558
Cabinet departments, listing of, 545
Cable news, 415–416. *See also* CNN;
    News
CAFE. *See* Corporate Average Fuel
    Economy law
Cain, James David, 144
Calhoun, John C., 118
California
    Democratic party in (1991), 334
    election costs in, 363
    federalism and, 121
California v. Acevedo, 597
California v. Hodari D., 597
Campaign(s), 357–360
    character images in, 244–245
    contributions to, 290–292

and elections, 345–385
financing, 360–369
media in 1992, 371–374
in 1992, 242–244
organization for, 360
Campaign finance system, reform
of, 307, **380**–381, 493–494, 498
Campbell, Ben Nighthorse, *256*
Canada
health care in, 644–645
judiciary in, 573
poverty and economic trends in,
663
Quebec separatism and federalism
in, 120, 121
trade agreement with, 725
Candidates. *See also* Elections
character of, 244–245
marketing of, 369–371
media coverage of, 346–347
nomination procedures for,
331–334
political parties and, 329–335
Cannon, Joseph, 490
Cantwell v. Connecticut (1940), 157,
161
Capitol Building, *78*
Cardozo, Benjamin, 155
Career management system, in
Congress, 468-**470**
Carlson, Peter, 288
Carlucci, Frank, *301*
Carroll, Eugene, *390*
Carswell, G. Harold, 599
Carter, Hodding, 390
Carter, Jimmy, 131, 502–503, 504
character of, *530*
educational policy and, *651*
executive style of, 520
gridlock and, 431
modern vice presidency and, 513
press and, 406
Carville, James, *332*
Case Act (1972), 720
Casework, congressional, **457**
Casey v. Planned Parenthood, 578
Categorical grant, 131
Caucuses, 331–333
nomination and, 353
Celebrities, public opinion and, 194,
194
Censorship, 157
Census Bureau, sampling by, 218
Central Intelligence Agency (CIA),
559
Iran-*contra* affair and, 77
Character, presidential, 244–245,
530–533. *See also* Ethics
Character types, presidential,
532-533
Checks and balances, 75-77, *76*

judicial review and, 82–83
Cheney, Dick, 298
Chicago, voter registration in, 250
Chief executive, and Articles of
Confederation, 52. *See also*
Executive branch; Presidency
Chief Justice, 583. *See also* Supreme
Court
Child care, corporate sponsorship of,
664
Child labor, federal division of powers
and, *116*
Children
and political agenda, 606–607
political learning by, 199–200
Children's Defense Fund, *275*
Chile, 559, 715
China
Bush policy toward, 722
Nixon policy toward, 717, *717*
revolt in Tiananmen Square, 722,
723
Choices. *See* Political parties
Christian right movement, 256,
262–263
Christopher, Warren, *558*
Churchill, Winston, 710–711, *712*
CIA. *See* Central Intelligence Agency
Circuit Court of Appeals, 583–584
Cisneros, Henry, *74*
Cities
in colonial America, 39
urban poor and, *40*
Citizenship
dual, 154–155
rights of, 151
slavery and, 119
of state, 142
Civil disobedience, 175
Civilians
in government branches, 549
in national, state, and local
government, 550
Civil law, **574**
Civil liberties, 145–185
in Bill of Rights, 169
defined, 152
status of, 168
Supreme Court and, 571
U.S. and British, 153
Civil procedure, in federal courts, 582
Civil rights, 168–182
Court composition and, 595
defined, 152
expanding definition of, 177–178
Fourteenth Amendment and, 124
free speech and, 147
harassment and, 146–148
important laws, 176
Civil Rights Act, **651**
free speech and, 147–148

1957, 176
1964, 176, 651
Civil rights movement, 256
leaders of, 258
of 1950s and 1960s, 171–177, *173*
Parks, Rosa, and, *173*, 176, 177
Civil service. *See also* Bureaucracy
employment in, 544
rise of, 551
Civil War (1860–1865), *120*
Constitution and, *98*, 99
and federalist debate, 118–120
Class
as social characteristic, 204
voting and, 248
Clay, Henry, *317*, 318
Clean Air Act (1990), 300, 540, *540*,
564
Clear and present danger, **156**
Cleveland, Grover, 125
and interest groups, 273
Climates of opinion, 212–214
Clinton, Bill, *6*, *27*, *73*, 502–503, 630
agenda policy of, 625–626
big government and, 114
budget and, 4, 26, 27
bureaucracy and, *538*
cabinet of, *558*
campaign, *231*
campaign finance reform and, 498
character issue and, 244
and Congress, 513, *523*
defense spending and, 729
educational policy of, 652
electoral vote of, 358, *358*
Executive Office of, 560
executive style of, 520
fiscal policy of, 686
focus groups and, 221
gridlock and, 430–431, *430*
and interest groups, 274
issue voting and, *243*
Los Angeles riots and, *180*
mandate of, 17
media campaign of, 373–374
media coverage and, *407*
media management and, 408–409,
409
monetary policy of, 688
on MTV, *229*
New Federalism and, 109, 114, 133
1992 campaign and, 377–379, *378*
1992 election, 73, 367–369
nomination and, 356
party structure and, *332*
persuasion and, *529*
poverty policy of, 655
public relations and, 513
sexual preference in military and,
617, 627, *627*
U.S. power and, 734

Clinton, Hillary, 623
    health care reform and, 642, *658*
Closed primary, 333
Closed rule, **447**
Cloture rule, 477
Clubs, participation in, 24
CNN (Cable News Network), 357, 398, *398*, 415
Coercive Acts, 49
Cold War, 527, 702, **710**–715, *712*
    foreign policy during, 715–719
    United States role after, 730–734
Coleman v. Thompson, 597
Colfax, Schuyler, 676
Collective action, 283
Colonial America
    Constitution and, 34–36
    pre-Revolutionary, 43–45
    rebellion and revolution in, 38–43
    taxation of 48–49
Colonial system, revolution and, 41–43
Colorado, homosexuality proposition in, 350
Commander in Chief, 524
Commissions. *See* Bureaucracy
Committee on committees, 487–488
Committees
    congressional, 446–447, 481
    in French National Assembly, 483
    power in, 478–484
Committee system
    development of, 493
    pros and cons of, 484
    reforming, 492
Common Cause, 291, 307, *307*
Common law tradition, **572**
Common Sense, 50
Communication(s). *See also* Media; News
    interest groups and, 282
    social movements and, 258–260
Communications Office, of White House, 406
Communism, 710. *See also* Cold War
    blacklisting and, 157
    fear of, 155, *156*
    free speech crackdowns and, 157–158
Comparable worth, 170
Competitiveness Council, 564
Compromise
    agenda and politics of, 609–612
    and Constitution, *53*, 56–61
    as pragmatism, 67
    tradition of, 36–38
Concurring opinion, **576**–577
Confederation, 110, **51**
Confederation Congress, 52
Conference committee, **448**
Conferences (Supreme Court), **592**

Conflict, Constitution and, 34–36
Congress, 429–461. *See also* Gridlock; House of Representatives; Legislature; Lobbying; Political action committees (PACs); Senate
    budget and, 5–6
    Clinton's budget control plan and, 27–28
    committees in, 446–447, 478–484
    constitutional design of, 432–433
    cooperative federalism and, 129–130
    elastic clause and, 79
    executive oversight by, 452–455
    expressed powers of, 79
    and federal courts, 583–586
    first meeting of (1789), 66
    foreign policy and, 718–719, 721
    history of, 436–437
    how a bill becomes a law, 78, 446–450
    image of, 464–466
    impeachment and, 453–454
    incumbent campaigns and, 366–367
    industrial expansion and, 116
    internal organization of, 78
    law-making powers of, 442–458
    leadership and legislation, 450–452, *451*
    monitoring rule–making by, 454–455
    New Federalism and, 133
    New Jersey Plan and, 56–57
    103rd, *471*, 472
    party system in, 489
    pay raises in, 91
    performance of, 460
    political world in, 479
    power structure of, 466–490
    presidential relationship with, 521–524
    presidential victories on votes in (1953–1990), 523
    public's opinion of, 467
    Reagan foreign policy and, 722
    reelection and, 457–458
    reforming, 490–495
    representation in, 432–433
    rules of debate in, 476–477
    seniority in, 488
    social composition of, 439–442
    term limits and, 494–495
    Virginia Plan and, 56
    White House relations with, 452
Congressional Budget Office, 5, 453
Congressional election committees, 330
Connecticut Compromise, 58
Consalvo, Pasquale, *140*

Conservatism, **11**–12
Conservative, 210–211. *See also* Ideology; Political culture; Public opinion
Constituents, congressional service to, 456–457
Constitution, **74**
    unwritten British, 48, 49
Constitutional Convention (1787), 14, 34, *35*, 37
    delegates to, 52–55
Constitutional tradition, 48
Constitution of the U.S. *See also* Amendments; Bill of Rights; Federalism
    amendment process, 91–98
    amendments, listing of, 92–95
    Bill of Rights and, 64–66
    colonial culture and, 34–36
    contemporary significance of, 85–99
    delegates' attitudes toward, 60–61
    document, 86–90
    elitist view of, 54
    formal foreign policy powers and, 721
    Great Compromise and, 57–58
    institutions, federalism, and, 614–616
    intentions about Supreme Court and, 590–591
    interpretation process for, 98–99
    legislative article (Article I), 78–79
    New Jersey Plan and, 56–57
    personal liberties, rights, and, 145–185
    pluralist view of, 55
    as political framework, *97*
    as politics and political philosophy, 38
    politics of, 52–61
    power distribution in, 74–85
    presidency and 514–517
    ratification of, 61–68, *64*
    signing of, 61, *61*
    slavery and, 58–59
    Virginia Plan and, 56
    written, 151–152
Containment doctrine, **712**–713
Continental Congress, 34
    First, 41, *42*
    Second, 50–51, *50*
Contras, and Iran-*contra* affair, 76, 77, *454*, 714
Conventional participation, **232**–237
Conventions, *338*, 356–357
    delegate selection for, 334–335
    Democratic (1968), 352, *352*
    political, 329
    primaries and, 331–333

Convicts, rights of, 597
Cook, Carl, 179
Cooperative federalism, 117, 120–122, 508
 cultural, institutional, and social factors affecting, 128–129
 education and, 651–652
 1937–1968, 127–130
Corporate Average Fuel Economy (CAFE) law (1975), 298–302
Corporatism, 276, 277
Corruption
 Crédit Mobilier scandal and, 675–676
 savings and loan disaster and, 675–676
Costs. *See also* Financing
 of education, 648
 government spending and, 130–131, 132–134, 661
 of health care, 637–640
Council of Economic Advisers, **691**
Court of Claims, 584
Courtroom ritual, 582–583
Courts, 567–601. *See also* Judicial branch; Supreme Court
 civil liberties rulings and, 163–165
 federal, 581–583
 jargon in, 583
 jurisdiction of, 574
Coverdell, Paul, *486*
Cox, Archibald, 578, *580*
Cranston, Alan, *672*
Credibility gap, 402
Crimes, Congress, executive oversight, and, 454
Criminal justice amendments, 163–165
Criminal law, **573**
Criminal procedure, in federal courts, 581–582
Critical election period, 336
Cross of Gold speech, 356, *357*
Crossover sanctions, 137
Cruel and unusual punishment clause, 165
Crédit Mobilier scandal, 675–676
C-Span, 357
Cuban missile crisis, 504, 715
Cultural attitudes, about power, 7–8
Cultural conflicts, social problems and, *635*
Cultural symbols, **614**
Cultural themes, **10**, **612**. *See also* Political culture; specific subjects
Cultural values, *7*
 Constitution and, 34
Culture
 budget control and, 27

economic policy and, 674
 news and, 392
 political, 8–14
 poverty and, 656–659
 rights, order, and, 151
 and symbolic politics, 613–614, 706
 two-party system and, 324
 U.S. as world power and, 705–708
Cuomo, Mario, 211
Customs Court, 584
Cynicism, **263**

D
Dahl, Robert, 566
Daley, Richard J., *352*
Damage control, **374**
Darman, Richard, 560
Davidson, Roger H., 462
Day, Luke, 35
Dealignment, political parties and, 337
Death penalty, 165
Deaver, Michael, 390
Debate, 479
 elections and, 348
 rules for congressional, 476–477
Debs, Eugene V., *321*
Debt, **677**, 678. *See also* National debt
 cultural politics and, 12–14
Declaration of Independence, 34, *42*, *50*
 background of, 50–51
 document, 46–47
 rights in, **9**
Declaration of Rights, *42*
Defendant, **573**
Defense Department, lobbying by, 291. *See also* Pentagon
Defense PACs, 290–291
Defense Planning Guidance for the Fiscal Years 1994–1999, 730
Defense policy, 725–730
 and economy, 728–729
 foreign policy and, 701–735
Deficit, 4
DeJonge v. Oregon, 157
Delegate, **20**
 to Constitutional Convention, 52–55
 view of representation, **432**, 437–439
Democracy, 62
 direct vs. representative, 348–350
 elections and, 348–350
 evolution of, 48
 information and, 391–399
 institutions and, 14–15
 and interest–group politics, 271–278, 303–309

mass media and, 387–425
 in political parties, 334–335
 and public opinion, 193
Democratic National Convention (1968), 352, *352*, 720
Democratic party, 317. *See also* Political parties in 1992 election, 73
 civil rights movement and, 172
 civil rights orientation of, 246
 cooperative federalism and, 125–130
 delegate opinions and, 335
 gridlock and 430–431
 identification with, 239–242
 ideology of, 12
 nomination of 1992 candidate, 354
 presidents and, 502–503
 Roosevelt, Franklin Delano, and, 127–129
 support by race, 203
Democratic–Republican party, 317
Democratic system, participation in, 232
Demographic composition of Congress, **439**–441
Demonstrations, *255*
Denied powers, **85**
Denmark
 judiciary in, 573
 political parties in, 319
Department of Defense (DOD), 544–545
Departments, **544**. *See also* departments by name
 listing of, 545
 politics in, 554–558
Deregulation, **138**, **693**–694
Derrick, Butler, *468*
Détente, **721**–722
Deviating elections, 336
De Vries, Walter, 375
Dingell, John, 450
Direct democracy, **15**, **348**–350
 comparative, 350, 351
Disadvantaged groups, 170
Disclosure law, and lobbying, 286, 287
Discontent, political parties as channels for, 329
Discount rate, **690**
Discretionary spending, 660–662
Discrimination. *See also* Affirmative action
 civil rights and, 168–171
 voting and, 250
Dissent, 67–68
Dissenting opinion, **592**
Distribution, 216–217
District courts, **583**

Districts, voting, 250–251
DiVall, Linda, 191
Divisions of power, 75
Dockets, 588–589
DOD. *See* Department of Defense
Dole, Robert, 367, *486*, *658*
Donaldson, Sam, 371
Double jeopardy, 163
Douglas, William O., 165, 168, 594
Dowd, Maureen, 377
Draft resistance, free speech and,
     155–156
Dred Scott vs. Sanford, 118–119
Drinking. *See* Prohibition
Drinking age, regulation of, 137
Drugs, in religious ceremonies, 162
Dual citizenship, national and state,
     154–155
Dual federalism, 117, 120–122, 615
     1800–1937, 122–126
     end of, 126
Duberstein, Kenneth, 286, *301*
Due process clause, 155
Dukakis, Michael, 247
     character of, 245
     1988 campaign and, 375–377
Dulles, Allen, *196*
Dulles, John Foster, *196*
Durant, Thomas C., 675

E
Eastern Europe
     revolutions in, 702–704
     after World War II, 710–712
Economic equality, 10
Economic interests, military power
     and, 708–710
Economic laws, Supreme Court and,
     571
Economic patterns, poverty and, 663
Economic philosophy
     Keynesianism, 667–678
     laissez-faire, 123–126. *See also*
          Laissez–faire
     new (neo) conservatism, 680
     new ideas, 697
Economic policies, 669–699, **681**.
     See also Social policy
     fiscal, monetary, and regulatory,
          682–694
     institutions and, 673–674
Economic relations, colonial, 41
Economics, 676–682
     social movements and, *259*
Economics of information, 414–422
Economy. *See also* New Deal; Political
     economy
     of colonial America, 45
     compromise and, 611
     defense spending and, 728–729
     domestic, 681

involvement with, 698
     in 1990s, 686
     regulation of, 692–694
     world, 681
Edsall, Thomas and Mary, 182
Education
     Civil Rights Act (1964) and, 651
     comparative costs of, 648
     reform of, 647–652
     unemployment and, 648
Education Consolidation and
     Improvement Act (1982), 652
Education Department, 133, 651, *651*
Edwards, Mickey, 347
Eighteenth Amendment (1919), 98
Eighth Amendment, 163
Eisenhower, Dwight, 23, 174, *446*, 504
     civil rights movement and, *178*
     defense policy and, 728–729
     and interest groups, 274
Elastic clause, 79, 116
**Election laws and procedures,
     238**
Election of representatives, 348
Elections, 348–350. *See also* Political
     parties; Voting
     campaigns and, 345–385
     convention and, 356–357
     costs of presidential (1960–1992),
          363
     Democratic voting in, 241
     of 1800, 60
     history of, 350–352
     independents voting in, 241
     laws and procedures of, 249–252,
          253
     of 1968, 720
     of 1988, 238
     of 1992, 17, 73, 228–230, 238,
          242–244, 354, 355, 361, 632,
          706–707
     nomination and, 353–356
     number of, 252
     party identification and, 240, 241
     political reality of, 360–374
     reelection of Congress and,
          457–458
     reforming system of, 380–382, 384
     social movements and, 262–263
     voting patterns in (1976–1992),
          252–253
     wealth and, 248
Electoral college, 59–60
     campaigns and, 357–358
     popular and electoral vote trends
          (1932–1992), 359
Electoral connection, 458
Electoral vote, 357
Elector system, 320
Electronic age. *See* Media; News
Elementary and Secondary Education

Act (1965), 651
Elitist theory of power, 18, *19*,
     21–23, 100–101. *See also* Power
     elite
     and budget, 25–26
     economic policy and, 674–676
     and interest groups, 279
     New Federalism and, 133
     public opinion and, 196–197
     two-party system and, 325
Ellsberg, Daniel, 402
El Salvador, foreign policy toward, 722
Employment, in bureaucracy, 544
Employment Division v. Smith (1990),
     162
Empowerment, individual, 257–258
Energy, compromise and, 611
Energy Department, 133
England. *See* Britain; Colonial
     America
Engle v. Vitale (1962), 161
Entitlements, 660
Enumerated powers, 515
Environment
     compromise and, 611
     French policy-making and, 612
     public opinion on, *207*, 208
     regulation and, 132, 540–542, 564
Environmental movement, 256
Environmental politics, opinion and
     power in, 197
Environmental Protection Agency
     (EPA), 132, 540–542
Equality of opportunity, 10, 171
Equal protection clause, 155
Equal Rights Amendment, 96
Equal time provision, 400
Era of Good Feeling, 317
Escobedo v. Illinois (1964), 164
Espionage Act (1917), 155, 158
Establishment, 527
Establishment clause, 160–161,
     162
Ethics
     in Congress, 464–465
     public-interest group movement
          and, 307
Etzioni, Amitai, 159
Eure, Steve, 288–289, *289*
Europe
     broadcasting systems in, 401
     government research and
          development investments in,
          727
     health care in, 645
     poverty in, 652–653
     United States and, 732–734
Evans, Dan, 468–469
Everson v. Board of Education (1947),
     161
Exclusionary rule, 164

Executive agreements, **515**, **524**, 525
Executive branch, 56. *See also* Gridlock; Presidency; President(s)
  Article II, 80–81
  bureaucracy and, 537–565
  congressional oversight of, 452–455
  power and leadership in, 500–535
  presidency and, 508–513
  relationship to other branches, 548
  vice president and, 513–514
Executive departments, **544–546**
Executive Office of the President, **538**–539, 558–562
  staff of, 560–562
Executive orders, **515**, **519**
Executive oversight, **452**–455
  hearings and, 453–454, *454*
  research and information-gathering, 453
Expressed powers, **79**

F
Factions. *See* Interest groups; Political parties
Fair Housing Acts (1968, 1988), 176
Fairness doctrine, 400
Fair trials, 164
Falwell, Jerry, 596
Family
  political socialization in, 199–200, *200*
  poverty and, 653–654
Faulk, John Henry, 157
Fazio, Vic, 455, *468*, 490
FCC. *See* Federal Communications Commission
FDIC. *See* Federal Deposit Insurance Corporation
Fed. *See* Federal Reserve System
Federal aid, to state governments (1950–1990), 135–136
Federal Arts Project, *127*
Federal Communications Commission (FCC), 399–400
Federal courts
  Congress and, 583–586
  courtroom ritual in, 582–583
  law and procedure in, 581–583
  organization of, 583–585
Federal Deposit Insurance Corporation (FDIC), 547–548
Federal Election Campaign Act (1974), 366
Federal employees, on interest–group staffs, 303
Federal grants, 130–132
Federalism, **75**, **84**, 106. *See also* Cooperative federalism; Dual

  federalism; New Federalism
  in Canada, 121
  civil liberties and, 153
  Civil War and, 118–120
  competing theories of, 114–120
  constitutional design and, 614–616
  defined, 110–114
  division of powers in, 112
  models of, 120–122
  national and state government powers, 83–85
  nation-centered view of, 115–117
  politics of, 107–142
  and politics of education, 649–651
  and unitary systems, 111
Federalist, The, 55, 62–64, *63*, 275–276, 414
  No. 10, 55, 62, *63*, 275–276, 316
  No. 45, 84
  No. 51, 62, 276
  No. 57, 435
  No. 62, 435
  Madison and, 62–63, *63*
Federalists, 65, 317
  Bill of Rights, and, 66
Federal Open Market Committee, 689, 690
Federal Register, 542
Federal Reserve Banks, 689–690
Federal Reserve System (Fed), *683*, **688**
  monetary policy and, 688
  operation of, 689–691
Federal spending (1980–1990), 134
Feinstein, Dianne, *314*, 364, *364*, 442
Felonies, **573**–574
Feminist movement, 256
Feynman, Richard, *453*
Fifteenth Amendment (1870), *97*, 100, 119, 249
  voting rights and, 172
Fifth Amendment, 163
Filibuster, **448**, **476**
Financiers, lobbies of, *274*
Financing, campaign, 360–369
First Amendment
  freedom of the press and, 157
  free speech rights of, 147–148
  truth and, 402–403
First Continental Congress, 41, *42*
Fiscal policy, **682**–687, **693**
  groups and, 698
  monetary policy and, 691–693
  and unemployment, 687
Flag
  burning of, 158, *158*
  symbolism of, 159–160
Flag Protection Act (1989), 158
Fletcher, James, *453*
Floor debate, **447–448**
Floor managers, 452

Flynn, Raymond, 138
Focus groups, 220, 221, 371
Foley, Thomas, *6*, *73*, 464, 465, *468*, 494
Foods, lobbying and, 288–289
Food Stamp Act (1964), 662
Food stamps, *655*
Foreign policy, 701–735
  and Cold War, 710–715, 715–719
  domestication of process, 719–725
  formal constitutional powers over, 721
  leaders of, *723*
  in national security state, 714–715
  participating in, 733
  president and, 524–527
  after World War II, 709–710
Foreign policy establishment, **716**–718
Formal declaration of war, **524**
Formal powers, **515**
Founders
  basic documents and, *62*
  compromise among, *53*
  as power elite, 54
Fourteenth Amendment (1868), 91, 100, 119, 124, 175
  Bill of Rights and, 154, 155
  business and, 124–126
  and equal protection of the laws, 171
Fourth Amendment, 163
France
  education expenditures in, 648
  environmental policy in, 612
  presidency in, 509
Frankfurter, Felix, 590, *593*
Franklin, Benjamin, 57, 58, 60 , 70
Freedom(s)
  American attitudes toward, 8–10
  of assembly, 157
  as cultural theme, 151
  from injustice, 163–165
  vs. political order, 37
  of press, 157
  of religion, 157, 160–163
  of speech, 147, 155–160. *See also* Bill of Rights; First Amendment
Freedom-liberty-individualism, as cultural theme, 10
Freedom of the press. *See also* Media
Free exercise clause, **161**
Free rider problem, 283
Free states, 119
French National Assembly, committees in, 483
Friedman, Milton, 668
Friedman, Thomas, 704
Frontier, 39
Fuel economy laws, 298–302
Fulton, Robert, 116

Fund raising, *295*
Furman v. Georgia (1976), 165

G

Galbraith, John Kenneth, 211, 668
Gallup polls. *See* Polls; Public opinion
Gardner, John, 307, *307*
Garfield, James A., 676
Gender
    rights and, 169
    as social characteristic, 205
    voting and, 245–246
General Accounting Office (GAO), **453**
General Theory of Employment, Interest, and Money, The, 677
General welfare, housing and, *74*
Generation. *See* Age
George III (England), *42*, *43*, *43*, 44
Georgia v. McCollum, 597
Gephardt, Dick, *723*
Gergen, David, 406, *407*, 409
Germany, *703*
    economy of, 711
    education expenditures in, 648
    health care in, 645
    judiciary in, 573
    Nazis in, 212
Gerry, Elbridge, 251
Gerrymandering, **250**–251, 330, **490**
Gibbons v. Ogden (1824), 116
Gideon v. Wainwright (1963), 164, 568–570, 581–582, 587
Gilded Age (late 1800s), 125
Ginsburg, Douglas, 599
Ginsburg, Ruth Bader, *81*, *588*, 598, *599*
Gitlow v. New York, 156–157
Glorious Revolution, 48
Gorbachev, Mikhail, 702, *703*, *731*
Gore, Al, *6*, 247, 514, *538*
    and 1992 campaign, 379, *380*
    media coverage and, *407*
    party structure and, *332*
Government. *See also* Bureaucracy;
    Economics; Power(s); branches
    of government by name;
    departments by name
    arguments for strong national, 63
    branches of, 56
    civilian employees in, 549
    federal design of, 83–85
    ideological foundations of, 39
    institutions of, 14–18
    limited, 152
    location of power, 99–102
    news-based images of, *418*
    operation of, 7
    press and, 399–403
    public opinion about state and

    national, 113
    rationale for, 74
    resisting authority of, 68
    responsibility for poor, *13*
    setting agenda for, 413–414
    shared powers of, 8
Government agenda, **617**
Government policy, interest groups
    and, 271–273
Government regulation. *See*
    Regulation
Government spending, **677**
    for means-tested and non-means-
    tested social programs, 661
    Nixon and, 130–131
    Reagan and, 132–134
Government support programs, as
    welfare, 660–664
Grandfather clauses, 249
Grant, Ulysses, Crédit Mobilier
    scandal and, 675–676
Grants-in-Aid, 136
Grass-roots lobby, *271*, 283
    political agenda and, 619
Great Compromise, 57–58
Great Depression (1930s)
    federalism and, 117, 120
    government regulation and, 125
    national government and, *126*
    Roosevelt, Franklin, and, 127–129
Great Society, 130, *139*
Green, Celia, 2
Green, Mark, 375, 662
Greenberg, Stanley, 247, *332*, 371
Greenpeace, *261*, 410, 411
Greenspan, Alan, *683*
Greider, William, 386
"Gridlock," 15–16, *16*, 26–27, 72–73
    health care and, 637
    political parties and, 83, 430–431
Griswold v. Connecticut (1965), 165–166, 293–294
Grodzins, Martin, 310
Gross domestic product, budget
    deficits and, 679
Gross national product, national debt
    and, 678
Group power, pluralist theory of
    power as, 20–21
Groups. *See* Interest groups
Grunwald, Mandy, *332*
Guatemala, foreign policy toward, 722
Guidelines, policies and, 608
Gulf of Tonkin, *22*
    repeal of resolution, 721

H

Habeas corpus, 597
Habeas Corpus Act (1679), 48
Hacker, Andrew, 181

Hague v. CIO, 157
Haiti, 731
    boat people, *625*
Hamilton, Alexander, 22, 37, 60, 62,
    63, *689*
    and Constitution, *53*
    ideology of, 39
Hancock, John, 32
Handicapped workers, 178
Harassment, 146–148
    women and, 178
Harding, Warren G., *321*
Harkin, Tom, *378*
Harmelin v. Michigan, 597
Harrington, Michael, 654, 655
Harrison, E. Bruce, 302
Harrison, William Henry, *317*
Hatch Act (1939), 544
Hatter, Terry, 617
Hawaii, statehood of, *446*
Hayes, George, *175*
Haynsworth, Clement, 599
Health and Human Services
    Department, 554, 556
Health care, *139*
    alternate plans for, 646
    cost increases in, 640
    crisis in, 636–647
    and public agenda, 622–623
    reform proposals, 645–647
    spending on, by nation, 639
    U. S. *vs.* Germany, 645
Health policy, **634**
Hearings, congressional, 453–454, *454*
Hearst, William Randolph, 415
Heflin, Howell, *464*
Helms, Jesse, 475, 476
Henry, Patrick
    Bill of Rights and, 64–65
    special interests and, 100
Henson, James, 179
Heritage Foundation, 657
Herschensohn, Bruce, *364*
Herberg, Will, *205*
Hierarchy, bureaucratic, 543
High crimes and misdemeanors, 454
Hill, Anita, 146, *146*, 287, 439–441,
    598, *599*
Hill & Knowlton, 278, 297, 388
Hilton, Claude M., 147
Hine, Lewis, *116*
Hiring, discrimination in, 170
Hobbes, Thomas, 39
Holmes, Oliver Wendell, Jr., 156, 570,
    590, *593*
Homelessness, *40*, *635*, 653
    general welfare, housing, and, *74*
Home rule, **140**
Home style politics, **437**–439
Homosexuality
    antidiscrimination proposition and

policy and, *616*, 617, *618*, 627, *627*
public opinion on, 194–196
rights movement, 256, *259*
Honeymoon period, 504
Honeywell, 664
Horizontal federalism, 121–122, 136
Horton, Willie, 247, 377
House of Representatives, 78. *See also*
Congress; Law(s)
formal organization of, 474
norms and rules in, 475–476
party system in, 489
representation in, 432
size of, 496
Speaker of, 447, 486
spending in races for (1974–1992),
365
women and minorities in, 440
House Rules Committee, 477
Housing, and general welfare, *74*
Housing and Urban Development
Department (HUD), *74*, 176
Human rights, 150
movement, 256
Humphrey, Hubert, 130, *358*, 720
Hussein, Saddam, *213*, *388*, 702. *See
also* Persian Gulf War
Hutchison, Kay Bailey, 440

I

Iacocca, Lee, 300
Idealists, 732
Ideology
Cold War foreign policy and, 716
national ranking by, 211
political culture and, 10–12,
208–212
political party and, 326–327
self-definition of, 208–209, 210,
219
U. S. as world power and, 705–708
"I Have a Dream" speech,
commemoration of, *99*
Illiterate America, 647
Image, making of, 220. *See also*
Elections; Marketing
Impeachment, 453–454
Imperial presidency, 716, 717
Implied powers, 116, **515**
Impoundment, 519
Income. *See also* Class
changing distributions of, 653
poverty and, 653–654
Incumbency
advantages of, 365
spending and, 365
Independent agencies, 546
Independent candidates, Perot as, 319
**Independent regulatory
commission, 546**
Independent voters, 239–240, 241

Indians. *See* American Indians
Indicted, 581
Individual empowerment, 257–258
Individual freedoms, 8–10
Individual responsibility, cultural
attitudes toward, *11*
Industrial expansion, in 1880s,
115–117
Industrial nations, tax structures of,
685
Industrial policy, 681
Industry, Gilded Age of, 125
Inequalities, growing, 141–142
Inflation, 680. *See also* Economy
Information
economics of, 414–422
power, democracy, and, 391–399
Informational hearing, 453–454
Information–gathering,
congressional, 453, *453*
"Infotainment," 415
Inherent powers, 515, 519
Initiatives, 252, **348**, 350
Injustice, freedom from, 163–165
Insiders, in news, 411, 671
Institutional gridlock, 15–16, *16*
Institutional responsibilities,
Constitution and, 34
Institutions, 14–18
constitutional design of, 614–616
democracy and, 14–15
economic policy and, 673
governmental, 7–8
interest-groups and, 278
news and, 392
as part of system, 26–29
public confidence in, 412
two-party system and, 324
use of, 17–18
Integration, of public schools, *178*
Interest-group liberalism, 304
Interest-group politics, 23, 269–309
arguments for and against,
304–309
of automobile industry, 298–302
campaign contributions and,
290–292
characteristics of groups, 278–284
corporatism and, 276, 277
dilemmas of, 275–278
factors affecting, 279
group organization and resources,
302–303
groups and people in, *301*
history of, 273–274
membership maintenance in,
282–284
mobilizing public opinion,
295–297
operation of, 284–302
organizations with former federal

employees on staff, 303
political strategies in, 299
selected groups, 272
size of system, 278–281
Interest groups, 452
in bureaucracy, 552–554
and economy, 698
health reform politics and,
640–644
joining, 308
laws and, 445, 452
lobbying and, 284–286
member benefits of, 283–284, 285
public policy and, 619
state and local, 123
Internal Revenue Service (IRS), *547*
**Internationalism vs.
isolationism, 706**
Internationalists, 706
Interstate commerce,
clause, regulation and, 128
manufacturing and, 126
Interstate disputes, 122
Interstate relations (Article IV), 60, 85
Intolerable Acts, 49
Investments, in research and
development, 727
"Invisible hand,", 676
Iran-*contra* affair, 76, 77, *454*, 714
Iranian hostage crisis, *7*
Iraq, Persian Gulf War and, 212, *213*,
388–391, *388*
Iron Curtain, 710–711, *712*
Iron law of oligarchy, 490
Iron triangles, 23, 291–292, *454*,
552, 728
Air Force and, 553
Pentagon and Osprey (VTOL
airplane), 292–293
IRS. *See* Internal Revenue Service
Isolationism, 706, 707–708
Israel, Persian Gulf War and, *213*
Issue networks, 452
Issue voting, 242–244

J

Jackson, Andrew, 317
and interest groups, 273
Jackson, Jesse, 247, 330
James II (England), 48
Japan
economy of, 711
education expenditures in, 648
Jaworski, Leon, 578, *580*
Jay, John, 62, *63*
Jefferson, Thomas, 32, 37, 41, *42*, *50*
Constitution and, 566
election of 1800 and, 60
political parties and, 310, 317
Jewish religion, *205*
Jim Crow laws, 177, **249**

Jobs, blacks in, 182
Jogger, Plough, 34–35
John of England, 48, 49
Johnson, Calvin, 570
Johnson, Frank M., *173*
Johnson, John H., 144
Johnson, Lyndon, *175*, 504, *517*
 Great Society of, 130, *139*
 persuasiveness of, 530
 Vietnam War and, 214, 720
Joint committee, 482
Joint resolutions. *See* Law(s)
Journalism and journalists, 414–415.
 See also Media; News
 operations of, 416–420
 routine news and, 417–420
Judges Bill, 588
Judicial branch, 56, 567–601
 in Denmark, Canada, and
 Germany, 573
 role in politics, 572
Judicial review, 82–83, 575–578
 Marbury v. Madison and, 82–83, 576
Judiciary (Article III), 60, 81–83,
 567–601
Judiciary Act, 586, 588
Jurisdiction, 574, 575
 Supreme Court and, 586–588
Jurisprudence, 590
Jury trial, 581
Justice, freedom from injustice and,
 163–165
Justices. *See* Supreme Court; justices
 by name

K
Keating Five, *672*
Keeny v. Tamayo 597
Kemp, Jack, *74*, 211, 659
Kennan, George F., 712, 716
Kennedy, Anthony, 167, *588*, 595, 597
 nomination of, 598
Kennedy, John, *504*
 and Cuban missile crisis, 715
 war on poverty in, 129–130
Kennedy, Robert, *352*, 720
Kennedy, Ted, 475
Kerrey, Bob, *378*
Keynes, John Maynard, 677–678,
 677
King, Martin Luther, Jr., 174, *174*, 177,
 352
 assassination of, *131*
 commemoration of, *99*
 unconventional participation and,
 236
Kingsley, Gregory, *568*
Kirkland, Lane, 659
Kissinger, Henry, 559, *717*, 721
Know-Nothing party, 320, *321*
Kozol, Jonathan, 647

Krauthammer, Charles, 312
Krugman, Paul R., 630
Kuwait, Persian Gulf War and, 388

L
Labor, *125*
 campaign financing by, 368
 economy and, 681
 minimum wage and, 128
 poverty and, 659
 unions. *See* Unions
Labor movement, 265
LaFollette, Robert, 320
Laissez-faire, 123–126, 676–677
 courts and, 570–571
 federalism and, 117, 120
 and government activism,
 676–679
Lake, Anthony, *723*
Lake, Celinda, 442
Landmark ruling, 575
Landon, Alf, 218
Langford, Charles, *173*
Lapham, Lewis H., 700
Latin America, U.S. and, 705–706. *See
 also* Nicaragua
Latinos
 poverty and, 655
 as voters, 246
Law(s)
 bureaucratic implementation of,
 542–543
 campaign financing and, 364–366
 Congress and, 442–452
 declared unconstitutional, 577
 election, 249–252
 equal representation and, 568–570
 and federal court procedure,
 581–583
 judicial branch and, 567–601
 passage of, 446–452, *446*
 and politics, 574–581
 and politics of social protest,
 175–177
 procedure for bill to become,
 446–450
 resistance to, 68
 and society, 570–574
 truth in media and, 402
 types of, 572–574
Law and order, civil liberties and, 164
Lawrence, M. Larry, 362
Leaders, and Constitutional
 compromises, *53*
Leadership, 257–258
 colonial, 41
 congressional, 479, *481*
 elections and, 348
 legislation and, 450–452, *451*
 party politics and congressional,
 484–490

 of political parties, 329–335,
 486–488
Lebanon, peace-keeping force in, 721
Lee, Richard Henry, *50*
Legal counsel, right of, 164
Legal formalism, 590
Legal jurisdictions, 574
Legal realism, 590
Legal system. *See also* Courts; Judicial
 branch; Supreme Court; courts
 by name
 jurisdiction(s) and, 574, 575
 political aspects of, 600
Legislation
 debate over, 476–477
 presidential military action and,
 720–721
Legislative article (Article I), 78–79
Legislative branch, 56. *See also*
 Gridlock
 limits on, 432–433
Legislative process, Congress and,
 429–461
Legislative veto, 521
Legislature. *See also* Congress
 comparison of women in, 441
 history of, 433–434
 logic behind American, 435–436
Legitimacy, 66, 232
 of government, 67–68
 of policy, 621
Lemann, Nicholas, 536
"Lemon test," 161
Lemon v. Kurtzman, 161
Leviathan, 39
Levin, Carl, 300
Liberalism, 11, 12, 210. *See also*
 Ideology; Political culture;
 Public opinion
 economic theories, 681
 opinion leaders, 211
Libertarians, 12, 211
Liberty(ies), 8–10, 38
 perception of, *9*
 personal, 145–185. *See also* Civil
 liberties; Civil rights
Limbaugh, Rush, 211, *376*
Limited government, 152
Limits on legislative power, 432
Lincoln, Abraham, 32, 318
 and interest groups, 273
 as nation-centered president, 119
Lincoln, Benjamin, 35
Line of the day, 374
Lippmann, Walter, 215, 410
Liquor. *See* Prohibition
Literacy, 647. *See also* Education
Litigation, lobbying and, 293–294
Little Rock, Ark.
 National Guard sent into, 524–525
 school integration in, *178*

Lobbying and lobbyists, 23, 284–289, *284. See also* Interest- group politics
  campaign contributions and, 290–292
  disclosure of, 286, 287
  Eure, Steve, as lobbyist, 288–289, *289*
  by government, 286–287
  litigation and, 293–294
  number of lobbyists, 281
  political action committees (PACs) and, 290–291
Local government
  education and, 650
  interest groups of, 123
  New Federalism and, 140–141
Locke, John, 39
Logjams, policy, **625–626**, *626*
Logrolling, **452**, 473
Long, Huey, *439*
Long, Russell, *439*
Los Angeles
  bottom-up policymaking and, *619*
  riots in (1991), *180*, 191
Lotteries, state, 138, *140*
Louisiana, American flag and, 160
Lowi, Theodore, 322
Low-income programs. *See* Support programs
Loyalty. *See* Party politics

M
Machine politics, 250
MAD. *See* Mutual assured destruction
Madison, James, 37, 58, 66, 70
  congressional pay raises and, 91
  and Constitution, *53*, 61
  Federalist papers and, 55, 62–63, *63*, 84
  and interest groups, 275–276
  political parties and, 316
  Virginia Plan and, 56
Madison Avenue marketing, campaigns and, 370–371
Magna Carta, **48**, 49, 151
Maintaining elections, 336
Major, John, *434*
Majoritarian theory of power, **18**–20, *19*
  and budget, 24
  and economic policy, 674
  and interest groups, 279
  New Federalism and, 133
  public opinion and, 193
Majority leader, 487
  of Senate, 447
Majority view, two-party system and, 325
Malcolm X, 176
Management style, presidential,

562
Manifest destiny, **704**
Manufacturing productivity, military spending and, 708
Mapp v. Ohio (1961), 164
Marbury v. Madison, 82–83, 576
  Watergate ruling and, 579, 581
Marketing
  of George Bush as candidate (1988), 375–377, *376*
  of George Bush as candidate (1992), *376*, 377–379
  campaigns and, 360, 361
  of candidates, 369–371
  elections and, 368
  interest groups and, 282, 295, *295*
Markey, Edward, 458
Markup session, **447**
Marshall, George, 712
Marshall, John, 74–75, 82
  dual citizenship and, 154
  Gibbons v. Ogden and, 116
  judicial review and, 576
  McCulloch v. Maryland and, 115–116, 117–118
Marshall, Thurgood, 144, 168, 172, *175*, *588*
Marshall Plan, **710**, 712–713
Martin, Joseph W., 529
Martin, Lynn, 476
Marx, Karl, *712*
Marzio, Peter, 159
Mason, George, 66
Massachusetts, 35, 36
Mass media. *See* Media
Matching funds, and campaign financing, 367
McBride, Ann, 307
McCarthy, Eugene, 720
McCarthy, Joseph, 157, 453
McClesky v. Zant, 597
McClure, Frederick, 286
McCulloch v. Maryland (1819), 74, 79, 115–116, 117–118
McGovern, George, 130, 356
McLarty, Thomas "Mack," *562*
McNamara, Robert, *22*
Means-tested programs, **660**
Meat Inspection Act, *125*
Media. *See also* News
  ad campaign coverage by, 372–373
  campaigns and, 228–229, 360, 361
  characteristics of news in, 396–399
  Congress and, 470–473
  coverage of candidates and, 346–347
  coverage of political agenda by, 606–608
  damage control and, 374
  democracy and, 387–425

  economics of information and, 414–422
  elections and, 368, 371–374
  executive persuasion and, 528–530
  journalism, journalists, and, 414–420
  making news, 371–373, 405–409
  management of, 405–409
  and message, 395–396
  Persian Gulf War and, 388–391
  political socialization by, 201–202
  president and, 510
  public opinion and, 215
  public opinion polls and, 190–192
  setting political agenda by, 414
  social movements and, 260–261, *261*
  truth and, 402–403
  vocabulary of, 409
Media monopoly, 400
Medicaid, **644**, 662
Medicare, *139*, **644**
Medicine, health care and, 622–623. *See also* Health care
Meinhold, Keith, *616*, 617
Melton, Howell, 148
Melville, Herman, *120*
Member benefits, of interest–group membership, 283–284
Mexico
  federal system in, 111
  political bureaucracy in, 551
  trade aagreement with, 725
Military. *See also* Defense policy
  action, Congress and, 720–721
  and Clinton's policy agenda, 625–626
  homosexuality in, *616*, 617, *618*, 627, *627*
  new roles for, 730
  power, economic interests and, 708–710
  president and, 524–527
  stealth bomber and, *728*
Military industrial complex, 274, 728
  decline of jobs in, 729
Military spending
  and budget deficits, 707
  and manufacturing productivity, 708
Minimum wage, 128
Minorities
  in House and Senate, 440
  poverty and, 655–656
  racial, 202–204
  as voters, 246–247
Minority issue, majority opinion on, 194–196
Minority leaders, 487
Minow, Newton, 536
Miranda v. Arizona (1966), 164

Misdemeanors, 574
Missouri, as slave state, 119
Mitchell, George, *73*, 287–288, *314*
Monarchical systems, 62
Mondale, Walter, 347, 513
Monetarists, 680
Monetary policy, 682, 688–691, **693**
    and fiscal policy, 691–693
Money
    campaigning and, 360–369
    creation of, 690
    flow of, 690
Money, marketing, and media, elections and, **360**
Monopolies. *See also* Trusts
Monroe, James, 705
Monroe Doctrine, 705
    Roosevelt, Theodore, and, *705*
Montesquieu, Baron (Charles–Louis de Secondat), 39, 75, **75**, 144
Montgomery, boycott in, *173*, 177
Morgan, Edmund, 100
Mosbacher, Robert A., Jr., 368
Moseley Braun, Carol, *314*, 476
Mother Jones, 665
Mothers Against Drunk Driving (MADD), *271*
Movements. *See* Social movements
Moynihan, Daniel Patrick, 659
MTV, election of 1992 and, 228–229, *229*
Multipolar world, power in, 732–734
Munro, Richard, *401*
Murray, Charles, *139*
Murray, Patty, *334*
Mutual assured destruction (MAD), 715
Myers, Dee Dee, *404*
Myrdal, Gunnar, 172

N
NAACP. *See* National Association for the Advancement of Colored People
Nabrit, James, *175*
Nader, Ralph, *301*, 306, 662
NAFTA, 725
Napoleon, 700
NASA, Congress and, *453*
Natcher, William, 487
Nation, The (magazine), 665
National Association for the Advancement of Colored People (NAACP), 174, 176
National Commission on Children, 606, 663–664
National Commitments resolution (1969), 720
National committees, 330
National Committee to Preserve Social

Security and Medicare, 284
National convention, 329
National debt, *4*, 678
National Election Studies, 265
National government
    arguments for, 62
    education and, 650
    powers granted to, 112
    public opinion about, 113
    state authority and, 137
National Guard, 524–526
National health plan, 622–623
National Labor Relations Act, *126*
National Labor Relations Board v. Jones & Laughlin Steel, 128
National Organization for Women (NOW), 148
    Legal Defense Fund of, 147
National Review, 665
National Rifle Association, 287
National Security Act (1947), 402, **713**, 714
National Security Council (NSC), 559–560, *559*, **713**, 714
    foreign policy establishment and, 716
National security state, 713
National supremacy, vs. states' rights, 84
Native Americans. *See* American Indians
Nativity scenes, 161
NATO. *See* North Atlantic Treaty Organization
Navajo Code Talkers Association, *256*
Nazi Germany, spiral of silence in, 212
Near v. Minnesota, 157
Necessary and proper clause, 79, 116
Needs, poverty and, 657–658
Negro leagues, 172
Neo-Keynesian, 681
Networks. *See* Television networks
    conventions and, 357
    policy, 624
Neuhaus, John, 159
New American Poverty, The, 655
Newcomb, Theodore, 200–201
New (neo) conservatism, 680–681
New Deal, 117, 127–129, 172, 201
    Court philosophy and, 590
New Federalism, 108–109, 121–122, 615
    cultural, institutional, and social factors affecting, 133
    inequalities and, 141–142
    1968–present, 130–138
    Nixon and, 130–131
    political struggle for, 133
    state experimentation and, 138–140

New Hampshire, 35, *64*
New industrial policy, 681
New Jersey Plan, 56–57
New Left, 255
    flag burning and, 159
New (neo) liberalism, 681
New Republic, 665, 723
New Right, 255
News, 392–394. *See also* Media
    believability of sources, 395
    characteristics of, 394
    coverage of political agenda in, 606–608
    creation of, 403–410
    economics of information and, 414–422
    information characteristics of, 396–399
    making, 371–373
    map of U. S. by coverage, 419
    outsiders and insiders in, 409–410, 411, 671
    personalities in, *393*
    popular tastes and, 420–422
    public opinion and, 410–414
    routine, 417–420
    savings and loan bankruptcies and, 670
    White House and, 405–409
News conferences, presidential, 510
News media. *See* Media; News
Newspapers, 415
New Vistas school, 664
New World Order, foreign policy and, 702–704
New York, *64*
New York Times, The, v. United States (1971), 402
New York Times Company, The, v. Sullivan, 402
Nicaragua, 714
    Iran-*contra* affair and, 77
    National Security Council and, 559–560
Nicholas, Nicholas J., *401*
Nineteenth Amendment (1920), 98, 352
Ninth Amendment, 91
    privacy rights and, 165–168
Nixon, Richard, *446*, 504
    electoral vote and (1968), 358, *358*
    foreign policy of, *717*
    New Federalism and, 107, 114, 130–131
    NSC (National Security Council) and, 714–715
    Pentagon Papers and, 158
    Vietnam War and, 214
    Watergate scandal and, 578–581, *580*
    White House Office of

Communications and, 406
Nixon Doctrine, 721
Nomination
    of 1992 Democratic candidate, 354
    of 1992 Republican candidate, 355
    for president, 353–356
    procedures, 331–334
    to Supreme Court, 598–599
Non-interventionism, federalism and,
    117
Non-means tested programs, **660**
Nonparticipation, 263–264
Noonan, Peggy, 188, 386
Noriega, Manuel, 706
North, Oliver, 77, **454**, 560
North American Free Trade
    Agreement (NAFTA), 725
North Atlantic Treaty Organization
    (NATO), 702, 712, 732
"No taxation without representation,"
    34, 48
NOW. *See* National Organization for
    Women
NSC. *See* National Security Council
Nuclear arms
    Cold War and, 710, 715
    disarmament and, *259*, 721
    limitation treaty, *731*
Nullification, of national laws, 118
Nunn, Sam, 529, 617, *618*

O
Occupational Safety and Health Act
    (OSHA) (1970), 542, 545–546
O'Connor, Sandra Day, *81*, 162, 167,
    576–577, *588*, 594, 596–597
    nomination of, 598
Office of Management and Budget
    (OMB), 5, *682*
Offices (governmental). *See* office by
    name
Oil cartel, 722
Oil industry, 23
"Old boy" network, 479
Older Americans. *See* American
    Association of Retired Persons
    (AARP); Senior citizens
OMB. *See* Office of Management and
    Budget
Open Market Committee, 689, 690
Open primary, 333
Open rule, 447
"Operation Restore Hope," *420*
Opinion objects, 192
Opinion polls, in news, 190–192
Opinion rally, 505
Opinions
    impact of, 224
    by Supreme Court, 592
Opportunity
    equality of, 10, 171

right to, 169
Order, 38
    as cultural theme, 151
Ordered liberty, 155
Order–social control, as cultural
    theme, 10
Organization, social movements and,
    258–260
O'Rourke, P. J., 5
Osprey (VTOL airplane), 292
Other America, The, 654
Outsiders
    in news, 409–410, 411
    as president, 518
Oval Office, *80*. *See also* Media;
    Presidency; White House

P
PAC system, 364–367. *See also*
    Political action committees
Paine, Thomas, 50, *53*
Palko v. Connecticut (1937), 155, 163
Panama, 706
Parks, Rosa, *173*, 176, 177
Parliament, 49
Parliamentary system, 434
    in Britain, 103, *434*
Particpation, 227–267, **230**
    conventional and unconventional,
        232–237
    elections and, 348
    in groups, 254
    mobilizing people, 257–262
    and personal commitment,
        231–232
    and political change, 235–236
    in social movement activities,
        254–263
    varieties of, 264–266, *264*
    voting as, 228–230, 237–254
Party identification
    loyalty to, 240
    voting and, 239–242
Party politics, and congressional
    leadership, 484–490, *485*
Party realignment, 336, 337
Paterson, William, 56
Paths to policy, 619
Patriotism–national unity, as theme,
    10
Pay or play plans, **646**
Peace dividend, 726–728
Peace of Paris (1763), 44
Peer groups, political socialization in,
    200–201, *201*
Pendleton Act (1883), 544, 551
Pentagon, 23. *See also* Defense policy;
    Military
    lobbying by, 286, 291, 292
Pentagon Papers, 402
    free speech and, 158

"People-to-government" model, of
    policy, 619
Per curiam opinion, **592**
Perks. *See also* Pork barrel politics
Perot, Ross, 17, 211–212, 228, 229,
    259, 707
    campaign marketing of, 369
    issue voting and, *243*
    and 1992 campaign, 379
    political parties and, 312–313, *313*,
        322–323
    poverty and, 655
    on television, 346, *347*
    United We Stand America, Inc.,
        and, *339*
Persian Gulf War, 377, *378*, *526*, 719,
    731
    media and, 388–391, 423
    news coverage of, 397–39
    public opinion and, 190–191, *190*
        212, *213*
Personal liberties and rights, 145–185
Personal presidency, 534
Persuasion
    executive powers of, 528–530
    Roosevelt, Clinton, and, *529*
Peters, Charles, 536
Petitition for certiorari, **586**, 577
Philadelphia, Pa., Constitutional
    Convention in, 52
Photojournalists, *416*
Pine, Robert Edge, *50*
Pinochet, Augusto, 559
Plaintiff, 574
Planned Parenthood Federation of
    America, *283*
*Planned Parenthood of Southeastern
    Pennsylvania v. Casey* (1992), 167
Platforms, 315, 329
    in 1992 election, 327–328
Playing the electoral vote, 357
Playing the swing vote, 357,
    358–359
Plessy, Homer, 124, 171, *171*
Plessy v. Ferguson (1896), 171, *171*,
    174, 595
Pluralist theory of power, 18, *19*,
    20–21, 101
    and budget, 25
    and Constitution, 54–55
    economic policy and, 674
    interest groups and, 276–277, 279
    New Federalism and, 133
    and public opinion, 194
    two-party system and, 325
Pocket veto, 448, 522
Poindexter, John, 77, 560
Police, civil liberties rulings and,
    163–165
Policy, 605–629
    bottom-up path to, 619–620, 621

constitution and, 614–616
economic, 669–699
inside system, 612–616
involvement in making, 628
and politics, 608–609
social, 631–667
top-down path to, 620–622, 623
Policy agenda
building, 616–623
health care and, 622–623
implementation of, 624–627
social policy and, 632–633
Policy Committee, 487–488
Policy networks, 624
Policy problems
defined, 634
judging competing programs, 636
political nature of, 634–636
Political action, 227–267
Political action committees (PACs),
281–282
auto industry and, 300–302
campaign contributions to,
290–291
and health care reform, 641
and public-interest groups, 307
Political agenda, 606–608
Political change, participation and,
235–236
Political community, social
movements and, 258–260
Political culture, 8–14, 26. See also
Cultural themes
and big government, 115
budget control plan and, 27
cultural politics and, 12–14
foundations of, 39
ideology and, 10–12, 208–212
rights and, 150
voting and, 242
Political economy, 676–682
laissez-faire and, 123–126
of New Federalism, 134–136
Political equality, 10
Political gridlock, 26–27
Political leaders, as role models, 202
Political leadership, legislation and,
450–451
Political machines, 250
Political opinions. See Public opinion
Political order, freedom *vs.*, 37
Political parties, 12, 311–343. See also
Democratic party; Republican
party; Party politics
backing for new, 323
candidates and leadership of,
329–335
childhood learning and affiliation,
199
congressional leadership of,
486–488

crisis and change in, 336–339
critical realignment of, 337
dealignment of, 337
decline of, 315–316
defined, 314
elections and, 351–352
functions of, 326–336
governing by, 335–336
gridlock and, 83, 430
history of, 316–323
House system, 489
and interest groups, 281
law-making and, 444–445
loyalty to, 239–242
minor, 322
Perot and, 319
platforms in 1992, 327–328
president as leader of, 518
reforming, 490–491
Republican wins and (1968–1990),
331
Senate system, 489
third parties, 320–323
two-party system, 318–320
use of institutions by, 17–18
working for, 342
Political philosophy, Constitution as,
38
Political problem, 634
**Political question doctrine,
580–581**
Political strategies, of interest groups,
299
Political symbols, 214
Political system, 7. See also
Participation
aspects of participation in, 236
culture, institutions, and power,
6–14
news and, 392–394
setting agenda for, 413–414
Political views
choices for 1990s, 328–329
parties as channels for, 326–329
Politicians, press and, 404–405
Politics. See also political issues by
name
bureaucratic, 539–542, 552–554,
544
cultural, 12–14
in departments and cabinet,
554–558
and economic policies, 682
of educational reform, 649–651
of health care reform, 640–644
judicial branch and, 572
of judicial organization, 585–586
law and, 574–581
of passing legislation, 450–452
policy and, 608–609
pork barrel, 455–456

and poverty, 654–656
and social policies, 633–636
Polling places. See Elections; Voting
Polls. See Opinion rally; Public
opinion polls; Public relations
Pollution, regulation of, 540–542. See
also Environment
Polsby, Nelson, 226
Poor, government responsibility for,
13. See *also* Poverty
Popular representation, 62
Popular sovereignty, 62, 100
as cultural theme, 10
Popular vote, 357–358. See *also*
Electoral college
Population
Census Bureau and, 218
1700–1790, 38
Populists, 211, 321
Pork barrel politics, 431, **455**–456
Postal Service, 547
Poverty
economic patterns and, 663
growth of, 656
impact on population, 657
old *vs.* new, 655–656
social differences affecting public
opinions about, 203
welfare and, 653–665
Powell, Colin, *389, 390,* 617, 626
Powell v. Alabama (1932), 163
Power(s), 18–26, **613**. See *also*
Congress
in bureaucratic state, 553
Constitution and, 34, 72–105
denied top national and state
governments, 85
denied to Congress, 79
divisions of, 72–73
economic policy and, 674
federal divisions of, 112
federalism and, 109–110
governing and, 23–26
granted to Congress, 79
gridlock and, 72–73
implied, 116
information and, 391–399
majoritarian theory of, 18–20
military, 708–710
in multipolar world, 732–734
national and state, 83–85,
107–142. See *also* Federalism
news and, 392
of opinion, 193–197
party realignment and, 336–337
and policy, 613
political agenda and, 607
in political parties, 330–331
presidential, 503–508
structure of, 99–102
Power brokers, 450, 496

Power elite, 100
  Constitution and, 54
  thesis of. *See* Elitist theory of power
Power relations, 7–8
Power structure of Congress, 466–490
  individual *vs.* organization,
    468–473
PR. *See* Public relations
Pragmatism, 67, 211–212
Prayer, in schools, 161
Precedent, 582
Precincts, 250
Preemption, 138
Presidency. *See also* Campaigns;
    Candidates; Elections; Executive
    branch; Political parties; White
    House
  activist phase of, 509–513
  Constitution and, 59–60
  constraints on, 507
  enforcement powers of, 519–520
  in France, 509
  history of, 508–513
  institutional design of, 507,
    508–509
  legislative powers of, 520–524
  military and foreign policy arenas
    and, 524–527
  news conferences and, 510
  persuasion and, 528–530
  succession and, 98
  traditional roles of, *516*, 517–518
  "two presidencies" theory of, 527
President(s). *See also* presidents by
    name
  addresses by, 511
  approval of, 506–507
  assassinations and, 531
  character of, 530–533
  during Cold War, 717–718
  constitutional job description of,
    514–517
  election costs, 362
  Executive Office of, 558–562
  foreign policy powers of, 721
  formal powers vs. inside politics,
    518–528
  and interest groups, 273–274
  military commitments by, 720–721
  nation-centered view of federalism
    by, 115
  1992 election financing, 367–369
  nomination process (1992), 354,
    355
  personality classifications of,
    532–533
  personal staff of, 562–563
  political reality of getting elected,
    360–374
  power of, 503–508
  public appearances by, 510

  responsibilities of, 508
  roles of, 502–503
  selling of (1988), 375–377
  veto power of, 448–449
President pro tempore, 487
Press. *See also* Journalism and
    journalists; Media; News
  concept of fair, 415
  and government, 399–403
  and politicians, 404–405
  problems with, 413
Press conferences. *See* Media; News
    conferences
Press corps, 405
Press secretaries, *405*
Primary agents of socialization,
    families, schools, and peer
    groups as, 199– 201
Primary elections, 331–333, *357*
  delegate selection and, 334
  nomination and, 353
Primary principle, 198
Prior restraint, 157
Privacy rights, 165–168. *See also*
    Abortion
Privileges and immunities clause,
    153
Probability sampling, 219
Pro-choice movement, 166, 256, *294*.
    See also Abortion
Pro-life movement, 166, 167, 256,
    294. *See also* Abortion
Proclamations, 515
Procompetitive proposals, **646**
Progressive party, 320
Progressive taxes, 684
Prohibition, Eighteenth and Twenty-
    first amendments and, 98
Property rights, 169
Proportionate taxes, 684
Prosecutor, 573
Prosperity, political parties and, 340
Protest, 232
  politics of, 175–177
Protestors, *7*
Psychology of the voting choice,
    238–245
  candidate character and, 244–245
  issue voting and, 242–244
  party identification and, 239–242
Public agenda, 617
Public corporations, 546–547
Public disclosure, of lobbying
    activities, 286, 287
Public information campaigns, *295*,
    296, 297
Public-interest group movement,
    306–309
  Nader and, *301*
Public opinion, 189–225
  battle for, 212–215

  change in, 206–208
  defined, 192–193
  democracy and, 193
  describing, 215–217
  on fiscal options, 695
  on foreign policy, 719
  formation and change of, 198–208
  ideology and, 208–212
  measurement of, 218–221
  mobilizing, 295–297
  and news, 410–414
  policy and, 613–614
  politics of, 197–198
  polling techniques, 218–221
  polls on ideology, 209
  power of, 193–197
  and presidency, 509–513. *See also*
    Public relations
  racial differences in, 204
  social characteristics and, 202–206
  socialization and, 198–202
  about state and national
    government (1941–1993), 113
  on Vietnam War, 720
Public relations (PR), 297
  president and, 502–507
Public trial rights, 163
Publius, 62
Pure Food and Drug Act, *125*

Q
Quality of life, social policy and,
    631–667
Quartering Acts, 44, *48*
Quayle, Dan, 513–514, 564
Quebec, separatism of, 120
Quebec Act (1774), *40*
Quotas, 180

R
Race. *See also* African Americans; Civil
    War; Slavery
  free speech and, 147
  Jim Crow laws and, 249
  public opinion differences by, 204
  rights and, 169
  as social characteristic, 202–204
  views on, 183
  voting and, 246–247, 249, 250–251
Racial separation. *See* Separate but
    equal
Racism
  Fourteenth Amendment, 124
  Warren, Earl, and, 174–175
Radicalism, flag and, 159
Randolph, Edmund, 56, 60–61
Rather, Dan, *376*, *420*
Ratification, *64*, **91**–96
  of amendments, 91–96
  of Constitution, 61–68
  order of, 65

Rayburn, Sam, *446*, *487*, 536
Reagan, Ronald
    and auto industry, 299
    block grants and, 131–132
    Cold War and, *703*
    defense spending of, 729
    educational policy of, 651–652
    Executive Office of, 560
    executive style of, 520
    FCC and, 400
    government spending and,
        132–134
    and interest groups, 274
    Iran-*contra* affair and, 76, 77
    Lebanon and, 721
    media management and, 406–408
    national security state and, 714
    New Federalism of, *108*, 114
    at 1984 convention, *338*
    NSC and, 559–560
    public relations and, 504, 512
Reagan Doctrine, **722**
Realists, **732**
Reapportionment, 488–490
Rebellions
    Constitution and, 34
    of 1786 and 1787, 34–37
Recession, **680**
    of 1980s–1990s, 693–694
Reciprocity, **473**, 479
"Reconstruction" amendments
        (Thirteenth, Fourteeth,
        Fifteenth), *99*, 100
Redburn, Thomas, 536
Redistricting, **490**
    voting and, 250–251
"Red scare" (1917), 155
Reelection, congressional, 457–458
Referendum, 252, **348**, 350
Reform
    of Congress, 490–495, 498
    of election process, 380–382, 384
Region, race and, 246
Registration, 266
    national bill for, 250
    voting, *249*, 250
Regressive taxes, **684**
Regulation, **693**
    bureaucratic, 542
    constitutional principle for, 128
    crossover sanctions and, 137
    enforcing, *135*
    FCC (Federal Communications
        Commission) and, 399–400
    Great Depression and, 125
    of interest groups, 282
    of lobbyists, 286, 287
    preemption and, 138
    of press, 399–402
    reduction of, 132–133
    savings and loan industry and,

670
Regulatory agencies and
        commissions, 128
Regulatory policy, 682, 692–694,
    693
Rehabilitation Act (1973), 176
Rehnquist, William, 162, 582–583,
        588, 594, 596, *596*
    politics of court of, 597
    school prayer and, 591
Reich, Robert, *651*, 664, *696*, 697
Reilly, William K., 540, *540*
Religion
    flag and, 159–160
    freedom of, 157, 160–163
    importance of, in five democracies,
        207
    as social characteristic, 205–206
    social movements and, 255, 256
Religious right, 262–263. *See also*
        Christian right movement
Renier, James J., 664
Reporters, routine news and, 417–420.
        See also Media
Representation, **432**
    delegate and trustee roles in, 432,
        437–439
    Great Compromise and, 57–58
    interest groups and, 279
    and New Jersey Plan, 57
    popular, 62
Republican form of government,
        Madison and, 62
Republican party, *317*, 318. *See also*
        Political parties
    conservatives in, *327*
    conventions of, *338*
    gridlock and, 430
    identification with, 239–242
    ideology of, 12
    nomination of 1992 candidate,
        354
Research, congressional, 453
Research and development,
        government investments in,
        727
Reserved powers, **91**
Resources, of interest groups, 302–303
Respect, 479
    in Senate, **475**
Responsibility
    cultural attitudes toward, 11
    social welfare and, *13*
Retrospective voting, 244
Revenue sharing, **131**
Revolution
    in civil rights applications,
        168–171
    colonial system and, 41–43
    politics of, 43–45
    politics of colonialism and, 41–42

Revolutionary War, colonial divisions
        after, 51
Richards, Ann, *139*
Richardson, Elliott, *580*
Richmond, Va., Civil War and, *120*
Richmond v. Corson (1989), 180
Riegle, Don, 300
Rights. *See also* Civil liberties; Civil
        rights; Freedoms
    American tradition of, 151–152
    of citizens, 184
    in Declaration of Independence, *9*
    personal, 145–185
    politics of, 148–150, 181–182
    to privacy, 165–168
    of suspects and convicts, 597
Right to choose, 166
Right to life, 166
Riley, Richard, *651*
Riordan, Richard, *180*, *619*
Rise of the bureaucratic state,
    552
Robber Barons, 124, 125
Roberts, Cokie, 72
Robinson v. Jacksonville Shipyards, 148
Rockefeller, Jay, 17, 606, 663–664
Roe v. Wade (1973), 166–167, *167*, *294*,
    576–578
Rogich, Sig, 375, 408
Rohatyn, Felix, 659
Role models, political leaders as, 202
Roosevelt, Franklin Delano, 172, 218
    as activist president, 509
    bank reform bill and, *126*
    Bill of Rights and, *149*
    character type of, *532*
    cooperative federalism and,
        127–129
    federalism and, 117
    ideologies of parties and, 326
    and interest groups, 273
    persuasion and, 529
    public relations and, 512
    radio and, 415
    Supreme Court and, 83, 566, 585
    World War II and, 710
Roosevelt, Theodore, *125*, 320, 322,
        503, *610*, 709
    and Monroe Doctrine, *705*
Rose, Richard, 500
Rostenkowski, Dan, 465
Rousseau, Jean–Jacques, 39
Rule-making, congressional
        monitoring of, **454**–455
Rules Committee, **447**, 477
Rusk, Dean, 715
Russell, Benjamin, 251

S
Sampling procedures, 218–219
Samuelson, Paul, 681

Sanders, Bernie, 485
Sandinista regime, 560
"Saturday Night Massacre," 580
Saudi Arabia, 390. *See also* Persian
    Gulf War
Savage, Edward, *50*
Savings and loan (S&L) bankruptcies,
    670–672
    elitist influence and, 675–676
Scalia, Antonin, 162, 167, 575, 577,
    588, 595, 597
    nomination of, 598
Schenck v. United States (1919),
    155–156
Schlesinger, Arthur, Jr., 344
School-based management, 652
School prayer, 161–162, 163
    Court and, 591
Schools. *See also* Education
    political socialization in, 200, *201*
    religious observances in, 591,
    161–162, 163
Schroeder, Patricia, 465, *475*, 476
Schwarzkopf, Norman, *618*
SCLC. *See* Southern Christian
    Leadership Conference
Scott, Dred, 118–119, *118*
Scottsboro case, 163
Scowcroft, Brent, 702
Search and seizure, 163, 164
Search warrant, rights and, 149
SEATO. *See* Southeast Asia Treaty
    Organization
Secession, 119
    Quebec and, 120
Second Amendment, 168
Secondary agents of socialization,
    201–202
Secondat, Charles–Louis de. *See*
    Montesquieu, Baron
Second Continental Congress, *50*
Second Treatise on Government, 39
Secretaries, of departments, 554
Secretaries of state, backgrounds of,
    717
Sedition Act (1918), 155
Segregation, Dred Scott decision and,
    118
Seib, Gerald F., 386
Select committees, 479–481
Selective incorporation, 154–155
Senate, 78. *See also* Congress; Law(s)
    formal organization of, 474
    Keating Five affair and, *672*
    majority leader of, 447
    norms and rules in, 473–475
    party system in, 489
    president pro tempore of, 487
    representation in, 432
    vice president and, 486–487
    women and minorities in, 440

Senators, direct election of, 98
Senior citizens, 178
    AARP and, 297
    interest groups of, 283–284
    movement of, 256
Seniority, 488
Separate but equal, 124, 171–172, *171*
Separation of church and state,
    160–161. *See also* Religion;
    Schools
Separation of powers, 15–16, **75**,
    102–104
    Court cases over, 578–581
    political parties and, 83
Separatism, in Canada, 120, 121
Service to constituents, **456**–457
Seventeenth Amendment (1913), 98
Seventh Amendment, 168
Seward, William, 706
Sexism, 178
Sexual harassment, 147–148, 439–441
Sexual preference, in military, *616*,
    617, *618*, 627, *627*
Seymour, John, 363–364
Shays, Daniel, 35
Shays' Rebellion (1786–1787), 35–36,
    35
Sherman Antitrust Act, 124, *125*
Shield laws, 402
Shultz, George, 560
Sidey, Hugh, 531
Simpson, Alan K., *398*
Single-party government, 312
Single payer proposal, **646**
Sirica, John, 578
Sixth Amendment, 163
Slack, James D., 630
Slaughterhouse Cases, The, 154
Slavery
    communication and, 260
    Constitution and, 58–59
    Dred Scott decision and, 118–119
    federalism and, 118
    and Founders of U.S., 54
Slave states, 119
Smith, Adam, **677**
Smith, Alfred, 162
Smith Act, 157
Smoking, public opinion on, *214*
Snack Food Association, lobbying by,
    288–289
SNCC. *See* Student Nonviolent
    Coordinating Committee
Social characteristics and public
    opinion
    class, 204–205
    gender and, 204–205
    race, 202–204
    religion and, 204–205
Social characteristics of voters,
    238, 245–249

age, 247–248
class, 248
gender, 245–246
race, 246–247
Social differences, **264**
Social insurance programs, 660
Socialists, **12**
Socialization, and political learning,
    198–202
Socialized medicine, 622
Social movements, 232, **254**
    elections and, 262–263
    listing of recent, 256
    mass media and, 260–261
    mobilizing people for, 257–262
    participation in, 254–263
    women's movement as, 254
Social order, 151
Social policy, 631–667. *See also*
    Economic policy
    education, 647–652
    health care, 636–647
    politics and, 633–636
    poverty and welfare, 653–665
Social power
    in Gilded Age, 125
    two-party system and, 324–325
Social problems, **634**
    education, 647–652
    health care crisis as, 636–647
    personal impact of, 665
    poverty and welfare, 653–664
Social programs, local, 141
Social protest, politics of, 175–177
Social Security Act, *126*
Social Security Programs, 128, 660
    Medicaid, 662
    as stabilizer, 696
Social welfare system, 8, 10
Society
    law and, 570–574
    policy agenda and, 624–627
Somalia
    media coverage of, 420–422
    "Operation Restore Hope" in, *420*
Sontag, Susan, *517*
Sound bites, 205
Souter, David, *588*, 597
    nomination of, 598
South. *See* States' rights;
    State–centered view
South Carolina
    nullification and, 119
    slavery and, 118
Southeast Asia Treaty Organization
    (SEATO), 712
Southern Christian Leadership
    Conference (SCLC), *97*, 174
Soviet Union, 527, 702, *703*, *712*, 726
    Cold War and, 710–712
Spanish–American War, 709

Speaker of the House, 447, 486
Special interests, government by and for, 100–101. *See also* Interest groups
Specialization, 479
Speech. *See* Freedom of speech
Spending. *See also* Fiscal policy; Government spending
    defense, 728–729
    military, 707
    strategies of, 684–687
Spin doctors, **374**
Spiral of silence, 212
Spirit of the Laws, The, 39, 75
Spoils system, 550–551
Square Deal, 125
St. Clair, James, 579
Staff, congressional, 491–492. *See also* Bureaucracy; Executive Office of the President; White House
Stagflation, *677*, **680**
Stahl, Lesley, 407–408
Stalin, Joseph, 710, *712*
Stamp Act, 44
Standard Oil monopoly, 124
Standing committees, **446**, **478**, 479, 481, 493
Standing subcommittees, 493
Standing to sue, **582**
Stare decisis, **582**
Star system, in Congress, 479
State-centered view, of federalism, 117–118
State Department, 554, 555
State laws, First Amendment protections and, 157
State of the Union Address, *448*
State politics, 319–320
    reapportionment and, 488–490
States
    citizenship of, 142
    education and, 650, 652
    federal aid to (1950–1990), 135–136
    federalism and, 83–85
    inequalities among, 141–142
    interest groups of, 123
    national authority and, 137
    New Federalism and experimentation by, 138–140
    party wins in (1968–1990), 331
    powers granted to, 112
    public opinion about, 113
States' rights
    federalism and, 117–118
    federal system and, 84
Statutory law, **573**
Stealth bomber, *728*
Steering Committee, 487
Stephanopoulos, George, *404*
Stevens, John Paul, *588*

Stevenson, Adlai (candidate), 346
Stewart, Joseph, Jr., 604
Stewart, Potter, 162, 592
Stewart Machine Company v. Davis, 128
Stockman, David, 682, *682*
Straw polls, 218
Strict constructionism, **590**
Strict registration procedures, **250**
Student Nonviolent Coordinating Committee (SNCC), *173*
Subcommittees, **447**, 468, 479, 481–482
    power of, 482–484
    standing, 493
Sugar Act, 44
Sullivan ruling, 402
Sunday closings, state laws and, 163
Sununu, John, 285, 560, *561*
"Super Tuesday," 353
Supply-siders, **680**, *682*
Support programs, 660–664
Supremacy clause, **85**, 116
Supreme Court, 56, 60, *593*. *See also* Freedom(s); New Deal; justices by name
    activist *vs.* self-restraint philosophy of, 589–590
    caseload of, 587
    case selection by, 588–589
    and civil rights movement, 174–175
    composition of, 594–598
    constitutional intentions about, 590–591
    deciding cases and writing opinions by, 592–594
    economic and civil liberties laws overturned by, 571
    elastic clause and, 79
    federalism and, 115–117
    freedom from injustice and, 163–165
    Gideon v. Wainwright and, 568–570
    judicial review and, 82
    jurisdiction of, 574–581, 586–588
    justices on, 585, *588*
    lobbying for nominees to, 286–287
    monopolies and, 124–126
    nomination to, 586, 598–599
    operation of, 586–599
    Plessy decision and, 124
    representation before, 568–570
    Roosevelt, Franklin, and, 83
    women on, *81*
Suspects, rights of, 597
Sweden, government in, 8
Swing vote, 357, 358–360
Switzerland, direct democracy in, 351
Symbols
    cultural, 614

    political, 214
    president as, 517–518

T
Taney, Roger B., 118, 119
Targeted groups, opinion polls and, 221
"Tax-and-spend" Democrats, 431
"Tax-and-spend" government, 114
Taxation. *See also* Fiscal policy
    Articles of Confederation and, 51–52
    colonists and, 48–49
    Constitution and, 34
    in pre-Revolutionary America, 45, *45*
    strategies of, 684
Tax structure, of leading industrial nations, 685
Taylor, Zachary, *317*
Technology, 727
Technology Assessment Office, 453
Teeter, Robert, 375, 379, 527
Television, 415
    conventions and, 357
    coverage of candidates on, 346–347
    regulation of, 400
Television networks. *See* Broadcast media; CNN; Media; Television
Tenth Amendment, 126, 168
Tessier, Rick, 570
Thatcher, Margaret, *434*
Think tanks
    Heritage Foundation as, 657
    interest groups and, 278
Third Amendment, 168
Third parties, 320–323
Thirteen colonies, 38–43
Thirteenth Amendment (1865), 91, 100, 119
Thomas, Clarence, 286–287, *301*, *588*, *597*, *599*.
    alleged harassment and, 146, *146*
    nomination of, 598
    Senate behavior and, 475
Three-fifths Compromise, 58–59
Thurmond, Strom, *488*
Tiananmen Square, 722, *723*
Time Warner, Inc., *401*
Title IV, of Civil Rights Act, 651
Tocqueville, Alexis de, 226, 566
Top-down path, **620**–622, *623*
Tower Commission, 714
"Town-hall" meetings, *231*
Townshend Acts, 45, *48*
Train, George Francis, 675
Treason, 454
Treasury Building, *689*
Treaties, **515**, 525
Trials. *See* Federal courts

Trickle down economics, 697
Triumph of Politics, The, 682
Truly, Richard, *453*
Truman, Harry, 712
    character type of, *532*
Truman Doctrine, 712
Trustee, 20Trustee view of
    representation, **432**, 437– 439
Trusts, 124, 125
Truth, and First Amendment, 402
Tsongas, Paul, 377, *378*
Twelfth Amendment, 60, 351
Twenty-first Amendment (1933), 98
Twenty-fifth Amendment (1967), 98
Twenty-sixth Amendment, *97*
Twenty-seventh Amendment, 91
Two Nations, 181
Two-party system, 318–320
    factors promoting weak, 325
    politics behind, 324–325
"Two presidencies" theory, 527
Tyson, Laura D'Andrea, 691

U
"Un-American activities" hearings,
    453
Unconventional participation,
    232–237
    commitment to, 257
    demonstrations as, *255*
    promoting acceptance of, 262
    varieties of, 235, *259*
Undeclared wars, 524
Underclass, 659
Unemployment
    fiscal actions of presidents and,
        687
    rates by educational level, 648
Unicameral legislature, 57, **434**
Union. *See also* Civil War
    Civil War and, 119–120
    secession from, 119
Unions (labor), 124
Unitary system, 110
    federalism and, 111
United States
    debt structure of, 12–14
    Declaration of Independence,
        46–47
    Founders and basic documents of,
        62
    government research and
        development investments in,
        727
    and post-Cold War world order,
        731–734
    as world power, 704–710
    after World War II, 709–710
U.S. Court of Appeals circuits,
    583–584
United States v. Eichman (1990), 158

United States v. Nixon (1974), 578
United States v. Students Challenging
    Regulatory Agency Procedures
    (1973), 582
United We Stand America, Inc., *339*
University of California Regents v. Bakke
    (1978), 179–180
Urban poor, *40*

V
Valence issues, 242
Values, 26
Vaughs, Clifford, *173*
Veto, 448–449, *448*
    legislative, 521
    presidential (1789–1993), 522
Vice president, 513–514
    and Senate, 486–487
Vietnam War, *22*, 719–721, *720*
    demonstration against, *255*
    flag burnings and, 159
    free speech and, 158
    media and, 402, 403
    Nixon and, 214
    press during, 422–423
Vinson, Carl, 469–470, 589
Vinson, Fred, 595
Virginia Bill of Rights, 66
Virginia Plan, 56
Voluntary associations, 278
Volunteerism–altruism, as theme, 10
Voters, attitudes of, 17
Voting, 228–230, 237–254
    age and, 247–248
    character and, 244–245
    as citizen participation, 234–237
    class and, 248
    comparative turnout, 239
    creative redistricting and, 250–251
    by issues, 242–244
    by party identification, 239–242
    patterns in five presidential
        elections, 252–253
    personal commitment and,
        231–232
    psychological basis of, 238–245
    race and, 246–247, 249, 250–251
    registration and, *249*, 266
    social basis of, 245–249
    trends in, 237–238
    women and, 245–246
Voting districts, 250–251, 329–330
Voting graveyards, in Chicago, 250
Voting rights
    amendment and, *97*
    of Black Americans, 172
    Fifteenth Amendment and, 172
    voting age, *97*
    of women, 98
Voting Rights Act (1965), 176, 250,
    352

gerrymandering and, 251

W
Wage-and-price freeze, *677*
Wagner Act, 128
Wallace, George, 321, *358*
Wallace v. Jaffree (1985), 161–162, 163,
    591
Wallop, Malcolm, *464*
Walz v. Tax Commission (1970),
    162–163
War(s), declared and undeclared, 524
Warner, John, 538
War of Independence, *35. See also*
    Revolutionary War
War on Poverty, 129–130, 139
Warren, Earl, 165, 174, 590, 595, 600
Washington, Denzel, 176
Washington, George, 37, *64*
    on Constitution, 60
    and interest groups, 273
Watergate scandal, *338*, 403, 453
    Supreme Court and, 578–581
Waters, Maxine, Los Angeles riots
    and, *180*
Watkins, James, *540*
Wealthy
    as Founders of U.S., 54
    voting and, 248
Webster, Daniel, 318
Webster v. Reproductive Health Services
    (1989), 167, 576–578
Welfare, 653–665
    cultural resistance to, 654–655
    government support programs
        and, 660–664
Welfare state, *139*
West Coast Hotel Company v. Parrish,
    128
Westmoreland, William, 402, *403*
Weyrich, Paul, 268
Whig party, 317, *317*
Whips, 487
White, Byron, 579, *588*, 598
White Americans, affirmative action
    and, 179–180
White House, *80. See also* Executive
    Office of the President;
    Presidency; President(s)
    budget and, 5
    communications management by,
        406–409
    congressional relations with, 452
    presidential staff and, 562–563
    press corps, 405
    press secretaries, *405*
    staff of, 539, 561
White House correspondents, 510
White supremacist movements, 256
Whitten, Jamie, 488
Wildavsky, Aaron, 226

Will, George, 375, 635
William and Mary, 48
Williams, Harrison, *464*
Wilson, Pete, *139*, 290
Wilson, Woodrow, 322, 462
Wilson v. Seider, 597
Window of opportunity, policy
  agenda and, **626**
Wines, Michael, 373
Winner-take-all rule, 357
Wirth, Tim, 475
Wirthlin, Richard, 375
Women. *See also* House of
  Representatives, norms and
  rules in; NOW; Senate, norms
  and rules in
  abortion and, 166–167
  civil rights and, 178
  communication among, 260
  and composition of Congress,
    439–441
  Equal Rights Amendment and, 96
  gender gap and, 205

in House and Senate, 440
  percentage in legislatures, 441
  sexual harassment and, 146–148
  suffrage of, *97*
  on Supreme Court, *81*
Women's movement, 254, 256
Woodin, William, *126*
Woods, Harriet, 369
Woodson v. North Carolina (1976), 165
Workplace, equality in, 170
Works Progress Administration (WPA),
  127, 129
World economy, 681
  U. S. in, 713
World order, foreign policy and,
  702–703
World power, United States as,
  704–710
World War I, world power after, 709
World War II
  civil rights movement and, 172
  economic power and, 709–710
  free speech and, 157–158

ideology and, 709
  military power and, 709
  world economy after, 711
WPA. *See* Works Progress
  Administration
Writ of certiorari, **581**
Writ of mandamus, 82

Y
Yalta, 710
"Year of the Woman" (1992), 146,
  245–246, *364*
Yellow press, 415
Yeltsin, Boris, 702, 703, *731*
Youth groups, participation in, 254
Yugoslavia, fighting in former, 731

Z
Zenger, Peter, 39, 402
Zone of privacy, 166

PERMISSIONS

Box 2.2
Reprinted with the permission of the Macmillan Publishing Company from *An Economic Interpretation of the Constitution of the United States* by Charles A. Beard. Copyright © 1953 by Macmillan Publishing Company, renewed © 1963 by William Beard and Mrs. Miriam Beard Vagts.

Figure 4.1
From *The Public Perspective,* March/April 1993, Volume 4, Number 3. Copyright © 1993 The Public Perspective. Reprinted by permission of Roper Center.

Box 5.1
Excerpt from "Rights and Discipline" from *Polity Magazine,* Volume 24, Number 14, Summer 1992 by John Gilliom. Copyright © 1992 by John Gilliom. Reprinted by permission of The Northeastern Political Science Association.

Box 5.5
"U. S. Flag: Tussle Over the National Icon" from *The International Herald Tribune* by E. J. Dionne, Jr. Copyright © 1990 by International Herald Tribune. Reprinted by permission of The International Herald Tribune, Inc.

Box 5.7
Reprinted with the permission of The Free Press, a Division of Macmillan, Inc. from *The Origins of the Civil Rights Movement: Black Communities Organizing for Change* by Aldon D. Morris. Copyright © 1984 by The Free Press.

Figure 6.1
From *The Public Perspective,* March/April 1993, Volume 4, Number 3. Copyright © 1993 The Public Perspective. Reprinted by permission of Roper Center.

Figure 6.2
From *The Political Character of Adolescence: The Influence of Families and Schools* by M. Kent Jennings and Richard G. Niemi. Copyright © by M. Kent Jennings and Richard G. Niemi. Reprinted by permission of Princeton University Press.

Table 6.1
Adapted from *The Gallup Poll Monthly,* July 1990. Copyright © 1990 by The Gallup Poll Monthly. Reprinted by permission.

Box 6.2
From *The Public Perspective,* December 1991. Copyright © 1991 by The Public Perspective. Reprinted by permission of Roper Center.

Figure 6.4
From *The Public Perspective,* March/April 1993, Volume 4, Number 3. Copyright © 1993 The Public Perspective. Reprinted by permission of Roper Center.

Figure 6.5
From *The Public Perspective,* March/April 1993, Volume 4, Number 3. Copyright © 1993 The Public Perspective. Reprinted by permission of Roper Center.

Figure 6.9
From *The Public Perspective,* March/April 1993, Volume 4, Number 3. Copyright ©

1993 The Public Perspective. Reprinted by permission of Roper Center.

Box 8.3
Excerpt from "None Dare Call It Lobbying" from *Common Cause Magazine* by Richard Cowan. Copyright © 1989 by Common Cause Magazine, Washington, D. C. Reprinted with permission.

Figure 13.1
"Ranking the Issues by Lawmakers Party" from *The Washington Post National Weekly Edition* by John Anderson. Copyright © 1992 by The Washington Post. Reprinted with permission.

Figure 18.3
Adapted figure of "How the Middle Class is Shrinking" from *The Seattle Post-Intelligencer* by Ben Garrison. Copyright © 1992 by the Seattle Post-Intelligencer. Reprinted courtesy of the Seattle Post-Intelligencer.

Box 19.1
"It was a Bad Time Last Time Too: The Crédit Mobilier Scandal of 1872" from *American Heritage Magazine* by Roy Hoopes. Reprinted by permission of American Heritage Magazine, a division of Forbes Inc., © Forbes Inc., 1991.

PHOTO/CARTOON CREDITS

Chapter 1
p. 4 © Rick Maiman/Sygma; 6 AP/Wide World Photos; 7, **left** © Steiner/Sygma; 7, **right** © Alain Keler/Sygma; 9 AP/Wide World Photos; 16 UPI/Bettmann Newsphotos; 17 OLIPHANT © Universal Press Syndicate, Reprinted with permission. All rights reserved; 19, **top** © J. Sohm/The Image Works; 19, **middle** AP/Wide World Photos; 19, **bottom** © Les Stone/Sygma; 20 AP/Wide World Photos; 22 UPI/Bettmann Newsphotos; 27 Reuters/Bettmann Newphotos.

Chapter 2
p. 35 The Bettmann Archive; 40 Culver Pictures; 42 The Bettmann Archive; 43 Culver Pictures; 45 The Bettmann Archive; 48 The Bettmann Archive; 50 The Bettmann Archive; 53, **top** Culver Pictures; 53, **middle** Brown Brothers; 53, **bottom** The Bettmann Archive; 64 The Bettmann Archive.

Chapter 3
p. 73 Reprinted with special permission of King Features Syndicate; 74 © J. L. Atlan/Sygma; 75 Culver Pictures; 78 Bettmann Newsphotos; 80 © Charles Steiner/Sygma; 81 AP/Wide World Photos; 97, **top** UPI/Bettmann Newsphotos; 97, **middle** UPI/Bettmann Newsphotos; 97, **bottom** The Bettmann Archive; 98 UPI/Bettmann Newsphotos; 99 UPI/Bettmann Newsphotos.

Chapter 4
p. 108 UPI/Bettmann Newsphotos; 111 © Engleman/Rothco; 116 AP/Wide World Photos; 118 The Bettmann Archive; 120 The Bettmann Archive; 125 Culver Pictures; 126 UPI/Bettmann Newsphotos; 127 UPI/Bettmann Newsphotos; 131 AP/Wide World Photos; 135 AP/Wide World Photos; 139, **top** AP/Wide World Photos; 139, **middle** UPI/Bettmann Newsphotos; 139, **bottom** AP/Wide World Photos; 140 © G. Kanatous/Sygma.

Chapter 5
p. 146 © Paul Conklin/PhotoEdit; 147 FEIFFER © Universal Press Syndicate. Reprinted with permission. All rights reserved; 156 Culver Pictures; 158 © Les Stone/Sygma; 161 AP/Wide World Photos; 167 AP/Wide World Photos; 171 The Bettmann Archive; 173, **top** UPI/Bettmann Newsphotos; 173, **middle** UPI/Bettmann Newsphotos; 173, **bottom** © Danny Lyon/Magnum Photos; 174 UPI/Bettmann Newsphotos; 175 AP/Wide World Photos; 178 UPI/Bettmann Newsphotos; 180 © Allen Tannenbaum/Sygma.

Chapter 6
p. 190 © J. L. Atlan/Sygma; 191 AP/Wide World Photos; 194 Reuters/Bettmann Newsphotos; 196 AP/Wide World Photos; 200 © 1993 Tony Muscionico/Contact Press Images; 210 © R. Maiman/Sygma; 205 UPI/Bettmann Newsphotos; 207 © 1990 Dan Lamont/Matrix; 213, **top** ©

John Chiasson/The Gamma Liaison Network: **213, middle** UPI/Bettmann Newsphotos; **213, bottom** © J. L. Atlan/Sygma; **214** AP/Wide World Photos; **220** © 1989, Boston Globe, Distributed by the Los Angeles Times Syndicate. Reprinted with permission.

Chapter 7
p. 229, top AP/Wide World; **229, bottom** The 1992 MTV Voter Registration Drive Ad appears courtesy of MTV Networks, a division of Viacom International Inc. MTV: MUSIC TELEVISION and *Choose or Lose* are trademarks of MTV Networks. © 1993 MTV Networks. All rights reserved; **231** © 1993 David Burnett/Contact Press Images; **243** © A. Tannenbaum/Sygma; **248** By permission of Chip Bok and Creators Syndicate; **249** UPI/Bettmann Newsphotos; **251** Culver Pictures, Inc.; **255** © P. Laffont/Sygma; **256** © Brooks Kraft/Sygma; **259, top** UPI/Bettmann Newsphotos; **259, middle** © Allan Tannenbaum/Sygma; **259, bottom** © R. Maiman/Sygma; **261** © R. Bossu/Sygma; **264** AP/Wide World Photos.

Chapter 8
p. 271 UPI/Bettmann Newsphotos; **274** Culver Pictures; **275** Reproduced with the permission of The Children's Defense Fund; **280** By permission of Mike Luckovich and Creators Syndicate; **283** Planned Parenthood ® Federation of America, Inc.; **284** © Terry Ashe/Time Magazine; **289** © Brian Smale Photography; **294** UPI/Bettmann; **295** © Paul Hosefros/New York Times Pictures; **296** Courtesy of The Committee for National Health Insurance; **298** © Ed Pritchard/Tony Stone Worldwide; **301, top** AP/Wide World Photos; **301, middle** UPI/Bettmann Newsphotos; **301, bottom** © Les Stone/Sygma; **307** Courtesy Common Cause.

Chapter 9
p. 313 AP/Wide World Photos; **314** Reuters/Bettmann Newsphotos; **317, left** The Bettmann Archive; **317, right** The Bettmann Archive; **320** Culver Pictures, Inc.; **321, top** Culver Pictures, Inc.; **321, bottom** Culver Pictures, Inc.; **327** © 92 Ken Hawkins/Sygma; **334** © Jeffrey Markowitz/Sygma; **332, top** AP/Wide World Photos; **332, middle** Les Stone/Sygma; **332, bottom** © Brooks Kraft/Sygma; **338, top** Reuters/Bettmann Newsphotos; **338, bottom** © J.L. Atlan/Sygma; **339** © Tim Sharp/Sygma.

Chapter 10
p. 344 AP/Wide World Photos; **347** Reuters/Bettmann Newsphotos; **350** AP/Wide World Photos; **352** UPI/Bettmann Newsphotos; **357** AP/Wide World Photos; **358** UPI/Bettmann Newsphotos; **362** Reprinted by permission: Tribune Media Services; **364** © J. Patrick Forden/Sygma; **376, top** © Michael

Evans/Sygma; **376, middle** Reuters/Bettmann Newsphotos; **376, bottom** Reuters/Bettmann Newsphotos; **378** AP/Wide World Photos; **380** AP/Wide World Photos; **381** Reprinted by permission: Tribune Media Services.

Chapter 11
p. 388 AP/Wide World Photos; **389** AP/Wide World Photos; **390** © San Francisco Chronicle. Reprinted by permission; **393, top** © Douglas Kirkland/Sygma; **393, middle** UPI/Bettmann Newsphotos; **393, bottom** © Eddie Adams/Sygma; **398** Sygma; **401** Wide World Photos, Inc.; **403** © Tannenbaum/Sygma; **404** AP/Wide World Photos; **405** UPI/Bettmann Newsphotos; **407, left** © L. Downing/Sygma; **407, right** Reuters/Bettmann Newsphotos; **409** AP/Wide World Photos; **416** © Mike Stewart/Sygma; **420, left** © Les Stone/Sygma; **420, right** Wide World Photos; **421** © 1992 Los Angeles Times. Reprinted with permission.

Chapter 12
p. 430 Reuters/Bettmann; **434** © M. Polak/Sygma; **439** AP/Wide World Photos; **446** AP/Wide World Photos; **448** AP/Wide World Photos; **451, top** AP/Wide World Photos; **451, middle** AP/Wide World Photos; **451, bottom** UPI/Bettmann; **453** Wide World Photos, Inc.; **454** © G. Mathieson/Sygma.

Chapter 13
p. 456 Reprinted by permission: Tribune Media Services; **462** © Sygma; **464** AP/Wide World Photos; **468** © Paul Hosefros/The New York Times; **471** AP/Wide World Photos; **475** © Larry Downing/Sygma; **480, top** © Wally McNamee/Sygma; **480, middle** © P. F. Gero/Sygma; **480, bottom** © F. Lee Corkran/Sygma; **485** UPI/Bettmann Newsphotos; **486** Wide World Photos, Inc.; **487** AP/Wide World Photos; **488** © R. Maiman/Sygma; **492** © Steve Kelly/The San Diego Union-Tribune.

Chapter 14
p. 503 Reprinted with special permission of King Features Syndicate; **504** AP/Wide World Photos; **505** Tom Toles in *The Buffalo News;* **512** © D. Rodgers/Sygma; **514** AP/Wide World Photos; **516, top** © Sygma; **516, middle** © John Ficara/Sygma; **516, bottom** © Sygma; **517** UPI/Bettmann Newsphotos; **523** Reuters/Bettmann Newsphotos; **526** © Larry Downing/Sygma; **530** © Arthur Grace/Sygma; **532, left** © J. P. Laffont/Sygma; **532, right** © Sygma.

Chapter 15
p. 536 © John Ficara/Sygma; **538** AP/Wide World Photos; **540, left** AP/Wide World Photos; **540, right** AP/Wide World Photos; **546** © Harley L. Schwadron; **547** AP/Wide World Photos; **557, top** Wide

World Photos; **557, middle** AP/Wide World Photos; **557, bottom** © 1993 David Burnett/Contact Press Images; **558** Wide World Photos; **559** Wide World Photos; **561** © P. F. Gero/Sygma.

Chapter 16
p. 568 © Sygma; **569** UPI/Bettmann Newsphotos; **580, left** AP/Wide World Photos; **580, right** © J. P. Laffont/Sygma; **581** © Bob Schochet; **588** © Sygma; **593, top** AP/Wide World Photos; **593, middle** AP/Wide World Photos; **593, bottom** © Sygma; **596** © Abc Frajndlich/Sygma; **599, left** © Jean Louis Atlan/Sygma; **599, right** Reuters/Bettmann Newsphotos.

Chapter 17
p. 607 © William Campbell/Sygma; **609** © John Ficara/Sygma; **610** © N. Tully/Sygma; **614** © J. L. Atlan/Sygma; **616** AP/Wide World Photos; **618, top** Reuters/Bettmann Newsphotos; **618, middle** Reuters/Bettmann Newsphotos; **618, bottom** Wide World Photos; **619** © D. Kuroda/Sygma; **625** © Steve Sapp, USCG/Sygma; **627** © 1993, Los Angeles Times. Reprinted with permission.

Chapter 18
p. 623 © Patrick Forestier/Sygma; **635** UPI/Bettmann Newsphotos; **637** Tom Toles in *The Buffalo News;* **643, top** © Wally McNamee/Sygma; **643, middle** Reuters/Bettmann Newsphotos; **643, bottom** © C. Pablo Manners/New York Times Pictures; **646** Reprinted by permission of John Trever, Albuquerque Journal; **649** UPI/Bettmann Newsphotos; **651** © Jeffrey Markowitz/Sygma; **653** © Patrick Forestier/Sygma; **655** UPI/Bettmann Newsphotos; UPI/Bettmann Newsphotos; **658** AP/Wide World Photos.

Chapter 19
p. 672 © Les Stone/Sygma; **668** © Ted Thai/Sygma; **677** The Bettmann Archive; **682** UPI/Bettmann Newsphotos; **683, top** © Scott Carpenter/Sygma; **683, middle** UPI/Bettmann Newsphotos; **683, bottom** © Wally McNamee/Sygma; **689** © Wally McNamee/Sygma; **691** Wide World Photos; **692** *This Fabulous Century,* v. 3, Time/Life series. Cartoon originally appeared in *Life,* 9/22/21; **694** Wide World Photos; **696** Wide World Photos.

Chapter 20
p. 703 © P. Habans/Sygma; **705** The Bettmann Archive; **712** © Sygma; **717** © Ch. Simonpietri/Sygma; **720** UPI/Bettmann Newsphotos; **723, top** © John Ficara/Sygma; **723, middle** Wide World Photos; **723, bottom** Reuters/Bettmann Newsphotos; **724** © J. Langevin/Sygma; **725** © Dan Foote/Texas International Features; **728** © Wide World Photos; **731** © De Keerle/Grochowiak/ Sygma